New York

Yankee Stadium, One East 161st

2020 OFFICIAL MEDIA GUIDE &

Official Publication of the New Yor

Produced by the Yankees Media Relations Departme
Michael Margolis, Lauren Moran, Rob Morse, Kaitlyn Bre
Germania Dolores Hernandez-Simonetti and Jason Zillo

MW01421648

Additional updated information is available for accredited members of the media at www.yankeespressbox.com.
The Yankees Media Relations Department may be reached at (718) 579-4460 or via e-mail at media@yankees.com.
Media Guides can be purchased at www.yankees.com/mediaguide.

Contributors: Ken Adams, Ron Antonelli, Marty Appel, Baseball Reference, Rick Cerrone, Daniel Cohen, *Elias Sports Bureau*, Daniel Gil Feuchtwanger, Stephen Gager, Jon Goldberg, Ariele Goldman Hecht, Tom Hirdt, Joe Kalar, Paul A. Kopp, David Kronheim, John Labombarda, Dan Laverde, Kenny Leandry, Nathan Maciborski, Amanda Rae McLean, National Baseball Hall of Fame & Museum, Jim Petrozzello, Brian Richards, Alfred Santasiere III, Yoshiki Sato, Barrie Schneiderman, Jordan Sprechman, STATS Inc.
Special thanks to: The *Elias Sports Bureau* for their research assistance with this book and throughout the year.
Photos courtesy of: New York Yankees, National Baseball Hall of Fame & Museum, Getty Images, *New York Daily News*, Photo File, Library of Congress, Michael Ponzini
Cover Design: Michael Margolis, Marlon Abreu and Brian Spector • **Design of page backgrounds:** Aaron Babcock, www.hailvarsity.com
Printing: Blue Parachute, www.bluechute.com, (732) 767-1320
Note: All content, including the team roster and all statistics, is updated through Feb. 1, 2020, unless otherwise indicated.

Table of Contents

FRONT OFFICE **2**
Front Office Directory 2
Harold Z. (Hal) Steinbrenner 6
Henry G. (Hank) Steinbrenner 6
Jennifer Steinbrenner Swindal 7
Jessica Steinbrenner 7
Randy Levine 8
Lonn A. Trost 9
Brian Cashman 10
Jean Afterman 12
Michael Fishman 12
Tim Naehring 13
Damon Oppenheimer 13
Kevin Reese 13

HOPE WEEK **14**

COMMITMENT TO COMMUNITY **16**

2020 NEW YORK YANKEES **23**
Aaron Boone 24
Matt Blake 27
Mike Harkey 28
Carlos Mendoza 29
Phil Nevin 30
P.J. Pilittere 31
Tanner Swanson 32
Marcus Thames 33
Reggie Willits 34
Additional Coaching Staff 37
Player Health & Performance Staff 38
Medical Staff 40
Mental Conditioning Staff 41
Support Staff 42
How the Yankees Were Built 43
Birthdays, Players and Coaches 43
40-Man Roster 44
Non-Roster Invitees to Spring Training 45
Numerical Roster and Pronunciations 45

2020 PLAYER BIOGRAPHIES **47**

2019 IN REVIEW **217**
Postseason Summary 218
Regular Season Summary 221
Final MLB Standings 227
NYY Record vs. Opponents 227
Day-by-Day 228
Postponed/Delayed/Suspended Games 230
Transactions 231
Postseason Batting/Pitching Statistics 234
Reg. Season Batting Statistics/Team Splits 235
Pinch-Hitters/RISP 237
Home Run Charts 238
Pitching Statistics/Team Splits 239
Fielding Statistics 242
Replays and Reviews 242
Team & Indiv. Highs-Lows/Award Winners 243
Opening Day/I.L./ Ejections 244
Players Used/Starts by Position & Bat. Order 245
Game Records by the Numbers 245

OPPONENTS **247**
Opponents Batting Records 256
Yankees-Mets All-Time Transactions 257
Yankees-Mets Two-Stadium Doubleheaders 257
Played/Managed for Yankees and Mets 258
Played for Yankees/Dodgers/Giants/Mets 258
Most Recent Trades by Team 259
Opp. Pitching vs. NYY (Most Ks/30+ Wins) 259
Series Results vs. AL, Year-by-Year, All-Time 260
Interleague Play Series Results 261
Home/Road Records vs. AL since 1981 262

HISTORY AND RECORDS **265**
History of the Yankees 266
Uniform Design and NY Logo 272
Origin of Numbered Uniforms 273
Top Hat Logo 273
Origin of Names "Yankees" & "Highlanders" 273
Patches and Armbands 274
Important Dates in Yankees History 275
Lou Gehrig Appreciation Day/Babe Ruth Day 281
George M. Steinbrenner III 282
Ownership Chronology 283
Bob Sheppard 284
Other Yankees PA Announcers 285
1927 Yankees/"Murderers' Row" 286
1939 Yankees/"Culmination of a Dynasty" 287
1961 Yankees/Maris 61HR Season 288
1998 Yankees/"Most Wins in a Season" 289
Official Scoring at Yankee Stadium 290
Yankees in Cooperstown 291
National Baseball Hall of Fame and Museum 293
Retired Yankees Uniform Numbers 294
Player Roster, All-Time 297
Military, Yankees in the 301
Managers and Coaches Rosters, All-Time 302
Captains, All-Time 302
Numerical Roster, All-Time 303
Opening Day Ceremonial First Pitches 310
Opening Day All-Time Record / HRs / Grand Slams 310
Managers, All-Time Records 311
General Managers, Chronology of 311
Year-by-Year Results, All-Time 312
Team Hitting, Year-by-Year 314
Team Pitching, Year-by-Year 315
Saves Leaders, Year-by-Year 315
Hitting Leaders, Year-by-Year 316
Pitching Leaders, Year-by-Year 318
Single-Season Batting/Pitching Leaders, Top 10 319
Career Batting Leaders, Top 20 320
Single Season Batting Leaders by Position 320
Career Pitching Leaders, Top 20 321
Club Records, Team 322
Club Records, Individual 324
Youngest/Oldest Yankees Players, All-Time 324
Longest Games in Club History 325
Cycles, by Yankees and Opponents 325
Award Winners (MVP/CY/ROY/GG/SilverSLG) 326
Award Winners (Player of Month/Week) 328
AL/ML Batting Leaders (Avg/HR/RBI/200H) 330
AL/ML Batting Leaders (H/OBP/R/SLG/K/SB/TB/BB) 331
AL/ML Pitching Leaders (W/L/PCT/ERA/G/GS/CG/SHO/IP) 332
AL/ML Pitching Leaders (H/BB/K/R/ER/HR/SV) 333
20-Game Winners 333
Home Run Feats 334
Grand Slams/Pinch-Hit HRs 335
Triple Crown Winners 336
30HR/30SB Seasons 336
No-Hitters and Perfect Games 337
All-Star Game Selections (by Year) / HR Derby 340
All-Star Game Selections/Starts (by Player/Pos.) 341
All-Star Batting Register, All-Time 342
All-Star Pitching Register, All-Time 343
All-Star Single-Game Highs/Notable Events 343
All-Star Game Career Top 10 Leaders/MVP 344
All-Star Games Played at Yankee Stadium 345
Exhibitions vs. Mets/Dodgers/Giants 346
Head Athletic Trainers 347
Forfeited Games 347
Postseason Series Results 348
Postseason Record by Opponent 348
Postseason Series Summaries 349
Postseason Award Winners 358
Postseason Batting/Pitching Leaders 359
World Series Batting/Pitching Leaders 360
ALCS Batting/Pitching Leaders 361
ALDS Batting/Pitching Leaders 362

YANKEE STADIUM **363**
Green Initiatives at Yankee Stadium 366
Yankee Stadium Firsts/ Construction Timeline 369
Social Gathering Areas at Yankee Stadium 370
Yankee Stadium by the Numbers 371
Other Events at Yankee Stadium 372
New York City FC 376
Attendance Records 377
History of the Original Yankee Stadium 378
Original Yankee Stadium Firsts/Lasts/Leaders 381
Negro Leagues at Original Yankee Stadium 382
Other Events at Original Yankee Stadium 383
Previous Homes of the Yankees 384
College Football at Original Yankee Stadium 385
Monument Park, History of 387
Monument Park, Monuments and Plaques 388

PLAYER DEVELOPMENT **395**
Player Development and Scouting Directory 396
Player Development Staff 397
Yankees Around the Globe 401
2019 Draft Review 404
No. 1 Draft Picks, All-Time 405
2019 Organizational Summary 406
Kevin Lawn Award 407
Scranton/Wilkes-Barre RailRiders (AAA) 408
Trenton Thunder (AA) 409
Tampa Tarpons (A) 410
Charleston RiverDogs (A) 411
Staten Island Yankees (Short-Season A) 412
Pulaski Yankees (R) 413
Gulf Coast Yankees West (R) 414
Gulf Coast Yankees East (R) 415
DSL (R)/International Player Development 416
Arizona Fall League, Yankees Participants in 418

MINOR LEAGUE/NON-ROSTER INVITEES BIOS **419**

MEDIA INFORMATION **465**
Yankees Media Relations Staff 466
Media Services at Yankee Stadium 466
YES Network Television Broadcasters 468
WFAN Radio Broadcasters 472
WADO Spanish Radio Broadcasters 473
TV/Radio Broadcast Teams, All-Time 474
Spring Training & Steinbrenner Field 475
Steinbrenner Field Enhancements 476
2020 Spring Training Schedule 477
All-Time Spring Sites/Attendances 477
Yankee Stadium Batting Practice Times 477
Yankee Stadium Seating Map and Directions 478
2020 Regular Season Schedule 480

YANKEE DOODLES INDEX
1921 American League Champions 336
1923 World Series Champions 313
1978 World Series Champions 473
Batterymates, Most Common in NYY History 123
Brothers & Fathers/Sons to Play for Yankees 105
Championships, Consecutive 80
Championships, Most in Four Major Sports 78
Core Four 156
Dawson Award (Best Rookie in Spring Training) 48
Derek Jeter Orig. Yankee Stad. Farewell Speech 177
Dominican Republic Fire Equipment Donation 151
Films and Television, Yankee Stadium in 386
Futures Game, Yankees in 400
General Mgrs., Best MLB Win. Pcts. since 1950 10
Glossary, Baseball Statistics 101
Home Record, 28 Consec. Winning Seasons 211
Home Runs, First World Series At-Bat 207
Home Runs, First Yankees At-Bat 95
Home Runs, Franchise Firsts 336
Interleague Play, Yankees in 170
Milestone Wins in Franchise History 42
Murcer Indoor Training Facility at Okla. Christian Univ. 126
New York Yankees Museum pres. by Bank of America 87
No-hitters, Two by One Pitcher in a Season 113
Presidents, Yankees 9
Ralph Lauren Yankee Fashion 67
Scoring in Consecutive Games 203
Steinbrenner High School 60
Winning Team Record, 27 Consecutive Seasons 139

FRONT OFFICE
2020 YANKEES
2019 REVIEW
OPPONENTS
HISTORY & RECORDS
YANKEE STADIUM
PLAYER DEVELOPMENT
MEDIA

New York Yankees Directory

George M. Steinbrenner III
1930-2010

Yankee Stadium, One East 161st Street, Bronx, NY 10451 • (718) 293-4300

Managing General Partner* / Co-Chairperson, New York Yankees .... Harold Z. Steinbrenner
General Partner** / Co-Chairperson, New York Yankees .... Henry G. Steinbrenner
General Partner‡ / Vice Chairperson, New York Yankees .... Jennifer Steinbrenner Swindal
General Partner‡‡ / Vice Chairperson, New York Yankees .... Jessica Steinbrenner
of Martinique Holdings, Inc.   **of Bellaire Holdings, Inc.*   ‡ of Marsh Harbor Holdings, Inc.*   ‡‡ of JJS NYY Holdings, LLC*

YANKEES FAMILY
Ray Bartoszek, Frank Brenner, Grant Cagle, Jerry Cohen, Daniel M. Crown, James S. Crown, Lester Crown, Ike S. Franco, John H. Freund, Peter B. Freund, Leslie Gelber, Marvin S. Goldklang, Perry Golkin, Robert Gorman, Jason Halper, Jon Hanson, Richard Heitzmann, Barry Klarberg, Louis A. Lamoriello, David Levinson, Patrick McCarthy, Roberto Mignone, Thomas Murphy, James L. Nederlander, Robert E. Nederlander, Morton Olshan, Michael Price, Karen Pritzker, Dani Reiss, Bill Rose, Howard Rubenstein, Eric Scheuermann, Jerry Speyer, Mark Tabak, Beth Wilf, Halle Wilf, Leonard Wilf, Orin Wilf, Spencer Zwick

EXECUTIVES
President .... Randy Levine, Esq.
Chief Operating Officer .... Lonn A. Trost, Esq.
Senior Vice President, General Manager .... Brian Cashman
Senior Vice President, Assistant General Manager .... Jean Afterman, Esq.
Senior Vice President, Stadium Operations .... Doug Behar
Senior Vice President, Yankee Global Enterprises CFO .... Anthony Bruno
Senior Vice President & General Counsel .... Alan Chang, Esq.
Senior Vice President, Strategic Ventures .... Marty Greenspun
Senior Vice President, Chief Security Officer .... Sonny Hight
C.F.O. and S.V.P., Financial Operations .... Scott M. Krug
Senior Vice President, Chief Information Officer .... Mike Lane
Senior Vice President & Chief Legal Officer .... Mike Mellis, Esq.
Senior Vice President, Corporate/Community Relations .... Brian E. Smith
Senior Vice President, Partnerships .... Michael J. Tusiani
Senior Vice President, Marketing .... Deborah A. Tymon
Vice President & CFO, Accounting .... Robert B. Brown
Vice President, Ticket Sales, Service & Operations .... Kevin Dart
Vice President, Assistant General Manager .... Michael Fishman
Vice President, Events & Brand Experiences .... Emily Hamel
Vice President, Non-Baseball Sports Events .... Mark Holtzman
Vice President, Baseball Operations .... Tim Naehring
Vice President, Domestic Amateur Scouting .... Damon Oppenheimer
Vice President, Human Resources, Employment & Labor Law .... Aryn Sobo, Esq.
Vice President, Communications & Media Relations .... Jason Zillo

BASEBALL OPERATIONS (NEW YORK)
Special Assignment Scout .... Jim Hendry
Special Advisors .... Reggie Jackson, Hideki Matsui,
 .... Andy Pettitte, CC Sabathia, Nick Swisher
Directors, Pro Scouting .... Matt Daley, Dan Giese
Director, Quantitative Analysis .... David Grabiner
Director, Baseball Operations .... Matthew Ferry
Director, Baseball Systems .... Brian Nicosia
Senior Web Developer .... Nick Eby
Senior Mobile Engineer .... Michael Traverso
Senior Analyst, Quantitative Analysis .... Christopher Fonnesbeck
Coordinator, Baseball Operations .... Michael Pinsky
Coordinator, Pro Scouting .... Adam Charnin-Aker
Analysts, Quantitative Analysis .... Collin Erickson, Theodore Feder,
 .... Walker Harrison, John Morris,
 .... Christopher Pang, Justin Sims, Sam Waters
Assistant, Baseball Operations .... Jesse Lippin-Foster
Database Engineer, Baseball Operations .... Jesse Bradford
Data Engineer .... Samuel Grigo
Mobile Engineer .... Rakibul Islam
Full-Stack Software Engineers .... James Dunn, Benjamin Gilman
Web Developers .... Rick Rosser, Marc Tanis
Database Engineers .... Eric Fitton, Patrick Gilligan
Research Analyst, Quantitative Analysis .... John Benedetto
Administrative Assistant .... Mary Pellino

FIELD AND SUPPORT STAFF
Director, Mental Conditioning .... Chad Bohling
Director, Clubhouse Operations .... Lou Cucuzza Jr.
Director, Team Travel & Player Services .... Ben Tuliebitz
Director, Advance Scouting/Coaching Assistant .... Brett Weber
Equipment Manager .... Rob Cucuzza
Manager, Advance Scouting .... Tyler DeClerck
Major League Video Coordinator .... Dan Pane
Coaching Assistant/Bullpen Catcher .... Radley Haddad
Bullpen Catcher .... Aaron Barnett
Major League Batting Practice Pitcher .... Danilo Valiente
Analyst, Major League Coaching Staff .... Zac Fieroh
Major League Interpreter .... Shingo Horie

PLAYER HEALTH AND PERFORMANCE STAFF
Head Team Physician .... Christopher Ahmad, M.D.
Head Team Internist .... Paul Lee, M.D., M.P.H.
Team Internist .... William Turner, M.D.
Senior Advisor, Orthopedics .... Stuart Hershon, M.D.
Director of Player Health and Performance .... Eric Cressey
Assistant Director of Player Health and Performance .... Donovan Santas
Director of Sports Medicine & Rehabilitation (ATC/PT) .... Michael Schuk
Head Athletic Trainer .... Tim Lentych
Assistant Athletic Trainer .... Alfonso Malaguti
Major League Strength & Conditioning Coach .... Brett McCabe
Assistant Major League Strength & Conditioning Coach .... Matt Rutledge
Director of Medical Services .... Steve Donohue
Major League Dietitian .... Drew Weisberg
Massage Therapist .... Doug Cecil

ACCOUNTING
Manager, Ticket Accounting .... Jeff Kline
Accounts Payable/Payroll Clerk .... Maria Lee
General Ledger Accountant .... Leonard Bates

BUSINESS STRATEGY & ANALYTICS
Senior Advisor, Business Strategy & Analytics .... Pete Britt
Senior Analyst, Business Analytics .... Nate Silverstein
Senior Analyst, Business Analytics & CRM Strategy .... Will Harris
Analyst, Business Strategy .... Haley Durmer

COMMUNICATIONS & MEDIA RELATIONS
Director, Communications & Media Relations .... Michael Margolis
Assistant Director, Baseball Information .... Lauren Moran
Senior Coordinator, Communications & Media Relations .... Rob Morse
Coordinator, Communications & Media Relations .... Kaitlyn Brennan
Assistant, Media Services .... Mark Torres
Assistant, Communications & Media Relations .... Jon Butensky
Admin. Asst., Comm. & Media Relations .... Germania Dolores Hernandez-Simonetti
Bilingual Media Relations Coordinator .... Marlon Abreu
Japanese Media Advisor .... Yoshiki Sato

CORPORATE/COMMUNITY RELATIONS
Director, Corporate/Community Relations .... Kenny Leandry
Manager, Multicultural Affairs .... Lina Cruz
Manager, Corporate Diversity Initiatives .... Deyanirse Jourdain
Manager, Corporate/Community Relations .... Joseph Kalar
Coordinators, Corporate/Community Relations ... Manny Guzman, Amanda Rae McLean

CREATIVE SERVICES
Senior Director, Creative Services .... Kara Mooney

DIGITAL & SOCIAL MEDIA ANALYTICS
Senior Manager, Digital and Social Media Strategy .... Stephi Blank
Senior Coordinator, Social Media & Content .... Ryan Callahan

EXECUTIVE DEPARTMENT
Counsel .... Mark Bienstock, Esq.
Counsel .... Cody Nastasia, Esq.
Director, Financial Operations .... Michael Parker
Director, Financial Operations .... Allison Stewart
Analysts, Financial Operations .... Jack Donnelly, Ally Howe, Joseph Zelkowitz
Senior Executive Assistants .... Stephanie Fullam, Monica Pisacano
Legal & Financial Assistant .... Christine Sheridan
Assistant, Strategic Ventures .... Amy Ficke
Executive Coordinator .... Dylan Nolan

HUMAN RESOURCES
Assistant Director, Human Resources .... Andrea Dutt
Assistant Director, Human Resources .... Julia Langan
Human Resources Generalist .... Madalyn Savishinsky

MARKETING, PROMOTIONS & SPECIAL EVENTS
Senior Associate Director, Marketing, Event Prod. and
Fan Experience Specialist, Yankees Universe Prog. Devel. ..... Robert N. Bernstein
Senior Associate Director, Marketing, Promotions,
Stadium Event Production Specialist, Broadcast Marketing ..... Craig L. Cartmell
Senior Associate Director, Marketing, Outbound Marketing &
Advertising, Brand Strategist and Special Event Activation ...... Gregory D. King
Coordinator Marketing, Stadium Event Production,
Fan Development and Advertising Partnerships .... John Curto

PARTNERSHIPS

Executive Director, Partnership Sales .... Daniel Gallivan
Director, Partnership Activation .... Jillian Wright
Senior Managers, Partnership Sales .... Thomas Barry, Joshua Goldblatt
Senior Account Executives, Partnership Activation .... Michael Holley,
.... Kaitlyn Swingle, Haley Yeranossian
Account Executives, Partnership Activation .... Matt Ferrara,
.... Kathryn Lazarski, Brandon Matukas
Account Executives, Partnership Sales .... Connor Glenn, Nicole Sanczyk
Account Executive, Partnerships .... Alexander Washington
Administrative Assistant, Partnerships .... Wanda Edwards
Special Advisor, Corporate Opportunities .... Lee Mazzilli

PUBLICATIONS

Senior Director .... Alfred Santasiere III
Executive Editor .... Nathan Maciborski
Deputy Editor .... Jon Schwartz
Chief Photographer/Senior Photography Editor .... Ariele Goldman Hecht
Senior Editor .... Jake Kring-Schreifels
Associate Editor .... Gary Phillips
Staff Photographer/Photography Editor .... Barrie Schneiderman

SECURITY

Executive Director, Team Security .... Edward Fastook
Executive Director, Stadium/Event Security .... Todd Letcher
Director, Team Security .... Mark Kafalas
Dock Master .... Robert Gomez
Manager, Security Systems and Business Continuity .... Samuel Koenig
Executive Security .... Mike Fitzgerald^, Russell MacArthur,
.... Robert Schnebly, Dominic Zano
Senior Coordinator, Stadium Security .... Antonio Coppola

^ Employed by River Operating Company Inc.

STADIUM OPERATIONS

Stadium Superintendent .... Pete Pullara
Director, Stadium Operations .... Carol Laurenzano
Director, Stadium Planning & Special Projects .... Cindy Kamradt
Director, Archives & Records Management .... Tom Barbagallo
Director, Office Administration .... Debbie Nicolosi
Environmental Science Advisor .... Dr. Allen Hershkowitz
Head Groundskeeper .... Dan Cunningham
Manager, Disabled Services & Guest Relations .... Cristina Campana
Managers, Stadium Operations .... Eric Fritz, Kayla O'Donovan
Manager, Housekeeping .... Jhon Londono
Coordinator, Disabled Services & Guest Relations .... Eric Sarmiento
Coordinators, Stadium Operations .... Douglas Austin,
.... Patrick Callahan, Amanda Ivory, Daniel Weber
Administrative Assistant .... Josephine Doring
Junior Archivist .... Andra McCartney
Junior Mail Handler .... Javier Ramos
Reception .... Erin Finn, Lisset Gonzalez, Lena Macchia
Grounds Crew^ .... Priamo Alfonso, Jeffrey Antoniewicz,
.... Anthony Armato, Carlos Blanco, Peter Bodo,
.... Jose Cepeda-Savinon, Luis Fernandez, Christopher Glover,
.... Luis Hernandez, Daniel Hightower, Alejandro Manzueta,
.... Juan Martinez, Luis Martinez, Oswyn Neptune, Angel Nunez,
.... Cristian Pichardo, Michael Rodriguez, Zunnel Rosa, Jhon Salcedo,
.... Javon Treherne, Rushone Treherne, Jose Villao, Devin Wright
Engineers^ .... Kevin Clerkin, Nicholas Dolengewicz,
.... Allan Erazo, Christian Everts, Donald Faivre, Edward Gallagher,
.... James Marino, John McCrory, John McLean, Michael McMorrow,
.... James Plevrites, Michael Ryan, Michael Sciortino, Devin Singh,
.... William Smith, Gerard Triglia, Connor Tymon
Electricians** .... Matt Consiglio, Francis Ninivaggi, Ray West Jr.

^ Employed by River Operating Company, Inc.
*** Employed by Unity International Group*

TECHNOLOGY, SCOREBOARD & BROADCASTING

Senior Director, Scoreboard & Video Production .... Gregory Colello
Senior Director, Broadcasting & Technical Operations .... Brett Moldoff
Director, Information Technology .... Scott Swist
Assistant Director, Production, Yankees Productions .... Pete Gergely
Assistant Director, Scoreboard & Video Production .... Nima Ghandforoush
Assistant Director, Scoreboard .... Ben Mace
Assistant Director, Original Content, Yankees Productions .... Brandon Mihm
Assistant Director, Creative, Yankees Productions .... Brian Spector
Senior Network Administrator .... James Pepe
Network Administrator .... Jason Wong
Broadcast Engineer .... Paul Wolf
Senior Coordinator, Information Technology .... Jake Moran
Media Specialist, Yankees Productions .... Jillian LaConti
Video Editor, Scoreboard Production .... Joseph Oliveri
Producer, Scoreboard & Video Production .... Nick Tyrell
Associate Producer, Yankees Productions .... Jake Korinko
On-Air Talent/Coordinator, Yankees Productions .... Lacey Mazzilli
Associate Designer/Animator, Yankees Productions .... Sydney Worek
Production Assistant, Yankees Productions .... Alexander Day
Creative Coordinator, Scoreboard .... Robert Azzinari
Coordinator, Media Assets, Scoreboard & Video Production .... Kristie Osborne
Technical Services Coordinator .... Saad Baig
Junior Designer/Animator, Yankees Productions .... Matthew Subrizi
Public Address Announcer^ .... Paul Olden
Organists^ .... Paul Cartier, Ed Alstrom

^ Employed by River Operating Company, Inc.

TICKET SALES, SERVICE AND OPERATIONS

Exec. Director, Ticket Sales, Service and CRM Business Strategies .... Rose Barre
Senior Director, Ticket Operations .... Irfan Kirimca
Director, Premium Sales & Service .... Joe Leva
Director, Ticket Sales & Service .... Kyle Hutchinson
Director, Ticket Operations .... James Traynor

PREMIUM SALES & SERVICES

Assistant Director, Premium Ticket Sales & Service .... Tahlor Levine
Assistant Director, CRM & Database Strategist .... Scott Jeffer
Assistant Director, Premium Suite Services .... Samantha Giraud
Senior Specialists, Premium Sales & Service .... Daniel Caplan, Max Esh,
.... Juliana Furey, Matt Hansen, Steve Lynes, Cory Sigadel
Specialists, Premium Sales & Service .... Jarrett Brachfeld, Samuel Clark,
.... Peter DiPietrantonio, Josh Giffin, Dana Russ
Specialist, Premium Service and Contract Administration .... Carly Thea
Analyst, CRM Strategy .... Victoria Ham
Senior Coordinator, Premium Suite Services .... Michael Pereira
Season Tickets Coordinator, Ticket Services .... Joseph Bongiorno
Coordinator, Premium Sales & Service .... Mikayla Melendez
Coordinator, CRM and Brand Strategy .... William Reagan
Groups Coordinator, Ticket Services .... Paige Ryan

SEASON AND GROUP TICKET SALES & SERVICE

Assistant Director, Season Ticket Retention,
Group Sales & Service .... Mike Robbins
Assistant Director, Strategic Business Ventures .... Valerie Shields
Assistant Director, Season Ticket Sales & Service .... Mario Oliveri
Manager, Group Sales & Service .... David Sibelman
Manager, Inside Sales & Service .... John Madden
Manager, Season Ticket Sales, Retention & Service .... Ken Cleary
Manager, Ticket Services & Strategy .... Mackenzie Blondin
Assistant Manager, Group Sales & Service .... P.J. Davidson
Account Executives, Group Sales & Service .... Michael Androsiglio,
.... Nana Anyane-Yeboa, Nicholas Cinelli, Christopher Fast,
.... Daniel O'Connell, Robb Pearson, Gregory Petorak,
.... Zachary Reuveni, Joseph Stephens, Gianluca Vasta, Patrick Winton
Account Executives, Season Ticket Sales & Service .... Derek Bocanegra,
.... John Burbella, Matthew Hickey, Iain Hunter,
.... Justin Pintak, Ezra Rawdon, Zachary Schlau, Ryman Seeley,
.... Kimberly Stover, Josh Varughese, Peter Vaziri
Senior Retention Sales Specialist .... George Stone
Retention Sales Specialists .... Christopher DePalma, Joseph Rofrano,
.... Ian Rubin, Nathaniel Siegel,
Specialist, Strategic Business Ventures .... Esther Chao
Sales Associates, Inside Sales .... Brandon Angelo, Nico Basile
.... Cole Carnemark, Jordan Harris, Connor Monzo,
.... Jess Tighe, Ariella Vaakil, Victoria Zozzaro
Sales Associates, Group Inside Sales .... Michael Bown, Lucas D'Aversa,
.... Joshua DeMartino, Matthew Langlois,
.... Fletcher Reese, Joseph Salituro

TICKET OPERATIONS

Assistant Director, Ticket Operations .... Scott Liller
Assistant Manager, Ticket Operations .... Raymond Soriano
Senior Ticket Office Representatives .... Clifford Davis, Alfred Jahn
Ticket Office Representatives .... Jaron Clyne, Richard Granato,
.... Hank Grazioso, Daniel Ubl
Group Sales Processor .... Carlos Gomez

YANKEE STADIUM EVENTS, MUSEUM & TOURS

Director, College Football Development .... John Mosley
Director, Stadium Tours .... Brett Searson
Assistant Director, Major Events & Programs .... Lesley Mace
Assistant Director, Strategy and Brand Activation .... Frank O'Brien
Senior Museum Curator .... Brian Richards
Senior Manager, College Football Development .... Matt Fox
Senior Manager, Major Events & Programs .... Laura Nicoletti
Senior Sales Manager, Yankee Stadium Events .... Megan Corbett
Assistant Sales Manager, Yankee Stadium Events .... Jessica Harran
Senior Coordinator, Stadium Tours .... Marissa Grieco
Senior Coordinator, Major Events & Programs .... Brynne Murphy
Coordinator, Museum & Stadium Tours .... Daniel Cohen
Coordinators, Stadium Tours .... Dylan Murphy, Franklin Osorio
Coordinator, Strategy & Brand Activation .... Brooke Williams

LEGENDS HOSPITALITY
Yankee Stadium • One East 161st Street • Bronx, NY 10451
info@legends.net / www.legends.net / (646) 977-8080

Legends Hospitality is the exclusive provider of concessions, catering, fine dining and merchandising at Yankee Stadium.

President & CEO .... Shervin Mirhashemi
President, Hospitality .... Dan Smith
Chief Customer Officer .... Marty Greenspun
Regional Vice President .... Richard Porteus
Vice President & Corporate Controller .... Mark A. Pizzariello
Vice President, Facilities .... Jon Muscalo
Vice President, Operations .... Anthony Parnagian
Vice President, Merchandising & Licensing .... Michael Loparo
In-House Counsel .... Karen Monteros
Executive Assistant to Vice President of Operations .... Erin Nargi
General Manager, Concessions .... Christopher Buffa
Manager, Concessions .... Jared Finelli
Manager, Concessions Warehouse .... Lenny Middleton
Director, Concessions Warehouse .... Shiv Ally
Manager, In Seat .... Mary Cortez
Chef, Concessions .... Anna Young

Utility Manager .... Chabbilall Robert
General Manager, Retail .... David Rodriguez
Merchandise Buyer .... Saeed Ramsaroop
Director, Retail Operations .... Emanuel Morel
Manager, Merchandise Warehouse .... Emilio Heredia
Senior Executive Chef & General Mgr., Premium Services .... Matt Gibson
Assistant General Manager, Premium Services .... Mike Foster
Executive Chef .... James D'heron
Executive Sous Chef .... Michael Faccidomo
Manager, Audi Club & Pepsi Lounge .... Julia Kohn
Manager, Catering .... Jahaira Diaz
Manager, Legends In-Seat & Champions Suite .... Richard MacDonald
Manager, Legends Suite Club .... James Callahan
Manager, Premium Purchasing .... Cristy Reynoso
Manager, Suites .... Mia Gibson
Assistant Manager, Suites .... Alyssa Meyer
Director, Human Resources .... Daniel Kelly
Manager, Customer Service .... Odilys Paula
Manager, Human Resources .... John Patino
Director, Finance .... Richard DeJesus
Manager, Venue Technology .... Harsh Khamar
Manager, Accounts Payable .... Kenya Kendricks
Manager, Payroll .... Kevin O'Connor
Associate Manager, Finance .... Michael Barton

PLAYER DEVELOPMENT AND SCOUTING
Yankees Complex • 3102 N. Himes Ave. • Tampa, FL 33607
Phone: (813) 875-7569 • Fax: (813) 873-2302

BASEBALL OPERATIONS (TAMPA)
Vice President, Domestic Amateur Scouting .... Damon Oppenheimer
Senior Director, Player Development .... Kevin Reese
Director, Player Development .... Eric Schmitt
Manager, International Operations .... Victor Roldan
Manager, Minor League Operations .... Nick Avanzato
Assistant Director, Domestic Amateur Scouting, Analytics .... Scott Benecke
Assistant Director, Domestic Amateur Scouting, Operations ...... Mitch Colahan
Assistant Director, Player Development .... Stephen Swindal Jr.
Coordinator of Baseball Development .... Mario Garza
Coordinator of Instruction/Outfield Coordinator .... Pat McMahon
Complex Coordinator/Minor League Manager .... David Adams
Hitting Coordinator .... Dillon Lawson
Director of Pitching .... Sam Briend
Pitching Coordinator/Performance Science Consultant .... John Kremer
Manager, Pitch Development .... Desi Druschel
Infield Coordinator .... Miguel Cairo
Assistant Infield Coordinator/Minor League Manager .... Travis Chapman
Catching Coordinator .... Aaron Gershenfeld
Baserunning Coordinator/Roving Hitting Coach .... Matt Talarico
Rehab Pitching Instructor .... Greg Pavlick
Pitching Analyst, Amateur Scouting .... Scott Lovekamp
Analysts, Player Development .... Brad Smith, Daniel Walco
Assistant, International Operations .... Giuliano Montanez
Assistant, Minor League Operations .... Nick Leon
Baseball Solutions Engineer .... Rob Owens
Education Coordinator .... Joe Perez
Lead Teacher, Player Development Assistant .... Melissa Hernandez
Player Development Consultants .... Marc Bombard, Tino Martinez
Associate Director, Mental Conditioning .... Chris Passarella
Coordinator, Cultural Development .... Héctor González
Coordinator, Mental Conditioning .... Lauren Johnson
Mental Conditioning Coach .... Noel Garcia
Video Coordinator, Mental Conditioning .... David Schnabel

Video Coordinators, Player Development .... Chris Whiting, Joe Wielbruda
Assistant Video Coordinator, Player Development .... Zach Iannarelli
Assistant, Domestic Amateur Scouting, Operations & Analytics .... Tristam Osgood
Video Coordinator, Amateur Scouting .... Ricky Castle
Player Development Equipment Manager .... Ryan Ornstein
Clubhouse Manager, Player Development .... Jamie Ventura

PERFORMANCE SCIENCE
Director, Performance Science .... David Whiteside, Ph.D.
Manager, Peak Performance Programs .... Joe Siara, MS
Coordinator, Preventative Programs .... Mike Wickland
Junior Sports Scientist .... Patrick Hipes, MS
Analyst, Performance Science .... Christina Williamson
Minor League Nutrition Coordinator .... Sydney Boehnlein, R.D.
Minor League Dietitian .... Chandler Falcon, MS

INTERNATIONAL BASEBALL OPERATIONS
Director, International Scouting .... Donny Rowland
Director, Dominican Republic Baseball Operations .... Andrew Wright
Director, Latin Baseball Academy .... Joel Lithgow
Assistant Director, International Scouting .... Brady LaRuffa
Dominican Republic-U.S. Transition Coach/Infield Coach .... Luis Sojo
Assistant to Director, Latin America .... Edgar Mateo
Video Coordinator, International PD/DR BBOPS Asst .... Dan O'Connor
Video Coordinator, International Scouting .... Ethan Sander
Dominican Academy Supervisor .... Josias Cabrera
Assistants, International Baseball Operations .... Manuel Castillo, JT Hernandez

MEDICAL AND TRAINING STAFF (TAMPA)
Team Physician .... Norman J. Castellano, M.D.
Team Orthopedic Surgeon .... Daniel Murphy, M.D.
Team Chiropractor .... Scott Hegseth, D.C.
Medical Coordinator, Player Development .... Mark Littlefield
Assistant Head Athletic Trainer .... Greg Spratt
Draft Medical Coordinator .... Justin Sharpe
Physical Therapist, Player Development .... David Colvin
Strength & Conditioning Coordinator .... Rigo Febles
Assistant Physical Therapist, Player Development .... Joe Bello

MAJOR LEAGUE SPRING TRAINING FACILITY
George M. Steinbrenner Field • 1 Steinbrenner Dr. • Tampa, FL 33614
Phone: (813) 875-7753 or (800) 96-YANKS • FAX: (813) 879-0247

OPERATIONS (TAMPA)
Senior Vice President, Operations .... Dean Holbert
Vice President, Administration .... Diann Blanco
Vice President, Business Operations .... C. Vance Smith
V.P., Tampa Corporate Sales & Media Relations .... Howard Grosswirth
Controller .... Derrick Baio
Assistant Controller .... Krystal Woytisek
Senior Financial Manager .... Kevin Adler
Director of Accounting, Yankee Global Enterprises .... Cassie Donovan
Director, Business Development/Fantasy Camps .... Julie Kremer
Director, Grounds .... Ritchie Anderson
Director, Information Technology .... Rudy Ramirez
Director, Payroll .... Christian Ruiz
Director, Risk Management .... Leslie Hanley
Director, Tax .... Fleur Brenning
Stadium Supervisor .... Ronnie Kaufman
Manager, New York Yankees Tampa Foundation .... Timothy J. Guidry
Manager, Partnership and Community Activation .... Jessica Ventura
Manager, Premium Ticket Services .... Jennifer Magliocchetti
Manager, Security .... Phil Aprea
Manager, Stadium Operations .... Ralph Caputo
Manager, Stadium Services .... John Sibayan

Head Groundskeeper .... Jeff Eckert
General Manager, Tampa Tarpons .... Matthew Gess
Assistant General Manager, Tampa Tarpons .... Jeremy Ventura
Assistant Director, Fantasy Camps .... AmySue Manzione
Assistant Director, Information Technology ...... Dave Levy
Assistant Director, Stadium Operations-Tampa .... Robert Molloy
Coordinator, Non-Baseball Events .... Cassandra Franklin
Grounds Supervisor, Player Development .... Chris Connell
Executive Assistants to the General Partners .... Dawn A. Galuska,
 .... Jenette Sibayan Cruz, Julia Steinbrenner

TAMPA STAFF
ADMINISTRATION: Matt Aber, Nicholas Apuzzo, Irma Badillo, Eric Baio, Jeanine Bender, Dominic Caro, Madaline Erhardt, Mary Kate Harvey, Lauren Hyde, Devin Kowal, Jay Mastri Conley McMillan, Michael Molloy, Daniel Sampson, Nichole Swindle, Colby Vine, Jackie Williams, Sydney Witowski

GROUNDS: Miguel Amezquita, Kenneth Brayton, Francis Gonzalez, Francisco Hernandez, Marquis Hook, Ryan Marsh, Ralph Martinez, Louis Pastore, Eddie Rivera, Jimmy Skeens, Dennis Story

SECURITY: Michael J. Ansotegui, Romeo Cole, Leo Cruz, Dottie De La Garza, Luis Duran, Dennis Hancock, Ronald Henry, Charles Lazzaro, Sean Swindle, Bachir Touirbi, Richard Wolfram, Charles Woodruff

STADIUM OPERATIONS: Kevin Brown, Rolando Chavez, Miguelina Garcia Sanchez, Ricardo Gonzalez, Antonio Green, Juan Hernandez, Dennise Maurer, Matthew Nixon, Eliseo Perez, Charles Poole, Debra Stansell

THE CHASE FOR...

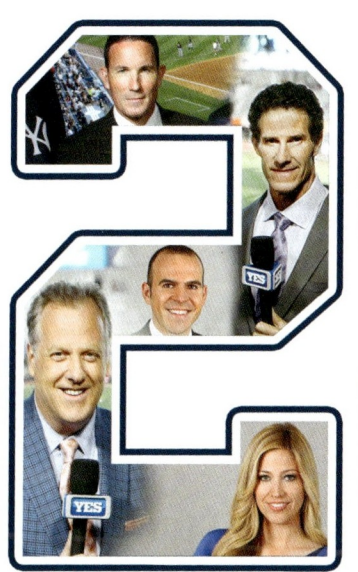

IT'S NOT JUST BASEBALL, IT'S THE *Yankees*™

CONE · CURRY · FLAHERTY · KAY · LORENZ · MARAKOVITS

NEWMAN · O'NEILL · RUOCCO · SHEARN · SINGLETON

Harold Z. (Hal) Steinbrenner
Managing General Partner / Co-Chairperson

Hal Steinbrenner begins his 30th season with the New York Yankees organization in 2020 and his 12th as Managing General Partner / Co-Chairperson. On November 20, 2008, Major League Baseball formalized Mr. Steinbrenner's role as the New York Yankees' Managing General Partner.

Under Mr. Steinbrenner's leadership, the Yankees have retained and enhanced their global popularity while continuing to field championship-caliber teams. Since taking the position of Managing General Partner, the Yankees' .575 combined winning percentage (1,024-758) is the best in all of baseball.

In 2019, the Yankees drew more than 3 million fans at home for the 21st consecutive season, extending their all-time Major League record. They also led the AL in average home attendance for the 16th time in the last 17 seasons. The club's Twitter, Facebook, and Instagram accounts each have the most followers among Major League Baseball teams, as the Yankees reach a global audience of more than 14 million fans over social media on a daily basis.

In recent years, Mr. Steinbrenner and the Yankees organization have focused on improving the experience for fans of all ages by providing more family-friendly and socially oriented spaces at the Yankees' spring training home — George M. Steinbrenner Field in Tampa — and at Yankee Stadium in the Bronx. Steinbrenner Field enhancements have included a complete modernization of the seating bowl and concession areas, and Yankee Stadium now features a dedicated children's zone as well as unique gathering areas for all ticketholders to enjoy.

The 51-year-old son of George Steinbrenner was elected General Partner by the New York Yankees Partnership in 1996, and he held that title for 13 seasons. In 2007, Mr. Steinbrenner was also named Chairman of Yankee Global Enterprises, LLC. In his first full year as Managing General Partner in 2009, the Yankees capped their historic inaugural season in Yankee Stadium with their 27th World Championship.

Along with General Partner / Co-Chairperson Hank Steinbrenner, his responsibilities include overseeing all areas of the club's business and baseball operations, and directing the financial aspects of the New York Yankees, Yankee Global Enterprises and their affiliates. He has also overseen the dynamic growth of Yankee Stadium as a marquee all-season entertainment venue for college football, soccer, hockey, concerts and other non-baseball events.

In 2019, Mr. Steinbrenner was appointed by Commissioner Rob Manfred to Major League Baseball's Advanced Media and Finance Committees. Mr. Steinbrenner previously served a four-year term on Major League Baseball's eight-owner Executive Council from 2015-19. The group functions as a sounding board for the Commissioner, advising him on all major issues. Mr. Steinbrenner also currently serves on the Board of Directors for Legends Hospitality, LLC, a holistic solution provider in the sports, music and entertainment industry which offers expertise in global planning, global sales and hospitality. Created with the Dallas Cowboys in 2008, Legends serves a diverse group of iconic venues, including Yankee Stadium, AT&T Stadium, One World Observatory, Golden 1 Center and the University of Notre Dame, among others. Additionally, he is Chairman and CEO of Steinbrenner Hotel Properties and holds a seat on both the Board of Directors of the Boys & Girls Club of Tampa Bay and the Special Operations Warrior Foundation.

Mr. Steinbrenner attended Culver Military Academy and graduated from Williams College in 1991 with a Bachelor of Arts degree. He earned a Master's degree in Business Administration from the University of Florida in 1994. Mr. Steinbrenner and his wife, Christina, currently reside in Tampa, Fla.

Henry G. (Hank) Steinbrenner
General Partner / Co-Chairperson

Henry G. (Hank) Steinbrenner begins his 13th season as General Partner and 11th season as Co-Chairperson of the New York Yankees. Along with Managing General Partner / Co-Chairperson Hal Steinbrenner, Hank, the oldest son of the late George Steinbrenner, is responsible for overseeing all areas of the club's business and baseball operations.

Mr. Steinbrenner is directly involved in player negotiations, setting long-term player recruitment goals and overall club strategy.

Mr. Steinbrenner serves as Vice President and a Director of Bay Farms Corporation, serves on the board of the YES Network and the Gold Shield Foundation, and has been a member of the board of the Ocala Breeders Sales Company. He has also been involved in a number of not-for-profit causes and children's charities in New York and Tampa Bay, including The Joshua House, St. Joseph's Children's Hospital, Gigi's Playhouse Tampa, The Children's Dream Fund and the New York Yankees' foundations.

In 2016, Mr. Steinbrenner, along with his son George Michael IV, made an entry into auto racing by contributing to the formation of Steinbrenner Racing. After racing two seasons in Indy Lights, a developmental circuit, the group announced in 2018 a partnership with Harding Racing. The 2019 season marked the inaugural year of Harding Steinbrenner Racing, which competes on the IndyCar circuit — with George Michael IV becoming the youngest team owner in IndyCar history.

Mr. Steinbrenner, who has four children and one granddaughter, attended Culver Military Academy and Central Methodist College and resides in Tampa, Fla.

Jennifer Steinbrenner Swindal
General Partner / Vice Chairperson

Jennifer Steinbrenner Swindal begins 2020 in her 12th full season in the role of General Partner / Vice Chairperson of the New York Yankees. She also serves as the President of the New York Yankees Foundation and the New York Yankees Tampa Foundation, overseeing numerous local, regional and national outreach efforts.

Within the scope of her roles, which include the implementation and integration of a wide range of community programs relating to the New York Yankees, Ms. Steinbrenner supervises three Tampa-area Children's Holiday Concerts that have been sponsored by the Steinbrenner family for more than 25 years. At least 5,000 children annually participate in the events, which provide musical education and exposure to the fine arts. She has also been instrumental in the development and growth of the Bronx Winter Wonderland event, which sees thousands of local youth visit the Stadium each year for a holiday extravaganza complete with decorations, festive music and food, and a holiday gift for each child in attendance.

Ms. Steinbrenner has a distinguished record of contributing to various community projects and initiatives, including current commitments on the Board of Directors of Mary Lee's House (a child protection and advocacy center in Tampa), St. Joseph's Children's Hospital Foundation, and Boys & Girls Club of Tampa Bay.

Ms. Steinbrenner also serves on the Executive Committee of the Gold Shield Foundation, which was established in 1981 by her father, George M. Steinbrenner III. The foundation, which currently covers seven counties in the Tampa Bay area, works to ensure that the families and dependent children of fallen police officers and firefighters receive early financial assistance and are guaranteed funds towards a college education.

In addition, Ms. Steinbrenner serves on the Board of Directors for Legends Hospitality, LLC, a holistic solution provider in the sports, music and entertainment industry, which offers expertise in global planning, sales and hospitality.

Having previously served in the Yankees Public Affairs Department in 1984-85 and spending 23 years actively participating in the philanthropic community, Ms. Steinbrenner has held prior board positions with the Children's Cancer Center of Tampa, Florida State Fair Authority (Executive Committee, Agricultural Committee, and Chairwoman of the Marketing Committee), H.B. Plant Museum at the University of Tampa, New York Pops, Harlem RBI, Florida Orchestra, Tampa Bay Salvation Army, Red Cross Angels of Tampa and Culver Academies. Additionally, Ms. Steinbrenner held the title of Senior Vice President of New Stadium Public Affairs in 2008.

A Morehead Scholar and 1981 graduate of the University of North Carolina with a Bachelor of Science degree in business administration, Ms. Steinbrenner previously served on the UNC Board of Visitors and Parents Council. Ms. Steinbrenner has two children, Haley Swindal Tantleff, and Stephen Swindal, who is the Yankees' Assistant Director of Player Development.

Ms. Steinbrenner was born in Cleveland, Ohio, and makes her home in Tampa, Fla.

Jessica Steinbrenner
General Partner / Vice Chairperson

Jessica Steinbrenner begins 2020 in her 12th full season as General Partner / Vice Chairperson for the New York Yankees. The younger daughter of George M. Steinbrenner previously served in the role of Senior Vice President for the team in 2008.

Ms. Steinbrenner is the owner of Bach Stables, LLC, a thoroughbred breeding and racing operation, and holds the position of Chief Executive Officer of the Steinbrenner-family-owned Bay Farms Corporation. She also served on the board of the Florida Thoroughbred Breeders' and Owners' Association. Ms. Steinbrenner is actively involved in the aftercare of retired thoroughbreds.

Ms. Steinbrenner served as the Executive Producer for the 2018 full length feature film *The Little Mermaid*, the live-action adaptation of Hans Christian Andersen's classic fairy tale. She has also authored two children's books: *My Sleepy Room* and *My Messy Room*.

Ms. Steinbrenner attended Culver Girls Academy and graduated from Sweet Briar College in Virginia. She has four children and three grandchildren, and currently resides in Tampa, Fla.

Randy Levine
President

Randy Levine begins his 21st season as President of the New York Yankees in 2020. He was named to his position in January 2000, becoming the first person to hold the post with the club since 1986.

Under his supervision and guidance, the franchise constructed the state-of-the-art Yankee Stadium, completing the facility on time for the beginning of the 2009 season, which culminated in the franchise's 27th World Championship. The Yankees have topped the American League in average home attendance in 16 of the last 17 seasons.

Mr. Levine was a principal founder of the YES Network, which is the most-watched regional sports network in the United States. He was also the lead negotiator in the sale of 80 percent of the network to 21st Century Fox and in 2019 led the negotiation to buy the YES Network from the Disney Company along with partners Amazon, Sinclair Broadcasting, Blackstone, Mubadala and Red Bird Capital. Today, Mr. Levine is the Chairman of the Board of the YES Network. In 2008, Mr. Levine was instrumental in creating Legends Hospitality, LLC, with the Dallas Cowboys, which currently operates at the Yankees' and Cowboys' stadiums, as well as many other world famous venues, including One World Observatory. In 2004, he helped organize Yankees-Steiner, a leading sports memorabilia company.

Mr. Levine has also spearheaded the Yankees' international brand expansion, including a transformational partnership in 2013 with Manchester City Football Club to acquire Major League Soccer's 20th expansion team. New York City Football Club (NYCFC) began play in 2015 at Yankee Stadium and has drawn more than 2 million fans in home attendance through its first five seasons. In 2010, Mr. Levine led a Yankees delegation that visited Tokyo, Beijing and Hong Kong with the 2009 World Series Trophy, marking the first-ever time that the Yankees brought one of their World Series trophies to Asia. In addition, Mr. Levine helped develop the joint venture agreement in Japan between the Yankees and Yomiuri Shimbun, which is the parent company of the Yomiuri Giants.

In 2007 alone, the Yankees became the first Major League organization to sign players from the Israel Baseball League, embarked on their first-ever large-scale outreach into Taiwan by holding a clinic for high school players and coaches in Taipei, Taiwan, and established a first-of-its-kind working relationship with the Chinese Baseball Association. Mr. Levine is also the Yankees' principal liaison to Major League Baseball and contributes to player negotiations and contract issues.

Mr. Levine has been at the forefront of bringing a diverse array of entertainment and special events to Yankee Stadium, transforming the venue into a year-round destination for a variety of college football, soccer, hockey, music, boxing and corporate events. Highlights have included the January 2014 Coors Light NHL Stadium Series featuring the New York Rangers, New York Islanders and New Jersey Devils; international soccer matches showcasing the likes of Manchester City, Liverpool, Real Madrid, AC Milan, Paris Saint-Germain and Chelsea; concerts by Paul McCartney, Madonna, Garth Brooks, JAY Z, Justin Timberlake, Eminem and Romeo Santos; as well as renewing the tradition of college football at the home of the Yankees with over a dozen games featuring iconic institutions such as Notre Dame, Army, Boston College, Syracuse and Penn State.

The Yankees president has also been the driving force behind the creation, organization and implementation of the New Era Pinstripe Bowl. The nationally broadcast contest — which has drawn approximately 40,000 fans per game since its inception in 2010 — provides the schools, their alumni and traveling supporters the unparalleled and thoroughly unique opportunity to enjoy a full week of bowl festivities in New York City during Christmas week. In 2018, Mr. Levine organized a Yankees investment in prominent esports company Vision Esports.

Before joining the Yankees, Mr. Levine served as New York City's Deputy Mayor for Economic Development, Planning and Administration. He also served as New York City's Labor Commissioner.

From 1995 through 1997, Mr. Levine was Chief Negotiator for Major League Baseball. In 1996, he negotiated the labor agreement that for the first time included revenue sharing, luxury taxes and Interleague play. Prior to that, Mr. Levine served as Principal Associate Deputy Attorney General and Principal Deputy Attorney General at the United States Department of Justice. He has also served as a special delegate to the United States Department of Labor and was vice chair and a board member for the Hudson River Park. Mr. Levine presently serves on the board of the Taylor Hooton Foundation and Hofstra University, and has served on the Boards of the ASPCA, George Washington University and the Yogi Berra Museum.

Mr. Levine has served on the Board of Directors of the New Jersey Nets and New Jersey Devils and is a member of the Board of Directors of the YES Network, Legends Hospitality, LLC, and NYCFC. He is also an officer of Yankee Global Enterprises, LLC. Additionally, Mr. Levine has served or serves on the International, Labor Policy, Diversity and Legislative Committees of Major League Baseball.

Mr. Levine has been a partner in the New York law firm of Proskauer Rose Goetz & Mendelson, was Counsel at the law firm of Akin Gump Strauss Hauer & Feld, and is presently Counsel at the law firm of Jackson Lewis P.C.

Born on February 22, 1955, in Brooklyn, N.Y., Mr. Levine received a Bachelor of Arts degree from George Washington University in 1977, and in 2011 was named as Chair of the school's athletic committee. His strategic plan led to the GW basketball team winning its first National Championship, the 2016 National Invitation Tournament. He now serves as vice chair of the Hofstra Athletic Committee. In 2018, *City & State* magazine named Mr. Levine one of its 50 over 50 leaders in New York, and *Business Week* listed him as one of the top 100 influential persons in sports. Mr. Levine has also garnered five Emmy Awards for his work with YES Network programming. He received his J.D. from Hofstra University School of Law in 1980. Mr. Levine and his wife, Mindy, reside in Manhattan.

New York Yankees Presidents
(Chief Executive Officers)

Joseph W. Gordon	1903-06	Michael Burke	1966-73
Frank J. Farrell	1907-14	Gabe Paul	1973-77
Jacob Ruppert	1915-39	Al Rosen	1978-79
Ed Barrow	1939-45	George M. Steinbrenner	1979-80
Larry MacPhail	1945-47	Lou Saban	1981-82
Daniel R. Topping	1947-53	Eugene McHale	1983-86
Dan Topping / Del E. Webb	1954-64	RANDY LEVINE	2000-present
Dan Topping	1964-66		

Yankees president Frank Farrell presents a trophy to Yankees manager Harry Wolverton as Red Sox and Yankees players look on at Hilltop Park on April 11, 1912.

Lonn A. Trost
Chief Operating Officer

Lonn A. Trost begins his 21st season as Chief Operating Officer of the New York Yankees in 2020. He was named to the position on January 10, 2000, after serving as the club's Executive Vice President from 1997-99. Mr. Trost was also Yankees General Counsel from 1997-2019, covering a span of 23 years.

Mr. Trost is responsible for the overall day-to-day functioning of the Yankees' operations. Under his direction, the Yankees have seen tremendous growth in brand recognition and sponsorship opportunities, while drawing more than 3 million fans at home for a Major League-record 21 consecutive seasons. During that stretch, the Yankees established single-season home attendance records nine times (1998-99; 2002-08). In addition, the Yankees have topped the American League in average home attendance in 16 of the last 17 seasons.

Additionally, Mr. Trost, along with Hal Steinbrenner and Randy Levine, spearheaded the most complex undertaking in New York Yankees history — construction and development of Yankee Stadium, which is the largest privately funded building project in the history of the Bronx. While remaining true to the architectural grandeur of the 1923 original, the current facility is one of the most technologically advanced sports venues in the world. In the 2016-17 offseason, Mr. Trost facilitated a series of major structural enhancements designed to improve the experience for all fans at Yankee Stadium. The new upgrades included a first-ever children's play zone and seven new social gathering spaces.

Mr. Trost has played a significant role in Yankee Stadium becoming a year-round multi-purpose home to special events. Since 2010, Yankee Stadium has played host to an array of landmark activities that transcend baseball, including the 2014 Coors Light NHL Stadium Series featuring the New York Rangers, New York Islanders and New Jersey Devils; concerts by Paul McCartney, Madonna, Garth Brooks, JAY Z, Romeo Santos, Justin Timberlake and Eminem; a world championship boxing match between Miguel Cotto and Yuri Foreman; as well as renewing the tradition of college football at the home of the Yankees with games featuring iconic institutions such as Notre Dame and Army. In addition, Mr. Trost has been an integral figure in the development and growth of the New Era Pinstripe Bowl — held annually for the last 10 years during Christmas week. The event has averaged approximately 40,000 fans since its inception in 2010.

Mr. Trost was also responsible for reintroducing a long-dormant Yankees tradition of hosting marquee professional soccer at Yankee Stadium. Since 2012, some of the most high-profile soccer teams in the world — AC Milan, Chelsea, Liverpool, Manchester City, Paris Saint-Germain and Real Madrid — have played summertime matches in front of more than 200,000 fans. In 2013, the Yankees established a partnership with Manchester City Football Club and jointly acquired Major League Soccer's 20th expansion team. New York City Football Club (NYCFC) began play in 2015 at Yankee Stadium and has drawn more than 2 million in MLS home attendance through its first five seasons.

Before joining the Yankees, Mr. Trost was a partner and member of the Executive Committee of the law firm of Shea and Gould from 1972 to 1994. He was also a partner at the New York law firm of Herrick, Feinstein from 1994 through 1997. While with these firms, he served as outside general counsel for numerous sports franchises, institutions and agents. Among his clients were the New York Yankees and Mets, the New Jersey Nets and Devils, the National Baseball Hall of Fame and Little League Baseball.

Mr. Trost was instrumental in the creation of the YES Network and is a member of its Board of Directors. In addition, he serves as an officer and on the Board of Directors for Yankee Global Enterprises and is on the Board of Directors for Legends Hospitality, both of which he participated in founding. While he maintains his responsibilities with the New York Yankees Partnership and the Yankees' other affiliates, he is also involved with the Tourette Syndrome Association.

Mr. Trost began his legal career in 1971 with the U.S. Justice Department, Office of Chief Counsel (Treasury Department). A 1968 graduate of Hunter College in the Bronx, Mr. Trost received his J.D. from Brooklyn Law School in 1971. It's interesting to note that Mr. Trost's initial employment with the Yankees was as a grandstand vendor in the mid-1960s in the original Yankee Stadium. He resides in Monroe Township, N.J., with his wife, Carol. They have two children, Evan and Audra, and four grandchildren, Ariella, Alexander, Bryn and Brooklyn.

Brian Cashman
Senior Vice President, General Manager

Brian McGuire Cashman has literally grown up in the Yankees family. He joined the organization in 1986 as a 19-year-old intern in the Minor League and Scouting Department and now holds one of the most demanding jobs in sports as Yankees Senior Vice President and General Manager.

Over the course of his 34 seasons with the team, he has earned five World Series rings, including four as General Manager. Since the Dodgers' Buzzie Bavasi in the 1950s and 60s, Mr. Cashman is the only general manager to win four World Series titles in that role. Notably, he has won his titles with two different managers — Joe Torre in 1998, 1999 and 2000, and Joe Girardi in 2009.

Mr. Cashman assumed his current post on February 3, 1998. At age 30, he became the second-youngest General Manager in Baseball history. In his first season, he became the youngest-ever GM to win a World Series, and with championships in 1999 and 2000, he became the only GM in Baseball history to win world titles in each of his first three seasons. A pennant in 2001 gave him four straight League Championships, placing him alongside Hall of Fame Yankees General Managers Ed Barrow (1936-39, four) and George Weiss (1949-53, five) as the only GMs in Baseball history to win four-or-more straight league titles at any point in their careers.

Among his peers, Mr. Cashman has achieved unparalleled success while carrying on the winning tradition of the Yankees. His lifetime winning percentage of .589 (2,098-1,462-2) is the highest of any General Manager with at least 10 seasons of experience whose career began in 1950 or later and marks the best team winning percentage in the Major Leagues during that same stretch. Now in his 23rd season, Mr. Cashman is the longest-tenured General Manager in baseball and is the longest-serving Yankees GM since Barrow led the team from October 28, 1920, through February 20, 1945.

With the start of Mr. Cashman's ascension to the GM role in 1998 and continuing through the 2019 season, the Yankees own the best record in Major League Baseball for any stretch of at least 10 seasons, including the most recent such stretch spanning the 2010 through 2019 seasons.

In all, his clubs have earned 18 berths in the playoffs, including 13 Division titles, six AL pennants and four World Series titles. His feat of reaching the playoffs in each of his first 10 seasons (1998-2007) remains unmatched in Baseball history. In addition, the Yankees have won at least 84 games in all 22 seasons of Mr. Cashman's tenure as General Manager, while the most any other team has reached that plateau over the stretch has been 18 times (Boston). Mr. Cashman has also overseen the growth of the Yankees' Player Development program that has consistently infused the Major League roster with young, elite talent in recent years. By producing the AL "Rookie of the Year" winner Aaron Judge in 2017, as well as runners-up Gary Sánchez in 2016 and Miguel Andújar in 2018, the Yankees were the first club to place a player in the top-two in "Rookie of the Year" voting in three consecutive seasons since the Seattle Mariners from 1999-2001.

There have been four women in Major League history to hold the position of Assistant General Manager, and Mr. Cashman has hired two of them: Jean Afterman, the Yankees' current Senior Vice President and Assistant General Manager; and Kim Ng, who worked for the Yankees from 1998-2001 and currently holds the position of Senior Vice President, Baseball & Softball Development for Major League Baseball.

Various groups have honored the achievements of the Yankees and Mr. Cashman. With the club's most recent World Series title, the Yankees were named "2009 Male Team of the Year" by the United States Sports Academy and were nominated as "Team of the Year" in the Laureus World Sports Awards competition. In both 1998 and 2000, the Yankees earned ESPY Awards — presented by ESPN — as "Outstanding Team of the Year," and were named "Organization of the Year" by *Baseball America* in 1998 and by *USA Today* in 1999.

Mr. Cashman has been honored as "Executive of the Year" six times: by *Baseball America* in 2017; the Boston Chapter of the BBWAA in 2000, 2009 and 2017; and in 1999 and 2003 by the New Jersey Sportswriters'

Best Winning Percentage for General Managers Whose Careers Began in 1950 or Later
(Min: 1,000 wins / *Active / Incl. Supervisors of Baseball Ops. with Other Titles / Excludes ties)

General Manager	Seasons (Years)	Record	Pct.
1. **BRIAN CASHMAN***	22 (1998-present)	2,098-1,462	.589
2. John Schuerholz	26 (1982-2007)	2,348-1,794	.567
3. Bob Howsam	15 (1964-77, '84)	1,294-1,010	.562
4. John Mozeliak*	12 (2008-present)	1,076-868	.553
5. Al Campanis	19 (1969-87)	1,576-1,283	.551
6. Theo Epstein*	17 (2003-present)	1,510-1,244	.548
7. Chub Feeney	20 (1950-69)	1,724-1,425	.547
8. Andrew Friedman*	14 (2006-present)	1,238-1,031	.546
9. Frank Cashen	15 (1972-75, '80-90)	1,265-1,093	.536
10. John McHale	16 (1957-66, '79-84)	1,317-1,144	.535

Credit: Bill Arnold of Sports Features Group

Association. In 2001, he received his third consecutive "40 Under 40" Award presented by *Street & Smith's Sports Business Journal* to recognize the top 40 people under the age of 40 who have made the greatest impact in the sports business industry. He has since been inducted into the publication's "40 Under 40" Hall of Fame. In 2003, Mr. Cashman was honored by the Latino Sports Writers and Broadcasters Association with their annual "Latino Achievement Award" for his contributions to the Latino media.

Philanthropy and community involvement play equally important roles in Mr. Cashman's scope of work. For the past 10 years he has served on the Board of Directors of Covenant House International, which provides services for homeless youth. He was honored by the organization with their Beacon of Hope Award in 2011, having participated in the group's CEO Solidarity Sleepout in each of the last nine years. In 2019, Cashman and the Yankees hosted the event at Yankee Stadium, where Covenant House supporters raised money and drew attention to the cause by sleeping outside in the Stadium's Great Hall.

In each of the last 10 offseasons, Mr. Cashman has rappelled down the 22-story Landmark Building in Stamford, Conn., as part of the Christmas-themed Heights and Lights Program, promoting activity in the city's downtown business district. In 2013, he joined the Board of Directors for TGEN (Translational Genomics Research Institute) Pancreatic Cancer. He also traveled to Vermont in November 2011 to join fellow GMs Theo Epstein and Neal Huntington at an event organized by ESPN's Buster Olney to support farm relief in the wake of Tropical Storm Irene.

For his efforts at work and in the community, Mr. Cashman was presented with the 2018 Joan Payson/Shannon Forde Community Service Award by the N.Y. Chapter of the BBWAA and the 2016 Jacob K. Javits Lifetime Achievement Award by the ALS Association Greater New York Chapter. He was also recognized by the Catholic Youth Organization of New York with the 2011 John V. Mara Sportsman of the Year Award and the 2005 Ossie Davis Award for Inspirational Leadership for promoting diversity in the workplace.

His career as a full-time Yankees employee began following his graduation from Catholic University in 1989, when Mr. Cashman became a full-time Assistant in Baseball Operations. He was later promoted and transferred to Tampa, Fla., where he served as Assistant Farm Director from 1990 to 1992. He returned to New York and became Assistant General Manager, Baseball Administration in November 1992.

Born on July 3, 1967, in Rockville Centre, N.Y., Mr. Cashman grew up in Lexington, Ky. He attended Georgetown Prep in Rockville, Md., and was inducted into the school's Athletic Hall of Fame in 2015. Mr. Cashman attended Catholic University in Washington, D.C., where he majored in history. He also played intercollegiate baseball for the Cardinals, breaking the then-team record for hits in a single season. Mr. Cashman will be inducted into Catholic University's Athletic Hall of Fame in 2020. His love for baseball developed when former Brooklyn Dodger Ralph Branca and his wife, Ann, arranged for him to serve as a batboy for the Los Angeles Dodgers in spring training in 1982.

NEW YORK YANKEES DURING BRIAN CASHMAN'S TENURE

Year	Record	Win%	Fin. in AL East
1998*	**114**-48-0	.704	1st (+22.0G)
1999*	**98**-64-0	.605	1st (+4.0G)
2000*	87-74-0	.540	1st (+2.5G)
2001*	95-65-1	.594	1st (+13.5G)
2002*	*103*-58-0	.640	1st (+10.5G)
2003*	**101**-61-1	.623	1st (+6.0G)
2004*	**101**-61-0	.623	1st (+3.0G)
2005*	95-67-0	.586	1st (tied)
2006*	**97**-65-0	.599	1st (+10.0G)
2007*	94-68-0	.580	2nd (-2.0G)
2008	89-73-0	.549	3rd (-8.0G)
2009*	**103**-59-0	.636	1st (+8.0G)
2010*	95-67-0	.586	2nd (-1.0G)
2011*	**97**-65-0	.599	1st (+6.0G)
2012*	**95**-67-0	.586	1st (+2.0G)
2013	85-77-0	.525	T3rd (-12.0G)
2014	84-78-0	.519	2nd (-12.0G)
2015*	87-75-0	.537	2nd (-6.0)
2016	84-78-0	.519	4th (-9.0)
2017*	91-71-0	.562	2nd (-2.0)
2018*	100-62-0	.617	2nd (-8.0)
2019*	103-59-0	.636	1st (+7.0G)
	2,098-1,462-2	.589	

Bold=most wins in AL
Italic=tied for most wins in AL
* Qualified for postseason (18 of 22 seasons)

Five times under Cashman, the Yankees have recorded the most wins in the Majors: 1998, 2002 (tied w/ OAK), 2003 (tied w/ ATL), 2006 (tied w/ NYM), 2009.

The Yankees' .589 winning pct. under Cashman marks the highest for any MLB team over the stretch (1998-present). Additionally, the club's 2,098 regular season wins over the span are 120 more than the second-best team (BOS-1,978).

For the past 10 years, **Brian Cashman** has served on the Board of Directors of Covenant House International, which provides services for homeless youth. He was honored by the organization with their Beacon of Hope Award in 2011. Additionally in each of the last nine years, Cashman has participated in the group's CEO Solidarity Sleepout to raise money and draw attention to its cause.

Jean Afterman
Senior Vice President, Assistant General Manager

Jean Afterman enters her 19th season as the Yankees' Assistant General Manager and ninth as Senior Vice President in 2020. She became only the third female to hold the position of Assistant General Manager in Major League Baseball history.

Ms. Afterman has been an integral part of the Yankees' efforts and operations in Asia. In her first year with the Yankees, she was instrumental in developing the club's relationship with the Yomiuri Giants of the Japan Central League and signing three-time MVP Hideki Matsui. In 2007, she joined team President Randy Levine and General Manager Brian Cashman on a week-long trip to Asia that concluded with a working agreement with the Chinese Baseball Association. She once again joined Levine and Cashman in 2010, when the Yankees brought the 2009 World Series trophy to Tokyo, Beijing and Hong Kong. While in Hong Kong, Ms. Afterman was given the honor of throwing out one of the ceremonial first pitches at the 2010 Phoenix Cup, an annual international women's baseball tournament.

Her contributions and leadership have been repeatedly recognized throughout her baseball career. Ms. Afterman was selected as one of the "50 Most Powerful Women in New York" by the *New York Post* in 2003 and 2007, and was named one of the 2004 "Power 100" by the *Sporting News*. In 2007, Ms. Afterman was profiled as one of *Crain's New York Business*' "100 Most Influential Women in New York Business," and in 2008, she was noted by *Forbes* as one of the top female executives in Baseball. In 2010, Ms. Afterman was named by WISE (Women in Sports and Events) as one of the "Women of the Year," and was tabbed by *New York Moves* magazine as a "Power Woman." In 2013, she was again profiled on the front page of her hometown newspaper, the *San Francisco Chronicle*. In 2017, she was named one of *Street & Smith's Sports Business Journal's* "Game Changers," and her story was featured on the YES Network and ESPN.com. Most recently, she was named one of *Crain's New York Business* "2019 Most Notable Women in the Business of Sports," and was awarded *Baseball America's* "2019 Trailblazer of the Year Award," becoming the inaugural winner of the honor.

Ms. Afterman is a frequent guest speaker on the topics of women in sports and the business of baseball, having participated in events sponsored by Major League Baseball, Columbia Business School, New York University, SABR, Beyond Sport, the Sports Lawyers Association and WISE, among others. In 2018 and 2019, Ms. Afterman was a member of the Steering Committee for the Integrity and Impact Award presented at the BT Sport Industry Awards in London.

Ms. Afterman joined the Yankees with a diverse business and legal background, focusing on international sports and licensing with an emphasis on U.S.-Japan matters. Prior to joining the Yankees, she managed her own practice, providing athletic representation and management with a specialization in arbitration proceedings. From 1994-99, Ms. Afterman was General Counsel at KDN Sports, Inc., and handled business and legal affairs for international baseball clients, including Hideo Nomo, Hideki Irabu, Masato Yoshii, Alfonso Soriano and more than 30 Major and Minor League players. In 1996, Ms. Afterman was appointed by the U.S. Secretary of Agriculture to a federal advisory committee, the National Organic Standards Board.

A graduate of the University of California at Berkeley in 1979, Ms. Afterman was the recipient of the Rosalynn Schneider Eisner Prize and the Mark Goodson Scholarship Grant. She received her J.D. from the University of San Francisco School of Law in 1991. In 2009, she was named "Alumni of the Year" by the Katherine Delmar Burke School in San Francisco.

Ms. Afterman maintains an active role in the Bronx community, working closely with P.S. 35, an elementary school within walking distance from Yankee Stadium. Over the last 12 years, she has organized Yankees-sponsored Read-A-Thons and directed a mentoring program which matches Yankees employees with fourth and fifth grade students. Additionally, she has worked with high school-aged students through New York City's Explorers program, which engages young people through career-orientation programs. She received the 2009 "Exploring Leadership Award" for her work with the group. In 2012 and 2013, she served on the Board of Trustees of the Women's Sports Foundation, and in 2015, she was appointed to serve on the advisory committee that oversees the Commissioner's Front Office and Field Staff Diversity Pipeline Program. In 2018, Ms. Afterman joined the Board of Directors of DREAM (formerly Harlem RBI), and in 2020, she joined the Board of the Major League Baseball Players Alumni Association.

Michael Fishman
Vice President, Assistant General Manager

Michael Fishman begins his third season as a Vice President and sixth season as an Assistant General Manager, working with General Manager Brian Cashman in all areas related to baseball operations, including player acquisitions and evaluation, roster management, staffing and personnel decisions, player contract negotiations and salary arbitration. In addition, he oversees all aspects of the club's baseball research, statistical analysis, and baseball information systems.

The 2020 season marks his 16th year with the Yankees organization, having been hired by the club in July 2005 as a Baseball Operations Analyst. From November 2006 through the 2014 season, he was the club's first Director of Quantitative Analysis, responsible for all of the Yankees' proprietary baseball operations systems and assembling a staff devoted to quantitative research. In this role, he oversaw all statistical research projects, providing information, recommendations and advance scouting reports to the baseball operations department and coaching staff. He also oversaw the baseball operations internship program.

Prior to joining the Yankees, Mr. Fishman was an actuarial associate with AXA Equitable Life Insurance Company.

Born in New York City and raised in Fairfield, Conn., Mr. Fishman graduated summa cum laude and Phi Beta Kappa from Yale University in 2001 with a Bachelor of Arts in Mathematics.

Over the last several seasons, Mr. Fishman has regularly given his time to school-age children and graduate students, speaking to them on a variety of topics related to the application of mathematics in the professional world.

He resides in Westchester Co., N.Y., with his wife, Sheryl, his daughter, JJ, and his son, Ellis.

Tim Naehring
Vice President, Baseball Operations

Tim Naehring begins his fifth season as Vice President of Baseball Operations with the Yankees, assisting General Manager Brian Cashman with player acquisitions, roster management and evaluation of all player personnel.

This season marks his 13th with the Yankees, having served as a professional scout from the fall of 2007 through the end of the 2015 season. After covering the minors and Majors in 2008, he was primarily responsible for covering the National League and crosschecking the American League from 2009-15.

Mr. Naehring began his front office career with the Cincinnati Reds during spring training in 1999, becoming a special assistant to general manager Jim Bowden. From October 2000 through 2005, he was the Reds' Director of Player Development, and he also held the role of Minor League Field Coordinator from October 2000 through 2003 and during the 2006 and 2007 seasons.

A native and current resident of Cincinnati, Mr. Naehring is a 1985 graduate of La Salle High School, where he was a three-sport athlete in baseball, soccer and basketball. He attended Miami (Ohio) University from 1985-88 and was named Mid-American Conference Player of the Year after his final season.

In June of 1988, he was drafted by the Boston Red Sox in the eighth round of the First-Year Player Draft. Mr. Naehring went on to play parts of eight Major League seasons with Boston from 1990-97, batting .282 (527-for-1,872) with 49 home runs and 250 RBI in 547 career games before a torn right elbow ligament ended his career on June 23, 1997.

In 1996, Mr. Naehring founded the Athletes Reaching Out Foundation (ARO), which has funded various good works in the greater Cincinnati area, including a mini-Fenway Park in Miamitown, Ohio.

He and his wife, Kris, have a daughter, Jamison, and a son, J.T.

Damon Oppenheimer
Vice President, Domestic Amateur Scouting

Damon Oppenheimer enters his 28th season with the Yankees and 18th as a Vice President in the organization's scouting department. Since 2005, Mr. Oppenheimer has fully directed the Yankees' efforts related to Major League Baseball's First-Year Player Draft, including the evaluation of all eligible players and the Yankees' selections. As part of his responsibilities, he manages all of the club's crosscheckers and area scouts throughout the United States, Canada and Puerto Rico.

Mr. Oppenheimer was twice honored during the 2018-19 offseason. He was first acknowledged by his scouting peers at the Baseball Winter Meetings with the 2018 "West Coast Scout of the Year Award." Then in January 2019, he received the "George Genovese Lifetime Achievement in Scouting Award" from the Professional Baseball Scouts Foundation at the 16th Annual "In the Spirit of the Game" Awards Dinner.

This season marks his sixth with the title of Vice President of Domestic Amateur Scouting. Between 2003 and 2014, he held various other Vice President titles, including those for Amateur Scouting (2007-14), Scouting (2005-06), Player Development and Scouting (2004) and Professional Scouting (2003).

A native of San Diego, Calif., Mr. Oppenheimer began his player development career as a part-time scout for the Padres while finishing his degree at the University of Southern California. He was hired as a full-time scout by San Diego in 1988, continuing in that role until he joined the Yankees as the Midwest crosschecker in 1993.

Mr. Oppenheimer became the team's Western crosschecker for the 1995 season and briefly joined the Texas Rangers as a national crosschecker from November 1995 through July 1996 before returning to the Yankees in August 1996 as a national crosschecker. He also served as the Yankees' director of player personnel from 2000-02.

The former USC catcher batted .364 in 1985, earning Pac-10 All-Conference honorable mention before being selected by Milwaukee in the 18th round of that June's First-Year Player Draft. He appeared in 12 games for Single-A Beloit in 1985 before getting injured the following year in spring training, ending his professional playing career. Mr. Oppenheimer returned to school and received his bachelor's degree in exercise science in 1987.

He and his wife, Tina, reside in Wesley Chapel, Fla., and have three children: A.J., Sierra and Gehrig.

Kevin Reese
Senior Director, Player Development

Kevin Reese begins his 19th year with the Yankees organization, his 13th as a scout or member of the front office, and his third as Senior Director of Player Development.

Mr. Reese joined the Yankees Pro Scouting Department at the conclusion of his playing career and held the title of Professional Scout from 2008 through 2014. For the three seasons from 2015-17, he was the Yankees' Director of Pro Scouting, overseeing the coordination of scout coverages and the intake of reports while using compiled information to help guide trade discussions and free agent signings. Additionally, Mr. Reese scouted the Yankees' own affiliates, organized advance scouting for the postseason and contributed to the construction of the Yankees' Major League and minor league rosters.

A native of San Diego, Mr. Reese was originally selected by the Padres in the 27th round of the 2000 First-Year Player Draft from the University of San Diego, where he was a two-time West Coast Conference first-team selection and later named to the West Coast Conference's 40th Anniversary All-Conference Team in 2007. On December 18, 2001, he was acquired by the Yankees in exchange for infielder Bernabel Castro.

Over 849 games across eight minor league seasons from 2000-07 (including 2000-01 with the Padres organization), Mr. Reese, a left-handed-hitting outfielder, posted a .292 (953-for-3,269) batting average with 546 runs scored, 192 doubles, 37 triples, 67 home runs, 395 RBI, 372 walks, 138 stolen bases, a .370 on-base percentage and an .804 OPS. Mr. Reese also appeared in 12 Major League games with the Yankees over two seasons (2005-06), batting .385 (5-for-13) with two runs scored, one RBI, two walks and one stolen base.

He and his wife, Laura, reside in Odessa, Fla., and have four children: Jackson, Kannon, Brooklyn and Gwynn.

Yankees HOPE Week 2019

Last year marked the Yankees' 11th annual HOPE Week (Helping Others Persevere & Excel) – an initiative rooted in the belief that acts of goodwill provide hope and encouragement to more than just the recipient of the gesture.

Each day during HOPE Week, the Yankees reach out to an individual, family or organization worthy of recognition and support. Whenever possible, the Yankees will attempt to personally connect with individuals in the settings of their greatest successes at locations that honor the spirit of their noble endeavors. All outreach in the community ultimately culminates with recognition at Yankee Stadium during a Yankees game.

HOPE Week is about people helping people. The one thing everybody has—no matter their background or financial situation—is time. By involving every one of our players and coaches, along with Manager Aaron Boone, General Manager Brian Cashman, our minor league affiliates and front office staff, we are sending the message that everyone can give of themselves to make their community a better place. Equally significant during HOPE Week is garnering publicity for the highlighted causes and organizations. The greatest challenge facing many not-for-profits is generating interest, awareness and funding for their missions.

The Yankees encourage all their fans to get involved … Give HOPE!

MONDAY, JUNE 17

The Yankees kicked off HOPE Week with a daytime reunion/party on the field at Yankee Stadium featuring the bulk of Yankees honoree alumni…**Bench Coach Josh Bard, Brett Gardner, Quality Control Coach/Infield Instructor Carlos Mendoza, 3B Coach Phil Nevin, CC Sabathia, Gary Sánchez, Hitting Coach Marcus Thames, Assistant Hitting Coach P.J. Pilittere** and **1B Coach Reggie Willits** joined the festivities for a morning filled with activities like running the bases, wiffle ball, face painting and carnival games. The group, composed of more than 200 Yankees honoree alumni, participated in the pregame ceremony by entering the field through center field and walking along the warning track. Prior to that evening's game, members of 2011 HOPE Week honoree **Daniel's Music Foundation** performed the national anthem, and the ceremonial first pitch was thrown by 2015 honoree **Chris Singleton**.

TUESDAY, JUNE 18

On Tuesday, the Yankees honored **Runway Heroes**, a New York City-based nonprofit that helps children with cancer forget about their illness for a few days and provides them a unique opportunity to feel like the stars they are. **General Manager Brian Cashman, Aroldis Chapman, Domingo Germán, Didi Gregorius, Kendrys Morales, Luis Severino** and **Masahiro Tanaka** joined the founder of Runway Heroes, Rachel Goldman, to surprise children with cancer and their families for a fashion show at Kleinfeld Bridal. With the help of the Yankees players and staff, the children got ready for their big day in the spotlight and were escorted down the runway.

Yankees players and staff hosted HOPE Week honorees at Yankee Stadium for the 10th anniversary reunion. The event honored more than 200 HOPE Week alumni.

Dressed to impress, Aroldis Chapman escorts a young Runway Hero during a fashion show held at the iconic Kleinfeld Bridal in Manhattan.

President's Volunteer Service Award

At the conclusion of each of the last 10 HOPE Weeks (2010-19), the Yankees and/or its affiliates were honored with the **President's Volunteer Service Award**, given "in recognition and appreciation of commitment to strengthening the Nation and for making a difference through volunteer service." The award was bestowed by the President's Council on Service and Civic Participation in conjunction with the Corporation for National and Community Service. Each of this year's HOPE Week honorees also received the award.

WEDNESDAY, JUNE 19

On Wednesday, the Yankees recognized **Olmedo Rentería "Olmedini el Mago."** Born in Ecuador in the 1940s, Olmedini has performed his magic routine throughout the New York City subways for three decades. Dressed in one of his trademark ornate tuxedos, the blind magician hops from train to train with his assistants by his side, a rabbit in his hat and who-knows-what up his sleeve, entertaining travelers in both Spanish and English throughout the day. **Luis Cessa, Nestor Cortes Jr., Chad Green, David Hale, Tommy Kahnle** and **James Paxton** surprised Olmedini at his home and assisted him with magic shows on the subway and for a class of P.S. 73 school children at Yankee Stadium. He was also presented with associate membership into the Society of American Magicians.

THURSDAY, JUNE 20

On Thursday, the Yankees celebrated the efforts of **Furniture Sharehouse**, a nonprofit organization that provides individuals and families with the basic household furnishings they need free of charge, enabling them to rebuild their lives with dignity. The nonprofit collects gently-used furniture and distributes it to individuals referred to them by social service agencies. **Zack Britton, J.A. Happ, Bullpen Coach Mike Harkey, Jonathan Holder, Austin Romine, Gleyber Torres, Gio Urshela** and **Luke Voit** surprised the staff and two families that had appointments to select furniture. The Yankees players assisted the families selecting their furniture while sharing stories and laughs. Following the selection process the players sat down with the Furniture Sharehouse staff and the families to eat lunch together.

Olmedo Rentería "Olmedini el Mago" performs a magic trick in front of P.S. 73 students at Plymouth Rock Kids Clubhouse inside Yankee Stadium.

Yankees players J.A. Happ [L] and Gleyber Torres [R] help select and label a piece of furniture for one of the families at the Furniture Sharehouse warehouse.

FRIDAY, JUNE 21

To cap off HOPE Week 2019, the Yankees recognized **Sandra Alfonzo**, founder of **AdaptAbility**. Born in Brooklyn and raised in Puerto Rico, Alfonzo created AdaptAbility to customize adaptive bicycles for children with special needs, allowing them to exercise, improve mobility, and experience the joy of bike riding. Each bicycle is tailored to the child's challenges and goals and donated to families free of charge, allowing them to increase their quality of life. **Manager Aaron Boone, Coach Jason Brown, Aaron Hicks, DJ LeMahieu, Cameron Maybin** and **Adam Ottavino** joined Kiko Mina and his family as he received a custom-built tandem bicycle for his first ride at a park in the South Slope section of Brooklyn.

Yankees players and staff (L to R) DJ LeMahieu, Cameron Maybin, Adam Ottavino, Manager Aaron Boone, Aaron Hicks and Coach Jason Brown share a laugh with Kiko Mina and his family, as well as founder of AdaptAbility Sandra Alfonzo.

Organizational Initiative

The Yankees are proud that 2019 marked the eighth consecutive year that each of their seven U.S.-based affiliates held their own HOPE Weeks, truly making the initiative one that the entire organization stands behind in words and in action.

Commitment to Community

*T*he New York Yankees are committed to promoting and sustaining cordial and cooperative relationships with their neighbors and community partners; working in conjunction with them to enhance the quality of life throughout the surrounding communities. On a consistent basis, the Yankees partner with community-based organizations to host events at Yankee Stadium and dedicate several millions of dollars in resources to support various outreach efforts that focus on providing positive educational, recreational and social outlets for New York City residents.

ARTS

El Museo del Barrio: In recognition of El Museo del Barrio's community initiatives and focus, the Yankees partnered with the museum to support their efforts associated with bilingual public programs, educational activities, festivals and special events. Located in the East Harlem section of New York City, El Museo's mission is to present and preserve the art of all Latin Americans in the United States and educate its diverse public in the richness of Caribbean and Latin American cultural history. To honor the 50th anniversary of El Museo del Barrio, the Yankees recognized students and staff during an on-field pregame ceremony on September 3, 2019, and invited the group to sit in the Judge's Chambers for that game.

LEAP: Learning through an Expanded Arts Program, Inc. (LeAp) is committed to countering illiteracy and improving the quality of public education for students through a unique, hands-on, arts-based approach to teaching the core curriculum. LeAp also implements an early childhood literacy program called Active Learning Leads to Literacy (ALLL) that is respectively endorsed by both the New York City and United States Departments of Education. ALLL provides in-school services for students to participate in sessions that enhance reading and writing skills, and workshops for parents to reinforce their children's learning at home. LeAp's programming reaches more than two million NYC students, K-12th grade. Through the consistent support of the New York Yankees Foundation and fundraising efforts, resources have been dedicated to enhance these efforts.

Highbridge Voices: The Yankees are committed to supporting efforts to ensure excellence in the lives of children through their active participation in the performing arts. In addition to being provided with various resources, local community group Highbridge Voices was invited to perform the National Anthem before a game on June 18, 2019 as well as perform holiday music during the Yankees annual Winter Wonderland event. Highbridge Voices in an extended-day music and academic program designed to inspire excellence in the lives of children.

On June 18, 2019, Highbridge Voices sang the national anthem prior to the Yankees' game vs. Tampa Bay.

EDUCATION

Bronx Education All-Star Day: For three consecutive years, the Yankees have partnered with the New York City Department of Education (DOE) to implement an incentive program that motivates and enhances the educational experience for students (grades 5-8) attending Bronx-based schools (Districts 7-12) and recognizes their accomplishments throughout the school year. From the beginning of the academic year in September until April, students are highlighted for their achievements and commitment to leadership, academics, community service and teamwork. On May 29, 2019, over 9,000 students were recognized at Yankee Stadium during a pregame celebration for excelling in the aforementioned areas of focus. In addition, all students, teachers and DOE officials were invited to stay and enjoy that afternoon's game.

On May 29, 2019, the Yankees held Bronx Education All-Star Day, which recognized over 9,000 local students for their achievements in their classrooms.

161st Street Merchants' Association's 18th Annual Back-to-School Jamm: The New York Yankees Foundation collaborated with the 161st Street Merchants' Association to provide 2,500 local youth with backpacks and back-to-school supply kits to ensure they started the 2019-2020 school year on a positive note. The Association is committed to promoting business growth and development along 161st Street in the Bronx and annually hosts a Back-to-School Jamm for local residents that provides attendees with health/educational resources, entertainment, and food and beverages. In addition to the resources dedicated to this initiative, the Yankees also provided another 2,500 backpacks to local community organizations.

Literacy Inc: On August 12, 2019, the Yankees partnered with Literacy, Inc. (LINC) to host the fifth annual Reading on the Rails event at Yankee Stadium. The program encourages youth and families to travel with a book and read, even when getting to and from locations in their normal, daily lives. The event began with a reading session for kids on their train ride to the stadium. Once there, children, parents and LINC staff gathered inside to take part in various literacy activities, including a parent workshop. Participants were then highlighted in an on-field pregame ceremony and invited to stay for that night's Yankees game. LINC reaches in excess of 9,000 children and 5,000 parents annually and is committed to addressing illiteracy among children growing up in poverty in New York City. Through the consistent support of the New York Yankees Foundation and fundraising efforts, resources have been dedicated to enhance these efforts.

Morris High School Campus Robotics Program: Since its inception in 1999, the Yankees have been proud supporters of the Morris High School Campus Robotics Program that sees students from the school participate in competitions where teams work together to create robots designed to complete various tasks. The program encourages students to pursue careers in science, math and engineering. On an annual basis, the Yankees recognize the students' accomplishments in various ways, including an on-field pregame ceremony, showcasing the Program's commitment to providing local youth with a superior educational experience.

NYPL Summer Reading Program: The Yankees and the New York Public Library (NYPL) partner together to encourage New York City students to exercise the reading skills they acquired during the previous academic year by challenging students to read during the summer months. On August 14, 2019, the Yankees rewarded the students who participated in the Summer Reading Program with tickets to attend that afternoon's game. In addition, the two students from each borough who read the most books met with Yankees first baseman Mike Ford prior to the game to discuss the importance of reading and were recognized during an on-field pregame ceremony.

Sport Management Mentoring Program: The Sport Management Mentoring Program was established to expose students throughout New York City to career options associated with professional sports. On a monthly basis, the Yankees work in conjunction with schools and community-based organizations that identify local youth to participate in a mentoring seminar at Yankee Stadium. At these sessions, Yankees front office personnel lead interactive discussions and share insightful information about their educational background, career paths and day-to-day responsibilities. They also provide an overview of what takes place off the field and away from public view, engaging students with supporting materials. In addition, students are treated to a working lunch and a private, behind-the-scenes tour of Yankee Stadium. At the conclusion of the seminar, students have a better understanding of the business side of a sports franchise and potential career opportunities that exist.

Yankees front office employees spoke with local students during the Yankees' Sport Management Mentoring Program at Yankee Stadium in 2019.

HEALTHY LIFESTYLE

Fans for the Cure: The Yankees teamed up with Fans for the Cure, New York-Presbyterian Hospital, Columbia University Medical Center and Weill Cornell Medicine to save the lives of their fans and employees from prostate cancer during Prostate Cancer Awareness Month. Prior to the Yankees game on September 3, 2019, fans, media members and employees 40 years of age or older were encouraged to visit medical professionals in a designated area of the stadium to undergo a quick prostate cancer screening.

Healthy Home Plate: The Yankees, Legends Hospitality, Ace Endico, Peapod and Food Bank for New York City partner to implement/host the Healthy Home Plate Program at Yankee Stadium. The Healthy Home Plate Program provides area youth with the opportunity to participate in a program focused on the importance of preparing affordable, healthy meals and incorporating these meals into their lifestyle. Kitchens located within Yankee Stadium become classrooms, where sous chefs engage youth with hands-on cooking demonstrations. During the interactive lesson, nutritionists from the Food Bank for New York City educate students about nutrition and the value of the ingredients in the recipes prepared. Ace Endico supplies the ingredients for the meals prepared in class. In recognition of the students' participation/completion of the program, their efforts are showcased during a pregame ceremony at Yankee Stadium. In addition, each participant receives a personalized chef's jacket, certificate, cookbook of healthy recipes, bag filled with provisions for students to prepare healthy meals at home, a gift card from Peapod and tickets to attend the game.

High School Blood Donor Championship: The Yankees and the New York Blood Center established a partnership to address the issue of a declining blood donor population. As a result, the New York Yankees High School Blood Donor Championship was created. High schools based in the metropolitan area are provided with incentives (tickets, promotional items, etc.) to motivate staff and students 16 years of age or older to donate blood at their school blood drives. The total number of donations collected at each school competing in the Blood Donor Championship is tallied at the conclusion of the academic year, and the top schools are invited to attend a game at Yankee Stadium, where they are honored during an on-field pregame ceremony. The New York Yankees High School Blood Donor Championship has surpassed approximately 1.2 million donations collected since the program's inception in 1996.

MULTICULTURAL

Hispanic Heritage Month: The Yankees proudly celebrated Hispanic Heritage Month during August and September by highlighting, recognizing and embracing Hispanic heritage, language, culture and traditions.

- **Better Money Habits:** The Yankees, Hispanic Federation and The Hispanic/Latino Organization for Leadership and Advancement (HOLA), under the Bank of America Diversity & Inclusion Framework, partnered to offer a financial education workshop to a group of students from Hispanic Federation's educational programs. Topics such as an economic way of thinking, money management, the basics of banking and savings were included. Moreover, Yankees third baseman Miguel Andújar spoke with students about his experiences and advised them of the importance of financial planning. HOLA's mission is to support financial wellness in the community and promote economic and social growth. The Yankees were proud to host this event at Yankee Stadium on September 16, 2019, as part of their various initiatives during the celebration of Hispanic Heritage Month.

Yankees third baseman Miguel Andújar [L] spoke to students about the importance of financial planning.

- **Community Achievement Awards:** The New York Yankees Hispanic Heritage Month Community Achievement Awards recognize organizations and individuals for their outstanding work and contributions to the betterment of the surrounding communities. The following individuals were recognized during an on-field pregame ceremony prior to the game on September 18, 2019.
    - Lisa Sorin (Business)
    - Richard Souto (Arts)
    - Elizabeth Toledo Cruz (Social Responsibility)
    - Leticia Rodriguez-Rosario (Education)
    - Salvador Cruz (Sports)
- **Legends Food Activation:** As part of a number of themed activities and festivities in 2019, Yankee Stadium's food service provider, Legends Hospitality, invited a chef from Café de Colombia Bakery to present two new items: "Rumba Shake," a Latin-inspired vanilla milkshake that includes guava puree, caramel sauce, New York cheesecake, and whipped cream, rimmed with toasted coconut and topped by a dedito de guayaba (a yucca pastry stuffed with white cheese and guava), and Colombian Empanadas (chicken or beef and potatoes) served with an ají sauce made of garlic, cilantro and jalapeño. Both items debuted on August 13, 2019.

- **Bronx Dominican Day Parade:** 2019 marked the 30th anniversary of the Bronx Dominican Day Parade's efforts to serve and cultivate Latin culture and traditions in the Bronx community. The Yankees were proud to once again participate in the scholarship program by providing 10 scholarships to local students selected by the Bronx Dominican Day Parade. The scholarship is intended to acknowledge the students' hard work, dedication and contributions to the community. The scholars were recognized during an on-field pregame ceremony on July 30, 2019, and were also invited to attend that evening's game with their families and friends.

The Yankees recognized the Bronx Dominican Day Parade with an on-field pregame ceremony on July 30, 2019.

- **National Puerto Rican Day Parade:** The National Puerto Rican Day Parade was established to create awareness and empower the Puerto Rican community by promoting culture, education, scholarships and civic engagement. The Yankees extended their educational outreach efforts by providing scholarships to seven students who exemplified the values of hard work and dedication in their communities. The students selected by the National Puerto Rican Day Parade, along with members of the Education Committee, were recognized in an on-field pregame ceremony on May 28, 2019, and were invited to watch that evening's game with their families and friends.

RECREATION

Pitch In For Baseball: Pitch In For Baseball provides new and gently used softball and baseball equipment to boys and girls around the world who want to play ball but lack the resources to do so. The Yankees and Pitch In For Baseball partner with the Public Schools Athletic League and New York City Parks and Recreation to ensure local youth have access to equipment needed to participate in organized baseball and softball programs. Annually, the Yankees and Pitch In For Baseball identify 10 Bronx-based high school teams and fully equip approximately 150 young athletes with all the gear needed to take the field during their seasons.

PLAY BALL, Stickball: Major League Baseball and the Yankees — in partnership with the Youth Stickball League (YSL) — hosted "The Bronx Stickball Classic" on River Avenue between 158th and 161st Streets in the Bronx, featuring youth participants from the Youth Stickball League. The event featured the 14U Stickball championship game on August 24, 2019. The winners of the championship game were recognized in a pregame ceremony prior to the Yankees game on August 30, 2019. Stickball, a modified game of baseball played with a broom stick and rubber ball, is a prominent street game within the Hispanic and Latino communities.

The Yankees partnered in hosting the "PLAY BALL: Stickball" tournament on Aug. 24, 2019.

London Meteorites Clinic: As part of Major League Baseball's inaugural series in London and in conjunction with the London Meteorites Baseball and Softball Club, the Yankees hosted a baseball clinic for 100 youth in the London community on June 27, 2019. Manager Aaron Boone and former Yankees players Carlos Beltrán, Reggie Jackson, Hideki Matsui, Andy Pettitte, Mariano Rivera, Alex Rodriguez and Nick Swisher served as coaches, instructing young players on hitting, fielding, base running and pitching. A BBQ-themed reception was held at the conclusion of the event where the Yankees presented the Meteorites with a legacy gift that included baseball and softball equipment. The evening prior, Dan Cunningham, head groundskeeper for the Yankees, hosted a Grounds Crew Shadowing Clinic for coaches and field maintenance workers from the Meteorites. The lessons included tips on maintaining, repairing and caring for baseball and softball fields.

The Yankees hosted a baseball clinic for approximately 100 children in the London community in conjunction with the London Meteorites Baseball and Softball Club.

2019 PSAL Championship Games: The Yankees partnered with the Public Schools Athletic League (PSAL) to host the PSAL Baseball & Football Championship Games at Yankee Stadium in 2019. Over the course of three games, approximately 10,000 tickets combined were distributed to guests who watched Lafayette Educational Complex and Inwood Campus compete for the AA Baseball Championship, Beacon High School and Gregorio Luperon High School compete for the AAA Baseball Championship and Erasmus Hall High School and Tottenville High School square off in the Football Championship game.

Erasmus Hall High School won the 2019 PSAL Football City Championship Game at Yankee Stadium on Dec. 4, 2019, defeating Tottenville High School, 27-0.

CHSAA All-Star Game: The Yankees partnered with the Catholic High Schools Athletic Association (CHSAA) to host the CHSAA's Baseball All-Star Game at Yankee Stadium. Approximately 1,000 tickets were distributed to fans as the American League All-Stars competed against the National League All-Stars.

SOCIAL RESPONSIBILITY

Yankees-Stonewall Scholars Initiative: In 2019, the Yankees collaborated with Stonewall Inn and the NYC Department of Education to implement the Yankees-Stonewall Scholars Initiative. This initiative commemorated the 50th anniversary of the Stonewall Inn uprising and celebrated the achievements of New York City Public School graduating seniors who demonstrated academic achievement, a commitment to equality and impactful support of the LGBTQ community. The Yankees provided five $10,000 scholarships to one student from each of the five boroughs of New York City. The recipients of the scholarships were honored during an on-field pregame ceremony at Yankee Stadium on June 25, 2019. In addition, a plaque was dedicated in Monument Park to commemorate the 50th Anniversary of the Stonewall Inn uprising and recognize the need for equality and acceptance for all.

In an on-field ceremony at Yankee Stadium on June 25, 2019, the Yankees honored the recipients of the Yankees-Stonewall Scholars Initiative.

Community Paint Project: The Yankees teamed up with Publicolor to transform PS 146 in the Bronx with color on August 6, 2019. Publicolor engages disconnected youth in their education through a continuum of design-based programs and academic support. The objective of this team project was to create a beautiful, warm, welcoming and student-centric environment. Yankees employees volunteered their time to paint the facility alongside area youth.

Line of Duty: During the 2019 season, the Yankees teamed up with the New York City Police Department to host the surviving children and widows/widowers of police officers killed in the line of duty. In honor of the legacy of these fallen heroes and over the course of 10 home games, the Yankees provided Line Of Duty families with complimentary tickets.

CC Sabathia's Softball Game: For the second consecutive year, the Yankees and the PitCCh In Foundation partnered to host CC Sabathia's Celebrity Softball Game on May 16, 2019, at Yankee Stadium. The event began with a red carpet VIP reception, followed by the softball game itself and a trophy presentation. All proceeds from the event benefited the PitCCh In Foundation's and the New York Yankees Foundation's efforts to enrich the lives of inner city children through education and athletics.

ALS Ride for Life: The Yankees and the ALS of Greater New York teamed up to kick off the Ride for Life, an annual event in which ALS patients embark on a 12-day, 100-mile electric wheelchair ride along highways and byways to raise awareness and funds for a cure for ALS. On May 17, 2019, approximately 150 students from Public School 346 gathered inside Monument Park at Yankee Stadium to pay tribute to Lou Gehrig's plaque and offer words of support/encouragement to Chris Pendergast, founder of Ride for Life, as he embarked on his 21st annual ride. On September 4, 2019, the Yankees and the ALS of Greater New York celebrated the event's success by recognizing Pendergast and other ride participants during an on-field pregame ceremony.

Make-A-Wish Foundation, Metro New York and Western New York: Since 1980, the Make-A-Wish Foundation has enriched the lives of children who have been diagnosed with life-threatening medical conditions through its wish-granting work. On an annual basis, the Yankees work in conjunction with the Make-A-Wish Foundation to grant approximately 30 wishes. In addition, resources dedicated through the New York Yankees Foundation support Make-A-Wish's efforts to lift children's spirits and convey the message that wishes can come true.

Yankees Manager Aaron Boone [L] and outfielder Brett Gardner [R] spent time with a young Make-A-Wish recipient during pre-game batting practice.

4 + 44 Awards Ceremony: The Yankees partnered with Bronx Community Board 4 (CB4) to host local police officers and firefighters at the 4 + 44 Police Officer and Firefighter Outstanding Service Award Ceremony at Yankee Stadium on December 5, 2019. Award recipients were acknowledged for their commitment to make a difference in the lives of local residents.

Covenant House Sleep Out: The Yankees partnered with Covenant House to host their annual Executive Sleep Out on November 14, 2019. Held at Yankee Stadium for the first time, Yankees Senior Vice President and General Manager Brian Cashman was joined by over 250 leaders from around the country who spent the night sleeping in the Great Hall in an effort to spread awareness about youth homelessness. Over $1.5 million was raised to help Covenant House continue its mission of providing housing and support services to youth in need.

Yankees General Manager Brian Cashman [R] participated in the ninth annual Covenant House Sleep Out, held in the Great Hall of Yankee Stadium on Nov. 14, 2019.

HOLIDAY CHEER

In celebration of the holiday season, the Yankees spread holiday cheer to their neighbors.

Thanksgiving Food Voucher Giveaway: The Yankees and Krasdale Foods teamed up to hold a Thanksgiving Food Voucher Giveaway at Yankee Stadium. Bronx residents were provided with a voucher that could be redeemed at a local C-Town or Bravo Supermarket to assist with expenses related to preparing a Thanksgiving meal. On November 21, 2019, approximately 3,000 food vouchers were distributed.

Thanksgiving Feast: The Yankees, Legends Hospitality and the Supportive Children's Advocacy Network New York collaborated to host a traditional Thanksgiving Feast on November 22, 2019, for several hundred local residents at the Mullaly Recreation Center, across the street from Yankee Stadium.

Winter Wonderland: Yankee Stadium transformed into the North Pole on December 13, 2019, when the Yankees hosted Winter Wonderland in conjunction with Walmart, Neil and Amanda Friedman, Legends Hospitality and American Foliage. Approximately 3,600 local youth were treated to a holiday extravaganza in Yankee Stadium's Great Hall, complete with festive decorations, music including caroling by the Highbridge Voices choir, and food and hot chocolate. In addition, and as a result of commitments from the New York Yankees Foundation, Walmart and Neil and Amanda Friedman, every child in attendance was presented with a holiday gift of their choosing.

Every year, Yankee Stadium's Great Hall is transformed for children during the Yankees' Winter Wonderland event.

Annual Holiday Food Drive: The Yankees partnered with members of the Bronx Clergy to host the annual Holiday Food Drive on December 18, 2019, at Yankee Stadium. Approximately 83,000 pounds of food was collected and distributed to families in need throughout the Bronx. In addition, 3,000 food vouchers were allocated to Bronx residents for redemption at local C-Town or Bravo Supermarkets to assist with the expenses related to preparing a holiday meal.

Several hundred children took part in the Yankees' Thanksgiving Feast at the Mullaly Recreation Center.

Yankees Community Partners

161st St. Merchants Assoc.
Actors Fund
A.C.E. Mentoring Program
AHRC NYC Foundation
Alliance for Lupus Research
ALS Association of Greater N.Y.
Alzheimer's Association
American Cancer Society
American Diabetes Association
American Red Cross
Armory Foundation
Autism Speaks
Blinknow Foundation
Breakthrough New York
Broadway Show League
Bronx Children's Museum
Bronx Colts Youth Football
Bronx Community Boards
Bronx Dominican Day Parade
Bronx Museum of the Arts
Bronx YMCA
BronxWorks
BuildOn
Catholic Charities of the
　Archdiocese of New York
Cerebral Palsy Foundation
Christopher Ricardo Cystic
　Fibrosis Foundation
Citymeals-on-Wheels
Connecticut Cancer Foundation
Covenant House
Dominican Day Parade
DREAM

Ed Randall's Fans for the Cure
El Museo del Barrio
Family Promise of Morris County
FDNY Foundation
Food Bank for NYC
Friends of Nassau County Recreation
Get in the Game Voter Registration
　Girls Inc.
Girl Scouts Council of Greater N.Y.
Greater N.Y. Councils, Boy
　Scouts of America
Highbridge Voices
Hispanic Federation
Immaculate Conception School
Impremedia
Joe Torre Safe at Home Foundation
Junior Achievement of N.Y.
Kipp New York
Kips Bay Boys & Girls Club
Lauren's Kids Foundation
Learning Through an
　Expanded Arts Program
Leukemia & Lymphoma Society
Literacy, Inc.
Little League Raiders Baseball
Madison Sq. Boys & Girls Club
Make-A-Wish Foundation
March of Dimes N.Y. Division
Mercy Center
Mid-Bronx Senior Citizen Council
Mindbuilders
Montefiore Medical Center
Morris High School Robotics

Multiple Sclerosis Assoc. of America
Museum of the City of New York
National Puerto Rican Day Parade
New York Blood Center
N.Y.C. Dept. of Education
N.Y.C. Hispanic Chamber of
　Commerce
N.Y.C. Police Foundation
New York League of Puerto
　Rican Women, Inc.
New York POPS
New York Public Library
New York Road Runners
N.Y. Society for the Prevention
　of Cruelty to Children
New York Urban League
Parkinson's Disease Foundation
Part of the Solution (POTS)
Pitch In For Baseball
PitCCh In Foundation
Police Athletic League
Positive Coaching Alliance
Pro. Baseball Scouts Foundation
Project Sunshine
Public Schools Athletic League
Publicolor
Quality Services for the Autism
　Community (QSAC)
Renaissance Youth Center
Ride for Life
Right to Play
Rising Ground
Rock and Wrap it Up!

Ronald McDonald House N.Y.
Safe Horizon
Salvation Army of Greater N.Y.
SCAN New York
Silver Shield Foundation
Somos El Futuro
South Bronx Physical Fitness
South Bronx United
Spanish Broadcasting Systems
Special Olympics New York
St. Francis Food Pantries & Shelters
Stamford Hospital Foundation
Sussman Family Fund
Taylor Hooton Foundation
Thurgood Marshall Junior
　Mock Trial Program
TM Baseball Academy
Tourette Assoc. of America
United Negro College Fund
U.S. Olympic Committee
United War Veterans Council
Univision Communications Inc.
USO of Metropolitan N.Y.
Vet Tix
Wheelchair Sports Federation
Whyhunger
Women in Sports and Events
Women's Housing and Economic
　Development Corp. (WHEDCo)
Women's Sports Foundation
Yogi Berra Museum &
　Learning Center

WILLIAMS Lumber & Home Centers

" The name you know and the name you trust "

Nail it right.
The first time.

74th ANNIVERSARY
1946-2020

We have everything you need!

- Lumber • Hardware • Paint • Electrical
- Plumbing • Windows & Doors
- Building Materials • Heating
- Power Tools • Hand Tools
- Lawn & Garden • Kitchen & Bath
- Housewares • Outdoor Living
- Boots & Apparel • Giftware
- Power Equipment & More!

845•876•WOOD
www.williamslumber.com

Rhinebeck • Hudson • Hopewell Junction • Tannersville
• Red Hook • Pleasant Valley • High Falls • Hyde Park

2020 Yankees

On December 18, 2019, the Yankees signed three-time All-Star **RHP Gerrit Cole** to a nine-year contract.

AARON BOONE • Manager

17

FULL NAME: Aaron John Boone
BIRTHDATE: 3/9/73 • **OPENING DAY AGE:** 47
BIRTHPLACE: La Mesa, Calif.
RESIDES: Scottsdale, Ariz.
COLLEGE: University of Southern California

STATUS
▸ Was named the 33rd manager in club history on December 4, 2017, signing a three-year contract through the 2020 season with a team option for 2021.

AT THE HELM IN 2019
▸ Placed second in AL Manager of the Year voting (received 13 first place votes, nine second place votes and four third place votes) after guiding the Yankees to a 103-59 record, the club's best mark since 2009 (also 103-59) and their Major League-record 21st 100-win season in franchise history…only one other franchise has 10 such seasons (Philadelphia/Kansas City/Oakland Athletics-10)…after going 100-62 in 2018, have back-to-back 100-win seasons for the second time since 1979 (also 2002-04)…the Yankees are one of two teams with consecutive 100-win seasons since 2010, joining the Houston Astros (2017-19).
▸ Yankees batters set a franchise record with 306HR, 1HR shy of the Major League mark set by the 2019 Minnesota Twins (307).
▸ Was ejected five times (4/20 vs. Kansas City by 2B umpire Jerry Meals, 5/1 at Arizona by HP umpire Paul Emmel, 7/18 Game 1 vs. Tampa Bay by HP umpire Brennan Miller, 8/17 vs. Cleveland by HP umpire Ben May, 9/21 vs. Toronto by 3B umpire Joe West)…has been ejected nine times as a manager (also four times in 2018).

MANAGERIAL/COACHING CAREER
▸ Is the first manager in Baseball history to guide his team to at least 100 wins in each of his first two seasons as skipper.
▸ Has 203 career managerial wins, trailing only Ralph Houk (205 wins with the Yankees from 1961-62) for most by any manager over his first two seasons at the helm.
▸ Joins Houk (all three seasons, 1961-63) as the only Yankees managers to lead the team to a postseason berth in each of his first two career managerial seasons.
▸ Made his managerial debut in 2018…placed fifth in AL "Manager of the Year" balloting, receiving two third-place votes…guided the Yankees to a 100-62 record, the club's best record since 2009 (103-59) and the 20th 100-win season in franchise history…became the sixth manager in Baseball history to lead his team to at least 100 wins in his rookie season, joining Ralph Houk (1961 Yankees, 109-53), Alex Cora (2018 Red Sox, 108-54), Dusty Baker (1993 Giants, 103-59), Sparky Anderson (1970 Reds, 102-60) and Mickey Cochrane (1934 Tigers, 101-53).
▸ Became the fourth Yankees manager to lead the team to a postseason berth in his rookie managerial season, joining Ralph Houk in 1961 (won World Series), Yogi Berra in 1964 (lost WS) and Dick Howser in 1980 (lost ALCS).
▸ In 2018, Yankees pitchers set franchise records for total strikeouts (1,634) and strikeouts by relievers (753).
▸ Made his managerial debut in 3/29/18 win at Toronto, becoming the 11th manager to win his Yankees managerial debut *on Opening Day* and the 18th to win his Yankees managerial debut *at any point during the season*…was the fourth consecutive manager to win his Yankees managerial debut (Joe Girardi in 2008 vs. Toronto, Joe Torre in 1996 at Cleveland and Buck Showalter in 1992 vs. Boston).
▸ Won his first home game as a manager on 4/3/18 vs. Tampa Bay, becoming the sixth straight Yankees manager to win his home Yankees managerial debut (also Girardi-2008, Torre-1996, Showalter-1992, Merrill-1990 and Dent-1989).
▸ With his father, Bob, became the fourth father-son duo to both serve as Major League managers, joining Connie and Earle Mack, George and Dick Sisler and Bob and Joel Skinner…were joined by Buddy and David Bell in 2019…in 2020, Mets' skipper Luis Rojas and his father, Felipe Alou, will become the sixth father-son duo to each manage in the Majors…Bob Boone spent parts of six seasons as a Major League skipper, leading the Kansas City Royals from 1995-97, then guiding the Reds from 2001-03, a stint during which he managed Aaron.
▸ Is the 18th Yankees manager to have also played for the club…is one of seven active managers (as of Feb. 1, 2020) to have played for the franchise he currently manages, joining Kevin Cash (Tampa Bay), Craig Counsell (Milwaukee), Terry Francona (Cleveland), Dave Martinez (Washington/Montreal), Dave Roberts (Los Angeles-NL) and David Ross (Chicago-NL).

PLAYING CAREER

- Is part of the first family in Baseball history to produce three generations of Major League players...his father, Bob, played 19 seasons from 1972-90, and his grandfather, Ray, had a 13-year playing career from 1948-60...his older brother, Bret, played 14 seasons (1992-2005), including two with Aaron in Cincinnati from 1997-98...all four reached 1,000H at the Major League level.
- He (126) and brother, Bret (252) are one of nine sets of brothers to each hit at least 100HR, joining Roberto and Sandy Alomar Jr., Ken and Clete Boyer, Joe and Vince DiMaggio, Stephen and J.D. Drew, Bob and Irish Meusel, Yadier and Bengie Molina, Melvin Jr. and Justin Upton and Delmon and Dmitri Young (credit: *Elias*).
- The 2003 NL All-Star hit .263 (1,017-for-3,871) with 519R, 216 doubles, 126HR, 555RBI and 107SB in 1,152 games over 12 Major League seasons as an infielder with the Cincinnati Reds (1997-2003), Yankees (2003), Cleveland Indians (2005-06), Florida Marlins (2007), Washington Nationals (2008) and Houston Astros (2009).
- Made his Major League debut with Cincinnati on 6/20/97 to replace his brother, Bret, who was optioned in what is believed to be the first transaction involving brothers...made his Major League debut that night at St. Louis, going 1-for-3 with 1RBI...collected his first hit and RBI in his third plate appearance with an infield single off Matt Morris in the sixth inning...was ejected from the game by HP umpire Gary Darling for throwing his helmet (was just the fourth player in Baseball history to be ejected in his Major League debut).

CAREER HIGHLIGHTS

NL All-Star Team
▸ 2003

- Made his first Opening Day roster with the Reds in 1998...hit his first career HR on 8/26 vs. the Cubs (Kerry Wood).
- Had arthroscopic surgery to clean out his left knee on 12/8/99, which was performed by Dr. Timothy Kremchek...underwent reconstructive surgery to repair a torn anterior cruciate ligament in his left knee on 8/8/00...the surgery was performed by Kremchek and Dr. James Andrews...suffered the injury on 7/5/00 at St. Louis.
- Played 103 games with the Reds in 2001, despite being placed on the D.L. with broken bones suffered after being hit by pitches: 5/15-6/14 with a broken hamate bone in his right hand (suffered on 5/14 vs. Houston when he was hit by a Wade Miller pitch and had surgery the next day to remove the bone, performed by hand specialist Dr. Greg Sommerkamp and Dr. Timothy Kremchek); 8/15-31 with a broken right wrist (suffered on 8/14 at St. Louis when he was hit by a pitch by Matt Morris) and 9/24-the end of the season with a broken left thumb (suffered on 9/23 at Milwaukee when hit by a Jamey Wright pitch and had surgery to insert a pin and a wire into the thumb, also performed by Sommerkamp and Kremchek, on 9/27).
- Hit a career-high 26HR with the Reds in 2002...homered three times on 8/9/02 vs. San Diego, including two in the first inning off Padres starter Brett Tomko...later homered off Tomko in the fourth inning...hit the last of 4,652HR at Cincinnati's Riverfront Stadium/Cinergy Field on 9/22/02 off Philadelphia's Dan Plesac.
- Helped the Yankees clinch the American League pennant in 2003, hitting a series-ending, "walk-off" home run off Boston's Tim Wakefield in the bottom of the 11th inning of Game 7 in the ALCS...in 54 regular season games with the Yankees—all in 2003—hit .254 (48-for-189) with 31R, 13 doubles, 6HR and 31RBI...was acquired by the Yankees from Cincinnati in exchange for LHP Brandon Claussen, LHP Charlie Manning and cash considerations on 7/31/03...overall, set career highs with 158H, 92R and 96RBI over 160G with the Reds and Yankees in 2003.
- Missed the entire 2004 season after having two surgeries on his left knee...prior to the season, had surgery on the knee after tearing the anterior cruciate ligament playing in a pick-up basketball game in January in Newport Beach, Calif....the surgery was performed by Dr. Lewis Yocum in Anaheim, Calif., on 2/16...at the time of the injury, was on the Yankees' 40-man roster, but was released on 3/1.
- Signed a Major League contract with Cleveland as a free agent on 6/26/04...joined Cleveland in July and began experiencing pain and swelling in the surgically repaired knee...underwent a second procedure on 8/20/04 to remove loose bodies and promote cartilage growth in the left knee joint.
- Reached the 1,000H and 500R plateau for his career in 2008 with Washington.
- On 3/26/09, underwent open-heart surgery to replace his bicuspid aortic valve, then returned to play for Houston in September 2009...is believed to be the first player to appear in a Major League game following open-heart surgery...played his final Major League game on 10/4/09 at the Mets.
- Was selected by the Cincinnati Reds in the third round of the 1994 First-Year Player Draft...was selected by the California Angels in the 43rd round of the 1991 First-Year Player Draft, but did not sign.
- Appeared in 580 minor league games, batting .271 (585-for-2,158) with 346R, 133 doubles, 67HR and 325RBI...was a Pioneer League All-Star in 1994, a Carolina League All-Star in 1995 and a Southern League All-Star in 1996.

PERSONAL/MISCELLANEOUS

- Is married to Laura...the couple has four children: Jeanel (JOHN-el), Sergot (SIR-go), Brandon and Bella.
- Is an active supporter of Chances for Children, a 501(c)(3) non-profit organization providing hope for children and communities in Haiti. Through the generosity of private funding, C4C works in 14 communities throughout Haiti, empowering families with programs that strengthen communities through church renovation, pastor/church leader training, feeding programs, medical clinics, education assistance, economic programs for women, and an orphanage for orphaned/abandoned children...provided the opening remarks at the organizations 7th Annual Night of Hope charity dinner and adoption benefit in November 2018...his wife serves as a Board Member and Night of Hope Committee Member...the Boones adopted two brothers, Jeanel and Sergot from Haiti in 2014.
- Was named a recipient of the Thurman Munson Award in February 2019.

- Graduated from Villa Park (Calif.) High School in 1991, where he played baseball, basketball and football.
- Played three seasons at the University of Southern California from 1992-94, hitting .302 with 11HR and 94RBI.
- Following his retirement as a player, spent eight years as a broadcaster for ESPN, appearing as a studio analyst on *Baseball Tonight* from 2010-14 before serving as a color analyst on game broadcasts in 2015 and on *Sunday Night Baseball* telecasts for the 2016-17 seasons.
- Was named the 2005 recipient of the Gibbons/Olin "Good Guy Award" presented by the Cleveland Chapter of the BBWAA to a player who best exhibits a professional and courteous manner with the media.

Boone's Major League Playing Career

Year	Club	AVG	G	AB	R	H	2B	3B	HR	RBI	SH	SF	HP	BB	SO	SB	CS	E	OBP	SLG
1997	CINCINNATI	.245	16	49	5	12	1	0	0	5	1	0	0	2	5	1	0	3	.275	.265
1998	CINCINNATI	.282	58	181	24	51	13	2	2	28	3	2	5	15	36	6	1	8	.350	.409
1999	CINCINNATI	.280	139	472	56	132	26	5	14	72	5	5	8	30	79	17	6	15	.330	.445
2000	CINCINNATI - a	.285	84	291	44	83	18	0	12	43	2	4	10	24	52	6	1	8	.356	.471
2001	CINCINNATI - b, c, d	.294	103	381	54	112	26	2	14	62	3	6	8	29	71	6	3	19	.351	.483
2002	CINCINNATI	.241	162	606	83	146	38	2	26	87	9	4	10	56	111	32	8	22	.314	.439
2003	CINCINNATI	.273	106	403	61	110	19	3	18	65	3	0	5	35	74	15	3	17	.339	.469
	YANKEES - e	.254	54	189	31	48	13	0	6	31	3	2	3	11	30	8	0	6	.302	.418
2004						Did Not Play - Injured - f, g														
2005	CLEVELAND	.243	143	511	61	124	19	1	16	60	4	6	9	35	92	9	3	18	.299	.378
2006	CLEVELAND	.251	104	354	50	89	19	1	7	46	4	1	6	27	62	5	4	16	.314	.370
2007	FLORIDA - h, i	.286	69	189	27	54	11	0	5	28	1	4	13	21	41	2	0	5	.388	.423
2008	WASHINGTON - j, k	.241	104	232	23	56	13	1	6	28	1	2	2	18	52	0	1	2	.299	.384
2009	HOUSTON - l	.000	10	13	0	0	0	0	0	0	0	0	1	0	2	0	0	0	.071	.000
Minor League Totals		**.271**	**580**	**2158**	**346**	**585**	**133**	**19**	**67**	**325**	**9**	**26**	**29**	**199**	**362**	**71**	**31**	**--**	**.337**	**.443**
AL Totals		**.248**	**301**	**1054**	**142**	**261**	**51**	**2**	**29**	**137**	**11**	**9**	**18**	**73**	**184**	**22**	**7**	**40**	**.305**	**.382**
NL Totals		**.268**	**851**	**2817**	**377**	**756**	**165**	**15**	**97**	**418**	**28**	**27**	**62**	**230**	**523**	**85**	**23**	**99**	**.334**	**.441**
Major League Totals		**.263**	**1152**	**3871**	**519**	**1017**	**216**	**17**	**126**	**555**	**39**	**36**	**80**	**303**	**707**	**107**	**30**	**139**	**.326**	**.425**

Selected by the California Angels in the 43rd round of the 1991 First-Year Player Draft, but did not sign.
Selected by the Cincinnati Reds in the third round of the 1994 First-Year Player Draft.

a - Placed on the 15-day disabled list on July 12, 2000 and transferred to the 60-day disabled list from September 5-October 4, 2000, with a torn left ACL.
b - Placed on the 15-day disabled list from May 15-June 15, 2001 with a broken right hand.
c - Placed on the 15-day disabled list from August 15-September 1, 2001 with a fractured right wrist.
d - Placed on the 15-day disabled list from September 24-October 11, 2001 with a fractured left thumb.
e - Acquired by the Yankees from the Cincinnati Reds in exchange for LHP Brandon Claussen, LHP Charlie Manning and cash considerations on July 31, 2003.
f - Signed by the Cleveland Indians as a free agent on June 26, 2004.
g - Placed on the 60-day disabled list from June 26-November 15, 2004 with a torn left ACL.
h - Signed by the Florida Marlins as a free agent on January 4, 2007.
i - Placed on the 15-day disabled list on June 25, 2007 and transferred to the 60-day disabled list from September 12-October 30, 2007, recovering from left knee surgery.
j - Signed by the Washington Nationals as a free agent on December 10, 2007.
k - Placed on the 15-day disabled list from July 7-August 14, 2008 with a strained left calf.
l - Signed by the Houston Astros as a free agent on December 19, 2008.

Boone's Postseason Record

Year	Club/Opponent	AVG	G	AB	R	H	2B	3B	HR	RBI	BB	SO	SB
2003	NYY vs. MIN (ALDS)	.200	4	15	1	3	1	0	0	0	0	3	1
	NYY vs. BOS (ALCS)	.176	7	17	2	3	0	0	1	2	1	6	1
	NYY vs. FLA (WS)	.143	6	21	1	3	0	0	1	2	0	6	0
POSTSEASON TOTALS		**.170**	**17**	**53**	**4**	**9**	**1**	**0**	**2**	**4**	**1**	**15**	**2**

Boone's All-Star Game Record

Year	Club, Site	AVG	G	AB	R	H	2B	3B	HR	RBI	BB	SO	SB
2003	CIN, Chicago-AL	.000	1	1	0	0	0	0	0	0	0	0	0

MATT BLAKE • Pitching Coach

67

FULL NAME: Matthew Blake
BIRTHDATE: 5/14/85 • **OPENING DAY AGE:** 34
BIRTHPLACE: Concord, N.H.
RESIDES: Cleveland, Ohio
COLLEGE: College of the Holy Cross

COACHING CAREER

- Begins his first season in the Yankees organization as the team's pitching coach in 2020, having been named to the position on 11/14/19…is his first coaching experience at the Major League level.
- Spent the last four seasons with Cleveland (2016-19), where he was promoted to Director of Pitching Development prior to joining the Yankees…began his time with the Indians as the Lower Level Pitching Coordinator in 2016…from 2017-19, served as the organization's Assistant Director of Player Development, a role in which he oversaw the formation of pitching strategy for the club, collaborating with coaches, coordinators and front office personnel…he also assisted with leadership of the organization's player development staff and the design and execution of the staff's programs, policies and curricula.
- In 2019, five young starters he worked with contributed for Cleveland at the Major League level…each member of that group—Mike Clevinger, Shane Bieber, Zach Plesac, Adam Plutko and Aaron Civale—were developed in the Indians' farm system, including three (Bieber, Plesac and Civale) who spent their entire minor league careers under his instruction since being drafted together in 2016…the five pitchers combined to produce 13.3 WAR (FanGraphs) over 107 games (105 starts) in 2019, anchoring the starting rotation for a 93-win team.
- Prior to joining the Indians, spent seven years as the Pitching Coordinator for Cressey Sports Performance in Hudson, Mass., working under current Yankees' Director of Player Health and Performance, Eric Cressey… also coached the Yarmouth-Dennis Red Sox of the Cape Cod League and was the pitching coach at Lincoln-Sudbury High School in Sudbury, Mass. in 2015.
- Served as an associate scout for the Yankees from 2009-15.

PLAYING CAREER

- Did not play baseball professionally.

PERSONAL

- Grew up in Concord, N.H.…graduated from Concord High School in 2003.
- Attended the College of the Holy Cross in Worcester, Mass., where he graduated in 2007 with a degree in psychology and philosophy…pitched four seasons and was a co-captain as a senior in 2007.

MIKE HARKEY • Bullpen Coach

FULL NAME: Michael Anthony Harkey
BIRTHDATE: 10/25/66 • **OPENING DAY AGE:** 53
BIRTHPLACE: San Diego, Calif.
RESIDES: Chino Hills, Calif.
COLLEGE: Cal State University Fullerton

COACHING CAREER

- The 2020 season marks his 11th as the Yankees' bullpen coach, having held the position from 2008-13 before returning prior to the 2016 season (rejoined the team on 11/17/15)…in 2019, the Yankees bullpen ranked third in the Majors with a 10.16K/9.0IP ratio, tied for second in saves (50) and ranked fifth in strikeouts (750)…in 2018, Yankees relievers set a Major League bullpen record with an 11.40 K/9.0IP ratio (753/594.2IP), surpassing the mark of 10.92 set by the 2017 Yankees…their 753K were then-second-most by a bullpen in Baseball history behind the 2018 Rays (754K in 824.1IP)…became the first bullpen in Major League history to strike out at least 30.0% of its batters faced (30.2%), surpassing the 2017 Yankees (29.0%) for the all-time record…their 9.7 WAR was best by a bullpen in Major League history…in 2017, Yankees relievers struck out 653 batters, eclipsing the 600K mark for the first time in franchise history…their 10.92 K/9.0IP ratio was a Major League record and their 9.1 WAR is now third-best by a bullpen in Major League history (Los Angeles-NL, 9.6 in 2003)…in 2016, Yankees relievers ranked third in the Majors (second in the AL) with 578K…led the Majors with a 10.15 K/9.0IP ratio (578K/512.1IP).
- Yankees relievers led the Majors in K/9.0IP ratio out of the bullpen each season from 2014-18: 2014 (10.25), 2015 (10.11), 2016 (10.15), 2017 (10.92) and 2018 (MLB-record 11.40).
- Served as the pitching coach for the Arizona Diamondbacks from 2014-15…over the two-year span, the team's bullpen tied for second in the Majors with 1,041K.
- During his first tenure with the Yankees (2008-13), the bullpen led the AL in strikeout-to-walk ratio (2.49), wins (173), saves (279) and strikeouts (2,775), ranked second in opponents' batting average (.237) and third in ERA (3.56)…over the same span, the Yankees went 491-17 when leading at the end of the eighth inning.
- Yankees relievers combined for 49 saves in 2013, fifth-most in the Majors, and recorded 9.01 K/9.0IP…in 2012, Yankees relievers tossed 444.0 innings, fewest in the AL and third-lowest in the Majors…Yankees relievers combined for a 3.12 ERA in 2011, the lowest mark in the AL and the lowest by a Yankees bullpen since 1985 (2.91)…in 2010, the Yankees bullpen combined for the second-lowest opponents' BA (.230) among AL teams…filled in as pitching coach from 6/4-29/10…Yankees relievers led the Majors in 2009 with 40 wins and tied for first with 51 saves…in 2008, the Yankees' bullpen collected a Major League-high 523K.
- Served as bullpen coach with the Florida Marlins in 2006.
- Spent six seasons (2000-05) as a pitching coach in the Padres organization, making stops at Single-A Rancho Cucamonga (2000), Single-A Fort Wayne (2001, '03), Single-A Lake Elsinore (2002, '04) and Double-A Mobile (2005)…was pitching coach for the 2007 Triple-A Iowa Cubs.

PLAYING CAREER

- Appeared in 131 career Major League games (104 starts) over eight seasons with the Cubs (1988-93), Rockies (1994), Athletics (1995), Angels (1995) and Dodgers (1997), going 36-36 with a 4.49 ERA (656.0IP, 327ER).
- Was named *Sporting News* 1990 "NL Rookie Pitcher of the Year" after posting a 12-6 record with a 3.26 ERA in 27 starts for the Cubs…selected as *USA Today* "Minor League Player of the Year" in 1988…made his Major League debut at age 21 on 9/5/88 at Wrigley Field, recording a no-decision in Game 2 of a doubleheader vs. the Phillies.
- Was a first-round pick (fourth overall) by the Cubs in the 1987 First-Year Player Draft…was selected by the San Diego Padres in the 18th round of the 1984 First-Year Player Draft, but chose to attend college.

PERSONAL

- Married (Nikki) and has two sons, Tony and Cory, and a daughter, Miani…Tony is an infielder for Concordia University and a member of the 2011 NAIA World Series championship team…Cory had a four-year college football career with UCLA and played five seasons with the St. Louis/Los Angeles Rams as a tight end from 2012-16…Miani majored in Business Management and Hospitality at Loyola Marymount University.
- Attended Cal State Fullerton from 1985-87, where he played baseball and earned All-American honors as a junior…graduated from Ganesha High School in Pomona, Calif.

Harkey's Major League Career Pitching Record

Year	Club	W-L	ERA	G	GS	CG	SHO	SV	IP	H	R	ER	BB	SO
1988	CHICAGO-NL	0-3	2.60	5	5	0	0	0	34.2	33	14	10	15	18
1990	CHICAGO-NL	12-6	3.26	27	27	2	1	0	173.2	153	71	63	59	94
1991	CHICAGO-NL	0-2	5.30	4	4	0	0	0	18.2	21	11	11	6	15
1992	CHICAGO-NL	4-0	1.89	7	7	0	0	0	38.0	34	13	8	15	21
1993	CHICAGO-NL	10-10	5.26	28	28	1	0	0	157.1	187	100	92	43	67
1994	COLORADO	1-6	5.79	24	13	0	0	0	91.2	125	61	59	35	39
1995	OAKLAND	4-6	6.27	14	12	0	0	0	66.0	75	46	46	31	28
	CALIFORNIA	4-3	4.55	12	8	1	0	0	61.1	80	32	31	16	28
1997	LOS ANGELES-NL	1-0	4.30	10	0	0	0	0	14.2	12	8	7	5	6
Major League Totals		**36-36**	**4.49**	**131**	**104**	**4**	**1**	**0**	**656.0**	**720**	**356**	**327**	**225**	**316**

CARLOS MENDOZA • Bench Coach

64

FULL NAME: Carlos Enrique Mendoza
BIRTHDATE: 11/27/79 • **OPENING DAY AGE:** 40
BIRTHPLACE: Barquisimeto, Venezuela
RESIDES: Wesley Chapel, Fla.

COACHING CAREER
- The 2020 season marks his 12th with the Yankees organization and first as the team's bench coach…served two seasons as the Yankees' Major League quality control and infield coach (2018-19)…made his Major League coaching debut in 2018 after being named to the role on 2/5/18…became the first person to hold the position for the Yankees.
- Served as the Yankees' lower level field coordinator in 2017 and infield coordinator from 2013-17…was Single-A Charleston's manager in 2012 after making his managerial debut with the GCL Yankees in 2011, leading the team to its fourth league championship…prior to that, served as a coach with short-season Single-A Staten Island in 2009 and Charleston in 2010.
- Served as manager of the Scottsdale Scorpions of the Arizona Fall League in both 2012 and 2016.

PLAYING CAREER
- Played 13 minor league seasons (1997-2009) as a utility infielder in the Giants and Yankees organizations, as well as three years for the independent Pensacola Pelicans…the switch-hitter owned a .232 batting average with 97 doubles, 15 triples, 19HR and 200RBI in 706 career affiliated minor league games.
- Was originally signed by San Francisco as a non-drafted free agent in 1996.

PERSONAL
- Is married to Francis…the couple has two sons, Adrian and Andres.
- Attended U.E. Colegio Andrés Bello in Barquisimeto, Venezuela.

Mendoza's Career Playing Record

Year	Club	AVG	G	AB	R	H	2B	3B	HR	RBI	BB	SO	SB
1997	Salem-Keizer	.208	33	106	10	22	0	0	0	6	11	19	6
1998	San Jose	.214	110	365	36	78	7	3	0	20	19	64	11
1999	Shreveport	.202	111	332	35	67	16	4	3	34	36	65	1
2000	San Jose	.256	112	394	52	101	16	4	5	45	49	82	25
	AZL Giants	.300	6	20	1	6	2	1	0	0	2	2	1
2001					Did Not Play - Injured								
2002	Shreveport	.244	111	377	44	92	20	2	2	28	68	42	12
2003	Norwich	.233	58	180	22	42	10	0	5	19	13	28	1
	Fresno	.250	9	24	3	6	2	0	0	0	0	4	0
2004	Pensacola (IND)	.314	88	328	55	103	21	3	6	44	49	42	11
2005	Pensacola (IND)	.293	89	352	61	103	21	1	10	59	40	56	7
2006	Pensacola (IND)	.346	68	260	40	90	20	0	3	34	40	35	21
	Tampa	.270	31	115	19	31	4	0	4	16	11	18	3
2007	Trenton	.210	84	267	27	56	13	0	0	17	40	54	4
2008	Trenton	.280	30	75	10	21	5	1	0	13	14	15	1
2009	Scranton/WB	.222	3	9	1	2	1	0	0	1	1	3	0
	Trenton	.286	8	14	2	4	1	0	0	1	0	3	0
Minor League Totals*		**.232**	**706**	**2278**	**262**	**528**	**97**	**15**	**19**	**200**	**264**	**399**	**65**

*(*Totals include affiliated minor league baseball only)*

PHIL NEVIN • 3B Coach

FULL NAME: Phillip Joseph Nevin
BIRTHDATE: 1/19/71 • **OPENING DAY AGE:** 49
BIRTHPLACE: Fullerton, Calif.
RESIDES: Poway, Calif.
COLLEGE: Cal State University Fullerton

COACHING CAREER

- Begins his third season as Yankees' third base coach, having been named to the position on 2/5/18…spent the 2017 season as the third base coach for the San Francisco Giants in his Major League coaching debut.
- Owns a .478 (481-525) managerial record over seven minor league seasons with Double-A Erie (2010), Triple-A Toledo (2011-13) and Triple-A Reno (2014-16).
- In his first managerial season with Reno (2014), guided the Aces to a franchise-tying-best record of 81-63 (.562), while leading them to the PCL Championship Series against Omaha before dropping the series.
- Spent the 2009 season managing the Orange County Flyers in the independent Golden Baseball League.

PLAYING CAREER

- In 12 Major League seasons, hit .270 (1,131-for-4,188) with 584R, 209 doubles, 6 triples, 208HR, 743RBI and 449BB over 1,217 games for the Houston Astros (1995), Detroit Tigers (1995-97), Anaheim Angels (1998), San Diego Padres (1999-2005), Texas Rangers (2005-06), Chicago Cubs (2006) and Minnesota Twins (2006).

CAREER HIGHLIGHTS
- NL All-Star Team
  - 2001

- Played five different positions during his career (third base, first base, catcher, left field, right field), starting at least 35 games at each…in 2001 with the Padres, was named to the NL All-Star Team and set career highs with a .306 batting average, 41HR and 126RBI.
- Appeared in one career postseason game, going 0-for-3 as the DH for the Twins in Game 1 of the 2006 ALDS.
- Was originally selected first overall by Houston in the 1992 First-Year Player Draft…is the first former No. 1 overall pick to serve as a Yankees coach.

PERSONAL

- Is married to Kristin and has three children: Koral, Tyler and Kyle…Tyler was drafted by the Colorado Rockies in the first round (38th overall) of the 2015 First-Year Player Draft.
- After retiring as a player in 2007, joined the Padres' pregame radio show and also served as an analyst for the college baseball regionals during the College World Series.
- Attended Cal State Fullerton where he played football and baseball…in 1992, won the Golden Spikes Award and National Player of the Year honors by *Baseball America* and Collegiate Baseball.

Nevin's Career Major League Playing Record

Year	Club	AVG	G	AB	R	H	2B	3B	HR	RBI	BB	SO	SB
1995	HOUSTON	.117	18	60	4	7	1	0	0	1	7	13	1
	DETROIT	.219	29	96	9	21	3	1	2	12	11	27	0
1996	DETROIT	.292	38	120	15	35	5	0	8	19	8	39	1
1997	DETROIT	.235	93	251	32	59	16	1	9	35	25	68	0
1998	ANAHEIM	.228	75	237	27	54	8	1	8	27	17	67	0
1999	SAN DIEGO	.269	128	383	52	103	27	0	24	85	51	82	1
2000	SAN DIEGO	.303	143	538	87	163	34	1	31	107	59	121	2
2001	SAN DIEGO	.306	149	546	97	167	31	0	41	126	71	147	4
2002	SAN DIEGO	.285	107	407	53	116	16	0	12	57	38	87	4
2003	SAN DIEGO	.279	59	226	30	63	8	0	13	46	21	44	2
2004	SAN DIEGO	.289	147	547	78	158	31	1	26	105	66	121	0
2005	SAN DIEGO	.256	73	281	31	72	11	1	9	47	19	67	1
	TEXAS	.182	29	99	15	18	5	0	3	8	8	30	2
2006	TEXAS	.216	46	176	26	38	8	0	9	31	21	39	0
	CHICAGO-NL	.274	67	179	26	49	4	0	12	33	17	52	0
	MINNESOTA	.190	16	42	2	8	1	0	1	4	10	15	0
AL Totals		**.228**	**326**	**1021**	**126**	**233**	**46**	**3**	**40**	**136**	**100**	**285**	**3**
NL Totals		**.284**	**891**	**3167**	**458**	**898**	**163**	**3**	**168**	**607**	**349**	**734**	**15**
Major League Totals		**.270**	**1217**	**4188**	**584**	**1131**	**209**	**6**	**208**	**743**	**449**	**1019**	**18**

P.J. PILITTERE • Asst. Hitting Coach

FULL NAME: Peter John Pilittere
BIRTHDATE: 11/23/81 • **OPENING DAY AGE:** 38
BIRTHPLACE: San Dimas, Calif.
RESIDES: Indio, Calif.
COLLEGE: Cal State University Fullerton

COACHING CAREER
- Begins his third season as the Yankees' assistant hitting coach in 2020…made his Major League coaching debut in 2018 after being named to the role on 2/5/18…is the third person to hold the position, joining Alan Cockrell in 2015 and Marcus Thames from 2016-17.
- The 2020 season marks his ninth with the Yankees organization (third in his current role) after previously serving as the hitting coach at four different levels over five years from 2013-17: Triple-A Scranton/Wilkes-Barre (2017), Double-A Trenton (2015-16), Single-A Tampa (2014) and Single-A Charleston (2013)…began his coaching career with the GCL Yankees in 2012.
- In 2017—his only season coaching with Scranton/WB—the RailRiders established a Yankees-era franchise record with a league-high 153HR, surpassing the previous team high of 133, set in 2013.
- In 2014, served as the hitting coach for the Scottsdale Scorpions of the Arizona Fall League.

PLAYING CAREER
- Played eight minor league seasons as a catcher in the Yankees system from 2004-11, hitting .264 (424-for-1,605) with 77 doubles, 16HR and 183RBI in 470 games.
- Twice led his league in fielding percentage at catcher, producing a .995 mark with Double-A Trenton in 2007 and a .998 mark with Single-A Tampa in 2006…posted a .995 career fielding pct. as a catcher, making just 18 errors in 3,306 total chances behind the plate.
- Was signed by Arizona to a minor league contract as a free agent in November 2010, but was released by the Diamondbacks prior to the start of the 2011 season and re-signed with the Yankees.
- Was originally selected by the Yankees in the 13th round of the 2004 First-Year Player Draft.

PERSONAL
- Last name is pronounced "pill-ih-TAIR-ee"…is married to Shannon.
- Was a team captain at Cal State Fullerton, helping lead the Titans to a College World Series Championship in 2004…hit .351 with 18 doubles, 4HR and 49RBI in 69 games during his senior season.
- Graduated from Bishop Amat H.S. (Calif.)…earned first-team All-Del Rey League and honorable mention All-San Gabriel Valley honors…was the starting catcher in the 1999 San Gabriel Valley All-Star Game.

Pilittere's Career Playing Record

Year	Club	AVG	G	AB	R	H	2B	3B	HR	RBI	BB	SO	SB
2004	Staten Island	.215	34	121	9	26	6	0	0	11	3	18	1
2005	Staten Island	.250	53	176	18	44	11	0	4	25	12	17	0
2006	Tampa	.302	87	291	39	88	14	2	5	38	20	24	3
2007	Trenton	.261	100	348	43	91	16	2	2	34	26	42	0
2008	Trenton	.277	97	364	46	101	15	1	3	48	20	32	0
2009	Scranton/WB	.244	28	86	8	21	6	0	1	9	3	9	0
	Trenton	.198	27	96	5	19	3	0	0	8	7	8	0
2010	Scranton/WB	.357	22	56	6	20	4	0	1	5	5	13	0
2011	Scranton/WB	.209	22	67	4	14	2	0	0	5	8	10	1
Minor League Totals		**.264**	**470**	**1605**	**178**	**424**	**77**	**5**	**16**	**183**	**104**	**173**	**5**

TANNER SWANSON • Coach

68

FULL NAME: Tanner James Swanson
BIRTHDATE: 8/31/82 • **OPENING DAY AGE:** 37
BIRTHPLACE: Seattle, Wash.
RESIDES: Seattle, Wash.
COLLEGE: Central Washington University

COACHING CAREER
- Begins his first season as the Yankees' quality control coach in 2020 after being named to the position on 1/14/20…also serves as the team's catching coach and the organization's Director of Catching, in which he oversees the Yankees' catching operation at all levels and consults with the player development catching coordinator.
- Spent the last two seasons (2018-19) as the Minnesota Twins' minor league catching coordinator.
- Prior to joining the Twins, spent nine seasons at various levels of collegiate baseball, including a five-year stint as a volunteer assistant coach at the University of Washington (2013-17), where he also briefly served as the school's Director of Baseball Operations for one season (2012)…during his tenure as a coach at Washington, his catchers garnered three All-Pac-12 Conference selections, with two also being selected in the first three rounds of the Major League First-Year Player Draft.
- Served as head coach at Green River Community College (Wash.) in 2011…was a lecturer in the School of Physical Education and School Health, while also serving as an assistant coach at his alma mater, Central Washington University, in 2010…in 2009, was an assistant coach at Everett Community College (Wash.), and in 2008, he taught and coached baseball at Sultan High School.

PLAYING CAREER
- Did not play baseball professionally.

PERSONAL
- Is married to Laura…the couple has two daughters, Tatum and Harper.
- Grew up in Roslyn, Wash., and graduated from Cle Elum-Roslyn High School in 2001.
- Attended Green River Community College (Wash.) for one year and Everett Community College (Wash.) for one year, earning All-NWAACC honors as a sophomore in 2003…graduated from Central Washington University in 2006 with a Bachelor of Science degree in Physical Education and School Health…while at CWU, was an academic all-conference selection.
- Attended Seattle University and is in the process of earning a Masters in Sports Administration and Leadership.

MARCUS THAMES • Hitting Coach

62

FULL NAME: Marcus Markley Thames
BIRTHDATE: 3/6/77 • **OPENING DAY AGE:** 43
BIRTHPLACE: Louisville, Miss.
RESIDES: Tampa, Fla.
COLLEGE: Texas State University

COACHING CAREER
- Begins his third season as the Yankees' hitting coach in 2020 after being named to the position on 2/5/18…spent the previous two seasons (2016-17) as the club's assistant hitting coach.
- In 2019, Yankees batters set a franchise record with 306HR, one shy of the Major League record set by the 2019 Minnesota Twins (307)…had a Major League-record 14 players hit at least 10HR, surpassing their own 2018 record (12)…tied club records with five players hitting 25HR and seven players with at least 20HR…Yankees batters scored 943R, their most since 2007 (968) and most in the Majors in 2019…was ejected by HP umpire Jeremie Rehak on 9/21 vs. Toronto.
- In 2018, Yankees batters set a then-single-season Major League record with 267HR, surpassing the 1997 Mariners (264) for the all-time team record (the 267HR record was surpassed by four clubs in 2019)…their 1.65HR/G and 20.66AB/HR ratios were also best in Major League history (also since surpassed)…ranked second in the Majors with 851R and 5.25R/G, trailing only Boston in both categories (876R, 5.41R/G)…tied a then-Major League record with 24 individual multi-HR games (also the 1961 Yankees and 1966 Braves, all surpassed in 2019)…became the first team in Baseball history to have 12 players hit at least 10HR in the same season…had five players with at least 25HR, matching the franchise record (also 2009 and '19)…according to *Elias*, became the first team in Major League history to hit at least 20HR from all nine batting order spots.
- In 2017, Yankees batters led the Majors with 241HR, the sixth-highest total in franchise history…scored 858R and averaged 5.30R/G, second to only Houston (896R, 5.53R/G)…outscored the Yankees' 2016 club (680R) by 178 runs, their largest year-over-year scoring increase since improving 247R from 1936-37 (excludes strike years).
- In 2016, helped three players record their first career 20HR seasons (Castro, Gregorius and Sánchez).
- Was a minor league hitting coach in the Yankees organization for three seasons, serving the role for Single-A Tampa in 2013, Double-A Trenton in 2014 and Triple-A Scranton/Wilkes-Barre in 2015…in 2015, the RailRiders offense led the International League with a .271 BA (1,332-for-4,915), 622 runs scored and a .727 OPS.

PLAYING CAREER
- Was selected by the Yankees in the 30th round of the 1996 First-Year Player Draft…played in parts of 10 Major League seasons with the Yankees (2002, '10), Texas (2003), Detroit (2004-09) and Los Angeles-NL (2011), combining to hit .246 (450-for-1,827) with 115HR and 301RBI.
- Made his Major League debut and homered off Randy Johnson in his first career at-bat on 6/10/02 vs. Arizona.
- Hit a career-high 26HR in 110 games with the AL Champion Detroit Tigers in 2006.

PERSONAL
- Last name is pronounced "tims"…he and his wife, Danna, have three daughters, Deja, Jade and Ella Grace, and two sons, Marcus Jr. and Kole…attended East Central Community College (Miss.) and Texas State University.
- Participated in and sponsored youth baseball organizations throughout his career, including Gloves for Kids and Play Baseball Detroit…also sponsored youth baseball teams during the annual Negro Leagues Weekend.
- Was a member of the National Guard from 1994-98.

Thames' Career Major League Playing Record

Year	Club	AVG	G	AB	R	H	2B	3B	HR	RBI	BB	SO	SB
2002	YANKEES	.231	7	13	2	3	1	0	1	2	0	4	0
2003	TEXAS	.205	30	73	12	15	2	0	1	4	8	18	0
2004	DETROIT	.255	61	165	24	42	12	0	10	33	16	42	0
2005	DETROIT	.196	38	107	11	21	2	0	7	16	9	38	0
2006	DETROIT	.256	110	348	61	89	20	2	26	60	37	92	1
2007	DETROIT	.242	86	269	37	65	15	0	18	54	13	72	2
2008	DETROIT	.241	103	316	50	76	12	0	25	56	24	95	0
2009	DETROIT	.252	87	258	33	65	11	1	13	36	29	72	0
2010	YANKEES	.288	82	212	22	61	7	0	12	33	19	61	0
2011	LOS ANGELES-NL	.197	36	66	4	13	1	1	2	7	4	16	0
Minor League Totals		.278	911	3344	580	928	207	28	147	545	367	645	51
Major League Totals		.246	640	1827	256	450	83	4	115	301	159	510	3

REGGIE WILLITS • 1B Coach

FULL NAME: Reggie Gene Willits
BIRTHDATE: 5/30/81 • **OPENING DAY AGE:** 38
BIRTHPLACE: Chickasha, Okla.
RESIDES: Fort Cobb, Okla.
COLLEGE: University of Oklahoma

COACHING CAREER
- Begins his third season as the Yankees' first base coach and outfield instructor in 2020…made his Major League coaching debut in the role in 2018 after being named to the position on 2/5/18.
- Spent the previous three seasons (2015-17) serving as an outfield and baserunning coordinator in the organization's player development system…during his tenure, Yankees minor leaguers were successful on 70.3 percent of their stolen base attempts.
- Prior to joining the Yankees organization, served as the head coach of both fall and spring baseball at Binger-Olney H.S. (Okla.) from August 2012 to January 2015…his team qualified for the state tournament in four of his five seasons and captured the state championship twice.

PLAYING CAREER
- Played six seasons as a switch-hitting outfielder for the Los Angeles Angels (2006-11), batting .258 (218-for-844) with 146R, 35 doubles, 58RBI and 40SB in 414 Major League games…in 2007, he led all AL rookies with 69BB and a .391 OBP and ranked in the top five in batting average (second, .293), stolen bases (second, 27), runs (third, 74) and hits (fifth, 126).
- Was originally selected by the Angels in the seventh round of the 2003 First-Year Player Draft out of the University of Oklahoma.

PERSONAL
- Is married to Amber…the couple has three children: Jaxon, Eli and Hunter.
- His father named him Reggie after Reggie Jackson…his sister, Wendi, was a professional basketball player and won a championship with the Los Angeles Sparks.
- Played for the University of Oklahoma after transferring from Seminole State College (Okla.).
- Attended Fort Cobb-Broxton H.S. (Okla.).

Willits' Career Playing Record

Year	Club	AVG	G	AB	R	H	2B	3B	HR	RBI	BB	SO	SB
2003	Provo	.300	59	230	53	69	14	4	4	27	37	52	14
2004	Rancho Cucamonga	.285	135	526	99	150	17	5	5	52	73	112	44
2005	Arkansas	.304	123	487	75	148	23	6	2	46	54	78	40
2006	Salt Lake	.327	97	352	85	115	18	4	3	39	77	50	31
	LOS ANGELES-AL	.267	28	45	12	12	1	0	0	2	11	10	4
2007	LOS ANGELES-AL	.293	136	430	74	126	20	1	0	34	69	83	27
2008	LOS ANGELES-AL	.194	82	108	21	21	4	0	0	7	21	26	2
	Salt Lake	.378	10	37	7	14	2	1	0	4	5	6	1
	Rancho Cucamonga	.357	4	14	4	5	0	0	0	0	2	1	2
2009	Salt Lake	.261	62	234	40	61	10	1	1	27	34	44	11
	LOS ANGELES-AL	.213	49	80	16	17	2	0	0	6	5	17	5
2010	Rancho Cucamonga	.267	5	15	3	4	1	0	0	1	4	2	2
	LOS ANGELES-AL	.258	97	159	23	41	7	0	0	8	19	26	2
2011	Inland Empire	.200	5	20	1	4	1	0	0	3	3	5	0
	LOS ANGELES-AL	.045	22	22	0	1	1	0	0	1	4	7	0
	Salt Lake	.260	65	227	36	59	5	2	0	15	44	46	5
Minor League Totals		.294	565	2142	403	629	91	23	15	214	333	396	150
Major League Totals		.258	414	844	146	218	35	1	0	58	129	169	40

SHARE THE GAME WITH THE NEXT GENERATION
GET INVOLVED AT PLAYBALL.org AND FOLLOW @PLAYBALL

2020 Major League Baseball Properties, Inc. All rights reserved. Major League Baseball trademarks and copyrights are proprietary to MLB entities. Visit MLB.com

complete your collection at **YANKEES BOOKSHELF**

YANKEES MAGAZINE
1-year subscription
Eight issues
$34.99
special offer

YEARBOOKS
2020 **$20.00** '05–'19 **$15.00**

$20.00

YANKEES MAGAZINE:
DEREK JETER COMMEMORATIVE EDITION
(EXPANDED EDITION)

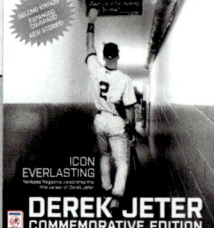

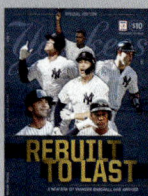

YANKEES MAGAZINE: 2018 SPECIAL EDITION
ALSO AVAILABLE: YANKEES MAGAZINE: MONUMENT PARK EDITION
YANKEES MAGAZINE: HOME RUN EDITION

$10.00

$19.95 | 2020 MEDIA GUIDE & RECORD BOOK

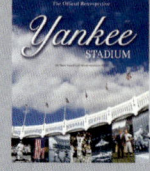

YANKEE STADIUM: THE OFFICIAL RETROSPECTIVE   **$50.00**

Call (800) GO-YANKS

or visit www.yankees.com/publications

Follow Yankees Magazine on Twitter @YanksMagazine

Additional Yankees Coaching Staff

Brett Weber
Advance Scouting Director and Coaching Assistant
The 2020 season marks his third as the Yankees' Advance Scouting Director and Coaching Assistant…joined the Major League coaching staff in 2009…handles advance materials in preparation for upcoming series, working directly with the coaching staff to provide analytical information…also coordinates all Yankees aspects of the MLB replay system…was drafted by the Phillies in 1997 (did not sign) and Yankees in 1998, spending three seasons pitching in the Yankees' minor league system (1998-2000)…also pitched for the Schaumburg Flyers in independent league baseball from 2003-04…a 1998 graduate of the University of Illinois, Weber worked in finance at Smith Barney Citigroup between his pitching and coaching career…is married to Tara and the couple has a son, Brady.

Zac Fieroh
Analyst, Major League Coaching Staff
Enters his third season as the Yankees' Major League Analyst…is responsible for integrating the use of quantitative information with on-field performance and preparation, serving as a conduit between the quantitative analysis department and the Major League players and coaches…worked in the Yankees' quantitative analysis department in 2017…was a software consultant prior to joining the Yankees…graduated from the University of Michigan with a degree in Industrial & Operations Engineering in 2012…he and his wife, Caroline, live in Manhattan.

Radley Haddad
Coaching Assistant and Bullpen Catcher
Enters his fourth season as the Yankees' Coaching Assistant and Bullpen Catcher after transitioning from a player to the coaching staff at the start of the 2017 season…works closely with Yankees coaches to aid in the development of Yankees pitchers and catchers…played four minor league seasons as a catcher with the Yankees (2013-16) after being signed by the organization as a non-drafted free agent in June 2013…also served as a player/coach with Staten Island in 2016…the Carmel, Ind., native graduated from Butler University with a finance degree in 2013…he and his wife, Arielle, live in New Jersey.

Aaron Barnett
Bullpen Catcher
Begins his first season as Yankees Bullpen Catcher…spent the 2019 season interning in the Mariners' player development department…played baseball at Pepperdine University from 2013-17, where he graduated with a degree in economics and a minor in applied mathematics…following his graduation, worked at Deloitte & Touche as a transfer pricing consultant from August 2017 through April 2018…underwent "Tommy John" surgery in Dec. 2017 as he looked to get back into baseball…prior to joining Seattle's front office, worked as a sales analyst at MDF Instruments, a medical device company…resides in his native Orange County, Calif., during the offseason.

Player Health & Performance Staff

Eric Cressey • Director, Player Health and Performance

The 2020 season will mark his first with the Yankees, having been named the club's Director of Player Health and Performance…is the first person to hold the title with the organization and will play a role in staffing, assessments, facility enhancements, equipment, continuing education, and technology across strength and conditioning and sports medicine…is president and co-founder of Cressey Sports Performance, which has facilities in Palm Beach Gardens, Fla. and Hudson, Mass., and specializes its training programs on kinesiology and biomechanics…has worked with athletes of all ages and levels, ranging from youth sports to professionals and Olympians, helping them to reach the pinnacle in performance in their sports…has worked most extensively with baseball players, with more than 100 professional players training with him each offseason…newly appointed Yankees pitching coach Matt Blake previously worked as a pitching coordinator for the company…is host of the "Elite Baseball Development" podcast and has served as an invited guest speaker nationally and internationally…has also authored more than 500 articles and published five books…is a Certified Strength and Conditioning Specialist (CSCS) through the National Strength and Conditioning Association…received his Master's degree in kinesiology with a concentration in exercise science through the University of Connecticut…his Master's thesis was published in the Journal of Strength and Conditioning Research…while at UConn, was involved in varsity strength and conditioning and research in the human performance laboratory…completed his undergraduate work at the University of New England with a double major in exercise science and sports and fitness management…currently serves on the advisory boards for the International Youth Conditioning Association, OnBaseU, and Precision Nutrition, and is a baseball consultant to New Balance…served as the strength and conditioning coach for the USA Baseball Under-18 National Team that won the gold medal at the 2015 World Cup in Osaka, Japan…as a competitive powerlifter, holds several state, national and world records…resides in Jupiter, Fla., with his wife, Anna, and three daughters, Lydia, Addison, and Teagan.

Donovan Santas • Assistant Director, Player Health and Performance

Will begin his first season as the Yankees' Assistant Director of Player Health and Performance in 2020, the first person to hold the position for the club…will be his 20th season working in professional baseball, having spent the last 17 with the Blue Jays…most recently served as Toronto's Head of Strength and Conditioning, overseeing all areas of the field for the organization…earned a Bachelor of Science degree in exercise and sports science from the University of Wisconsin-La Crosse and is a National Strength and Conditioning Association Registered Strength and Conditioning Coach with Distinction…serves on the Board of Directors for the Professional Baseball Strength Coaches Society…resides in Tampa, Fla., with his wife, Dana, and son, Luke.

Michael Schuk • Director, Sports Medicine & Rehabilitation

Begins his seventh season with the Yankees and first as Director of Sports Medicine & Rehabilitation…spent six seasons (2014-19) as the team's Physical Therapist/Assistant Athletic Trainer…spent time from 2012-14 working on the THOR[3] initiative, a program designed to aid the physical and mental abilities of Army Special Forces…prior to his work with the Army, served as an athletic trainer in the Cleveland Indians' minor league system in 2006 and again in 2010…earned a Doctor of Physical Therapy degree at Nova Southeastern University in Fort Lauderdale, Fla., in 2010…graduated from the University of Central Florida in 2005…resides in Manhattan.

Tim Lentych • Head Athletic Trainer

The 2020 season is his first as the Yankees' Head Athletic Trainer and 17th with the organization…spent four seasons (2016-19) as the Yankees' Assistant Athletic Trainer…was the Yankees' Minor League Head Athletic Trainer from 2012-15…spent four seasons as the head trainer for Double-A Trenton (2008-11) and was named the 2009 Eastern League "Athletic Trainer of the Year"…was the trainer with Single-A Charleston from 2005-07 after serving the same role for short-season Single-A Staten Island in 2004…earned his Bachelor's degree in applied sciences and technology with a concentration in athletic training from Ball State University in 2001 and worked as an athletic training intern with Baltimore that year…earned his Master's degree from the University of Tennessee in 2004…he and his wife, Katie, live in Tampa.

Steve Donohue • Director, Medical Services

Begins his 42nd consecutive season in the Yankees organization in 2020 and first as Director of Medical Services...spent the prior eight seasons as the team's Head Athletic Trainer (2012-19)...spent 26 years (1986-2011) as the Yankees' Assistant Athletic Trainer under Gene Monahan, sharing MLB's "Athletic Training Staff of the Year" honors in 1990 and 2010...in January 2020, was inducted into the New York State Athletic Trainers Association Hall of Fame...in January 2018, was named the winner of the "Most Distinguished Athletic Trainer Award" by the National Athletic Trainers Association...served as an athletic trainer for the American League squad at the 2018 All-Star Game at Nationals Park in Washington D.C., the 2006 All Star Game at Pittsburgh's PNC Park and the 1999 All-Star Game at Boston's Fenway Park...began his athletic training career in 1979 at the Yankees' Double-A West Haven affiliate before being promoted to Double-A Nashville (1980-81) and Triple-A Columbus (1982-85)...was promoted to the New York Yankees in 1986...is a 1974 graduate of Cardinal Spellman High School in the Bronx and a 1979 graduate of the University of Louisville...was the trainer for the NCAA Champion University of Louisville men's basketball team in 1980...is a member of the National Athletic Trainers Association and on the organization's public relations committee...is also a member of the Eastern Athletic Trainers Association...also pens the annual Professional Baseball Athletic Trainers Society's *Confidential Directory*...he and his wife, Paula, have two daughters, Shannon and Margaret...was born in Bronxville, N.Y.

Alfonso Malaguti • Assistant Athletic Trainer

Begins his first season as the Yankees' Assistant Athletic Trainer and ninth in the Yankees organization...most recently served as the Yankees' International Player Development Athletic Trainer from 2018-19...joined the Yankees as an Athletic Trainer Intern with Single-A Tampa in 2010 and served in the same role with Player Development in 2011...was the GCL Yankees East Athletic Trainer in 2012 before becoming the Latin America Medical Coordinator and GCL athletic trainer from 2012-15...served as the U.S. Men's National Softball Team Athletic Trainer from 2017-19, which included the 2019 Lima Pan American games and tournaments in the Czech Republic, U.S.A. and Dominican Republic...in 2016, founded Centro de Medicina Deportiva Malaguti, a sports medicine clinic and rehab center in Juan Dolio, D.R. that works with patients of all ages and specializes in the examination and program development of professional and amateur baseball players...won the GCL Athletic Trainer of the Year Award in 2014...earned a Bachelor's degree in athletic training from the University of South Florida in 2011...is a native of Maracay, Venezuela.

Brett McCabe • Major League Strength and Conditioning Coach

Begins his first season as the Yankees' Major League Strength and Conditioning Coach in 2020...spent six seasons (2013-18) in the same role with the San Diego Padres...prior to joining the Padres, spent seven seasons (2006-12) with the Arizona Diamondbacks, where, as the minor league strength and conditioning coordinator, he oversaw the strength and conditioning programs for each of the organization's affiliates...from 2003-05, was a strength and conditioning coach in the Blue Jays system, working at Double-A New Haven in 2003 and Triple-A Syracuse from 2004-05...earned a Bachelor of Science degree in movement science at Grand Valley State University (Mich.) in 2002...is a licensed massage therapist, registered strength and conditioning coach and certified strength and conditioning specialist...resides in San Diego, Calif., with his wife, Krystle, and their daughter, Ella.

Matt Rutledge • Major League Assistant Strength and Conditioning Coach

Begins his first season as the Yankees' Major League Assistant Strength and Conditioning Coach...spent the last five seasons in the Athletics organization...from 2018-19, served as the organization's minor league assistant strength and conditioning coordinator...served as a minor league strength and conditioning coach in the A's system from 2015-17...earned a Bachelor of Science degree in community health sciences from the University of Nevada-Reno in 2013, and is a native of Carson City, Nevada.

Drew Weisberg • Major League Dietitian

Begins his fourth season in the Yankees organization and first as the Major League Dietitian...spent the previous three seasons (2017-19) as the team's Assistant Strength and Conditioning Coach...prior to joining the Yankees, worked as an intern in the nutrition department for the Green Bay Packers from 2015-17...completed his undergraduate degree at Rutgers University in 2014 and became a registered dietitian through schooling at NYU in 2018...is also a certified strength and conditioning specialist...is a lifelong resident of Bergen County, N.J.

Doug Cecil • Massage Therapist

Begins his 10th season as the Yankees' Massage Therapist in 2020, having joined the organization in 2011...prior to his time with the Yankees, held the same role for the Tampa Bay Devil Rays (2005), Toronto Blue Jays (2006) and Texas Rangers (2007-10)...attended Florida State University and later graduated from the Suncoast School of Massage for Sports Medicine in 2005...grew up in Elizabethtown, Ky., and later spent 20 years living in Tampa, Fla....currently resides in Manhattan.

Yankees Medical Staff

Dr. Christopher Ahmad, M.D.
Head Team Physician

Dr. Christopher S. Ahmad begins his 12th season as Yankees Head Team Physician in 2020…holds the same position with NYCFC…has been an Assistant Attending Orthopaedic Surgeon in the Sports Medicine and Shoulder Service at New York Orthopaedic Hospital since 2001…has also served as an Associate Professor of Orthopaedic Surgery at Columbia University since 2007 after having been an Assistant Professor beginning in 2001…trained in sports medicine at the Kerlan-Jobe Orthopaedic Clinic from 2000-01, which included team physician coverage for the Dodgers (MLB), Lakers (NBA), Kings (NHL), Galaxy (MLS) and Fullerton College football…was Administrative Chief Resident of Orthopaedic Surgery from 1999-2000 at Columbia University, where he served his orthopaedic surgery residency from 1996-99…completed the Frank E. Stinchfield Orthopaedic Research Fellowship at Columbia from 1994-95…received his M.D. from the NYU School of Medicine in 1994 and a B.S. in Mechanical Engineering from Columbia University in 1990…has been elected into the American Orthopaedic Society for Sports Medicine and the American Shoulder and Elbow Surgeons Society…his practice specializes in advanced arthroscopic surgical techniques for sports-related injuries of the knee, shoulder and elbow.

Dr. Paul Lee, M.D., M.P.H.
Head Team Internist

Dr. Paul Gene Lee has served as the Head Team Internist for the New York Yankees since 2007…has held the same position with New York City Football Club since 2015…is the Harry C. and Misook Doolittle Professor of Medicine at Columbia University…received his B.A. degree from Cornell University, his M.D. degree from Mount Sinai School of Medicine and his M.P.H. degree from Columbia University…after serving as a chief resident at Columbia Presbyterian Medical Center, he joined the faculty in 2001…among his current functions, he serves as Medical Director of the Hospitalist Program, Medical Director for Columbia Crown Health, a concierge medicine program, and Medical Director for Global (International) Patient Services at the NewYork-Presbyterian Hospital.

Dr. Stuart J. Hershon, M.D., P.C.
Senior Advisor, Orthopedics

Born December 18, 1937, in Brooklyn, N.Y., Hershon, begins his 33rd season as part of the Yankees medical staff, serving as the team's Head Physician from 1988-2008…is an orthopedic surgeon affiliated with NYU Langone Medical Center and Hospital for Joint Diseases, where he is Assistant Clinical Professor of Sports Medicine and Orthopedic Surgery…was formerly Chief of Sports Medicine at Roosevelt Hospital and North Shore University Medicine…graduated from Harvard (1959) and New York Medical College (1963) before serving as a medical officer with the U.S. Navy from 1964-66…was a starting tight end for Harvard and their leading receiver in 1958…was a *Newsday* "All-Scholastic" player at Long Beach (N.Y.) High School in 1954…has also served as team physician for the New York Arrows of the Major Indoor Soccer League and Nassau Community College…Dr. Hershon and his wife, Judy, reside in Cove Neck, N.Y., and have two children, Joanna and Jordan, and several grandchildren.

Dr. Norman Castellano, M.D.
Team Physician, Tampa

Dr. Will Turner, M.D.
Team Internist

Dr. Daniel Murphy, M.D.
Team Orthopedic Surgeon, Tampa

Additional Medical Staff
T. Sean Lynch - Orthopedic
Arnold Ramirez - Family Practice/Sports Medicine, Tampa
Scott Levy, D.D.S. - Dentist
Darrell Rigel, M.D. - Dermatologist
Louis Bisogni, D.C. - Chiropractor
Gil Chimes, D.C. - Chiropractor
Scott Hegseth, D.C. - Team Chiropractor, Tampa

Yankees Mental Conditioning Staff

The Mental Conditioning Department educates, challenges, and supports players, coaches, and staff on the mental side of the game by emphasizing the right mindset that contributes to elite performance, on and off the field.

Chad Bohling
Director, Mental Conditioning
Begins his 16th season in the Yankees organization, overseeing the club's mental conditioning department…was named to his position in 2009 and works with the Major League club throughout the season…also assists with scouting interviews for the Major Leaue Baseball First-Year Player Draft…outside of the Yankees, consults with the Dallas Cowboys in the NFL (since 2012) and Wheels Up Aviation Company (since 2019), and serves in an advisory role for both the Michael Johnson Performance Center and LEADERS in Sport…prior to joining the Yankees, served as the Director of Mental Conditioning for the IMG Academies in Bradenton, Fla., from 1997-2005, working with many athletes, including Olympians and MLB, NBA, NFL, ATP and WTA professionals…with IMG, specifically worked with 27 NFL first-round draft picks from 2001-05 and the Jacksonville Jaguars from 2002-05…also while at IMG Academies, served as an Adjunct Professor for Manatee Community College, teaching Mental Training and Development…earned a B.A. in Psychology from Wichita State University and an M.A. in Exercise and Nutritional Sciences with specialization in Sport Psychology from San Diego State University.

Chris Passarella
Associate Director, Mental Conditioning
Begins his 13th season with the Yankees organization, having joined the club in 2008…is based out of the Yankees' Player Development Complex in Tampa, but travels throughout the team's minor league system during the season…oversees the organization's mental conditioning program as it relates to the annual Major League Baseball First-Year Player Draft, conducting interviews with prospective amateur players prior to the June draft…earned a B.A. of Psychology from the University of Indianapolis in 1999 and an M.S. in Sport Behavior and Performance from Miami University (Ohio) in 2001.

Héctor González
Coordinator, Cultural Development
The 2020 season marks his 12th as the Yankees' Cultural Development Coordinator…is based out of the Yankees' Player Development Complex in Tampa…travels throughout the minor league system during the season to work with the organization's prospects, while also assisting Latin American players as they adjust to life in the United States…the former infielder is a native of Estado Miranda, Venezuela, and was selected by the Yankees in the 35th round of the 2003 First-Year Player Draft…played in the Yankees' minor league system for three seasons (2003-05)…graduated from Brito Miami Private School in Miami, Fla., and is currently attending Hillsborough Community College (Fla.).

David Schnabel
Video Coordinator, Mental Conditioning
Begins his 11th season with the Yankees organization…produces motivational, educational and highlight videos for individual players and for use in team and group meetings…also assists other departments within the Yankees organization with video needs (i.e. front office, scouting and player development)…attended Vanderbilt University, where he earned a Bachelor of Music degree.

Lauren Johnson
Coordinator, Mental Conditioning
The 2020 season marks her fourth with the Yankees organization…travels throughout the organization's minor league system during the season…also assists with the interview process in preparation for the Major League Baseball First-Year Player Draft in June…earned her M.A. in Performance Psychology from National University in 2014.

Noel Garcia
Mental Conditioning Coach
Begins his second season in the Yankees organization, having been hired in February 2019…in his role, assists with domestic and Latin players on the mental side of the game, as well as guiding Latin players in their transition to the United States…earned a Masters of Science in Sports Exercise and Performance Psychology from Barry University (Fla.) in May 2018.

Yankees Support Staff

Rob Cucuzza
Equipment Manager
Begins his 23rd season as home clubhouse manager…was named the 2010 MLB "Home Clubhouse Manager of the Year" as voted by his peers…has been a member of the Yankees organization since 1984, working as a bat boy (1984-86), assistant visiting clubhouse manager (1987-89) and assistant equipment manager (1990-97)…was born on 1/4/68 in the Bronx, N.Y., and is a 1985 graduate of Mount St. Michael Academy…resides in White Plains, N.Y., and is the son of former Visiting Clubhouse Manager, Lou Cucuzza, Sr.

Lou Cucuzza, Jr.
Director, Clubhouse Operations
The 2020 season marks his 42nd year in the New York Yankees organization, having started as a bat boy in 1979…served as equipment manager on the 2014 MLB Japan Tour…was named the 2010 MLB "Visiting Clubhouse Manager of the Year" as voted by his peers, earning the title for the second straight season and third time over a five-year span (also 2006)…currently serves as President of the Major League Baseball Clubhouse Managers Association…earned a B.A. in public accounting from Iona College…worked five years as an auditor for the accounting firm of KPMG Peat Marwick (1987-91) and five years as budgeting manager for Melville Corporation (1992-96)…was born on 8/5/64 in the Bronx, N.Y.…resides in Yonkers, N.Y., with his wife, Joanna, and their children, Anthony and Kathryn…is the son of former Visiting Clubhouse Manager, Lou Cucuzza, Sr.

Clubhouse Assistants
Cesar Caceres ◆ Chris Cruz ◆ Rich Davis ◆ Doug Fiedler ◆ Joe Lee ◆ Chris Manzione ◆ Matt Nimer ◆ Aaron Patella Ryan

Danilo Valiente
Major League
Batting Practice Pitcher

Dan Pane
Major League
Video Coordinator

Milestone Wins in Franchise History

1 . . . . 4/23/1903 at Washington, 7-2	5,000 . . . . 9/11/1959 vs. Detroit, 9-3
100 . . . . 6/19/1904 at St. Louis (G1), 4-3	6,000 . . 5/8/1971 at Chicago-AL, 2-1 (11 innings)
500 . . . . .8/31/1909 at Cleveland (G1), 4-1	7,000 . . . . .8/4/1982 vs. Chicago-AL, 6-2
1,000 . . . . 9/9/1916 at Philadelphia (G1), 4-1	8,000 . . . . 7/21/1994 at California, 11-7
2,000 . . . . 6/2/1928 at Detroit, 5-2 (10 innings)	9,000 . . . . .5/17/2005 at Seattle, 6-0
3,000 . . . . 8/27/1938 vs. Cleveland (G1), 8-7	10,000 . . . . 10/1/2015 vs. Boston, 4-1
4,000 . . . . 6/30/1949 at Boston, 6-3	

*With their 10,000th win, the Yankees became the first AL team to reach 10,000 regular season victories…with a 10,378-7,240 (.570) franchise record through 2019, the Yankees are the all-time winningest AL team.

How the Yankees Were Built

SIGNED AS A FREE AGENT (9):
Zack Britton...January 11, 2019
Aroldis Chapman..............................December 15, 2016
Gerrit Cole...December 18, 2019
Brett Gardner*....................................January 11, 2020
J.A. Happ..December 17, 2018
Kyle Higashioka*.............................November 18, 2015
DJ LeMahieu......................................January 14, 2019
Jonathan Loaisiga.............................February 9, 2016
Adam Ottavino....................................January 24, 2019

SIGNED AS A NON-DRAFTED FREE AGENT (9):
Miguel Andújar..July 2, 2011
Thairo Estrada..August 2, 2012
Estevan Florial..March 19, 2015
Mike Ford..July 17, 2013
Deivi García...July 2, 2015
Luis Medina...July 8, 2015
Gary Sánchez..July 2, 2009
Luis Severino....................................December 26, 2011
Miguel Yajure..March 5, 2015

SELECTED IN FIRST-YEAR PLAYER DRAFT (6):
Jonathan Holder..........................June 2014, 6th round
Aaron Judge................................June 2013, 1st round
Brooks Kriske..............................June 2016, 6th round
Jordan Montgomery...................June 2014, 4th round
Nick Nelson.................................June 2016, 4th round
Tyler Wade..................................June 2013, 4th round

ACQUIRED THROUGH THE MLB/JAPAN POSTING SYSTEM (1):
Masahiro Tanaka...............................January 22, 2014

(40-man roster and restricted list as of 2/1/20)

* Originally selected by the Yankees in the First-Year Player Draft.
\+ Acquired with cash considerations or international signing bonus pool money.
NOTE: Free agent dates listed are for a player's most recent contract

ACQUIRED BY TRADE (16):

PLAYER	FROM	DATE	IN EXCHANGE FOR
Albert Abreu-a	Houston	November 17, 2016	C Brian McCann
Luis Cessa-b	Detroit	December 9, 2015	LHP Justin Wilson
Clint Frazier-c	Cleveland	July 31, 2016	LHP Andrew Miller
Domingo Germán-d	Miami	December 19, 2014	RHP David Phelps, INF Martin Prado
Luis Gil	Minnesota	March 16, 2018	OF Jake Cave
Chad Green-b	Detroit	December 9, 2015	LHP Justin Wilson
Ben Heller-c	Cleveland	July 31, 2016	LHP Andrew Miller
Aaron Hicks	Minnesota	November 11, 2015	C John Ryan Murphy
Tommy Kahnle*-e	Chicago-AL	July 18, 2017	Four players
Michael King-f+	Miami	November 20, 2017	INF Garrett Cooper, LHP Caleb Smith
James Paxton-g	Seattle	November 19, 2018	Three players
Giancarlo Stanton-h+	Miami	December 11, 2017	Three players
Mike Tauchman	Colorado	March 23, 2019	LHP Phillip Diehl
Gleyber Torres-i	Chicago-NL	July 25, 2016	LHP Aroldis Chapman
Gio Urshela-k	Toronto	August 4, 2018	Cash considerations
Luke Voit-j+	St. Louis	July 28, 2018	RHP Giovanny Gallegos, LHP Chasen Shreve

a — Acquired from Houston along with RHP Jorge Guzman in exchange for C Brian McCann and cash considerations.
b — RHPs Luis Cessa and Chad Green acquired from Detroit in exchange for LHP Justin Wilson.
c — OF Clint Frazier, LHP Justus Sheffield, RHP J.P. Feyereisen and RHP Ben Heller acquired from Cleveland in exchange for LHP Andrew Miller.
d — Acquired from Miami along with RHP Nathan Eovaldi and INF Garrett Jones in exchange for RHP David Phelps and INF Martin Prado (was later non-tendered by the Yankees on December 3, 2015 and signed with the club as a minor league free agent on December 11, 2015).
e — Acquired from Chicago-AL with RHP David Robertson and INF Todd Frazier in exchange for RHP Tyler Clippard, LHP Ian Clarkin, OF Blake Rutherford and OF Tito Polo.
f — Acquired from Miami with 2017-18 international signing bonus pool money in exchange for INF Garrett Cooper and LHP Caleb Smith.
g — Acquired from Seattle in exchange for LHP Justus Sheffield, RHP Erik Swanson and RHP Dom Thompson-Williams.
h — Acquired from Miami with cash considerations in exchange for 2B Starlin Castro, RHP Jorge Guzman and INF Jose Devers.
i — Acquired from Chicago-NL along with RHP Adam Warren, OF Billy McKinney and OF Rashad Crawford in exchange for LHP Aroldis Chapman.
j — Acquired from St. Louis with international signing bonus pool money in exchange for LHP Chasen Shreve and RHP Giovanny Gallegos.
k — Acquired from Toronto on August 4, 2018 and re-signed by the Yankees on October 24, 2018 before becoming a minor league free agent.

2020 Yankees Birthdays

January
Phil Nevin..................... 1/19/1971

February
Brooks Kriske.................. 2/3/1994
Luke Voit....................... 2/13/1991
Luis Severino................. 2/20/1994
Thairo Estrada................ 2/22/1996
Aroldis Chapman............. 2/28/1988

March
Miguel Andújar................. 3/2/1995
Marcus Thames................ 3/6/1977
Aaron Boone................... 3/9/1973

April
Kyle Higashioka.............. 4/20/1990
Luis Cessa..................... 4/25/1992
Aaron Judge................... 4/26/1992

May
Miguel Yajure................... 5/1/1998
Luis Medina.................... 5/3/1999
Matt Blake...................... 5/14/1985
Deivi García................... 5/19/1999
Chad Green.................... 5/24/1991
Michael King.................. 5/25/1995
Reggie Willits................. 5/30/1981

June
Luis Gil............................ 6/3/1998
Jonathan Holder.............. 6/9/1993

July
Mike Ford........................ 7/4/1992
DJ LeMahieu.................. 7/13/1988

August
Domingo Germán............. 8/4/1992
Ben Heller....................... 8/5/1991
Tommy Kahnle................ 8/7/1989
Brett Gardner................ 8/24/1983
Tanner Swanson............ 8/31/1982

September
Clint Frazier................... 9/6/1994
Gerrit Cole...................... 9/8/1990
Albert Abreu................. 9/26/1995

October
Aaron Hicks.................. 10/2/1989
Gio Urshela................. 10/11/1991
J.A. Happ.................... 10/19/1982
Mike Harkey................ 10/25/1966

November
Masahiro Tanaka............ 11/1/1988
Jonathan Loaisiga.......... 11/2/1994
James Paxton............... 11/6/1988
Giancarlo Stanton........ 11/8/1989
Adam Ottavino............ 11/22/1985
P.J. Pilittere................. 11/23/1981
Tyler Wade.................. 11/23/1994
Estevan Florial........... 11/25/1997
Carlos Mendoza........... 11/27/1979

December
Gary Sánchez.............. 12/2/1992
Mike Tauchman........... 12/3/1990
Nick Nelson................. 12/5/1995
Gleyber Torres........... 12/13/1996
Zack Britton............... 12/22/1987
Jordan Montgomery.... 12/27/1992

(Includes all coaches and players on the 40-man roster or restricted list as of 2/1/20)

2020 New York Yankees 40-Man Roster

MANAGER: Aaron Boone (17)
COACHES: Matt Blake (67, Pitching), Mike Harkey (60, Bullpen), Carlos Mendoza (64, Bench), Phil Nevin (88, Third Base), P.J. Pilittere (63, Assistant Hitting), Tanner Swanson (68, Quality Control/Catching), Marcus Thames (62, Hitting), Reggie Willits (50, First Base)
DIRECTOR HEALTH & PERFORMANCE: Eric Cressey **ASST. DIRECTOR HEALTH & PERFORMANCE:** Donovan Santas **DIRECTOR SPORTS MEDICINE & REHAB.:** Michael Schuk
HEAD TRAINER: Tim Lentych **DIRECTOR MEDICAL SERVICES:** Steve Donohue **HEAD TEAM PHYSICIAN:** Dr. Christopher Ahmad
MAJOR LEAGUE STRENGTH AND CONDITIONING: Brett McCabe **DIRECTOR OF MENTAL CONDITIONING:** Chad Bohling
EQUIPMENT MANAGER: Rob Cucuzza **CLUBHOUSE MANAGER:** Lou Cucuzza, Jr. **DIRECTOR OF TEAM TRAVEL & PLAYER SERVICES:** Ben Tuliebitz
VP OF COMMUNICATIONS & MEDIA RELATIONS: Jason Zillo **TEAM SECURITY:** Edward Fastook, Mark Kafalas **MAJOR LEAGUE COACHING ASSISTANTS:** Brett Weber, Radley Haddad
MAJOR LEAGUE VIDEO COORDINATOR: Dan Pane

(Roster as of 2/1/20)

#	PITCHERS (23)	B-T	HT.	WT.	BORN	BIRTHPLACE	2019 CLUB(S)	W-L	ERA	G	GS	CG	SV	IP	H	R	ER	BB	SO	SVC
84	Abreu, Albert	R-R	6-2	190	9/26/95	Guayubín, D.R.	Trenton	5-8	4.28	23	20	0	0	96.2	103	62	46	53	91	0.000
53	Britton, Zack	L-L	6-1	200	12/22/87	Panorama City, Calif.	YANKEES	3-1	1.91	66	0	0	3	61.1	38	13	13	32	53	7.158
85	Cessa, Luis	R-R	6-0	208	4/25/92	Córdoba, México	YANKEES	2-1	4.11	43	0	0	1	81.0	75	42	37	31	75	2.131
54	Chapman, Aroldis	L-L	6-4	218	2/28/88	Holguín, Cuba	YANKEES	3-2	2.21	60	0	0	37	57.0	38	18	14	25	85	9.009
45	Cole, Gerrit	R-R	6-4	220	9/8/90	Newport Beach, Calif.	HOUSTON	20-5	2.50	33	33	0	0	212.1	142	66	59	48	326	6.111
83	García, Deivi	R-R	5-9	163	5/19/99	Bonao, D.R.	Tampa	0-2	3.06	4	4	0	0	17.2	14	10	6	8	33	0.000
							Trenton	4-4	3.86	11	11	0	0	53.2	43	23	23	26	87	
							Scranton/WB	1-3	5.40	11	6	0	0	40.0	39	25	24	20	45	
55	Germán, Domingo*	R-R	6-2	181	8/4/92	San Pedro de Macorís, D.R.	YANKEES	18-4	4.03	27	24	0	0	143.0	125	69	64	39	153	2.017
							Scranton/WB	0-0	9.00	1	1	0	0	4.0	4	4	4	2	5	
81	Gil, Luis	R-R	6-2	185	6/3/98	Azua, D.R.	Charleston	4-5	2.39	17	17	0	0	83.0	60	29	22	39	112	0.000
							Tampa	1-0	4.85	3	3	0	0	13.0	11	7	7	8	11	
57	Green, Chad	L-R	6-3	215	5/24/91	Greenville, S.C.	YANKEES	4-4	4.17	54	15	0	2	69.0	66	35	32	19	98	3.050
							Scranton/WB	0-0	2.45	3	0	0	0	7.1	5	2	2	2	14	
33	Happ, J.A.	L-L	6-5	205	10/19/82	Spring Valley, Ill.	YANKEES	12-8	4.91	31	30	0	0	161.1	160	88	88	49	140	11.047
61	Heller, Ben	R-R	6-3	210	8/5/91	Milwaukee, Wisc.	Tampa	0-0	0.00	2	2	0	0	2.2	3	0	0	1	2	2.096
							Scranton/WB	0-0	0.82	9	4	0	1	11.0	5	1	1	3	13	
							YANKEES	0-0	1.23	6	0	0	0	7.1	4	1	1	3	9	
56	Holder, Jonathan	R-R	6-2	232	6/9/93	Gulfport, Miss.	YANKEES	5-2	6.31	34	1	0	0	41.1	43	32	29	11	46	2.124
							Scranton/WB	1-1	2.92	9	0	0	2	12.1	13	5	4	2	15	
48	Kahnle, Tommy	R-R	6-1	230	8/7/89	Latham, N.Y.	YANKEES	3-2	3.67	72	0	0	0	61.1	45	27	25	20	88	4.131
73	King, Michael	R-R	6-3	210	5/25/95	Rochester, N.Y.	GCL West	0-0	0.00	1	1	0	0	5.2	3	3	3	2	7	0.011
							Staten Island	0-0	0.00	1	0	0	0	4.0	4	0	0	0	6	
							Trenton	0-1	9.95	3	2	0	0	12.2	20	15	14	2	8	
							Scranton/WB	3-1	4.18	4	4	0	0	23.2	20	12	11	6	28	
							YANKEES	0-0	0.00	1	1	0	0	2.0	2	1	0	0	1	
82	Kriske, Brooks	R-R	6-3	190	2/3/94	Scottsdale, Ariz.	Tampa	1-1	0.00	7	0	0	1	12.0	4	1	0	5	16	0.000
							Trenton	2-2	2.59	36	0	0	11	48.2	30	14	14	23	64	
43	Loaisiga, Jonathan	R-R	5-11	165	11/2/94	Managua, Nicaragua	YANKEES	2-2	4.55	15	4	0	0	31.2	31	16	16	16	37	1.022
							Scranton/WB	0-2	6.32	5	4	0	0	15.2	14	11	11	5	19	
							Trenton	0-0	0.00	1	1	0	0	2.0	1	0	0	0	3	
80	Medina, Luis	R-R	6-1	175	5/3/99	Nagua, D.R.	Charleston	1-8	6.00	20	20	0	0	93.0	86	65	62	67	115	0.000
							Tampa	0-0	0.84	2	2	0	0	10.2	7	5	1	3	12	
47	Montgomery, Jordan	L-L	6-6	228	12/27/92	Sumter, S.C.	Tampa	0-0	0.00	1	1	0	0	2.0	0	0	0	0	2	2.153
							Scranton/WB	0-0	0.00	1	1	0	0	1.2	2	1	0	0	3	
							YANKEES	0-0	6.75	2	1	0	0	4.0	7	3	3	0	1	
79	Nelson, Nick	R-R	6-1	205	12/5/95	Panama City, Fla.	Trenton	7-2	2.35	13	12	1	0	65.0	48	18	17	35	83	0.000
							Tampa	0-0	0.00	1	1	0	0	3.2	4	0	0	1	7	
							Scranton/WB	1-1	4.71	4	4	0	0	21.0	20	11	11	7	24	
0	Ottavino, Adam	S-R	6-5	246	11/22/85	New York, N.Y.	YANKEES	6-5	1.90	73	0	0	2	66.1	47	17	14	40	88	8.087
65	Paxton, James	L-L	6-4	227	11/6/88	Ladner, B.C., Can.	YANKEES	15-6	3.82	29	29	0	0	150.2	138	71	64	55	186	5.151
40	Severino, Luis	R-R	6-2	218	2/20/94	Sabana de la Mar, D.R.	Scranton/WB	0-0	18.00	1	1	0	0	1.0	3	2	2	0	2	3.170
							YANKEES	1-1	1.50	3	3	0	0	12.0	6	2	2	6	17	
19	Tanaka, Masahiro	R-R	6-3	218	11/1/88	Itami, Japan	YANKEES	11-9	4.45	32	31	1	0	182.0	186	95	90	40	149	6.000
89	Yajure, Miguel	R-R	6-1	175	5/1/98	Cabimas, Ven.	Tampa	8-6	2.26	22	18	1	0	127.2	110	47	32	28	112	0.000
							Trenton	0-0	0.82	2	2	0	0	11.0	9	1	1	2	11	

#	CATCHERS (2)	B-T	HT.	WT.	BORN	BIRTHPLACE	2019 CLUB(S)	AVG	G	AB	R	H	2B	3B	HR	RBI	BB	SO	SB	SVC
66	Higashioka, Kyle	R-R	6-1	202	4/20/90	Huntington Beach, Calif.	Scranton/WB	.278	70	241	42	67	13	0	20	56	24	53	0	1.005
							YANKEES	.214	18	56	8	12	5	0	3	11	0	26	0	
24	Sánchez, Gary	R-R	6-2	230	12/2/92	Santo Domingo, D.R.	YANKEES	.232	106	396	62	92	12	1	34	77	40	125	0	3.086
							Charleston	.000	1	3	0	0	0	0	0	0	0	0	0	
							Scranton/WB	.200	2	5	1	1	0	0	0	1	0	1	0	

#	INFIELDERS (8)	B-T	HT.	WT.	BORN	BIRTHPLACE	2019 CLUB(S)	AVG	G	AB	R	H	2B	3B	HR	RBI	BB	SO	SB	SVC
41	Andújar, Miguel	R-R	6-0	211	3/2/95	San Cristóbal, D.R.	YANKEES	.128	12	47	1	6	0	0	0	1	1	11	0	2.020
							Tampa	.300	3	10	1	3	0	0	1	4	0	0	0	
71	Estrada, Thairo	R-R	5-10	185	2/22/96	Bejuma, Ven.	Scranton/WB	.266	60	241	39	64	17	2	8	32	14	50	3	0.099
							YANKEES	.250	35	64	12	16	3	0	3	12	3	15	4	
72	Ford, Mike	L-R	6-0	225	7/4/92	Belle Mead, N.J.	Scranton/WB	.303	79	294	59	89	20	0	23	60	46	55	0	0.080
							YANKEES	.259	50	143	30	37	7	0	12	25	17	28	0	
26	LeMahieu, DJ	R-R	6-4	220	7/13/88	Visalia, Calif.	YANKEES	.327	145	602	109	197	33	2	26	102	46	90	5	7.128
25	Torres, Gleyber	R-R	6-1	205	12/13/96	Caracas, Ven.	YANKEES	.278	144	546	96	152	26	0	38	90	48	129	5	1.162
29	Urshela, Gio	R-R	6-0	215	10/11/91	Cartagena, Colombia	Scranton/WB	.444	5	18	2	8	0	0	0	1	0	2	0	2.127
							YANKEES	.314	132	442	73	139	34	0	21	74	25	87	1	
59	Voit, Luke	R-R	6-3	255	2/13/91	Wildwood, Mo.	YANKEES	.263	118	429	72	113	21	1	21	62	71	142	0	1.169
14	Wade, Tyler	L-R	6-1	188	11/23/94	Murrieta, Calif.	YANKEES	.245	43	94	16	23	3	1	2	11	11	28	7	1.093
							Scranton/WB	.296	79	301	51	89	19	4	4	38	23	76	13	

#	OUTFIELDERS (7)	B-T	HT.	WT.	BORN	BIRTHPLACE	2019 CLUB(S)	AVG	G	AB	R	H	2B	3B	HR	RBI	BB	SO	SB	SVC
90	Florial, Estevan	L-R	6-1	195	11/25/97	Barahona, D.R.	Tampa	.237	74	274	38	65	10	3	8	38	24	98	9	0.000
77	Frazier, Clint	R-R	5-11	212	9/6/94	Decatur, Ga.	YANKEES	.267	69	225	31	60	14	0	12	38	16	70	1	1.163
							Trenton	.333	1	3	1	1	0	0	0	0	0	1	0	
							Scranton/WB	.247	61	247	35	61	20	1	8	26	17	56	1	
11	Gardner, Brett	L-L	5-11	195	8/24/83	Holly Hill, S.C.	YANKEES	.251	141	491	86	123	26	7	28	74	52	108	10	11.072
31	Hicks, Aaron	S-R	6-1	205	10/2/89	San Pedro, Calif.	Tampa	.000	3	11	0	0	0	0	0	1	3	0	0	6.041
							Scranton/WB	.429	2	7	4	3	0	0	0	1	1	1	1	
							YANKEES	.235	59	221	41	52	10	0	12	36	31	72	1	
99	Judge, Aaron	R-R	6-7	282	4/26/92	Linden, Calif.	YANKEES	.272	102	378	75	103	18	1	27	55	64	141	3	3.051
							Scranton/WB	.125	5	16	5	2	2	0	0	1	2	3	0	
27	Stanton, Giancarlo	R-R	6-6	245	11/8/89	Panorama City, Calif.	YANKEES	.288	18	59	8	17	3	0	3	13	12	24	0	9.118
							Tampa	.500	3	10	4	5	0	0	0	4	5	0	0	
							HOUSTON	.091	3	11	2	1	0	0	1	1	0	3	0	
39	Tauchman, Mike	L-L	6-2	220	12/3/90	Pallatine, Ill.	YANKEES	.277	87	260	46	72	18	1	13	47	34	71	6	1.055
							Scranton/WB	.274	28	95	22	26	10	3	5	16	8	16	4	

*Restricted list, not on 40-man roster

2020 Yankees Spring Training Invitees

#	PITCHERS (8)	B-T	HT.	WT.	BORN	BIRTHPLACE	2019 CLUB(S)	W-L	ERA	G/GS	IP	R/ER	SO	SVC
95	Acevedo, Domingo	R-R	6-7	240	3/6/94	Villa Los Almácigos, D.R.	Trenton	7-1	3.86	22/0	35.0	17/15	33	0.001
							Scranton/WB	1-0	5.40	10/0	16.2	10/10	21	
70	Avilán, Luis	L-L	6-2	220	7/19/89	Caracas, Ven.	NEW YORK-NL	4-0	5.06	45/0	32.0	18/18	30	6.146
							Syracuse	0-0	0.00	2/0	2.1	0/0	4	
							St. Lucie	1-0	4.50	2/0	2.0	1/1	2	
75	Hale, David	R-R	6-2	210	9/27/87	Atlanta, Ga.	Scranton/WB	3-2	4.13	7/7	32.2	17/15	30	2.163
							YANKEES	3-0	3.11	20/0	37.2	13/13	23	
36	Otero, Dan	R-R	6-3	205	2/19/85	Miami, Fla.	CLEVELAND	0-0	4.85	25/0	29.2	17/16	16	6.124
							Mahoning Valley	0-0	0.00	1/1	0.2	0/0	1	
							Akron	0-0	9.00	3/0	3.0	3/3	1	
							Columbus	0-0	0.73	11/0	12.1	1/1	8	
58	Lyons, Tyler	l-l	6-2	210	2/21/88	Lubbock, Tex.	Indianapolis	4-3	3.35	35/0	45.2	20/17	55	4.064
							PITTSBURGH	1-1	11.25	3/0	4.0	5/5	5	
							Scranton/WB	0-0	1.93	3/0	4.2	1/1	5	
							YANKEES	0-1	4.15	11/0	8.2	4/4	12	
86	Schmidt, Clarke	R-R	6-1	200	2/20/96	El Toro, Calif.	Tampa	4-5	3.84	13/12	63.1	35/27	69	0.000
							GCL Yankees East	0-0	3.24	3/3	8.1	3/3	14	
							Trenton	2-0	2.37	3/3	19.0	5/5	19	
35	Tropeano, Nick	R-R	6-4	225	8/27/90	West Islip, N.Y.	Salt Lake	4-6	5.87	17/15	79.2	55/52	85	3.105
							LOS ANGELES-AL	0-1	9.88	3/1	13.2	15/15	10	
87	Vizcaíno, Alexander	R-R	6-2	160	5/22/97	San Cristóbal, D.R.	Charleston	5-5	4.41	16/16	87.2	47/43	101	0.000
							Tampa	1-1	4.28	5/5	27.1	14/13	27	

#	CATCHERS (5)	B-T	HT.	WT.	BORN	BIRTHPLACE	2019 CLUB(S)	AVG	G	AB	H	HR	RBI	BB	SO	SVC
78	Deglan, Kellin	L-R	6-2	205	5/3/92	Langley, B.C., Can.	Scranton/WB	.158	6	19	3	1	2	2	6	0.000
							Trenton	.265	65	230	61	8	30	17	73	
22	Iannetta, Chris	R-R	6-0	230	4/8/83	Providence, R.I.	COLORADO	.222	52	144	32	6	21	18	54	12.154
							Hartford	.000	3	8	0	0	1	0	2	
38	Kratz, Erik	R-R	6-4	245	6/15/80	Telford, Pa.	SAN FRANCISCO	.125	15	32	4	1	3	2	6	5.054
							TAMPA BAY	.059	6	17	1	0	0	0	8	
							Scranton/WB	.299	46	154	46	7	31	17	21	
94	Sawyer, Wynston	R-R	6-3	215	11/14/91	San Diego, Calif.	Rochester	.260	43	154	40	2	20	11	48	0.000
30	Thole, Josh	L-R	6-1	230	10/28/86	Breese, Ill.	Tulsa	.292	22	65	19	0	10	7	16	5.165
							Oklahoma City	.203	25	74	15	1	4	14	19	
							Salt Lake	.241	25	87	21	2	12	16	25	

#	INFIELDERS (2)	B-T	HT.	WT.	BORN	BIRTHPLACE	2019 CLUB(S)	AVG	G	AB	H	HR	RBI	BB	SO	SVC
92	Gittens, Chris	R-R	6-4	250	2/4/94	Sherman, Tex.	Trenton	.281	115	398	112	23	77	71	139	0.000
76	Holder, Kyle	L-R	6-1	204	5/25/94	San Diego, Calif.	Trenton	.265	112	412	109	9	40	41	65	0.000

#	OUTFIELDERS (4)	B-T	HT.	WT.	BORN	BIRTHPLACE	2019 CLUB(S)	AVG	G	AB	H	HR	RBI	BB	SO	SVC
91	Amburgey, Trey	R-R	6-2	210	10/24/94	Lake Worth, Fla.	Scranton/WB	.274	124	470	129	6	22	62	32	112	0.000
74	Granite, Zack	L-L	6-1	175	9/17/92	Staten Island, N.Y.	Nashville	.290	119	504	146	3	37	31	45	0.070
13	Herrera, Rosell	S-R	6-3	200	10/16/92	Santo Domingo, D.R.	MIAMI	.200	63	105	21	2	11	11	27	1.046
							New Orleans	.309	48	165	51	5	24	14	32	
93	Milone, Thomas	L-L	5-11	190	1/26/95	Monroe, Conn.	Montgomery	.214	28	84	18	1	7	12	19	0.000
							Charlotte	.309	55	204	63	3	28	20	42	

New York Yankees Pronunciation Guide

Domingo Acevedo	ahh-suh-VAY-doh
Trey Amburgey	AMM-burr-ghee
Miguel Andújar	ahn-DOO-har
Luis Avilán	ah-vee-LAHN
Luis Cessa	SESS-uh
Thairo Estrada	TYE-row
Deivi García	DAY-vee
Domingo Germán	hurr-MAHN
Luis Gil	HEEL
J.A. Happ	JAY
Chris Iannetta	aye-ah-NETT-ah
Kyle Higashioka	he-GAH-shi-Oh-kah
Tommy Kahnle	CAIN-lee
Brooks Kriske	KRISS-key
DJ LeMahieu	leh-MAY-hyoo
Jonathan Loaisiga	loh-AYE-see-gah
Thomas Milone	mill-OHN
Dan Otero	oh-TAIR-oh
Adam Ottavino	ah-tah-VEE-noh
Mike Tauchman	TOCK-min
Josh Thole	TOLL-ee
Gleyber Torres	GLAY-burr
Nick Tropeano	troh-pee-AH-noh
Gio Urshela	urr-SHELL-ah
Miguel Yajure	zha-HOO-ray

Numerical Roster

- 0 Adam Ottavino . . . . RHP
- 11 Brett Gardner . . . . OF
- 13 Rosell Herrera* . . . . OF
- 14 Tyler Wade . . . . INF
- 17 Aaron Boone . . . . . MANAGER
- 19 Masahiro Tanaka . . . . RHP
- 22 Chris Iannetta* C
- 24 Gary Sánchez C
- 25 Gleyber Torres . . . . INF
- 26 DJ LeMahieu . . . . INF
- 27 Giancarlo Stanton . . . . OF
- 29 Gio Urshela . . . . INF
- 30 Josh Thole* C
- 31 Aaron Hicks . . . . OF
- 33 J.A. Happ . . . . LHP
- 35 Nick Tropeano* . . . . RHP
- 36 Dan Otero* . . . . RHP
- 38 Erik Kratz* C
- 39 Mike Tauchman . . . . OF
- 40 Luis Severino . . . . RHP
- 41 Miguel Andújar . . . . INF
- 43 Jonathan Loaisiga . . . . . . RHP
- 45 Gerrit Cole . . . . RHP
- 47 Jordan Montgomery . . . LHP
- 48 Tommy Kahnle . . . . RHP
- 50 Reggie Willits . . . FIRST BASE
- 53 Zack Britton . . . . LHP
- 54 Aroldis Chapman . . . . . . LHP
- 56 Jonathan Holder . . . . RHP
- 57 Chad Green . . . . RHP
- 58 Tyler Lyons* . . . . LHP
- 59 Luke Voit . . . . INF
- 60 Mike Harkey . . . . . . BULLPEN
- 61 Ben Heller . . . . RHP
- 62 Marcus Thames . . . . HITTING
- 63 P.J. Pilittere . . . ASST. HITTING
- 64 Carlos Mendoza . . . . . BENCH
- 65 James Paxton . . . . LHP
- 66 Kyle Higashioka C
- 67 Matt Blake . . . . PITCHING
- 68 Tanner Swanson . . QUAL. CTRL.
- 70 Luis Avilán* . . . . LHP
- 71 Thairo Estrada . . . . INF
- 72 Mike Ford . . . . INF
- 73 Michael King . . . . RHP
- 74 Zack Granite* . . . . OF
- 75 David Hale* . . . . RHP
- 76 Kyle Holder* . . . . INF
- 77 Clint Frazier . . . . OF
- 78 Kellin Deglan* C
- 79 Nick Nelson . . . . RHP
- 80 Luis Medina . . . . RHP
- 81 Luis Gil . . . . RHP
- 82 Brooks Kriske . . . . RHP
- 83 Deivi García . . . . RHP
- 84 Albert Abreu . . . . RHP
- 85 Luis Cessa . . . . RHP
- 86 Clarke Schmidt* . . . . RHP
- 87 Alexander Vizcaíno* . . . . RHP
- 88 Phil Nevin . . . . THIRD BASE
- 89 Miguel Yajure . . . . RHP
- 90 Estevan Florial . . . . OF
- 91 Trey Amburgey* . . . . OF
- 92 Chris Gittens* . . . . INF
- 93 Thomas Milone* . . . . OF
- 94 Wynston Sawyer* C
- 95 Domingo Acevedo* . . . . RHP
- 99 Aaron Judge . . . . OF

*Non-roster invitee

NISSAN
Innovation that excites

NISSAN **I**NTELLIGENT **M**OBILITY

Weather. Or not.

⌐ **INTELLIGENT**
  ALL-WHEEL DRIVE ⌐

THE 2020
NISSAN **ALTIMA**

Drive confidently, no matter what's the forecast, with the 2020 Nissan Altima, featuring available Intelligent All-Wheel Drive.* This is instant confidence. This is Nissan Intelligent Mobility.

Check out the latest in Nissan Intelligent Mobility technologies at your local Nissan store and shop ChooseNissan.com.

*Intelligent All-Wheel Drive cannot prevent collisions or provide enhanced traction in all conditions. Always monitor traffic and weather conditions.

ALBERT ABREU • RHP

84

HT: 6-2 • **WT:** 190 • **BATS:** R • **THROWS:** R
BIRTHDATE: 9/26/95 • **OPENING DAY AGE:** 24
BIRTHPLACE: Guayubín, D.R.
RESIDES: Guayubín, D.R.
M.L. SERVICE: None (Rookie)

STATUS
- Acquired by the Yankees with RHP Jorge Guzman from the Houston Astros in exchange for C Brian McCann on November 17, 2016.

2019
- Spent the entire season with Double-A Trenton, going 5-8 with a 4.28 ERA (96.2IP, 46ER) and 91K in 23 games (20 starts)…marked a career high in wins and starts and his highest totals in games played, innings pitched and strikeouts since 2016 (24G, 101.2IP, 115K).
- Following the season, was tabbed by *Baseball America* as the Yankees' No. 10 prospect…was named the organization's No. 6 prospect by MLB Pipeline.

2018
- Combined with Single-A Tampa, the GCL Yankees East and West and Double-A Trenton to go 4-6 with a 5.20 ERA (72.2IP, 42ER) in 17 starts.
- Missed nearly two and a half months of the season over two stints on the minor league disabled list (4/5-29 and 6/29-8/11)…pitched for the GCL Yankees East and West as part of his rehab assignment (3GS).
- Spent the majority of the season with Tampa, going 4-3 with a 4.16 ERA (62.2IP, 29ER) in 13 starts.
- Made one start with Trenton on 9/3 vs. Reading, tossing 5.0 hitless and scoreless innings (1BB, 4K).
- Pitched for the Tigres del Licey in the Dominican Winter League, making six starts and going 0-2 with a 1.80 ERA (20.0IP, 4ER).
- Following the season, was tabbed by *Baseball America* as the Yankees' No. 9 prospect.

2017
- Combined with Single-A Charleston, Single-A Tampa and the GCL Yankees East to go 2-3 with a 3.38 ERA (53.1IP, 20ER) in 14 games (13 starts).
- Began the season with Charleston, going 1-0 with a 1.84 ERA (14.2IP, 3ER) in three games (two starts) before being promoted to Tampa on 4/23, where he went 1-3 with a 4.19 ERA (34.1IP, 16ER) in nine starts.
- Missed nearly three months over two stints on the minor league disabled list…made two rehab starts with the GCL Yankees East, allowing 1ER in 4.1IP.
- Pitched for Scottsdale in the Arizona Fall League, going 1-2 with a 2.60 ERA (27.2IP, 8ER) in six starts…was named the AFL "Pitcher of the Week" for the period from 10/16-21.
- Following the season, was tabbed by *Baseball America* as the Yankees' No. 6 prospect and No. 77 prospect in baseball.
- Was added to the Yankees' 40-man roster on 11/20/17.

2016
- Combined at Single-A Quad Cities and Single-A Lancaster to go 3-8 with four saves and a 3.72 ERA (101.2IP, 42ER) and 115K in 24 games (16 starts)…posted a 0.65 ERA (27.2IP, 13H, 4R/2ER, 13BB, 39K) in eight relief appearances.
- Began the season with Quad Cities and pitched to a 2-8 record with four saves and a 3.50 ERA (90.0IP, 35ER) and 104K in 21 games (14 starts)…led Midwest League pitchers (min. 75.0IP) in opponents' BA (.193, 62-for-321) and ranked fifth in K/9.0IP ratio (10.40)…earned Midwest League "Pitcher of the Week" honors for 6/27-7/3.
- Was promoted on 8/19 to Lancaster, going 1-0 with a 5.40 ERA (11.2IP, 7ER) in three games (two starts).
- Was acquired by the Yankees with RHP Jorge Guzman from Houston in exchange for C Brian McCann on 11/17/16.

2015
- Spent the season with Rookie-level Greeneville and was 2-3 with one save, one complete game and a 2.51 ERA (46.2IP, 13ER) in 13 games (seven starts).
- Went 1-2 with a 3.55 ERA (25.1IP, 10ER) as a starter and 1-1 with a 1.27 ERA (21.1IP, 3ER) in six relief appearances.

2014
▸ Made his professional debut with the DSL Astros Blue, going 3-2 with a 2.78 ERA (68.0IP, 21ER) in 14 starts.

PERSONAL
▸ Full name is Albert Enmanuel Abreu Dias.

Abreu's Career Pitching Record

Year	Club	W	L	ERA	G	GS	CG	SHO	SV	IP	H	R	ER	HR	HP	BB	SO	WP	BK
2014	DSL Astros Blue	3	2	2.78	14	14	0	0	0	68.0	48	25	21	1	3	29	54	8	1
2015	Greeneville	2	3	2.51	13	7	1	0	1	46.2	35	18	13	2	5	21	51	3	0
2016	Quad Cities	2	8	3.50	21	14	0	0	4	90.0	62	40	35	5	10	49	104	15	2
	Lancaster	1	0	5.40	3	2	0	0	0	11.2	12	7	7	2	0	9	11	1	0
2017	Charleston - a	1	0	1.84	3	2	0	0	0	14.2	9	3	3	1	2	3	22	1	0
	Tampa	1	3	4.19	9	9	0	0	0	34.1	33	17	16	2	2	15	31	6	1
	GCL Yankees East	0	0	2.08	2	2	0	0	0	4.1	3	3	1	0	1	0	8	1	0
2018	Tampa	4	3	4.16	13	13	0	0	0	62.2	54	34	29	9	7	29	65	6	0
	GCL Yankees East	0	1	18.00	1	1	0	0	0	2.0	4	4	4	0	1	0	2	3	0
	GCL Yankees West	0	2	27.00	2	2	0	0	0	3.0	10	10	9	0	1	2	3	4	0
	Trenton	0	0	0.00	1	1	0	0	0	5.0	0	0	0	0	0	1	4	0	0
2019	Trenton	5	8	4.28	23	20	0	0	0	96.2	103	62	46	9	7	53	91	7	2
Minor League Totals		19	30	3.77	105	87	1	0	5	439.0	373	223	184	31	39	211	446	55	6

Signed by Houston as a non-drafted free agent on August 5, 2013.

a - Acquired by the Yankees from Houston with RHP Jorge Guzman in exchange for C Brian McCann on November 17, 2016.

James P. Dawson Award

Each spring training, the Yankees present the James P. Dawson Award to the outstanding Yankees rookie in spring training, as voted on by the New York Yankees beat writers. The award was established in honor of James P. Dawson (1896-1953), who began a 45-year career with *The New York Times* as a copy boy in 1908. Eight years later, he became boxing editor and covered boxing and baseball until his death during spring training in 1953.

Two winners of the honor, Tony Kubek in 1957 and Tom Tresh in 1962, went on to win the American League "Rookie of the Year" Award. Prior winners are listed below:

Manager Casey Stengel presents Norm Siebern the first Dawson Award in 1956.

1956… Norm Siebern, OF
1957… Tony Kubek, SS
1958… John Blanchard, C
1959… Gordon Windhorn, OF
1960… John James, RHP
1961… Rollie Sheldon, RHP
1962… Tom Tresh, SS
1963… Pedro González, 2B
1964… Pete Mikkelsen, RHP
1965… Arturo López, OF
1966… Roy White, OF
1967… Bill Robinson, OF
1968… Mike Ferraro, 3B
1969… Jerry Kenney, OF
        Bill Burbach, RHP
1970… John Ellis, 1B/C
1971… None Selected
1972… Rusty Torres, OF
1973… Otto Velez, OF
1974… Tom Buskey, RHP
1975… Tippy Martinez, LHP
1976… Willie Randolph, 2B

1977… George Zeber, INF
1978… Jim Beattie, RHP
1979… Paul Mirabella, RHP
1980… Mike Griffin, RHP
1981… Gene Nelson, RHP
1982… Andre Robertson, SS
1983… Don Mattingly, 1B
1984… José Rijo, RHP
1985… Scott Bradley, C
1986… Bob Tewksbury, RHP
1987… Keith Hughes, OF
1988… Al Leiter, LHP
1989… None Selected
1990… Alan Mills, RHP
1991… Hensley Meulens, OF
1992… Gerald Williams, OF
1993… Mike Humphreys, OF
1994… Sterling Hitchcock, LHP
1995… None Selected
1996… Mark Hutton, RHP
1997… Jorge Posada, C
1998… Homer Bush, INF

1999… None Selected
2000… None Selected
2001… Alfonso Soriano, 2B
2002… Nick Johnson, 1B
2003… Hideki Matsui, OF
2004… Bubba Crosby, OF
2005… Andy Phillips, INF
2006… Eric Duncan, INF
2007… Kei Igawa, LHP
2008… Shelley Duncan, INF/OF
2009… Brett Gardner, OF
2010… Jon Weber, OF
2011… Manny Bañuelos, LHP
2012… David Phelps, RHP
2013… Vidal Nuno, LHP
2014… Masahiro Tanaka, RHP
2015… Slade Heathcott, OF
2016… Johnny Barbato, RHP
2017… Gleyber Torres, INF
2018… Miguel Andújar, INF
2019… Stephen Tarpley, LHP

MIGUEL ANDÚJAR • INF

41

HT: 6-0 • **WT:** 211 • **BATS:** R • **THROWS:** R
BIRTHDATE: 3/2/95 • **OPENING DAY AGE:** 25
BIRTHPLACE: San Cristóbal, D.R.
RESIDES: San Cristóbal, D.R.
M.L. SERVICE: 2 years, 20 days

STATUS
▸ Signed by the Yankees as a non-drafted free agent on July 2, 2011.

CAREER NOTES
▸ Has 78XBH through his first 166 career games, fourth-most in Yankees history through 166G (Joe DiMaggio-102XBH, Bob Meusel-83, Gary Sánchez-81).
▸ Is one of 15 players in Baseball history with 16G with at least 2XBH within his first 166G and one of three such Yankees (Joe DiMaggio, 23 and Bob Meusel, 16).
▸ His 49 doubles through his first 166 career games are third-most in franchise history (Meusel-54, DiMaggio-51).
▸ Has hit safely in each of his last 18 games vs. Baltimore (since 4/7/18)…had a streak of seven straight multi-hit games vs. the Orioles (from 8/1-9/23/18), tied for the fifth-longest multi-hit game streak vs. the Orioles since the franchise moved to Baltimore in 1954.

CAREER HIGHLIGHTS
Sporting News AL "Rookie of the Year"
▸ 2018

2019
▸ Hit .128 (6-for-47) with 1R and 1RBI in 12 games with the Yankees.
▸ Made his first career Opening Day roster…had a team-leading 17H in spring training.
▸ Had a career-best nine-game hitting streak from 9/27/18-5/5/19.
▸ Was placed on the 10-day injured list from 4/1-5/4 with a right shoulder strain, missing 28 team games…in three rehab games with Single-A Tampa, hit .300 (3-for-10) with 1R, 1HR and 4RBI.
▸ Hit .088 (3-for-34) with 1BB in nine games following his first I.L. stint.
▸ Was placed back on the 10-day I.L. on 5/13 with a right labrum tear…underwent right shoulder labral repair on 5/20 performed by Dr. Christopher Ahmad at NewYork Presbyterian Hospital…was transferred to the 60-day I.L. on 5/21, missing the remainder of the season.

2018
▸ Was tabbed by *Sporting News* as the AL "Rookie of the Year" as voted on by his peers after hitting .297 (170-for-573) with 83R, 47 doubles, 27HR and 92RBI in 149 games (132GS at 3B, 13 at DH) with the Yankees…led all Major League rookies in hits, doubles, RBI, extra-base hits (76) and multi-hit games (53), tied for first in HR and ranked second in runs and batting average…was the 15th Yankees rookie with at least 150H in a season.
▸ Ranked second in AL "Rookie of the Year" voting to the Angels' Shohei Ohtani, collecting five first-place votes, 20 second-place votes and four third-place votes…was named to *Baseball Digest's* 2018 Rookie All-Star team.
▸ Set the Yankees' single-season rookie record with 47 doubles (previous: Joe DiMaggio, 44 in 1936)…were tied with Boston's Fred Lynn (1975) for the most ever by an AL rookie and the second-most by any rookie in Major League history behind only Brooklyn's Johnny Frederick in 1929 (52).
▸ Had 76XBH, third-most in a season by a rookie in Yankees history behind Joe DiMaggio (88 in 1936) and Aaron Judge (79 in 2017).
▸ Became the first rookie third baseman (min. 50% of games at 3B) in Major League history with at least 40 doubles and 25HR in his rookie season…is the seventh rookie, age 23-or-younger, to reach the marks, joining Hal Trosky in 1934, Joe DiMaggio in 1936, Ted Williams in 1939, Nomar Garciaparra in 1997, Albert Pujols in 2001 and Corey Seager in 2016.
▸ Joins Joe DiMaggio (1936) as the only rookies in Yankees history to hit at least 40 doubles and 20HR in a season…joins the Dodgers' Corey Seager (2016) as the only rookies to accomplish the feat since 2007.
▸ With teammate Gleyber Torres hitting 24HR, became the first pair of Yankees rookies to hit 20HR in the same season…according to *Elias*, were the eighth set of rookie teammates to both hit 20HR, the first since Cincinnati's Joey Votto and Jay Bruce in 2008…the Yankees are the sixth team in Major League history with multiple rookies with at least 20HR and 60RBI, joining the 2006 Marlins (Mike Jacobs, Dan Uggla, Josh Willingham), 1982 Twins (Gary Gaetti, Kent Hrbek), 1977 Athletics (Wayne Gross, Mitchell Page), 1975 Red Sox (Fred Lynn, Jim Rice) and 1960 Orioles (Jim Gentile, Ron Hansen).

- Is one of four Yankees rookies to hit at least 25HR in a season, joining Aaron Judge (52HR in 2017), Joe DiMaggio (29HR in 1936) and Joe Gordon (25HR in 1938)…is one of four Yankees rookies with at least 20HR since 2016 (also Gary Sánchez-20HR in 2016, Aaron Judge-52HR in 2017 and Gleyber Torres-24HR in 2018).
- Was the fifth Yankees rookie with multiple grand slams in the same season (6/5 at Toronto and 9/15 vs. Toronto), joining Shane Spencer (three in 1998), Russ Derry (two in 1945), Yogi Berra (two in 1947) and Hideki Matsui (two in 2003).

MOST DOUBLES BY A ROOKIE, MAJOR LEAGUE HISTORY		
PLAYER	YEAR	2B
Johnny Frederick (BRO)	1929	52
MIGUEL ANDÚJAR (NYY)	2018	47
Fred Lynn (BOS)	1975	47
Albert Pujols (STL)	2001	47
Ryan Zimmerman (WAS)	2006	47

- Was the second Yankee since 1952 to hit .290-or-better with at least 50XBH *in a rookie season*, joining Robinson Canó in 2005 (.297, 52XBH)…was the eighth Yankees rookie with 90RBI in a season, the third since 1963 (Judge-114 in 2017, Matsui-106 in 2003).
- Is one of seven Yankees since 1913 to collect at least 50 multi-hit games in his rookie season, joining Joe DiMaggio (66 in 1936), Earle Combs (65 in 1925), Tom Tresh (54 in 1962), Ben Chapman (52 in 1930), Derek Jeter (50 in 1996) and Phil Rizzuto (50 in 1941)…marked the third-most by an AL rookie over the last 15 seasons (since 2004) behind Mike Trout (56 in 2012) and Delmon Young (55 in 2007).
- Of his 27HR, 12 tied the game (four) or gave the Yankees the lead (eight)…nine of his HRs came in the seventh inning or later…hit 14 of his 27HR when behind in the count, four more than any other Major League player this season.
- Was the first Yankee, age-23 or younger, to hit 25HR in a season since Bobby Murcer (26HR) at age-23 in 1969.
- Had 12HR during the first half, one of five Yankees rookies all time to hit at least 10HR before the All-Star break, joining Aaron Judge (30HR in 2017), Gleyber Torres (15HR in 2018), Joe DiMaggio (11HR in 1936) and Nick Johnson (11HR in 2002)—credit: *Elias*…joined Torres as the first Yankees rookies with at least 10HR before the All-Star break in the same season (first team to do so since the 2016 Dodgers: Corey Seager-17, Trayce Thompson-13).
- Hit 27 doubles in the "first half," the most by a Yankee before the All-Star break since Hideki Matsui collected 30 in 2003.
- Was recalled from Triple-A Scranton/Wilkes-Barre on 4/1 without appearing in a game with the RailRiders…remained at the Major League level for the rest of the season.
- Had at least one extra-base hit in seven straight games from 4/13-23 (8 doubles, 1 triple, 3HR), collecting multiple XBH in five of those games…was the second-youngest Yankee in franchise history with at least 1XBH in seven straight games (DiMaggio, 7G, 6/4-11/37, ending at age 22y, 198d according to *Elias*)…was one of six players his age (23y, 52d) or younger to have as long a streak from 1999-2018, joining Ronald Acuña, 8G in 2018; Cody Bellinger, 7G in 2017; Corey Seager, 7G in 2016; Freddy Freeman, 8G in 2012 and Albert Pujols, 7G in 2001.
- Tied a Yankees franchise record with three straight games with multiple extra-base hits (28th time) from 4/13-17…was the second Yankees 3B with at least 2XBH in three consecutive games, joining Bob Meusel (7/9-11/1920).
- Hit solo HR—the first home run of his Major League career—in the ninth in 4/17 loss vs. Miami.
- Was 4-for-4 with 1R, 2 doubles and 1RBI in 4/22 win vs. Toronto…at 23 years, 51 days old, was the youngest Yankee to have at least 4H in a game since Melky Cabrera (21y, 292d) on 5/30/06 at Detroit…was the youngest Yankee to go 4-for-4 or better since Derek Jeter on 7/2/96 vs. Boston (4-for-4 at 22 years, 6 days)…was the youngest Yankee to go 4-for-4 or better with *at least 2XBH* since Thurman Munson, who went 4-for-4 with 1 double and 1HR on 7/28/70 at California, at exactly the same age as Andújar (23.051).
- Hit "walk-off" RBI single—his first career "walk-off" hit—in the ninth and was 2-for-5 with 2R in 5/4 win vs. Cleveland…at 23 years, 63 days old, was the second-youngest Yankee with a "walk-off" hit since 2010 (Clint Frazier, 22y, 305d on 7/8/17 vs. Milwaukee)…Gleyber Torres (21y, 144d) hit a "walk-off" HR two days later.
- Was named AL "Rookie of the Month" for June, his first career monthly award…in 25G, hit .264 (24-for-91) with 10R, 6 doubles, 7HR and 20RBI, leading all Major League rookies in home runs and extra-base hits (13) and tying for first in RBI (first in the AL)…was the sixth Yankee (ninth time) to win AL "Rookie of the Month" and the fourth current Yankee to do so, joining Gary Sánchez (Aug. 2016), Aaron Judge (four times in 2017) and Gleyber Torres (May 2018).
- Hit first career grand slam in 6/5 win at Toronto…at age 23y, 95d, became the youngest Yankee to hit a grand slam since Melky Cabrera (age 21y, 328d) on 7/5/06 at Cleveland…according to the YES Network, was the third Yankees rookie third baseman to hit a grand slam, joining Horace Clarke 9/21/65 and Mike Pagliarulo 9/18/1984.
- Recorded his 100th career hit in his 92nd career game (7/23 at Tampa Bay)…among players to debut since 1942, is tied with Gary Sánchez for the third-fastest Yankees to reach 100 career hits, behind Hideki Matsui (81G) and Robinson Canó (87G).
- Was named AL "Rookie of the Month" for August after batting .320 (39-for-122) with 21R, 7 doubles, 10HR, 29RBI, 4BB and 1SB in 30 games…tied for the AL lead in HRs (with Oakland's Khris Davis), tied for the MLB lead in RBI (with Texas' Rougned Odor) and tied for second in the Majors in hits…marked the fifth time in Yankees history a rookie hit at least 10HR in a calendar month, following Aaron Judge (15HR in Sept. 2017, 10HR in April 2017, 10HR in June 2017) and Gary Sánchez (11HR in August 2016)…was the third rookie in Yankees history to hit .320-or-better with at least 10HR in a month (Judge, June 2017 and Sánchez, August 2016)…was tied for the third-highest RBI total by a Yankees rookie in a month, joining Bob Meusel (42RBI in July 1920), Judge (32RBI in Sept. 2017), Hideki Matsui (29RBI in June 2003), Bill Johnson (29RBI in July 1943) and Joe DiMaggio (29RBI in June 1936)…are tied for the fourth-most RBI by any Yankee in a calendar month since the start of 2012 trailing only Aaron Judge (32 in Sept. 2017), Alfonso Soriano (31 in August 2013) and Didi Gregorius (30 in April 2018).

- Hit game-tying solo HR in the seventh and hit game-winning single in the 13th on 8/7 at Chicago-AL, going 3-for-5 with 1HP…was the first Yankees rookie with multiple go-ahead/game-tying hits in the seventh inning or later since Bernie Williams on 10/5/91 vs. Cleveland (go-ahead single in seventh, game-tying single in ninth)…was tied for the latest go-ahead hit by a Yankees rookie since Mike Blowers hit a two-run single in the 15th inning on 6/22/90 at Toronto (Brett Gardner also hit a "walk-off" single in the 13th inning on 8/16/08 vs. Kansas City).
- Reached base safely in a career-high 17 straight games from 8/17-9/3, batting .333 (23-for-69) with 14R, 4 doubles, 4HR, 17RBI and 5BB over the span.
- Collected multiple hits in all four games of the Yankees' series at Baltimore from 8/24 26, going 9-for-19 (.474) with 3R, 1 double, 1HR and 6RBI…were tied for the most hits by a Yankee in a single series since the start of 2014 (also Carlos Beltrán, 9-for-18 from 5/19-22/16 at Oakland; and Didi Gregorius, 9-for-15 from 7/27-30/15 at Texas).
- Hit his 44th double of the season in the fourth inning of 9/28 win at Boston, tying Joe DiMaggio (44 in 1936) for most in a single season by a Yankees rookie…surpassed DiMaggio in the fifth inning of 9/29 win at Boston.
- Made his postseason debut, starting four of the Yankees' five playoff games at 3B and going 2-for-10 with 2BB.
- In 15 spring training games with the Yankees, hit .267 (12-for-45) with 8R, 2 doubles, 1 triple, 4HR, 10RBI, 3BB with a .928 OPS…was named the recipient of the 2018 James P. Dawson Award, given annually to the outstanding Yankees rookie in spring training.

2017
- Saw his first Major League action, appearing in five games (1 start at DH) over three stints with the Yankees (6/28-29, 6/30-7/1 and 9/16-10/1) and hitting .571 (4-for-7) with 2 doubles and 4RBI.
- Made his Major League debut in 6/28 win at Chicago-AL, starting at DH and going 3-for-4 with 1 double, 4RBI, 1BB and 1SB…collected his first Major League hit with a bases-loaded single off Carlos Rodón in the first inning…set a Yankees record in RBI in a Major League debut (previously 3RBI, Marv Throneberry on 9/25/55-G1 and Billy Martin on 4/18/50)…according to ESPN Stats & Info, was the third player to notch 4RBI in his Yankees debut, joining Roger Maris (4/19/60 at Boston) and Raúl Ibañez (4/6/12 at Tampa Bay)…became the 12th player in Major League history (ninth in the AL) to record at least 3H and 4RBI in his Major League debut…since 1949, was only the second Yankee with 3H in his Major League debut (also Mike Pagliarulo, 3-for-5 on 7/7/84 at Minnesota)…became the sixth Yankee to make his Major League debut as the starting DH and, at 22 years, 118 days old, the second-youngest (Jesus Montero - 21y, 277d on 9/1/11 at Boston).
- With Tyler Wade's debut on 6/27, his on 6/28 and Dustin Fowler debuting on 6/29, the Yankees had position players make their Major League debuts on three straight days for the first time since Jack Little, John Dowd and Bill Otis from 7/2-4/1912 (credit: *Elias*).
- Was named the winner of the Kevin Lawn "Player of the Year" Award, presented annually to the organization's top performer…the award is dedicated to Kevin O'Brien Lawn—the son of longtime Yankees Vice President and Chief of Operations Jack Lawn—who passed away in 1999.
- Led all Yankees minor leaguers in season batting average (.315) and doubles (36), ranked third in RBI (82) and tied for fourth…struck out in just 13.6% of his 522PA (71K).
- Began the season with Double-A Trenton, hitting .312 (79-for-253) with 30R, 23 doubles, 7HR and 52RBI in 67G.
- Was promoted to Scranton/WB on 6/19 and hit .317 (72-for-227) with 36R, 13 doubles, 9HR and 30RBI in 58 games…in eight postseason games for the RailRiders, hit .235 (8-for-34) with 1R, 4 doubles, 1HR and 5RBI.
- Following the season, played for the Cibao Giants in the Dominican Winter League.
- Was tabbed by *Baseball America* as the Yankees' No. 5 prospect and the No. 59 prospect in Baseball following the season…was also named an MiLB.com Organization All-Star.

2016
- Split the season between Single-A Tampa and Double-A Trenton, batting a combined .273/.332/.410 (140-for-512) with 62R, 26 doubles, 4 triples, 12HR, 83RBI and 39BB in 130 games…ranked second among Yankees minor leaguers in RBI…was named an Organization All-Star by MiLB.com.
- Started the season in Tampa and made the FSL Mid-Season All-Star Team…was promoted to Trenton in June.
- In 72 games with Trenton, hit .266 (75-for-282) with 28R, 16 doubles, 2 triples, 2HR and 42RBI.
- Following the season, played for Scottsdale in the Arizona Fall League…was named to the league's Fall Stars Game.
- Was added to the Yankees' 40-man roster on 11/18/16.

2015
- Batted .243 (118-for-485) with 54R, 24 doubles, 5 triples, 8HR and 57RBI in 130 games for Single-A Tampa…stole 12 bases in 13 chances (92.3%)…was named a Florida State League Mid-Season All-Star.
- Following the season, was tabbed by *Baseball America* as the No. 10 third baseman in the minors.

2014
- Spent the entire season with Single-A Charleston, batting .267 (129-for-484) with 75R, 25 doubles, 4 triples, 10HR, 70RBI and 35BB in 127 games…ranked third in the Yankees organization in RBI.
- Following the season was tabbed by *Baseball America* as the No. 10 prospect in the Yankees organization.

2013
- Spent the season with the GCL Yankees 2, batting .323/.368/.496 (43-for-133) with 18R, 11 doubles, 4HR and 25RBI in 34 games.

2012
- Made his professional debut with the GCL Yankees, hitting .232 (41-for-177) with 21R, 9 doubles, 1HR and 19RBI in 50 games.

PERSONAL
- Was named a recipient of the Thurman Munson Award in February 2019.

Andújar's Career Playing Record

Year	Club	AVG	G	AB	R	H	2B	3B	HR	RBI	SH	SF	HP	BB	SO	SB	CS	E	OBP	SLG
2012	GCL Yankees	.232	50	177	21	41	9	0	1	19	0	0	1	13	37	1	3	14	.288	.299
2013	GCL Yankees 2	.323	34	133	18	43	11	0	4	25	0	1	3	7	21	4	1	11	.368	.496
2014	Charleston	.267	127	484	75	129	25	4	10	70	2	3	3	35	83	5	1	26	.318	.397
2015	Tampa	.243	130	485	54	118	24	5	8	57	0	3	3	29	90	12	1	26	.288	.363
2016	Tampa	.283	58	230	34	65	10	2	10	41	0	0	3	18	30	1	3	7	.343	.474
	Trenton	.266	72	282	28	75	16	2	2	42	0	9	7	21	42	2	1	15	.323	.358
2017	Trenton	.312	67	253	30	79	23	1	7	52	0	5	2	12	38	2	3	10	.342	.494
	Scranton/WB	.317	58	227	36	72	13	1	9	30	0	4	2	17	33	3	0	7	.364	.502
	YANKEES	.571	5	7	0	4	2	0	0	4	0	0	0	1	0	1	0	0	.625	.857
2018	Scranton/WB	-	-	-	-	-	-	-	-	-	-	-	-	-	-	-	-	-	-	-
	YANKEES	.297	149	573	83	170	47	2	27	92	0	4	4	25	97	2	1	15	.328	.527
2019	YANKEES - a, b	.128	12	47	1	6	0	0	0	1	0	1	0	1	11	0	0	3	.143	.128
	Tampa	.300	3	10	1	3	0	0	0	4	0	0	0	0	0	0	0	2	.300	.600
Minor League Totals		**.274**	**599**	**2281**	**297**	**625**	**131**	**15**	**52**	**340**	**2**	**25**	**24**	**152**	**374**	**30**	**13**	**118**	**.323**	**.413**
Major League Totals		**.287**	**166**	**627**	**84**	**180**	**49**	**2**	**27**	**97**	**0**	**5**	**4**	**27**	**108**	**3**	**1**	**18**	**.318**	**.501**

Signed by the Yankees as a non-drafted free agent on July 2, 2011.

a - Placed on the 10-day injured list from April 1 - May 4, 2019 with a right shoulder strain.
b - Placed on the 10-day injured list on May 13, 2019 with a right labrum tear…transferred to the 60-day injured list on May 20, 2019, missing the remainder of the season.

Andújar's Postseason Record

Year	Club vs. Opp.	AVG	G	AB	R	H	2B	3B	HR	RBI	SH	SF	HP	BB	SO	SB	CS	E	OBP	SLG
2018	NYY vs. OAK (WC)	1.000	1	1	0	1	0	0	0	0	0	0	0	1	0	0	0	1	1.000	1.000
	NYY vs. BOS (DS)	.111	3	9	0	1	0	0	0	0	0	0	0	1	2	0	0	0	.200	.111
Wild Card Game Totals		**1.000**	**1**	**1**	**0**	**1**	**0**	**0**	**0**	**0**	**0**	**0**	**0**	**1**	**0**	**0**	**0**	**1**	**1.000**	**1.000**
LDS Totals		**.111**	**3**	**9**	**0**	**1**	**0**	**0**	**0**	**0**	**0**	**0**	**0**	**1**	**2**	**0**	**0**	**0**	**.200**	**.111**
POSTSEASON TOTALS		**.200**	**4**	**10**	**0**	**2**	**0**	**0**	**0**	**0**	**0**	**0**	**0**	**2**	**2**	**0**	**0**	**1**	**.333**	**.200**

Andújar's Career Fielding Record

Position	PCT	G	PO	A	E	TC	DP
Third Base	.940	143	94	186	18	298	6

Andújar's Career Home Run Chart
MULTI-HOMER GAMES: None. **TWO-HOMER GAMES:** None. **GRAND SLAMS:** 2, last on 9/15/18 vs. TOR (Tyler Clippard). **PINCH-HIT HR:** None. **INSIDE-THE-PARK HR:** None. **WALK-OFF HR:** None. **LEADOFF HR:** None.

Andújar's Career Bests and Streaks
HITS: 4, 4/22/18 vs. TOR. **RUNS:** 3 - 3 times (last on 9/2/18 vs. DET). **2B:** 2 - 8 times (last on 9/29/18 at BOS). **3B:** 1 - 2 times (last on 5/20/18 at KC). **HR:** 1 - 27 times (last on 9/27/18 at TB). **RBI:** 4 - 4 times (last on 9/15/18 vs. TOR). **BB:** 2, 6/6/18 at TOR. **SO:** 3 - 2 times last on 5/12/19 at TB). **SB:** 1, 3 times (last on 8/8/18 at CWS). **HIT STREAK:** 9g, 9/27/18-5/5/19. **"WALK-OFF" HITS:** 1, 5/4/18 vs. CLE (single).

Player of the Month: None   **Player of the Week:** None   **Rookie of the Month:** 2 times (last: August 2018)

ZACK BRITTON • LHP

53

HT: 6-1 • **WT:** 200 • **BATS:** L • **THROWS:** L
BIRTHDATE: 12/22/87 • **OPENING DAY AGE:** 32
BIRTHPLACE: Panorama City, Calif.
RESIDES: Weatherford, Tex.
M.L. SERVICE: 7 years, 158 days

STATUS
- On January 11, 2019, was signed by the Yankees to a three-year contract extending through the 2021 season with a team option for 2022, which the club must exercise or decline following 2020…if the Yankees decline the 2022 team option following 2020, he may elect to become a free agent for the 2021 season…was originally acquired by the Yankees from Baltimore for RHP Dillon Tate, RHP Cody Carroll and LHP Josh Rogers on July 24, 2018.

CAREER NOTES
- His 1.81 career ERA *as a reliever* is the lowest among all active relievers (min. 100.0IP in relief).
- His 89.5% save percentage (145-for-162) is third-highest among active pitchers (min. 100 saves) behind Craig Kimbrel (90.3%) and Aroldis Chapman (89.5%).
- Since the start of 2014, leads all Major League pitchers (min. 200.0IP) with a 1.83 ERA (348.1IP, 71ER)…over the same six-season span, leads all pitchers with a 77.1% groundball rate, holding the lead in each of those six seasons (2014-19)…his 8.20 groundball to fly ball ratio leads all Major Leaguer relievers over the stretch.
- Pitched for the Orioles over parts of eight seasons from 2011-18, going 30-22 with 139 saves, a 3.22 ERA (516.2IP, 185ER) and 425K.
- Recorded at least 36 saves each season from 2014-16 and was named to the AL All-Star team in 2015 and '16.
- Converted 60 consecutive save chances from 10/1/15–8/21/17, the second-longest streak in Major League history (Éric Gagné, 84 straight from 2002-04).
- Did not allow an earned run in 43 consecutive games from 5/5-8/22/16, the longest such streak in Major League history (since earned runs became an official stat in 1913).
- Was named the Mariano Rivera AL "Reliever of the Year" in 2016 after going a perfect 47-for-47 in save opportunities, the third-highest save total without a blown save in Major League history behind only Éric Gagné (55-for-55 in 2003) and José Valverde (49-for-49 in 2011)…led all Major League relievers with a 0.54 ERA (67.0IP, 4ER), the lowest season ERA in Major League history (min. 50.0IP)…tied for second in saves (led the AL).
- In 43 career *relief appearances* vs. Boston, has posted a 0.76 ERA (47.1IP, 34H, 8R/4ER, 26BB, 42K, 2HR)…has not allowed an earned run in his last 23 relief appearances vs. the Red Sox since 6/1/16 (22.0IP, 2R/0ER).
- Has made five career Opening Day rosters (2014-17 w/ Baltimore and 2019 w/ the Yankees)…began the 2012 and '18 seasons on the disabled list.

CAREER HIGHLIGHTS
AL All-Star Team
- 2015, 2016

Mariano Rivera AL Reliever of the Year
- 2016

2019
- Went 3-1 with three saves, a 1.91 ERA (61.1IP, 13ER) and 53K in 66 relief appearances in his first full season with the Yankees…posted his lowest ERA since a career-best 0.54 ERA in 2016…had a 78.5% groundball percentage, his highest since 2016 w/ Baltimore (79.4%) and the best mark among all Major League relievers.
- Did not allow an earned run over a 14-appearance stretch (9/4/18-4/4/19), holding opponents to 6H in 13.2IP over the span (2R, 6BB, 12K)…had a season-high 13.1IP scoreless streak spanning parts of 14 games from 5/6-6/5… was the third-longest scoreless streak by a Yankees reliever in 2019 (Ottavino-17.1IP; Nestor Cortes Jr.-15.2IP).
- Pitched in both games of a doubleheader for the first time in his career on 5/15 vs. Baltimore (2.0IP, 1H, 3K).
- Struck out 7-of-9 batters faced over three games from 7/14-18 after fanning only 1-of-50BF in his previous 13 games from 6/5-7/13 (11.0IP).
- Exited 8/31 win vs. Oakland with right calf cramping in the eighth inning after recording two outs and getting to a 3-1 count on his third batter.
- Posted a 1.13 ERA (8.0IP, 1ER) in seven postseason relief appearances, allowing his only run on a solo HR in ALDS Game 3 at Minnesota…tossed 1.2 perfect innings in ALCS Game 5 vs. Houston, his longest outing since 2018 ALDS Game 4 vs. Boston (2.0IP).

2018
- Combined to go 2-0 with seven saves (in 10 chances), a 3.10 ERA (40.2IP, 14ER) and 34K in 41 relief appearances with Baltimore and the Yankees.
- Went 1-0 with a 2.88 ERA (25.0IP, 8ER) and 21K in 25 relief appearances with the Yankees.
- Went 1-0 with four saves and a 3.45 ERA (15.2IP, 6ER) in 16 relief appearances with the Orioles.
- Began the season on the 60-day disabled list recovering from right Achilles surgery…combined to make five rehab relief appearances with Single-A Frederick, Double-A Bowie and Triple-A Norfolk…was returned from rehab and reinstated from the D.L. on 6/11.
- Made his season debut on 6/12 vs. Boston, tossing 1.0 scoreless inning (3BB, 1K).

- Blew his first save of the season on 6/27 vs. Seattle after allowing a two-run HR to Kyle Seager…was his second career home run surrendered to a left-handed hitter as a reliever (also Matt Olson on 8/13/17 at Oakland)…also allowed a HR to LHH Chris Davis on 8/24 at Baltimore.
- Made nine consecutive scoreless appearances from 6/30-7/26, going 1-0 with three saves (9.0IP, 3H, 4BB, 7K).
- Was acquired by the Yankees from Baltimore for RHP Dillon Tate, RHP Cody Carroll and LHP Josh Rogers on 7/24 and added to the 25-man roster on 7/26…at the time of his trade from Baltimore (29-73 record) to the Yankees (64-36 at the time of his Yankees debut), gained 36 games in the standings…according to *Elias*, marked the largest win-loss improvement for a player switching teams during the season since 1904, when C/OF Doc Marshall gained 37.5 games by being traded from the Philadelphia Phillies (21-60) to the New York Giants (59-23).
- Made his Yankees debut in 7/26 win vs. Kansas City, tossing a perfect eighth inning (1.0IP, 1K).
- Earned his first save as a Yankee in 8/24 win at Baltimore, allowing 1ER in 1.0IP (2H, 1HR).
- In 10 outings in September, he held opponents to a .088 BA (3-for-34) without allowing an earned run (9.2IP, 2R).
- Appeared in four of the Yankees' five postseason games, posting a 5.40 ERA (5.0IP, 3ER).
- On 1/11/19, was signed by the Yankees to a three-year contract extending through the 2021 season with a team option for 2022, which the club must exercise or decline following the 2020 season…if the Yankees decline the 2022 team option following 2020, he may elect to become a free agent for the 2021 season.

2017

- Went 2-1 with 15 saves and a 2.89 ERA (37.1IP, 12ER) in 38 relief appearances with the Orioles.
- Converted 60 consecutive save opportunities from 10/1/15-8/21/17, the second-longest streak in Major League history (Éric Gagné, 84 consecutive, 8/28/02-7/3/04).
- Was placed on the 10-day disabled list from 4/16-5/2 with a left forearm strain…returned to the 10-day D.L. on 5/6 (retro. to 5/5) with a left forearm strain…was transferred to the 60-day D.L. on 6/20 and reinstated on 7/5.
- Combined to allow 2ER in 8.2IP over nine rehab games (two starts) with Double-A Bowie, short-season Single-A Aberdeen, Single-A Delmarva and Single-A Frederick.
- Converted his 55th consecutive save opportunity on 7/23 vs. Houston, surpassing RHP Tom Gordon (54, 4/19/98-5/31/99) to set a new American League consecutive converted save opportunities record.
- Allowed a home run to Matt Olson on 8/13 at Oakland…was his first home run allowed of the season, and first since 4/11/16 at Boston (Mookie Betts), a span of 88 appearances…marked his first home run allowed to a left-handed hitter since Michael Saunders on 4/29/13.

2016

- Went a perfect 47-for-47 in save opportunities, the third-highest save total without a blown save in Major League history behind only Éric Gagné (55-for-55 in 2003) and José Valverde (49-for-49 in 2011)…his 47 saves led the AL and were tied for second in the Majors…was the only qualifying reliever in the Majors with a 100.0% save pct.
- Led all Major League relievers with a 0.54 ERA (67.0IP, 4ER) in 69 relief appearances, the lowest season ERA in Major League history (min. 50.0IP) en route to being named the Mariano Rivera "American League Reliever of the Year"…was the only qualifying reliever in the Majors with a sub-1.00 ERA.
- Led all Major League relievers in ground ball/fly ball ratio (9.77) and in ground ball percentage (79.4%).
- Posted a Major League-record 43 consecutive relief appearances (41.1IP) without surrendering an earned run from 5/5-8/22, according to STATS, LLC (since 1913).
- Recorded a career-long 21.2-inning scoreless streak from 6/22-8/22.
- Was selected to the 2016 All-Star Game, earning the save for the AL squad (1.0IP, 1H).
- With his save on 8/3 vs. Texas, set the Major League record (since 1969) for most consecutive saves (33) in as many chances to begin a season by a left-handed pitcher (finished with 47).
- Earned the 100th save of his career on 7/10 vs. Los Angeles-AL, becoming the fourth pitcher in club history (since saves became an official statistic) to record 100 or more career saves with the Orioles.
- Posted his 106th career save on 8/3 vs. Texas, passing Tippy Martinez for the Orioles club record for saves by a LHP.
- Appeared on the Orioles' AL Wild Card Game roster, but did not pitch.

2015

- Went 4-1 with 36 saves and a 1.92 ERA (65.2IP, 14ER) in 64 relief appearances with Baltimore…tied for third among AL relievers in saves…led Major League relievers in ground ball percentage (80.4%) and ground ball/fly ball ratio (8.47)…ranked fifth among AL relievers in ERA (1.92) and tied for eighth in strikeouts (79).
- Converted 24 consecutive save opportunities from 5/3-8/10.
- Was selected to the AL All-Star team for the first time in his career…was chosen by AL manager Ned Yost in conjunction with Major League Baseball…tossed 0.2 scoreless innings in the game (1H, 1K).
- Snapped a 96-game stretch in which he did not record a win after earning the victory on 7/10 vs. Washington…is the longest winless stretch in terms of games in his career.
- Posted a 13-game scoreless streak from 5/17-6/17 (13.2IP)…tied for the AL lead with nine saves in June…was one of two AL relievers to go 9-for-9 in save opportunities during the month (also Kansas City's Greg Holland).

2014

- Went 3-2 with 37 saves and a 1.65 ERA (76.1IP, 14ER) in 71 relief appearances, pitching exclusively out of the bullpen for the first time in his career…finished fourth in the AL in saves…led all relievers in groundball/flyball ratio (6.68) and ground ball percentage (75.8%).
- Tossed at least 1.0 inning in 64 of 71 appearances (eighth-most in the Majors, third-most in the AL).
- Posted a 0.84 ERA (21.1IP, 2ER) in his first 16 appearances from 3/31-5/10.
- Earned his first career save on 5/15 at Kansas City (1.0IP).
- Posted a franchise record 35.1 consecutive scoreless innings at home from 9/27/13-8/3/14…his stretch of 27 straight scoreless home outings tied the club record.
- Made his postseason debut, appearing in six postseason games and recording a 3.86 ERA (4.2IP, 2ER) with two saves (Games 2 and 3 of the ALDS).

2013
- Went 2-3 with a 4.95 ERA (40.0IP, 22ER) in eight games (seven starts) over four stints with the Orioles (4/25-30, 6/18-7/9, 9/2-5 and 9/21-29).
- Spent the majority of the season with Triple-A Norfolk, going 6-5 with a 4.27 ERA (103.1IP, 49ER) in 19 starts.

2012
- In 12 appearances (11 starts) with Baltimore, went 5-3 with a 5.07 ERA (60.1IP, 34ER).
- Began season on the 15-day disabled list with a left shoulder impingement and transferred to the 60-day disabled list on 6/3…combined to make three rehab starts with Triple-A Norfolk and Double-A Bowie…was reinstated from the D.L. on 6/6 and optioned to Norfolk.
- In nine total starts for Norfolk (including rehab), went 4-2 with a 4.91 ERA (51.1IP, 28ER)…went 2-0 with a 2.14 ERA (21.0IP, 5ER) in three July starts for the Tides.
- Made five starts while posting an 8.10 ERA (23.1IP, 21ER) in his first stint with Baltimore (7/17-8/7).
- Tossed a season-high 8.0IP and struck out a career-high 10 batters on 8/30 vs. Chicago-AL.
- Made his first career relief appearance on 10/3 at Tampa Bay (1.0IP, 1K).

2011
- Saw his first Major League action, going 11-11 with a 4.61 ERA (154.1IP, 79ER) in 28 starts with Baltimore.
- Went 5-for-8 with 3R, 1 double, 1HR and 2RBI as a hitter in his three Interleague starts…according to *Elias*, his 5H were the most in one season by an AL pitcher since the creation of the designated hitter in 1974.
- Had his contract selected from Triple-A Norfolk on 4/3 and made his Major League debut that night at Tampa Bay, earning the win after allowing 1ER in 6.0IP…struck out six batters, including Elliot Johnson in the first inning for his first career strikeout.
- Allowed 1ER in 13.2IP over his first two Major League appearances (4/3 at Tampa Bay, 4/9 vs. Texas), earning the win in both…according to *Elias*, joined Tom Phoebus as the only two pitchers to win their first two Major League games as an Oriole (since 1954), both as a starter, while also allowing no more than 1ER combined.
- Had a streak of 15.1 scoreless innings over three starts from 5/6-18.
- Tossed 9.0 scoreless innings without a decision in 5/12 12-inning win vs. Seattle (3H, 0BB, 5K)…was the first Oriole to throw 9.0 shutout innings and not factor in the decision since Mike Morgan on 4/16/88 vs. Cleveland.
- In starts on 7/8 at Boston (0.2IP, 8R/7ER) and 7/30 at the Yankees (0.1IP, 9R/6ER), became the first player in Major League history to allow at least 8R while lasting less an an inning in each of two consecutive starts.
- Was placed on the 15-day disabled list from 8/5-22/11 with a left shoulder strain…made one rehab relief appearance with Triple-A Norfolk.
- Also made three starts for Double-A Bowie from 7/15-25, going 0-2 with a 5.40 ERA (11.2IP, 7ER).

2010
- Split the season between Double-A Bowie and Triple-A Norfolk…received the Jim Palmer Award for the Orioles' "Minor League Pitcher of the Year."
- Began the season with Bowie, going 7-3 with a 2.48 ERA (87.0IP, 24ER) in 15 games (14 starts)…was named to the All-Star Futures Game.
- Was named the Orioles "Organizational Pitcher of the Month" for June, going 3-0 with a 0.66 ERA in four starts.
- Was promoted to Norfolk on 7/1 and went 3-4 with a 2.98 ERA (66.1IP, 22ER) in 12 starts.
- Following the season, was tabbed by *Baseball America* as the No. 2 prospect in the Orioles system.

2009
- In 25 games (24 starts) with Single-A Frederick, went 9-6 with a 2.70 ERA (140.0IP, 42ER) en route to being named the Carolina League "Pitcher of the Year"…was named to the CL Mid-Season and Postseason All-Star Teams.
- Ranked second in the league in ERA (2.70) and strikeouts (131), fourth in IP (140.0) and tied for fifth in wins (nine).
- Following the season, was tabbed by *Baseball America* as the No. 3 prospect in the Orioles system.

2008
- Spent the entire season with Single-A Delmarva, going 12-7 with a 3.12 ER (147.1IP, 51ER) in 27 starts…ranked seventh in the South Atlantic League in ERA, fourth in opp. BA (.219) and tied for fourth in innings pitched.
- Among Orioles farmhands, tied for second in wins and ranked eighth in ERA.
- Made 15 quality starts and struck out a season-high nine batters on 6/25 at Lake County.

2007
- Went 6-4 with a 3.68 ERA (63.2IP, 26ER) in 15 starts for short-season Single-A Aberdeen.
- Posted an 8.00 ERA in June (9.0IP, 8ER), but had a 2.96 ERA (54.2IP, 18ER) from 7/1 through the end of the season.

2006
- Made his professional debut, going 0-4 with a 5.29 ERA (34.0IP, 20ER) in 11 starts with Rookie-level Bluefield.

PERSONAL
- Full name is Zackary Grant Britton…is married to Courtney…the couple has three children: one son, Zander, and two daughters, Zilah and Cienna.
- His brother, Buck, managed the Bowie Baysox and was named Eastern League "Manager of the Year" in 2019.
- Graduated from Weatherford (Tex.) High School…was born in California, but moved to Weatherford, Tex., during his sophomore year of high school…went to high school with Clayton Kershaw and was going to room with him at Texas A&M.
- Shares the same hometown of Panorama City, Calif., as teammate Giancarlo Stanton.
- For Players' Weekend in 2018, wore the nickname "Anglada" on his jersey as a nod to his family and grandmother's Dominican heritage…Anglada is his maternal grandmother's maiden name.

Britton's Career Pitching Record

Year	Club	W	L	ERA	G	GS	CG	SHO	SV	IP	H	R	ER	HR	HP	BB	SO	WP	BK
2006	Bluefield	0	4	5.29	11	11	0	0	0	34.0	35	22	20	4	2	20	21	5	0
2007	Aberdeen	6	4	3.68	15	15	0	0	0	63.2	64	33	26	1	5	22	45	4	0
2008	Delmarva	12	7	3.12	27	27	1	0	0	147.1	118	68	51	9	6	49	114	13	0
2009	Frederick	9	6	2.70	25	24	0	0	0	140.0	123	64	42	6	9	55	131	21	0
2010	Bowie	7	3	2.48	15	14	0	0	0	87.0	76	33	24	4	3	28	68	6	0
	Norfolk	3	4	2.98	12	12	0	0	0	66.1	63	31	22	3	1	23	56	8	0
2011	BALTIMORE - a	11	11	4.61	28	28	0	0	0	154.1	162	93	79	12	1	62	97	7	0
	Bowie	0	2	5.40	3	3	0	0	0	11.2	14	11	7	3	1	2	15	1	1
	Norfolk	0	1	1.80	1	1	0	0	0	5.0	3	1	1	0	0	1	3	0	0
2012	Bowie	1	0	0.75	2	2	0	0	0	12.0	8	4	1	0	1	3	11	2	0
	Norfolk	4	2	4.91	9	9	0	0	0	51.1	49	29	28	5	0	20	37	7	0
	BALTIMORE - b	5	3	5.07	12	11	0	0	0	60.1	61	37	34	6	2	32	53	4	0
2013	Norfolk	6	5	4.27	19	19	0	0	0	103.1	112	59	49	5	5	46	75	9	0
	BALTIMORE	2	3	4.95	8	7	0	0	0	40.0	52	23	22	4	1	17	18	1	0
2014	BALTIMORE	3	2	1.65	71	0	0	0	37	76.1	46	17	14	4	1	23	62	0	0
2015	BALTIMORE	4	1	1.92	64	0	0	0	36	65.2	51	16	14	3	1	14	79	5	0
2016	BALTIMORE	2	1	0.54	69	0	0	0	47	67.0	38	7	4	1	0	18	74	10	0
2017	BALTIMORE - c, d	2	1	2.89	38	0	0	0	15	37.1	39	12	12	1	0	18	29	4	0
	Bowie	0	0	4.91	4	0	0	0	0	3.2	4	2	2	1	0	2	5	0	0
	Aberdeen	0	0	0.00	1	1	0	0	0	1.0	0	0	0	0	0	1	1	0	0
	Delmarva	0	0	0.00	2	1	0	0	0	2.0	1	0	0	0	0	1	2	0	0
	Frederick	0	0	0.00	2	0	0	0	0	2.0	1	0	0	0	0	1	2	0	0
2018	Frederick	1	0	0.00	1	0	0	0	0	1.0	1	0	0	0	0	0	3	0	0
	Bowie	0	0	0.00	1	0	0	0	0	1.0	0	0	0	0	0	0	0	0	0
	Norfolk	0	0	2.70	3	0	0	0	0	3.1	3	1	1	0	1	0	3	0	0
	BALTIMORE- e	1	0	3.45	16	0	0	0	4	15.2	11	6	6	1	0	10	13	2	0
	YANKEES - f	1	0	2.88	25	0	0	0	3	25.0	18	10	8	2	2	11	21	5	0
2019	YANKEES	3	1	1.91	66	0	0	0	3	61.1	38	13	13	3	1	32	53	3	0
Minor League Totals		49	38	3.35	153	139	1	0	0	735.2	675	358	274	41	34	274	592	76	1
Major League Totals		34	23	3.07	397	46	0	0	145	603.0	516	234	206	37	10	237	499	41	0
NYY Totals		4	1	2.19	91	0	0	0	6	86.1	56	23	21	5	3	43	74	8	0

Was selected by the Orioles in the third round of the 2006 First-Year Player Draft.

a – Placed on the 15-day disabled list from August 5-22, 2011 with a left shoulder strain.
b – Placed on the 15-day disabled list on March 26, 2012 with a left shoulder impingement…was transferred to the 60-day disabled list on June 3 and reinstated on June 6, 2012.
c – Placed on the 10-day disabled list from April 16-May 2, 2017 with a left forearm strain.
d – Placed on the 10-day disabled list on May 6, 2017 (retroactive to May 5) with a left forearm strain…was transferred to the 60-day disabled list on June 20 and reinstated on July 5, 2017.
e – Placed on the 60-day disabled list from February 15-June 11, 2018 recovering from right Achilles surgery.
f – Acquired by the Yankees from the Baltimore Orioles for RHP Dillon Tate, RHP Cody Carroll and LHP Josh Rogers on July 24, 2018.

Britton's Postseason Record

Year	Club vs. Opp.	W	L	ERA	G	GS	CG	SHO	SV	IP	H	R	ER	HR	HP	BB	SO	WP	BK
2014	BAL vs. DET (DS)	0	0	3.86	3	0	0	0	0	2.1	2	1	1	0	0	1	2	0	0
	BAL vs. KC (CS)	0	0	3.86	3	0	0	0	0	2.1	3	1	1	0	0	4	3	0	0
2016	BAL at TOR (WC)						On Roster - Did Not Pitch												
2018	NYY vs. OAK (WC)	0	0	18.00	1	0	0	0	0	1.0	2	2	2	1	0	1	0	0	0
	NYY vs. BOS (DC)	0	0	2.25	3	0	0	0	0	4.0	3	1	1	1	0	1	4	0	0
2019	NYY vs. MIN (DS)	0	0	3.86	2	0	0	0	0	2.1	1	1	1	0	1	1	1	0	0
	NYY vs. HOU (CS)	0	0	0.00	5	0	0	0	0	5.2	1	0	0	0	2	5	5	1	0
Wild Card Game Totals		0	0	18.00	1	0	0	0	0	1.0	2	2	2	1	0	1	0	0	0
Division Series Totals		0	0	3.12	8	0	0	0	2	8.2	6	3	3	2	0	3	7	1	0
LCS Totals		0	0	1.13	8	0	0	0	0	8.0	4	1	1	0	0	9	8	1	0
POSTSEASON TOTALS		0	0	3.06	17	0	0	0	2	17.2	12	6	6	3	0	13	15	2	0

Britton's All-Star Game Record

Year	Club, Site	W	L	ERA	G	GS	CG	SHO	SV	IP	H	R	ER	HR	HP	BB	SO	WP	BK
2015	BAL, Cincinnati	0	0	0.00	1	0	0	0	0	0.2	1	0	0	0	0	0	1	0	0
2016	BAL, San Diego	0	0	0.00	1	0	0	0	1	1.0	1	0	0	0	0	0	0	0	0
All-Star Game Totals		0	0	0.00	2	0	0	0	1	1.2	2	0	0	0	0	0	1	0	0

Britton's Career Fielding Record

Position	PCT	G	PO	A	E	TC	DP
Pitcher	.965	397	29	110	5	144	7

Britton's Regular Season Batting Record

Year	Team	AVG	G	AB	R	H	2B	3B	HR	RBI	SH	SF	HP	BB	SO	SB	CS
2019	NYY					Did Not Bat											
Major League Totals		.625	397	8	3	5	1	0	1	2	0	0	0	1	0	0	0

Britton's Career Bests and Streaks

COMPLETE GAMES: None. **LOW-HIT COMPLETE GAME:** N/A. **IP (START):** 9.0, 5/12/11 vs. SEA. **IP (RELIEF):** 3.2, 9/27/13 vs. BOS. **HITS:** 12, 8/4/11 at KC. **RUNS:** 9, 7/30/11 at NYY. **WALKS:** 6, 7/17/12 at MIN. **STRIKEOUTS:** 10, 8/30/12 vs. CWS. **HOME RUNS:** 2 - 4x (last on 7/9/13 vs. TEX). **WINNING STREAK:** 4g - 3x (last on 7/10/18-5/20/19). **LOSING STREAK:** 5g, 6/22-8/4/11. **SCORELESS STREAK (IP):** 21.2, 6/22-8/22/16.

Pitcher of the Month: None   **Pitcher of the Week:** None   **Rookie of the Month:** None

LUIS CESSA • RHP

85

HT: 6-0 • **WT:** 208 • **BATS:** R • **THROWS:** R
BIRTHDATE: 4/25/92 • **OPENING DAY AGE:** 27
BIRTHPLACE: Córdoba, México
RESIDES: Cardenas, México
M.L. SERVICE: 2 years, 131 days

STATUS
- Acquired by the Yankees from the Detroit Tigers along with RHP Chad Green in exchange for LHP Justin Wilson on December 9, 2015.

CAREER NOTES
- Born in Córdoba, Veracruz, is one of five México-born pitchers to start a game in Yankees history, joining Jaime García (8GS), Esteban Loaiza (6GS), Alfredo Aceves (5GS) and Alfonso Pulido (3GS)…leads México-born Yankees with 19 starts and 232.0IP in pinstripes.
- Has made two career Opening Day rosters (2016, '19).

2019
- Spent the entire season at the Major League level for the first time in his career, going 2-1 with one save, a 4.11 ERA (81.0IP, 37ER) and 75K in 43 relief appearances with the Yankees.
- Tossed at least 2.0 innings in 11 straight relief appearances from 4/17/18-4/7/19…had at least 3.0IP with 1ER-or-fewer in four straight relief outings from 9/14/18-3/31/19.
- Made his season debut in 3/31 loss vs. Baltimore (3.1IP, 2H, 2R/1ER, 2BB, 5K).
- Allowed 12ER in 11.1IP from 6/2-23.
- Tied his career high with 5ER allowed (fourth time) on 6/2 vs. Boston (1.0IP, 5H, 1BB)…his 3ER allowed in the seventh snapped a 24.1-inning scoreless streak by Yankees relievers.
- Had a 1.11 ERA (24.1IP, 4R/3ER) with 24K over 9G from 6/19-8/4, tossing at least 3.0 innings in five of those nine outings and at least 2.0 innings in five straight from 7/18-8/4.
- Matched his season high with 4.0IP on 6/30 at Boston in London (4H, 0R, 2K)…was his fourth career relief appearance of at least 4.0 innings (6/23/19 vs. Houston, 4.0IP, 1ER; 7/4/17 vs. Toronto, 4.2IP, 0R; 5/28/16 at Tampa Bay, 4.0IP, 1ER).
- Set a relief appearance career high with 6K on 7/22 at Minnesota.
- Earned his first save of the season on 8/8 at Toronto (3.0IP, 2H, 1ER, 1BB, 5K, 1HR).
- Made a career-high four consecutive scoreless appearances from 8/22-9/4 (9.0IP, 7H, 0BB, 6K)…tossed multiple innings in each of those outings.
- Allowed a solo HR to García in the eighth inning on 9/25 at Tampa Bay, becoming the fifth Yankees pitcher since 1908 to allow a home run on his only pitch thrown (also Chasen Shreve in 2018, Boone Logan in 2012, Mike Stanton in 2005 and Graeme Lloyd in 1998).
- Made two postseason relief appearances, combining to toss 4.0 scoreless innings…made his postseason debut in ALCS Game 3 vs. Houston (2.0IP, 1H, 3K, 1HP).

2018
- Went 1-4 with two saves and a 5.24 ERA (44.2IP, 26ER) in 16 games (five starts) over eight stints with the Yankees (4/7-15, 4/17-6/27, 7/9, 7/25-26, 8/2-3, 8/15, 8/25 and 9/1-30)…was 1-4 with a 6.50 ERA (18.0IP, 13ER) in five starts and posted a 4.39 ERA (26.2IP, 13ER) with two saves in his 11 relief appearances.
- Tossed at least 2.0IP in nine of his 11 relief appearances and 3.0IP in six of those 11 games.
- Started the season with Triple-A Scranton/Wilkes-Barre but did not make an appearance before being recalled on 4/7…made his season debut that day vs. Baltimore, closing out the game with a perfect ninth (1.0IP, 2K).
- Was placed on the 10-day disabled list from 4/19 (retroactive to 4/18) - 6/21 with a left oblique strain, missing 55 team games…was removed from 4/17 loss vs. Miami in the eighth inning with the injury…in two rehab starts (1GS with Single-A Tampa, 1GS with Double-A Trenton), went 0-1 with a 3.18 ERA (5.2IP, 3R/2ER).
- Earned the win in a spot start in Game 2 of a doubleheader on 7/9 at Baltimore (6.0IP, 3H, 0R, 3BB, 4K), his first win as a starter since 8/26/16 vs. Baltimore…snapped his 13-start winless streak, tied for the longest by a Yankees starter (excluding openers) since 2002 (also Severino and Hughes).
- Recorded a career-long 12.0 scoreless inning streak from 6/27-7/25.
- Started on 7/25 at Tampa Bay and took the loss (5.1IP, 4H, 2ER, 0BB, 3K, 1HR)…retired the leadoff batters over the first five innings…retired 11 straight batters faced from the second out in the second to the end of the fifth, then allowed a leadoff single in the sixth and a subsequent two-run HR to Kiermaier.

- Tossed the final 3.0 innings of 8/25 Game 1 win at Baltimore to earn his first career save (3H, 1ER, 1BB, 2K)…was the Yankees' "26th Man" for the doubleheader.
- Made the start on 9/30 at Boston and took the loss (0.1IP, 5H, 4R/3ER)…exited the game in the first inning after colliding with Eduardo Núñez at first base.
- In six games (five starts) for Scranton/WB, went 3-0 with a 2.73 ERA (26.1IP, 8ER).

2017
- Went 0-3 with a 4.75 ERA (36.0IP, 19ER) in 10 games (five starts) over four stints with the Yankees (5/1, 6/15-7/8, 7/18-30 and 8/14-10/1)…was 0-3 with a 5.82 ERA (21.2IP, 14ER) in five starts and posted a 3.14 ERA (14.1IP, 5ER) without recording a decision in his five relief appearances.
- Tossed 4.2 scoreless innings (5H, 3K) in 7/4 loss vs. Toronto in the longest relief outing by a Yankee in 2017…was the longest scoreless relief appearance by a Yankee since Diego Moreno tossed 5.1 scoreless innings on 7/28/15 at Texas…became just the third Yankee since 1998 to toss at least 4.2IP with no runs or walks: Alfredo Aceves (5.1IP on 5/4/14 vs. Tampa Bay) and Aaron Small (6.2IP on 9/24/05 vs. Toronto).
- Made his final appearance of the season on 8/14 vs. the Mets, starting and allowing 2ER in 4.1IP (5H, 1BB, 5K, 2HR) without recording a decision…allowed solo HRs to Granderson and Céspedes in the third, his second career multi-HR inning (also allowed 2HR in the sixth inning of a start on 9/11/16 vs. Tampa Bay)…recorded all three outs in the first inning via strikeout…was his first career appearance vs. the Mets, the organization that originally signed him as a non-drafted free agent infielder in 2008.
- Was placed on the 10-day disabled list on 8/15 with a ribcage injury and transferred to the 60-day D.L. on 9/1…was reinstated on 11/3…missed the team's final 45 games of the season.
- In 14 games (13 starts) with Triple-A Scranton/Wilkes-Barre, went 4-6 with a 3.45 ERA (78.1IP, 30ER) with 67K.

2016
- Made his first career Opening Day roster and saw his first Major League action, going 4-4 with a 4.35 ERA (70.1IP, 34ER) in 17 games (nine starts) over four stints with the Yankees (4/4-15, 5/17-6/7, 6/26-7/5, 8/11-10/2)…made his first career Opening Day roster…won his first four career decisions.
- Allowed 24 of his 36R on his 16HR (10 solo HRs, four two-run HRs, two three-run HRs)…his 2.05 HR/9.0IP ratio (16HR/70.1IP) was fifth-highest in the Majors among pitchers with at least 70.0IP.
- Made his first eight appearances out of the bullpen, going 2-0 with a 5.30 ERA (18.2IP, 11ER)…permitted five of his 11ER in his final relief outing on 8/14 vs. Tampa Bay…tossed at least 2.0IP in 6-of-8 relief outings.
- Made his Major League debut on 4/8 loss at Detroit, entering the game in relief and allowing 2H and 1ER in 2.0IP (2K, 1HR)…struck out Justin Upton (swinging) in the seventh for his first career strikeout.
- Earned his first Major League win on 6/29 vs. Texas, allowing 1ER in 3.0IP (1H, 2BB, 2K, 1HR) to close out the game.
- Joined the rotation on 8/20 and was 2-4 with a 4.01 ERA (51.2IP, 23ER) in nine starts…his 1.06 WHIP as a starter was fifth-lowest among AL starters (min. 50.0IP)…since 1913, only four Yankees rookie starters threw at least 50.0IP and had lower WHIPs (Tiny Bonham-0.97 in 1940, José Contreras-0.99 in 2003, Masahiro Tanaka-1.06 in 2014, Stan Bahnsen-1.06 in 1968)…completed 6.0IP in 5-of-9 starts, permitted 3ER-or-fewer in 7-of-9, and allowed 6H-or-fewer in all nine…permitted HRs in 7-of-9 starts (11HR total, accounting for 15-of-24R).
- Became the second pitcher in Yankees history to toss at least 5.0IP and allow 6H-or-fewer in each of his first nine career starts (Rollie Sheldon, first nine starts, 4/30-7/9/61)…was the second Yankees pitcher since 2009 to record quality starts in each of his first three career starts, joining Masahiro Tanaka (AL-record first 16 starts)…was one of two Yankees pitchers since 2004 to win each of his first two career starts (Shane Greene, first 2GS in 2014).
- Earned the win in his first Major League start on 8/20 at Los Angeles-AL, tossing 6.0 scoreless innings (3H, 1BB, 5K, 1HP)…was the first Yankee with at least 6.0 scoreless innings in his first career start since Jorge De Paula on 9/26/03 (G2) vs. Baltimore…at 24 years, 117 days old, was the youngest Yankees pitcher to toss at least 6.0 scoreless innings with 3H-or-fewer since Joba Chamberlain (23y, 309d) allowed 3H over 8.0IP on 7/29/09 at Tampa Bay.
- Went 6-3 with a 3.03 ERA (77.1IP, 26ER) in 15 games (14GS) with the RailRiders…allowed 1ER-or-fewer in six of his last eight starts, going 6-2 with a 2.06 ERA (48.0IP, 11ER) over the span.

2015
- Combined to go 8-10 with a 4.52 ERA (139.1IP, 70ER) and 119K in 25 starts between Double-A Binghamton and Triple-A Las Vegas in the Mets organization and Triple-A Toledo in the Tigers organization.
- Began the season with the B-Mets and went 7-4 with a 2.56 ERA (77.1IP, 22ER) in 13 starts…ranked eighth in the Eastern League in ERA and tied for sixth in wins at the time of his 7/3 promotion…allowed one-or-zero runs in 8-of-13 starts…in his season debut on 4/12 at Akron, faced the minimum and permitted only 1H over 7.0 scoreless innings to earn the win (0BB, 8K)…was 0-3 with an 8.51 ERA (24.1IP, 23ER) in five starts for the 51s.
- Was traded to the Tigers along with RHP Michael Fulmer in exchange for OF Yoenis Céspedes on 7/31…made seven starts for the Mud Hens, going 1-3 with a 5.97 ERA (37.2IP, 25ER).
- Was added to the Tigers' 40-man roster on 11/3/15.
- Was acquired by the Yankees from Detroit with RHP Chad Green in exchange for LHP Justin Wilson on 12/9/15.

2014
- Posted a 7-8 record, a 4.00 ERA (114.2IP, 51ER) and one complete game in 20 starts at Single-A St. Lucie…also made one spot start for Double-A Binghamton, taking the loss on 5/21 at Portland (3.2IP, 5ER).
- Recorded a season-high 10K and did not walk a batter in a 6/4 win at Dunedin (7.0IP, 5H, 3ER).

2013
- Went 8-4 with a 3.12 ERA (130.0IP, 45ER) and one complete game in 21 starts at Single-A Savannah…ranked eighth in the South Atlantic League in ERA…among SAL pitchers who threw at least 125.0IP, finished third in K/BB ratio (6.53) and BB/9.0IP ratio (1.32) and fifth in K/9.0IP ratio (8.58).
- Allowed 2ER-or-fewer in 13-of-21 outings and issued 1BB-or-fewer in 16-of-21 starts.
- Was named SAL "Pitcher of the Week" for 5/27-6/3…over his final 13 starts (from 6/1), was 6-2 with a 2.46 ERA (84.0IP, 23ER).

2012
- Spent the season with short-season Single-A Brooklyn, posting a 5-4 record while ranking 10th in the New York-Penn League with a 2.49 ERA (72.1IP, 20ER) in 13 starts.
- Allowed 2R-or-fewer in 11-of-13 starts, including his final start of the year, in which he permitted 1R over a career-high 8.2 innings (6H, 1BB, 2K) in a win on 9/3 vs. Lowell.

2011
- Split his first season as a pitcher between the DSL Mets 2 and the GCL Mets, going 4-3 with one save and a 3.19 ERA (53.2IP, 19ER) in 15 games (six starts).
- Went 0-1 with a 2.49 ERA (21.2IP, 6ER) in five starts in the DSL…was promoted to the GCL on 6/29 and was 4-2 with one save and a 3.66 ERA (32.0IP, 13ER) in 10 games (one start).

2010
- Batted .162 (11-for-68) with 2R, 2 doubles and 3RBI in 23 games with the DSL Mets 1…committed 3E in 82TC (.963) while splitting time between 2B (10G/10GS) and 3B (10G/9GS).

2009
- Made his professional debut as an infielder with the DSL Mets, batting .191 (17-for-89) with 17R, 1 double, 1 triple, 1HR, 9RBI, 19BB and 8SB in 34 games…posted a .379 on-base percentage.
- Committed 8E in 98TC (.918) while playing 3B (22G/21GS), 2B (8G/4GS) and SS (1G/0GS).

PERSONAL
- Full name is Luis Enrique Cessa (pronounced "SESS-uh").
- Was a color analyst for FOX Latin America's broadcast of the 2016 World Series.

Cessa's Career Pitching Record

Year	Club	W	L	ERA	G	GS	CG	SHO	SV	IP	H	R	ER	HR	HP	BB	SO	WP	BK
2011	DSL Mets 2	0	1	2.49	5	5	0	0	0	21.2	19	8	6	0	1	3	23	1	0
	GCL Mets	4	2	3.66	10	1	0	0	1	32.0	29	15	13	1	1	10	23	2	0
2012	Brooklyn	5	4	2.49	13	13	0	0	0	72.1	64	21	20	4	2	13	44	0	0
2013	Savannah	8	4	3.12	21	21	1	0	0	130.0	136	53	45	11	0	19	124	4	1
2014	St. Lucie	7	8	4.00	20	20	1	0	0	114.2	110	54	51	7	3	27	83	6	0
	Binghamton	0	1	12.27	1	1	0	0	0	3.2	7	5	5	2	1	2	3	1	0
2015	Binghamton	7	4	2.56	13	13	0	0	0	77.1	77	25	22	2	0	17	61	4	0
	Las Vegas - a	0	3	8.51	5	5	0	0	0	24.1	40	25	23	3	1	4	24	0	0
	Toledo - b	1	3	5.97	7	7	0	0	0	37.2	46	27	25	2	2	15	34	1	1
2016	YANKEES	4	4	4.35	17	9	0	0	0	70.1	64	36	34	16	3	14	46	2	0
	Scranton/WB	6	3	3.03	15	14	1	1	0	77.1	66	33	26	8	0	23	69	3	0
2017	Scranton/WB	4	6	3.45	14	13	0	0	0	78.1	75	37	30	7	2	26	67	0	0
	YANKEES - c	0	3	4.75	10	5	0	0	0	36.0	36	21	19	7	3	17	30	2	0
2018	YANKEES - d	1	4	5.24	16	5	0	0	2	44.2	51	27	26	5	0	13	39	7	0
	Tampa	0	1	10.80	1	1	0	0	0	1.2	3	2	2	0	0	4	1	0	0
	Trenton	0	1	2.70	2	2	0	0	0	10.0	6	4	3	0	1	1	12	0	0
	Scranton/WB	3	0	2.73	6	5	0	0	0	26.1	19	9	8	1	0	4	25	3	0
2019	YANKEES	2	1	4.11	43	0	0	0	1	81.0	75	42	37	14	3	31	75	1	0
Minor League Totals		45	41	3.55	133	121	3	1	1	707.1	697	318	279	48	13	168	593	25	2
Major League Totals		7	12	4.50	86	19	0	0	3	232.0	226	126	116	42	9	75	190	12	0

Signed by the New York Mets as a non-drafted free agent on July 9, 2008.

a - Acquired by the Tigers from the Mets along with RHP Michael Fulmer in exchange for OF Yoenis Céspedes on July 31, 2015.
b - Acquired by the Yankees from the Tigers along with RHP Chad Green in exchange for LHP Justin Wilson on December 9, 2015.
c - Placed on the 10-day disabled list on August 15, 2017 with a ribcage injury…was transferred to the 60-day disabled list on September 1 and reinstated on November 3, 2017.
d - Placed on the 10-day disabled list from April 19 (retroactive to April 18) - June 21, 2018 with a left oblique strain.

Cessa's Postseason Record

Year	Club vs. Opp.	W	L	ERA	G	GS	CG	SHO	SV	IP	H	R	ER	HR	HP	BB	SO	WP	BK
2019	NYY vs. MIN (DS)							On Roster - Did Not Pitch											
	NYY vs. HOU (CS)	0	0	0.00	2	0	0	0	0	4.0	2	0	0	0	1	0	4	0	0
Wild Card Game Totals		-	-	-	-	-	-	-	-	-	-	-	-	-	-	-	-	-	-
Division Series Totals		-	-	-	-	-	-	-	-	-	-	-	-	-	-	-	-	-	-
LCS Totals		0	0	0.00	2	0	0	0	0	4.0	2	0	0	0	1	0	4	0	0
POSTSEASON TOTALS		0	0	0.00	2	0	0	0	0	4.0	2	0	0	0	1	0	4	0	0

Cessa's Career Fielding Record

Position	PCT	G	PO	A	E	TC	DP
Pitcher	.951	86	10	29	2	41	1

Cessa's Regular Season Batting Record

Year	Team	AVG	G	AB	R	H	2B	3B	HR	RBI	SH	SF	HP	BB	SO	SB	CS
2019	NYY	.000	43	1	0	0	0	0	0	0	0	0	0	0	1	0	0
Major League Totals		.000	86	2	0	0	0	0	0	0	0	0	0	0	2	0	0

Cessa's Career Bests and Streaks

COMPLETE GAMES: None. **LOW-HIT COMPLETE GAME:** N/A. **IP (START):** 6.0 - 6 times (last on 7/9/18 at BAL-G2). **IP (RELIEF):** 4.2, 7/4/17 vs. TOR. **HITS:** 7 - 2 times (last on 8/15/18 vs. TB). **RUNS:** 5 - 4 times (last on 6/2/19 vs. BOS). **WALKS:** 4 - 3 times (last on 9/28/19 at TEX). **STRIKEOUTS:** 8, 6/24/17 vs. TEX. **HOME RUNS:** 3, 9/11/16 vs. TB. **WINNING STREAK:** 4g, 6/29-8/26/16. **LOSING STREAK:** 8g, 9/11/16-6/27/18. **SCORELESS STREAK (IP):** 12.0, 6/27-7/25/18.

Pitcher of the Month: None   **Player of the Week:** None   **Rookie of the Month:** None

Steinbrenner High School

Named for the late Yankees Principal Owner, George M. Steinbrenner High School opened in August 2009 on Lutz Lake Fern Road just north of Tampa.

"Over the years, Mr. Steinbrenner has been deeply involved in the community, particularly with the schools and the school system," said Steven Ayers, director of community relations for Hillsborough County public schools. "He has been very involved and very philanthropic. He has probably donated tens of millions over the length of time. He's had a significant amount of money and significant amount of involvement in the community."

In addition to regular classroom curriculum, the school also offers classes for students preparing for a career in sports with sports marketing, sports medicine and the business of sports (BOSS). The school's teams are named the Warriors, featuring navy and gold coloring.

AROLDIS CHAPMAN • LHP

54

HT: 6-4 • **WT:** 218 • **BATS:** L • **THROWS:** L
BIRTHDATE: 2/28/88 • **OPENING DAY AGE:** 32
BIRTHPLACE: Holguín, Cuba
RESIDES: Davie, Fla.
M.L. SERVICE: 9 years, 9 days

STATUS
- Signed by the Yankees on December 15, 2016 to a five-year contract extending through the 2021 season with a player opt-out after the 2019 season…signed a contract extension extending through the 2022 season on November 3, 2019.

CAREER NOTES
- Has averaged 14.84 K/9.0IP in his career (535.2IP, 883K), the best ratio in the Major Leagues since at least 1900 (min. 300.0IP)…since 2010, leads all Major League relievers in K/9.0IP ratio and ranks third in strikeouts, trailing only Kenley Jansen (903) and Craig Kimbrel (898).
- Led all National League relievers in strikeouts each season from 2012-15.
- Reached 500K in 292.0IP (on 7/19/15), becoming the fastest to 500K (by IP) in Major League history, surpassing Craig Kimbrel's record (305.0IP), set in 2015.
- Struck out at least one batter in a Major League-record 49 consecutive relief appearances from 8/21/13-8/13/14 (50.2IP, 100K)…the next six such streaks are by Corey Knebel (46G, 10/2/16-7/15/17), Dellin Betances (44G, 5/29-9/22/18), Bruce Sutter (39G, 6/1-10/2/77), Eric Gagne (35G, 7/18/03-4/10/04), Josh Hader (35G, 9/4/17-6/22/18) and Chapman (34G, 9/15/11-6/16/12)…extended the streak by striking out his final batter faced on nine occasions.
- Ranks 34th on Baseball's all-time list with 273 saves…surpassed Ugueth Urbina (237), Dan Quisenberry (244), Dave Righetti (252), Todd Worrell (256) and Bob Wickman (267) in 2019.
- Is the only pitcher in Major League history with four seasons of at least 30 saves and 100K, having accomplished the feat each season from 2012-15…only Craig Kimbrel (2011-12, '17), Eric Gagne (2002-04), Kenley Jansen (2014, '16-17) and Billy Wagner (1999, 2003, '10) have had as many as three such seasons in their careers.
- Has reached 20 saves in eight straight seasons (since 2012) and is one of 31 pitchers with at least eight 20-save seasons all time.
- Is one of two pitchers with at least 20 saves in each of the last eight seasons (2012-19), joining Kenley Jansen…is one of two pitchers to record 30 saves at least seven times (2012-16, '18-19) in the last eight years (since 2012), joining Kimbrel, who had at least 30 saves in eight consecutive seasons from 2011-18.
- Is one of 17 pitchers to record at least 30 saves in seven different seasons…has seven career 25-save seasons (2012-16, '18-19).
- Has four 20-save seasons as a Yankee (2016-19)…is one of 11 pitchers in franchise history to reach the mark at least once…in 2016, became the fifth different pitcher in as many seasons to earn at least 20 saves (also Andrew Miller-36 in 2015, David Robertson-39 in 2014, Mariano Rivera-44 in 2013 and Rafael Soriano-42 in 2012).
- Owns the most career saves by a Cuba-born pitcher (273), surpassing Danys Báez's record (114) on 4/10/15 vs. St. Louis…had 146 saves with Cincinnati, fourth-most on the Reds' all-time saves list behind Danny Graves (182), Francisco Cordero (150) and John Franco (148).
- Has held opponents to a .161 batting average (300-for-1,864) in his career, the second-lowest of any pitcher since 1900 with at least 1,000 opponent at-bats behind Craig Kimbrel (.158).
- Has held left-handers to a .134 (64-for-478) batting average with just 3HR in his Major League career.
- Held opponents scoreless in September in 2014, '16 and '17 (30.2IP)…was named AL "Reliever of the Month" in September 2017…owns a 1.58 ERA (85.2IP, 15ER) in 87 career September appearance.
- Has nine career postseason saves, tied for seventh-most all time…has posted a 1.65 ERA (16.1IP, 3ER) with five saves, 7BB/1IBB and 29K in 14 postseason relief appearances as a Yankee.
- Converted 56 consecutive save opportunities at Great American Ball Park from 9/25/12-8/4/15, the longest home saves streak by any pitcher since the stat became official in 1969.
- Was the only relief pitcher ever to be named to four All-Star teams while playing for the Reds.
- Has made seven career Opening Day rosters (2011-13, '15 w/ Cincinnati and '17-19 w/ the Yankees).

CAREER HIGHLIGHTS

AL All-Star Team
- 2018, 2019

NL All-Star Team
- 2012, 2013, 2014, 2015

Mariano Rivera AL Reliever of the Year
- 2019

2019

- Went 3-2 with 37 saves (in 42 chances) and a 2.21 ERA (57.0IP, 14ER) in 60 relief appearances…was named to the Inaugural 2019 All-MLB Second Team.
- Ranked fourth American League relievers with a 13.42 K/9.0IP ratio (57.0IP, 85K)…struck out 36.2% of his batters faced (85K, 235BF).
- Tied for third in the Majors—and ranked second in the AL—with 37 saves, one shy of his career high (38 in both 2012 and 2013 w/ Cincinnati).
- Reached the 25-saves plateau for the seventh time in his career (also 2012-16, '18).
- Had at least 1K in 27 straight appearances from 9/20/18-5/25/19 (G2), the third-longest stretch of his career.
- Converted 15 straight save opportunities from 4/24-6/6.
- Made his 500th career appearance on 4/24 at Los Angeles-AL, tossing a scoreless ninth.
- Recorded a save and had at least 1K with 0BB in seven consecutive appearances from 4/27-5/15 (G2), tied for the longest such streak in Yankees history (also John Wetteland from 9/14-29/95).
- Earned his 79th save as a Yankee on 4/27 at San Francisco, surpassing Steve Farr (78 saves) for fifth-most in franchise history.
- Was named AL "Reliever of the Month" in May after leading the Majors with 11 saves (12G, 0.79 ERA, 11.1IP, 1ER, 18K)…was his second career "Reliever of the Month" Award…was the fifth calendar month by a Yankees pitcher with at least 11 saves and a sub-1.00 ERA (Mariano Rivera, 3x, August 1999, June 2003, June '04 and Chapman also June 2018).
- Earned the save in both games of a doubleheader for the second time in his career on 5/15 vs. Baltimore (also 8/16/16 vs. Milwaukee w/ Chicago-NL)…was the first Yankee to do so since Rafael Soriano on 9/19/12 vs. Toronto.
- Had saves in seven straight appearances from 5/20-6/6 and 14-of-15 from 4/27-6/6.
- Collected his 250th career save in 5/25 Game 2 win at Kansas City (37th pitcher with 250SV, most by a Cuba-born pitcher).
- Reached 500.0 career innings pitched on 5/27 vs. San Diego.
- Had a 6.39 ERA (12.2IP, 9ER) over 13G (from 6/24-7/31) after posting a 1.24 ERA (29.0IP, 4ER) over his first 31 games of the season (thru 6/21).
- On 6/25 vs. Toronto, allowed his first earned runs since 5/9 and had his 17-game streak with 0ER snapped (16.1IP, 8H, 3R/0ER, 6BB, 23K over the span).
- Was named to his sixth career All-Star team (also 2012-15 and '18, 2x in the AL) via the player ballot and recorded his first career All-Star save with a scoreless ninth (3BF, 3K), the fifth All-Star save by a Yankee (Mariano Rivera-4).
- Had consecutive blown save chances (7/15 vs. Tampa Bay and 7/23 at Minnesota) for the fifth time in his career and first since 7/1-14/17.
- Earned a save in nine consecutive appearances from 7/31-8/17, tying Kansas City's Ian Kennedy, Minnesota's Taylor Rogers and Milwaukee's Josh Hader for the longest streak in the Majors in 2019…was the third-longest streak of his career (16 from 7/15-8/12/12 and 10 from 5/30-6/18/18).
- Was named AL "Reliever of the Month" for August, his third career monthly honor and second of the season (also May)…retired 33-of-41 batters across 11.0 shutout innings (3H, 5BB, 20K) and earned an AL-high nine saves in 11 appearances during the month…were the Majors' most innings pitched in August without allowing a run… opponents hit .083/.195/.083 (3-for-36)…became the second Yankee to record at least nine saves and not allow a run in a calendar month, joining Mariano Rivera, who did it three times: 11SV in August 1999, 10SV in July 2009 and 9SV in September 2003.
- Threw just 4.1 innings and 70 pitches over five appearances in September.
- Closed out the game with a scoreless ninth inning in the Yankees' AL East-clinching win on 9/19 vs. Los Angeles-AL.
- Made the postseason for the seventh time in his career and third with the Yankees…tossed 1.2 scoreless innings in ALDS Game 3 at Minnesota, his longest outing since 2017 ALDS Game 5 at Cleveland (2.0IP)…in ALCS Game 5 vs. Houston, moved into a tie for seventh place on the all-time postseason saves list with nine…allowed a "walk-off" two-run HR to Jose Altuve in the ninth inning of ALCS Game 6 to record the loss in the Astros series clinching win.
- Following the season, signed a contract extension, extending through 2022.

2018

- Went 3-0 with 32 saves (in 34 chances) and a 2.45 ERA (51.1IP, 14ER) in 55 relief appearances…was named via the Player Ballot to his fifth career All-Star team (also 2012-15) and first as a member of the AL (did not pitch).
- Led all Major League relievers with a 16.31 K/9.0IP ratio (51.1IP, 93K)…struck out 43.9% of his batters faced (93K, 212BF).
- Collected 26 saves before the All-Star break…only one Yankee since 2005 had more saves in the "first half" (Mariano Rivera, 30 in 2013).
- Converted 22 straight save chances from 5/8-7/31…was the third-longest streak of his career (29 straight from 7/4/14-5/30/15; 27 straight from 6/26-9/4/12) and the longest streak by a Yankee since Andrew Miller converted 24 in a row from 4/8-8/6/15.

- Earned a save in 10 straight appearances from 5/30-6/18, matching the longest streak by a Yankee since 2011 (Mariano Rivera, 11 straight from 8/29-9/21/11 and 10 straight from 4/12-5/1/13).
- Allowed 1ER in 11.2IP (4H, 4BB, 19K, 1HP, 1HR) in 12 appearances in June...his 11 saves in June were tied for third-most in a calendar month in Yankees history, trailing only John Wetteland (15 in June 1996) and Sparky Lyle (12 in June 1973)...is just the second Yankee since 2005 to record 11 saves in a month (Rafael Soriano, 11 in June 2012).
- Allowed his first HR of the season to Maikel Franco with two outs in the ninth inning on 6/25 at Philadelphia...marked his first regular season HR allowed since 8/25/17 vs. Seattle (Yonder Alonso)...snapped a streak of 176BF without a HR...his 33.2IP had been the most by any pitcher who had not yet allowed a HR in 2018.
- Threw his fastest pitch of the season at 104.4 mph to Acuña (Statcast) in 7/2 loss vs. Atlanta.

MOST STRIKEOUTS BY A RELIEVER, 2011-19
1. AROLDIS CHAPMAN 864
2. Kenley Jansen 862
3. Craig Kimbrel 858
4. David Robertson 710
5. Tyler Clippard 694

HIGHEST SINGLE-SEASON K/9.0IP RATIO BY A RELIEVER, ALL TIME (min. 50.0IP)

Rk.	Player	Year	K/9.0IP (IP, K)
1.	AROLDIS CHAPMAN	2014	17.67 (54.0, 106)
2.	Craig Kimbrel	2012	16.66 (62.2, 116)
3.	Craig Kimbrel	2017	16.43 (69.0, 126)
4.	Josh Hader	2019	16.41 (75.2, 138)
5.	AROLDIS CHAPMAN	2018	16.31 (51.1, 93)
6.	Kenley Jansen	2011	16.10 (53.2, 96)
7.	Carlos Marmol	2010	15.99 (77.2, 138)
8.	AROLDIS CHAPMAN	2013	15.83 (63.2, 112)
9.	Josh Hader	2018	15.82 (81.1, 143)
10.	AROLDIS CHAPMAN	2015	15.74 (66.1, 116)

- Struck out only his batter faced in the ninth before being removed with left knee discomfort in 7/7 win at Toronto.
- Struck out a career-high-tying eight straight batters from his final batter faced on 7/28 (Game 2) vs. Kansas City through his first batter on 8/5 at Boston...prior to the streak, had struck out only two of his previous 15BF...was part of a streak of 10 straight recorded via strikeout.
- Had 25K in 11.1IP over his final 13 relief appearances (beginning in 7/28 Game 2)...collected multiple strikeouts in 10 of those games.
- Was placed on the 10-day D.L. from 8/22-9/19 with left knee tendinitis...was removed from 8/21 win at Miami after allowing 1BB and throwing one pitch to his second batter faced before being removed with left knee soreness...threw a total of 22 pitches to Kyle Higashioka and Tyler Wade in a simulated game at Yankee Stadium on 9/17.
- During his D.L. stint (8/22-9/18), four different Yankees recorded saves, each saving at least two games: Dellin Betances (3), Zack Britton (2), Luis Cessa (2), David Robertson (2).
- Allowed 1H in 3.0 scoreless innings (1BB, 4K) over three postseason relief appearances.

2017
- Went 4-3 with 22 saves (in 26 chances) and a 3.22 ERA (50.1IP, 18ER) in 52 relief appearances.
- According to MLB's Statcast, 345 of his 879 pitches were thrown at 100 mph or faster (39.2%)...also posted the highest average fastball velocity in the Majors (100.0 mph).
- Allowed homers by two left-handed batters (Rafael Devers on 8/13 vs. Boston and Yonder Alonso on 8/25 vs. Seattle)...allowed just 1HR to a left-handed hitter in his first 418 career appearances.
- Was placed on the 10-day disabled list on 5/14 (retroactive to 5/13) - 6/18 with left shoulder rotator cuff inflammation (missed 33 team games)...made one rehab appearance with Double-A Trenton.
- On 8/13 vs. Boston, allowed a game-tying solo HR to Rafael Devers in the ninth and the winning run in the 10th (1.1IP, 1H, 2ER, 1BB, 3K, 1HR, 1HP)...the homer to Devers was just the second HR allowed to a left-handed hitter in either a regular season or postseason game in his career (also Luke Scott on 6/26/11 at Baltimore w/ Cincinnati)...faced 405 left-handed batters between homers (regular and postseason)...also snapped a career-long 76-appearance streak without a HR overall...had not allowed a regular season HR since giving up back-to-back HRs to Eduardo Escobar and Kurt Suzuki on 6/18/16 at Minnesota...48 of the 76G during the streak came as a Yankee.
- Over his final 14 appearances (8/20-9/30), posted a 0.61 ERA (14.2IP, 1ER) with 19K.
- Was named AL "Reliever of the Month" for the first time in his career in September...retired 36-of-41 batters faced, tossing 12.0 scoreless innings with six saves in 11G in September (3H, 2BB, 17K).
- Earned his 200th career save in 9/13 win against Tampa Bay at Citi Field, the 49th pitcher to reach the milestone.
- In six postseason relief appearances, went 0-1 with three saves, a 1.13 ERA (8.0IP, 1ER) and 16K...closed out ALDS Game 5 at Cleveland with 2.0 scoreless innings (1BB, 4K) to earn his longest save of 2017.

2016
- Combined with the Yankees and Cubs to go 4-1 with 36 saves (in 39 chances) and a 1.55 ERA (58.0IP, 32H, 12R/10ER, 18BB, 90K) in 59 relief appearances...among relievers, ranked third in opponents' batting average (.158), fourth in ERA, sixth in save percentage (92.3%), seventh in K/9.0IP (13.97) and tied for 11th in saves.
- Threw the 30 fastest pitches in the Majors in 2016 (Statcast), with the fastest coming on a 105.1 mph fastball on 7/18 vs. Baltimore...posted the Majors' highest average fastball velocity (100.9 mph).
- In 31 relief appearances with the Yankees, went 3-0 with 20 saves (in 21 chances), a 2.01 ERA (31.1IP, 7ER) and 44K...posted a 12.64 K/9.0IP ratio and a 36.7% strikeout rate (44K, 120BF).

- Began the season on the restricted list after accepting a 30-game suspension from Commissioner Manfred on 3/1 for violating Major League Baseball's Joint Domestic Violence, Sexual Assault and Child Abuse Policy.
- Made his Yankees debut in 5/9 win vs. Kansas City…was reinstated from the restricted list before the game.
- In 5/27 win at Tampa Bay, closed out the game with 2K in 0.1IP…was first Yankees pitcher since at least 1913 to finish an appearance with 2K in 0.1IP and fourth since 1913 with more strikeouts than outs (David Robertson, 8/6/09 vs. Boston, 0.2IP, 3K; Sterling Hitchcock, 6/30/94 at Boston, 0.0IP, 1K; Ron Davis, 9/17/80 vs. Toronto, 0.2IP, 3K).
- Threw the five fastest pitches ever tracked by MLB Statcast (at the time) in 7/18 win vs. Baltimore, ranging from 104.0 to 105.1 mph…his 105.1 mph fastball (on the sixth pitch to J.J. Hardy) matched his Major League-record 105.1 mph fastball clocked by Pitch f/x on 9/24/10 w/ Cincinnati at San Diego.
- Was traded by the Yankees to the Cubs on 7/25 in exchange for RHP Adam Warren, INF Gleyber Torres, OF Billy McKinney and OF Rashad Crawford.
- In 28 games for the Cubs, went 1-1 with 16 saves (in 18 chances), a 1.01 ERA (26.2IP, 3ER), 46K and a 15.53 K/9.0IP ratio…his ERA ranked as the fourth-lowest mark by a Cubs reliever all-time in the season's second half (min. 20G)…ranked fourth in the NL in saves after his Cubs debut.
- Following the All-Star break, recorded a 0.83 ERA (32.2IP, 3ER) in 33 appearances…held opponents to a .127 (14-for-110) batting average and did not allow a homer…surrendered just 1H over 9.0 scoreless innings in September, holding batters to a .036 (1-for-28) BA with 16K in eight games.
- During the postseason, went 2-0 with four saves, a 3.45 ERA (15.2IP, 6ER) and 21K in 13 relief appearances…no other pitcher appeared in more than 11 postseason contests…his 15.2IP trailed only Cleveland's Andrew Miller (19.1IP) among relievers…finished Game 6 of the NLCS against the Dodgers, tossing 1.2 hitless innings (1BB, 1K) to send the Cubs to their first World Series since 1945…with the Cubs facing elimination in World Series Game 5 against Cleveland, tossed a career-high 2.2 innings to earn the save (1H, 1HP, 4K)…recorded the win in the Cubs' 10-inning World Series Game 7 victory to secure the club's first championship since 1908.

2015

- Went 4-4 with 33 saves (in 36 chances) and a 1.63 ERA (66.1IP, 12ER) in 65 relief appearances with the Reds…received the Johnny Vander Meer Award as Cincinnati's "Most Outstanding Pitcher" as voted on by the local chapter of the BBWAA…was named to his fourth straight NL All-Star Team as voted on by his peers.
- Led all Major League relievers with a 15.74 K/9.0IP ratio (66.1IP, 116K) and ranked second in strikeouts behind only Dellin Betances (131)…led all National League relievers in ERA and strikeouts.
- According to MLB's Statcast, threw the 62 fastest pitches in the Majors, with a high of 103.92 mph on 6/29 vs. Minnesota (a pitch fouled off by Brian Dozier)…posted the highest average fastball velocity in the Majors (99.96 mph), ahead of Kansas City's Kelvin Herrera (98.46).
- Recorded his 115th career save on 4/10 vs. St. Louis, surpassing Danys Báez (114) for the most career saves by a Cuba-born pitcher in Baseball history…his hat from the game was sent to the Hall of Fame in Cooperstown.
- Did not allow a run over a 28-appearance stretch from 8/21/14-5/6/15 (16 saves, 28.1IP, 10H, 12BB, 54K).
- Converted 29 consecutive save chances from 7/4/14-5/30/15, the longest active streak in the Majors at the time…also tied a Reds record for consecutive converted saves (Francisco Cordero, 7/23/08-6/9/09)…snapped a 74.1-inning homerless streak (5/13/14-6/3/15) with a game-tying HR to Maikel Franco on 6/3 at Philadelphia.
- Struck out all three batters on 14 pitches for the NL in the All-Star Game at Great American Ball Park.
- Recorded his 500th career strikeout on 7/19 vs. Cleveland…reached the plateau in 292.0IP to become the fastest to 500K (by IP) in Baseball history, surpassing Craig Kimbrel's record of 500K in 305.0IP, set earlier in 2015.
- Allowed a game-tying leadoff HR to Ben Zobrist in the ninth inning on 8/18 vs. Kansas City, snapping a streak of 56 straight converted save chances at Great American Ball Park dating back to a blown save on 9/7/12 vs. Houston…was the Majors' longest home save streak since saves became an official statistic in 1969.
- Scored from first base—his first career run scored—on a Jason Bourgeois double on 8/31 at Chicago-NL.

2014

- Went 0-3 with 36 saves (in 38 chances), a 2.00 ERA (54.0IP, 12ER) and 106K in 54 relief appearances with the Reds…his 94.7% conversion rate was best in the National League and second-best in the Majors behind only Kansas City's Greg Holland (46-for-48, 95.8%)…was named to his third straight All-Star Game (0.2IP).
- Established Major League records *by a reliever* with 17.67 K/9.0IP (106K, 54.0IP), a 5.05-to-1 strikeouts-to-hits ratio (106K, 21H) and a 52.5% strikeout rate (106K, 202 BF).

- Became the first pitcher to average at least 100 mph (100.3) for an entire season (Pitch f/x)…hit at least 100 mph in 53 of his 54 appearances, including a high of 104.53 mph to Paul Goldschmidt on 7/28 vs. Arizona.
- Was placed on the 15-day disabled list from 3/30-5/9 following surgery to insert a three-inch titanium plate and 12 screws to stabilize the bones around his left eye (performed on 3/20)…the injury was suffered during spring training on 3/19 at Kansas City, when he was hit in the face by a line drive off the bat of Salvador Pérez in the sixth inning…suffered fractures of his eye and nose and a concussion…his vision was unaffected…had staples in his scalp removed on 4/2…made four rehab appearances (3GS) with Single-A Dayton and Triple-A Louisville.
- Earned his 100th career save on 7/29 vs. Arizona.
- Had at least 1K in a Major League-record 49 straight relief appearances from 8/21/13-8/13/14 (50.2IP, 100K).

2013
- Went 4-5 with 38 saves (in 43 chances), a 2.54 ERA (63.2IP, 18ER) and 112K in 68 relief appearances with Cincinnati…was named to his second straight NL All-Star team (1.0IP, 1BB, 1K).
- Posted a 0.66 ERA (41.0IP, 3ER) with 20 saves (in 20 opps.) and 79K in 40 games at Great American Ball Park.
- Recorded his first career plate appearance on 8/21 vs. Arizona, striking out vs. Brad Ziegler.
- Was on the Reds' roster for the NL Wild Card Game at Pittsburgh, but did not pitch.

2012
- Was 5-5 with 38 saves (in 43 chances), a 1.51 ERA (71.2IP, 12ER) and 122K in 68 relief appearances with the Reds…ranked second in the NL with a 15.32 K/9.0IP ratio…finished eighth in NL Cy Young Award voting and 12th in NL MVP voting…was elected by his peers to his first career All-Star Game.
- Went to spring training in competition for a spot in the starting rotation, but spent the entire regular season in the bullpen after RHPs Ryan Madson and Nick Masset were placed on the disabled list prior to Opening Day.
- Did not allow an earned run over his first 24 appearances of the season (29.0IP) from 4/5-6/6, the longest scoreless appearance stretch to begin a season in Reds history (surpassed John Hudek's 1998 record of 18G).
- Converted 27 consecutive save chances from 6/26-9/4 (0.29 ERA, 30.2IP, 1ER)…threw 23 consecutive scoreless appearances from 6/26-8/17, recording 20 saves over the span (22.2IP, 9H, 3BB, 45K).
- Led the Majors with 13 saves in July and 11 saves in August and was named MLB's "Delivery Man of the Month" following each of those two months.
- Made his All-Star Game debut, walking one batter in 0.1IP (1K) at Kauffman Stadium.
- Made three postseason relief appearances in the NLDS vs. San Francisco, posting a 3.00 ERA (3.0IP, 1ER).

2011
- Went 4-1 with a 3.60 ERA (50.0IP, 20ER) and 71K in 54 relief appearances with the Reds.
- Reached 106 mph on a pitch on the Great American Ball Park scoreboard radar gun on 4/18 vs. Pittsburgh (pitch speed was unofficial).
- Was placed on the 15-day disabled list from 5/16-6/23 with left shoulder inflammation.
- Earned his first Major League save in a 13-inning, 9-8 win on 7/6 at St. Louis.
- Following the season, made two relief appearances in the Arizona Fall League (2.2IP, 1H, 1ER, 2BB, 2K), but did not pitch for the rest of the winter while recovering from general shoulder stiffness.

2010
- Saw his first Major League action, going 2-2 with a 2.03 ERA (13.1IP, 3ER) and 19K in 15 relief outings with the Reds.
- Was recalled from Triple-A Louisville on 8/31 and made his Major League debut that night vs. Milwaukee, tossing a perfect eighth inning (1.0IP, 1K)…struck out his first batter faced (Jonathan Lucroy).
- Earned his first career win on 9/1 vs. Milwaukee in his second Major League appearance (1.0IP, 2K).
- Reached 100 mph on all 25 of his pitches on 9/24 at San Diego, with a high of 105 mph against Tony Gwynn Jr.
- Made his postseason debut, going 0-1 with a 0.00 ERA (1.2IP, 3R/0ER) in two relief appearances.
- Began the season with Louisville, going 9-6 with eight saves, a 3.57 ERA (95.2IP, 38ER) and 125K in 39G/13GS.
- Made his first 13 appearances for the Bats as a starter (5-5, 4.11 ERA) and his final 26 appearances in relief (4-1, 2.40 ERA)…over his final 20 games from 7/10-8/27, posted a 0.83 ERA (21.2IP, 2ER)…in his final minor league appearance (8/27 vs. Columbus), reached 105 mph on the radar gun.
- Was voted by *Baseball America* as having the "Best Fastball" and "Best Breaking Pitch" in the IL.

2005-09
- Over four seasons with Holguín of the Cuban National Series in Cuba (2005-08), went 24-19 with a 3.74 ERA (327.2IP, 136ER) and 365K in 76 games (63 starts)…led the league with 100K in 2006 and 130K in 2008…was named the top left-handed pitcher in the 2007 Baseball World Cup…according to published reports, threw a pitch on 12/20/08 that reached 102 mph to break Maels Rodríguez's record for the fastest in Cuban baseball history…pitched for Cuba in the 2009 World Baseball Classic.

PERSONAL

- Full name is Albertin Aroldis de la Cruz Chapman…has two daughters and one son.
- Defected from Cuba in July 2009 before the start of the World Port Tournament in Rotterdam, The Netherlands…established residence in the Principality of Andorra, making him a free agent eligible to be signed by any Major League team…at 181 square miles with an estimated population of 77,000, Andorra is the seventh-smallest nation in Europe…it is located in the eastern Pyrenees Mountains, bordered by Spain and France…became a United States citizen in April 2016.
- Along with Andrew Miller and teammate Dellin Betances, was honored with the "Willie, Mickey and the Duke" Award from the New York BBWAA, presented at the annual writers dinner in January 2017.

Chapman's Career Pitching Record

Year	Club	W	L	ERA	G	GS	CG	SHO	SV	IP	H	R	ER	HR	HP	BB	SO	WP	BK
2010	Louisville	9	6	3.57	39	13	1	0	8	95.2	77	46	38	7	5	52	125	14	0
	CINCINNATI	2	2	2.03	15	0	0	0	0	13.1	9	4	3	0	0	5	19	2	0
2011	CINCINNATI - a	4	1	3.60	54	0	0	0	1	50.0	24	21	20	2	2	41	71	4	0
	Louisville	0	1	11.12	4	1	0	0	0	5.2	9	7	7	0	0	2	9	2	1
	Carolina	1	1	6.14	5	2	0	0	0	7.1	5	5	5	1	0	6	11	2	0
2012	CINCINNATI	5	5	1.51	68	0	0	0	38	71.2	35	13	12	4	4	23	122	4	0
2013	CINCINNATI	4	5	2.54	68	0	0	0	38	63.2	37	18	18	7	3	29	112	6	0
2014	Dayton	0	0	0.00	2	2	0	0	0	2.0	0	0	0	0	0	1	3	0	0
	Louisville	0	1	72.00	2	1	0	0	0	1.0	7	8	8	0	1	2	2	1	0
	CINCINNATI - b	0	3	2.00	54	0	0	0	36	54.0	21	12	12	1	2	24	106	4	0
2015	CINCINNATI - c	4	4	1.63	65	0	0	0	33	66.1	43	13	12	3	5	33	116	7	0
2016	YANKEES - d, e	3	0	2.01	31	0	0	0	20	31.1	20	8	7	2	0	8	44	2	1
	CHICAGO-NL	1	1	1.01	28	0	0	0	16	26.2	12	4	3	0	0	10	46	6	0
2017	YANKEES - f	4	3	3.22	52	0	0	0	22	50.1	37	20	18	3	3	20	69	5	0
	Trenton	0	0	13.50	1	1	0	0	0	0.2	0	1	1	0	0	2	2	2	0
2018	YANKEES - g	3	0	2.45	55	0	0	0	32	51.1	24	15	14	2	5	30	93	9	0
2019	YANKEES	3	2	2.21	60	0	0	0	37	57.0	38	18	14	3	1	25	85	6	0
Minor League Totals		10	9	4.73	53	20	1	0	8	112.1	98	67	59	8	6	65	152	21	1
AL Totals		13	5	2.51	198	0	0	0	111	190.0	119	61	53	10	9	83	291	22	1
NL Totals		20	21	2.08	352	0	0	0	162	345.2	181	85	80	17	16	165	592	33	0
Major League Totals		33	26	2.23	550	0	0	0	273	535.2	300	146	133	27	25	248	883	55	1

Signed by Cincinnati as a non-drafted free agent to a six-year Major League contract through the 2015 season on January 11, 2010.

a – Placed on the 15-day disabled list from May 16-June 23, 2011 with left shoulder inflammation.
b – Placed on the 15-day disabled list from March 30-May 9, 2014 following surgery to insert a plate and screws to stabilize the bones around his left eye.
c – Acquired by the Yankees from the Cincinnati Reds in exchange for RHPs Caleb Cotham and Rookie Davis and INFs Eric Jagielo and Tony Renda on December 28, 2015.
d – Placed on the restricted list to start the 2016 season after accepting a 30-game suspension for violating Major League Baseball's Joint Domestic Violence, Sexual Assault and Child Abuse Policy…was suspended by Commissioner Manfred on March 1 and reinstated on May 9.
e – Acquired by the Chicago Cubs from the Yankees in exchange for RHP Adam Warren, INF Gleyber Torres, OF Billy McKinney and OF Rashad Crawford on July 25, 2016.
f – Placed on the 10-day disabled list from May 14 (retroactive to May 13) - June 18, 2017 with left shoulder rotator cuff inflammation.
g – Placed on the 10-day disabled list from August 22 - September 19, 2018 with left knee tendinitis.

Chapman's Postseason Record

Year	Club vs. Opp.	W	L	ERA	G	GS	CG	SHO	SV	IP	H	R	ER	HR	HP	BB	SO	WP	BK
2010	CIN vs. PHI (DS)	0	1	0.00	2	0	0	0	0	1.2	3	3	0	0	1	0	1	0	0
2012	CIN vs. SF (DS)	0	0	3.00	3	0	0	0	0	3.0	2	1	1	0	0	2	3	2	0
2013	CIN vs. PIT (WC)							On Roster - Did Not Pitch											
2016	CHC vs. SF (DS)	0	0	2.70	4	0	0	0	3	3.1	3	1	1	0	0	1	7	0	0
	CHC vs. LAD (CS)	1	0	3.86	4	0	0	0	0	4.2	3	2	2	0	0	3	3	0	0
	CHC vs. CLE (WS)	1	0	3.52	5	0	0	0	1	7.2	5	3	3	1	1	2	11	0	0
2017	NYY vs. MIN (WC)	0	0	0.00	1	0	0	0	0	1.0	1	0	0	0	0	0	3	0	0
	NYY vs. CLE (DS)	0	0	0.00	3	0	0	0	2	5.2	4	0	0	0	0	2	10	0	0
	NYY vs. HOU (CS)	0	0	6.75	2	0	0	0	1	1.1	2	1	1	0	0	0	3	0	0
2018	NYY vs. OAK (WC)	0	0	0.00	1	0	0	0	0	1.0	1	0	0	0	0	0	2	0	0
	NYY vs. BOS (DS)	0	0	0.00	2	0	0	0	0	2.0	0	0	0	0	0	1	2	0	0
2019	NYY vs. MIN (DS)	0	0	0.00	2	0	0	0	0	2.2	1	0	0	0	0	2	4	0	0
	NYY vs. HOU (CS)	0	1	6.75	3	0	0	0	1	2.2	1	2	2	1	0	2	5	0	0
Wild Card Game Totals		0	0	0.00	2	0	0	0	0	2.0	2	0	0	0	0	0	5	0	0
Division Series Totals		0	1	0.98	16	0	0	0	6	18.1	13	5	2	0	1	8	27	2	0
LCS Totals		1	2	5.19	9	0	0	0	2	8.2	6	5	5	1	0	5	11	0	0
World Series Totals		1	0	3.52	5	0	0	0	1	7.2	5	3	3	1	1	2	11	0	0
POSTSEASON TOTALS		2	3	2.45	32	0	0	0	9	36.2	26	13	10	2	2	15	54	2	0

Chapman's All-Star Game Record

Year	Club, Site	W	L	ERA	G	GS	CG	SHO	SV	IP	H	R	ER	HR	HP	BB	SO	WP	BK
2012	CIN, Kansas City	0	0	0.00	1	0	0	0	0	0.1	0	0	0	0	0	1	1	0	0
2013	CIN, New York-NL	0	0	0.00	1	0	0	0	0	1.0	0	0	0	0	0	1	1	0	0
2014	CIN, Minnesota	0	0	0.00	1	0	0	0	0	0.2	0	0	0	0	0	0	0	0	0
2015	CIN, Cincinnati	0	0	0.00	1	0	0	0	0	1.0	0	0	0	0	0	0	3	0	0
2018	NYY, Washington							Selected, Did Not Pitch (Injured)											
2019	NYY, Cleveland	0	0	0.00	1	0	0	0	1	1.0	0	0	0	0	0	0	3	0	0
All-Star Game Totals		0	0	0.00	5	0	0	0	1	4.0	0	0	0	0	0	2	8	0	0

Chapman's World Baseball Classic Game Record

Year	Country, Site	W	L	ERA	G	GS	CG	SHO	SV	IP	H	R	ER	HR	HP	BB	SO	WP	BK
2009	Cuba, Mexico	0	1	5.68	2	2	0	0	0	6.1	6	4	4	0	0	4	8	1	1
WBC Totals		0	1	5.68	2	2	0	0	0	6.1	6	4	4	0	0	4	8	1	1

Chapman's Career Fielding Record

Position	PCT	G	PO	A	E	TC	DP
Pitcher	.867	550	17	35	8	60	1

Chapman's Regular Season Batting Record

Year	Team	AVG	G	AB	R	H	2B	3B	HR	RBI	SH	SF	HP	BB	SO	SB	CS
2019	NYY					Did Not Bat											
Major League Totals		.000	550	2	1	0	0	0	0	0	0	0	0	1	0	0	0

Chapman's Career Bests and Streaks

COMPLETE GAMES: None. **LOW-HIT COMPLETE GAME:** N/A. **IP (START):** N/A. **IP (RELIEF):** 2.1, 7/9/16 at CLE. **HITS:** 4 - 2 times (last on 5/3/13 at CHC). **RUNS:** 4 - 3 times (last on 8/17/14 at COL-G1). **WALKS:** 4 - 2 times (last on 8/17/14 at COL-G1). **STRIKEOUTS:** 5 - 2 times, last on 7/19/15 vs. CLE). **HOME RUNS:** 2 - 2 times (last on 6/18/16 at MIN). **WINNING STREAK:** 6g, 8/23/11-5/23/12. **LOSING STREAK:** 4g, 2 times (last from 5/19-8/16/13). **SCORELESS STREAK (IP):** 28.1, 8/21/14-5/6/15.

Pitcher of the Month: None **Pitcher of the Week:** None **Reliever of the Month:** 3 times, last: August 2019

Yankees Have a Fan in Fashion

Growing up as the youngest of Frank and Frieda Lifshitz's four children, Ralph Lauren didn't know what a fashion designer was and preferred to be either a movie star or a ballplayer. As homage to his baseball passion, the numbers 3, 4, 5, and 7 appear on the sleeves of his "Big Pony" line of shirts, representing the Yankees uniform numbers of Babe Ruth, Lou Gehrig, Joe DiMaggio and Mickey Mantle.

In recognition of the 50th anniversary of the Ralph Lauren company in 2018, Ralph Lauren and Major League Baseball partnered to create a limited-edition Ralph Lauren Yankees collection. The collaboration featured a classic baseball jacket, a New Era baseball cap, a Wilson baseball glove, and a Rawlings commemorative baseball.

In honor of the event, Ralph Lauren threw out a ceremonial first pitch prior to a Yankees vs. Red Sox game at Yankee Stadium in September 2018.

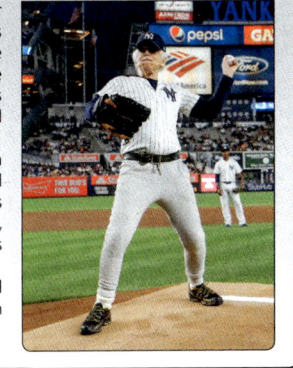

GERRIT COLE • RHP

45

HT: 6-4 • **WT:** 220 • **BATS:** R • **THROWS:** R
BIRTHDATE: 9/8/90 • **OPENING DAY AGE:** 29
BIRTHPLACE: Newport Beach, Calif.
RESIDES: Newport Beach, Calif.
COLLEGE: UCLA
M.L. SERVICE: 6 years, 111 days

STATUS
- Signed to a nine-year contract extending through the 2028 season with a player opt-out following the 2024 season on December 18, 2019.

CAREER NOTES
- In 192 starts across seven Major League seasons with the Pittsburgh Pirates (2013-17) and Houston Astros (2018-19), is 94-52 with a 3.22 ERA (1,195.0IP, 1,034H, 461R/427ER, 315BB, 1,336K, 115HR).
- Is a three-time All-Star (2018-19 with Houston, 2015 with Pittsburgh)…has finished in the top-five of Cy Young Award voting three times (second in 2019, fifth in 2018, fourth in 2015).
- In two seasons with the Astros (2018-19), was 35-10 with a 2.68 ERA (412.2IP, 285H, 134R/123ER, 112BB, 602K, 48HR) over 65 starts…led the Majors in strikeouts during that span, just the seventh pitcher in the Modern Era (since 1900) to record at least 600K over two consecutive seasons (also Randy Johnson, Curt Schilling, J.R. Richard, Nolan Ryan, Sandy Koufax, Rube Waddell)…ranks second in the last two seasons in wins and K/9.0IP ratio (13.13, min. 300.0IP).
- Led the Majors with 326 strikeouts in 2019, the 14th-highest total in Baseball's Modern Era (since 1900)…also set the Major League record with a 13.82 K/9.0IP ratio (326K/212.1IP)…led the AL in ERA.
- Has reached 10 wins in six of his seven Major League seasons (since 2013)…is one of 14 pitchers to reach double-digit wins at least six times in that span (only Zack Greinke, Jon Lester and Max Scherzer have done it in all seven).
- Has eclipsed the 200.0-innings pitched mark in each of the last three seasons and is one of five pitchers to hit the mark in four of the last five seasons (Zack Greinke, Corey Kluber, Max Scherzer, Justin Verlander).
- Was the first overall pick of the 2011 First-Year Player Draft, the 15th pitcher (and 11th right-hander) to be chosen first…would become the fifth player selected first overall to play for the Yankees, joining Alex Rodriguez (1993, Seattle; 2004-13, '15-16 with the Yankees), Darryl Strawberry (1980, New York-NL; 1995-99 with the Yankees), Tim Foli (1968, New York-NL; 1984 with the Yankees) and Ron Blomberg (1967, Yankees; 1969, '71-76 with the Yankees).
- With a 40-20 record from 2013-15, became just the second Pirates pitcher since 1930 to collect at least 40 wins over his first three Major League seasons, joining John Candelaria (44-18 from 1975-77)…is one of three Pirates pitchers to collect at least 10 wins in each of his first three seasons, joining Bill Swift (first five, 1932-36) and Ray Kremer (first eight, 1924-31).
- Including the postseason, became the first pitcher ever to win 19 consecutive decisions in a single season, accomplishing the feat from 5/27/19 vs. Chicago-NL to ALCS Game 3 at the Yankees on 10/15/19 (16-0 over 22 reg. season starts; 3-0 over three postseason starts).
- Is 6-4 with a 2.60 ERA (65.2IP, 41H, 20R/19ER, 16BB, 78K, 9HR) in 10 career postseason starts with Pittsburgh (2013, '15) and Houston (2018-19)…has allowed 1R-or-fewer six times, completing 7.0IP in five of those outings…his 10.69 K/9.0IP ratio is sixth-highest in postseason history (min. 50.0IP), behind Stephen Strasburg (11.55), Jake Arrieta (11.28), Ryan Madson (11.25), Rich Hill (11.04) and Max Scherzer (11.01)…is one of five pitchers in postseason history with multiple starts with at least 12K, joining Bob Gibson, Jim Palmer, Tom Seaver and Stephen Strasburg.
- Is 4-1 with a 1.34 ERA (33.2IP, 14H, 5ER, 5BB, 47K, 4HR) in five Division Series starts…owns the fourth-lowest ERA in Division Series history (min. 25.0IP), behind Mariano Rivera (0.32), Curt Schilling (0.93) and Kevin Brown (0.98)…leads all Division Series pitchers all-time (min. 100BF) with a .124 opponents' BA (14-for-113), 12.56 K/9.0IP ratio and 39.8% strikeout rate.

CAREER HIGHLIGHTS

AL All-Star Team
- 2018, 2019

NL All-Star Team
- 2015

All-MLB First Team
- 2019

2019

- In his second year with Houston, finished second in American League Cy Young Award voting after going 20-5 with an AL-best 2.50 ERA (212.1IP, 142H, 66R/59ER, 48BB, 326K, 29HR) in 33 starts…set career highs in wins, innings pitched and strikeouts…posted a 2.64 FIP (FanGraphs)…opponents hit .186 (142-for-762, 29HR); LH .175 (67-for-383, 17HR); RH .198 (75-for-379, 12HR).
- Led Major League pitchers in strikeouts, K/9.0IP ratio (13.82), strikeout rate (39.9%) and WAR (7.4, FanGraphs), while ranking second in wins and WHIP (0.89) and fourth in innings…led the AL in ERA and opponent OPS (.579) and ranked second in opponents' BA.
- Was one of five pitchers named to the inaugural All-MLB First Team.
- Was named to his third All-Star team, but did not pitch in the AL's 4-3 win in Cleveland.
- His 326K were an Astros single-season record and the 14th-highest total in Baseball's Modern Era (since 1900)…was just the sixth pitcher in that span to reach the mark, joining Randy Johnson (5x), Nolan Ryan (5x), Bob Feller, Sandy Koufax and Rube Waddell…marked the Majors' highest strikeout total since Arizona's Randy Johnson (334) in 2002 and the highest by an AL pitcher since California's Nolan Ryan (341) in 1977…was the third pitcher in Astros history to record 300K in a season, following J.R. Richard (313 in 1979; 303 in 1978) and Mike Scott (306 in 1986); was joined by Justin Verlander (300K) in 2019.
- Set a Major League record with a 13.82 K/9.0IP ratio (326K/212.1IP), surpassing Arizona's Randy Johnson (13.41) in 2001…marked the fewest innings in a 300-strikeout season in Baseball history.
- Became the fourth pitcher in Major League history to notch double-digit strikeouts at least 21 times in one season, joining Arizona's Randy Johnson (23 in 1999, 23 in 2000, 23 in 2001), Los Angeles-NL's Sandy Koufax (21 in 1965) and California's Nolan Ryan (23 in 1973)…beginning 8/7, became the first pitcher ever to compile a streak of nine consecutive double-digit-strikeout performances…recorded at least 10K with 0BB a Major League-record seven times.
- Over his final 22 regular-season starts (beg. 5/27), went 16-0 with a 1.78 ERA (146.2IP, 88H, 32R/29ER, 31BB, 226K, 18HR)…is tied for the 10th-longest winning streak in Baseball history, the longest since Washington's Stephen Strasburg also won 16 straight from 9/15/15-7/15/16…marked the longest winning streak in Astros history, surpassing the previous record of 12 consecutive wins, held by Wade Miller (2002) and Mark Portugal (1993)…was tied for the third-longest streak of winning decisions in a single season in Major League history, behind the New York Giants' Rube Marquard's 19 consecutive wins in 1912 and Pittsburgh's Roy Face's 17 straight in 1959…was the longest in a season since the Yankees' Roger Clemens also won 16 consecutive decisions (over 20 starts) in 2001…is tied with Clemens (final 22 starts in 1998 with Toronto) for the Majors' longest single-season streak of unbeaten starts since Baltimore's Dave McNally was unbeaten in his first 26 starts of 1969.
- Finished runner-up in AL Cy Young Award voting to teammate Justin Verlander (171-159)…Verlander received 17 first-place and 13 second-place votes, while Cole received 13 first-place and 17 second-place votes…marked the fifth time in Cy Young Award history that teammates occupied the first two places, after Arizona's Randy Johnson (winner) and Curt Schilling (runner-up) in both 2001 and 2002, the Los Angeles Dodgers' Mike Marshall (winner) and Andy Messersmith (runner-up) in 1974, and the Brooklyn Dodgers' Don Newcombe (winner) and Sal Maglie (runner-up; acquired midseason from Cleveland) in 1956.
- Took home three of the AL's six "Pitcher of the Month" Awards in 2019, in June, July and September…was the third AL pitcher in five years to take home three "Pitcher of the Month" awards in one season, following Cleveland's Corey Kluber in 2017 and Houston's Dallas Keuchel in 2015.
- Held left-handed hitters to .175/.235/.352 (67-for-383) with 17HR, 30BB and 182K…his 43.6% strikeout rate vs. lefties is the highest by any pitcher since data was first tracked in 1974 (min. 300BF), eclipsing his own mark of 41.1% in 2018.
- According to Statcast, threw 1,048 fastballs of at least 97.0 mph, second-most in the Majors to the Mets' Noah Syndergaard (1,392)…registered a 97.2 mph average velocity on the pitch (FanGraphs), second to Syndergaard (97.7) among qualified Major League pitchers.
- Allowed one-or-zero runs in 17-of-33 starts, tied with St. Louis's Jack Flaherty for the most in the Majors (excluding "openers").
- Surrendered a career-high 9R and 8ER over 4.1IP in 4/20 loss at Texas…had gone his first 36 starts as an Astro without allowing more than 4R, tying Philadelphia's Tommy Greene (1990-92) for the longest streak by a pitcher to start his tenure with a club in Major League history (excluding 'openers').

STRIKEOUTS, SEASON, AMERICAN LEAGUE HISTORY

SO	PITCHER-TEAM	YEAR
383	Nolan Ryan-CAL	1973
367	Nolan Ryan-CAL	1974
349	Rube Waddell-PHA	1904
348	Bob Feller-CLE	1946
341	Nolan Ryan-CAL	1977
329	Nolan Ryan-CAL	1972
327	Nolan Ryan-CAL	1976
326	**GERRIT COLE-HOU**	**2019**
325	Sam McDowell-CLE	1965

K/9.0IP RATIO, SEASON, MLB HISTORY

K/9.0IP	PITCHER-TEAM	YEAR
13.82	**GERRIT COLE-HOU**	**2019**
13.41	Randy Johnson-ARI	2001
13.20	Pedro Martinez-BOS	1999
12.93	Chris Sale-BOS	2017
12.69	Max Scherzer-WAS	2019
12.58	Kerry Wood-CHC	1998
12.56	Randy Johnson-ARI	2000
12.49	José Fernández-MIA	2016
12.40	**GERRIT COLE-HOU**	**2018**
12.35	Randy Johnson-SEA	1995

- In 4/30 win at Minnesota, allowed 1H with 11K over 7.0 scoreless innings (3BB, 1WP)…was the ninth game in Astros history with at least 7.0 scoreless innings, 11K and 1H-or-fewer.
- With 65K in his first seven starts (3/29-4/30), tied Philadelphia's Curt Schilling (1998) for the most strikeouts prior to May in Major League history.
- Was named the AL "Pitcher of the Month" for June after going 3-0 with a 1.89 ERA (38.0IP, 8ER) in six starts…was his second career "Pitcher of the Month" award (also April 2015 with Pittsburgh)…was named the AL "Pitcher of the Month" for July after going 4-0 with a 1.85 ERA (34.0IP, 7ER) in five starts, his second consecutive "Pitcher of the Month" award.

COLE'S 2019 PITCHING LINES

Date/Opp	Score	W/L	IP	H	R	ER	HR	BB	K	NP/S	ERA	Left Game
3/29 at TB	2-4	L	6.0	5	4	1	1	0	10	101/71	1.50	Trailing 4-2
4/3 at TEX*	0-4	L	6.0	4	3	3	0	3	9	105/70	3.00	Trailing 3-0
4/9 vs. NYY	6-3	ND	7.0	4	3	3	1	3	6	99/64	3.32	Trailing 3-2
4/14 at SEA	3-2	W	6.0	4	2	2	1	0	11	101/64	3.24	Leading 3-2
4/20 at TEX	4-9	L	4.1	9	9	8	1	3	8	104/68	5.22	Trailing 7-2
4/25 vs. CLE	1-2	L	7.0	3	2	2	2	3	10	103/63	4.71	Trailing 2-1
4/30 at MIN*	11-0	W	7.0	1	0	0	0	3	11	104/71	3.95	Leading 11-0
5/6 vs. KC	6-4	W	6.1	7	4	4	2	0	9	107/77	4.17	Leading 5-4
5/11 vs. TEX	11-4	W	6.0	4	1	1	1	0	12	97/68	3.88	Leading 6-1
5/17 at BOS	3-1	ND	5.0	6	0	0	0	1	7	99/62	3.56	Tied 0-0
5/22 vs. CWS	4-9	L	5.0	7	6	6	2	1	7	92/62	4.11	Trailing 4-3
5/27 vs. CHC*	6-5	W	6.0	3	2	2	1	1	12	99/69	4.02	Leading 6-2
6/2 at OAK	6-4 (12)	ND	6.0	4	2	2	2	2	4	104/67	3.94	Leading 4-2
6/7 vs. BAL	4-3 (11)	ND	7.0	4	3	1	0	1	14	113/80	3.72	Tied 3-3
6/14 vs. TOR*	15-2	W	6.0	3	2	2	0	1	10	100/64	3.67	Leading 10-2
6/19 at CIN*	2-3	ND	6.0	6	1	1	1	3	8	94/64	3.54	Leading 2-1
6/25 vs. PIT	5-1	W	6.0	7	1	1	0	2	3	104/69	3.42	Leading 3-1
6/30 at SEA	6-1	W	7.0	5	1	1	1	1	10	109/74	3.28	Leading 3-1
7/6 vs. LAA*	4-0	W	7.0	3	0	0	0	2	9	110/70	3.09	Leading 4-0
7/12 at TEX*	8-9	ND	6.0	5	4	4	3	2	13	101/74	3.23	Leading 8-5
7/17 at LAA*	11-2	W	7.0	7	1	1	1	1	11	109/76	3.12	Leading 11-1
7/22 vs. OAK	11-1	W	7.0	2	1	1	1	0	11	106/67	3.03	Leading 11-1
7/27 at STL*	8-2	W	7.0	4	1	1	1	3	7	101/65	2.94	Leading 8-1
8/1 at CLE*	7-1	W	7.0	4	1	1	0	2	4	95/65	2.87	Leading 4-1
8/7 vs. COL	14-3	W	6.0	3	2	2	2	0	10	103/69	2.87	Leading 11-2
8/22 vs. DET*	6-3	W	7.0	2	0	0	0	1	12	94/65	2.75	Leading 6-0
8/28 vs. TB	8-6	ND	6.2	6	4	4	1	1	14	112/78	2.85	Trailing 4-3
9/2 at MIL	3-2 (10)	ND	6.0	3	1	1	1	2	14	105/65	2.81	Leading 2-1
9/8 vs. SEA	21-1	W	8.0	1	1	1	1	0	15	96/68	2.73	Leading 21-1
9/13 at KC*	4-1	W	8.0	4	1	0	0	2	11	101/70	2.62	Leading 4-1
9/18 vs. TEX	3-2	W	8.0	6	2	2	1	1	10	101/73	2.61	Leading 3-2
9/24 at SEA	3-0	W	7.0	2	0	0	0	0	14	101/63	2.52	Leading 3-0
9/29 at LAA	8-5	W	5.0	4	1	1	1	2	10	92/59	2.50	Leading 8-1
Totals (33GS)	20-5		212.1	142	66	59	29	48	326		2.50	

*start came after a team loss / **Bold** - season high

- In 7/22 win vs. Oakland, recorded 11K to reach 200K on the season (in 133.1IP), the second-fewest innings needed to reach 200 strikeouts in a season in Major League history, trailing only Arizona's Randy Johnson (130.2IP in 2001).
- Was scratched from his scheduled start on 8/13 at Chicago-AL with right hamstring discomfort…missed two turns in the rotation but did not go on the I.L.
- Was named AL "Pitcher of the Month" for September after going 5-0 with a 1.07 ERA (42.0IP, 20H, 6R/5ER, 7BB, 74K, 4HR) in six starts…his 74K were tied for the 10th-highest total in a calendar month in the Modern Era (since 1900), and the second-most since 1978 (Chicago-AL's Chris Sale-75K in June 2015)…were the most strikeouts in a month without a loss in Baseball history (previously Boston's Pedro Martinez-70K in September 1999).
- In a 21-1 win on 9/8 vs. Seattle, celebrated his 29th birthday by recording a season-high 15 strikeouts over 8.0IP (1H, 1ER, 1HR, 0BB)…was the second-highest total of his career (16K on 5/4/18 at Arizona w/ Houston)…his only base runner allowed was a one-out solo HR in the fourth by Shed Long…set a Major League record for strikeouts on a pitcher's birthday, surpassing the 14K by Arizona's Randy Johnson on 9/10/00 at Florida…was one of three double-digit-strikeout performances by a pitcher on his birthday during the 2010s, also Washington's Max Scherzer (11K on 7/27/18 at Miami) and the Angels' Dan Haren (10K on 9/17/10 at Tampa Bay)…joined St. Louis' Chris Carpenter (12K, 0BB on 4/27/05 vs. Milwaukee) as the only two pitchers ever to record

STRIKEOUTS, MONTH, MLB HISTORY

SO	PITCHER-TEAM	MONTH
87	Nolan Ryan-CAL	June 1977
85	Nolan Ryan-CAL	Aug. 1974
83	Nolan Ryan-CAL	July 1972
79	Bill Bailey-BAL	Sept. 1914
76	Nolan Ryan-CAL	Sept. 1972
76	Sam McDowell-CLE	May 1968
76	Sandy Koufax-LAD	May 1965
75	Chris Sale-CWS	June 2015
75	Nolan Ryan-CAL	Aug. 1973
74	**GERRIT COLE-HOU**	**Sept. 2019**
74	Ed Walsh-CWS	Sept. 1908

at least 10K with 0BB on his birthday…was the first Astros starter to earn a win on his birthday since Roy Oswalt on 8/29/07 vs. St. Louis…was the first pitcher ever to receive at least 20R of support on his birthday.
- On 8/28 vs. Tampa Bay (6.2IP, 4ER, 14K), 9/2 at Milwaukee (6.0IP, 1ER, 14K) and 9/8 vs. Seattle (8.0IP, 1ER, 15K), became the second pitcher in Major League history to record at least 14K in three consecutive starts, joining Boston's Pedro Martinez from 9/4-15/99 (15K, 17K, 14K)…according to *Elias*, became the first pitcher since 1893 to record at least 14K in fewer than 7.0IP in consecutive games…the 9/2 start came one day after Justin Verlander's 14-strikeout no-hitter, making the duo the first pair of teammates in Major League history to register at least 14K in consecutive games.
- From 8/22-9/8 became the first pitcher in Astros history and fourth in Major League history to record at least 12K in four consecutive starts (Pedro Martinez-3x, Randy Johnson, Chris Sale).

- Was named AL "Player of the Week" for 9/23-29 after earning wins on 9/24 at Seattle (7.0IP, 2H, 0R, 0BB, 14K) and 9/29 at Los Angeles-AL (5.0IP, 4H, 1ER, 2BB, 10K, 1HR)…was his first career weekly award.
- In 9/24 win at Seattle, surpassed J.R. Richard's 1979 Houston franchise record of 313 strikeouts.
- In 9/29 win at Los Angeles-AL (5.0IP, 4H, 1ER, 2BB, 10K, 1HR), set a Major League record with his ninth consecutive start with at least 10K…marked his career-high 20th win.
- Went 4-1 with a 1.72 ERA (36.2IP, 21H, 7ER, 11BB, 47K, 4HR) in five postseason starts to lead Houston to the American League pennant…tied the AL record for strikeouts in a postseason (also Texas's Cliff Lee in 2010)…is tied for the second-highest strikeout total by any pitcher in a postseason behind Arizona's Curt Schilling's 56K in 2001…opponents hit .165 (21-for-127).
- Set a Major League Division Series record with 25K in two starts vs. Tampa Bay (2-0, 0.57 ERA, 15.2IP, 6H, 1ER, 3BB, 1HR)…broke the previous mark of 22K shared by Washington's Stephen Strasburg in 2017 and Detroit's Justin Verlander in 2012…was the eighth postseason series in Major League history with at least 25K, following St. Louis's Bob Gibson (35K in 1968 World Series, 31K in 1964 World Series, 26K in 1967 World Series), Los Angeles-NL's Sandy Koufax (29K in 1965 World Series), Boston's Bill Dineen (28K in 1903 World Series), Arizona's Curt Schilling (26K in 2001 World Series) and Baltimore's Mike Mussina (25K in 1997 ALCS)…joined Washington's Stephen Strasburg (2017 NLDS), Detroit's Justin Verlander (2012-13 ALDS), Texas's Cliff Lee (2010 ALDS), Mussina (1997 ALCS), Gibson (1967-68 World Series) and Koufax (1965 World Series) as the seventh pitcher (ninth occurrence) to record two double-digit-strikeout efforts in one postseason series.
- In ALDS Game 2 win vs. Tampa Bay, recorded 15K over 7.2 scoreless innings (4H, 1BB)…set an Astros postseason strikeout record, tied for the third-highest strikeout total in Major League postseason history, behind St. Louis's Bob Gibson (17K in 1968 World Series Game 1 vs. Detroit) and San Diego's Kevin Brown (16K in 1998 NLDS Game 1 at Houston)…was the seventh pitcher with 15K in a postseason game, his 15K also tied with the Yankees' Roger Clemens (2000 ALCS Game 4 at Seattle), Florida's Livan Hernández (1997 ALCS Game 5 vs. Atlanta), Baltimore's Mike Mussina (1997 ALCS Game 3 at Cleveland) and Los Angeles-NL's Sandy Koufax (1963 World Series Game 1 at the Yankees)…joined Gibson (17K, 1BB) as the only pitchers with 15K and 1BB-or-fewer in a postseason game.
- In ALDS Game 5 win vs. Tampa Bay, earned the series-clinching victory with a postseason career-high 8.0IP (2H, 1ER, 2BB, 10K, 1HR)…allowed his only run on a solo HR by Eric Sogard in the second inning…became the third pitcher to complete 8.0IP and allow 2H-or-fewer in a winner-take-all postseason game, joining Kansas City's Johnny Cueto (8.0IP, 2H, 2ER, 0BB, 8K, 1HR) in 2015 ALDS Game 5 vs. Houston and Detroit's Justin Verlander (8.0IP, 2H, 0R, 1BB, 10K) in 2013 ALDS Game 5 at Oakland.
- In ALCS Game 3 win at the Yankees, tossed 7.0 scoreless innings (4H, 5BB, 7K) to earn his 19th consecutive win (reg. season and postseason), a Major League record…his 5BB tied his regular season career high…snapped his streak of 11 consecutive starts (reg. season and postseason) with double-digit strikeouts…became the third Astros pitcher to win each of his first three starts of a postseason, joining Justin Verlander (first 4GS in 2017) and Roy Oswalt (2005), and the first to do so while allowing 1R-or-fewer in all three.
- Had his record streak of 19 consecutive winning decisions snapped with a loss in World Series Game 1 vs. Washington (7.0IP, 8H, 5ER, 1BB, 6K, 2HR)…marked his first career World Series start.
- Earned his first World Series win in Game 5 at Washington (7.0IP, 3H, 1ER, 2BB, 9K, 1HR)…marked his AL-record fourth start of the 2019 postseason with at least 7.0IP and 1R-or-fewer.

STRIKEOUTS, SINGLE POSTSEASON, MLB HISTORY

SO	PITCHER-TEAM	YEAR
56	Curt Schilling-ARI	2001
47	**GERRIT COLE-HOU**	**2019**
47	Stephen Strasburg-WSH	2019
47	Cliff Lee-TEX	2010
47	Josh Beckett-FLA	2003
47	Randy Johnson-ARI	2001
46	Kevin Brown-SD	1998

STRIKEOUTS, POSTSEASON SERIES, MLB HISTORY

SO	PITCHER-TEAM	SERIES
35	Bob Gibson-STL	1968 World Series
31	Bob Gibson-STL	1964 World Series
29	Sandy Koufax-LAD	1965 World Series
28	Bill Dineen-BOS	1903 World Series
26	Curt Schilling-ARI	2001 World Series
26	Bob Gibson-STL	1967 World Series
25	**GERRIT COLE-HOU**	**2019 ALDS**
25	Mike Mussina-BAL	1997 ALCS

2018

- In his first season with Houston, went 15-5 with a 2.88 ERA (200.1IP, 143H, 68R/64ER, 64BB, 276K, 19HR) in 32 starts…opponents hit .198 (143-for-723, 19HR); LH .162 (56-for-346, 7HR); RH .231 (87-for-377, 12HR)…had a 6.0 WAR (FanGraphs) and 2.70 FIP.
- Finished fifth in AL Cy Young voting…led the Majors in K/9.0IP ratio (12.40)…ranked second in the AL in strikeouts, strikeout rate (34.5%), opponents' BA and WAR, tied for third in winning percentage (.750), fourth in ERA and WHIP (1.03), tied for fourth in quality starts (20) and fifth in innings pitched.
- Was named to his second career All-Star team, his first in the AL…did not pitch in the AL's 8-6 win in Washington.
- His 276K were 74 more than his previous career high (202K in 2015)…he and Justin Verlander (290K in 2018) were the third and fourth pitchers in Astros history to eclipse 275K in a season, following J.R. Richard (313 in 1979, 303 in 1978) and Mike Scott (306 in 1986)…set a then-franchise record for K/9.0IP ratio (12.40), topping Nolan Ryan's 11.48 in 1987…was the then-third-best mark in AL history, behind Boston's Pedro Martinez (13.20 in 1999) and Boston's Chris Sale (12.93 in 2017).

- Was the fifth pitcher in Astros history to post an opponents' BA under .200, joining Mike Scott (.186 in 1986), Nolan Ryan (.188 in 1981, .188 in 1986, .195 in 1983), J.R. Richard (.196 in 1978) and Roger Clemens (.198 in 2005).
- Held left-handed hitters to .162/.250/.269 (56-for-346) with 7HR, 38BB and 160K...is the fourth-lowest opponents' BA vs. lefties (min. 300AB) since 1974, when data was first available...the only pitchers with lower marks are Boston's Pedro Martinez (.150 in 2000), Chicago-NL's Jake Arrieta (.159 in 2015) and Milwaukee's Mike Caldwell (.160 in 1978)...his 41.1% strikeout rate vs. left-handed hitters surpassed Pedro Martinez (33.0% in 1999) for the Majors' highest mark in that span (min. 300BF), which he then broke himself in 2019 (43.6%).
- Tied for the sixth in the Majors with eight double-digit-strikeout games, recording at least 11K in all eight...had just six double-digit-strikeout games in 127 starts over five seasons with the Pirates, and just two games with at least 11K.

\multicolumn{3}{l}{STRIKEOUTS, BACK-TO-BACK SEASONS, MLB, MODERN ERA (since 1900)}
SO	PITCHER-TEAM	YEARS
750	Nolan Ryan-CAL	1973-74
719	Randy Johnson-ARI	2000-01
712	Nolan Ryan-CAL	1972-73
711	Randy Johnson-ARI	1999-00
706	Randy Johnson-ARI	2001-02
699	Sandy Koufax-LAD	1965-66
693	Randy Johnson-SEA/HOU/ARI	1998-99
668	Nolan Ryan-CAL	1976-77
651	Rube Waddell-PHA	1903-04
636	Rube Waddell-PHA	1904-05
620	Randy Johnson-SEA/HOU	1997-98
619	Curt Schilling-PHI	1997-98
616	J.R. Richard-HOU	1978-79
609	Curt Schilling-ARI	2001-02
605	Sandy Koufax-LAD	1964-65
602	**GERRIT COLE-HOU**	**2018-19**

- Combined with Justin Verlander (290K) to post 566K, then the most by a duo in Astros history, surpassing the 503K by Nolan Ryan and Mike Scott in 1987...also became the second pair of teammates in the Modern Era (since 1900) to both record at least 270K in the same season, joining Arizona's Randy Johnson and Curt Schilling, who did it in both 2001 and 2002.
- Set an Astros record for strikeouts over a pitcher's first three games with the club (36K), besting the previous record of 33K held by Randy Johnson in 1998...according to STATS Inc., marked the second-highest strikeout total over a pitcher's first three games of a season in the live-ball era (since 1920), behind California's Nolan Ryan (37K in 1973)...his 41K set a club record for strikeouts through any pitcher's first four starts of a season, and tied for the fourth-most over a pitcher's first four starts with a team in Major League history (Arizona's Randy Johnson-44K in 1999, Boston's Pedro Martinez-44K in 1998, Boston's Chris Sale-42K in 2017, Washington's Stephen Strasburg-41K in 2010)...per *Elias*, his 61K were tied for the third-most over a pitcher's first six starts with a team in Major League history (Arizona's Johnson-63K in 1999, Boston's Sale-63K in 2017, Houston's Johnson-61K in 1998)...his 77K set a Major League record for strikeouts over a pitcher's first seven starts with a team...his 93K were the third-most over a pitcher's first nine starts with a team in Major League history (Houston's Johnson-96K in 1998, Boston's Sale-95K in 2017)...his 101K were tied for the second-most over a pitcher's first 10 starts with a team in Major League history (Houston's Johnson-108K in 1998, Boston's Sale-101K in 2017).
- Went 10-2 with a 2.52 ERA (128.1IP, 81H, 39R/36ER, 45BB, 177K, 14HR) in 20 starts before the All-Star break...set a franchise record for strikeouts prior to the break (prev. Mike Scott-167K in 1986).
- Made his Astros debut in 4/1 win at Texas (7.0IP, 2H, 1ER, 3BB, 11K, 1HR)...per *Elias*, became the fourth pitcher in Astros history to record 11 strikeouts in his Astros debut (J.R. Richard-15K on 9/5/71-G2 at San Francisco, Randy Johnson-12K on 8/2/98 at Pittsburgh, Collin McHugh-12K on 4/22/14 at Seattle).
- In his Astros home debut on 4/7 vs. San Diego, recorded 11K over 7.0 scoreless innings (5H, 0BB)...became the first pitcher to have 11K in each of his first two starts with Houston...his 22K are a club record for a pitcher's first two starts with the Astros...became the first Astros pitcher to post 11K in back-to-back games since Wade Miller from 4/5-11/01.
- In his third start on 4/13 vs. Texas (7.0IP, 3H, 2ER, 1BB, 14K, 2HR, 1HP), recorded 14K for the first time in his career...tied the then-record for strikeouts by an Astros pitcher at Minute Maid Park...became the first Major League pitcher since pitch count data was first tracked to strike out at least 14 batters on 93 pitches or fewer...joined California's Nolan Ryan (1973) as the only pitchers in Major League history to start a season with at least 11K in three consecutive games...was the fourth pitcher in Astros history to record 11K in three consecutive starts at any point in a season.
- Set the AL strikeout record for April with 61K, topping the previous mark of 60K set by Boston's Roger Clemens in 1988...was just the seventh time a pitcher tallied at least 60K in April, also Randy Johnson (4x: 64K in 2000, 63K in 1999, 61K in 2002, 61K in 2001), Clemens and Curt Schilling (61K in 2002)...became the fourth Astros pitcher with 61K in a single calendar month, joining Randy Johnson (61K in Aug. 1998), J.R. Richard (69K in Sept. 1979, 62K in Aug. 1979) and Mike Scott (64K in May 1986).
- Compiled a career-best 19.0-inning scoreless streak from 4/1-13.
- From 4/1-5/9, became the first pitcher to start his tenure with the Astros with eight straight quality starts.

- Threw his first career shutout on 5/4 at Arizona, striking 16-of-29 batters and allowing just one hit (Chris Owings double in the fifth) and one walk (David Peralta in the fourth)…marked his second career complete game…threw 114 pitches (82 strikes)…struck out six consecutive batters in the second and third, and 9-of-10 from the second through fourth…retired his final 14 batters…set a career high in strikeouts, tied for the second-most in Astros history (Don Wilson-18K on 7/14/68-G1 at Cincinnati, Randy Johnson-16K on 8/28/98 vs. Pittsburgh, Nolan Ryan-16K on 9/9/87 vs. San Francisco, Don Wilson-16K on 9/10/68-G1 at Cincinnati)…marked the 10th game in Major League history that a pitcher recorded at least 16K with 1H-or-fewer in a shutout (also Nolan Ryan-4x, Max Scherzer-2x, Brandon Morrow, Curt Schilling, Kerry Wood)…went 0-for-5 with 5K at the plate, the 16th pitcher since 1900 to strike out five times in a game and first since Chicago-NL's Ted Lilly (0-for-5, 5K) on 6/30/08 at San Francisco.
- Won seven consecutive decisions from 5/4-6/24, the third-longest winning streak of his career.
- Recorded his 1,000th career strikeout on 9/21/18 vs. Los Angeles-AL (Kaleb Cowart in the third)…reached the mark in his 158th career game…at the time, only 12 pitchers all-time had hit the milestone in fewer games: Kerry Wood, Tim Lincecum, Corey Kluber, Roger Clemens, Stephen Strasburg, Hideo Nomo, Dwight Gooden, Randy Johnson, Clayton Kershaw, Chris Archer, Frank Tanana and Yu Darvish.
- Made two postseason starts, going 1-1 with a 3.46 ERA (13.0IP, 9H, 6R/5ER, 2BB, 17K, 1HR)…in ALDS Game 2 win vs. Cleveland (7.0IP, 3H, 1ER, 0BB, 12K, 1HR), became the second pitcher in postseason history to record at least 12K with 0BB, joining New York-NL's Tom Seaver in 1973 NLCS Game 1 at Cincinnati (8.1IP, 6H, 2ER, 0BB, 13K, 2HR)…his lone run allowed was a solo HR by Francisco Lindor in the third…took the loss in ALCS Game 2 at Boston (6.0IP, 5R/4ER).

2017
- In his final season with Pittsburgh, posted a 12-12 record and career-high 4.26 ERA (203.0IP, 199H, 98R/96ER, 55BB, 196K, 31HR) in 33 starts…opponents hit .254 (199-for-784, 31HR); LH .268 (101-for-377, 18HR); RH .241 (98-for-407, 13HR)…had a 3.4 WAR (FanGraphs) and 4.08 FIP.
- Tied for the NL lead in starts, tied for second in home runs allowed and ranked third in innings pitched and 10th in strikeouts…finished with the NL's seventh-lowest BB/9.0IP ratio (2.44)…set career highs in starts, hits, runs, earned runs and home runs allowed…was the second-highest home run total in Pirates history (32HR by Murry Dickson in 1951).
- Made his first career Opening Day start on 4/3 at Boston (L, 5.0IP, 5ER).
- Allowed a then-career-high 7ER three times in June: 6/2 at New York-NL (5.0IP), 6/8 vs. Miami (4.2IP), 6/30 vs. San Francisco (5.1IP)…had not previously allowed more than 5ER in any Major League start.
- In a 1-0 win on 8/26 at Cincinnati (7.0IP, 5H, 0R, 0BB, 6K), hit his third career home run off Luis Castillo in the sixth…marked the first time in team history that a Pittsburgh pitcher accounted for all the team's runs with a home run in a shutout victory.
- From 6/2-8/26, became the first Pirates starter to win eight consecutive road decisions since Steve Blass in 1972…from 6/2-8/10, became the first to win seven straight road starts since Don Robinson in 1982.
- Was acquired by Houston in exchange for RHP Michael Feliz, OF Jason Martin, INF Colin Moran and RHP Joe Musgrove on 1/13/18.

2016
- Went 7-10 with a 3.88 ERA (116.0IP, 131H, 57R/50ER, 36BB, 98K, 7HR) in 21 starts with the Pirates, the only season of his career without double-digit wins…opponents hit .289 (131-for-454, 7HR); LH .329 (70-for-213, 3HR); RH .253 (61-for-241, 4HR)…had a 2.5 WAR (FanGraphs) and 3.33 FIP.
- In 5/26 win vs. Arizona, went 2-for-2 with a three-run HR in the second off Patrick Corbin, his second career HR…added a double in the fourth, the first Pirates pitcher with six total bases in a game since Danny Darwin on 5/29/96 vs. Houston.
- Left his 6/10 start vs. St. Louis (2.0IP, 0R) in the third inning due to right arm discomfort…was placed on the 15-day D.L. on 6/14 (retro to 6/11) with a strained right triceps…made two rehab starts with Triple-A Indianapolis, tossing 8.0 scoreless innings (4H, 0BB, 12K)…was reinstated on 7/16.
- Recorded his 500th career strikeout in 7/16 loss at Washington (Bryce Harper in the third).
- Tossed his first career complete game in just 93 pitches on 7/27 vs. Seattle (9.0IP, 3H, 1ER, 0BB, 6K, 1HP).
- Went a career-best 10 consecutive starts without surrendering a home run from 5/26-8/13…the homerless streak totaled 60.0IP from the seventh inning on 5/20 to the fifth inning on 8/19.
- Was placed on the 15-day D.L. on 8/29 (retro to 8/25) with posterior inflammation of his right elbow…was reinstated on 9/12…made one start on 9/12 at Philadelphia (2.0IP, 5ER) and was placed on the 60-day D.L. on 9/13, missing the remainder of the season.

2015

- Went 19-8 with a 2.60 ERA (208.0IP, 183H, 71R/60ER, 44BB, 202K, 11HR) in 32 starts with the Pirates…opponents hit .239 (183-for-765, 11HR); LH .227 (85-for-374, 5HR); RH .251 (98-for-391, 6HR)…had a 5.1 WAR (FanGraphs) and 2.66 FIP.
- Finished fourth in AL Cy Young Award balloting…tied for second in the NL in wins and ranked fifth in ERA, seventh in innings and 10th in strikeouts…was one of three finalists for the Rawlings Gold Glove Award for NL pitchers.
- Was named to his first National League All-Star Team…pitched a scoreless third inning in the NL's 6-3 loss in Cincinnati, striking out Mike Trout and walking Josh Donaldson.
- He and teammate Francisco Liriano (205K in 2015) became the fifth and sixth pitchers in Pirates history to post a 200-strikeout season, also Bob Veale (4x: 1964-66, '69), Ed Morris (2x: 1885-86), A.J. Burnett (2013) and Oliver Pérez (2004)…joined Burnett as the first two right-handers to do it.
- His 19 wins were the most by a Pittsburgh pitcher since John Smiley (20-8) in 1991, and the most by a right-hander since Doug Drabek (22-6) in 1990.
- Was named National League "Pitcher of the Month" for April after going 4-0 with a 1.76 ERA (30.2IP, 22H, 8R/6ER, 8BB, 35K, 1HR) in five starts…was his second career monthly award, and his first "Pitcher of the Month" honor…was the first Pittsburgh pitcher to win the award since Randy Tomlin in June 1992.
- Became the 2015 season's first 10-game winner on 6/13 vs. Philadelphia (6.0IP, 2R/1ER)…was the first Pirate to earn his 10th win prior to 6/14 of a season since Bob Friend on 6/8/56 and the first to record 10 wins in the team's first 61 games since Vernon Law in Game 56 in 1960.
- Won a career-high-tying six consecutive starts from 5/22-6/18.
- Prior to the All-Star break, went 13-3 with a 2.30 ERA (117.1IP, 30ER) in 18 starts…was the third Pirate to lead the Majors in wins at the All-Star break, joining Roy Face (12-0, tied for lead) in 1959 and Rip Sewell (12-2) in 1943…became just the second Pittsburgh pitcher to win 13 games prior to the All-Star break, also Dock Ellis (14-3 in 1971).
- Took the loss in the NL Wild Card Game vs. Chicago-NL (5.0IP, 4ER).
- Received the Steve Blass Award, given by the Pittsburgh chapter of the BBWAA to the team's most outstanding pitcher.

2014

- Made just 22 starts with Pittsburgh, going 11-5 with a 3.65 ERA (138.0IP, 127H, 58R/56ER, 40BB, 138K, 11HR)…opponents hit .248 (127-for-512, 11HR); LH .249 (60-for-241, 6HR); RH .247 (67-for-271, 5HR)…had a 2.1 WAR (FanGraphs) and 3.23 FIP.
- Was placed on the 15-day D.L. on 6/8 (retro to 6/4) with right arm fatigue…was reinstated on 6/28.
- Was placed on the 15-day D.L. on 7/8 (retro to 7/5) with right lat soreness…was reinstated on 8/20…made four rehab starts with Triple-A Indianapolis, logging a 3-1 record and 2.01 ERA (22.1IP, 5ER).
- In 9/7 win at Chicago-NL, hit his first career home run, a two-run HR off Blake Parker in the seventh.

2013

- Made his Major League debut with Pittsburgh, posting a 10-7 record and 3.22 ERA (117.1IP, 109H, 43R/42ER, 28BB, 100K, 7HR) in 19 starts…ranked sixth among NL rookies in wins and ERA (min. 100.0IP), seventh in innings and eighth in strikeouts…was the first Pirates rookie with at least 10 wins since Josh Fogg (12-12) in 2002…opponents hit .253 (109-for-431, 7HR); LH .249 (48-for-193, 2HR); RH .256 (61-for-238, 5HR)…had a 2.4 WAR (FanGraphs) and 2.91 FIP.
- Was selected to the Major League roster on 6/11 and made his Major League debut that night vs. San Francisco, earning the win (6.1IP, 7H, 2ER, 0BB, 2K)…struck out his first batter faced on three pitches (Gregor Blanco)…became the third Pirates pitcher since 1900 to toss at least 6.0 walk-less innings in his debut, joining Len Gilmore on 10/1/1944-G2 at Philadelphia and George Merritt on 9/6/1901 at the New York Giants.
- In his debut, hit a two-run single off Tim Lincecum in his first career at-bat in the second inning, his first hit since high school…became the fourth starting pitcher since RBI became an official stat in 1920 to earn a win and record at least 2RBI in his Major League debut (Colorado's Jason Jennings on 8/23/01 at New York-NL; Boston-NL's Jim Turner on 4/30/37 at Philadelphia-NL; Philadelphia-AL's George Caster on 9/10/34 at Cleveland).
- Became the first Pirates pitcher to start and win each of his first four Major League games since Nick Maddox in 1907…also won his final four starts of the season.
- In 7/23 win at Washington (7.0IP, 2H, 1ER, 1BB, 4K, 1HR, 1HP), also went 2-for-3 with 1RBI…was the first Pirates rookie starter to collect at least 2H while allowing 2H-or-fewer since Hank Gornicki on 8/27/42 vs. Boston-NL.
- Was the first Pirate since Joe Conzelman in 1913-14 to permit 3R-or-fewer in each of his first 10 career starts.
- Was named National League "Rookie of the Month" for September after going 4-0 with a 1.69 ERA (32.0IP, 24H, 6ER, 10BB, 39K, 0HR) in five starts.
- In 9/19 win vs. San Diego (6.0IP, 4H, 1ER, 3BB, 12K), recorded his first career double-digit-strikeout effort…were the most strikeouts by a Pirates rookie since José DeLeón had 13K on 8/20/83 vs. Cincinnati.

- Earned the win in his postseason debut in NLDS Game 2 at St. Louis (6.0IP, 2H, 1ER, 1BB, 5K, 1HR)…also drove in the first run of the game with an second-inning RBI single…according to *Elias*, was the third rookie to record both a victory and a game-winning RBI in a postseason game, joining the Yankees' Spec Shea in 1947 World Series Game 5 at Brooklyn and St. Louis's Paul (Daffy) Dean in 1934 World Series Game 6 at Detroit…in his first career winner-take-all game, took the loss in NLDS Game 5 at St. Louis (5.0IP, 3H, 2ER, 1BB, 5K, 1HR).
- Was named to the *Baseball America* National League All-Rookie Team.
- Began the season with Triple-A Indianapolis and was 5-3 with a 2.91 ERA (68.0IP, 44H, 23R/22ER, 28BB, 47K, 4HR) in 12 starts.
- Entered the season ranked by *Baseball America* as the Pirates' No. 1 prospect and No. 7 prospect in baseball…was also tabbed by MLB.com as the No. 9 overall prospect.

2012
- In his first professional season, went 9-7 with a 2.80 ERA (132.0IP, 113H, 55R/41ER, 45BB, 136K, 7HR) in 26 starts between Single-A Bradenton, Double-A Altoona and Triple-A Indianapolis…ranked second in strikeouts and fourth in ERA among Pirates minor leaguers…was a non-roster invitee to Major League spring training with Pittsburgh.
- Was named a Florida State League Mid-Season All-Star, going 5-1 with a 2.55 ERA (67.0IP, 53H, 24R/19ER, 21BB, 69K, 5HR) in 13 starts with Bradenton…made his pro debut with the Marauders on 4/9 at Palm Beach (4.0IP, 4H, 1ER, 1BB, 7K).
- Was promoted to Altoona on 6/20 and went 3-6 with a 2.90 ERA (59.0IP, 54H, 28R/19ER, 23BB, 60K, 2HR) in 12 starts with the Curve…finished the season by winning his lone start with Indianapolis on 9/1 vs. Toledo (6.0IP, 6H, 3ER, 1BB, 7K)…made one postseason start for Indianapolis, taking the loss in Game 2 of the International League Division Series vs. Charlotte (2.0IP, 8ER).
- Pitched in the 2012 SiriusXM All-Star Futures Game in Kansas City.
- Was named an MiLB.com Organization All-Star.
- Entered the season ranked by *Baseball America* as Pittsburgh's No. 1 prospect and the No. 12 prospect in all of baseball…was also tabbed as having the "Best Fastball" and "Best Slider" among Pirates farmhands.

2011
- Pitched for the Mesa Solar Sox in the Arizona Fall League, going 2-0 with a 3.00 ERA (15.0IP, 10H, 6R/5ER, 4BB, 16K, 1HR) in five starts…started for the East Division in the AFL Rising Stars Game.

PERSONAL
- Is married to Amy.
- Pitched three seasons at UCLA (2009-11), going 21-20 with five complete games and a 3.38 ERA (322.1IP, 252H, 143R/121ER, 114BB, 376K, 22HR) in 50 appearances (49 starts)…finished his career at UCLA ranked second in strikeouts, third in starts and fifth in innings pitched…was the first pitcher in school history to record three 100-strikeout seasons…in 2009, earned Freshman All-America honors from *Collegiate Baseball*…in 2010, was a consensus All-American, landing on the Collegiate Baseball second team and the *Baseball America* and NCBWA third team…finished third in the nation with 153K.
- Pitched for the USA Collegiate National Team in 2009 and 2010, combining to go 6-0 with a 0.92 ERA (59.0IP, 6ER) and 69K in 11 games (nine starts)…tossed 7.0 scoreless innings Team USA's loss to Cuba in the Gold Medal Game of the 2010 FISU World University Baseball Championships…was rated the No. 1 prospect on the team in both years by *Baseball America*.
- Is a 2008 graduate of Orange Lutheran (Calif.) H.S.…as a senior, went 8-2 with a 0.47 ERA (75.2IP, 4ER) in 13 games (12 starts) and 121K while hitting .310 with 7HR and 25RBI…was named to the 2008 *USA Today* All-USA High School First Team, the EA Sports All-America First Team and *Baseball America* All-America Second Team…was selected as an AFLAC All-American as a junior in 2007…following his senior season, was rated as the top high school prospect in his class by Perfect Game Crosschecker, and the No. 17 prospect by *Baseball America* (No. 4 prep prospect)…was selected by the Yankees in the first round (28th overall) of the 2008 First-Year Player Draft but did not sign.
- Wife, Amy, is the younger sister of multiple-time NL All-Star SS Brandon Crawford, currently of the San Francisco Giants…both Crawford (2006-08) and Cole (2009-11) played at UCLA.

Cole's Career Pitching Record

Year	Club	W	L	ERA	G	GS	CG	SHO	SV	IP	H	R	ER	HR	HP	BB	SO	WP	BK
2012	Bradenton	5	1	2.55	13	13	0	0	0	67.0	53	24	19	5	3	21	69	3	1
	Altoona	3	6	2.90	12	12	0	0	0	59.0	54	28	19	2	2	23	60	3	1
	Indianapolis	1	0	4.50	1	1	0	0	0	6.0	6	3	3	0	0	1	7	0	0
2013	Indianapolis	5	3	2.91	12	12	0	0	0	68.0	44	23	22	4	4	28	47	4	1
	PITTSBURGH	10	7	3.22	19	19	0	0	0	117.1	109	43	42	7	3	28	100	4	0
2014	PITTSBURGH - a,b	11	5	3.65	22	22	0	0	0	138.0	127	58	56	11	9	40	138	9	1
	Indianapolis	3	1	2.01	4	4	0	0	0	22.1	21	5	5	1	1	5	16	0	0
2015	PITTSBURGH	19	8	2.60	32	32	0	0	0	208.0	183	71	60	11	10	44	202	7	0
2016	PITTSBURGH - c,d,e	7	10	3.88	21	21	1	0	0	116.0	131	57	50	7	6	36	98	5	1
	Indianapolis	0	0	0.00	2	2	0	0	0	8.0	4	0	0	0	1	0	12	0	0
2017	PITTSBURGH - f	12	12	4.26	33	33	0	0	0	203.0	199	98	96	31	4	55	196	7	0
2018	HOUSTON	15	5	2.88	32	32	1	1	0	200.1	143	68	64	19	7	64	276	9	0
2019	HOUSTON - g	20	5	2.50	33	33	0	0	0	212.1	142	66	59	29	3	48	326	4	3
Minor League Totals		17	11	2.66	44	44	0	0	0	230.1	182	83	68	12	11	78	211	10	3
AL Totals		35	10	2.68	65	65	1	1	0	412.2	285	134	123	48	10	112	602	13	3
NL Totals		59	42	3.50	127	127	1	0	0	782.1	749	327	304	67	32	203	734	32	2
Major League Totals		94	52	3.22	192	192	2	1	0	1195.0	1034	461	427	115	42	315	1336	45	5

Selected by the New York Yankees in the first round (28th overall) of the 2008 First-Year Player Draft but did not sign.
Selected by the Pittsburgh Pirates in the first round (first overall) of the 2011 First-Year Player Draft.

a – Placed on the 15-day disabled list from June 8 (retroactive to June 4) – June 28, 2014 with right arm fatigue.
b – Placed on the 15-day disabled list from July 8 (retroactive to July 5) – Aug. 20, 2014 with right lat soreness.
c – Placed on the 15-day disabled list from June 14 (retroactive to June 11) – July 16, 2016 with a strained right triceps.
d – Placed on the 15-day disabled list from Aug. 29 (retroactive to Aug. 25) – Sept. 12, 2016 with right elbow inflammation.
e – Placed on the 60-day disabled list from Sept. 13 – Nov. 4, 2016 with right elbow inflammation.
f – Acquired by the Houston Astros from the Pittsburgh Pirates in exchange for RHP Michael Feliz, OF Jason Martin, INF Colin Moran and RHP Joe Musgrove on Jan. 13, 2018.
g – Signed by the Yankees as a free agent on Dec. 18, 2019.

Cole's Postseason Record

Year	Club vs. Opp.	W	L	ERA	G	GS	CG	SHO	SV	IP	H	R	ER	HR	HP	BB	SO	WP	BK
2013	PIT vs. CIN (WC)						On Roster - Did Not Pitch												
	PIT vs. STL (DS)	1	1	2.45	2	2	0	0	0	11.0	5	3	3	2	0	2	10	0	0
2015	PIT vs. CHC (WC)	0	1	7.20	1	1	0	0	0	5.0	6	4	4	2	0	1	4	0	0
2018	HOU vs. CLE (DS)	1	0	1.29	1	1	0	0	0	7.0	3	1	1	1	0	0	12	0	0
	HOU vs. BOS (CS)	0	1	6.00	1	1	0	0	0	6.0	6	5	4	0	0	2	5	0	0
2019	HOU vs. TB (DS)	2	0	0.57	2	2	0	0	0	15.2	6	1	1	1	0	3	25	0	0
	HOU vs. NYY (CS)	1	0	0.00	1	1	0	0	0	7.0	4	0	0	0	0	5	7	0	0
	HOU vs. WAS (WS)	1	1	3.86	2	2	0	0	0	14.0	11	6	6	3	0	3	15	0	0
Wild Card Game Totals		0	1	7.20	1	1	0	0	0	5.0	6	4	4	2	0	1	4	0	0
Division Series Totals		4	1	1.34	5	5	0	0	0	33.2	14	5	5	4	0	5	47	0	0
LCS Totals		1	1	2.77	2	2	0	0	0	13.0	10	5	4	0	0	7	12	0	0
World Series Totals		1	1	3.86	2	2	0	0	0	14.0	11	6	6	3	0	3	15	0	0
POSTSEASON TOTALS		6	4	2.60	10	10	0	0	0	65.2	41	20	19	9	0	16	78	0	0

Cole's All-Star Game Record

Year	Club, Site	W	L	ERA	G	GS	CG	SHO	SV	IP	H	R	ER	HR	HP	BB	SO	WP	BK
2015	PIT, Cincinnati	0	0	0.00	1	0	0	0	0	1.0	0	0	0	0	0	1	1	0	0
2018	HOU, Washington						Selected, Did Not Pitch												
2019	HOU, Cleveland						Selected, Did Not Pitch												
All-Star Game Totals		0	0	0.00	1	0	0	0	0	1.0	0	0	0	0	0	1	1	0	0

Cole's Career Fielding Record

Position	PCT	G	PO	A	E	TC	DP
Pitcher	.966	192	75	155	8	238	12

Cole's Regular Season Batting Record

Year	Team	AVG	G	AB	R	H	2B	3B	HR	RBI	SH	SF	HP	BB	SO	SB	CS
2019	HOU	.000	33	7	0	0	0	0	0	0	0	0	0	0	5	0	0
Major League Totals		.163	192	251	17	41	2	0	3	15	28	0	1	6	112	0	0

Cole's Career Bests and Streaks

COMPLETE GAMES: 2, last on 5/4/18 at ARI. **LOW-HIT COMPLETE GAME:** 1, 5/4/18 at ARI. **IP (START):** 9.0 - 2 times (last on 5/4/18 at ARI). **IP (RELIEF):** N/A. **HITS:** 12 - 2 times (last on 8/19/16 vs. MIA). **RUNS:** 9, 4/20/19 at TEX. **EARNED RUNS:** 8, 4/20/19 at TEX. **WALKS:** 5, 6/18/18 vs. TB. **STRIKEOUTS:** 16, 5/4/18 at ARI. **HOME RUNS:** 3 - 4 times (last on 7/12/19 at TEX). **WINNING STREAK:** 16g, 5/27/19-current. **LOSING STREAK:** 5g, 8/7/16-4/3/17. **SCORELESS STREAK (IP):** 19.0, 4/1-13/17.

Pitcher of the Month: 4 times, last: Sept. 2019   **Player of the Week:** 9/23-29/19   **Rookie of the Month:** Sept. 2013

THAIRO ESTRADA • INF

71

HT: 5-10 • **WT:** 185 • **BATS:** R • **THROWS:** R
BIRTHDATE: 2/22/96 • **OPENING DAY AGE:** 24
BIRTHPLACE: Bejuma, Venezuela
RESIDES: Bejuma, Venezuela
M.L. SERVICE: 99 days

STATUS
- Signed by the Yankees as a non-drafted free agent on August 2, 2012.

2019
- Saw his first Major League action, hitting .250/.294/.438 (16-for-64) with 12R, 3 doubles, 3HR, 12RBI, 3BB and 4SB in 35 games over four stints with the Yankees (4/4-6, 4/21-6/6, 6/29-30, 8/14-9/29).
- Made his Major League debut as a 10th-inning pinch-hitter for Ford in 4/21 win vs. Kansas City, hitting a sacrifice bunt.
- Collected his first Major League hit with a second-inning single on 4/23 at Los Angeles-AL.
- Started in LF on 4/26 at San Francisco, his first professional appearance (Majors and minors) at a position outside the infield.
- Hit his first Major League HR off fellow Venezuelan Félix Hernández on 5/6 vs. Seattle.
- Served as the Yankees' "26th Man" for the London Series against Boston from 6/29-30, but did not play.
- Was placed on the 10-day injured list from 8/18-9/8 with a right hamstring strain.
- In 60 games with Triple-A Scranton/Wilkes-Barre, hit .266 (64-for-241) with 39R, 17 doubles, 2 triples, 8HR and 32RBI.

2018
- Was limited to 18 total games with Single-A Tampa and Triple-A Scranton/Wilkes-Barre, combining to hit .192 (15-for-78) with 5R, 3 doubles and 8RBI…spent the majority of the season on the minor league disabled list over two stints (4/6-18 and 5/8-9/24).
- Following the season, played for the Arizona Fall League's Glendale Desert Dogs, batting .238 (19-for-80) with 9R, 2 doubles and 7RBI in 19 games.

2017
- Spent the entire season with Double-A Trenton, batting .301 (149-for-495) with 72R, 19 doubles, 4 triples, 6HR and 48RBI in 122 games…ranked second in the Eastern League in hits, tied for fourth in in runs scored and ranked sixth in batting average…ranked among Yankees farmhands in hits (149, second) and batting average (.301, fourth)…played primarily SS (90G), but also saw time at 2B (23G) and 3B (3G).
- At 21 years and two months, was the seventh-youngest player to make a 2017 Opening Day roster in the EL.
- Was named to the EL Mid-Season and Postseason All-Star teams.
- Following the season, played for Scottsdale in the Arizona Fall League, batting .342 (27-for-79) with 13R, 2 doubles, 1 triple, 1HR and 10RBI in 20 games…was named to the league's Fall Stars Game and the AFL's 2017 Top Prospects Team.
- Was tabbed by *Baseball America* as the Yankees' No. 9 prospect following the season.
- Was added to the Yankees' 40-man roster on 11/20/17.

2016
- Split the season between Single-A Charleston and Single-A Tampa and hit .290/.346/.391 (132-for-455) with 63R, 18 doubles, 2 triples, 8HR and 49RBI in 118 games…stole 18 bases in 26 attempts (69.2%)…was named an MiLB.com Organization All-Star…ranked sixth among Yankees farmhands in batting average.
- Began the season by batting .286/.324/.429 (40-for-140) with 11R, 3 doubles, 1 triple, 5HR and 19RBI in 35 games for the RiverDogs before a promotion to Tampa on 5/23.
- In 83 games with Tampa, hit .292/.355/.375 (92-for-315) with 52R, 15 doubles, 1 triple, 3HR and 30RBI…overall, saw time at 2B (57G/56GS), 3B (47GS) and SS (8G/7GS).

2015
- Batted .267 (66-for-247) with 37R, 17 doubles, 2HR, 23RBI and 8SB in 63 games with short-season Single-A Staten Island…was named a NYPL Mid-Season All-Star…reached base safely in 20 consecutive games from 7/26-8/22 (G1), hitting .351 (27-for-77) over that stretch…batted .356 (26-for-73) against lefties.

2014
▸ Combined at short-season Single-A Staten Island and the GCL Yankees 1 to bat .272 (22-for-81) with 13R, 3 doubles, 6RBI and 7BB in 23 games.

2013
▸ Made his professional debut with the GCL Yankees 2, batting .278 (49-for-176) with 28R, 11 doubles, 5 triples, 2HR, 17RBI and 7SB in 50 games…ranked 10th among Yankees minor leaguers in batting average.

PERSONAL
▸ Full name is Thairo Jose Estrada Villegas.

Estrada's Career Playing Record

Year	Club	AVG	G	AB	R	H	2B	3B	HR	RBI	SH	SF	HP	BB	SO	SB	CS	E	OBP	SLG
2013	GCL Yankees 2	.278	50	176	28	49	11	5	2	17	2	1	8	12	30	7	5	11	.350	.432
2014	Staten Island	.271	17	59	11	16	1	0	0	2	1	0	1	6	7	8	1	2	.348	.288
	GCL Yankees 1	.273	6	22	2	6	2	0	0	4	0	0	0	1	4	0	0	0	.304	.364
2015	Staten Island	.267	63	247	37	66	17	0	2	23	1	3	5	23	30	8	3	11	.338	.360
2016	Charleston	.286	35	140	11	40	3	1	5	19	0	0	0	8	21	11	3	8	.324	.429
	Tampa	.292	83	315	52	92	15	1	3	30	2	2	3	29	46	7	5	8	.355	.375
2017	Trenton	.301	122	495	72	149	19	4	6	48	1	4	8	34	56	8	11	17	.353	.392
2018	Tampa	.222	10	45	4	10	2	0	0	5	0	1	1	0	9	0	0	0	.234	.267
	Scranton/WB	.152	8	33	1	5	1	0	0	3	0	0	1	0	8	0	0	1	.176	.182
2019	Scranton/WB	.266	60	241	39	64	17	2	8	32	0	1	3	14	50	3	1	4	.313	.452
	YANKEES - a	.250	35	64	12	16	3	0	3	12	1	0	1	3	15	4	0	1	.294	.438
Minor League Totals		**.280**	**454**	**1773**	**257**	**497**	**88**	**13**	**26**	**183**	**7**	**12**	**30**	**127**	**261**	**52**	**29**	**62**	**.337**	**.389**
Major League Totals		**.250**	**35**	**64**	**12**	**16**	**3**	**0**	**3**	**12**	**1**	**0**	**1**	**3**	**15**	**4**	**0**	**1**	**.294**	**.438**

Signed by the Yankees as a non-drafted free agent on August 2, 2012.

a – Placed on the 10-day injured list from August 18 – September 8, 2019 with a right hamstring strain.

Estrada's Career Fielding Record

Position	PCT	G	PO	A	E	TC	DP
Second Base	1.000	17	24	18	0	42	6
Shortstop	.950	9	7	12	1	20	1
Outfield	1.000	4	2	0	0	2	0

Estrada's Career Home Run Chart
MULTI-HOMER GAMES: None. **TWO-HOMER GAMES:** None. **GRAND SLAMS:** None. **PINCH-HIT HR:** None. **INSIDE-THE-PARK HR:** None. **WALK-OFF HR:** None. **LEADOFF HR:** None.

Estrada's Career Bests and Streaks
HITS: 2 - 5 times (last on 9/14/19 at TOR). **RUNS:** 1 - 12 times (last on 9/14/19 at TOR). **2B:** 1 - 3 times (last on 5/25/19 at KC, Game 1). **3B:** None. **HR:** 1 - 3 times (last on 5/22/19 at BAL). **RBI:** 3, 5/19/19 vs. TB. **BB:** 1 - 3 times (last on 5/28/19 vs. SD). **SO:** 3, 5/12/19 at TB. **SB:** 1 - 4 times (last on 9/10/19 at DET). **HIT STREAK:** 4g, from 4/23-28/19. **"WALK-OFF" HITS:** None.

Player of the Month: None   **Player of the Week:** None   **Rookie of the Month:** None

---

Most Championships, in the Four Major Sports

MLB – New York Yankees (27)
NHL – Montreal Canadiens (24)
NBA – Boston Celtics (17)
NFL – Green Bay Packers (13)

as of 2/1/20

ESTEVAN FLORIAL • OF

HT: 6-1 • **WT:** 195 • **BATS:** L • **THROWS:** R
BIRTHDATE: 11/25/97 • **OPENING DAY AGE:** 22
BIRTHPLACE: Barahona, D.R.
RESIDES: Santo Domingo Este, D.R.
M.L. SERVICE: None (Rookie)

STATUS
- Signed by the Yankees as a non-drafted free agent on March 19, 2015.

2019
- Hit .237 (65-for-274) with 38R, 10 doubles, 3 triples, 8HR, 38RBI, 24BB and 9SB in 74 games with Single-A Tampa.
- Attended spring training with the Yankees as a non-roster invitee, batting .355 (11-for-31) with 7R, 2 doubles, 1HR, 4RBI and 5SB in 13 games…had his spring cut short after colliding with the outfield wall on 3/16…underwent X-rays that day revealing a non-displaced right wrist fracture…had an MRI two days later, revealing a second break in a different bone in his hand…was reassigned to minor league camp on 3/23.
- Made his season debut on 6/3 after missing the season's first two months on the minor league injured list…homered and drove in three of the Tarpons' four runs in the game.
- Was tabbed by *Baseball America* as being the "Fastest Baserunner" among Yankees farmhands…was named the Yankees' No. 3 prospect by MLB Pipeline.
- Was added to the Yankees' 40-man roster on 11/20.

2018
- In 84 games between Single-A Tampa and both GCL Yankees squads, hit .283/.377/.422 (92-for-325) with 55R, 19 doubles, 4 triples, 6HR, 35RBI, 48BB and 16SB.
- Hit .255/.354/.361 (75-for-294) with 45R, 16 doubles, 3 triples, 3HR and 27RBI in 75 games with Tampa.
- Played in nine GCL games on a rehab assignment (7/5-17) and hit .548 (17-for-31) with 10R, 3 doubles, 1 triple, 3HR, 8RBI and 5SB.
- Following the season, was named the "Fastest Baserunner," "Best Athlete," "Best Defensive Outfielder" and "Best Outfield Arm" in the Yankees organization by *Baseball America*.
- At the end of the season, was tabbed by *Baseball America* as the top prospect in the Yankees organization.
- Following the season, hit .178 (13-for-73) with 10R, 2 doubles, 2 triples, 8RBI and 2SB in 21 games for Glendale in the Arizona Fall League.

2017
- Combined at Single-A Charleston and Single-A Tampa to bat .298/.372/.479 (125-for-420) with 77R, 23 doubles, 7 triples, 13HR, 57RBI, 50BB and 23SB in 110 games…ranked fifth among Yankees minor leaguers in batting average and stolen bases.
- Spent the majority of the season with Charleson, hitting .297 (102-for-344) with 64R, 21 doubles, 5 triples, 11HR, 43RBI, 41BB and 17SB in 91 games…was named a South Atlantic League Mid-Season and Postseason All-Star…was tabbed the No. 2 prospect in the SAL by *Baseball America*.
- Ranked third in the SAL in OBP (.373) and SLG (.483) and fourth in BA.
- Was selected to the SiriusXM Futures All-Star Game in Miami.
- Was promoted to Tampa on 8/1 and batted .303 (23-for-76) with 13R, 2 doubles, 2 triples, 2HR, 14RBI, 9BB and 6SB in 19 games.
- Following the season, was tabbed an Organization All-Star by MiLB.com…was also named the "Fastest Baserunner," "Best Athlete," "Best Defensive Outfielder" and "Best Outfield Arm" among Yankees farmhands by *Baseball America*…the publication also tabbed him the No. 2 prospect in the Yankees organization and No. 38 prospect in all of baseball.
- Appeared in 19 games for Scottsdale of the Arizona Fall League, hitting .286 (20-for-70) with 14R, 5 doubles, 2 triples and 4RBI…was named to the AFL Top Prospects Team.

2016
- Combined at three levels to hit .227 (60-for-264) with 40R, 10 doubles, 8HR and 30RBI in 67 games.
- Spent the majority of the season with Rookie-level Pulaski, hitting .225 (53-for-236) with 36R, 10 doubles, 1 triple, 7HR, 25RBI and 10SB in 60 games.

- Was ranked by *Baseball America* as the No. 3 prospect in the Appalachian League.
- Also played in two games with Single-A Tampa (1-for-8) and five games with Single-A Charleston (.300, 6-for-20, 4R, 1 triple, 1HR, 5RBI).

2015
- Made his professional debut with the DSL Yankees 1, batting .313/.394/.527 (70-for-224) with 51R, 11 doubles, 8 triples, 7HR, 53RBI and 30BB in 57 games.
- Ranked second in the DSL in slugging and third in RBI and OPS (.921)…batted .337 (57-for-169) against righties.

PERSONAL
- Full name is Estevan Haniel Florial.

Florial's Career Batting Record

Year	Club	AVG	G	AB	R	H	2B	3B	HR	RBI	SH	SF	HP	BB	SO	SB	CS	E	OBP	SLG
2015	DSL Yankees 1	.313	57	224	51	70	11	8	7	53	2	6	4	30	61	15	5	3	.394	.527
2016	Tampa	.125	2	8	0	1	0	0	0	0	0	0	0	0	2	0	0	0	.125	.125
	Pulaski	.225	60	236	36	53	10	1	7	25	1	0	3	28	78	10	2	4	.315	.364
	Charleston	.300	5	20	4	6	0	1	1	5	0	1	0	2	5	0	0	0	.348	.550
2017	Charleston	.297	91	344	64	102	21	5	11	43	0	2	2	41	124	17	7	4	.373	.483
	Tampa	.303	19	76	13	23	2	2	2	14	0	2	0	9	24	6	1	0	.368	.461
2018	Tampa	.255	75	294	45	75	16	3	3	27	0	0	1	44	87	11	10	3	.354	.361
	GCL Yankees West	.429	4	14	5	6	0	0	1	3	0	0	0	2	3	2	0	0	.500	.643
	GCL Yankees East	.647	5	17	5	11	3	1	2	5	0	0	0	2	2	3	0	0	.684	1.294
2019	Tampa	.237	74	274	38	65	10	3	8	38	1	2	0	24	98	9	5	4	.297	.383
Minor League Totals		.273	392	1507	261	412	73	24	42	213	4	13	10	182	484	73	30	18	.353	.437

Signed by the Yankees as a non-drafted free agent on March 19, 2015.

Consecutive World Championships

NEW YORK YANKEES (5)	1949-53
NEW YORK YANKEES (4)	1936-39
NEW YORK YANKEES (3)	1998-2000
Oakland Athletics (3)	1972-74
Toronto Blue Jays (2)	1992-93
NEW YORK YANKEES (2)	1977-78
Cincinnati Reds (2)	1975-76
NEW YORK YANKEES (2)	1961-62
Philadelphia Athletics (2)	1929-30
NEW YORK YANKEES (2)	1927-28
New York Giants (2)	1921-22
Boston Red Sox (2)	1915-16
Philadelphia Athletics (2)	1910-11
Chicago Cubs (2)	1907-08

MIKE FORD • INF

#72

HT: 6-0 • **WT:** 225 • **BATS:** L • **THROWS:** R
BIRTHDATE: 7/4/92 • **OPENING DAY AGE:** 27
BIRTHPLACE: Belle Meade, N.J.
RESIDES: Belle Meade, N.J.
COLLEGE: Princeton University
M.L. SERVICE: 80 days

STATUS

- Signed by the Yankees as a non-drafted free agent on July 17, 2013…was selected by the Seattle Mariners from the Yankees in the first round of the Major League phase of the 2017 Rule 5 Draft on December 14, 2017…was returned to the Yankees on March 24, 2018.

2019

- Saw his first Major League action, batting .259/.350/.559 (37-for-143) with 30R, 7 doubles, 12HR, 25RBI and 17BB in 50 games over three stints with the Yankees (4/16-5/3, 7/2-5, 8/3-9/29)…made 24 starts at 1B and 12 starts at DH…hit .333/.389/1.000 (11-for-33) with 1 double, 7HR and 3BB vs. left-handed pitchers…was 5-for-11 with 1 double, 2HR and 3RBI as a pinch-hitter, the most pinch-hits by a Yankee since Ichiro Suzuki (6-for-13) in 2014.
- Reached safely in each of his first 14 career games with a plate appearance from 4/18-8/6, tied with Jesse Hill (14G in 1935) for the third-longest career-opening on-base streak in Yankees history, behind Truck Hannah (38G in 1918) and George Selkirk (17G in 1934)…was the Majors' longest such streak since the Yankees/Toronto's Billy McKinney reached in his first 19G from 3/30-9/9/18.
- Made his Major League debut on 4/18 vs. Kansas City, starting at DH (0-for-3, 1BB)…born in Belle Mead, N.J., is the first New Jersey-born player to make his Major League debut for the Yankees since LHP Steve Garrison (Trenton) on 7/25/11 vs. Seattle and the first position player since SS Derek Jeter (Pequannock) on 5/29/95 at Seattle.
- Collected his first career hit with a second-inning double on 4/21 vs. Kansas City…is just the third New Jersey native since 1991 have collected a hit for the Yankees: Jeter (3,465H, 1995-2014) and INF Todd Frazier (43H, 2017).
- Hit his first Major League HR in the fifth inning on 4/23 at Los Angeles-AL (two-run HR off Stratton).
- Tossed the game's final 2.0 innings (6H, 5ER, 1K, 2HR) on 8/15 vs. Cleveland, becoming the second Yankees position player to pitch in 2019 (also Austin Romine on 7/25 at Boston)…was his first professional pitching appearance at any level…struck out Roberto Pérez to end the ninth.
- Homered in back-to-back games for the first time in his career on 8/25 at Los Angeles-NL and 8/26 at Seattle…recorded his first career multi-HR game on 8/26 at Seattle.
- Hit .371/.426/.839 (23-for-62) with 14R, 5 doubles, 8HR, 17RBI and 6BB over his final 24 games (from 8/21-9/29).
- Hit his first career "walk-off" home run on 9/1 vs. Oakland…was his first career pinch-hit HR…was the first rookie in Yankees history to hit a pinch-hit "walk-off" home run (credit: STATS)…was the sixth pinch-hit, "walk-off" HR in the Majors in 2019, and first by a Yankee since Neil Walker on 8/28/18 vs. Chicago-AL (off Dylan Covey).
- Hit .303/.401/.605 (89-for-294) with 59R, 20 doubles, 23HR and 60RBI in 79 games with Triple-A Scranton/Wilkes-Barre and was tabbed an International Mid-Season All-Star…was named IL "Player of the Week" for 6/24-30, batting .414 (12-for-29) with 7R, 5 doubles, 3HR, 10RBI and 7BB in eight games.

2018

- Played most of the season with Triple-A Scranton/Wilkes-Barre, hitting .253/.327/.433 (93-for-367) with 48R, 21 doubles, 15HR, 52RBI and 37BB in 102 games.
- Hit .211 (4-for-19) with 2R, 1 double, 1HR and 2RBI in six games with short-season Single-A Staten Island.
- Spent spring training in Major League camp with Seattle before being returned to the Yankees as a Rule 5 Draft selection on 3/24.

2017

- Split the season between Triple-A Scranton/Wilkes-Barre and Double-A Trenton, batting .270/.404/.471 (116-for-429) with 80R, 24 doubles, 1 triple, 20HR and 86RBI in 126 games…drew 94BB against 72K.
- Tied for third in all of minor league baseball in walks…was named an Eastern League Mid-Season All-Star, leading the league in OBP (.410) and walks (76)…was an MiLB.com Organization All-Star.
- Was selected by the Seattle Mariners from the Yankees in the first round of the Major League phase of the 2017 Rule 5 Draft on 12/14/17.

2016

- Combined with Single-A Tampa, short-season Single-A Staten Island and Double-A Trenton to hit .289/.411/.479 (55-for-190) with 26R, 12 doubles, 8HR and 43RBI in 56 games…drew 41BB against just 29K.
- Began the season by hitting .371 (13-for-35) with 3R, 1 double, 2HR, 14RBI and 5BB in 10 games with Tampa.

- Joined Staten Island for four games (7/16-19) and went 2-for-12 with 2R, 1 double, 1HR and 3RBI.
- Finished the season by hitting .280/.417/.455 (40-for-143) with 21R, 10 doubles, 5HR, 26RBI, 34BB and 25K in 42 games at Trenton...ranked second in the Eastern League in walks during his stint with the Thunder (7/21-end of the season)...reached safely via H/BB/HP in 37-of-42 games with Trenton and drew at least 1BB in 27-of-42.
- In seven Eastern League playoff games, hit .200 (5-for-25) with 3R, 3 doubles, 1HR and 3RBI.
- Made his Triple-A debut with Scranton/Wilkes-Barre in the Triple-A National Championship Game win, going 0-for-3 with 1BB.

2015
- In 123 games with Single-A Tampa, batted .260 (113-for-435) with 62R, 23 doubles, 3 triples, 6HR, 55RBI and 60BB...was named an FSL Mid-Season All-Star...ranked fourth in the FSL in walks...was named the FSL "Player of the Week" for 8/3-9 (.389, 7-for-18, 7R, 3 doubles, 2HR, 6RBI, 7BB).

2014
- Combined with Single-A Charleston and Single-A Tampa to bat .292/.383/.458 (109-for-373) with 47R, 19 doubles, 2 triples, 13HR, 56RBI and 52BB in 105 games.
- Began the season with Charleston, batting .283 (92-for-325) with 40R, 15 doubles, 2 triples, 11HR and 46RBI in 93 games...was named a SAL Mid-Season All-Star...on 5/25 at Hickory, went 4-for-5 with 4R, 4HR and 5RBI in a 17-10 win, becoming the third player in SAL history to hit 4HR in a game.
- Was promoted to Tampa on 8/19 and hit .354 (17-for-48) with 7R, 4 doubles, 2HR and 10RBI in 12 games.

2013
- Made his professional debut with short-season Single-A Staten Island, batting .235 (27-for-115) with 19R, 7 doubles, 3HR, 17RBI and 20BB in 33 games.

PERSONAL
- Graduated from and attended The Hun School (N.J.) for three years after one year at Montgomery H.S. (N.J.).
- Played two ways at Princeton for three seasons (2011-13)...hit .299 (132-for-442) with 78R, 22 doubles, 2 triples, 10HR, 100RBI and 72BB in 123 games as a first baseman...also went 15-8 with a 2.83 ERA (184.2IP, 176H, 78R/58ER, 47BB, 96K) in 29 games (28 starts) on the mound...as a junior in 2013, hit .320 with 6HR and 38RBI and went 6-0 with a 0.98 ERA in nine starts to win both the Ivy League Player of the Year and Pitcher of the Year Awards, becoming the first player in Ivy League history to win both awards in the same season...was also an NCBWA Third-Team All-American, a finalist for the John Olerud Two-Way Player of the Year Award and a semifinalist for the Gregg Olson Award in 2013...in 2011, was named the Ivy League Rookie of the Year and a *College Baseball* Louisville Slugger Freshman All-American...was a three-time All-Ivy selection (First Team in 2013, Second Team in 2011-12).

Ford's Career Playing Record

Year	Club	AVG	G	AB	R	H	2B	3B	HR	RBI	SH	SF	HP	BB	SO	SB	CS	E	OBP	SLG
2013	Staten Island	.235	33	115	19	27	7	0	3	17	0	1	0	20	23	0	0	5	.346	.374
2014	Charleston	.283	93	325	40	92	15	2	11	46	0	3	5	48	39	2	0	7	.381	.443
	Tampa	.354	12	48	7	17	4	0	2	10	0	0	0	4	7	0	0	0	.404	.563
2015	Tampa	.260	123	435	62	113	23	3	6	55	0	5	0	60	75	1	0	15	.346	.368
2016	Tampa	.371	10	35	3	13	1	0	2	14	0	1	0	5	4	0	1	1	.439	.571
	Staten Island	.167	4	12	2	2	1	0	1	3	0	1	0	2	0	0	0	0	.267	.500
	Trenton	.280	42	143	21	40	10	0	5	26	0	2	1	34	25	0	0	1	.417	.455
2017	Trenton	.272	101	335	61	91	19	1	13	65	0	2	4	76	56	1	0	5	.410	.451
	Scranton/WB	.266	25	94	19	25	5	0	7	21	0	2	1	18	16	0	0	1	.383	.543
2018	Scranton/WB - a	.253	102	367	48	93	21	0	15	52	0	2	4	37	70	1	0	1	.327	.433
	Staten Island	.211	6	19	2	4	1	0	1	2	0	0	1	2	3	0	0	0	.318	.421
2019	Scranton/WB	.303	79	294	59	89	20	0	23	60	0	4	5	46	55	0	1	3	.401	.605
	YANKEES	.259	50	143	30	37	7	0	12	25	0	0	3	17	28	0	0	3	.350	.559
Minor League Totals		**.273**	**630**	**2222**	**343**	**606**	**127**	**6**	**89**	**371**	**0**	**23**	**21**	**352**	**373**	**5**	**2**	**39**	**.374**	**.455**
Major League Totals		**.259**	**50**	**143**	**30**	**37**	**7**	**0**	**12**	**25**	**0**	**0**	**3**	**17**	**28**	**0**	**0**	**3**	**.350**	**.559**

Signed by the Yankees as a non-drafted free agent on July 17, 2013.

a – Selected by Seattle from the Yankees in the first round of the Major League phase of the 2017 Rule 5 Draft on December 14, 2017...was returned to the Yankees on March 24, 2018.

Ford's Career Fielding Record

Position	PCT	G	PO	A	E	TC	DP
First Base	.985	29	191	9	3	203	22
Pitcher	1.000	1	0	1	0	1	0

Ford's Career Home Run Chart
MULTI-HOMER GAMES: 1, 8/26/19 at SEA. **TWO-HOMER GAMES:** 1, 8/26/19 at SEA. **GRAND SLAMS:** None. **PINCH-HIT HR:** 2, last on 9/14/19 at TOR (Justin Shafer). **INSIDE-THE-PARK HR:** None. **WALK-OFF HR:** 1, 9/1/19 vs. OAK (Liam Hendriks). **LEADOFF HR:** None.

Ford's Career Bests and Streaks
HITS: 3 - 2 times (last on 9/21/19 vs. TOR). **RUNS:** 3, 9/27/19 at TEX. **2B:** 1 - 7 times (last on 9/27/19 at TEX). **3B:** None. **HR:** 2, 8/26/19 at SEA. **RBI:** 4, 9/27/19 at TEX. **BB:** 2 - 2 times (last on 4/22/19 at LAA). **SO:** 3, 4/24/19 at LAA. **SB:** None. **HIT STREAK:** 7g, from 8/25-9/2/19. **"WALK-OFF" HITS:** 1, 9/1/19 vs. OAK (HR).

Player of the Month: None   **Player of the Week:** None   **Rookie of the Month:** None

CLINT FRAZIER • OF

77

HT: 5-11 • **WT:** 212 • **BATS:** R • **THROWS:** R
BIRTHDATE: 9/6/94 • **OPENING DAY AGE:** 25
BIRTHPLACE: Decatur, Ga.
RESIDES: Marietta, Ga.
M.L. SERVICE: 1 year, 163 days

STATUS
- Acquired by the Yankees with LHP Justus Sheffield, RHP Ben Heller and RHP J.P. Feyereisen from Cleveland in exchange for LHP Andrew Miller on July 31, 2016.

2019
- Hit .267 (60-for-225) with 31R, 14 doubles, 12HR, 38RBI, 16BB and 1SB in 69 games (31 starts in RF, 14 starts in LF and 14 at DH) over two stints with the Yankees (4/1-6/16, 9/1-29)…set career highs in hits, doubles, home runs, RBI, walks and games played…the Yankees went 9-1 when he homered (had two multi-HR games).
- Batted .362/.411/.787 (17-for-47) with 5 doubles, 5HR, 28RBI and 5BB with RISP.
- Since 1987, became the third Yankees outfielder (min. 50% of games in OF), in his age-24 season or younger, to reach double digits in HR (also Melky Cabrera, 13HR in 2009 and Bernie Williams, 12HR in 1993, both age 24).
- Hit a go-ahead, three-run HR in the eighth inning of 4/6 win at Baltimore…marked his first HR since 7/28/17 vs. Tampa Bay.
- Collected his first career multi-HR game, set a career high with 4H and had 4RBI in 4/7 win at Baltimore…at 24 years, 213 days, was the second Yankee under age-25 to collect at least 2HR and 4H in a game in the span of three games (also Gleyber Torres, 4-for-4, 2HR, 4RBI on 4/4/19 at Baltimore)…prior to Torres, no Yankee under age-25 had accomplished the feat since Joe Pepitone at 23 years, 221 days on 5/17/64-G2 vs. Kansas City-AL…with DH Gary Sánchez hitting 3HR in the game, became the third and fourth Yankees to collect multi-HR games during the three-game series at Baltimore, joining Gleyber Torres (2HR on 4/4) and Aaron Judge (2HR on 4/6)…marked the fourth time ever that two Yankees combined for 5HR in a game, the first since 7/28/40-G1 at Chicago-AL (Charlie Keller-3HR, Joe DiMaggio-2HR)…were the first Yankees teammates to hit multiple HRs in the same game since Sánchez and Judge on 9/10/17 at Texas.
- Was placed on the 10-day injured list with a left ankle sprain from 4/25 (retroactive to 4/23) - 5/6…missed 11 team games…went 1-for-3 with 1R, 1BB and 1SB in one rehab game with Double-A Trenton.
- Collected his second career multi-HR game (also 4/7/19 at Baltimore) and had a career-high 5RBI on 5/21 at Baltimore.
- Doubled in four straight games from 6/7-11 (G1), the first Yankee to do so since Didi Gregorius from 3/30-4/3/18.
- Hit .247 (61-for-247) with 35R, 20 doubles, 1 triple, 8HR and 26RBI in 61 games with the RailRiders.

2018
- Hit .265 (9-for-34) with 9R, 3 doubles and 1RBI in 15 games (7 starts in LF, one in CF and one at DH) over four stints with the Yankees (5/15-20, 6/4, 6/18-25 and 7/7-15).
- Began the season on the 7-day concussion disabled list…in six rehab games (four with Single-A Tampa, two with Triple-A Scranton/Wilkes-Barre), combined to hit .217 (5-for-23) with 6R, 1 double, 2HR and 3RBI…was returned from rehab, reinstated from the concussion disabled list and optioned to Triple-A Scranton/WB on 5/2.
- Scored a run in each of his first seven games of the season (5/19-6/21), tied for the third-longest run-scoring streak to start a season by a Yankee since 1908: Babe Ruth (first 13G in 1931), Derek Jeter (first 8G in 1999), Bernie Williams (first 7G in 2003)…was tied for the Majors' longest season-opening runs streak since 2008 (Cincinnati's Shin-Soo Choo, first 7G in 2013; Toronto's Marco Scutaro, first 7G in 2009)…is the longest run-scored streak of his career.
- Hit safely in each of his first six games with an at-bat (5/19-6/21), a career-long hit streak.
- Was again placed on the 7-day concussion disabled list on 7/16 and transferred to the 10-day D.L. on 7/25 (post-concussion migraines)…began a rehab assignment with Single-A Tampa on 8/30 and played in one game (1-for-3)…was transferred to the 60-day D.L. on 9/18 with post-concussion migraines, missing the remainder of the season.
- In 48 games with Scranton/WB, hit .311/.389/.574 (59-for-190) with 38R, 14 doubles, 3 triples, 10HR, 21RBI and 23BB.
- Played in just two spring training games…suffered a concussion on 2/24 at Pittsburgh.

2017
- Hit .231 (31-for-134) with 16R, 9 doubles, 4 triples, 4HR and 17RBI in 39 games (27 starts in LF, 6 in RF and 2 at DH) with the Yankees…of his 31H, 17 went for extra bases (54.8%).
- His first 4H were a double, HR, triple and single, becoming the second Yankee to hit for the cycle in his first 4H (also RHP Johnny Allen in 1932, who went 17-3 with a 3.70 ERA in his rookie season as the Yankees swept the Cubs in the World Series) and the first Major Leaguer to do so since Atlanta's Tyler Pastornicky in 2012—credit: *Elias*.

83

- Of his first 7H, six went for extra-bases (1 double, 2 triples, 3HR)…was the fourth Yankee ever to hit at least 3HR within his first seven Major League games, joining Jesús Montero in 2011 (3HR), Shelley Duncan in 2007 (4HR) and Steve Whitaker in 1966 (3HR)…only three players under age-23 hit *more* HR in their first seven Major League games (Houston's Yordan Alvarez-2019, Los Angeles-NL's Yasiel Puig-2013, St. Louis' Joe Cunningham-1954, 4HR each).
- Had 11 extra-base hits (6 doubles, 2 triples, 3HR) through his first 16 career games (7/1-23)…according to *Elias*, the only other Yankee with at least 11XBH through 16G is Joe DiMaggio (13)…had 14 extra-base hits (7 doubles, 3 triples, 4HR) through his first 25 games (7/1-8/3)…only four other players in Yankees history have as many as 14XBH through 25 career games: DiMaggio (22), Gary Sánchez (19), Miguel Andújar (18) and Shane Spencer (14).
- Had 16RBI through his first 20G (7/1-28), becoming the fifth Yankee in franchise history to accomplish the feat according to the YES Network (Hideki Matsui-20RBI, Joe DiMaggio-17, George Selkirk-17 and Mickey Mantle-16).
- Made his Major League debut in 7/1 loss at Houston, hitting his first career home run (off Tony Sipp) in the seventh inning…was the 12th Yankee to homer in his Major League debut and first since Tyler Austin and Aaron Judge went back-to-back on 8/13/16 vs. Toronto…his sixth-inning double off Francis Martes was his first Major League hit…became the third Yankee ever with multiple extra-base hits in his Major League debut (also Dixie Walker in 1931: 2 doubles in a 14-inning game and Mike Pagliarulo in 1984: 2 doubles) and the first to do so while hitting a homer—credit: *Elias*…was signed to a Major League contract and selected to the Yankees' 25-man roster from Triple-A Scranton/Wilkes-Barre prior to the game.
- Hit ninth-inning "walk-off" three-run HR and was 3-for-4 with 1 triple and 4RBI in 7/8 win vs Milwaukee (his sixth career game)…at 22 years, 305 days old, was the youngest Yankee with a "walk-off" HR since Melky Cabrera (21y, 341d) on 7/18/06 vs. Seattle and the youngest Yankee ever with a "walk-off" HR *when the team was trailing*…was his second career HR, making him the fifth Yankee to hit a "walk-off" HR within his first 2HR: Alfonso Soriano (1st HR on 9/24/99 vs. Tampa Bay) Mike Hegan (1st HR on 9/1/67 vs. Washington-AL), Bob Grim (2nd HR on 9/5/57 vs. Boston) and Frank LaPorte (2nd HR on 5/3/1906 vs. Philadelphia-AL)…was the third Yankee with a "walk-off" HR within his first 10 Major League games — Phil Rizzuto (10th game, 4/23/41 vs. Boston, two-run HR in the 11th off starter Charlie Wagner) and Alfonso Soriano (sixth game, 9/24/99 vs. Tampa Bay, solo HR in the 11th off Norm Charlton)—credit: *Elias*.
- Started in LF with Todd Frazier starting at 3B in 7/21 win at Seattle…it marked the first time the Yankees had two fielders with the same last name in the starting lineup since 9/19/08 vs. Baltimore, when 3B Alex Rodriguez and C Iván Rodríguez started in the first game of the final series at the original Yankee Stadium.
- Was placed on the 10-day disabled list from 8/10 (retroactive to 8/9) - 9/11 with a left oblique strain…missed 31 team games…played in four postseason rehab games with Double-A Trenton (2-for-17, 1R, 2RBI).
- Was on the Yankees' Wild Card Game roster, but did not play…was not on the roster for the ALDS or ALCS.
- In 74 games with the RailRiders, hit .256/.344/.473 (70-for-273) with 46R, 19 doubles, 12HR, 42RBI and 9SB.

2016

- Combined at Double-A Akron, Triple-A Columbus and Triple-A Scranton/Wilkes-Barre to bat .263/.335/.447 (122-for-463) with 75R, 27 doubles, 5 triples, 16HR, 55RBI and 13SB in 119 games…played in the MLB All-Star Futures Game in San Diego.
- Overall, saw action at all three OF positions — 41 starts in LF, 21 starts in CF, 40 starts in RF — committing 13E in 221TC (.941) with 11 outfield assists…was named by *Baseball America* as the No. 8 prospect in the Eastern League.
- Began the season with the RubberDucks, hitting .276/.356/.469 (94-for-341) with 56R, 25 doubles, 13HR, 48RBI, 41BB and 13SB in 89 games…was named to the Eastern League Mid-Season All-Star Team…was promoted to Columbus on 7/25 and went 5-for-21 (.238) with 2R and 1 triple in five games.
- Was traded to the Yankees on 7/31 and batted .228 (23-for-101) with 17R, 2 doubles, 3HR and 7RBI in 25G with Scranton/WB.
- Following the season, was ranked by *Baseball America* as the No. 2 prospect in the Yankees organization.

2015

- In 133 games at Single-A Lynchburg, hit .285/.377/.465 (143-for-501) with 88R, 36 doubles, 3 triples, 16HR, 72RBI, 68BB and 15SB…led the Carolina League in hits, doubles, extra-base hits (55) and total bases (233) and placed among league leaders in home runs (second), runs scored (second), RBI (third), walks (third), OPS (third, .842), BA (fourth), OBP (fourth) and slugging pct. (fourth)…ranked among Indians organizational leaders in runs scored (first), hits (second) and RBI (fourth)…was named a CL Postseason All-Star and MiLB.com Organization All-Star.
- Earned MiLB.com CL "Player of the Month" honors in July (.363, 37-for-102, 21R, 7 doubles, 3HR, 17RBI, 6SB in 28G).
- After the season, played for the Scottsdale Scorpions of the Arizona Fall League and hit .281/.347/.438 (25-for-89) with 15R, 1 double, 3HR, 8RBI and 4SB in 22G…was named to the AFL Rising Stars Game and the AFL All-Prospect Team.
- Following the season, was ranked by *Baseball America* as the No. 44 overall prospect and No. 2 prospect in the Indians organization…was tabbed by *Baseball America* as the No. 5 prospect in the Carolina League.

2014

- Spent the season with Single-A Lake County and hit .266/.349/.411 (126-for-474) with 70R, 18 doubles, 6 triples, 13HR, 50RBI, 56BB and 12SB in 120 games.
- Following the season, was ranked by *Baseball America* as the No. 3 prospect in the Indians organization and the No. 9 prospect in the Midwest League.

2013
- Made his professional debut with the AZL Indians, batting .297 (51-for-172) with 32R, 11 doubles, 5 triples, 5HR and 28RBI in 44 games…was an Arizona League Postseason All-Star.
- Was tabbed by *Baseball America* as the No. 1 prospect in the Arizona League…following the season, was ranked by the same publication as the No. 48 overall prospect and No. 2 prospect in the Indians organization.

PERSONAL
- Full name is Clint Jackson Frazier…graduated in 2013 from Loganville H.S. (Ga.)…was named the 2013 Gatorade National Baseball Player of the Year after hitting .485/.561/1.134 with 56R, 17HR and 45RBI as a senior…earned 2012 All-America honors from Under Armour and AFLAC as a junior.
- Was the first high school position player chosen in the 2013 First-Year Player Draft…was the top-ranked player in the nation by Perfect Game USA and MaxPreps entering the draft.
- Was signed to play at the University of Georgia prior to signing with the Indians.

Frazier's Career Playing Record

Year	Club	AVG	G	AB	R	H	2B	3B	HR	RBI	SH	SF	HP	BB	SO	SB	CS	E	OBP	SLG
2013	AZL Indians	.297	44	172	32	51	11	5	5	28	0	4	3	17	61	3	2	2	.362	.506
2014	Lake County	.266	120	474	70	126	18	6	13	50	1	4	7	56	161	12	6	8	.349	.411
2015	Lynchburg	.285	133	501	88	143	36	3	16	72	5	5	9	68	125	15	7	6	.377	.465
2016	Akron	.276	89	341	56	94	25	1	13	48	3	3	3	41	86	13	4	8	.356	.469
	Columbus	.238	5	21	2	5	0	1	0	0	0	0	0	0	6	0	0	1	.238	.333
	Scranton/WB - a	.228	25	101	17	23	2	3	3	7	0	0	0	7	30	0	0	4	.278	.396
2017	Scranton/WB	.256	74	273	46	70	19	2	12	42	0	7	3	37	69	9	2	4	.344	.473
	YANKEES - b	.231	39	134	16	31	9	4	4	17	0	1	0	7	43	1	0	2	.268	.448
2018	YANKEES - c, d	.265	15	34	9	9	3	0	0	1	0	0	2	5	13	0	0	0	.390	.353
	Tampa	.250	6	20	6	5	1	0	1	3	0	1	1	4	3	2	0	0	.385	.450
	Scranton/WB	.311	48	190	38	59	14	3	10	21	0	1	2	23	52	4	2	1	.389	.574
2019	YANKEES - e	.267	69	225	31	60	14	0	12	38	0	3	2	16	70	1	2	3	.317	.489
	Trenton	.333	1	3	1	1	0	0	0	0	0	0	0	1	0	1	0	0	.500	.333
	Scranton/WB	.247	61	247	35	61	20	1	8	26	0	1	4	17	56	1	2	4	.305	.433
Minor League Totals		**.272**	**606**	**2343**	**391**	**638**	**146**	**25**	**81**	**297**	**9**	**26**	**32**	**271**	**649**	**60**	**25**	**38**	**.352**	**.460**
Major League Totals		**.254**	**123**	**393**	**56**	**100**	**26**	**4**	**16**	**56**	**0**	**4**	**4**	**28**	**126**	**2**	**2**	**5**	**.308**	**.463**

Selected by Cleveland in the first round (fifth overall) of the 2013 First-Year Player Draft.

a - Acquired by the Yankees with LHP Justus Sheffield, RHP Ben Heller and RHP J.P. Feyereisen from Cleveland in exchange for LHP Andrew Miller on July 31, 2016.
b - Placed on the 10-day disabled list from August 10 (retroactive to August 9) - September 11, 2017 with a left oblique strain.
c - Placed on the 7-day concussion disabled list from March 29 (retroactive to March 26) - May 2, 2018.
d - Placed on the 7-day concussion disabled list on July 16, 2018…was transferred to the 10-day disabled list on July 25 with post-concussion migraines and transferred to the 60-day disabled list from September 18, 2018 through the end of the season.
e - Placed on the 10-day injured list from April 25 (retroactive to April 23) - May 6, 2019 with a left ankle sprain.

Frazier's Postseason Record

Year	Club vs. Opp.	AVG	G	AB	R	H	2B	3B	HR	RBI	SH	SF	HP	BB	SO	SB	CS	E	OBP	SLG
2017	NYY vs. MIN (WC)								On Roster - Did Not Play											
Wild Card Game Totals		-	-	-	-	-	-	-	-	-	-	-	-	-	-	-	-	-	-	-
POSTSEASON TOTALS		-	-	-	-	-	-	-	-	-	-	-	-	-	-	-	-	-	-	-

Frazier's Career Fielding Record

Position	PCT	G	PO	A	E	TC	DP
Outfield	.966	100	136	6	5	147	1

Frazier's Career Home Run Chart
MULTI-HOMER GAMES: 2. **TWO-HOMER GAMES:** 2, last on 5/21/19 at BAL. **GRAND SLAMS:** None. **PINCH-HIT HR:** None. **INSIDE-THE-PARK HR:** None. **WALK-OFF HR:** 1, 7/8/17 vs. MIL (Corey Knebel). **LEADOFF HR:** None.

Frazier's Career Bests and Streaks
HITS: 4, 4/7/19 at BAL. **RUNS:** 2 - 6 times (last on 5/25/19 at KC-G2). **2B:** 2, 7/17/17 at MIN. **3B:** 1 - 4 times (last on 9/20/17 vs. MIN). **HR:** 2 - 2 times (last on 5/21/19 at BAL). **RBI:** 5, 5/21/19 at BAL. **BB:** 2 - 3 times (last on 5/21/19 at KC). **SO:** 3 - 7 times (last on 5/28/19 vs. SD). **SB:** 1 - 2 times (last on 5/25/19 at KC-G2). **HIT STREAK:** 6g, 5/19-6/21/18. **"WALK-OFF" HITS:** 1, 7/8/17 vs. MIL (HR).

Player of the Month: None **Player of the Week:** None **Rookie of the Month:** None

DEIVI GARCÍA • RHP

83

HT: 5-9 • **WT:** 163 • **BATS:** R • **THROWS:** R
BIRTHDATE: 5/19/99 • **OPENING DAY AGE:** 20
BIRTHPLACE: Bonao, D.R.
RESIDES: Bonao, D.R.
M.L. SERVICE: None (Rookie)

STATUS
- Signed by the Yankees as a non-drafted free agent on July 2, 2015.

2019
- Went 5-9 with a 4.28 ERA (111.1IP, 96H, 58R/53ER, 54BB, 165K, 10HR) in 26 games (21 starts) between Single-A Tampa, Double-A Trenton and Triple-A Scranton/Wilkes-Barre.
- Posted the fourth-highest K/9.0IP ratio (13.34) among all minor league pitchers (min. 75.0IP) and led all Yankees farmhands in strikeouts.
- Began the season with Tampa (0-2, 3.06 ERA) and made four starts before being promoted to Trenton on 4/30…in 11 starts with Trenton, went 4-4 with a 3.86 ERA (53.2IP, 23ER).
- Earned Eastern League "Pitcher of the Week" honors from 6/17-23…struck out a career-high 15 batters over six scoreless frames on 6/18 vs. Richmond.
- Was one of three pitchers (RHP Domingo Acevedo, RHP Daniel Alvarez) to throw a combined no-hitter on 6/24 in a 7-0 win vs. Reading (5.0IP, 0ER, 2BB, 9K, 1HP).
- Was named a 2019 Eastern League Mid-Season All-Star and was selected to the SiriusXM All-Star Futures Game in Cleveland…started the game for the American League and pitched a 1-2-3 first inning (1.0IP, 1K).
- Was promoted to Scranton/Wilkes-Barre on 7/11…went 1-3 with a 5.40 ERA (40.0IP, 24ER) in 11 games (six starts).
- Following the season, was tabbed by *Baseball America* as the Yankees' No. 3 prospect and the No. 5 prospect in the Eastern League…was listed by MLB Pipeline as the organization's No. 1 prospect and as having the "best curveball" among all minor league prospects…was also tabbed by *Baseball America* as having the "best slider" among Yankees farmhands.
- Was added to the Yankees' 40-man roster on 11/20.

2018
- Split the season between Single-A Tampa, Single-A Charleston and Double-A Trenton to go 5-4 with a 2.55 ERA (74.0IP, 50H, 25R/21ER, 20BB, 105K, 5HR) in 14 starts.
- His 12.77 K/9.0IP was second highest among Yankees farmhands (min 50.0IP) .
- Limited batters to a .189 BA (50-for-265); LH .221 (25-for-113), RH .164 (25-for-152).
- Began his season with a spot start for Tampa (4.2IP, 1ER) on 6/5…made eight starts with Charleston from 6/11-7/31…during his eight-start stint at Charleston, was 2-4 with a 3.76 ERA (40.2IP, 31H, 19R/17ER, 10BB, 63K, 5HR).
- Was assigned back to Tampa on 8/6, going 2-0 with a 1.14 ERA (23.2IP, 17H, 4R/3ER, 5BB, 28K) in four starts.
- Was named FSL "Pitcher of the Week" for 8/6-12 after retiring all 21BF over 7.0 perfect innings with 12K in Game 2 on 8/6 vs. Clearwater.
- In his Double-A debut on 9/2 vs. Reading pitched 5.0 no-hit innings (2BB, 7K).
- Following the season, was ranked by *Baseball America* as the No. 6 prospect in the Yankees organization.

2017
- Combined with the DSL Yankees, the GCL Yankees West and Rookie-level Pulaski to go 6-2 with a 3.30 ERA (60.0IP, 42H, 23R/22ER, 19BB, 85K, 7HR) in 13 games (10 starts).
- Posted a 12.75 K/9.0IP ratio, the second-highest among Yankees farmhands (min. 50.0IP)
- Held opponents to a .202 BA (42-for-208).
- Started the season with the DSL Yankees, going 1-1 with a 1.17 ERA (15.1IP, 10H, 3R/2ER, 2BB, 18K, 1HR) in three starts.
- Was transferred to the GCL Yankees West on 6/26 and went 3-0 with a 3.24 ERA (16.2IP, 9H, 6ER, 4BB, 24K, 3HR) in four games (two starts).
- Was promoted to Pulaski on 7/24 and went 2-1 with a 4.50 ERA (28.0IP, 23H, 14ER, 13BB, 43K, 3HR) in six games (five starts).

2016
- Made his professional debut with the DSL Yankees 2, going 1-5 with a 2.61 ERA (48.1IP, 23H, 17R/14ER, 32BB, 61K, 1HR) in 12 starts.
- Led DSL starters (min. 10GS) with an 11.36 K/9.0IP ratio.

PERSONAL
- Full name is Deivi Anderson García (pronounced DAY-vee).

García's Career Pitching Record

Year	Club	W	L	ERA	G	GS	CG	SHO	SV	IP	H	R	ER	HR	HP	BB	SO	WP	BK
2016	DSL Yankees 2	1	5	2.61	12	12	0	0	0	48.1	23	17	14	1	6	32	61	7	0
2017	DSL Yankees 1	1	1	1.17	3	3	0	0	0	15.1	10	3	2	1	1	2	18	2	2
	GCL Yankees W	3	0	3.24	4	2	0	0	0	16.2	9	6	6	3	2	4	24	1	0
	Pulaski	2	1	4.50	6	5	0	0	0	28.0	23	14	14	3	1	13	43	4	0
2018	Tampa	2	0	1.27	5	5	0	0	0	28.1	19	6	4	0	1	8	35	2	0
	Charleston	2	4	3.76	8	8	0	0	0	40.2	31	19	17	5	6	10	63	3	1
	Trenton	1	0	0.00	1	1	0	0	0	5.0	0	0	0	0	0	2	7	0	0
2019	Tampa	0	2	3.06	4	4	0	0	0	17.2	14	10	6	0	0	8	33	1	0
	Trenton	4	4	3.86	11	11	0	0	0	53.2	43	23	23	2	6	26	87	3	3
	Scranton/WB	1	3	5.40	11	6	0	0	0	40.0	39	25	24	8	4	20	45	1	1
Minor League Totals		17	20	3.37	65	57	0	0	0	293.2	211	123	110	23	27	125	416	24	7

Signed by the Yankees as a non-drafted free agent on July 2, 2015.

New York Yankees Museum Presented by Bank of America

"Nobody has a story like the New York Yankees," says Yankees Museum Curator Brian Richards.

The New York Yankees Museum Presented by Bank of America is located on Yankee Stadium's Main Level (near Section 210). The museum presents the history of baseball's most legendary franchise through rotating displays of historic artifacts.

Displays include a "Ball Wall" containing autographed baseballs from Yankees past and present; Thurman Munson's locker from the original Yankee Stadium; and all seven World Series trophies won by the Yankees since the Steinbrenner family assumed principal ownership in 1973.

On game days, fans are welcome to visit the museum from 90 minutes prior to first pitch until the end of the eighth inning. On non-game days, visitors may visit the museum as part of Yankee Stadium tours.

The museum presents exhibits on key players, teams, and achievements in Yankees history. In addition to permanent displays, the museum has featured rotating exhibits including: "Five Great Teams: The 1927, 1939, 1961, 1977, and 1998 New York Yankees"; "Babe Ruth and Lou Gehrig: Baseball's Hardest-Hitting Teammates"; "Yankees by the Numbers"; and "Bronx Bombers: The New York Yankees' Home Run Heritage."

Featured artifacts have included Roger Maris' 61st home run jersey; Mickey Mantle's 1964 World Series bat and 1956 game-used glove; Derek Jeter's jersey from the first inning of his 3,000th hit game; Babe Ruth's bat from Yankee Stadium's inaugural home run on April 18, 1923; 1932 game-worn Babe Ruth and Lou Gehrig jerseys; Chris Chambliss's bat from his game-winning home run in 1976 ALCS Game 5; and baseballs autographed by all 27 World Series-winning Yankees teams.

BRETT GARDNER • OF

11

HT: 5-11 • **WT:** 195 • **BATS:** L • **THROWS:** L
BIRTHDATE: 8/24/83 • **OPENING DAY AGE:** 36
BIRTHPLACE: Holly Hill, S.C.
RESIDES: Holly Hill, S.C.
COLLEGE: College of Charleston
M.L. SERVICE: 11 years, 72 days

STATUS
- Selected by the Yankees in the third round of the 2005 First-Year Player Draft…signed a one-year contract for the 2020 season with a club option for 2021 on January 11, 2020.

CAREER NOTES
- Is the Yankees' longest-tenured player, having been drafted by the club in the third round of the 2005 First-Year Player Draft and making his Major League debut with the Yankees in 2008…is one of five players drafted by the Yankees to collect at least 1,000H with the club (also Thurman Munson, Don Mattingly, Derek Jeter and Jorge Posada), all of whom spent their entire careers in pinstripes.
- Is one of four players in Yankees history to collect at least 1,000H and 200SB with the club over his first 10 seasons: also Derek Jeter, Willie Randolph and Hal Chase.
- Is one of two players with at least 100HR and 250SB with the club (also Derek Jeter - 260HR/358SB).
- Is the 30th player in club history to play in at least 12 seasons…is looking to become the sixth outfielder in Yankees history to appear in at least part of 13 different seasons with the club, joining Mickey Mantle (16), Bernie Williams (16), Babe Ruth (15), Roy White (15) and Joe DiMaggio (13)…among all outfielders in franchise history, his 37.0 WAR ranks ninth (FanGraphs).
- Is one of only 11 players to play for the same team in each season since 2008, joining Ryan Braun (MIL), Miguel Cabrera (DET), Alex Gordon (KC), Félix Hernández (SEA), Clayton Kershaw (LAD), Yadier Molina (STL), Dustin Pedroia (BOS), Joey Votto (CIN), Adam Wainwright (STL) and Ryan Zimmerman (WSH).
- Is the only current Yankee to appear with the club in both the current and original Yankee Stadiums.
- Is one of four Major Leaguers to appear in at least 140 games in each of the last seven seasons (2013-19), joining Brandon Crawford, Anthony Rizzo and Carlos Santana…is one of six players in franchise history with at least six such seasons in his age-30 season or older…trails only Derek Jeter (9) and Dave Winfield (7) in Yankees history.
- Is one of two players with at least 80R each season since 2013 (also Mike Trout).
- Has hit 124 home runs in his career, with the Yankees going 84-31 in those 115 contests (has nine multi-HR games)…of his 124HR, 58 have either tied the game (11) or given the Yankees the lead (47).
- Is one of 16 players drafted and signed by the Yankees to reach 100HR in the Majors and one of seven to hit at least 100HR with the Yankees (also Jorge Posada-275, Derek Jeter-260, Don Mattingly-222, Thurman Munson-113, Aaron Judge-110 and Mike Pagliarulo-105).
- Has 15 career leadoff home runs, tied with Chuck Knoblauch for fifth-most on the Yankees' all-time list…of his 15 leadoff HR, eight have come vs. the AL East (three vs. Baltimore, three vs. Tampa Bay, two vs. Toronto).
- Had a 32.55 AB/HR ratio (3,288AB/101HR) over six seasons from 2014-19…posted an 84.00 AB/HR ratio (1,932AB/23HR) over the first six seasons of his career (2008-13).
- Has recorded at least 10HR and 10SB in the same season five times (2014-15, '17-19)…is one of four Yankees with at least five such seasons at age-30 or older, joining Derek Jeter (7), Paul O'Neill (5) and Alex Rodriguez (5).
- Has stolen 267 bases in 328 career attempts…his 81.4% success rate is highest among players with at least 300 career stolen base attempts who appeared in a game in 2019.
- Ranks third on the Yankees' all-time list with 267SB behind Derek Jeter (358) and Rickey Henderson (326)…has 11 seasons with double-digit steals (2008-11, '13-19), fourth-most in Yankees history behind Derek Jeter (17), Roy White (13) and Willie Randolph (12)…had led the club in steals six times in his career (2010-11, '13, '17-19).
- Has seven seasons with at least 20SB (2009-11, '13-15, '17), the third-most 20SB seasons in Yankees history, trailing Derek Jeter (eight: 1997-98, 2000-02, '04, '06 and '09) and Hal Chase (eight: 1905-12).
- Collected 103SB within his first three years in the Majors (6/30/08-6/29/11)…according to *Elias*, were the most SB by a Yankee within three years of his debut since Ben Chapman, who had 113SB from 4/16/30-4/15/33.
- Stole his 100th career base on 6/14/11…came in his 364th game and 124th career attempt…according to *Elias*, during the Live Ball Era (since 1920, the same year caught stealing became an official stat in the AL), only Rickey Henderson (162 games) and Ben Chapman (313) reached 100SB in fewer games for the Yankees…*Elias* also notes his 24CS at the time of his 100th stolen base were the fewest among players who made their Major League debut with the Yankees in the Live Ball Era…broke the previous record held by Mickey Mantle, who had 27CS at the time of his 100th stolen base in 1960…overall, became the third Yankee since 1920 with as few as 24CS at the time of his 100th stolen base with the club, joining Rickey Henderson and Alex Rodriguez.
- Recorded his 50th stolen base in his 171st career game, the first Yankee to reach the plateau in as few games from the start of his career since Fritz Maisel on 6/21/1914 (102 games)—credit: *Elias*.

CAREER HIGHLIGHTS
AL All-Star Team
- 2015

AL Gold Glove
- 2016

Wilson Defensive Player of the Year in LF
- 2016

- Is one of three Yankees all-time with at least 45SB in back-to-back seasons (2010-11), joining Fritz Maisel (1914-15) and Rickey Henderson (1985-86).
- Since the start of 2016, has hit .385 (15-for-39) with 43RBI with the bases loaded.
- Since the start of 2014, the Yankees have played 19 doubleheaders…over that same span, he has appeared in 34 games that are part of DHs (all except G1 on 9/12/14 at Baltimore, G2 on 10/3/15 at Baltimore, G1 on 6/4/18 at Detroit and G1 on 9/12/19 at Detroit), hitting .345 (41-for-119) with 25R, 8 doubles, 5 triples, 7HR, 26RBI, 14BB, 3SB and 3HP…has reached safely in 28-of-34 games…hit .326 (14-for-43) with 9R, 2 doubles, 3 triples, 1HR, 7RBI, 5BB and 2SB in 13 games that were part of doubleheaders in 2019.
- Has made 11 career Opening Day rosters, all for the Yankees (2009-19)…has made seven Opening Day starts in LF, tying Babe Ruth for the second most O.D. starts at that position in Yankees history (Roy White, 9)…his 10 O.D. starts in the outfield are tied for the fourth-most in Yankees history (Mickey Mantle-16, Babe Ruth-13, Bernie Williams-11).

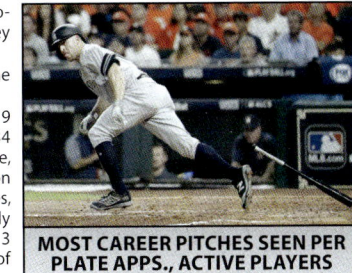

MOST CAREER PITCHES SEEN PER PLATE APPS., ACTIVE PLAYERS (min. 3,000PA)
1. Matt Carpenter 4.27
2. Mike Trout 4.26
3. **BRETT GARDNER** 4.25

2019
- Set career highs in home runs, RBI and slugging pct., hitting .251/.325/.503 (123-for-491) with 86R, 26 doubles, 7 triples, 28HR, 74RBI, 52BB and 10SB in 141 games with the Yankees…of his 123H, 61 went for extra bases…hit more home runs than doubles for the first time in his career.
- Collected his second career season with at least 20HR and 10SB (also 2017 - 21HR, 23SB)…is the first Yankee with multiple such seasons since Curtis Granderson did it in three straight years from 2010-12.
- Turned 36 years old on 8/24…was the oldest player in the Majors to make at least 100 outfield starts in 2019.
- Hit in every spot in the starting lineup except cleanup…hit third in the starting lineup 12 times, with his only prior appearances there coming in Sept. 2014 (9x)…had never hit fifth in the lineup before 2019.
- According to FanGraphs, was the seventh-most valuable base runner in the American League.
- Hit his 15th career leadoff HR on 4/10 at Houston, tying Chuck Knoblauch for fifth place on the Yankees' all-time leadoff HR list…also homered on 4/12 vs. Chicago-AL, his first homers in consecutive games since 7/27-28/17.
- Hit his 100th career HR on 4/17 vs. Boston, a go-ahead grand slam in the seventh inning…became the fourth Yankee all time to hit a grand slam for his 100th homer, joining Jacoby Ellsbury (4/28/17 vs. Baltimore), Matt Nokes (5/13/92 vs. Seattle) and Eric Soderholm (9/26/80 at Detroit)…was the first Major Leaguer to do so since Texas' Rougned Odor on 8/3/18 vs. Baltimore…was the 15th player drafted and signed by the Yankees to reach 100HR in the Majors and the sixth to hit at least 100HR with the Yankees (also Jorge Posada-275, Derek Jeter-260, Don Mattingly-222, Thurman Munson-113 and Mike Pagliarulo-105)…Judge later joined the group in 2019.
- Collected his 16th career game with a HR and SB on 5/19 vs. Tampa Bay, third of the season.
- Had a career-high 3 doubles on 5/22 at Baltimore, his sixth career game with 3XBH.
- Hit a two-run HR on 5/27 vs. San Diego off Matt Strahm, his first HR off a left-handed pitcher since 8/10/18 (snapped a streak of nine straight HRs off RHPs).
- Homered in three straight games (7/5-7, all at Tampa Bay) for the second time in his career (also 7/28-30/14)…hit a three-run HR in the 11th inning on 7/5 and a solo HR in the second inning on 7/6.
- Missed nine games on the 10-day injured list from 7/25 (retro. to 7/22) - 8/2 with left knee inflammation…was his first stint on the I.L. since 2012.
- Over his final 46 games of the season (from 8/4), 28 of his 44H went for extra-bases (13 doubles, 2 triples, 13HR)…had at least 1XBH in a career-best five straight games from 8/4-9 (4 doubles, 2HR).
- Was ejected by HP umpire Chris Segal in the top of the fourth inning on 8/9 at Toronto…was his fifth career ejection and first since 9/9/18.
- Hit a bases-clearing triple in the first inning of Game 2 vs. Baltimore on 8/12, the first by a Yankee since Jacoby Ellsbury on 8/6/17 at Cleveland…collected his 500th career RBI on the hit.
- Was ejected in the bottom of the sixth inning of 8/17 win vs. Cleveland…was his sixth career ejection and second of the season.
- Tied for second in the Majors (tied for first in the AL) with 10HR in September (trailed only the Mets' Pete Alonso), his highest total in a calendar month in his career (previous: 9HR in May 2017)…in 129 September games over the previous six seasons (2013-18), hit just 6HR while slugging .357.
- Led off the ninth inning of 9/1 win vs. Oakland with a game-tying HR…marked his seventh career game-tying or go-ahead HR in the ninth inning or later and first since 5/29/18 vs. Houston (two-run game-tying HR off Devenski in the ninth).
- Stole his 10th base of the season on 9/7 at Boston, his 11th season with double-digit steals (2008-11,'13-19).
- Homered in the first and second innings on 9/10 at Detroit, his eighth career multi-HR game and first of 2019.
- Collected his second multi-HR game of the road trip on 9/14 at Toronto…his 5RBI in the game were a season high and his most in a single game since 6/30/17 at Houston (6RBI).
- In nine postseason games, hit .176 (6-for-34) with 4R, 1HR and 4RBI…hit a solo HR in ALDS Game 1 vs. Minnesota, his second career playoff HR (also a solo HR in the 2017 AL Wild Card Game vs. Minnesota).
- Signed a one-year contract for the 2020 season with a club option for 2021 on 1/11/20.

2018

- Hit .236 (125-for-530) with 95R, 20 doubles, 7 triples, 12HR, 45RBI and 16SB in 140 games (101 starts in LF, 29 in CF) with the Yankees…was a finalist for the AL Gold Glove Award in LF.
- Hit three leadoff HRs (5/26 vs. Los Angeles-AL, 5/29 vs. Houston, 7/7 at Toronto)…had two multi-HR games (5/29 vs. Houston and 7/12 at Cleveland).
- Turned 35 years old on 8/24…was the oldest player in the Majors to make at least 100 outfield starts in 2018.
- According to FanGraphs, was the second-most valuable base runner in the Majors…with 16SB in 18 attempts (88.9%), was third-highest SB success rate in the AL (min. 15 att.).
- Hit solo HR in 3/29 Opening Day win…was his second career O.D. homer (also 4/6/15 vs. Toronto).
- Hit 4HR over a 10-game span from 5/26-6/8 after hitting just 1HR over his first 43 games of the season.
- Hit leadoff HR in 5/26 loss vs. Los Angeles-AL…was his first HR since the Yankees' season opener on 3/29 at Toronto, snapping a 159AB homerless stretch.
- In 5/29 win vs. Houston, hit his 13th career leadoff HR and a ninth-inning, game-tying two-run HR, collecting his sixth career multi-HR game (first since 5/30/17 at Baltimore)…according to STATS, became the second Yankee ever to hit a leadoff HR and a game-tying or go-ahead HR in the ninth inning or later in the same game, joining Snuffy Stirnweiss, who did so with a go-ahead HR in the 10th inning on 8/27/47 at St. Louis.
- Missed five games from 6/17-21 with right knee soreness.
- Played in all 11 games on the Yankees' road trip from 7/6-15, hitting 4HR with 12RBI…prior to the trip, had just 4HR and 8RBI over his previous 36 games (5/11-7/4) and 0RBI over his prior 17 games (6/9-7/4).
- Hit leadoff HR on the first pitch of the game (his first such leadoff HR) in 7/7 win at Toronto.
- His steal of second base in 7/11 win at Baltimore was the 250th stolen base of his career, surpassing Hal Chase (249) for fourth place on the Yankees all-time list.
- Collected his 252nd career stolen base in the first inning on 8/18 vs. Toronto, surpassing Willie Randolph (251) for third place on the Yankees' all-time list.
- Was ejected by HP Umpire Jeremie Rehak (arguing balls/strikes) on 9/9 at Seattle following his ninth-inning strikeout.
- Appeared in all five of the Yankees' playoff games (0-for-8, 1R, 1RBI, 3BB, 1SF).

2017

- Hit .264 (157-for-594) with 96R, 26 doubles, 4 triples, 21HR, 63RBI and 23SB in 151 games (116 starts in LF, 18 in CF, 5 at DH) with the Yankees…hit five leadoff HRs (4/29 vs. Baltimore, 5/30 at Baltimore, 7/23 at Seattle, 7/28 vs. Tampa Bay, 9/28 vs. Tampa Bay)…the Yankees went 16-2 when he homered, winning each of the first 16 such games…became the fifth Yankee to hit 20HR from the leadoff spot in a single season (seventh time) and first since Johnny Damon (24HR) in 2006.
- Became the 13th Yankee with at least 20HR and 20SB in a single season, joining Alex Rodriguez (3x), Rickey Henderson (2x), Derek Jeter (2x), Alfonso Soriano (2x), Bobby Abreu (1x), Bobby Bonds (1x), Johnny Damon (1x), Curtis Granderson (1x), Roberto Kelly (1x), Mickey Mantle (1x), Paul O'Neill (1x) and Roy White (1x).
- Each of his first 13RBI of the season came via the HR (7HR)…overall, 31 of his 63RBI came via the HR.
- Collected three double-digit hitting streaks after not having any from 2012-16…had three from 2008-11.
- Had 12 outfield assists, tied for fourth-most in the Majors.
- Reached on a throwing error in 4/12 win vs. Tampa Bay and was removed from the game with a bruised jaw and strained neck following a collision with Weeks at 1B on the play (missed one game).
- Hit leadoff HR and three-run HR and was 2-for-4 in 4/29 win vs. Baltimore…was his third career multi-HR game, first since 9/12/15 vs. Toronto (G2)…was his first leadoff HR since 8/31/14 at Toronto and his first homer overall since 7/30/16 at Tampa Bay, snapping a 261AB homerless stretch…his 66-game streak without a HR was the second-longest in his career (84G from 7/5/10-4/19/11)…snapped an 18G stretch without an RBI to begin the season.
- His 21RBI in May were his most in any calendar month and his 9HR and 23R were his second-highest (10HR in Sept. 2019, 27R in June 2015)…hit .327 (33-for-101) with 23R, 6 doubles and 12BB in 26 games during the month.
- Hit game-winning three-run HR with two strikes and two outs in the ninth, with the Yankees trailing 2-0 on 5/5 at Chicago-NL…was the first go-ahead HR by a Yankee with the team trailing in the ninth inning or later on the road since Alex Rodriguez's two-out, three-run HR off Koji Uehara on 9/17/10 at Baltimore.
- Hit leadoff HR in the first and solo HR in the fourth in 5/30 win at Baltimore…was his third multi-HR game of the season, all in a span of 27 games played (4/29-5/30)…had just two multi-HR games over his first 1,085 games.
- Collected his 1,000th career hit with a fourth-inning single on 6/1 at Toronto, becoming the 41st Yankee to reach the milestone.
- Had career-long 14-game hitting streak from 7/18-8/2, batting .317/.397/.583 (19-for-60) with 10R, 2 doubles, 1 triple, 4HR and 7RBI.
- Scored the game-tying run in the ninth after leading off the inning with a triple and hit "walk-off" solo HR to lead off the 11th in 7/27 win vs. Tampa Bay…was his third career "walk-off" HR and fourth career go-ahead HR in the ninth inning or later…became the first Yankee with multiple extra-base hits in the ninth inning or later since Raúl Ibañez did it twice in 2012—once in the regular season on 9/22/12 vs. Oakland (12th-inning double and 13th-inning HR) and once in the postseason in ALDS Game 3 vs. Baltimore (ninth-inning HR and 12th-inning HR)…according to STATS Inc., became the first Yankee to score the game-tying run in the ninth inning or later, then hit a "walk-off" homer later in the game since Joe Gordon on 8/11/40 vs. the A's (scored the tying run in the ninth, when Joe DiMaggio singled and homered in the 11th).
- Hit his 10th career leadoff HR (fourth of the season) in 7/28 win vs. Tampa Bay…after hitting a "walk-off" HR on 7/27, became the third Yankee in franchise history with a leadoff HR in the next team game following a "walk-off HR," joining Roberto Kelly (8/5-6/90, both vs. Cleveland) and Joe Gordon (8/12/40 vs. Philadelphia, 8/13/40 vs. Boston).

- Hit ninth-inning "walk-off" single in 7/29 win vs. Tampa Bay…was his eighth career "walk-off" hit and second in three days…according to *ESPN Stats & Info*, became the first Yankees player with two "walk-off" hits in the same series since he did so on 8/9/13 and 8/11/13 vs. Detroit.
- Hit his fifth leadoff HR of the season in 9/28 loss vs. Tampa Bay, the first of consecutive homers (also Judge) in the bottom of the first inning…became the first pair of Yankees with back-to-back HRs to lead off a game since Derek Jeter and Curtis Granderson did so on 4/16/12 vs. Minnesota.
- Batted .231 (12-for-52) with 7R, 2 doubles, 1HR and 4RBI in 13 playoff games…hit his first career postseason HR and scored 3R in the Yankees' AL Wild Card win vs. Minnesota…with Aaron Judge, became the seventh set of Yankees teammates to each score at least 3R in a postseason game, and only the second since 1962 (Rodriguez/Matsui/Sheffield in 2004 ALCS Game 3 at Boston)…had two 12-pitch at-bats in ALDS Game 5 at Cleveland, including a two-run single off Indians closer Cody Allen to give the Yankees a 5-2 lead in the ninth inning.

2016
- Hit .261 (143-for-547) with 80R, 22 doubles, 6 triples, 7HR, 41RBI and 16SB in 148 games (137 starts in LF, 2 in CF) with the Yankees.
- Won his first career Gold Glove Award and was named the Wilson Defensive Player of the Year in LF for the first time following the season…was the first Yankees Gold Glove Award winner since 2012 (Teixeira-1B/Canó-2B) and the first Yankees outfielder to win the award since Bernie Williams won four straight from 1997-2000…had nine OF assists, the most by a Yankee since 2011 (Granderson-11/Swisher-9).
- Reached base safely in 22 straight games vs. Boston from 9/3/14-4/29/16, hitting safely in 21 of 22G over the span.
- Hit .323 (30-for-93) with 20R, 4 doubles and 3RBI in 25G in June.
- In his final 99 games of the season (6/3-10/2), hit .282 (109-for-386) with 55R, 17 doubles, 2HR and 29RBI…in his first 49 games (4/5-6/2), batted .211 (34-for-161) with 25R, 5 doubles, 5HR and 12RBI.
- Played in his 1,000th career game in 7/9 win at Cleveland.
- Hit .250 (8-for-32) with 2HR and 5RBI in 12 spring training games…did not play until 3/15 (left wrist).

2015
- Batted .259 (148-for-571) with 94R, 26 doubles, 3 triples, 16HR, 66RBI and 20SB in 151 games (104 starts in LF, 36 in CF) with the Yankees…reached 20SB in a season for the sixth time in his career (2009-11 and '13-15).
- Was selected to his first career All-Star Game after being named by AL/Royals Manager Ned Yost as a replacement for injured OF Alex Gordon on 7/9, becoming just the fifth position player drafted by the Yankees to make the All-Star team as a Yankee, joining Thurman Munson, Don Mattingly, Derek Jeter and Jorge Posada…was 0-for-2 in 7/14 AL win in Cincinnati, pinch-hitting for Adam Jones in the fifth and remaining in the game in LF before moving to CF in the seventh…was originally selected as one of five players on the AL Final Vote.
- Hit his first career Opening Day home run and the 100th Opening Day HR by a Yankee in franchise history (first since Raúl Ibañez on 4/6/12 at Tampa Bay) in 4/6 loss vs. Toronto.
- Missed two games (4/14-15) with bruised right wrist…had an MRI in Tampa on 4/16, reconfirming a bone bruise as previously diagnosed by an X-ray…sustained injury on 4/13 at Baltimore after first inning HP (left game in seventh).
- Hit .351 (39-for-111) with 27R, 11 doubles, 2 triples, 5HR and 18RBI in 26 games in June, leading the Majors in runs, tying for first in doubles and ranking second in hits.
- Was named AL "Player of the Week" for the period from 6/22-28 after batting .500 (13-for-26) with 9R, 4 doubles, 2HR and 6RBI in six games…was his third career weekly honor.
- Hit two-run HR, tied a team record with a career-high 5R and reached safely a career-high six times in 7/28 win at Texas (3-for-4, 3RBI, 3BB)…was the 11th time since 1913 a Yankee had at least 5R and 3RBI in a game.
- Was 0-for-4 in the Yankees' 10/6 AL Wild Card Game loss vs. Houston.

2014
- Batted .256 (142-for-555) with 87R, 25 doubles, 8 triples, 17HR, 58RBI and 21SB in 148 games (120 starts in LF, 20 in CF, one in RF and one at DH) with the Yankees.
- Hit an AL-best five leadoff HRs (7/2 vs. Tampa Bay, 7/13 at Baltimore, 7/29 at Texas, 7/30 at Texas and 8/31 at Toronto), tied with Milwaukee's Carlos Gomez and Colorado's Charlie Blackmon for most such HRs in the Majors…tied Los Angeles-AL's Kole Calhoun for the most HR in the AL out of the leadoff spot in the lineup (17).
- Scored 4R on 3BB without a hit in 4/24 win at Boston…became just the second Yankee in franchise history with at least 4R in a single game without a hit (also Bert Daniels on 5/10/1913 at Detroit, 0-for-3 with 4R)—credit: *Elias*.
- Was named AL "Player of the Week" after batting .478 (11-for-23) with 8R, 3 doubles, 5HR, 7RBI, 5BB and a Major League-leading 1.261 slugging percentage in six games from 7/28-8/3…all of his games during his "Player of the Week"-winning stretch came during the Yankees' six-game road trip to Texas and Boston…became the first player to hit at least .478 with 5HR on one road trip since Mickey Mantle hit .550 (11-for-20) with 8HR on a six-game road trip to Boston and Washington from 6/28-7/3/66 (credit: *Elias*).
- Homered in three consecutive games (7/28-30) for the first time in his career (4HR total over the stretch)…hit two solo HRs—his first career multi-HR game—in 7/28 loss at Texas.
- Hit leadoff HRs on 7/29 and 7/30 at Texas, becoming the third Yankee in 50 years (since 1965) to hit a leadoff HR in consecutive team games (also Chuck Knoblauch, 7/30-31/99, and Derek Jeter, 8/17-18/01).
- Was ejected from 9/2 loss vs. Boston by HP umpire Tim Timmons in the fifth inning (arguing a called third strike)…was his third career ejection (also 7/21/10 vs. Los Angeles-AL and 7/19/13 at Boston).
- Missed six games from 9/6-12 (Game 1) with a lower abdominal strain.
- Hit the 15,000th home run in Yankees franchise history with a fifth-inning solo shot in 9/21 win vs. Toronto.
- Underwent surgery to repair a core muscle injury to his right rectus abdominis muscle on 10/16…the surgery was performed by Dr. William Meyers at the Philadelphia Vincera Institute in Philadelphia.

- Signed a four-year contract extension with the Yankees on 2/24/14, beginning in the 2015 season and extending through 2018, with a club option for 2019.

2013
- Hit .273 (147-for-539) with 81R, 33 doubles, 10 triples, 8HR, 52RBI and 24SB in 145 games (130 starts in CF, one at DH) with the Yankees…was the first Yankee to lead the AL in triples since Hank Bauer and Gil McDougald each had an AL-leading 9 triples in 1957…was the first Yankee since Snuffy Stirnweiss in 1945 with at least 30 doubles, 10 triples and 20SB in a single season.
- Was named AL "Player of the Week" for 6/4-9, batting .520 (13-for-25) with 5R, 5 doubles, 1HR and 6RBI during the stretch…was his first career "Player of the Week" award.
- With his 10th-inning "walk-off" single in 8/9 win vs. Detroit and ninth-inning "walk-off" HR in 8/11 win vs. Detroit, became the first Yankee with two "walk-off" hits in a span of three-days-or-fewer since Claudell Washington in 1988 (credit: *Elias*)…the solo HR was his first career "walk-off" HR.
- Collected his 500th career hit with a fifth-inning single in 8/26 loss at Toronto.
- Did not play in the Yankees' final 15 games of the season (9/13-29) with a left oblique strain…left 9/12 win at Baltimore after the top of the first inning with the injury, which was suffered on a checked swing.

2012
- Was limited to 16 games (8GS in LF) with the Yankees, batting .323 (10-for-31) with 7R, 2 doubles and 3RBI.
- Was placed on the 15-day D.L. on 4/19 (retro. to 4/18) with a right elbow strain…was transferred to the 60-day D.L. on 6/26 and reinstated on 9/25, missing 142 team games…was scratched from the lineup prior to 4/18 loss vs. Minnesota…the injury occurred during 4/17 win vs. Minnesota, on a diving catch to end the third inning.
- Began a rehab assignment with Triple-A Scranton/Wilkes-Barre on 5/8…played in two rehab games before being returned from rehab on 5/10 after experiencing soreness and swelling…played in an additional rehab game with Single-A Charleston on 6/8…was again returned from rehab after experiencing right elbow stiffness.
- Met with Dr. Timothy Kremchek on 6/14, who agreed with the Yankees' previous diagnosis of an elbow muscle strain, bone bruise and joint inflammation which had not fully healed…underwent arthroscopic surgery on the elbow on 7/24, performed by Dr. Christopher Ahmad at NewYork-Presbyterian Hospital.
- Made his first appearance since 4/17 in 9/26 win at Minnesota, entering as a ninth-inning defensive replacement in LF…his pinch-hit at-bat in 10/1 win vs. Boston and pinch-hit single in 10/3 win vs. Boston were his first plate appearance and hit, respectively, since 4/17 vs. Minnesota.
- Appeared in five postseason games for the Yankees, going 0-for-8 with 2SB…started ALCS Game 3 (in LF) and Game 4 (in CF), both at Detroit.

2011
- Hit .259 (132-for-510) with 87R, 19 doubles, 7HR, 36RBI and 60BB in 159 games (124 starts in LF and 10 in CF) with the Yankees…tied for the AL lead and tied for second in the Majors with 49 stolen bases (in 62 attempts).
- Along with Coco Crisp, was the co-recipient of the Negro Leagues Baseball Museum's James "Cool Papa" Bell Award, given annually to the AL and NL leaders in stolen bases…was successful in 44 of his last 51 steal attempts (86.3%), beginning on 5/20, after having just 5SB in his first 11 tries.
- Hit his first career leadoff HR—and the Yankees' only leadoff HR in 2011—in 6/19 win at Chicago-NL.
- Successfully stole a base in 22 straight attempts from 6/25-8/9, the longest such streak by a Yankee since Derek Jeter's 22 in-a-row from 7/20/01-6/2/02 (credit: *Elias*)…*Elias* also notes it was the longest single-season streak by a Yankee since Rickey Henderson's franchise record of 28 straight steals without being caught in 1988.
- Recorded 13SB in July, tied with Rajai Davis for most in the AL for the month…was the first Yankee since 1920 (when the AL began tracking caught stealing) with 13-or-more SB in a calendar month without being caught…his total was the highest for a Yankee in a calendar month since Tony Womack stole 14 bases in May 2005.
- Hit .412 (7-for-17) with 3R, 1 double and 5RBI in the ALDS loss vs. Detroit…tied for team lead in hits for the series.

2010
- Hit .277 (132-for-477) with 97R, 20 doubles, 7 triples, 5HR, 47RBI and 47SB in 150 games (96 starts in LF, 38 in CF) with the Yankees…stole 47 bases in 56 attempts (83.9%).
- Led all Major Leaguers with 4.61 pitches seen per PA…swung at only 7.6% of first pitches, the lowest such mark in the Majors.
- Became the seventh Yankee since 1941 to reach the 40-steal plateau in a season (also Rickey Henderson, Roberto Kelly, Mickey Rivers, Steve Sax, Alfonso Soriano and Snuffy Stirnweiss)…marked the most steals by a Yankee in a season since Rickey Henderson in 1988 (93SB)…recorded 45.6% of the Yankees' 103SB in 2010, the highest percentage by a Yankee since Henderson in 1988 (63.7%, 93-of-147)—credit: *Elias*.
- Stole home on the back end of a double steal in the fourth inning of 4/4 Opening Day loss at Boston…became the first Yankee to steal home since Alex Rodriguez on 7/31/04 vs. Baltimore (also part of a double steal) and the first player to steal home on Opening Day since Oakland's Mike Bordick on 4/6/92 vs. Kansas City (credit: *Elias*).
- Was removed from 6/8 win at Baltimore for PH (Thames) in the eighth with a sore left thumb and missed the next two games…underwent X-rays on 6/9 (results were negative)…was hit by a pitch in 6/27 loss at Los Angeles-NL and left with a bruised right wrist (missed 6/29-7/1)…hit .233 (56-for-240) over the remainder of the season.
- Played all 20 innings in 10/2 doubleheader at Boston…had 2SB in Game 1 and a career-high-tying 3SB in Game 2, becoming the first player in franchise history to steal five bases in a single day (credit: *Elias*).
- Underwent surgery on 12/8/10 to have inflamed tissue removed from his right wrist…the procedure was performed by Dr. Melvin Rosenwasser at NewYork-Presbyterian Hospital.

2009
- Hit .270 (67-for-248) with 48R, 3HR, 23RBI and 26SB in 108 games (63 starts in CF) with the Yankees…went 26-for-31 in stolen base attempts (83.9%), ranking third among Major League rookies in stolen bases…became the third Yankees rookie since 1960 to steal at least 26 bases in a season, joining Alfonso Soriano (43SB in 2001) and Willie Randolph (37SB in 1976).
- Hit his first Major League home run—a two-run HR in the second inning—and was 2-for-3 with 2R, 1 triple, 3RBI and 1BB in 5/13 win at Toronto…along with Ramiro Peña, became the first pair of Yankees rookies to both triple in the same game since 8/31/70, when Thurman Munson and Johnny Ellis did so off Mike Cuellar—credit: *Elias*.
- Hit an inside-the-park solo HR and tripled in 5/15 win vs. Minnesota after entering defensively in the fourth in CF when Johnny Damon was ejected…was the first inside-the-park HR by a Yankee since Ricky Ledee on 8/29/99 vs. Seattle…was the fifth Yankees rookie since 1969 with an inside-the-park HR (Johnny Ellis-1969, Deion Sanders-1990, Derek Jeter-1996 and Ricky Ledee-1999).
- Homered and was 5-for-6 in 6/26 win at the Mets…was the third Yankees rookie in club history with at least 5H and 1HR in the same game, joining Joe DiMaggio in 1936 (5H, 1HR) and Shane Spencer in 1998 (5H, 2HR).
- Was placed on the 15-day D.L. from 7/26-9/7 with a fractured left thumb (missed 40 team games).
- Appeared in 14 of the Yankees' postseason games, going 2-for-13 with 3R and 1SB…started the final two games (WS Games 5 and 6) in CF when Melky Cabrera was removed from the roster with a hamstring strain.
- Won the James P. Dawson Award, given by the BBWAA to the most outstanding Yankees rookie in spring training.

2008
- Saw his first Major League action, hitting .228 (29-for-117) with 5 doubles, 2 triples, 16RBI and 13SB in 42 games (17 starts in CF, 15 starts in LF) over two stints with the Yankees (6/30-7/25 and 8/15-9/28).
- Was signed to a Major League contract and selected to the Yankees' 25-man active roster from Triple-A Scranton/Wilkes-Barre on 6/30, making his Major League debut that night in a loss vs. Texas and going 0-for-3 with 1SB as the leadoff hitter…according to *Elias*, was the first Yankee to make his Major League debut in the leadoff spot since Roberto Kelly on 7/29/87 vs. Kansas City.
- Was 8-for-8 in SB attempts before his first CS on 9/15 win vs. Chicago-AL…according to *Elias*, was the first Yankee to begin his Major League career with eight straight successful SB attempts since Andy Fox (8-for-8 in 1996).
- Recorded his first Major League hit—a seventh-inning single off Warner Madrigal—and was 1-for-4 with 2R, 1RBI, 1BB and 1SB in 7/2 win vs. Texas, also recording his first run and RBI.
- Notched his first career "walk-off" hit in 7/6 win vs. Boston, going 2-for-5 with 1R, 1RBI and 1SB…became the first Yankee to record a "walk-off" hit in his sixth career game or earlier since Alfonso Soriano (also in his sixth game) in 1999—credit: *Elias*…*Elias* also notes he was the first Yankees rookie to provide a "walk-off" hit vs. Boston since Derek Jeter hit a 10th-inning single off Joe Hudson in a 12-11 Yankees victory on 9/21/96.
- In 94 games with Scranton/WB, hit .296 (101-for-341) with 68R, 12 doubles, 11 triples, 3HR, 32RBI, 70BB, 11SH and 37SB, while recording 27 multi-hit games…led all Yankees farmhands in SB and tied for fourth in BA.
- Hit the first "walk-off" HR in Scranton/WB Yankees history on 4/23 vs. Buffalo, a solo HR in the bottom of the ninth.

2007
- Hit .281 (108-for-384) with 80R, 18 doubles, 8 triples, 1HR and 35RBI in 99 combined games with Double-A Trenton and Triple-A Scranton/Wilkes-Barre…led Yankees minor leaguers with 39SB.
- Began the year at Trenton (54G, .300, 61-for-203, 18SB).
- Was promoted to Scranton/WB on 7/13 and hit .260 (47-for-181)…successfully stole a base in 21-of-24 attempts.
- Following the season, played with the Peoria Javelinas, hitting safely in 24-of-26 contests and leading the Arizona Fall League in runs (27) and stolen bases (16), while ranking second in hits (37), tying for third in walks (17) and placing fifth in batting average (.343)…was named to the 2007 Arizona Fall League Top Prospects Team.

2006
- Hit .298 (134-for-449) with 16 doubles, 8 triples, 35RBI and 58SB in 118 combined games with Single-A Tampa and Double-A Trenton…ranked second among all Yankees prospects in stolen bases and was tied for second in batting average…was selected to the West Division All-Star Team for the Florida State League.
- Played in 27 games with the Peoria Saguaros in the Arizona Fall League, batting .250 (27-for-108) with 6SB.

2005
- Made his professional debut, hitting .284 (80-for-282) with 62R, 5HR, 32RBI and 19SB in 73G with short-season Single-A Staten Island…reached safely in a team-best 24 straight games from 7/17-8/10…hit .235 (4-for-17) in four playoff games for the NYPL Champions.

PERSONAL
- He and his wife, Jessica, have two children, Hunter Thomas and Miller Mack…his father, Jerry, played minor league baseball with the Phillies in the 1970s…growing up, helped work on his father's 2,600-acre farm, which produces corn, soybeans and wheat…played golf and tennis as a child, then played baseball and football in high school.
- Graduated from the College of Charleston and was the highest-drafted player in the school's history after walking on the baseball team…in his senior year at Charleston, led the Cougars with a .447 batting average (122-for-273) and helped guide the team to a 48-15 regular season record and an NCAA tournament berth.
- Was named the winner of the "Heart and Hustle Award" in 2017, an award presented annually by the MLB Players Alumni Association to honor one Major Leaguer who demonstrates a passion for baseball and embodies the values, spirit and tradition of the game…has been named the Yankees' "Heart and Hustle Award" nominee five times in his career (2010, '13-15, '17), most by a Yankee since the award's inception in 2005.

- Was named the Yankees' nominee for the 2017 Roberto Clemente Award, his second nomination (also 2016)…the award recognizes a player from each MLB club who "best represents the game of Baseball through extraordinary character, community involvement, philanthropy and positive contributions, both on and off the field"…three Yankees have won the award since its inception in 1971: Derek Jeter (2009), Don Baylor (1985) and Ron Guidry (1984).
- Wore two pairs of specially designed New Balance cleats (one gold pair, one multi-colored pair) on 9/1/17 vs Boston, which were auctioned off as a fundraiser for Children's Cancer Awareness Month…proceeds from the auction went to Memorial Sloan Kettering Pediatric Center.
- In 2016, he and his wife hosted a surprise Thanksgiving lunch for 100 active duty members of the 15th Airlift Squadron at Charleston Air Force Base in South Carolina.
- Was named the 2014 "Ben Epstein - Dan Castellano 'Good Guy'" award winner by members of the New York chapter of the BBWAA…received his award at the annual writers dinner on 1/24/15 in Manhattan.
- Was named the Yankees' 2014 Hank Aaron Award nominee, recognizing the most outstanding offensive performers in each league…received the Thurman Munson Award in 2014.
- In 2014, became a charter member of the Taylor Hooton Foundation's Advisory Board, made up exclusively of active Major League players…the foundation educates young people about the dangers of appearance and performance enhancing drugs…as an advisory board member, works to create the most effective ways of educating youth about the dangers of anabolic steroids and other appearance and performance enhancing drugs.
- Supports Ronald McDonald House in South Carolina and New York…provides lodging and holiday gifts to families living at the house…in December 2013, bought a puppy named "Gardy" for the Ronald McDonald House that is a therapy dog for the children and families…his wife, Jessica, prepares home-cooked meals that are delivered regularly to families staying at the Ronald McDonald House…took part in the Ronald McDonald House's 30th anniversary campaign…also visits with children at Medical University of South Carolina (MUSC) and Maria Fareri Children's Hospital at Westchester Medical Center in Valhalla, N.Y.
- Supports the Salvation Army and their Angel Tree, providing holiday gifts to children…hosts select groups of children at Yankee Stadium and meets with them before games.
- Has served as an ambassador for the annual Damon Runyon 5K at Yankee Stadium.
- Gave free haircuts to underprivileged kids at Jordan's Barber Shop in the Bronx on 7/8/08…makes regular visits to ailing children at NewYork-Presbyterian Morgan Stanley Children's Hospital.

Gardner's Career Batting Record

Year	Club	AVG	G	AB	R	H	2B	3B	HR	RBI	SH	SF	HP	BB	SO	SB	CS	E	OBP	SLG
2005	Staten Island	.284	73	282	62	80	9	1	5	32	3	5	6	39	49	19	3	0	.377	.376
2006	Tampa	.323	63	232	46	75	12	5	0	22	1	0	2	43	51	30	7	0	.433	.418
	Trenton	.272	55	217	41	59	4	3	0	13	1	4	2	27	39	28	5	0	.352	.318
2007	Trenton	.300	54	203	43	61	14	5	0	17	1	4	0	33	32	18	4	1	.392	.419
	Scranton/WB	.260	45	181	37	47	4	3	1	9	3	0	2	21	43	21	3	2	.343	.331
2008	Scranton/WB	.296	94	341	68	101	12	11	3	32	11	3	1	70	76	37	9	0	.414	.422
	YANKEES	.228	42	127	18	29	5	2	0	16	3	1	2	8	30	13	1	0	.283	.299
2009	YANKEES - a	.270	108	248	48	67	6	6	3	23	6	1	3	26	40	26	5	2	.345	.379
	Scranton/WB	.091	4	11	3	1	0	0	0	0	0	0	0	5	1	3	0	0	.375	.091
2010	YANKEES	.277	150	477	97	132	20	7	5	47	5	3	5	79	101	47	9	1	.383	.379
2011	YANKEES	.259	159	510	87	132	19	8	7	36	8	2	8	60	93	49	13	5	.345	.369
2012	YANKEES - b	.323	16	31	7	10	2	0	0	3	1	0	0	5	7	2	2	0	.417	.387
	Scranton/WB	.600	2	5	1	3	0	1	0	0	0	0	0	2	1	0	0	0	.714	1.000
	Charleston	.333	1	3	1	1	0	0	0	0	0	0	0	0	1	1	0	0	.333	.333
2013	YANKEES	.273	145	539	81	147	33	10	8	52	7	3	8	52	127	24	8	3	.344	.416
2014	YANKEES	.256	148	555	87	142	25	8	17	58	13	6	6	56	134	21	5	2	.327	.422
2015	YANKEES	.259	151	571	94	148	26	3	16	66	8	3	6	68	135	20	5	2	.343	.399
2016	YANKEES	.261	148	547	80	143	22	6	7	41	4	5	8	70	106	16	4	3	.351	.362
2017	YANKEES	.264	151	594	96	157	26	4	21	63	5	3	8	72	122	23	5	0	.350	.428
2018	YANKEES	.236	140	530	95	125	20	7	12	45	4	5	5	65	107	16	2	3	.322	.368
2019	YANKEES - c	.251	141	491	86	123	26	7	28	74	0	3	4	52	108	10	2	1	.325	.503
Minor League Totals		.290	391	1475	302	428	55	29	9	125	20	16	13	240	293	157	31	3	.390	.385
Major League Totals		.260	1499	5220	876	1355	230	68	124	524	64	35	63	613	1110	267	61	22	.342	.401

Selected by the Yankees in the third round of the 2005 First-Year Player Draft.

a – Placed on the 15-day disabled list from July 26 – September 7, 2009 with a left thumb fracture.
b – Placed on the 15-day disabled list on April 19, 2012 (retroactive to April 18) with a right elbow strain…was transferred to the 60-day disabled list on June 26 and reinstated on September 25, 2012.
c – Placed on the 10-day injured list from July 25 (retroactive to July 22) - August 2, 2019 with left knee inflammation.

Gardner's Postseason Record

Year	Club vs. Opp.	AVG	G	AB	R	H	2B	3B	HR	RBI	SH	SF	HP	BB	SO	SB	CS	E	OBP	SLG
2009	NYY vs. MIN (DS)	---	3	0	0	0	0	0	0	0	0	0	0	0	0	1	0	0	---	---
	NYY vs. LAA (CS)	.667	6	3	2	2	0	0	0	0	1	0	0	0	0	0	2	0	.667	.667
	NYY vs. PHI (WS)	.000	5	10	1	0	0	0	0	0	0	0	0	4	0	0	0	0	.000	.000
2010	NYY vs. MIN (DS)	.200	3	10	1	2	0	0	0	1	0	1	0	1	3	1	0	0	.250	.200
	NYY vs. TEX (CS)	.176	6	17	1	3	0	0	0	1	1	0	0	2	5	1	0	0	.263	.176
2011	NYY vs. DET (DS)	.412	5	17	3	7	1	0	0	5	0	0	0	1	4	0	0	0	.444	.471
2012	NYY vs. BAL (DS)	---	2	0	0	0	0	0	0	0	0	0	0	0	0	0	0	0	---	---
	NYY vs. DET (CS)	.000	3	8	0	0	0	0	0	0	0	0	0	0	1	2	0	0	.000	.000
2015	NYY vs. HOU (WC)	.000	1	4	0	0	0	0	0	0	0	0	0	3	0	0	0	0	.000	.000
2017	NYY vs. MIN (WC)	.500	1	4	3	2	0	0	1	1	0	0	0	1	0	0	0	0	.600	1.250
	NYY vs. CLE (DS)	.286	5	21	2	6	1	0	0	2	1	1	0	1	3	1	1	0	.304	.333
	NYY vs. HOU (CS)	.148	7	27	2	4	1	0	0	1	0	0	1	1	9	0	0	0	.207	.185
2018	NYY vs. OAK (WC)	---	1	0	0	0	0	0	0	0	0	0	0	0	0	0	0	0	---	---
	NYY vs. BOS (DS)	.000	4	8	1	0	0	0	0	1	0	1	0	3	1	0	0	0	.250	.000
2019	NYY vs. MIN (DS)	.250	3	12	3	3	0	0	1	3	0	0	1	1	5	0	0	0	.357	.500
	NYY vs. HOU (CS)	.136	6	22	1	3	0	0	0	1	0	0	0	2	10	0	0	0	.208	.136
Wild Card Game Totals		.250	3	8	3	2	0	0	1	1	0	0	0	1	3	0	0	0	.333	.625
LDS Totals		.265	25	68	10	18	2	0	1	12	1	3	1	7	16	3	1	0	.329	.338
LCS Totals		.156	28	77	6	12	1	0	0	3	2	0	1	5	25	3	2	0	.217	.169
World Series Totals		.000	5	10	1	0	0	0	0	0	0	0	0	4	0	0	0	0	.000	.000
POSTSEASON TOTALS		.196	61	163	20	32	3	0	2	16	3	3	2	13	48	6	3	0	.260	.252

Gardner's All-Star Game Record

Year	Club, Site	AVG	G	AB	R	H	2B	3B	HR	RBI	SH	SF	HP	BB	SO	SB	CS	E	OBP	SLG
2015	NYY, Cincinnati	.000	1	2	0	0	0	0	0	0	0	0	0	0	2	0	0	0	.000	.000
All-Star Game Totals		.000	1	2	0	0	0	0	0	0	0	0	0	0	2	0	0	0	.000	.000

Gardner's Career Fielding Record

Position	PCT	G	PO	A	E	TC
Outfield	.992	1449	2795	75	22	2892

Gardner's Career Home Run Chart

MULTI-HOMER GAMES: 9. **TWO-HOMER GAMES:** 9, last on 9/14/19 at TOR. **GRAND SLAMS:** 4, last on 4/17/19 vs. BOS (Ryan Brasier). **PINCH-HIT HR:** None. **INSIDE-THE-PARK HR:** 2, last on 7/4/10 vs. TOR (Brandon Morrow). **WALK-OFF HR:** 3, last on 7/27/17 vs. TB (Andrew Kittredge). **LEADOFF HR:** 15, last on 4/10/19 at HOU (Colin McHugh).

Gardner's Career Bests and Streaks

HITS: 5, 6/26/09 at NYM. **RUNS:** 5, 7/28/15 at TEX. **2B:** 3, 5/22/19 at BAL. **3B:** 1 - 68 times (last on 8/26/19 at SEA). **HR:** 2 - 9 times (last on 9/14/19 at TOR). **RBI:** 6 - 2 times (last on 6/30/17 at HOU). **BB:** 4 - 2 times (last on 7/7/17 vs. MIL). **SO:** 4 - 2 times (last on 9/12/19 at DET-G2). **SB:** 3 - 2 times (last on 10/2/10 at BOS-G2). **HIT STREAK:** 14g, 7/18-8/2/17. **WALK-OFF HITS:** 8, last on 7/29/17 vs. TB (single).

Player of the Month: None   **Player of the Week:** 3 times, last: 6/22-28/15   **Rookie of the Month:** None

Home Runs in First At-Bat with the Yankees
Since 1961 (Expansion Era)

John A. Miller .... 9/11/1966 at BOS^	Nick Green .... 7/2/2006 vs. NYM*
Graig Nettles .... 4/6/1973 at BOS*†	Wilson Betemit .... 8/2/2007 vs. CWS
Jimmy Wynn .... 4/7/1977 vs. MIL†	Cody Ransom .... 8/17/2008 vs. KC**
Barry Foote .... 4/28/1981 at DET	Curtis Granderson .... 4/4/2010 at BOS†
Glenallen Hill .... 7/24/2000 at BAL	Andruw Jones .... 4/5/2011 vs. MIN
Ron Coomer .... 4/6/2002 vs. TB	Mark Reynolds .... 8/16/2013 at BOS
Marcus Thames .... 6/10/2002 vs. ARI^	Tyler Austin .... 8/13/2016 vs. TB (b2b w/ Judge)^
Todd Zeile .... 4/2/2003 at TOR	Aaron Judge ..... 8/13/2016 vs. TB (b2b w/ Austin)^
Bubba Crosby .... 4/9/2004 vs. CWS	Giancarlo Stanton .... 3/29/2018 at TOR†
Andy Phillips .... 9/26/2004 at BOS^	

*All players except Nettles and Green homered in their first plate appearance as a Yankee.
**Ransom also homered in his second PA (and AB) with the Yankees, and is the only Yankee ever to accomplish the feat.
†Opening Day / ^First career plate appearance

DOMINGO GERMÁN • RHP

#55

HT: 6-2 • **WT:** 181 • **BATS:** R • **THROWS:** R
BIRTHDATE: 8/4/92 • **OPENING DAY AGE:** 27
BIRTHPLACE: San Pedro de Macorís, D.R.
RESIDES: San Pedro de Macorís, D.R.
M.L. SERVICE: 2 years, 17 days

STATUS
- Was signed by the Yankees as a minor league free agent on December 11, 2015.

CAREER NOTES
- Won 18 games in 2019, nine times as many wins as he totaled in 28 games (14 starts) in his first two Major League seasons (2017-18).
- Has held opponents to a .201 BA (86-for-427) at Yankee Stadium compared to .258 (131-for-507) on the road.
- Has a 2.48 ERA (40.0IP, 11ER) in 17 career relief appearances…has thrown 15.1 scoreless innings (8H, 3BB, 20K) over his last six relief appearances (since 5/1/18).

2019
- Made 27 appearances (24 starts), going 18-4 with a 4.03 ERA (143.0IP, 125H, 69R/64ER, 39BB, 153K, 30HR)…posted a 2.0 WAR and 4.72 FIP (FanGraphs)…made his first career Opening Day roster…held opponents to a .228 BA (125-for-548); LH .242 (75-for-310, 20HR); RH .210 (50-for-238, 10HR).
- His 18 wins were tied for fourth-most in the Majors…were the second-highest total by a Yankee in eight seasons (since 2012), behind only Luis Severino (19-8 in 2018).
- Led the Majors with a .818 winning percentage…is tied for the sixth-highest winning percentage in Yankees history (min. 20 decisions), the highest since Roger Clemens (20-3, .870) in 2001.
- In 24 starts, went 16-4 with a 4.28 ERA (134.2IP, 122H, 69R/64ER, 37BB, 142K, 30HR)…made three relief appearances, retiring 26-of-32 batters faced in 8.1 scoreless innings (3H, 2BB, 11K, 1HP).
- Held right-handed batters to a .210/.265/.387 (50-for-238) line…was the AL's sixth-lowest BA and was the fifth-lowest OBP (min. 250 RHB faced).
- Went 8-1 with a 2.26 ERA (63.2IP, 45H, 17R/16ER, 19BB, 76K, 10HR) in 12 games (10 starts) at Yankee Stadium…posted the AL's second-lowest home ERA (min. 60.0IP), behind Cleveland's Mike Clevinger (1.78)…tied for the fourth-best home record in the Majors (min. 7 decisions)…opposing batters hit .195 (45-for-231) at Yankee Stadium, the fourth-lowest opponents' BA at home in the AL (min. 200AB).
- Was 10-3 with a 5.45 ERA (79.1IP, 48ER) in 15 road games (14 starts)…tied for second in the Majors in road wins despite having the fifth-highest road ERA (min. 75.0IP)…were the most road wins by a Yankee since CC Sabathia went 11-5 in 2011…won his first five road starts, the fourth Yankee since 1965 to accomplish the feat, joining Aaron Small (five) in 2005, Roger Clemens (six) in 2003 and Ron Guidry (five) in 1982.
- Earned at least four wins in four different months, going 5-1 in April, 4-0 in May, 4-0 in July and 4-1 in August.
- Went 5-0 with a 4.63 ERA (35.0IP, 18ER) in six Sunday starts.
- Went 10-1 with a 3.74 ERA (67.1IP, 28ER) in 12 starts vs. the AL East…tied for the second-most wins vs. one division in 2019: Justin Verlander, 13-2 vs. AL West; Stephen Strasburg, 10-1 vs. NL East; Gerrit Cole, 10-2 vs. AL West.
- On 4/7 at Baltimore, earned his first career road win (6.0IP, 2H, 2ER, 2BB, 3K), in his eighth road start…took a no-hitter into the sixth before allowing a one-out single to Hanser Alberto.
- Was the third Yankees pitcher to complete at least 5.0IP and allow 2H-or-fewer in each of his first two appearances in a season, joining Pascual Perez (first 2GS in 1991) and Tom Hughes (first 2G in 1910).
- Won a career-best six consecutive starts from 4/23-5/21.
- Was the second Yankees pitcher since 1981 to earn seven wins in the team's first 38 games of the season (also Mike Mussina-2003).
- Went 9-1 in his first 10 games (nine starts)…was the first Yankees pitcher to record nine wins in his first 10 appearances of a season since Tommy John went 9-0 in his first 10 games (nine starts) in 1979.
- Went 9-1 with a 3.43 ERA (60.1IP, 23ER) in 11 games (10 starts) through the end of May…according to *Elias*, became the fourth Yankees pitcher ever to earn at least nine wins before the start of June (Herb Pennock-10 in 1926, Tommy John-9 in 1979, and Jack Chesbro-9 in 1904).
- Was on the 10-day I.L. from 6/9 (retroactive to 6/8) – 7/3 with a left hip flexor strain…made a rehab start with Triple-A Scranton/WB on 6/27 vs. Buffalo (ND, 4.0IP, 4H, 4ER, 2BB, 5K, 2HR, 65 pitches/41 strikes).

- Won a career-high seven consecutive decisions over eight starts from 7/3-8/13, his first eight starts off the I.L.
- On 8/25 at Los Angeles-NL, defeated Clayton Kershaw to earn his 17th win (6.0IP, 1ER)...at the time, Kershaw (13-2) and Germán (16-3) ranked first and second, respectively, in the Majors in winning percentage.
- Led the Majors in wins through the end of August, going 17-3 in 24 games (23 starts).
- Made his final two appearances out of the bullpen, on 9/12 at Detroit (4.0IP, 0R) and 9/18 vs. Los Angeles-AL (2.1IP, 0R).
- Went 1-2 with a 4.11 ERA (15.1IP, 16H, 8R/7ER, 2BB, 22K, 3HR) in five games (three starts) this spring...tied for sixth in the Grapefruit League in strikeouts, second-most on the Yankees (Tanaka-23K).
- On 9/19, was placed on administrative leave by the Office of the Commissioner of Baseball and was placed on the restricted list...on 1/2/20, accepted an 81-game suspension under Major League Baseball's Joint Domestic Violence, Sexual Assault and Child Abuse Policy (served the first 18 games during the 2019 season).

GERMÁN'S 2019 PITCHING LINES

Date/Opp	Score	W/L	IP	H	R	ER	HR	BB	K	NP/S	ERA	Left game
4/1 vs. DET*	3-1	W	5.0	1	1	0	0	5	7	79/44	0.00	Leading 3-1
4/7 at BAL	15-3	W	6.0	2	2	2	0	2	3	89/60	1.64	Leading 9-0
4/13 vs. CWS	4-0	W	2.0	0	0	0	0	0	4	25/19	1.38	*relief*
4/18 at KC	1-6	L	6.0	6	3	3	2	0	9	88/62	2.37	Trailing 3-1
4/23 at LAA	7-5	W	6.2	4	1	0	0	1	5	99/65	1.75	Leading 6-1
4/28 at SF	11-5	W	6.0	5	4	4	0	1	4	87/63	2.56	Leading 8-4
5/5 vs. MIN*	4-1	W	6.2	4	1	1	0	3	7	**108/69**	2.35	Leading 4-1
5/10 at TB	4-3	W	5.0	5	3	3	2	2	5	84/54	2.70	Leading 4-3
5/15 vs. BAL (G2)	3-1	W	7.0	6	1	1	0	1	8	85/64	2.50	Leading 3-1
5/21 at BAL	11-4	W	5.0	5	3	2	1	1	5	93/62	2.60	Leading 11-3
5/26 at KC	7-8 (10)	ND	5.0	**9**	**7**	**7**	**4**	0	6	84/55	3.43	Trailing 7-4
6/1 vs. BOS	5-3	ND	3.2	6	3	3	1	2	8	87/54	3.66	Tied 3-3
6/7 at CLE	2-5	L	6.0	6	4	4	2	1	6	92/60	3.86	Trailing 4-2
7/3 at NYM*	5-1	W	6.0	5	1	1	1	0	6	80/56	3.67	Leading 5-1
7/12 vs. TOR*	4-0	W	6.0	3	0	0	0	0	7	78/54	3.40	Leading 4-0
7/18 vs. TB (G1)	6-2	W	6.0	4	2	2	2	2	5	90/56	3.38	Leading 6-2
7/23 at MIN*	14-12 (10)	ND	3.2	**9**	**8**	**8**	3	2	3	82/50	4.03	Trailing 8-2
7/28 at BOS*	9-6	W	5.1	4	3	3	1	1	**9**	77/57	4.08	Leading 6-3
8/3 vs. BOS (G1)	9-2	W	**7.0**	5	2	2	2	0	7	97/55	3.98	Leading 9-2
8/8 at TOR	12-6	W	5.0	8	4	3	2	1	3	90/64	4.05	Leading 10-4
8/13 vs. BAL	8-3	W	**7.0**	5	2	2	2	1	7	93/65	3.96	Leading 8-2
8/20 at OAK*	2-6	L	5.1	8	6	5	2	2	7	99/62	4.15	Trailing 6-1
8/25 at LAD*	5-1	W	6.0	5	1	1	1	2	5	85/53	4.03	Leading 3-1
8/31 vs. OAK*	4-3 (11)	ND	5.0	4	2	2	1	3	5	90/55	4.01	Tied 2-2
9/6 at BOS	1-6	L	4.1	3	5	5	1	4	5	92/56	4.21	Trailing 4-1
9/12 at DET (G2)	6-4	W	4.0	2	0	0	0	0	5	50/37	4.09	*relief*
9/18 vs. LAA	2-3	--	2.1	1	0	0	0	2	2	44/25	4.03	*relief*
Totals (27G/24GS)		**18-4**	**143.0**	**125**	**69**	**64**	**30**	**39**	**153**		**4.03**	
As Starter (24GS)		16-4	134.2	122	69	64	30	37	142		4.28	
As Reliever (3G)		2-0	8.1	3	0	0	0	2	11		0.00	

*start came after a Yankees loss / **Bold**=season high

2018
- Went 2-6 with a 5.57 ERA (85.2IP, 81H, 55R/53ER, 33BB, 102K, 15HR) in 21 games (14 starts) over two stints with the Yankees (4/7-7/20 and 9/18-30)...opponents hit .242 (81-for-335, 15HR); LH .256 (42-for-164, 8HR), RH .228 (39-for-171, 7HR).
- Had a 2-5 record and a 6.19 ERA (68.1IP, 47ER) in 14 starts, completing 6.0IP six times.
- Went 0-1 with a 3.12 ERA (17.1IP, 6ER) in seven relief appearances.
- Became the first pitcher in Yankees history to record at least 3K in seven consecutive relief appearances (9/20/17-5/1/18)...had 25K in 18.0IP (14H, 7ER, 9BB) over the span.
- Made his first career Major League start on 5/6 vs. Cleveland, tossing 6.0 hitless, scoreless innings with 9K and 2BB in a no-decision...retired his first 11 batters faced before walking José Ramírez with two outs in the fourth...overall, retired 18-of-20 batters...per Elias, was the first Major League pitcher since the mound was moved to 60'6" in 1893 to throw at least 6.0 hitless innings with at least 9K in his first career start...was the first Yankee ever to record a hitless start of at least 6.0IP in his first career start...was the fourth Yankee to record at least 9K in his first career start, joining Hideki Irabu (9K on 7/10/97 vs. Detroit), Dan Tripple (10K on 9/25/1915-G2 vs. Cleveland) and Russ Ford (9K on 4/21/1910 at Philadelphia-AL).
- Recorded 9K and 0BB in 6/9 no-decision at the Mets (6.0IP, 5H, 3ER, 2HR, 1HP, 1WP)...became the seventh rookie in Yankees history with a start with 0BB and at least 9K...went 0-for-1 with 1BB at the plate, his first professional plate appearances.
- Earned his first career win on 6/14 vs. Tampa Bay and set a career high with 10K (6.0IP, 5H, 3ER, 2BB, 10K, 1HR, 1WP)...recorded 26 swinging strikes, tied for the fifth-highest single-game total by a Major League pitcher in 2018 (James Paxton-31, Max Scherzer-29, Jacob deGrom-27, Paxton-27).
- In 6/19 win vs. Seattle, allowed 2H and 0BB and set a career high with 7.0IP (2R/1ER, 9K, 1HR)...was his third straight start with at least 9K, matching Luis Severino (3G, 8/28-9/9/17) for the longest such streak by a Yankee since 2012...became the first Yankees rookie to record multiple starts with 0BB and at least 9K in a single season.
- Combined to make four minor league appearances (three starts) with Triple-A Scranton/Wilkes-Barre, the GCL Yankees East and Single-A Tampa, going 0-1 with a 7.56 ERA (8.1IP, 7ER)...missed a month on the minor league D.L....also made two postseason starts with the RailRiders and was 0-1 with a 4.76 ERA (5.2IP, 3ER).

2017
- Went 0-1 with a 3.14 ERA (14.1IP, 5ER) in seven relief appearances over four stints with the Yankees in his first Major League action (6/11, 6/15-7/4, 7/16 and 9/17-10/1).
- Made his Major League debut in 6/11 win vs. Baltimore, tossing 2.2 scoreless innings (2H, 1BB, 1K)…recorded his first career strikeout to end the seventh inning (Jonathan Schoop, swinging).
- Tossed 4.0 shutout innings in 6/17 loss at Oakland (4H, 3BB, 6K)…became the first reliever in Yankees history to strike out at least six batters and not allow a run within one of his first two Major League games…three Yankees starters did so in their second career outing: Jonathan Loaisiga (6K in 5.0IP on 6/15/18 vs. Tampa Bay), Phil Hughes (6K in 6.1IP on 5/1/07 at Texas) and Bill Burbach (7K in 9.0 shutout innings on 4/20/69-G2 vs. Detroit)…with Masahiro Tanaka (10K in 4.0IP), became the fourth pair of Yankees teammates to both tally at least 6K in a nine-inning game, joining Rick Rhoden (7K)/Tim Stoddard (6K) on 8/23/87 at Oakland; Doc Medich (6K)/Lindy McDaniel (6K) on 4/23/73 at Milwaukee; and Stan Williams (6K)/Steve Hamilton (6K) on 7/17/64 vs. Cleveland.
- In 20 games (19 starts) between Double-A Trenton (6GS) and Triple-A Scranton/Wilkes-Barre (14G/13GS), combined to go 8-6 with a 2.88 ERA (109.1IP, 35ER) and 119K…in two postseason starts with the RailRiders, went 1-0 with a 3.65 ERA (12.1IP, 5ER) and 10K.
- Following the season, played for Toros del Este of the Dominican Winter League, posting a 21.60 ERA (1.2IP, 4ER) and 4K in three relief appearances.

2016
- Began the season on the minor league disabled list recovering from "Tommy John" surgery performed on 3/31/15…was reinstated from the D.L. on 6/26 and assigned to Single-A Charleston…in five starts with the RiverDogs, went 1-1 with a 3.12 ERA (26.0IP, 9ER).
- Was promoted to Single-A Tampa on 7/24 and went 0-2 with a 3.04 ERA (23.2IP, 8ER) in five starts.
- Was added to the Yankees' 40-man roster on 11/4/16.

2015
- Missed the entire season after undergoing "Tommy John" surgery on his right elbow on 3/31…the surgery was performed by Yankees Head Team Physician Dr. Christopher Ahmad at NewYork-Presbyterian Hospital…was placed on the minor league disabled list on 4/9…was reinstated from the minor league D.L., recalled from Single-A Tampa and placed on the Yankees' 60-day disabled list on 9/1…was reinstated on 11/4.
- Was non-tendered by the Yankees on 12/3 before signing with the club as a minor league free agent on 12/11.

2014
- Spent the entire season with Single-A Greensboro, going 9-3 with a 2.48 ERA (123.1IP, 34ER) and 113K in 25 starts for the Grasshoppers.
- Led all Marlins minor leaguers in ERA and ranked fourth in strikeouts…finished second in the South Atlantic League in ERA and third in WHIP (1.14)…his 1.82 BB/9.0IP ratio (25BB/123.1IP) was fourth-lowest among SAL starters, and his 8.25 K/9.0IP ratio (113K/123.1IP) ranked fifth.
- Was named to the All-Star Futures Game World Team, striking out two batters in 1.0 scoreless inning of relief in the 3-2 Team USA win at Target Field.
- Was added to the Marlins' 40-man roster on 11/20/14.
- Was acquired by the Yankees from the Miami Marlins along with RHP Nathan Eovaldi and INF Garrett Jones in exchange for RHP David Phelps and INF Martín Prado on 12/19/14.

2013
- Combined with the GCL Marlins and short-season Single-A Batavia to go 5-3 with a 1.61 ERA (67.0IP, 12ER) in 13 starts.
- Began the season with the GCL Marlins, going 3-0 with a 1.38 ERA (26.0IP, 4ER) in five starts.
- Was promoted to Batavia on 7/23 and went 2-3 with a 1.76 ERA (41.0IP, 8ER) in eight starts.

2012
- Went 2-0 with a 1.61 ERA (22.1IP, 4ER) and 29K in 13 relief appearances for the GCL Marlins.

2011
- Made eight appearances (six starts) with the DSL Marlins, going 2-1 with a 1.82 ERA (34.2IP, 7ER)…posted a 10.38 K/9.0IP ratio (40K/34.2IP).

2010
- Made his professional debut, going 2-3 with six saves and a 3.69 ERA (46.1IP, 19ER) in 18 relief appearances with the DSL Marlins.

PERSONAL
- Full name is Domingo Polanco Germán (pronounced "hurr-MAHN").

Germán's Career Pitching Record

Year	Club	W	L	ERA	G	GS	CG	SHO	SV	IP	H	R	ER	HR	HP	BB	SO	WP	BK
2010	DSL Marlins	2	3	3.69	18	0	0	0	6	46.1	29	22	19	1	7	27	43	4	0
2011	DSL Marlins	2	1	1.82	8	6	0	0	0	34.2	38	19	7	0	6	13	40	5	0
2012	GCL Marlins	2	0	1.61	13	0	0	0	0	22.1	17	5	4	0	0	16	29	2	0
2013	GCL Marlins	3	0	1.38	5	5	0	0	0	26.0	15	4	4	1	2	5	27	0	0
	Batavia	2	3	1.76	8	8	0	0	0	41.0	33	14	8	0	4	5	34	2	1
2014	Greensboro - a	9	3	2.48	25	25	0	0	0	123.1	116	43	34	6	11	25	113	9	1
2015							Did Not Pitch - b												
2016	Charleston	1	1	3.12	5	5	0	0	0	26.0	15	11	9	2	2	2	18	2	0
	Tampa	0	2	3.04	5	5	0	0	0	23.2	26	10	8	1	1	9	20	4	1
2017	Trenton	1	4	3.00	6	6	1	0	0	33.0	32	13	11	4	2	10	38	2	0
	Scranton/WB	7	2	2.83	14	13	0	0	0	76.1	59	26	24	5	6	22	81	4	0
	YANKEES	0	1	3.14	7	0	0	0	0	14.1	11	6	5	1	0	9	18	3	0
2018	YANKEES	2	6	5.57	21	14	0	0	0	85.2	81	55	53	15	5	33	102	7	1
	Scranton/WB	0	0	18.00	1	1	0	0	0	1.0	2	2	2	1	0	0	0	0	0
	GCL Yankees East	0	1	33.75	1	0	0	0	0	1.1	3	5	5	1	0	2	2	2	0
	Tampa	0	0	0.00	2	2	0	0	0	6.0	3	1	0	0	0	2	8	0	0
2019	YANKEES - c, d	18	4	4.03	27	24	0	0	0	143.0	125	69	64	30	5	39	153	5	0
	Scranton/WB	0	0	9.00	1	1	0	0	0	4.0	4	4	4	2	0	2	5	0	0
Minor League Totals		29	20	2.69	112	77	1	0	6	465.0	392	179	139	24	41	140	458	36	3
Major League Totals		20	11	4.52	55	38	0	0	0	243.0	217	130	122	46	10	81	273	15	1

Signed by the Florida Marlins as a non-drafted free agent on August 8, 2009.

a - Acquired by the Yankees from the Miami Marlins along with RHP Nathan Eovaldi and INF Garrett Jones in exchange for RHP David Phelps and INF Martin Prado on December 19, 2014.
b - Placed on the 60-day disabled list from September 1 – November 4, 2015 recovering from "Tommy John" surgery.
c - Placed on the 10-day injured list from June 9 (retroactive to June 8) – July 3, 2019 with a left hip flexor strain.
d - Placed on administrative leave by the Office of the Commissioner of Baseball and placed on the restricted list on September 19, 2019.

Germán's Career Fielding Record

Position	PCT	G	PO	A	E	TC	DP
Pitcher	.897	55	9	17	3	29	1

Germán's Regular Season Batting Record

Year	Team	AVG	G	AB	R	H	2B	3B	HR	RBI	SH	SF	HP	BB	SO	SB	CS
2019	NYY	.000	27	8	0	0	0	0	0	0	0	0	0	0	7	0	0
Major League Totals		.000	55	9	0	0	0	0	0	0	0	0	0	1	8	0	0

Germán's Career Bests and Streaks

COMPLETE GAMES: None. **LOW-HIT COMPLETE GAME:** None. **IP (START):** 7.0 - 4 times (last on 8/13/19 vs. BAL). **IP (RELIEF):** 4.0 - 3 times (last on 9/12/19-G2 at DET). **HITS:** 9 - 3 times (last on 7/23/19 at MIN). **RUNS:** 8, 7/23/19 at MIN. **BB:** 5, 4/1/19 vs. DET. **SO:** 10, 6/14/18 vs. TB. **HR:** 4, 5/26/19 at KC. **WINNING STREAK:** 7g, 7/3-8/13/19. **LOSING STREAK:** 5g, 10/1/17-6/4/18. **SCORELESS STREAK (IP):** 15.0, 4/26-5/12/18.

Pitcher of the Month: None   **Player of the Week:** None   **Rookie of the Month:** None

LUIS GIL • RHP

81

HT: 6-2 • **WT:** 185 • **BATS:** R • **THROWS:** R
BIRTHDATE: 6/3/98 • **OPENING DAY AGE:** 21
BIRTHPLACE: Azua, D.R.
RESIDES: Azua, D.R.
M.L. SERVICE: None (Rookie)

STATUS
▸ Acquired by the Yankees from the Minnesota Twins in exchange for OF Jake Cave on March 16, 2018.

2019
▸ Combined with Single-A Charleston and Single-A Tampa to go 5-5 with a 2.72 ERA (96.0IP, 29ER) in 20 starts… posted the second-lowest ERA among Yankees minor leaguers.
▸ Began the season with Charleston, going 4-5 with a 2.39 ERA (83.0IP, 22ER) in 17 starts before being promoted to Tampa on 7/25…in three starts with Tampa, went 1-0 with a 4.85 ERA (13.0IP, 7ER).
▸ Was named a 2019 South Atlantc League Mid-Season All-Star with Charleston.
▸ Earned SAL "Pitcher of the Week" honors from 6/10-16…compiled a 0.75 ERA (12.0IP, 11H, 1ER, 3BB, 18K) in two starts over that span.
▸ Was placed on the minor league injured list from 8/12 (retroactive to 8/10)…was reinstated on 9/13.
▸ Following the season, was tabbed by *Baseball America* as the Yankees' No. 4 prospect and No. 14 prsopect in the South Atlantic League…was also named the Yankees' No. 4 prospect by MLB Pipeline.
▸ Was added to the Yankees' 40-man roster on 11/20/19.

2018
▸ Combined with Rookie-level Pulaski and short-season Single-A Staten Island to go 2-3 with a 1.96 ERA (46.0IP, 10ER) in 12 starts…his 13.30 K/9.0IP ratio (68K/46.0IP) led all Yankees farmhands with at least 40.0IP.
▸ Began the season with Pulaski, going 2-1 with a 1.37 ERA (39.1IP, 6ER) and 58K in 10 starts…led the Appalachican League (min. 35.0IP) in ERA, opponents' BA (.154, 21-for-136) and K/9.0IP ratio (13.27)…earned *Baseball America* Rookie-level All-Star team honors with Pulaski.
▸ Was promoted to Staten Island on 8/22, posting a 0-2 record with a 5.40 ERA (6.2IP, 4ER) in two starts.
▸ Following the season, was named by *Baseball America* as the Yankees' No. 26 propsect and No. 19 prospect in the Appalachian League.
▸ Was aquired by the Yankees from the Minnesota Twins in exchange for OF Jake Cave on 3/16/18.

2017
▸ Spent the season with the DSL Twins and was 0-2 with a 2.59 ERA (41.2 IP, 31H, 15R/12ER, 20BB, 49K, 2HR) in 14 starts.

2016
▸ Missed the entire 2016 season recovering from right shoulder surgery, performed on 4/27/16 by Dr. Leroy McCarty…was placed on the minor league disabled list on 6/6 and reinstated on 9/7.

2015
▸ Made his professional debut with the DSL Twins, going 1-2 with two saves and a 4.63 ERA (23.1IP, 15H, 15R/12ER, 26BB, 24K) in 16 relief appearances.

PERSONAL
▸ Full name is Luis Angel Gil (pronounced "HEEL").

Gil's Career Pitching Record

Year	Club	W	L	ERA	G	GS	CG	SHO	SV	IP	H	R	ER	HR	HP	BB	SO	WP	BK
2015	DSL Twins	1	2	4.63	16	0	0	0	2	23.1	15	15	12	2	1	26	24	5	0
2016								Did Not Pitch											
2017	DSL Twins	0	2	2.59	14	14	0	0	0	41.2	31	15	12	2	5	20	49	5	0
2018	Pulaski - a	2	1	1.37	10	10	0	0	0	39.1	21	10	6	1	0	25	58	8	0
	Staten Island	0	2	5.40	2	2	0	0	0	6.2	11	7	4	1	0	6	10	3	1
2019	Charleston	4	5	2.39	17	17	0	0	0	83.0	60	29	22	1	4	39	112	13	1
	Tampa	1	0	4.85	3	3	0	0	0	13.0	11	7	7	0	1	8	11	2	0
Minor League Totals		**8**	**12**	**2.74**	**62**	**46**	**0**	**0**	**2**	**207.0**	**149**	**83**	**63**	**7**	**11**	**124**	**264**	**36**	**2**

Signed by Minnesota as a non-drafted free agent on February 13, 2015.

a – Acquired by the Yankees from the Minnesota Twins in exchange for OF Jake Cave on March 16, 2018.

Baseball Glossary

HOW TO FIGURE...

Batting Average: (H/AB) Hits divided by at-bats.

ERA: (ERx9/IP) Multiply earned runs by nine and divide the total by innings pitched.

Slugging Percentage: (TB/AB) Total bases (1B=1, 2B=2, 3B=3, HR=4) divided by at-bats.

On-Base Percentage: (H+BB+HBP)/(AB+BB+HBP+SF) Add hits, walks, hit by pitch and divide by the total of at-bats plus walks plus hit-by-pitch plus sacrifice flies.

Fielding Percentage: (PO+A)/(PO+A+E) Total putouts plus assists divided by total chances.

Winning Percentage: The number of games won divided by the total games played (not including ties).

Magic Number: Determine the number of games yet to be played, add one, then subtract the number of games ahead in the loss column of the standings from the closest opponent.

QUALIFYING RULES

Batting Championship: To qualify for a batting title, a player must make 502 or more plate appearances (calculated by 3.1 plate appearances per team game scheduled, which is 162).

Pitching Championship: To qualify for the lowest ERA, a pitcher must throw at least 162.0 innings.

Fielding Championship: To qualify as the top fielder:
 (a) a catcher must have played in at least 81 games at catcher.
 (b) an infielder or outfielder must have played at his position in at least 108 games.
 (c) a pitcher must have 162.0 innings pitched.

Rookie: A player shall be considered a rookie unless, during a previous season or seasons, he has (a) exceeded 130 at-bats or 50 innings pitched in the Major Leagues; or (b) accumulated more than 45 days on the active roster of a Major League club or clubs during the period of the 25-player limit.

Save: Credit a pitcher with a save when:
 (1) He is the finishing pitcher in a game won by his club;
 (2) He is not the winning pitcher, and
 (3) He qualifies under one of the following conditions:
  a. He enters the game with a lead of no more than three runs and pitches for at least one inning, or
  b. He enters the game with the potential tying run either on base, at bat or on deck, or
  c. He pitches effectively for at least three innings
 *No more than one save may be credited each game.

CHAD GREEN • RHP

#57

HT: 6-3 • **WT:** 215 • **BATS:** L • **THROWS:** R
BIRTHDATE: 5/24/91 • **OPENING DAY AGE:** 28
BIRTHPLACE: Greenville, S.C.
RESIDES: Louisville, Ky.
COLLEGE: University of Louisville
M.L. SERVICE: 3 years, 50 days

STATUS
- Acquired by the Yankees from the Detroit Tigers with RHP Luis Cessa in exchange for LHP Justin Wilson on December 9, 2015.

CAREER NOTES
- Has four games with at least 5K and no base runners since 2015 (2G in 2019, 2G in '17), the only such games by a Yankees pitcher in that span and tied for the most such games in the Majors during that stretch (also Milwaukee's Josh Hader)…is second in the Majors with seven games of at least 4K and zero base runners since the start of 2017 (Josh Hader-8).
- Has made two career Opening Day rosters (2018-19).

2019
- Went 4-4 with a 4.17 ERA (69.0IP, 32ER) and 98K in 54 appearances (15 starts) over two stints (3/28-4/23, 5/12-9/29) with the Yankees.
- Had three appearances with at least 4K and no base runners, tied for the Major League lead (also John Brebbia, Josh Hader and Drew Pomeranz).
- Went 0-1 with a 3.72 ERA (19.1IP, 8ER) and 32K in his 15 opening assignments…the Yankees went 11-4 in those games…marked his first starts since 6/11/17 vs. Baltimore…retired 50-of-70 batters faced over his final 13 opening assignments (16.2IP, 12H, 6R/5ER, 7BB, 31K, 2HR) beginning on 5/27.
- Went 4-3 with two saves, a 4.35 ERA (49.2IP, 24ER) and 66K in 39 relief appearances.
- Allowed a grand slam to Justin Bour on 4/23 at Los Angeles-AL, his most earned runs (4) allowed since 9/2/16 at Baltimore (4ER)…was optioned to Triple-A Scranton/Wilkes-Barre following the game.
- Over his 10 relief appearances before being optioned to Scranton/WB, posted a 16.43 ERA (7.2IP, 14ER) with 4HR…matched his earned runs allowed in 46.0IP over 36 appearances prior to the All-Star break in 2018.
- Was recalled from Scranton/WB on 5/12…posted a 2.64 ERA (61.1IP, 18ER) with 91K in 44 appearances (15 starts) over the remainder of the season, all at the Major League level.
- Made his first start of the season on 5/19 vs. Tampa Bay (1.2IP, 3H, 2ER, 1BB, 1K, 2HR, 1HP), becoming the seventh pitcher to start a game for the Yankees in 2019.
- Posted a 0.69 ERA (26.0IP, 23H, 2ER, 3BB, 38K, 1HR) in 19 games from 5/27-7/23…had an 11.2-inning scoreless streak from 6/9-7/3.
- Retired 37-of-46BF over nine opening assignments from 5/27-8/12 (12.1IP, 4H, 0R, 4BB, 22K).
- Earned his second career save on 7/23 at Minnesota (also 7/24/16 vs. San Francisco) after entering in the 10th with the bases loaded and retiring his only batter faced.
- Started and took his fourth loss on 8/15 vs. Cleveland (0.1IP, 4H, 5ER, 1BB, 1K, 2HR), allowing back to back homers to Ramírez (grand slam) and Kipnis (solo).
- Over his final 11 appearances, struck out 34 batters while walking just six in 17.2IP (from 8/24).
- Earned the win in Game 1 of 9/12 doubleheader at Detroit (2.1IP, 1H, 1ER, 2K) but snapped his season-high-tying 11.2 scoreless inning streak.
- Struck out five of his six batters faced in extra innings on 9/24 at Tampa Bay (2.0IP).
- Went 1-0 with a 6.75 ERA (6.2IP, 5ER) in six postseason games (one start)…earned his second career postseason win in ALDS Game 3 at Minnesota…retired all 6BF in ALCS Game 2 at Houston (2.0IP, 2K)…made his first career postseason start as the Yankees' "opener" in ALCS Game 6 (1.0IP, 2H, 3ER, 1BB, 1K, 2HR).
- In three starts with the RailRiders, posted a 2.45 ERA (7.1IP, 2ER) with 14K and just 2BB.

2018
- Went 8-3 with a 2.50 ERA (75.2IP, 21ER) and 94K in 63 relief appearances with the Yankees…spent the entire season at the Major League level for the first time in his career.
- Over the span of 21 appearances from 8/23/17-4/13/18, posted a 0.99 ERA (27.1IP, 3ER), allowing just 15H with 4BB, 44K and a .400 OPS against.
- Allowed a game-winning two-run HR to Soto in the sixth inning of 6/18 resumption of 5/15 game at Washington to record the loss (1.0IP, 3H, 2ER, 2K, 1HR)…the homer is credited to Soto on 5/15, despite him not making his Major League debut until 5/20.

- Posted a career-long 17.1-inning scoreless streak (over 13G) from 5/25-7/8 (11H, 3BB, 18K)…does not include his 2ER allowed in 6/18 resumption of 5/15 loss at Washington…had the streak snapped on 7/10 at Baltimore (2ER).
- Posted a 0.55 ERA (16.1IP, 1ER) with 18K over a 12-game stretch from 8/13-9/18…from 8/13 through the end of the season, allowed 3ER in 21.1IP over 17 appearances (15H, 4BB, 28K)…was the Majors' seventh-lowest ERA over the span (min. 20.0IP).
- Made his 100th career relief appearance in 9/15 loss vs. Toronto, tossing 2.1 scoreless innings (3H, 3K).
- Allowed 1ER in 3.2IP over two postseason relief appearances.

2017

- Went 5-0 with a 1.83 ERA (69.0IP, 14ER) and 103K in 40 games (one start) over two stints with the Yankees (5/8-9 and 5/14-10/1)…allowed 4-of-31 inherited runners (12.9%), the second-lowest mark among qualifying relievers.
- Out of the bullpen, recorded a 13.43 K/9.0IP ratio, 10th-best among all Major League relievers (fifth in the AL)…ranked third among all relievers with a 41.0% strikeout rate (244BF, 100K) and .207 opponents' OBP and fifth with a 1.61 ERA, .143 opp. BA and .233 opp. SLG…his 2.3 WAR was sixth among relievers (FanGraphs).
- Is one of eight pitchers in franchise history with at least 100K in relief in a season, joining Dellin Betances (5x), Goose Gossage (3x), Jay Howell (1x), Andrew Miller (1x), Joe Page (1x), Mariano Rivera (1x) and David Robertson (1x).
- With Dellin Betances (100K), became the second pair of Yankees to each strike out at least 100 batters in relief in the same season (also Betances/Andrew Miller in 2015).
- Made 29 relief appearances of more than 1.0IP (second-most in the Majors) and 16 of at least 2.0IP…made three scoreless relief appearances of at least 3.0IP…had multiple strikeouts in 30 of his 40 total appearances.
- Had six relief appearances with at least 5K…since 1992, is one of six relievers with at least six 5K games in a season, joining Felix Pena (10G in 2019), Mariano Rivera (9G in 1996), Octavio Dotel (7G in 2001), Tommy Milone (7G in 2019) and Ryan Yarbrough (6G in 2018).
- Made nine straight relief appearances of at least 1.1IP from 5/14 (G1) - 6/21, posting a 1.77 ERA (20.1IP, 4ER) with 23K over the stretch.
- Made his only start of the season in 6/11 win vs. Baltimore (ND, 2.0IP, 2H, 2ER, 1BB, 3K).
- Had multiple strikeouts in eight straight games from 6/25-7/19, tied for the Majors' second-longest streak of the season by a reliever (C. Kimbrel-9, C. Devenski-8)…was one shy of the Yankees relief record of nine: Dellin Betances (4/17-5/10/14), Mariano Rivera (6/4-7/2/96) and Lindy McDaniel (7/27-8/29/73).
- Over a six-outing stretch from 7/9-23, tossed 9.1 scoreless and hitless innings, retiring 28-of-32 batters (3BB, 1HP, 16K)…is tied for the fourth-longest single-season streak of scoreless, hitless relief appearances of at least 1.0IP in Yankees history behind Dellin Betances (9G, 6/8-25/18), David Robertson (8G, 9/15-30/17) and Mariano Rivera (7G, 6/3-20/10).
- Following the All-Star break, struck out 46.2% (61-of-132) of his batters faced, the second-highest pct. in the Majors (min. 100BF) behind Craig Kimbrel (48.3%).
- From 8/23 through the end of the season, allowed just 1ER with 2BB and 28K (60BF) in 17.0IP over 12 games.
- Struck out seven of eight batters faced in 2.2 scoreless innings (1H) in 8/30 Game 1 loss vs. Cleveland…marked the most strikeouts in a single game by any pitcher in Major League history when facing eight-or-fewer batters…marked the fewest non-Ks by a pitcher facing eight-or-more batters since the Yankees' Ron Davis struck out eight-of-nine batters on 5/4/81 at California (credit: *Elias*).
- Collected his 100th strikeout of the season *as a reliever* in the seventh inning of 9/30 win vs. Toronto (Jose Bautista, swinging)…according to *Elias*, the only other Yankees with 100K within their first 50 relief appearances of a season were Dellin Betances (2017), Mariano Rivera (1996) and Joe Page (1947).
- Began the season with Single-A Tampa, making one start (0-1, 2.25 ERA, 4.0IP, 2H, 1ER, 5K)…was transferred to Triple-A Scranton/Wilkes-Barre and went 2-1 with a 4.73 ERA (26.2IP, 14ER) and 33K in five starts.
- Went 1-0 with a 4.15 ERA (8.2IP, 4ER) and 11K in five postseason relief appearances…made his playoff debut in the Yankees' AL Wild Card win vs. Minnesota, entering with one out in the first inning (2.0IP, 1H, 1ER, 2BB, 4K)…became the first Yankee to strike out his first four career postseason batters faced, and the first Major League pitcher to do so since Colorado's Jeff Francis in 2007 NLDS Game 1 at Philadelphia…allowed a grand slam to Francisco Lindor in ALDS Game 2 loss at Cleveland…earned his first postseason win in ALCS Game 4 vs. Houston (2.0IP, 1H, 1R/0ER, 2K).

2016

- Went 2-4 with one save and a 4.73 ERA (45.2IP, 24ER) and 52K over five stints with the Yankees (5/14-17, 6/10-12, 7/2-9, 7/21-8/4 and 8/15-10/2)…in eight starts, went 2-4 with a 5.94 ERA (36.1IP, 24ER)…in four relief appearances, tossed 9.1 scoreless innings without recording a decision (6H, 3BB, 8K).
- Recorded a 10.25 K/9.0IP ratio, eighth-best among Major League rookies (min. 40.0IP) and fourth among AL rookies (Seattle's Edwin Diaz-15.33, Houston's Michael Feliz-13.15, Baltimore's Mychal Givens-11.57).
- Tossed 6.0IP with 1R-or-fewer in 3-of-8 starts…had a 10.90 K/9.0IP ratio (44K/36.1IP) in his starts, eighth-highest among Major League pitchers with at least 30.0IP as a starter (third-highest in AL).
- Made his Major League debut on 5/16 at Arizona, recording the loss (4.0IP, 8H, 6R/4ER, 2HR, 1BB, 5K)…was the first Yankees pitcher drafted by another organization to make his Major League debut as a Yankees starter since RHP Christian Parker—who was selected by Montreal and traded to the Yankees—debuted on 4/6/01 vs. Toronto…was signed to a Major League contract and selected to the Yankees' 25-man roster from Triple-A Scranton/Wilkes-Barre on 5/14.

- Became the fourth Yankees pitcher since 2000 to record at least 5K in each of his first three Major League starts, joining Masahiro Tanaka (2014, first 11GS), Phil Hughes (2007, first 4GS) and José Contreras (2003, first 7GS).
- Made his first Major League relief appearance in 6/12 loss vs. Detroit, tossing a perfect ninth (1.0IP).
- Earned his first Major League win on 7/3 at San Diego (his third career game), allowing 1ER in 6.0IP (3H, 0BB, 8K, 1HR)…was only the third Yankee since 1913 to record at least 8K without walking a batter within his first three career games…joined Rich Beck (7.0IP and 8K on 9/14/65) and Masahiro Tanaka (7.0IP and 8K on 4/4/14) who both did so in their Major League debuts…became the first Yankees pitcher since 1913 to toss at least 6.0IP with 3H-or-fewer and no walks in one of his first three career games.
- Earned his first Major League save in 7/24 win vs. San Francisco, tossing 2.1 scoreless innings (3H, 1K).
- Had a career-high 11K in 6.0 scoreless innings in his start on 8/15 vs. Toronto (2H, 0BB), the most by a Yankees rookie since Masahiro Tanaka had 11K on 6/11/14 at Seattle…retired his first 13 batters, including six via strikeout, before Tulowitzki's one-out single to left in the fifth…had streaks of five consecutive strikeouts and four straight strikeouts…became the second rookie pitcher in Yankees history to record at least 11K with no walks and no runs in a game, joining Stan Bahnsen on 8/1/68 at Boston (CG SHO, 3H, 12K)…was the 12th Yankees pitcher (of any experience level) since 1913 to do it, the first since Randy Johnson on 7/26/05 vs. Minnesota (8.0IP, 2H, 11K)…matched the most strikeouts by an AL rookie in 2016 (Detroit's Michael Fulmer, 11K on 5/21/16 vs. Tampa Bay).
- Was removed from 9/2 loss at Baltimore after 1.2IP with right elbow pain (5H, 4ER, 2BB, 1HR, 3K)…underwent an MRI on 9/3 in Baltimore, revealing a sprained right UCL and a strained flexor tendon…was placed on the 15-day disabled list on 9/7 (retro. to 9/3) with a right forearm tendon injury…was transferred to the 60-day D.L. on 9/18.
- In 16 starts for Scranton/WB, was 7-6 with a 1.52 ERA and team-leading 100K (94.2IP, 68H, 21R/16ER, 21BB, 3HR)…was named to the International League Mid-Season All-Star Team…led IL pitchers (min. 90.0IP) in ERA and WHIP, and had the third-lowest ERA among all minor league pitchers (min. 90.0IP)…allowed one-or-zero runs in 10-of-16GS…issued one-or-zero walks in 12-of-16GS and allowed 4H-or-fewer in 10-of-16…compiled a 26.0-inning scoreless streak from 6/15-8/9.

2015
- Spent the season with Double-A Erie, going 5-14 with a 3.93 ERA (148.2IP, 170H, 84R/65ER, 43BB, 137K, 9HR) in 27 starts…over his final eight starts, posted a 3-0 record with a 1.70 ERA (47.2IP, 42H, 9ER, 11BB, 49K, 1HR) and a .237 (42-for-177) opponents' BA.
- Was named the Eastern League "Pitcher of the Week" for 8/24-30 after going 1-0 with a 0.69 ERA (13.0IP, 12H, 1ER, 0BB, 14K) over two starts, including a seven-inning complete game.
- Was acquired by the Yankees from Detroit with RHP Luis Cessa in exchange for LHP Justin Wilson on 12/9/15.

2014
- Went 6-4 with a 3.11 ERA (130.1IP, 121H, 51R/45ER, 28BB, 125K) in 23 starts with Single-A West Michigan…ranked third in the Midwest League in WHIP (1.14) and ninth in ERA…went 4-1 with a 2.03 ERA (44.1IP, 35H, 10ER, 9BB, 50K) in his final eight starts of the season.

2013
- In his professional debut, combined to go 4-0 with a 3.54 ERA (20.1IP, 19H, 7ER, 6BB, 10K) in 12 games (two starts) with the Rookie-level GCL Tigers and Single-A Lakeland.
- Went 1-0 with a 3.00 ERA (3.0IP, 3H, 1ER, 0BB, 6K) in two relief appearances before being promoted on 7/12…in 10G/2GS with Lakeland, went 3-0 with a 3.63 ERA (17.1IP, 16H, 7ER, 6BB, 10K).

PERSONAL
- Full name is Chad Keith Green…is married to Jenna…his twin brother, Chase, is three minutes younger than Chad and is an assistant baseball coach at McKendree University (Ill.).
- In three seasons at Louisville (2011-13), went 16-6 with a 2.38 ERA (193.0IP, 175H, 51ER, 66BB, 139K) in 61 appearances (26 starts)…finished his collegiate career as the school's record holder in career ERA…earned Second Team All-BIG EAST honors after finishing his junior season going 10-4 with 2.42 ERA (104.1IP, 28ER).
- Graduated from Effingham (Ill.) H.S., where he earned all-state honors as a senior…also lettered for three seasons in basketball.

Green's Career Pitching Record

Year	Club	W	L	ERA	G	GS	CG	SHO	SV	IP	H	R	ER	HR	HP	BB	SO	WP	BK
2013	GCL Tigers	1	0	3.00	2	0	0	0	0	3.0	3	1	1	1	0	0	6	0	0
	Lakeland	3	0	3.63	10	2	0	0	1	17.1	16	7	7	0	0	6	10	0	0
2014	West Michigan	6	4	3.11	23	23	0	0	0	130.1	121	51	45	8	3	28	125	5	0
2015	Erie - a	5	14	3.93	27	27	1	0	0	148.2	170	84	65	9	7	43	137	5	0
2016	Scranton/WB	7	6	1.52	16	16	0	0	0	94.2	68	21	16	3	1	21	100	2	0
	YANKEES - b	2	4	4.73	12	8	0	0	1	45.2	49	26	24	12	1	15	52	1	0
2017	Tampa	0	1	2.25	1	0	0	0	0	4.0	2	1	1	1	0	0	5	0	0
	Scranton/WB	2	1	4.73	5	5	0	0	0	26.2	32	15	14	1	0	11	33	0	0
	YANKEES	5	0	1.83	40	1	0	0	0	69.0	34	14	14	4	2	17	103	3	0
2018	YANKEES	8	3	2.50	63	0	0	0	0	75.2	64	22	21	9	1	15	94	3	0
2019	YANKEES	4	4	4.17	54	15	0	0	2	69.0	66	35	32	10	6	19	98	2	0
	Scranton/WB	0	0	2.45	3	3	0	0	0	7.1	5	2	2	0	0	2	14	0	0
Minor League Totals		24	26	3.15	87	76	1	0	1	432.0	417	182	151	23	11	111	430	12	0
Major League Totals		19	11	3.16	169	24	0	0	3	259.1	213	97	91	35	10	66	347	9	0

Selected by the Toronto Blue Jays in the 37th round of the 2010 First-Year Player Draft, but did not sign.
Selected by the Detroit Tigers in the 11th round of the 2013 First-Year Player Draft.

a – Acquired by the Yankees from the Detroit Tigers with RHP Luis Cessa in exchange for LHP Justin Wilson on December 9, 2015.
b – Placed on the 15-day disabled list from September 7 (retroactive to September 3) – October 2, 2016 with a right forearm tendon injury…transferred to the 60-day disabled list on September 18.

Green's Postseason Record

Year	Club vs. Opp.	W	L	ERA	G	GS	CG	SHO	SV	IP	H	R	ER	HR	HP	BB	SO	WP	BK
2017	NYY vs. MIN (WC)	0	0	4.50	1	0	0	0	0	2.0	1	1	1	0	0	2	4	0	0
	NYY vs. CLE (DS)	0	0	81.00	1	0	0	0	0	0.1	2	3	3	1	1	0	0	0	0
	NYY vs. HOU (CS)	1	0	0.00	3	0	0	0	0	6.1	3	1	0	0	0	1	7	0	0
2018	NYY vs. OAK (WC)						On Roster - Did Not Pitch												
	NYY vs. BOS (DS)	0	0	2.45	2	0	0	0	0	3.2	4	1	1	0	0	3	1	0	0
2019	NYY vs. MIN (DS)	0	0	0.00	2	0	0	0	0	2.0	2	0	0	0	0	0	1	0	0
	NYY vs. HOU (CS)	0	0	9.64	4	0	1	0	0	4.2	4	5	5	2	0	1	5	0	0
Wild Card Game Totals		0	0	4.50	1	0	0	0	0	2.0	1	1	1	0	0	2	4	0	0
LDS Totals		1	0	6.00	5	0	0	0	0	6.0	8	4	4	1	1	3	1	0	0
LCS Totals		1	0	4.09	7	0	1	0	0	11.0	7	6	5	2	0	2	12	0	0
POSTSEASON TOTALS		2	0	4.74	13	0	1	0	0	19.0	16	11	10	3	1	7	17	0	0

Green's Career Fielding Record

Position	PCT	G	PO	A	E	TC	DP
Pitcher	1.000	169	6	13	0	19	2

Green's Regular Season Batting Record

Year	Team	AVG	G	AB	R	H	2B	3B	HR	RBI	SH	SF	HP	BB	SO	SB	CS
2019	NYY	.000	54	1	0	0	0	0	0	0	0	0	0	1	0	0	0
Major League Totals		.000	169	5	0	0	0	0	0	0	0	0	0	0	5	0	0

Green's Career Bests and Streaks

COMPLETE GAMES: None. **LOW-HIT COMPLETE GAME:** N/A. **IP (START):** 6.0 - 3 times (last on 8/21/16 at LAA). **IP (RELIEF):** 3.2 - 2 times (last on 5/14/17 vs. HOU-G1). **HITS:** 8 - 2 times (last on 8/3/16 vs. NYM). **RUNS:** 7, 7/8/16 at CLE. **WALKS:** 4, 8/3/16 vs. NYM. **STRIKEOUTS:** 11, 8/15/16 vs. TOR. **HOME RUNS:** 4, 7/8/16 at CLE. **WINNING STREAK:** 7g, 7/23/17-4/25/18. **LOSING STREAK:** 3g, 9/20/18-4/9/19. **SCORELESS STREAK (IP):** 17.1, 5/25-7/10/18.

Pitcher of the Month: None   **Player of the Week:** None   **Rookie of the Month:** None

---

ALL IN THE FAMILY

There have been eight sets of brothers to each play for the Yankees…Homer (1912) and Tommy (1912) **Thompson**; Bobby (1957-60) and Billy (1960) **Shantz**; Felipe (1971-73) and Matty (1973) **Alou**; Phil (1984-85) and Joe (1985-87) **Niekro**; Al (1987-89, 2005) and Mark (1990) **Leiter**; Pascual (1990-91) and Mélido (1992-95) **Pérez**; Marcus (1989) and Matt (2005) **Lawton**; and Donzell (2001) and Darnell (2012) **McDonald**.

1B Ike Davis made his Yankees debut in 2016 and his father, Ron Davis was a relief pitcher for the team from 1978-81. According to the *Elias Sports Bureau*, the duo joins Yogi and Dale Berra as the only father/son player combos in Yankees history.

J.A. HAPP • LHP

33

HT: 6-5 • WT: 205 • BATS: L • THROWS: L
BIRTHDATE: 10/19/82 • OPENING DAY AGE: 37
BIRTHPLACE: Spring Valley, Ill.
RESIDES: Clearwater, Fla.
COLLEGE: Northwestern University
M.L. SERVICE: 11 years, 47 days

STATUS

- Signed by the Yankees on December 17, 2018, to a two-year contract through the 2020 season with a vesting option for 2021…was originally acquired from the Toronto Blue Jays in exchange for INF Brandon Drury and OF Billy McKinney on July 26, 2018.

CAREER NOTES

- Has pitched in 13 Major League seasons with the Phillies (2007-10), Astros (2010-12), Blue Jays (2012-14, '16-18), Mariners (2015), Pirates (2015) and Yankees (2018-19)…is 121-90 with a 3.99 ERA (1,692.0IP, 751ER) in 315 career games (289 starts)…ranks sixth among active left-handed pitchers in wins, seventh in starts and eighth in innings pitched…has 1,497 career strikeouts, and needs three strikeouts to reach 1,500.
- Has made 10 Opening Day rosters with five teams: Philadelphia (2009-10), Houston (2011-12), Toronto (2013, '16-18), Seattle (2015) and the Yankees (2019).
- Is one of six pitchers to earn at least 10 wins in each of the last six seasons (2014-19), along with teammate Masahiro Tanaka, Jon Lester, Max Scherzer, Stephen Strasburg and Zack Greinke.
- Is one of 14 pitchers to make at least 25 starts in each of the last five seasons (2015-19).
- Over the last five seasons (2015-19), his .654 winning percentage (70-37) ranks ninth in the Majors (min. 50 decisions).
- Left-handed batters are hitting .201 (80-for-398) in the last three seasons, fourth-lowest among Major League starting pitchers (min. 300AB) in that span.
- Since the start of 2017, is 17-10 with a 3.13 ERA (218.2IP, 76ER) in 40 games (39 starts) vs. AL East clubs…has held opponents to a .222 BA (182-for-821) in that span…is 11-3 with a 3.71 ERA (119.0IP, 49ER) in 22 games (21 starts) vs. the AL East as a Yankee, with the team going 16-5 in those starts.
- Went 7-0 in his first 11 starts with the Yankees (7/29-9/28/18), the first Yankees pitcher to go unbeaten in his first 11 starts in pinstripes since Joe Cowley was 8-0 in 12 starts from 7/16/84-4/23/85…was the first pitcher to win his first seven decisions as a Yankee since Dellin Betances started his career 9-0 from 2011-15.
- Won seven consecutive starts at Yankee Stadium from 5/26/16-8/19/18 (three w/ Toronto, four w/ Yankees), tied for the longest such streak in Yankee Stadium history (Masahiro Tanaka, seven straight from 8/7/16-5/2/17).
- Is 11-4 with a 3.00 ERA (141.0IP, 47ER) in 25 regular season games (24 starts) vs. Boston…from 5/15/15-9/18/18, became the third pitcher since earned runs became an official statistic in the AL in 1913 to allow 2ER-or-fewer in 11 consecutive starts vs. Boston, joining the Yankees' Bob Shawkey (14 starts from 6/29/21-4/15/24) and Cleveland's Gaylord Perry (11 starts from 9/9/72-9/11/74)…was 4-1 with a 1.62 ERA (66.2IP, 12ER) during the stretch…is 6-2 with a 2.91 ERA (58.2IP, 19ER) in 11 career games (10 starts) at Fenway Park.
- Made his first career AL All-Star Team in 2018.
- Has been traded at four July non-waiver trading deadlines (2010, '12, '15, '18)…in 45 post-trade games (41 starts) with his new clubs, has compiled a 22-8 record with one complete game and a 3.12 ERA (239.1IP, 198H, 87R/83ER, 81BB, 239K)…following his 7/26/18 trade from Seattle to the Yankees, went 7-0 with a 2.69 ERA (63.2IP, 19ER) in 11 starts to help the Yankees advance to the ALDS…on 7/31/15, was acquired by Pittsburgh from Seattle and went 7-2 with a 1.85 ERA (63.1IP, 13ER) in 11 starts as the Pirates reached the NL Wild Card Game…on 7/20/12, was acquired by Toronto from Houston and went 3-2 with a 4.69 ERA (40.1IP, 21ER) in 10 games (six starts) for the Blue Jays…on 7/29/10, was acquired by Houston from Philadelphia and went 5-4 with a 3.75 ERA (72.0IP, 30ER) in 13 starts for the Astros.
- Finished sixth in 2016 AL Cy Young Award voting after going 20-4 with Toronto and tying for the second-most wins in the Majors.
- Started for Philadelphia in the 22nd game in Yankee Stadium history on 5/23/09, yielding 2ER in 6.0IP (4H, 0BB, 4K, 1HR) in a no-decision.
- Finished second in 2009 BBWAA NL "Rookie of the Year" balloting to Florida's Chris Coghlan…appeared on all 32 ballots, receiving 10 first-place votes…won the 2009 Players' Choice Award for "NL Outstanding Rookie"…was named 2009 NL "Rookie of the Year" by The Sporting News.
- Has reached the postseason five times with three different clubs: Philadelphia (2008-09), Toronto (2016) and the Yankees (2018-19)…is 1-3 with a 5.04 ERA (25.0IP, 31H, 14ER, 13BB, 24K, 4HR) in 14 career postseason appearances (four starts)…earned his lone postseason win in 2016 ALDS Game 2 at Texas (5.0IP, 1ER)…in 10 postseason appearances as a reliever, has posted a 2.70 ERA (10.0IP, 9H, 3ER, 8BB, 9K, 2HR).

CAREER HIGHLIGHTS

AL All-Star Team
- 2018

- Won the 2008 World Series with Philadelphia but did not pitch in the World Series vs. Tampa Bay...made two relief appearances for the Phillies in the 2009 World Series vs. the Yankees (2.2IP, 1ER)...made his Yankees postseason debut in 2018 ALDS Game 1 at Boston (L, 2.0IP, 5ER).

2019

- Made 31 appearances (30 starts) for the Yankees, going 12-8 with a 4.91 ERA (161.1IP, 160H, 88ER, 49BB, 140K, 34HR)...opponents hit .258 (160-for-621, 34HR); LH .228 (36-for-158, 6HR); RH .268 (124-for-463, 28HR)...the Yankees went 20-10 in his starts (11-4 vs. the AL East).
- From the start of August through the end of the regular season, held lefties to a .078/.161/.098 (4-for-51) with 1XBH (1 double), 4BB and 19K...lefties had an 0-for-29 stretch with 4BB from 8/9-9/12 (G1).
- Allowed a career-high 34HR, tied for sixth-most in the Majors and tied for fourth-most in Yankees history.
- In Game 1 win on 5/25 at Kansas City (6.0IP, 4H, 3ER, 0BB, 10K, 1HR), recorded his 10th career double-digit-strikeout game and first as a Yankee...was his fifth with 0BB.
- From 5/9-6/18, went 6-0 with a 4.29 ERA (42.0IP, 20ER) over eight starts...was his second streak of at least six wins as a Yankee.
- Made his 300th career Major League appearance and 275th career start on 6/23 vs. Houston.
- Was on the paternity list from 8/2-4.
- Became the second player to go unbeaten in his first 13 road starts as a Yankee (Whitey Ford, first 15 road starts from 1950-53)...the streak was snapped with a loss on 8/9 at Toronto...was 6-0 with a 3.96 ERA (72.2IP, 32ER) during the streak.
- On 9/1 vs. Oakland (6.0IP, 1H, 0R, 4BB, 5K), recorded his fourth career start with at least 6.0 scoreless innings and one-or-zero hits, also 8/14/18 vs. Tampa Bay w/ the Yankees (7.0IP, 1H), 7/24/16 vs. Seattle (6.0IP, 1H) and 9/28/15 vs. St. Louis (6.0IP, 1H)...is the only Yankee since 2011 with multiple such starts.
- On 9/1 vs. Oakland (6.0IP, 1H, 4BB, 5K) and 9/7 at Boston (6.1IP, 2H, 1BB, 7K), became the fifth pitcher in Yankees history to toss at least 6.0 shutout innings with 2H-or-fewer in consecutive starts, joining Freddy Garcia (4/16 and 4/24/11), David Cone (4/6 and 4/11/97), Ron Guidry (9/9 and 9/15/78) and Allie Reynolds (9/22/53 and 5/6/54)...Bob Shawkey (5/8 and 5/12/1919) also did so in one start and one relief appearance.
- Compiled a career-best 19.1-inning scoreless streak from 8/26-9/12-G1, the AL's eighth-longest scoreless streak in 2019 and longest by a Yankee.
- Left his start on 9/12-G1 at Detroit with left biceps tendinitis...was examined by team physician Dr. Christopher Ahmad.
- Made his lone relief appearance on 9/25 at Tampa Bay, allowing 1ER over 5.0IP (4H, 1BB, 6K, 1WP)...was his first game out of the bullpen since 7/27/15 vs. Arizona with Seattle (1.0IP, 2K)...matched the longest relief appearance by a Yankee in 2019 (also Nestor Cortes-5.0IP on 6/15 at Chicago-AL).
- Went 1-0 with a 1.65 ERA (27.1IP, 5ER) in five September outings (four starts)...was his only monthly ERA under 4.00.
- Made three relief appearances in the postseason, going 0-1 with a 2.45 ERA (3.2IP, 1ER)...took the loss in ALCS Game 2 at Houston, allowing a "walk-off" solo HR to Carlos Correa in the 11th inning.
- Went 2-0 with a 7.94 ERA (11.1IP, 10ER) in four official spring training appearances (three starts).

HAPP'S 2019 PITCHING LINES

Date/Opp	Score	W/L	IP	H	R	ER	HR	BB	K	NP/S	ERA	Left Game
3/31 vs. BAL*	5-7	L	4.0	5	4	4	2	1	3	75/50	9.00	Trailing 4-3
4/6 at BAL	6-4	ND	4.1	5	2	2	1	2	5	88/55	6.48	Leading 3-1
4/12 at CWS*	6-9 (7)	L	4.0	9	6	6	1	2	5	88/54	8.76	Tied 5-5
4/17 vs. BOS	5-3	ND	6.1	6	3	3	2	1	4	84/58	7.23	Trailing 3-1
4/22 at LAA	4-3 (14)	ND	**7.0**	3	2	2	1	2	5	89/54	5.96	Tied 2-2
4/27 at SF	6-4	W	**7.0**	5	0	0	0	0	2	95/63	4.68	Leading 6-0
5/4 vs. MIN	3-7	L	5.2	7	4	4	2	1	3	81/51	4.93	Trailing 4-0
5/9 vs. SEA*	3-1	W	5.0	1	0	0	0	3	7	94/55	4.36	Leading 1-0
5/15 vs. BAL (G1)	5-3	W	5.1	5	3	3	2	0	3	64/42	4.44	Leading 5-3
5/20 at BAL	10-7	ND	3.2	9	6	6	2	1	3	77/47	5.16	Trailing 6-1
5/25 at KC (G1)	7-3	W	6.0	4	3	3	1	0	**10**	82/59	5.09	Leading 5-3
5/31 vs. BOS	4-1	W	5.0	3	1	1	1	2	5	84/47	4.83	Leading 4-1
6/6 at TOR*	6-2	W	**7.0**	4	1	1	1	0	4	**102/69**	4.48	Leading 6-1
6/13 at CWS*	4-5	ND	5.0	5	4	4	1	**4**	2	91/53	4.66	Tied 4-4
6/18 vs. TB	6-3	W	5.0	7	2	2	0	0	3	87/58	4.59	Leading 4-2
6/23 vs. HOU	4-9	L	4.0	**11**	**8**	**8**	**3**	0	2	68/43	5.23	Trailing 8-0
7/4 at TB	8-4	ND	5.1	3	1	1	0	3	5	92/54	5.02	Leading 2-1
7/13 at TOR	1-2	L	5.1	5	2	2	0	1	5	89/56	4.93	Tied 0-0
7/19 vs. COL	8-2	W	5.0	8	2	2	1	2	8	90/59	4.86	Leading 5-2
7/24 at MIN	10-7	ND	3.1	6	6	6	2	2	3	74/46	5.23	Leading 9-5
7/30 vs. ARI	2-4	L	6.0	8	3	3	1	1	2	94/63	5.19	Trailing 3-1
8/4 vs. BOS	7-4	W	5.2	7	4	4	2	1	2	91/54	5.24	Leading 7-4
8/9 at TOR	2-8	L	5.0	4	6	6	**3**	3	4	99/58	5.48	Trailing 6-1
8/14 vs. BAL	6-5	W	5.0	6	2	2	0	3	6	95/58	5.40	Leading 4-2
8/21 at OAK*	4-6	L	4.0	4	5	5	2	2	4	80/45	5.58	Trailing 4-1
8/26 vs. SEA	5-4	W	5.0	2	3	3	1	3	7	95/55	5.57	Leading 5-3
9/1 vs. OAK	5-4	ND	6.0	1	0	0	0	**4**	5	98/55	5.34	Tied 0-0
9/7 at BOS*	5-1	W	6.1	2	0	0	0	1	7	92/62	5.10	Leading 4-0
9/12 at DET (G2)*	10-4	ND	4.2	7	2	2	1	3	6	99/64	5.07	Leading 4-2
9/20 vs. TOR	3-4	ND	5.1	4	2	2	1	0	4	82/53	5.01	Leading 3-2
9/25 at TB*		-	5.0	4	1	1	0	1	6	77/51	4.91	*relief*
Totals (31G/30GS)		12-8	161.1	160	88	88	34	49	140		4.91	

*start came after a team loss / **Bold** - season high / *italics* - relief

2018

- Combined to go 17-6 with a 3.65 ERA (177.2IP, 150H, 81R/72ER, 51BB, 193K, 27HR) in 31 starts between the Blue Jays and Yankees…held opponents to a .225 BA (150-for-668, 27HR); LH .171 (22-for-129, 2HR), RH .237 (128-for-539, 25HR)…his teams were 21-10 in his starts…posted a 3.2 WAR and 3.98 FIP (FanGraphs)…made his ninth Opening Day roster.
- According to STATS, was the fourth pitcher to make starts for both the Yankees and Blue Jays in the same season, and the first since David Cone in 1995.
- Tied for fourth in the AL (and tied for seventh in the Majors) in wins…posted the second-highest win total of his career (20-4 in 2016).
- Set career highs in strikeouts, K/9.0IP ratio (9.78) and strikeout rate (26.3%)…finished eighth in the AL in K/9.0IP ratio…had a season-high 10K twice, on 4/24 vs. Boston and 5/16 at the Mets.
- His .171 opponents' BA vs. left-handed batters was the Majors' fourth-lowest mark by a starting pitcher.
- Made his first career All-Star Game, selected by MLB as Toronto's lone representative…pitched the 10th inning and earned a save in the AL's 8-6 win despite allowing a solo HR to Joey Votto (1.0IP, 1H, 1ER, 1K)…at the age of 35, was the fourth-oldest player in the game behind Nelson Cruz (38), Shin-Soo Choo (36) and Yadier Molina (35).
- Was 10-6 with a 4.18 ERA (114.0IP, 53ER) in 20 starts with Toronto.
- Was acquired by the Yankees from the Blue Jays in exchange for INF Brandon Drury and OF Billy McKinney on 7/26.
- Made 11 starts with the Yankees, going 7-0 with a 2.69 ERA (63.2IP, 51H, 20R/19ER, 16BB, 63K, 10HR)…was the third pitcher in Yankees history to go 7-0 or better in a season, joining Tom Zachary (12-0 in 1929) and Aaron Small (10-0 in 2005)…the Yankees were 9-2 in his starts…tied for sixth in the Majors in wins from the day of his Yankees debut on 7/29 through the end of the season, one of two pitchers at 7-0 or better in that span (Tampa Bay's Blake Snell, 9-0)…held opponents to a .143 BA (6-for-42) with RISP as a Yankee.
- Won his first five starts as a Yankee (7/29-8/25), the first Yankees pitcher since Bob Turley in 1955 to both start and win each of his first five appearances as a Yankee according to the *Elias Sports Bureau*…was the first Yankee to win his first five starts with the club since Rob Gardner, who had relief appearances mixed in among his first five Yankees starts stretching from 1970-72…was the first Yankee to go undefeated in his first 12 starts with the club since Joe Cowley (8-0 in 12 starts from 7/16/84-4/23/85)…was the first pitcher to win his first seven decisions as a Yankee since Dellin Betances started his career 9-0 from 2011-15.
- Finished the season on a 12-start unbeaten streak (since 7/22, including his final start with Toronto)…was tied for the Majors' fourth-longest active streak of unbeaten starts as of the end of the 2018 season…was tied for the second-longest unbeaten streak of his career (15 straight starts from 7/4/08-7/19/09).
- Was placed on the 10-day disabled list on 8/2 (retroactive to 7/30) with hand, foot and mouth disease…was reinstated on 8/9.
- Tied for second in the Majors in home wins, going 10-4 with a 4.31 ERA (108.2IP, 52ER) in 19 starts…was 4-0 with a 2.72 ERA (39.2IP, 12ER) in seven home starts as a Yankee.
- Was 7-2 with a 2.61 ERA (69.0IP, 20ER) in 12 road starts, including 3-0 with a 2.63 ERA (24.0IP, 7ER) in four road starts with the Yankees…was 11-2 with a 2.65 ERA (108.2IP, 32ER) in 19 starts outside of Rogers Centre.
- Opponents batted .160 (15-for-94) in at-bats ending in a slider and .203 (71-for-350) in at-bats ending with a four-seam fastball (Brooks Baseball).
- Made his first career Opening Day start on 3/29 vs. the Yankees (L, 4.2IP, 4H, 3R/2ER, 1BB, 5K, 1HR)…according to the YES Network, was the second pitcher ever to start against the Yankees on Opening Day and later pitch for the club in the same season…on 4/23/1919, Carl Mays tossed a four-hit shutout for Boston at the Polo Grounds, then was traded to the Yankees on 7/30/1919…Mays, however, did not start for the Yankees against his former club that season.
- In 5/16 win at the Mets, went 2-for-3 with 2R and 1BB at the plate, becoming the first pitcher in Blue Jays history to reach base safely three times in a game…was the third multi-hit game by a pitcher in franchise history (Roy Halladay, Drew Hutchison)…tied Halladay's club record for runs scored by a pitcher…also allowed just 2H over 7.0 scoreless innings (0BB, 10K), becoming the first AL pitcher to record at least as many hits as his opponent while tossing at least 7.0IP since California's Clyde Wright on 9/14/72 vs. Texas.
- Earned his 100th career win on 6/8 vs. Baltimore.
- Made his Yankees debut on 7/29 vs. Kansas City, starting and earning the win (6.0IP, 1ER).
- In 8/14 win vs. Tampa Bay, allowed 1H over 7.0 scoreless innings (4BB, 4K, 1HP), his first career start with at least 7.0IP and 1H-or-fewer.
- Made one postseason start, taking the loss in ALDS Game 1 at Boston (2.0IP, 4H, 5ER, 1BB, 2K, 1HR)…was on the roster for the Yankees' AL Wild Card Game win vs. Oakland but did not pitch.

2017

- Posted a 10-11 record and 3.53 ERA (145.1IP, 145H, 64R/57ER, 46BB, 142K, 18HR) in 25 starts with Toronto…held opponents to a .252 BA (145-for-575); LH .198 (22-for-111), RH .265 (123-for-464)…posted a 2.8 WAR and 3.76 FIP (FanGraphs)…made his eighth Opening Day roster.
- His .198 opponents' BA vs. left-handed batters was fifth-lowest among AL starting pitchers (min. 100AB).
- Exited his 4/16 start vs. Baltimore with left elbow tightness…was placed on the 10-day disabled list on 4/18 (retroactive to 4/17) with left elbow inflammation…made one rehab start with Single-A Dunedin (3.0IP, 3ER)…was reinstated on 5/30.
- Went 7-3 with a 2.81 ERA (67.1IP, 21ER) in his final 11 starts (beg. 8/2), permitting 1ER in 8-of-11 turns.

2016

- Went 20-4 with a 3.18 ERA (195.0IP, 168H, 72R/69ER, 60BB, 163K, 22HR) in his first season back in Toronto…set career highs in wins, starts, innings and quality starts (21)…held opponents to a .231 BA (168-for-726); LH .245 (36-for-147), RH .132-for-579)…Toronto was 24-8 in his 32 starts…posted a 3.1 WAR and 3.96 FIP (FanGraphs)…made his seventh Opening Day roster.
- Finished sixth in AL Cy Young voting, accumulating 14 points on six ballots (3 third-place votes, 2 fourth-place votes, 1 fifth-place vote)…was the highest finish by a pitcher who spent the entire season in Toronto since Roy Halladay placed fifth in 2009.
- Became the sixth Toronto pitcher to win 20 games in a single season, joining Roy Halladay (2003, '08), Roger Clemens (1997-98), David Wells (2000), Pat Hentgen (1996) and Jack Morris (1992)…was tied for the fourth-highest win total by a Blue Jays pitcher behind Halladay (22-7 in 2003), Clemens (21-7 in 1997) and Morris (21-6 in 1992)…joined Wells (20-8 in 2000) as the only Toronto left-handers to win 20 games…was one of three 20-game winners in 2016, joining Boston's Rick Porcello (22-4) and Washington's Max Scherzer (20-7)…with a .833 winning percentage, he and teammate Aaron Sanchez (.882, 15-2 in 2016) posted the two highest marks in Blue Jays history (min. 15 decisions)…was the third-highest clip in the Majors in 2016 behind Sanchez (.882, 15-2) and Porcello (.846).
- Went 12-3 with a 3.36 ERA (112.1IP, 42ER) in 18 starts before the All-Star break, tied for the third-most wins in the Majors…became the fourth pitcher in Blue Jays history to earn 12 wins prior to the All-Star break, joining Roy Halladay (2003, '05-06), David Wells (2000) and Roger Clemens (1997).
- Earned his 15th win on 8/4 vs. Houston, becoming the first pitcher in the AL to reach the total in 2016 (second in the Majors to Washington's Stephen Strasburg, who earned his 15th win on 8/1).
- Went 11-0 with a 2.53 ERA (74.2IP, 21ER) over 12 starts from 6/11-8/17, the longest winning streak of his career…tied for the third-longest winning streak in Blue Jays history behind Roy Halladay (15 straight in 2003) and Roger Clemens (15 straight in 1998)…was the AL's longest and the Majors' second-longest winning streak in 2016 (Washington's Stephen Strasburg, 13-0 from 4/6-7/15)…won a career-best six straight starts from 6/11-7/8.
- Recorded his 1,000th career strikeout on 8/30 at Baltimore (Chris Davis in the second inning).
- Made two postseason starts as the Blue Jays advanced to the ALCS, going 1-1 with a 2.70 ERA (10.0IP, 3ER)…defeated the Rangers in ALDS Game 2 at Texas to earn his first career postseason victory (5.0IP, 9H, 1ER, 1BB, 5K)…took the loss in ALCS Game 2 at Cleveland (5.0IP, 4H, 2ER, 1BB, 4K, 1HR).

2015

- Split the season between Seattle and Pittsburgh, combining to go 11-8 with a 3.61 ERA (172.0IP, 173H, 71R/69ER, 45BB, 151K, 16HR) in 32 games (31 starts)…held opponents to a .259 BA (173-for-668); LH .267 (47-for-176), RH .256 (126-for-492)…posted a career-high 3.4 WAR and career-best 3.41 FIP (FanGraphs)…made his sixth Opening Day roster, with his fourth different club (Philadelphia, Houston, Toronto, Seattle).
- In four months with the Mariners, went 4-6 with a 4.64 ERA (108.2IP, 56ER) in 21 games (20 starts)…went 3-1 with a 3.31 ERA (65.1IP, 24ER) in his first 11 starts, then was 1-5 with a 6.65 ERA (43.1IP, 32ER) in his next 10 games (nine starts)…earned just one win in his final 15 games (14 starts) with Seattle.
- Became the second Seattle pitcher to allow 2R-or-fewer in each of his first six home starts (4/17-6/5), joining Joel Piñeiro (6GS, 7/26/01-5/10/02).
- Was acquired by the Pirates from the Mariners in exchange for RHP Adrian Sampson on 7/31.
- Went 7-2 with a 1.85 ERA (63.1IP, 13ER) in 11 starts with Pittsburgh…yielded one-or-zero runs in 7-of-11 starts, including five scoreless outings.
- From 8/14 through the end of the season, was 7-1 with a 1.37 ERA (59.0IP, 43H, 9ER, 11BB, 63K, 3HR), the second-lowest ERA in the Majors behind Chicago-NL's Jake Arrieta (0.49).

2014

- Went 11-11 with a 4.22 ERA (158.0IP, 160H, 79R/74ER, 51BB, 133K, 22HR) in 30 games (26 starts) for the Blue Jays…held opponents to a .261 BA (160-for-614); LH .268 (33-for-123), RH .259 (127-for-491).
- Began the season on the 15-day disabled list with back soreness…made one rehab start each with Single-A Dunedin and Triple-A Buffalo, combining for a 1-0 record and 2.79 ERA (9.2IP, 3ER).
- Was reinstated on 4/13 and joined the bullpen, posting a 4.15 ERA (4.1IP, 2ER) in three appearances…made a fourth relief appearance later in the season on 7/12 at Tampa Bay (0.2IP, 2ER).
- Was inserted into the starting rotation on 5/5…in 26 starts, went 11-11 with a 4.12 ERA (153.0IP, 70ER).
- On 8/7 vs. Baltimore, set a career high with 12K but took the loss (8.0IP, 5H, 2ER, 1BB, 1HR, 1HP).
- Was acquired by the Seattle Mariners from the Blue Jays in exchange for OF Michael Saunders on 12/3/14.

2013

- Made just 18 starts for Toronto, logging a 5-7 record with a 4.56 ERA (92.2IP, 91H, 53R/47ER, 45BB, 77K, 10HR)…held opponents to a .250 BA (91-for-364); LH .304 (31-for-102), RH .229 (60-for-262)…made his fifth Opening Day roster, his first with Toronto.
- Recorded his 500th career strikeout on 4/6 vs. Boston (Mike Napoli in the first inning).
- On 5/7 at Tampa Bay, suffered a skull fracture and right knee sprain after being struck in the head by a line drive off the bat of Desmond Jennings…was placed on the 15-day disabled list on 5/8…was transferred to the 60-day D.L. on 5/24…the stint was due primarily to the right knee sprain…made five rehab starts with the GCL Blue Jays (1GS), Single-A Dunedin (1GS) and Triple-A Buffalo (3GS), going 0-2 with a 4.22 ERA (21.1IP, 10ER)…was reinstated from the 60-day D.L. on 8/5.
- Had a 2-2 record and 4.91 ERA (33.0IP, 18ER) in seven starts prior to going on the disabled list…went 3-5 with a 4.37 ERA (59.2IP, 29ER) in 11 starts following the D.L. stint.

2012

- Combined to go 10-11 with a 4.79 ERA (144.2IP, 147H, 79R/77ER, 56BB, 144K, 19HR) in 28 games (24 starts) between the Astros and Blue Jays…held opponents to a .264 BA (147-for-556); LH .259 (38-for-147), RH .267 (109-for-409)…made his fourth Opening Day roster.
- In 18 starts for Houston, logged a 7-9 record and 4.83 ERA (104.1IP, 56ER).
- Set a career high with 11 hits allowed and tied a career high with 8ER allowed in 6/13 loss at San Francisco (3.1IP).
- Was acquired by Toronto along with RHP David Carpenter and RHP Brandon Lyon from the Astros in exchange for RHP Asher Wojciechowski, C Carlos Perez, LHP David Rollins, RHP Joe Musgrove, RHP Francisco Cordero, OF Ben Francisco and a player to be named later (RHP Kevin Comer) on 7/20.
- Went 3-2 with a 4.69 ERA (40.1IP, 21ER) in 10 games (six starts) with Toronto…made his first four appearances out of the bullpen, posting a 5.14 ERA (7.0IP, 4ER)…in his six starts, was 3-2 with a 4.59 ERA (33.1IP, 17ER).
- On 8/17 vs. Texas, tied a Blue Jays club record by striking out six consecutive batters.
- Was placed on the 15-day disabled list on 9/7 (retroactive to 9/4) with a right foot fracture…underwent surgery and missed the rest of the season.

2011

- Made 28 starts for the Astros and compiled a 6-15 record with a 5.35 ERA (156.1IP, 157H, 103R/93ER, 83BB, 134K, 21HR)…held opponents to a .265 BA (157-for-592); LH .270 (31-for-115), RH .264 (126-for-477)…set career highs in losses, runs and walks…made his third Opening Day roster and first with Houston.
- Ranked third in the NL in losses and fourth in walks.
- On 5/29 vs. Arizona, hit his first Major League home run, a solo shot off Josh Collmenter…hit .389 (7-for-18) through this game before going 0-for-25 over the remainder of the season.
- Lost a career-worst seven consecutive decisions over 10 starts from 5/19-7/7.
- Was optioned to Triple-A Oklahoma City on 8/6…in three starts with the RedHawks, went 1-0 with a 1.50 ERA (18.0IP, 3ER)…was recalled on 8/24.
- In six starts following his trip to the minors, went 2-1 with a 2.43 ERA (37.0IP, 10ER)…was 4-14 with a 6.26 ERA (119.1IP, 83ER) in 22 starts prior to the stint.

2010

- Split the season between Philadelphia and Houston, posting a 6-4 record with 1CG and a 3.40 ERA (87.1IP, 73H, 37R/33ER, 47BB, 70K, 8HR) in 16 starts…limited opponents to a .230 BA (73-for-317); LH .179 (12-for-67), RH .244 (61-for-250)…made his second Opening Day roster.
- Made only three starts with the Phillies before the trade, going 1-0 with a 1.76 ERA (15.1IP, 3ER).
- Was placed on the 15-day disabled list on 4/16 with a left forearm strain…appeared in six rehab games (five starts) with Triple-A Lehigh Valley, Double-A Reading and Single-A Clearwater before being reinstated from the D.L. on 7/6 and optioned to Lehigh Valley, where he made three more starts…overall, went 1-2 with a 5.97 ERA (37.2IP, 25ER) in nine minor league appearances (eight starts) with Lehigh Valley (5G/4GS), Reading (3GS) and Clearwater (1GS)…was recalled by the Phillies on 7/25.
- Was acquired by the Astros along with INF Jonathan Villar and OF Anthony Gose from the Phillies in exchange for RHP Roy Oswalt and cash considerations on 7/29.
- In 13 starts with Houston, went 5-4 with a 3.75 ERA (72.0IP, 30ER).
- On 7/30 vs. Milwaukee (W, 6.0IP, 2H, 0R, 4BB, 6K), became the seventh pitcher in Astros history to throw at least 6.0 shutout innings in his team debut.
- Earned wins both for and against the two clubs he played for in 2010, on 4/9 at Houston (5.0IP, 0R) and 8/25 at Philadelphia (6.1IP, 2ER).
- On 8/30 vs. St. Louis, tossed a two-hit complete game shutout (1BB, 4K)…marked the fourth complete game and third shutout of his career…marked his fewest hits allowed in a complete game in his career…was the first Houston left-hander to allow 2H-or-fewer in a complete game since Bob Knepper threw a one-hit shutout on 9/21/88 vs. Atlanta.

2009
- In his first full Major League season, was 12-4 with 3CG and a 2.93 ERA (166.0IP, 149H, 55R/54ER, 56BB, 119K, 20HR) in 35 games (23 starts) with the Phillies...held opponents to a .244 BA (149-for-610); LH .216 (32-for-148), RH .253 (117-for-462)...made his first career Opening Day roster.
- Finished second in NL "Rookie of the Year" voting to Florida's Chris Coghlan, garnering 94 points across 32 ballots (10 first-place votes, 11 second-place votes, 11 third-place votes)...was named NL "Rookie of the Year" by both The Sporting News and MLB.com...won the Players' Choice Award for NL Outstanding Rookie...was named to both the Baseball America and TOPPS All-Rookie Teams...earned the Steve Carlton "Pitcher of the Year" Award as the top Phillies pitcher, from the Philadelphia chapter of the BBWAA.
- Ranked eighth in the NL in ERA.
- Led NL rookies in innings and strikeouts, was tied for the lead in wins, and ranked second in ERA (min. 100.0IP)...was the first Phillies rookie to win 12 games in a season since Tom Underwood (14-13) in 1975.
- Went 7-2 with a 1.99 ERA (95.0IP, 21ER) in 18 road games (13 starts), the lowest road ERA in the NL...allowed 2R-or-fewer in 11-of-13 road starts.
- Began the year in the bullpen, going 2-0 with a 2.49 ERA (21.2IP, 6ER) in 12 appearances.
- Was moved to the rotation on 5/23 at the Yankees...in 23 starts, was 10-4 with a 2.99 ERA (144.1IP, 48ER).
- Won his first seven decisions of the season before taking his first loss on 7/24 vs. St. Louis.
- Compiled a career-best 15-start unbeaten streak from 7/4/08-7/19/09...was 6-0 with a 2.63 ERA (96.0IP, 28ER) in those 15 starts.
- On 6/27 at Toronto, tossed his first career complete game and shutout (9.0IP, 5H, 0BB, 4K).
- On 7/2 at Atlanta, recorded his first Major League hit with an infield single off Javier Vazquez.
- On 8/5 vs. Colorado, tossed his second career shutout and recorded his first double-digit-strikeout game (9.0IP, 4H, 2BB, 10K)...also collected his first extra-base hit, an eighth-inning double off Josh Fogg.
- On 9/5 at Houston, suffered a right intercostal strain during batting practice and missed his next two starts.
- Recorded his first career RBI on 9/24 at Milwaukee with a single off Jeff Suppan.
- Made six postseason appearances (one start), compiling a 5.68 ERA (6.1IP, 8H, 4ER, 6BB, 8K, 1HR)...made his first career postseason start in NLDS Game 3 at Colorado (ND, 3.0IP, 3ER)...appeared in two World Series games vs. the Yankees, allowing a solo HR to Nick Swisher in Game 3 in Philadelphia (1.2IP, 1ER) and throwing a scoreless inning in Game 6 in the Bronx.

2008
- In three stints for the Phillies (7/4-10, 7/29-8/8, 9/1-end of season), compiled a 1-0 record and 3.69 ERA (31.2IP, 13ER) in eight appearances (four starts).
- Earned his first Major League win on 9/17 at Atlanta, throwing 6.0 scoreless innings (3H, 1BB, 2K)...marked his first career scoreless start.
- Went 8-7 with a 3.60 ERA (135.0IP, 54ER) in 24 games (23 starts) with Triple-A Lehigh Valley...ranked second in the International League with 151K and was eighth in ERA...earned the Paul Owens Award as the Phillies' best minor league pitcher...was named a Baseball America Triple-A All-Star.
- Made his postseason debut, entering in relief in an NLCS Game 3 loss at Los Angeles-NL (3.0IP, 4H, 1ER, 2BB, 2K)...was his only postseason appearance in 2008...was on the roster for Philadelphia's NLDS win over Milwaukee and World Series win over Tampa Bay.
- Following the season, was rated as the No. 9 prospect in the Phillies organization by Baseball America.

2007
- Made his Major League debut for Philadelphia with a start on 6/30 vs. the Mets (L, 4.0IP, 7H, 5ER, 2BB, 5K, 3HR)...recorded his first career strikeout (Carlos Beltrán in the first)...became the fourth pitcher in Phillies history to allow at least 3HR in his debut (Paul Lo Duca two-run HR in the first, David Wright solo HR in the first, Carlos Beltrán two-run HR in the fifth)...had his contract selected earlier that day...was optioned back to Triple-A Ottawa after the game.
- Pitched the balance of the season with Ottawa, where he went 4-6 with a 5.02 ERA (118.1IP, 66ER) in 24 starts.

2006
- Split the season between Single-A Clearwater, Double-A Reading and Triple-A Scranton/Wilkes-Barre...in 26 starts, went 10-9 with a 2.69 ERA (160.2IP, 48ER)...ranked third among Phillies farmhands with 162K.
- Was named a Florida State League Mid-Season All-Star after posting a 3-7 record and a 2.81 ERA (80.0IP, 25ER) in 13 starts at Clearwater.
- Pitched for the Peoria Saguaros in the Arizona Fall League, going 1-0 with a 5.02 ERA (14.1IP, 8ER) in five games (four starts).
- Following the season, was rated as the No. 8 prospect in the Phillies organization by Baseball America.

2005
- Combined with Single-A Lakewood and Double-A Reading to go 5-4 with a 2.30 ERA (78.1IP, 20ER) in 15 games (13 starts)...pitched a majority of the season with Lakewood before making one start for Reading.

2004
- Made his professional debut with short-season Single-A Batavia, going 1-2 with a 2.02 ERA (35.2IP, 8ER) in 11 starts.

PERSONAL
- Full name is James Anthony (J.A.) Happ…his first name is pronounced "JAY."
- Played three seasons at Northwestern University (Ill.)…became the first player in school history to be named All-Big Ten in three straight seasons…led the Big Ten in ERA (2.68) and strikeouts (106) as a senior.
- Graduated from St. Bede H.S. in Chicago…was named Bureau County "Athlete of the Year" as a senior…also played basketball for four seasons, becoming the school's all-time leading scorer.

Happ's Career Pitching Record

Year	Club	W	L	ERA	G	GS	CG	SHO	SV	IP	H	R	ER	HR	HP	BB	SO	WP	BK
2004	Batavia	1	2	2.02	11	11	0	0	0	35.2	22	8	8	1	3	18	37	0	0
2005	Lakewood	4	4	2.36	14	12	0	0	0	72.1	57	26	19	3	5	26	70	4	1
	Reading	1	0	1.50	1	1	0	0	0	6.0	3	1	1	0	0	2	8	1	0
2006	Clearwater	3	7	2.81	13	13	0	0	0	80.0	63	35	25	9	2	19	77	1	2
	Reading	6	2	2.65	12	12	0	0	0	74.2	58	27	22	2	3	29	81	0	0
	Scranton/WB	1	0	1.50	1	1	0	0	0	6.0	3	1	1	1	1	4	0	0	0
2007	Ottawa	4	6	5.02	24	24	0	0	0	118.1	118	74	66	12	0	62	117	2	1
	PHILADELPHIA	1	0	11.25	1	1	0	0	0	4.0	7	5	5	3	0	2	5	0	0
2008	Lehigh Valley	8	7	3.60	24	23	0	0	0	135.0	116	58	54	14	1	48	151	4	0
	PHILADELPHIA	1	0	3.69	8	4	0	0	0	31.2	28	13	13	3	1	14	26	1	0
2009	PHILADELPHIA	12	4	2.93	35	23	0	0	0	166.0	149	55	54	20	5	56	119	2	0
2010	PHILADELPHIA - a	1	0	1.76	3	3	0	0	0	15.1	13	4	3	1	0	12	9	1	0
	Lehigh Valley	0	1	4.84	5	4	0	0	0	22.1	26	12	12	3	0	15	22	0	0
	Clearwater	0	1	6.00	1	1	0	0	0	3.0	3	2	2	0	0	0	2	1	0
	Reading	1	0	8.03	3	3	0	0	0	12.1	18	11	11	3	1	4	10	1	0
	HOUSTON	5	4	3.75	13	13	1	1	0	72.0	60	33	30	7	1	35	61	3	0
2011	HOUSTON	6	15	5.35	28	28	0	0	0	156.1	157	103	93	21	2	83	134	3	2
	Oklahoma City	1	0	1.50	3	3	0	0	0	18.0	11	5	3	0	0	9	16	0	0
2012	HOUSTON	7	9	4.83	18	18	0	0	0	104.1	112	58	56	17	1	39	98	5	0
	TORONTO - c, d	3	2	4.69	10	6	0	0	0	40.1	35	21	21	2	1	17	46	2	0
2013	TORONTO - e	5	7	4.56	18	18	0	0	0	92.2	91	53	47	10	2	45	77	5	0
	GCL Blue Jays	0	0	0.00	1	1	0	0	0	3.0	4	2	0	0	0	0	0	0	0
	Dunedin	0	0	0.00	1	1	0	0	0	5.0	3	0	0	0	0	0	7	0	0
	Buffalo	0	2	6.75	3	3	0	0	0	13.1	17	10	10	2	0	8	13	1	0
2014	Dunedin - f	1	0	3.60	1	1	0	0	0	5.0	3	2	2	0	0	1	5	0	0
	Buffalo	0	0	1.93	1	1	0	0	0	4.2	5	1	1	1	0	2	6	0	0
	TORONTO	11	11	4.22	30	26	0	0	0	158.0	160	79	74	22	2	51	133	1	0
2015	SEATTLE - g	4	6	4.64	21	20	0	0	0	108.2	121	58	56	13	2	32	82	4	0
	PITTSBURGH - h	7	2	1.85	11	11	0	0	0	63.1	52	13	13	3	0	13	69	2	0
2016	TORONTO - i	20	4	3.18	32	32	0	0	0	195.0	168	72	69	22	6	60	163	3	2
2017	TORONTO - j	10	11	3.53	25	25	0	0	0	145.1	145	64	57	18	0	46	142	4	0
	Dunedin	0	0	9.00	1	1	0	0	0	3.0	7	3	3	0	0	0	3	0	0
2018	TORONTO	10	6	4.18	20	20	0	0	0	114.0	99	61	53	17	4	35	130	1	0
	YANKEES - k, l, m	7	0	2.69	11	11	0	0	0	63.2	51	20	19	10	5	16	63	3	1
2019	YANKEES	12	8	4.91	31	30	0	0	0	161.1	160	88	88	34	5	49	140	3	0
Minor League Totals		31	32	3.50	120	116	0	0	0	617.2	537	278	240	51	16	244	629	15	4
AL Totals		82	55	4.04	198	188	0	0	0	1079.0	1030	516	484	148	27	351	976	26	3
NL Totals		39	35	3.92	117	101	4	3	0	613.0	578	284	267	75	10	254	521	17	2
Major League Totals		121	90	3.99	315	289	4	3	0	1692.0	1608	800	751	223	37	605	1497	43	5
NYY Totals		19	8	4.28	42	41	0	0	0	225.0	211	108	107	44	10	65	203	6	1

Selected by the Philadelphia Phillies in the third round in the 2004 First-Year Player Draft.

a - Placed on the 15-day disabled list from April 16 - July 6, 2010 with a left forearm strain.
b - Acquired by the Houston Astros along with INF Jonathan Villar and OF Anthony Gose from the Philadelphia Phillies in exchange for RHP Roy Oswalt and cash considerations on July 29, 2010.
c - Acquired by the Toronto Blue Jays along with RHP David Carpenter and RHP Brandon Lyon from the Houston Astros in exchange for RHP Asher Wojciechowski, C Carlos Perez, LHP David Rollins, RHP Joe Musgrove, RHP Francisco Cordero, OF Ben Francisco and a player to be named later (RHP Kevin Comer) on July 20, 2012.
d - Placed on the 15-day disabled list from September 7, 2012 (retroactive to September 4) - rest of the season with a right foot fracture.
e - Placed on the 15-day disabled list from May 8 - August 5, 2013 with a skull fracture and right knee sprain…was transferred to the 60-day disabled list on May 24, 2013.
f - Placed on the 15-day disabled list from March 26 - April 13, 2014 with back soreness.
g - Acquired by the Seattle Mariners from the Toronto Blue Jays in exchange for OF Michael Saunders on December 3, 2014.
h - Acquired by the Pittsburgh Pirates from the Seattle Mariners in exchange for RHP Adrian Sampson on July 31, 2015.
i - Signed by the Toronto Blue Jays as a free agent on November 27, 2015.
j - Placed on the 10-day disabled list from April 18 (retroactive to April 17) - May 30, 2017 with left elbow inflammation.
k - Acquired by the Yankees from the Toronto Blue Jays in exchange for INF Brandon Drury and OF Billy McKinney on July 26, 2018.
l - Placed on the 10-day disabled list from August 2 (retroactive to July 30) - August 9, 2018 with hand, foot and mouth disease.
m- Signed by the Yankees as a free agent on December 17, 2018.

Happ's Postseason Record

Year	Club vs. Opp.	W	L	ERA	G	GS	CG	SHO	SV	IP	H	R	ER	HR	HP	BB	SO	WP	BK
2008	PHI vs. MIL (DS)							On Roster - Did Not Pitch											
	PHI vs. LAD (CS)	0	0	3.00	1	0	0	0	0	3.0	4	1	1	0	0	2	2	0	0
	PHI vs. TB (WS)							On Roster - Did Not Pitch											
2009	PHI vs. COL (DS)	0	0	9.00	2	1	0	0	0	3.0	6	3	3	0	0	2	4	0	0
	PHI vs. LAD (CS)	0	0	0.00	3	0	0	0	0	0.2	0	0	0	0	0	3	0	0	0
	PHI vs. NYY (WS)	0	0	3.38	2	0	0	0	0	2.2	2	1	1	1	0	1	4	0	0
2016	TOR vs. TEX (DS)	1	0	1.80	1	1	0	0	0	5.0	9	1	1	0	0	1	5	0	0
	TOR vs. CLE (CS)	0	1	3.60	1	1	0	0	0	5.0	4	2	2	1	0	1	4	1	0
2018	NYY vs. OAK (WC)							On Roster - Did Not Pitch											
	NYY vs. BOS (DS)	0	1	22.50	1	1	0	0	0	2.0	4	5	5	1	0	1	2	0	0
2019	NYY vs. MIN (DS)	0	0	0.00	1	0	0	0	0	1.0	1	0	0	0	0	1	2	0	0
	NYY vs. HOU (CS)	0	1	3.38	2	0	0	0	0	2.2	1	1	1	1	0	1	1	0	0
Wild Card Totals		-	-	-	-	-	-	-	-	-	-	-	-	-	-	-	-	-	-
LDS Totals		1	1	7.36	5	3	0	0	0	11.0	20	9	9	1	0	5	13	0	0
LCS Totals		0	2	3.18	7	1	0	0	0	11.1	9	4	4	2	0	7	7	1	0
WS Totals		0	0	3.38	2	0	0	0	0	2.2	2	1	1	1	0	1	4	0	0
POSTSEASON TOTALS		1	3	5.04	14	4	0	0	0	25.0	31	14	14	4	0	13	24	1	0

Happ's All-Star Game Record

Year	Club, Site	W	L	ERA	G	GS	CG	SHO	SV	IP	H	R	ER	HR	HP	BB	SO	WP	BK
2018	TOR, Washington	0	0	9.00	1	0	0	0	1	1.0	1	1	1	1	0	0	1	0	0
All-Star Game Totals		0	0	9.00	1	0	0	0	1	1.0	1	1	1	1	0	0	1	0	0

Happ's Career Fielding Record

Position	PCT	G	PO	A	E	TC	DP
Pitcher	.970	315	45	179	7	231	2

Happ's Regular Season Batting Record

Year	Team	AVG	G	AB	R	H	2B	3B	HR	RBI	SH	SF	HP	BB	SO	SB	CS
2019	NYY	.000	32	3	1	0	0	0	0	1	0	0	0	0	0	0	0
Major League Totals		.102	315	197	13	20	2	0	1	6	31	0	0	10	86	0	0

Happ's Career Bests and Streaks

COMPLETE GAMES: 4, last on 8/30/10 vs. STL. **LOW-HIT COMPLETE GAME:** 2, 8/30/10 vs. STL. **IP (START):** 9.0 - 3 times (last on 8/30/10 vs. STL). **IP (RELIEF):** 5.0, 9/25/19 at TB. **HITS:** 11 - 2 times (last on 6/23/19 vs. HOU). **RUNS:** 8 - 5 times (last on 6/23/19 vs. HOU). **BB:** 7 - 2 times (last on 5/2/13 vs. BOS). **SO:** 12, 8/7/14 vs. BAL. **HR:** 3 - 10 times (last on 8/9/19 at TOR). **WINNING STREAK:** 11g, 6/11-8/17/16. **LOSING STREAK:** 7g, 5/19-7/7/11. **SCORELESS STREAK (IP):** 19.1, 8/26-9/12/19.

Pitcher of the Month: None   **Player of the Week:** None   **Rookie of the Month:** None

---

No Hits For You

Former Yankee Allie Reynolds (pictured) is one of only five pitchers to record two regular-season no-hitters in the same season, accomplishing the feat in 1951…prior to Reynolds, Cincinnati's Johnny Vander Meer was the first pitcher to hurl two no-hitters in the same season, doing so in back-to-back starts in June 1938…Detroit's Virgil Trucks (1952), California's Nolan Ryan (1973) and Washington's Max Scherzer (2015) are the only other pitchers to match the record.

Reynolds' first no-hitter of the 1951 season came on July 12 vs. Cleveland…his second no-hitter, took place in Game 1 of a doubleheader on Sept. 28 vs. Boston in an 8-0 win…notably with the Yankees' subsequent victory in Game 2, they clinched the American League pennant.

BEN HELLER • RHP

61

HT: 6-3 • **WT:** 210 • **BATS:** R • **THROWS:** R
BIRTHDATE: 8/5/91 • **OPENING DAY AGE:** 28
BIRTHPLACE: Milwaukee, Wisc.
RESIDES: Brookfield, Wisc.
COLLEGE: Olivet Nazarene University
M.L. SERVICE: 2 years, 96 days (Rookie)

STATUS
- Acquired by the Yankees from Cleveland, along with OF Clint Frazier, LHP Justus Sheffield and RHP J.P. Feyereisen, in exchange for LHP Andrew Miller on July 31, 2016.

2019
- Posted a 1.23 ERA (7.1IP, 1ER) in six relief appearances with the Yankees.
- Missed the Yankees' first 145 games of the season after being placed on the 10-day injured list on 3/28 (retroactive to 3/25) recovering from "Tommy John" surgery, performed on 4/6/18…was transferred to the 60-day I.L. on 4/4…combined with Single-A Tampa and Triple-A Scranton/Wilkes-Barre to post a 0.57 ERA (15.2IP, 1ER) with 20K in 12 rehab games (six starts), including one playoff appearance with the RailRiders…struck out a rehab-high five batters in 2.0 scoreless innings of relief (1BB) in Game 3 of the first round of the Governor's Cup playoffs on 9/7 vs. Durham.
- Was reinstated from the 60-day injured list on 9/10 after being returned from rehab on 9/8.
- Made his season debut in Game 1 of 9/12 doubleheader at Detroit (1.0IP, 2H, 1ER, 1BB, 1K, 1HR)…was his first Major League appearance since 10/1/17 vs. Toronto…tossed 6.1 scoreless innings over his final five outings (8K).
- Was added to the Yankees' ALCS roster as an injury replacement for LHP CC Sabathia prior to ALCS Game 5 (did not pitch).

2018
- Missed the entire season after undergoing "Tommy John" surgery on 4/6, which also involved removing a bone spur from his right elbow…the procedure was performed by Yankees Head Team Physician Dr. Christopher Ahmad…was placed on the 10-day disabled list on 4/2 (retroactive to 3/27) with a right elbow bone spur…was transferred to the 60-day disabled list on 4/3 and reinstated on 11/1.

2017
- Was 1-0 with a 0.82 ERA (11.0IP, 1ER) in nine relief appearances over three stints with the Yankees (6/12-14, 7/8-16 and 9/1-10/1).
- Made his season debut in 6/13 loss at Los Angeles-AL, allowing a "walk-off" infield single in the 11th (0.1IP, 1H, 1BB).
- Tossed a career-high 2.1 scoreless innings in 9/28 loss vs. Tampa Bay (1BB, 2K).
- Made 41 relief appearances for Triple-A Scranton/Wilkes-Barre, going 5-4 with six saves, a 2.88 ERA (56.1IP, 18ER) and 82K…led Yankees farmhands (min. 50.0IP) with a 13.10 K/9.0IP ratio…at the time of his final call-up, his .172 (34-for-198) opponents' BA and 13.10 K/9.0IP ratio (56.1IP, 82K) ranked second among relievers in the International League.

2016
- Went 1-0 with a 6.43 ERA (7.0IP, 5ER) in 10 relief appearances over two stints with the Yankees (8/11-13 and 8/23-10/2).
- Was signed to a Major League contract and selected to the Yankees' 25-man roster from Triple-A Scranton/Wilkes-Barre on 8/11…made his Major League debut in 8/26 win vs. Baltimore, tossing a scoreless eighth inning (1.0IP).
- Allowed a two-run HR in 0.2IP (3H, 1BB, 1K) in 8/28 loss vs. Baltimore, recording his first career strikeout (Chris Davis, swinging).
- Earned his first Major League win on 8/31 at Kansas City, tossing a perfect 12th inning (1.0IP).
- In six games with Scranton/Wilkes-Barre, was 0-1 with one save and a 1.42 ERA (6.1IP, 1ER, 7K).
- Was acquired by the Yankees from Cleveland on 7/31 with OF Clint Frazier, LHP Justus Sheffield and RHP J.P. Feyereisen in exchange for LHP Andrew Miller.
- Combined to go 3-2 with 12 saves in 13 chances and a 1.73 ERA (41.2IP, 23H, 8ER, 12BB, 48K, 2HR) in 43 relief appearances with Triple-A Columbus (28G) and Double-A Akron (15G), holding batters to a combined .159 (23-for-145) batting average with a 0.84 WHIP.

2015
- Combined with Single-A Lynchburg and Double-A Akron to go 0-2 with 12 saves, a 4.02 ERA (40.1IP, 18ER) and 58K in 41 relief appearances…tied for fourth among Indians minor leaguers with 12 saves.
- Following the season, was tabbed by *Baseball America* as having the "Best Fastball" in the Indians organization.

2014
- Combined with Single-A Lake County and Single-A Carolina to go 5-1 with five saves, a 2.38 ERA (53.0IP, 14ER) and 81K in 45 relief appearances.
- Led all Midwest League pitchers (min. 30.0IP) with a 15.57 K/9.0IP ratio (37.0IP, 64K).
- Following the season, was tabbed by MiLB.com as an Organization All-Star.

2013
- Made his professional debut, going 1-3 with a 3.13 ERA (37.1IP, 13ER) and 39K in 21 games (one start) with short-season Single-A Mahoning Valley.

PERSONAL
- Is married to Martha…the couple has a son.
- Graduated from Whitewater High School (Wisc.), where he pitched, caught and played SS and 3B…attended Olivet Nazarene University in Bourbonnais , Ill. (pronounced "BURR-buh-nay"), approximately 50 miles south of Chicago.
- In December 2017, he and his wife traveled to Guatemala, delivering Christmas gifts to children in a local orphanage and donating ovens and water filters to families living in impoverished communities.

Heller's Career Pitching Record

Year	Club	W	L	ERA	G	GS	CG	SHO	SV	IP	H	R	ER	HR	HP	BB	SO	WP	BK
2013	Mahoning Valley	1	3	3.13	21	1	0	0	2	37.1	37	16	13	0	2	14	39	4	0
2014	Lake County	4	1	2.43	28	0	0	0	4	37.0	19	10	10	3	2	16	64	4	1
	Carolina	1	0	2.25	17	0	0	0	1	16.0	8	6	4	1	3	13	17	2	0
2015	Lynchburg	0	2	4.46	36	0	0	0	12	34.1	30	18	17	0	2	13	43	6	0
	Akron	0	0	1.50	5	0	0	0	0	6.0	5	1	1	0	0	1	15	5	0
2016	Akron	1	0	0.55	15	0	0	0	7	16.1	3	1	1	1	2	5	23	0	0
	Columbus	2	2	2.49	28	0	0	0	5	25.1	20	7	7	1	4	7	25	2	1
	Scranton/WB - a	0	1	1.42	6	0	0	0	1	6.1	3	1	1	0	0	2	7	0	0
	YANKEES	1	0	6.43	10	0	0	0	0	7.0	11	5	5	3	2	4	6	0	0
2017	Scranton/WB	5	4	2.88	41	0	0	0	6	56.1	34	21	18	6	3	21	82	8	0
	YANKEES	1	0	0.82	9	0	0	0	0	11.0	5	1	1	0	0	6	9	1	0
2018	YANKEES							Did Not Pitch - Injured - b											
2019	Tampa - c	0	0	0.00	2	2	0	0	0	2.2	3	0	0	0	0	1	2	1	0
	Scranton/WB	0	0	0.82	9	4	0	0	1	11.0	5	1	1	0	1	3	13	1	0
	YANKEES	0	0	1.23	6	0	0	0	0	7.1	6	1	1	1	0	3	9	0	0
Minor League Totals		**14**	**13**	**2.64**	**208**	**7**	**0**	**0**	**39**	**248.2**	**167**	**82**	**73**	**12**	**19**	**96**	**330**	**33**	**2**
Major League Totals		**2**	**0**	**2.49**	**25**	**0**	**0**	**0**	**0**	**25.1**	**22**	**7**	**7**	**4**	**2**	**13**	**24**	**1**	**0**

Selected by Cleveland in the 22nd round of the 2013 First-Year Player Draft.

a - Acquired by the Yankees from the Cleveland Indians, along with OF Clint Frazier, LHP Justus Sheffield and RHP J.P. Feyereisen, in exchange for LHP Andrew Miller on July 31, 2016.
b - Placed on the 10-day disabled list on April 2, 2018 (retroactive to March 27) with a right elbow bone spur…was transferred to the 60-day disabled list on April 3, 2018, missing the entire season.
c - Placed on the 10-day injured list on March 28, 2019 (retroactive to March 25) recovering from "Tommy John" surgery…was transferred to the 60-day injured list on April 4, returned from rehab on September 8 and reinstated from the 60-day injured list on September 10, 2019.

Heller's Postseason Record

Year	Club vs. Opp.	W	L	ERA	G	GS	CG	SHO	SV	IP	H	R	ER	HR	HP	BB	SO	WP	BK
2019	NYY vs. HOU (CS)							On Roster - Did Not Pitch											
Wild Card Totals		-	-	-	-	-	-	-	-	-	-	-	-	-	-	-	-	-	-
LDS Totals		-	-	-	-	-	-	-	-	-	-	-	-	-	-	-	-	-	-
LCS Totals		-	-	-	-	-	-	-	-	-	-	-	-	-	-	-	-	-	-
POSTSEASON TOTALS		-	-	-	-	-	-	-	-	-	-	-	-	-	-	-	-	-	-

Heller's Career Fielding Record

Position	PCT	G	PO	A	E	TC	DP
Pitcher	.800	25	1	3	1	5	0

Heller's Regular Season Batting Record

Year	Team	AVG	G	AB	R	H	2B	3B	HR	RBI	SH	SF	HP	BB	SO	SB	CS
2019	NYY							Did Not Bat									
Major League Totals		---	25	-	-	-	-	-	-	-	-	-	-	-	-	-	-

Heller's Career Bests and Streaks

COMPLETE GAMES: None. **LOW-HIT COMPLETE GAME:** None. **IP (START):** None. **IP (RELIEF):** 2.1, 9/28/17 vs. TB. **HITS:** 3, 8/28/16 vs. BAL. **RUNS:** 2 - 2 times (last: 9/23/16 at TOR). **WALKS:** 2, 9/16/17 vs. BAL. **STRIKEOUTS:** 3 - 2 times (last on 9/15/19 at TOR). **HOME RUNS:** 1 - 4 times (last: 9/12/19 at DET-G1). **WINNING STREAK:** 2g, 8/31/16-present. **LOSING STREAK:** None. **SCORELESS STREAK (IP):** 7.0, 9/16/17-10/1/17.

Pitcher of the Month: None   **Player of the Week:** None   **Rookie of the Month:** None

AARON HICKS • OF

31

HT: 6-1 • **WT:** 205 • **BATS:** S • **THROWS:** R
BIRTHDATE: 10/2/89 • **OPENING DAY AGE:** 30
BIRTHPLACE: San Pedro, Calif.
RESIDES: Phoenix, Ariz.
M.L. SERVICE: 6 years, 41 days

STATUS
- Signed a seven-year contract extending through the 2025 season with a team option for 2026 on February 25, 2019…was originally acquired by the Yankees from the Minnesota Twins in exchange for C John Ryan Murphy on November 11, 2015.

CAREER NOTES
- Has appeared at all three outfield positions in his career, posting a .994 fielding percentage (1,392TC, 9E) with 30 assists…from 2013-15, led all Twins outfielders in assists (22) and games played in the outfield (243).
- Of his 62HR hit since joining the Yankees in 2016, 38 have been hit at Yankee Stadium…has 59HR in 317 games since 8/5/16 after hitting just 3HR in his first 90 games as a Yankee.
- Ranked third among Major League switch-hitters with 27HR in 2018…was the seventh switch-hitter in Yankees history to hit at least 25HR in a season, joining Mickey Mantle (10x), Bernie Williams (5x), Mark Teixeira (4x), Tom Tresh (3x), Jorge Posada (2x) and Nick Swisher (2x).
- Since joining the Yankees in 2016, the Yankees have gone 47-10 when he homers.
- From 2017-18, posted an .838 OPS and a .368 OBP…was one of just eight American Leaguers over the stretch to reach both of those marks with at least 200 games played (also Jose Altuve, Mookie Betts, Alex Bregman, Aaron Judge, J.D. Martinez, José Ramirez and Mike Trout).
- His 8.4 WAR (FanGraphs) from 2017-18 ranked 10th among all Major League outfielders.
- Has made five career Opening Day rosters (2013-14, '16-18), including three as a Yankee…began the 2019 season on the 10-day injured list.

2019
- Hit .235 (52-for-221) with 41R, 10 doubles, 12HR, 36RBI and 31BB in 59 games (55 starts in CF, 1 at DH) in his fourth season with the Yankees.
- Had six game-tying or go-ahead RBI when trailing in the ninth inning or later (go-ahead two-run HR with two outs in the ninth on 7/23 at Minnesota, game-tying solo HR with two outs in the ninth on 7/6 at Tampa Bay, game-tying two-run single with two outs in the ninth on 5/26 at Kansas City, and a sac fly with one out in the ninth on 5/20 at Baltimore).
- Missed the Yankees' first 40 games of the season from 3/28 (retroactive to 3/25) - 5/12 on the 10-day injured list with a lower left back strain…combined to hit .167 (3-for-18) with 4R, 2 doubles, 1HR and 1RBI in five rehab games with Single-A Tampa and Triple-A Scranton/WB, with all 3H coming on 5/11.
- Made his season debut in Game 2 on 5/15 vs. Baltimore…recorded his first hits of the year on 5/18 vs. Tampa Bay…hit his first HR of the season on 5/19 vs. Tampa Bay.
- Hit a game-tying two-run single with two outs in the ninth on 5/26 at Kansas City…since 1999, was the seventh *game-tying or go-ahead hit by a Yankee with two outs when trailing by multiple runs in the ninth inning or later*, joining Brett Gardner (HR on 5/5/17 at Chicago-NL), Didi Gregorius (1B on 4/30/17 vs. Baltimore), Mark Teixeira (grand slam on 9/28/16 vs. Boston), Alex Rodriguez (HR on 9/17/10 at Baltimore), Shelley Duncan (HR on 8/15/07 vs. Baltimore) and Paul O'Neill (HR on 5/13/01 vs. Baltimore).
- Doubled and homered on 6/4 at Toronto after not collecting an extra-base hit over his prior 10 games.
- Homered in three straight games with a plate appearance from 6/4-7, just the second time in his career he homered in three straight (also 6/17-19/18).
- His first inning two-run HR on 6/29 at Boston at London Stadium was the first Major League homer ever hit in London.
- Hit game-tying solo HR in the eighth inning on 7/5 at Tampa Bay, his third career pinch-hit home run.
- Hit a game-tying ninth-inning solo HR on 7/6 at Tampa Bay…was his fifth career home run in the eighth inning-or-later that either tied the game or gave his team the lead, and his second in as many days.
- Collected his 500th career hit with a third-inning single on 7/23 at Minnesota…hit go-ahead, two-out, two-run HR in the ninth inning to give the Yankees a 12-11 lead…was his second game-tying or go-ahead HR in the ninth inning or later of the season and third of his career (also game-tying solo HR in the ninth on 7/6 at Tampa Bay and go-ahead two-run HR on 9/26/16 at Toronto).
- Was placed on the 10-day injured list on 8/4 with a right flexor strain…was transferred to the 60-day I.L. on 9/28… was removed from Game 2 vs. Boston in the middle of the eighth on 8/3 with an elbow injury…was 2-for-3 with 2R and 1BB in the game after entering in an 0-for-17 drought.

- Was reinstated from the 60-day injured list and added to the Yankees' postseason roster prior to the start of the ALCS vs. Houston…reached three times (1H, 2BB) in ALCS Game 4 and collected his first hit since 8/3-Game 2 vs. Boston…hit his second career postseason home run in ALCS Game 5, a three-run HR in the first inning off Justin Verlander that provided the margin of victory…both of his career postseason HRs have been tie-breaking three-run homers off Cy Young winners (broke a 3-3 tie in the third inning of 2017 ALDS Game 2 at Cleveland with a three-run HR off Corey Kluber).
- Underwent UCL reconstruction surgery on his right elbow on 10/30…the surgery was performed by Dr. Neal ElAttrache in Los Angeles.
- Signed a seven-year contract extending through the 2025 season with a club option for 2026 on 2/25.

Aaron Hicks' first-inning home run on 6/29/19 against Boston at London Stadium marked the first MLB homer ever hit in Europe.

2018
- Hit .248 (119-for-480) with 90R, 18 doubles, 3 triples, 27HR, 79RBI, 90BB and 11SB in 137 games (129 starts in CF, 2 at DH)…set single-season career highs in runs scored, hits, home runs, extra-base hits (48), RBI and walks (previous: 54R, 15HR, 33XBH, 52RBI, 51BB in 2017; 90H in 2015)…ranked fifth in the Majors (min. 500PA) with a 15.5% walk rate and his 20.9% chase rate was seventh-lowest.
- Ranked third among Major League switch-hitters with 27HR (José Ramírez-39 and Francisco Lindor-38)…was the highest total by a switch-hitting centerfielder (min. half of games at the position) since Carlos Beltrán hit 27HR in 2008…was the seventh switch-hitter in Yankees history to hit at least 25HR in a season, joining Mickey Mantle (10x), Bernie Williams (5x), Mark Teixeira (4x), Tom Tresh (3x), Jorge Posada (2x) and Nick Swisher (2x).
- Was the fourth centerfielder (min. 50.0% of games in CF) in American League history to post a season with at least 25HR and a walk rate of 15.0% or better, joining Mickey Mantle (9 times), Mike Trout (4) and Larry Doby (2).
- Hit 11HR in 31G as a leadoff hitter and 16HR in 106G in all other spots in the lineup…had 21HR over his final 88G after hitting just 6HR in his first 49G.
- Was the first Yankee with multiple inside-the-park HRs in the same season (4/13 at Detroit and 5/19 at Kansas City) since Mickey Mantle (three in 1958)…became the sixth player in the last 20 seasons (since 1999) to have multiple ITP HR in the same season, joining Charlie Blackmon (2017), Brandon Barnes (2014), Tony Gwynn Jr. (2010), Mark Teahen (2008) and Jimmy Rollins (2004).
- Joined Didi Gregorius as the first pair of Yankees each with at least 20HR and 10SB in the same season since 2009 (Damon/Rodriguez).
- Hit .636/.690/1.045 (14-for-22) with 9R, 1 double, 1 triple, 2HR, 5RBI and 6BB in seven games against Kansas City, the third-highest BA by any player against a single opponent in 2018 (min. 15AB) behind only Steve Pearce (.667, 10-for-15 vs. Kansas City) and Scooter Gennett (.654, 17-for-26 vs. Los Angeles-NL)…had multiple hits and reached safely at least three times in each of his six starts vs. Kansas City, tying the Yankees' Roy White (8/15/70-6/4/71) for the longest such streak by an opponent in Royals history.
- Was placed on the 10-day disabled list from 3/30-4/12 with a right intercostal muscle strain (missed 11 team games)…played two rehab games with Triple-A Scranton/Wilkes-Barre.
- Hit two-run inside-the-park HR and solo HR in 4/13 win at Detroit…was his first career inside-the-park HR and first by a Yankee since Curtis Granderson on 8/21/11 at Minnesota…it had been 1,022 games since Granderson's homer, the Yankees' second-longest drought with no inside-the-park HRs in team history (1,523 games from 8/30/99-5/14/09)…is the first Yankee to hit both an inside-the-park HR and a homer over the fence in the same game since Hank Bauer on 5/30/56-G2 vs. Washington at Yankee Stadium (*STATS Inc.*)…Bauer homered off Camilo Pascual leading off the first inning and hit a two-run inside-the-park home run off Tex Clevenger in the eighth…was his fourth career multi-HR game (first since 6/9/17 at Baltimore).
- Hit .279 (24-for-86) with 6HR in 24 games in June…had a season batting average of .230 (32-for-139) with 5HR in 39 games through the end of May.
- Played in his 500th Major League game in 6/4 Game 1 win at Detroit (0-for-4, 1BB).
- Hit leadoff HR in 6/26 win at Philadelphia…was his third career leadoff HR and first as a Yankee (first since 9/7/15 at Kansas City w/ Minnesota).
- Hit two-run HR and two solo HRs and was 3-for-4 with 1BB in 7/1 win vs. Boston…was his first career 3HR game and the first by a Yankee since Alex Rodriguez on 7/25/15 at Minnesota…became the fourth player (second Yankee) with 3HR in a game at the current Yankee Stadium, joining Curtis Granderson on 4/19/12 vs. Minnesota, Detroit's J.D. Martinez on 6/21/15 and Kansas City's Lorenzo Cain on 5/10/16…was joined by Texas' Ronald Guzmán on 8/10/18…is the first Yankees leadoff hitter ever to hit 3HR in a game and just the 27th instance in Major League history (joined by St. Louis' Matt Carpenter on 7/20/18)…homered from both sides of the plate for the second time in his career (also 4/13/17 vs. Tampa Bay)…was his fifth career multi-HR game and second of the season (also 4/13 at Detroit-2HR).
- Had 49BB in 61 games following the All-Star break, tied for second-most in the Majors (tied for first in the AL)… drew at least 1BB in 10 consecutive starts from 7/15-8/2 (13BB total), tied for the longest such streak by a Yankee since Jorge Posada's 11-start walk streak from 5/11-29/04.

- Scored a career-high-tying 4R in 9/21 win vs. Baltimore (also 8/12/15 vs. Texas), going 2-for-3 with 1HR, 2RBI and 2BB…hit in the leadoff spot in the starting lineup for the first time since 8/30 vs. Detroit.
- Recorded his first "walk-off" hit as a Yankee and the third of his career (also singles on 5/15/14 vs. Boston and 9/16/14 vs. Detroit) with an 11th-inning double on 9/22 vs. Baltimore to clinch the Yankees' postseason berth.
- Was removed from 9/24 win at Tampa Bay in the bottom of the fourth inning with a tight left hamstring…missed the following three games with the injury.
- Hit .222 (2-for-9) with 1R, 1 double and 1RBI in three postseason games…was removed from ALDS Game 1 at Boston in the fourth inning with right hamstring tightness and missed the following two games.

2017

- Hit .266 (80-for-301) with 54R, 18 doubles, 15HR, 52RBI, 51BB and 10SB in 88 games (50 starts in CF, 16 in LF and 10 in RF) in his second season with the Yankees…of his 15HR, 12 were hit at Yankee Stadium.
- Had his second career multi-HR game (also 5/13/13 vs. Chicago-AL w/ Minnesota) in 4/13 win vs. Tampa Bay…homered from both sides of the plate, the first Yankee to do so since Mark Teixeira on 7/31/15 at Chicago-AL.
- Hit his first career pinch-hit HR in the eighth inning of 4/19 win vs. Chicago-AL.
- Reached base safely in a career-high 21 consecutive games from 5/23-6/14…hit .342/.413/.595 (27-for-79) with 16R, 11 doubles, 3HR, 17RBI and 11BB during the stretch.
- Established career highs with 6RBI and 3 doubles in 6/1 win at Toronto, going 4-for-5 with 2R…was the third Yankee since 1954 with at least 6RBI without a home run (also Jorge Posada-6RBI on 6/6/98 vs. Kansas City and Joe Girardi-7RBI on 8/23/99 at Texas).
- Was placed on the 10-day disabled list from 6/26-8/10 with a right oblique strain (missed 39 games)…combined to appear in seven rehab games with Triple-A Scranton/Wilkes-Barre and Double-A Trenton from 8/2-9.
- At the time he was placed on the D.L. on 6/26, had a .398 OBP, ninth-best in the Majors and second-highest in the AL behind only teammate Aaron Judge (.440).
- Was placed on the 10-day disabled list from 9/3-25 with a left oblique strain (missed 21 team games)…was removed in the seventh inning of 9/2 win vs. Boston with the injury.
- Hit his second career pinch-hit home run in 9/28 loss vs. Tampa Bay (also 4/19/17 vs. Chicago-AL).
- Made his postseason debut…in 13 playoff games, hit .196 (9-for-46) with 5R, 2 doubles, 1HR and 5RBI…hit safely in each of his first six postseason games, the sixth-longest hitting streak to begin a postseason career in Yankees history: Thurman Munson (11G), Chris Chambliss (10G), Derek Jeter (9G), George Selkirk (9G) and Earle Combs (7G).
- Hit his first career postseason homer in ALDS Game 2 loss at Cleveland, a go-ahead three-run HR off Corey Kluber.

2016

- Hit .217 (71-for-327) with 32R, 13 doubles, 8HR and 31RBI in 123 games (52 starts in RF, 20 in LF and 20 in CF) in his first season with the Yankees…was the only Major League player to make at least 20 starts at all three outfield positions in 2016…was the first Yankee to do so since Joe DiMaggio in 1936.
- Of the 16 outfield throws of at least 100 mph tracked by MLB Statcast in 2016, three were by Hicks…had an outfield assist to nab Danny Valencia at the plate to end the fourth inning on 4/20 vs. Oakland, with a throw recorded at 105.5 mph by MLB Statcast (the fastest throw by an outfielder in 2016).
- Made his Yankees debut in 4/5 Opening Day loss vs. Houston, starting in LF…collected his first hit as a Yankee with a seventh-inning single in 4/6 win vs. Houston.
- Missed four games from 4/23-26 with left shoulder bursitis…suffered the injury in 4/22 win vs. Tampa Bay diving for a fly ball in the fourth inning.
- Hit game-winning solo HR—his first HR as a Yankee—in the seventh and was 1-for-2 in 5/6 win vs. Boston.
- Hit .280 (23-for-82) with 4HR and 9RBI in 26 games in August…over the first four months of the season, batted just .187 (39-for-209) with 3HR and 19RBI in 86 games.
- Was placed on the 15-day D.L. from 9/5 (retroactive to 9/1) – 9/20 with a Grade 2 right hamstring strain…suffered the injury in 8/31 win at Kansas City and underwent an MRI in Baltimore on 9/1.
- Hit a go-ahead two-run HR in the ninth inning of 9/26 win at Toronto…was his first career game-tying or go-ahead HR in the ninth or later…was his first home run on the road since 9/7/15 at Kansas City w/ Minnesota.

2015

- Hit .256 (90-for-352) with 48R, 11 doubles, 11HR and 33RBI in 97 games with the Twins…batted .307 (31-for-101) with 6HR and a .870 OPS off left-handed pitching…following the season, was named the 2015 Charles O. Johnson Award winner for "Most Improved Twin" by the Twin Cities Chapter of the BBWAA.
- Posted a .996 fielding percentage (254TC, 1E)…tied for 11th in the AL with nine outfield assists.
- Was placed on the 15-day disabled list on 6/14 with a right forearm strain…played in six rehab games with Triple-A Rochester…was returned from rehab and reinstated from the D.L. on 7/3.
- Hit .346 (27-for-78) with 15R, 2 doubles, 2 triples, 4HR, 16RBI, 11BB and a .424 OBP in 23 games in July.
- Hit his first career leadoff HR (off Nick Martinez) in 8/12 win vs. Texas.
- Was placed on the 15-day disabled list on 8/20 with a left hamstring strain, suffered running to first base to beat out a ground ball on 8/19 at Yankee Stadium…was returned from rehab and reinstated from the D.L. on 9/4.
- Began the season with Rochester, batting .342 (51-for-149) with 2R, 13 doubles, 3HR and 20RBI in 38 games.
- Was traded to the Yankees on 11/11 in exchange for C John Ryan Murphy.

2014
- In 69 games with the Twins, batted .215 (40-for-186) with 22R, 8 doubles, 1HR and 18RBI.
- Was placed on the 7-day concussion disabled list from 5/2-9 with concussion-like symptoms after colliding with the centerfield wall on 5/1 vs. Los Angeles-NL.
- Was placed on the 15-day disabled list from 6/13 (retroactive to 6/10)-7/2 with a right shoulder strain, suffered diving for a ball on 6/7 vs. Houston…went on a rehab assignment with Double-A New Britain and was optioned there after being reinstated from the D.L.
- Hit .297 (44-for-148) with 30R, 11 doubles, 4HR and 21RBI in 43G with New Britain…hit .347 (35-for-101) in July.
- Also saw time with Triple-A Rochester after being transferred from New Britain on 8/5, batting .278 (20-for-72) with 9R, 5 doubles, 1HR and 8RBI in 24 games.

2013
- Made his first career Opening Day roster and saw his first Major League action, hitting .192 (54-for-281) with 37R, 11 doubles, 8HR and 27RBI in 81 games…had a team-best nine outfield assists…among AL rookies, tied for fifth in homers, tied for sixth in walks (24), was eighth in runs scored and tied for 10th in doubles.
- Made his Major League debut on 4/3 vs. Detroit, going 0-for-4 with 1BB as the Twins' leadoff hitter and starting centerfielder…became the fourth different Twins player to make his Major League debut as the Opening Day leadoff hitter, joining Sergio Ferrer on 4/5/74, Hosken Powell on 4/5/78 and Jim Eisenriech on 4/6/82.
- Recorded his first Major League hit and RBI with a two-run single off Brayan Villarreal in the eighth inning on 4/4 vs. Detroit…hit his first career home run on 5/4 at Cleveland, a solo HR off Scott Kazmir…recorded his first career multi-HR game on 5/13 vs. Chicago-AL.
- Was placed on the 15-day disabled list from 6/10-7/2 with a left hamstring strain…played in six games on a rehab assignment with Triple-A Rochester.
- Was optioned to Rochester on 8/1…in 22 total games with the club, hit .222 (16-for-72) with 7R, 4 doubles and 5RBI…was placed on the minor league disabled list from 8/13-20 with a right heel bruise.
- Entered the season ranked by *Baseball America* as the Twins' fifth-best prospect, "Best Defensive Outfielder," "Best Outfield Arm" and as having the "Best Strike-Zone Discipline."

2012
- In 129 games with Double-A New Britain, hit .286 (135-for-472) with 100R, 21 doubles, 11 triples, 13HR, 61RBI and 32SB…set New Britain single-season records and led the Eastern League in runs scored and triples…led Twins farmhands in runs and SB, ranked second in triples and walks, fourth in total bases (217) and fifth in hits.
- Hit .318 (35-for-110) with a .433 OBP in 30 games in July and .319 (36-for-113) with a .402 OBP in 28 games in August.
- Was named to the EL Postseason All-Star team…was also selected to the *Baseball America* Double-A All-Star team and tabbed by the publication as the eighth-best prospect in the Eastern League.
- Following the season, played for the Bravos de Margarita in the Venezuelan Winter League.
- Was added to the Twins' 40-man roster on 11/20/12.

2011
- In 122 games with Single-A Fort Myers, hit .242 (107-for-443) with 79R, 31 doubles, 5HR and 38RBI.
- Following the season, played for the Mesa Solar Sox in the Arizona Fall League.
- Was named the fourth-best prospect, "Best Defensive Outfielder" and "Best Outfield Arm" in the Twins minor league system by *Baseball America*, and as having the "Best Outfield Arm" in the Florida State League.

2010
- Spent the entire season with Single-A Beloit, batting .279 (118-for-423) with 86R, 27 doubles, 8HR, 49RBI and 21SB in 115 games…was a Mid-Season All-Star.
- Following the season, was tabbed by *Baseball America* as the fifth-best prospect in the Midwest League…was also named by the publication as the second-best prospect, "Best Defensive Outfielder," "Best Outfield Arm" and as having the "Best Strike-Zone Discipline" in the Twins system.

2009
- Hit .251 (63-for-251) with 43R, 15 doubles, 4HR and 29RBI in 67 games with Single-A Beloit.
- Following the season, was ranked by *Baseball America* as the best prospect in the Midwest League…was also ranked by the publication as the Twins' top prospect, "Best Athlete," "Best Defensive Outfielder," "Best Outfield Arm" and as having the "Best Strikezone Discipline."

2008
- Made his professional debut, hitting .318 (55-for-173) with 32R, 10 doubles, 4HR and 27RBI in 45 games for the GCL Twins…led the team in hits, home runs, walks (28) and stolen bases (12) and tied for the team lead in RBI.
- Following the season, was tabbed by *Baseball America* as a Rookie-level All-Star and the GCL's Top Prospect.

PERSONAL

- Full name is Aaron Michael Hicks...has a son, Aaron Michael Hicks Jr.
- Graduated from Woodrow Wilson High School in Long Beach, Calif. in 2008, where he hit .407 (114-for-280) with 24 doubles, 10 triples and 6HR in 97 games...also pitched, going 11-2 with a 1.11 ERA (94.1IP, 15ER) and 144K in 13 games started...played in the 2007 AFLAC All-American High School Baseball Classic...was named to the *Baseball America* All-American Second Team in 2008.
- Is a product of Major League Baseball's Urban Youth Academy in Compton, Calif.
- Played golf growing up and has participated in numerous charity golf tournaments.
- In September 2018, joined Didi Gregorius to serve as ambassadors for the PitCCh In Foundation's "Welcome Back to School" assembly and backpack giveaway in the Bronx at PS/MS 71.

Hicks' Career Batting Record

Year	Club	AVG	G	AB	R	H	2B	3B	HR	RBI	SH	SF	HP	BB	SO	SB	CS	E	OBP	SLG
2008	GCL Twins	.318	45	173	32	55	10	4	4	27	1	2	0	28	32	12	2	2	.409	.491
2009	Beloit	.251	67	251	43	62	14	3	4	29	2	3	1	40	55	10	8	7	.353	.382
2010	Beloit	.279	115	423	86	118	27	6	8	49	4	3	0	88	112	20	11	6	.401	.428
2011	Fort Myers	.242	122	443	79	107	31	5	5	38	3	3	1	78	110	17	9	8	.354	.368
2012	New Britain	.286	129	473	100	135	21	11	13	61	3	8	1	78	115	32	11	8	.384	.460
2013	MINNESOTA - a	.192	81	281	37	54	11	3	8	27	4	2	2	24	84	9	3	0	.259	.338
	Rochester	.222	22	72	7	16	4	2	0	5	0	0	0	10	21	1	0	0	.317	.333
2014	MINNESOTA - b, c	.215	69	186	22	40	8	0	1	18	2	1	0	36	56	4	3	2	.341	.274
	New Britain	.297	43	148	30	44	11	1	4	21	0	2	0	28	27	2	3	2	.404	.466
	Rochester	.278	24	72	9	20	5	0	1	8	1	2	0	9	13	1	1	0	.349	.389
2015	Rochester	.342	38	149	26	51	13	4	3	20	0	2	0	17	30	2	1	0	.408	.544
	MINNESOTA - d, e, f	.256	97	352	48	90	11	3	11	33	0	2	2	34	66	13	3	2	.323	.398
2016	YANKEES - g	.217	123	327	32	71	13	1	8	31	1	3	0	30	68	3	4	1	.281	.336
2017	YANKEES - h, i	.266	88	301	54	80	18	0	15	52	1	5	3	51	67	10	5	2	.372	.475
	Scranton/WB	.375	5	16	4	6	2	1	0	1	0	0	0	2	2	1	0	0	.444	.625
	Trenton	.250	2	8	3	2	1	0	1	2	0	0	0	1	1	0	0	0	.333	.750
2018	YANKEES - j	.248	137	480	90	119	18	3	27	79	2	6	3	90	111	11	2	2	.366	.467
	Scranton/WB	.333	2	6	0	2	1	0	0	0	0	0	0	1	0	0	0	0	.429	.500
2019	Tampa	.000	3	11	0	0	0	0	0	0	0	0	0	1	3	0	0	0	.083	.000
	Scranton/WB	.429	2	7	4	3	2	0	1	1	0	0	0	1	1	1	0	0	.500	1.143
	YANKEES - k, l	.235	59	221	41	52	10	0	12	36	0	3	0	31	72	1	2	1	.325	.443
Minor League Totals		**.276**	**619**	**2252**	**423**	**621**	**142**	**37**	**44**	**262**	**14**	**25**	**3**	**382**	**522**	**99**	**46**	**33**	**.378**	**.430**
Major League Totals		**.236**	**654**	**2148**	**324**	**506**	**89**	**10**	**82**	**276**	**10**	**22**	**10**	**296**	**524**	**51**	**22**	**9**	**.328**	**.401**
NYY Totals		**.242**	**407**	**1329**	**217**	**322**	**59**	**4**	**62**	**198**	**4**	**17**	**6**	**202**	**318**	**25**	**13**	**6**	**.341**	**.433**

Selected by Minnesota in the first round (14th pick overall) of the 2008 First-Year Player Draft.

a – Placed on the 15 day disabled list from June 10-July 2, 2013 with a left hamstring strain.
b – Placed on the 7-day concussion disabled list from May 2-9, 2014.
c – Placed on the 15-day disabled list from June 13 (retroactive to June 10) - July 2, 2014 with a right shoulder strain.
d – Placed on the 15-day disabled list from June 14-July 3, 2015 with a right forearm strain.
e – Placed on the 15-day disabled list from August 20-September 4, 2015 with a left hamstring strain.
f – Acquired by the Yankees from the Minnesota Twins in exchange for C John Ryan Murphy on November 11, 2015.
g – Placed on the 15-day disabled list from September 5 (retroactive to September 1) - September 20, 2016 with a right hamstring strain.
h – Placed on the 10-day disabled list from June 26-August 10, 2017 with a right oblique strain.
i – Placed on the 10-day disabled list from September 3-25, 2017 with a left oblique strain.
j – Placed on the 10-day disabled list from March 30 - April 12, 2018 with a right intercostal muscle strain.
k – Placed on the 10-day injured list from March 28 (retroactive to March 25) - May 13, 2019 with a lower left back strain.
l – Placed on the 10-day injured list on August 4, 2019 with a right flexor strain...was transferred to the 60-day injured list on September 28, 2019 through the end of the season.

Hicks' Postseason Record

Year	Club vs. Opp.	AVG	G	AB	R	H	2B	3B	HR	RBI	SH	SF	HP	BB	SO	SB	CS	E	OBP	SLG
2017	NYY vs. MIN (WC)	.333	1	3	0	1	0	0	0	1	0	0	0	1	0	0	0	0	.500	.333
	NYY vs. CLE (DS)	.316	5	19	3	6	1	0	1	4	0	0	0	1	6	0	0	0	.350	.526
	NYY vs. HOU (CS)	.083	7	24	2	2	1	0	0	0	0	0	0	2	8	0	0	0	.154	.125
2018	NYY vs. OAK (WC)	.250	1	4	1	1	1	0	0	1	0	0	0	0	0	0	0	0	.250	.500
	NYY vs. BOS (DS)	.200	2	5	0	1	0	0	0	0	0	0	0	1	1	0	0	0	.333	.200
2019	NYY vs. HOU (CS)	.154	5	13	1	2	0	0	1	3	0	0	0	4	5	1	0	0	.353	.385
Wild Card Totals		**.286**	**2**	**7**	**1**	**2**	**1**	**0**	**0**	**2**	**0**	**0**	**0**	**1**	**0**	**0**	**0**	**0**	**.375**	**.429**
LDS Totals		**.292**	**7**	**24**	**3**	**7**	**1**	**0**	**1**	**4**	**0**	**0**	**0**	**2**	**7**	**0**	**0**	**0**	**.346**	**.458**
LCS Totals		**.108**	**12**	**37**	**3**	**4**	**1**	**0**	**1**	**3**	**0**	**0**	**0**	**6**	**13**	**1**	**0**	**0**	**.233**	**.216**
POSTSEASON TOTALS		**.191**	**21**	**68**	**7**	**13**	**3**	**0**	**2**	**9**	**0**	**0**	**0**	**9**	**20**	**1**	**0**	**0**	**.286**	**.324**

Hicks' Career Fielding Record

Position	PCT	G	PO	A	E	TC	DP
Outfield	.994	635	1353	30	9	1392	8

Hicks' Career Home Run Chart

MULTI-HOMER GAMES: 5. **TWO-HOMER GAMES:** 4, last on 4/13/18 at DET. **THREE-HOMER GAMES:** 7/1/18 vs. BOS. **GRAND SLAMS:** None. **PINCH-HIT HR:** 3, last on 7/5/19 at TB (Pagán). **INSIDE-THE-PARK HR:** 2, last on 5/19/18 at KC. **WALK-OFF HR:** None. **LEADOFF HR:** 3, last on 6/26/18 at PHI.

Hicks' Career Bests and Streaks

HITS: 4 - 5 times (last on 8/30/17 vs. CLE). **RUNS:** 4 - 2 times, last on 9/21/18 vs. BAL. **2B:** 3, 6/1/17 at TOR. **3B:** 1 - 10 times (last on 9/19/18 vs. BOS). **HR:** 3, 7/1/18 vs. BOS. **RBI:** 6, 6/1/17 at TOR. **BB:** 3 - 3 times (last on 9/26/17 vs. TB). **SO:** 4, 5/7/17 at CHC. **SB:** 1 - 51 times (last on 6/11/19 vs. NYM). **HIT STREAK:** 9g, 5/28-6/6/17. **"WALK-OFF" HITS:** 3, last on 9/22/18 vs. BAL (double).

Player of the Month: None   **Player of the Week:** None   **Rookie of the Month:** None

KYLE HIGASHIOKA • C

66

HT: 6-1 • **WT:** 202 • **BATS:** R • **THROWS:** R
BIRTHDATE: 4/20/90 • **OPENING DAY AGE:** 29
BIRTHPLACE: Huntington Beach, Calif.
RESIDES: Bend, Ore.
M.L. SERVICE: 1 year, 5 days

STATUS
- Signed by the Yankees as a minor league free agent on November 18, 2015…was selected by the Yankees in the seventh round of the 2008 First-Year Player Draft.

CAREER NOTES
- In his minor league career (since 2008), has caught 29.9% of potential base stealers (205-of-685).
- The 2008 seventh-round Yankees draft pick made his Major League debut in 2017 after spending parts of 10 seasons in the minors…matches the club record for the longest gap from draft to debut by a player drafted by and debuting with the Yankees…shares the record with INF George Zeber, who was chosen in the fifth round of the 1968 First-Year Player Draft and made his debut for the team in the 1977 season.

2019
- Hit .214 (12-for-56) with 8R, 5 doubles, 3HR and 11RBI in 18 games over three stints with the Yankees (4/12-23, 7/24-8/9, 9/8-29)…made 14 starts at C.
- Hit doubles in the second and third innings on 8/4 vs. Boston, his first career game with 2XBH…had 4 doubles in 46 career games coming into the day.
- Collected his first career multi-HR game and set a career high with 5RBI on 8/7 at Baltimore…had never had more than 2RBI in a game entering the night.
- In 70 games with Triple-A Scranton/Wilkes-Barre, hit .278/.348/.581 (67-for-241) with 42R, 13 doubles, 20HR and 56RBI…ranked fifth among Yankees minor leaguers in home runs…hit .350 (14-for-40) with 4HR and 8RBI in 13 games in July.
- Hit 2HR—including a grand slam—and had 7RBI on 5/5 at Syracuse, going 3-for-4 with 3R…was his second career minor league game with 2HR and 7RBI (also 6/26/16 at Akron w/ Trenton).

2018
- Hit .167 (12-for-72) with 6R, 2 doubles, 3HR and 6RBI in 29 games (20 starts at C) over two stints with the Yankees (6/25-7/19 and 7/24-9/30).
- Hit solo HR off David Price—the first hit and HR of his Major League career—and was 1-for-4 in 7/1 win vs. Boston…snapped an 0-for-22 stretch to begin his career, the longest drought by a Yankee to start his career since RHP Hal Reniff (0-for-25 from 1961-64)…was the first Yankee to homer for his first MLB hit since Tyler Austin and Aaron Judge hit back-to-back HRs in their first PAs on 8/13/16 vs. Tampa Bay…was the first Yankee to homer against Boston for his first MLB hit since Andy Phillips on 9/26/04 at Fenway Park.
- With solo HRs on 7/1, 7/3 and 7/4, became the second Yankee in franchise history to have his first three Major League hits go for HRs, joining Alfonso Soriano (first 3H were HRs from 9/24/99-4/9/00)…was the first Major Leaguer whose first three Major League hits were HRs since Colorado's Trevor Story in April 2016 (first 4H were HRs).
- Threw out a runner trying to steal second in the bottom of the 12th inning to end 8/21 win at Miami.
- Was on the Yankees' AL Wild Card Game roster, but did not play.
- In 53 games with the RailRiders, hit .202 (38-for-188) with 16R, 10 doubles, 5HR and 22RBI.

2017
- In nine games (5GS at C) over two stints with the Yankees (4/9-5/5, 6/16-18), did not record a hit in 18AB (2R, 2BB).
- Made his Major League debut as ninth-inning defensive replacement at C in 4/10 home-opening win vs. Tampa Bay (did not bat)…became the first Yankee to make his Major League debut at catcher since Austin Romine on 9/11/11 at Los Angeles-AL.
- Made his first Major League start at C in 4/12 win vs. Tampa Bay, going 0-for-4 with 1R…was behind the plate for LHP Jordan Montgomery's Major League debut that day, making the duo the first Yankees battery to each make their first Major League starts in the same game since RHP Jorge De Paula and C Michel Hernandez on 9/26/03 vs. Baltimore (Game 2).
- In 14 games with Scranton/WB, hit .264 (14-for-53) with 5R, 4 doubles, 2HR and 11RBI…in six postseason games, hit .100 (2-for-20) with 2R, 1 double and 1RBI…missed nearly half the season with three stints on the minor league disabled list…appeared with short-season Single-A Staten Island and Rookie-level Pulaski as part of rehab assignments, combining to hit 7HR with 12RBI in seven games (.524, 11-for-21, 10R, 3 doubles).
- Following the season, was tabbed by *Baseball America* as the Yankees' "Best Defensive Catcher."

2016
- Combined with Double-A Trenton and Triple-A Scranton/Wilkes-Barre to bat .276 (102-for-370) with 55R, 24 doubles, 21HR and 81RBI in 102 games…set career highs in runs, hits, doubles and RBI and walks (38)…entered the season with just 30HR in 411 career minor league games and his previous single-season career high was 8HR in 2011…caught 30.2% of potential base stealers (29-of-96).
- Among Yankees farmhands, tied Chris Gittens for the lead in home runs (21) and ranked third in RBI (81).
- Began the season with Trenton, batting .293 (65-for-222) with 31R, 15 doubles, 11HR and 51RBI in 63 games…was named an EL Mid-Season All-Star…also played for Scranton/WB, hitting .250 (37-for-148) with 24R, 9 doubles, 10HR and 30RBI in 39 games…combined between Trenton and Scranton/WB to bat .420 (29-for-69) with 21R, 8 doubles, 9HR and 32RBI in 18 games in June.
- Played in seven playoff games for the Governors' Cup-champion RailRiders (.250, 6-for-24, 1R, 2 doubles, 7RBI).
- Was added to the 40-man roster on 11/4/16.

2015
- Combined at Single-A Tampa and Triple-A Scranton/Wilkes-Barre to hit .250 (81-for-324) with 27R, 19 doubles, 2 triples, 5HR and 37RBI in 93 games…threw out 40-for-136 potential base stealers (29.4%).
- Began the season with Tampa, batting .254 (78-for-307) with 25R, 18 doubles, 2 triples, 5HR and 36RBI in 88 games and was named a FSL Mid-Season All-Star.
- Was promoted to Scranton/WB on 9/1, batting .176 (3-for-17) with 2R, 1 double and 1RBI in five games.
- After becoming a free agent in November, re-signed with the Yankees to a minor league contract on 11/18/15.

2014
- Split time with the GCL Yankees 1 and Single-A Tampa to bat .224 (11-for-49) with 8R, 4 doubles, 1HR, 3RBI and 7BB in 17 games…caught 6-of-24 (25.0%) potential base stealers.
- Started the season with the GCL Yankees 1 and hit .217 (5-for-23) with 3R, 1 double, 1RBI and 3BB in eight games.
- Was transferred to Tampa on 8/5 and batted .231 (6-for-26) with 5R, 3 doubles, 1HR, 2RBI and 4BB in nine games.
- Following the season, hit .409 (9-for-22) with 4R, 3 doubles, 1HR and 2RBI in 6G with the AFL's Scottsdale Scorpions.

2013
- Appeared in seven games with Double-A Trenton and batted .320 (8-for-25) with 1R, 3 doubles, 1HR and 5RBI…threw out 4-of-16 (25.0%) potential base stealers.

2012
- Combined at Single-A Tampa and Double-A Trenton to bat .170 (25-for-147) with 14R, 5 doubles, 6HR and 23RBI in 44 games…appeared in 29 games as a catcher and threw out 15-of-34 (44.1%) potential base stealers.

2011
- Combined at Single-A Tampa and Single-A Charleston to hit .231 (68-for-294) with 35R, 16 doubles, 8HR and 29RBI in 82 games…caught 27-of-73 (37.0%) potential base stealers.
- Spent the first half of the season with Single-A Tampa, batting .238 (39-for-164) with 21R, 10 doubles, 4HR and 16RBI in 46 games…was transferred to Single-A Charleston on 6/23 and batted .223 (29-for-130) with 14R, 6 doubles, 4HR and 13RBI in 36 games.

2010
- Spent the entire season with Single-A Charleston, hitting .225 (72-for-320) with 35R, 18 doubles, 6HR and 24RBI in 90 games…threw out 27-of-83 (32.5%) potential base stealers.

2009
- Played the entire season with short-season Single-A Staten Island, batting .253 (55-for-217) with 24R, 11 doubles, 2HR and 32RBI in 60 games…caught 19-of-75 (25.3%) potential base stealers.

2008
- Made his professional debut with the GCL Yankees, batting .261 (12-for-46) with 5R, 1 double, 1HR and 3RBI in 18 games.

PERSONAL
- Last name is pronounced "he-GAH-shi-Oh-kah"…married Alyse in November 2016.
- Graduated from Edison (Calif.) High School in 2008, where he batted .382 with 7HR and 31RBI as a senior and earned All-County honors…was selected as the starting catcher for the 2008 Orange County All-Star South team…was the 2006 All-Sunset League "Rookie of the Year."

Higashioka's Career Playing Record

Year	Club	AVG	G	AB	R	H	2B	3B	HR	RBI	SH	SF	HP	BB	SO	SB	CS	E	OBP	SLG
2008	GCL Yankees	.261	18	46	5	12	1	0	1	3	0	1	1	2	8	0	0	0	.300	.348
2009	Staten Island	.253	60	217	24	55	11	0	2	32	1	2	1	26	31	0	1	5	.333	.332
2010	Charleston	.225	90	320	35	72	18	0	6	24	2	1	5	31	64	0	2	6	.303	.338
2011	Tampa	.238	46	164	21	39	10	0	4	16	0	1	1	14	22	1	0	6	.300	.372
	Charleston	.223	36	130	14	29	6	0	4	13	1	2	2	9	19	0	0	1	.280	.362
2012	Tampa	.185	37	124	13	23	5	0	6	21	2	2	0	10	34	1	1	2	.243	.371
	Trenton	.087	7	23	1	2	0	0	0	2	0	1	0	2	8	0	0	0	.154	.087
2013	Trenton	.320	7	25	1	8	3	0	1	5	1	0	0	0	5	0	0	0	.320	.560
2014	GCL Yankees 1	.217	8	23	3	5	1	0	0	1	0	1	0	3	7	0	0	1	.296	.261
	Tampa	.231	9	26	5	6	3	0	1	2	0	1	0	4	4	0	0	0	.323	.462
2015	Tampa	.254	88	307	25	78	18	2	5	36	0	1	1	22	49	0	0	8	.305	.375
	Scranton/WB	.176	5	17	2	3	1	0	0	1	0	0	0	0	4	0	0	0	.176	.235
2016	Trenton	.293	63	222	31	65	15	0	11	51	0	8	0	26	42	0	1	9	.355	.509
	Scranton/WB	.250	39	148	24	37	9	0	10	30	0	0	0	12	31	0	1	0	.306	.514
2017	Scranton/WB	.264	14	53	5	14	4	0	2	11	0	0	0	4	7	0	0	4	.316	.453
	YANKEES	.000	9	18	2	0	0	0	0	0	0	0	0	2	6	0	0	0	.100	.000
	Staten Island	.438	5	16	7	7	2	0	4	8	0	0	0	2	5	0	0	0	.500	1.313
	Pulaski	.800	2	5	3	4	1	0	3	4	0	1	0	1	0	0	0	0	.714	2.800
2018	YANKEES	.167	29	72	6	12	2	0	3	6	0	0	1	6	16	0	0	1	.241	.319
	Scranton/WB	.202	53	188	16	38	10	1	5	22	0	2	3	17	44	2	0	6	.276	.346
2019	Scranton/WB	.278	70	241	42	67	13	0	20	56	0	2	3	24	53	0	0	6	.348	.581
	YANKEES	.214	18	56	8	12	5	0	3	11	0	1	0	0	26	0	0	0	.211	.464
Minor League Totals		.246	657	2295	277	564	131	3	85	338	7	26	17	209	437	4	6	54	.310	.417
Major League Totals		.164	56	146	16	24	7	0	6	17	0	1	1	8	48	0	0	1	.212	.336

Selected by the Yankees in the seventh round of the 2008 First-Year Player Draft.

Higashioka's Career Fielding Record

Position	PCT	G	PO	A	E	TC	PB
Catcher	.998	53	426	24	1	451	3

Higashioka's Career Home Run Chart

MULTI-HOMER GAMES: 1. **TWO-HOMER GAMES:** 1, 8/7/19 at BAL. **GRAND SLAMS:** None. **PINCH-HIT HR:** None. **INSIDE-THE-PARK HR:** None. **WALK-OFF HR:** None. **LEADOFF HR:** None.

Higashioka's Career Bests and Streaks

HITS: 2 - 2 times (last on 8/7/19 at BAL). **RUNS:** 2, on 8/7/19 at BAL. **2B:** 2, on 8/4/19 vs. BOS. **3B:** None. **HR:** 2, on 8/7/19 at BAL. **RBI:** 5, on 8/7/19 at BAL. **BB:** 1 - 8 times (last on 8/30/18 vs. DET). **SO:** 3 - 3 times (last on 7/30/19 vs. ARI). **SB:** None. **HIT STREAK:** 4G - 3 times (last from 4/19-7/27/19). **"WALK-OFF" HITS:** None.

Player of the Month: None   **Player of the Week:** None   **Rookie of the Month:** None

---

Howdy, Partner

RHP Red Ruffing and **C Bill Dickey** started 281 games together, marking the most starts by batterymates in New York Yankees history, and the fifth-most of any pairing all time. According to SABR's Walt Wilson, the second-most frequent Yankees battery featured Dickey and LHP Lefty Gomez (247).

MOST COMMON STARTING BATTERYMATES ALL TIME

1. Mickey Lolich and Bill Freehan, Detroit Tigers..................325
2. Warren Spahn and Del Crandall, Atlanta Braves...............318
3. Red Faber and Ray Schalk, Chicago White Sox 307
4. Don Drysdale and Johnny Roseboro, Los Angeles Dodgers 283
5. RED RUFFING and BILL DICKEY, YANKEES 281

JONATHAN HOLDER • RHP

56

HT: 6-2 • **WT:** 232 • **BATS:** R • **THROWS:** R
BIRTHDATE: 6/9/93 • **OPENING DAY AGE:** 26
BIRTHPLACE: Gulfport, Miss.
RESIDES: Gulfport, Miss.
COLLEGE: Mississippi State University
M.L. SERVICE: 2 years, 124 days

STATUS
- Selected by the Yankees in the sixth round of the 2014 First-Year Player Draft.

CAREER NOTES
- Has made three career Opening Day rosters, all with the Yankees (2017-19).

2019
- Went 5-2 with a 6.31 ERA (41.1IP, 29ER) in 34 games (one start) over three stints with the Yankees (3/28-6/24, 7/22-23, 7/31-9/29)…allowed at least 1R in 15 of his 34 games with the Yankees…tossed at least 2.0 innings in nine of his 34 appearances.
- Earned his first win of the season on 4/22 at Los Angeles-AL after tossing 2.0 scoreless innings (1IBB, 3K).
- Did not allow a run or extra-base hit over a seven-appearance stretch from 4/22-5/7 (8.0IP), his first consecutive scoreless outings of the season…had allowed at least 1R in six of his first seven appearances of the season immediately prior to the stretch, including 6XBH over the span (4 doubles, 2HR).
- Allowed 5H, 5ER and 2HR—including a grand slam—without retiring a batter on 6/24 vs. Toronto and was optioned to Triple-A Scranton/Wilkes-Barre following the game…matched career highs in hits and home runs allowed…posted a 21.94 ERA (5.1IP, 13ER) with 6HR over his final six appearances before being optioned (6/8-24).
- Made his second career start on 8/6 at Baltimore (also 9/24/18 at Tampa Bay), allowing 2ER in 2.2IP.
- Was placed on the 10-day injured list with right shoulder inflammation on 8/10 (retroactive to 8/7)…was transferred to the 60-day I.L. on 9/15, missing the remainder of the season.
- Went 1-1 with two saves, a 2.92 ERA (12.1IP, 4ER) and 15K in nine relief appearances w/ the RailRiders.
- Went 1-0 with a 0.79 ERA (11.1IP, 1ER) in 10 spring training appearances (one start), the lowest ERA among Yankees pitchers with at least 10.0IP.

2018
- Was 1-3 with a 3.14 ERA (66.0IP, 23ER) with 60K in 60 appearances (one start) over two stints with the Yankees (3/29-4/6 and 4/21-9/30).
- Allowed a 14th-inning grand slam to Álvarez on 4/6 vs. Baltimore to record the loss (2.0IP, 2H, 4R/3ER, 1BB, 2K).
- Did not allow an earned run over 23 relief appearances from 4/21-6/27, the AL's second-longest such streak of the season, and tied for third-longest in the Majors…was the second-longest streak by a Yankee since 2012 (Betances, 27G from 9/23/14-6/2/15)…retired 83-of-97 batters over the span (27.2IP, 10H, 3R/0ER, 3BB/1IBB, 26K, 1HP).
- In his first 35 appearances after being recalled (4/21-8/1), posted a 0.88 ERA (41.0IP, 7R/4ER), holding opponents without an earned run 31 times…had the Majors' lowest ERA and third-lowest WHIP (0.73, 24H, 6BB) over the span (min. 25.0IP).
- Had a career-long 10.2-inning scoreless streak over eight appearances from 6/8-27…the streak was snapped in 6/30 loss vs. Boston (1.0IP, 2H, 1ER).
- Allowed 5H and 7ER (1BB, 1HR) without retiring a batter in the fourth inning to suffer the loss on 8/2 at Boston.
- Made the first start of his Major League career in 9/24 win at Tampa Bay, tossing a scoreless first (1.0IP, 2BB, 1K)…came after making his first 102 Major League appearances as a reliever…*Elias* confirmed the 102 relief outings were the most before a pitcher's first career start in Yankees history…prior to Holder, Pete Mikkelsen held the club record with 69 relief appearances before his first start on 7/8/65 at Detroit…also, Brian Bruney made his lone career start on 4/9/08 at Kansas City after 157 relief appearances with Arizona (77) and the Yankees (80).
- Made his postseason debut in ALDS Game 3 loss vs. Boston, allowing 1ER in 2.0IP (2H, 1BB, 1K)…was his only playoff appearance.
- Made four appearances (one start) with Scranton/WB, going 1-0 with a 3.00 ERA (6.0IP, 5H, 2ER, 1BB, 8K, 1HR).

2017
- Was 1-1 with a 3.89 ERA (39.1IP, 17ER) in 37 relief appearances over four stints with the Yankees (4/2-6/27, 7/8-16, 7/31 and 9/16-10/1)…made his first career Opening Day roster.
- Earned his first Major League win on 5/5 at Chicago-NL (1.0IP, 1H, 1K).

- Set a career high with 3.0 scoreless innings (also 3.0IP on 7/15 at Boston) in the Yankees' 18-inning win on 5/7 at Chicago-NL (1H, 1BB, 3K).
- In 12 regular season relief appearances with Triple-A Scranton/Wilkes-Barre, had one save and posted a 1.69 ERA (16.0IP, 3ER) with 21K...in three postseason relief appearances with the RailRiders, posted a 3.60 ERA (5.0IP, 3H, 2ER, 1HR, 2BB) and a team-leading 12K.

2016
- Posted a 5.40 ERA (8.1IP, 5ER) over eight relief appearances in his only stint with the Yankees (9/2-10/2).
- Made his Major League debut in 9/2 loss at Baltimore, tossing a perfect sixth inning (1.0IP, 1K)...struck out his first batter faced (Adam Jones, swinging)...was signed to a Major League contract and selected to the active roster from Triple-A Scranton/Wilkes-Barre prior to the game.
- Spent the majority of the season in the minors with Single-A Tampa, Double-A Trenton and Scranton/Wilkes-Barre, going 5-1 with 16 saves, a 1.65 ERA (65.1IP, 12ER), 101K and just 7BB in 42 relief appearances.
- Led all minor league pitchers (min. 60.0IP) with a 42.4% strikeout rate (101K/238BF) and ranked third with a 13.91 K/9.0IP ratio (101K/65.1IP)...led full-season minor league pitchers (min. 60.0IP) with a 14.43 K/BB ratio (101K/7BB).
- Went 2-0 with six saves, a 0.89 ERA (20.1IP, 2ER), 0BB and 35K in 12 relief appearances for the RailRiders...on 8/28 at Rochester, struck out 12 of his 13 batters faced, including his first 11 straight before allowing a single to former Yankee John Ryan Murphy (4.0IP, 1H).

2015
- Combined with Single-A Tampa, the GCL Yankees 2 and Triple-A Scranton/Wilkes-Barre to go 7-6 with a 2.52 ERA (118.0IP, 33ER) and 90K in 23 games (21 starts)...recorded the fourth-lowest ERA among all Yankees farmhands...allowed 2ER-or-fewer in 19 of his 21 starts.
- Spent the majority of the season with Tampa, going 7-5 with a 2.44 ERA (103.1IP, 28ER) in 19 games (18 starts)...was named a FSL Mid-Season All-Star...tied for Tampa's team lead in wins.

2014
- Made his professional debut, combining with the GCL Yankees 2 and short-season Single-A Staten Island to go 2-3 with a 3.96 ERA (36.1IP, 16ER) and 34K in 12 games (eight starts).

PERSONAL
- Is married to Nicole...graduated from Gulfport H.S. (Miss.) in 2011, where he lettered three times as a pitcher and first baseman.
- Played three seasons for Mississippi State, owning a 1.59 ERA in 91 relief appearances...set the school's career (37) and single-season saves records (21)...was named a 2013 consensus All-American and earned 2012 consensus Freshman All-America honors.
- In January 2018, hosted a youth baseball clinic in Biloxi, Miss., with other professional and collegiate baseball players, with proceeds benefiting local youth undergoing cancer treatment.

Holder's Career Pitching Record

Year	Club	W	L	ERA	G	GS	CG	SHO	SV	IP	H	R	ER	HR	HP	BB	SO	WP	BK
2014	GCL Yankees 2	1	1	12.27	2	1	0	0	0	3.2	7	5	5	0	0	3	4	0	0
	Staten Island	1	2	3.03	10	7	0	0	0	32.2	35	16	11	1	0	10	30	3	0
2015	Tampa	7	5	2.44	19	18	1	0	0	103.1	92	33	28	3	5	21	78	2	0
	GCL Yankees 2	0	0	1.00	3	3	0	0	0	9.0	5	1	1	0	0	0	8	0	0
	Scranton/WB	0	1	6.35	1	0	0	0	0	5.2	4	4	4	1	0	4	4	0	0
2016	Tampa	0	0	0.00	2	0	0	0	0	4.0	2	0	0	0	1	0	7	0	0
	Trenton	3	1	2.20	28	0	0	0	10	41.0	27	10	10	2	3	7	59	0	0
	Scranton/WB	2	0	0.89	12	0	0	0	6	20.1	7	2	2	1	0	0	35	0	0
	YANKEES	0	0	5.40	8	0	0	0	0	8.1	8	5	5	1	0	4	5	0	0
2017	YANKEES	1	1	3.89	37	0	0	0	0	39.1	45	17	17	5	3	8	40	2	0
	Scranton/WB	0	0	1.69	12	0	0	0	1	16.0	15	3	3	1	1	8	21	0	0
2018	YANKEES	1	3	3.14	60	1	0	0	0	66.0	53	27	23	4	1	19	60	1	0
	Scranton/WB	1	0	3.00	4	1	0	0	0	6.0	5	2	2	1	0	1	8	1	0
2019	YANKEES - a	5	2	6.31	34	1	0	0	0	41.1	43	32	29	8	2	11	46	0	0
	Scranton/WB	1	1	2.92	9	0	0	0	2	12.1	13	5	4	1	0	2	15	1	0
Minor League Totals		16	11	2.48	102	30	1	0	19	254.0	212	81	70	11	10	56	269	7	0
Major League Totals		7	6	4.30	139	2	0	0	0	155.0	149	81	74	18	6	42	151	3	0

Selected by the Yankees in the sixth round of the 2014 First-Year Player Draft.

a - Placed on the 10-day injured list on August 10, 2019 (retroactive to August 7) with right shoulder inflammation...was transferred to the 60-day injured list on September 15, 2019, missing the remainder of the season.

Holder's Postseason Record

Year	Club vs. Opp.	W	L	ERA	G	GS	CG	SHO	SV	IP	H	R	ER	HR	HP	BB	SO	WP	BK
2018	NYY vs. OAK (WC)							On Roster - Did Not Pitch											
	NYY vs. BOS (DS)	0	0	4.50	1	0	0	0	0	2.0	2	1	1	0	0	1	1	0	0
Wild Card Totals		-	-	-	-	-	-	-	-	-	-	-	-	-	-	-	-	-	-
LDS Totals		0	0	4.50	1	0	0	0	0	2.0	2	1	1	0	0	1	1	0	0
POSTSEASON TOTALS		0	0	4.50	1	0	0	0	0	2.0	2	1	1	0	0	1	1	0	0

Holder's Career Fielding Record

Position	PCT	G	PO	A	E	TC	DP
Pitcher	1.000	139	5	8	0	13	1

Holder's Regular Season Batting Record

Year	Team	AVG	G	AB	R	H	2B	3B	HR	RBI	SH	SF	HP	BB	SO	SB	CS
2019	NYY					Did Not Bat											
Major League Totals		-	139	-	-	-	-	-	-	-	-	-	-	-	-	-	-

Holder's Career Bests and Streaks

COMPLETE GAMES: None. **LOW-HIT COMPLETE GAME:** None. **IP (START):** 2.2IP, 8/6/19 at BAL. **IP (RELIEF):** 3.0 - 2 times (last on 7/15/17 at BOS). **HITS:** 5 - 2 times (last on 6/24/19 vs. TOR). **RUNS:** 7, 8/2/18 at BOS. **WALKS:** 2 - 5 times (last on 5/23/19 at BAL). **STRIKEOUTS:** 4, 8/12/18 vs. TEX. **HOME RUNS:** 2 - 2 times (last on 6/24/19 vs. TOR). **WINNING STREAK:** 2g - 2 times (last: 5/29/19-present). **LOSING STREAK:** 2g - 2 times (last on 8/2-8/5/18). **SCORELESS STREAK (IP):** 10.2, 6/8-27/18.

Pitcher of the Month: None   **Player of the Week:** None   **Rookie of the Month:** None

---

Bobby Murcer Recognized

Oklahoma Christian University dedicated the new Bobby Murcer Indoor Training Facility on September 23, 2011.

OCU officials and members of Bobby Murcer's family were on hand to celebrate the opening of the $503,000 facility, named after the Oklahoma City native and New York Yankees player and broadcaster, who died in July 2008 at age 62 after battling brain cancer.

Although he never attended Oklahoma Christian, Murcer—who attended Southeast High School in Oklahoma City and was one of the state's most famous baseball players before being drafted by the Yankees—had strong ties with many people associated with the university, as he and his wife, Kay, attended Memorial Road Church of Christ, which is located immediately southwest of the OCU campus.

The Bobby Murcer Indoor Training Facility is located on the northwest corner of the Oklahoma Christian campus, next to Dobson Field, where the Eagles' baseball team plays its home games. The 12,800-square-foot facility includes 8,000 square feet of workout space, including batting cages. The facility also includes a clubhouse with showers, an athletic training area, a weight training area and laundry facilities.

The lobby of the facility includes photos from Murcer's playing and broadcasting careers, special wallpaper depicting various scenes from OCU's baseball history and plaques honoring the Oklahoma Christian players who have received NAIA All-America honors through the years.

AARON JUDGE • OF

99

HT: 6-7 • **WT:** 282 • **BATS:** R • **THROWS:** R
BIRTHDATE: 4/26/92 • **OPENING DAY AGE:** 27
BIRTHPLACE: Linden, Calif.
RESIDES: Linden, Calif.
COLLEGE: Fresno State
M.L. SERVICE: 3 years, 51 days

STATUS
▸ Selected by the Yankees in the first round (32nd overall) of the 2013 First-Year Player Draft.

CAREER NOTES
▸ Has been among the fastest in Baseball history to reach all of his career home runs (in terms of games played).
▸ Has hit 110HR in 396 career Major League games…the Yankees have gone 72-29 in his career when he homers…had 56HR in 348 games in the minor leagues prior to his Major League debut.
▸ Is one of seven players drafted and signed by the Yankees to hit at least 100HR with the club (Gardner, Posada, Jeter, Mattingly, Munson and Pagliarulo).
▸ Among players drafted by the organization since 1997, his 110 career home runs trail only Brett Gardner (124HR) for most hit as a member of the Yankees.
▸ Has 65HR in 201 career home games, sixth-most in Yankee Stadium history and four behind Brett Gardner (69HR) and Curtis Granderson (69HR)…is a career .315/.433/.647 (220-for-699) hitter at home.
▸ Has a 10.75 AB/HR ratio at home (699AB, 65HR), the third-best such ratio in home games in Major League history (min. 300AB) behind only Joey Gallo (10.43) and Mark McGwire (10.56)…is the best mark by any player at the current Yankee Stadium (min. 100AB).
▸ With 52HR in 2017, established a rookie single-season home run record (surpassing Mark McGwire-49HR in 1987)…was surpassed by the Mets' Pete Alonso (53) in 2019.
▸ Hit a total of 14HR in the first 50 games of his career, tied with Gleyber Torres (in 2018) for third-most by a Yankee through 50 career games since 1913, behind only Gary Sánchez-19 and Kevin Maas-15.
▸ Reached base safely in 31 straight home games from 9/3/17-5/4/18, the second-longest home on-base streak at the current Yankee Stadium (Mark Teixeira, 33G, 6/3-8/16/10)…hit .346/.493/.860 (37-for-107) with 34R, 7 doubles, 16HR, 39RBI and 33BB over the stretch.
▸ Is one of six position players drafted by the Yankees to make the All-Star team as a Yankee (also Thurman Munson, Don Mattingly, Derek Jeter, Jorge Posada and Brett Gardner).
▸ Reached base safely in 32 straight games vs. the Orioles (w/ a PA) from 9/3/16-9/22/18…is one of eight players with as long an on-base streak vs. the O's since 1994…had an 18-game run-scoring streak vs. the O's (4/9/17-4/5/18), the second-longest by any player vs. the Baltimore/St. Louis Browns franchise since 1913, behind Boston's Jimmie Foxx's 19-game streak from 6/1/38-5/9/39…reached safely in 35 straight starts vs. the Orioles from 9/3/16-3/31/19, matching the longest such streak by a Major League player since Jacoby Ellsbury's 40-game streak vs. Baltimore from 4/17/09-9/29/12…hit .346/.494/.708 (45-for-130) with 40R, 8 doubles, 13HR, 34RBI, 37BB and 1HP in those games.
▸ Has 8HR in 27 career postseason games…with 4HR in 14 postseason home games, is tied with Robinson Canó (4HR in 20G) for the most postseason HRs at the current Yankee Stadium…has four career ALCS homers, tied for the fifth-most in Yankees history behind Bernie Williams (9HR), Derek Jeter (7HR), Graig Nettles (5HR) and Alex Rodriguez (5HR).
▸ Hit 4HR in the 2017 postseason and 3HR in the 2018 playoffs…is the second Yankee to hit at least three postseason HRs in consecutive years (Reggie Jackson: 5HR in 1977, 4HR in 1978).
▸ Is the only player ever to homer in multiple Wild Card Games (2017 vs. Minnesota and 2018 vs. Oakland).
▸ Has made three Opening Day rosters in his career (2017-19)…is 5-for-11 with 4R, 2 doubles, 1RBI and 3BB in his three career Opening Day games.

CAREER HIGHLIGHTS

AL All-Star Team
▸ 2017, 2018

AL "Rookie of the Year"
▸ 2017

Baseball America MLB "Rookie of the Year"
▸ 2017

Sporting News AL "Rookie of the Year"
▸ 2017

AL Silver Slugger
▸ 2017

Wilson Defensive Player of the Year in RF
▸ 2019

2019
▸ In 102 games with the Yankees, hit .272 (103-for-378) with 75R, 18 doubles, 27HR and 55RBI…reached the 20HR plateau for the third straight season…of his 27HR, 19 tied the game (four) or gave the Yankees the lead (15).
▸ Was named the winner of the 2019 Wilson Defensive Player of the Year Award in RF, his first such award and the second by a Yankee in the six years of its current format (LF Brett Gardner in 2016)…his seven assists were fourth-most among outfielders who did not commit an error, while his 12.7 UZR (Ultimate Zone Rating) and 19 Defensive Runs Saved ranked third and fifth, respectively, among all outfielders (FanGraphs).

- Went 2-for-3 with 3R and 2BB in 3/28 Opening Day win vs. Baltimore…with Luke Voit going 1-for-1 with 1R, 1HR, 4RBI, 2BB and 1HP in the game, the duo became the first Yankees to reach base safely at least four times on Opening Day since Alex Rodriguez on 4/6/12 at Tampa Bay and the first Yankees teammates to do so in the same Opening Day game since Rodriguez and Hideki Matsui on 4/3/06 at Oakland.
- Recorded his eighth career multi-HR game in 4/6 win at Baltimore, his first since 9/25/17 vs. Kansas City (also 2HR).
- Hit a solo HR in the first inning of 4/20 win vs. Kansas City…was his second extra-base hit in as many days (doubled on 4/19) after collecting just 1XBH over his previous eight games (solo HR on 4/13 vs. Chicago-AL)…singled to right field in the sixth inning and was removed from the game for a pinch-runner after suffering a left oblique injury…was sent New York-Presbyterian Hospital for further evaluation and an MRI.
- Was placed on the 10-day injured list from 4/21-6/21 with a left oblique strain…missed 54 team games…hit .125 (2-for-16) with 2R, 1HR, 2RBI and 3BB in five rehab games with Triple-A Scranton/Wilkes-Barre.
- Hit leadoff in the starting lineup for the first time in his career on 6/21 vs. Houston (0-for-4).
- Hit two solo HRs on 7/5 at Tampa Bay, his ninth career multi-HR game…his 11th-inning, game-winning, first-pitch HR had an exist velocity of 116.3 mph…was his second career go-ahead HR in extra innings (also a two-run HR on 6/6/18 at Toronto).
- Went 7-for-11 (.636) in the Toronto series immediately following the All-Star break from 7/12-14 after entering the break with just 3H in 21AB in July…marked the beginning of a stretch in which he had eight straight hits go for singles, his longest career streak of hits without an extra-base hit.
- Hit game-winning, two-run HR in the eighth inning on 7/16 vs. Tampa Bay, his fifth career go-ahead HR in the eighth inning or later.
- Hit a solo HR on 8/4 vs. Boston, snapping a season-long 14-game homerless stretch (first HR since 7/19 vs. Colorado)…marked his first RBI since 7/23 at Minnesota, ending a career-long-tying 10-game RBI drought.
- Reached in 24-of-57PA in 13 games from 8/16-31 (21H, 3BB) after reaching in 6-of-34PA over his prior 8G (3H, 3BB).
- Played in each of the Yankees' nine games on their west coast road trip from 8/20-28 (at Oakland, Los Angeles-NL and Seattle), hitting .359/.375/.897 (14-for-39) with 7R, 3 doubles, 6HR and 9RBI.
- Homered in each of the Yankees' 10 series from 8/20-9/22, hitting 14HR in 29 games during the stretch…was homerless over a 13-game span from 8/5-18 leading into the streak.
- Had a season-best nine-game hitting streak from 8/22-31, batting .432 (16-for-37) with 7R, 3 doubles, 6HR and 9RBI during the stretch…homered in three straight games from 8/23-25, tying the longest streak of his career (fourth time and first since 7/4-7/17).
- Hit his 100th career home run on 8/27 at Seattle (off Yusei Kikuchi)…came in his 371st career game, becoming the third-fastest player to reach the mark (in terms of games played) in Baseball history behind only Philadelphia's Ryan Howard (Game No. 325 on 6/27/07) and teammate Gary Sánchez (Game No. 355 on 8/23/19)…was the fourth Yankee to hit career HR No. 100 in 2019 (Gardner, Gregorius, Sánchez)…is the seventh player drafted and signed by the Yankees to hit at least 100HR with the club (Gardner, Posada, Jeter, Mattingly, Munson and Pagliarulo).
- Hit a game-tying solo HR with two outs in the eighth inning on 8/31 vs. Oakland…was his seventh career HR to tie the game or give the Yankees the lead in the eighth inning or later and third of the season (also a go-ahead solo HR in the top of the 11th inning on 7/5 at Tampa Bay and a go-ahead two-run HR in the bottom of the eighth on 7/16 vs. Tampa Bay).
- Reached base four times in Game 1 of 9/12 doubleheader at Detroit, scoring a career-high-tying 4R and recording a season-high-tying 3BB…hit a two-run HR in Game 2.
- Started in RF in each of the Yankees' nine postseason games…hit a two-run HR in the fourth inning of ALCS Game 2 at Houston…marked his eighth career postseason HR (in his 23rd career playoff game), becoming the fourth Yankee to hit 8HR within his first 23 postseason games (also Lou Gehrig-9HR, Mickey Mantle-8HR and Bernie Williams-8HR).

2018

- In 112 games with the Yankees (88 starts in RF, 19 at DH, 1 in CF), hit .278 (115-for-413) with 77R, 22 doubles, 27HR, 67RBI, 76BB and 6SB…the Yankees went 21-6 when he homered in 2018.
- Was a finalist for the AL Gold Glove Award in RF.
- Hit .352/.471/.699 (69-for-196) with 47R, 14 doubles, 18HR, 45RBI and 20 multi-hit games in 56 contests at Yankee Stadium…did not go consecutive home games without a hit over a 59-game stretch at Yankee Stadium (9/17/17-7/26/18)…hit safely in 17 consecutive home games from 9/17/17-4/16/18…had at least 1RBI in a franchise-record 14 straight home games from 9/18/17-4/7/18…was tied for the fourth-longest such streak in the Majors since RBI became an official statistic in 1920.
- Appeared in each of the Yankees' first 56 games of the season from 3/29 through Game 2 on 6/4.
- Hit 25HR before the All-Star break, becoming the fourth player to hit at least 25HR before the break in two different seasons as a Yankee and just the second to do so in consecutive years, joining Roger Maris (1960-61), Mickey Mantle (1956 and '61) and Jason Giambi (2003 and '06).
- Had a career-long 14-game hitting streak from 9/17/17-3/29/18…had an eight-game streak of drawing at least one walk from 9/24/17-3/29/18, matching the longest streak of his career (also 6/6-13/17).
- Made his first Major League start (and appearance) in CF in 3/31 loss at Toronto.
- Reached base safely in 23 of his 25 games in April (all except 4/27 and 4/29 at Los Angeles-AL), including each of his first 21 games of the month.

- Was 3-for-3 with a HR off Red Sox starter Chris Sale on 4/10…entered 0-for-12 with 10K in his career vs. Sale…became the first player to record 3H off Sale in one game since he joined the Red Sox before the 2017 season…prior to Judge, the last player with a three-hit game vs. Sale was Detroit's Miguel Cabrera, who went 4-for-4 with two solo HRs against him on 9/5/16 at Chicago-AL.
- Had at least 1RBI in seven straight games from 5/6-13 (14RBI), tying the longest RBI streak of his career.
- Hit game-winning two-run HR in the 13th on 6/6 at Toronto…was his first career extra-inning HR and was the latest Yankees HR to break a 0-0 tie since Alex Rodriguez's 15th-inning two-run "walk-off" HR on 8/7/09 vs. Boston.
- Hit game-winning solo HR in the eighth inning on 6/9 at the Mets…was the third straight game the Yankees hit a go-ahead HR in the eighth-inning-or-later, their first time doing so since 8/29-31/77 (three straight - Chambliss, Rivers and Nettles)…Judge hit two of those homers after having just one go-ahead HR in the eighth-inning-or-later over his first 239 career games.
- Started in LF and went 1-for-2 with 1R, 1HR, 1RBI and 1BB in the AL's All-Star Game win on 7/17…his solo HR off Scherzer to lead off the second inning was the first of 10HR hit in the game and the first All-Star homer by a Yankee since Jason Giambi in 2003…became the third Yankee to homer in an All-Star Game at age 26-or-younger, joining Joe DiMaggio (1936) and Mickey Mantle (1955 and '56)…was selected by fans to his second straight All-Star team…is one of five position players drafted by the Yankees to make the All-Star team multiple times as a Yankee (also Thurman Munson, Don Mattingly, Derek Jeter and Jorge Posada)…received a fan-elected starting assignment for the second straight year and is the *first Yankee to start at least two straight ASGs* since Robinson Canó (2010-13) and *first Yankees OF to start two straight* since Curtis Granderson (2011-12).
- Was 1-for-1 with 1R in 7/26 win vs. Kansas City before being removed from the game in the fourth for PH (Andújar) after being hit by a pitch in the first inning…underwent an MRI at New York-Presbyterian Hospital and was diagnosed with a chip fracture of the right wrist (ulnar styloid bone)…was placed on the 10-day disabled list with the injury from 7/27-9/14 (missed 45 team games)…in a simulated game at Yankee Stadium on 9/17, had 11 live at-bats off of RHP A.J. Cole, RHP Chance Adams and minor-league LHP Phillip Diehl.
- Hit the Yankees' 264th home run of the season with a solo HR in the eighth inning of 9/28 win at Boston, tying the single-season Major League record (1997 Seattle Mariners)…the record has since been surpassed…was his first HR since 7/21 vs. the Mets, snapping a 15-game homerless stretch (49AB) and 11-game stretch without a homer since returning from the D.L.
- Hit .421/.500/.947 (8-for-19) with 6R, 1 double, 3HR, 4RBI and 3BB in five postseason games…homered in each of the first 3G, joining Hank Bauer (1958 World Series Games 1-3) as the only Yankees to homer in each of the team's first three postseason games in a year (note: Johnny Mize homered in 1952 World Series Games 3-5 after missing the first 2G of the Series)…became the third player to begin a postseason with 3G with at least 2H and 1HR, joining St. Louis' Matt Carpenter in 2014 and the Yankees' Hank Bauer in 1958.
- Hit a two-run HR in the first inning of the Wild Card Game…with an exit velocity of 116.1 mph, was briefly the hardest-hit postseason HR of the Statcast era (since 2015), until Stanton's HR surpassed it later in the game.

2017

- In 155 games with the Yankees (141 starts in RF, 10 at DH), hit .284 (154-for-542) with 128R, 24 doubles, 3 triples, 52HR, 114RBI, 127BB and 9SB…according to MLB Statcast, his 94.9 mph average exit velocity on balls in play was highest among all Major League hitters…received his first career Silver Slugger Award.
- Placed second in AL Most Valuable Player voting, totaling 279 points (2 first place votes, 27 second place votes, 1 third place vote)…was the second rookie all time to finish second in MVP voting, joining Mike Trout in 2012 (won by Miguel Cabrera).
- Was unanimously named AL Jackie Robinson "Rookie of the Year" by the BBWAA…was the ninth Yankee to win the award and second by a unanimous vote (also Derek Jeter in 1996)…was the only player listed on every ballot.
- Was named MLB "Rookie of the Year" by *Baseball America*, the first Yankee to win the award since Derek Jeter (1996)…was also named 2017 *Sporting News* AL "Rookie of the Year," as voted on by a panel of AL players…was selected to the Topps MLB All-Star Rookie Team.
- Led the American League in runs scored (128, 2nd MLB), home runs (52, 2nd MLB), walks (127, 2nd MLB) and on-base pct. (.422, 3rd MLB) and slugging pct. (.627, 2nd MLB)…led the Majors in RBI (114, 6th MLB)…led the Majors with an 8.2 WAR, the highest by a Yankee since Alex Rodriguez in 2007 (9.6).
- With a 1.049 OPS, was the fourth rookie in the Modern Era (since 1900) with an OPS of 1.000-or-better: St. Louis' Albert Pujols (1.013) in 2001, Boston's Ted Williams (1.045) in 1939 and Cleveland's Joe Jackson (1.058) in 1911.
- Had 186 balls hit at least 95 mph, accounting for 55.0% of his balls put in play, the highest pct. in the Majors…hit 7HR with an exit velocity of 117 mph or higher (rest of the Majors: two, both by Giancarlo Stanton).
- Became the 13th Yankee to lead the AL (or tie for the lead) in home runs and first since Mark Teixeira (tied) in 2009…is the first Yankee to lead outright since Alex Rodriguez in 2007.
- Held at least a share of the AL HR lead every day from 5/28 through the end of the season except one (end of play on 9/6).
- At the outset, his 52HR were the most ever by a Major League rookie (Mark McGwire, 49HR in 1987) and surpassed Joe DiMaggio (29HR in 1936) for most by a Yankees rookie…was surpassed by the Mets' Pete Alonso (53) in 2019.
- His 52HR were then-tied with Mickey Mantle (52HR in 1956) and Alex Rodriguez (52HR in 2001) for third-most by a player 25-or-younger in Baseball history, trailing only Jimmie Foxx (58HR in 1932) and Babe Ruth (54HR in 1920)…was the fifth Yankee age 25-or-younger to hit at least 40HR in a season.
- Tied Mickey Mantle (52HR in 1956) for the eighth-most single-season homers in Yankees history and had the second-most by a right-handed hitter (Alex Rodriguez-54HR in 2007).

- Homered against every AL opponent, the first Yankee to do so since the AL expanded to 15 teams in 2013.
- Had 33HR at Yankee Stadium, most by a Yankee in a single season at a home venue in franchise history, ahead of Babe Ruth (32 in 1921)…in 77 home games, hit .312/.440/.725 (84-for-269) with 73R, 10 doubles, 33HR, 68RBI and 62BB.
- Had seven multi-HR games (all 2HR games): 4/28 vs. Baltimore, 5/2 vs. Toronto, 6/11 vs. Baltimore, 9/10 at Texas, 9/14 vs. Baltimore, 9/24 at Toronto and 9/25 vs. Kansas City), tied for fourth-most by a Yankee in a single season at the time (Gleyber Torres notched eight in 2019)…matched Mark McGwire (7G in 1987) for the most ever by a rookie in a single season…at the time, were tied for the fifth-most in a season by any player, age 25-or-younger behind only Ralph Kiner (10G in 1947), Willie Mays (9G in 1955), Reggie Jackson (8G in 1969) and Vladimir Guerrero (8G in 2000)…Gleyber Torres recorded eight such games in 2019.
- Had 52HR, while Gary Sánchez had 33HR…was just the second time in Yankees history that two teammates, age 25-or-younger, hit at least 30HR in the same season, joining Joe DiMaggio (31HR) and Joe Gordon (30HR) in 1940…with a combined 85HR, set the Major League record for homers by two teammates, each 25-or-younger (surpassed the 2007 Milwaukee Brewers' Prince Fielder-50 and Ryan Braun-34).
- Hit 30HR before the All-Star Game, one of three rookies ever to reach 30HR prior to the All-Star break (since 1933), joining Mark McGwire (33 in 1987) and Pete Alonso (30 in 2019)…is one of three Yankees ever to hit at least 30HR by the break, joining Roger Maris (33HR in 1961) and Alex Rodriguez (30HR in 2007)…marked the seventh time a Yankee led the Majors in homers at the All-Star break (since 1933): Rodriguez (30) in 2007, Maris (33) in 1961, Mantle (27) in 1960, Mantle (29) in 1956, DiMaggio/Keller (19 each) in 1941 and DiMaggio (20) in 1937.
- His 128R were most by a Major League rookie since Mike Trout in 2012 (129R)…were second-most by a Yankees rookie (Joe DiMaggio-132R in 1936)…the Yankees went 58-27 when he scored a run.
- His 114RBI were most by a Yankee since Curtis Granderson (119) and Robinson Canó (118) in 2011…the Yankees were 44-20 when he had at least 1RBI and 23-5 when he had multiple RBI.
- Is the fourth rookie in Yankees history with at least 100RBI in a season, joining Joe DiMaggio (125 in 1936), Tony Lazzeri (114 in 1926) and Hideki Matsui (106 in 2003).
- Became the eighth player in Yankees history with at least 100R, 100RBI and 100BB in a season, joining Lou Gehrig (11x: 1926-27, '29-32, '34-38), Babe Ruth (10x: 1920-21, '23-24, '26-28, '30-32), Mickey Mantle (3x: 1954, '56, '61), Charlie Keller (2x: 1941-42), George Selkirk (1939), Bernie Williams (1999) and Jason Giambi (2002)…only Ruth (10x), Gehrig (5x), Mantle (2x) and Giambi accomplished the feat while also hitting at least 40HR…is the fourth Yankee ever with at least 110R, 110RBI and 110BB in a season (Ruth-10x, Gehrig-5x, Mantle-2x).
- Joined Boston's Ted Williams (1939) as the only players ever with at least 100R, 100RBI and 100BB as a rookie.
- Had 38 games with at least 1R, 1RBI and 1BB, most by a Yankee since Lou Gehrig in 1936 (43).
- Became the fourth rookie all-time to draw 100BB *and* score 100R in a season, joining Ted Williams in 1939 (131R, 105BB), Lu Blue in 1921 (103R, 103BB) and Jim Gilliam in 1953 (125R, 100BB).
- Is one of three players in Baseball history, age 25-or-younger, with at least 125R and 125BB in a season, joining Babe Ruth (1920, age 25) and Ted Williams (1941 and '42, ages 22 and 23).
- His 127BB set a Major League rookie record, surpassing Cleveland's Les Fleming (106BB in 1942) on 9/10 at Texas (credit: *Elias*)…surpassed Charlie Keller (81BB in 1939) for the Yankees' rookie walk record on 8/9 at Toronto.
- Is the fifth Yankee in franchise history—and only right-handed batter—with at least 125BB in a season (Ruth-10x, Gehrig-3x, Mantle-3x, Giambi-1x).
- Was twice named AL "Player of the Week:" 6/5-11 and 9/18-24.
- Hit .426/.588/1.049 (26-for-61) with 31R, 5 doubles, 11HR, 24RBI and 24BB in 19 games vs. Baltimore…his 31R were the most by any player vs. any opponent in one season since Boston's Ted Williams scored 31R in 1947 vs. St. Louis-AL…*Elias* notes it marked the most by a rookie vs. one team since Joe DiMaggio in 1936 vs. the Browns (31R)…his 11HR were the most by a Yankee vs. a single opponent in a season since 1961, when Roger Maris hit 13HR vs. Chicago-AL and Mickey Mantle hit 11HR vs. Washington-AL…according to *Elias*, tied Cleveland's Hal Trosky (11HR in 22G vs. Chicago-AL in 1934) for the most homers by a rookie against one team in a single season…his 24BB were the most by a Yankee vs. an opponent since 1959.
- Was the only Major Leaguer to post an OPS higher than 1.000 in each of the season's first three months: April (1.161), May (1.084) and June (1.167)…led the AL in OPS in April and June.

MOST HR IN A SEASON BY A YANKEE

HR	PLAYER	YEAR
61	Roger Maris	1961
60	Babe Ruth	1927
59	Babe Ruth	1921
54	Alex Rodriguez*	2007
54	Mickey Mantle	1961
54	Babe Ruth	1928
54	Babe Ruth	1920
52	AARON JUDGE*	2017
52	Mickey Mantle	1956

*right-handed batter

HR IN A SEASON, YANKEES, AGE 25-OR-YOUNGER

HR	PLAYER	YEAR
54	Babe Ruth	1920
52	AARON JUDGE	2017
52	Mickey Mantle	1956

HR, MLB ROOKIE, ALL TIME

HR	PLAYER	YEAR
53	Pete Alonso	2019
52	AARON JUDGE	2017
49	Mark McGwire	1987

100RBI, YANKEES ROOKIE

RBI	PLAYER	YEAR
125	Joe DiMaggio	1936
114	AARON JUDGE	2017
114	Tony Lazzeri	1926
106	Hideki Matsui	2003

WAR, MLB, 2017 (FanGraphs)

WAR	PLAYER	YEAR
8.2	OF AARON JUDGE	NYY
7.7	LHP Chris Sale	BOS
7.5	2B José Altuve	HOU
7.3	RHP Corey Kluber	CLE

WAR, MLB ROOKIES, MODERN ERA (FanGraphs)

WAR	PLAYER	YEAR
10.3	Mike Trout-LAA*	2012
9.3	Joe Jackson-CLE	1911
8.3	Doc Gooden-NYM*	1984
8.2	AARON JUDGE-NYY*	2017
8.2	Dick Allen-PHI*	1964

*Won Rookie of the Year Award

- Was named AL "Rookie of the Month" for April, batting .303 (23-for-76) with 23R, 10HR and 20RBI in 22 games...was the third Yankee ever to hit at least 10HR in March/April (Alex Rodriguez: 14HR in 2007 and Graig Nettles: 11HR in 1974)...ranked among all AL leaders with 23R (1st), a .750 SLG (1st), 10HR (T1st) and 20RBI (T5th) in April...tied a Major League rookie record for the most home runs in April, previously set by Chicago-AL's José Abreu in 2014 and tied by Colorado's Trevor Story in 2016 (credit: ESPN Stats & Info)...was the fourth Yankee ever to win the award (also Hideki Matsui-June 2003, Robinson Canó-September 2005 and Gary Sánchez-August 2016).

- In April, became the 10th rookie in Major League history with at least 10HR, 10BB, and a .300 batting average in any calendar month...the only other rookies to do so in the prior 40 years were Mike Trout (July 2012) and Gary Sánchez (August 2016)...also accomplished the feat in June and September, while Rhys Hoskins did so in August.

- Posted a .411 OBP in April (in 22G), a .441 OBP in May (26G) and a .481 OBP in June (28G)...became the third rookie in Major League history to have an OBP of at least .400 in April, May and June (min. 75PA in each month): also St. Louis' Albert Pujols in 2001 and Houston's Greg Gross in 1974.

- Became the youngest player in Major League history—and the only rookie—to hit at least 13HR through his team's first 26G of the season...was the second Yankee to do so (also Alex Rodriguez-14HR in 2007).

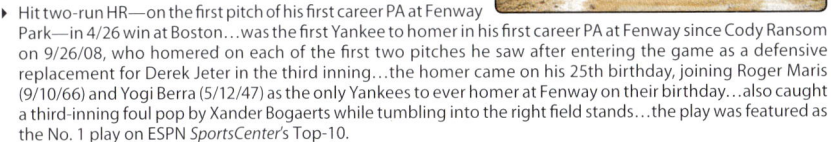

- Hit two-run HR—on the first pitch of his first career PA at Fenway Park—in 4/26 win at Boston...was the first Yankee to homer in his first career PA at Fenway since Cody Ransom on 9/26/08, who homered on each of the first two pitches he saw after entering the game as a defensive replacement for Derek Jeter in the third inning...the homer came on his 25th birthday, joining Roger Maris (9/10/66) and Yogi Berra (5/12/47) as the only Yankees to ever homer at Fenway on their birthday...also caught a third-inning foul pop by Xander Bogaerts while tumbling into the right field stands...the play was featured as the No. 1 play on ESPN *SportsCenter*'s Top-10.

- Recorded his first career multi-HR game in 4/28 win vs. Baltimore, hitting solo HR in the fifth and two-run HR in the sixth...at 25 years, 2 days old, was the youngest Yankees outfielder with 2HR in a game since Melky Cabrera (24y, 254d on 4/22/09 vs. Oakland)...collected his second career multi-HR game in 5/2 win vs. Toronto...at 25 years, 6 days old, became the youngest Yankees outfielder with multiple 2HR games since Dan Pasqua (23y, 268d on 7/12/85 and 24y, 217d on 5/22/86).

- Was named AL "Rookie of the Month" for May after batting .347/.441/.642 (33-for-95) with 17R, 5 doubles, 7HR and 17RBI in 26 games and leading all AL rookies in BA, runs, hits, HR, RBI and OBP, while ranking second in SLG...was his second straight "Rookie of the Month" honor, having also won the award in April...became the first Yankee ever to win the award twice...was the first Yankee to win any monthly award in consecutive months since Don Mattingly was named AL "Player of the Month" in both August and September of 1985.

- Had a career-long 32-game on-base streak from 5/28-6/30, batting .339/.483/.720 (40-for-118) with 34R, 7 doubles, 1 triple, 12HR, 32RBI and 32BB over the span...was the longest single-season streak by a Yankee since Derek Jeter had a 34-game streak to end the 2012 season (8/27-10/3/12) and the longest single-season streak for a Yankees rookie since Charlie Keller in 1939 (40 games)...reached base safely in 42 consecutive *starts* from 5/28-7/16 (G1), batting .321 (51-for-159) with 39R, 8 doubles, 15HR, 36RBI and 38BB in his starts over the span...was the longest single-season streak by a Yankee since Mark Teixeira (42G, 6/6-7/26/10).

- Was named AL "Player of the Month" and "Rookie of the Month" for June, batting .324/.481/.686 (33-for-102) with 30R, 5 doubles, 10HR, 25RBI and 30BB in 28G and reaching safely in every game...was his first career "Player of the Month" nod and his third "Rookie of the Month" honor, having also won the award in April and May...became the first Yankee ever to win three consecutive monthly awards and the first AL player with three straight "Rookie of the Month" honors in a single season since Chicago-AL's José Abreu in 2014...was the first AL player to win three "Rookie of the Month" awards in a row since Mike Trout won four straight from May-August 2012...was the 10th player all time (in either league) to win both awards in the same calendar month and second Yankee (also Gary Sánchez in August 2016).

- Hit safely in 17 straight *home* games from 6/10-7/28 (.379/.461/.864, 25-for-66, 20R, 2 doubles, 10HR, 17RBI, 9BB), matching the second-longest single-season streak by a Yankee at the current Yankee Stadium (since 2009): Carlos Beltrán, 18G (7/19-8/26/15) and Robinson Canó, 17G (5/17-6/17/10)...was the longest home hitting streak *by a rookie* in franchise history (previous: Hideki Matsui, 16G in 2003)—credit: *Elias*.

- His first-inning solo HR in 6/10 win vs. Baltimore had an exit velocity of 121.1 mph, setting a record for hardest hit HR in the Statcast-era (since 2015)...was surpassed by Giancarlo Stanton's 121.7 mph HR on 8/9/18.

- Hit his Major League-leading 20th home run of the season on 6/11 vs. Baltimore, becoming the first rookie in Major League history to be the first player to 20HR in a season...hit solo HR and two-run HR and went 4-for-4 with 4R, 1 double and 1BB in the game...at 25 years, 46 days old, became the youngest Yankee to go 4-for-4 or better with 2HR since Mickey Mantle (24 years, 211 days) went 4-for-4 with 2HR on 5/18/56 at Chicago-AL...his sixth-inning solo HR went 495' (per Statcast), the longest measured HR hit in the Majors in 2017.

131

- Through the end of play on 6/11, led the AL in all three Triple Crown categories…since RBI became an official stat, was the first time a rookie led his league in each of those categories on 6/1 or later (credit: *Elias*).
- Was selected to his first career All-Star team after leading the AL with 4,488,702 votes…was the first Yankee to lead the AL in All-Star voting since Jeter in 2009…at age 25, was the youngest player to lead the AL in voting since Ken Griffey Jr. (24) in 1994…was the leading vote-getter in all of Baseball via the Player Ballot…was the third Yankees rookie elected to start an All-Star Game (Hideki Matsui-2003, Joe DiMaggio-1936)…eight other Yankees rookies were AL All-Star Team reserves: Dellin Betances (2014), Masahiro Tanaka (2014), Willie Randolph (1976), Tom Tresh (1962), Ryne Duren (1958), Bobby Richardson (1957), Spec Shea (1947) and Joe Page (1944)…is the sixth position player drafted by the Yankees to make the All-Star team as a Yankee (Munson, Mattingly, Jeter, Posada and Gardner).
- Won the Home Run Derby, defeating Minnesota's Miguel Sanó in the final round, 11HR-to-10HR…became the fourth Yankee to win a Derby, joining Robinson Canó (2011), Jason Giambi (2002) and Tino Martinez (1997)…was pitched to by Yankees BP pitcher Danilo Valiente…hit 23HR in the first round, topping Miami's Justin Bour (22HR)…in the semifinals, out-homered NL Rookie of the Year, Cody Bellinger of the Dodgers, 13HR-to-12HR…his 47 total homers hit (in 76 swings) were most ever by a Yankee in the Home Run Derby, surpassing Canó's 32HR in 2011 and second-most in Derby history at the time (2016 winner Giancarlo Stanton hit 61)…four of Judge's homers went at least 500 ft…is the first rookie ever to win the Derby outright (the Angels' Wally Joyner was a co-champion in 1986)…became the first player ever to win both the College and MLB Home Run Derby.
- Started in RF and went 0-for-3 for the AL in the All-Star Game on 7/11…was the second consecutive Yankees RF to be an All-Star (Carlos Beltrán)…at 25, was 14 years younger than Beltrán (39) in 2016…was the first Yankee to serve as the AL's starting right fielder since Paul O'Neill in 1997.
- Ended his single-season Major League-record 37-game strikeout streak (7/8-8/20) in 8/22 win at Detroit.
- Was named September AL "Player of the Month" (second, also June 2017) and "Rookie of the Month" (fourth, also April, May and June 2017)…hit .311/.463/.889 (28-for-90) with 29R, 7 doubles, 15HR, 32RBI and 28BB in 27G, his most HR and RBI in a calendar month in his career…were the most homers by a Yankee in a calendar month since Roger Maris hit 15HR in June 1961…was the fifth Yankee in franchise history to hit at least 15HR in a calendar month (Babe Ruth-4x, Joe DiMaggio-1x, Mickey Mantle-1x and Roger Maris-1x)…led the Majors in runs and walks and led the AL in RBI (2nd MLB), home runs (2nd MLB), slugging pct. (2nd MLB) and on-base pct. (3rd MLB).
- Reached base safely in his final 25 games (from 9/3), batting .329/.487/.951 (27-for-82) with 29R, 15HR, 31RBI and 28BB…hit 9HR over his final 12 games (from 9/18) and 15HR over his final 25 games (from 9/3).
- Hit 2HR in 9/10 win at Texas…with Gary Sánchez (2HR) also hitting multiple homers, the duo became the fourth pair of Yankees teammates, both age-25 or younger, with multiple HRs in the same game (also Ron Blomberg-2HR/Otto Velez-2HR on 9/23/73-G1 at Cleveland; Charlie Keller-3HR/Joe DiMaggio-2HR on 7/28/40-G1 at Chicago-AL; and Joe Gordon-2HR/Tommy Henrich-2HR on 8/27/38-G2 vs. Cleveland)…also collected his 107th walk of the season, surpassing Cleveland's Les Fleming (106BB in 1942) to set the all-time Major League rookie walks record.
- Had eight straight games with an extra-base hit (9/20-28), the longest ever by a Yankees rookie.
- Hit his 49th and 50th home runs of the season in 9/25 win vs. Kansas City, tying and surpassing Mark McGwire (49HR in 1987) for the single-season rookie home run record…was surpassed by the Mets' Pete Alonso in 2019.
- Made his postseason debut, batting .188 (9-for-48) with 9R, 3 doubles, 4HR and 11RBI in 13 playoff games…his 4HR were the most ever by a Yankees rookie in a single postseason (credit: ESPN Stats & Info) and were tied with Miguel Cabrera (2003) for the third-most by a rookie in a single postseason behind Evan Longoria (6HR in 2008) and Kyle Schwarber (5HR in 2015)…was the 15th player in Baseball history (and second Yankee) to have 4HR in a single postseason at age 25-or-younger (also Lou Gehrig-4HR in 1928).
- Made his postseason debut in the Yankees' AL Wild Card win vs. Minnesota, hitting a two-run HR in the fourth…according to *Elias*, became the third Yankees rookie to homer in his postseason debut, joining Shane Spencer (1998 ALDS Game 2 vs. Texas) and Elston Howard (1955 World Series Game 1 vs. Brooklyn)…was the first postseason HR by any Yankees rookie since Hideki Matsui in 2003 World Series Game 2 vs. Florida…both he and Brett Gardner scored 3R, becoming the seventh set of Yankees teammates to each score at least 3R in a postseason game, and only the second since 1962 (Rodriguez/Matsui/Sheffield in 2004 ALCS Game 3 at Boston).
- Leapt at the right field wall to rob Francisco Lindor of a potential two-run HR for the second out in the top of the sixth in ALDS Game 3 vs. Cleveland…was the first time in his career he robbed a homer (ESPN Stats & Info).
- Had multiple RBI in three straight home games (ALDS Game 4, ALCS Game 3 and ALCS Game 4), going 4-for-11 with 3R, 2 doubles, 2HR, 7RBI and 2BB in those games…became the second player in Yankees postseason history to record at least 2RBI in three consecutive home games, joining Lou Gehrig (3G, 1928 World Series Game 1 through 1932 World Series Game 1).
- Homered in consecutive games (ALCS Games 3 and 4 vs. Houston), becoming the seventh Yankee, age 25-or-younger, to homer in back-to-back playoff games (also Lou Gehrig, three straight; Mickey Mantle, two straight twice; Greg Bird; Derek Jeter; Gil McDougald and Charlie Keller)…was the third Yankees rookie to homer in consecutive playoff games, joining Keller (Games 3-4 in the 1939 World Series vs. Cincinnati) and Shane Spencer (Games 2-3 of the 1998 ALDS vs. Texas)—credit: *Elias*.
- In ALCS Games 3-5, became the seventh player (second Yankee) in postseason history to tally at least 1RBI, 1XBH and 1BB in three straight playoff games (Gehrig: MLB-record 4G from 1928 World Series Game 2-1932 World Series Game 1)…in each of his four games from ALCS Games 3-6, had at least 1R, 1RBI and 1XBH, becoming the third Yankee to do so in four straight postseason games (also Reggie Jackson and Lou Gehrig).
- Underwent arthroscopic surgery on his left shoulder on 11/20…the procedure involved a loose-body removal and cartilage clean-up, and was performed by Dr. Neal ElAttrache in Los Angeles at the Kerlan-Jobe Orthopaedic Clinic.

2016
- In 27 games with the Yankees (24 starts in RF), hit .179 (15-for-84) with 10R, 2 doubles, 4HR and 10RBI…according to MLB Statcast, had a 95.5 mph average exit velocity, second-highest among all Major League hitters (min. 40 batted ball events) behind only the Mariners' Nelson Cruz (95.9).
- Became the first player in Yankees history to record an extra-base hit in each of his first three career games (Game 1 - HR, Game 2 - HR, Game 3 - double)…became the ninth AL player since 1913 to accomplish the feat.
- According to ESPN Stats & Info, is the first player in AL history to record at least 1XBH and 1RBI in each of his first three career games…became the seventh player in Yankees history to record RBI in five of his first seven games to begin a Major League career, joining Yangervis Solarte (2014), Hideki Matsui (2003), Joe Buzas (1945), Joe DiMaggio (1936), George Selkirk (1934) and Norm McMillan (1922).
- Made his Major League debut in 8/13 win vs. Tampa Bay, hitting solo HR in the second off Matt Andriese…the HR came in his first career PA, becoming the fifth Yankee in franchise history (and second in the inning immediately following Tyler Austin's solo HR) to accomplish the feat (also John Miller, Marcus Thames and Andy Phillips)…per ESPN Stats & Info, was the longest HR by a Yankee at Yankee Stadium since 6/10/11 (Alex Rodriguez vs. Cleveland off Fausto Carmona)…became the third player in the history of the current Yankee Stadium to hit a ball into or over the centerfield batters eye glass (also Seattle's Russell Branyan on 7/2/09 and Houston's Carlos Correa on 4/6/16)…with Austin also making his Major League debut in the game, became the first pair of teammates in Major League history to each homer in their Major League debuts in the same game…there had been just one other game in Baseball history in which two players each hit HRs in their first Major League at-bats, but they were on opposing teams (Brooklyn at Philadelphia on 4/19/38 – the Phillies' Emmett "Heinie" Mueller and the Dodgers' Ernie Koy – both in the first inning)…became the first pair of Yankees to make their Major League debuts as starters in the same game since C Johnny Ellis and CF Jim Lyttle on 5/17/69 vs. California…was signed to a Major League contract and selected to the Yankees' 25-man roster prior to the game.
- Hit solo HR—his second in as many career games—in 8/14 loss vs. Tampa Bay…according to *Elias*, became the second player in Baseball history to homer in his first at-bat in each of his first two Major League games, joining the Cardinals' Keith McDonald in 2000…is the second player in Yankees history to homer in each of his first two Major League games, joining Joe Lefebvre, who did so from 5/22-23/80…joined Colorado's Trevor Story (first 4G, 6HR from 4/4-8) as the only two players to accomplish the feat in 2016.
- Was placed on the 15-day disabled list on 9/14 with a Grade 2 right oblique strain…injury occurred on a swing taken in the bottom of the fourth in 9/13 win vs. Los Angeles-NL (was removed in the top of the fifth).
- In 93 games with Scranton/WB, hit .270 (95-for-352) with 62R, 18 doubles, 19HR and 65RBI…at the time of his call up, ranked second in the IL in RBI and HR/AB ratio (1HR/18.53AB) and fourth in runs scored, home runs and slugging percentage (.489)…was an IL Mid-Season and Postseason All-Star, and an MiLB.com Organization All-Star.
- Following the season, was named the 2016 Kevin Lawn Award winner as the Yankees' minor league "Player of the Year"…was also tabbed by *Baseball America* as the Yankees' No. 6 prospect, as well as the IL's "Best Power Prospect" and the league's 19th-best prospect.

2015
- Split the season with Double-A Trenton and Triple-A Scranton/Wilkes-Barre, batting .255 (122-for-478) with 63R, 26 doubles, 3 triples, 20HR, 72RBI and 53BB in 124 games…led all Yankees minor leaguers in home runs and RBI.
- Played in the SiriusXM All-Star Futures Game in Cincinnati and went 1-for-4 with 1R.
- Appeared in three postseason games for the RailRiders, batting .364 (4-for-11) with 1RBI and 1BB.
- Following the season, was ranked by *Baseball America* as the No. 3 prospect in the Yankees organization, the No. 10 prospect in the International League and the No. 15 prospect in the Eastern League…was tabbed by MiLB.com as an Organization All-Star.

2014
- Made his professional debut, combining at Single-A Charleston and Single-A Tampa to bat .308 (144-for-467) with 80R, 24 doubles, 4 triples, 17HR, 78RBI and a .419 OBP in 131 games…finished the season ranked third among all minor leaguers with 89BB…led all Yankees farmhands in RBI, ranked fifth in HR and sixth in batting average.
- Was named a SAL Mid-Season All-Star with Charleston…following the season, was tabbed by *Baseball America* as the Yankees' second-best prospect…was also named an Organization All-Star by MiLB.com.
- After the season, played for Scottsdale in the Arizona Fall League, batting .278 (25-for-90) with 15R, 5 doubles, 4HR and 15RBI in 24G…was selected to the Fall Stars Game and was named AFL "Player of the Week" from 10/28-11/3.

2013
- Did not appear in a game after being selected by the Yankees in the first round of the First-Year Player Draft.
- Following the season, was ranked by *Baseball America* as the Yankees' sixth-best prospect.

PERSONAL
- Full name is Aaron James Judge…he and his older brother, John, were both adopted…his brother is an English teacher in South Korea…graduated from Linden High School (Calif.) in 2010.
- Played baseball for three seasons at Fresno State, where he was a three-time All-Conference first team selection and a 2013 All-America honoree…in his three years, hit .346 (201-for-581) with 41 doubles, 17HR and 35SB…won the 2012 TD Ameritrade College Baseball Home Run Derby in Omaha…was named a Louisville Slugger Freshman All-American and the WAC Freshman of the Year in 2011.

- Played for the Brewster Whitecaps of the Cape Cod League in 2012, earning the team's Citizenship Award for being a positive team member.
- Has hosted annual ALL RISE Foundation Baseball ProCamps at Fresno State each November since 2018.
- Launched the Aaron Judge ALL RISE Foundation in January 2019…ALL RISE inspires children and youth to become responsible citizens by engaging and encouraging them to reach unlimited possibilities…phase one of the foundation aims to support youth in California and phase two will reach youth in the New York area…over time, its goal is also to honor those who have had a positive influence on these children, while creating a legacy to continue to guide future generations…additionally, the foundation will provide financial support so eligible students can attend California Association of Directors of Activities (CADA) leadership conferences as well as California Association of Student Leader (CASL) conferences.
- Partners with #ICANHELP and the "I Can Help Delete Negativity" intiative to combat toxic behavior on social media by spreading positivity online.
- Was on the cover of the MLB: The Show video game in 2018…appeared on CONAN and played the game with the late-night talk show host in May 2018.
- For 2017, was named the New York Player of the Year and selected as the Joe DiMaggio Toast of the Town Award winner, as voted on by the BBWAA…received the awards, along with his 2017 AL Rookie of the Year Award, at the BBWAA dinner in New York on 1/28/18.
- Has finished each of the last three seasons (2017-19) with the top-selling jersey among all Major League players…in 2017, became the second rookie ever to wear Baseball's most popular jersey (also Kris Bryant in 2015).

Judge's Career Batting Record

Year	Club	AVG	G	AB	R	H	2B	3B	HR	RBI	SH	SF	HP	BB	SO	SB	CS	E	OBP	SLG
2013							Did Not Play													
2014	Charleston	.333	65	234	36	78	15	2	9	45	0	3	2	39	59	1	0	4	.428	.530
	Tampa	.283	66	233	44	66	9	2	8	33	0	1	1	50	72	0	0	4	.411	.442
2015	Trenton	.284	63	250	36	71	16	3	12	44	0	3	3	24	70	1	0	3	.350	.516
	Scranton/WB	.224	61	228	27	51	10	0	8	28	0	3	0	29	74	6	2	0	.308	.373
2016	Scranton/WB	.270	93	352	62	95	18	1	19	65	0	3	8	47	98	5	0	3	.366	.489
	YANKEES - a	.179	27	84	10	15	2	0	4	10	0	1	1	9	42	0	1	1	.263	.345
2017	YANKEES	.284	155	542	128	154	24	3	52	114	0	4	5	127	208	9	4	5	.422	.627
2018	YANKEES - b	.278	112	413	77	115	22	0	27	67	0	5	4	76	152	6	3	3	.392	.528
2019	YANKEES - c	.272	102	378	75	103	18	1	27	55	0	1	3	64	141	3	2	0	.381	.540
	Scranton/WB	.125	5	16	2	2	0	0	1	2	0	0	0	3	7	0	0	0	.263	.313
Minor League Totals		**.276**	**353**	**1313**	**207**	**363**	**68**	**8**	**57**	**217**	**0**	**13**	**14**	**192**	**380**	**13**	**2**	**14**	**.371**	**.471**
Major League Totals		**.273**	**396**	**1417**	**290**	**387**	**66**	**4**	**110**	**246**	**0**	**11**	**13**	**276**	**543**	**18**	**10**	**9**	**.394**	**.558**

Selected by Oakland in the 31st round of the 2010 First-Year Player Draft, but did not sign.
Selected by the Yankees in the first round (32nd overall) of the 2013 First-Year Player Draft.
a – Placed on the 15-day disabled list on September 14, 2016 – the end of the season with a Grade 2 right oblique strain.
b – Placed on the 10-day disabled list from July 27 - September 14, 2018 with a chip fracture of the right wrist (ulnar styloid bone).
c – Placed on the 10-day injured list from April 21 - June 21, 2019 with a left oblique strain.

Judge's Postseason Record

Year	Club vs. Opp.	AVG	G	AB	R	H	2B	3B	HR	RBI	SH	SF	HP	BB	SO	SB	CS	E	OBP	SLG
2017	NYY vs. MIN (WC)	.500	1	4	3	2	0	0	1	2	0	0	0	1	0	0	0	0	.600	1.250
	NYY vs. CLE (DS)	.050	5	20	1	1	1	0	0	2	0	0	0	4	16	0	0	0	.208	.100
	NYY vs. HOU (CS)	.250	7	24	5	6	2	0	3	7	0	0	0	4	11	0	1	0	.357	.708
2018	NYY vs. OAK (WC)	.667	1	3	2	2	1	0	1	2	0	0	0	1	1	0	0	0	.750	2.000
	NYY vs. BOS (DS)	.375	4	16	4	6	0	0	2	2	0	0	0	2	2	0	0	0	.444	.750
2019	NYY vs. MIN (DS)	.333	3	9	3	3	0	0	0	0	0	0	0	4	1	0	0	0	.538	.333
	NYY vs. HOU (CS)	.240	6	25	3	6	0	0	1	2	0	0	0	3	10	2	0	0	.321	.360
Wild Card Game Totals		**.571**	**2**	**7**	**5**	**4**	**1**	**0**	**2**	**4**	**0**	**0**	**0**	**2**	**1**	**0**	**0**	**0**	**.667**	**1.571**
LDS Totals		**.222**	**12**	**45**	**8**	**10**	**1**	**0**	**2**	**4**	**0**	**0**	**0**	**10**	**19**	**0**	**0**	**0**	**.364**	**.378**
LCS Totals		**.245**	**13**	**49**	**8**	**12**	**2**	**0**	**4**	**9**	**0**	**0**	**0**	**7**	**21**	**2**	**1**	**0**	**.339**	**.531**
POSTSEASON TOTALS		**.257**	**27**	**101**	**21**	**26**	**4**	**0**	**8**	**17**	**0**	**0**	**0**	**19**	**41**	**2**	**1**	**0**	**.375**	**.535**

Judge's All-Star Game Record

Year	Club, Site	AVG	G	AB	R	H	2B	3B	HR	RBI	SH	SF	HP	BB	SO	SB	CS	E	OBP	SLG
2017	NYY, Miami	.000	1	3	0	0	0	0	0	0	0	0	0	1	0	0	0	0	.000	.000
2018	NYY, Washington	.500	1	2	1	1	0	0	1	1	0	0	0	0	1	0	0	0	.667	2.000
All-Star Game Totals		**.200**	**2**	**5**	**1**	**1**	**0**	**0**	**1**	**1**	**0**	**0**	**0**	**1**	**1**	**0**	**0**	**0**	**.333**	**.800**

Judge's Career Fielding Record

Position	PCT	G	PO	A	E	TC	DP
Outfield	.987	351	648	23	9	680	4

Judge's Career Home Run Chart
MULTI-HOMER GAMES: 9. **TWO-HOMER GAMES:** 9, last on 7/5/19 at TB. **GRAND SLAMS:** 1, 5/28/17 vs. OAK (Andrew Triggs). **PINCH-HIT HR:** None. **INSIDE-THE-PARK HR:** None. **WALK-OFF HR:** None. **LEADOFF HR:** None.

Judge's Career Bests and Streaks
HITS: 4 - 2 times (last on 7/13/19 vs. TOR). **RUNS:** 4 - 3 times (last on 9/12/19 at DET-G1). **2B:** 2 - 3 times (last on 8/28/19 at SEA). **3B:** 1 - 4 times (last on 9/28/19 at TEX). **HR:** 2 - 9 times (last on 7/5/19 at TB). **RBI:** 6, 9/14/19 vs. BAL. **BB:** 4, 9/4/17 at BAL. **SO:** 5, 6/4/18 at DET-G2. **SB:** 2, 7/3/18 vs. ATL. **HIT STREAK:** 14g, 9/17/17-3/29/18. **"WALK-OFF" HITS:** None.

Player of the Month: 2 times (last: Sept. '17)   **Player of the Week:** 2 times (last: 9/18-24/17)   **Rookie of the Month:** 4 times (last: Sept. '17)

TOMMY KAHNLE • RHP

48

HT: 6-1 • **WT:** 230 • **BATS:** R • **THROWS:** R
BIRTHDATE: 8/7/89 • **OPENING DAY AGE:** 30
BIRTHPLACE: Latham, N.Y.
RESIDES: Albany, N.Y.
COLLEGE: Lynn University
M.L. SERVICE: 4 years, 131 days

STATUS
- Was acquired by the Yankees with INF Todd Frazier and RHP David Robertson from the Chicago White Sox in exchange for RHP Tyler Clippard, LHP Ian Clarkin and OFs Blake Rutherford and Tito Polo on July 18, 2017…was originally selected by the Yankees in the fifth round of the 2010 First-Year Player Draft.

CAREER NOTES
- Owns a 2.33 ERA (19.1IP, 5ER) with 18K in 15 career postseason relief appearances, all with the Yankees.
- Has made four career Opening Day rosters (2014, '17-19), including each of the last two with the Yankees.

2019
- Went 3-2 with a 3.67 ERA (61.1IP, 25ER) and 88K in a career-high 72 relief appearances with the Yankees after posting a 6.56 ERA in 2018…tied for sixth in the AL in relief appearances.
- Of his 72 relief appearances, 42 were hitless *and* scoreless.
- Tossed 1.2 scoreless innings on 4/4 at Baltimore, his longest scoreless outing since 4/6/18 vs. Baltimore (2.0IP).
- Had a stretch of 11 straight appearances without allowing a hit or run from 4/14-5/5, the longest in Yankees history (surpassed the mark of 10 held by Dellin Betances in 2018, Boone Logan in 2010, Edwar Ramirez in 2008, Kyle Farnsworth in 2008 and Paul Assenmacher in 1993)…retired 28-of-30 batters faced over the span (2BB)…also had at least 1K in all 11G and was the third pitcher in Major League history to record at least 1K without allowing a hit or run in at least 11 straight relief outings, joining Los Angeles-AL's Ernesto Frieri (13 straight from 5/5-6/1/12) and Boston's Koji Uehara (11 straight from 8/21-9/13/13).
- Had an 0-for-29 hitless streak (2BB) by opposing batters snapped by a Haniger single on 5/7 vs. Seattle.
- Allowed 4ER—including 2HR—on 6/9 at Cleveland, matching his total erned runs allowed over his first 28G of the season.
- Had an 11-game scoreless streak from 6/30-7/27, one of five career scoreless streaks of at least 10G in his career and two in 2019 (11G from 4/14-5/5).
- Was named AL July "Reliever of the Month" after posting a 0.77 ERA (11.2IP, 5H, 1ER, 2BB, 17K) in 12G…limited opponents to a .128/.171/.154 slash during the month…was his first career monthly award and the third AL "Reliever of the Month" award won by a Yankee, joining Aroldis Chapman (Sept. 2017, May 2019).
- Allowed 3ER in 1.0IP on 8/30 vs. Oakland, his second outing with at least 3ER in 2019 (4ER on 6/9 at Cleveland).
- Made the postseason for the second time in his career (2017, '19)…appeared in eight of the Yankees' nine playoff games, posting a 2.25 ERA (8.0IP, 2ER) and retiring 25-of-32 batters faced…retired 16 consecutive batters faced from his final two batters in ALDS Game 3 at Minnesota through his first batter in ALCS Game 5 vs. Houston…appeared in each of the Yankees' three ALDS games, earning his first postseason win in ALDS Game 1 vs. Minnesota…tossed 2.1 perfect innings (25 pitches) in ALCS Game 2 at Houston, his longest outing since the 2017 AL Wild Card Game vs. Minnesota.

2018
- Went 2-0 with one save and a 6.56 ERA (23.1IP, 17ER) in 24 relief appearances over three stints with the Yankees (3/29-6/4, 8/3-4, 8/16-9/30).
- Tossed 48 pitches in 4/6 loss vs. Baltimore, the second-most in a single game in his career (threw 53 pitches on 6/20/14 vs. Milwaukee w/ Colorado).
- Was ejected in the seventh inning of 4/11 win at Boston…was his second career ejection (also 8/24/17 at Detroit).
- Was placed on the 10-day disabled list from 4/17 (retroactive to 4/16) - 5/25 with right shoulder tendonitis (missed 33 team games)…in two rehab appearances (one start) with Single-A Charleston (1GS) and Triple-A Scranton/WB (1G), combined to go 1-1 with a 6.00 ERA (3.0IP, 5H, 2ER, 0BB, 2K, 1HR).
- Tossed 1.0 perfect inning (1K) in 8/21 win at Miami, earning his fourth career save and first since 9/4/16 at Minnesota w/ Chicago-AL.
- In 25 total relief appearances with the RailRiders (including his rehab assignment), went 2-2 with one save, a 4.01 ERA (24.2IP, 11ER) and 37K.

2017
- Combined with the Yankees and White Sox to go 2-4 with a 2.59 ERA (62.2IP, 18ER) in 69 relief appearances…ranked eighth among relievers (third in the AL) with a 13.79 K/9.0IP ratio (96K, 62.2IP).
- Had at least 1K in 29 straight games from 5/6-7/22, the Majors' second-longest streak of the season by a reliever behind Milwaukee's Corey Knebel's 45-game stretch from 4/3-7/15.
- Was acquired by the Yankees with INF Todd Frazier and RHP David Robertson from Chicago-AL on 7/18 in exchange for RHP Tyler Clippard, LHP Ian Clarkin and OFs Blake Rutherford and Tito Polo.
- In 32 games with the Yankees, went 1-1 with a 2.70 ERA (26.2IP, 8ER).
- Was added to the Yankees' active roster on 7/19 and made his Yankees debut in that day's loss at Minnesota, tossing a perfect eighth (1.0IP, 2K)…became the fourth New York-born pitcher to appear for the Yankees in as many seasons (also RHP Dellin Betances, New York City; RHP Danny Burawa, Riverhead; and RHP Matt Daley, New York City).
- Earned his first win as a Yankee on 8/16 at the Mets (BS, 0.2IP).
- In 8/24 loss at Detroit, struck out three batters in 1.0IP before being ejected by HP umpire Carlos Torres with two outs in the sixth for throwing behind Miguel Cabrera…was his first career ejection.
- Recorded a career-long 13.1-inning scoreless streak over 14 games from 8/24-9/26 (9H, 5BB, 20K).
- Made his postseason debut, posting a 2.38 ERA (11.1IP, 3ER) with one save in seven relief appearances…had four multi-inning scoreless playoff outings, one of four relievers in Yankees history with at least four such appearances in one postseason (also Mariano Rivera-6G in 2003, 5G in 1996, 4G in 2001; Goose Gossage-5G in 1981 and David Robertson-4G in 2017).
- Retired all 7BF over 2.1 scoreless innings in AL Wild Card win vs. Minnesota (2.1IP, 1K)…was the longest perfect outing by a Yankees reliever in the postseason since Mariano Rivera (2.2IP) in 1996 ALDS Game 2 vs. Texas.
- Earned his first save as a Yankee in ALDS Game 4 vs. Cleveland, entering with two on and no one out in the eighth and retiring all 3BF, then striking out all 3BF in the ninth…became the third pitcher (fourth occurrence) to record at least 5K in a postseason appearance of 6BF-or-fewer, joining St. Louis' Todd Worrell in 1985 World Series Game 5 vs. Kansas City (2.0IP, 6K, 6BF) and Cleveland's Andrew Miller twice in the 2016 ALCS vs. Toronto: Game 1 (1.2IP, 5K, 6BF) and Game 2 (2.0IP, 5K, 6BF)…is the only one of the three to also earn a save in the appearance.
- In 37 relief appearances with the White Sox, went 1-3 with a 2.50 ERA (36.0IP, 10ER) and 60K, while walking just seven batters.

2016
- Made his White Sox debut, going 0-1 with a 2.63 ERA (27.1IP, 8ER) in 29 relief appearances over five stints with the club (4/29-4/30, 5/5-8, 5/23-29, 6/3 and 7/9-10/2).
- Of his 29 appearances with Chicago-AL, 24 were scoreless…tossed at least 1.0 inning 22 times.
- Posted a 0.51 ERA (17.2IP, 1ER) and 18K over his final 17 appearances from 8/7-9/30.
- Began the season with Triple-A Charlotte, combining to go 1-1 with a 3.00 ERA (27.0IP, 9ER) in 23 relief outings.

2015
- Went 0-1 with a 4.86 ERA (33.1IP, 18ER) in 36 relief appearances with Colorado.
- Earned his first career save on 8/7 at Washington, tossing a scoreless ninth inning (1BB, 2K).
- Began the season with Triple-A Albuquerque, going 1-3 with a 4.67 ERA (27.0IP, 14ER) in 21 relief appearances.
- Was traded to Chicago-AL in exchange for RHP Yency Almonte on 11/24/15.

2014
- Saw his first Major League action, spending the entire season with Colorado and going 2-1 with a 4.19 ERA (68.2IP, 32ER) and 63K in 54 relief appearances…became the first Rockies Rule 5 draft selection to make the team and remain with the club for the entire season since INF Luis Gonzalez in 2003.
- Made his Major League debut on 4/3 at Miami (1.2IP, 1ER)…recorded his first career strikeout in the sixth inning (Reed Johnson)…earned his first Major League win on 4/5 vs. Arizona, tossing 1.2 scoreless innings.
- Struck out a career-high five batters in 2.0IP on 4/21 vs. San Francisco, becoming the sixth reliever in Rockies history with at least 5K in 2.0IP-or-less…matched his career high in strikeouts on 6/13 at San Francisco.

2013
- Spent the season with Double-A Trenton, going 1-3 with a 2.85 ERA (60.0IP, 19ER) and 74K in 46 relief appearances…led all Yankees farmhands with 15 saves.
- Was selected by Colorado in the Major League phase of the Rule 5 draft on 12/12/13.

2012
- Appeared in 30 games with Single-A Tampa, going 2-1 with a 2.45 ERA (55.0IP, 15ER), striking out 72 batters…led all Tampa relievers in strikeouts.
- Was promoted to Double-A Trenton on 9/2, making one regular season relief appearance (2.0IP, 2H, 2K)…made three postseason appearances out of the bullpen for the Thunder, tossing 3.0 scoreless innings (2H, 3BB, 3K).

2011
- Spent the entire season with Single-A Charleston, going 3-5 with a 4.22 ERA (81.0IP, 38ER) in 40 relief appearances…led all Charleston relievers with 112K and posted the fifth-most strikeouts among all Yankees minor league pitchers.

2010
- Made his professional debut with short-season Single-A Staten Island, posting a 0.56 ERA (16.0IP, 1ER) with just 3H and 25K in 11 relief appearances…posted a .061 opponents' batting average (3-for-49).

PERSONAL
- Full name is Thomas Robert Kahnle ("CAIN-lee")…is married to Veronica.
- Graduated from Shaker High School in Latham, N.Y.…lettered in baseball, basketball and football.
- Attended Lynn University in Boca Raton, Fla.…became the highest drafted player from the Division II University…led the team in ERA, strikeouts and opp. BA as a sophomore in 2010…tossed the third no-hitter in the school's history on 3/13/10…was part of the school's NCAA Division II Championship team in 2009, tossing 12.2 scoreless innings in the postseason as a freshman.

Kahnle's Career Pitching Record

Year	Club	W	L	ERA	G	GS	CG	SHO	SV	IP	H	R	ER	HR	HP	BB	SO	WP	BK
2010	Staten Island	0	0	0.56	11	0	0	0	3	16.0	3	1	1	0	3	5	25	2	0
2011	Charleston	3	5	4.22	40	0	0	0	2	81.0	69	50	38	1	1	49	112	11	1
2012	Tampa	2	1	2.45	30	0	0	0	6	55.0	30	16	15	3	2	24	72	4	1
	Trenton	0	0	0.00	1	0	0	0	0	2.0	2	0	0	0	0	0	2	0	0
2013	Trenton	1	3	2.85	46	0	0	0	15	60.0	38	20	19	4	0	45	74	7	0
2014	COLORADO - a, b	2	1	4.19	54	0	0	0	0	68.2	51	39	32	7	1	31	63	7	0
2015	Albuquerque	1	3	4.67	21	0	0	0	6	27.0	19	14	14	3	1	12	28	5	0
	COLORADO	0	1	4.86	36	0	0	0	2	33.1	31	22	18	3	0	28	39	3	0
2016	Charlotte - c	1	1	3.00	23	0	0	0	7	27.0	17	9	9	0	1	12	36	2	0
	CHICAGO-AL	0	1	2.63	29	0	0	0	1	27.1	21	8	8	2	0	20	25	3	0
2017	CHICAGO-AL	1	3	2.50	37	0	0	0	0	36.0	28	12	10	3	0	7	60	2	0
	YANKEES - d	1	1	2.70	32	0	0	0	0	26.2	25	8	8	1	2	10	36	3	0
2018	YANKEES - e	2	0	6.56	24	0	0	0	0	23.1	23	22	17	3	0	15	30	2	0
	Charleston	0	1	4.50	1	1	0	0	0	2.0	3	1	1	1	0	0	2	0	0
	Scranton/WB	2	2	4.01	25	0	0	0	0	24.2	23	14	11	2	1	11	37	0	0
2019	YANKEES	3	2	3.67	72	0	0	0	0	61.1	45	27	25	9	2	20	88	8	0
Minor League Totals		10	16	3.30	198	1	0	0	40	294.2	204	125	108	14	9	158	388	31	2
AL Totals		7	7	3.50	194	0	0	0	2	174.2	142	77	68	18	4	72	239	18	0
NL Totals		2	2	4.41	90	0	0	0	2	102.0	82	61	50	10	1	59	102	10	0
Major League Totals		9	9	3.84	284	0	0	0	4	276.2	224	138	118	28	5	131	341	28	0
NYY Totals		6	3	4.04	128	0	0	0	1	111.1	93	57	50	13	4	45	154	13	0

Selected by the Yankees in the fifth round of the 2010 First-Year Player Draft.

a – Selected by Colorado in the Major League phase of the 2013 Rule 5 Draft on December 12, 2013.
b – Placed on the 15-day disabled list from August 13 - September 2, 2014 with right shoulder inflammation.
c – Acquired by Chicago-AL from Colorado in exchange for RHP Yency Almonte on November 24, 2015.
d – Acquired by the Yankees from the Chicago White Sox with INF Todd Frazier and RHP David Robertson in exchange for RHP Tyler Clippard, LHP Ian Clarkin and OFs Blake Rutherford and Tito Polo on July 18, 2017.
e – Placed on the 10-day disabled list from April 17 (retroactive to April 16) - May 25, 2018 with right shoulder tendonitis.

Kahnle's Postseason Record

Year	Club vs. Opp.	W	L	ERA	G	GS	CG	SHO	SV	IP	H	R	ER	HR	HP	BB	SO	WP	BK
2017	NYY vs. MIN (WC)	0	0	0.00	1	0	0	0	0	2.1	0	0	0	0	0	1	0	0	0
	NYY vs. CLE (DS)	0	0	0.00	2	0	0	0	1	2.2	0	0	0	0	0	0	5	0	0
	NYY vs. HOU (CS)	0	1	4.26	4	0	0	0	0	6.1	6	3	3	1	0	2	4	0	0
2019	NYY vs. MIN (DS)	1	0	3.86	3	0	0	0	0	2.1	2	1	1	1	0	1	3	0	0
	NYY vs. HOU (CS)	0	0	1.59	5	0	0	0	0	5.2	2	1	1	0	0	2	5	0	0
Wild Card Game Totals		0	0	0.00	1	0	0	0	0	2.1	0	0	0	0	0	1	0	0	0
Division Series Totals		1	0	1.80	5	0	0	0	1	5.0	2	1	1	1	0	1	8	0	0
LCS Totals		0	0	3.00	9	0	0	0	0	12.0	8	4	4	1	0	4	9	0	0
POSTSEASON TOTALS		1	0	2.33	15	0	0	0	1	19.1	10	5	5	2	0	5	18	0	0

Kahnle's Career Fielding Record

Position	PCT	G	PO	A	E	TC	DP
Pitcher	.938	284	25	20	3	48	2

Kahnle's Regular Season Batting Record

Year	Team	AVG	G	AB	R	H	2B	3B	HR	RBI	SH	SF	HP	BB	SO	SB	CS
2019	NYY					Did Not Bat											
Major League Totals		.000	284	3	0	0	0	0	0	1	0	0	0	1	0	0

Kahnle's Career Bests and Streaks

COMPLETE GAMES: None. **LOW-HIT COMPLETE GAME:** N/A. **IP (START):** N/A. **IP (RELIEF):** 3.0, 6/13/14 at SF. **HITS:** 4 - 8 times (last on 6/9/19 at CLE). **RUNS:** 5, 4/10/18 at BOS. **WALKS:** 4 - 2 times (last on 8/7/16 vs. BAL). **STRIKEOUTS:** 5 - 2 times (last on 6/13/14 at SF). **HOME RUNS:** 2, on 6/9/19 at CLE. **WINNING STREAK:** 5g, 4/3/18-8/3/19. **LOSING STREAK:** 6g, 4/30/14-7/4/17. **SCORELESS STREAK (IP):** 13.1IP, 8/24-9/26/17.

Reliever of the Month: July 2019 **Player of the Week:** None **Rookie of the Month:** July 2019

MICHAEL KING • RHP

#73

HT: 6-3 • **WT:** 210 • **BATS:** R • **THROWS:** R
BIRTHDATE: 5/25/95 • **OPENING DAY AGE:** 24
BIRTHPLACE: Rochester, N.Y.
RESIDES: Warwick, R.I.
COLLEGE: Boston College
M.L. SERVICE: 11 days (Rookie)

STATUS
- Was acquired by the Yankees from Miami along with 2017-18 international signing bonus pool money in exchange for INF Garrett Cooper and LHP Caleb Smith on November 20, 2017.

CAREER NOTES
- Has the 11th-lowest ERA (2.93) among minor league pitchers with at least 350.0IP since 2016.

2019
- Saw his first Major League action, making just one appearance (2.0IP, 2H, 1R/0ER, 1K) in his only stint with the Yankees (9/19-29).
- Was signed to a Major League contract and selected to the Yankees' active roster on 9/19.
- Made his Major League debut in 9/27 win at Texas, allowing 1R/0ER in 2.0IP (2H, 1K)…collected his first career strikeout (Shin-Soo Choo, swinging) in the eighth.
- Spent the first four months of the season on the minor league injured list…combined with the GCL Yankees West, short-season Single-A Staten Island, Double-A Trenton and Triple-A Scranton/Wilkes-Barre to go 3-2 with a 5.48 ERA (46.0IP, 28ER) and 44K in 11 games (eight starts).
- Also made two postseason appearances, one with the RailRiders (start at Durham on 9/6, L, 5.0IP, 6H, 4ER, 4BB, 4K, 2HR) and one with the Thunder (relief appearance at Bowie on 9/12, W, 4.0IP, 1H, 2BB, 5K).
- Attended spring training as a non-roster invitee with the Yankees, but did not pitch.

2018
- Combined to go 11-5 with two complete games and a 1.79 ERA (161.1IP, 118H, 43R/32ER, 29BB, 152K, 8HR) in 25 games (24 starts) with Single-A Tampa (7GS), Double-A Trenton (12G/11GS) and Triple-A Scranton/Wilkes-Barre (6GS)… allowed 2ER-or-fewer in 21-of-24 starts.
- Was named the winner of the Kevin Lawn "Pitcher of the Year" Award, presented annually to the organization's top performer…the award is dedicated to Kevin O'Brien Lawn—the son of longtime Yankees Vice President and Chief of Operations Jack Lawn—who passed away in 1999.
- Ranked second among all minor leaguers in ERA (min. 100.0IP)…his 5.24 K/BB ratio ranked sixth among all minor leaguers (min. 100.0IP)…was the lowest season ERA recorded by a Yankees farmhand (min. 20GS) since Dietrich Enns in 2016 (1.73 ERA with Trenton and Scranton/WB)…among Yankees farmhands, led in strikeouts and ERA and was second in wins.
- Started the season with Single-A Tampa and was named a Florida State League Mid-Season All-Star after going 1-3 with a 1.79 ERA (40.1IP, 8ER) in seven starts.
- Was promoted to Double-A Trenton on 5/19 and went 6-2 with a 2.09 ERA (82.0IP, 19ER) and 76K…earned Eastern League "Pitcher of the Week" honors from 6/25-7/1 after throwing his first 9.0-inning complete game shutout win on 6/30 vs. New Hampshire (3H, 0BB, 11K).
- Went undefeated in his final 4GS with Trenton from 7/14-31, going 4-0 with a 1.93 ERA (28.0IP, 6ER) and 24K.
- Was transferred to Scranton/WB on 8/4 and went 4-0 with a 1.15 ERA (39.0IP, 5ER) with 31K.
- Allowed more than 1R in just one-of-six starts with the RailRiders and had a 16.1IP scoreless streak from 8/18-29.
- Earned International League's August "Pitcher of the Month" honors after going 3-0 with a 1.09 ERA (33.0IP, 4ER) in five August starts with the RailRiders.
- Made two postseason starts for the RailRiders, going 0-1 with a 3.38 ERA (13.1IP, 5ER) and 12K.
- Following the season, was named to *Baseball America's* Minor League All-Star Second Team…was named an MiLB.com Organization All-Star…was also tabbed by *Baseball America* as the No. 5 prospect in the Yankees system and as having the organization's "Best Control."

2017
- Went 11-9 with a 3.14 ERA (149.0IP, 141H, 55R/52ER, 21BB, 106K, 14HR) in 26 games (25 starts) with Single-A Greensboro…was tied for second in the South Atlantic League in wins, ranked third in innings pitched and was 10th in ERA…posted the fifth-highest K/BB ratio (5.05) in the SAL (min. 100.0IP).
- Was third in ERA and wins among Miami farmhands…posted a 2.08 ERA (60.2IP, 14ER) in 10 starts from 6/8-8/4.

2016
- Made his professional debut, combining with the GCL Marlins, short-season Single-A Batavia and Single-A Greensboro to go 3-3 with a 4.11 ERA (30.2IP, 37H, 16R/14ER, 9BB, 20K) in 15 games (one start).
- Made his first four appearances with the GCL Marlins, going 1-1 with a 10.80 ERA (5.0IP, 6ER).
- Was transferred to Batavia on 7/16 and went 2-2 with one save and a 3.38 ERA (21.1IP, 8ER) in 10 appearances (one start).
- Made his final appearance of the season with Greensboro on 9/2 (4.1IP, 2R/0ER).

PERSONAL
- Full name is Michael McRae King.
- Graduated from Bishop Hendricken (R.I.) High School, where he was named the 2013 Rhode Island Gatorade "Player of the Year" as a senior…was also a Louisville Slugger First-Team All-American and the Rhode Island Baseball Coaches Association "Player of the Year."
- In three seasons with Boston College (2014-16), went 11-11 with four saves and a 3.14 ERA (209.1IP, 73ER) in 47 games (27 starts)…his 3.14 career ERA ranks second all-time at Boston College.

King's Career Pitching Record

Year	Club	W	L	ERA	G	GS	CG	SHO	SV	IP	H	R	ER	HR	HP	BB	SO	WP	BK
2016	GCL Marlins	1	1	10.80	4	0	0	0	0	5.0	11	6	6	0	0	2	3	0	0
	Batavia	2	2	3.38	10	1	0	0	1	21.1	22	8	8	0	1	6	15	3	0
	Greensboro	0	0	0.00	1	0	0	0	0	4.1	4	2	0	0	0	1	2	0	0
2017	Greensboro	11	9	3.14	26	25	2	1	0	149.0	141	55	52	14	11	21	106	6	0
2018	Tampa - a	1	3	1.79	7	7	0	0	0	40.1	33	15	8	1	2	10	45	2	2
	Trenton	6	2	2.09	12	11	1	1	0	82.0	65	23	19	4	3	13	76	4	0
	Scranton/WB	4	0	1.15	6	6	1	1	0	39.0	20	5	5	3	0	6	31	1	0
2019	GCL Yankees West	0	0	4.76	3	2	0	0	0	5.2	3	3	3	0	1	2	8	1	0
	Staten Island	0	0	0.00	1	1	0	0	0	4.0	4	0	0	0	0	0	0	0	0
	Trenton	0	1	9.95	3	2	0	0	0	12.2	20	15	14	1	2	2	8	0	0
	Scranton/WB	3	1	4.18	4	3	0	0	0	23.2	20	12	11	3	3	6	28	0	0
	YANKEES	0	0	0.00	1	0	0	0	0	2.0	2	1	0	0	0	0	1	0	0
Minor League Totals		28	19	2.93	77	58	4	2	1	387.0	343	144	126	26	23	69	322	17	2
Major League Totals		0	0	0.00	1	0	0	0	0	2.0	2	1	0	0	0	0	1	0	0

Selected by the Marlins in the 12th round of the 2016 First-Year Player Draft.

a – Was acquired by the Yankees from Miami along with 2017-18 international signing bonus pool money in exchange for INF Garrett Cooper and LHP Caleb Smith on November 20, 2017.

King's Career Fielding Record

Position	PCT	G	PO	A	E	TC	DP
Pitcher	.000	1	0	0	1	1	0

King's Regular Season Batting Record

Year	Team	AVG	G	AB	R	H	2B	3B	HR	RBI	SH	SF	HP	BB	SO	SB	CS
2019	NYY					Did Not Bat											
Major League Totals		-	1	-	-	-	-	-	-	-	-	-	-	-	-	-	-

Pitcher of the Month: None **Player of the Week:** None **Rookie of the Month:** None

Above Board

The Yankees have finished with a winning record in each of the last 27 seasons (1993-2019), marking the second-longest such stretch in Major League history behind only the franchise's unprecedented streak of 39 straight winning seasons from 1926-1964.

At Right: The Yankees celebrate after winning the 2009 World Series title.

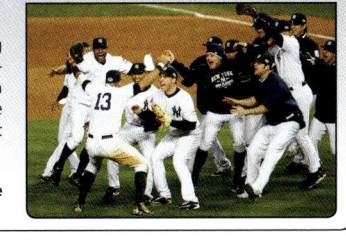

BROOKS KRISKE • RHP

82

HT: 6-3 • **WT:** 190 • **BATS:** R • **THROWS:** R
BIRTHDATE: 2/3/94 • **OPENING DAY AGE:** 26
BIRTHPLACE: Scottsdale, Ariz.
RESIDES: La Quinta, Calif.
COLLEGE: University of Southern California
M.L. SERVICE: None (Rookie)

STATUS
- Selected by the Yankees in the sixth round of the 2016 First-Year Player Draft.

2019
- Combined to go 3-3 with 12 saves and a 2.08 ERA (60.2IP, 34H, 15R/14ER, 80K) in 43 relief appearances between Single-A Tampa and Double-A Trenton…opponents batted .161 (34-for-211, 3HR); LHH .206 (22-for-107), RHH .115 (12-for-104)…his 12 saves between Tampa and Trenton were a career-high…his 11 saves with Trenton ranked 10th among Eastern League pitchers.
- Started the year with Tampa, going 1-1 and allowing just one unearned run in seven relief appearances (12.0IP, 4H, 5BB, 16K)…limited Florida State League hitters to a .111 average (4-for-36, 0HR)…allowed 1H-or-fewer and recorded 1K-or-more in each of his seven outings with Tampa, including five outings in which he registered multiple strikeouts…named a Florida State League Midseason All-Star.
- Was promoted to Double-A Trenton on 4/27 and went 2-2 with 11 saves and a 2.59 ERA (48.2IP, 30H, 14ER, 23BB, 64K) in 36 relief appearances…went 1-1 with a 0.79 ERA (11.1IP, 3H, 1ER, 7BB, 17K, 0HR) while limiting opposing batters to a .081 average (3-for-37) over nine games in June.

2018
- Made his return to pitching after missing the entire 2017 season to recover from Tommy John surgery, making his first appearance with short-season Single-A Staten Island on 6/18 at Lowell…combined to go 2-2 with three saves and a 1.57 ERA (28.2IP, 5ER, 39K) in 16 relief appearances between Staten Island and Single-A Charleston.
- In 14 games with Staten Island to begin the season, went 2-2 with three saves and a 1.09 ERA (24.2IP, 3ER, 33K)…did not allow an earned run in 11 of his 14 outings with Staten Island and never allowed more than one earned run…tossed 2.1 scoreless innings and struck out a career-high six batters in a relief outing on 8/8 vs. Lowell.
- Earned a promotion to Charleston on 8/23…made two relief appearances with Charleston to end the season, allowing 2ER in 4.0IP (4H, 1BB, 6K).

2017
- Missed entire season to recover from "Tommy John" surgery performed in 2016.

2016
- Made his professional debut and spent the season with Single-A Staten Island, going 0-2 with four saves and a 2.25 ERA (16.0IP, 4ER, 16K) in 13 relief outings…allowed one XBH all season (double by Jonathan Popadics on 7/4 vs. Hudson Valley).
- Underwent "Tommy John" surgery in August and missed the remainder of the season.

PERSONAL
- Full name is Brooks Joseph Kriske.
- In three seasons at USC (2014-16), went 4-3 with six saves and a 2.98 ERA (99.2IP, 90H, 33ER, 45BB, 92K) in 58 appearances (five starts)…finished his collegiate career tied for sixth on the school's all-time leaders list with 64 relief appearances.
- Graduated from Palm Desert H.S. (Calif.) in 2012, where he earned all-state honors as a junior and senior…helped team to win two state titles in 2010 and 2012, and threw a complete game shutout in the CIF championship game in 2012.

Kriske's Career Pitching Record

Year	Club	W	L	ERA	G	GS	CG	SHO	SV	IP	H	R	ER	HR	HP	BB	SO	WP	BK
2016	Staten Island	0	2	2.25	13	0	0	0	4	16.0	12	8	4	0	0	6	16	6	0
2017								Did Not Pitch - Injured											
2018	Staten Island	2	2	1.09	14	0	0	0	3	24.2	21	4	3	0	0	8	33	2	0
	Charleston	0	0	4.50	2	0	0	0	0	4.0	4	2	2	0	0	1	6	0	0
2019	Tampa	1	1	0.00	7	0	0	0	1	12.0	4	1	0	0	1	5	16	0	0
	Trenton	2	2	2.59	36	0	0	0	11	48.2	30	14	14	3	1	23	64	5	0
Minor League Totals		**5**	**7**	**1.97**	**72**	**0**	**0**	**0**	**19**	**105.1**	**71**	**29**	**23**	**3**	**2**	**43**	**135**	**13**	**0**

Selected by the Yankees in the sixth round of the 2016 First-Year Player Draft.

DJ LeMAHIEU • INF

26

HT: 6-4 • **WT:** 220 • **BATS:** R • **THROWS:** R
BIRTHDATE: 7/13/88 • **OPENING DAY AGE:** 31
BIRTHPLACE: Visalia, Calif.
RESIDES: Birmingham, Mich.
COLLEGE: Louisiana State University
M.L. SERVICE: 7 years, 128 days

STATUS
- Signed by the Yankees to a two-year contract on January 14, 2019.

CAREER NOTES
- Is one of four active players to win a batting title (2016) and earn multiple Gold Glove awards (2014, '17 and '18), joining Mookie Betts, Carlos González and Albert Pujols.
- In his Major League career, has appeared in games defensively at 2B (967G/923GS), 3B (93G/71GS), 1B (44G/29GS) and SS (4G/0GS)…ranks second among active second basemen (min. 500G) with a .991 fielding pct. in his career, trailing only Dustin Pedroia (a higher .991)…over his final five seasons with Colorado (2014-18), led NL second basemen (12th among all Major League defenders) with 48 defensive runs saved.
- Among 88 hitters with at least 2,500 plate appearances over the last five seasons (2015-19), has the fourth-lowest swing-and-miss rate (5.3%), the sixth-highest contact rate (87.6%) and the eighth-highest line-drive rate (24.4%)—FanGraphs.
- Has 260 multi-hit games since 2015, fifth-most in the Majors.
- Has made six career Opening Day rosters (2014-18 w/ Colorado and 2019 w/ the Yankees)…started at 2B in all five of his Opening Day games with the Rockies.

CAREER HIGHLIGHTS

AL All-Star Team
- 2019

NL All-Star Team
- 2015, 2017

NL Batting Title
- 2016

AL Silver Slugger Award
- 2019

NL Gold Glove Award
- 2014, 2017, 2018

All-MLB First Team
- 2019

Wilson Defensive Player of the Year
- 2013, 2017, 2018

2019
- Placed fourth in AL MVP balloting, hitting .327 (197-for-602) with 109R, 33 doubles, 2 triples, 26HR and 102RBI in 145 games in his first season with the Yankees…set career highs in runs, hits, doubles, home runs, RBI, extra-base hits (61), slugging pct. (.518) and multi-hit games (61), surpassing previous highs of 104R, 192H, 66RBI, 51 extra-base hits and 59 multi-hit games in 2016, 15HR in 2018 and 32 doubles (twice)…was the highest batting average by a Yankee since Derek Jeter hit .334 in 2009…was named to the Inaugural 2019 All-MLB First Team.
- Earned his first career Silver Slugger Award after finishing second in the AL in batting average (.327) and fourth in hits (197)…was the fourth Yankee to win the award at second base, joining Robinson Canó (2006, '10-13), Alfonso Soriano (2002) and Willie Randolph (1980).
- Became the first player in Yankees history to start at least 25 games at three different infield positions in one season (28 starts at 1B, 66 starts at 2B, 47 starts at 3B)…also made one start at DH.
- Was a finalist for the AL Gold Glove Award at 2B…among second baseman (min. 50GS at 2B), ranked second in the Majors and led the AL with a .993 fielding pct. (2E, 275 TC)…was his third straight season leading 2B in his league in fielding pct. (also 2017-18 in the NL).
- Led the Majors with 61 multi-hit games, tied for third with 18 games of 3-or-more hits and ranked fourth (second in the AL) in batting average…led the Majors with a .389 (49-for-126) batting average with runners in scoring position and a .667 (10-for-15) average with the bases loaded…was the best batting average with RISP by a Yankee since Paul O'Neill's .428 mark in 1997.
- Ranked 11th in the AL with a team-leading 102RBI, the second-most by a Yankee in the last six seasons since 2014 (Aaron Judge-114 in 2017).
- Reached base safely in 122 of his 142 starts…reached multiple times in 78 of those starts.
- Reached 100R for the second time in his career (104R in 2016).
- His 197H were the most by a Yankee since 2012, when Derek Jeter had 216H…had the most multi-hit games (61) by a Yankee since Derek Jeter had 64 in 2012.
- Hit six leadoff HR (5/29 vs. San Diego, 6/25 vs. Toronto, 7/21 vs. Colorado, 8/3 vs. Boston-G1, 8/13 vs. Baltimore, 8/25 at Los Angeles-NL), most by a Yankee since Alfonso Soriano's club-record 13 leadoff HRs in 2003…hit .325 (175-for-539) with 98R, 29 doubles, 25HR and 92RBI as a leadoff hitter overall, collecting the fifth 25HR season by a Yankees leadoff hitter (also Alfonso Soriano: 38HR in 2002 and 35HR in 2003; Rickey Henderson: 28HR in 1986 and Bobby Bonds: 25HR in 1975)…his 92RBI from the leadoff spot were second-most in Yankees history behind Alfonso Soriano (99RBI in 2002).
- Had four hitting streaks of at least 10G (14G from 6/14-30; 12G from Game 2 on 9/12-27; 11G from Game 2 on 5/25-6/6 and 11G from 4/24-5/9), tied with Tim Anderson for most in the Majors…was the first Yankee with four double-digit hitting streaks in one year since Robinson Canó had four in 2011.

141

- Made his Yankees debut in 3/30 loss vs. Baltimore…started at 3B, his first appearance at the position since 6/13/14 at San Francisco w/ Colorado.
- Reached base safely in all 5PA of 3/31 loss vs. Baltimore, matching a career high (fifth time, first since 8/3/17 vs. the Mets w/ Colorado)…joined Robinson Canó (2010) as the only two Yankees since 2006 with at least 2H, 1R and 1RBI in each of his first two games of the season.
- Hit safely in six straight at-bats from the second inning on 4/10 through the fourth inning on 4/13.
- Hit third in the starting lineup for just the second time in his career on 4/13 (also 8/2/15 at St. Louis w/ Colorado).
- Snapped an 0-for-15 stretch with a fourth-inning solo HR on 4/20 vs. Kansas City, his first HR as a Yankee (first HR since 9/12/18 vs. Arizona).
- Was removed from 4/28 win at San Francisco in the bottom of the third with right knee inflammation (X-rays were negative)…underwent an MRI on 4/29, confirming inflammation in his right knee from his original contusion suffered in 4/26 win at San Francisco…missed three games (4/30-5/3) with the injury.
- Hit "walk-off" RBI single in the ninth on 5/7 vs. Seattle, his second career "walk-off" hit (also 9/12/18 vs. Arizona w/ Colorado).
- Started at 1B and batted leadoff on 5/9 vs. Seattle, the first Yankee to do both in the same game since Wade Boggs on 8/29/95 vs. California.
- Played in his 1,000th career game on 5/23 at Baltimore.
- Hit his third career leadoff HR on 5/29 vs. San Diego (first since 6/17/18 at Texas)…was the first of back-to-back HRs with Voit to lead off the game, marking the 10th instance in Yankees history they led off a game with consecutive homers (first since Gardner and Judge on 7/7/18 at Toronto)…was his fourth career HR on an 0-2 pitch (last: 4/15/18 at Washington).
- Was voted AL "Player of the Month" for June after leading the Majors in hits and pacing the AL in runs and RBI during the month, batting .395/.434/.658 (45-for-114) with 26R, 8 doubles, 2 triples, 6HR, 29RBI and 8BB in 25G…were the most hits by a Yankee in a calendar month since Derek Jeter had 46H in August 2009, and the most by an AL player since Baltimore's Tim Beckham had 50H in August 2017…became the seventh different Yankee (22nd time) to amass at least 45H, 16 extra-base hits and 29RBI in a calendar month, and first since Don Mattingly in September/October 1985…marked his first career monthly honor.
- Had a season-long 14-game hitting streak from 6/14-30, his longest since a 16-game streak from 8/23-9/8/17 with Colorado.
- Had at least 1H and 1R in 12 consecutive games from 6/16-30, tied for the sixth-longest streak in franchise history, trailing only Hall of Famers Lou Gehrig (15, 1930), Joe DiMaggio (14, 1941) and Babe Ruth (14, 1926; 13, 1921), as well as Bernie Williams (13, 2000)…hit .519 (27-for-52) with 19R, 3 doubles, 2 triples, 5HR, 20RBI and 6BB over the span.
- Collected 25H and 20RBI over an 11-game span from 6/17-30…according to *Elias*, the only other Yankee to ever record as many hits and RBI over an 11-game span was Lou Gehrig, who had 27H and 26RBI from 6/7-19/1930 (since RBI became an official statistic in 1920).
- Reached base safely multiple times in a career-high-tying 10 straight games from 6/18-30.
- Had a career-best six-game multi-hit streak from 6/23-30, the first Yankee since Carlos Beltrán in 2014 to post a multi-hit streak of six-or-more games…according to *Elias*, his 18H during the streak tied a Yankees franchise record for most hits in a six-game span, set by Bernie Williams (18-for-29) from 8/14-20/02.
- Was named AL "Player of the Week" for the first time in his career from 6/24-30, batting .625 (15-for-24) with 8R, 3 doubles, 1 triple, 2HR, 10RBI and a 1.083 SLG pct. in 5G.
- Tied his career high in hits on both 6/24 vs. Toronto (4-for-4, 2R, 1BB) and 6/29 at Boston in London (4-for-6, 2R, 1 double, 5RBI)…his 5RBI on 6/29 tied a career high (also 6/28/18 at San Francisco).
- Hit 2 doubles in the Yankees' nine-run seventh on 6/30 at Boston in London, the first Yankee with 2XBH in one frame since Brendan Ryan hit 2 doubles in the second inning on 7/28/15 at Texas.
- Hit a two-run single with the bases loaded in the 10th inning on 7/4 at Tampa Bay, his third career go-ahead hit in extras (also an RBI single on 9/15/15 at Los Angeles-NL and a solo HR on 8/18/18 at Atlanta, both w/ Colorado).
- Led the AL in the "first half" with a .336 batting average, the second-highest in the "first half" by a Yankee since 2000, behind Derek Jeter's .345 in 2006.
- Was voted by fans to his third career All-Star team (also 2015 and '17 in the NL)…batted second in the AL's starting lineup (0-for-2), the highest spot in the starting lineup by a Yankee since Derek Jeter in 2014 (led off for the AL).
- Hit his fifth career leadoff HR and third of the season (also 5/29 vs. San Diego and 6/25 vs. Toronto) on 7/21 vs. Colorado…hit his first two career leadoff homers *for the Rockies* (4/12/18 at Washington and 6/17/18 at Texas).
- Missed four games from 7/27-31 (groin).
- Hit 9HR in 28 games in August, a career high for homers in a calendar month…prior to 2019, had never hit 5HR in a month in his career.

- Recorded his third career 2HR game and first since 4/12/18 at Washington w/ Colorado in Game 1 on 8/3 vs. Boston (3-for-5, 2R, 2HR, 4RBI)…set a new career high with his 16th and 17th HRs of the season…also hit his fourth leadoff HR of 2019 in the first inning (sixth career)…was his third game with at least 4RBI of the season, matching his career total entering 2019 (all three in 2018 with Colorado)…his 4RBI were his most ever in a home game…was the second 4RBI game by a Yankees first baseman this season (LeMahieu-5RBI on 6/29 at Boston in London).
- Hit a first-pitch leadoff HR on 8/13 vs. Baltimore, the second time he homered on the first pitch of the first inning this season (also 7/21 vs. Colorado).
- Hit a first pitch "walk-off" solo HR to lead off the 11th inning on 8/31 vs. Oakland…was his third career "walk-off" hit and second of the season (also a ninth-inning single on 5/7/19 vs. Seattle and a ninth-inning two-run HR on 9/12/18 vs. Arizona w/ Colorado)…was the Yankees' first "walk-off" HR since Neil Walker on 8/28/18 vs. Chicago-AL.
- Scored his 100th run of the season on 9/9 at Boston.
- Drove in three runs on 9/27 at Texas, surpassing the 100RBI mark for the first time in his career.
- Started at 1B in each of the Yankees' nine postseason games, batting .325 (13-for-40) with 10R, 3 doubles, 3HR and 7RBI…hit safely in eight of his nine games and reached safely multiple times in six of those.
- Hit a solo HR in the sixth inning of ALDS Game 1 win vs. Minnesota, his first career postseason HR and RBI…also hit a bases-clearing double in the seventh…his 3H in the game matched his total from his first five career postseason contests…became the second player in Yankees history to record 4RBI in his first postseason game with the club, joining Bobby Abreu (4RBI in 2006 ALDS Game 1 vs. Detroit)…was the first player to collect 3H in his first postseason game with the Yankees since Jason Giambi in 2002 ALDS Game 1 vs. Anaheim…was the first Yankee with at least 3H and 4RBI in a postseason game since Robinson Canó (3H, 6RBI) in 2011 ALDS Game 1 vs. Detroit…was the fourth Yankees leadoff hitter with 4RBI in a postseason game, joining Johnny Damon (4RBI in 2007 ALDS Game 3 vs. Cleveland), Hank Bauer (4RBI in 1958 World Series Game 3 vs. Milwaukee-NL) and Frankie Crosetti (1938 World Series Game 4 vs. Chicago-NL).
- Scored a playoff career-high 3R in ALCS Game 1 at Houston…hit a leadoff HR in ALCS Game 5 vs. Houston, the first by a Yankee in the playoffs since Derek Jeter in 2009 ALCS Game 3 at Los Angeles-AL…was the seventh leadoff HR in Yankees history (Derek Jeter-3, Johnny Damon-1, Phil Rizzuto-1, Gene Woodling-1).
- Tied the game with a two-run HR with one out in the top of the ninth inning in ALCS Game 6 at Houston.

2018

- Hit .276 (147-for-533) with 90R, 32 doubles, 15HR and 62RBI in 128 games with Colorado…had 12 go-ahead homers, five of which came in the eighth inning or later…of his 15HR, 11 came on the road…his 128 games were his fewest since 2013 (109 games).
- Earned his third career Gold Glove (also 2014 and '17) and was named the Wilson "Defensive Player of the Year" for the third time (also 2013 and '17)…led all Major League second basemen with a .993 fielding pct. (4E, 591 TC)…was his second straight season leading NL second baseman in fielding pct.
- Collected his second career multi-HR game and tied his career high with 4H on 4/12 at Washington…also had 2 doubles in the game, marking the eighth time in Rockies history a player had at least four extra-base hits in a game and the first since Corey Dickerson did so on 5/10/14 at Cincinnati…hit his first career leadoff HR in the game.
- Was placed on the 10-day disabled list from 4/30 (retroactive to 4/28)-5/8 with a right hamstring strain…was his first career D.L. stint…returned to the D.L. the following week (on 5/14) with a left thumb sprain and was reinstated on 6/1.
- Set a career high with 5RBI on 6/28 at San Francisco…hit a game-winning HR in the ninth inning.
- Was placed on the 10-day disabled list from 7/21-8/2 with a left oblique strain.
- Hit his first career grand slam on 8/27 at Los Angeles-AL.
- Collected his 1,000th career hit on 9/8 vs. Los Angeles-NL…reached 1,000 hits *as a Rockie* on 9/21 at Arizona, becoming the eighth player in franchise history to reach the plateau.
- Hit a two-run "walk-off" HR on 9/12 vs. Arizona…was his first career "walk-off" RBI.
- Started at second base in all four of the Rockies' postseason games, batting .200 (3-for-15) with 2 doubles.

2017

- Hit .310 (189-for-609) with 95R, 28 doubles, 8HR and 64RBI in a career-high 155 games with Colorado…ranked fifth in the NL in hits, seventh in batting average and tied for 10th in runs scored…was his third consecutive season with a batting average over .300…had a NL-best five games with at least 4H and tied for second in the NL with 19 games of at least 3H…tied for fifth in the NL with 52 multi-hit games.
- Led all NL second basemen with a .989 fielding pct. (8E, 729 TC)…earned his second career Gold Glove Award (also 2014) and was named the Wilson "Defensive Player of the Year" for the second time (also 2013).
- Was selected to his second career NL All-Star team (did not play due to a right groin injury).
- From 6/15 through the end of the season, hit an NL-best .335 (114-for-340).
- Had consecutive four-hit games on 6/15 and 6/16 vs. San Francisco, becoming the 11th player (12th time) in Rockies history to collect at least 4H in consecutive games.
- Hit safely in a season-high 16 straight games from 8/23-9/8, the second-longest hitting streak of his career.
- Collected his first career multi-HR game on 8/26 at Atlanta…three of his 8HR came over a four-game span from 8/26-29.
- Went 0-for-5 in the National League Wild Card Game at Arizona, his first career postseason appearance.

2016
- Won the National League batting title after leading the Majors with a .348 (192-for-552) batting average with 104R, 32 doubles, 8 triples, 11HR and 66RBI in 146 games…was the highest batting average in the NL since Chipper Jones (.364) and Albert Pujols (.357) in 2008…was the highest by a second baseman since Rod Carew batted .359 in 1975 (min. 50.0% of games at 2B)…was the eighth player in Rockies history (10th time) to win the NL batting title…was the highest by a Rookie since Todd Helton hit .358 in 2003.
- Ranked second in the NL in on-base percentage (.416), third in hits (192) and sixth in runs scored (104)…led all NL players in multi-hit games (59), tied for second in three-hit games (20) and tied for fifth in triples (eight).
- Batted a Major League-best .439 (43-for-98) in August…his 43H during the month were most in any calendar month by a Rookie since Todd Helton had 50H and Neifi Pérez had 44H in August 2000.
- Posted a career-long 38-game on-base streak from 8/9-9/22…hit .420 (63-for-150) with 32R, 10 doubles, 4HR and 26RBI during the stretch.

2015
- Hit .301 (170-for-564) with 85R, 21 doubles, 6HR, 61RBI and 23SB in 150 games with the Rockies…his 88.5% stolen base percentage (23SB, 3CS) was tied for the highest in the NL.
- Was one of five NL players with at least 20 doubles, 20SB and a batting average over than .300.
- Was selected to his first career NL All-Star team…started at 2B for the NL and went 0-for-2.
- Hit .406 (28-for-69) in April, the third-highest batting average in the Majors during the month…hit .400 (36-for-90) in July, becoming the first Rockies player to hit at least .400 in two calendar months during the same season since Larry Walker in 2002 (credit: *Elias*).
- Had a career-high 18-game hitting streak from 7/4-28, batting .444 (32-for-72) over the streak.

2014
- Spent the entire season at the Major League level for the first time in his career, batting .267 (132-for-494) with 59R, 15 doubles, 5HR and 42RBI in 149 games with Colorado.
- Earned his first career Gold Glove Award, posting a .991 fielding pct. (6E, 676 TC) at 2B…became the first Rockies second baseman in franchise history to win a Gold Glove Award.
- Made his first career Opening Day roster, starting at 2B in Colorado's 3/31 loss at Miami.

2013
- Spent the majority of the season with the Rockies, batting .280 (113-for-404) with 39R, 21 doubles, 2HR, 28RBI and 18SB in 109 games…was recalled from Triple-A Colorado Springs on 5/16 and spent the remainder of the season at the Major League level.
- Was named the Wilson "Defensive Player of the Year" for the first time after posting a .993 fielding pct. (3E, 442 TC) at second base.
- In 33 games with Colorado Springs, hit .364 (52-for-143) with 34R, 8 doubles, 1HR and 22RBI.

2012
- Batted .297 (68-for-229) with 26R, 12 doubles, 2HR and 22RBI in 81 games during his first season with Colorado…spent the season's final two months as the Rockies' starting second baseman.
- Hit his first Major League home run on 8/11 at San Francisco (off Matt Cain).
- Played for Triple-A Colorado Springs, batting .314 (80-for-255) with 33R, 14 doubles, 1HR and 31RBI in 61 games.

2011
- Saw his first Major League action, batting .250 (15-for-60) with 3R, 2 doubles and 4RBI in 37 games over two stints with Chicago-NL (5/30-6/28 and 9/6-28).
- Made his Major League debut on 5/30 vs. Houston as an eighth-inning pinch-hitter…collected his first career hit on 6/3 at St. Louis with a single off Jaime García.
- Spent the majority of the season between Double-A Tennessee and Triple-A Iowa, combining to hit .319 (132-for-414) with 55R, 22 doubles, 5HR and 50RBI in 108 games…was named an MiLB.com Organization All-Star.
- Following the season, played for Mesa in the Arizona Fall League, batting .302 (38-for-126) in 31 games.
- Was traded from Chicago-NL to Colorado on 12/8/11 along with OF Tyler Colvin in exchange for 3B Ian Stewart and RHP Casey Weathers.

2010
- Spent the entire season with Single-A Daytona, batting .314 (174-for-554) with 63R, 24 doubles, 2HR and 73RBI in 135 games…was named a Florida State League All-Star.

2009
- Made his professional debut with the rookie-level AZL Cubs, going 5-for-12 with 2R and 4RBI in three games before being transferred to Single-A Peoria…with Peoria, hit .316 (48-for-152) with 19R, 4 doubles and 30RBI.
- Following the season, was named the Cubs' 10th-best prospect by *Baseball America*.

PERSONAL

- Full name is David John LeMahieu…is married to Jordan.
- Has twice been named his team's "Heart and Hustle Award" winner (2019 with the Yankees and 2015 with Colorado)…the award honors active players who demonstrate a passion for the game of baseball and best embody the values, spirit and traditions of the game.
- For 2019, was named the Sid Mercer/Dick Young New York Player of the Year, as voted on by the BBWAA.
- Attended Louisiana State University…was named to the 2009 College World Series All-Tournament Team as the LSU Tigers' leadoff hitter.
- Attended Brother Rice High School in Bloomfield Hills, Mich., where he received All-America honors from Rawlings and Louisville Slugger…was twice named Gatorade "Player of the Year" in Michigan.
- Lived in California until he was seven years old, then lived in Las Vegas for one year, Madison, Wis., for five years and Bloomfield Hills, Mich., for five years.

LeMahieu's Career Batting Record

Year	Club	AVG	G	AB	R	H	2B	3B	HR	RBI	SH	SF	HP	BB	SO	SB	CS	E	OBP	SLG
2009	AZL Cubs	.417	3	12	2	5	0	1	0	4	0	1	0	1	3	1	0	1	.429	.583
	Peoria	.316	38	152	19	48	4	2	0	30	1	1	2	12	22	2	2	3	.371	.368
2010	Daytona	.314	135	554	63	174	24	5	2	73	10	6	1	29	61	15	7	13	.346	.386
2011	Tennessee	.358	50	187	32	67	15	2	2	27	0	4	0	11	22	4	3	4	.386	.492
	CHICAGO-NL	.250	37	60	3	15	2	0	0	4	1	0	0	1	12	0	0	4	.262	.283
	Iowa	.286	58	227	23	65	7	1	3	23	0	4	2	14	27	5	5	1	.328	.366
2012	Colorado Springs	.314	61	255	33	80	14	2	1	31	0	2	0	23	29	13	6	7	.368	.396
	COLORADO - a	.297	81	229	26	68	12	4	2	22	3	2	0	13	42	1	2	2	.332	.410
2013	Colorado Springs	.364	33	143	34	52	8	5	1	22	0	3	2	10	19	8	2	4	.405	.510
	COLORADO	.280	109	404	39	113	21	3	2	28	7	3	1	19	67	18	7	3	.311	.361
2014	COLORADO	.267	149	494	59	132	15	5	5	42	7	2	2	33	97	10	10	6	.315	.348
2015	COLORADO	.301	150	564	85	170	21	5	6	61	3	2	1	50	107	23	3	9	.358	.388
2016	COLORADO	.348	146	552	104	192	32	8	11	66	8	6	3	66	80	11	7	6	.416	.495
2017	COLORADO	.310	155	609	95	189	28	4	8	64	3	5	6	59	90	6	5	8	.374	.409
2018	COLORADO - b, c, d	.276	128	533	90	147	32	2	15	62	2	7	2	37	82	6	5	4	.321	.428
2019	YANKEES	.327	145	602	109	197	33	2	26	102	1	4	2	46	90	5	2	8	.375	.518
Minor League Totals		.321	378	1530	206	491	72	18	9	210	11	21	7	100	183	48	25	33	.361	.409
Major League Totals		.302	1100	4047	610	1223	196	33	75	451	35	31	17	324	667	80	41	50	.354	.423

Selected by Detroit in the 41st round of the 2007 First-Year Player Draft (did not sign).
Selected by Chicago-NL in the second round of the 2009 First-Year Player Draft.

a – Acquired by Colorado from Chicago-NL with OF Tyler Colvin on December 8, 2011 in exchange for 3B Ian Stewart and RHP Casey Weathers.
b – Placed on the 10-day disabled list from April 30 (retroactive to April 29) - May 8, 2018 with a right hamstring strain.
c – Placed on the 10-day disabled list from May 14 - June 1, 2018 with a left thumb sprain.
d – Placed on the 10-day disabled list from July 21 - August 2, 2018 with a left oblique strain.

LeMahieu's Postseason Batting Record

Year	Club vs. Opp.	AVG	G	AB	R	H	2B	3B	HR	RBI	SH	SF	HP	BB	SO	SB	CS	E	OBP	SLG
2017	COL vs. ARI (WC)	.000	1	5	0	0	0	0	0	0	0	0	0	0	2	0	0	0	.000	.000
2018	COL vs. CHC (WC)	.167	1	6	0	1	1	0	0	0	0	0	0	0	1	0	0	0	.167	.333
	COL vs. MIL (DS)	.222	3	9	0	2	1	0	0	0	0	0	0	3	2	0	1	0	.417	.333
2019	NYY vs. MIN (DS)	.286	3	14	4	4	2	0	0	4	0	0	0	1	4	0	0	1	.333	.643
	NYY vs. HOU (CS)	.346	6	26	6	9	1	0	2	3	0	0	0	3	2	0	0	2	.414	.615
Wild Card Game Totals		.091	2	11	0	1	1	0	0	0	0	0	0	0	3	0	0	0	.091	.182
LDS Totals		.261	6	23	4	6	3	0	0	4	0	0	0	4	6	0	1	1	.370	.522
LCS Totals		.346	6	26	6	9	1	0	2	3	0	0	0	3	2	0	0	2	.414	.615
POSTSEASON TOTALS		.267	14	60	10	16	5	0	3	7	0	0	0	7	11	0	1	3	.343	.500

LeMahieu's All-Star Game Record

Year	Club, Site	AVG	G	AB	R	H	2B	3B	HR	RBI	SH	SF	HP	BB	SO	SB	CS	E	OBP	SLG
2015	COL, Cincinnati	.000	1	2	0	0	0	0	0	0	0	0	0	0	0	0	0	0	.000	.000
2017	COL, Miami					Selected - Did Not Play (Injured)														
2019	NYY, Cleveland	.000	1	2	0	0	0	0	0	0	0	0	0	0	0	0	0	0	.000	.000
All-Star Game Totals		.000	2	4	0	0	0	0	0	0	0	0	0	0	0	0	0	0	.000	.000

LeMahieu's Career Fielding Record

Position	PCT	G	PO	A	E	TC	DP
First Base	.992	44	226	19	2	247	25
Second Base	.991	967	1,700	2,787	40	4,527	634
Shortstop	-	4	0	0	0	0	0
Third Base	.955	93	34	136	8	178	14

LeMahieu's Career Home Run Chart

MULTI-HOMER GAMES: 3. **TWO-HOMER GAMES:** 3 (last in Game 1 on 8/3/19 vs. BOS). **GRAND SLAMS:** 1, 8/27/18 at LAA (Jim Johnson). **PINCH-HIT HR:** None. **INSIDE-THE-PARK HR:** None. **WALK-OFF HR:** 2, last on 8/31/19 vs. OAK (Lou Trivino). **LEADOFF HR:** 8, last on 8/25/19 at LAD (Clayton Kershaw).

LeMahieu's Career Bests and Streaks

HITS: 4 - 14 times (last on 9/14/19 at TOR). **RUNS:** 4 - 3 times (last on 7/11/18 vs. ARI). **2B:** 2 - 16 times (last on 9/27/19 at TEX). **3B:** 1 - 33 times (last on 6/25/19 vs. TOR). **HR:** 2 - 3 times (last in Game 1 on 8/3/19 vs. BOS). **RBI:** 5 - 2 times (last on 6/29/19 at BOS). **BB:** 3 - 5 times (last on 3/30/18 at ARI). **SO:** 5, 8/3/15 vs. SEA. **SB:** 2, 9/6/14 vs. SD. **HIT STREAK:** 18g, 7/4-28/15. **"WALK-OFF" HITS:** 3, last on 8/31/19 vs. OAK (HR).

Player of the Month: June 2019 **Player of the Week:** 6/24-30/19 **Rookie of the Month:** None

JONATHAN LOAISIGA • RHP

43

HT: 5-11 • **WT:** 165 • **BATS:** R • **THROWS:** R
BIRTHDATE: 11/2/94 • **OPENING DAY AGE:** 25
BIRTHPLACE: Managua, Nicaragua
RESIDES: Managua, Nicaragua
M.L. SERVICE: 1 year, 22 days

STATUS
- Signed by the Yankees as a minor league free agent on February 9, 2016.

2019
- Went 2-2 with a 4.55 ERA (31.2IP, 16ER) and 37K in 15 games (four starts) over four stints with the Yankees (4/3-9, 4/23-4/24, 5/8-8/23, 8/31-9/29).
- Made four starts (4/3 vs. Detroit, 4/9 at Houston, 5/8 vs. Seattle and 9/25 at Tampa Bay), going 0-2 with a 6.75 ERA (12.0IP, 9ER)…served as the Yankees' opener on 9/25 at Tampa Bay.
- Earned his first win of the season on 4/24 at Los Angeles-AL, tossing 3.0 scoreless innings of relief (2H, 1BB, 1K).
- Was placed on the 10-day injured list on 5/13 (retroactive to 5/10) with a right shoulder strain…was transferred to the 60-day I.L. on 5/14…was returned from rehab and reinstated from the 60-day I.L. on 8/13…combined in three rehab starts with Double-A Trenton and Triple-A Scranton/Wilkes-Barre to allow 3ER in 5.2IP (5H, 1BB, 8K, 1HR, 1HP).
- Had 5K on 9/21 vs. Toronto, setting a relief appearance career high…touched 100.0 mph in the outing according to Statcast.
- Posted a 3.38 ERA (2.2IP, 1ER) in four postseason relief appearances…made his postseason debut in ALDS Game 2 vs. Minnesota, allowing 1ER in 1.0IP (2H, 2K)…became the fifth Nicaragua-born player to appear in a postseason game, joining Dennis Martínez, David Green, Marvin Benard and Vicente Padilla, and the first to do so with the Yankees.
- Combined with Trenton and Scranton/WB to go 0-2 with a 5.60 ERA (17.2IP, 11ER) in six total appearances (five starts).

2018
- Went 2-0 with a 5.11 ERA (24.2IP, 26H, 17R/14ER, 12BB, 33K, 3HR) in nine appearances (four starts) over two stints with the Yankees (6/15-7/2 and 9/2-30)…became the first Nicaragua-born player in Yankees history and the 15th Nicaraguan player (11th pitcher) in Baseball history.
- Was 2-0 with a 3.00 ERA (18.0IP, 6ER) in four starts…posted a 10.80 ERA (6.2IP, 8ER) without recording a decision in five relief appearances.
- Made his Major League debut on 6/15 vs. Tampa Bay, tossing 5.0 shutout innings (3H, 4BB, 6K) to earn the win…was the 11th pitcher (eighth starter) in Yankees history to toss at least 5.0 scoreless innings in his Major League debut, just the second since 1943 (Sam Militello-7.0IP in a start on 8/9/92 vs. Boston)…was the first Yankees pitcher since 1908 to record at least 6K and not allow a run in his Major League debut…was the first Yankees pitcher to record a win in his first career game since Masahiro Tanaka on 4/4/14 at Toronto…was recalled from Double-A Trenton prior to the game, and per *Elias*, was the first player to make his Major League debut with the Yankees (excluding Masahiro Tanaka) without having ever appeared at the Triple-A level since INF Ramiro Peña on 4/6/09 at Baltimore…was the first pitcher to do so since LHP Chase Wright on 4/17/07 vs. Cleveland.
- On 6/25 at Philadelphia, took a no-hitter into the sixth inning and earned his second win (5.1IP, 1H, 0R, 2BB, 8K)…allowed his only hit on a leadoff single by Jorge Alfaro in the sixth…retired the first 12BF in order…became the second Yankees pitcher since 1908 to toss at least 5.0 shutout innings twice within his first three career games, joining Johnny Allen (5/3/32 at Washington-AL, 5/11/32 vs. St. Louis-AL).
- Combined with Single-A Tampa, Double-A Trenton and the GCL Yankees West to go 6-1 with a 2.89 ERA (56.0IP, 57H, 18ER, 8BB, 67K) in 14 minor league starts…had two stints on the minor league disabled list.
- Was named Florida State League "Pitcher of the Week" for 4/5-15 (2-0, 10.0IP, 0R in 2GS).
- Made one spring training relief appearance with the Yankees, tossing 1.0 scoreless inning (1HP, 2K).
- Following the season, was tabbed by *Baseball America* as the No. 2 prospect in the Yankees organization…was named by MLB.com as the No. 66 overall prospect.

2017
- Combined with the GCL Yankees East, GCL Yankees West and short-season Single-A Staten Island to go 1-1 with a 1.38 ERA (32.2IP, 17H, 7R/5ER, 3BB, 33K, 1HR) in 11 starts.
- Made his season debut in June with the GCL Yankees East, going 0-1 with a 2.63 ERA (13.2IP, 4ER) in six starts…also made one start with the GCL Yankees West, tossing 2.0 perfect innings.

- Was promoted to short-season Single-A Staten Island on 8/16, where he went 1-0 with a 0.53 ERA (17.0IP, 1ER) in four starts.
- Was added to the Yankees' 40-man roster on 11/20/17.

2016
- Made one start with Single-A Charleston on 5/13 at Lexington-G2, allowing 2ER in 2.1IP.

2015
- Did not pitch.
- Was released by San Francisco on 5/28/15.

2014
- Spent the season on the minor league disabled list and did not pitch.

2013
- Made his professional debut with the DSL Giants and was 8-1 with a 2.75 ERA (68.2IP, 21ER) in 13 starts.

PERSONAL
- Full name is Jonathan Stanley Loaisiga (pronounced "loh-AYE-see-gah").
- Is the first Nicaragua-born player in Yankees history and one of 15 Nicaraguan players (one of 11 pitchers) in Baseball history.

Loaisiga's Career Pitching Record

Year	Club	W	L	ERA	G	GS	CG	SHO	SV	IP	H	R	ER	HR	HP	BB	SO	WP	BK
2013	DSL Giants	8	1	2.75	13	13	0	0	0	68.2	60	29	21	4	2	16	40	6	0
2014								Did Not Pitch											
2015								Did Not Pitch											
2016	Charleston - a	0	0	7.71	1	1	0	0	0	2.1	2	2	2	1	0	1	2	0	0
2017	GCL Yankees East	0	1	2.63	6	6	0	0	0	13.2	10	5	4	1	0	2	15	0	0
	GCL Yankees West	0	0	0.00	1	1	0	0	0	2.0	0	0	0	0	0	0	0	0	0
	Staten Island	1	0	0.53	4	4	0	0	0	17.0	7	2	1	0	1	1	18	1	0
2018	Tampa	3	0	1.35	4	4	0	0	0	20.0	19	3	3	0	1	1	26	2	0
	Trenton	3	1	3.93	9	9	0	0	0	34.1	37	15	15	6	2	6	40	1	0
	YANKEES	2	0	5.11	9	4	0	0	0	24.2	26	17	14	3	0	12	33	0	0
	GCL Yankees West	0	0	0.00	1	1	0	0	0	1.2	1	0	0	0	1	1	1	0	0
2019	YANKEES - b	2	2	4.55	15	4	0	0	0	31.2	31	16	16	6	1	16	37	1	0
	Scranton/WB	0	2	6.32	5	4	0	0	0	15.2	14	11	11	3	1	5	19	2	0
	Trenton	0	0	0.00	1	1	0	0	0	2.0	1	0	0	0	1	0	3	1	0
Minor League Totals		15	5	2.89	45	44	0	0	0	177.1	151	67	57	15	9	33	164	13	0
Major League Totals		4	2	4.79	24	8	0	0	0	56.1	57	33	30	9	1	28	70	1	0

Signed by San Francisco as a non-drafted free agent on September 13, 2012.
a – Signed by the Yankees as a minor league free agent on February 9, 2016.
b – Placed on the 10-day injured list on May 13, 2019 (retroactive to May 10) with a right shoulder strain…was transferred to the 60-day injured list on May 14 and reinstated on August 13, 2019.

Loaisiga's Postseason Record

Year	Club vs. Opp.	W	L	ERA	G	GS	CG	SHO	SV	IP	H	R	ER	HR	HP	BB	SO	WP	BK
2019	NYY vs. MIN (DS)	0	0	9.00	1	0	0	0	0	1.0	2	1	1	0	0	0	2	0	0
	NYY vs. HOU (CS)	0	0	0.00	3	0	0	0	0	1.2	1	1	0	0	0	3	1	2	0
POSTSEASON TOTALS		0	0	3.38	4	0	0	0	0	2.2	3	2	1	0	0	3	3	2	0

Loaisiga's Regular Season Batting Record

Year	Team	AVG	G	AB	R	H	2B	3B	HR	RBI	SH	SF	HP	BB	SO	SB	CS
2019	NYY							Did Not Bat									
Major League Totals		.000	24	2	0	0	0	0	0	0	0	0	0	0	2	0	0

Loaisiga's Career Fielding Record

Position	PCT	G	PO	A	E	TC	DP
Pitcher	1.000	24	3	4	0	7	3

Loaisiga's Career Bests and Streaks

COMPLETE GAMES: None. **LOW-HIT COMPLETE GAME:** N/A. **IP (START):** 5.1, 6/25/18 at PHI. **IP (RELIEF):** 3.0, 4/24/19 at LAA. **HITS:** 6 - 2 times (last on 5/8/19 vs. SEA). **RUNS:** 6, 9/11/18 at MIN. **WALKS:** 4, 6/15/18 vs. TB. **STRIKEOUTS:** 8, 6/25/18 at PHI. **HOME RUNS:** 2, 8/15/19 vs. CLE. **WINNING STREAK:** 3g, 6/15/18-4/24/19. **LOSING STREAK:** 1g, 2 times (last from 9/25/19-present). **SCORELESS STREAK (IP):** 8.0, 6/15-20/18.

Pitcher of the Month: None   **Pitcher of the Week:** None   **Rookie of the Month:** None

LUIS MEDINA • RHP

#80

HT: 6-1 • **WT:** 175 • **BATS:** R • **THROWS:** R
BIRTHDATE: 5/3/99 • **OPENING DAY AGE:** 20
BIRTHPLACE: Nagua, D.R.
RESIDES: Santo Domingo, D.R.
M.L. SERVICE: None (Rookie)

STATUS
- Signed by the Yankees as a non-drafted free agent on July 8, 2015.

2019
- Combined with Single-A Charleston and Single-A Tampa to go 1-8 with a 5.47 ERA (103.2IP, 63ER) in 22 starts.
- Spent the majority of the season with Charleston, going 1-8 with a 6.00 ERA (93.0IP, 62ER) in 20 starts.
- Made two starts with Tampa, receiving no-decisions in both with 5R/1ER in 10.2IP.
- Finished fifth among Yankee minor league pitchers with 127 strikeouts.
- Was named SAL "Pitcher of the Week" for 8/12-18 after tossing 7.0 scoreless innings on 8/13 vs. Columbia (2H, 1B, 10K).
- Following the season, was tabbed by *Baseball America* as the Yankees' No. 7 prospect and No. 15 prospect in the South Atlantic League…was touted as having the "Best Fastball" among organization farmhands.
- Was added to the Yankees' 40-man roster on 11/20/19.

2018
- Went 1-3 with a 6.25 ERA (36.0IP, 32H, 35R/25ER, 46BB, 47K) in 12 starts with Rookie-level Pulaski.
- Had a career-high 11.75 K/9.0IP ratio.
- Following the season, was named by *Baseball America* as having the "Best Fastball" and the "Best Curveball" in the Yankees organization.

2017
- Combined with the DSL Yankees and Rookie-level Pulaski to go 2-2 with a 5.35 ERA (38.2 IP, 31H, 29R/23ER, 24BB, 39K) in 10 games (nine starts).
- Appeared in four games (three starts) with the DSL Yankees, going 1-1 with a 5.74 ERA (15.2IP, 17H, 15R/10ER, 10BB, 17K).
- Was promoted on 7/24 to Pulaski, going 1-1 with a 5.09 ERA (23.0IP, 14H, 14R/13ER, 14BB, 22K) in six starts.
- Following the season, was ranked the No.8 prospect in the Yankees organization by *Baseball America*.

2016
- Did not record a decision and posted a 1.93 ERA (4.2 IP, 2H, 1ER, 4BB, 4K) in three starts in his professional debut with the DSL Yankeees.

PERSONAL
- Full name is Luis Angel Medina.

Medina's Career Pitching Record

Year	Club	W	L	ERA	G	GS	CG	SHO	SV	IP	H	R	ER	HR	HP	BB	SO	WP	BK
2016	DSL Yankees	0	0	1.93	3	3	0	0	0	4.2	2	1	1	0	1	4	4	3	0
2017	DSL Yankees	1	1	5.74	4	3	0	0	0	15.2	17	15	10	0	0	10	17	11	2
	Pulaski	1	1	5.09	6	6	0	0	0	23.0	14	14	13	1	2	14	22	7	0
2018	Pulaski	1	3	6.25	12	12	0	0	0	36.0	32	35	25	3	2	46	47	12	2
2019	Charleston	1	8	6.00	20	20	0	0	0	93.0	86	65	62	9	9	67	115	26	1
	Tampa	0	0	0.84	2	2	0	0	0	10.2	7	5	1	0	0	3	12	1	0
Minor League Totals		4	13	5.51	47	46	0	0	0	183.0	158	135	112	13	14	144	217	60	5

Signed by the Yankees as a non-drafted free agent on July 8, 2015.

JORDAN MONTGOMERY • LHP

47

HT: 6-6 • **WT:** 228 • **BATS:** L • **THROWS:** L
BIRTHDATE: 12/27/92 • **OPENING DAY AGE:** 27
BIRTHPLACE: Sumter, S.C.
RESIDES: Sumter, S.C.
COLLEGE: University of South Carolina
M.L. SERVICE: 2 years, 153 days

STATUS
- Selected by the Yankees in the fourth round of the 2014 First-Year Player Draft.

CAREER
- Is one of three pitchers ever drafted by the Yankees (since 1965) to post an ERA under 4.00 in 25-or-more starts in pinstripes (also Joba Chamberlain-3.85 ERA, 2006 draft; and Andy Pettitte-3.94 ERA, 1990 draft).
- Recorded his 100th career strikeout in his 20th career game (7/30/17 vs. Tampa Bay), tied for the fifth-fastest to the mark in Yankees history.
- Never allowed more than 4R in any of his 64 career minor league games (60 starts), going 25-14 with a 2.54 ERA (304.1IP, 86ER).

2019
- Made two appearances (one start) with the Yankees, posting a 6.75 ERA (4.0IP, 3ER).
- Was placed on the 60-day injured list on 3/23 recovering from left elbow UCL surgery (performed on 6/7/18), missing the Yankees' first 150 games of the season…began a rehab assignment on 8/25 and combined with Single-A Tampa and Triple-A Scranton/Wilkes-Barre (one regular season start with each), and Double-A Trenton (two postseason starts) to make four rehab starts, posting a 2.79 ERA (9.2IP, 9H, 5R/3ER, 1BB, 11K).
- Was reinstated from the injured list and made his season debut on 9/15 at Toronto, allowing 3ER in 2.0IP (4H, 2K, 1HR) in relief…was his first appearance at the Major League level since 5/1/18 at Houston and his first career relief appearance.
- Made his only start of the season on 9/24 at Tampa Bay (2.0IP, 3H, 3K).

2018
- Made just six starts with the Yankees, going 2-0 with a 3.62 ERA (27.1IP, 25H, 11ER, 12BB, 23K, 3HR)…held opponents to a .125 BA (3-for-24) with RISP…the Yankees went 5-1 in his starts…made his first career Opening Day roster.
- Left his 5/1 start at Houston after 1.0IP with left elbow tightness…was placed on the 10-day disabled list on 5/2 with a left elbow strain…was transferred to the 60-day disabled list on 8/13.
- On 6/7, underwent "Tommy John" surgery on his left elbow, performed by Yankees Head Team Physician Dr. Christopher Ahmad at NewYork-Presbyterian Hospital…a loose bone chip was also removed from the elbow.

2017
- In his first Major League season, went 9-7 with a 3.88 ERA (155.1IP, 140H, 72R/67ER, 51BB, 144K, 21HR) in 29 starts over five stints with the Yankees (4/12-7/8, 7/14-8/6, 8/11-19, 8/30, 9/1-end of season)…opponents hit .236 (140-for-592); LH .195 (17-for-87); RH .244 (123-for-505)…had 2.7 WAR and a 4.07 FIP (FanGraphs).
- Finished sixth in AL Rookie of the Year voting, receiving one second-place vote and one third-place vote (4 pts.)…was also named to the Topps MLB All-Star Rookie Team.
- Led AL rookies in starts, strikeouts and innings pitched…tied for second in wins…finished second in strikeouts among MLB rookies to Colorado's Germán Marquez (147), tied Marquez for the most starts, was fourth in innings pitched and tied for fifth in wins…led Major League rookie pitchers in WAR (FanGraphs).
- His 144K were the sixth-highest single-season total by a rookie in Yankees history: Russ Ford (209 in 1910), Al Downing (171 in 1963), Stan Bahnsen (162 in 1968), Doc Medich (145 in 1973), Ray Caldwell (145 in 1911).
- His 29 starts were fifth-most by a rookie pitcher in a single season in Yankees history, second among left-handers to Fritz Peterson (32 starts in 1966)…were the most by any Yankees rookie since Doc Medich (32) in 1973.
- Was the third Yankees rookie in 45 seasons (since 1974) to throw at least 150.0IP in a season, joining Iván Nova (165.1IP in 2011) and Andy Pettitte (175.0IP in 1995).
- Limited LHB to a .195 BA (17-for-87), sixth-lowest among AL starters (min. 75AB by LHB)…faced just 96 LHB (14.8% of batters faced), compared to 553 RHB (85.2%).
- Held opponents to a .221 BA (27-for-122) with RISP, eighth-lowest in the AL (min. 100AB with RISP).

- Opponents swung at 33.2% of his pitches outside the strike zone, the ninth-highest "chase rate" among Major League pitchers with at least 150.0IP (FanGraphs)…according to Brooks Baseball, opponents batted a combined .185 (67-for-362) with 121K against his three offspeed pitches (changeup/slider/curveball).
- Was 6-3 with a 3.43 ERA (81.1IP, 31ER) in 15 starts at home…posted a 0.77 HR/9.0IP ratio (7HR/81.1IP) at Yankee Stadium.
- Made his Major League debut in 4/12 win vs. Tampa Bay (ND, 4.2IP, 5H, 3R/2ER, 2BB, 7K, 1HR, 1HP)…struck out his first two batters faced (Steven Souza Jr., Kevin Kiermaier)…was the first Yankees left-hander to make his Major League debut as a starter since Chase Wright on 4/17/07 vs. Cleveland…his 7K were the second-most by a Yankees left-hander in his MLB debut since 1908, behind only Al Leiter (8K on 9/15/87 vs. Milwaukee)…along with C Kyle Higashioka (first career start in second career game), became the first Yankees battery to each make their first Major League starts in the same game since RHP Jorge De Paula and C Michel Hernandez on 9/26/03 vs. Baltimore.
- Earned his first career win in his second start on 4/17 vs. Chicago-AL, taking a shutout into the seventh inning.
- Was 4-0 with a 2.59 ERA (31.1IP, 9ER) in five June starts…was the first Yankees rookie starter to go 4-0 or better with an ERA under 3.00 in a calendar month since Stan Bahnsen in May 1968 (4-0, 1.93).
- Was 6-4 with a 3.53 ERA (81.2IP, 32ER) in 14 starts from April-June and 3-3 with a 4.28 ERA (73.2IP, 35ER) in 15 starts from July-October.
- On 8/12 vs. Boston, was hit on the head by a flyball during Red Sox batting practice, but made his start the next day.
- Went 0-for-3 with 2BB at the plate…drew a walk in his first Major League plate appearance on 4/23 at Pittsburgh…had not batted in an official game since high school.
- Went 0-0 with a 1.13 ERA (8.0IP, 1ER) in two minor league starts…made his first start of the season with Single-A Tampa on 4/6 vs. Lakeland (5.0IP, 3H, 1R/0ER, 1BB, 8K)…also started for Triple-A Scranton/Wilkes-Barre on 8/24 at Rochester (3.0IP, 2H, 1ER, 0BB, 3K).

2016
- Combined with Double-A Trenton and Triple-A Scranton/Wilkes-Barre to go 14-5 with 2.13 ERA (139.1IP, 122H, 39R/33ER, 45BB, 134K) in 25 starts…recorded the seventh-lowest ERA among all minor leaguers (min. 125.0IP)…tied for the most wins among all Yankees minor leaguers, was second in strikeouts and third in ERA.
- Began the season with Trenton, going 9-4 with a 2.55 ERA (102.1IP, 94H, 35R/29ER, 36BB, 97K) in 19 starts…was named an Eastern League Mid-Season and Postseason All-Star…allowed 2ER-or-fewer in 13-of-19 starts with Trenton…recorded a career-high 11K on 6/15 vs. Harrisburg.
- Was promoted to Scranton/WB on 8/1 and went 5-1 with a 0.97 ERA (37.0IP, 28H, 4ER, 9BB, 37K) in six starts…recorded a 29.1-inning scoreless streak from 8/7-31…recorded at least 8K in three of his six starts.
- Went 1-1 with a 3.52 ERA (7.2IP, 3ER) in two postseason starts for Scranton/WB…also earned the win in the franchise's first Triple-A National Championship vs. El Paso (5.0IP, 6H, 1ER, 0BB, 5K).
- Following the season, was tabbed by *Baseball America* as having the Eastern League's "Best Breaking Pitch."

2015
- Led Yankees farmhands with 132K, combining with Single-A Charleston and Single-A Tampa to post a 10-8 record with a 2.95 ERA (134.1IP, 118H, 51R/44ER, 36BB, 132K, 5HR) and one complete game in 25 games (24 starts)…had the seventh-lowest ERA in the organization…allowed 1ER-or-fewer in 11-of-25 games.
- Logged a 4-3 record and 2.68 ERA (43.2IP, 36H, 15R/13ER, 12BB, 55K) in nine starts at Charleston…earned South Atlantic League "Pitcher of the Week" honors for 5/18-24 after going 1-0 with a 0.79 ERA (11.1IP, 4H, 1ER, 0BB, 15K) in two starts…allowed 2H over 7.0 shutout innings (0BB, 8K) on 5/23 at Greenville.
- Was promoted to Tampa on 6/1 and went 6-5 with a 3.08 ERA (90.2IP, 82H, 36R/31ER, 24BB, 77K) and 1CG in 16 games (15 starts)…retired 20-of-22 batters faced in his Tampa debut on 6/3-G2 at Lakeland, issuing 1HP and allowing a runner to reach on an error (6.2IP, 0H, 1R/0ER, 0BB, 6K)…was named Florida State League "Pitcher of the Week" for 8/24-30 after throwing 6.0 perfect innings with 8K on 8/28 at Daytona.

2014
- In his professional debut, combined with the GCL Yankees 2 (three starts) and short-season Single-A Staten Island (seven games/four starts) to go 1-1 with a 3.79 ERA (19.0IP, 16H, 10R/8ER, 6BB, 20K).

PERSONAL
- Played three seasons at the University of South Carolina (2012-14), going 20-7 with a 2.87 ERA (253.2IP, 81ER) in 44 appearances (42 starts)…also made five postseason starts, going 5-0 with a 0.93 ERA.
- Graduated from Sumter H.S. (S.C.), earning 2011 Gatorade State "Player of the Year" honors after going 11-0 with a 0.38 ERA as a senior.
- In January 2018, spent two weeks with patients at Palmetto Children's Hospital in Columbia, S.C., promoting a virtual book drive on behalf of "Reach Out & Read," an organization which helps build home libraries for children at clinics located at various pediatric hospitals in South Carolina.
- Visited and played games with patients at the NYU Hassenfeld Children's Hospital in August 2018.

Montgomery's Career Pitching Record

Year	Club	W	L	ERA	G	GS	CG	SHO	SV	IP	H	R	ER	HR	HP	BB	SO	WP	BK
2014	GCL Yankees 2	0	1	4.76	3	3	0	0	0	5.2	5	4	3	0	0	2	5	0	0
	Staten Island	1	0	3.38	7	4	0	0	0	13.1	11	6	5	0	0	4	15	2	0
2015	Charleston	4	3	2.68	9	9	0	0	0	43.2	36	15	13	1	0	12	55	6	1
	Tampa	6	5	3.08	16	15	1	0	0	90.2	82	36	31	4	1	24	77	9	0
2016	Trenton	9	4	2.55	19	19	1	1	0	102.1	94	35	29	5	2	36	97	9	0
	Scranton/WB	5	1	0.97	6	6	0	0	0	37.0	28	4	4	0	0	9	37	1	0
2017	Tampa	0	0	0.00	1	1	0	0	0	5.0	3	1	0	0	0	1	8	0	0
	Scranton/WB	0	0	3.00	1	1	0	0	0	3.0	2	1	1	0	0	0	3	0	0
	YANKEES	9	7	3.88	29	29	0	0	0	155.1	140	72	67	21	1	51	144	7	1
2018	YANKEES - a	2	0	3.62	6	6	0	0	0	27.1	25	11	11	3	0	12	23	0	0
2019	Tampa - b	0	0	0.00	1	1	0	0	0	2.0	0	0	0	0	0	0	2	0	0
	Scranton/WB	0	0	0.00	1	1	0	0	0	1.2	2	1	0	0	0	0	3	0	0
	YANKEES	0	0	6.75	2	1	0	0	0	4.0	7	3	3	1	0	0	5	0	0
Minor League Totals		25	14	2.54	64	60	2	1	0	304.1	263	103	86	10	3	88	302	27	1
Major League Totals		11	7	3.91	37	36	0	0	0	186.2	172	86	81	25	1	63	172	7	1

Selected by the Yankees in the fourth round of the 2014 First-Year Player Draft.

a - Placed on the 10-day disabled list from May 2, 2018 through the end of the season with a left elbow strain…transferred to the 60-day disabled list on August 13, 2018.

b - Placed on the 60-day injured list from March 23-September 15, 2019 recovering from left elbow UCL surgery.

Montgomery's Postseason Record

Year	Club vs. Opp.	W	L	ERA	G	GS	CG	SHO	SV	IP	H	R	ER	HR	HP	BB	SO	WP	BK
2017	NYY vs. CLE (DS)							On Roster - Did Not Pitch											
	NYY vs. HOU (CS)							On Roster - Did Not Pitch											
POSTSEASON TOTALS		-	-	-	-	-	-	-	-	-	-	-	-	-	-	-	-	-	-

Montgomery's Regular Season Batting Record

Year	Team	AVG	G	AB	R	H	2B	3B	HR	RBI	SH	SF	HP	BB	SO	SB	CS
2019	NYY		2					Did Not Bat									
Major League Totals		.000	37	3	0	0	0	0	0	0	0	0	0	2	2	0	0

Montgomery's Career Fielding Record

Position	PCT	G	PO	A	E	TC	DP
Pitcher	.900	37	2	7	1	10	0

Montgomery's Career Bests and Streaks

COMPLETE GAMES: None. **LOW-HIT COMPLETE GAME:** N/A. **IP (START):** 7.0 - 2 times (last on 6/26/17 at CWS). **IP (RELIEF):** 2.0IP, 9/15/19 at TOR. **HITS:** 10, 4/8/18 vs. BAL. **RUNS:** 6, on 7/19/17 at MIN. **WALKS:** 4 - 4 times (last on 4/3/18 vs. TB). **STRIKEOUTS:** 8 - 2 times (last on 6/26/17 at CWS). **HOME RUNS:** 2 - 4 times (last on 9/4/17 at BAL). **WINNING STREAK:** 4g - 2 times (last from 9/16/17-present). **LOSING STREAK:** 3g, 5/12-29/17. **SCORELESS STREAK (IP):** 9.0 - 2 times (last from 7/19-25/17).

Pitcher of the Month: None   **Pitcher of the Week:** None   **Rookie of the Month:** None

Yankees Donate Firefighting and Medical Equipment

In a ceremony which took place on October 9, 2013, the Yankees donated a fire truck and ambulance, along with firefighting and medical equipment, to the city of Boca Chica in the Dominican Republic. The city is home to the Yankees Latin Béisbol Academy.

Distinguished guests at the event included members of the Boca Chica Fire Department, officials from Boca Chica City Hall and other recognized community members.

NICK NELSON • RHP

#79

HT: 6-1 • **WT:** 205 • **BATS:** R • **THROWS:** R
BIRTHDATE: 12/5/95 • **OPENING DAY AGE:** 24
BIRTHPLACE: Panama City, Fla.
RESIDES: Panama City, Fla.
COLLEGE: Gulf Coast State College
M.L. SERVICE: None (Rookie)

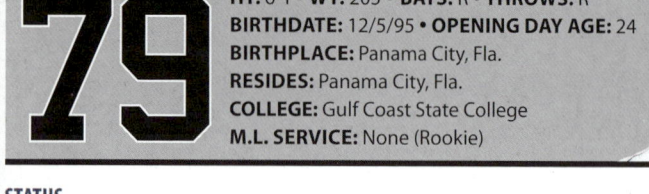

STATUS
- Selected by the Yankees in the fourth round of the 2016 First Year Player Draft.

2019
- Split the season with Single-A Tampa, Double-A Trenton and Triple-A Scranton/Wilkes-Barre to go 8-3 with a 2.81 ERA (89.2IP, 72H, 29R/28ER, 43BB, 114K, 6HR) in 18 games (17 starts)…ranked third in the entire Yankees organization in ERA.
- Began the season with Trenton, appearing in 13 games (12 starts) and going 7-2 with a 2.35 ERA (65.0IP, 48H, 18R/17ER, 35BB, 83K, 4HR).
- Was placed on the 7-day minor league injured list from 4/19 (retroactive to 4/17) - 6/1…made one start with Tampa on 6/1 (3.2IP, 4H, 0ER, 1BB, 7K) before returning to Trenton on 6/7.
- Was promoted to Scranton/Wilkes-Barre on 8/13…went 1-1 with a 4.71 ERA (21.0IP, 20H, 11ER, 7BB, 24K) in four starts.
- Was added to the Yankees 40-man roster on 11/20.

2018
- Combined to go 8-6 with a 3.55 ERA (121.2IP, 97H, 53R/48ER, 63BB, 144K, 3HR) in 26 games (25 starts) with Single-A Charleston, Single-A Tampa, and Double-A Trenton…his 144K were the second-most among all Yankees farmhands.
- Started the season with Charleston…made five starts, going 1-1 with a 3.65 ERA (24.2IP, 10ER)…collected a career-high 12K (5.0IP, 2H, 1R/1ER, 3BB) on 4/13 vs. Kannapolis.
- Also pitched for Tampa, going 7-5 with a 3.36 ERA (88.1IP, 69H, 37R/33ER, 47BB, 99K, 1HR) in 18 games (17 starts).
- Made his Double-A debut with Trenton on 7/22, posting a 5.19 ERA (8.2IP, 5ER) without recording a decision.
- Following the season, was tabbed by *Baseball America* as the No. 19 prospect in the Yankees organization.

2017
- Spent the entire season with Single-A Charleston, going 3-12 with a 4.56 ERA (100.2IP, 103H, 54R/51ER, 50BB, 110K, 5HR) in 22 starts.
- Appeared on the minor league disabled list on two separate occasions: 4/24 (retroactive to 4/23) - 5/5 and 6/2 (retroactive to 6/1) - 6/16.

2016
- Made his professional debut with rookie-level Pulaski, going 0-3 with a 3.38 ERA (21.1IP, 14H, 14R/8ER, 22BB, 19K, 0HR) in 10 starts.

PERSONAL
- Played two seasons (2015-16) at Gulf Coast State College (Fla.), where he went 13-5 with a 4.16 ERA (114.2IP, 108H, 64R/53ER, 49BB, 121K) in 22 games (21 starts)…had committed to play at the University of Florida before signing with the Yankees.
- Graduated from Rutherford H.S. (Fla.) in 2014.

Nelson's Career Pitching Record

Year	Club	W	L	ERA	G	GS	CG	SHO	SV	IP	H	R	ER	HR	HP	BB	SO	WP	BK
2016	Pulaski	0	3	3.38	10	10	0	0	0	21.1	14	14	8	0	6	22	19	3	1
2017	Charleston	3	12	4.56	22	22	0	0	0	100.2	103	54	51	5	12	50	110	16	1
2018	Charleston	1	1	3.65	5	5	0	0	0	24.2	18	10	10	1	2	7	35	2	0
	Tampa	7	5	3.36	18	17	0	0	0	88.1	69	37	33	1	4	47	99	11	0
	Trenton	0	0	5.19	3	3	0	0	0	8.2	10	6	5	1	0	9	10	3	0
2019	Trenton	7	2	2.35	13	12	1	0	0	65.0	48	18	17	4	5	35	83	6	1
	Tampa	0	0	0.00	1	1	0	0	0	3.2	4	0	0	0	1	7	0	0	0
	Scranton/WB	1	1	4.71	4	4	0	0	0	21.0	20	11	11	2	0	7	24	1	0
Minor League Totals		**19**	**24**	**3.65**	**76**	**74**	**1**	**0**	**0**	**333.1**	**286**	**150**	**135**	**14**	**29**	**178**	**387**	**42**	**3**

Selected by the San Francisco Giants in the 31st round of the 2014 First Year Player Draft (did not sign).
Selected by the New York Yankees in the fourth round of the 2016 First Year Player Draft.

ADAM OTTAVINO • RHP

HT: 6-5 • **WT:** 246 • **BATS:** S • **THROWS:** R
BIRTHDATE: 11/22/85 • **OPENING DAY AGE:** 34
BIRTHPLACE: New York, N.Y.
RESIDES: New York, N.Y.
COLLEGE: Northeastern University
M.L. SERVICE: 8 years, 87 days

STATUS
- Signed by the Yankees to a three-year contract extending through 2021 on January 24, 2019.

CAREER
- Ranks on the Rockies' all-time lists with 361 appearances (fourth), 3.41 ERA (sixth among relievers, min. 100.0IP) and 452K (11th)…has a career 3.36 ERA (206.0IP, 77ER) at Coors Field, the lowest mark at the ballpark in club history (min. 100.0IP).
- Set a Rockies franchise record with 37 consecutive scoreless appearances from 9/7/14-8/24/16 (31.0IP).
- Has made six career Opening Day rosters (2013-15 and '17-18 w/ Colorado, 2019 w/ the Yankees)…began 2016 on the 60-day disabled list.

2019
- Went 6-5 with two saves, a 1.90 ERA (66.1IP, 14ER) and 88K in 73 relief appearances in his first season with the Yankees…tied his career high in wins (also 2018) and set a career best in ERA…tied for third in the AL in relief appearances.
- Held opponents scoreless in 61-of-73 appearances, tied for the fourth-most scoreless outings in the Majors (tied for second-most in the AL)…had multiple strikeouts in 24-of-73G, including at least 3K in six of his games.
- His 38.6% swing rate was third-lowest in the Majors (min. 50.0IP, FanGraphs) behind only Clay Holmes (37.4%) and Chaz Roe (37.6%).
- Made his Yankees debut in 3/28 Opening Day win vs. Baltimore, striking out three of his four batters faced (1.1IP).
- Earned his first win as a Yankee on 4/6 at Baltimore.
- Struck out Kansas City RF Terrance Gore (No. 0) on 4/19, the first time in Major League history a pitcher wearing No. 0 faced a batter wearing No. 0.
- Had an 18-appearance (17.1IP) scoreless streak from 4/22-6/5, matching the longest scoreless streak by a Yankee since 2018: Dellin Betances (18G, 5/27-7/7/18)…was the third-longest streak of his career (37G from 9/7/14-8/24/16 and 20G from 9/11/13-4/27/14).
- Collected his 500th career strikeout on 6/5 at Toronto (Grichuk swinging).
- Allowed 1HR in consecutive appearances (6/9-13) for the fifth time in his career and allowed a run in back-to-back games for the first time in 2019.
- Earned his first save of 2019 on 8/6 at Baltimore, tossing a season-high-tying 2.0 scoreless innings (1H, 2K).
- Recorded the loss on 8/10 at Toronto (1.0IP, 2H, 2ER, 1BB, 2K), allowing his first runs since 7/2 at the Mets (snapped a 15-appearance scoreless streak)…had not allowed a run in his first 28 games vs. AL East opponents (24.0IP) before the outing.
- Earned his sixth win of the season on 9/1 vs. Oakland (1.0IP, 1BB, 1K), matching his career high in wins (went 6-4 with Colorado in 2018).
- Allowed a run in four straight appearances from 9/8-18 for the first time since 7/20-8/3/13 (career-high-tying five straight).
- Appeared in eight of the Yankees' nine postseason games, posting an 8.10 ERA (3.1IP, 3ER)…did not record an out in four of his nine appearances, becoming the first pitcher in Baseball history to fail to retire a batter in at least four outings in the same postseason…in ALCS Game 2 at Houston, became the first pitcher in postseason history to record more strikeouts than outs in a playoff game (0.1IP, 2K)…struck out Michael Brantley in the fifth, but Brantley advanced to first base on a wild pitch.

2018
- Went 6-4 with six saves and a 2.43 ERA (77.2IP, 21ER) in 75 relief appearances with Colorado, setting a career high in wins and surpassing 100K for the first time in his career.
- His 112K ranked second in the NL and fourth in the Majors among relievers, and set a new Rockies' single-season record for strikeouts by a reliever (previous: Curtis Leskanic, 107K in 1995)…among NL relievers, ranked fifth with a .158 opponents' BA and 36.2% strikeout rate (112K/309BF), tied for fifth in appearances (75) and tied for sixth in innings pitched (77.2).
- Held opponents scoreless in 60-of-75 appearances…had multiple strikeouts in 36-of-75 appearances, including at least 3K in 12 of his games.

- Over his first 18 appearances from 3/29-5/6, posted a 0.47 ERA (19.0IP, 1ER) with 35K (5H, 6BB, 2HP).
- Had a 15.0-inning scoreless streak over 14 appearances from 5/11-6/26.
- Was placed on the 10-day disabled list from 5/28-6/14 with a left oblique strain.
- Made his postseason debut, going 0-1 with a 4.91 ERA (3.2IP, 2ER) over three relief appearances…took the loss in NLDS Game 1 at Milwaukee after allowing a "walk-off" RBI single to Mike Moustakas in the 10th inning.

2017
- In 63 relief appearances, went 2-3 with a 5.06 ERA (53.1IP, 30ER) for Colorado.
- Held opponents scoreless in 46-of-63 appearances, including 21-of-27 outings following the All-Star break.
- Was placed on the 10-day disabled list from 5/30-6/9 with right shoulder inflammation.
- Allowed 6ER on 6/25 at Los Angeles-NL, his most since allowing a career-high 7ER on 9/16/12 at San Diego…his four wild pitches in the game tied the Rockies' franchise record.

2016
- Went 1-3 with a 2.67 ERA (27.0IP, 8ER) and career-high seven saves in 34 relief appearances with the Rockies.
- Set a Rockies franchise record with 37 consecutive scoreless appearances from 9/7/14-8/24/16 (31.0IP)…is tied for the third-longest streak by games in Baseball history (Ryan Pressly, 40 games from 8/15/18-5/20/19; Craig Kimbrel, 38 games from 6/14-9/8/11)…did not allow a run in his first 21 games of the season, the second-longest scoreless game streak to start a season in franchise history…the streaks snapped on 8/27 at Washington.
- Began the season on the 60-day disabled list recovering from "Tommy John" surgery, performed in May 2015… was returned from rehab and reinstated from the D.L. on 7/5 and made his season debut that night at San Francisco…combined to make 10 rehab relief appearances with Single-A Modesto and Triple-A Albuquerque.
- Allowed 5ER in 1.0IP to record the loss in Game 2 of 8/31 DH vs. Los Angeles-NL, his first loss since 8/15/14 vs. Cincinnati…allowed a grand slam to Andrew Toles, his first HR allowed since 8/29/14 at Arizona (a span of 35.0IP).

2015
- Went 1-0 with three saves while tossing 10.1 scoreless innings over 10 relief appearances with Colorado.
- Was placed on the 15-day disabled list on 4/27 (retroactive to 4/26) with right triceps inflammation…underwent "Tommy John" surgery on 5/7, performed by Dr. James Andrews…missed the remainder of the season.

2014
- Went 1-4 with one save and a 3.60 ERA (65.0IP, 26ER) in 75 relief appearances with the Rockies…tied for seventh in the Majors in appearances…had 70K with 16BB, marking the sixth time in Rockies history a pitcher appeared in at least 75 games while issuing no more than 22 walks in a single season.
- Began the season with a 13-game scoreless streak spanning 11.1 innings (6H, 1BB, 15K)…at the time, was the fourth-longest scoreless game streak by a Rockies reliever to open the season and longest since Randy Flores began the 2010 season with a 16-game scoreless streak.
- Earned his first career save on 7/30 at Chicago-NL, tossing a scoreless 10th inning (1.0IP, 1H, 1K).

2013
- Made 51 relief appearances for Colorado, going 1-3 with a 2.64 ERA (78.1IP, 23ER).
- Made his first career Opening Day roster and spent the entire season at the Major League level.
- Tossed at least 1.0 inning in 42-of-51 appearances and at least 2.0 innings in 24 of those games…his 24 appearances of two or more innings in relief are a Rockies single-season record, surpassing Curtis Leskanic (1995) and Jerry Dipoto (1999), who held the record with 22 games.
- His 2.00 ERA (45.0IP, 10ER) at Coors Field led all Rockies relievers.

2012
- Went 5-1 with a 4.56 ERA (79.0IP, 40ER) and 81K over 53 relief appearances in his first season with the Rockies… ranked fourth among NL relievers in innings pitched.
- Was claimed off waivers by Colorado from St. Louis on 4/3 and assigned to Triple-A Colorado Springs before making his Rockies debut on 5/6 vs. Atlanta (2.0IP, 2K).
- Made two appearances (2.2IP, 0H, 0BB, 4K) before being optioned on 5/9…was again recalled on 5/20 and remained in the Majors for the remainder of the season.
- Earned his first Major League win on 6/1 vs. Los Angeles-NL, tossing 1.2 scoreless innings (2H, 3K).
- Made 13 relief appearances for Colorado Springs, posting a 3.20 ERA (19.2IP, 7ER) without recording a decision.

2011
- Spent the entire season with Triple-A Memphis, going 7-8 with a 4.85 ERA (141.0IP, 76ER) and 120K in 26G/25GS… tied for third among Cardinals farmhands in starts and ranked sixth in innings pitched and eighth in strikeouts.

2010
- Saw his first Major League action, going 0-2 with an 8.46 ERA (22.1IP, 21ER) in five games (three starts) over two stints with St. Louis (5/29-6/13, 6/25-10/3).

- Made his Major League debut on 5/29 at Chicago-NL, starting and recording the loss (5.2IP, 5H, 4ER, 6BB, 5K).
- Was placed on the 15-day disabled list on 7/7 (retroactive to 7/4) with a right shoulder strain...was transferred to the 60-day D.L. on 8/16 and reinstated on 9/29.
- Began the season with Triple-A Memphis, going 5-3 with a 3.97 ERA (47.2IP, 21ER) in nine starts.

2009
- Spent the entire season with Triple-A Memphis, going 7-12 with a 4.63 ERA (144.0IP, 74ER) in 27 starts...led all Cardinals minor leaguers in starts, tied for second with 119K and ranked sixth in innings pitched.
- Prior to the season, pitched for Italy in the World Baseball Classic vs. Venezuela, tossing 3.0 scoreless innings.

2008
- Made 24 starts for Double-A Springfield, going 3-7 with a 5.23 ERA (115.1IP, 67ER).
- Went 0-3 in four April starts before being placed on the minor league disabled list from 4/29-5/10 with right shoulder inflammation...in five June starts, was 1-0 with a 3.27 ERA (22.0IP, 8ER).
- Following the season, went 3-1 with a 6.17 ERA (23.1IP, 16ER) in eight starts for Peoria in the Arizona Fall League.

2007
- Spent the entire season with Single-A Palm Beach, going 12-8 with a 3.08 ERA (143.1IP, 49ER) in 27 starts.
- Was named to the Florida State League's Mid-Season and Postseason All-Star teams.

2006
- Made his professional debut, combining with short-season Single-A St. College and Single-A Quad Cities to go 4-5 with a 3.31 ERA (65.1IP, 24ER) in 14 starts.

PERSONAL
- Full name is Adam Robert Ottavino...is married to Brette...the couple has two daughters, Bradley and Oakley.
- Is the first player in franchise history to wear No. 0...is the first player to wear a single-digit uniform number since Derek Jeter's retirement in 2014.
- Grew up a Yankees fan in Park Slope, Brooklyn...played baseball in the 78th Precinct Youth Council Little League and graduated from the Berkeley Carroll High School in Brooklyn in 2003...was in attendance at Yankee Stadium for David Wells' perfect game in 1998.
- Attended Northeastern University...was the second-highest Major League draft pick in Northeastern history behind Carlos Peña (10th overall by Texas in 1998).
- Is an avid photographer and documented his "Tommy John" surgery rehab for *The Players' Tribune*.
- His mother, Eve, is an elementary school teacher at P.S. 39 in Brooklyn...his father, John, is an actor who has appeared on Broadway and in movies and television shows, including 17 episodes of *Law & Order* and *Law & Order: SVU*...his father also coached Adam's baseball teams while he was growing up and now serves as an umpire for youth and high school games throughout New York City...more than 100 years ago, his paternal great grandfather, Adamo Ottavino, founded the A. Ottavino Corporation, a stone and granite company that has restored several buildings in Manhattan.

Ottavino's Career Pitching Record

Year	Club	W	L	ERA	G	GS	CG	SHO	SV	IP	H	R	ER	HR	HP	BB	SO	WP	BK
2006	State College	2	2	3.14	6	6	0	0	0	28.2	23	12	10	1	1	13	26	0	0
	Quad Cities	2	3	3.44	8	8	0	0	0	36.2	28	21	14	3	4	19	38	3	0
2007	Palm Beach	12	8	3.08	27	27	1	0	0	143.1	130	63	49	10	8	63	128	6	0
2008	Springfield	3	7	5.23	24	24	1	0	0	115.1	133	75	67	16	10	52	96	6	0
2009	Memphis	7	12	4.63	27	27	0	0	0	144.0	140	80	74	12	10	82	119	13	1
2010	Memphis	5	3	3.97	9	9	0	0	0	47.2	43	23	21	5	3	12	43	3	0
	ST. LOUIS - a	0	2	8.46	5	3	0	0	0	22.1	37	21	21	5	0	9	12	1	0
2011	Memphis	7	8	4.85	26	25	0	0	0	141.0	154	85	76	14	9	71	120	8	1
2012	Colorado Springs	0	0	3.20	13	0	0	0	0	19.2	22	8	7	2	0	7	25	1	0
	COLORADO - b	5	1	4.56	53	0	0	0	0	79.0	76	42	40	9	1	34	81	8	0
2013	COLORADO	1	3	2.64	51	0	0	0	0	78.1	73	27	23	5	2	31	78	9	1
2014	COLORADO	1	4	3.60	75	0	0	0	1	65.0	67	26	26	6	4	16	70	4	0
2015	COLORADO - c	1	0	0.00	10	0	0	0	3	10.1	3	0	0	0	1	2	13	0	0
2016	Modesto	0	0	6.75	4	0	0	0	0	2.2	6	2	2	0	0	2	6	2	0
	Albuquerque	0	1	4.76	6	0	0	0	0	5.2	2	3	3	1	0	3	6	0	0
	COLORADO - d	1	3	2.67	34	0	0	0	7	27.0	28	9	8	3	2	7	35	4	0
2017	COLORADO - e	2	3	5.06	63	0	0	0	0	53.1	48	30	30	8	4	39	63	8	0
2018	COLORADO - f	6	4	2.43	75	0	0	0	6	77.2	41	25	21	5	6	36	112	7	0
2019	YANKEES	6	5	1.90	73	0	0	0	2	66.1	47	17	14	5	2	40	88	3	1
Minor League Totals		**38**	**44**	**4.25**	**150**	**126**	**2**	**0**	**1**	**684.2**	**681**	**372**	**323**	**64**	**45**	**324**	**607**	**42**	**2**
AL Totals		**6**	**5**	**1.90**	**73**	**0**	**0**	**0**	**2**	**66.1**	**47**	**17**	**14**	**5**	**2**	**40**	**88**	**3**	**1**
NL Totals		**17**	**20**	**3.68**	**366**	**3**	**0**	**0**	**17**	**413.0**	**363**	**180**	**169**	**41**	**20**	**174**	**464**	**41**	**1**
Major League Totals		**23**	**25**	**3.44**	**439**	**3**	**0**	**0**	**19**	**479.1**	**410**	**197**	**183**	**46**	**22**	**214**	**552**	**44**	**2**

Selected by Tampa Bay in the 30th round of the 2003 First-Year Player Draft (did not sign).
Selected by St. Louis in the first round (30th overall) of the 2006 First-Year Player Draft.

a – Placed on the 15-day disabled list on July 7, 2010 (retroactive to July 4, 2010) with a right shoulder strain…transferred to the 60-day disabled list on August 16 and reinstated on September 29, 2010.
b – Claimed off waivers by Colorado on April 3, 2012.
c – Placed on the 15-day disabled list with right triceps inflammation on April 27, 2015 (retroactive to April 26, 2015)…transferred to the 60-day disabled list from May 14 through the end of the season.
d – Placed on the 60-day disabled from February 18, 2016 through July 5, 2016 recovering from "Tommy John surgery."
e – Placed on the 10-day disabled list from May 30 - June 9, 2017 with right shoulder inflammation.
f – Placed on the 10-day disabled list from May 28 - June 14, 2018 with a left oblique strain.

Ottavino's Postseason Record

Year	Club vs. Opp.	W	L	ERA	G	GS	CG	SHO	SV	IP	H	R	ER	HR	HP	BB	SO	WP	BK
2018	COL vs. CHC (WC)	0	0	9.00	1	0	0	0	0	1.0	2	1	1	0	0	1	2	1	0
	COL vs. MIL (DS)	0	1	3.38	2	0	0	0	0	2.2	1	1	1	0	0	2	1	1	0
2019	NYY vs. MIN (DS)	0	0	0.00	3	0	0	0	0	1.0	1	0	0	0	0	2	1	0	0
	NYY vs. HOU (CS)	0	0	11.57	5	0	0	0	0	2.1	6	4	3	1	0	1	3	1	0
Wild Card Totals		0	0	9.00	1	0	0	0	0	1.0	2	1	1	0	0	1	2	1	0
Division Series Totals		0	1	2.45	5	0	0	0	0	3.2	2	1	1	0	0	4	2	1	0
LCS Totals		0	0	11.57	5	0	0	0	0	2.1	6	4	3	1	0	1	3	1	0
POSTSEASON TOTALS		0	1	6.43	11	0	0	0	0	7.0	10	6	5	1	0	6	7	3	0

Ottavino's World Baseball Classic Record

Year	Country, Site	W	L	ERA	G	GS	CG	SHO	SV	IP	H	R	ER	HR	HP	BB	SO	WP	BK
2009	Italy, Toronto	0	0	0.00	1	1	0	0	0	3.0	1	0	0	0	0	1	3	0	0
WBC Totals		0	0	0.00	1	1	0	0	0	3.0	1	0	0	0	0	1	3	0	0

Ottavino's Regular Season Batting Record

Year	Team	AVG	G	AB	R	H	2B	3B	HR	RBI	SH	SF	HP	BB	SO	SB	CS
2019	NYY									Did Not Bat							
Major League Totals		.083	439	24	1	2	0	0	0	3	0	0	1	17	0	0

Ottavino's Career Fielding Record

Position	PCT	G	PO	A	E	TC	DP
Pitcher	.938	439	37	39	5	81	2

Ottavino's Career Bests and Streaks

COMPLETE GAMES: None. **LOW-HIT COMPLETE GAME:** N/A. **IP (START):** 5.2, on 5/29/10 at CHC. **IP (RELIEF):** 4.1, on 6/27/10 at KC. **HITS:** 9 - 3 times (last on 7/3/10 vs. MIL). **RUNS:** 7, on 9/16/12 at SD. **WALKS:** 6, 5/29/10 at CHC. **STRIKEOUTS:** 5 - 2 times (last on 6/28/12 vs. WAS). **HOME RUNS:** 3, 6/12/10 at ARI. **WINNING STREAK:** 4g, 8/24/17-4/15/18. **LOSING STREAK:** 5g, 9/9/13-8/15/14. **SCORELESS STREAK (IP):** 31.1, 9/7/14-8/27/16.

Pitcher of the Month: None **Pitcher of the Week:** None **Rookie of the Month:** None

Core Four

According to *Elias*, Hall of Famers Derek Jeter and Mariano Rivera, alongside Jorge Posada became the first trio of teammates in MLB, NBA, NFL and NHL history to appear in at least one game together in each of 17 consecutive seasons from 1995-2011. The second-longest trios in Yankees franchise history played 13 years together (Bill Dickey, Lefty Gomez and Red Ruffing from 1930-42; and Whitey Ford, Elston Howard and Mickey Mantle from 1955-67).

Jeter and Posada appeared in 1,693 regular season games together for the Yankees, surpassing Lou Gehrig and Tony Lazzeri (1,659 games) for the most games played together by any pair of teammates in franchise history.

Elias also notes that, in 2013, Rivera and Jeter each played in their 19th season with the Yankees, becoming the first pair of players to be teammates in 19 or more consecutive seasons since Alan Trammell and Lou Whitaker with Detroit, who were also together 19 straight seasons from 1977-95.

The first game in which Derek Jeter, Jorge Posada and Mariano Rivera appeared together was Sept. 28, 1996 at Fenway Park. Jeter started and went 0-for-4. Andy Pettitte also appeared in his first career game with the trio that day, starting and going 2.0IP. Rivera allowed 1ER in 1.0IP. Posada also pinch-hit in the contest, striking out. The Yankees won, 4-2, and the losing pitcher was Roger Clemens.

JAMES PAXTON • LHP

65

HT: 6-4 • **WT:** 227 • **BATS:** L • **THROWS:** L
BIRTHDATE: 11/6/88 • **OPENING DAY AGE:** 31
BIRTHPLACE: Ladner, B.C., Canada
RESIDES: Eau Claire, Wisc.
COLLEGE: University of Kentucky
M.L. SERVICE: 5 years, 151 days

STATUS
▶ Was acquired by the Yankees from the Seattle Mariners in exchange for LHP Justus Sheffield, RHP Erik Swanson and OF Dom Thompson-Williams on November 19, 2018.

CAREER NOTES
▶ Has pitched seven Major League seasons (2013-18 with Seattle, 2019 with the Yankees), going 56-32 with a 3.50 ERA (733.0IP, 661H, 315R/285ER, 223BB, 803K, 77HR) in 131 starts...has recorded a sub-4.00 ERA in every season of his career.
▶ His 11.07 K/9.0IP ratio (550K/447.0IP) since 2017 ranks sixth among pitchers with at least 300.0IP in that span (Chris Sale-13.21, Max Scherzer-12.29, Robbie Ray-12.09, Gerrit Cole-11.67 and Justin Verlander-11.32).
▶ Has recorded 13 of his 16 career games with double-digit strikeouts in the last two seasons (eight in 2018 with Seattle, five in 2019 with the Yankees), tied for seventh-most in the Majors.
▶ Finished his Mariners tenure in 2018 in 10th place on the franchise's all-time strikeouts list (617).
▶ Has made five career Opening Day rosters (2014-15 and '17-18 w/ Seattle, 2019 w/ the Yankees).
▶ Was the eighth Canadian-born pitcher to appear in a game for the Yankees, following LHP Jeff Francis (2014), RHP Chris Leroux (2014), RHP Paul Quantrill (2004-05), RHP Dave Pagan (1973-76), RHP Ralph Buxton (1949), RHP Russ Ford (1909-13) and Bill Hogg (1905-08).
▶ Is 1-0 with a 3.46 ERA (13.0IP, 13H, 5ER, 7BB, 20K, 2HR) in three postseason starts (all in 2019 with the Yankees)...is the third pitcher in Yankees history to record at least 20K in his first three career postseason starts, joining Red Ruffing (22K from 1932-36) and Monte Pearson (20K from 1936-38)...is the all-time postseason strikeout leader among Canadian pitchers (next-most: John Axford-18K)...his 9K in 2019 ALCS Game 5 vs. Houston were the most by a Canadian pitcher in a postseason game.

CAREER HIGHLIGHTS
No-Hitter
▶ May 8, 2018 at Toronto

2019
▶ In his first season with the Yankees, went 15-6 with a 3.82 ERA (150.2IP, 138H, 71R/64ER, 55BB, 186K, 23HR) in a career-high 29 starts...opponents hit .242 (138-for-570, 23HR); LH .266 (38-for-143, 2HR); RH .234 (100-for-427, 21HR)...had a 3.86 FIP and 3.5 WAR (FanGraphs)...set career highs in wins and starts...tied for eighth in the AL in wins.
▶ His 11.11 K/9.0IP ratio ranked seventh in the AL (min. 125.0IP)...was the highest single-season K/9.0IP in Yankees history (min. 125.0IP), surpassing Luis Severino (10.71 in 2017).
▶ Was one of five Yankees pitchers (sixth time) to record at least 12K three times in a season, joining Al Downing (4 in 1963, 3 in 1967), Masahiro Tanaka (3 in 2017), Mike Mussina (3 in 2001) and David Cone (3 in 1997)...tied for fourth-most in the Majors in 2019 (Gerrit Cole-9, Chris Sale-6, Justin Verlander-6)...was the second Yankee to record at least 11K five times in a season (David Cone 7 in 1998)...tied for fifth-most in the Majors in 2019.
▶ In 4/16 win vs. Boston, recorded 12K and allowed just 2H over 8.0 shutout innings (1BB, 1HP)...was the second-highest strikeout total of his career (16K on 5/2/18 vs. Oakland w/ Seattle), a feat he matched two more times in 2019...was the first Yankee to throw at least 8.0 scoreless innings and record at least 12K since Mike Mussina tossed a two-hit shutout with 12K on 9/24/02 vs. Tampa Bay.
▶ Also had 12K over 6.0 shutout innings (3H, 1BB, 1WP) in his next start on 4/21 vs. Kansas City, becoming the second pitcher in Yankees history to record back-to-back games with at least 12K (also David Cone, 6/7/98 vs. Florida-14K, 6/14/98 vs. Cleveland-12K)...was the first Yankee ever (and the 11th pitcher all-time) to strike out at least 12 batters and allow zero runs in consecutive appearances.
▶ Made five April starts, going 3-1 with a 3.72 ERA (29.0IP, 12ER) and 46K...tied for second in the Majors in strikeouts (Gerrit Cole-55K in 6GS, Trevor Bauer-46K in 6GS)...was also tied for the second-highest April strikeout total in Yankees history (David Cone-49K in April 1997, Masahiro Tanaka-46K in April 2014).
▶ Was on the 10-day I.L. with left knee inflammation from 5/4-29...left his start on 5/3 vs. Minnesota after 3.0IP with left knee soreness.
▶ On 7/7 at Tampa Bay (6.0IP, 7H, 2ER, 0BB, 11K), became the third pitcher in Yankees history to take a loss despite registering 11K and 0BB (Masahiro Tanaka-13K on 5/26/17 vs. Oakland; Roger Clemens-13K on 5/28/00 vs. Boston).

- Won a career-best 10 consecutive starts from 8/2-9/21, posting a 2.25 ERA (60.0IP, 35H, 16R/15ER, 20BB, 68K, 5HR) during the streak...was the first Major League pitcher to win at least 10 consecutive starts in one season since Detroit's Justin Verlander won 12 straight from 7/21-9/18/11...was the sixth Yankees pitcher (seventh occurrence) to win 10 consecutive starts, joining Jack Chesbro (14 in 1904), Russ Ford (12 in 1910), Ron Guidry (11 in 1979, 10 in 1978), Whitey Ford (11 in 1961) and Lefty Gomez (10 in 1932).
- Was presented with his 2018 Tip O'Neill Award by the Canadian Baseball Hall of Fame & Museum in a pregame ceremony on 8/9 in Toronto.
- Recorded 29 swings-and-misses in 8/23 win at Los Angeles-NL (6.2IP, 5H, 2ER, 0BB, 11K)...were

PAXTON'S 2019 PITCHING LINES

Date/Opp	Score	W/L	IP	H	R	ER	HR	BB	K	NP/S	ERA	Left game
3/30 vs. BAL	3-5	L	5.2	4	2	1	0	1	5	82/57	1.59	Trailing 2-1
4/4 at BAL*	8-4	W	5.1	8	4	4	1	2	9	99/63	4.09	Leading 5-4
4/10 at HOU*	6-8	L	4.0	8	5	5	2	3	5	95/60	6.00	Trailing 4-2
4/16 vs. BOS*	8-0	W	**8.0**	2	0	0	0	1	12	110/78	3.91	Leading 8-0
4/21 vs. KC	7-6 (10)	ND	6.0	3	0	0	0	1	12	104/67	3.10	Leading 5-0
4/26 at SF*	7-3	W	5.2	5	3	3	0	2	8	106/70	3.38	Leading 5-3
5/3 vs. MIN*	6-3	ND	3.0	2	1	0	0	3	1	64/32	3.11	Leading 2-1
5/29 vs. SD*	7-0	ND	4.0	0	0	0	0	2	7	66/40	2.81	Leading 3-0
6/5 at TOR*	7-11	ND	4.2	4	3	3	1	3	4	83/55	3.11	Tied 4-4
6/11 vs. NYM (G2)	4-10	L	2.2	7	6	6	1	2	1	63/39	4.04	Trailing 6-0
6/16 at CWS	10-3	W	6.0	8	2	2	1	1	7	108/73	3.93	Leading 9-2
6/21 vs. HOU	4-1	W	5.0	5	1	1	0	3	7	100/60	3.75	Leading 4-1
6/26 vs. TOR	8-7	ND	4.1	8	6	6	3	4	3	91/55	4.34	Trailing 6-5
7/2 at NYM	2-4	ND	6.0	8	1	1	1	2	3	103/61	4.09	Leading 2-1
7/7 at TB*	1-2	L	6.0	7	2	2	0	0	11	99/68	4.01	Trailing 2-1
7/15 vs. TB	4-5	ND	6.0	7	2	2	2	2	7	107/67	3.94	Trailing 2-1
7/21 vs. COL	4-8	L	3.1	5	7	4	1	3	6	77/47	4.20	Trailing 5-1
7/26 at MIN	5-10	L	4.0	**9**	**7**	**7**	**4**	0	9	99/67	4.72	Trailing 7-0
8/2 vs. BOS	4-2	W	6.0	2	2	2	1	3	6	100/60	4.61	Leading 4-2
8/7 at BAL	14-2	W	6.2	5	1	1	1	0	7	108/75	4.40	Leading 11-1
8/12 vs. BAL (G1)	8-5	W	6.0	5	3	3	2	2	7	107/78	4.40	Leading 7-3
8/17 vs. CLE	6-5	W	5.0	6	4	4	0	3	4	88/53	4.53	Leading 5-4
8/23 at LAD*	10-2	W	6.2	5	2	2	0	0	11	109/71	4.43	Leading 8-1
8/28 at SEA	7-3	W	5.0	1	2	2	1	**5**	4	86/45	4.39	Leading 6-2
9/3 vs. TEX*	10-1	W	7.0	1	0	0	0	1	12	95/66	4.16	Leading 10-0
9/9 at BOS	5-0	W	6.2	4	0	0	0	3	7	107/70	3.96	Leading 4-0
9/14 at TOR*	13-3	W	5.0	3	1	1	0	2	3	101/62	3.88	Leading 9-1
9/21 at TOR*	7-2	W	6.0	3	1	0	0	0	7	87/63	3.73	Leading 6-1
9/27 at TEX*	14-7	ND	1.0	3	2	2	1	0	1	21/14	3.82	Tied 2-2
Totals (29GS)		**15-6**	**150.2**	**138**	**71**	**64**	**23**	**55**	**186**		**3.82**	

*start came after a team loss / **Bold** - season high

the most by a Yankee in the Statcast era (since 2015) and tied for the most in a game in 2019, also Houston's Gerrit Cole (6/7 vs. Baltimore) and Houston's Justin Verlander (6/12 vs. Milwaukee).
- Went 6-0 in August, one of just two Yankees to go 6-0 or better in August since 1979 (also Andy Pettitte, 6-0 in 6GS in August 2007).
- Allowed 1H in consecutive starts on 8/28 at Seattle (5.0IP) and 9/3 vs. Texas (7.0IP)...became the fourth pitcher in Yankees history to complete 5.0IP and allow 1H-or-fewer in consecutive starts within a season, joining Don Larsen (9/20 & 9/28/58), Whitey Ford (9/2 and 9/7/55) and Vic Raschi (9/9 and 9/14/51).
- On 9/3 vs. Texas, struck out 12 and allowed 1H over 7.0 scoreless innings (1BB) to win his seventh consecutive start...the only hit was a two-out single by Isiah Kiner-Falefa in the fifth inning...recorded the third start in Yankees history with at least 12K and 1H-or-fewer, joining Mike Mussina (9.0IP, 1H, 0R, 0BB, 13K) on 9/2/01 at Boston and CC Sabathia (7.0IP, 1H, 1ER, 3BB, 14K) on 7/26/11 vs. Seattle.
- In five September starts, went 4-0 with a 1.05 ERA (25.2IP, 14H, 4R/3ER, 6BB, 30K, 1HR)...was the lowest September ERA in the AL (min. 25.0IP) and second-lowest in the Majors to St. Louis' Jack Flaherty (0.82)...was the lowest September ERA by a Yankee over a full month since Ron Guidry in 1978 (0.96).
- Had a season-long 18.2-inning scoreless streak from 8/28-9/14.
- Left his final start of the season after 1.0IP on 9/27 at Texas with left glute tightness...an MRI revealed nerve irritation.
- In five spring training starts, went 3-0 with a 2.08 ERA (17.1IP, 4ER).
- Made his postseason debut, going 1-0 with a 3.46 ERA (13.0IP, 13H, 5ER, 7BB, 20K, 2HR) in three starts...is the third pitcher in Yankees history to record at least 20K in his first three career postseason starts, joining Red Ruffing (22K from 1932-36) and Monte Pearson (20K from 1936-38).
- Made his first postseason start in ALDS Game 1 vs. Minnesota (ND, 4.2IP, 5H, 3ER, 1BB, 8K, 2HR)...was the fourth pitcher in Yankees history to record at least 8K in his postseason debut, joining Dave Righetti (10K in 1981 ALDS G2), Red Ruffing (10K in 1932 World Series G1) and Lefty Gomez (8K in 1932 World Series G2)...according to the YES Network, was the seventh Yankees pitcher to start the club's first postseason game in his first season with the club, joining CC Sabathia (2009 ALDS), David Cone (1995 ALDS), Jim Beattie (1978 ALCS), Don Gullett (1977 ALCS), Spec Shea (1947 World Series) and Bullet Joe Bush (1922 World Series).
- Was 1-0 with a 2.16 ERA (8.1IP, 8H, 2ER, 6BB, 12K) in two ALCS starts vs. Houston...went just 2.1IP (ND, 4H, 1ER, 2BB, 3K) in ALCS Game 2 at Houston...earned his first career postseason win in ALCS Game 5 vs. Houston (6.0IP, 4H, 1ER, 4BB, 9K, 1WP)...threw 112 pitches, the most by any Yankees pitcher in 2019...was the first Yankee with at least 9K and 1R-or-fewer in a postseason game since Sabathia (9.0IP, 4H, 1ER, 2BB, 9K) in 2012 ALDS Game 5 vs. Baltimore, and only the fourth Yankee ever to do it in an elimination game.

2018

- Made 28 starts in his final season with Seattle, going 11-6 with 2CG and a 3.76 ERA (160.1IP, 134H, 67ER, 42BB, 208K, 23HR)…held opponents to a .224 BA (134-for-598); LH .330 (34-for-103), RH .202 (100-for-495)…set career highs in innings pitched and strikeouts…had a 3.24 FIP (FanGraphs)…ranked 10th among AL pitchers with 3.8 WAR (FanGraphs).
- Ranked ninth in the AL in strikeouts…was the sixth Mariners pitcher to reach 200K in a season…his 42BB were the fewest by a Mariners pitcher in a 200-strikeout season…was the seventh Canadian-born pitcher to record a 200-strikeout season.
- Logged eight double-digit-strikeout efforts, tied for sixth in the Majors (tied for fourth in the AL)…was the third Mariners pitcher to have eight such outings in one season (Randy Johnson-6x, Mark Langston-2x).
- Among pitchers with 150.0IP, his 11.68 K/9.0IP ratio and 32.2% strikeout rate ranked fifth in the Majors (fourth in the AL), and 4.95 K/BB ratio was 10th in the Majors (fifth in the AL)…his 1.10 WHIP was eighth-lowest in the AL among that group.
- Limited right-handed batters to a .202 BA, third-lowest among Major League left-handers (min. 500BF) behind Boston's Chris Sale (.183) and Tampa Bay's Blake Snell (.188).
- On 5/2 vs. Oakland, recorded a career-high 16K over 7.0 shutout innings (5H, 1BB)…was tied for the highest strikeout total in the Majors in 2018 (also Houston's Gerrit Cole on 5/4 at Arizona)…marked the most strikeouts by a Seattle pitcher since Randy Johnson had 19K on 8/8/97 vs. Chicago-AL…joined Johnson (twice) as the second Mariner to record at least 16K in a scoreless outing of 7.0IP-or-longer…had at least 2K in all seven frames, the first Mariners pitcher to record multiple strikeouts in the first seven innings of a game.
- On 5/8 at Toronto, threw the sixth no-hitter in Mariners history (9.0IP, 3BB, 7K) in Seattle's 5-0 win…was the fifth by an individual pitcher, joining Hisashi Iwakuma, Félix Hernández (perfect game), Chris Bosio and Randy Johnson…completed the feat in 99 pitches, becoming the 12th pitcher to throw a no-hitter in fewer than 100 pitches since 1988 (the first year that pitch counts are complete)…marked his first career complete game.
- Was the second Canadian-born pitcher to throw a no-hitter, also Philadelphia-AL's Dick Fowler on 9/9/45 (G2) vs. St. Louis-AL…marked the sixth no-hitter to take place in Canada.
- According to STATS, Inc., was the first AL pitcher to record at least 16K and throw a no-hitter in the same season since Texas's Nolan Ryan accomplished both in the same game on 5/1/91 vs. Toronto.
- Was named AL co-"Player of the Week" for 5/7-13 with Cleveland's Francisco Lindor…went 1-0 with a 1.80 ERA (15.0IP, 6H, 3ER, 3BB, 11K, 1HR) in two starts, including his no-hitter on 5/8 at Toronto…marked his third career weekly award.
- In 5/19 win vs. Detroit, tossed his second career complete game (9.0IP, 3H, 2ER, 1BB, 8K, 1HR).
- Was placed on the 10-day disabled list on 7/13 with lower back inflammation…left 7/12 start at Los Angeles-AL with lower back stiffness…was reinstated on 7/30.
- Was placed on the 10-day disabled list on 8/15 with a left forearm contusion…left 8/14 start at Oakland after being struck on the left forearm by a line drive hit by Jed Lowrie…was reinstated on 9/1.
- Made his 100th career start in 9/7 loss vs. the Yankees (6.0IP, 4ER).
- Missed two starts from 9/12-23 while recovering from pneumonia.
- Was acquired by the Yankees in a four-player trade on 11/19/18.

2017

- Went 12-5 with a 2.98 ERA (136.0IP, 113H, 47R/45ER, 37BB, 156K, 9HR) in 24 starts with Seattle…held opponents to a .223 BA (113-for-506); LH .198 (17-for-86), RH .229 (96-for-420)…had a 2.61 FIP (FanGraphs)…made his third career Opening Day roster…his 4.6 WAR (FanGraphs) ranked 10th among Major League pitchers…tied for the AL lead with 15 wild pitches.
- Was named Mariners "Pitcher of the Year" by the Seattle chapter of the BBWAA.
- Recorded a career-long 23.0-inning scoreless streak to open the season (4/5-20), the longest season-opening scoreless streak in Mariners history…reliever Mark Lowe (17.2IP in 2006) previously held the mark for all Seattle pitchers, while Félix Hernández (17.0IP in 2007) had the record for starters…allowed his first 3R of the season in the third inning on 4/20 at Oakland (Adam Rosales RBI single, run-scoring error, Ryon Healy RBI double).
- Began the season with three consecutive scoreless starts: 4/5 at Houston (6.0IP), 4/10 vs. Houston (7.0IP) and 4/15 vs. Texas (8.0IP)…became the 10th pitcher in the Modern Era (since 1900) to start a season with three scoreless starts of at least 6.0IP, joining Detroit's Jordan Zimmermann (2016), St. Louis' Woody Williams (2003), Philadelphia's Tommy Greene (1991), Cleveland's Luis Tiant (1966), St. Louis' Harry Brecheen (1948), the Yankees' George Mogridge (1916), the Yankees' Ray Caldwell (1914), Pittsburgh's Lefty Leifield (1907) and Philadelphia's George McQuillan (1907).
- Was placed on the 10-day disabled list on 5/5 (retroactive to 5/3) with a left forearm strain…made one rehab start for Double-A Arkansas at Frisco on 5/26 (4.0IP, 5H, 2ER, 0BB, 5K, 1HR)…was reinstated on 5/31.
- Recorded a 21.0-inning scoreless streak from 7/19-8/4…was the third pitcher in Mariners history to compile multiple scoreless streaks of at least 20.0IP in the same season (Hisashi Iwakuma-2013, Freddy García-2001).
- Won seven consecutive starts from 7/2-8/4, tying Jamie Moyer (5/6-6/8/03) and Scott Bankhead (6/18-7/20/89) for the longest streak in Mariners history…was tied for the AL's longest streak of winning starts in 2017 (also Texas's Martín Perez and Kansas City's Jason Vargas)…during the streak, went 7-0 with a 1.59 ERA (45.1IP, 29H, 8ER, 7BB, 53K, 0HR)…completed 6.0IP and allowed 2R-or-fewer in all seven starts, tied for the fourth-longest such streak in Mariners history.

- Was named AL "Pitcher of the Month" for July after going 6-0 with a 1.37 ERA (39.1IP, 25H, 6ER, 6BB, 46K, 0HR) in six starts…marked his first career monthly award…was the first pitcher in Mariners history to tally six wins in a calendar month…led Major League pitchers in wins during the month and ranked fourth in ERA and tied for fourth in strikeouts.
- In 7/24 win at Boston, collected his third career double-digit-strikeout game (7.0IP, 4H, 0R, 0BB, 10K).
- Left his 8/10 start vs. Los Angeles-AL with a left arm injury…was placed on the 10-day disabled list on 8/11 with a left pectoral muscle strain…was reinstated on 9/15.

2016
- Went 6-7 with a 3.79 ERA (121.0IP, 134H, 62R/51ER, 24BB, 117K, 9HR) in 20 starts for Seattle…held opponents to a .279 BA (134-for-480), LH .284 (21-for-74), RH .278 (113-for-406)…recorded a 3.5 WAR and 2.80 FIP (FanGraphs).
- Began the season with Triple-A Tacoma and went 4-3 with a 3.97 ERA (47.2IP, 21ER) in 10 starts…including his rehab start on 8/20, was 4-3 with a 3.73 ERA (50.2IP, 21ER) in 11 total starts with the Rainiers.
- Was recalled by Seattle on 6/1 and made his Mariners season debut later that day at San Diego (L, 3.2IP, 8R/3ER).
- Recorded his second career double-digit-strikeout game on 6/6 vs. Cleveland (L, 6.0IP, 5H, 3R/1ER, 1BB, 10K, 1HR).
- Was placed on the 15-day D.L. on 8/16 (retroactive to 8/8) with a left elbow contusion…made one rehab start with Tacoma on 8/20 vs. Las Vegas (3.0IP, 2H, 0R, 1BB, 3K)…was reinstated on 8/25.
- In 9/6 loss vs. Texas, became the fourth pitcher in Mariners history record four strikeouts in one inning, fanning Delino DeShields, Ian Desmond (reached on WP), Jonathan Lucroy and Elvis Andrus…also allowed three singles in the frame…joined Félix Hernández (2010), Kaz Sasaki (2003) and Matt Young (1990).

2015
- Went 3-4 with a 3.90 ERA (67.0IP, 67H, 34R/29ER, 29BB, 56K, 8HR) in 13 starts with Seattle…made his second straight Opening Day roster.
- Was placed on the 15-day disabled list on 5/29 with a tendon strain in his left middle finger…made three rehab starts with Triple-A Tacoma and went 0-1 with an 8.10 ERA (6.2IP, 6ER)…was reinstated on 9/13.
- Left his final start on 9/24 at Kansas City with a torn fingernail on his left hand.
- Following the season, pitched for the Peoria Javelinas of the Arizona Fall League, going 2-4 with a 4.60 ERA (29.1IP, 15ER) in seven starts.

2014
- Made 13 starts for Seattle, going 6-4 with a 3.04 ERA (74.0IP, 60H, 29R/25ER, 29BB, 59K, 3HR)…made his first career Opening Day roster.
- Permitted just 3HR, posting a 0.36 HR/9.0IP ratio…did not allow a HR over his final 10 starts (57.2IP), tied for the third-longest such streak in Mariners history.
- In his first start of the season on 4/2 at Los Angeles-AL, threw 7.0 shutout innings (2H, 2BB, 9K) in an 8-2 win…was his fifth career Major League game…became the fifth pitcher in Major League history to toss at least 6.0 shutout frames in his first five games, and the first since Chicago-AL's Cisco Carlos in 1967.
- Was placed on the 15-day disabled list on 4/9 with a left lat strain…was transferred to the 60-day D.L. on 6/9…made four rehab starts, going 0-2 with a 4.85 ERA (13.0IP, 7ER)…started three times at Triple-A Tacoma (0-1, 4.35 ERA, 10.1IP, 5ER) and once at short-season Single-A Everett (0-1, 6.75 ERA, 2.2IP, 2ER)…was reinstated on 8/2…permitted 2ER-or-fewer in each of his first eight starts off the D.L. (8/2-9/12), going 4-2 with a 1.91 ERA (47.0IP, 10ER).
- Suffered his first career loss on 8/20 at Philadelphia (4.0IP, 7H, 4R/1ER, 2BB, 5K) to fall to 6-1 lifetime…his six wins without a loss were the second-most to begin a career by a Mariners pitcher (Eric O'Flaherty, 7-0 in 2006-07), and the most among Seattle starting pitchers…the loss came in his 10th career start, the longest streak of unbeaten starts to begin a career in Mariners history, surpassing Joel Piñeiro (eight from 2000-01).
- Threw a career-high 118 pitches (68 strikes) in 8/26 win vs. Texas (6.2IP, 4H, 0R, 3BB, 4K).
- Did not allow an extra-base hit to 142 consecutive batters from 8/20-9/22, the second Mariners pitcher to record a streak of that length, also Jim Beattie, 157BF in 1982.
- Set career highs by allowing 9R, 8ER and 6BB in 9/22 loss at Toronto (2.2IP, 7H, 1K).

2013
- Made his MLB debut with Seattle, going 3-0 with a 1.50 ERA (24.0IP, 15H, 5R/4ER, 7BB, 21K, 2HR) in four starts.
- Had his contract selected from Triple-A Tacoma on 9/3 and made his Major League debut on 9/7 vs. Tampa Bay, earning a win (6.0IP, 4H, 2R/1ER, 1BB, 3K, 1HR) in a 6-2 victory…became the third Mariners pitcher to complete 6.0IP and allow one-or-zero earned runs in his Major League debut, joining Blake Beavan (7/3/11 vs. San Diego) and Erik Hanson (9/5/88 at Minnesota)…recorded his first career strikeout (Desmond Jennings, third inning).
- Also won his second Major League game, tossing 6.0 scoreless innings (2H, 2BB, 5K) on 9/14 at St. Louis…was the fifth Mariners pitcher to throw at least 6.0 scoreless frames within his first two career games (Doug Fister, Félix Hernández, Clint Nageotte, Erik Hanson).
- In his final start of the season on 9/24 vs. Kansas City, recorded 10K without issuing a walk over 7.0 scoreless innings (4H) in a 4-0 win…became the third pitcher in Major League history to tally double-digit strikeouts with no runs or walks in one of his first four career games; the Mets' Dennis Ribant had 10K in a four-hit shutout in his third game on 8/17/1964 vs. Pittsburgh; the Washington Senators' Doc Ayers recorded 11K in a four-hit shutout in his fourth game on 9/30/1913 vs. Philadelphia-AL.

- Was the first pitcher in Mariners history to toss at least 6.0 scoreless innings multiple times within his first four career games.
- Began the season with Triple-A Tacoma and posted an 8-11 record with 2CG and a 4.45 ERA (145.2IP, 72ER) in 28 games (26 starts)…tied for third in the Pacific Coast League in strikeouts (131) and tied for fourth in starts…was named PCL "Pitcher of the Week" for 6/17-23…was named an MiLB.com Organization All-Star.
- Following the season, was ranked by *Baseball America* as the Mariners' No. 3 prospect and the No. 99 overall prospect in baseball.

2012
- Went 9-4 with a 3.05 ERA (106.1IP, 36ER) in 21 starts with Double-A Jackson.
- Was named Southern League "Pitcher of the Week" for 4/5-15.
- Was named an MiLB.com Organization All-Star.
- Following the season, pitched for the Peoria Javelinas in the Arizona Fall League and went 1-1 with a 5.68 ERA (12.2IP, 8ER) in five starts…was named to the Rising Stars Game.
- Following the season, was ranked by *Baseball America* as the Mariners' No. 4 prospect and the No. 87 overall prospect in baseball.

2011
- Made his professional debut, combining to go 6-3 with a 2.37 ERA (95.0IP, 25ER) in 17 starts between Single-A Clinton and Double-A Jackson…his 131K were tied for second-most among Mariners farmhands, while his 12.41 K/9.0IP ratio was second-highest among all minor league pitchers with at least 90.0IP.
- Was named a Midwest League Mid-Season All-Star at Clinton.
- Was named Southern League "Pitcher of the Week" for 8/1-7 with Jackson.
- Pitched for the World Team in the All-Star Futures Game at Arizona's Chase Field…was named an MiLB.com Organization All-Star.
- Following the season, was ranked by *Baseball America* as the Mariners' No. 3 prospect and the No. 52 overall prospect in baseball.

2010
- Was selected by Toronto in the supplemental round (37th overall) of the 2009 First-Year Player Draft but did not sign…did not return to the University of Kentucky, but instead made four starts for Grand Prairie of the independent American Association, going 1-2 with a 4.08 ERA (17.2IP, 15H, 9R/8ER, 7BB, 18K, 1HR).

PERSONAL
- Full name is James Alston Paxton…is married to Katie.
- Was born in Ladner, B.C., Canada, a suburb of Vancouver located 22 miles from the U.S. border…was the eighth Canadian-born pitcher in Yankees history.
- Was named the winner of the 2018 James Tip O'Neill Award, presented annually by the Canadian Baseball Hall of Fame and Museum to the Canadian player judged to have excelled in individual achievement and team contribution while adhering to baseball's highest ideals.
- Received the 2018 Best of B.C. Award, presented by the Province of British Columbia to the individual or team thought to have best represented B.C., nationally or internationally, in either a professional or amateur sport.
- Pitched three seasons (2007-09) for the University of Kentucky, going 11-5 with 4.91 ERA (148.1IP, 81ER) in 55 games (24 starts) for Wildcats…made the SEC Academic Honor Roll three times as an accounting major.
- Graduated in 2006 from Delta Secondary School (B.C.)…helped Delta win the B.C.'s Best Tournament Championship both as a junior and senior.
- Pitched for Team Canada's bronze medal-winning U-18 squad in the 2006 World Junior Championships in Sancti Spiritus, Cuba.

Paxton's Career Pitching Record

Year	Club	W	L	ERA	G	GS	CG	SHO	SV	IP	H	R	ER	HR	HP	BB	SO	WP	BK
2011	Clinton	3	3	2.73	10	10	0	0	0	56.0	45	21	17	1	1	30	80	6	0
	Jackson	3	0	1.85	7	7	0	0	0	39.0	28	10	8	2	1	13	51	3	1
2012	Jackson	9	4	3.05	21	21	0	0	0	106.1	96	43	36	5	1	54	110	13	1
2013	Tacoma	8	11	4.45	28	26	2	1	0	145.2	158	84	72	10	3	58	131	14	0
	SEATTLE	3	0	1.50	4	4	0	0	0	24.0	15	5	4	2	0	7	21	0	0
2014	SEATTLE - a	6	4	3.04	13	13	0	0	0	74.0	60	29	25	3	1	29	59	7	0
	Tacoma	0	1	4.35	3	3	0	0	0	10.1	13	7	5	2	0	6	14	0	0
	Everett	0	1	6.75	1	1	0	0	0	2.2	2	2	2	1	0	1	2	1	0
2015	SEATTLE - b	3	4	3.90	13	13	0	0	0	67.0	67	34	29	8	0	29	56	5	0
	Tacoma	0	1	8.10	3	3	0	0	0	6.2	12	6	6	0	0	3	4	2	0
2016	Tacoma	4	3	3.73	11	11	0	0	0	50.2	43	24	21	6	0	15	53	4	0
	SEATTLE - c	6	7	3.79	20	20	0	0	0	121.0	134	62	51	9	1	24	117	5	0
2017	SEATTLE - d, e	12	5	2.98	24	24	0	0	0	136.0	113	47	45	9	3	37	156	15	1
	Arkansas	0	0	4.50	1	1	0	0	0	4.0	5	2	2	1	0	0	5	1	0
2018	SEATTLE - f, g, h	11	6	3.76	28	28	2	1	0	160.1	134	67	67	23	1	42	208	5	0
2019	YANKEES - i	15	6	3.82	29	29	0	0	0	150.2	138	71	64	23	2	55	186	7	1
Minor League Totals		27	24	3.61	85	83	2	1	0	421.1	402	199	169	28	6	180	450	44	2
Major League Totals		56	32	3.50	131	131	2	1	0	733.0	661	315	285	77	8	223	803	47	2

Selected by the Toronto Blue Jays in the supplemental round (37th overall) of the 2009 First-Year Player Draft but did not sign.
Selected by the Seattle Mariners in the fourth round of the 2010 First-Year Player Draft.

a - Placed on the 15-day disabled list from April 9 - August 2, 2014 with a left lat strain…transferred to the 60-day disabled list on June 9, 2014.
b - Placed on the 15-day disabled list from May 29 - September 13, 2015 with a tendon strain in his left middle finger.
c - Placed on the 15-day disabled list from August 16 (retroactive to August 8) - August 25, 2016 with a left elbow contusion.
d - Placed on the 10-day disabled list from May 5 (retroactive to May 3) - May 31, 2017 with a left forearm strain.
e - Placed on the 10-day disabled list from August 11 - September 15, 2017 with a left pectoral muscle strain.
f - Placed on the 10-day disabled list from July 13-30, 2018 with lower back inflammation.
g - Placed on the 10-day disabled list from August 15 - September 1, 2018 with a left forearm contusion.
h - Acquired by the Yankees from the Seattle Mariners in exchange for LHP Justus Sheffield, RHP Erik Swanson and OF Dom Thompson-Williams on November 19, 2018.
i - Placed on the 10-day injured list from May 4-29 with left knee inflammation.

Paxton's Postseason Record

Year	Club vs. Opp.	W	L	ERA	G	GS	CG	SHO	SV	IP	H	R	ER	HR	HP	BB	SO	WP	BK
2019	NYY vs. MIN (DS)	0	0	5.79	1	1	0	0	0	4.2	5	3	3	2	0	1	8	0	0
	NYY vs. HOU (CS)	1	0	2.16	2	2	0	0	0	8.1	8	2	2	0	0	6	12	1	0
Division Series Totals		0	0	5.79	1	1	0	0	0	4.2	5	3	3	2	0	1	8	0	0
LCS Totals		1	0	2.16	2	2	0	0	0	8.1	8	2	2	0	0	6	12	1	0
POSTSEASON TOTALS		1	0	3.46	3	3	0	0	0	13.0	13	5	5	2	0	7	20	1	0

Paxton's Regular Season Batting Record

Year	Team	AVG	G	AB	R	H	2B	3B	HR	RBI	SH	SF	HP	BB	SO	SB	CS
2019	NYY	.000	29	5	0	0	0	0	0	1	3	0	0	0	5	0	0
Major League Totals		.000	131	12	1	0	0	0	0	1	4	0	0	2	12	0	0

Paxton's Career Fielding Record

Position	PCT	G	PO	A	E	TC	DP
Pitcher	.908	131	8	51	6	65	2

Paxton's Career Bests and Streaks

COMPLETE GAMES: 2 (last on 5/19/18 vs. DET). **LOW-HIT COMPLETE GAME:** 0, 5/8/18 at TOR. **IP (START):** 9.0 - 2 times (last on 5/19/18 vs. DET). **IP (RELIEF):** N/A. **HITS:** 11, 6/21/19 at DET. **RUNS:** 9, 9/22/14 at TOR. **WALKS:** 6, 9/22/14 at TOR. **STRIKEOUTS:** 16, 5/2/18 vs. OAK. **HOME RUNS:** 4, 7/26/19 at BOS. **WINNING STREAK:** 10g, 8/2/19-present. **LOSING STREAK:** 4g - 2 times (last from 5/28/15-6/6/16). **SCORELESS STREAK (IP):** 23.0, 4/5-20/17.

Pitcher of the Month: July 2017 **Player of the Week:** Three times (last: 5/7-13/18) **Rookie of the Month:** None

GARY SÁNCHEZ • C

#24

HT: 6-2 • **WT:** 230 • **BATS:** R • **THROWS:** R
BIRTHDATE: 12/2/92 • **OPENING DAY AGE:** 27
BIRTHPLACE: Santo Domingo, D.R.
RESIDES: Santo Domingo, D.R.
M.L. SERVICE: 3 years, 86 days

STATUS
- Was signed by the Yankees as a non-drafted free agent on July 2, 2009.

CAREER NOTES
- In 2016, became the fastest player in Major League history to reach 11HR in his career (23G), 18HR (45G) and 19HR (45G)… tied for the fastest to reach 20HR (51G)…has since been matched or surpassed by Philadelphia's Rhys Hoskins (11HR through 18G), Los Angeles-NL's Cody Bellinger (20HR through 51G) and Cincinnati's Aristides Aquino (11HR through 17G; 18HR through 34G)…has been among the fastest in Baseball history to reach most of his career home run totals (in terms of games played).
- Hit career HRs 54-71 in 2018…was tied for most HR through 212G (63HR); had the second-most HRs through 201G (60), 203G (61), and 216G (65); and was tied for second-most HRs through 187G (56), 198G (59) and 206G (62).
- Is the ninth catcher all time with at least three 20HR seasons prior to his age-27 season, joining Johnny Bench (6), Brian McCann (4), Gary Carter (4), Joe Torre (4), Mike Piazza (3), Earl Williams (3), Yogi Berra (3) and Rudy York (3).
- Is one of four catchers all-time with multiple 30HR seasons prior to his age-27 season (Johnny Bench-3, Mike Piazza-2, Rudy York-2).
- Is the sixth catcher in Yankees history with at least three 20HR seasons (2016-17, '19), joining Yogi Berra (10), Jorge Posada (8), Bill Dickey (4), Elston Howard (3) and Brian McCann (3).
- Hit his 30th career home run in his 90th Major League game (6/11/17), all with the Yankees…according to Elias, only two other players hit 30-or-more homers within their first 90 games with the Yankees, but both had previously played for other teams: Roger Maris (his 30th HR with the Yankees came in his 78th game with the team) and Babe Ruth (30th Yankees HR in his 82nd game).
- With 33HR in 2017 and 34HR in 2019, owns two of the five 30HR seasons by a Yankees catcher in franchise history (min. 50.0% of games at C), along with Jorge Posada (2003) and Yogi Berra (1952 and '56).
- Hit his 33rd career HR in his 100th career game, tied with Rudy York and Pete Alonso for the third-most homers through 100G in Major League history (Mark McGwire-37, Cody Bellinger-34).
- His 105 career homers are second-most by a player through 372 career games (Ryan Howard-115).
- Has 14 career multi-HR games, the second-most by any player in Baseball history through 372 career games behind only Ralph Kiner (17)…reached the 10 career multi-HR games on 5/19/18 at Kansas City (in his 216th career game), surpassing Bob Horner (267th game) to become the fastest to reach the mark in Baseball history.
- Had nine multi-HR games through his 200th career game played, most in Baseball history (next: five players with seven multi-HR games each—Aaron Judge, Zeke Bonura, Ryan Braun, Joe DiMaggio and Mark McGwire).
- His 6HR in 27 career playoff games are third-most by a Yankees catcher in the postseason behind Jorge Posada (11) and Yogi Berra (10).
- His 262RBI through his first 372 career games are 10th-most in franchise history.
- Of his 343 career hits, 167 have gone for extra bases (61 doubles, 1 triple, 105HR)…of his 60H in 2016, 32 went for extra-bases…according to Elias, became the first player to debut with the Yankees and have at least 32 of the first 60H of his career go for extra bases since Gerald Williams from 1992-95 (also 32-of-60)…is tied with teammate Aaron Judge for the fifth-most XBH by a Yankee through 372 career games.
- Collected 20XBH within his first 27 career games, becoming the third Major League player since 1908 to accomplish the feat (also Joe DiMaggio-24 and Mandy Brooks-23)…Toronto's Bo Bichette (22G) joined the group in 2019…according to Elias, was the first Yankee to have at least 20 of his first 37 career hits go for extra bases since Frank Fernández from 1967-69 (21-of-37).
- In 71 career games in August, has hit .316/.388/.706 (86-for-272) with 51R, 13 doubles, 31HR and 60RBI.
- Has made three career Opening Day rosters (2017-19).

CAREER HIGHLIGHTS

AL All-Star Team
- 2017, 2019

AL Silver Slugger
- 2017

2019
- Hit .232 (92-for-396) with 62R, 12 doubles, 34HR, 1 triple, 77RBI and 40BB in 106 games with the Yankees…led all Major League catchers in homers…surpassed his own 2017 club record (33) for homers in a season by a Yankees catcher (min. 50.0% of games at C).
- Became the first catcher with multiple 30HR seasons (33HR in 2017) since Atlanta's Javy Lopez in 1998 (34HR) and 2003 (43HR)…is one of four catchers all-time with multiple 30HR seasons prior to his age-27 season (Johnny Bench-3, Mike Piazza-2, Rudy York-2).

- Hit a career-high 19HR with exit velocities of at least 110.0 mph (Statcast), tied with the Mets' Pete Alonso for most in the Majors.
- Hit .364 (20-for-55) with 10HR and 22RBI in 14 games against the Orioles…homered in five straight games against Baltimore from 4/7-5/22 (7HR), the ninth player in Orioles/Browns history to do so in a single season…hit 7HR in 7G at Camden Yards…according to STATS, LLC, became the fourth Yankee to hit at least 6HR in his first 5G in a ballpark in one season, joining Lou Gehrig (7HR at League Park in 1930), Babe Ruth (6HR at Shibe Park in 1930) and Tony Lazzeri (6HR at Shibe Park in 1936)…is the first visiting player to record at least 4RBI in three consecutive games (4/7-5/21) against the Baltimore Orioles franchise since RBI became an official stat in 1920…according to the YES Network, with Gleyber Torres hitting 13HR vs. the O's, became the 10th set of teammates in Major League history (fifth set of Yankees) to hit at least 9HR against the same team in a single season and the first since San Francisco's Barry Bonds and Rich Aurilia (9HR each) in 2001 vs. Arizona…the last set of Yankees to do so was Mickey Mantle (11HR) and Roger Maris (9HR) in 1961 vs. the Washington Senators.
- Hit 24HR prior to the All-Star break, the most ever by a Yankees catcher before the break (surpassed Yogi Berra-18HR in 1956)…was the first Major League catcher to hit 24HR prior to the break since the Rangers' Iván Rodríguez (26) and Mets' Mike Piazza (24) in 2000.
- Through 50 team games (Game 1 on 5/25), hit 15HR…with Gleyber Torres (12HR) and Luke Voit (13HR), became the second trio in Yankees history to reach 12HR apiece by the club's 50th game of the season, joining Mickey Mantle (21HR), Yogi Berra (16HR) and Hank Bauer (13HR) in 1956 (credit: STATS, LLC.).
- Hit 7HR in April despite playing just 13 games…is only the fourth player in the Expansion Era (since 1961) to hit at least 7HR in April in fewer than 15G, joining Philadelphia's Mike Schmidt (11HR in 14G in 1976), Pittsburgh's Willie Stargell (7HR in 13G in 1973) and San Francisco's Willie Mays (7HR in 11G in 1964).
- Set a career high with 6RBI and hit three, two-run HRs in 4/7 win at Baltimore, his first career three-homer game…marked the Yankees' first 3HR game since Aaron Hicks (7/1/18 vs. Boston)…was their first 3HR game on the road since Alex Rodriguez on 7/25/15 at Minnesota…marked the first time a Yankee has ever hit 3HR in a game in Baltimore (note: Joe DiMaggio hit 3HR on 6/13/37-G2 at St. Louis-AL)…at 26 years, 126 days, became the youngest Yankee to hit 3HR in a game since Bobby Murcer (24 years, 35 days) on 6/24/70-G2 vs. Cleveland…became the third Yankee ever to hit 6HR through nine team games, joining Alex Rodriguez (6HR) in 2007 and Graig Nettles (6HR) in 1974…marked his 11th career multi-HR game…is the fastest player in Major League history to reach 11 multi-HR games (274G)…with Clint Frazier hitting 2HR in the game, marked the fourth time ever that two Yankees combined for 5HR in a game, the first since 7/28/40 (G1) at Chicago-AL (Charlie Keller-3HR, Joe DiMaggio-2HR)…were the first Yankees teammates to hit multiple HRs in the same game since Sánchez and Judge on 9/10/17 at Texas.
- Was placed on the 10-day injured list from 4/12 (retroactive to 4/11)-4/24 with a left calf strain…played one rehab game with Single-A Charleston, going 0-for-3.
- Hit his first career grand slam in 4/27 win at San Francisco.
- Hit 9HR in 22 games in May, the fifth time in his career he hit at least 9HR in a calendar month (also August 2016, September 2016, June 2017 and August 2017)…became the first player in Yankees history to record at least 10XBH (also hit 1 triple) in a calendar month without hitting a double (in July 1925, Babe Ruth hit .301, 28-for-93, with 1 triple and 8HR)…was the first player to do so since Baltimore's Mark Trumbo had all 10XBH go for homers in August 2016.
- Had his 12th career multi-HR game in 5/3 win vs. Minnesota…is the second-fastest player to reach 12 multi-HR games (in 284G), behind only Ralph Kiner (282G).
- Hit his 11th HR in his 19th game of the season (5/4 vs. Minnesota)…is the third-fastest Yankees player to reach 11HR in a season (in terms of games played), following Alex Rodriguez (12HR in 15G in 2007, had 2HR in Game 15) and Glenallen Hill (11HR in 18G in 2000 as a mid-season acquisition).
- Hit his first career triple on 5/19, the first triple by a Yankees catcher since Austin Romine on 8/13/17 vs. Boston…according to Elias, his 1,101 at-bats were the second-most among active players without a triple, behind Seattle's Ryon Healy (1,501).
- Joined Gleyber Torres in homering in three straight team games from 6/19-21, becoming the first pair of teammates in Yankees history to homer in three consecutive games together (confirmed by Elias).
- His three-run HR in the 10th inning—his first career extra-inning HR—on 7/4 at Tampa Bay traveled an estimated 461 ft. (Statcast).
- Was voted by fans to his second career AL All-Star team (also 2017) and went 1-for-2 with 1R and 1 double as the AL's starting catcher.
- On 7/15 vs. Tampa Bay, picked off Willy Adames at second base in the fifth…the pickoff was his third of the season and came through 504.2 innings, matching his total from the previous two seasons (2017-18) combined (in 1,534.0 innings caught).
- In Game 1 on 7/18 vs. Tampa Bay, collected his first multi-hit game since 6/21 vs. Houston…snapped a 16-game stretch with 1H-or-fewer, the second-longest such streak of his career (20G from 5/22-6/19/18).
- Was placed on the 10-day injured list from 7/24-8/10 with a left groin strain…was removed from 7/23 win at Minnesota in the eighth inning with the injury…went 1-for-5 with 1R in two rehab starts at C with Triple-A Scranton/Wilkes-Barre.
- Hit 10HR with 19RBI in 27 games after returning from the I.L. before suffering a groin injury on 9/12…had just 1RBI (0HR) in his prior 12 games (7/5-23) before being placed on the I.L.
- Hit his 25th home run of the season on 8/10 at Toronto after being reinstated from the 10-day injured list prior to the game.

- Went 3-for-3, including a three-run HR, on 8/14 vs. Baltimore, matching his RBI total from his previous 16 games combined (3RBI from 7/5-8/13).
- Hit his 100th career home run on 8/23 at Los Angeles-NL, in his 355th game…became the second-fastest player in Major League history to reach 100HR, behind Philadelphia's Ryan Howard (325G)…at 26 years, 264 days old, was the seventh-youngest catcher in Major League history to reached the milestone, behind Johnny Bench, Yogi Berra, Gary Carter, Brian McCann, Lance Parrish and Joe Torre…is the sixth catcher in Yankees history to reach 100HR, joining Yogi Berra (358), Jorge Posada (275), Bill Dickey (202), Elston Howard (161) and Thurman Munson (113)…according to *Elias*, prior to Sánchez, the fewest games by a Yankee to reach 100 career homers was 395 by Joe DiMaggio.
- Recorded his 13th career multi-HR game and third of the season in his 362nd career game on 8/31 vs. Oakland…became the second-fastest player to reach 13 multi-HR games in Baseball history (in terms of games played) behind only Ralph Kiner (308).
- Collected his 14th career multi-HR, fourth of the year and second in four games on 9/3 vs. Texas…came in his 365th career game, becoming the second-fastest player to reach 14 multi-HR games in Baseball history (in terms of games played) behind Ralph Kiner (313).
- Was removed from Game 2 of 9/12 doubleheader at Detroit in the fourth inning with left groin tightness…missed the following 11 games with the injury.
- Was the Yankees' starting catcher in each of their nine playoff games, batting .129 (4-for-31) with 2R, 1HR, 3RBI and 4BB…hit a two-run HR in the sixth inning of ALCS Game 4 vs. Houston.

2018

- Hit .186 (60-for-323) with 51R, 17 doubles, 18HR, 53RBI and 46BB in 89 games (74 starts at C, 12 at DH).
- Posted a 3.47 catcher's ERA…threw out 12-of-40 potential base stealers (30.0%).
- Had at least 3RBI in six of the Yankees' first 29 games (3/29-5/1), becoming the fourth Yankee (fifth time) to accomplish the feat (Gehrig-8G in 1934, Ruth-6G in 1926, '32, Rodriguez-6G in 2007).
- Missed two games (4/7-8) with right calf cramps…was removed from 4/6 loss vs. Baltimore during the top of the 14th with the injury.
- Hit two two-run HRs in 4/11 win at Boston…was his eighth career two-homer game (first since 9/10/17 at Texas).
- Homered five times over an eight-game stretch from 4/24-5/1…hit 9HR from 4/24-5/19, tied for the second-most HR in the Majors over the span.
- Hit solo HR and two-run HR in 4/24 win vs. Minnesota (in his 196th career game)…was his ninth career multi-HR game and second of the season (also 4/11 at Boston).
- Hit ninth-inning three-run "walk-off" HR in 4/26 win vs. Minnesota…was his first career "walk-off" hit…since 2003, was the Yankees' third "walk-off" HR when trailing by at least 2R: also Mark Teixeira on 9/28/16 vs. Boston (grand slam off Joe Kelly, down 3-1) and Chris Young on 9/11/14 vs. Tampa Bay (three-run HR off Jake McGee, down 4-2).
- Hit two-run HR in the fourth inning to account for all of the Yankees offense in 4/29 win at Los Angeles-AL…was the first Yankee to drive in all the runs in a winning effort with one homer since Greg Bird hit a solo HR in a 1-0 win in 2017 ALDS Game 3 vs. Cleveland, and the first to do it in the regular season since Brett Gardner hit a three-run HR in the ninth inning of a 3-2 win on 5/5/17 at Chicago-NL.
- Hit ninth-inning, game-winning three-run HR to break a scoreless tie on 5/1 at Houston…was the seventh Yankee since 1974 to homer to break a scoreless tie in the ninth inning or later, the first since Chris Young hit a solo HR in the 11th inning on 9/12/14-G1 at Baltimore.
- Recorded his 10th career multi-HR game on 5/19 at Kansas City (in his 216th career game)…is the fastest to reach the mark in Baseball history (previous: Bob Horner-267th career game)…is one of five Yankees with 10 multi-HR game at age 25 or younger, joining Joe DiMaggio (17), Mickey Mantle (14), Lou Gehrig (13) and Gleyber Torres (10)…was 4-for-5 with 2R, 1 double and 3RBI in the game, tying his career high in hits (also 8/10/16 at Boston).
- Hit solo HR in 6/16 win vs. Tampa Bay, his first HR since 5/19 at Kansas City…snapped a career-long 18-game homerless stretch (5/21-6/15) that spanned 66AB.
- Was placed on the 10-day disabled list from 6/25-7/19 with a right groin strain (missed 20 team games)…was removed from 6/24 loss at Tampa Bay with the injury…played three rehab games with Triple-A Scranton/WB.
- Was placed back on the 10-day disabled list with a recurrence of his right groin strain from 7/24-9/1 (missed 37 team games)…played five rehab games (one with the GCL Yankees East and four with Triple-A Scranton/WB).
- Hit .167 (3-for-18) with 3R, 1 double, 2HR and 5RBI in five postseason games.
- Hit 2HR and had 4RBI in ALDS Game 2 at Boston, becoming the second Yankees catcher to hit multiple HRs in a postseason game (also Yogi Berra, who hit 2HR in the 1956 World Series-clinching Game 7 win at Brooklyn on 10/10/56)…was the 10th catcher in Major League history with a postseason multi-HR game (first since Cleveland's Roberto Pérez in 2016 World Series Game 1 vs. Chicago-NL)…was the fourth postseason multi-HR game by a Yankees right-handed hitter (also Chad Curtis, 1999 WS Game 3 vs. Atlanta; Scott Brosius, 1998 WS Game 3 at San Diego; Tony Lazzeri, 1932 WS Game 4 at Chicago-NL)…was the fifth multi-HR game by a Yankee (first since Didi Gregorius, 2HR in Game 5 of the 2017 ALDS at Cleveland)…was the first 4RBI game by a Yankee in the playoffs since Robinson Canó had 6RBI in 2001 ALDS Game 1 vs. Detroit and the first on the road since Melky Cabrera in 2009 ALCS Game 4 at Los Angeles-AL (4RBI).
- Underwent left shoulder debridement performed by Yankees Head Team Physician Dr. Christopher Ahmad at NewYork-Presbyterian Hospital in Manhattan on 11/8.

2017

- Hit .278/.345/.531 (131-for-471) with 79R, 20 doubles, 33HR and 90RBI in 122 games (99 starts at C, 18 at DH).
- Earned his first Silver Slugger Award…his 79R, 33HR, 90RBI and .531 SLG% were best in the Majors among catchers.
- Ranked fourth in the Majors (third in the AL) with a 3.43 catcher's ERA…the last Yankee with a lower catcher's ERA was Joe Girardi in 1997 (3.42)…threw out 19-of-56 potential base stealers (33.9%).
- In his first 64 games behind the plate (through 8/4), permitted 12 passed balls in 553.2 innings (1PB every 46.1 innings) and threw out just 27.8% of attempted base stealers (10-of-36)…over his final 40 games from 8/8 (when he returned from three days off defensively), allowed just four passed balls in 327.1 innings (1PB every 81.8 innings) and threw out 45.0% of base stealers (9-for-20).
- His 33HR were most by any catcher since Atlanta's Javy Lopez (43) in 2003 and the most by a C, 24-or-younger, since the Dodgers' Mike Piazza hit 35HR in 1993…were the most HR in a single-season by a Dominican-born catcher (previous: Wilin Rosario, 28HR in 2012).
- Is the youngest catcher in Yankees history to hit at least 25HR in a season, one of seven Yankees catchers overall to reach the mark (also: Yogi Berra-6x, Bill Dickey-2x, Jorge Posada-2x, Brian McCann, Mike Stanley and Elston Howard)…was the third catcher in AL history to hit at least 25HR in his age-24 season or younger, joining Detroit's Rudy York (2x: 35HR in 1937, 33HR in 1938) and Detroit's Matt Nokes (32HR in 1987)…was one of two Major League catchers since 1994 to accomplish the feat (also Colorado's Wilin Rosario-28HR in 2012)…was the first Yankee to hit at least 25HR in a season age at 24-or-younger since Don Mattingly (35HR) in 1985.
- Joined Aaron Judge as the first Yankees age 25-or-younger to hit at least 30HR in a season since Don Mattingly in 1986 (31HR at age 25).
- Had 33HR, while Aaron Judge had 52HR…was just the second time in Yankees history that two teammates, age 25-or-younger, hit at least 30HR in a season (also Joe DiMaggio, 31HR and Joe Gordon, 30HR in 1940)…with a combined 85HR, set the Major League record for home runs by two teammates, each 25-or-younger (surpassed the 2007 Milwaukee Brewers' Prince Fielder-50 and Ryan Braun-34).
- Had four multi-HR games (6/1 at Toronto, 6/8 vs. Boston, 8/22 at Detroit and 9/10 at Texas), while teammate Aaron Judge had seven…became the second pair of Yankees teammates, each age 25-or-younger, with at least four multi-HR games in the same season (DiMaggio/Gordon, four each in 1939).
- Was placed on the 10-day disabled list from 4/8-5/5 with a right biceps strain (missed 21 team games)…an MRI on 4/10 revealed a Grade 1 right biceps strain…played three rehab games with Triple-A Scranton/Wilkes-Barre.
- Hit .307/.390/.659 with 21R, 9HR and 27RBI in 23 games in June…his 27RBI were tied for second-most in the Majors during the month and the most by a Yankees catcher in a calendar month since Jorge Posada had 29RBI in August 2000…at 24 years old, was the third-youngest Yankee in 61 years (since 1957) with at least 27RBI in a calendar month (Robinson Canó, 28RBI in Sept. 2006; Don Mattingly, 37RBI in Sept. 1985 and 27RBI in July 1985)…Miguel Andújar had 28RBI in August 2018 at age 23…drove in or scored 22.0% of the Yankees' 177R in June.
- Collected his fourth career multi-HR game—and first of the season—in 6/1 win at Toronto…his first homer was the 25th of his career (in his 300th career AB)…according to Elias, became the fifth player all time to hit at least 25HR in 300-or-fewer AB: Rudy York (256th at-bat, 1937 season), Mark McGwire (264th, 1987 season), José Abreu (264th, 2014 season) and Wally Berger (284th, 1930 season).
- Was named via the Player Ballot to his first career All-Star team…was the third Yankees catcher to make the All-Star team at age 24-or-younger, joining Munson (24 years old in 1971) and Berra (23-24 years old in 1948-49)…was 0-for-2 as a defensive replacement at C…participated in the Home Run Derby on 7/10, hitting 17HR in the first round to defeat reigning-champion Giancarlo Stanton (16HR) before hitting 10HR to fall shy of Miguel Sanó (11HR) in the semifinals…was pitched to by Yankees BP pitcher Danilo Valiente.
- In 28 August games, hit .287/.347/.648 (31-for-108) with 19R, 3 doubles, 12HR, 26RBI and 8BB…his 12HR were tied for the most in the AL and tied for second-most in the Majors during the month (Giancarlo Stanton-18HR)…were the most HRs by a Yankee in a calendar month since Mark Teixeira hit 13HR in May 2009…was the fourth Yankee to hit at least 12HR in a month prior to turning 25, joining Mickey Mantle (3x–13HR in Aug. 1956, 16HR in May 1956, 12HR in August 1955), Joe DiMaggio (2x–14HR in Aug. 1939, 15HR in July 1937) and Lou Gehrig (13HR in June 1927)…tied Yogi Berra's June 1952 record for HRs by a Yankees catcher in a single month…was the second catcher in Major League history to hit at least 12HR in a calendar month before turning 25 (Detroit's Rudy York hit 18HR in August 1937, and 24 years old on 8/17/37).
- From 7/27 through the end of the season, hit 19HR in 55 games, after hitting just 3HR in his previous 30 games (6/15-7/26)…had 12HR with 31RBI over his final 36 games beginning on 8/17.
- Hit two two-run HRs in 8/22 win at Detroit…his first-inning HR was measured at an estimated 493 ft. by Statcast—the second-longest HR in the Majors in 2017 (Judge - 495 ft. on 6/11), the longest HR of his career.
- Served a three-game suspension during the Yankees' series at Baltimore from 9/4-7…was suspended for his actions during a fight on 8/24 at Detroit.
- Hit two solo HRs and established a career high with 4R in 9/10 win at Texas…with RF Aaron Judge also hitting 2HR, the duo became the fourth pair of Yankees teammates, both age 25-or-younger, to each hit multiple HRs in the same game (also Ron Blomberg-2HR/Otto Velez-2HR on 9/23/73-G1 at Cleveland; Charlie Keller-3HR/Joe DiMaggio-2HR on 7/28/40-G1 at Chicago-AL; and Joe Gordon-2HR/Tommy Henrich-2HR on 8/27/38-G2 vs. Cleveland).
- Played in his 162nd career game on 9/11 against Tampa Bay at Citi Field…had 50HR through his first 162 games, third-most in Baseball history at the time (Rudy York-55, Mark McGwire-51).
- Hit his 31st HR of the season in 9/14 win vs. Baltimore, setting a single-season franchise record for homers by a catcher (previous: Yogi Berra, 30 in 1952 and '56 and Jorge Posada, 30 in 2003)…surpassed his own record with 34HR in 2019.

- Made his postseason debut, hitting .208 (11-for-53) with 5R, 2 doubles, 3HR and 8RBI in 13 playoff games.
- With Greg Bird (3HR), became the first pair of Yankees teammates, age 24-or-younger, to each hit multiple HRs in the same postseason…hit his first career postseason HR off Corey Kluber in ALDS Game 2 loss at Cleveland.
- Made seven starts in the cleanup spot, becoming the third catcher in Major League history to bat cleanup in a playoff game at age 24-or-younger (also Johnny Bench and Buster Posey)…was the fourth Yankees catcher to hit in the cleanup spot in the playoffs (also Yogi Berra, Elston Howard and Jorge Posada).
- With his tie-breaking two-run double in ALCS Game 4 vs. Houston (at age 24y, 319d), became the youngest Yankee with a go-ahead hit in the eighth inning or later in a playoff game since Tom Tresh (age 24y, 20d) hit a tie-breaking three-run HR off San Francisco's Jack Sanford in the bottom of the eighth inning in 1962 World Series Game 5.

2016

- Hit .299/.376/.657 (60-for-201) with 34R, 12 doubles, 20HR and 42RBI in 53 games (36 starts at C, 17 at DH) over two stints with the Yankees (5/13-14 and 8/3-10/2)…threw out 12-of-31 potential base stealers (38.7%).
- Placed second in AL "Rookie of the Year" voting behind Detroit's Michael Fulmer (142 total points), receiving four first-place votes, 23 second-place votes and two third-place votes (91 points)…was named on 29-of-30 ballots.
- His 3.2 WAR (FanGraphs) ranked fifth among Major League catchers and was tops in the AL (Jonathan Lucroy-4.5, Buster Posey-4.0, J.T. Realmuto-3.5 and Wilson Ramos-3.5)…led all AL rookies and ranked fifth among Major League rookies in WAR (Corey Seager-7.5, Jon Gray-3.7, Trea Turner-3.3 and Kenta Maeda-3.3).
- According to *Elias*, his 20HR were the most in Major League history by a player who did not hit one prior to 8/1 of that season (did not homer prior to 8/10)…*Elias* notes the only other Yankees to hit at least 20HR from 8/10 until the end of the season were Babe Ruth (25 in 1927) and Roger Maris (20 in 1961)…his 20HR from 8/10-10/2 were most in the Majors…his 53 games were fewest by any player who hit at least 20HR in a season in Major League history (previous was Giancarlo Stanton, 27HR in 74G in 2015).
- With Brian McCann (also 20HR), the Yankees became the third team in Major League history to have two players, who each played at least half of their games at C, hit at least 20HR in the same season…joined the 1965 Milwaukee Braves (Joe Torre-27HR/Gene Oliver-21HR) and the 1961 Yankees (Elston Howard-21HR/Johnny Blanchard-21HR).
- Made his season debut in 5/13 loss vs. Chicago-AL, starting at DH and going 0-for-4…at 23 years, 163 days old, was the fifth-youngest player to start at DH for the Yankees at the time—Jesús Montero (14 starts at age 21), Terry Whitfield (1GS at age 22), Juan Bernhardt (2GS at age 22) and Nick Johnson (3GS at age 22, 3GS at a "younger" 23)…was joined by Clint Frazier in 2017, Miguel Andújar in 2018 and Gleyber Torres in 2019.
- Was named AL "Player of the Month" and "Rookie of the Month" for August, hitting .389/.458/.832 (37-for-95) with 20R, 9 doubles, 11HR, 21RBI and 11BB in 24G…was the first Yankees catcher to win either award…was the first Yankees "Player of the Month" since Curtis Granderson in August 2011 and the first "Rookie of the Month" since Robinson Canó in September 2005…was the first Yankee to win both awards in the same month and the first AL player to do so since Chicago-AL's José Abreu in July 2014…was the first catcher to be named the AL "Player of the Month" since Joe Mauer in May 2009…was the first AL catcher to win both awards in the same month.
- Hit 11HR in 24G in August, the most in a month by any rookie since Milwaukee's Ryan Braun (11HR in July 2007)…were the most by an AL rookie since Oakland's Mark McGwire hit 15HR in May 1987.
- Became the first catcher in Yankees history to record at least 20XBH in a calendar month (9 doubles, 11HR in August)…was the third Yankees rookie to record at least 20XBH in a calendar month (fifth time), joining Joe DiMaggio (23 in May 1936 and 22 in August 1936) and Bob Meusel (20 in June 1920 and 24 in July 1920)…was joined by teammate Aaron Judge in September 2017 (22).
- Collected his first Major League hit with a single off Hansel Robles in 8/3 win vs. the Mets…from 2012-16, the only Yankees younger than Sánchez (23 years, 245 days) at the time of their first Major League hit were Ramón Flores (23y, 66d in 2015), Greg Bird (22y, 279d in 2015) and John Ryan Murphy (22y, 112d in 2013).
- Hit his first Major League HR in the eighth (solo HR off Junichi Tazawa) and was 4-for-5 with 2R in 8/10 win at Boston (his 14th career game)…became the ninth Yankee since 1913 with a 4H game within the first 9G of his career (last: D'Angelo Jiménez, 9/19/99 at Cleveland).
- Reached base safely in 21 straight games from 8/14-9/6…hit safely in 18 of the 21 games, batting .380/.473/.835 (30-for-79) with 14R, 6 doubles, 10HR, 17RBI, 13BB and 1SB over the streak.
- Was named AL "Player of the Week" for the period from 8/15-21, batting an AL-best .524 (11-for-21) with 4R, 2 doubles, 4HR and 6RBI in 6G…became the second catcher in franchise history to win the award (Thurman Munson on 5/4/75 and 7/25/76)…was the first Yankees rookie to win the award since Robinson Canó on 9/19/05.
- Hit 10HR over a 12-game span from 8/14-27, most by a Yankee in 12G since Alex Rodriguez (10HR, 8/29-9/9/07)…had 9HR in 10G from 8/16-27, most by a Yankee since Tino Martinez (9HR, 4/5-15/05)—credit: *Elias*.
- Recorded his first career multi-HR game in 8/16 loss vs. Toronto (solo HR and three-run HR)…came in his 14th career game, becoming the seventh Yankee since at least 1913 with a multi-HR game within his first 14 career games and first since Greg Bird on 8/19/15 vs. Minnesota (2HR)…according to *Elias*, at 23 years, 258 days old, became the second-youngest Yankees catcher with a multi-homer game, behind Bill Dickey, who homered twice on 7/26/29 vs. St. Louis (22y, 50d)…became the first Yankees rookie catcher with a multi-HR game since Aaron Robinson on 9/6/45 vs. Detroit (2HR)…Toronto's Russell Martin also hit 2HR, marking the first time in AL history (fourth in Major League history) that two catchers each hit multiple home runs in the same game.
- Hit cleanup in the starting lineup for the first time and homered in 8/17 loss vs. Toronto…at 23 years, 259 days old, was the third Yankee since 1975 to start in the cleanup spot before turning 24 (also Jay Buhner: 23y, 52d, 10/4/87 vs. Baltimore and Don Mattingly: 23y, 102d, 7/31/84 vs. Milwaukee)…according to the YES Network, was the youngest Yankee to homer out of the No. 4 spot in the starting lineup since Bobby Murcer (23y, 101d) on 8/29/69.

- Was named AL "Player of the Week" for the period from 8/22-28—his second straight POTW award...became the first rookie in Major League history to win back-to-back POTW awards...was the first AL player with consecutive "Player of the Week" awards since Chicago-AL's Albert Belle in July 1998...hit .522 (12-for-23) with 7R, 3 doubles, 5HR, 9RBI and a 1.304 slugging pct. in six games during the week.
- His seventh and eighth HRs came in his 19th game (8/22 loss at Seattle), the fewest games by a Yankee to reach 8HR in franchise history...became the fastest player in Yankees history (19G) with at least two multi-HR games...collected his 25th career hit in the game, 13 of which were XBH (5 doubles, 8HR), becoming the first Yankee with at least 13XBH in his first 25H since Alfonso Soriano in 2001 (also 13XBH).
- Hit his 11th career home run in his 23rd career game (8/27 win vs. Baltimore), becoming the fastest player in Major League history to reach the mark...was passed by Rhys Hoskins in 2017 (18 games) and Aristides Aquino in 2019 (17 games).
- Became the first rookie in Yankees history to homer in four straight games (9/17-21, 5HR total)—credit: *Elias*.
- Hit his 18th and 19th career HRs (in his 45th career game) on 9/21 at Tampa Bay, becoming the fastest player in Baseball history to reach 19HR (previous: Wally Berger in 1930, 19th HR in his 51st game).
- Hit his 20th career homer in his 51st game on 9/27, tying Wally Berger (1930 Boston Braves) for the fastest by any player to reach 20HR in Baseball history...Cody Bellinger hit his 20th and 21st HRs in his 51st game in 2017.
- In 71 games with Triple-A Scranton/Wilkes-Barre, hit .282 (80-for-284) with 39R, 21 doubles, 10HR and 50RBI...was named to the International League Postseason All-Star Team.
- Following the season, was tabbed by *Baseball America* as the International League's "Best Defensive Catcher."

2015

- Was 0-for-2 in two games in his only stint with the Yankees (9/12-10/4)...made his Major League debut in 10/3 Game 1 loss at Baltimore, going 0-for-1 as a ninth-inning pinch-hitter for Greg Bird.
- Was on the Yankees' active roster for the AL Wild Card Game vs. Houston, but did not play.
- Began the season with Double-A Trenton, batting .262 (61-for-233) with 33R, 14 doubles, 12HR and 36RBI in 58G.
- Was promoted to Triple-A Scranton/Wilkes-Barre on 7/18 and hit .295 (39-for-132) with 17R, 9 doubles, 6HR and 26RBI in 35 games...was on the minor league disabled list from 8/27-9/9 (hamstring).
- Started at catcher for the World Team in the All-Star Futures Game in Cincinnati, going 1-for-2 with 1 double.
- Following the season, played for the Surprise Saguaros of the Arizona Fall League, batting .295 (26-for-88) with 16R, 6 doubles, 1 triple, 7HR and 21RBI in 22 games...was named MVP of the AFL Fall Stars Game (1-for-3, 1HR, 2RBI)...was tabbed by *Baseball America* as the No. 2 prospect in the AFL.
- After the season, was ranked by *Baseball America* as the No. 2 prospect in the Yankees organization and No. 36 in Baseball overall...was named an MiLB.com Organization All-Star.

2014

- Spent the season at Double-A Trenton, batting .270 (116-for-429) with 48R, 19 doubles, 13HR and 65RBI in 110 games...caught 37-of-95 (38.9%) potential base stealers, the second-highest caught stealing pct. in the EL.
- Was named to the EL's Mid-Season All-Star Team after batting .270 (79-for-293) with 9HR and 45RBI in the first half.
- Following the season, was ranked by *Baseball America* as the No. 5 prospect in the Yankees organization.

2013

- Combined to bat .253 (115-for-454) with 50R, 27 doubles, 15HR and 71RBI in 117 games with Single-A Tampa and Double-A Trenton...began the season with Tampa, batting .254 (92-for-362) with 38R, 21 doubles, 13HR and 61RBI in 94 games...was named to the Florida State League's Mid-Season All-Star Team.
- Was promoted to Trenton on 8/3, batting .250 (23-for-92) with 12R, 6 doubles, 2HR and 10RBI in 23 games.
- Appeared in 12 games with Toros del Este of the Dominican Winter League after the season, batting .179 (5-for-28) with 1R, 1 double, 2RBI and 3BB.
- Following the season, was ranked by *Baseball America* as the top prospect in the Yankees organization and the No. 35 prospect in all of baseball...was also named the organization's "Best Power Hitter."
- Was added to the Yankees' 40-man roster on 11/20/13.

2012

- Combined at Single-A Charleston and Single-A Tampa to hit .290 (126-for-435) with 48 extra-base hits (29 doubles, 1 triple, 18HR) and 85RBI in 116 games...tied for the lead among all Yankees minor leaguers in RBI.
- Began the year with the RiverDogs, batting .297 (78-for-263) with 44R, 19 doubles, 13HR and 56RBI in 68 games...was named to the South Atlantic League Mid-Season All-Star team.
- Was twice named a SAL "Player of the Week" (5/28-6/3 and 6/11-17).
- Was promoted to Tampa on 7/3, hitting .279 (48-for-172) with 21R, 10 doubles, 1 triple, 5HR and 29RBI in 48 games.
- Played seven games with the Leones del Escogido of the Dominican Winter League.
- Following the season, was ranked by *Baseball America* as the No. 3 prospect in the Yankees organization...was also selected as an Organization All-Star by MiLB.com and a Top 100 Prospect for the 2013 Season by MLB.com, being named the No. 36 overall prospect in all of Baseball...was also a *Baseball America* "Minor League All-Star."

2011
- Batted .256 (77-for-301) with 49R, 16 doubles, 17HR and 52RBI in 82 games with Single-A Charleston…led the team and ranked fourth among all Yankees farmhands in home runs…was named South Atlantic League "Player of the Week" twice (6/13-19 and 8/1-7).
- Played eight games with Escogido in the Dominican Winter League after the season.
- Following the season, was ranked by *Baseball America* as the No. 4 prospect in the Yankees organization.

2010
- Made his professional debut, combining with the GCL Yankees and short-season Single-A Staten Island to bat .329 (57-for-173) with 33R, 13 doubles, 8HR and 43RBI in 47 games.
- Spent the majority of the season with the GCL Yankees, hitting .353 (42-for-119) with 25R, 11 doubles, 6HR and 36RBI in 31 games.
- Hit safely in each of his first 10 games, batting .459 (17-for-37) over the stretch…hit a grand slam in his second professional at-bat on 6/21 vs. the GCL Pirates.
- Was promoted to Staten Island on 8/19, where he hit .278 (15-for-54) with 2HR and 7RBI in 16 games over the remainder of the season.
- Following the season, was named to the Topps Short-Season/Rookie All-Star Team…was also named the second-best prospect in the Yankees organization by *Baseball America*.

PERSONAL
- Is married to Sahaira…the couple has a daughter, Sarah.
- His older brother, Miguel, spent six seasons (2009-14) in the Mariners' minor league system.
- Received a 2017 Thurman Munson Award for success on the field and in the philanthropic community.

Sánchez's Career Batting Record

Year	Team	AVG	G	AB	R	H	2B	3B	HR	RBI	SH	SF	HP	BB	SO	SB	CS	E	OBP	SLG
2010	GCL Yankees	.353	31	119	25	42	11	0	6	36	0	2	4	11	28	1	1	7	.419	.597
	Staten Island	.278	16	54	8	15	2	0	2	7	0	1	1	3	16	1	1	1	.333	.426
2011	Charleston	.256	82	301	49	77	16	1	17	52	0	4	2	36	93	2	1	8	.335	.485
2012	Charleston	.297	68	263	44	78	19	0	13	56	0	2	2	22	65	11	4	12	.353	.517
	Tampa	.279	48	172	21	48	10	1	5	29	0	0	3	10	41	4	0	4	.330	.436
2013	Tampa	.254	94	362	38	92	21	0	13	61	0	4	5	28	71	3	1	7	.313	.420
	Trenton	.250	23	92	12	23	6	0	2	10	0	1	4	13	16	0	0	4	.364	.380
2014	Trenton	.270	110	429	48	116	19	0	13	65	0	3	2	43	91	1	1	17	.338	.406
2015	Trenton	.262	58	233	33	61	14	0	12	36	0	1	2	18	50	6	0	8	.319	.476
	Scranton/WB	.295	35	132	17	39	9	0	6	26	0	2	1	11	28	1	2	2	.349	.500
	YANKEES	.000	2	2	0	0	0	0	0	0	0	0	0	0	1	0	0	0	.000	.000
2016	Scranton/WB	.282	71	284	39	80	21	1	10	50	0	3	5	21	45	7	1	5	.339	.468
	YANKEES	.299	53	201	34	60	12	0	20	42	0	2	2	24	57	1	0	3	.376	.657
2017	YANKEES - a	.278	122	471	79	131	20	0	33	90	0	4	10	40	120	2	1	13	.345	.531
	Scranton/WB	.385	3	13	3	5	2	0	1	3	0	0	0	0	3	0	0	0	.385	.769
2018	YANKEES - b, c	.186	89	323	51	60	17	0	18	53	0	2	3	46	94	1	0	6	.291	.406
	Scranton/WB	.179	7	28	4	5	0	0	4	4	0	0	0	0	10	0	0	0	.179	.607
	GCL Yankees East	.000	1	3	1	0	0	0	0	0	0	0	0	1	0	0	0	0	.250	.000
2019	YANKEES - d, e	.232	106	396	62	92	12	1	34	77	0	1	9	40	125	0	1	15	.316	.525
	Charleston	.000	1	3	0	0	0	0	0	0	0	0	0	0	0	0	0	0	.000	.000
	Scranton/WB	.200	2	5	1	1	0	0	0	0	0	0	0	1	1	0	0	1	.333	.200
Minor League Totals		**.274**	**650**	**2493**	**343**	**682**	**150**	**3**	**104**	**435**	**0**	**23**	**31**	**218**	**558**	**37**	**12**	**76**	**.337**	**.461**
Major League Totals		**.246**	**372**	**1393**	**226**	**343**	**61**	**1**	**105**	**262**	**0**	**9**	**24**	**150**	**397**	**4**	**2**	**37**	**.328**	**.518**

Signed by the Yankees as a non-drafted free agent on July 2, 2009.

a – Placed on the 10-day disabled list from April 8 (postgame) - May 4, 2017 with a right biceps strain.
b – Placed on the 10-day disabled list from June 25 - July 19, 2018 with a right groin strain.
c – Placed on the 10-day disabled list from July 24 - September 1, 2018 with a right groin strain.
d – Placed on the 10-day injured list from April 12 (retroactive to April 11) - April 24, 2019 with a left calf strain.
e – Placed on the 10-day injured list from July 24 - August 10, 2019 with a left groin strain.

Sánchez's Postseason Record

Year	Club vs. Opp.	AVG	G	AB	R	H	2B	3B	HR	RBI	SH	SF	HP	BB	SO	SB	CS	E	OBP	SLG
2015	NYY vs. HOU (WC)						On Roster - Did Not Play													
2017	NYY vs. MIN (WC)	.500	1	4	1	2	1	0	0	0	0	0	0	0	0	0	0	0	.500	.750
	NYY vs. CLE (DS)	.174	5	23	3	4	0	0	2	3	0	0	0	0	10	0	0	0	.174	.435
	NYY vs. HOU (CS)	.192	7	26	1	5	1	0	1	5	0	1	0	1	9	0	0	0	.214	.346
2018	NYY vs. OAK (WC)	.000	1	3	0	0	0	0	0	0	0	0	0	0	0	0	0	0	.000	.000
	NYY vs. BOS (DS)	.200	4	15	3	3	1	0	2	5	0	1	0	1	5	0	0	0	.235	.667
2019	NYY vs. MIN (DS)	.125	3	8	1	1	0	0	0	0	0	1	0	3	4	0	0	0	.417	.125
	NYY vs. HOU (CS)	.130	6	23	1	3	0	0	1	3	0	0	0	1	12	0	0	0	.167	.261
Wild Card Game Totals		**.286**	**2**	**7**	**1**	**2**	**1**	**0**	**0**	**0**	**0**	**0**	**0**	**0**	**0**	**0**	**0**	**0**	**.286**	**.429**
Division Series Totals		**.174**	**12**	**46**	**7**	**8**	**1**	**0**	**4**	**8**	**0**	**1**	**1**	**4**	**19**	**0**	**0**	**0**	**.250**	**.457**
LCS Totals		**.163**	**13**	**49**	**2**	**8**	**1**	**0**	**2**	**8**	**0**	**1**	**0**	**2**	**21**	**0**	**0**	**0**	**.192**	**.306**
POSTSEASON TOTALS		**.176**	**27**	**102**	**10**	**18**	**3**	**0**	**6**	**16**	**0**	**2**	**1**	**6**	**40**	**0**	**0**	**0**	**.225**	**.382**

Sánchez's All-Star Game Record

Year	Club, Site	AVG	G	AB	R	H	2B	3B	HR	RBI	SH	SF	HP	BB	SO	SB	CS	E	OBP	SLG
2017	NYY, Miami	.000	1	2	0	0	0	0	0	0	0	0	0	0	1	0	0	0	.000	.000
2019	NYY, Cleveland	.500	1	2	1	1	1	0	0	0	0	0	0	0	0	0	0	0	.500	1.000
All-Star Game Totals		.250	2	4	1	1	1	0	0	0	0	0	0	0	1	0	0	0	.250	.500

Sánchez's Career Fielding Record

Position	PCT	G	PO	A	E	TC	PB
Catcher	.988	306	2,763	161	37	2,961	47
First Base	1.000	2	7	0	0	7	-

Sánchez's Career Home Run Chart

MULTI-HOMER GAMES: 14. **TWO-HOMER GAMES:** 13, last on 9/3/19 vs. TEX. **THREE-HOMER GAMES:** 1, 4/7/19 at BAL. **GRAND SLAMS:** 1, 4/27/19 at SF (Derek Holland). **PINCH-HIT HR:** None. **INSIDE-THE-PARK HR:** None. "WALK-OFF" **HR:** 1, 4/26/18 vs. MIN (Fernando Rodney). **LEADOFF HR:** None.

Sánchez's Career Bests and Streaks

HITS: 4 - 2 times (last on 5/19/18 at KC). **RUNS:** 4, 9/10/17 at TEX. **2B:** 2 - 3 times (last on 5/15/18 at WAS). **3B:** 1, 5/19/19 vs. TB. **HR:** 3, 4/7/19 at BAL. **RBI:** 6, 4/7/19 at BAL. **BB:** 2 - 24 times (last on 9/7/19 at BOS). **SO:** 4 - 4 times (last on 7/6/19 at TB). **SB:** 1 - 4 times (last on 9/12/18 at MIN). **HIT STREAK:** 9g, 8/22-31/16. **"WALK-OFF" HITS:** 1, 4/26/18 vs. MIN (home run).

Player of the Month: August 2016   **Player of the Week:** 2 times, last: 8/22-28/16   **Rookie of the Month:** August 2016

Yankees in Interleague Play

Year	Opponents	Record	Year	Opponents	Record
1997	(NYM, ATL, MON, FLA, PHI)	5-10	2009	(NYM, PHI, WAS, FLA, ATL)	10-8
1998	(NYM, ATL, MON, FLA, PHI)	13-3	2010	(NYM, HOU, PHI, ARI, LAD)	11-7
1999	(NYM, ATL, MON, FLA, PHI)	9-9	2011	(NYM, CHC, CIN, COL, MIL)	13-5
2000	(NYM, ATL, MON, FLA, PHI)	11-6	2012	(NYM, CIN, ATL, WAS)	13-5
2001	(NYM, ATL, MON, FLA, PHI)	10-8	2013	(NYM, ARI, COL, LAD, SD, SF)	9-11
2002	(NYM, SF, ARI, COL, SD)	11-7	2014	(NYM, CHC, CIN, MIL, PIT, STL)	13-7
2003	(NYM, CIN, CHC, HOU, STL)	13-5	2015	(NYM, ATL, MIA, PHI, WAS)	11-9
2004	(NYM, COL, SD, ARI, LAD)	10-8	2016	(NYM, ARI, COL, LAD, SD, SF)	8-12
2005	(NYM, MIL, STL, PIT, CHC)	11-7	2017	(NYM, CHC, CIN, MIL, PIT, STL)	15-5
2006	(NYM, WAS, PHI, FLA, ATL)	10-8	2018	(NYM, ATL, MIA, PHI, WAS)	11-9
2007	(NYM, PIT, ARI, COL, SF)	10-8	2019	(NYM, ARI, COL, LAD, SD, SF)	12-8
2008	(NYM, HOU, SD, CIN, PIT)	10-8			

The Yankees are second in the Majors in all-time Interleague winning percentage (.590, 249-173) and wins, trailing only Boston in both categories (.598, 253-170)…went 12-8 vs. the NL in 2019, marking their fifth winning Interleague season series in six years and 19th in 23 seasons since the inception of Interleague play in 1997…posted a Major League-record 15-year stretch of a .500-or-better record in Interleague games from 1998-2012—credit: *Elias Sports Bureau*.

Since the current Yankee Stadium opened in 2009, the Yankees have gone 64-42 (.604) in Interleague games in the Bronx.

In 2020, the Yankees will play the NL Central for the first time since 2017…the Yankees went 15-5 in their 20 Interleague contests that year, their highest-ever single-season win total in Interleague play.

LUIS SEVERINO • RHP

#40

HT: 6-2 • **WT:** 218 • **BATS:** R • **THROWS:** R
BIRTHDATE: 2/20/94 • **OPENING DAY AGE:** 26
BIRTHPLACE: Sabana de la Mar, D.R.
RESIDES: Santo Domingo, D.R.
M.L. SERVICE: 3 years, 170 days

STATUS
- On 2/15/19, was signed to a four-year contract extending through the 2022 season, with a club option for the 2023 season.

CAREER NOTES
- Is a two-time AL All-Star (2017-18).
- Finished third in 2017 AL Cy Young Award voting, the highest finish by a Yankees pitcher since CC Sabathia also got third in 2010.
- Has made three career Opening Day rosters (2016-18), all as a member of the Yankees' starting rotation…began the 2019 season on the injured list.
- Has two of the top-six single-season strikeout totals in Yankees history (230K in 2017, 220K in 2018)…is one of three pitchers in Yankees history with multiple 200-strikeout seasons (also David Cone, 1997-98 and Ron Guidry, 1978-79)…his 450K from 2017-18 were the most over a two-season span in Yankees history (previously Guidry, 449K from 1978-79).
- With his 500th strikeout on 7/23/18 at Tampa Bay, became just the third Yankees pitcher to reach the mark prior to his 25th birthday (Al Downing, Lefty Gomez).
- Has five games with at least 10K and 0BB, tied with David Cone and Masahiro Tanaka for the second-most in Yankees history behind Mike Mussina (seven).
- Since 1908, his 85 regular season starts prior to turning 25 years old were the fourth-most by a Yankees pitcher (Waite Hoyt-121, Al Downing-102, Lefty Gomez-93)…was the first Yankees pitcher to have multiple 30-start seasons in his age-24 seasons or younger since Steve Kline in 1971-72.
- The Yankees are 46-20 in his 66 starts in the last three seasons (since 2017)…are 39-11 in his last 50 starts since 7/8/17…from 7/8/17-7/12/18, the Yankees went 31-4 in his 35 starts, the first time the Yankees won at least 31 games in a pitcher's 35-start span since going 31-4 over 35 Ron Guidry starts from 8/10/77-8/15/78 (*Elias*).
- Has allowed 1ER-or-fewer in 31-of-66 starts (47.0%) since the start of 2017.
- Made his Major League debut as a 21-year-old in 2015, going 5-3 with a 2.89 ERA (62.1IP, 20ER) in 11 starts…was just the fourth pitcher in Yankees history to record at least five wins and post an ERA of 3.00-or-lower in his age-21 season or younger, joining Whitey Ford (1950), Hank Thormahlen (1918) and Ray Keating (1914).
- Was the first Yankee to allow 1ER-or-fewer in each of his first three career starts at the current Yankee Stadium.
- Is 6-2 with a 1.46 ERA (61.2IP, 10ER) in 11 career Interleague appearances (nine starts)…is the fifth-lowest Interleague ERA among active pitchers (min. 50.0IP), behind Craig Kimbrel (1.13), Justin Wilson (1.29), Dellin Betances (1.35) and Blake Snell (1.43).
- In 82 career minor league games (79 starts), held opponents to a .220 batting average (328-for-1,489) while averaging more than a strikeout per inning (405K/402.1IP)…allowed a total of 13HR in the minors (1,617BF)…pitched in the 2014 MLB All-Star Futures Game in Minnesota.
- Is 1-3 with a 5.17 ERA (31.1IP, 18ER) in eight career postseason starts (4GS in 2017, 2GS in 2018, 2GS in 2019)…with starts in the 2017 and 2018 AL Wild Card Games, joined Madison Bumgarner and Jon Lester as the only three pitchers to start two Wild Card Games…is one of two pitchers in Yankees history to start four postseason games prior to turning 24 years old (Waite Hoyt, 4GS), and one of two to start six postseason games prior to turning 25 (Andy Pettitte, 6GS) and eight prior to turning 26 (Pettitte, 8GS)…made his postseason debut in the 2017 AL Wild Card Game vs. Minnesota (ND, 0.1IP, 3ER), matching the shortest start by a Yankees pitcher in postseason history (also Art Ditmar in 1960 WS Game 1 at Pittsburgh and Bob Turley in 1958 WS Game 2 at Milwaukee)…at 23 years, 225 days old, was the youngest Yankee to start a postseason game since Andy Pettitte (23.111) in 1995 ALDS Game 2 vs. Seattle…with 9K in 2017 ALDS Game 4 vs. Cleveland, was the second-youngest Yankee (23 years, 231 days) to record 9K in a postseason game, behind Dave Righetti (22 years, 314 days for 1981 ALDS Game 2 at Milwaukee-10K)…started two potential elimination games at age-23; only two other such games in Yankees history were started by pitchers 23-or-younger: Mel Stottlemyre (22 years, 337 days in 1964 WS Game 7 at St. Louis) and Waite Hoyt (22 years, 34 days in 1921 WS Game 8 vs. New York Giants)…recorded scoreless starts in the 2018 AL Wild Card Game vs. Oakland (4.0IP) and 2019 ALDS Game 3 at Minnesota (4.0IP).

CAREER HIGHLIGHTS
AL All-Star Team
- 2017, 2018

2019

- Made just three starts after returning from the 60-day I.L. in September, going 1-1 with a 1.50 ERA (12.0IP, 6H, 2ER, 6BB, 17K, 0HR)…opponents hit .146 (6-for-41); LH .148 (4-for-27); RH .143 (2-for-14).

SEVERINO'S 2019 PITCHING LINES											
Date/Opp	Score	W/L	IP	H	R	ER	HR	BB	K	NP/S	ERA	Left game
9/17 vs. LAA*	8-0	ND	4.0	2	0	0	0	2	4	67/47	0.00	Leading 8-0
9/22 vs. TOR	8-3	W	**5.0**	3	0	0	0	0	**9**	80/54	0.00	Leading 8-0
9/28 at TEX	4-9	L	3.0	1	**2**	**2**	0	4	4	72/44	1.50	Trailing 2-1
Totals (3GS)		1-1	12.0	6	2	2	0	6	17		1.50	

*start came after a Yankees loss / **Bold**-season high

- On 2/15, was signed to a four-year contract extending through the 2022 season, with a club option for the 2023 season.
- Was placed on the 10-day I.L. with right shoulder rotator cuff inflammation on 3/28 (retroactive to 3/25)…was transferred to the 60-day I.L. on 4/25…was reinstated on 9/17 after missing the team's first 151 games…was just his second career I.L. stint (first was 5/14-30/16).
- Made three rehab starts, all in September, going 0-1 with a 4.70 ERA (7.2IP, 13H, 7R/4ER, 0BB, 11K, 2HR)…on 9/1 with Triple-A Scranton/WB, allowed 2ER in 1.0IP…on 9/6 with Double-A Trenton, permitted 1ER in 3.0IP in an Eastern League postseason game…on 9/11 with Trenton, allowed 4R/1ER in 3.2IP in another postseason game.
- Made his season debut in a 9/17 start vs. Los Angeles-AL, throwing 4.0 scoreless innings (2H, 2BB, 4K).
- On 9/22 vs. Toronto, started the Yankees' final home game of the 2019 regular season, tossing 5.0 shutout innings (3H, 0BB, 9K, 1HP) to earn his first win since 9/25/18 at Tampa Bay…became the second Yankees pitcher in the last 52 seasons (since 1968) to toss at least 4.0 shutout innings in each of his first two appearances of a season, joining Pascual Perez in 1991.
- In his three starts, his 119 fastballs averaged 96.2 mph (Statcast).
- Made two postseason starts, going 0-1 with a 2.16 ERA (8.1IP, 9H, 2ER, 5BB, 10K, 2HR)…tossed 4.0 scoreless innings (ND, 4H, 2BB, 4K) in ALDS Game 3 at Minnesota, his second career scoreless postseason start (also 4.0IP in 2018 ALWCG vs. Oakland)…took the loss in ALCS Game 3 vs. Houston (4.1IP, 5H, 2ER, 3BB, 6K, 2HR), allowing solo HRs to Jose Altuve in the first and Josh Reddick in the second.

2018

- Went 19-8 with a 3.39 ERA (191.1IP, 173H, 76R/72ER, 46BB, 220K, 19HR) and one complete game in 32 starts…held opponents to a .238 BA (173-for-726); LH .252 (81-for-321), RH .227 (92-for-405)…ranked seventh among Major League pitchers and fourth among AL pitchers with 5.7 WAR (FanGraphs).
- Was named via the Player Ballot to his second career All-Star team (also 2017)…was the first Yankees starting pitcher to be named to consecutive All-Star teams since CC Sabathia made it to three straight from 2010-12…tossed a scoreless second inning (1H, 2K) in the AL's 8-6, 10-inning win, allowing a double to Matt Kemp and striking out Bryce Harper and Brandon Crawford.
- Ranked third in the Majors (and AL) in wins, behind Tampa Bay's Blake Snell (21-5) and Cleveland's Corey Kluber (20-7)…were tied for the second-most wins by a Yankee since 2009, behind CC Sabathia (21-7 in 2010)…was the first Yankee to win 15 games since 2012 (Phil Hughes-16, Hiroki Kuroda-16, CC Sabathia-15)…in 14 seasons since 2006, tied for the second-highest win total by any pitcher in his age-24 season or younger, behind Clayton Kershaw (21-5 in 2011), and was the first AL pitcher that young to win at least 19 games since David Price (19-6) in 2010…were the second-most wins by a Yankees pitcher, age-24-or-younger, in the last 51 seasons (since 1969), behind Andy Pettitte (21-8 in 1996).
- Finished eighth in the AL with 220 strikeouts…was the sixth-highest single-season strikeout total in Yankees history…ranked fourth in the AL with a 4.78 K/BB ratio and seventh with a 10.35 K/9.0IP ratio…had five double-digit-strikeout games, tied for 10th-most by a Yankee in a single season, and tied for the most since CC Sabathia had six in 2012.
- Tied for sixth in the AL in starts and ranked ninth in the AL in ERA…was sixth among qualified AL pitchers with 2.95 FIP (FanGraphs).
- His 32 starts tied for the most by a Yankee in the last seven seasons (since 2013).

YANKEES SINGLE-SEASON STRIKEOUT LEADERS		
RK PITCHER	YEAR	K
1 Ron Guidry	1978	248
2 Jack Chesbro	1904	239
3 **LUIS SEVERINO**	**2017**	**230**
CC Sabathia	2011	230
5 David Cone	1997	222
6 **LUIS SEVERINO**	**2018**	**220**

- The Yankees went 24-8 in his 32 starts, tied for the most team wins started by one pitcher in 2018…were the second-most Yankees wins started by one pitcher in a season in the last 21 years (since 1999) behind Roger Clemens (27) in 2001…the Yankees won 10 straight Severino starts from 4/16-6/4…the Yankees were 18-2 in his first 20 starts; according to STATS, Inc., was only the second time in the Live Ball Era that the Yankees won at least 18 of a pitcher's first 20 starts of a season (were 18-2 in Ron Guidry's first 20 starts in 1978).
- Led Major League starters with an average fastball velocity of 97.6 mph (FanGraphs)…per Statcast, threw 50 pitches in the sixth inning or later that registered at 99.0 mph-or-faster, the most by a starter in the Majors (Chris Sale was second with 16)…threw first-pitch strikes to 68.9 percent of batters, the highest mark in the AL and third-highest in the Majors…opponents hit .191 (56-for-293) with 11BB, 119K and 6HR in ABs ending in a slider (Brooks Baseball).

- Became the fifth pitcher in Yankees history to record at least 10K with 0BB three times in a single season, joining Mike Mussina (4 in 2001), David Cone (3 in 1998), Masahiro Tanaka (3 in 2017) and David Wells (3 in 1998).
- Led the Majors in wins before the All-Star break, going 14-2 with a 2.31 ERA (128.1IP, 33ER) in 20 starts…was the fourth pitcher in franchise history to record at least 14 wins prior to the All-Star break, joining Mel Stottlemyre (14-7 in 24GS in 1969), Whitey Ford (16-2 in 21GS in 1961) and Lefty Gomez (14-2 in 19G/17GS in 1934)…was only the fourth Major League pitcher in 16 seasons (since 2003) to record at least 14 wins prior to the All-Star break, joining Los Angeles-NL's Clayton Kershaw (14-2 in 19GS in 2017), Chicago-AL's Chris Sale (14-3 in 18GS in 2016) and Colorado's Ubaldo Jimenez (15-1 in 18GS in 2010)…went just 5-6 with a 5.57 ERA (63.0IP, 39ER) in 12 starts after the break.
- Went 10-2 with a 2.74 ERA (92.0IP, 28ER) in 15 starts at Yankee Stadium…was the fourth pitcher to earn at least 10 wins in a season at the current Yankee Stadium, joining CC Sabathia (11-2 in 2010, 10-5 in 2013), Phil Hughes (11-4 in 2010, 11-4 in 2012) and Hiroki Kuroda (11-6 in 2012).
- From 9/3/17-7/1/18, went 11-0 with a 1.83 ERA (88.2IP, 18ER) over 14 home starts, all Yankees wins…the 11 wins were the most consecutive winning decisions at home by a Yankee since CC Sabathia was 16-0 from 7/18/09-9/2/10…marked the Yankees' longest winning streak in a pitcher's starts at the current Yankee Stadium and the longest since winning 16 consecutive David Cone home starts from 8/17/97-8/27/98.
- Went 9-6 with a 3.99 ERA (99.1IP, 44ER) in 17 road starts, tying for fourth in the AL in road wins.
- From 4/7/17-6/26/18, recorded at least 6K in 23 consecutive road starts, the fourth-longest streak in Major League history (Randy Johnson-33GS from 8/22/98-8/14/00; Pedro Martinez-28GS from 8/24/99-6/21/01; Randy Johnson-25GS from 8/30/00-5/11/02)…was nearly triple the length of the next-longest streak in Yankees history (eight, by Roger Clemens and Melido Perez).
- Made his first career Opening Day start on 3/29 at Toronto, allowing just 1H over 5.2 scoreless innings (3BB, 7K) to earn the win…was the first Yankees starter to earn a win on Opening Day since Chien-Ming Wang on 4/1/08 vs. Toronto…was the first scoreless Opening Day start by a Yankee since Roger Clemens (6.0IP, 3H) on 3/31/03 at Toronto…the 1H marked the fewest by a Yankees Opening Day starter since at least 1908…at 24 years, 37 days, was the youngest Yankees Opening Day starter since Lefty Gomez (23 years, 138 days) on 4/12/32 at Philadelphia-AL…only three pitchers younger than Severino have started for the Yankees on Opening Day: Gomez, Ray Caldwell (23 years, 351 days on 4/11/1912 vs. Boston) and Hippo Vaughn twice (23 years, 3 days on 4/12/1911 at Philadelphia-AL; 22 years, 5 days on 4/14/1910 vs. Boston)…was the fifth-youngest pitcher since 1908 to allow 1H-or-fewer in a scoreless Opening Day start…was the youngest since 21-year-old Bob Feller threw a no-hitter for Cleveland on 4/16/40 at Chicago-AL…was the first Dominican-born pitcher and fourth foreign-born pitcher to start for the Yankees on Opening Day, joining Masahiro Tanaka (Japan) in 2015-17 and '19, Chien-Ming Wang (Taiwan) in 2008 and Orlando Hernandez (Cuba) in 2000.
- From 4/16-6/4, went 7-0 with a 1.85 ERA (68.0IP, 14ER) over 10 starts, the longest winning streak and longest streak of unbeaten starts of his career…turned in a quality start in each outing, the longest QS streak by a Yankee since Masahiro Tanaka had 14QS in his first 14 Major League starts from 4/4-6/28/14.
- In 5/2 win at Houston, tossed his first career complete game and shutout (5H, 1BB, 10K)…marked the most strikeouts in a shutout by a Yankees pitcher since Mike Mussina on 9/24/02 vs. Tampa Bay (12K, 2H)…at 24 years, 71 days old, was the second-youngest Yankee in the last 47 seasons (since 1972) to toss a shutout, behind Sterling Hitchcock (24 years, 22 days) on 5/21/95 vs. Baltimore (4H)…was the youngest Yankee with at least 10K in a CGSHO since Stan Bahnsen (23 years, 230 days) on 8/1/68 at Boston (12K, 3H)…was the second Yankee since 2004 to throw a shutout against the defending World Series champion (also Iván Nova, 6H on 9/21/13 vs. San Francisco).
- In six May starts, went 4-0 with a 2.03 ERA (40.0IP, 9ER) and 50K…was the fifth 50-strikeout calendar month by a Yankee in the last 50 seasons since 1969 (Ron Guidry, 64K in June 1978; David Cone, 56K in June 1997; CC Sabathia, 50K in July 2011; Randy Johnson, 50K in July 2005)…was the first Yankee with at least 50K and zero losses in a calendar month since David Cone in June 1997 (2-0, 56K).
- Won a career-best five consecutive starts from 6/16-7/7.
- Allowed 3R-or-fewer in 16 consecutive starts from 4/16-7/7, the second-longest streak by a Yankees starter in franchise history, behind Russ Ford's 20-start streak over two seasons from 1910-11.
- In 7/23 loss at Tampa Bay, recorded his 500th career strikeout in the second inning (Willy Adames), just the third Yankees pitcher to reach the mark prior to his 25th birthday, also Al Downing (644K) and Lefty Gomez (511K).
- In 9/5 loss at Oakland, reached 500.0 career innings pitched, becoming the 11th Yankee to reach the milestone prior to his 25th birthday, and the first to do it since Dave Righetti from 1979-83.
- In 9/19 win vs. Boston, induced seven pop-ups, tied for the most by a Yankees pitcher in a single game in the last 12 seasons (since 2008), with Bartolo Colon (8/11/11 vs. Los Angeles-AL).

2017

- In his first full Major League season, went 14-6 with a 2.98 ERA (193.1IP, 150H, 73R/64ER, 51BB, 230K, 21HR) in 31 starts…held opponents to a .208 BA (150-for-720); LH .221 (72-for-326), RH .198 (78-for-394)…pitched the entire season at 23 years old, the seventh-youngest AL pitcher to start a game.
- Finished third in AL Cy Young Award voting behind winner Corey Kluber and runner-up Chris Sale…appeared on 27-of-30 ballots and receiving 73 points (3 third place votes, 6 fourth place votes, 1 fifth place vote)…was the highest finish by a Yankees pitcher since CC Sabathia also got third in 2010.

- Ranked third in the AL in ERA and fourth in strikeouts…his 5.6 WAR (FanGraphs) was third among AL pitchers and fourth in the Majors…was the highest WAR by a Yankees pitcher since CC Sabathia's 6.4 WAR in 2011…was third among qualified AL pitchers with a 3.07 FIP…finished second in the AL in opponents' SLG (.338) and OPS (.603), third in opp. BA (.208) and OBP (.266), and third in WHIP (1.04)…his 10.71 K/9.0IP ratio was fourth-best in the AL and his 4.51 K/BB ratio was fifth.
- Posted the lowest ERA by a qualified Yankee since David Cone (2.82) and Andy Pettitte (2.88) in 1997.
- Recorded the highest K/9.0IP ratio by a qualifying pitcher in Yankees history (10.71)…had the lowest opp. BA by a qualified Yankee since Ron Guidry (.193) in 1978, the lowest opp. OBP since David Wells (.265) in 1998, the lowest opp. SLG since David Cone (.332) and Andy Pettitte (.335) in 1997, and the lowest opp. OPS since Ron Guidry (.585) in 1981…marked the best WHIP by a qualified Yankee since Ron Guidry (0.99) in 1981.
- Was named to his first career AL All-Star Team via the Player Ballot, but did not pitch in the game…at age 23, was the youngest Yankees All-Star pitcher since Mel Stottlemyre (also 23) in 1965.
- Ranked sixth in the Majors (fourth in the AL) with 230K…was the fourth Yankees pitcher to record 230K in a season, joining Ron Guidry (248 in 1978), Jack Chesbro (239 in 1904) and CC Sabathia (230 in 2011)…were the most by a Yankee, age-23 or younger, surpassing Al Downing's 217 in 1964…were the second-most strikeouts by an AL pitcher, age-23 or younger, in 31 years (since 1987), behind Tampa Bay's Scott Kazmir (239) in 2007.
- Was the second AL pitcher in 41 years (since 1977) to post a sub-3.00 ERA with at least 225K at age-23 or younger, joining Boston's Roger Clemens (2.48, 238K, age-23) in his AL MVP and Cy Young-winning 1986 season.
- Recorded his first five career double-digit-strikeout games, tied for fourth-most among AL pitchers…was tied for 10th-most in a season by a Yankees pitcher and second-most at age-23 or younger (Al Downing, eight at age-22 in 1963)…had at least 7K in a Yankees-record 21 games.
- His 16 starts with 1R-or-fewer led the Majors…were tied for the third-most such starts by a Yankee in a single season since 1908 (Ron Guidry-18 in 1978, Whitey Ford-18 in 1964, Mike Mussina-16 in 2001, Spud Chandler-16 in 1943, Russ Ford-16 in 1910)…allowed 1ER-or-fewer in 17 starts, tied for the Major League lead…were the most by a Yankee since Ron Guidry (21 in 1978).
- Led the AL with a 2.24 road ERA (96.1IP, 24ER) while going 6-1 in 15 starts…was also the fifth-lowest road ERA in the Majors…was the first Yankee ever to allow 1R-or-fewer in 11 different road starts…went 4-0 with a 0.89 ERA (40.2IP, 4ER) in six road starts after the All-Star break, becoming the second Yankees pitcher in 100 years to allow 1R-or-fewer in at least six consecutive road starts within a single season (Al Downing, seven straight from 5/14-9/14/68)…from 7/15/17-3/29/18, compiled a streak of seven consecutive road starts with 1R-or-fewer, tied for the AL's second-longest such streak since 1908 (Minnesota's Johan Santana, eight starts from 7/17-9/29/04).
- On 4/13 vs. Tampa Bay (7.0IP, 5H, 2ER, 1BB, 11K, 1HR) and 4/18 vs. Chicago-AL (8.0IP, 3H, 4R/3ER, 0BB, 10K, 2HR), became the third of four pitchers in Yankees history to record at least 10K and one-or-zero walks in consecutive games, joining James Paxton (4/16/19 and 4/21/19), Masahiro Tanaka (4/9/14 and 4/16/14) and David Wells (9/1/98 and 9/7/98)–credit: *Elias*.
- On 6/27 at Chicago-AL, recorded a career-high 12 strikeouts and did not walk a batter over 7.0IP…at 23 years, 127 days old, was the second-youngest Yankees pitcher to fan at least 12 batters in a game, behind Al Downing, who did it six times at age-22 in 1963-64…was the youngest pitcher in club history with at least 12K and 0BB, breaking the mark previously held by Stan Bahnsen (23y, 230d) on 8/1/68 at Boston (12K in 9.0IP CG SHO).
- On 8/17 at the Mets, recorded his first Major League hit with a bunt single off Steven Matz and scored his first run in the fourth inning.
- Made his first four postseason starts, going 1-1 with a 5.63 ERA (16.0IP, 10ER)…made his postseason debut in the AL Wild Card Game vs. Minnesota (ND, 0.1IP, 3ER), matching the shortest start by a Yankees pitcher in postseason history (also Art Ditmar in 1960 WS Game 1 at Pittsburgh and Bob Turley in 1958 WS Game 2 at Milwaukee)…earned his first postseason win in ALDS Game 4 vs. Cleveland (7.0IP, 3ER, 9K), also becoming the second-youngest Yankee (23 years, 231 days) to record 9K in a postseason game, behind Dave Righetti (22 years, 314 days in 1981 ALDS Game 2 at Milwaukee-10K)…made two road starts in the ALCS vs. Houston, taking a no-decision in Game 2 (4.0IP, 1ER) and a loss in Game 6 (4.2IP, 3ER).

2016
- Went 3-8 with a 5.83 ERA (71.0IP, 78H, 48R/46ER, 25BB, 66K, 11HR, 3HP, 3WP) in 22 games (11 starts) with the Yankees over four stints with the Yankees (4/4-5/30, 7/25-8/10, 8/12-14 and 9/2-10/2)…had 0.6 WAR (FanGraphs)…was the second-youngest AL pitcher to start a game, behind Minnesota's José Berrios.
- Was placed on the 15-day D.L. from 5/14-30 with a right triceps strain.
- Was 3-0 with a 0.39 ERA (23.1IP, 8H, 2R/1ER, 10BB, 25K) in 11 Major League relief appearances…led Major League relievers (min. 20.0 relief innings) in ERA, the second-lowest ERA by a reliever in Yankees history (min. 20.0 relief innings) to Joba Chamberlain's 0.38 ERA (24.0IP, 1ER) in 2007…also led Major League relievers in opp. BA (.105), opp. slugging (.158) and opp. OPS (.367).
- Went 0-8 with an 8.50 ERA (47.2IP, 70H, 46R/45ER, 15BB, 41K, 11HR) in 11 starts…was the second pitcher in Yankees history to make at least 11 starts in a season without earning a win as a starter (Fred Talbot, 0-8 in 11 starts in 1968)…the Yankees were 2-9 in his 11 starts, losing each of his first nine.
- Lost six consecutive starts from 4/26-8/14, the longest single-season losing streak by a Yankee since Tim Leary also lost six straight starts from 5/28-6/23/90.
- Earned his first career ejection on 9/26 at Toronto (by Todd Tichenor, for throwing at Justin Smoak).
- In 13 games (12 starts) with the RailRiders, went 8-1 with a 3.49 ERA (77.1IP, 30ER).

2015
- In his first Major League season, went 5-3 with a 2.89 ERA (62.1IP, 20ER) in 11 starts…opponents hit .229 (53-for-231); LH .244 (30-for-123), RH .213 (23-for-108)…recorded a 0.7 WAR (FanGraphs).
- Was the fourth pitcher in Yankees history to record at least five wins and post an ERA of 3.00-or-lower in his age-21 season or younger, joining Whitey Ford (1950), Hank Thormahlen (1918) and Ray Keating (1914)…since 2009, only five other Major League pitchers have accomplished that feat: Mike Soroka (2019), José Fernandez (2013), Madison Bumgarner (2010), Stephen Strasburg (2010) and Clayton Kershaw (2009)…was the first AL starting pitcher to do so since the Royals' Bret Saberhagen (20-6, 2.87) won the AL Cy Young Award as a 21-year-old in 1985.
- Went 3-2 with a 2.04 ERA (35.1IP, 8ER) and 34K in his first six career starts…was the first Yankees pitcher since 1913 to record at least 30K and an ERA as low as 2.04 in his first six career games…his 2.04 ERA was the lowest by a Yankees pitcher through six career appearances (min. 30.0IP) since Bob Porterfield had a 1.94 ERA (46.1IP, 10ER) in his first six career games (two starts) in 1948.
- Made his Major League debut at 21 years, 166 days old on 8/5 vs. Boston and took the loss in the Yankees' 2-1 defeat (5.0IP, 2H, 2R/1ER, 0BB, 7K, 1HR)…recorded his first career strikeout (Xander Bogaerts)…was the youngest pitcher to make a start in the Majors in 2015 and the youngest Yankees pitcher to start a game since Phil Hughes was 21 years, 95 days old in his final start of 2007…became the first pitcher in AL history with 2H-or-fewer, no walks and at least 7K in his Major League debut…was the sixth Major League pitcher (third starter) to do it in the Modern Era (since 1900), joining five NL pitchers: Atlanta's Manny Banuelos (5.2IP, 2H, 0BB, 7K on 7/2/15 vs. Washington); Arizona's Max Scherzer (4.1IP, 0H, 0BB, 7K in relief on 4/29/08 vs. Houston); Cincinnati's Johnny Cueto (7.0IP, 1H, 0BB, 10K on 4/3/08 vs. Arizona); Los Angeles-NL's Pete Richert (3.1IP, 0H, 0BB, 7K in relief on 4/12/62 vs. Cincinnati); and the Milwaukee Braves' Don McMahon (4.0IP, 2H, 0BB, 7K in relief on 6/30/57-G2 vs. Pittsburgh)…was the third pitcher in Yankees history to record at least 7K and no walks in his Major League debut, joining Masahiro Tanaka (7.0IP, 0BB, 8K on 4/14 at Toronto) and Rich Beck (7.0IP, 0BB, 8K on 9/14/65 at Washington-AL)…was the first Yankees starter since 1913 to take a loss while throwing at least 5.0IP and allowing two baserunners-or-fewer (via H/BB/HP).
- Debuted in the same series as the Red Sox' Henry Owens (8/4/15), as the two became just the second pair of Yankees and Red Sox pitchers since 1913 to make their MLB debuts as starting pitchers in the same series, joining the Red Sox' Jim Bagby (4/18/38 vs. New York) and the Yankees' Atley Donald (4/21/38 at Boston).
- Earned his first Major League win on 8/22 vs. Cleveland (6.0IP, 1ER)…at 21 years, 183 days, was the second-youngest Yankee in 30 years (since 1985) to earn a win, behind Phil Hughes, who earned five wins at a younger age in 2007.
- Went 9-2 with a 2.45 ERA (99.1IP, 72H, 35R/27ER, 27BB, 98K, 2HR) in 19 starts between Double-A Trenton and Triple-A Scranton/Wilkes-Barre…after the season, was named to *Baseball America*'s 2015 Triple-A Post-Season All-Star Team…was named an MiLB.com Organization All-Star.

2014
- Combined with Single-A Charleston, Single-A Tampa and Double-A Trenton to go 6-5 with a 2.46 ERA (113.1IP, 31ER, 27BB, 127K) in 24 starts…opponents batted .220 (93-for-423, 3HR); RH .236 (59-for-250); LH .197 (34-for-173)…led all Yankees minor leaguers in strikeouts…was tabbed an Organization All-Star by MiLB.com…competed for the World Team in the SiriusXM All-Star Futures Game at Minnesota.
- Began the season with Charleston, going 3-2 with a 2.79 ERA (67.2IP, 21ER) in 14 starts…was promoted to Tampa on 6/20 and went 1-1 with a 1.31 ERA (20.2IP, 3ER) in four starts…was named FSL "Pitcher of the Week" on 6/30 after throwing 6.0 hitless innings on 6/25 at Clearwater (1BB, 6K)…allowed 0ER in his final three starts with Tampa (16.0IP, 6H)…was promoted to Trenton on 7/16 and made six starts with the Thunder, going 2-2 with a 2.52 ERA (25.0IP, 7ER).
- Following the season, was rated by *Baseball America* as the Yankees' top prospect and the No. 35 overall prospect (No. 16 pitcher)…was tabbed by MLB.com as the No. 23 prospect in baseball.

2013
- Combined with GCL Yankees 1 and Single-A Charleston to go 4-2 with a 2.45 ERA (44.0IP, 12ER, 10BB, 53K) in 10 appearances (eight starts)…produced a 1.37 ERA (26.1IP, 4ER) and .172 opponents' BA (16-for-93) in six games (four starts) in the GCL…was promoted to Charleston on 7/29 and went 1-1 with a 4.08 ERA (17.2IP, 8ER) in four starts.
- Following the season, was tabbed by *Baseball America* as the No. 9 prospect in the Yankees organization.

2012
- Made his professional debut with DSL Yankees 1, going 4-2 with a 1.68 ERA (64.1IP, 12ER, 45K) in 14 starts.

PERSONAL
- Is married to Rosmaly…the couple has a daughter, Abigail (born July 2015).
- He and Rosmaly established the Luis & Rosmaly Severino Foundation in 2018, with the mission of supporting the educational and technological development of teenagers in their communities, and improving the quality of life in those communities through the development of educational projects and social action programs.
- Is one of several Major Leaguers from Latin America who learned English partially by way of watching episodes of the critically-acclaimed sitcom series, *Friends*.

Severino's Career Pitching Record

Year	Club	W	L	ERA	G	GS	CG	SHO	SV	IP	H	R	ER	HR	HP	BB	SO	WP	BK
2012	DSL Yankees 1	4	2	1.68	14	14	0	0	0	64.1	46	19	12	2	3	17	45	3	0
2013	GCL Yankees 1	3	1	1.37	6	4	0	0	0	26.1	16	5	4	0	2	6	32	1	0
	Charleston	1	1	4.08	4	4	0	0	0	17.2	21	9	8	1	0	4	21	2	0
2014	Charleston	3	2	2.79	14	14	0	0	0	67.2	62	24	21	2	3	15	70	4	0
	Tampa	1	1	1.31	4	4	0	0	0	20.2	11	4	3	0	0	6	28	0	0
	Trenton	2	2	2.52	6	6	0	0	0	25.0	20	8	7	1	0	6	29	0	1
2015	Trenton	2	2	3.32	8	8	0	0	0	38.0	32	17	14	2	2	10	48	1	1
	Scranton/WB	7	0	1.91	11	11	0	0	0	61.1	40	18	13	0	3	17	50	3	0
	YANKEES	5	3	2.89	11	11	0	0	0	62.1	53	21	20	9	2	22	56	3	1
2016	YANKEES - a	3	8	5.83	22	11	0	0	0	71.0	78	48	46	11	3	25	66	3	0
	Tampa	0	0	0.00	1	1	0	0	0	3.0	2	0	0	0	0	0	2	0	0
	Scranton/WB	8	1	3.49	13	12	0	0	0	77.1	75	31	30	4	2	18	78	5	0
2017	YANKEES	14	6	2.98	31	31	0	0	0	193.1	150	73	64	21	6	51	230	6	0
2018	YANKEES	19	8	3.39	32	32	1	1	0	191.1	173	76	72	19	5	46	220	8	0
2019	Scranton/WB	0	0	18.00	1	1	0	0	0	1.0	3	2	2	1	0	0	2	0	0
	YANKEES - b	1	1	1.50	3	3	0	0	0	12.0	6	2	2	0	1	6	17	0	0
Minor League Totals		31	12	2.55	82	79	0	0	0	402.2	328	137	114	13	15	99	405	19	2
Major League Totals		42	26	3.46	99	88	1	1	0	530.0	460	220	204	60	17	150	589	19	1

Signed by the Yankees as a minor league free agent on December 26, 2011.

a – Placed on the 15-day disabled list from May 14-30, 2016, with a right triceps strain.
b – Placed on the 10-day injured list from March 28 (retroactive to March 25) – September 17, 2019 with right shoulder rotator cuff inflammation…was transferred to the 60-day injured list on April 25.

Severino's Postseason Record

Year	Club vs. Opp.	W	L	ERA	G	GS	CG	SHO	SV	IP	H	R	ER	HR	HP	BB	SO	WP	BK
2015	NYY vs. HOU (WC)					On Roster - Did Not Pitch													
2017	NYY vs. MIN (WC)	0	0	81.00	1	1	0	0	0	0.1	4	3	3	2	0	1	0	0	0
	NYY vs. CLE (DS)	1	0	3.86	1	1	0	0	0	7.0	4	3	3	2	0	1	9	0	0
	NYY vs. HOU (CS)	0	1	4.15	2	2	0	0	0	8.2	5	4	4	1	0	6	3	0	0
2018	NYY vs. OAK (WC)	0	0	0.00	1	1	0	0	0	4.0	2	0	0	0	0	4	7	0	0
	NYY vs. BOS (DS)	0	1	18.00	1	1	0	0	0	3.0	7	6	6	0	0	2	2	0	0
2019	NYY vs. MIN (DS)	0	0	0.00	1	1	0	0	0	4.0	4	0	0	0	0	2	4	0	0
	NYY vs. HOU (CS)	0	1	4.15	1	1	0	0	0	4.1	5	2	2	2	0	3	6	0	0
Wild Card Game Totals		0	0	6.23	2	2	0	0	0	4.1	6	3	3	2	0	5	7	0	0
Division Series Totals		1	1	5.79	3	3	0	0	0	14.0	15	9	9	2	0	5	15	0	0
LCS Totals		0	2	4.15	3	3	0	0	0	13.0	10	6	6	3	0	9	9	0	0
POSTSEASON TOTALS		1	3	5.17	8	8	0	0	0	31.1	31	18	18	7	0	19	31	0	0

Severino's All-Star Game Record

Year	Club, Site	W	L	ERA	G	GS	CG	SHO	SV	IP	H	R	ER	HR	HP	BB	SO	WP	BK
2017	NYY, Miami					Selected - Did Not Pitch													
2018	NYY, Washington	0	0	0.00	1	0	0	0	0	1.0	1	0	0	0	0	0	2	0	0
All-Star Game Totals		0	0	0.00	1	0	0	0	0	1.0	1	0	0	0	0	0	2	0	0

Severino's Career Fielding Record

Position	PCT	G	PO	A	E	TC	DP
Pitcher	.924	99	22	75	8	105	7

Severino's Regular Season Batting Record

Year	Team	AVG	G	AB	R	H	2B	3B	HR	RBI	SH	SF	HP	BB	SO	SB	CS
2019	NYY					Did Not Bat											
Major League Totals		.083	99	12	1	1	0	0	0	0	0	0	0	0	5	0	0

Severino's Career Bests and Streaks

COMPLETE GAMES: 1, 5/2/18 at HOU. **LOW-HIT COMPLETE GAME:** 5, 5/2/18 at HOU. **IP (START):** 9.0, 5/2/18 at HOU. **IP (RELIEF):** 4.1, 8/3/16 vs. NYM. **HITS:** 11, 7/23/18 at TB. **RUNS:** 10, 8/12/17 vs. BOS. **BB:** 4 - 5 times (last on 9/28/19 at TEX). **SO:** 12, 6/27/17 at CWS. **HR:** 3 - 2 times (last on 8/28/17 vs. CLE). **WINNING STREAK:** 7g, 4/16-6/4(G1)/18. **LOSING STREAK:** 6g, 4/8-5/13/16. **SCORELESS STREAK (IP):** 17.0 - 2 times (last from 7/15-26/17).

Pitcher of the Month: None   **Player of the Week:** None   **Rookie of the Month:** None

DEREK JETER'S FAREWELL SPEECH FOLLOWING FINAL GAME AT THE ORIGINAL YANKEE STADIUM
September 21, 2008

"For all of us up here, it's a huge honor to put this uniform on every day and come out here and play. Every member of this organization, past and present, has been calling this place home for 85 years. There's a lot of tradition, a lot of history, and a lot of memories. Now, the great thing about memories, is you're able to pass [them] along from generation to generation. And although things are going to change next year – we're going to move across the street – there are a few things with the New York Yankees that never change. That's pride, it's tradition, and most of all, we have the greatest fans in the world.

"We're relying on you to take the memories from this Stadium, add them to the new memories that come at the new Yankee Stadium and continue to pass them on from generation to generation. So, on behalf of the entire organization, we just want to take this moment to salute you, the greatest fans in the world."

GIANCARLO STANTON • OF

27

HT: 6-6 • **WT:** 245 • **BATS:** R • **THROWS:** R
BIRTHDATE: 11/8/89 • **OPENING DAY AGE:** 30
BIRTHPLACE: Panorama, Calif.
RESIDES: Miami, Fla.
M.L. SERVICE: 9 years, 118 days

STATUS
- Was acquired by the Yankees from the Miami Marlins along with cash considerations in exchange for 2B Starlin Castro, RHP Jorge Guzman and INF José Devers on December 11, 2017…contract extends through the 2027 season, with an opt-out following the 2020 season.

CAREER NOTES
- Has homered against every Major League team in his career except Miami.
- Hit 270HR through his first 1,000 career games…only three players hit as many home runs through their first 1,000 career games: Ryan Howard (279), Ralph Kiner (277) and Harmon Killebrew (272).
- Hit his 300th career homer in his 1,119th career game, becoming the fifth-fastest player to reach the mark in Baseball history, trailing only Ralph Kiner (1,087G), Ryan Howard (1,093), Juan González (1,096) and Alex Rodriguez (1,117)…at 28 years, 295 days old, was the ninth-youngest player to reach the mark in Baseball history.
- His 308HR are third-most in the Majors since 2010 (Nelson Cruz-346, Edwin Encarnación-335)…is the 15th-highest total all-time for a player before his 30th birthday.
- Was one of two players with at least 20HR in each season from 2010-18, joining Nelson Cruz…was the 11th player ever to hit at least 20HR in at least each of his first nine Major League seasons.
- Is one of six players with at least four 35HR seasons since 2012…was one of six players (also Mike Trout, Nelson Cruz, Edwin Encarnación, Anthony Rizzo and Justin Upton) to hit at least 25HR in each season from 2014-18…has done so seven times in 10 career seasons (2011-12, '14-18).
- His 32 career multi-homer games are sixth-most among active players behind Albert Pujols (59), Miguel Cabrera (39), Edwin Encarnación (36), Nelson Cruz (34) and Ryan Braun (33)…is one of 11 players in Baseball history with at least 32 multi-HR games prior to turning 30 years old.
- Since the start of his career in 2010, his 13.81 AB/HR ratio leads the Majors (min. 1,500AB)…is the fifth-best mark all-time, behind Mark McGwire (10.61), Babe Ruth (11.76), Barry Bonds (12.92) and Jim Thome (13.76).
- In the Statcast era (since 2015), owns seven of the eight hardest hits, 14 of the top 18 and 20 of the top 28.
- With his trade from the Marlins to the Yankees on 12/11/17, became the second reigning league MVP in Major League history to be traded prior to the start of the following season; on 2/16/04, the Yankees acquired reigning AL MVP Alex Rodriguez from Texas in exchange for Alfonso Soriano and a PTBNL (Joaquin Arias)…*Elias* notes that the only other MVP to change teams in the season following his award was Barry Bonds, who won the NL MVP with Pittsburgh in 1992 and signed with San Francisco as a free agent prior to the 1993 season.
- Was the fifth player to be acquired by the Yankees the year immediately after leading or tying for a league lead in HRs, joining Babe Ruth (acquired in 1920), Johnny Mize (1949), Alex Rodriguez (2004) and Chris Carter (2017).
- His acquisition made the 2018 Yankees the second team in Major League history to acquire Baseball's reigning home run champion after leading the Majors in team homers the prior year; the 1919 Yankees led the Majors with 45 home runs, then acquired Babe Ruth (29HR in 1919) from Boston prior to the 1920 season (credit: *Elias*).
- Made his postseason debut in 2018…his 1,144 career regular season games at the time of his first playoff game were second-most among active players who have never reached the postseason, behind Seattle's Kyle Seager (1,155G at the time of Stanton's playoff debut)…his 305 regular season home runs led that group, 112 more than second-place Khris Davis (193HR), who also made his playoff debut in the 2018 AL Wild Card Game.
- Wears an extended helmet flap to protect his face after suffering facial lacerations, small fractures and dental damage when he was hit in the face by a pitch thrown by Milwaukee's Mike Fiers on 9/11/14.
- His 267HR with the Marlins are most in franchise history…enters 2020 as one of only four active players who hold a franchise's all-time home run lead, joining Ryan Braun (344HR with Milwaukee), Evan Longoria (261HR with Tampa Bay) and Ryan Zimmerman (270HR with Washington).
- Is also the Marlins' all-time leader in RBI (672), extra-base hits (479) and total bases (1,983)…ranks second in walks (487), third in runs scored (576), doubles (202) and games played (986) and fifth in hits (960)…his 34.6 WAR are the most by any player in Marlins history (FanGraphs)…his 60 assists lead all Marlins outfielders.
- Led the Marlins in home runs each season from 2011-17…according to *Elias*, is one of two active players to outright lead the same franchise in home runs in at least seven consecutive seasons, joining Albert Pujols, who led St. Louis in homers in seven straight seasons from 2001-07.
- Has made nine Opening Day rosters, seven with the Marlins (2011-17) and two with the Yankees (2018-19)…has reached base safely in 6-of-10 Opening Day plate appearances with the Yankees, going 4-for-8 with 4R, 1 double, 2HR, 4RBI and 2BB.

CAREER HIGHLIGHTS

NL Most Valuable Player
- 2017

NL All-Star Team
- 2012, 2014, 2015, 2017

NL Silver Slugger
- 2014, 2017

2019
- Hit .288 (17-for-59) with 8R, 3 doubles, 3HR, 13RBI and 12BB in 18 games with the Yankees.
- Reached base safely three times in 3/28 Opening Day win vs. Baltimore…according to Statcast, his first-inning single to right field had an exit velocity of 120.6 mph, the fifth-hardest-hit base hit in the Statcast era (since 2015).
- Was placed on the 10-day injured list on 4/1 with a left biceps strain…began a rehab assignment on 5/20, but was returned from rehab on 5/22 with left calf tightness after appearing in just one game…began a second rehab assignment on 6/11…in six total rehab appearances with Single-A Tampa and Triple-A Scranton/Wilkes-Barre, hit .286 (6-for-21) with 5R, 5HR and 8RBI…was returned from rehab and reinstated from the 10-day I.L. on 6/18.
- Hit his first HR of the season on 6/24 vs. Toronto (estimated at 445 ft.).
- Was placed on the 10-day injured list on 6/26 with a right knee sprain…left 6/25 game with a right knee contusion…was transferred to the 60-day injured list on 8/11…was reinstated on 9/18, missing 73 team games…played in just six Major League games between I.L. stints.
- Went 8-for-28 with 4R, 2 doubles, 2HR and 6RBI in nine games after returning from his second I.L. stint.
- Doubled in his first plate appearance on 9/18 (1-for-3) after being reinstated from the 60-day I.L. prior to the game.
- Hit the Yankees' 300th home run of the season in the first inning on 9/27 at Texas…reached base five times in the game (3-for-3, 1R, 1HR, 3RBI, 2BB), his 11th career game reaching safely at least five times.
- Hit .231 (3-for-13) with 1R, 1HR, 2RBI and 4BB in five postseason games, with the Yankees going 5-0 in those contests…had 3BB in ALDS Game 1 vs. Minnesota (had 1BB in 22PA in 2018 postseason)…hit a solo HR in ALCS Game 1 at Houston…missed four games in the ALCS with a low Grade 2 quad strain.

2018
- Hit .266/.343/.509 (164-for-617) with 102R, 34 doubles, 38HR, 100RBI and 70BB in 158 games (85GS at DH, 37 in RF and 35 in LF) in his first season with the Yankees…reached the 100RBI plateau for the second straight season and third time in his career (105RBI in 2014 and 132RBI in 2017)…reached 100R for the second time (123R in 2017).
- Was the Yankees' nominee for the 2018 Hank Aaron Award…won the award in both 2014 and '17 with Miami.
- Batted .316/.391/.645 (48-for-152) with 9 doubles, 1 triple, 13HR and 28RBI off left-handed pitching.
- His 38HR were fifth-most by a player in his first season as a Yankee, trailing Babe Ruth (54HR in 1920), Jason Giambi (41HR in 2002), Mark Teixeira (39HR in 2009) and Roger Maris (39HR in 1960).
- With 38HR and 34 doubles, was one of nine Majors Leaguers to reach 30 doubles and 35HR in 2018…was the first Yankee to reach those benchmarks in the same season since Mark Teixeira in 2009 (39HR, 43 doubles).
- Had a Major League-leading 74 batted balls with an exit velocity of at least 110 mph according to MLB Statcast (next: Nelson Cruz-50)…had five of the Majors' 10 hardest-hit home runs of 2018.
- Had 102R, 38HR and 100RBI, the 12th player in franchise history to reach each of those totals in a single season…was just the fourth to reach those totals in his first season with the club, joining Mark Teixeira in 2009 (39HR, 122RBI, 103R), Jason Giambi in 2002 (41HR, 122RBI, 120R) and Babe Ruth in 1920 (54HR, 136RBI, 158R).
- Had six games of at least 4H in 2018, tied with Arizona's David Peralta for second-most in the Majors (Boston's Mookie Betts-7)…were the most 4H games by a Yankee since Bernie Williams (7 in 1999).
- Became the first Yankee to hit at least 20HR before the All-Star break during his first season with the club since Mark Teixeira in 2009 (21HR before the break)…is the first Yankee to do so after being traded to the team since Alex Rodriguez in 2004 (22HR)…was the only player with at least 20HR before the break each season from 2014-18.
- Went 3-for-5 with 3R, 1 double, 2HR and 4RBI in his Yankees debut in 3/29 win at Toronto, marking his 29th career multi-HR game…according to *Elias*, was just the second player in Yankees history to homer twice in his first game with the club, joining Roger Maris, who began his 1960 AL MVP Award-winning season by going 4-for-5 with 2R, 1 double, 2HR and 4RBI on 4/19/60 at Boston…was the first player to homer in his first plate appearance as a Yankee since Tyler Austin and Aaron Judge did so in consecutive at-bats on 8/13/16 vs. Tampa Bay.
- Became the second Yankee since 1908 to collect at least 3XBH and 4RBI on Opening Day, joining Roger Maris (3XBH, 4RBI) on 4/19/60 at Boston…along with Chicago-AL's Matt Davidson (3-for-4, 4R, 3HR, 5RBI in 2018), became the first Major League hitters to accomplish the feat since Toronto's J.P. Arencibia (3XBH, 5RBI) on 4/1/11 vs. Minnesota…became the seventh Yankee to hit 2HR on Opening Day, the first since Joe Pepitone on 4/9/63 at the Kansas City A's…his ninth-inning homer to center was measured at 109.4 mph.
- Hit .218 in April, .264 in May, .298 in June and .323 in July…was the third player in Yankees history to improve his monthly averages by 25 or more points in every month, April through July (min. 50AB each month), joining Melky Cabrera in 2007 (.200, .254, .298, .368) and Didi Gregorius in 2015 (.206, .232, .258, .317)—credit: *Elias*.
- Hit his third HR of the season in 4/4 win vs. Tampa Bay, becoming the first player ever to hit at least 3HR in the first six team games in his first season as a Yankee.
- His first-inning single in 4/6 loss vs. Baltimore was his 2,000th career total base.
- Struck out a career-high, and franchise-record-tying, five times twice on the Yankees' first homestand (4/3 win vs. Tampa Bay and 4/8 loss vs. Baltimore).
- Played his 1,000th career game on 4/13 at Detroit, becoming the fourth player from the 2007 First-Year Player Draft to reach the 1,000-game milestone, joining OF Jason Heyward, C Matt Wieters and 1B Freddie Freeman…his 270HR were the fourth-most HRs through a player's first 1,000 career games, behind Ryan Howard (279), Ralph Kiner (277) and Harmon Killebrew (272).
- Hit two-run HR and solo HR and was 3-for-4 with 1 double and 4RBI on 5/2 at Houston, driving in all of the Yankees' runs in their 4-0 shutout victory…was his 30th career two-homer game (and second of the season)…became the ninth player in Major League history to record at least 30 multi-homer games prior to turning 29 years old…was the third player in Baseball history to reach 30 multi-HR games through his first 1,016 career games (also Ralph Kiner-35 and Juan González-30).

- Hit two solo HRs in 5/8 win vs. Boston…was his 31st career two-homer game, becoming the second player in Baseball history to reach 31 multi-HR games through his first 1,021 career games (Ralph Kiner-35).
- His fifth-inning single in 5/15 loss at Washington was the 1,000th hit of his Major League career…through his first 1,000 career hits, 499 went for extra bases (211 doubles, 11 triples, 277HR)…was the third player in Baseball history with at least 499 extra-base hits through his first 1,000 career hits (Babe Ruth-517, Adam Dunn-507)—credit: *Elias*.
- Hit solo HR in 5/19 win at Kansas City…the homer was his 500th career extra-base hit…at 28 years, 192 days old, was the fourth-youngest player to debut since 2000 to reach 500XBH (at that time), trailing: Albert Pujols (26 years, 208 days), Miguel Cabrera (27 years, 40 days) and Prince Fielder (28 years, 141 days)…was later surpassed by Mike Trout (27 years, 36 days) and Nolan Arenado (28 years, 147 days).
- Made 85 consecutive starts from 5/28-9/1 (46 at DH, 26 in RF, 13 in LF), the longest streak of consecutive starts by a Yankee since Robinson Canó started 176 in-a-row from 8/17/12-8/27/13…acccording to *Elias*, was the first Yankee to *appear* in at least 85 consecutive team games since Starlin Castro appeared in 96 consecutive games from 6/2-9/17/16.
- Hit two-run "walk-off" HR in the ninth of 6/20 win vs. Seattle…was his sixth career "walk-off" hit (first since a single on 8/19/14 vs. Texas) and fourth career "walk-off" HR (first since 4/18/14 vs. Seattle off Yoervis Medina)…was just the second "walk-off" HR by a Yankee on an 0-2 count since 2000 (also Jason Giambi on 6/5/08 vs. Toronto off B.J. Ryan)…was the first such homer in the Majors since 4/30/17 (Arizona's Daniel Descalso off Colorado's Jordan Lyles)…had an exit velocity of 117.9 mph and an estimated distance of 453 feet.
- Hit game-tying solo HR in the eighth and was 5-for-5 with 2R, 2 doubles, 2RBI and 1BB in 6/24 loss at Tampa Bay, tying his career high in hits (also 8/11/17 at Washington) and times on base (6, also 7/9/17 at San Francisco: 3H, 2BB, 1HP)…was the first 5H game by a Yankee since Curtis Granderson on 4/19/12 vs. Minnesota (5H)…was the first Yankee to reach safely at least six times since Stephen Drew on 8/30/15 at Atlanta (4H, 2BB).
- Went 9-for-9 with 4R, 3 doubles, 1HR, 4RBI and 2BB over consecutive games at Tropicana Field (6/24 and 7/23)…according to *Elias*, became the first Yankee to record hits in nine consecutive at-bats at one road venue since Lou Piniella also had nine straight hits at Kansas City's Kauffman Stadium from 9/3/82-5/3/83…was the first MLB player to reach safely (via H/BB/HP) at least five times without making an out in consecutive games at one road venue since Cleveland's Michael Brantley on 6/9/14 and 5/15/15 at Texas' Globe Life Park (credit: *Elias*).
- Was one of five AL All-Star "Final Vote" candidates…was the 10th Yankee to appear on the Final Vote ballot, joining SS Didi Gregorius (2017), OF Brett Gardner (2017), RHP David Robertson (2013), OF Nick Swisher (2010), 1B Jason Giambi (2008), SS Derek Jeter and OF Hideki Matsui (2005), Matsui (2004) and Giambi (2003).
- Reached base safely in 21 straight games from 8/4-8/25 (G2), tied for the third-longest streak of his career…was his longest such streak since reaching safely in a career-high 27 straight games from 7/24-8/22/17 with Miami…reached base safely multiple times in seven straight games from 8/16-24.
- Scored at least 1R in a career-high nine straight games from 8/6-14, matching Didi Gregorius (nine straight, 4/20-28) for the longest streak by a Yankee in 2018.
- Hit his sixth career grand slam (first since a "walk-off" grand slam on 4/18/14 vs. Seattle) in 8/8 win at Chicago-AL…hit 170HR between grand slams.
- His solo HR in 8/9 win vs. Texas had an exit velocity of 121.7 mph, surpassing Aaron Judge's 121.1 mph HR on 6/10/17 vs. Baltimore for the hardest-hit HR in the Statcast era (since 2015).
- Hit the 300th homer of his career off Francisco Liriano in 8/30 loss vs. Detroit…came in his 1,119th career game, becoming the fifth-fastest player to reach the mark in Baseball history, trailing Ralph Kiner (1,087G), Ryan Howard (1,093), Juan González (1,096) and Alex Rodriguez (1,117).
- Made his postseason debut, hitting .238 (5-for-21) with 4R, 1HR and 1RBI in five games…played in his first postseason after 1,144 career regular season games…were second-most among active players who had never reached the postseason (Kyle Seager-1,155G through 2018)…his 305HR were the most in that group, 112 more than Oakland's Khris Davis (193HR), who also debuted in the 2018 AL Wild Card Game.
- Homered and stole a base in his postseason debut in the AL Wild Card Game vs. Oakland…the HR had an exit velocity of 117.4 mph, the hardest-hit postseason HR of the Statcast era (since 2015), surpassing Judge's 116.1 mph HR from seven innings earlier…was the first Yankee and eighth player ever (Longoria, Podsednik, Beltrán, Edmonds, Alicea, Grace, Versailles) to record both a HR and SB in his postseason debut.

2017

- Won the National League Most Valuable Player Award after leading the Majors with 59HR and 132RBI and hitting .281/.376/.631 (168-for-597) with 123R, 32 doubles and 85BB in 159 games with the Marlins…tied for the Major League lead with an NL-high 91 extra-base hits and ranked second in Baseball in total bases (377), third in runs scored and fourth in OPS (1.007)…was seventh in the NL in walks…led the Majors with a 10.12 AB/HR ratio…finished sixth in the Majors (fourth among position players) with 6.9 WAR (FanGraphs).
- Received 302 points in NL MVP balloting to edge Cincinnati's Joey Votto (300 points) in the fourth-closest MVP race in Major League history (third-closest NL MVP race)…received 10 first-place votes, 10 second-place votes, 5 third-place votes, 3 fourth-place votes, 1 fifth-place vote and 1 sixth-place vote…was the first MVP in Marlins franchise history, making the Marlins the 27th current franchise to have an MVP winner.
- Set career highs in runs, hits, homers, RBI, games played, extra-base hits and total bases…homered in a Major League-best 49 different games, ahead of Aaron Judge (45).
- Earned his second career NL Hank Aaron Award (most outstanding offensive performer), his second NL Silver Slugger Award and his second Players' Choice Award for Outstanding NL Player.
- Was the sixth player in Major League history to hit at least 59HR in a season (10th occurrence)…marked the most HRs by any Major League player since 2001, when San Francisco's Barry Bonds hit 73 and the Cubs' Sammy Sosa hit 64…was the sixth-highest total by a right-handed batter in Major League history, behind Mark McGwire (70 in 1998, 65 in 1999) and Sammy Sosa (66 in 1998, 64 in 2001, 63 in 1999)…set a new Marlins club record for homers and was the first Marlin to win the Major League HR title.

- With 59HR, finished 7HR ahead of the AL HR leader Aaron Judge (52HR) and 20HR ahead of the NL runner-up, the Dodgers' Cody Bellinger (39HR)…was the largest margin ever for an NL home run champion over the runner-up, besting the previous mark of 19HR in 1923 (Cy Williams' 41HR to Jack Fournier's 22HR)…according to *Elias*, was tied for the fifth-largest margin by a home run champion in either league, behind four Babe Ruth seasons: 1920 AL (35, Ruth's 54HR to George Sisler's 19HR); 1921 AL (35, Ruth's 59HR to Bob Meusel/Ken Williams' 24HR); 1926 AL (28, Ruth's 47HR to Al Simmons' 19HR); 1928 AL (27, Ruth's 54HR to Lou Gehrig's 27HR)…matched the 1956 AL (20, Mickey Mantle's 52HR to Vic Wertz's 32HR).
- Became the ninth player (10th time) in Major League history to record at least 10 multi-homer games in one season…was tied for the third-highest single-season total, one behind the Cubs' Sammy Sosa (11 in 1998) and Detroit's Hank Greenberg (11 in 1938)—credit: *Elias*…marked the most multi-homer games since St. Louis' Albert Pujols had 10 in 2009…had 2 in April, 1 in May, 4 in July, 2 in August and 1 in September.
- Hit 86 batted balls (33HR) with an exit velocity of at least 110 mph according to MLB Statcast, marking the most batted balls (and most HRs) of at least 110 mph by a player in a single season since Statcast began tracking that data in 2015…his third-inning single on 10/1/17 vs. Atlanta left his bat at 122.2 mph, marking the highest exit velocity on a base hit in the Majors over the past three seasons (2015-17)…had four of the Majors' 12 hardest-hit home runs of 2017; his 59th and final HR on 9/28 vs. Atlanta (off Rex Brothers) had an exit velocity of 118.9 mph, the third-hardest-hit home run in the Majors in 2017 (behind two Aaron Judge HRs).
- Of his 59HR, a Major League-high 39 traveled a projected distance of at least 400 feet…his 34th HR on 8/4 at Atlanta (off R.A. Dickey) was his longest of the season, projected at 477 feet.
- His 132RBI set a Marlins franchise record, breaking Preston Wilson's mark of 121RBI in 2000…was the first player in Marlins history to lead the Majors in RBI…teammate Marcell Ozuna placed third in the Majors with 124RBI, as the Marlins were the first NL club to produce two of the Majors' top-three RBI leaders since the 1976 Reds (George Foster-121, first; Joe Morgan-111, second)…also led the Majors with 38 go-ahead RBI and was third with 18 game-winning RBI…tied for third in the Majors with 32 multi-RBI games (5RBI-1x, 4RBI-5x, 3RBI-13x, 2RBI-13x).
- Hit 26 go-ahead HRs, the most by any Major League hitter since St. Louis' Mark McGwire hit 30 in 1998…ranked second in the Majors with 23HR with runners on base, trailing only Aaron Judge (24HR with runners on).
- Hit a franchise-record 31HR in 76 home games (prev.: Stanton, 24 in 2014)…were second in the Majors to the Aaron Judge (33HR) and the most by an NL player at home since 2001 (Barry Bonds-37HR, Sammy Sosa-34HR).
- In 83 road games, hit a franchise-record 28HR (previously Gary Sheffield, 23 in 1996)…led the Majors in road HRs, the most by any player since San Diego's Adrián González also hit 28HR on the road in 2009…the Marlins had a three-game home series vs. the Brewers (9/13-15) moved from Miami to Milwaukee due to Hurricane Irma.
- Hit 30HR vs. NL East opponents (8 vs. Atlanta, 8 vs. New York, 8 vs. Philadelphia, 6 vs. Washington)…since intra-divisional play was expanded in 2001, became the fourth player to hit at least 30HR vs. a single division, joining Sammy Sosa in 2001 (37 vs. NL Central), Barry Bonds in 2001 (36 vs. NL West) and Brian Dozier in 2016 (31 vs. AL Central).
- Hit a Major League-record 47HR from the No. 2 spot in the batting order (previously Milwaukee-NL's Eddie Mathews, 46HR in 1959).
- Earned three NL "Player of the Week" Awards, second-most weekly awards in the Majors in 2017 (J.D. Martinez-4)—8/6-12 (.346, 9-for-26, 8R, 1 double, 5HR, 10RBI in 7G); 8/20-26 (.387, 12-for-31, 7R, 2 doubles, 5HR, 11RBI in 7G) and 9/17-23 (.318, 7-for-22, 6R, 1 double, 3HR, 12RBI in 6G), co-winner with Marcell Ozuna.
- On 6/2 vs. Arizona, hit a solo HR off Patrick Corbin to collect his 579th career RBI, moving past Mike Lowell (578) for sole possession of first place on the Marlins' all-time RBI list.
- Led the Majors with 12HR in July, matching a then-club record for HRs in a calendar month (fourth time, first since Stanton in June 2015).
- From 7/5-8/29, hit 30HR in a 48-game stretch…according to *Elias*, became the second player ever to homer 30 times in a stretch of 50G-or-fewer within a season (Barry Bonds, 30HR in 47G from 4/12-6/5 and from 4/13-6/7)…also hit 23HR in a 35-game stretch from 7/5-8/15, tied for the third-highest total in a 35-game span in Major League history…homered in 10-of-12 games from 8/4-15 (11HR total), including a club-record 9HR in a 10-game span from 8/4-13.
- Was named via the Player Ballot to his fourth career NL All-Star Team, tying Miguel Cabrera (2004-07) for the most All-Star appearances in Marlins history…started at DH and went 0-for-3 in the game at Marlins Park.
- Participated in his third Home Run Derby…was eliminated in Round 1 by the Yankees' Gary Sánchez, 17-16.
- From 7/24-8/22, reached base in a career-best 27 consecutive games, hitting .343/.463/.889 (34-for-99) with 29R, 6 doubles, 16HR, 34RBI and 19BB.
- Was named NL "Player of the Month" after tying the Major League August record with 18HR…hit .349/.433/.899 (38-for-109) with 28R, 6 doubles, 37RBI and 14BB in 29 games…shares the mark with Detroit's Rudy York, who hit 18HR in August 1937…tied York for the second-highest HR total in any month in Major League history, behind the Cubs' Sammy Sosa, who hit 20HR in June 1998…broke Hanley Ramirez's single-month club RBI record of 33 in June 2009…was his third career monthly award.
- Became the second player in Major League history to combine for at least 30HR over the span of two consecutive calendar months…joined Cleveland's Albert Belle, who hit 31HR in August/September 1995.
- From 8/1-15, tied the Major League record by hitting 11HR in the first 15 days of a calendar month, matching Troy Tulowitzki (Sept. 2010), Sammy Sosa (June 1998) and Ralph Kiner (Sept. 1949).
- From 8/10-15, set a Marlins record by homering in six consecutive games…tied for the then-seventh-longest home run streak in Major League history, two shy of the record of eight games, shared by Ken Griffey, Jr., Don Mattingly and Dale Long.
- Hit his 43rd HR on 8/14 vs. San Francisco (off Ty Blach), breaking Gary Sheffield's club record of 42HR in 1996…had tied Sheffield with his 42nd HR the previous day, 8/13 vs. Colorado (off Germán Márquez).

- On 8/27 vs. San Diego, hit his 50th HR (off Clayton Richard), becoming the 28th player to reach the milestone in a single season…with 50HR in the Marlins' first 129 games, was the seventh-fastest player to the number, behind San Francisco's Barry Bonds in 2001 (117th team game), the Cubs' Sammy Sosa in 1999 (121st), St. Louis' Mark McGwire in 1999 (124th) and 1998 (125th), the Yankees' Roger Maris in 1961 (125th) and the Yankees' Babe Ruth in 1921 (125th)…was the eighth-fastest player, by date, to hit 50HR, and the first player to reach the 50-homer mark in August since 2001 (Bonds/Sosa).
- On 9/28 vs. Atlanta, hit home runs No. 58 (third PA) and No. 59 (fifth and final PA)…in 14PA with a chance to hit a 60th HR, went 5-for-14 (.357) with one double.
- Was acquired by the Yankees from the Marlins along with cash considerations in exchange for 2B Starlin Castro, RHP Jorge Guzman and INF Jose Devers on 12/11.

2016
- In 119 games with the Marlins, hit .240/.326/.489 (99-for-413) with 56R, 20 doubles, 1 triple, 27HR, 74RBI and 50BB…marked a career low in batting average but led Miami in home runs for the sixth consecutive season.
- Won the Home Run Derby at San Diego's PETCO Park, defeating the defending champion, Chicago-AL's Todd Frazier, in the final round to become the first Marlin to win the event…set a then-Derby record with 61 home runs over three rounds (24HR in Round 1, 17HR in semifinals, 20HR in finals), topping the previous mark of 41 by Philadelphia's Bobby Abreu at Detroit's Comerica Park in 2005…according to MLB Statcast, his home runs traveled an estimated combined distance of 27,187 feet (5.15 miles)…hit the 10 longest homers and 18 of the 19 longest homers in the contest…also had the 20 hardest-hit homers.
- Became the first player in Marlins history to homer in four consecutive at-bats, doing so in his final 2PA on 7/5 at the Mets and first 2AB (3PA) on 7/6 at the Mets (walked in his first PA on 7/6)…was the second player in Marlins history to record consecutive 2HR games (also Derrek Lee, 6/9-10/02).
- Hit his 200th career HR on 7/6 at the Mets (off Jacob deGrom)…at 26 years, 241 days, was the 12th-youngest player in Baseball history to reach the milestone at the time…according to STATS, Inc., was the seventh-fastest ever to reach 200HR, doing so in his 781st game…was the first player in Marlins history to hit 200HR.
- Won NL "Player of the Week" Award for 7/3-9 (.391, 9-for-23, 6R, 1 double, 1 triple, 4HR, 8RBI, 3BB in 6G).
- Was placed on the 15-day disabled list from 8/14-9/6 with a left groin strain.

2015
- Tied for 10th in the NL in home runs despite playing in just 74 games, hitting .265/.346/.606 (74-for-279) with 47R, 12 doubles, 1 triple, 27HR, 67RBI and 34BB for the Marlins.
- On 4/16 at Atlanta, hit his first HR of the season and 155th of his career, surpassing Dan Uggla (154) to become the Marlins' all-time home run leader.
- Earned the NL "Player of the Month" Award for June after batting .344/.404/.800 (31-for-90) with 18R, 5 doubles, 12HR and 23RBI in 24 games…was his second career monthly award…during the month, led the Majors in SLG (min. 50PA) and OPS (1.204), tied for the NL lead in homers, was third in XBHs (17) and total bases, and tied for fourth in RBI…set a Marlins record for homers in June, and tied a then-franchise record for HRs in any month.
- Was named NL "Player of the Week" for 6/8-14 (.520, 13-for-25, 7R, 4 doubles, 5HR, 12RBI, 4BB in 7G).
- On 6/26 vs. Los Angeles-NL, suffered a hamate bone fracture in his left wrist while taking a swing and missed the final 87 games of the season…was placed on the 15-day D.L. from 6/27-10/5…underwent surgery to remove the bone on 6/28, performed by hand specialist Dr. Patrick Owens at the University of Miami Hospital…played in one rehab game with Single-A Jupiter on 9/1, going 0-for-2 with 1BB.
- Was elected by the fans as a starting outfielder for the NL in the All-Star Game in Cincinnati, his third career All-Star nomination and first as a fan-elected starter…missed the game due to injury.

2014
- Led the NL with 37HR, hitting .288/.395/.555 (155-for-539) with 89R, 31 doubles, 1 triple, 105RBI and 94BB in 145 games with Miami…was the first player in Marlins history to lead the league in home runs…also paced the league in slugging pct., total bases (299) and intentional walks (24)…had a career-high 13SB…tied for the NL lead in extra-base hits (69) and go-ahead RBI (31) and ranked second in RBI, walks and on-base pct.
- Finished as the runner-up for the NL Most Valuable Player Award (298 points), behind the Dodgers' Clayton Kershaw (355 points)…received 8 first-place votes, 10 second-place votes and 12 third-place votes.
- Earned his first career NL Hank Aaron Award (most outstanding offensive player), first career NL Silver Slugger Award, and first career Players' Choice Award for Outstanding NL Player…was one of three finalists for the NL Gold Glove for right field.
- Recorded RBI in each of his first seven games from 3/31-4/6, tied for the second-longest season-opening streak in Marlins history…set a Marlins record with 31RBI prior to 5/1, tallying at least 1RBI in 14 of his first 27 games.
- From 3/31-4/18, delivered the game-winning RBI in six of the Marlins' first seven wins…according to *Elias*, was the first player with at least 6GWRBI in a team's first seven wins since the stat was first kept starting in 1980.
- On 4/18 vs. Seattle, hit his second career "walk-off" grand slam—and the fifth in Marlins history—in the ninth inning off Yoervis Medina…marked his fifth career grand slam, tied with Hanley Ramirez for second-most in Marlins history behind Jeff Conine (6).
- Compiled a career-best 17-game hitting streak from 4/29-5/15, batting .417/.514/.700 (25-for-60) with 11R, 5 doubles, 4HR, 13RBI and 12BB during the streak.
- Was named named via the Player Ballot to his second All-Star team…started at DH and went 0-for-3 in the game at Minnesota's Target Field…participated in his first Home Run Derby, losing in the semifinals to Cincinnati's Todd Frazier, 1-0.

- On 8/11 vs. St. Louis, hit 2HR, setting a new franchise record with his 13th career multi-HR game and surpassing Hanley Ramirez (12).
- On 9/8 at Milwaukee, homered off Yovani Gallardo in the third inning to tie Dan Uggla's record for the most homers in Marlins history (154).
- Left game on 9/11 at Milwaukee after being hit in the face by a pitch thrown by Mike Fiers in the fifth inning…suffered facial lacerations, small fractures and dental damage…missed the Marlins' final 17 games.

2013
- Hit .249/.365/.480 (106-for-425) with 62R, 26 doubles, 24HR, 62RBI and 74BB in 116 games for the Marlins.
- Batted .302 (61-for-202) in 57 home games and .202 (45-for-223) in 59 road games, the largest home-road batting average split in the Majors in 2013…hit 15HR at home, tied for fifth-most in the NL.
- Was placed on the 15-day D.L. from 4/30-6/10 with a right hamstring strain…in five rehab games with Single-A Jupiter from 6/4-9, went 0-for-15 with 2BB and 1SB…the Marlins went 11-25 in the 36 games he missed.
- Hit career home runs No. 99 and No. 100 on 6/17 at Arizona…was the fastest player in Marlins history to reach the milestone (400 games), breaking Dan Uggla's record of 509 games…was the ninth player in Major League history to hit at least 100HR in his first 400 career games…at 23 years, 221 days, was the 11th-youngest player at the time to reach the milestone.
- Drew a Major League-leading 27BB in 26 games in July, setting a Marlins record for the month…was the Majors' highest walk total in July since San Francisco's Barry Bonds drew 33BB in 24G in July 2004.

2012
- In 123 games with Miami, hit .290/.361/.608 (130-for-449) with 75R, 30 doubles, 1 triple, 37HR, 86RBI and 46BB…led the NL in slugging pct., finished second in home runs to Milwaukee's Ryan Braun (41) and was seventh with 68 extra-base hits…received seven votes in NL MVP voting.
- Was named to his first career All-Star team, selected as a reserve by NL Manager Tony La Russa…was also chosen to participate in the Home Run Derby…did not participate in either event due to injury.
- Became the fifth player in Major League history to record two seasons with at least 30 doubles and 30HR in each at age-22 or younger (also 2011)…joined Florida's Miguel Cabrera (2004-05), St. Louis' Albert Pujols (2001-02), Seattle's Alex Rodriguez (1996, '98) and Boston's Ted Williams (1939, '41).
- Earned the Wilson "Defensive Player of the Year" Award for the Marlins.
- Was named NL "Player of the Month" for May after hitting .343/.432/.769 (37-for-108) with 23R, 10 doubles, 12HR, 30RBI, 16BB and 3SB in 29 games…tied for the Major League lead in home runs and extra-base hits (22), ranked third in RBI and tied for sixth in runs scored…tied Marlins franchise records for home runs and RBI in May…the 12HR tied a then-franchise record for HRs in any month.
- On 5/13 vs. the Mets, hit the third "walk-off" grand slam in Marlins history, a two-out, tie-breaking shot off Manny Acosta…joined Dan Uggla (6/11/08 vs. Philadelphia) and Bobby Bonilla (9/16/97 vs. Colorado).
- Was placed on the 15-day D.L. from 7/8-8/7 after undergoing arthroscopic surgery to remove loose bodies from his right knee…was his first career D.L. stint…the Marlins went 8-17 in the 25 games he missed.
- Homered in the first 3G of a four-game series at Colorado's Coors Field from 8/16-19, becoming the first player in Major League history to homer in each of his first six career games at any ballpark (also 8/15-17/11)—credit: Elias…became the first visiting player to homer in six straight games at Coors Field (8/15/11-8/18/12)…on 8/19, went 0-for-2 with 2BB in his bid to tie the Major League record for consecutive games with a HR at one park.
- Was named NL "Player of the Week" for 8/20-26 (.286, 8-for-28, 7R, 1 double, 5HR, 8RBI in 7G).
- Missed nine games from 9/17-27 with a left intercostal muscle strain.
- Finished the season with 93 career home runs, at the time tied with Frank Robinson for fifth-most by a player prior to turning 23, trailing Mel Ott (115), Eddie Mathews (112), Tony Conigliaro (104) and Alex Rodriguez (95)—credit: Elias…was later surpassed by Bryce Harper (97HR).

2011
- In his first full Major League season, hit .262/.356/.537 (135-for-516) with 79R, 30 doubles, 5 triples, 34HR, 87RBI and 70BB in 150 games with Florida…finished fifth in the NL in home runs, sixth in extra-base hits (69) and eighth in slugging…received one vote in NL MVP voting.
- Tied for fifth in the NL with 10 outfield assists…was the third player in franchise history to collect at least 10 outfield assists in consecutive seasons, joining Mark Kotsay (1998-2000) and Miguel Cabrera (2004-05).
- Became the 10th player in Major League history to collect at least 30 doubles and 30HR in a season at age-21 or younger…was the second Marlin to do so (also Miguel Cabrera in 2004).
- Had a career-best eight-game RBI streak from 5/11-20.
- On 8/1 at the Mets, hit a 10th-inning grand slam (second career), just the second extra-inning slam in Marlins history (also Greg Colbrunn on 7/18/95 at San Francisco)…at 21 years, 266 days, was the youngest player to hit an extra-inning grand slam since Cincinnati's Johnny Bench (21 years, 249 days) on 8/13/69 at Montreal.
- From 8/14-17, tied a then-Marlins franchise record by homering in four consecutive games.

2010
- Made his Major League debut with Florida, hitting .259/.326/.507 (93-for-359) with 45R, 21 doubles, 1 triple, 22HR, 59RBI and 34BB in 100 games…led Major League rookies in home runs.
- Tied for the lead among Major League rookies with 10 outfield assists…committed just 4E in 98 games (97 starts), all in right field.
- On 6/8, was signed to a Major League contract and selected to the Marlins' active roster…was in the starting lineup that night at Philadelphia, batting seventh, in right field…at 20 years, 212 days, was the third-youngest player (at the time) to make his Major League debut with the Marlins (Edgar Renteria: 19 years, 277 days; Miguel Cabrera: 20 years, 63 days)…went 3-for-5 with 2R…in his first plate appearance, recorded his first Major League hit with an infield single off Kyle Kendrick…according to *Elias*, was the youngest player to collect at least 3H in his Major League debut since Toronto's Danny Ainge (20 years, 65 days) on 5/21/79 vs. Cleveland.
- Hit his first Major League home run on 6/18 vs. Tampa Bay, a first-inning grand slam off Matt Garza…became the sixth player in Marlins history to hit a grand slam for his first career home run (also Jeremy Hermida, Craig Counsell, Quilvio Veras, Chuck Carr and Jeff Conine).
- On 8/11 at Washington, went 5-for-5 with 2R, 2 doubles, 1HR and 4RBI…was the second player in franchise history to collect at least 5H and 4RBI in a game (Gary Sheffield, 9/17/95 at Colorado)…according to *Elias*, was the second-youngest player (20y, 276d) with at least 5H and 4RBI in a game since RBI became an official statistic in 1920…only Chicago-NL's Phil Cavarretta had done so at a younger age (19y, 33d on 8/21/35 at Philadelphia).
- Earned his first career NL "Player of the Week" Award for 8/9-15 (.583, 14-for-24, 5R, 5 doubles, 4HR, 8RBI, 3BB in 6G).
- Started the season with Double-A Jacksonville, batting .313/.442/.729 (60-for-192) with 42R, 13 doubles, 2 triples, 21HR, 52RBI and 44BB in 53 games…led all minor leaguers in home runs at the time of his Major League promotion on 6/8…was named an MiLB.com Organization All-Star.
- Was the first player to hit at least 20HR in both the minors and Majors in the same season since at least 1988…in 2017, Oakland's Matt Olson matched the feat with 24HR in the Majors and 23HR in the minors.

2009
- In 129 games between Single-A Jupiter and Double-A Jacksonville, hit .254/.341/.500 (122-for-480) with 76R, 24 doubles, 5 triples, 28HR, 92RBI and 59BB…led Marlins minor leaguers in home runs, RBI and total bases.
- Began the season with Jupiter, earning a place on the Florida State League Mid-Season All-Star Team, as he hit .294/.390/.578 (53-for-180) with 27R, 9 doubles, 3 triples, 12HR, 39RBI and 28BB in 50 games.
- Was promoted to Jacksonville on 6/5 and hit .231/.311/.455 (69-for-299) with 49R, 15 doubles, 2 triples, 16HR, 53RBI and 31BB in 79 games…ranked fifth in the Southern League in home runs.
- Was named to the U.S. Team for the All-Star Futures Game in St. Louis.
- Played for Mesa in the Arizona Fall League, hitting .478 (11-for-23) with 2R, 1HR, 2RBI and 4SB in six games.
- Following the season, was named the No. 3 overall prospect and No. 1 prospect in the Marlins organization by *Baseball America*…was also labeled by the publication as the "Best Power Prospect" in both the FSL and SL.

2008
- Led the South Atlantic League in home runs (39) with Single-A Greensboro while hitting .293/.381/.611 (137-for-468) with 89R, 26 doubles, 3 triples, 97RBI and 58BB in 125 games…also topped the league in extra-base hits (68), total bases (286), slugging percentage and AB/HR ratio (12.00), was third in RBI and tied for third in runs scored…led Marlins farmhands in total bases and ranked second in home runs and RBI.
- Was named to the SAL Postseason All-Star Team and MiLB.com's Single-A Offensive Player of the Year…appeared on *Baseball America*'s Minor League All-Star Team and Single-A All-Star Team.
- Following the season, was named the No. 16 overall prospect and No. 2 prospect in the Marlins organization by *Baseball America*.

2007
- Made his professional debut, combining with the GCL Marlins and short-season Single-A Jamestown to bat .161 (9-for-56) with 8R, 3 doubles, 1HR and 3RBI in 17 games.

PERSONAL
- Full name is Giancarlo Cruz-Michael Stanton ("jawn-KAHR-loh").
- Graduated from Notre Dame H.S. (Calif.) in 2007…earned All-Southern Section honors in baseball, football and basketball as a senior…was named the 2007 Cal-Hi Sports Boys State Athlete of the Year.
- Following his 2014 dental surgery after being hit in the face by a pitch, co-founded the All-Star Smiles Foundation to fight child tooth decay by providing free dental care to children in need…the foundation held events in 2015 and 2016, and has assisted approximately 1,000 Miami-area children to date.
- Was on a cover of *Sports Illustrated* in March 2018 with teammate Aaron Judge.
- Appeared on the *Tonight Show Starring Jimmy Fallon* in May 2018…also appeared on the *TODAY Show* in June 2018 to help launch the Yankees' 10th annual HOPE Week.

Stanton's Career Batting Record

Year	Team	AVG	G	AB	R	H	2B	3B	HR	RBI	SH	SF	HP	BB	SO	SB	CS	E	OBP	SLG
2007	GCL Marlins	.269	8	26	6	7	2	0	0	1	0	0	1	1	6	0	0	0	.321	.346
	Jamestown	.067	9	30	2	2	1	0	1	2	1	0	3	15	0	0	0	.147	.200
2008	Greensboro	.293	125	468	89	137	26	3	39	97	0	3	11	58	153	4	2	5	.381	.611
2009	Jupiter	.294	50	180	27	53	9	3	12	39	0	1	1	28	45	2	2	3	.390	.578
	Jacksonville	.231	79	299	49	69	15	2	16	53	0	5	6	31	99	1	1	7	.311	.455
2010	Jacksonville	.313	53	192	42	60	13	2	21	52	0	2	2	44	53	1	0	0	.442	.729
	FLORIDA	.259	100	359	45	93	21	1	22	59	0	1	2	34	123	5	2	4	.326	.507
2011	FLORIDA	.262	150	516	79	135	30	5	34	87	0	6	9	70	166	5	3	6	.356	.537
2012	MIAMI - a	.290	123	449	75	130	30	1	37	86	0	1	5	46	143	6	2	7	.361	.608
	Jupiter	.313	4	16	2	5	1	0	2	5	0	0	0	1	0	0	1	.313	.750
2013	MIAMI - b	.249	116	425	62	106	26	0	24	62	0	1	4	74	140	1	0	8	.365	.480
	Jupiter	.000	5	15	0	0	0	0	0	0	0	0	0	2	5	1	0	0	.118	.000
2014	MIAMI	.288	145	539	89	155	31	1	37	105	0	2	3	94	170	13	1	6	.395	.555
2015	MIAMI - c	.265	74	279	47	74	12	1	27	67	0	3	2	34	95	4	2	3	.346	.606
	Jupiter	.000	1	2	0	0	0	0	0	0	0	0	1	1	0	0	0	.333	.000
2016	MIAMI - d	.240	119	413	56	99	20	1	27	74	0	2	4	50	140	0	0	4	.326	.489
2017	MIAMI - e	.281	159	597	123	168	32	0	59	132	0	3	7	85	163	2	2	4	.376	.631
2018	YANKEES	.266	158	617	102	164	34	1	38	100	0	10	8	70	211	5	0	1	.343	.509
2019	YANKEES - f, g	.288	18	59	8	17	3	0	3	13	0	1	0	12	24	0	0	1	.403	.492
	Tampa	.500	3	10	4	5	0	0	4	5	0	0	0	3	0	0	0	.500	1.700
	Scranton/WB	.091	3	11	1	1	0	0	1	3	0	0	0	7	0	0	0	.091	.364
Minor League Totals		.271	340	1250	222	339	67	10	96	257	1	12	21	168	388	9	5	16	.364	.571
AL Totals		.268	176	676	110	181	37	1	41	113	0	11	8	82	235	5	0	2	.349	.507
NL Totals		.268	986	3577	576	960	202	10	267	672	0	19	36	487	1140	36	14	42	.360	.554
Major League Totals		.268	1162	4253	686	1141	239	11	308	785	0	30	44	569	1375	41	14	44	.358	.547

Selected by the Florida Marlins in the second round of the 2007 First-Year Player Draft.

a – Placed on the 15-day disabled list from July 8 – August 7, 2012 after undergoing arthroscopic surgery to remove loose bodies from his right knee.
b – Placed on the 15-day disabled list from April 30 – June 10, 2013 with a right hamstring strain.
c – Placed on the 15-day disabled list from June 27 – October 5, 2015 with a left hamate bone fracture.
d – Placed on the 15-day disabled list from August 14 – September 6, 2016 with a left groin strain.
e – Acquired by the Yankees from the Miami Marlins along with cash considerations in exchange for 2B Starlin Castro, RHP Jorge Guzman and INF Jose Devers on December 11, 2017.
f – Placed on the 10-day injured list from April 1 – June 18, 2019 with a left biceps strain.
g – Placed on the 10-day injured list on June 26, 2019 with a right knee sprain…was transferred to the 60-day injured list on August 11 and reinstated on September 18, 2019.

Stanton's Postseason Record

Year	Club vs. Opp.	AVG	G	AB	R	H	2B	3B	HR	RBI	SH	SF	HP	BB	SO	SB	CS	E	OBP	SLG
2018	NYY vs. OAK (WC)	.333	1	3	2	1	0	0	1	1	0	0	0	1	1	1	0	0	.500	1.333
	NYY vs. BOS (DS)	.222	4	18	2	4	0	0	0	0	0	0	0	0	6	0	0	0	.222	.222
2019	NYY vs. MIN (DS)	.167	3	6	0	1	0	0	0	1	0	1	0	4	2	0	0	0	.455	.167
	NYY vs. HOU (CS)	.286	2	7	1	2	0	0	1	1	0	0	0	0	3	0	0	0	.286	.714
Wild Card Totals		.333	1	3	2	1	0	0	1	1	0	0	0	1	1	1	0	0	.500	1.333
Division Series Totals		.208	7	24	2	5	0	0	0	1	0	1	0	4	8	0	0	0	.310	.208
LCS Totals		.286	2	7	1	2	0	0	1	1	0	0	0	0	3	0	0	0	.286	.714
POSTSEASON TOTALS		.235	10	34	5	8	0	0	2	3	0	1	0	5	12	1	0	0	.325	.412

Stanton's All-Star Game Record

Year	Club, Site	AVG	G	AB	R	H	2B	3B	HR	RBI	SH	SF	HP	BB	SO	SB	CS	E	OBP	SLG
2012	MIA, Kansas City								Selected - Did Not Play											
2014	MIA, Minnesota	.000	1	3	0	0	0	0	0	0	0	0	0	1	0	0	0	.000	.000
2015	MIA, Cincinnati								Selected - Did Not Play											
2017	MIA, Miami	.000	1	3	0	0	0	0	0	0	0	0	0	2	0	0	0	.000	.000
All-Star Game Totals		.000	2	6	0	0	0	0	0	0	0	0	0	3	0	0	0	.000	.000

Stanton's World Baseball Classic Record

Year	Country, Site	AVG	G	AB	R	H	2B	3B	HR	RBI	SH	SF	HP	BB	SO	SB	CS	E	OBP	SLG
2013	USA, Miami	.235	5	17	0	4	0	0	0	1	0	0	0	4	3	0	0	0	.381	.235
2017	USA, Miami	.227	7	22	3	5	2	0	1	4	0	0	1	2	10	0	0	0	.320	.455
WBC Totals		.231	12	39	3	9	2	0	1	5	0	0	1	6	13	0	0	0	.348	.359

Stanton's Career Fielding Record

Position	PCT	G	PO	A	E	TC	DP
Outfield	.980	1,027	2,120	66	44	2,230	9

Stanton's Career Home Run Chart

MULTI-HOMER GAMES: 32. **TWO-HOMER GAMES:** 32, last on 9/27/18 at TB. **THREE-HOMER GAMES:** None. **GRAND SLAMS:** 7, last on 9/20/18 vs. BOS (Heath Hembree). **PINCH-HIT HR:** None. **INSIDE-THE-PARK HR:** None. **"WALK-OFF" HR:** 4, last on 6/20/18 vs. SEA (Ryan Cook). **LEADOFF HR:** None.

Stanton's Career Bests and Streaks

HITS: 5 - 2 times (last on 6/24/18 at TB). **RUNS:** 4, 7/9/17 at SF. **2B:** 3, 5/20/17 at LAD. **3B:** 1 - 11 times (last on 4/11/18 at BOS). **HR:** 2 - 32 times (last on 9/27/18 at TB). **RBI:** 5 - 5 times (last on 8/25/17 vs. SD). **BB:** 4, 9/19/17 vs. NYM. **SO:** 5 - 2 times (last on 4/8/18 vs. BAL). **SB:** 1 - 41 times (last on 8/19/18 vs. TOR). **HIT STREAK:** 17g, 4/29-5/15/14. **"WALK-OFF" HITS:** 6 (last on 6/20/18 vs. SEA).

Player of the Month: 3 times (Last: August 2017)   **Player of the Week:** 7 times (Last: 9/18-24/17)   **Rookie of the Month:** None

MASAHIRO TANAKA • RHP

19

HT: 6-3 • **WT:** 218 • **BATS:** R • **THROWS:** R
BIRTHDATE: 11/1/88 • **OPENING DAY AGE:** 31
BIRTHPLACE: Itami, Japan
RESIDES: Miyagi Prefecture, Japan
M.L. SERVICE: 6 years

STATUS

▸ Acquired by the Yankees via the posting system from the Tohoku Rakuten Golden Eagles of Japan and signed to a seven-year contract on January 22, 2014…contract extends through the 2020 season…declined to exercise his opt-out clause following the 2017 season.

CAREER NOTES

▸ Is 75-43 (.636) with a 3.75 ERA (1,006.1IP, 419ER) in 164 games (163 starts) over his first six Major League seasons, all with the Yankees…is tied for eighth among active pitchers in winning percentage (min. 75 decisions).

▸ Is a two-time AL All-Star (2014, '19)…is one of five Japanese players (three pitchers) to make multiple All-Star teams (OF Ichiro Suzuki-10, RHP Yu Darvish-4, OF Hideki Matsui-2, RHP Kaz Sasaki-2)…in 2019, became the fifth Yankees pitcher to record a win in the All-Star Game, joining Lefty Gomez (three: 1933, '35, '37), Spud Chandler (1942), Spec Shea (1947) and Vic Raschi (1948).

▸ Is the second pitcher in Yankees history to reach double-digit wins in each of his first six Major League seasons, joining Andy Pettitte, who did it in each of his first nine campaigns (1995-2003)…is one of six pitchers with at least 10 wins in each of the last six seasons, joining Zack Greinke, J.A Happ, Jon Lester, Max Scherzer and Stephen Strasburg…among players who debuted since 1950, was the fifth to win at least 12 games in each of his first five seasons, joining Pettitte (1995-99), Dwight Gooden (1984-88), Dennis Eckersley (1975-79) and Tom Seaver (1967-71).

▸ Has 174 career wins between Major League Baseball (75) and Nippon Professional Baseball (99)…ranks third in wins by a Japanese pitcher in Major League history behind Hideo Nomo (123-109) and Hiroki Kuroda (79-79)…joins Hideo Nomo as the only two Japanese pitchers to earn at least 10 wins in six different Major League seasons (Hideo Nomo-7x) and is the first to do it over his first six MLB seasons.

▸ His 947K are the most by a Yankees pitcher through his first six Major League seasons and the most by any Yankee through his first 164 career games…is the fourth Japanese pitcher to reach 900K (Hideo Nomo-1,918K, Yu Darvish-1,299K, Hiroki Kuroda-986K)…his 14 games with at least 10K are tied with Whitey Ford for fifth-most in franchise history…is one of three Japanese pitchers with at least three 13K games (Hideo Nomo-7x, Yu Darvish-7x, Tanaka-3x).

▸ His 4.74 career K/BB ratio (947K/200BB) is the fourth-highest (min. 700.0IP) in the Modern Era (since 1900).

CAREER HIGHLIGHTS

AL All-Star Team
▸ 2014, 2019

HIGHEST CAREER K/BB RATIO, MODERN ERA (SINCE 1900)
1. Chris Sale 5.37
2. Corey Kluber 5.00
3. Josh Tomlin 4.74
4. **MASAHIRO TANAKA** 4.74
5. Jacob deGrom 4.72

Min. 700.0 innings pitched

▸ The Yankees are 103-60 in his 163 career starts, third-most team wins in a pitcher's starts in the AL since 2014.

▸ Is one of three pitchers to record three complete-game shutouts in the last three seasons since 2017 (Corey Kluber-4, Ervin Santana-3).

▸ His four shutouts are third-most among Japanese-born players (Hideo Nomo-9, Hiroki Kuroda-5).

▸ Is one of three pitchers in Yankees history to make at least 20 starts in each of his first six Major League seasons, joining Fritz Peterson (first eight, 1966-73) and Andy Pettitte (first nine, 1995-2003).

▸ Is 42-20 (.677) with a 3.36 ERA (516.2IP, 193ER) and 510K in 82 career starts at Yankee Stadium, the second-highest winning percentage at the current Yankee Stadium (min. 20 decisions), behind J.A. Happ (15-7, .682)…ranks second in wins, starts and strikeouts at the venue…is the third-highest winning percentage among active pitchers (min. 50 decisions) at any ballpark, behind Max Scherzer (47-13, .783 at Comerica Park) and Clayton Kershaw (93-36, .721 at Dodger Stadium).

▸ Has made four Opening Day starts for the Yankees (2015-17, '19)…was the first right-hander to start consecutive openers for the club since Roger Clemens from 2001-03…is one of four foreign-born Yankees pitchers to start on Opening Day, joined by RHP Luis Severino (Dominican Republic) in 2018, RHP Chien-Ming Wang (Taiwan) in 2008 and RHP Orlando Hernandez (Cuba) in 2000…is the only foreign-born pitcher to make multiple Opening Day starts for the Yankees…his four Opening Day starts are the most among five Japanese Opening Day starters in Major League history: Hideo Nomo (3x–2000 w/ Detroit, 2003-04 w/ Los Angeles-NL), Yu Darvish (2017 w/ Texas), Hiroki Kuroda (2009 w/ Los Angeles-NL) and Daisuke Matsuzaka (2008 w/ Boston).

- Has pitched head-to-head against an opposing Japanese starting pitcher four times as a Yankee, going 3-0 with a 0.62 ERA (29.0IP, 17H, 3R/2ER, 4BB, 27K, 0HR), with the Yankees winning all four...defeated Hisashi Iwakuma on 4/16/16 vs. Seattle and 8/24/16 at Seattle, took a no-decision against Yu Darvish on 6/23/17 vs. Texas, and defeated Yusei Kikuchi on 8/27/19 at Seattle.
- Is one of seven Japan-born players to appear in a game for the Yankees, joining Hideki Irabu (1997-99), Hideki Matsui (2003-09), Kei Igawa (2007-08), Hiroki Kuroda (2012-14), Ryota Igarashi (2012) and Ichiro Suzuki (2012-14).
- With Tanaka and Hiroki Kuroda, the Yankees had two Japan-born pitchers in their starting rotation in 2014, becoming the first team to do so since the Dodgers had Hideo Nomo and Kazuhisa Ishii starting for them in 2004.

TANAKA'S 2019 PITCHING LINES

Date/Opp	Score	W/L	IP	H	R	ER	HR	BB	K	NP/S	ERA	Left Game
3/28 vs. BAL	7-2	W	5.2	6	2	1	0	0	5	83/56	1.59	Leading 6-2
4/2 vs. DET	1-3	ND	6.2	8	1	1	0	0	7	87/63	1.46	Tied 1-1
4/8 at HOU	3-4	ND	6.0	3	1	1	1	2	3	78/50	1.47	Leading 3-1
4/14 vs. CWS	2-5	L	4.0	7	5	5	1	**3**	6	81/49	3.22	Trailing 4-2
4/20 vs. KC	9-2	W	7.0	4	1	1	1	**3**	7	94/59	2.76	Leading 9-1
4/25 at LAA	5-11	L	5.2	6	6	5	**2**	**3**	2	89/55	3.60	Tied 4-4
5/1 at ARI*	2-3	L	4.0	5	3	3	1	1	6	74/47	3.92	Trailing 3-0
5/7 vs. SEA	5-4	ND	6.1	5	2	2	1	2	4	95/61	3.77	Trailing 2-1
5/12 at TB*	7-1	W	7.0	5	1	1	1	0	7	73/55	3.44	Leading 3-1
5/18 vs. TB	1-2 (11)	ND	6.0	3	0	0	0	0	6	88/60	3.09	Leading 1-0
5/23 at BAL	6-5	ND	6.0	5	1	1	0	1	5	95/70	2.94	Leading 4-1
5/28 vs. SD	4-5	L	6.0	9	5	5	1	1	7	100/67	3.20	Trailing 5-1
6/4 at TOR*	3-4	L	6.0	6	4	**2**	**2**	2	5	85/57	3.42	Trailing 4-2
6/11 vs. NYM	12-5	W	6.2	7	5	4	1	0	7	101/74	3.58	Leading 9-5
6/17 vs. TB	3-0	W	**9.0**	2	0	0	0	1	**10**	111/76	3.23	CG
6/22 at HOU	7-5	ND	6.0	8	2	2	1	1	1	88/55	3.21	Leading 4-2
6/29 at BOS (Lon.)	17-13	ND	0.2	4	6	6	1	2	0	37/24	3.74	Tied 6-6
7/5 at TB	8-4 (11)	ND	6.1	6	4	4	**2**	2	5	101/68	3.86	Leading 3-3
7/14 at TOR*	4-2	W	6.0	4	2	2	**2**	0	5	79/56	3.81	Leading 3-2
7/20 vs. COL	11-5	W	6.0	7	5	5	1	3	5	85/55	4.00	Leading 9-5
7/25 at BOS	3-19	L	3.1	**12**	**12**	**12**	**2**	**3**	4	87/54	4.79	Trailing 11-2
7/31 vs. ARI*	7-5	ND	4.0	5	2	2	0	**3**	4	82/52	4.78	Leading 2-0
8/5 at BAL	9-6	ND	5.1	10	5	5	1	2	4	92/60	4.93	Leading 6-4
8/11 at TOR*	1-0	W	8.0	3	0	0	0	0	4	94/66	4.64	Leading 1-0
8/16 vs. CLE*	3-2	W	6.1	4	2	**2**	0	0	2	83/56	4.56	Leading 3-2
8/22 at OAK*	3-5	L	6.0	8	5	5	0	2	5	109/72	4.68	Trailing 5-2
8/27 at SEA	7-0	W	7.0	2	0	0	0	1	7	106/67	4.47	Leading 6-0
9/2 vs. TEX	0-7	L	6.0	7	2	2	1	2	5	103/68	4.42	Trailing 2-0
9/8 at BOS	10-5	ND	4.0	8	4	4	1	0	2	80/63	4.53	Leading 8-4
9/13 at TOR	5-6	ND	5.0	8	4	4	1	0	6	88/64	4.60	Leading 5-4
9/19 vs. LAA*	9-1	W	7.0	4	1	1	1	0	6	86/60	4.47	Leading 6-1
9/29 at TEX	1-6	L	3.0	5	2	1	0	1	2	53/35	4.45	*relief*
Totals (32G/31GS)			182.0	186	95	90	28	40	149		4.45	

*start came after a Yankees loss / **Bold** - season high

- Was the sixth pitcher all-time to record at least 25 wins and 300K through his first 50 career appearances.
- Recorded quality starts in each of his first nine career Interleague starts (4/16/14-7/22/16), the longest streak to begin a career in Interleague history (since 1997).
- In eight career postseason starts, is 5-3 with a 1.76 ERA (46.0IP, 25H, 10R/9ER, 11BB, 37K, 4HR)...has the third-lowest postseason ERA among Major League starting pitchers (min. 8GS) since earned runs became an official stat in 1912, trailing only Stephen Strasburg (1.46) and George Earnshaw (1.58)...is the 10th-lowest ERA among all pitchers with at least 40.0IP...leads all Japanese pitchers in postseason wins...according to *Elias*, is the first pitcher in Major League history to allow 4H-or-fewer in each of his first eight postseason starts...*Elias* also notes that prior to allowing 4R/3ER in 2019 ALCS Game 4 vs. Houston, was the first pitcher in Major League history to allow 2R-or-fewer in each of his first seven postseason starts (prev. Sandy Koufax, first six starts from 1959-65)...won four consecutive postseason starts from 2017 ALCS Game 5 – 2019 ALCS Game 1...with postseason starts in 2015 (1), 2017 (3), 2018 (1) and 2019 (3), is the first pitcher to make a start in four consecutive Yankees postseasons since CC Sabathia started in four straight from 2009-12.
- Is 2-2 with a 1.88 ERA (24.0IP, 6R/5ER) in four ALCS starts...is the sixth-lowest ERA in LCS history (min. 4GS).

2019

- Went 11-9 with a 4.45 ERA (182.0IP, 186H, 95R/90ER, 40BB, 149K, 28HR) in a career-high 32 appearances (31 starts)...opponents hit .261 (186-for-713, 28HR); LH .285 (101-for-354, 15HR); RH .237 (85-for-359, 13HR)...tied a career high in starts (also 2016)...had a 3.3 WAR and 4.27 FIP (FanGraphs).
- Was named to his second career All-Star Game (also 2014) and made his All-Star debut, tossing a scoreless second inning (1H, 1K) and earning the win in the AL's 4-3 victory in Cleveland...faced Cody Bellinger (K), Nolan Arenado (F8), Josh Bell (infield single) and Willson Contreras (1-3 putout)...was the fifth Yankees pitcher to record a win in the All-Star Game, joining Lefty Gomez (three: 1933, '35, '37), Spud Chandler (1942), Spec Shea (1947) and Vic Raschi (1948)...was named to the AL squad on 7/6 as an injury replacement for Toronto's Marcus Stroman.
- Went 8-3 with a 3.10 ERA (98.2IP, 90H, 37R/34ER, 18BB, 85K, 13HR) in a career-high 16 home starts...allowed 2R-or-fewer in 12-of-16 turns.
- Opponents hit .192 (50-for-260) with 81K in at-bats ending in a slider (Brooks Baseball).
- Made his fourth career Opening Day start on 3/28 vs. Baltimore (5.2IP, 6H, 2R/1ER, 0BB, 5K), earning his first Opening Day win...was the first Yankee to record at least 5K with 0BB in an Opening Day start since Catfish Hunter (5K) on 4/7/77 vs. Milwaukee.

- Recorded his 800th career strikeout in the second inning on 3/28 vs. Baltimore (Joey Rickard)…recorded his 900th career strikeout in the fourth inning on 7/25 at Boston (J.D. Martinez).
- Left his 5/18 start vs. Tampa Bay with a right shin contusion.
- Was on the paternity leave list from 6/8-9 after the birth of his daughter.
- On 6/17 vs. Tampa Bay, threw the first two-hitter of his Major League career (9.0IP, 2H, 0R, 1BB, 10K)…marked only the second two-hitter by a Yankees pitcher since the start of 2009 (Hiroki Kuroda, 9.0IP, 2H, 2BB, 5K on 8/14/12 vs. Texas)…was the Yankees' first two-hitter with at least 10K since Mike Mussina on 9/24/02 vs. Tampa Bay (9.0IP, 2H, 2BB, 12K)…marked his seventh career complete game and fourth complete-game shutout, the first since a three-hit shutout on 7/24/18 at Tampa Bay.
- Made his 150th career start on 7/5 at Tampa Bay.
- On 7/25 at Boston, allowed a career-high 12ER and 12H (3.1IP, 3BB, 4K, 2HR) in a loss…marked the second-most earned runs allowed by a Yankee in franchise history (Carl Mays, 13ER on 7/17/1923 at Cleveland)…were the most hits allowed by a Yankee since A.J. Burnett gave up 13H on 8/3/11 at Chicago-AL.
- On 8/27 at Seattle, faced Seattle's Yusei Kikuchi in the Majors for the first time, tossing 7.0 shutout innings (2H, 1BB, 7K) to earn the win…marked the 16th game in Major League history featuring two Japanese-born starting pitchers, the eighth involving the Yankees, most of any team (are 7-1 in those games).
- Made his first career relief appearance in the regular-season finale on 9/29 at Texas (L, 3.0IP, 5H, 2R/1ER, 1BB, 2K)…his 163 starts to begin his career were the most in Yankees history prior to a pitcher making his first career appearance as a reliever.
- Made five spring training starts, going 2-0 with a 2.65 ERA (17.0IP, 14H, 5ER, 3BB, 23K, 3HR)…ranked fifth in the Grapefruit League in strikeouts.
- Made three postseason starts, going 2-1 with a 2.25 ERA (16.0IP, 8H, 5R/4ER, 4BB, 12K, 1HR)…earned the win in ALDS Game 2 vs. Minnesota (5.0IP, 3H, 1ER, 1BB, 7K, 1HP)…allowed 1H over 6.0 shutout innings (1BB, 4K) to earn the win in ALCS Game 1 at Houston…was the fourth pitcher in Yankees history to yield 1H-or-fewer over at least 6.0 shutout innings in a postseason game, joining Roger Clemens (9.0IP, 1H in 2000 ALCS Game 4 at Seattle), David Cone (7.0IP, 1H in 1999 World Series Game 2 at Atlanta) and Don Larsen (perfect game in 1956 World Series Game 5 vs. Brooklyn)…took the loss in ALCS Game 4 vs. Houston (5.0IP, 4H, 4R/3ER, 2BB, 1K, 1HR).
- On 10/23/19, had arthroscopic surgery on his right elbow to remove bone spurs…the procedure was done by Dr. David Altchek at the Hospital for Special Surgery in Manhattan.

2018

- Went 12-6 with a 3.75 ERA (156.0IP, 141H, 68R/65ER, 35BB, 159K, 25HR) and one complete game in 27 starts…held opponents to a .240 BA (141-for-588, 25HR); LH .236 (61-for-259, 8HR), RH .243 (80-for-329, 17HR)…the Yankees were 16-11 in his starts…had a 2.4 WAR and 4.01 FIP (FanGraphs).
- Ranked seventh among AL pitchers (min. 150.0IP) in K/BB ratio (4.54) and ninth in BB/9.0IP ratio (2.02).
- Among pitchers with at least 150.0IP, led the AL and ranked third in the Majors with a 37.6% "chase rate" (FanGraphs)…his 14.1% swinging strike rate was sixth-highest in the AL (ninth-highest in the Majors)…had a 68.2% first-strike rate, third in the AL.
- Was placed on the 10-day D.L. from 6/9-7/10 with mild left and right hamstring strains…made one rehab start with Triple-A Scranton/Wilkes-Barre on 7/4 vs. Buffalo (5.0IP, 3H, 2ER, 0BB, 4K, 1HR).
- Was 7-1 with a 3.47 ERA (85.2IP, 33ER) in 15 road starts…his .875 road winning percentage was the best by a Yankee (min. 8 decisions) since Jimmy Key went 10-0 in 1994…was tied for the third-best mark in the Majors in 2018 behind St. Louis' Miles Mikolas (10-0) and Cleveland's Shane Bieber (7-0)…went 7-0 in his first 14 starts before a loss on 9/26 at Tampa Bay, tied for the sixth-longest road unbeaten streak in Yankees history.
- From 4/23-8/5, went 7-0 with a 3.12 ERA (80.2IP, 28ER) over 14 starts, the longest unbeaten streak of his career…was tied for the longest streak in the Majors in 2018…was the third-longest unbeaten streak by a Yankee since 2005 (Iván Nova-20, CC Sabathia-15).
- Had the two longest scoreless streaks of his career: 21.1IP from 7/15-8/5 and 20.0IP from 9/1-14…*Elias* confirmed that he is the first Yankees pitcher to record multiple scoreless streaks of at least 20.0IP in a single season since Ron Guidry in 1983 (22.2IP, 5/11-22/83; 21.1IP, 5/26/6/83)…the 21.1-inning streak was the longest single-season streak by a Yankee since CC Sabathia's 23.2-inning streak from 6/30-7/10/2011.
- In 12 starts after the All-Star break, went 5-4 with a 2.85 ERA (72.2IP, 23ER), the AL's seventh-lowest ERA (min. 50.0IP)…was 7-2 with a 4.54 ERA (83.1IP, 42ER) in 15 starts prior to the break.
- On 3/30 at Toronto and 4/5 vs. Baltimore, became the first Yankee since 1908 (and just the eighth MLB pitcher) to record at least 7K and not walk a batter in each of his first two starts of a season.
- In 7/24 win at Tampa Bay, tossed a three-hit shutout (1BB, 9K), his third career shutout and sixth career complete game…was the first Yankee to allow 3H-or-fewer with at least 9K in a CG SHO since Mike Mussina on 8/17/03 at Baltimore…retired the first 12 batters of the game.
- Went 0-3 in five August starts, the first winless month in his Major League career.
- In 9/7 win at Seattle, recorded a season-high 10K over 8.0 shutout innings (3H, 0BB) and retired 24-of-27 batters…was his fifth game with at least 10K and 0BB, tied with David Cone and Luis Severino for second-most in Yankees history (Mike Mussina-7).

2017

- Went 13-12 with a 4.74 ERA (178.1IP, 94ER) and one complete game in 30 starts for the Yankees…held opponents to a .257 BA (180-for-700); LH .252 (75-for-298), RH .261 (105-for-402)…had a 2.7 WAR and 4.34 FIP (FanGraphs).
- Was placed on the 10-day D.L. from 8/12 (retroactive to 8/10) to 8/22 with right shoulder inflammation.
- Ranked eighth in the AL in strikeouts, seventh in K/9.0IP ratio (9.79), fourth in K/BB ratio (4.73) and third in BB/9.0IP ratio (2.07)…had the second-highest run-support average (6.51) in the Majors (Boston's Drew Pomeranz-6.63).
- Batters swung at 37.8% of his pitches outside the strike zone, highest in the Majors (FanGraphs)…his career-high 15.1% swinging strike rate was third-highest in the Majors.
- Allowed 35HR, tied for third-most in the AL and tied for fourth in the Majors…was tied with Phil Hughes (35 in 2012) for the second-highest single-season total in Yankees history behind Ralph Terry (40 in 1962).
- Became the first pitcher in Yankees history to record at least 14K multiple times in a season (15K on 9/29 vs. Toronto, 14K on 7/28 vs. Tampa Bay), and the first to collect at least 13K three times in a season (also 13K on 5/26 vs. Oakland…joined David Cone (6/23/97 at Detroit-16K, 6/7/98 vs. Florida-14K) and Ron Guidry (7/11/87 vs. Chicago-AL-14K, 6/17/78 vs. California-18K) as the only pitchers with multiple 14K starts during their Yankees careers…was the fourth AL pitcher to record 14K and 0BB in multiple starts in a single season, following Texas' Yu Darvish (3x in 2013), Boston's Roger Clemens (3x in 1997) and Boston's Pedro Martinez (2x in 1999 and 2x in 2000).
- Went 9-5 with a 3.22 ERA (95.0IP, 34ER) in 15 home starts…his 112K were the third-highest total in a season at the current Yankee Stadium…became the first pitcher to win seven consecutive starts at the current Yankee Stadium (8/7/16-5/2/17)…was the longest streak of winning home starts since Roger Clemens won seven straight from 4/29-7/23/01.
- Made his third consecutive Opening Day start in 4/2 loss at Tampa Bay (2.2IP, 7ER).
- Won five consecutive starts from 4/14-5/8, then lost five consecutive starts from 5/14-6/6…was the third Yankees pitcher since 1913 to win at least five consecutive starts and lose at least five consecutive starts within the same season, joining Bob Turley (5-0, 0-5) in 1955 and Bullet Joe Bush (5-0, 0-5) in 1924…Tanaka is the only one to have one streak immediately follow the other.
- In 4/27 win at Boston, tossed the second shutout of his career (3H, 0BB, 3K)…threw just 97 pitches (72 strikes) and faced 29 batters…was the first complete-game shutout by a Yankee since Brandon McCarthy on 8/21/14 vs. Houston…snapped a streak of 380 consecutive starts by the Yankees without a CGSHO (the Yankees' franchise record is 414 games without a CGSHO)…was the first complete-game shutout by a Yankee at Fenway Park since Mike Mussina on 8/28/02…was the first Yankee to toss a nine-inning complete-game shutout by a Yankee in fewer than 100 pitches since David Wells (96 pitches) on 4/10/03 vs. Minnesota.
- In 5/26 loss at Oakland, set a then-career high with 13K (and 0BB) but took a loss in the Yankees' 4-1 defeat (7.1IP, 5H, 1ER)…was his eighth career double-digit strikeout game…tied a Yankees record for most strikeouts while taking a loss (third time, also Roger Clemens twice: 5/28/00 vs. Boston-13K; 6/17/99 vs. Texas-13K).
- In 6/17 loss at Oakland, became the first pitcher in Yankees history to record 10K without completing 5.0IP (4.0IP, 8H, 5ER, 1BB, 10K, 3HR, 1WP)…was the seventh pitcher in Major League history to last 4.0IP-or-less in a game with double-digit strikeouts.
- In 6/23 win vs. Texas, tossed 8.0 scoreless innings (3H, 2BB, 9K) but took a no-decision in a matchup with the Rangers' Yu Darvish…marked the 15th game in Major League history featuring two Japanese-born starting pitchers…marked the first time that Tanaka and Darvish matched up stateside after four meetings in NPB from 2007-11…Darvish also threw 7.0 scoreless innings as the two pitchers combined for 15.0 scoreless innings (5H, 2BB, 19K).
- In 7/28 win vs. Tampa Bay, set a then-career high with 14K (8.0IP, 2H, 1ER, 0BB, 1HR)…retired the first 17 batters of the game before Adeiny Hechavarria's two-out single in the sixth broke up the perfect game bid.
- Recorded his 500th career strikeout on 5/31 at Baltimore (Manny Machado in the third inning)…was the 27th Major League pitcher since 1908 to reach 500K within 86 career games.
- Made his 100th Major League start on 8/27 vs. Seattle…recorded his 600th career strikeout.
- In 9/29 win vs. Toronto, set a Major League career high with 15K over 7.0 shutout innings (3H, 0BB)…became the seventh Yankees pitcher to record at least 15K in a game…was the second-highest strikeout total without a walk in Yankees history (Michael Pineda, 16K on 5/10/15 vs. Baltimore)…was the first Yankees pitcher to record at least 15K with 0BB in a scoreless start, the 21st such game (18th different pitcher) in Major League history…was the highest strikeout total by an AL pitcher in 2017, one of two 15K games in the Majors (Washington's Stephen Strasburg, 15K on 5/27/17 vs. San Diego)…was tied for the third-highest single-game strikeout total by a Japanese pitcher (Nomo-17K on 4/13/96 with the Dodgers vs. Florida and 16K on 6/14/95 with the Dodgers at Pittsburgh; Darvish-15K on 8/12/13 with Texas at Houston).
- Made three postseason starts, going 2-1 with a 0.90 ERA (20.0IP, 10H, 2ER, 3BB, 18K)…was the second-lowest ERA by a Yankees starter in a single postseason (min. 3GS), trailing only Waite Hoyt's 0.00 ERA (27.0IP, 2R/0ER) in 1921…in ALDS Game 3 vs. Cleveland, tossed 7.0 scoreless innings (3H, 1BB, 7K) to earn his first career postseason win…was the first Yankee to record 7.0 scoreless innings with at least 7K in the postseason since Roger Clemens in 2000 World Series Game 2 vs. the Mets (8.0IP, 9K)…took the loss in ALCS Game 1 at Houston (6.0IP, 4H, 2ER, 1BB, 3K)…tossed 7.0 shutout innings (3H, 1BB, 8K) in a win in ALCS Game 5 vs. Houston…was the third Yankees pitcher to record multiple scoreless starts of at least 7.0IP in a single postseason, joining Roger Clemens (2000) and Whitey Ford (1960)…was the fifth pitcher in Baseball history with multiple scoreless starts with at least 7.0IP and 3H-or-fewer in one postseason, joining San Diego's Kevin Brown (1998), the Yankees' Roger Clemens (2000), Arizona's Randy Johnson (2001) and Detroit's Kenny Rogers (2006).

2016

- In his third season with the Yankees, went 14-4 with a 3.07 ERA (199.2IP, 68ER) in 31 starts…set career highs in wins, innings pitched, starts and quality starts (19)…opponents hit .236 (179-for-759); LH .237 (88-for-372), RH .235 (91-for-387)…was sixth among AL pitchers with a career-best 4.7 WAR (FanGraphs)…the Yankees went 23-8 in his starts.
- Ranked third in the AL in ERA behind Toronto's Aaron Sanchez (3.00) and Detroit's Justin Verlander (3.04)…ranked third in the AL in opponents' OBP (.272) and BB/9.0IP ratio (1.62), fourth in K/BB ratio (4.58) and fifth in winning percentage (.778).
- Led the AL with a 2.34 road ERA (104.0IP, 92H, 33R/27ER, 19BB, 75K, 9HR), while going 7-3 in 16 road starts…trailed only the Mets' Noah Syndergaard (2.29) among Major League pitchers.
- On 4/5 vs. Houston, made his second career Opening Day start (ND, 5.2IP, 2ER).
- On 4/17 vs. Seattle and 8/24 at Seattle, Tanaka and the Mariners' Hisashi Iwakuma faced each other in the 12th and 13th games in Major League history featuring two Japanese-born starting pitchers…Tanaka earned the win in both games…the two pitchers were teammates on the Tohoku Rakuten Golden Eagles from 2007-11, as it marked the first instances of two Japanese former NPB teammates starting against one another in a Major League game.
- Went 4-1 with 3.00 ERA (39.0IP, 34H, 14R/13ER, 1BB, 38K, 5HR) in six starts in August…was the fourth pitcher in Major League history to record at least 38K with one-or-zero walks in a calendar month.
- From 8/7-19, became the first pitcher in Yankees history (and ninth in Major League history) to record at least 8K and 0BB in three consecutive starts…was the first pitcher in AL history (and the second in Major League history) to record at least 8K with no walks and earn a win in three consecutive starts (Clayton Kershaw, 7/8-23/15).
- In a win on 9/21 at Tampa Bay (6.0IP, 4ER), surrendered four solo HRs in the third inning, the first Yankees pitcher to allow 4HR in an inning since Chase Wright on 4/22/07 at Boston.
- Finished the season on his first career seven-game winning streak (8/7-end of the season) while logging a 2.28 ERA (59.1IP, 15ER) over the nine-start span.
- Was scratched from his final two scheduled starts with a mild strain to the flexor mass in his right forearm.

2015

- Went 12-7 with a 3.51 ERA (154.0IP, 60ER) and one complete game in 24 starts…recorded a 2.2 WAR and 3.98 FIP (FanGraphs)…allowed a .221 (126-for-571, 25HR) opponents' average; LH .223 (60-for-269, 13HR), RH .219 (66-for-302, 12HR)…the Yankees went 15-9 in his 24 starts.
- Was placed on the 15-day D.L. from 4/29-6/3 with right wrist tendinitis and a right forearm strain…missed a start in late September after suffering a right hamstring strain while running out a groundball on 9/18 at the Mets.
- His 0.99 WHIP led the AL and was sixth-lowest in the Majors (min. 150.0IP)…was the eighth pitcher in Yankees history to post a WHIP under 1.00 (min. 150.0IP) and one of just two since 1945, joining Ron Guidry (0.95 in 1978)…led AL pitchers (min. 150.0IP) with a .254 opponents' OBP, while his .221 opponents' BA ranked fifth…ranked fourth with a 1.58 BB/9.0IP ratio (154.0IP, 27BB) and fifth with a 5.15 K/BB ratio (139K, 27BB)…his 1.46 HR/9.0IP ratio (25HR/154.0IP) was fourth-highest in the AL, but 19 of his 25HR allowed were solo HRs…did not allow a three-run HR or grand slam until his final start of the season on 9/30 vs. Boston (three-run HR by Travis Shaw).
- On 4/6 vs. Toronto, became the fourth Japanese-born pitcher in Major League history to start on Opening Day (and the first in Yankees history)…at 26 years and 156 days, was the second Yankees pitcher under age-27 to start on Opening Day since 1975 (Andy Pettitte, 25 years, 290 days in 1998)…had started only once on Opening Day during his seven-year career with the Tohoku Rakuten Golden Eagles in Japan (2012).
- When John Ryan Murphy replaced Brian McCann in the second inning on 6/3 at Seattle, it marked the first time in Tanaka's Major League career that he pitched to a catcher other than McCann…he had McCann as his starting catcher for each of his first 32 career starts (through his 7/17/15 start), becoming the first Yankees pitcher in the last 100 years to make his first 32 MLB starts all with the same catcher (credit: *Elias*)…was the longest such streak in the Majors since the Dodgers' Chad Billingsley (first 36 career starts from 2006-07 with Russell Martin).
- On 6/21 vs. Detroit and 6/27 at Houston, allowed 6R and 3HR in consecutive starts, joining Orlando Hernández (5/25/01 and 8/21/01) as the only Yankees pitchers since 1908 to do so…did it again in consecutive starts on 5/14/17 and 5/20/17.
- Made his MLB postseason debut in the AL Wild Card Game, taking the loss in the Yankees' 3-0 defeat vs. Houston (5.0IP, 4H, 2ER, 3BB, 3K, 2HR)…allowed solo HRs to Colby Rasmus leading off the second inning and Carlos Gómez leading off the fourth.
- On 10/20/15, had arthroscopic surgery to remove a bone spur from his right elbow…the bone spur was pre-existing, dating back to his pitching career in Japan…the procedure was performed by Dr. David Altchek at the Hospital for Special Surgery in New York.

2014

- Made 20 starts in his first Major League season, going 13-5 with a 2.77 ERA (136.1IP, 123H, 47R/42ER, 21BB, 141K, 15HR) and three complete games…finished fifth in AL Rookie of the Year voting…marked the lowest ERA by a Yankees rookie (min. 15GS) since Dave Righetti went 8-4 with a 2.05 ERA (105.1IP, 24ER) in 1981…recorded a 2.9 WAR and 3.04 FIP (FanGraphs).
- Became the fifth rookie to lead the Yankees in wins, joining Fritz Peterson (12-11 in 1966, tied), Bob Grim (20-6 in 1954), Bill Bevens (13-9 in 1945) and Russ Ford (26-6 in 1910)…also led the club in complete games.
- Paced all Major League rookies in complete games and ranked third in wins and ninth in innings pitched…no other rookie recorded more than one complete game…led MLB rookies (min. 100.0IP) in K/BB ratio (6.71) and BB/9.0IP ratio (1.39), was second in K/9.0IP ratio (9.31), third in ERA and fourth in opponents' BA (.240).
- Was selected via the Player Ballot to his first AL All-Star Team…was one of three Yankees chosen as All-Stars (also SS Derek Jeter and RHP Dellin Betances)…according to *Elias*, Tanaka and Betances became the first pair of rookie teammates in Yankees history to be named to the same All-Star Game…the duo also became the ninth and 10th Yankees rookies to earn All-Star selections, following Joe DiMaggio (1936), Joe Page (1944), Spec Shea (1947), Bobby Richardson (1957), Ryne Duren (1958), Tom Tresh (1962), Willie Randolph (1976) and Hideki Matsui (2003)–credit: *Elias*.
- Completed at least 6.0IP in each of his first 18 starts (4/4-7/8)…according to *Elias*, became the first pitcher to record at least 6.0IP in each of his first 18 Major League starts since John Farrell (21 straight w/ Cleveland from 8/21/87-6/6/88)…was also the first Yankees pitcher to accomplish the feat…became the first pitcher to record at least 6.0IP in each of his first 18-or-more starts *as a Yankee* since Carl Mays from 1919-20 (18GS).
- Produced a quality start in each of his first 16 games, tied with Montreal's Steve Rogers (1973) for the longest such streak to begin a Major League career (since earned runs became an official stat in 1912)–credit: *Elias*…was also the longest quality starts streak to begin a season since Greg Maddux (16) in 1994…tied CC Sabathia (6/3-8/22/10) for the longest QS streak in Yankees history.
- His five double-digit-strikeout games led MLB rookies…according to *Elias*, joined Al Downing (8x in 1963) as the only Yankees rookies to produce at least three 10K games in a season.
- Was the first Yankees rookie to record at least 3CG since Orlando Hernández in 1998 (also 3CG).
- Made his Major League debut in 4/4 win at Toronto (7.0IP, 6H, 3R/2ER, 1HR, 0BB, 8K)…according to *Elias*, became the sixth pitcher since 1900 to earn a win in his Major League debut while completing at least 7.0IP with at least 8K and 0BB…the only other Yankees pitcher to accomplish the feat was Rich Beck on 9/14/65 at Washington (7.0IP, 8K).
- Recorded 10K on 4/9 vs. Baltimore and on 4/16 vs. Chicago-NL, becoming only the fourth pitcher since 1908 to record at least 10K twice within his first three MLB games (also Stephen Strasburg, Daisuke Matsuzaka and Karl Spooner)…according to *Elias*, became the first rookie pitcher ever to register at least 10K in consecutive games for the Yankees…*Elias* also notes that Tanaka joined Washington's Stephen Strasburg as the only two pitchers since 1900 to record at least 8K in each of their first three career games…became the second Yankee to record at least 10K and 7.0IP with 1BB-or-fewer in consecutive starts (David Wells on 9/1/98 vs. Oakland and 9/7/98 at Boston; since joined by Luis Severino, in 2017 and in 2018).
- Improved to 6-0 and recorded his first Major League shutout in his eighth career start on 5/14 at the Mets (4H, 0BB, 8K)…joined Andy Pettitte (6/30/00) as the only Yankees starters to throw a complete-game shutout against the Mets (credit: *Elias*)…became the first Yankees rookie to begin his career 6-0 as a starter since Whitey Ford went 9-0 in 12 starts in 1950…according to *Elias*, became the first pitcher since 1900 to earn at least six wins and record at least 60K in his first eight appearances in the Majors…became the first pitcher since 1900 to register at least 60K while issuing fewer than 10BB in his first eight career games (66K, 7BB).
- Went 1-for-4 in 5/14 win at the Mets, hitting a two-out single off José Valverde in the ninth inning…became the first pitcher to record his first MLB shutout and first career hit in the same game since Pittsburgh's Jeff Karstens on 8/6/08 at Arizona (credit: *Elias*)…became the first Yankees pitcher to accomplish the feat since Ron Klimkowski on 9/18/70 at Detroit.
- Suffered his first career Major League loss in his ninth career start, a Yankees' 6-1 defeat on 5/20 at Chicago-NL (6.0IP, 8H, 4R/3ER, 1BB, 7K)…had been unbeaten in his previous 42 regular season starts (34-0) in Nippon Professional Baseball and Major League Baseball…marked his first regular season loss since 8/19/12, when the Seibu Lions defeated the Rakuten Golden Eagles at the Seibu Dome.
- Was named AL "Pitcher of the Month" for May after going 5-1 with a 1.88 ERA (43.0IP, 9ER), one shutout, 6BB and 42K over six appearances…became the first Yankees rookie to win an AL "Pitcher of the Month" award since its inception in 1979…became the third Japan-born pitcher to win the award, joining Hideo Nomo (June 1995 and September 1996) and Hideki Irabu (May 1998 and July 1999).
- According to *Elias*, became only the fifth pitcher since 1900 to record at least 100K through his first 13 career games (103K), joining Hideo Nomo (119K), Kerry Wood (118K), Herb Score (107K) and José DeLeón (106K).
- Improved to 11-1 and lowered his ERA to 1.99 following 6/17 win vs. Toronto…became the first Yankees pitcher to win at least 11 of his first 12 decisions in a season since Roger Clemens went 11-1 to begin the 2001 season.
- Was placed on the 15-day disabled list with right elbow inflammation on 7/9…was transferred to the 60-day D.L. on 9/2…missed 65 games from 7/9-9/20.

191

- Returned from the 60-day disabled list on 9/21 and started that day vs. Toronto, earning his 13th win in a 5-2 Yankees victory (5.1IP, 5H, 1ER, 0BB, 4K)…made his final start in 9/27 loss at Boston (1.2IP, 7H, 7R/5ER, 2BB, 2K).
- Made five official spring training appearances (three starts), going 2-0 with a 2.14 ERA (21.0IP, 15H, 5ER, 3BB, 26K)…earned the "James P. Dawson Award" as the Yankees' top rookie in spring training, as voted on by the club's beat writers…led Yankees pitchers in strikeouts.

JAPANESE CAREER NOTES
- In 175 games (172 starts) over seven seasons (2007-13) with the Tohoku Rakuten Golden Eagles in Japan's Pacific League, went 99-35 with a 2.30 ERA (1,315.0IP, 336ER), 53 complete games and 18 shutouts…in his final three seasons (2011-13), combined to go 53-9 with a 1.44 ERA (611.1IP, 98ER), 30 complete games and 11 shutouts in 77 games (76 starts), recording 593K and only 78BB over the stretch.
- Won his final 28 decisions in his Japanese regular season career, going 4-0 over his final four starts in 2012 and 24-0 in 2013…surpassed Kiyoshi Matsuda from 1951-52 and Kazuhisa Inao in 1957 (20 each) for most consecutive wins in NPB history.
- Was a two-time winner (2011 and '13) of the prestigious Sawamura Award as Nippon Professional Baseball's best pitcher…was named Pacific League MVP in 2013…was named "Pitcher of the Month" a Nippon Professional Baseball-record 12 times…was a seven-time NPB All-Star (2007-13)…earned three Gold Glove Awards (2011-13)…was the recipient of the Pacific League's 2011 and '13 "Best Nine Award" as the league's best pitcher…was named "Rookie of the Year" in 2007.
- Pitched for Japan in the 2009 and '13 World Baseball Classics, combining to make eight appearances (one start) and post a 2.89 ERA (9.1IP, 13H, 4R, 3ER, 0BB, 1HR, 17K), helping guide the 2009 team to a championship…also competed on Japan's national team in the 2008 Olympics, tossing 7.0 scoreless innings over three games.
- Posted NPB's lowest ERA and most wins in 2011 (1.27, 19) and '13 (1.27, 24) and the most strikeouts in 2012 (169).

2013
- Went 24-0 with one save and a 1.27 ERA (212.0IP, 30ER) and 183K in 28 games (27 starts) with Rakuten…tossed eight complete games and two shutouts…led NPB in wins and ERA, setting an NPB record in victories.
- Earned the Pacific League MVP Award, was named to the "Best Nine" and won a Gold Glove Award.
- Was his third straight season with an ERA under 2.00…his 1.27 ERA was the third-lowest in Pacific League history (fractionally higher than his ERA in 2011) and the sixth-lowest in NPB history.
- Earned the Sawamura Award as NPB's best pitcher at the conclusion of the season…was named "Pitcher of the Month" five times (May-September).
- Set a Rakuten club record for most consecutive wins to start the season with his ninth victory on 6/16…set an NPB record with his 16th straight win to open the season on 8/9…on 9/13 vs. the Orix Buffaloes, won his NPB-record 21st straight decision.
- Went 1-1 with a 2.37 ERA (19.0IP, 5ER) in three games (two starts) with 21K and 4BB in the Japan Series vs. the Yomiuri Giants…was given the honor of throwing the final pitches in Game 7 of the best-of-seven series, earning the save as Rakuten won its first title in franchise history.
- Prior to the season, pitched for Japan in the World Baseball Classic, allowing 2ER in 7.0IP over four appearances (one start)…recorded 12K without walking a batter.

2012
- Was 10-4 with a 1.87 ERA (173.0IP, 36ER) in 22 starts with Rakuten…posted an ERA under 2.00 for the second straight year…led the Pacific League with 169K and eight complete games and tied for the league lead with three shutouts…his 19BB were fewest among qualifying pitchers…recorded a 0.99 BB/9.0IP ratio.
- Won his second career Gold Glove Award (also 2011).

2011
- Went 19-5 with a 1.27 ERA (226.1IP, 32ER) in 27 starts with Rakuten…struck out 241 batters with just 27BB…his 226.1IP and 241K marked his highest totals while playing in Japan…recorded 14 complete games, including six shutouts…of his 27 starts, 12 were scoreless…his 1.27 ERA was the second-lowest in Pacific League history and fifth-lowest since the advent of the two-league system in Japan.
- Won the Sawamura Award, given annually to NPB's best pitcher…led the Pacific League in ERA and was tied for first in wins and complete-game shutouts…led NPB in complete games.
- Was selected to the "Best Nine" and won the Gold Glove Award…with his catcher, the duo won the Most Valuable Battery Award.
- Won consecutive "Pitcher of the Month" Awards in June and July and a third award in October, becoming the first pitcher ever to receive the award three times in the same season.
- Struck out 18 batters on 8/27 vs. Softbank, the second-most strikeouts in a single game in NPB history.
- Following the season, was chosen as the "Georgia Spirit Award" winner for 2011, a prize given annually from Georgia Can Coffee to the player who most "gives his all for his team."

2010
- Was 11-6 with a 2.50 ERA (155.0IP, 43ER) in 20 starts with Rakuten…led the team in wins and ERA.
- Won his third career "Pitcher of the Month" award in May and led his team with eight wins in June.

2009
- Went 15-6 with a 2.33 ERA (189.2IP, 49ER) in 25 appearances (24 starts) for Rakuten…led Rakuten pitchers and tied for second in the Pacific League in wins…finished third in the league in ERA.
- Was named Pacific League "Pitcher of the Month" for April, going 4-0 with a 0.50 ERA and 37K in four starts.
- Went 4-0 with four complete games over his first four starts of the season…tossed a four-hit shutout vs. the Hawks on 4/7, allowed one run vs. the Chiba Lotte Marines on 4/14, tossed a three-hit shutout vs. the Marines on 4/22 and struck out 11 batters while allowing 1ER vs. the Fighters on 4/29…became the first pitcher to start the season with four consecutive complete-game wins since 1993.
- Went 4-0 with a 1.44 ERA and 30K in August, winning his second career "Pitcher of the Month" Award.
- Made his first career postseason start on 10/17 in the clinching game of the First Stage of the Climax Series vs. the Softbank Hawks, allowing 7H and 1ER with 9K in a complete-game win…on 10/23, made a start in an elimination game of the Second Stage with his team down 2-games-to-none against the Nippon Ham Fighters, tossing a complete-game win (6H, 2ER, 1BB, 6K) in Rakuten's only victory of the series.
- Prior to the season, pitched for the World Baseball Classic-champion Japan team, making four relief appearances and allowing 1ER in 2.1IP (3H, 1HR, 0BB, 5K)…pitched in the semifinals against the United States team, allowing a triple to Jimmy Rollins before striking out David Wright.

2008
- Went 9-7 with a 3.49 ERA (172.2IP, 67ER) in 25 appearances (24 starts) with Rakuten.
- With 159K in 2008 and 196K in 2007, became the first high school draftee in Nippon Professional Baseball to reach 150K in two consecutive seasons since 1970.
- Made his first career relief appearance on 6/22 in an Interleague game vs. the Hiroshima Carp, earning the save.
- Participated in the 2008 Beijing Olympics in August as a member of the Japanese national team, combining to toss 7.0 scoreless innings over three appearances.

2007
- Made his professional debut, going 11-7 with a 3.82 ERA (186.1IP, 79ER) and 196K in 28 starts with Rakuten en route to being named the Pacific League "Rookie of the Year"…became the first pitcher to record double-digit wins in Eagles franchise history and the first to do so as a rookie out of high school in Japanese professional baseball since Daisuke Matsuzaka…led the Pacific League in games started and ranked fourth in innings pitched.
- His 196K were the second-most by any pitcher in either the Pacific League or the Central League (trailing only Yu Darvish) and the fourth-most as a rookie out of high school in Japanese professional baseball history.
- Made his first career start—and appearance—on 3/29/07 against the Fukuoka Softbank Hawks, allowing 6H and 6ER in 1.2IP in a no-decision after being named to the Eagles' Opening Day roster during spring training.
- Earned the first win of his Japanese career on 4/18 vs. the Hawks, tossing a complete game (2ER, 13K).
- On 6/13, started an Interleague game against the Chunichi Dragons and became the first pitcher since Yu Darvish to throw a complete-game shutout as a rookie out of high school.
- Became the first pitcher since Daisuke Matsuzaka (1999) to be voted the starter of the NPB All-Star Game (representing the Pacific League) as a rookie out of high school, starting in Game 2 on 7/22 (2.0IP, 6ER).

PERSONAL
- Married Mai Satoda in March 2012…Mai is a well-known singer and pop star in Japan…the couple has a son and a daughter.
- Attended Komazawa University Tomakomai High School…over the course of his high school career (2004-06), struck out 458 batters, surpassing Daisuke Matsuzaka's previous national high school record with Yokohama Senior High School (423K)…in the summer of his junior year, was the top pitcher in the Summer Koshien Tournament and was chosen to represent the Japanese team at the U18 Asia Baseball Championships…led Tomakomai to the Meiji Jingu Tournament in the fall of his junior year…began playing baseball in first grade as a catcher…did not pitch until junior high school.
- Was selected to the All-Japan team in 2006 and traveled to play an American All-Star team…while on the trip, visited the original Yankee Stadium and met then-Yankees outfielder Hideki Matsui.
- On 9/25/06, the Nippon Ham Fighters, Orix Buffaloes, Yokohama Baystars and Tohoku Rakuten Golden Eagles all selected him as their first-round draft pick…Rakuten won the lottery and the rights to negotiate with him…signed with the Golden Eagles on 11/2/06…was given uniform No. 18, the traditional number given to the ace pitcher of a professional team in Japan.

Tanaka's Career Pitching Record

Year	Club	W	L	ERA	G	GS	CG	SHO	SV	IP	H	R	ER	HR	HP	BB	SO	WP	BK
2007	Rakuten	11	7	3.82	28	28	4	1	0	186.1	183	83	79	17	7	68	196	10	1
2008	Rakuten	9	7	3.49	25	24	5	2	1	172.2	171	71	67	9	2	54	159	6	0
2009	Rakuten	15	6	2.33	25	24	6	3	0	189.2	170	51	49	13	7	43	171	3	0
2010	Rakuten	11	6	2.50	20	20	8	1	0	155.0	159	47	43	9	5	32	119	1	0
2011	Rakuten	19	5	1.27	27	27	14	6	0	226.1	171	35	32	8	5	27	241	7	0
2012	Rakuten	10	4	1.87	22	22	8	3	0	173.0	160	45	36	4	2	19	169	4	0
2013	Rakuten	24	0	1.27	28	27	8	2	1	212.0	168	35	30	6	3	32	183	9	0
2014	YANKEES - a	13	5	2.77	20	20	3	1	0	136.1	123	47	42	15	4	21	141	4	0
2015	YANKEES - b	12	7	3.51	24	24	1	0	0	154.0	126	66	60	25	1	27	139	4	0
	Scranton/WB	0	0	4.50	2	2	0	0	0	6.0	6	3	3	1	0	2	6	0	0
2016	YANKEES	14	4	3.07	31	31	0	0	0	199.2	179	75	68	22	3	36	165	7	0
2017	YANKEES - c	13	12	4.74	30	30	1	1	0	178.1	180	100	94	35	7	41	194	7	0
2018	YANKEES - d	12	6	3.75	27	27	1	1	0	156.0	141	68	65	25	7	35	159	3	0
	Scranton/WB	0	0	3.60	1	1	0	0	0	5.0	3	2	2	1	0	0	4	0	0
2019	YANKEES	11	9	4.45	32	31	1	0	0	182.0	186	95	90	28	2	40	149	7	0
Japan Totals		99	35	2.30	175	172	53	18	3	1315.0	1182	367	336	66	31	275	1238	40	1
Minor League Totals		0	0	4.09	3	3	0	0	0	11.0	9	5	5	2	0	2	10	0	0
Major League Totals		75	43	3.75	164	163	7	4	0	1006.1	935	451	419	150	24	200	947	32	0

Acquired by the Yankees via the posting system from the Tohoku Rakuten Golden Eagles of Japan on January 22, 2014.

a - Placed on the 15-day disabled list from July 9 – September 21, 2014 with right elbow inflammation…transferred to the 60-day disabled list on September 2.
b - Placed on the 15-day disabled list from April 29 – June 2, 2015 with right wrist tendinitis/right forearm strain.
c - Placed on the 10-day disabled list from August 12 (retroactive to August 10) – August 22, 2017 with right shoulder inflammation.
d - Placed on the 10-day disabled list from June 9 – July 10, 2018 with mild left and right hamstring strains.

Tanaka's Postseason Record

Year	Club vs. Opp.	W	L	ERA	G	GS	CG	SHO	SV	IP	H	R	ER	HR	HP	BB	SO	WP	BK
2015	NYY vs. HOU (WC)	0	1	3.60	1	1	0	0	0	5.0	4	2	2	2	0	3	3	0	0
2017	NYY vs. CLE (DS)	1	0	0.00	1	1	0	0	0	7.0	3	0	0	0	0	1	7	0	0
	NYY vs. HOU (LS)	1	1	1.38	2	2	0	0	0	13.0	7	2	2	0	0	2	11	2	0
2018	NYY vs. OAK (WC)							On Roster - Did Not Pitch											
	NYY vs. BOS (DS)	0	1	1.80	1	1	0	0	0	5.0	3	1	1	1	0	1	4	0	0
2019	NYY vs. MIN (DS)	1	0	1.80	1	1	0	0	0	5.0	3	1	1	0	1	1	7	0	0
	NYY vs. HOU (CS)	1	1	2.45	2	2	0	0	0	11.0	5	4	3	1	0	3	5	0	0
Wild Card Totals		0	1	3.60	1	1	0	0	0	5.0	4	2	2	2	0	3	3	0	0
Division Series Totals		3	0	1.06	3	3	0	0	0	17.0	9	2	2	1	1	3	18	0	0
LCS Totals		2	2	1.88	4	4	0	0	0	24.0	12	6	5	1	0	5	16	2	0
POSTSEASON TOTALS		5	3	1.76	8	8	0	0	0	46.0	25	10	9	4	1	11	37	2	0

Tanaka's World Baseball Classic Record

Year	Country, Site	W	L	ERA	G	GS	CG	SHO	SV	IP	H	R	ER	HR	HP	BB	SO	WP	BK
2009	Japan, Japan	0	0	3.86	4	0	0	0	0	2.1	3	1	1	1	0	0	5	0	0
2013	Japan, Japan	0	0	2.57	4	1	0	0	0	7.0	10	3	2	0	0	0	12	0	0
WBC Totals		0	0	2.89	8	1	0	0	0	9.1	13	4	3	1	0	0	17	0	0

Tanaka's All-Star Game Record

Year	Club, Site	W	L	ERA	G	GS	CG	SHO	SV	IP	H	R	ER	HR	HP	BB	SO	WP	BK
2014	NYY, Minnesota					Selected - Did Not Pitch Due to Injury													
2019	NYY, Cleveland	1	0	0.00	1	0	0	0	0	1.0	1	0	0	0	0	0	1	0	0
All-Star Game Totals		1	0	0.00	1	0	0	0	0	1.0	1	0	0	0	0	0	1	0	0

Tanaka's Career Fielding Record

Position	PCT	G	PO	A	E	TC	DP
Pitcher	.980	164	65	127	4	196	12

Tanaka's Regular Season Batting Record

Year	Team	AVG	G	AB	R	H	2B	3B	HR	RBI	SH	SF	HP	BB	SO	SB	CS
2019	NYY	.000	32	1	0	0	0	0	0	0	0	0	0	0	0	0	0
Major League Totals		.037	164	27	1	1	0	0	0	1	0	0	1	12	0	0

Tanaka's Career Bests and Streaks

COMPLETE GAMES: 7, last on 6/17/19 vs. TB. **LOW-HIT COMPLETE GAME:** 2, 6/17/19 vs. TB. **IP (START):** 9.0 - 7 times (last on 6/17/19 vs. TB). **IP (RELIEF):** 3.0, 9/29/19 at TEX. **HITS:** 12, 7/25/19 at BOS. **RUNS:** 12, 7/25/19 at BOS. **WALKS:** 5, 8/9/17 at TOR. **STRIKEOUTS:** 15, 9/29/17 vs. TOR. **HOME RUNS:** 4 - 2 times (last on 5/14/17-G2 vs. HOU). **WINNING STREAK:** 7g - 2 times (last from 4/23-7/31/18). **LOSING STREAK:** 6g, 5/14-6/17/17. **SCORELESS STREAK (IP):** 21.1, 7/15-8/5/18.

Pitcher of the Month: May 2014   **Player of the Week:** None   **Rookie of the Month:** None

MIKE TAUCHMAN • OF

39

HT: 6-2 • **WT:** 220 • **BATS:** L • **THROWS:** L
BIRTHDATE: 12/3/90 • **OPENING DAY AGE:** 29
BIRTHPLACE: Pallatine, Ill.
RESIDES: Chicago, Ill.
COLLEGE: Bradley University
M.L. SERVICE: 1 year, 55 days

STATUS
- Acquired by the Yankees from the Colorado Rockies in exchange for LHP Phillip Diehl on March 23, 2019.

2019
- Hit .277/.361/.504 (72-for-260) with 46R, 18 doubles, 1 triple, 13HR and 47RBI in 87 games over four stints with the Yankees (3/28-5/12, 5/15, 6/13-17, 6/26-9/29)…made 55 starts in LF, 11 in CF and 11 in RF.
- Of his 72H, 32 went for extra bases…hit 13HR with the first seven coming at Yankee Stadium and the final six coming on the road…hit .324 (24-for-74) with 5HR and 36RBI with runners in scoring position.
- Hit .357 (25-for-70) off left-handed pitching…of his 13HR, 12 came vs. right-handers.
- Made his second career Opening Day roster (also 2018)…made his Yankees debut as ninth-inning PR for Voit on 3/30 vs. Baltimore…collected his first hit as a Yankee with a second-inning double on 4/2 vs. Detroit.
- Hit a three-run HR in the sixth inning of 4/16 win vs. Boston, the first Major League homer of his career…was the fifth Yankee since 2014 to hit his first Major League homer against the Red Sox, joining Kyle Higashioka (7/1/18), Gary Sánchez (8/10/16), Rob Refsnyder (7/12/15) and Dean Anna (4/10/14).
- Hit fifth in the lineup for the first time in his career on 4/21 vs. Kansas City…batted fifth five times in 2019.
- Hit two-run HR on 5/5, snapping an 11-game streak without an extra-base hit from 4/22-5/4.
- Batted .423/.474/.750 (22-for-52) with 16R, 6 doubles, 1 triple, 3HR and 13RBI in 16G in July, becoming the third Yankee to hit at least .420 and slug .700 in a calendar month (min. 50PA) since 1990 (Bernie Williams, June 2001 and Paul O'Neill, April 1994)…the only other Yankees to reach those numbers in July are Joe DiMaggio (2x) and Babe Ruth (4x)…led the Majors in batting average and on-base pct. during July and ranked fifth in SLG.
- Hit .315 (46-for-146) with 29R, 10 doubles, 9HR and 30RBI in 45 games following the All-Star break.
- Tied his career high with a six-game run scoring streak from 7/19-24 (10R)…also scored a run in six straight from 4/14-21 (8R)…had a career-best five-game RBI streaks from 7/20-24 and 7/31-8/6.
- Had multiple RBI in six of 7G with a plate appearance from 7/31-8/8, including five straight games (with an AB) from 7/31-8/6…the five-game streak was tied for the third-longest streak by a Yankee (since RBI became an official stat in 1920), trailing only Tino Martinez (6G, 4/10-18/98) and Lou Gehrig (6G, 8/28-9/1/31)…was the longest by a Yankee since Bernie Williams' five-game streak from 4/19-23/03.
- Hit 5HR over a five-game span from 8/5-9…collected his first career multi-HR game on 8/5 at Baltimore, his first career homers on the road (first 7HR came at Yankee Stadium)…had a career-high-tying 4RBI on 8/8 at Toronto.
- Was placed on the 10-day injured list on 9/10 (retroactive to 9/9) with a left calf strain, missing the remainder of the season.
- Was acquired by the Yankees from Colorado in exchange for LHP Phillip Diehl on 3/23.
- Hit .274 (26-for-95) with 22R, 10 doubles, 3 triples, 2HR and 16RBI in 28 games with Triple-A Scranton/Wilkes-Barre.

2018
- Made his first career Opening Day roster and hit .094 (3-for-32) with 5R, 1 double, 4BB and 1SB in 21 games over two stints (3/29-4/21 and 6/5-12) with the Rockies.
- Spent the majority of the season with Triple-A Albuquerque, batting .323/.408/.571 (130-for-403) with 84R, 26 doubles, 7 triples, 20HR, 81RBI, 60BB and 12SB in 112 games en route to being named to the Pacific League's Mid-Season and Postseason All-Star teams…ranked fourth in RBI and seventh in BA among Rockies minor leaguers…ranked among league leaders in the PCL in OBP (third), SLG (third), runs (fifth) and batting average (sixth).
- Was tabbed the PCL "Player of the Month" for May after batting .379/.426/.698 (44-for-116) with 31R, 9 doubles, 2 triples, 8HR, 24RBI and 11BB in 29 games…was named the PCL "Player of the Week" for 5/14-20 after hitting .417/.462/1.125 (10-for-24) with 8R, 1 triple, 5HR and 8RBI in six games.
- Following the season, was named an Organization All-Star by MiLB.com.

2017
- Saw his first Major League action with the Rockies, hitting .222 (6-for-27) with 2R, 1 triple, 2RBI, 5BB and 1SB in 31 games over three stints (6/27-7/7, 8/18-22 and 9/1-10/1).
- In 110 games with Triple-A Albuquerque, hit .331 (139-for-420) with 82R, 30 doubles, 8 triples, 16HR, 80RBI, 40BB and 16SB…was named a PCL Postseason All-Star…ranked fifth in BA among Rockies minor leaguers.
- Following the season, was named an Organization All-Star by MiLB.com.

2016
- Hit .286/.342/.373 (136-for-475) with 72R, 24 doubles, 7 triples, 1HR, 51RBI, 40BB and 23SB in 129 games with Triple-A Albuquerque.
- Following the season, appeared in 31 games for the Aguilas del Zulia of the Venezuelan Winter League, batting .269 (32-for-119) with 21R, 4 doubles, 1HR, 9RBI, 11BB and 5SB.

2015
- Spent the entire season with Double-A New Britain, batting .294/.355/.381 (149-for-507) with 62R, 23 doubles, 6 triples, 3HR, 43RBI, 47BB and 25SB in 131 games…was named an Eastern League Postseason All-Star.
- Tied for fourth in the Eastern League in triples and ranked fourth in hits and seventh in BA.

2014
- Combined with short-season Single-A Tri-City and Single-A Modesto to hit .293/.384/.437 (65-for-222) with 38R, 12 doubles, 4 triples, 4HR, 22RBI, 33BB and 15SB in 60 games.
- Began the season with Tri-City, batting .280 (7-for-25) with 5R, 1 double, 4RBI, 4BB and 6SB in seven games…was promoted to Modesto on 6/26 and hit .294 (58-for-197) with 33R, 11 doubles, 4 triples, 4HR, 18RBI, 29BB and 9SB in 53 games.

2013
- Made his professional debut with short-season Single-A Tri-City, hitting .297 (70-for-236) with 38R, 13 doubles, 3 triples, 23RBI, 33BB and 20SB in 64 games…was named a North West League Mid-Season All-Star…ranked ninth in BA among Rockies minor leaguers.
- Tied for third in the Northwest League in stolen bases and tied for fourth in hits…also ranked fourth in BA and fifth in OBP (.388) and runs.
- Was tabbed the NWL "Player of the Week" from 7/29-8/4 after hitting .480/.533/.720 (12-for-25) with 9R, 4 doubles, 1 triple, 4RBI, 4BB and 2SB in seven games.

PERSONAL
- Full name is Michael Robert Tauchman…is married to Eileen.
- Attended William Fremd High School in Palatine, Ill., where he played football and baseball…named all-conference in baseball three times, including the Conference Player of the Year as a senior.
- Played collegiately at Bradley University, where he majored in business management and administration.

Tauchman's Career Batting Record

Year	Team	AVG	G	AB	R	H	2B	3B	HR	RBI	SH	SF	HP	BB	SO	SB	CS	E	OBP	SLG
2013	Tri-City	.297	64	236	38	70	13	3	0	23	1	1	3	33	55	20	7	3	.388	.377
2014	Tri-City	.280	7	25	5	7	1	0	0	4	0	1	0	4	2	6	0	0	.367	.320
	Modesto	.294	53	197	33	58	11	4	4	18	0	1	1	29	41	9	3	2	.386	.452
2015	New Britain	.294	131	507	62	149	23	6	3	43	5	2	2	47	69	25	13	2	.355	.381
2016	Albuquerque	.286	129	475	72	136	24	7	1	51	6	4	2	40	77	23	10	5	.342	.373
2017	COLORADO	.222	31	27	2	6	0	1	0	2	0	0	0	5	10	1	2	1	.344	.296
	Albuquerque	.331	110	420	82	139	30	8	16	80	1	10	4	40	73	16	7	3	.386	.555
2018	COLORADO	.094	21	32	5	3	1	0	0	0	1	0	0	4	15	1	0	0	.194	.125
	Albuquerque	.323	112	403	84	130	26	7	20	81	0	6	2	60	70	12	10	3	.408	.571
2019	YANKEES - a, b	.277	87	260	46	72	18	1	13	47	0	1	1	34	71	6	0	1	.361	.504
	Scranton/WB	.274	28	95	22	26	10	3	2	16	0	1	2	16	16	4	0	0	.386	.505
Minor League Totals		**.303**	**634**	**2358**	**398**	**715**	**138**	**38**	**46**	**316**	**13**	**26**	**16**	**269**	**403**	**115**	**50**	**18**	**.375**	**.453**
AL Totals		**.277**	**87**	**260**	**46**	**72**	**18**	**1**	**13**	**47**	**0**	**1**	**1**	**34**	**71**	**6**	**0**	**1**	**.361**	**.504**
NL Totals		**.153**	**52**	**59**	**7**	**9**	**1**	**1**	**0**	**2**	**1**	**0**	**0**	**9**	**25**	**2**	**2**	**1**	**.265**	**.203**
Major League Totals		**.254**	**139**	**319**	**53**	**81**	**19**	**2**	**13**	**49**	**1**	**1**	**1**	**43**	**96**	**8**	**2**	**2**	**.343**	**.448**

Selected by the Colorado Rockies in the 10th round of the 2013 First-Year Player Draft.

a – Acquired by the Yankees from the Colorado Rockies in exchange for LHP Phillip Diehl on March 23, 2019.
b – Placed on the 10-day injured list from September 10 (retroactive to September 9) - September 29, 2019 with a left calf strain.

Tauchman's Career Fielding Record

Position	PCT	G	PO	A	E	TC	DP
Outfield	.988	104	168	3	2	173	1

Tauchman's Career Home Run Chart
MULTI-HOMER GAMES: 1. **TWO-HOMER GAMES:** 1, 8/5/19 at BAL. **THREE-HOMER GAMES:** None. **GRAND SLAMS:** None. **PINCH-HIT HR:** None. **INSIDE-THE-PARK HR:** None. **"WALK-OFF" HR:** None. **LEADOFF HR:** None.

Tauchman's Career Bests and Streaks
HITS: 3 - 4 times (last on 8/5/19 at BAL). **RUNS:** 3, 8/5/19 at BAL. **2B:** 1 - 19 times (last on 9/8/19 at BOS). **3B:** 1 - 2 times (last on 7/24/19 at MIN). **HR:** 2, 8/5/19 at BAL. **RBI:** 4 - 2 times (last on 8/8/19 at TOR). **BB:** 3, 8/10/19 at TOR. **SO:** 3 - 3 times (last on 4/3/19 vs. DET). **SB:** 1 - 8 times (last on 8/25/19 at LAD). **HIT STREAK:** 6g, 7/21-26/19. **"WALK-OFF" HITS:** None.

Player of the Month: None   **Player of the Week:** None   **Rookie of the Month:** None

GLEYBER TORRES • INF

25

HT: 6-1 • **WT:** 205 • **BATS:** R • **THROWS:** R
BIRTHDATE: 12/13/96 • **OPENING DAY AGE:** 23
BIRTHPLACE: Caracas, Venezuela
RESIDES: Caracas, Venezuela
M.L. SERVICE: 1 year, 162 days

STATUS
- Acquired by the Yankees from the Chicago Cubs along with RHP Adam Warren, OF Billy McKinney and OF Rashad Crawford in exchange for LHP Aroldis Chapman on July 25, 2016.

CAREER NOTES
- With 24HR in his 2018 rookie season and 38HR in 2019, became the third Yankee all-time with multiple 20HR seasons *before turning 23 years old* (also Mickey Mantle, three seasons from 1952-54 and Joe DiMaggio, two seasons from 1936-37)…is one of five middle infielders in Baseball history with multiple 20HR seasons by his age 22 season, joining Cal Ripken Jr. (two, 1982-83), Alex Rodriguez (three, 1996-98), Carlos Correa (three, 2015-17) and Ozzie Albies (2018-19).

CAREER HIGHLIGHTS

AL All-Star Team
▸ 2018, 2019

- Has hit 62HR in 267 career games, the second-highest total for a Yankee in his first two Major League seasons (Joe DiMaggio, 75HR in 1936-37).
- Of his 62 career home runs, 27 have come with runners on base…of his 62HR, 21 have tied the game (4) or given the Yankees the lead (17)…has 27HR in his career against the AL East, including 16 vs. the Baltimore Orioles.
- Has 10 career multi-HR games, tied for second-most by any player in Baseball history prior to turning 23 (Eddie Mathews-13; Mel Ott, Bob Horner and Bryce Harper-10 each).
- Has a Major League-high 13 three-run HRs since the start of 2018.
- Is a career .357 (10-for-28) batter with two grand slams and 26RBI with the bases loaded.
- Has made one career Opening Day roster (2019).

2019
- Hit .278 (152-for-546) with 96R, 26 doubles, 38HR, 90RBI and 48BB in 144 games…set career highs in almost every offensive category…is the second Yankees middle infielder in the last 100 years to lead the club in home runs (Robinson Canó-27HR in 2013)…received one fifth place and one ninth place vote in AL MVP balloting.
- Is the second-youngest Yankee to have at least 30HR in a season behind only Joe DiMaggio…his 90RBI were most by a Yankee in a season at age 22-or-younger since Mickey Mantle had 102RBI in 1954.
- His 38HR were tied for second-most by a middle infielder in team history (min. 50% of G at 2B/SS): 2B Alfonso Soriano (39HR in 2002, 38HR in 2003).
- Of his 38HR, 21 came vs. the AL East…hit 13HR vs. Baltimore, the most ever by a player vs. a single opponent in a single season in the divisional era (since 1969).
- Had 16 of his 38HR come in his Major League-best eight multi-HR games…tied the Yankees' franchise record for multi-HR games in a season, joining Alex Rodriguez (2007), Mickey Mantle (1961) and Babe Ruth (1927)…were second-most by any Major Leaguer since 2011 behind Giancarlo Stanton (10) with Miami in 2017…was the first player under the age of 23 to record eight multi-HR games in a season (previous record set by Texas's Juan Gonzalez-7 in 1992)…is the second player ever to record eight multi-HR games as a middle infielder in a season, joining Texas's Alex Rodriguez (10 in 2002).
- Hit 20HR at Yankee Stadium, fifth-most home runs at home by an AL player in 2019…became the sixth player (eighth time) to hit 20 homers at the current Yankee Stadium in a single season and third since 2017 (Aaron Judge-33HR in 2017 and Giancarlo Stanton-20HR in 2018).
- Batted .394/.467/1.045 (26-for-66) with 22R, 4 doubles, 13HR and 20RBI in 18 games vs. the Orioles, hitting safely in 15 of those contests…his 13HR surpassed Chicago-NL's Sammy Sosa (12HR in 1998 vs. Milwaukee) for the most by any player vs. a single opponent in one season in the divisional era (since 1969)…is one of six players ever to hit at least 13HR vs. a single opponent in a season (Yankees' Lou Gehrig-Major League-record 14HR vs. Cleveland in 1936; Yankees' Roger Maris-13HR vs. Chicago-AL in 1961, Milwaukee-NL's Joe Adcock-13HR vs. Brooklyn in 1956, Chicago-NL's Hank Sauer-13HR vs. Pittsburgh in 1954, Philadelphia-AL's Jimmie Foxx-13HR vs. Detroit in 1932)…had five multi-HR games vs. Baltimore, establishing a new Major League record for multi-HR games vs. one opponent in a single season, previously held by Roy Sievers (1955 vs. Kansas City A's), Gus Zernial (1951 vs. St. Louis-AL) and Ralph Kiner (1947 vs. Boston-AL)…*STATS, LLC*, notes he became the first player in Major League history to hit 10 of his first 12 home runs of a season against the same team…according to STATS, Inc., was the first player to homer in both games of two doubleheaders vs. the same opponent (5/15 and 8/12, both vs. Baltimore) in one year since Philadelphia's Mike Schmidt in 1983 vs. Montreal.

197

- Hit two grand slams, becoming the fourth Yankee to hit multiple grand slams in the same season before turning 23 years old, joining Joe DiMaggio (3 in 1937), Mickey Mantle (2 in 1952) and Yogia Berra (2 in 1947).
- According to the YES Network, with Gary Sánchez hitting 10HR vs. the O's, became the 10th set of teammates in Major League history (fifth set of Yankees) to hit at least 9HR against the same team in a single season and the first since San Francisco's Barry Bonds and Rich Aurilia (9HR each) in 2001 vs. Arizona…the last set of Yankees to do so was Mickey Mantle (11HR) and Roger Maris (9HR) in 1961 vs. the Washington Senators.
- Hit .338 (25-for-74) with 8R, 6 doubles, 3HR and 14RBI in 19 Interleague games, reaching safely in 16 of those 19 contests…became just the fifth player in Interleague history (since 1998) to begin a season with XBHs in each of his first six Interleague contests (also Milwaukee's Keon Broxton-2017, Texas' Nomar Mazara-2017, Toronto's Matt Stairs-2007 and Philadelphia's Doug Glanville-1999, all 6G streaks).
- Is one of only two players in Yankees history to have multiple games in the same season in which he went 4-for-4 or better with 2HR (4/4 at Baltimore, 8/22 at Oakland), joining Lou Gehrig in 1934.
- Through 50 team games (Game 1 on 5/25), hit 12HR…with Gary Sánchez (15HR) and Luke Voit (13HR), became the second trio in Yankees history to reach 12HR apiece by the club's 50th game of the season, joining Mickey Mantle (21HR), Yogi Berra (16HR) and Hank Bauer (13HR) in 1956 (credit: *STATS, LLC.*).
- Made his first career Opening Day roster…at 22 years, 105 days old, was the eighth-youngest player to make an Opening Day roster in 2019, older than only Atlanta's Ronald Acuña Jr., Ozzie Albies and Bryse Wilson, Toronto's Elvis Luciano, Washington's Victor Robles and Juan Soto and San Diego's Fernando Tatis Jr.
- Became the first Yankee to hit safely in the team's first three games of the season at age 22-or-younger since Bobby Murcer in 1969 (first 9G at age 22).
- Collected his third career multi-HR game on 4/4 at Baltimore (also 5/21/18 at Texas and 8/1/18 vs. Baltimore), going 4-for-4 with 2R, 1 double and 4RBI, setting a career high in hits…joined Didi Gregorius (4/3/18 vs. Tampa Bay) as just the second Yankee to collect at least 4H, 2HR and 4RBI in a game since 2013…became the seventh player in franchise history to collect at least three multi-HR games through his first 130 career games, joining teammates Gary Sánchez (5) and Aaron Judge (3), Aaron Robinson (4), Joe DiMaggio (3), Joe Gordon (3) and Joe Pepitone (3)…joined DiMaggio and Pepitone as the only three Yankees to do so before turning 23 years old…at 22 years, 112 days old, became the youngest Yankee with 4H, including at least 3XBH, in a single game since DiMaggio on 6/28/36 (Game 1) at St. Louis-AL (21y, 216d).
- Had a career-high 12-game hitting streak from 4/23-5/7, hitting .347 (17-for-49) with 6R, 4 doubles, 1HR, 7RBI, 2BB and 2SB…was the first Yankee, age-22 or younger, to compile at least a 10-game hitting streak since 22-year-old Melky Cabrera had both a 15-game and a 13-game streak in 2007.
- Played in his 100th career win on 5/9 vs. Seattle (his 159th career game), becoming the quickest Yankees position player to appear in 100 wins since Brett Gardner reached 100 team wins in his 155th game on 4/11/10.
- Hit 9HR—including three multi-HR games—in 15 games from 5/15 (Game 1) through 5/29…had 1HR over his previous 22 games from 4/17-5/11.
- Hit 3HR in 5/15 doubleheader vs. Baltimore, the first Yankee with 3HR in a doubleheader since Brett Gardner on 9/12/15 vs. Toronto…at 22 years, 153 days old, joined Joe DiMaggio as the only Yankees under 23 years old to hit 3HR in one day (DiMaggio had 3HR in a DH on 9/13/36 and a 3HR game on 6/13/37, both at St. Louis-AL's Sportsman's Park)…was the seventh-youngest Yankee to homer in both games of a doubleheader and youngest since Johnny Ellis on 5/24/70 (21y, 276d)…hit 2HR in Game 1, his fourth career multi-HR game…at 22y, 153d, became the youngest Yankee to reach four multi-HR games (prev.: Joe DiMaggio, 22y, 166d on 5/10/37 at Chicago-AL).
- Went 2-for-4 with two solo HRs on 5/20 at Baltimore…marked his fifth career 2HR game, third of the season and second in six games…at 22 years, 158 days, was the youngest Yankee to reach five career multi-HR games, surpassing Joe DiMaggio by 40 days (22 years, 198 days on 6/11/37 at St. Louis-AL)…was the 12th-youngest player in Major League history to reach five multi-HR games (has since been surpassed).
- Collected his sixth career multi-HR game (fifth vs. Baltimore) on 5/22…at 22y, 160d, became the youngest Yankee to reach six multi-HR games (prev.: Joe DiMaggio, 22y, 200 on 6/13/37-G2 vs. St. Louis-AL).
- Led the Majors with a .462 OBP in June, batting .333/.462/.569 (24-for-72) with 21R, 2 doubles, 5HR, 17RBI and 19BB in 22G…had a 20.4% walk rate (19BB/93PA) after posting a 5.8% walk rate (13BB/226PA) from March-May.
- Hit his first career grand slam on 6/19 vs. Tampa Bay.
- Had multiple RBI in three straight games from 6/19-21…hit a homer in each game, homering in at least three straight games for the second time in his career (homered in four straight from 5/21-25/18)…with Gary Sánchez also homering in each of those games, became the first pair of teammates in Yankees history to homer in three consecutive games together (confirmed by *Elias*).
- Hit a "walk-off" single in the ninth inning on 6/26 vs. Toronto, his third career "walk-off" hit.
- Collected his 200th career hit on 6/30 in London…at 22 years, 199 days, was the youngest player to collect 200H with the Yankees since Mickey Mantle reached the mark as a 20-year-old in 1952.
- Was named to his second career AL All-Star team (also 2018) and went 1-for-2…according to *Elias*, was the third Yankee to make two All-Star teams before turning 23, joining Joe DiMaggio and Mickey Mantle…was the third Yankee to record multiple seasons with at least 20HR prior to turning 23, joining Mickey Mantle (3x, 1952-54) and Joe DiMaggio (2x, 1936-37).
- Hit his 20th homer on 7/24 at Minnesota…with 24HR in his 2018 rookie season, became the third Yankee all-time with multiple 20HR seasons *before turning 23 years old* (also Mickey Mantle, three seasons from 1952-54 and Joe DiMaggio, two seasons from 1936-37)…became the fourth middle infielder in Baseball history with multiple 20HR seasons by his age 22 season, joining Cal Ripken Jr. (two, 1982-83), Alex Rodriguez (three, 1996-98) and Carlos Correa (three, 2015-17)…was joined by Ozzie Albies later in 2019…was his first homer since 6/25 vs. Toronto, snapping a career-long 19-game homerless stretch (6/26-7/23) during which he hit .333 (24-for-72).

- Hit 13HR in 26 games in August, second-most in the Majors behind only Cincinnati's Aristides Aquino (14HR)…were the most by a Yankee in a calendar month since Aaron Judge hit 15HR in Sept. 2017 and most by a Yankees middle infielder in a month since 2B Joe Gordon hit 13HR in July 1940…had four multi-HR games, the most in a month by a Yankee since Judge (four), also in Sept. 2017.
- Hit his second career grand slam on 8/2 and drove in all four Yankees runs in the team's 4-2 win vs. Boston.
- Collected his fifth 2HR game of the season—and seventh of his career—in Game 2 on 8/3 vs. Boston…at 22 years, 233 days old, was the second-youngest player in AL history (and seventh-youngest in Major League history) to reach seven career multi-HR games, one week older than the Yankees' Joe DiMaggio (22 years, 226 days on 7/9/37 vs. Washington-AL)…is the second player in Yankees history (and eighth in Major League history) to record five multi-HR games in a season prior to turning 23 years old, joining Joe DiMaggio (5x in 1937 at age 22).
- Hit 15HR over his final 38 games of the season (from Game 1 on 8/12).
- Reached base safely in a career-best 22 straight games from 8/12 (Game 1) through 9/4, batting .306/.355/.718 (26-for-85) with 18R, 2 doubles, 11HR, 17RBI and 6BB over the span…since 1955, was the second-longest streak by a Yankee at age-22 or younger, behind Derek Jeter's 23-game streak from 8/31-9/25/96.
- Went 4-for-8 with 4R, 3HR and 7RBI in 8/12 doubleheader vs. Baltimore, homering once in Game 1 and hitting two three-run HRs in Game 2…at 22 years, 242 days old, became the youngest player in AL history (and fourth-youngest in Major League history) to reach eight career multi-HR games…was his sixth multi-HR game of the season…was his second career doubleheader with 3HR (also 5/15/19 vs. Baltimore) and just the eighth such instance by a Yankee in the last 50 seasons…became the only player in the last 50 seasons to hit 3HR in a doubleheader twice as a Yankee (credit: *Elias*)…according to STATS, Inc., is the first player to homer in both games of a doubleheader vs. the same opponent twice in one year since Philadelphia's Mike Schmidt in 1983 vs. Montreal.
- His second HR in Game 2 on 8/12 vs. Baltimore was his 50th career home run…at age 22 years, 242 days, was the third-youngest Yankee to reach the plateau, older than only Mickey Mantle (21 years, 279 days on 7/26/53, Game 1) and Joe DiMaggio (22 years, 226 days on 7/9/37).
- Went 3-for-4 with 3R, 2HR and 6RBI in Game 2 on 8/12 vs. Baltimore, the third-youngest (22y, 242d) Yankee to record at least 2HR and 6RBI in a game (since RBI became an official stat in 1920), behind Joe DiMaggio (22y, 226d on 7/9/37 vs. Washington-AL) and Lou Gehrig (22y, 34d on 7/23/25 vs. Washington-AL).
- Hit two solo HRs on 8/17 vs. Cleveland at 22 years, 247 days old, becoming the youngest player in Major League history to record seven multi-HR games in the same season.
- Hit two solo HRs on 8/22 at Oakland (4-for-4, 3R, 1 double, 2HR, 2RBI), his eighth multi-home run game of the season…at 22 years, 252 days, became the second-youngest player in Baseball history to reach 10 career multi-HR games behind only the New York Giants' Mel Ott (22 years, 163 days)…was his second career game going 4-for-4 or better with at least 2HR (also 4/4/19 at Baltimore)…no other player in Major League history had two such games before turning 24 years old.
- Hit his 60th career home run on 9/10 at Detroit…at 22 years, 271 days, was the third-youngest Yankee to reach 60HR (Mickey Mantle - 22 years, 199 days; Joe DiMaggio - 22 years, 249 days)…his 256 games were the fourth-fewest by a Yankee to reach 60 career homers (Aaron Judge-197G; Sánchez-201G; DiMaggio-223G).
- Started at 2B in each of the Yankees' nine postseason games, hitting .324/.375/.703 (12-for-37) with 8R, 5 doubles, 3HR and 10RBI…became the first Yankee to hit 3HR in a single postseason at age-22 or younger and the third-youngest Yankee to hit multiple postseason HRs: Mickey Mantle hit 4HR prior to turning 22 years old (2HR in 1952 World Series at age-20, 2HR in 1953 World Series at age-21); Tony Kubek hit 2HR in 1957 World Series Game 3 at Milwaukee at 21 years, 358 days…led all playoff participants in slugging and OPS (1.078), tied for third with 8XBH, ranked fourth in OBP and tied for sixth in RBI…had a 10-game postseason hitting streak from 2018 ALDS Game 1 at Boston through 2019 ALCS Game 3 vs. Houston, batting .378/.452/.730 (14-for-37) with 8R, 4 doubles, 3HR, 10RBI, 5BB and 2SB during the span…was the second player under age-23 to compile a 10-game postseason hitting streak, joining Texas' Elvis Andrus (12G in 2010)…was the longest by any Yankee since Derek Jeter (11G in 2009-10)…became the first AL player (and seventh Major Leaguer) to collect 7XBH (4 doubles, 3HR) through his team's first six postseason games in a season…his 8XBH are tied for the fourth-highest total in a single postseason in Yankees history…are tied for the most in a postseason by any player age-22 or younger (Los Angeles-NL's Cody Bellinger, 8XBH in 2017; Washington's Juan Soto, 8XBH in 2019)…had at least 1RBI in four straight games from ALDS Game 1 through ALCS Game 1, tied for the second-longest streak to begin a postseason in club history (Alex Rodriguez-7G in 2009).
- In ALDS Game 1 vs. Minnesota, hit a go-ahead two-run double in the fifth…in ALDS Game 3 at Minnesota, hit his first career postseason HR and collected his first postseason multi-hit game (3-for-4, 3R, 2 doubles, 1HR, 1RBI, 1SB)…at 22 years, 298 days old, became the second player under the age of 23 in Major League history to record three extra-base hits in a postseason game, joining Houston's Carlos Correa (1 double, 2HR) in 2015 ALDS Game 4 vs. Kansas City at 21 years, 20 days old…was the seventh Yankee of any age to do so, joining Babe Ruth (twice), Robinson Canó, Derek Jeter, Reggie Jackson, Hideki Matsui and Alex Rodriguez.
- In ALCS Game 1 win at Houston (3-for-5, 1R, 1 double, 1HR, 5RBI), had 3H for the second consecutive game and set a Yankees single-game RBI record for a player 22 years old or younger…at 22 years, 303 days old, became the third-ever player under the age of 23 to record 5RBI in a postseason game (Atlanta's Andruw Jones (5RBI) in 1996 World Series Game 1 at the Yankees at 19 years, 180 days old, and Chicago-NL's Addison Russell (6RBI) in 2016 World Series Game 6 at Cleveland at 22 years, 283 days old)…tied the Yankees' ALCS RBI record, joining Hideki Matsui, who did it twice (2004 ALCS Game 1 vs. Boston and 2004 ALCS Game 3 at Boston)…along with his ALDS Game 3 at Minnesota (3-for-4, 3R, 2 doubles, 1HR, 1RBI, 1SB), became the second player in Major League history with at least 3H, including a double and a HR, in consecutive postseason games, joining Brooklyn's Roy Campanella in 1955 World Series Games 3-4 vs. the Yankees…was the 12th Yankee with 3H in consecutive postseason games and ninth to do so within the same postseason…in ALCS Game 3 vs. Houston, supplied the Yankees' only run with an eighth-inning solo HR…batted cleanup in ALCS Game 4 vs. Houston, becoming the first Yankee under age 23 to bat fourth in the starting lineup in a playoff game.

2018

- Hit .271 (117-for-431) with 54R, 16 doubles, 24HR, 77RBI and 42BB in 123 games (104GS at 2B, 15 at SS)…ranked second among Major League rookies in RBI and fourth in HR…hit .538 (7-for-13) with 15RBI with the bases loaded.
- Ranked third in AL "Rookie of the Year" voting, collecting three second-place votes and 16 third-place votes…was a finalist for the *Sporting News* AL "Rookie of the Year."
- Of his 24HR, 13 came with runners on base…ranked third in the Majors with seven three-run HR…of his 24HR, 12 tied the game (2) or gave the Yankees the lead (10)…hit 13HR from the ninth spot in the lineup, the most by a Yankee in a single season from the No. 9 spot in franchise history.
- Is one of nine rookies in Yankees history to hit 20HR in a season and one of four to do so since 2016 (also Gary Sánchez-20HR in 2016, Aaron Judge-52HR in 2017 and Miguel Andújar-27HR in 2018).
- With teammate Miguel Andújar hitting 27HR, became the first pair of Yankees rookies to hit 20HR in the same season…according to *Elias*, were the eighth set of rookie teammates to both hit 20HR, and the first since Cincinnati's Joey Votto and Jay Bruce in 2008…the Yankees became the sixth team in Major League history with multiple rookies with at least 20HR and 60RBI, joining the 2006 Marlins (Mike Jacobs, Dan Uggla, Josh Willingham), 1982 Twins (Gary Gaetti, Kent Hrbek), 1977 Athletics (Wayne Gross, Mitchell Page), 1975 Red Sox (Fred Lynn, Jim Rice) and 1960 Orioles (Jim Gentile, Ron Hansen).
- His 24HR marked the second-highest single-season total by a Yankee in his age-21 season or younger, behind 21-year-old Joe DiMaggio (29HR in 1936)…owns the third-most career HRs by a Yankee prior to turning 22, trailing only Mickey Mantle (57) and DiMaggio (29).
- Had 15HR during the first half, one of five Yankees rookies to hit at least 10HR before the All-Star break, joining Aaron Judge (30HR in 2017), Miguel Andújar (12HR in 2018), Joe DiMaggio (11HR in 1936) and Nick Johnson (11HR in 2002)—credit: *Elias*…joined Andújar as the first Yankees rookies with at least 10HR before the All-Star break in the same season (first team to do so since the 2016 Dodgers: Corey Seager-17, Trayce Thompson-13).
- His 15HR before the All-Star Game were tied with Robinson Canó (15HR in 2011) for fourth-most by a Yankees second baseman entering the break, trailing only Canó (21HR in 2013, 20HR in 2012 and 16HR in 2010).
- Was twice named AL "Player of the Week:" 5/21-27 and 8/27-9/2.
- Started at 2B in first 20 games after his recall, with the Yankees going 17-3…became the first position player in the Modern Era (since 1900) to start and be on the winning side in 16 of his first 17 Major League games.
- Is the second-youngest Yankee to record at least 17H in his first 15 career games (4/22-5/6), just two weeks older than Ben Chapman, who collected 17H from 4/19-5/4/30…is one of three 21-year-olds in Yankees history to record hits in 12 of his first 15 career games (Joe DiMaggio, Frankie Crosetti)…is the youngest Yankee to collect at least 11RBI through his first 15 games.
- Made his Major League debut on 4/22 at 21y, 130d old and was the ninth-youngest player to appear in a game in 2018 (Atlanta's Ozzie Albies, a "younger" 21 years old, Kolby Allard-20 years, Ronald Acuña-20 years, Mike Soroka-20 years, and Bryson Wilson-20 years, San Diego's Luis Urías-a "younger" 21 and Washington's Víctor Robles-a "younger" 21 and Juan Soto-19 years)…was the youngest position player to appear in a game for the Yankees since Melky Cabrera (age 20) in 2005.
- Made his Major League debut in 4/22 win vs. Toronto, going 0-for-4…was recalled from Triple-A Scranton/WB prior to the game…collected his first Major League hit in 4/23 win vs. Minnesota (single off Tyler Kinley)…at 21 years, 131 days old, was the youngest Yankee to record a hit since Melky Cabrera (20y, 338d) on 7/15/05 at Boston.
- Doubled in 4/25 win vs. Minnesota…at 21 years, 133 days old, became the youngest Yankee to record an extra-base hit since Derek Jeter doubled on 9/26/95 at Milwaukee at 21 years, 92 days old.
- Stole his first career base in 4/30 loss at Houston…at 21 years, 138 days, was the youngest Yankee to steal a base since Bobby Murcer on 9/23/66 vs. Boston (20 years, 126 days)…the loss marked his first time being on the losing side of a Major League game, snapping a career-opening eight-game winning streak…became the fourth position player in the Modern Era (since 1900) to start and be on the winning side in each of his first eight Major League games, joining Atlanta C Evan Gattis (won and started his first 10G in 2013), Washington-AL OF Babe Ganzel (first 9G in 1927) and Philadelphia SS Dave Bancroft (first 8G in 1915)…two pitchers also started team wins in their first 8G: St. Louis' Allen Watson (1993) and Chicago-AL's John Whitehead (1935).
- Was named AL "Rookie of the Month" for May…in 24G, hit .325/.380/.663 (27-for-83) with 13R, 9HR and 24RBI, leading all Major League rookies in batting average, HR and RBI during the month (min. 75AB)…was the fifth Yankee (eighth time) to win AL "Rookie of the Month" and the third current Yankee to do so, joining Gary Sánchez (Aug. 2016) and Aaron Judge (four times in 2017)…teammate Miguel Andújar won in June and August 2018.
- Hit safely in nine straight games (5/2-11), the youngest Yankee to tally as long a hitting streak since Mickey Mantle had a 10G hitting streak from 6/24-7/3/52 (G1), ending at 20y, 257d.
- Had 3RBI, including a game-tying two-run ninth-inning single in 5/3 win at Houston…became the youngest Yankee (age 21y, 141d) with a game-tying or go-ahead hit in the ninth inning-or-later since Bobby Murcer (20y-134d) on 10/1/66 at Chicago-AL (RBI single in the ninth in a 5-3 win)…had 3RBI on 5/4, becoming the youngest Yankee (21y, 141d - 21y, 142d) ever with at least 3RBI in consecutive games (prev. Jerry Priddy, 21 years, 179 days, 5/6-7/41).
- Hit three-run HR—the first of his Major League career—in 5/4 win vs. Cleveland…at age 21y, 142d, became the youngest Yankee to homer since John Ellis hit an inside-the-park HR on 5/17/69 vs. California (20y, 269d)…was the youngest Yankee to homer over the fence since Bobby Murcer (19y, 117d) on 9/14/65 at Washington-AL…became the youngest player born outside the U.S. to homer for the Yankees (prev. Jesús Montero, 21y, 281d on 9/5/11 vs. Baltimore)…was the youngest Yankees 2B ever to hit a HR (prev. Jerry Priddy, 21 years, 178 days on 5/6/41 vs. Detroit)…was the second Yankee since 1999 to hit a HR with at least two runners on for his first career homer (also Colin Curtis, three-run HR, on 7/21/10 vs. Los Angeles-AL; and Hideki Matsui, grand slam, on 4/8/03 vs. Minnesota).

- Hit a three-run "walk-off" home run in the ninth inning to win 5/6 game vs. Cleveland, becoming the youngest player in franchise history (21 years, 144 days) to hit a "walk-off" HR (prev. Mickey Mantle, 21y, 185d on 4/23/53 vs. Boston)…according to *Elias*, is the third-youngest Yankee ever with a "walk-off" RBI, older than only Mark Koenig (age 21y, 76d on 10/3/1925 vs. Philadelphia) and Ben Chapman (age 21y, 121d on 4/25/1930 vs. Boston)…was the sixth Yankee with a "walk-off" HR within his first two career HRs, joining Clint Frazier (2017), Alfonso Soriano (1999), Mike Hegan (1967), Bob Grim (1957) and Frank LaPorte (1906).
- Became the youngest player in AL history ever to homered in four straight games (5/21-25)…at 21 years and 163 days old, was the fourth-youngest player in the Modern Era (since 1900) to homer in four consecutive games (Miguel Cabrera in 2004 at 20y, 362d; Andruw Jones in 1998 at 21y, 138d; Albert Pujols in 2001 at 21y 147d)—credit: *Elias*…Ronald Acuña joined the group later in 2018 (5 straight at age 20y, 239d)…was the second Yankees rookie to accomplish the feat (also Gary Sánchez, 4G from 9/17-21/16)…his four-game HR streak was tied for the longest by a second baseman in franchise history (also Joe Gordon from 7/24-27/40 and Tony Lazzeri from 5/21-24/36).
- Collected his first career multi-HR game in 5/21 win at Texas, hitting a two-run HR and solo HR…at 21y, 159d old, became the second-youngest player in Yankees history with a multi-HR game (Mickey Mantle hit 2HR on 8/11/52 vs. Boston at 20y, 296d)…both HR came off RHP Bartolo Colon (44.362), who is 23y, 203d older than Torres…according to STATS, marked the third-largest age difference between an older pitcher and younger batter on a HR in Yankees history, behind a Mickey Mantle HR off Satchel Paige (25y, 105d difference) in 1951 and Bobby Murcer HR off Hoyt Wilhelm (23y, 298d difference) in 1969.
- Collected his second career "walk-off" hit with a 10th-inning RBI single on 5/29 vs. Houston at age 21y, 167d (also a three-run "walk-off" HR on 5/6 vs. Cleveland, age 21y, 144d)…is the youngest player in franchise history with two "walk-off" RBI in the same season…was his first career extra-inning hit.
- Homered at age 21 years, 182 days on 6/13 vs. Washington, in the same game as Nationals OF Juan Soto (19y, 231d)…according to STATS, their combined age of 41y, 48d was the youngest by opposing players to homer in the same game since Indianapolis' Egyptian Healy and the New York Giants' Mike Tiernan on 5/19/1887.
- Reached 50 career games on 6/19 vs. Seattle…through his 50th game, had 14HR and 35RBI…at the time, his 14HR were tied for seventh-most in AL history through a player's first 50 career games…were tied with Aaron Judge for third-most by a Yankee through 50G (Gary Sánchez-19 and Kevin Maas-15)…his 35RBI were eighth-most by a Yankee through his first 50 career games.
- Hit cleanup for the first time in his career on 6/30…at 21 years, 199 days, became the third-youngest cleanup hitter in Yankees history, behind Mickey Mantle (27G from 1951-53, first on 9/29/51-G1 vs. Boston at 19y, 344d) and Lou Gehrig (4G in 1923, first on 9/27/23 at Boston at 20y, 100d)…was the youngest since Mantle hit cleanup on 5/5/53 at Cleveland at 21 years, 197 days.
- Was the first Yankee—and sixth Major Leaguer—ever to hit at least 15HR in his first 60 career games at age 21-or-younger, joining Cody Bellinger (24), Adam Dunn (17), Willie Mays (17), Albert Pujols (17) and Frank Robinson (16)…became the second rookie in Yankees history to hit 15HR before the All-Star break (Judge-30HR in 2017)…his 42RBI were eighth-most by a Yankee through his first 60 career games.
- Was placed on the 10-day disabled list from 7/4 (effective 7/5) - 7/25 with a right hip strain…was removed from 7/4 win vs. Atlanta in the fifth with the injury…played three rehab games with Single-A Tampa.
- Was named via the Player Ballot to his first career All-Star team (did not play due to injury)…became the fourth Yankee to be named to the AL All-Star team at age 21-or-younger, joining Joe DiMaggio (age 21 in 1936), Mickey Mantle (ages 20-21 from 1952-53) and Willie Randolph (age 21 in 1976)…was the 12th Yankees rookie selected to an AL All-Star team, joining starters Aaron Judge (2017), Hideki Matsui (2003) and Joe DiMaggio (1936) and reserves Dellin Betances (2014), Masahiro Tanaka (2014), Willie Randolph (1976), Tom Tresh (1962), Ryne Duren (1958), Bobby Richardson (1957), Spec Shea (1947) and Joe Page (1944)…was the fourth Yankee to make the All-Star team as a rookie since 2014 (Betances, Judge and Tanaka) after the team had just one rookie All-Star from 1977-2013 (Matsui in 2003).
- Hit solo HR and three-run HR in 8/1 loss vs. Baltimore…was his second career 2HR game (also 5/21 at Texas)…became the second player in Yankees history to record at least two multi-HR games before turning 22 years old, joining Joe DiMaggio, who had three in 1936…at 21 years, 231 days old, was the youngest Yankee ever to record a second career multi-HR game, 10 days younger than DiMaggio was on 7/23/36 at St. Louis-AL (21 years, 241 days).
- Collected his 50th career RBI with a sacrifice fly on 8/5 at Boston…reached the mark in his 74th game, the seventh-fastest Yankee to 50RBI, behind Joe DiMaggio (46th game), Joe Gordon (53rd), Tony Lazzeri (57th), Bob Meusel (65th), Gary Sánchez (69th) and Mickey Mantle (73rd).
- Reached 20HR in his 93rd game on 8/27 vs. Chicago-AL, at the age of 21y, 257d…at the time, only eight other players as young as Torres in Major League history reached the milestone in as few games (Ronald Acuña Jr., Tony Conigliaro, Carlos Correa, Bob Horner, Albert Pujols, Frank Robinson, Giancarlo Stanton, Darryl Strawberry)…became the third Yankee ever to hit 20HR prior to turning 22 years old (Mickey Mantle-57, Joe DiMaggio-29).
- Had a career-long streak of four straight games with multiple RBI from 8/30-9/2 (2RBI in each game)…collected the game-winning RBI in consecutive games (two-run HR in the fifth on 9/1, two-run single in the eighth on 8/31).
- Hit two-run HR and was 1-for-4 in 9/7 win at Seattle…the homer was his 100th career hit and at 21 years, 268 days of age, became the fourth-youngest Yankees player to reach the milestone behind Mickey Mantle (20 years, 193 days), Ben Chapman (21 years, 207 days) and Joe DiMaggio (21 years, 230 days).
- Hit a two-run home run off Eduardo Rodriguez in the fourth inning of 9/29 win at Boston…was the 265th by a Yankee in 2018, surpassing the 1997 Mariners (264) for most by any team in Major League history (has since been surpassed)…was also the 20th HR by a Yankee from the ninth spot in the batting order, making the Yankees the first team in Baseball history with at least 20HR from all nine spots in the lineup (credit: *Elias*).
- Made his postseason debut, batting .250 (4-for-16) with 1R in five playoff games.

- At age 21y, 294d, on the day of the AL Wild Card Game, became just the third Yankee since 1958 to appear in a postseason game at age 21-or-younger (also Jesús Montero at age 21y, 310d in ALDS Game 4 on 10/4/11 and Phil Hughes at age 21y, 102d in ALDS Game 1 on 10/4/07)…was the youngest position player to appear in a postseason game for the Yankees since INF Tom Carroll (age 19y, 15d) in World Series Game 5 on 10/2/55.
- Collected his first playoff hit in ALDS Game 1 at Boston, becoming the second-youngest player in Yankees history (21 years, 296 days) to record a postseason hit, behind Mickey Mantle (first postseason hit at 19 years old in 1951 World Series Game 2 vs. the New York Giants)…hit safely in all four games of the ALDS, the second-longest hitting streak by a Yankee, age-21 or younger, behind Mickey Mantle (6G: 4G in 1952 at age-20, 2G in 1953 at age 21).
- Batted .347 (17-for-49) with 6R, 3 doubles, 1 triple, 1HR and 11RBI in 14 games with the RailRiders, appearing at 2B, SS and 3B…was named International League "Player of the Week" for 4/5-15 after hitting .385/.405/.564 (15-for-39) with 5R, 2 doubles, 1 triple, 1HR, 10RBI, 2BB and 1SB in 10 games.

2017

- Played in 55 games between Double-A Trenton and Triple-A Scranton/Wilkes-Barre before missing the remainder of the season with a torn ulnar collateral ligament in his left elbow…combined to hit .287/.383/.480 (58-for-202) with 31R, 14 doubles, 2 triples, 7HR, 34RBI, 30BB and 7SB…recorded a .973 fielding percentage (5E/187TC) while playing in 28G at SS, 15G at 3B and 10G at 2B.
- Began the year with Trenton and hit .273/.367/.496 (33-for-121) with 22R, 10 doubles, 1 triple, 5HR, 18RBI, 17BB and 5SB in 32 games…reached safely in 27-of-32 games with the Thunder…at 20 years and 4 months, was the youngest player to make a 2017 Opening Day roster in the Eastern League.
- Was placed on the minor league D.L. from 4/19 (retroactive to 4/18) to 4/28 with mild right rotator cuff tendinitis.
- Was promoted to Scranton/WB on 5/22 and hit .309/.406/.457 (25-for-81) with 9R, 4 doubles, 1 triple, 2HR, 16RBI and 13BB in 23 games…reached safely in 21-of-23 games with the RailRiders.
- Suffered a torn UCL in his left (non-throwing) elbow on a slide at home plate in a 6-2 win in Game 1 of a doubleheader on 6/17 at Buffalo…underwent "Tommy John" surgery on 6/21.
- Attended his first Major League spring training as a non-roster invitee, hitting .448/.469/.931 (13-for-29) with 8R, 6 doubles, 1 triple, 2HR and 9RBI in 19 games…was named the recipient of the 2017 James P. Dawson Award, given annually to the outstanding Yankees rookie in spring training.
- Following the season, was tabbed by *Baseball America* as the Yankees' top prospect for the second consecutive season and the No. 6 overall prospect in baseball…*Baseball America* also labeled him as the Yankees' "Best Defensive Infielder" and as having the "Best Infield Arm."

2016

- Split the season with Single-A Myrtle Beach and Single-A Tampa, batting .270 (129-for-478) with 81R, 29 doubles, 5 triples, 11HR, 66RBI and 21SB in 125 games.
- Began the season with Myrtle Beach and hit .275 (98-for-356) with 62R, 23 doubles, 3 triples, 9HR and 47RBI in 94G.
- Was traded to the Yankees from the Cubs on 7/25 and played in 31 games for Tampa, batting .254 (31-for-122) with 19R, 6 doubles, 2 triples, 2HR and 19RBI.
- After the season, played in 18 games for the Scottsdale Scorpions of the Arizona Fall League and was the recipient of the AFL's 2016 Joe Black MVP Award…was the youngest MVP in AFL history (at the time) as he batted .403/.513/.645 (25-for-62) with 15R, 4 doubles, 1 triple, 3HR, 11RBI and 14BB…was also named the AFL "Player of the Week" twice and was named to the AFL Top Prospects Team and AFL Fall Stars Game.
- Following the season, was named by *Baseball America* as the No. 1 prospect in the Yankees organization, Baseball's No. 5 prospect overall, the FSL's No. 2 prospect and the Carolina League's "Best Defensive Shortstop" and "Best Infield Arm"…was ranked the No. 3 overall prospect by MLB Pipeline and No. 4 overall prospect by ESPN.

2015

- Combined with Single-A South Bend and Single-A Myrtle Beach to bat .287 (140-for-487) with 54R, 24 doubles, 5 triples, 3HR, 64RBI and 22SB in 126G…was fifth among all Cubs farmhands in batting average and stolen bases.
- Was named to the Midwest League Mid-Season and Postseason All-Star teams and was tabbed the Midwest League Prospect of the Year.
- Following the season, was named the top prospect in the Cubs organization by *Baseball America*, as well as the No. 41 overall prospect in baseball.

2014

- In his professional debut, combined to bat .297 (54-for-182) with 37R, 8 doubles, 6 triples, 2HR, 33RBI, 29BB and 10SB in 50 games with the AZL Cubs and short-season Single-A Boise…his .297 BA was the third-highest among all Cubs minor leaguers.
- Following the season, was tabbed by *Baseball America* as the No. 8 prospect in the Cubs organization.

2013

- Was signed by the Cubs as a non-drafted free agent on 7/2/13…was ranked by *Baseball America* as the No. 2 prospect in the 2013 international free agent class.

PERSONAL
- Full name is Gleyber David Torres Castro ("GLAY-burr").
- Was named a recipient of the Thurman Munson Award, presented in February 2020.
- Was honored in November 2018 with the Community Service Award by Hamilton-Madison House, a non-profit organization dedicated to providing non-English speaking residents with the lessons English language, computer and career skills…spoke to event attendees about learning English after coming to the United States from Venezuela.

Torres' Career Batting Record

Year	Club	AVG	G	AB	R	H	2B	3B	HR	RBI	SH	SF	HP	BB	SO	SB	CS	E	OBP	SLG
2014	AZL Cubs	.279	43	154	33	43	6	3	1	29	0	4	0	25	33	8	7	14	.372	.377
	Boise	.393	7	28	4	11	2	3	1	4	0	0	0	4	7	2	0	5	.469	.786
2015	South Bend	.293	119	464	53	136	24	5	3	62	1	4	2	43	108	22	13	26	.353	.386
	Myrtle Beach	.174	7	23	1	4	0	0	0	2	0	0	0	1	7	0	1	1	.208	.174
2016	Myrtle Beach	.275	94	356	62	98	23	3	9	47	5	1	5	42	87	19	10	19	.359	.433
	Tampa - a	.254	31	122	19	31	6	2	2	19	0	0	0	16	23	2	3	4	.341	.385
2017	Trenton	.273	32	121	22	33	10	1	5	18	0	0	1	17	21	5	4	0	.367	.496
	Scranton/WB	.309	23	81	9	25	4	1	2	16	0	1	1	13	26	2	2	5	.406	.457
2018	Scranton/WB	.347	14	49	6	17	3	1	1	11	0	2	0	5	10	1	1	2	.393	.510
	YANKEES - b	.271	123	431	54	117	16	1	24	77	1	5	5	42	122	6	2	17	.340	.480
	Tampa	.333	3	9	3	3	1	0	0	0	0	0	0	2	3	0	0	2	.455	.444
2019	YANKEES	.278	144	546	96	152	26	0	38	90	1	6	3	48	129	5	2	20	.337	.535
Minor League Totals		.285	373	1407	212	401	79	19	24	208	6	12	9	168	325	61	41	78	.362	.419
Major League Totals		.275	267	977	150	269	42	1	62	167	2	11	8	90	251	11	4	37	.338	.511

Signed by the Chicago Cubs as a non-drafted free agent on July 2, 2013.
a - Acquired by the Yankees from the Chicago Cubs along with RHP Adam Warren, OF Billy McKinney and OF Rashad Crawford in exchange for LHP Aroldis Chapman on July 25, 2016.
b - Placed on the 10-day disabled list from July 4 (effective July 5) - July 25, 2018 with a right hip strain.

Torres' Postseason Record

Year	Club vs. Opp.	AVG	G	AB	R	H	2B	3B	HR	RBI	SH	SF	HP	BB	SO	SB	CS	E	OBP	SLG
2018	NYY vs. OAK (WC)	.000	1	3	0	0	0	0	0	0	0	0	0	1	0	0	0	0	.000	.000
	NYY vs. BOS (DS)	.308	4	13	1	4	0	0	0	0	0	0	0	2	2	0	0	0	.400	.308
2019	NYY vs. MIN (DS)	.417	3	12	5	5	3	0	1	4	0	0	0	1	2	2	0	0	.462	.917
	NYY vs. HOU (CS)	.280	6	25	3	7	2	0	2	6	0	0	0	2	4	0	0	2	.333	.600
Wild Card Totals		.000	1	3	0	0	0	0	0	0	0	0	0	1	0	0	0	0	.000	.000
Division Series Totals		.360	7	25	6	9	3	0	1	4	0	0	0	3	4	2	0	0	.429	.600
LCS Totals		.280	6	25	3	7	2	0	2	6	0	0	0	2	4	0	0	2	.333	.600
POSTSEASON TOTALS		.302	14	53	9	16	5	0	3	10	0	0	0	6	8	2	0	2	.362	.566

Torres' All-Star Game Record

Year	Club, Site	AVG	G	AB	R	H	2B	3B	HR	RBI	SH	SF	HP	BB	SO	SB	CS	E	OBP	SLG
2018	NYY, Washington					Selected - Did Not Play (Injured)														
2019	NYY, Cleveland	.500	1	2	0	1	0	0	0	0	0	0	0	1	0	0	0	0	.500	.500
All-Star Game Totals		.500	1	2	0	1	0	0	0	0	0	0	0	1	0	0	0	0	.500	.500

Torres' Career Fielding Record

Position	PCT	G	PO	A	E	TC	DP
Second Base	.969	174	276	377	21	674	88
Shortstop	.954	98	113	222	16	351	48

Torres' Career Home Run Chart
MULTI-HOMER GAMES: 10. **TWO-HOMER GAMES:** 10, last on 8/22/19 at OAK. **THREE-HOMER GAMES:** None. **GRAND SLAMS:** 2, last on 8/2/19 vs. BOS (Eduardo Rodriguez). **PINCH-HIT HR:** None. **INSIDE-THE-PARK HR:** None. **"WALK-OFF" HR:** 1, 5/6/18 vs. CLE (Dan Otero). **LEADOFF HR:** None.

Torres' Career Bests and Streaks
HITS: 4 - 2 times (last on 8/22/19 at OAK). **RUNS:** 3 - 5 times (last on 8/22/19 at OAK). **2B:** 1 - 42 times (last on 9/27/19 at TEX). **3B:** 1, 6/29/18 vs. BOS. **HR:** 2 - 10 times (last on 8/22/19 at OAK). **RBI:** 6, 8/12/19 vs. BAL-G2. **BB:** 3 - 2 times (last on 6/24/19 vs. TOR). **SO:** 3 - 9 times (last in Game 2 on 9/12/19 at DET). **SB:** 1 - 11 times (last on 9/8/19 vs BOS). **HIT STREAK:** 12g, 4/23-5/7/19. **"WALK-OFF" HITS:** 3, last on 6/26/19 vs. TOR (single).

Player of the Month: None   **Player of the Week:** 2 times (last: 8/27-9/2/18)   **Rookie of the Month:** May 2018

Scoring Machine

The Yankees hold the Major League record for consecutive games without being shut out, scoring at least one run in 308 straight contests from 8/3/31-8/2/33…the streak was broken by a 7-0 shutout by Philadelphia's Lefty Grove.

The Yankees scored a run in 220 consecutive games between shutouts on 6/30/18 vs. Boston and 9/2/19 vs. Texas, marking the Majors' second-longest streak in the Modern Era (since 1900) behind the clubs' own record listed above. During the span, there were 368 shutouts in the Majors.

GIO URSHELA • INF

#29

HT: 6-0 • **WT:** 215 • **BATS:** R • **THROWS:** R
BIRTHDATE: 10/11/91 • **OPENING DAY AGE:** 28
BIRTHPLACE: Cartagena, Colombia
RESIDES: Cartagena, Colombia
M.L. SERVICE: 2 years, 127 days

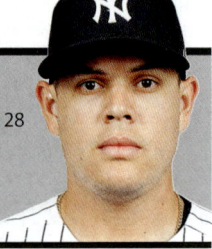

STATUS
- Acquired by the Yankees from the Toronto Blue Jays in exchange for cash considerations on August 4, 2018 and re-signed on October 24, 2018.

2019
- Hit .314/.355/.534 (139-for-442) with 73R, 34 doubles, 21HR, 74RBI and 25BB in 132 games with the Yankees after joining the team on 4/6 and remaining with the club for the rest of the season…entered the year with 8HR and 39RBI in his first 167 career games…led the team in doubles.
- Made 112 starts (109 at 3B, 3 at DH), reaching safely in 93 of those starts.
- Hit .333 (36-for-108) with runners in scoring position…ranked second in the Majors with a .625 (5-for-8) average with the bases loaded (min. 10PA)…hit .272 (66-for-243) with two strikes, the third-best such average in the Majors.
- Was one of 10 American Leaguers to hit at least .300 (min. 400AB) and collect 50 extra-base hits.
- Was signed to a Major League contract and selected to the Yankees' 25-man roster from Triple-A Scranton/WB on 4/6 and made his Yankees debut that night.
- Collected his first hit as a Yankee with a fourth-inning double and set a career high by reaching safely four times (2H, 1BB, 1HP) in 4/7 win at Baltimore.
- Went 2-for-5 with 2RBI, 1SF and 1SB in 4/22 win at Los Angeles-AL, recording a go-ahead sac fly in the 12th inning and a game-winning RBI single in the 14th inning.
- Hit his first HR as a Yankee on 4/25 at Los Angeles-AL (first since 5/19/18 vs. Oakland w/ Toronto).
- Batted cleanup on 4/26 at San Francisco, his first career start in that spot in the starting lineup.
- Was removed from 4/28 win at San Francisco after being hit by a pitch on the left hand (X-rays were negative).
- Hit a game-tying two-run HR in the ninth inning on 5/7 vs. Seattle, his first career game-tying hit in the ninth-or-later (has two tie-breaking, go-ahead hits in extra innings)…the HR had a Win Probability Added (WPA) of +47%, taking the Yankees' chances of winning from 11% to 58%…was the Yankees' first go-ahead or game-tying HR when trailing in the ninth inning or later since 5/29/18 vs. Houston (Brett Gardner game-tying two-run HR in the ninth off Chris Devenski).
- On 5/12, made his first career start in the No. 3 spot in the lineup, hitting a two-run double in the ninth.
- Collected his first career "walk-off" hit with a two-out RBI single over the CF Kevin Kiermaier's head to cap a three-run ninth inning on 5/17 vs. Tampa Bay.
- Had a career-high 4BB on 6/9 at Cleveland, most by a Yankee since Aaron Judge on 9/4/17 at Baltimore (also 4BB)…had just 4BB over his prior 28 games.
- Matched his career high with 4RBI in Game 1 on 6/11 vs. the Mets…doubled and homered in the game.
- Made his first career appearance in the OF as a left-field defensive replacement on 7/25 at Boston.
- Had a career-best 22-game on-base streak from 7/22-8/16, batting .467/.489/.900 (42-for-90) with 23R, 12 doubles, 9HR, 21RBI and 4BB over the stretch…reached multiple times in 16 of those 22G.
- Had a career-high-tying 13-game hitting streak from 7/22-8/8 (also 13G from 6/20-7/4/15)…had 16XBH during the streak (.444, 24-for-54, 15R, 9 doubles, 7HR, 14RBI)…doubled in five straight games from 7/22-28, the longest such streak by a Yankee since Robinson Canó in 2005 (also five straight).
- Over a 32-game stretch from 7/27-9/9, hit .408/.431/.728 (51-for-125) with 25R, 13 doubles, 9HR and 22RBI…during the span, led the Majors in batting average and ranked third in on-base pct., slugging and OPS (1.159).
- Hit safely in 12 consecutive home games from 7/30-8/16, batting .489/.510/.702 (23-for-47) with 10R, 4 doubles, 2HR and 7RBI.
- Homered in five of seven games from 8/4-12 (Game 1), hitting 7HR with 14RBI total over the span.
- Collected his first career multi-HR game on 8/7 at Baltimore…also homered twice the following night at Toronto (8/8)…was one of six players with consecutive multi-HR games in 2019 (also Oakland's Khris Davis and Matt Chapman, Toronto's Lourdes Gurriel Jr., Minnesota's Eddie Rosario and Los Angeles-NL's Joc Pederson)…was the first Yankee to accomplish the feat since Aaron Judge in 2017…became the second player in Yankees history to record his first two career multi-HR games on back-to-back days, joining Bill Skowron (7/28-29/56)—credit: *STATS, Inc*.…was part of a stretch in which he homered in a career-best three straight games from 8/6-8 (5HR total)…according to *Elias*, became the seventh player in Yankees history to hit 5HR over a three-game span and first since Alex Rodriguez from 9/5-8/07.

- Had multiple hits in four straight games from 8/11-13…had 3H in each of 3G from 8/12-13 (including both games of 8/12 doubleheader vs. Baltimore), the first Yankee to record three consecutive three-hit games since Alfonso Soriano did so in four straight from 8/13-16/13…was the first Yankee since Brett Gardner (5/14/17 vs. Houston) to collect 3H in both ends of a doubleheader.
- Went 10-for-18 (.556) with 6R, 2 doubles, 1HR and 3RBI during the Yankees' four-game series vs. Baltimore from 8/12-14…was the first Yankee to record at least 10H in a series since Robinson Canó and Alfonso Soriano both had 10H in a four-game series vs. Los Angeles-AL from 8/12-15/13.
- Each of his 17 games played from 8/20-9/15 came on the road.
- Was placed on the 10-day injured list from 8/30 (retroactive to 8/29) through 9/8 with a left groin injury.
- Hit his first career pinch-hit home run in Game 2 on 9/12 at Detroit, one of four pinch-hit HR by a Yankee in 2019 (also Aaron Hicks on 7/5 at Tampa Bay and Mike Ford on 9/1 vs. Oakland and 9/14 at Toronto)…was his 20th home run of the season, becoming the seventh Yankee to reach the plateau in 2019.
- Was removed from the game in the seventh inning on 9/24 at Tampa Bay after being hit by a pitch on his left hand in the sixth…X-rays were negative.
- Was removed from the Yankees' season finale on 9/29 at Texas for precautionary reasons in the fourth inning with a mild left ankle sprain.
- Started each of the Yankees' nine postseason games at 3B, hitting .242 (8-for-33) with 4R, 1 double, 2HR and 2RBI…hit his first career postseason home run in ALCS Game 1 at Houston…reached base safely four times in ALCS Game 6 at Houston (3-for-3, 2R, 1HR, 1RBI, 1BB), hitting a fourth-inning solo HR.

2018
- Began the year on the Indians' disabled list with a right hamstring strain from 3/29 (retro 3/26) to 5/4…played in 11 rehab games with Triple-A Columbus and hit .324 (12-for-37) with 6R, 4 doubles, 7RBI and 5BB…was reinstated from the 10-day D.L. and designated for assignment on 5/4.
- Was traded to Toronto on 5/9 in exchange for future considerations…appeared in 19 games for the Blue Jays, hitting .233 (10-for-43) with 7R, 1 double, 1HR and 3RBI…was designated for assignment on 6/26 and outrighted to Triple-A Buffalo on 7/3…hit .244 (21-for-86) with 7R, 3 doubles, 5RBI and 4BB in 24 games with Buffalo.
- Was acquired by the Yankees on 8/4 in exchange for cash considerations…finished the season with Triple-A Scranton/Wilkes-Barre, batting .307 (31-for-101) with 14R, 7 doubles, 2 triples, 2HR and 12RBI in 27 games.
- Hit .382/.475/.588 (13-for-34) with 5R, 4 doubles, 1HR, 3RBI and 5BB in nine playoff games for the RailRiders.
- Following the season, batted .229 (22-for-96) with 11R, 9 doubles, 1HR, 10RBI and 4BB in 26 games for the Tigres del Licey of the Dominican Winter League.

2017
- Hit .224 (35-for-156) with 14R, 7 doubles, 1HR, 15RBI and 8BB in 67 games (60G/36GS at 3B, 5G/3GS at 2B, 5G/1GS at SS and 2G at 1B) over two stints with Cleveland (6/17, 7/9-end of season).
- Made his playoff debut, starting all five games in the ALDS vs. the Yankees and hitting .167 (2-for-12) with 1RBI.
- Appeared in 76 games for Triple-A Columbus, batting .266 (79-for-297) with 34R, 12 doubles, 6HR and 34RBI.
- Played for Colombia in the WBC prior to the season, batting .143 (2-for-14) with 1RBI in three games.

2016
- Spent the entire season with Triple-A Columbus, batting .274 (128-for-468) with 54R, 24 doubles, 1 triple, 8HR and 57RBI in 117 games.
- Was named the International League "Batter of the Week" for 4/25-5/1 (.455, 10-for-22, 7R, 3 doubles, 1HR and 10RBI in 7G) and 8/1-7 (.500, 14-for-28, 4R, 4 doubles, 2HR and 12RBI in 7G).
- Following the season, played for the Aguilas del Zulia in the Venezuelan Winter League and hit .337 (57-for-169) with 23R, 16 doubles, 3HR and 33RBI in 43 games.

2015
- Saw his first Major League action, hitting .225 (60-for-267) with 25R, 8 doubles, 1 triple, 6HR and 21RBI in 81 games (76 starts at 3B) in his only stint with Cleveland (6/9-end of season).
- Was recalled from Triple-A Columbus on 6/9 and made his Major League debut that day vs. Seattle…collected his first hit (third-inning RBI single off Tom Wilhelmsen) and first home run (solo shot off Vidal Nuño in the fifth inning) on 6/11 vs. Seattle.
- Hit a game-winning two-run HR in the 12th inning on 8/4 at Los Angeles-AL, becoming the second player in Indians history to break a 0-0 tie with an extra-inning HR (also Brook Jacoby on 4/15/91 at Boston).
- Reached base safely in a season-high 21 straight games from 6/11-7/4…recorded a season-high 13-game hitting streak from 6/20-7/4, batting .295 (13-for-44) with 4R, 1HR and 3RBI in that span.
- Did not play from 9/18-30 due to right shoulder soreness.
- Started the season on the Triple-A disabled list with lower back inflammation…returned to the Triple-A D.L. with lower back inflammation from 5/8-21…hit .272 (22-for-81) with 12R, 5 doubles, 1 triple, 3HR, 9RBI and 3BB in 22 games with Columbus.

2014
- Combined with Double-A Akron and Triple-A Columbus to bat .280 (136-for-485) with 78R, 36 doubles, 6 triples, 18HR, 84RBI and 36BB in 128 games…ranked second among Indians farmhands in RBI and fourth in home runs.
- Started the year with Akron, hitting .300/.347/.567 (27-for-90) with 15R, 9 doubles, 5HR and 19RBI in 24 games.
- Was promoted to Columbus on 5/3 and hit .276/.331/.473 (109-for-395) with 63R, 27 doubles, 6 triples, 13HR, 65RBI and 30BB in 104 games.
- Following the season, appeared in 27 games for the Aguilas del Zulia of the Venezuelan Winter League, batting .398/.424/.556 (43-for-108) with 18R, 2 doubles, 3 triples, 3HR, 22RBI and 5BB…was also tabbed an Organization All-Star by MiLB.com.
- Was added to the Indians' 40-man roster on 11/20.

2013
- Spent the entire season with Double-A Akron, batting .270 (120-for-445) with 42R, 23 doubles, 2 triples, 8HR and 43RBI in 116 games.

2012
- In 114 games with Single-A Carolina, hit .278 (122-for-439) with 50R, 30 doubles, 1 triple, 14HR and 59RBI.
- Was named the Carolina League "Batter of the Week" from 8/6-12 after batting .520/.520/1.080 (13-for-25) with 6R, 5 doubles, 3HR and 6RBI.
- Following the season, was tabbed the "Best Infield Arm" in the organization by *Baseball America*.
- Hit .250 (3-for-12) with 2R, 1 doubles, 1HR and 3RBI in three games for Colombia in the WBC qualifiers.

2011
- Hit .238 (120-for-505) with 57R, 24 doubles, 2 triples, 9HR and 46RBI in 126 games with Single-A Lake County.
- Was tabbed the "Best Defensive Third Baseman" in the Midwest League by *Baseball America*.

2010
- Spent the season with short-season Single-A Mahoning Valley, hitting .290 (64-for-221) with 22R, 8 doubles, 3HR, 35RBI and 5SB in 58 games…ranked ninth among all Indians minor leaguers in batting average.
- Was named the New York-Penn League "Batter of the Week" from 8/2-8 after hitting .464 (13-for-28) with 6R, 2 doubles, 2HR and 7RBI in seven games over that span.
- Following the season, was named the "Best Infield Arm" in the organization by *Baseball America*.

2009
- Made his professional debut, splitting the season with the AZL Indians and DSL Indians and combining to bat .263 (56-for-213) with 20R, 10 doubles, 1 triple, 1HR and 35RBI in 59 games.
- Began the season with the DSL Indians, batting .269 (29-for-108) with 10R, 8 doubles, 1 triple, 1HR and 24RBI in 27 games.
- Was transferred to the AZL Indians on 7/10 and hit .257 (27-for-105) with 10R, 2 doubles and 11RBI in 32 games.

PERSONAL
- Last name is pronounced "urr-SHEL-lah"…has a son, Thiago.
- Is only the fifth player with a surname starting with 'U' to play for the Yankees…joins RHP George Uhle (1933-34), LHP Tom Underwood (1980-81), INF Bob Unglaub (1904) and RHP Cecil Upshaw (1974).

Urshela's Career Batting Record

Year	Team	AVG	G	AB	R	H	2B	3B	HR	RBI	SH	SF	HP	BB	SO	SB	CS	E	OBP	SLG
2009	DSL Indians	.269	27	108	10	29	8	1	1	24	0	1	1	7	14	2	2	10	.316	.389
	AZL Indians	.257	32	105	10	27	2	0	0	11	1	2	1	10	12	3	0	11	.322	.276
2010	Mahoning Valley	.290	58	221	22	64	8	0	3	35	1	6	3	12	32	5	3	8	.326	.367
2011	Lake County	.238	126	505	57	120	24	2	9	46	2	4	4	14	69	3	0	22	.262	.347
2012	Carolina	.278	114	439	50	122	30	1	14	59	5	8	7	16	60	1	1	10	.309	.446
2013	Akron	.270	116	445	42	120	23	2	8	43	4	2	1	14	48	1	1	12	.292	.384
2014	Akron	.300	24	90	15	27	9	0	5	19	0	1	1	6	16	1	1	4	.347	.567
	Columbus	.276	104	395	63	109	27	6	13	65	1	1	3	30	51	0	2	5	.331	.473
2015	Columbus	.272	22	81	12	22	5	1	3	9	0	0	0	3	12	0	0	3	.298	.469
	CLEVELAND	.225	81	267	25	60	8	1	6	21	1	0	2	18	58	0	1	6	.279	.330
2016	Columbus	.274	128	468	54	128	24	1	8	57	1	6	1	15	58	0	0	9	.294	.380
2017	Columbus	.266	76	297	34	79	12	1	6	34	1	2	5	20	45	0	0	6	.321	.374
	CLEVELAND	.224	67	156	14	35	7	0	1	15	1	0	0	8	22	0	0	5	.262	.288
2018	Columbus - a	.324	11	37	6	12	4	0	0	7	0	0	0	5	9	0	0	1	.405	.432
	TORONTO - b	.233	19	43	7	10	1	0	1	3	0	0	1	2	10	0	0	1	.283	.326
	Buffalo	.244	24	86	7	21	3	0	0	5	0	1	0	4	9	0	0	3	.275	.279
	Scranton/WB - c	.307	27	101	14	31	7	2	2	12	1	0	1	4	13	0	0	1	.340	.475
2019	Scranton/WB	.444	2	9	2	4	2	0	0	1	0	0	0	0	2	0	0	0	.444	.667
	YANKEES - d	.314	132	442	73	139	34	0	21	74	0	4	5	25	87	1	1	13	.355	.534
	Minor League Totals	.270	880	3387	398	915	188	17	72	427	17	34	28	160	450	16	10	105	.306	.399
	Major League Totals	.269	299	908	119	244	50	1	29	113	2	4	8	53	177	1	2	25	.313	.422

Signed by the Cleveland Indians as a non-drafted free agent on July 2, 2008.

a – Placed on the 10-day disabled list from March 29 (retroactive to March 26) - May 4, 2018 with a right hamstring strain.
b – Acquired by Toronto from Cleveland on May 9, 2018 in exchange for future considerations.
c – Acquired by the Yankees from Toronto on August 4, 2018 in exchange for cash considerations.
d – Placed on the 10-day injured list from August 30 (retroactive to August 29) - September 8, 2019 with a left groin injury.

Urshela's Postseason Record

Year	Club vs. Opp.	AVG	G	AB	R	H	2B	3B	HR	RBI	SH	SF	HP	BB	SO	SB	CS	E	OBP	SLG
2017	CLE vs. NYY (DS)	.167	5	12	0	2	0	0	0	1	1	0	0	0	6	0	0	2	.167	.167
2019	NYY vs. MIN (DS)	.250	3	12	1	3	1	0	0	0	0	0	0	2	2	0	0	0	.250	.333
	NYY vs. HOU (CS)	.238	6	21	3	5	0	0	2	2	0	0	0	2	2	0	0	0	.304	.524
Wild Card Totals		-	-	-	-	-	-	-	-	-	-	-	-	-	-	-	-	-	-	-
Division Series Totals		.208	8	24	1	5	1	0	0	1	1	0	0	0	8	0	0	2	.208	.250
LCS Totals		.238	6	21	3	5	0	0	2	2	0	0	0	2	2	0	0	0	.304	.524
POSTSEASON TOTALS		.222	14	45	4	10	1	0	2	3	1	0	0	2	10	0	0	2	.255	.378

Urshela's World Baseball Classic Stats

Year	Country, Site	AVG	G	AB	R	H	2B	3B	HR	RBI	SH	SF	HP	BB	SO	SB	CS	E	OBP	SLG
2017	Colombia, Miami	.143	3	14	0	2	0	0	0	1	0	0	0	0	3	0	0	0	.143	.143
WBC Totals		.143	3	14	0	2	0	0	0	1	0	0	0	0	3	0	0	0	.143	.143

Urshela's Career Fielding Record

Position	PCT	G	PO	A	E	TC	DP
First Base	1.000	3	10	0	0	10	2
Second Base	.909	5	2	8	1	11	2
Shortstop	.963	13	7	19	1	27	2
Third Base	.961	273	131	435	23	589	44
Outfield	1.000	1	2	0	0	2	0

Urshela's Career Home Run Chart

MULTI-HOMER GAMES: 2. **TWO-HOMER GAMES:** 2 - 2 times (last on 8/8/19 at TOR). **THREE-HOMER GAMES:** None. **GRAND SLAMS:** None. **PINCH-HIT HR:** 1, on 9/12/19 at DET-G2 (Gregory Soto). **INSIDE-THE-PARK HR:** None. **"WALK-OFF" HR:** None. **LEADOFF HR:** None.

Urshela's Career Bests and Streaks

HITS: 4, 7/27/19 at BOS. **RUNS:** 3 - 3 times (last on 8/8/19 at TOR). **2B:** 2 - 6 times (last on 8/23/19 at LAD). **3B:** 1, 7/26/15 vs. CWS. **HR:** 2 - 2 times (last on 8/8/19 at TOR). **RBI:** 4 - 4 times (last on 8/8/19 at TOR). **BB:** 4, on 6/9/19 at CLE. **SO:** 4 - 2 times (last on 8/22/19 at OAK). **SB:** 1, 4/22/19 at LAA. **HIT STREAK:** 13g - 2 times (last from 7/22-8/8/19). **"WALK-OFF" HITS:** 1, 5/17/19 vs. TB (single).

Player of the Month: None   **Player of the Week:** None   **Rookie of the Month:** None

---

YANKEES TO HOMER IN THEIR FIRST CAREER WORLD SERIES AT-BAT
According to the Elias Sports Bureau

Chick Fewster.....................10/11/21, Game 6 loss vs. NY Giants (off Jesse Barnes, 2nd inning, 1 on)*
George Selkirk.......................9/30/36, Game 1 loss at NY Giants (off Carl Hubbell, 3rd inning, solo)
Elston Howard.............9/28/55, Game 1 win vs. Brooklyn (off Don Newcombe, 2nd inning, 1 on)
Roger Maris.........................10/5/60, Game 1 loss at Pittsburgh (off Vern Law, 1st inning, solo)
Jim Mason......................10/19/76, Game 3 loss vs. Cincinnati (off Pat Zachry, 7th inning, solo)
  -Mason's pinch-hit homer was his only career World Series plate appearance
Bob Watson..................10/20/81, Game 1 win vs. Los Angeles-NL (off Jerry Reuss, 1st inning, 2 on)

All but Fewster homered in their first plate appearance.

IN A PINCH

There have been 25 pinch-hit home runs all time in World Series play, eight of which have been hit by a member of the Yankees…the first pinch-hit home run during a World Series game was hit by Yogi Berra on 10/2/47 in a Game 3 loss at Brooklyn…Berra's solo homer came in the seventh inning off Ralph Branca and was his first career postseason hit…the most recent such home run by a Yankee was hit by Hideki Matsui in Game 3 of the 2009 World Series at Philadelphia.

LUKE VOIT • INF

59

HT: 6-3 • **WT:** 255 • **BATS:** R • **THROWS:** R
BIRTHDATE: 2/13/91 • **OPENING DAY AGE:** 29
BIRTHPLACE: Wildwood, Mo.
RESIDES: Wildwood, Mo.
COLLEGE: Missouri State University
M.L. SERVICE: 1 year, 169 days

STATUS
- Was acquired along with international signing bonus pool money from the St. Louis Cardinals on July 28, 2018 in exchange for LHP Chasen Shreve and RHP Giovanny Gallegos.

2019
- Hit .263 (113-for-429) with 72R, 21 doubles, 1 triple, 21HR and 62RBI in 118 games with the Yankees in his first full season at the Major League level…set career highs in home runs and RBI.
- Hit .292 (61-for-209) with 45R, 13 doubles, 14HR and 34RBI in 55 road games…had two road hitting streaks of at least 9G: 17G from 9/24/18-4/26/19 (11G in 2019) and 9G from 6/14-7/27.
- Hit .377 (20-for-53) with 9R, 8 doubles, 1HR and 5RBI in 14 games vs. Boston, hitting safely in 11 of those games.
- Through 50 team games (Game 1 on 5/25), hit 13HR…with Gary Sánchez (15HR) and Gleyber Torres (12HR), became the second trio in Yankees history to reach 12HR apiece by the club's 50th game of the season, joining Mickey Mantle (21HR), Yogi Berra (16HR) and Hank Bauer (13HR) in 1956 (credit: *STATS, LLC.*).
- Made his first career Opening Day roster…hit a three-run HR in the first inning and went 1-for-1 with 4RBI, 2BB and 1HP, becoming the second Yankee in as many seasons to collect 4RBI on Opening Day (Giancarlo Stanton-4RBI on 3/29/18 at Toronto)…with Aaron Judge going 2-for-3 with 3R and 2BB in the game, the duo became the first Yankees to reach base safely at least four times on Opening Day since Alex Rodriguez (2-for-3, 2BB) on 4/6/12 at Tampa Bay and the first Yankees teammates to do so in the same Opening Day game since Rodriguez and Hideki Matsui on 4/3/06 at Oakland.
- Homered in a career-best four straight games from 9/27/18-3/28/19…had a career-long seven-game RBI streak from 9/25/18-3/30/19 (13RBI total).
- Had a career-best 42-game on-base streak from 9/19/18-5/3/19 (.316/.416/.658, 50-for-158, 35R, 6 doubles, 16HR, 43RBI, 24BB, 3HP)…was tied for the longest streak by a Yankee since 2005 with Mark Teixeira's 42-game streak from 6/6-7/26/10…*Elias* noted that Voit is one of four Yankees (also Babe Ruth-46G/54RBI in 1921, Lou Gehrig-4x and Joe DiMaggio-52G/63RBI in 1937) to average at least 1RBI per game in an on-base streak of at least 40G (since RBI became an official stat in 1920).
- His 31-game on-base streak *to start the season* was tied for sixth-longest by a Yankee since 1913 (when walks were first compiled in both leagues)…was the longest since Derek Jeter's club-record 53-game streak to begin the 1999 season.
- Had a career-best 13-game hitting streak from 4/13-26, batting .367 (18-for-49) with 10R, 3 doubles, 4HR and 10RBI.
- Was named AL "Player of the Week" for 4/22-28, batting .433/.528/.867 (13-for-30) with 10R, 1 double, 4HR, 10RBI, 5BB and 1HP with four multi-hit contests (1-2H, 3-3H) over seven games…was his second career weekly honor (also 9/24-30/18) and the first by a Yankee in 2019.
- Collected his third career multi-HR game on 4/23 at Los Angeles-AL (also 8/24/18 at Baltimore and 9/19/18 vs. Boston).
- Went 22 games before his first multi-hit game (4/23 at Los Angeles-AL), compiled the Majors' longest *season-opening on-base streak without a multi-hit game* since walks were first tracked in 1913 (when walks were first tracked in both leagues), surpassing Philadelphia-AL's Max Bishop (first 18G of 1932)…was the longest such streak at any point in a season since Philadelphia-NL's Clay Dalrymple did so in 25 straight games from 5/19-6/22/62.
- Hit a 470-foot HR (Statcast) in Game 1 on 5/25 at Kansas City, the second-longest HR by a Yankee in 2019.
- Hit his first career triple on 5/29 vs. San Diego…also homered in the game—the second of back-to-back HRs with LeMahieu to lead off the game, marking the 10th instance in Yankees history they led off a game with consecutive homers (first since Gardner and Judge on 7/7/18 at Toronto).
- Tied a career high in hits while going 4-for-4 on 6/29 at Boston at London Stadium…included 3 doubles, his first career multi-double game.
- Was placed on the 10-day injured list from 7/2 (retro to 6/30)-7/13 with an abdominal strain (missed eight team games).
- Hit a solo HR in Game 2 on 7/18 vs. Tampa Bay, snapping a 17-game homerless streak, the second-longest of his career and longest as a Yankee (38 games from 7/14-9/23/17 w/ St. Louis).
- Left 7/20 win vs. Colorado in the top of the fifth inning after being hit by a pitch in the face in the fourth inning.

- Was placed on the 10-day injured list from 7/31-8/30 with a sports hernia (missed 29 team games)…was removed in the fifth inning of 7/30 loss vs. Arizona with a core muscle injury…in four rehab games with Triple-A Scranton/Wilkes-Barre, hit .471 (8-for-17) with 5R, 2 doubles, 2HR and 4RBI.
- Hit an RBI single in the ninth inning on 9/9 at Boston, his first RBI since 7/26 (snapped a career-long 11-game stretch without driving in a run).
- Was on the Yankees' ALDS roster, but did not play…was not on the club's ALCS roster.
- Underwent surgery to repair bilateral core muscle injuries on 10/24…the surgery was performed by Dr. William Meyers in Philadelphia.

2018
- Combined with the Cardinals and Yankees to hit .322/.398/.671 (46-for-143) with 30R, 5 doubles, 15HR and 36RBI in 47 games.
- Hit .333/.405/.689 (44-for-132) with 28R, 5 doubles, 14HR, 33RBI and 15BB in 39 games (31GS at 1B, 4 at DH) over two stints with the Yankees (8/2-13, 8/21-9/30)…of his 44H, 19 went for extra bases (43.2%)…batted .393 (11-for-28) with 3 doubles, 3HR and 17RBI with runners in scoring position as a Yankee.
- Led all AL hitters (min. 50AB) with a 9.43AB/HR ratio (132AB, 14HR)…the next best was Oakland's Khris Davis (12.00)…of his 14HR with the Yankees, five tied the game (two) or gave the Yankees the lead (three).
- Was acquired by the Yankees with international signing bonus pool money from St. Louis on 7/28 in exchange for LHP Chasen Shreve and RHP Giovanny Gallegos.
- Made his Yankees debut in 8/2 loss at Boston, starting at DH and going 0-for-4…collected his first Yankees hit with his 13th-inning single in 8/7 win at Chicago-AL.
- Had 41H in 116AB (.353 BA) after being recalled on 8/21.
- Hit an AL-high 14HR in 32G from 8/24 through the end of the season, the second-highest total in the Majors over the span behind only Milwaukee's Christian Yelich (15).
- Hit 7HR over his final 11G, 10HR over his last 23G and 14HR over his final 32G.
- Recorded his first career multi-HR game and went 3-for-5 with 4RBI in 8/24 win at Baltimore…hit a game-tying two-run HR—his first HR as a Yankee—in the fourth and a two-run shot in the 10th…his 4RBI tied his career high.
- Hit go-ahead HRs in the seventh inning on 8/30 vs. Detroit and the eighth inning on 9/4 vs. Oakland.
- Homered in three straight games for the first time in his career from 9/2-4.
- Over his final 11 games (from 9/19), hit .419 (18-for-43) with 12R, 3 doubles, 7HR and 16RBI.
- Had multiple RBI in three straight games from 9/19-21 (7RBI total)…marked his first time collecting multiple RBI in consecutive games in his career.
- Hit solo HR and two-run HR and went 4-for-4 with 4R in 9/19 win vs. Boston…was his second career multi-HR game (also 8/24 at Baltimore) and set career highs in runs and hits…became the second Yankee since 2008 to go 4-for-4 or better with at least 4R in a game, joining Aaron Judge (4-for-4, 4R, 1 double, 2HR, 3RBI, 1BB on 6/11/17 vs. Baltimore).
- His two-run HR in 9/20 loss vs. Boston was the Yankees' 246th homer of the year, surpassing the previous club record (245HR in 2012).
- Was named AL "Player of the Week" for 9/24-30, batting .458/.519/.958 (11-for-24) with 5R, 3 doubles, 3HR and 8RBI…led the AL in total bases (23) and tied for AL lead in hits, HRs, RBI and XBH (6)…was his first career weekly award.
- Ended the season with a five-game RBI streak (9/25-30), driving in eight runs over the span…extended the streak to seven games with 2RBI in each of his first two playoff contests.
- Made his postseason debut, starting all five Yankees games at 1B and batting .235 (4-for-17) with 2R, 1 triple, 4RBI and 4BB.
- Hit a two-run triple in the sixth inning of the AL Wild Card Game vs. Oakland, his first career triple (regular or postseason)…also had 2RBI in ALDS Game 1 at Boston, becoming third Yankee since 1908 with at least 2RBI in each of his first two career postseason games (also Ben Chapman and Bill Dickey, each in Games 1 and 2 of the 1932 World Series vs. the Cubs).
- In nine games with the RailRiders, hit .310 (9-for-29) with 2R, 2 doubles, 1HR and 3RBI.
- Appeared in eight games for the Cardinals, hitting .182 (2-for-11) with 1HR and 3RBI…also saw time with Triple-A Memphis (67 games) and Double-A Springfield (two games), combining to bat .300 (72-for-240) with 36R, 16 doubles, 2 triples, 10HR, 37RBI, 32BB, a .392 OBP and a .900 OPS in 69 games.

2017
- Saw his first Major League action, batting .246 (28-for-114) with 18R, 9 doubles, 4HR and 18RBI in 62 games (18 starts at 1B, 1 at DH) over two stints with St. Louis (6/25-8/21 and 8/27-10/1).
- Batted .300 (10-for-33) with 1HR as a pinch-hitter, one of three Cardinals with 10 pinch-hits in 2017 (also Greg Garcia and Jose Martinez).
- Was signed to a Major League contract and selected to the Cardinals' 25-man roster from Triple-A Memphis on 6/25…made his Major League debut as a pinch-hitter that night vs. Pittsburgh and was hit by a pitch.
- Started at 1B and collected his first Major League hit with a double on 6/26 vs. Cincinnati.
- Hit his first career home run on 7/3 vs. Miami off Jarlin Garcia…hit 3HR over a seven-game span from 7/3-9.
- Hit his first career pinch-hit home run with a solo HR off Brian Duensing on 9/25 vs. Chicago-NL.

- Appeared in 74 games with Triple-A Memphis, batting .327 (88-for-269) with 35R, 23 doubles, 13HR and 50RBI.
- At the time of his first call-up, was ranked among the Pacific Coast League leaders in batting (.322, 10th), hits (82, T11th), doubles (23, T1st), RBI (48, T9th), OBP (.406, 4th), slugging pct. (.561, 6th) and OPS (.967, 4th).
- Was named Cardinals Minor League "Player of the Month" for April after batting .360 (27-for-75) with 8R, 7 doubles, 5HR and 16RBI…of his 27H during the month, 13 went for extra bases.
- Homered in three straight games from 4/9-11…hit 2HR on 4/28 vs. Round Rock and 6/14 vs. Colorado Springs.

2016
- Spent the entire season with Double-A Springfield, batting .297 (143-for-482) with 70R, 20 doubles, 5 triples, 19HR and 74RBI in 134 games…was named to the Texas League Mid-Season and Postseason All-Star teams.
- Led the Texas League in batting average, games played and hits, ranked second in on-base pct. (.372), third in runs and total bases (230), tied for third in triples (5), ranked fourth in RBI and seventh in extra-base hits (53)…among Cardinals minor leaguers, tied for second in runs, ranked second in hits and RBI, tied for third in home runs, tied for fourth in triples, ranked sixth in walks (52) and slugging pct. (.477), eighth in OPS (.849) and tied for ninth in doubles…ranked 10th among all Double-A players in hits.
- Was named Cardinals Minor League "Player of the Month" for August, batting .366 (34-for-93) with 7 doubles, 1 triple, 4HR and 20RBI in 26 games.

2015
- Batted .273 (126-for-462) with 52R, 18 doubles, 5 triples, 11HR and 77RBI in 130 games with Single-A Palm Beach…was named a Midseason Florida State League All-Star…his 77RBI were tied for second in the FSL and tied the Palm Beach Cardinals single-season RBI record (also Allen Craig in 2007)…ranked second in the league in walks (63) and third in on-base pct. (.360).
- Hit .330 (34-for-103) with 9R, 5 doubles, 5HR and 31RBI in August, the third-most RBI by any minor leaguers during the month.
- Went 3-for-9 with 3 doubles and 2RBI in the FSL playoffs.

2014
- Spent the season with Single-A Palm Beach, batting .276 (97-for-351) with 57R, 21 doubles, 5 triples, 9HR and 51RBI in 93 games…ranked fifth in the Florida State League with a .442 slugging pct. (min. 350AB)…ranked 10th among Cardinals minor leaguers in doubles and slugging pct.
- Had two 4H games (5/28 at Daytona and 6/17 vs. Jupiter)…hit 2HR on 7/13 at Clearwater.

2013
- Made his professional debut with short-season Single-A State College, hitting .242 (36-for-149) with 14R, 7 doubles, 2HR and 16RBI in 46 games…started 43 games at catcher and threw out 38.0% (19-of-50) of attempted base stealers (fourth in the NY-Penn League).
- Hit his first professional home run vs. Mahoning Valley on 7/9 with a solo HR off Robert Whitenack.

PERSONAL
- Full name is Louis Linwood Voit III…is married to Tori.
- Was originally drafted as a catcher…started 43 games at catcher in the N.Y.-Penn League in 2013 before being converted to an infielder.
- Played collegiate baseball at Missouri State University and was a member of the 2012 team that qualified for an NCAA Regional.
- Graduated from Lafayette High School (Mo.)…Major Leaguers David Freese and Ryan Howard also attended the school.
- Wears No. 59 in honor of his brother, John, who wore the number when he played collegiate football at the United States Military Academy at West Point and served as team captain.

Voit's Career Batting Record

Year	Team	AVG	G	AB	R	H	2B	3B	HR	RBI	SH	SF	HP	BB	SO	SB	CS	E	OBP	SLG
2013	State College	.242	46	149	14	36	7	0	2	16	0	1	6	21	29	1	0	3	.356	.329
2014	Palm Beach	.276	93	351	57	97	21	5	9	51	1	2	4	32	79	1	1	14	.342	.442
2015	Palm Beach	.273	130	462	52	126	18	5	11	77	0	9	5	63	104	2	0	16	.360	.405
2016	Springfield	.297	134	482	70	143	20	5	19	74	0	4	8	52	83	1	2	8	.372	.477
2017	Memphis	.327	74	269	35	88	23	1	13	50	0	1	8	29	53	1	1	5	.407	.565
	ST. LOUIS	.246	62	114	18	28	9	0	4	18	0	0	3	7	31	0	0	0	.306	.430
2018	Memphis	.299	67	234	35	70	16	2	9	36	0	1	5	31	49	0	1	5	.391	.500
	Springfield	.333	2	6	1	2	0	0	1	1	0	0	0	1	0	0	0	0	.429	.833
	ST. LOUIS - a	.182	8	11	2	2	0	0	1	3	0	0	0	2	4	0	0	0	.308	.455
	Scranton/WB	.310	9	29	2	9	2	0	1	3	0	0	0	3	7	0	0	2	.375	.483
	YANKEES	.333	39	132	28	44	5	0	14	33	0	0	1	15	39	0	0	2	.405	.689
2019	YANKEES - b, c	.263	118	429	72	113	21	1	21	62	0	1	9	71	142	0	0	7	.378	.464
	Scranton/WB	.471	4	17	5	8	2	0	2	4	0	0	0	2	2	0	0	0	.526	.941
Minor League Totals		**.290**	**559**	**1999**	**271**	**579**	**109**	**18**	**67**	**312**	**1**	**18**	**36**	**234**	**406**	**6**	**5**	**53**	**.371**	**.463**
AL Totals		**.280**	**157**	**561**	**100**	**157**	**26**	**1**	**35**	**95**	**0**	**1**	**10**	**86**	**181**	**0**	**0**	**9**	**.384**	**.517**
NL Totals		**.240**	**70**	**125**	**20**	**30**	**9**	**0**	**5**	**21**	**0**	**0**	**3**	**9**	**35**	**0**	**0**	**0**	**.307**	**.432**
Major League Totals		**.273**	**227**	**686**	**120**	**187**	**35**	**1**	**40**	**116**	**0**	**1**	**13**	**95**	**216**	**0**	**0**	**9**	**.371**	**.501**

Selected by the St. Louis Cardinals in the 22nd round of the 2013 First-Year Player Draft.

a – Acquired by the Yankees with cash considerations in exchange for LHP Chasen Shreve and RHP Giovanny Gallegos.
b – Placed on the 10-day injured list from July 2 (retroactive to June 30) – July 13, 2019 with an abdominal strain.
c – Placed on the 10-day injured list from July 31 - August 30, 2019 with a sports hernia.

Voit's Postseason Record

Year	Club vs. Opp.	AVG	G	AB	R	H	2B	3B	HR	RBI	SH	SF	HP	BB	SO	SB	CS	E	OBP	SLG
2018	NYY vs. OAK (WC)	.250	1	4	1	1	0	1	0	2	0	0	0	0	2	0	0	0	.250	.750
	NYY vs. BOS (DS)	.231	4	13	1	3	0	0	0	2	0	0	0	4	4	0	0	0	.412	.231
2019	NYY vs. MIN (DS)								On Roster - Did Not Play											
Wild Card Totals		.250	1	4	1	1	0	1	0	2	0	0	0	0	2	0	0	0	.250	.750
Division Series Totals		.231	4	13	1	3	0	0	0	2	0	0	0	4	4	0	0	0	.412	.231
POSTSEASON TOTALS		.235	5	17	2	4	0	1	0	4	0	0	0	4	6	0	0	0	.381	.353

Voit's Career Fielding Record

Position	PCT	G	PO	A	E	TC	DP
First Base	.991	149	963	58	9	1,030	92
Outfield	-	1	0	0	0	0	0

Voit's Career Home Run Chart

MULTI-HOMER GAMES: 2. **TWO-HOMER GAMES:** 2 - 3 times (last on 4/23/19 at LAA). **THREE-HOMER GAMES:** None. **GRAND SLAMS:** None. **PINCH-HIT HR:** 2, last on 6/7/18 vs. MIA (Adam Conley). **INSIDE-THE-PARK HR:** None. **"WALK-OFF" HR:** None. **LEADOFF HR:** None.

Voit's Career Bests and Streaks

HITS: 4 - 2 times (last on 6/29/19 at BOS). **RUNS:** 4, 9/19/18 vs. BOS. **2B:** 3, on 6/29/19 at BOS. **3B:** 1, on 5/29/19 vs. SD. **HR:** 2 - 3 times (last on 4/23/19 at LAA). **RBI:** 4 - 4 times (last on 3/28/19 vs. BAL). **BB:** 3, on 5/12/19 at TB. **SO:** 4 - 3 times (last on 9/20/19 vs. TOR). **SB:** None. **HIT STREAK:** 13g, 4/13-26/19. **"WALK-OFF" HITS:** None.

Player of the Month: None   **Player of the Week:** 2 times (last: 4/22-28/19)   **Rookie of the Month:** None

---

Home Sweet Home

The Yankees went 57-24 (.704) at Yankee Stadium in 2019. It marked the Yankees' 28th consecutive winning season at home (since 1992)…according to *Elias*, it is the longest current streak of any team in the Majors and the longest such streak by any team since a Major League-record 47-year streak for the Yankees from 1918-64.

The Yankees collected at least 50 wins at home in each of their first four seasons at the current Yankee Stadium (2009-12)…in 2012, Yankee Stadium became the second ballpark to host the postseason in each of the first four years of its existence, joining Atlanta's Turner Field (first six)—credit: *Elias*.

The Yankees own the two highest single-season home winning percentages all time: .805 (62-15) in 1932 and .802 (65-16) in 1961.

TYLER WADE • INF/OF

14

HT: 6-1 • **WT:** 188 • **BATS:** L • **THROWS:** R
BIRTHDATE: 11/23/94 • **OPENING DAY AGE:** 25
BIRTHPLACE: Murrieta, Calif.
RESIDES: Murrieta, Calif.
M.L. SERVICE: 1 year, 93 days

STATUS
- Selected by the Yankees in the fourth round of the 2013 First-Year Player Draft.

2019
- Hit .245 (23-for-94) with 16R, 3 doubles, 1 triple, 2HR, 11RBI, 11BB and 7SB in 43 games over three stints with the Yankees (4/1-5/7, 7/28-8/2 and 8/18-9/29).
- Has played at 2B, SS, 3B and all three outfield positions in his Major League career.
- Singled, stole second base and scored the game-winning run in the ninth inning on 4/24 at Los Angeles-AL.
- Had his first career multi-SB game on 4/25 at Los Angeles-AL (2SB).
- Hit his second career homer on 7/30 vs. Arizona (also 7/11/18 at Baltimore)…became the 22nd player to homer for the Yankees in 2019, marking the fourth time in franchise history the team had at least 22 different players homer in the same season.
- Hit .297/.366/.486 (11-for-37) with 6R, 2 doubles, 1 triple, 1HR, 5RBI, 4BB and 1SB in 18 games in September.
- Hit a two-run triple on 9/10 at Detroit, the first triple of his career and third career multi-RBI game.
- Collected at least 1H and 1R in three straight games with an AB from 9/15-21 (4-for-8, 3R, 1 double, 1HR, 2RBI).
- Was on the Yankees' ALDS roster vs. Minnesota, but did not play.
- Hit .296 (89-for-301) with 51R, 19 doubles, 4 triples, 4HR, 38RBI and 13SB in 79 games with Triple-A Scranton/Wilkes-Barre.
- Had five consecutive multi-hit games with Scranton/WB from 6/28-7/2 (11-for-23)…from 6/28 through his 7/28 recall, batted a team-best .358 (38-for-106) with 20R, 9 doubles, 1 triple, 2HR and 15RBI in 26 games…was the fifth-best batting average in the International League over the span.

2018
- Hit .167 (11-for-66) with 8R, 4 doubles, 1HR, 5RBI and 1SB in 36 games (13 starts at 2B, 1 at SS and 1 at LF) over four stints with the Yankees (3/29-4/22, 7/6-25, 7/27-8/2, 9/1-9/30).
- Made his first career Opening Day roster…at age 23y, 126d, was the youngest player on the Yankees' Opening Day roster and the youngest position player to make a Yankees O.D. roster since Melky Cabrera in 2007 (age 22y, 234d).
- During his second stint with the Yankees, hit .368 (7-for-19) with 5R, 2 doubles, 1HR and 1RBI in 10 games.
- Hit his first Major League home run (a solo shot in the sixth off Wright Jr.) and set a career high in hits in 7/11 win at Baltimore, going 3-for-5 with 1 double.
- Was on the Yankees' AL Wild Card Game roster, but did not play.
- In 91 games with Triple-A Scranton/WB, hit .255 (93-for-364) with 46R, 18 doubles, 4 triples, 4HR, 27RBI, 37BB and 11SB…saw time at SS (51 games/48 starts), LF (12 starts), 2B (10 starts), CF (10 starts), RF (eight starts) and 3B (three games/two starts).

2017
- Saw his first Major League action and hit .155 (9-for-58) with 7R, 4 doubles and 2RBI in 30 games (11 starts at 2B, 1 at SS, 1 in LF and 1 in RF) over three stints with the Yankees (6/27-7/15, 7/23-8/25 and 9/4-10/1).
- Made his Major League debut in 6/27 loss at Chicago-AL, pinch-hitting for Refsnyder in the eighth and remaining in the game in LF (0-for-1, 1R, 1BB)…scored the game-tying run in the eighth inning after drawing a walk in his first career PA…became the second Yankee since 1997 to make his Major League debut *as a substitute* and still score a run (also Brandon Laird on 7/22/11 vs. Oakland)…was signed to a Major League contract and selected to the Yankees' 25-man roster from Triple-A Scranton/Wilkes-Barre prior to the game.
- With his debut on 6/27, Miguel Andújar's debut on 6/28 and Dustin Fowler debuting on 6/29, the Yankees had position players make their Major League debuts on three straight days for the first time since Jack Little, John Dowd and Bill Otis from 7/2-4/1912 (credit: *Elias*).
- Collected his first Major League hit with a sixth-inning double off Jake Petricka in 6/28 win at Chicago-AL.
- In 85 games with Scranton/WB, hit .310/.382/.460 (105-for-339) with 68R, 22 doubles, 4 triples, 7HR, 31RBI and 26SB (in 31 chances), winning the International League batting title…was named to the International League Postseason All-Star Team…appeared at 2B, SS, 3B, LF, CF and RF.
- Was on the Yankees' AL Wild Card Game roster, but did not play.

2016
- Hit .259 (131-for-505) with 90R, 16 doubles, 7 triples, 5HR, 27RBI, 66BB and 27SB (in 35 attempts) in 133 games with Double-A Trenton…was named to both the Eastern League Mid-Season and Postseason All-Star teams…ranked third in the Eastern League in walks and runs scored and fourth in games played and at-bats.
- Following the season, hit .241 (13-for-54) with 17R, 1 triple, 4RBI and 13BB in 18 games with the Arizona Fall League Scottsdale Scorpions, while going 10-for-11 in stolen base attempts…played 16 of his 18G in the outfield.

2015
- Combined with Single-A Tampa (98G) and Double-A Trenton (29G) to bat .262 (126-for-481) with 57R, 15 doubles, 5 triples, 3HR and 31RBI in 127 games…stole 33 bases in 49 attempts (67.3%), third-most among Yankees minor leaguers…earned spots on both the FSL Mid-Season and Postseason All-Star teams.
- In 98 games at Tampa, hit .280 (103-for-368) with 51R, 11 doubles, 5 triples, 2HR, 28RBI and 31SB.
- Was promoted to Trenton on 8/5 and hit .204 (23-for-113) in 29 games with the Thunder.
- Following the season, was ranked by *Baseball America* as the Yankees' No. 7 prospect…was ranked by *Baseball America* as the No. 18 prospect in the Florida State League following the season.
- After the season, batted .220 (9-for-41) with 6R, 2 doubles, 6RBI and 6BB in 14 games with the Surprise Saguaros of the Arizona Fall League.

2014
- Spent the entire season with Single-A Charleston, batting .272 (138-for-507) with 77R, 24 doubles, 6 triples, 1HR and 51RBI in 129 games…tied for third among Yankees minor leaguers in stolen bases (22)…played 94G at SS, 20G at DH, 15G at 2B and 1G at 3B…following the season, was tabbed an Organization All-Star by MiLB.com.

2013
- Made his professional debut with the GCL Yankees 1 and played his first 46 games there, batting .309 (50-for-162) with 10 doubles, 37R, 12RBI, 32BB and a .429 on-base percentage…stole 11 bases in 12 attempts (91.7%).
- Was transferred to short-season Single-A Staten Island on 8/28 and went 1-for-13 (.077) in 4G…ranked fourth among Yankees minor league hitters in season batting average (.291).

PERSONAL
- Full name is Tyler Dean Wade…graduated in 2013 from Murrieta Valley H.S. (Calif.), hitting .524 as a senior.

Wade's Career Batting Record

Year	Club	AVG	G	AB	R	H	2B	3B	HR	RBI	SH	SF	HP	BB	SO	SB	CS	E	OBP	SLG
2013	GCL Yankees 1	.309	46	162	37	50	10	0	0	12	2	0	2	32	42	11	1	7	.429	.370
	Staten Island	.077	4	13	0	1	0	0	0	1	0	0	0	2	4	0	0	0	.200	.077
2014	Charleston	.272	129	507	77	138	24	6	1	51	2	4	6	57	118	22	13	22	.350	.349
2015	Tampa	.280	98	368	51	103	11	5	2	28	5	4	2	39	65	31	15	28	.349	.353
	Trenton	.204	29	113	6	23	4	0	1	3	1	0	1	2	24	2	1	7	.224	.265
2016	Trenton	.259	133	505	90	131	16	7	5	27	4	1	7	66	103	27	8	26	.352	.349
2017	Scranton/WB	.310	85	339	68	105	22	4	7	31	1	4	4	38	75	26	5	15	.382	.460
	YANKEES	.155	30	58	7	9	4	0	0	2	0	0	0	5	19	1	1	3	.222	.224
2018	YANKEES	.167	36	66	8	11	4	0	1	5	0	0	0	4	23	1	0	1	.214	.273
	Scranton/WB	.255	91	364	46	93	18	4	4	27	2	2	3	37	82	11	8	13	.328	.360
2019	YANKEES	.245	43	94	16	23	3	1	2	11	2	0	1	11	28	7	0	1	.330	.362
	Scranton/WB	.296	79	301	51	89	19	4	4	38	4	2	4	23	76	13	5	10	.352	.425
Minor League Totals		**.274**	**694**	**2672**	**426**	**733**	**124**	**30**	**24**	**218**	**21**	**17**	**29**	**296**	**589**	**143**	**56**	**128**	**.351**	**.370**
Major League Totals		**.197**	**109**	**218**	**31**	**43**	**11**	**1**	**3**	**18**	**2**	**0**	**1**	**20**	**70**	**9**	**1**	**5**	**.268**	**.298**

Selected by the Yankees in the fourth round of the 2013 First-Year Player Draft.

Wade's Postseason Record

Year	Club vs. Opp.	AVG	G	AB	R	H	2B	3B	HR	RBI	SH	SF	HP	BB	SO	SB	CS	E	OBP	SLG
2017	NYY vs. MIN (WC)				On Roster - Did Not Play															
2018	NYY vs. OAK (WC)				On Roster - Did Not Play															
2019	NYY vs. MIN (DS)				On Roster - Did Not Play															
POSTSEASON TOTALS		-	-	-	-	-	-	-	-	-	-	-	-	-	-	-	-	-	-	-

Wade's Career Fielding Record

Position	PCT	G	PO	A	E	TC	DP
Second Base	.981	59	66	85	3	154	24
Shortstop	1.000	13	3	8	0	11	0
Third Base	1.000	6	5	5	0	10	0
Outfield	.929	32	25	1	2	28	0

Wade's Career Home Run Chart
MULTI-HOMER GAMES: None. **TWO-HOMER GAMES:** None. **GRAND SLAMS:** None. **PINCH-HIT HR:** None. **INSIDE-THE-PARK HR:** None. **WALK-OFF HR:** None. **LEADOFF HR:** None.

Wade's Career Bests and Streaks
HITS: 3, 7/11/18 at BAL. **RUNS:** 2 - 2 times (last on 4/24/19 at LAA). **2B:** 1 - 11 times (last on 9/21/19 vs. TOR). **3B:** 1, 9/10/19 at DET. **HR:** 1 - 3 times (last on 9/20/19 vs. TOR). **RBI:** 2 - 4 times (last on 9/20/19 vs. TOR). **BB:** 2, 4/5/18 vs. BAL. **SO:** 3 - 3 times (last on 4/12/18 at BOS). **SB:** 2, 4/25/19 at LAA. **HIT STREAK:** 3g - 3 times (last from 9/15-21/19). **"WALK-OFF" HITS:** None.

Player of the Month: None   **Player of the Week:** None   **Rookie of the Month:** None

MIGUEL YAJURE • RHP

89

HT: 6-1 • **WT:** 175 • **BATS:** R • **THROWS:** R
BIRTHDATE: 5/1/98 • **OPENING DAY AGE:** 21
BIRTHPLACE: Cabimas, Venezuela
RESIDES: Cabimas, Venezuela
M.L. SERVICE: None (Rookie)

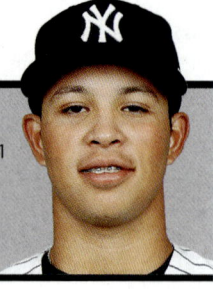

STATUS
- Signed by the Yankees as a non-drafted free agent on March 5, 2015.

2019
- Led all of minor league baseball in ERA (min. 125.0IP), going 9-6 with a 2.14 ERA (138.2IP, 119H, 48R/33ER, 30BB, 133K, 5HR) in 24 games (20 starts) between Single-A Tampa and Double-A Trenton…his 133 strikeouts ranked second among Yankees minor leaguers, while his nine wins were tied for third and his 138.2IP ranked fifth.
- Spent the majority of the season with Tampa, going 8-6 with a 2.26 ERA (127.2IP, 32ER) in 22 games (18 starts)…ranked among Florida State League pitchers in strikeouts (tied for second, 122), WHIP (second, 1.08) and average against (fourth, .233)…set career-highs with 10 strikeouts in two starts, 6/7 vs. Florida (6.0IP, 2H, 0R, 2BB) and 7/30 vs. Lakeland (7.0IP, 5H, 1R/0ER, 0BB)…was named a Florida State League Postseason All-Star.
- Earned a promotion to Trenton on 8/25, going 1-0 with a 0.82 ERA (11.0IP, 9H, 1ER, 2BB, 11K, 0HR) in two starts.
- Following the season, was named by *Baseball America* as having the "best control" among Yankees farmhands.
- Was added to the Yankees' 40-man roster on 11/20/19.

2018
- Missed the start of the season recovering from "Tommy John" surgery and made his first start with Single-A Charleston on 6/8 at Greenville.
- Spent the entire season with Charleston and went 4-3 with a 3.90 ERA (64.2IP, 64H, 38R/28ER, 15BB, 56K, 3HR) in 14 starts…tossed 5.0 hitless innings and struck out a season-high nine batters in his start on 6/14 vs. Asheville (1R/0ER, 1BB).

2017
- Missed entire season recovering from "Tommy John" surgery.

2016
- Spent the season with the GCL Yankees East, going 1-2 with a 2.87 ERA (31.1IP, 24H, 10ER, 5BB, 21K) in nine games (six starts).
- Held opposing batters to a .211 average (24-for-114), with right-handers batting just .163 (13-for-80) against him.

2015
- Made his professional debut with the DSL Yankees 2, posting an 0-2 record and 1.42 ERA (57.0IP, 54H, 20R/9ER, 20BB, 36K, 1HR) in 14 starts…had the sixth-lowest ERA among Dominican Summer League pitchers who threw at least 50.0IP.
- Recorded a 0.82 ERA (33.0IP, 27H, 9R/3ER, 9BB, 22K) over his final eight starts from 7/7-8/18, allowing one earned run or fewer in each of those starts.

PERSONAL
- Full name is Miguel Ángel Yajure (last name is pronounced zha-HOO-ray)

Yajure's Career Pitching Record

Year	Club	W	L	ERA	G	GS	CG	SHO	SV	IP	H	R	ER	HR	HP	BB	SO	WP	BK
2015	DSL Yankees 2	0	2	1.42	14	14	0	0	0	57.0	54	20	9	1	4	20	36	7	1
2016	GCL Yankees East	1	2	2.87	9	6	0	0	0	31.1	24	10	10	1	2	5	21	1	0
2017								Did Not Pitch - Injured											
2018	Charleston	4	3	3.90	14	14	0	0	0	64.2	64	38	28	3	0	15	56	3	2
2019	Tampa	8	6	2.26	22	18	1	0	0	127.2	110	47	32	5	7	28	122	9	1
	Trenton	1	0	0.82	2	2	0	0	0	11.0	9	1	1	0	0	2	11	1	0
Minor League Totals		**14**	**13**	**2.47**	**61**	**54**	**1**	**0**	**0**	**291.2**	**261**	**116**	**80**	**10**	**13**	**70**	**246**	**21**	**4**

Signed by the Yankees as a non-drafted free agent on March 5, 2015.

New York Community Bank

PROUDLY CALLING NEW YORK OUR HOME

— SINCE 1859 —

myNYCB.com • (877) 786-6560

NYCB — *Now Your* **COMMUNITY** *Bank*®

The strength behind the names you know!

©2020 New York Community Bank – Member FDIC

AACSB ACCREDITED

FAU

FLORIDA ATLANTIC UNIVERSITY
MBA IN SPORT MANAGEMENT
AVAILABLE ONLINE OR ON-CAMPUS IN BOCA RATON, FL

BEST ONLINE PROGRAMS — U.S. News — MBA PROGRAMS 2019

BEST GRAD SCHOOLS — U.S. News — BUSINESS PART-TIME MBA 2020

BEST ONLINE PROGRAMS — U.S. News — VETERANS MBA 2019

SportBusiness POSTGRADUATE COURSE RANKINGS 2019 — TOP 20 COURSE

WHY FAU MBASPORT?

- Extensive internship and employment opportunities and networking
- Complete the degree online or in sunny Boca Raton, FL
- Sport courses taught by seasoned industry practitioners
- Finish the program in 23 months
- GMAT/GRE waiver available based on credentials evaluation

PREVIOUS EMPLOYERS INCLUDE:

New York Yankees

Tampa Bay Lightning

Amalie Arena

University of South Florida

Florida Panthers

Miami Dolphins

FAU.EDU/MBASPORT • 561.297.6000

Contact us today to learn more about our curriculum, admissions, financial aid, and more!

2019 in Review

INF DJ LeMahieu was the 2019 AL Silver Slugger Award winner at 2B, setting career highs with 109R, 197H, 26HR and 102RBI in 145 games, and was the first player in Yankees history to make at least 25 starts at three different infield positions.

2019 Postseason Summary

PLAYOFF RETURN: The Yankees clinched the 55th playoff appearance in franchise history (117 seasons, 47.0%) with a 103-59 record...qualified for the postseason for the 21st time in 25 seasons since 1995 (missed in 2008, '13-14, '16).
- After sweeping Minnesota in their three-game ALDS, were eliminated by Houston in the ALCS, 4-games-to-2.
- Won their first four games of a postseason for the 11th time in franchise history...became the first team in postseason history to win each of their first four playoff games in a season by at least 4R...were the fifth team ever to win four straight playoff games by 4R-or-more and just the third to do it within one postseason: San Francisco (2012 NLCS/WS), Boston (2007 ALCS/WS), the Yankees (1936-37 WS) and the Yankees (1928-32 WS).
- Marked only the second postseason in franchise history that they won 3G by at least 6R, also the 1960 World Series vs. Pittsburgh.

BRONX BOMBERS: The Yankees' 15HR were hit by 10 different **Yankees batters**, tying the club record for a single postseason set in 1999 (Brosius, Curtis, Jeter, Knoblauch, Ledee, Leyritz, Martinez, Posada, Strawberry, Williams)...homered in all 9G, matching the longest postseason streak in Yankees history, done four times.

GLEYBER DAY: INF **Gleyber Torres** started at 2B in all nine Yankees postseason games, hitting .324 (12-for-37) with 8R, 5 doubles, 3HR and 10RBI...at 22 years, 303 days old, became the third-youngest Yankee to hit multiple postseason HRs, following Mickey Mantle (4HR prior to turning 22) and Tony Kubek (2HR prior to turning 22)...was the first Yankee (and eighth player ever) to hit 3HR in a postseason at age-22 or younger.
- Hit safely in 10 consecutive playoff games from 2018 ALDS Game 1 through 2019 ALCS Game 3, batting .378 (14-for-37) with 8R, 4 doubles, 3HR and 10RBI over the span...was the Majors' second-longest postseason hitting streak by a player age-22 or younger.
- In ALDS Game 3 at Minnesota, was 3-for-4 with 3R, 2 doubles, 1HR, 1RBI and 1SB...at 22y, 298d old, became the second player age-22 or younger in Major League history to record three extra-base hits in a postseason game and the seventh Yankee of any age to do so.
- In ALCS Game 1 at Houston, went 3-for-5 with 1R, 1 double, 1HR and 5RBI...tied the Yankees' ALCS RBI record set by Hideki Matsui, who did it twice (2004 ALCS Game 1 vs. Boston, 2004 ALCS Game 3 at Boston)...was 1RBI shy of the team's postseason record of 6RBI, shared by four players...at 22y, 303d old, became the third player age-22 or younger to record 5RBI in a postseason game...joined Atlanta's Andruw Jones (5RBI in 1996 World Series Game 1 at the Yankees at 19y, 180d old, and Chicago-NL's Addison Russell (6RBI) in 2016 World Series Game 6 at Cleveland at 22y, 283d.
- Hit fourth in ALCS Game 4 vs. Houston, the first cleanup hitter age-22 or younger in Yankees postseason history.

IN THE ALDS: The Yankees swept the Twins, 3-0, in the ALDS...swept the ALDS for the fifth time in franchise history (also 1998, '99, 2009 and '10).
- Outscored the Twins, 23-7, in the series...**Yankees batters** hit .293/.403/.525 (29-for-99) with 8 doubles, 5HR and 17BB in 3G, the fourth-highest OBP in Division Series history...their 7.67 runs/game average was the Majors' highest in a Division Series since the 2005 White Sox scored 24R in a three-game sweep of Boston (8.00)...hit .324/.442/.500 (11-for-34) with 3 doubles, 1HR and 6BB with RISP in the ALDS.
- The Yankees used the same lineup (by both batting order and fielding position) in all three games in the ALDS...had just one stretch during the regular season in which they used the same batting order in consecutive games (three straight from 9/6-8 at Boston).
- Eight of the Yankees' nine starting position players in the ALDS reached base at least five times, with only Gio Urshela (3-for-12) falling short.
- The Yankees' ALDS roster featured players born in 10 different countries: United States (14), Dominican Republic (3), Canada, Colombia, Cuba, Japan, México, The Netherlands, Nicaragua, Venezuela.

KEEPIN' IT 100: In Minnesota (101-61), the Yankees faced a 100-win team in the ALDS for the third straight postseason (2018 vs. Boston, 2017 vs. Cleveland).
- Became the first team ever to sweep a 100-win team in the Division Series...were the first team to sweep a 100-win opponent in the first round of the postseason since the 1980 Royals swept the Yankees, three-games-to-none, in the ALCS.

TWIN KILLING: The Yankees improved to 6-0 all-time in postseason series vs. Minnesota...also won the 2017 AL Wild Card Game (1-0), 2010 ALDS (3-0), 2009 ALDS (3-0), 2004 ALDS (3-1) and 2003 ALDS (3-1)...is their best postseason series record vs. any Major League club...the Twins have been their first opponent in six of their 13 postseason trips since 2003...are 16-2 (.889) all-time in postseason games against the Twins (8-2 at home, 8-0 on the road).
- Have won 13 consecutive postseason games vs. Minnesota (since 10/6/04), the longest postseason winning streak by any team vs. any single opponent in Baseball history.

PAX-10: LHP **James Paxton** made his postseason debut in ALDS Game 1 vs. Minnesota, allowing 3ER in 4.2IP...according to the YES Network, became the seventh Yankees pitcher to start the club's first postseason game *in his first season with the club*, joining CC Sabathia (2009 ALDS), David Cone (1995 ALDS), Jim Beattie (1978 ALCS), Don Gullett (1977 ALCS), Spec Shea (1947 World Series) and Bullet Joe Bush (1922 World Series).

LeMACHINE: INF **DJ LeMahieu** went 3-for-5 with 2R, 1 double, 1HR and 4RBI in ALDS Game 1...his sixth-inning solo HR marked his first career postseason HR and RBI...added a bases-clearing double in the seventh...his 3H matched his total from his first five career postseason games (3-for-20, 0R, 2 doubles, 0RBI w/ Colorado).
- Became the second player in Yankees history to record 4RBI in his first postseason game with the club, joining Bobby Abreu (4RBI in 2006 ALDS G1 vs. Detroit)...was the first player to record 3H in his first postseason game with the Yankees since Jason Giambi (3-for-4 with 1HR, 3RBI in 2002 ALDS G1 vs. Anaheim)...became the first Yankee with at least 3H and 4RBI in a postseason game since Robinson Canó (3-for-5, 1R, 2 doubles, 1HR, 6RBI in 2011 ALDS G1 vs. Detroit).
- Was the fourth Yankees leadoff hitter to collect 4RBI in a postseason game, joining Johnny Damon (4RBI in 2007 ALDS G3 vs. Cleveland), Hank Bauer (4RBI in 1958 World Series G3 vs. Milwaukee-NL) and Frankie Crosetti (4RBI in 1938 World Series G4 vs. Chicago-NL).

IN THE ALCS: The Yankees fell to the Astros, 4-games-to-2 in the ALCS...marked the Yankees' 17th trip to the ALCS, the most by any franchise...was the fourth postseason meeting of 100-win teams prior to the World Series in the last two seasons (also the Yankees vs. Boston in the 2018 ALDS, Boston vs. Houston in the 2018 ALCS and the Yankees vs. Minnesota in the 2019 ALDS), after there had not been any since the Yankees defeated Kansas City in the 1977 ALCS.

TANAKTOBER: RHP **Masahiro Tanaka** allowed 1H over 6.0 shutout innings (1BB, 4K) to earn the win in ALCS Game 1 at Houston...became the fourth pitcher in Yankees history to yield 1H-or-fewer over at least 6.0 shutout innings in a postseason game, joining Roger Clemens (9.0IP, 1H in 2000 ALCS Game 4 at Seattle), David Cone (7.0IP, 1H in 1999 World Series Game 2 at Atlanta) and Don Larsen (perfect game in 1956 World Series Game 5 vs. Brooklyn).
- Is 5-3 with a 1.76 ERA (46.0IP, 25H, 10R/9ER, 11BB, 37K, 4HR) in eight career postseason starts...is the fourth-lowest postseason ERA among pitchers with at least eight playoff starts since earned runs became an official stat in 1912.
- Was the first pitcher in Major League history to allow 2R-or-fewer in each of his first seven career postseason starts...also allowed 4H-or-fewer in all seven.

Postseason Game Summaries

Yankees def. Twins 3-games-to-0

GAME 1 – October 4, 2019 at Yankee Stadium

	1 2 3	4 5 6	7 8 9		R	H	E
MIN	1 0 1	0 1 1	0 0 0	-	4	7	1
NYY	0 0 3	0 2 2	3 0 x	-	10	8	1

WP: Tommy Kahnle; **LP**: Zack Littell; **SV**: None

HR: NYY — LeMahieu (inning: 6, 1 out, 0 on, off Stashak), Gardner (inning: 6, 2 out, 0 on, off Stashak). MIN — Polanco (inning: 1, 1 out, 0 on, off Paxton), Cruz (inning: 3, 2 out, 0 on, off Paxton), Sanó (inning: 6, 0 out, 0 on, off Kahnle).

The Yankees took a 1-0 series lead in the ALDS with a 10-4 win over Minnesota in Game 1 at Yankee Stadium…scored 10R in a postseason game for the first time since 2011 ALDS G4 at Detroit (10-1 win)…at 4 hours, 15 minutes, was the second-longest nine-inning postseason game in Yankees history, behind 2004 ALCS Game 3 at Boston (4:20)…was surpassed by ALCS Game 6 vs. Houston (4:19)…**LHP James Paxton** (4.2IP, 5H, 3ER, 1BB, 8K, 2HR) made his postseason debut and took a no-decision…**1B DJ LeMahieu** (3-for-5, 2R, 1 double, 1HR, 4RBI) hit a solo HR in the sixth, his first career postseason HR, and added a bases-clearing double in the seventh…**CF Brett Gardner** (1-for-4, 2R, 1HR, 1RBI) hit a solo HR in the sixth…**2B Gleyber Torres** (1-for-3, 1R, 1 double, 2RBI, 1BB, 1SB) hit a go-ahead two-run double in the fifth.

GAME 2 – October 5, 2019 at Yankee Stadium

	1 2 3	4 5 6	7 8 9		R	H	E
MIN	0 0 0	1 0 0	0 0 1	-	2	6	0
NYY	1 0 7	0 0 0	0 0 x	-	8	11	0

WP: Masahiro Tanaka; **LP**: Randy Dobnak; **SV**: None

HR: NYY — Gregorius (inning: 3, 1 out, 3 on, off Duffey).

The Yankees took a 2-0 series lead in the ALDS with an 8-2 win over Minnesota in Game 2 at Yankee Stadium…scored 7R in the third inning, their highest-scoring frame in the postseason since plating 7R in the eighth inning of their 2000 ALCS Game 2 win vs. Seattle…**RHP Masahiro Tanaka** (5.0IP, 3H, 1ER, 1BB, 7K, 1HP) earned his fourth career postseason win…**SS Didi Gregorius** (2-for-3, 1R, 1HR, 4RBI, 1BB) hit a grand slam in the third inning, the 12th in Yankees postseason history, the first since Robinson Canó in 2011 ALDS Game 1 vs. Detroit, and the first ever by a shortstop.

GAME 3 – October 7, 2019 at Target Field

	1 2 3	4 5 6	7 8 9		R	H	E
NYY	0 1 1	0 0 0	1 0 2	-	5	10	0
MIN	0 0 0	0 0 0	0 1 0	-	1	9	1

WP: Chad Green; **LP**: Jake Odorizzi; **SV**: Aroldis Chapman

HR: NYY — Torres (inning: 2, 1 out, 0 on, off Odorizzi), Maybin (inning: 9, 1 out, 0 on, off Romo). MIN — Rosario (inning: 8, 0 out, 0 on, off Britton).

The Yankees finished a three-game sweep in the ALDS with a 5-1 win at Minnesota in Game 3…**RHP Luis Severino** started and threw 4.0 scoreless innings (4H, 2BB, 4K)…**Yankees pitchers** held the Twins to 1-for-12 with RISP…**2B Gleyber Torres** (3-for-4, 3R, 2 doubles, 1HR, 1RBI, 1SB) hit his first career postseason HR in his first postseason multi-hit game…at 22 years, 298 days old, became the second player under the age of 23 in Major League history with 3XBH in a playoff game…**LF Cameron Maybin** (1-for-1) entered as a defensive replacement and hit his first career postseason HR.

2B Gleyber Torres hit his first career postseason homer as part of a 3-for-4 night in ALDS Game 3 at Minnesota…he also scored 3R, hit 2 doubles and stole a base in the game.

Astros def. Yankees 4-games-to-2

GAME 1 – October 12, 2019 at Minute Maid Park

	1 2 3	4 5 6	7 8 9		R	H	E
NYY	0 0 0	1 0 2	2 0 2	-	7	13	0
HOU	0 0 0	0 0 0	0 0 0	-	0	3	1

WP: Masahiro Tanaka; **LP**: Zack Greinke; **SV**: None

HR: NYY — Torres (inning: 6, 1 out, 0 on, off Greinke), Stanton (inning: 6, 2 out, 0 on, off Greinke), Urshela (inning: 9, 0 out, 0 on, off Abreu).

The Yankees claimed a 7-0 win in ALCS Game 1 at Houston…**RHP Masahiro Tanaka** allowed 1H over 6.0 shutout innings (1BB, 4K)…became the fourth pitcher in Yankees postseason history to allow 1H-or-fewer over at least 6.0 shutout innings (also Roger Clemens, David Cone and Don Larsen)…**2B Gleyber Torres** (3-for-5, 1R, 1 double, 1HR, 5RBI) had 3H for the second consecutive game and set a Yankees single-game RBI record for a player age-22 or younger…**LF Giancarlo Stanton** (2-for-4) and **3B Gio Urshela** (2-for-4) drove in the other 2R with solo HRs…**1B DJ LeMahieu** (2-for-4, 3R, 1BB) and **RF Aaron Judge** (2-for-5, 1SB) each contributed two of the team's 13H.
- Marked their largest shutout win ever in an ALCS game and their largest shutout win in the postseason since 1999 ALDS Game 1 vs. Texas (8-0)…was their largest shutout win on the road since 1961 World Series Game 4 at Cincinnati (7-0).

GAME 2 – October 13, 2019 at Minute Maid Park

	1 2 3	4 5 6	7 8 9	10 11	R	H	E
NYY	0 0 0	2 0 0	0 0 0	0 2	2	6	0
HOU	0 1 0	0 1 0	0 0 0	0 1	3	7	0

WP: Josh James; **LP**: J.A. Happ; **SV**: None

HR: NYY — Judge (inning: 4, 0 out, 1 on, off Verlander). HOU — Springer (inning: 5, 1 out, 0 on, off Ottavino), Correa (inning 11, 0 out, 0 on, off Happ).

The Yankees suffered their first postseason loss of 2019 with a 3-2, 11-inning defeat at Houston…**LHP James Paxton** (2.1IP, 4H, 1ER, 2BB, 3K) took a no-decision in his first career ALCS start…**RF Aaron Judge** (1-for-4, 1R, 1HR, 2RBI, 1BB) plated both runs with a two-run HR in the fourth…**CF/LF Brett Gardner** (2-for-5) had the Yankees' only multi-hit effort…**RHP Chad Green** (2.0IP, 2K) retired all 6BF…**RHP Tommy Kahnle** (2.1IP, 2K) retired all 7BF.
- The Yankees used eight relievers, a franchise record for a postseason game, who combined to allow 2ER over 7.2IP (3H, 4BB, 11K, 2HR, 1WP).

219

LHP James Paxton earned his first career postseason win in ALCS Game 5 vs. Houston, striking out nine batters and holding the Astros to 1R in 6.0IP.

GAME 3 – October 15, 2019 at Yankee Stadium

	1 2 3	4 5 6	7 8 9		R	H	E
HOU	1 1 0	0 0 0	2 0 0	-	4	7	0
NYY	0 0 0	0 0 0	0 1 0	-	1	5	1

WP: Gerrit Cole; **LP**: Luis Severino; **SV**: Roberto Osuna

HR: NYY — Torres (inning: 8, 1 out, 0 on, off Smith). HOU — Altuve (inning: 1, 1 out, 0 on, off Severino), Reddick (inning: 2, 0 out, 0 on, off Severino).

The Yankees returned to Yankee Stadium for ALCS Game 3 and lost, 4-1, to Houston…**RHP Luis Severino** (4.1IP, 5H, 2ER, 3BB, 6K, 2HR) started and took the loss…**2B Gleyber Torres** (1-for-2, 1R, 1HR, 1RBI, 2BB) supplied the Yankees' only run with an eighth-inning solo HR…**1B DJ LeMahieu** (2-for-5) had his third multi-hit effort in six postseason games…**RHP Luis Cessa** threw 2.0 scoreless innings (1H, 3K, 1HP) in his postseason debut.

GAME 4 – October 17, 2019 at Yankee Stadium

	1 2 3	4 5 6	7 8 9		R	H	E
HOU	0 0 3	0 0 3	0 1 1	-	8	8	1
NYY	1 0 0	0 0 2	0 0 0	-	3	5	4

WP: Ryan Pressly; **LP**: Masahiro Tanaka; **SV**: None

HR: NYY — Sánchez (inning: 6, 0 out, 1 on, off James). HOU — Springer (inning: 3, 0 out, 2 on, off Tanaka), Correa (inning: 6, 1 out, 2 on, off Green).

The Yankees lost their third straight game in the ALCS, an 8-3 defeat in Game 4 vs. Houston…at 4 hours, 19 minutes, it edged out ALDS Game 1 (4:15) for the second-longest nine-inning game in Yankees postseason history…was one minute shy of 2004 ALCS Game 3 at Boston (4:20)….**RHP Masahiro Tanaka** (5.0IP, 4H, 4R/3ER, 2BB, 1K, 1HR) suffered the loss…**C Gary Sánchez** (1-for-4) hit a two-run HR in the sixth…**CF Aaron Hicks** (1-for-3, 2BB) reached three times in his second start after missing two months due to injury…**LHP CC Sabathia** (0.2IP, 1HP) made the final appearance of his 19-year career…exited after three pitches to his fifth batter, George Springer, with a left shoulder subluxation…**Yankees fielders** committed 4E in a postseason game for the first time since 1976 ALCS Game 2 at Kansas City (5E).

GAME 5 – October 18, 2019 at Yankee Stadium

	1 2 3	4 5 6	7 8 9		R	H	E
HOU	1 0 0	0 0 0	0 0 0	-	1	5	0
NYY	4 0 0	0 0 x		-	4	5	0

WP: James Paxton; **LP**: Justin Verlander; **SV**: Aroldis Chapman

HR: NYY — LeMahieu (inning: 1, 0 out, 0 on, off Verlander), Hicks (inning: 1, 1 out, 2 on, off Verlander).

The Yankees extended the ALCS with a 4-1 win in Game 5 vs. Houston at Yankee Stadium…at 2 hours, 59 minutes, was their shortest postseason game since 2012 ALDS Game 5 vs. Baltimore (2:52)…**LHP James Paxton** (6.0IP, 4H, 1ER, 4BB, 9K, 1WP) earned his first career postseason win…his 112 pitches were the most by a Yankee in 2019 (regular or postseason)…was the first Yankee with at least 9K and 1R-or-fewer in a playoff game since CC Sabathia (9.0IP, 4H, 1ER, 2BB, 9K) in 2012 ALDS Game 5 vs. Baltimore and only the fourth Yankee to do it in a potential elimination game…**Yankees batters** scored all 4R and collected four of their 5H in the first inning…**1B DJ LeMahieu** (1-for-4) hit the seventh leadoff HR in Yankees history…**CF Aaron Hicks** (1-for-3) hit his second career postseason HR, a three-run shot in the first…after Hicks's HR, only 1-of-24 Yankees batters reached base…following **SS Didi Gregorius**'s (1-for-3) fourth-inning single, the final 13 Yankees batters were retired in order…**LHP Aroldis Chapman** (1.0IP, 1K) moved into a tie for seventh place on the all-time postseason saves list with his ninth.

▸ According to the *Elias Sports Bureau*, ALCS Game 5 was the first game in postseason history in which both teams scored in the first inning and neither team scored thereafter.

GAME 6 – October 19, 2019 at Minute Maid Park

	1 2 3	4 5 6	7 8 9		R	H	E
NYY	0 1 0	1 0 0	0 0 2	-	4	10	0
HOU	3 0 0	0 0 1	0 0 2	-	6	6	0

WP: Roberto Osuna; **LP**: Aroldis Chapman; **SV**: None

HR: NYY — Urshela (inning: 4, 1 out, 0 on, off Urquidy), LeMahieu (inning: 9, 1 out, 1 on, off Osuna). HOU — Gurriel (inning: 1, 2 out, 2 on, off Green), Altuve (inning: 9, 2 out, 1 on, off Chapman).

The Yankees were eliminated by the Astros with a 6-4 loss at Minute Maid Park…**RHP Chad Green** started the game as an "opener," allowing 3ER in 1.0IP (2H, 1HR, 1BB, 1K)…**3B Gio Urshela** (3-for-3, 2R, 1BB) hit a solo HR in the fourth to cut the deficit to 3-2…**LHP J.A. Happ** (2.0IP, 0H, 0R, 1BB), **RHP Luis Cessa** (2.0IP, 1H, 0R, 1K), **RHP Adam Ottavino** (1.0IP, 0H, 0R, 1K) and **LHP Zack Britton** (1.0IP, 1H, 0R, 2BB) each provided scoreless relief…trailing, 4-2, with one out in the ninth, **1B DJ LeMahieu** (1-for-5) hit a game-tying, two-run HR off Roberto Osuna for his third home run of the 2019 postseason…**LHP Aroldis Chapman** (0.2IP, 1H, 2ER, 1BB, 1K) took the loss after allowing a two-out, two-run "walk-off" HR to Jose Altuve in the ninth…marked the sixth "walk-off" home run allowed in Yankees postseason history and the second to end a series (Pittsburgh's Bill Mazeroski in 1960 World Series Game 7 off Ralph Terry).

2019 Regular Season Summary

EASTERN STANDARD: The Yankees clinched the 2019 AL East division title, their first since 2012…ended their third-longest drought (six seasons) in the Divisional Era (since 1969); also went 12 seasons from 1982-93 and seven seasons from 1969-75…are the fourth different AL East champion in the last six years (Baltimore–2014, Toronto–2015, Boston–2016-18).
- Is their third consecutive postseason berth and their 21st trip to the postseason in the last 25 years (since 1995)…is the 55th playoff appearance in franchise history (117 seasons, 47.0%).
- The only two Yankees to play for both the 2012 and 2019 AL East champions were **OF Brett Gardner** and **LHP CC Sabathia**.

TOP OF THE TABLE: The Yankees finished 7.0G ahead of Tampa Bay (96-66), their largest division title since 2009 (+8.0G)…clinched the division with their win on 9/19 vs. Los Angeles-AL, the second team to clinch a division in 2019 (Los Angeles-NL).
- With their win on 6/15, took possession of first place in the AL East and did not relinquish it over the final 106 days of the season…led the division by a season-high 11.5G at the end of play on 8/28, their largest lead since the end of play on 9/29/06 (12.0G).
- Started the season 5-8 and were 5.5G behind first-place Tampa Bay at the end of play on 4/12…marked the fewest games into a season they were at least 5.5G back since 4/14/84, when they were 3-6 and 5.5G behind Detroit (8-0).

KEEPIN' IT 100: The Yankees won 103 games, their most since 2009 (103-59)…have consecutive 100-win seasons (100-62 in 2018) for the second time in the last 41 years since 1979 (also 2002-04)…were one of a Major League-record four teams to win 100 games in 2019 (Houston, 107-55; Los Angeles-NL, 106-56; Minnesota, 101-61).
- Was their Major League-record 21st 100-win season in their 117-year history (17.9%)…only one other franchise has 10 such seasons (Philadelphia/Kansas City/Oakland Athletics-10)…join Houston (2017-19) as the only two clubs with multiple 100-win seasons this decade (since 2010).
- Had sole possession of the best record in Baseball as late as 9/14 (98-52)…was the latest in a season that they had the outright best record in the Majors since the end of play on 7/27/12 (*Elias*).

ABOVE BOARD: With a 103-59 (.636) record in 2019, the Yankees posted their 27th consecutive season with a winning record (1993-2019), the second-longest such stretch in Major League history, behind only the Yankees' own streak of 39 straight winning seasons from 1926-64.
- Reached 47G over .500 on 9/22 for the first time since ending the 1998 season with a 114-48 record (66G over).
- Their +204 run differential ranked third in the Majors.

THE HUNDREDS: Manager Aaron Boone became the first manager in Major League history to earn 100 wins in each of his first two seasons…with 203 wins, joins Ralph Houk (205 wins with the Yankees from 1961-62) as the only Major League managers to earn 200 wins over their first two career seasons at the helm.
- Joined Houk (three seasons, 1961-63) as the only Yankees managers to lead the team to postseason berths in each of his first two career seasons as a Major League skipper.

TO BE THE BEST: The Yankees went an AL-best 43-32 (.573) vs. opponents with records of .500 or better, second-highest in the Majors to Los Angeles-NL (45-32, .584).
- Went 23-18 (.561) vs. clubs that qualified for the postseason (12-7 vs. Tampa Bay, 4-2 vs. Minnesota, 2-1 vs. Los Angeles-NL, 3-4 vs. Houston, 2-4 vs. Oakland), including 15-5 at home.

FEAST ON THE EAST: The Yankees went 54-22 (.711) vs. the AL East, the best record ever by an AL East team within the division…broke the mark previously held by the 1998 Yankees (33-15, .688)…was the sixth-best record by any club vs. its own division in the Divisional Era (since 1969), behind the 2019 Astros (56-20, .737 vs. AL West), the 1994 Mariners (19-7, .731 vs. AL West), the 1995 Indians (37-14, .725 vs. AL Central), the 1995 Reds (35-14, .714 vs. NL Central) and the 1996 Cardinals (37-15, .712 vs. NL Central).
- Marked the most divisional wins by an AL East team in the six-division era (since 1994), breaking the mark set by the 2018 Red Sox (52-24).
- Compiled an 11-game winning streak vs. AL East opponents from 6/6-7/5, their longest since a 13-game streak from 5/26-7/3/99.
- Went 30-7 (.811) at home, their most home wins in the division in Division Era (since 1969)…after dropping their first series (1-2 vs. Baltimore, 3/28-31), won their final 11 series…swept six of the 12 series, including at least one vs. all four AL East opponents…won 11 straight home games vs. AL East teams from 7/16-8/14, their longest such winning streak since a 12-game streak from 6/1-7/22/04.
- Went 24-15 (.615) on the road, their best road mark in the division since going 24-13 in 2006.
- Won the season series over all four AL East opponents for the first time since 2006 (17-2 vs. Baltimore, 14-5 vs. Boston, 12-7 vs. Tampa Bay, 11-8 vs. Toronto).
- Went 49-37 outside the AL East: 18-15 vs. the AL Central, 19-14 vs. the AL West and 12-8 vs. the National League.

A BRONX TALE: The Yankees went 57-24 (.704) at Yankee Stadium, tying 2009 for their best single-season record at the current Yankee Stadium…also tied 2004 and '09 for their best home record mark in the last 21 seasons (since 1999)…was the Majors' third-best home record (Houston, 60-21, .741; Los Angeles-NL, 59-22, .728)…have won at least 50 home games in seven of their first 11 seasons at Yankee Stadium and in 14-of-19 in the Bronx since 2001.
- Posted a winning home record for the 28th consecutive season (1992-2019), the second-longest such streak in Major League history, trailing only the Yankees' 47-year streak of winning home records from 1918-64 (*Elias*).
- Did not lose any of their final 23 home series (20-0-3) after dropping their first three series of the season to Baltimore, Detroit and Chicago-AL through 4/14…marks their longest unbeaten-series streak at home since going 20-0-5 from 9/15/97-8/16/98…went 20-3-3 in 26 series, their first season with three-or-fewer home series losses since 1998 (21-2-6)…lost first three home series of a season for the first time since 1982.
- From 4/16-6/2, won eight consecutive home series, their second-longest streak of winning home series at the current Yankee Stadium (nine series from 6/10-8/11/11).
- Went 18-8 in home series openers…lost six of their last 10.
- Won nine consecutive home games from 7/31-8/14, the longest home winning streak in the AL in 2019…was their second home winning streak of at least 9G in the last nine seasons (since 2011), also an 11-game home winning streak from 4/21-5/9/18.

RAIN, RAIN, GO AWAY: The Yankees had 20 games affected by rain: 7 postponements, 7 pre-game delays, 6 in-game delays (including 2 games called early)…16 of the 20 occurred at Yankee Stadium.

SHORT STOP: The Yankees lost a season-high four straight games twice, from 4/8-12 and 8/18-22…were one of three Major League teams that did not lose five straight games in 2019 (Atlanta, Minnesota)…marked the first time since 2012 that they did not have a five-game losing streak.

DON'T CALL IT A COMEBACK: The Yankees tied for fourth in the Majors with 43 comeback wins, behind Los Angeles-NL (48), Philadelphia (45) and Oakland (44).

221

ROAD RULES: The Yankees went 46-35 (.568) on the road, tied for the Majors' sixth-best road record...tied for their second-best road mark in the last 13 seasons (since 2007), going 47-34 in 2018 and 46-35 in 2009...won a season-high seven consecutive road games from 5/12-25, tied for their longest road winning streak in 10 seasons since 2010...played 24 of their final 36G on the road (12-12).
- **Yankees batters** led the Majors with 503R and 6.21 runs/game on the road...was the Majors' fourth-highest run total since 1940, behind the 1996 Seattle Mariners (520R), 1996 Baltimore Orioles (511R) and 1999 Cleveland Indians (509R)...was their seventh season in club history with at least 500R on the road, first since 1939 (585R)...their 163HR on the road were the second-most in Major League history (2019 Twins, 170HR)...from 7/28-8/8, tied a club record by scoring at least 9R in five consecutive road games (fourth time, first since 9/14-29/74).
- **Yankees pitchers** posted a 5.01 road ERA, sixth-highest in the Majors in 2019, and fourth-highest in club history...from 8/23-9/7, held opponents to 6H-or-fewer in eight consecutive road games for the first time since at least 1908...were the first team to accomplish the feat since the 1968 Baltimore Orioles did so in 9G from 6/23-7/19/68.

LET'S PLAY TWO: The Yankees swept six of their seven doubleheaders (went 6-0-1), becoming the first team to sweep six doubleheaders in a season since Boston (7) and Pittsburgh (6) did so in 1979 (STATS, Inc.)...were the most by a Yankees club since 1973, when they swept 7-of-15 twinbills...last played as many as seven doubleheaders in 1982 (1-3-3)...are 7-0-4 in twin bills since the start of 2018.

WE WERE ON A BREAK: The Yankees went 57-31 (.648) before the break, their 24th consecutive season with a pre-All-Star record of .500-or-better (1996-2019)...was their fourth-best record at the All-Star break in the last 61 seasons (since 1959), behind 1998 (61-20, .753), 1980 (51-27, .654) and 2018 (62-33, .653).
- Had the AL's best record at the break for the first time since 2012 (52-33, .612)...trailed Los Angeles-NL (60-32, .652) for the best mark in the Majors.
- Were 46-28 (.622) after the All-Star break...was their 27th consecutive season with a winning record after the break (1993-2019)...is the second-longest such streak in Major League history, after their own 32-year streak from 1933-64.
- Their 53-28 record at the midway point of the season was their third-best mark through 81G in the last 61 seasons (since 1959), behind a 61-20 record in 1998 and 54-27 record in 2018...went 50-31 in the second half.

CALENDAR DAYS: The Yankees have recorded 13 consecutive winning calendar months (excl. March and October), tied with Houston for the longest active streak in the Majors...have not had a losing month since August 2017...is tied for their second-longest streak of winning full months since a 20-month streak from September 1996 to April 2000...also reeled off 13 straight months with a winning record from April 2001 to April 2003.
- Went 21-9 (.700) in August, their most wins in a calendar month since August 2009 (21-7)...tied for the most wins in a month in the Majors in 2019 (Minnesota, 21-8 in May)...with a Major League-best 20-7 record (.741) in May, had two of the Majors' six 20-win months in 2019, the only club with multiple 20-win months.

FAN FAVORITES: With a total home attendance of 3,304,404, the Yankees drew at least 3 million fans for the 21st consecutive year (1999-2019), extending their Major League record...had an average home attendance of 41,828 per date over 79 dates...hosted two single-admission doubleheaders...ranked third in the Majors in both average and total home attendance behind Los Angeles-NL (49,066 / 3,974,309) and St. Louis (42,968 / 3,480,393).
- Also led the AL in average road attendance (30,759), the only AL team above 30,000.

ROLL CALL: The Yankees used 54 players in 2019 (P-30, C-3, INF-14, OF-7), their most since 2015 (56)...trailed only Tampa Bay (57) among playoff teams, the only two teams with winning records to use at least 54 players.
- Had 22 position players make at least 10 starts, their second-highest total in club history (26 in 2013)...were the most by a 100-win team in Major League history (Elias)...three other 100-win teams had 20 players make 10 starts: 2019 Astros, 2018 Yankees, 2001 Athletics.
- 22 players made their Yankees debuts in 2019.
- 10 players remained on the active roster for the entire season: LeMahieu, Romine, Torres among position players, and Britton, Chapman, Cessa, Happ*, Kahnle, Ottavino and Tanaka* among pitchers (* - Happ and Tanaka each spent three days on the paternity list).

WELCOME TO THE SHOW: The Yankees used 13 rookies in 2019, including six who made their Major League debuts (*): Chance Adams, Nestor Cortes Jr., Thairo Estrada*, Mike Ford*, Joseph Harvey*, Ben Heller, Michael King*, Brady Lail*, Jonathan Loaisiga, Joe Mantiply, Adonis Rosa*, Stephen Tarpley, Breyvic Valera...marked their second straight season with just six MLB debuts.

MISSING IN ACTION: The Yankees placed 30 different players on the I.L. for a total of 39 I.L. stints, both the highest single-season totals on record for any Major League team...accounted for a total of 2,129 player-games missed...seven players made multiple I.L. trips: Sabathia (4), Andújar (2), Betances (2), Hicks (2), Sánchez (2), Stanton (2), Voit (2).
- Utilized the 60-day I.L. 16 times...four players began the year on the I.L. before making their season debuts in September (Betances, Heller, Montgomery, Severino)...Ellsbury spent the entire season on the I.L. for the second consecutive year.

NATIONAL ENQUIRERS: The Yankees went 12-8 (.600) against the National League, facing the Mets and all five NL West clubs...have posted a winning record in 19-of-23 Interleague season series since the advent of Interleague play in 1997 (19-3-1).
- Went 6-4 at home and 6-4 on the road.
- Went 2-2 against the Mets...have won or split six consecutive season series since 2014...with a 71-51 record in the Subway Series, have the most victories by any team over a single opponent in Interleague history (next-most: Los Angeles Angels, 70-54 vs. Los Angeles Dodgers).
- Took 2-of-3 from the Dodgers in Los Angeles in August, improving to 8-8 all-time against them...have at least a .500 all-time record against every NL team (are also 15-15 vs. Philadelphia).

SWEEPSTAKES: The Yankees recorded 12 series sweeps for the second consecutive season, matching 2018 for their most since 2009 (14)...swept four-game series at Baltimore (5/20-23), vs. Baltimore (8/12-14) and vs. Boston (8/2-4)...was their first 4G sweep over Boston since 8/6-9/09.
- Swept five of their six series vs. Baltimore, the first time they have recorded at least five sweeps over one opponent in a season since 1957 (six vs. Kansas City A's).

SURVEY SAYS...: The Yankees' 69.6% success rate on replay challenges was second-highest in the Majors in 2019 (23 challenges: 16 overturned, 0 confirmed, 7 stand)...were the only club not to have a challenge confirmed, while their seven non-overturned challenges were fewest in the Majors.

2019 HOPE WEEK: The Yankees celebrated the 10th Anniversary of HOPE Week from 6/17-21...went 5-0 during the week, completing the fourth HOPE Week sweep in its 11-year history (also 5-0 in 2009 and '16; 4-0 in '14)...outscored opponents, 35-11, hitting multiple HRs in all 5G and posting a 2.20 ERA (45.0IP, 11ER).
- Are 38-13 (.745) all-time during HOPE Week, having won seven consecutive HOPE Week games (since 6/14/18).

BRONX BOMBERS: Yankees batters hit 306HR, the second-highest home run total in Major League history…joined the 2019 Minnesota Twins (307HR) as the first two clubs to hit 300HR in one season…broke the previous club record (267HR in 2018) in their 144th game on 9/8 at Boston (Aaron Judge's fifth-inning solo HR).

- Hit 143HR at home and 163HR on the road…joined the 2019 Twins (170HR) as the first two teams in Major League history to hit at least 140 HRs on the road.
- Set a Major League record by homering in 139 games, one of three teams in 2019 to top the previous record of 131 games shared by the 2018 and 2012 Yankees…HRs by game: 0HR (23G), 1HR (54G), 2HR (41G), 3HR (21G), 4HR (13G), 5HR (6G), 6HR (3G), 7HR (1G)…set a Major League record with 23 games with at least 4HR.
- HRs by position: C (38HR), 1B (27HR), 2B (22HR), 3B (32HR), SS (43HR), LF (29HR), CF (34HR), RF (37HR), DH (40HR), PH (4HR)…the 43HR by shortstops were a club record and fifth-most in Major League history…the 38HR by catchers were a club record…hit 100HR as an outfield for the first time in club history.
- Hit a Major League-record 223HR batting right-handed, and 83HR batting left-handed.
- Scored 51.1 percent of their runs on home runs (482-of-943), the fourth-highest rate in the Majors (Toronto-53.2%, Milwaukee-51.5%, Minnesota-51.2%)…hit 178 solo HRs, 87 two-run HRs, 34 three-run HRs and 7 grand slams.
- Their 74HR in 30G in August set a Major League record for home runs in a calendar month…broke the previous record of 58HR, shared by Baltimore in May 1987 (28G) and Seattle in May 1999 (27G)…Minnesota (59HR in August 2019) also surpassed the old mark…the previous club record was 54HR (August 1998, July 1940).
- Hit 52HR in 25G in September, second-most in the Majors behind Houston's 58HR (MLB record for September)…tied the previous mark (52HR by Toronto in September 2010)…led the Majors with 126HR in 56G since the start of August (next-most: Houston-111HR).
- Hit 4HR in March (3G), 42HR in April (26G), 45HR in May (27G), 47HR in June (26G), 42HR in July (25G), 74HR in August (30G) and 52HR in September (25G).
- Hit 157 home runs after the All-Star break, the most in Major League history (prev. 127HR, by Oakland in 1999 and Minnesota in 1963)…hit 149HR before the break.

RAKER'S DOZEN: The Yankees set a Major League record with 14 players with 10HR…were the third team ever with at least 12 players with 10HR (also the 2019 Blue Jays-13 and 2018 Yankees-12).

- Had seven players with at least 20HR (Torres, Sánchez, Gardner, Judge, LeMahieu, Voit, Urshela), matching the club record for players reaching the mark (also 2009)…also tied a club record with five players with at least 25HR…for the second straight year, had at least 20HR from all nine spots in the lineup (credit: YES Network); the Twins are the only other franchise to do it ever (2019).
- The Yankees had 22 different players homer for the fourth time in franchise history (23 in 2013, 22 in 2000 and 22 in 1965).

DOUBLE-DIPPING: Yankees batters recorded 28 multi-HR games in 2019, the second-highest total in Major League history (Minnesota-33 in 2019)…broke their previous club record of 24 (2018, 1961).

- Recorded 12 individual multi-HR games in August, setting a Major League record for a calendar month (previously Minnesota-9 in June 2019)…also became the first team in Major League history to have eight different players collect a multi-HR game in one month (credit: Elias) – Torres (4), Urshela (2), Ford, Gregorius, Higashioka, LeMahieu, Sánchez, Tauchman…had just 12 multi-HR games as a team from March-July, and four in September.
- Got multi-HR games from all nine spots in the order, and from every position, with at least two from every position but second base.

TATER TROTS: Yankees batters set a Major League record by hitting a home run in 31 consecutive games from 5/26-6/30…broke the previous record of 27 consecutive games, by Texas from 8/11-9/9/02…the Yankees' previous record was a 25-game HR streak from 6/1-29/41…14 different Yankees hitters combined to hit 57HR during the streak, their highest HR total in a team homer streak…hit multiple HRs in 17 of the 31G: 4HR (3x), 3HR (3x), 2HR (11x), 1HR (14x).

- Tied a Yankees record by hitting multiple HRs in nine consecutive games from 8/3 (G1) to 8/10 (hit 29HR)…first accomplished the feat from 5/15-23/09…fell 1G shy of the Major League record of 10G, set by Baltimore from 7/17-27/19.
- With 5HR on 8/5, 6HR on 8/6, and 5HR on 8/7 at Baltimore, became the second team in Major League history to hit at least 5HR in three consecutive games, joining the 1977 Red Sox (6/17-19/77 vs. the Yankees)…the 16HR tied the Major League record for a three-game series, also set by Boston vs. the Yankees from 6/17-19/77…surpassed the club record of 15HR set from 7/31-8/2/07 vs. Chicago-AL.
- Set a Major League record for home runs over a four-game stretch with 19HR from 8/5-8 (5, 6, 5, 3)…tied the Major League record for a five-game stretch from 8/4-8 (2, 5, 6, 5, 3) and 8/5-9 (5, 6, 5, 3, 2).

BLANK SPACE: The Yankees scored a run in 220 consecutive games, between shutouts on 6/30/18 vs. Boston (11-0 loss) and 9/2/19 vs. Texas (7-0 loss)…was the Majors' second-longest streak in the Modern Era (since 1900), behind only a 308-game streak by the Yankees from 8/3/1931-8/2/1933.

- During the streak, there were 368 shutouts in the Majors, including 10 thrown by Yankees pitchers…28 of the 29 other Major League teams were shut out at least seven times (Oakland-3x)…Miami (26x) and Detroit (21x) were both blanked more than 20 times in that span…there were also four no-hitters…as a team, hit .263/.338/.474 (1,980-for-7,530) with 362 doubles, 26 triples and 392HR during the streak, while scoring 1,247 runs (5.67 runs/game)…scored at least 10 runs 29 times during the streak…had a 137-83 (.623) record.
- Only twice during the streak were they held scoreless into the ninth inning…in a 2-1 loss on 7/13/19 vs. Toronto, DJ LeMahieu and Aaron Judge hit back-to-back two-out singles to score Aaron Hicks…in a 4-1 loss on 8/4/18 at Boston: Giancarlo Stanton and Didi Gregorius hit back-to-back doubles with two outs (Stanton's double came on a 1-2 pitch).

SWINGING AWAY: Yankees batters led the Majors with 943 runs scored, the most by any Major League team since the 2007 Yankees (968R)…led the Majors with 5.82 runs/game, their fourth-highest scoring average over a full season since 1940 (excl. strike seasons), behind 5.98 in 2007, 5.96 in 1998 and 5.90 in 1950.

- Hit .267/.339/.490 as a team with 290 doubles, 17 triples, 306HR, 904RBI and 569BB…their franchise-record .490 SLG was the fourth-highest in Major League history behind the 2019 Astros (.495), 2019 Twins (.494) and 2003 Red Sox (.491)…broke the club mark of .489 set in 1927…set a club record with 613 extra-base hits, fourth-most in 2019 and sixth-most in Major League history.
- Scored double-digit runs in 25 games, second-most in the Majors (Houston-27).
- Were shut out a Major League-low two times (9/2 vs. Texas, 9/25 at Tampa Bay).
- From July-September, hit .300/.369/.588 vs. left-handed pitching, the Majors' highest OBP, SLG and OPS (.957) in that span…from March-June, had hit .236/.314/.394, ranking 24th in OPS (.707).

EXIT VELO CITY: Yankees batters had 99 batted balls with exit velocities of at least 110.0 mph this season (Statcast), third-most in the Majors (Minnesota-112, Chicago-NL-108)…had a Major League-best 35HR with exit velocities of 110.0 mph or higher.

RISP-Y BUSINESS: Yankees batters led the Majors with a .294 BA (374-for-1271) and .518 SLG with runners in scoring position…was their third-highest BA with RISP in the 46 seasons since 1974 that it has been tracked (.300 in 1998, .298 in 1997).
- **INF DJ LeMahieu** led the Majors with a .389 BA (49-for-126) with RISP, while **INF Gleyber Torres** (.344, 44-for-128) ranked 10th (sixth in AL).

PACK YOUR BAGS: With the bases loaded in 2019, **Yankees batters** hit .361/.390/.609 (48-for-133) with 10 doubles, 1 triple and 7HR…was their second-highest BA with the bases loaded in club history (.371 in 1976), and the highest OPS (.999)…led the AL and ranked second in the Majors to Colorado (.389).
- **INF DJ LeMahieu** (.667, 10-for-15) and **INF Gio Urshela** (.625, 5-for-8) ranked first and second in the Majors in BA with the bases loaded.

THE SANCHINO: C Gary Sánchez hit three, two-run HRs on 4/7 vs. Baltimore, his first career three-homer game and the only 3HR game by a Yankee in 2019…at 26 years, 126 days, was the youngest Yankee to hit 3HR in a game since Bobby Murcer (24 years, 35 days) on 6/24/70-G2 vs. Cleveland.

HOMER BOTH WAYS: From 5/31-6/16, the Yankees became the first team in Major League history to both hit and allow home runs in 15 consecutive games, breaking Philadelphia's record of 14G from 5/17-31/2006.

LONDON SERIES: On 6/29 and 6/30, the Yankees and Red Sox played a two-game series at London Stadium, site of the 2012 Olympic Games…were the first two Major League games ever played in Europe…marked the Yankees' first games played outside the U.S. or Canada since opening the 2004 season against Tampa Bay at the Tokyo Dome in Japan.
- Won, 17-13, on 6/29…the teams combined for 30 runs on 37 hits, including 10 doubles and 6HR, in the second-highest-scoring game in series history…marked the first time the Yankees scored and allowed at least 13R in the same game since a 14-13 win on 5/16/06 vs. Texas…was the second nine-inning game in the Majors in the last 11 seasons (since 2009) in which both teams collected at least 18H (also Arizona at Colorado on 9/22/13)…both teams scored 6R in the first inning, the first game in which both teams did so since 6/23/89 (Toronto at Oakland)…was the first game in which both the Yankees' and their opponents' starting pitchers were knocked out in the first inning since 9/5/72 at Baltimore (Doc Medich/Dave McNally)…at 4 hours, 42 minutes, was the third-longest nine-inning game in Major League history, behind Yankees-Red Sox games at Fenway Park on 8/18/06-G2 (4 hours, 45 minutes) and 9/14/07 (4 hours, 43 minutes).
- Won, 12-8, on 6/30…became the first team to sweep a two-game series despite allowing at least 21R since 9/23-24/85, when Montreal defeated the Chicago Cubs at Wrigley Field, 10-7, and 17-15.

BLASTING OFF: The Yankees both hit and allowed leadoff HRs in a game for the seventh time in franchise history on 7/21 vs. Colorado, as Charlie Blackmon homered on the second pitch of the game off James Paxton, and **INF DJ LeMahieu** homered on the first pitch of the bottom of the first off German Márquez…also accomplished the feat on 8/17/2006 vs. Baltimore (Johnny Damon and Brian Roberts-BAL), 8/1/2001 vs. Texas (Chuck Knoblauch and Michael Young-TEX), 7/27/1985 at Texas (Rickey Henderson and Oddibe McDowell-TEX), 8/15/1980 at Baltimore (Willie Randolph and Al Bumbry-BAL), 9/3/1955 vs. Washington-AL (Hank Bauer and Eddie Yost-WSH) and 6/25/1920 vs. Boston (Roger Peckinpaugh and Harry Hooper-BOS).

OPENING ACT: The Yankees used an 'opener' in 20 games, going 13-7 in those contests…won the first 11 before going 2-7 in the last nine…openers posted a 5.72 ERA (28.1IP, 38H, 21R/18ER, 9BB, 41K, 8HR), recording scoreless appearances in 12 outings.

- **RHP Chad Green** made 15 starts as an opener (11-4 team record), posting a 3.72 ERA (19.1IP, 4ER on 6/30 at Boston in London); **RHP Jonathan Holder** (2.2IP, 2ER on 8/6 at Baltimore); **LHP Nestor Cortes Jr.** (2.1IP, 4R/2ER on 9/10 at Detroit); **LHP Jordan Montgomery** (2.0IP, 0R on 9/24 at Tampa Bay); **RHP Jonathan Loaisiga** (1.0IP, 2ER on 9/25 at Tampa Bay).

PEN PALS: Yankees relievers had a 4.08 ERA, ninth-lowest in the Majors but their highest since 2007 (4.37)…ranked fifth with 750K, 3K shy of their club record (753K in 2018)…struck out 26.4% of batters, third-highest in the Majors…threw a club-record 664.2IP, seventh-most in the Majors…also set club records with 610H, 267BB, 96HR and 61GIDP.
- Tied for second in the Majors with 50 saves, their most since 2012 (51)…tied a club record with 25 blown saves (also 1997)…had just two saves (both by Chapman) in their final 37 games of the season after recording 48 saves in their first 125 games.
- Used a club-record 30 different pitchers in relief (previously 26 relievers, in 2011, '14, '15), including the first career relief appearances by **LHP CC Sabathia** and **RHP Masahiro Tanaka**.

THE FOUR HORSEMEN: The Yankees were the first team in Major League history to have four pitchers each make at least 60 appearances and limit opponents to a .200 BA or lower, with **LHP Zack Britton** (.182 in 66G), **LHP Aroldis Chapman** (.185 in 60G), **RHP Tommy Kahnle** (.200 in 72G) and **RHP Adam Ottavino** (.198 in 73G).
- The quartet combined to hold batters to a .192/.289/.299 (168-for-876) line while posting a 2.41 ERA (246.0IP, 168H, 75R/66ER, 117BB, 314K, 20HR) in 271 appearances.

NEW YORK STATE OF MIND: Four pitchers born in New York state pitched for the Yankees in 2019: **RHP Dellin Betances** (born in New York City), **RHP Tommy Kahnle** (Latham), **RHP Michael King** (Rochester) and **RHP Adam Ottavino** (New York City)…marked the first time that four New York natives pitched for the club in the same season since 1965 (Whitey Ford, Mike Jurewicz, Pete Mikkelsen, Bill Stafford).

SEEING RED: The Yankees went 14-5 vs. Boston (8-1 at Yankee Stadium, 4-4 at Fenway, 2-0 in London)…were the most defeats any team has handed the Red Sox in one season since Detroit went 15-3 against them in 1973…were just the fifth team to win at least 14 games over Boston in the Expansion Era: 1973 Tigers (15-3), 1965 Twins (17-1), 1965 White Sox (14-4), 1964 White Sox (14-4)…were their most wins vs. Boston since going 15-7 in 1960.
- Have won seven consecutive home series over the Red Sox (since 8/31/17), their longest such streak since an eight-series streak from 6/3/60-7/26/62…went 8-1 at home vs. Boston, their most home wins over the Red Sox since going 8-1 in 2001.
- Yankees pitchers permitted 44R in 4G at Boston from 7/25-28, the most runs allowed in a series of 4G-or-fewer by either pitching staff in the rivalry's history.

GAME OF THRONES: The Yankees are 56-31 (.644) against reigning AL champions since 2010, when they were the defending AL (and World Series) champions themselves…went 14-5 vs. Boston in 2019, 5-2 vs. Houston in 2018, 2-5 vs. Cleveland in 2017, 5-2 vs. Kansas City in 2016, 4-2 vs. Kansas City in 2015, 12-7 vs. Boston in 2014, 3-3 vs. Detroit in 2013, 4-3 vs. Texas in 2012 and 7-2 vs. Texas in 2011.

CASHING IN: Yankees Senior VP/GM Brian Cashman led the Yankees to the 2,000th regular season win of his tenure as General Manager on 4/7 at Baltimore…the club has a Major League-best .589 winning percentage (2,098-1,462-2) over 3,562 games in Cashman's tenure (since 2/3/98), with 120 more wins than the second-best team (Boston: 1,978-1,585).

O' YEAH!: The Yankees went 17-2 vs. Baltimore, their most wins vs. a single opponent since going 17-5 vs. the Kansas City A's in 1959…was their third-best record vs. an opponent in a season (min. 15G), behind 21-1 vs. St. Louis-AL in 1927 and 18-2 vs. Philadelphia-AL in 1919…were one of three teams in 2019 to win at least 17 games over one opponent, joining Cleveland (18-1 vs. Detroit) and Houston (18-1 vs. Seattle).
- Won their final 16 games against Baltimore, tied for their third-longest winning streak vs. a single opponent in franchise history…was their longest since a 19-game winning streak over the Philadelphia A's from 1938-39…their last longer single-season streak was a franchise-record 21-game winning streak over the St. Louis Browns in 1927.
- **Yankees batters** hit 61HR vs. Baltimore in 2019, setting a Major League record for home runs vs. one opponent in a single season…broke the previous mark of 48HR by the Yankees vs. Kansas City A's in 1956…their 151R were their second-most vs. one opponent in the divisional era (since 1969), trailing their 154R in 2017 vs. Baltimore…hit .303/.386/.632 (204-for-673) with 34 doubles, 2 triples, 61HR and 88BB vs. the O's in 2019.
- Had 12 individual multi-HR games vs. Baltimore (Torres-5, Frazier-2, Higashioka-1, Judge-1, Sánchez-1, Tauchman-1, Urshela-1), setting a Major League record for the most individual multi-HR games vs. one opponent in a season…broke the previous mark of 10 by San Francisco vs. Los Angeles-NL in 1958…10 of those multi-HR games came at Camden Yards, breaking the Major League record for a team at any road park in a season, previously held by the 1958 Giants, who had eight at the L.A. Coliseum (credit: STATS, LLC).
- Their nine-game multi-HR streak vs. Baltimore from 5/20-8/12(G2) was the longest vs. one opponent in franchise history (prev. 8G, done three times).
- From 8/5-13, scored at least 8R in six consecutive games vs. Baltimore, their longest streak vs. one opponent since a six-game streak vs. Washington-AL from 7/1-8/9/56.
- Hit 13HR off RHP David Hess, tied for their second-most against one pitcher in a season in club history (15HR off Cleveland's Jim Perry in 1960, 13HR off Washington-AL's Camilo Pascual in 1956)…was tied for the third-most HRs by one team off a pitcher in Major League history (also trailed Cleveland's 14HR off Detroit's Fred Hutchinson in 1948).

CHARMED LIFE: The Yankees went 10-0 at Baltimore's Camden Yards, becoming the second team since 1955 to go 10-0 or better at a ballpark in one season (Boston, 10-0 at Tampa Bay's Tropicana Field in 2002).
- Have won 15 straight games at Camden Yards (since 7/11/18), a franchise-best road winning streak at any opponent…is tied for the second-longest winning streak by an AL team all-time, behind Boston's 18-game winning streak at the Yankees from 10/3/1911 (G1) to 6/2/1913 (G2), which included one tie.
- **Yankees batters** hit 43HR in 10G at Camden Yards in 2019, setting a Major League record for home runs hit by a visiting team in a ballpark…broke the record previously held by the Milwaukee Braves (29HR at Cincinnati's Crosley Field in 1957).
- Had 5G with at least 5HR at Camden Yards, marking the first time in Major League history that a team has had five 5HR games vs. one opponent in a single season…were the first team ever to record more than 2G with 5HR in an opponent's park in one season (5G)…from 4/4-5/22, became the first Major League team ever to hit at least 3HR in six straight games at at any park (credit: STATS, LLC).
- Hit 16HR at Baltimore from 8/5-7, tying the Major League record for a three-game series, set by Boston vs. the Yankees at Fenway Park from 6/17-19/77…surpassed the previous club record of 15HR set from 7/31-8/2/07 vs. Chicago-AL…had six different players homer on 8/6 at Baltimore, tied for their second-highest total in a game in franchise history, behind a club-record seven players on 7/31/07 vs. Chicago-AL.

- On 4/7 at Baltimore, hit 7HR in a game for the fifth time in franchise history, also 7/31/2007 vs. Chicago-AL (8HR), 6/28/1939-G1 at Philadelphia-AL (8HR), 5/30/1961 at Boston (7HR) and 6/3/1932 at Philadelphia-AL (7HR)…**DH Gary Sánchez** (3HR) and **LF Clint Frazier** (2HR) became the fourth pair of Yankees teammates to combine for 5HR in a game, the first since 7/28/40-G1 at Chicago-AL (Charlie Keller-3HR, Joe DiMaggio-2HR)…marked the only 3HR game by a Yankee in 2019.

UN-RIOLE: INF **Gleyber Torres** hit 13HR vs. Baltimore, the most by any player vs. a single opponent in one season in the divisional era (since 1969), surpassing Chicago-NL's Sammy Sosa (12HR in 1998 vs. Milwaukee)…is one of six players ever to hit at least 13HR vs. a single opponent in a season…in 18 games vs. Baltimore, hit .394/.467/1.045 (26-for-66) with 22R, 4 doubles, 13HR, 20RBI and 9BB…was the third Yankee since 1943 to record at least 17 extra-base hits vs. one opponent in a season, joining Roger Maris, who had 18XBH in 1961 vs. Chicago-AL (4 doubles, 1 triple, 13HR), and Mickey Mantle, who had 18XBH in 1957 vs. Chicago-AL (8 doubles, 3 triples, 7HR).
- Had five multi-HR games vs. Baltimore in 2019, setting a Major League record for multi-HR games vs. one opponent in a season…broke the mark of four, previously held by Roy Sievers (1955 vs. Kansas City A's), Gus Zernial (1951 vs. St. Louis-AL) and Ralph Kiner (1947 vs. Boston-AL).
- Along with **C Gary Sánchez** (10HR), became the second pair of teammates in Major League history to hit double-digit home runs against the same opponent in the same season, joining the 1927 Yankees' Lou Gehrig and Babe Ruth, who both hit 11HR vs. Boston…their 23 combined home runs are the most vs. one opponent in a season in Major League history.

ZERO TO 500 REAL QUICK: The Yankees earned their 500th regular season win at the current Yankee Stadium on 4/1 vs. Detroit…were the quickest team to reach 500 wins at a new stadium (in terms of decisions) since the Atlanta Braves went 500-305 from 1997-2006 to begin their stay at Turner Field…the all-time record for fewest losses at a stadium at the time of a team's 500th win was set by the Yankees at the original Yankee Stadium (500-264).
- Since Yankee Stadium opened in 2009, the Yankees' 555-336 (.623) home record is the best in Baseball.

SERIES-LY SPEAKING: The Yankees won nine consecutive series from 5/3-6/2, their longest such streak since a nine-series winning streak from 7/20-8/20/98.

HIST-0-RY: When **RHP Adam Ottavino** faced Royals RF Terrance Gore to begin the seventh inning on 4/19 vs. Kansas City, it marked the first time in Major League history that a pitcher wearing No. 0 faced a batter wearing No. 0 (credit: MLB).

FIRST IMPRESSION: On 5/27, the Yankees hosted San Diego for the first time at the current Yankee Stadium (since 2009), as the Padres became the 29th and final different opponent to play there…defeated the Padres, 5-2.
- Went 24-5 in opponents' first-ever games at the current Yankee Stadium, winning each of their final 11 such games (Milwaukee in 2011; Cincinnati and Atlanta in 2012; Arizona, Los Angeles-NL and San Francisco in 2013; Chicago-NL and Pittsburgh in 2014; Miami in 2015; St. Louis in 2017; San Diego in 2019)…went 14-2 vs. NL opponents' debuts, losing to only Philadelphia in 2009 and Colorado in 2011.

G&G UNIT: On 6/19 vs. Tampa Bay and 6/20-21 vs. Houston, **C Gary Sánchez** and **INF Gleyber Torres** became the first pair of teammates in Yankees history to homer in three consecutive games together.

BOMBS IN THE BRONX: On 8/15 at Yankee Stadium, the Yankees (3HR) and Indians (7HR) combined to hit 10HR, a record for a Yankees home game (credit: *Elias*)...the previous record for the current Yankee Stadium was 9HR, set on 6/20/12 vs. Atlanta (Yankees-4HR, Braves-5HR)...were the most in any Yankees game since 6/23/50, when the Yankees (6HR) and Detroit (5HR) combined for 11HR at Tiger Stadium.

CAN'T TOUCH THIS: Yankees pitchers recorded 42K in a 3G series vs. Toronto from 9/20-22, their most ever in a three-game series without any extra-inning games...was their third three-game set with at least 42K, also 43K in 31.0IP from 8/6-8/18 at Chicago-AL and 42K in 36.0IP from 5/5-7/17 at Chicago-NL.

NEXT MAN UP, LITERALLY: In a 12-inning loss at Tampa Bay on 9/24, the Yankees used 26 players (15 position players, 11 pitchers)...*Elias* confirms that it was the fourth time in franchise history they have used more than 25 players in a game, also doing so on 9/22/12 vs. Oakland (26), 9/28/11 at Tampa Bay (27) and 9/29/56 vs. Boston (26), all extra-inning contests...the 11 pitchers used tied a franchise record, first set on 9/28/11 at Tampa Bay...a club-record nine different pitchers recorded at least 1K.

HEY NOW, YOU'RE AN ALL-STAR: The Yankees placed five players on the 2019 AL All-Star team: **LHP Aroldis Chapman** (player vote), **INF DJ LeMahieu** (fan vote) **C Gary Sánchez** (fan vote) and **INF Gleyber Torres** (player vote) were elected, while **RHP Masahiro Tanaka** was named a replacement...marked the third straight year they had at least four players selected.

▸ All five appeared in the game: Tanaka (1.0IP, 1H, 1K) tossed a scoreless second inning to earn the win, the fifth Yankees pitcher to record a win in the All-Star Game, joining Lefty Gomez (three: 1933, '35, '37), Spud Chandler (1942), Spec Shea (1947) and Vic Raschi (1948)...Chapman (1.0IP, 3K) recorded his first career All-Star save, the eighth by a Yankee (Mariano Rivera-4, Bob Grim, Joe Page, Vic Raschi)...Sánchez (1-for-2) doubled and scored in the fifth inning...LeMahieu (0-for-2) started and was replaced by Torres (1-for-2) in the fifth.

▸ **LHP CC Sabathia** was also honored at the All-Star Game in Cleveland, in recognition of his contributions to the game of baseball and his longtime service to the community.

SHOWCASE SHOWDOWN: The Yankees (83-46) and Dodgers (85-44) entered their three-game series in Los Angeles (8/23-25) with the Majors' two best records, as well as the best record in each league...*Elias* confirmed that it marked the latest in a season in the Interleague era (since 1997) that the teams with the best record in each league faced each other in the regular season, a mark previously held by Kansas City and St. Louis on 7/23/15.

▸ **Yankees batters** hit 9HR in the series, only the second visiting team ever to hit 9HR off the Dodgers in a three-game series at Dodger Stadium (opened 1962), joining the 1973 Pittsburgh Pirates (10HR in 3G, 5/7-9/73).

WALK-OFF FAME: The Yankees had six "walk-off" wins in 2019: 4/21 vs. Kansas City (Romine RBI single), 5/7 vs. Seattle (LeMahieu RBI single), 5/17 vs. Tampa Bay (Urshela RBI single), 6/26 vs. Toronto (Torres RBI single), 8/31 vs. Oakland (LeMahieu solo HR), 9/1 vs. Oakland (Ford PH solo HR).

▸ On 9/1 vs. Oakland, **CF Brett Gardner** and **PH Mike Ford** hit back-to-back home runs, with Ford's a "walk-off" HR...was the third time in franchise history that the Yankees hit back-to-back HRs, including a "walk-off" HR: also 8/8/2000 vs. Oakland (Bernie Williams/David Justice) and 8/6/1949 vs. St. Louis-AL (Tommy Henrich/Joe DiMaggio)...Ford was the first rookie in Yankees history to hit a pinch-hit, "walk-off" home run.

OLDIES BUT GOODIES: The Yankees hosted the 73rd annual Old-Timers' Day on 6/23 vs. Houston...making his Old-Timers' Day debut was **Mariano Rivera**, who was inducted into Cooperstown a month later as the first player unanimously elected to the Baseball Hall of Fame...Rivera hit an inside-the-park home run in his first career Old-Timers' Day at-bat...along with Rivera, the Old-Timers' Day roster featured fellow Hall of Famer **Reggie Jackson**, and **Yankees Manager Aaron Boone** and **Hitting Coach Marcus Thames**...**Jason Grimsley** and **Jerry Hairston Jr.** also made their Old-Timers' Day debuts.

PAYING TRIBUTE: The Yankees wore a black armband on the left sleeve of their jerseys for the 2019 season to honor the life of former Yankees pitching coach and RHP Mel Stottlemyre, who passed away on January 13, 2019, at the age of 77.

NEW JERSEY, OLD NAME: For the third consecutive season, **RF Aaron Judge** had the most popular player jersey in the Majors, based on sales of Majestic jerseys at MLBShop.com during the 2019 season.

DOWN ON THE FARM: For the fourth consecutive season in 2019, the Yankees qualified their top two minor league affiliates for their respective league's postseasons...Triple-A Scranton/Wilkes-Barre was eliminated by Durham for the second straight year, this time in the International League Semifinals...Double-A Trenton dropped just one game en route to winning the Eastern League Championships for the fourth time in franchise history and first since 2013.

GRAPEFRUIT JUICE: The Yankees completed their 2019 spring training schedule with a 17-10-4 record (.630), the best mark among Grapefruit League clubs and second-best spring mark in the Majors (Chicago-AL, 14-8, .636)...over the last three springs, have a 59-32-6 record (.648)...**Yankees batters** tied for the Grapefruit League lead and tied for second in the Majors with 49HR...**RF Aaron Judge** tied for second in the Majors and the Grapefruit League with 6HR and tied for fourth in the Majors with 11XBH...tied for third in the Grapefruit League with 15RBI and tied for fourth with 13R...**1B Greg Bird** led the GL with 13BB, tied for second in the Majors...**RHP Masahiro Tanaka** (fifth, 23K) and **RHP Domingo Germán** (T-sixth, 22K) ranked among GL leaders in strikeouts...**RHP Luis Cessa** posted a 2-0 record and 0.98 ERA (18.1IP, 11H, 2ER, 2BB, 19K) in six games (three starts)...**LHP Stephen Tarpley** won the 2019 James P. Dawson Award as the most outstanding rookie in camp after going 1-1 with one save and a 1.42 ERA (12.2IP, 8H, 2ER, 1BB, 9K, 1HR) in 11 games (two starts)...the Yankees drew a total of 142,459 fans to George M. Steinbrenner Field, their 9,497 average ranking second in the Grapefruit League...Steinbrenner Field hosted four sellouts on the spring.

2019 Major League Standings

AMERICAN LEAGUE

East	W	L	Pct	GB	Home	Road	East	Cent	West	NL	RS	RA	Diff
x-New York Yankees	103	59	.636	-	57-24	46-35	54-22	18-15	19-14	12-8	943	739	+204
y-Tampa Bay Rays	96	66	.593	7.0	48-33	48-33	44-32	20-13	18-15	14-6	769	656	+113
Boston Red Sox	84	78	.519	19.0	38-43	46-35	35-41	21-11	18-16	10-10	901	828	+73
Toronto Blue Jays	67	95	.414	36.0	35-46	32-49	33-43	17-18	14-17	3-17	726	828	-102
Baltimore Orioles	54	108	.333	49.0	25-56	29-52	24-52	12-20	11-23	7-13	729	981	-252

Central	W	L	Pct	GB	Home	Road	East	Cent	West	NL	RS	RA	Diff
x-Minnesota Twins	101	61	.623	-	46-35	55-26	20-12	50-26	23-11	8-12	939	754	+185
Cleveland Indians	93	69	.574	8.0	49-32	44-37	18-16	48-28	19-13	8-12	769	657	+112
Chicago White Sox	72	89	.447	28.5	39-41	33-48	15-18	38-37	13-20	6-14	708	832	-124
Kansas City Royals	59	103	.364	42.0	31-50	28-53	10-23	31-45	9-24	9-11	691	869	-178
Detroit Tigers	47	114	.292	53.5	22-59	25-55	14-19	22-53	6-27	5-15	582	915	-333

West	W	L	Pct	GB	Home	Road	East	Cent	West	NL	RS	RA	Diff
x-Houston Astros	107	55	.660	-	60-21	47-34	19-13	21-13	56-20	11-9	920	640	+280
y-Oakland Athletics	97	65	.599	10.0	52-29	45-36	17-16	25-8	44-32	11-9	845	680	+165
Texas Rangers	78	84	.481	29.0	45-36	33-48	18-14	18-16	33-43	9-11	810	878	-68
Los Angeles Angels	72	90	.444	35.0	38-43	34-47	17-18	13-18	30-46	12-8	769	868	-99
Seattle Mariners	68	94	.420	39.0	35-46	33-48	14-19	18-15	27-49	9-11	758	893	-135

NATIONAL LEAGUE

East	W	L	Pct.	GB	Home	Road	East	Cent	West	AL	RS	RA	Diff
x-Atlanta Braves	97	65	.599	-	50-31	47-34	46-30	20-13	18-15	13-7	855	743	+112
y-Washington Nationals	93	69	.574	4.0	50-31	43-38	44-32	17-15	18-16	14-6	873	724	+149
New York Mets	86	76	.531	11.0	48-33	38-43	40-36	14-19	17-16	15-5	791	737	+54
Philadelphia Phillies	81	81	.500	16.0	45-36	36-45	36-40	20-13	14-19	11-9	774	794	-20
Miami Marlins	57	105	.352	40.0	30-51	27-54	24-52	10-24	14-18	9-11	615	808	-193

Central	W	L	Pct	GB	Home	Road	East	Cent	West	AL	RS	RA	Diff
x-St. Louis Cardinals	91	71	.562	-	50-31	41-40	18-15	46-30	18-15	9-11	764	662	+102
y-Milwaukee Brewers	89	73	.549	2.0	49-32	40-41	21-11	45-31	15-19	8-12	769	766	+3
Chicago Cubs	84	78	.519	7.0	51-30	33-48	17-17	37-39	18-14	12-8	814	717	+97
Cincinnati Reds	75	87	.463	16.0	41-40	34-47	17-17	33-43	16-16	9-11	701	711	-10
Pittsburgh Pirates	69	93	.426	22.0	35-46	34-47	11-21	29-47	17-17	12-8	758	911	-153

West	W	L	Pct	GB	Home	Road	East	Cent	West	AL	RS	RA	Diff
x-Los Angeles Dodgers	106	56	.654	-	59-22	47-34	23-10	22-11	51-25	10-10	886	613	+273
Arizona Diamondbacks	85	77	.525	21.0	44-37	41-40	17-17	16-16	38-38	14-6	813	743	+70
San Francisco Giants	77	85	.475	29.0	35-46	42-39	14-19	14-19	38-38	11-9	678	773	-95
Colorado Rockies	71	91	.438	35.0	43-38	28-53	16-17	15-18	32-44	8-12	835	958	-123
San Diego Padres	70	92	.432	36.0	36-45	34-47	14-18	14-20	31-45	11-9	682	789	-107

KEY: x-Division winner, y-Wild Card

POSTSEASON

American League — ALWC: TB def. OAK; ALDS: NYY def. MIN, 3-0; HOU def. TB, 3-2; ALCS: HOU def. NYY, 4-2
National League — NLWC: WAS def. MIL; NLDS: WAS def. LAD, 3-2; STL def. ATL, 3-2; NLCS: WAS def. STL, 4-0
World Series — WAS def. HOU, 4-3

2019 Yankees vs. Opponents

AL East	Home	Road	Total	AL Central	Home	Road	Total	AL West	Home	Road	Total
vs. Baltimore	7-2	10-0	17-2	vs. Chicago	1-2	2-2	3-4	vs. Houston	3-1	0-3	3-4
vs. Boston	8-1	6-4	14-5	vs. Cleveland	2-2	1-2	3-4	vs. Los Angeles	2-1	3-1	5-2
vs. Yankees	--	--	--	vs. Detroit	1-2	2-1	3-3	vs. Oakland	2-1	0-3	2-4
vs. Tampa Bay	8-2	4-5	12-7	vs. Kansas City	3-1	2-1	5-2	vs. Seattle	3-1	3-0	6-1
vs. Toronto	7-2	4-6	11-8	vs. Minnesota	2-1	2-1	4-2	vs. Texas	2-1	1-2	3-3
Totals	30-7	24-15	54-22	Totals	9-8	9-7	18-15	Totals	12-5	7-9	19-14

NL	Home	Road	Total
vs. Arizona	1-1	0-2	1-3
vs. Colorado	2-1	0-0	2-1
vs. Los Angeles	0-0	2-1	2-1
vs. New York	1-1	1-1	2-2
vs. San Diego	2-1	0-0	2-1
vs. San Francisco	0-0	3-0	3-0
Totals	6-4	6-4	12-8

MLB	Home	Road	Total
vs. AL	51-20	40-31	91-51
vs. NL	6-4	6-4	12-8
2019 Totals	57-24	46-35	103-59

2019 Day-by-Day

Gm	Date	Opponent	W/L	Score	Winning Pitcher	Losing Pitcher	Save	Rec.	Pos.	GA/GB	Att.
1	3/28	vs. Baltimore	W	7-2	Tanaka (1-0)	Cashner (0-1)	-	1-0	1st	+1.0	*46,928 (1)
	3/29	OFF DAY							1st	+0.5	
2	3/30	vs. Baltimore	L	3-5	Yacabonis (1-0)	Paxton (0-1)	Wright (1)	1-1	T3rd	-0.5	42,203
3	3/31	vs. Baltimore	L	5-7	Means (1-0)	Happ (0-1)	Fry (1)	1-2	4th	-1.5	38,419
4	4/1	vs. Detroit	W	3-1	Germán (1-0)	Ross (1-1)	Chapman (1)	2-2	3rd	-1.5	32,036
5	4/2	vs. Detroit	L	1-3	Jiménez (1-0)	Chapman (0-1)	Greene (3)	2-3	3rd	-2.5	32,018
6	4/3	vs. Detroit	L	1-2	Farmer (1-0)	Green (0-1)	Greene (4)	2-4	4th	-2.5	33,038
7	4/4	at Baltimore	W	8-4	Paxton (1-1)	Wright (0-1)	-	3-4	3rd	-2.0	*44,182
	4/5	OFF DAY							3rd	-2.0	
8	4/6	at Baltimore	W	6-4	Ottavino (1-0)	Castro (0-1)	Chapman (2)	4-4	T2nd	-1.5	27,504
9	4/7	at Baltimore	W	15-3	Germán (2-0)	Hess (1-1)	-	5-4	2nd	-1.5	33,102
10	4/8	at Houston	L	3-4	Pressly (1-0)	Ottavino (1-1)	Osuna (3)	5-5	T2nd	-2.5	27,631
11	4/9	at Houston	L	3-6	Rondón (1-0)	Green (0-2)	Osuna (4)	5-6	T2nd	-3.5	31,009
12	4/10	at Houston	L	6-8	McHugh (2-1)	Paxton (1-2)	Pressly (1)	5-7	T2nd	-4.5	27,685
	4/11	OFF DAY							2nd	-4.5	
13	4/12	vs. Chicago-AL	L	6-9	Giolito (2-1)	Happ (0-2)	Jones (1)	5-8	2nd	-5.5	40,913
14	4/13	vs. Chicago-AL	W	4-0	Germán (3-0)	Nova (0-2)	-	6-8	2nd	-4.5	41,176
15	4/14	vs. Chicago-AL	L	2-5	Rodón (2-2)	Tanaka (1-1)	Colomé (3)	6-9	2nd	-5.5	40,104
	4/15	OFF DAY							3rd	-5.5	
16	4/16	vs. Boston	W	8-0	Paxton (2-2)	Sale (0-4)	-	7-9	2nd	-5.5	45,008
17	4/17	vs. Boston	W	5-3	Kahnle (1-0)	Workman (0-1)	Chapman (3)	8-9	2nd	-5.5	44,106
18	4/18	vs. Kansas City	L	1-6	Bailey (2-1)	Germán (3-1)	-	8-10	2nd	-5.5	39,106
19	4/19	vs. Kansas City	W	6-2	Sabathia (1-0)	Junis (1-2)	-	9-10	2nd	-4.5	39,668
20	4/20	vs. Kansas City	W	9-2	Tanaka (2-1)	Fillmyer (0-1)	-	10-10	2nd	-3.5	42,013
21	4/21	vs. Kansas City	W	7-6 (10)	Britton (1-0)	Diekman (0-1)	-	11-10	2nd	-2.5	40,523
22	4/22	at Los Angeles-AL	W	4-3 (14)	Holder (1-0)	Bard (0-1)	-	12-10	2nd	-2.5	35,403
23	4/23	at Los Angeles-AL	W	7-5	Germán (4-1)	Stratton (0-2)	Britton (1)	13-10	2nd	-2.5	38,016
24	4/24	at Los Angeles-AL	W	6-5	Loaisiga (1-0)	Buttrey (1-1)	Chapman (4)	14-10	2nd	-1.5	37,928
25	4/25	at Los Angeles-AL	L	5-11	Ramirez (1-0)	Tanaka (2-2)	-	14-11	2nd	-2.0	39,584
26	4/26	at San Francisco	W	7-3	Paxton (3-2)	Bumgarner (1-4)	-	15-11	2nd	-1.5	34,950
27	4/27	at San Francisco	W	6-4	Happ (1-2)	Holland (1-4)	Chapman (5)	16-11	2nd	-1.5	33,971
28	4/28	at San Francisco	W	11-5	Germán (5-1)	Rodríguez (3-3)	-	17-11	2nd	-1.5	34,540
	4/29	OFF DAY							2nd	-2.0	
29	4/30	at Arizona	L	1-3	Greinke (5-1)	Sabathia (1-1)	Holland (6)	17-12	2nd	-2.5	36,352
30	5/1	at Arizona	L	2-3	Kelly (3-2)	Tanaka (2-3)	Holland (7)	17-13	2nd	-2.5	31,365
	5/2	OFF DAY							2nd	-2.5	
31	5/3	vs. Minnesota	W	6-3	Holder (2-0)	Gibson (2-1)	Chapman (6)	18-13	2nd	-2.5	35,911
32	5/4	vs. Minnesota	L	3-7	Odorizzi (4-2)	Happ (1-3)	-	18-14	2nd	-2.5	43,123
33	5/5	vs. Minnesota	W	4-1	Germán (6-1)	Pineda (2-3)	Chapman (7)	19-14	2nd	-2.0	38,603
34	5/6	vs. Seattle	W	7-3	Sabathia (2-1)	Hernández (1-3)	-	20-14	2nd	-2.0	37,423
35	5/7	vs. Seattle	W	5-4	Harvey (1-0)	Swarzak (2-2)	-	21-14	2nd	-2.0	36,851
36	5/8	vs. Seattle	L	1-10	Kikuchi (2-1)	Loaisiga (1-1)	-	21-15	2nd	-2.0	38,774
37	5/9	vs. Seattle	W	3-1	Happ (2-3)	Leake (2-4)	Chapman (8)	22-15	2nd	-1.5	37,016
38	5/10	at Tampa Bay	W	4-3	Germán (7-1)	Glasnow (6-1)	Chapman (9)	23-15	2nd	-0.5	20,846
39	5/11	at Tampa Bay	L	2-7	Chirinos (5-1)	Holder (2-1)	-	23-16	2nd	-1.5	*25,025
40	5/12	at Tampa Bay	W	7-1	Tanaka (3-3)	Snell (3-4)	-	24-16	2nd	-0.5	*25,025
	5/13	vs. Baltimore	Ppd. rain (made up as Game 1 of a single-admission doubleheader on 5/15)						2nd	-0.5	
	5/14	vs. Baltimore	Ppd. rain (made up as Game 1 of a separate-admission doubleheader on 8/12)						2nd	-1.0	
41	5/15 (G1)	vs. Baltimore	W	5-3	Happ (3-3)	Hess (1-5)	Chapman (10)	25-16	2nd	-1.0	
42	5/15 (G2)	vs. Baltimore	W	3-1	Germán (8-1)	Cashner (4-2)	Chapman (11)	26-16	2nd	-0.5	41,138
	5/16	OFF DAY							2nd	-0.5	
43	5/17	vs. Tampa Bay	W	4-3	Holder (3-1)	Alvarado (0-3)	-	27-16	1st	+0.5	41,281
44	5/18	vs. Tampa Bay	L	1-2	Wood (1-0)	Cessa (0-1)	Alvarado (5)	27-17	2nd	-0.5	43,079
45	5/19	vs. Tampa Bay	W	13-5	Ottavino (2-1)	Castillo (0-3)	Adams (1)	28-17	1st	+0.5	43,032
46	5/20	at Baltimore	W	10-7	Britton (2-0)	Givens (0-1)	Chapman (12)	29-17	1st	+1.0	16,457
47	5/21	at Baltimore	W	11-4	Germán (9-1)	Hale (1)	-	30-17	1st	+2.0	17,389
48	5/22	at Baltimore	W	7-5	Sabathia (3-1)	Straily (1-4)	Chapman (13)	31-17	1st	+2.0	17,849
49	5/23	at Baltimore	W	6-5	Kahnle (2-0)	Givens (0-2)	Britton (2)	32-17	1st	+2.0	30,624
	5/24	at Kansas City	Ppd. rain (made up as Game 2 of a separate-admission doubleheader on 5/25)						1st	+2.5	
50	5/25 (G1)	at Kansas City	W	7-3	Happ (4-3)	Barlow (1-1)	-	33-17	1st	+3.0	25,243
51	5/25 (G2)	at Kansas City	W	6-5	Adams (1-0)	López (0-6)	Chapman (14)	34-17	1st	+3.0	18,599
52	5/26	at Kansas City	L	7-8 (10)	McCarthy (1-1)	Holder (3-2)	-	34-18	1st	+2.0	21,499
53	5/27	vs. San Diego	W	5-2	Hale (1-0)	Strahm (2-4)	Chapman (15)	35-18	1st	+2.0	*46,254 (2)
54	5/28	vs. San Diego	L	4-5	Lauer (4-4)	Tanaka (3-4)	Yates (21)	35-19	1st	+1.0	37,028
55	5/29	vs. San Diego	W	7-0	Holder (4-2)	Paddack (4-3)	-	36-19	1st	+1.0	40,918
	5/30	vs. Boston	Ppd. rain (made up as Game 2 of a separate-admission doubleheader on 8/3)						1st	+0.5	
56	5/31	vs. Boston	W	4-1	Happ (5-3)	Sale (1-7)	Chapman (16)	37-19	1st	+1.5	45,556
57	6/1	vs. Boston	W	5-3	Green (1-2)	Porcello (4-5)	Chapman (17)	38-19	1st	+2.5	*46,307 (3)
58	6/2	vs. Boston	L	5-8	Price (3-2)	Sabathia (3-2)	Workman (2)	38-20	1st	+2.5	40,068

KEY: Bold = Complete Game / * = Sellout (Home Sellout Number)

Gm	Date	Opponent	W/L	Score	Winning Pitcher	Losing Pitcher	Save	Rec.	Pos.	GA/GB	Att.
	6/3	OFF DAY							1st	+2.5	
59	6/4	at Toronto	L	3-4	Pannone (2-3)	Tanaka (3-5)	Giles (11)	38-21	1st	+2.5	20,671
60	6/5	at Toronto	L	7-11	Gaviglio (4-1)	Britton (2-1)	-	38-22	1st	+1.5	16,609
61	6/6	at Toronto	W	6-2	Happ (6-3)	Jackson (0-4)	Chapman (18)	39-22	1st	+1.5	25,657
62	6/7	at Cleveland	L	2-5	Plesac (1-1)	Germán (9-2)	Hand (19)	39-23	1st	+0.5	31,531
63	6/8	at Cleveland	L	4-8	Plutko (2-1)	Sabathia (3-3)	-	39-24	T1st	0.0	32,239
64	6/9	at Cleveland	W	7-6	Chapman (1-1)	Pérez (1-1)	Tarpley (1)	40-24	T1st	0.0	29,028
	6/10	vs. New York-NL		Ppd. rain (made up as Game 1 of a separate-admission doubleheader on 6/11)					2nd	-0.5	
65	6/11 (G1)	vs. New York-NL	W	12-5	Tanaka (4-5)	Wheeler (5-4)	-	41-24	T1st	0.0	41,538
66	6/11 (G2)	vs. New York-NL	L	4-10	Vargas (3-3)	Paxton (3-3)	-	41-25	T1st	0.0	44,698
	6/12	OFF DAY							1st	+0.5	
67	6/13	at Chicago-AL	L	4-5	Marshall (2-0)	Ottavino (2-2)	Bummer (1)	41-26	1st	+0.5	25,311
68	6/14	at Chicago-AL	L	2-10	Giolito (10-1)	Sabathia (3-4)	-	41-27	2nd	-0.5	31,438
69	6/15	at Chicago-AL	W	8-4	Cortes Jr. (1-0)	López (4-7)	-	42-27	1st	+0.5	*36,074
70	6/16	at Chicago-AL	W	10-3	Paxton (4-3)	Despaigne (0-2)	-	43-27	1st	+0.5	*37,277
71	6/17	vs. Tampa Bay	W	3-0	**Tanaka** (5-5)	Chirinos (7-3)	-	44-27	1st	+1.5	39,042
72	6/18	vs. Tampa Bay	W	6-3	Happ (7-3)	Roe (0-3)	Chapman (19)	45-27	1st	+2.5	40,479
73	6/19	vs. Tampa Bay	W	12-1	Sabathia (4-4)	Snell (4-6)	-	46-27	1st	+3.5	41,144
74	6/20	vs. Houston	W	10-6	Cortes Jr. (2-0)	Valdez (3-3)	Chapman (20)	47-27	1st	+4.5	41,030
75	6/21	vs. Houston	W	4-1	Paxton (5-3)	Peacock (6-5)	Chapman (21)	48-27	1st	+4.5	41,166
76	6/22	vs. Houston	W	7-5	Holder (5-2)	Pressly (1-1)	Britton (3)	49-27	1st	+5.5	46,034
77	6/23	vs. Houston	L	4-9	Verlander (10-3)	Happ (7-4)	-	49-28	1st	+4.5	*46,769 (4)
78	6/24	vs. Toronto	W	10-8	Sabathia (5-4)	Sanchez (3-10)	Chapman (22)	50-28	1st	+5.0	37,204
79	6/25	vs. Toronto	W	4-3	Cortes Jr. (3-0)	Richard (0-4)	Chapman (23)	51-28	1st	+6.0	40,119
80	6/26	vs. Toronto	W	8-7	Britton (3-1)	Kingham (3-2)	-	52-28	1st	+7.0	40,578
	6/27	OFF DAY							1st	+6.5	
	6/28	OFF DAY							1st	+7.0	
81	6/29	at Boston (London)	W	17-13	Green (2-2)	Wright (0-1)	-	53-28	1st	+7.0	*59,659
82	6/30	at Boston (London)	W	12-8	Ottavino (3-2)	Walden (6-1)	-	54-28	1st	+7.0	*59,059
	7/1	OFF DAY							1st	+6.5	
83	7/2	at New York-NL	L	2-4	Lugo (4-2)	Ottavino (3-3)	Díaz (18)	54-29	1st	+5.5	*42,150
84	7/3	at New York-NL	W	5-1	Germán (10-2)	Vargas (3-4)	-	55-29	1st	+6.5	*43,323
85	7/4	at Tampa Bay	W	8-4 (10)	Chapman (2-1)	Drake (0-1)	Hale (2)	56-29	1st	+7.5	21,974
86	7/5	at Tampa Bay	W	8-4 (11)	Hale (2-0)	Stanek (0-2)	Chapman (24)	57-29	1st	+8.5	22,182
87	7/6	at Tampa Bay	W	3-4	Poche (2-1)	Green (2-3)	-	57-30	1st	+7.5	21,477
88	7/7	at Tampa Bay	L	1-2	Morton (10-2)	Paxton (5-4)	Pagán (5)	57-31	1st	+6.5	20,091
	7/8-7/11	90th All-Star Game on 7/9 at Progressive Field (AL 4, NL 3)									
89	7/12	vs. Toronto	W	4-0	Germán (11-2)	Sanchez (3-13)	-	58-31	1st	+6.5	*47,162 (5)
90	7/13	vs. Toronto	L	1-2	Biagini (3-1)	Happ (7-5)	Hudson (2)	58-32	1st	+6.0	43,472
91	7/14	vs. Toronto	W	4-2	Tanaka (6-5)	Stroman (5-10)	Chapman (25)	59-32	1st	+6.0	42,303
92	7/15	vs. Tampa Bay	L	4-5	Kittredge (1-0)	Chapman (2-2)	Drake (1)	59-33	1st	+5.0	43,173
93	7/16	vs. Tampa Bay	W	8-3	Hale (3-0)	Poche (2-3)	-	60-33	1st	+6.0	40,401
	7/17	vs. Tampa Bay		Ppd. rain (made up as Game 1 of a single-admission doubleheader on 7/18)						1st	+6.0	
94	7/18 (G1)	vs. Tampa Bay	W	6-2	Germán (12-2)	Chirinos (8-5)	-	61-33	1st	+7.0	
95	7/18 (G2)	vs. Tampa Bay	W	5-1	Cessa (1-1)	Morton (11-3)	-	62-33	1st	+8.0	40,504
96	7/19	vs. Colorado	W	8-2	Happ (8-5)	Freeland (2-7)	Tarpley (3)	63-33	1st	+9.0	44,316
97	7/20	vs. Colorado	W	11-5	Tanaka (7-5)	Senzatela (8-7)	-	64-33	1st	+10.0	41,499
98	7/21	vs. Colorado	L	2-8	Márquez (9-5)	Paxton (5-5)	-	64-34	1st	+9.0	41,841
99	7/22	at Minnesota	L	6-8	Thorpe (1-1)	Sabathia (5-5)	Rogers (15)	64-35	1st	+9.0	34,627
100	7/23	at Minnesota	W	14-12 (10)	Chapman (3-2)	Stewart (2-2)	Green (1)	65-35	1st	+10.0	32,470
101	7/24	at Minnesota	W	10-7	Cortes Jr. (4-0)	Odorizzi (11-5)	Chapman (26)	66-35	1st	+10.0	*40,127
102	7/25	at Boston	L	3-19	Porcello (9-7)	Tanaka (7-6)	-	66-36	1st	+9.5	*37,591
103	7/26	at Boston	L	5-10	Cashner (10-5)	Paxton (5-6)	-	66-37	1st	+8.5	*37,095
104	7/27	at Boston	L	5-9	Rodríguez (13-4)	Sabathia (5-6)	-	66-38	1st	+8.0	*36,862
105	7/28	at Boston	W	9-6	Germán (13-2)	Sale (5-10)	-	67-38	1st	+8.5	*37,429
	7/29	OFF DAY							1st	+8.5	
106	7/30	vs. Arizona	L	2-4	Clarke (4-3)	Happ (8-6)	Bradley (1)	67-39	1st	+7.5	*47,281 (6)
107	7/31	vs. Arizona	W	7-5	Ottavino (4-3)	Hirano (3-5)	Chapman (27)	68-39	1st	+7.5	43,979
	8/1	OFF DAY							1st	+7.0	
108	8/2	vs. Boston	W	4-2	Paxton (6-5)	Rodríguez (13-5)	Chapman (28)	69-39	1st	+7.5	*46,932 (7)
109	8/3 (G1)	vs. Boston	W	9-2	Germán (14-2)	Sale (5-11)	-	70-39	1st	+8.0	*46,625 (8)
110	8/3 (G2)	vs. Boston	W	6-4	Kahnle (3-0)	Barnes (3-4)	Chapman (29)	71-39	1st	+8.0	*48,101 (9)
111	8/4	vs. Boston	W	7-4	Happ (9-6)	Price (7-5)	Green (2)	72-39	1st	+8.0	*47,267 (10)
112	8/5	at Baltimore	W	9-6	Ottavino (5-3)	Fry (1-4)	Chapman (30)	73-39	1st	+9.0	20,151
113	8/6	at Baltimore	W	9-4	Cortes Jr. (5-0)	Wojciechowski (2-5)	Ottavino (1)	74-39	1st	+9.0	17,201
114	8/7	at Baltimore	W	14-2	Paxton (7-6)	Means (8-7)	-	75-39	1st	+10.0	16,299
115	8/8	at Toronto	W	12-6	Germán (15-2)	Pannone (2-5)	Cessa (1)	76-39	1st	+10.5	34,108
116	8/9	at Toronto	L	2-8	Reid-Foley (2-2)	Happ (9-7)	-	76-40	1st	+9.5	25,782
117	8/10	at Toronto	W	4-5	Adam (1-0)	Ottavino (5-4)	Law (3)	76-41	1st	+8.5	33,903
118	8/11	at Toronto	W	1-0	Tanaka (8-6)	Thornton (4-8)	Chapman (31)	77-41	1st	+8.5	27,790

KEY: Bold = Complete Game / * = Sellout (Home Sellout Number)

Gm	Date	Opponent	W/L	Score	Winning Pitcher	Losing Pitcher	Save	Rec.	Pos.	GA/GB	Att.
119	8/12 (G1)	vs. Baltimore	W	8-5	Paxton (8-6)	Ynoa (1-7)	Chapman (32)	78-41	1st	+9.0	42,843
120	8/12 (G2)	vs. Baltimore	W	11-8	Mantiply (1-0)	Blach (0-1)	Ottavino (2)	79-41	1st	+9.0	40,354
121	8/13	vs. Baltimore	W	8-3	Germán (16-2)	Means (8-8)	-	80-41	1st	+9.0	41,284
122	8/14	vs. Baltimore	W	6-5	Happ (10-7)	Bundy (5-13)	Chapman (33)	81-41	1st	+10.0	43,909
123	8/15	vs. Cleveland	L	5-19	Plutko (5-3)	Green (2-4)	-	81-42	1st	+9.5	44,654
124	8/16	vs. Cleveland	W	3-2	Tanaka (9-6)	Civale (1-2)	Chapman (34)	82-42	1st	+10.5	45,015
125	8/17	vs. Cleveland	W	6-5	Paxton (9-6)	Plesac (1-4)	Chapman (35)	83-42	1st	+10.5	*47,347 (11)
126	8/18	vs. Cleveland	L	4-8	Clevinger (8-2)	Sabathia (5-7)	-	83-43	1st	+9.5	45,682
	8/19	OFF DAY							1st	+10.0	
127	8/20	at Oakland	L	2-6	Bailey (11-8)	Germán (16-3)	-	83-44	1st	+10.0	21,471
128	8/21	at Oakland	L	4-6	Fiers (12-3)	Happ (10-8)	Hendriks (15)	83-45	1st	+9.0	22,017
129	8/22	at Oakland	L	3-5	Roark (8-8)	Tanaka (9-7)	Soria (1)	83-46	1st	+8.0	24,758
130	8/23	at Los Angeles-NL	W	10-2	Paxton (10-6)	Ryu (12-4)	-	84-46	1st	+8.0	*53,775
131	8/24	at Los Angeles-NL	L	1-2	Gonsolin (2-1)	Sabathia (5-8)	Jansen (27)	84-47	1st	+8.0	*53,803
132	8/25	at Los Angeles-NL	W	5-1	Germán (17-3)	Kershaw (13-3)	-	85-47	1st	+9.0	*53,828
133	8/26	at Seattle	W	5-4	Happ (11-8)	Milone (3-8)	Chapman (36)	86-47	1st	+9.5	23,030
134	8/27	at Seattle	W	7-0	Tanaka (10-7)	Kikuchi (5-9)	-	87-47	1st	+10.5	23,129
135	8/28	at Seattle	W	7-3	Paxton (11-6)	Sheffield (0-1)	-	88-47	1st	+11.5	32,013
	8/29	OFF DAY							1st	+11.0	
136	8/30	vs. Oakland	L	2-8	Anderson (11-9)	Kahnle (3-1)	-	88-48	1st	+10.0	*47,265 (12)
137	8/31	vs. Oakland	W	4-3 (11)	Gearrin (1-2)	Trivino (4-6)	-	89-48	1st	+10.0	44,462
138	9/1	vs. Oakland	W	5-4	Ottavino (6-4)	Hendriks (4-2)	-	90-48	1st	+10.0	42,860
139	9/2	vs. Texas	L	0-7	Minor (12-8)	Tanaka (10-8)	-	90-49	1st	+9.0	40,015
140	9/3	vs. Texas	W	10-1	Paxton (12-6)	Vólquez (0-1)	-	91-49	1st	+9.5	33,711
141	9/4	vs. Texas	W	4-1	Cessa (2-1)	Lynn (14-10)	-	92-49	1st	+10.0	36,082
	9/5	OFF DAY							1st	+9.5	
142	9/6	at Boston	L	1-6	Walden (9-2)	Germán (17-4)	-	92-50	1st	+8.5	36,162
143	9/7	at Boston	W	5-1	Happ (12-8)	Weber (2-3)	-	93-50	1st	+8.5	*36,619
144	9/8	at Boston	W	10-5	Green (3-4)	Porcello (12-12)	-	94-50	1st	+8.5	35,681
145	9/9	at Boston	W	5-0	Paxton (13-6)	Rodríguez (17-6)	-	95-50	1st	+9.0	35,884
146	9/10	at Detroit	L	11-12	Jiménez (4-1)	Adams (1-1)	-	95-51	1st	+9.0	16,733
	9/11	at Detroit		Ppd. rain (made up as Game 1 of a single-admission doubleheader on 9/12)					1st	+8.5	
147	9/12	at Detroit (G1)	W	10-4	Green (4-4)	Boyd (8-11)	-	96-51	1st	+9.0	
148	9/12	at Detroit (G2)	W	6-4	Germán (18-4)	Turnbull (3-15)	Chapman (37)	97-51	1st	+10.0	17,807
149	9/13	at Toronto	L	5-6 (12)	Font (4-4)	Lyons (1-2)	-	97-52	1st	+9.0	23,915
150	9/14	at Toronto	W	13-3	Paxton (14-6)	Waguespack (4-5)	-	98-52	1st	+9.0	26,308
151	9/15	at Toronto	L	4-6	Zeuch (1-0)	Cortes Jr. (5-1)	Giles (20)	98-53	1st	+9.0	22,562
	9/16	OFF DAY							1st	+9.0	
152	9/17	vs. Los Angeles-AL	W	8-0	Loaisiga (2-1)	Ramírez (5-4)	-	99-53	1st	+10.0	41,026
153	9/18	vs. Los Angeles-AL	L	2-3	Bard (2-2)	Ottavino (6-5)	Robles (22)	99-54	1st	+9.0	38,106
154	9/19	vs. Los Angeles-AL	W	9-1	Tanaka (11-8)	Heaney (4-6)	-	100-54	1st	+9.5	42,056
155	9/20	vs. Toronto	L	3-4	Adam (2-0)	Kahnle (3-2)	Giles (21)	100-55	1st	+8.5	45,270
156	9/21	vs. Toronto	W	7-2	Paxton (15-6)	Zeuch (1-1)	-	101-55	1st	+8.5	43,602
157	9/22	vs. Toronto	W	8-3	Severino (1-0)	Font (4-5)	-	102-55	1st	+9.5	44,583
	9/23	OFF DAY							1st	+9.0	
158	9/24	at Tampa Bay	L	1-2 (12)	Fairbanks (2-3)	Gearrin (1-3)	-	102-56	1st	+8.0	16,699
159	9/25	at Tampa Bay	L	0-4	Morton (16-6)	Loaisiga (2-2)	-	102-57	1st	+7.0	20,390
	9/26	OFF DAY							1st	+7.0	
160	9/27	at Texas	W	14-7	Tarpley (1-0)	Palumbo (0-3)	-	103-57	1st	+7.0	35,168
161	9/28	at Texas	L	4-9	Hernández (2-1)	Severino (1-1)	-	103-58	1st	+7.0	42,870
162	9/29	at Texas	L	1-6	Lynn (16-11)	Tanaka (11-9)	-	103-59	1st	+7.0	*47,144

KEY: **Bold** = Complete Game / * = Sellout (Home Sellout Number)

Postponements and Rain Delays

Postponed (7) . . . . 5/13 vs. BAL (rain), 5/14 vs. BAL (rain), 5/24 at KC (rain), 5/30 vs. BOS (rain), 6/10 vs. NYM (rain), 7/17 vs. TB (rain), 9/11 at DET (rain)

Rain Delays at Start (7) . . . . 3/31 vs. BAL (3:17, rain), 6/15 at CHW (0:32, rain), 6/18 vs. TB (1:16, rain), 7/18 vs. TB (1:26, rain), 8/4 vs. BOS (1:09, rain), 8/6 at BAL (1:12, rain), 9/2 vs. TEX (2:52, rain)

Delays In-Game (7) . . . . 4/12 vs. CWS (0:41, rain), 5/5 vs. MIN (1:01, rain), 5/7 vs. SEA (1:12, rain), 5/12 at TB (0:43, power), 5/17 vs. TB (0:35, rain), 6/20 vs. HOU (0:37, rain), 7/31 vs. ARI (0:36, rain)

Games Called Early (2) . . . . 4/12 vs. CWS (7 inn., rain), 5/5 vs. MIN (8 inn., rain)

Suspended Game (0) . . . . Last on 5/15/18 at WAS (B6, resumed 6/18/18, 5-3 loss)

In 2018: Ppd. (9) / Delays at Start (5) / Delays In-Game (4)

2019 Transactions

Jan. 3	Signed **OF Billy Burns** to a minor league contract with an invitation to Major League Spring Training.
Jan. 4	Signed **INF Troy Tulowitzki** to a one-year contract…designated **RHP A.J. Cole** for assignment.
Jan. 5	Signed **OF Matt Lipka** to a minor league contract with an invitation to Major League Spring Training.
Jan. 10	Signed **RHP Drew Hutchison** to a minor league contract with an invitation to Major League Spring Training.
Jan. 11	Signed **LHP Zack Britton** to a three-year contract with a team option and player opt-out…designated **INF Hanser Alberto** for assignment…**INF Hanser Alberto** claimed off waivers by Baltimore…**RHP A.J. Cole** claimed off waivers by Cleveland…agreed to terms with **RHP Dellin Betances, 1B Greg Bird, RHP Sonny Gray, SS Didi Gregorius, OF Aaron Hicks, RHP Tommy Kahnle, LHP James Paxton** and **C Austin Romine** on one-year, non-guaranteed contracts, avoiding arbitration.
Jan. 14	Signed **INF DJ LeMahieu** to a two-year contract…designated **OF Tim Locastro** for assignment.
Jan. 16	Acquired **LHP Ronald Roman** and cash considerations from Arizona in exchange for OF Tim Locastro.
Jan. 21	Acquired **2B Shed Long** and a Competitive Balance Round A pick in the 2019 MLB First-Year Player Draft from Cincinnati in exchange for RHP Sonny Gray and LHP Reiver Sanmartín…acquired **OF Josh Stowers** from Seattle in exchange for 2B Shed Long…signed **RHP David Hale** and **RHP Danny Farquhar** to a minor league contract with an invitation to Major League Spring Training.
Jan. 24	Signed **RHP Adam Ottavino** to a three-year contract.
Feb. 1	Invited 21 non-roster players to spring training: **OF Trey Amburgey**, **LHP Rex Brothers**, **OF Billy Burns**, **LHP Nestor Cortes Jr.**, **RHP Cale Coshow**, **LHP Danny Coulombe**, **C Kellin Deglan**, **C Francisco Diaz**, **RHP Raynel Espinal**, **RHP Danny Farquhar**, **OF Estevan Florial**, **INF Mike Ford**, **RHP David Hale**, **INF Kyle Holder**, **RHP Drew Hutchison**, **RHP Michael King**, **RHP Brady Lail**, **C Ryan Lavarnway**, **OF Matt Lipka**, **C Jorge Saez** and **INF Gio Urshela**.
Feb. 15	Signed **RHP Luis Severino** to a four-year contract extending through the 2022 season with a team option for 2023.
Feb. 25	Signed **OF Aaron Hicks** to a seven-year contract extending through the 2025 season with a team option for 2026.
Mar. 6	Optioned **RHP Domingo Acevedo** to Double-A Trenton…reassigned **RHP Brady Lail** and **RHP Trevor Stephan** to minor league camp.
Mar. 10	Optioned **RHP Albert Abreu** to Double-A Trenton.
Mar. 12	Prior to the game, optioned **RHP Chance Adams** and **RHP Joe Harvey** to Triple-A Scranton/WB and reassigned **RHP Cale Coshow**, **RHP Danny Farquhar** and **C Kellin Deglan** to minor league camp…following the game, optioned **INF Thairo Estrada** to Triple-A Scranton/WB and reassigned **OF Trey Amburgey** and **INF Mike Ford** to minor league camp.
Mar. 16	Optioned **C Kyle Higashioka** to Triple-A Scranton/WB.
Mar. 20	Signed **LHP Gio Gonzalez** to a minor league contract with an invitation to Major League spring training.
Mar. 21	Reassigned **OF Billy Burns**, **OF Matt Lipka** and **C Ryan Lavarnway** to minor league camp.
Mar. 22	Prior to the game, optioned **OF Clint Frazier** to Triple-A Scranton/WB…reassigned **LHP Rex Brothers**, **LHP Danny Coulombe**, **LHP Phillip Diehl** and **RHP Drew Hutchison** to minor league camp…following the game, reassigned **INF Kyle Holder** and **INF Gio Urshela** to minor league camp.
Mar. 23	Prior to the game, optioned **RHP Jonathan Loaisiga** to Triple-A Scranton/WB…following the game, acquired **OF Mike Tauchman** from the Colorado Rockies in exchange for **LHP Phillip Diehl**…placed **LHP Jordan Montgomery** on the 60-day I.L.…reassigned **LHP Nestor Cortes Jr.**, **OF Estevan Florial** and **RHP David Hale** to minor league camp.
Mar. 24	Optioned **INF Tyler Wade** to Triple-A Scranton/WB…received **RHP Nick Green** as a Rule 5 Draft return from Arizona.
Mar. 28	Placed **RHP Dellin Betances** on the 10-day I.L. (retroactive to 3/25) with a right shoulder impingement…placed **RHP Ben Heller** on the 10-day I.L. (retroactive to 3/25) with right elbow UCL surgery recovery…placed **RHP Luis Severino** on the 10-day I.L. (retroactive to 3/25) with right shoulder rotator cuff inflammation…placed **INF Didi Gregorius** on the 10-day I.L. (retroactive to 3/25) with right elbow UCL surgery recovery…placed **OF Jacoby Ellsbury** on the 10-day I.L. (retroactive to 3/25) with left hip surgery recovery…placed **OF Aaron Hicks** on the 10-day I.L. (retroactive to 3/25) with a left lower back strain…**LHP CC Sabathia** was placed on MLB's Suspended List.
April 1	Placed **OF Giancarlo Stanton** on the 10-day I.L. with a left biceps strain…recalled **OF Clint Frazier** from Triple-A Scranton/WB…placed **INF Miguel Andújar** on the 10-day I.L. with a right shoulder strain…recalled **INF/OF Tyler Wade** from Triple-A Scranton/WB.
April 3	Reinstated **LHP CC Sabathia** from the MLB Suspended List…placed **LHP CC Sabathia** on the 10-day I.L. (rehab from cardiac surgery)…recalled **RHP Jonathan Loaisiga** from Triple-A Scranton/WB.
April 4	Placed **INF Troy Tulowitzki** on the 10-day I.L. with left calf strain…recalled **INF Thairo Estrada** from Triple-A Scranton/WB…acquired **RHP Jake Barrett** off waivers from Pittsburgh and transferred **RHP Ben Heller** to the 60-day I.L.
April 6	Selected **INF Gio Urshela** from Triple-A Scranton/Wilkes-Barre and signed him to a Major League contract…optioned **INF Thairo Estrada** to Triple-A Scranton/WB…transferred **INF Didi Gregorius** to the 60-day I.L. (right elbow UCL surgery recovery).
April 9	Following the game, optioned **RHP Jonathan Loaisiga** to Triple-A Scranton/WB.
April 10	Recalled **RHP Joe Harvey** from Triple-A Scranton/WB.
April 12	Placed **C Gary Sánchez** on the 10-day I.L. (retroactive to 4/11) with a left calf strain…recalled **C Kyle Higashioka** from Triple-A Scranton/WB…following the game, optioned **LHP Stephen Tarpley** to Triple-A Scranton/WB.
April 13	**LHP CC Sabathia** returned from rehab and reinstated from the 10-day I.L.
April 16	Placed **1B Greg Bird** on the 10-day I.L. (retroactive to 4/14) with a left plantar fascia tear…selected **1B Mike Ford** from Triple-A Scranton/WB and signed him to a Major League contract…transferred **OF Jacoby Ellsbury** to the 60-day I.L.
April 21	Placed **OF Aaron Judge** on the 10-day I.L. with a left oblique strain…recalled **INF Thairo Estrada** from Triple-A Scranton/WB.
April 22	Following the game, optioned **RHP Joseph Harvey** to Triple-A Scranton/WB.
April 23	Recalled **RHP Jonathan Loaisiga** from Triple-A Scranton/WB…following the game, optioned **RHP Chad Green** and **C Kyle Higashioka** to Triple-A Scranton/WB.
April 24	Recalled **LHP Stephen Tarpley** from Triple-A Scranton/WB and returned from rehab and reinstated **C Gary Sánchez** from the 10-day I.L.…following the game, optioned **RHP Jonathan Loaisiga** to Triple-A Scranton/WB.
April 25	Placed **OF Clint Frazier** on the 10-day I.L. with a left ankle sprain (retroactive to 4/23)…recalled **RHP Joseph Harvey** from Triple-A Scranton/WB…acquired **OF Cameron Maybin** from Cleveland for cash considerations, signed him to a Major League contract and selected him to the 25-man roster…transferred **RHP Luis Severino** to the 60-day I.L.…
May 3	Following the game, optioned **1B Mike Ford** to Triple-A Scranton/WB.
May 4	Returned from rehab and reinstated **INF Miguel Andújar** from the 10-day I.L.…placed **LHP James Paxton** on the 10-day I.L. with left knee inflammation…recalled **RHP Jake Barrett** from Triple-A Scranton/WB.
May 5	Following the game, optioned **LHP Stephen Tarpley** to Triple-A Scranton/WB.
May 6	Returned **OF Clint Frazier** from rehab and reinstated him from the 10-day I.L.
May 7	Following the game, optioned **INF/OF Tyler Wade** to Triple-A Scranton/WB.
May 8	Recalled **RHP Jonathan Loaisiga** from Triple-A Scranton/WB…following the game, optioned **RHP Jake Barrett** to Triple-A Scranton/WB.
May 9	Signed **LHP Nestor Cortes, Jr.** to a Major League contract and selected him from Triple-A Scranton/WB…transferred **RHP Dellin Betances** from the 10-day I.L. to the 60-day I.L.
May 11	Following the game, optioned **LHP Nestor Cortes, Jr.** to Triple-A Scranton/WB.

May 12	Recalled **RHP Chad Green** from Triple-A Scranton/WB…acquired **INF Breyvic Valera** off waivers from San Francisco…following the game, optioned **OF Mike Tauchman** to Triple-A Scranton/WB.
May 13	Returned **OF Aaron Hicks** from his rehab assignment and reinstated him from the 10-day I.L.…placed **RHP Jonathan Loaisiga** on the 10-day I.L. (retroactive to 5/10) with a right shoulder strain…recalled **RHP Chance Adams** from Triple-A Scranton/WB…placed **INF Miguel Andújar** on the 10-day I.L. with a right labrum tear…recalled **LHP Nestor Cortes Jr.** from Triple-A Scranton/WB.
May 14	Acquired **1B/DH Kendrys Morales** and cash considerations from Oakland in exchange for a player to be named later or cash considerations…transferred **RHP Jonathan Loaisiga** to the 60-day I.L.
May 15	Recalled **OF Mike Tauchman** from Triple-A Scranton/WB as the "26th Man"…returned **OF Mike Tauchman** to Triple-A Scranton/WB.
May 19	Following the game, optioned **RHP Chance Adams** to Triple-A Scranton/WB.
May 20	Recalled **RHP Jake Barrett** from Triple-A Scranton/WB…following the game, optioned **LHP Nestor Cortes Jr.** to Triple-A Scranton/WB.
May 21	Signed **RHP David Hale** to a Major League contract and selected him to the 25-man roster from Triple-A Scranton/WB…transferred **INF Miguel Andújar** to the 60-day I.L.
May 23	Placed **LHP CC Sabathia** on the 10-day I.L. with a right knee inflammation…recalled **LHP Nestor Cortes Jr.** from Triple-A Scranton/WB.
May 25	Recalled **RHP Chance Adams** from Triple-A Scranton/WB as the "26th Man"…returned **RHP Chance Adams** to Triple-A Scranton/WB.
May 26	Placed **RHP Jake Barrett** on the 10-day I.L. (retroactive to 5/23) with right elbow inflammation…recalled **RHP Joseph Harvey** from Triple-A Scranton/WB.
May 28	Following the game, optioned **RHP Joseph Harvey** to Triple-A Scranton/WB.
May 29	Reinstated **LHP James Paxton** from the 10-day I.L.
June 1	Following the game, optioned **LHP Nestor Cortes Jr.** to Triple-A Scranton/WB.
June 2	Reinstated **LHP CC Sabathia** from the 10-day I.L.
June 6	Optioned **INF Thairo Estrada** to Triple-A Scranton/WB.
June 7	Returned **SS Didi Gregorius** from rehab and reinstated him from the 60-day I.L. and transferred **INF Troy Tulowitzki** to the 60-day I.L.
June 8	Placed **RHP Masahiro Tanaka** on the paternity leave list…recalled **LHP Nestor Cortes Jr.** from Triple-A Scranton/WB.
June 9	Placed **RHP Domingo Germán** on the 10-day I.L. with a left hip flexor strain (retro. to 6/8)…recalled **LHP Stephen Tarpley** from Triple-A Scranton/WB…following the game, optioned **LHP Nestor Cortes Jr.** to Triple-A Scranton/WB.
June 10	Reinstated **RHP Masahiro Tanaka** from the paternity leave list.
June 11	Prior to the second game, appointed **RHP Chance Adams** as their "26th Man"…returned **RHP Chance Adams** "the 26th man" to Double-A Trenton…optioned **LHP Stephen Tarpley** to Triple-A Scranton/WB.
June 13	Placed **1B/DH Kendrys Morales** on the 10-day I.L. (retroactive to 6/12) with a left calf strain…recalled **LHP Nestor Cortes Jr.** and **OF Mike Tauchman** from Triple-A Scranton/WB.
June 15	Acquired **1B/DH Edwin Encarnación** and cash considerations from Seattle in exchange for RHP Juan Then.
June 16	Following the game, optioned **OF Clint Frazier** to Triple-A Scranton/WB.
June 17	Added **DH/1B Edwin Encarnación** to the 25-man roster.…following the game, optioned **OF Mike Tauchman** to Triple-A Scranton/WB.
June 18	Returned **OF Giancarlo Stanton** from rehab and reinstated him from the 10-day I.L..
June 20	Following the game, optioned **LHP Nestor Cortes Jr.** to Triple-A Scranton/WB.
June 21	Returned **RF Aaron Judge** from rehab and reinstated him from the 10-day I.L..
June 23	Placed **OF Cameron Maybin** on the 10-day I.L. with a left calf strain (retro. to 6/22)…recalled **LHP Nestor Cortes Jr.** from Triple-A Scranton/WB.
June 24	Following the game, optioned **RHP Jonathan Holder** to Triple-A Scranton/WB.
June 25	Reinstated **1B/OF Kendrys Morales** from the 10-day I.L. and designated him for assignment…recalled **LHP Stephen Tarpley** from Triple-A Scranton/WB.
June 26	Following the game, placed **OF Giancarlo Stanton** on the 10-day I.L. with a right knee sprain…recalled **OF Mike Tauchman** from Triple-A Scranton/WB.
June 29	Following the game, optioned **LHP Nestor Cortes Jr.** to Triple-A Scranton/WB.
June 30	Recalled **RHP Chance Adams** from Triple-A Scranton/WB…following the game, returned "26th Man" **INF Thairo Estrada** to Triple-A Scranton/WB…following the game, optioned **RHP Chance Adams** to Triple-A Scranton/WB.
July 2	Placed **INF Luke Voit** on the 10-day I.L. with an abdominal strain (retroactive to 6/30)…recalled **LHP Nestor Cortes Jr.** from Triple-A Scranton/WB…recalled **INF Mike Ford** from Triple-A Scranton/WB…following the game, optioned **LHP Stephen Tarpley** to Triple-A Scranton/WB.
July 3	Returned **RHP Domingo Germán** from rehab and reinstated him from the 10-day I.L..
July 5	Following the game, optioned **INF Mike Ford** to Triple-A Scranton/WB.
July 6	**LHP Daniel Camarena** was signed to a Major League contract and selected to the 25-man roster from Triple-A Scranton/WB…following the game, optioned **LHP Daniel Camarena** to Triple-A Scranton/WB.
July 7	Recalled **INF Breyvic Valera** from Triple-A Scranton/WB.
July 12	Following the game, optioned **INF Breyvic Valera** to Triple-A Scranton/WB.
July 13	Reinstated **1B/DH Luke Voit** from the 10-day I.L.
July 18	Prior to the second game of a doubleheader, appointed **LHP Stephen Tarpley** as their "26th Man."…following the second game, optioned **LHP Nestor Cortes Jr.** to Triple-A Scranton/WB.
July 21	Following the game, optioned **LHP Stephen Tarpley** to Triple-A Scranton/WB.
July 22	Recalled **RHP Jonathan Holder** from Triple-A Scranton/WB.
July 23	Following the game, optioned **RHP Jonathan Holder** to Triple-A Scranton/WB.
July 24	Placed **C Gary Sánchez** on the 10-day I.L. with a left groin strain…recalled **C Kyle Higashioka** from Triple-A Scranton/WB…recalled **LHP Nestor Cortes** from Triple-A Scranton/WB.
July 25	**INF Troy Tulowitzki** announced his retirement…placed **OF Brett Gardner** on the 10-day I.L. with left knee inflammation (retroactive to 7/22)…recalled **LHP Stephen Tarpley** from Triple-A Scranton/WB…optioned **LHP Stephen Tarpley** to Triple-A Scranton/WB following the game.
July 26	Returned **OF Cameron Maybin** from rehab and reinstated him from the 10-day I.L..
July 28	Placed **LHP CC Sabathia** on the 10-day I.L. with right knee inflammation…recalled **INF/OF Tyler Wade** from Triple-A Scranton/WB.
July 31	Placed **1B Luke Voit** on the 10-day I.L. with a sports hernia and placed **RHP David Hale** on the 10-day I.L. with a lumbar spine strain (retroactive to 7/28)…recalled **RHP Jonathan Holder** and **INF Breyvic Valera** from Triple-A Scranton/WB…acquired **LHP Alfredo Garcia** from Colorado for RHP Joseph Harvey.
Aug. 2	Placed **LHP J.A. Happ** on the Major League Paternity List…reinstated **OF Brett Gardner** from the 10-day I.L.…optioned **INF/OF Tyler Wade** to Triple-A Scranton/WB…recalled **LHP Stephen Tarpley** from Triple-A Scranton/WB.
Aug. 3	Appointed **RHP Chance Adams** as the "26th man" for the doubleheader…placed **1B/DH Edwin Encarnación** on the 10-day I.L. with a right wrist fracture…recalled **1B Mike Ford** from Triple-A Scranton/WB…returned "26th man" **RHP Chance Adams** to Triple-A Scranton/WB.

Aug. 4	Placed **OF Aaron Hicks** on the 10-day I.L. with a right flexor strain…returned **LHP J.A. Happ** from the paternity list.
Aug. 6	Following the game, optioned **LHP Stephen Tarpley** to Triple-A Scranton/WB.
Aug. 7	Recalled **RHP Chance Adams** from Triple-A Scranton/WB.
Aug. 9	Following the game, optioned **C Kyle Higashioka** to Triple-A Scranton/WB.
Aug. 10	Returned from rehab and reinstated **C Gary Sánchez** from the 10-day I.L.…recalled **LHP Stephen Tarpley** from Triple-A Scranton/WB…placed **RHP Jonathan Holder** on the 10-day I.L. with right shoulder inflammation (retroactive to 8/7).
Aug. 11	Placed **LHP Stephen Tarpley** on the 10-day I.L. with a left elbow impingement…signed **RHP Brady Lail** and **LHP Joe Mantiply** to Major League contracts and selected them to the 25-man roster from Triple-A Scranton/WB…transferred **OF Giancarlo Stanton** to the 60-day I.L.
Aug. 12	Appointed **INF Breyvic Valera** as the "26th man" for the doubleheader…returned "26th man" **INF Breyvic Valera** to Triple-A Scranton/WB…following the game, optioned **LHP Joe Mantiply** and **RHP Brady Lail** to Triple-A Scranton/WB.
Aug. 13	Designated **LHP Joe Mantiply** for assignment…released **LHP Daniel Camarena** from the roster…returned **RHP Jonathan Loaisiga** from rehab and reinstated him from the 60-day I.L.…signed **RHP Adonis Rosa** to a Major League contract and selected him to the 25-man roster from Triple-A Scranton/WB…following the game, optioned **RHP Adonis Rosa** to Triple-A Scranton/WB.
Aug. 14	Recalled **INF Thairo Estrada** from Triple-A Scranton/WB…acquired **RHP Ryan Dull** off waivers from San Francisco and added him to the 40-man roster…designated **RHP Brady Lail** for assignment.
Aug. 16	Recalled **RHP Ryan Dull** from Triple-A Scranton/WB.
Aug. 17	Optioned **RHP Ryan Dull** to Triple-A Scranton/WB.
Aug. 18	Reinstated **LHP CC Sabathia** from the 10-day I.L…placed **INF Thairo Estrada** on the 10-day I.L. with a right hamstring strain…recalled **INF/OF Tyler Wade** from Triple-A Scranton/WB.
Aug. 23	Acquired **RHP Cory Gearrin** off waivers from Seattle…released **RHP Domingo Acevedo**…following the game, optioned **RHP Jonathan Loaisiga** to Triple-A Scranton/WB.
Aug. 24	Added **RHP Cory Gearrin** to the active roster.
Aug. 30	Returned from rehab and reinstated **1B Luke Voit** from the 10-day I.L.…placed **INF Gio Urshela** on the 10-day I.L. with a left groin injury (retroactive to 8/28).
Aug. 31	Placed **LHP CC Sabathia** on the 10-day I.L. with right knee inflammation…recalled **RHP Jonathan Loaisiga** from Triple-A Scranton/WB.
Sept. 1	Recalled **RHP Chance Adams, RHP Ryan Dull** and **OF Clint Frazier** from Triple-A Scranton/WB…signed **LHP Tyler Lyons** to an MLB contract and selected him from Triple-A Scranton/WB…transferred **RHP David Hale** to the 60-day I.L.
Sept. 3	Returned from rehab and reinstated **1B/DH Edwin Encarnación** from the 10-day I.L.
Sept. 8	Reinstated **INF Gio Urshela** from the 10-day I.L.…returned **INF Thairo Estrada** from his rehab assignment and reinstated him from the 10-day I.L.…recalled **C Kyle Higashioka** and **INF Breyvic Valera** from Triple-A Scranton/WB.
Sept. 10	Reinstated **RHP Ben Heller** from the 60-day I.L.…placed **OF Mike Tauchman** on the 10-day I.L. (retroactive 9/9) with a left calf strain…designated **RHP Adonis Rosa** for assignment.
Sept. 11	Reinstated **LHP CC Sabathia** from the 10-day I.L.…returned **LHP Stephen Tarpley** from rehab.
Sept. 12	Reinstated **LHP Stephen Tarpley** from the 10-day I.L.
Sept. 13	Returned **LHP Jordan Montgomery** and **RHP Luis Severino** from rehab…outrighted **RHP Adonis Rosa** off the Major League roster.
Sept. 14	Returned **RHP Dellin Betances** from rehab.
Sept. 15	Reinstated **RHP Dellin Betances** and **LHP Jordan Montgomery** from the 60-day I.L.…transferred **RHP Jonathan Holder** to the 60-day I.L.…designated **RHP Ryan Dull** for assignment.
Sept. 17	Reinstated **RHP Luis Severino** from the 60-day I.L.…designated **INF Breyvic Valera** for assignment.
Sept. 18	Reinstated **OF Giancarlo Stanton** from the 60-day I.L.…**RHP Dellin Betances** on the 60-day I.L. with a partial tear of the left Achilles' tendon…**RHP Ryan Dull** claimed off waivers by Toronto.
Sept. 19	**RHP Domingo Germán** placed on administrative leave by the Office of the Commissioner of Baseball and placed on the Restricted List…signed **RHP Michael King** to a Major League contract and selected him to the active roster.
Sept. 20	**INF Breyvic Valera** claimed off waivers by Toronto.
Sept. 28	Reinstated **RHP David Hale** from the 60-day I.L.…and transferred **OF Aaron Hicks** to the 60-day I.L.
Oct. 12	Reinstated **OF Aaron Hicks** from the 60-day injured list and designated **RHP David Hale** for assignment.
Oct. 18	Replaced **LHP CC Sabathia** on the ALCS roster with **RHP Ben Heller**…**LHP CC Sabathia** suffered a subluxation of his left shoulder joint.
Oct. 31	Declined the 2020 club option on **1B/DH Edwin Encarnación**.
Nov. 3	Signed **LHP Aroldis Chapman** to a contract extension through the 2022 season…the club had previously signed Chapman on 12/15/16, to a five-year contract through 2021 with a player opt-out following the 2019 season.
Nov. 4	Reinstated **3B Miguel Andújar, 1B Greg Bird, OF Jacoby Ellsbury** and **RHP Jonathan Holder** from the 60-day injured list…reinstated **RHP Jake Barrett** from the 60-day injured list and outrighted him to Triple-A Scranton/Wilkes-Barre…**LHP Tyler Lyons** elected free agency in lieu of accepting an outright assignment to Scranton/WB.
Nov. 14	Announced the hiring of **Pitching Coach Matt Blake**.
Nov. 20	Added **OF Estevan Florial, RHP Deivi García, RHP Luis Gil, RHP Brooks Kriske, RHP Luis Medina, RHP Nick Nelson** and **RHP Miguel Yajure** to the Major League roster…released **OF Jacoby Ellsbury**…designated **1B Greg Bird** and **LHP Nestor Cortes Jr.** for assignment.
Nov. 25	Traded **LHP Nestor Cortes Jr.** to Seattle for international signing bonus pool money.
Nov. 27	**1B Greg Bird** elected free agency in lieu of accepting an outright assignment to Triple-A Scranton/Wilkes-Barre.
Dec. 12	In the first round of the Major League phase of the 2019 Rule 5 Draft, Detroit selected **RHP Rony Garcia** from the Yankees…in the first round of the Triple-A phase, Toronto selected **RHP Hobie Harris**, Chicago-AL selected **RHP Will Carter**, Boston selected **RHP Raynel Espinal** and Atlanta selected **INF Wendell Rijo** from the Yankees.
Dec. 18	Signed **RHP Gerrit Cole** to a nine-year contract extending through the 2028 season with a player opt-out following the 2024 season.…designated **RHP Chance Adams** for assignment.
Dec. 23	Acquired minor league **INF Cristian Perez** from Kansas City in exchange for RHP Chance Adams.

2020

Jan. 10	Agreed to terms with **RHP Luis Cessa, RHP Chad Green, RHP Jonathan Holder, OF Aaron Judge, RHP Tommy Kahnle, LHP Jordan Montgomery, LHP James Paxton, C Gary Sánchez** and **3B Gio Urshela** on one-year, non-guaranteed contracts, thus avoiding arbitration.
Jan. 11	Signed **OF Brett Gardner** to a one-year contract with a club option for 2021…designated **LHP Stephen Tarpley** for assignment.
Jan. 14	Announced his coaching staff for the 2020 season, naming **Quality Control and Catching Coach Tanner Swanson**, along with **Pitching Coach Matt Blake** (previously announced), **Bullpen Coach Mike Harkey** (returning), **Bench Coach Carlos Mendoza** (promoted), **Third Base Coach Phil Nevin** (returning), **Assistant Hitting Coach P.J. Pilittere** (returning), **Hitting Coach Marcus Thames** (returning) and **First Base Coach Reggie Willits** (returning).
Jan. 15	Acquired minor league **3B James Nelson** and cash considerations from Miami in exchange for LHP Stephen Tarpley.

2019 Postseason Statistics

Overall Hitting	AVG	G	PA	AB	R	H	TB	2B	3B	HR	RBI	BB	IBB	SO	SB	CS	SH	SF	HP	GIDP	OBP	SLG	OPS
E. Encarnación	.161	8	36	31	2	5	8	3	0	0	2	5	0	13	0	0	0	0	0	0	.278	.258	.536
Brett Gardner	.176	9	38	34	4	6	9	0	0	1	4	3	0	15	0	0	0	0	1	0	.263	.265	.528
Didi Gregorius	.273	9	35	33	4	9	13	1	0	1	6	2	0	6	0	0	0	0	0	0	.314	.394	.708
Aaron Hicks	.154	5	17	13	1	2	5	0	0	1	3	4	0	5	1	0	0	0	0	0	.353	.385	.738
Aaron Judge	.265	9	42	34	6	9	12	0	0	1	2	7	0	11	2	0	0	0	0	0	.390	.353	.743
DJ LeMahieu	.325	9	44	40	10	13	25	3	0	3	7	4	0	6	0	0	0	0	0	0	.386	.625	1.011
C. Maybin	.333	5	7	6	2	2	5	0	0	1	1	1	0	4	2	0	0	0	0	0	.429	.833	1.262
Gary Sánchez	.129	9	36	31	2	4	7	0	0	1	3	4	0	16	0	0	0	0	1	0	.250	.226	.476
G. Stanton	.231	5	18	13	1	3	6	0	0	1	2	4	0	5	0	0	0	1	0	1	.389	.462	.850
Gleyber Torres	.324	9	40	37	8	12	26	5	0	3	10	3	0	6	2	0	0	0	0	0	.375	.703	1.078
Gio Urshela	.242	9	35	33	4	8	15	1	0	2	2	2	0	4	0	0	0	0	0	1	.286	.455	.740
Post. Totals	.239	9	348	305	44	73	131	13	0	15	42	39	0	91	7	0	0	1	2	5	.329	.430	.758

ALDS	AVG	G	PA	AB	R	H	TB	2B	3B	HR	RBI	BB	IBB	SO	SB	CS	SH	SF	HP	GIDP	OBP	SLG	OPS
E. Encarnación	.308	3	14	13	2	4	6	2	0	0	2	1	0	2	0	0	0	0	0	0	.357	.462	.819
Brett Gardner	.250	3	14	12	3	3	6	0	0	1	3	1	0	5	0	0	0	0	1	0	.357	.500	.857
Didi Gregorius	.400	3	12	10	2	4	7	0	0	1	6	2	0	3	0	0	0	0	0	0	.500	.700	1.200
Aaron Judge	.333	3	14	9	3	3	3	0	0	0	0	4	0	1	0	0	0	0	0	0	.538	.333	.872
DJ LeMahieu	.286	3	15	14	4	4	9	2	0	1	4	1	0	4	0	0	0	0	0	0	.333	.643	.976
C. Maybin	.333	3	3	3	2	1	4	0	0	1	1	0	0	2	2	0	0	0	0	0	.333	1.333	1.667
Gary Sánchez	.125	3	12	8	1	1	1	0	0	0	3	0	0	4	0	0	0	0	1	0	.417	.125	.542
G. Stanton	.167	3	11	6	0	1	1	0	0	0	1	4	0	2	0	0	0	1	0	1	.455	.167	.621
Gleyber Torres	.417	3	13	12	5	5	11	3	0	1	4	1	0	2	2	0	0	0	0	2	.462	.917	1.378
Gio Urshela	.250	3	12	12	1	3	4	1	0	0	0	0	0	2	0	0	0	0	0	1	.250	.333	.583
ALDS Totals	.293	3	120	99	23	29	52	8	0	5	21	17	0	27	4	0	0	1	2	4	.403	.525	.929

ALCS	AVG	G	PA	AB	R	H	TB	2B	3B	HR	RBI	BB	IBB	SO	SB	CS	SH	SF	HP	GIDP	OBP	SLG	OPS
E. Encarnación	.056	5	22	18	0	1	2	1	0	0	0	4	0	11	0	0	0	0	0	0	.227	.111	.338
Brett Gardner	.136	6	24	22	1	3	3	0	0	0	1	2	0	10	0	0	0	0	0	0	.208	.136	.345
Didi Gregorius	.217	6	23	23	2	5	6	1	0	0	0	0	0	3	0	0	0	0	0	0	.217	.261	.478
Aaron Hicks	.154	5	17	13	1	2	5	0	0	1	3	4	0	5	1	0	0	0	0	0	.353	.385	.738
Aaron Judge	.240	6	28	25	3	6	9	0	0	1	2	3	0	10	2	0	0	0	0	0	.321	.360	.681
DJ LeMahieu	.346	6	29	26	6	9	16	1	0	2	3	3	0	2	0	0	0	0	0	0	.414	.615	1.029
C. Maybin	.333	2	4	3	0	1	1	0	0	0	0	1	0	2	0	0	0	0	0	0	.500	.333	.833
Gary Sánchez	.130	6	24	23	1	3	6	0	0	1	3	1	0	12	0	0	0	0	0	1	.167	.261	.428
G. Stanton	.286	2	7	7	1	2	5	0	0	1	1	0	0	3	0	0	0	0	0	0	.286	.714	1.000
Gleyber Torres	.280	6	27	25	3	7	15	2	0	2	6	2	0	4	0	0	0	0	0	0	.333	.600	.933
Gio Urshela	.238	6	23	21	3	5	11	0	0	2	2	2	0	2	0	0	0	0	0	0	.304	.524	.828
ALCS Totals	.214	6	228	206	21	44	79	5	0	10	21	22	0	64	3	0	0	0	0	1	.289	.383	.673

Overall Pitching	W-L	ERA	G	GS	CG	SHO	SV	SVO	IP	H	R	ER	HR	HP	BB	IBB	SO	WP	BK	AVG	WHIP	BF
Zack Britton	0-0	1.13	7	0	0	0	0	0	8.0	2	1	1	1	0	6	1	6	2	0	.080	1.00	32
Luis Cessa	0-0	0.00	2	0	0	0	0	0	4.0	2	0	0	0	1	0	0	4	0	0	.154	0.50	14
A. Chapman	0-1	3.38	5	0	0	0	2	2	5.1	2	2	2	1	0	4	0	9	0	0	.111	1.13	22
Chad Green	1-0	6.75	6	1	0	0	0	0	6.2	6	5	5	2	0	1	0	6	0	0	.231	1.05	27
J.A. Happ	0-1	2.45	3	0	0	0	0	0	3.2	2	1	1	1	0	2	0	3	0	0	.154	1.09	15
Tommy Kahnle	1-0	2.25	8	0	0	0	0	0	8.0	4	2	2	1	0	3	0	8	0	0	.138	0.88	32
J. Loaisiga	0-0	3.38	4	0	0	0	0	0	2.2	3	2	1	0	0	3	0	3	2	0	.250	2.25	15
Tyler Lyons	0-0	0.00	2	0	0	0	0	0	1.2	0	0	0	0	0	0	0	4	0	0	.000	0.00	5
Adam Ottavino	0-0	8.10	8	0	0	0	0	1	3.1	7	4	3	1	0	3	0	4	1	0	.389	3.00	21
James Paxton	1-0	3.46	3	3	0	0	0	0	13.0	13	5	5	2	0	7	0	20	1	0	.255	1.54	58
CC Sabathia	0-0	0.00	2	0	0	0	0	0	1.0	0	0	0	0	1	0	0	0	0	0	.000	0.00	5
Luis Severino	0-0	2.16	2	2	0	0	0	0	8.1	9	2	2	2	0	5	0	10	0	0	.265	1.68	39
M. Tanaka	2-1	2.25	3	3	0	0	0	0	16.0	8	5	4	1	1	4	0	12	0	0	.148	0.75	59
Post. Totals	5-4	2.87	9	9	0	0	2	3	81.2	58	29	26	12	3	38	1	89	6	0	.192	1.18	344

ALDS	W-L	ERA	G	GS	CG	SHO	SV	SVO	IP	H	R	ER	HR	HP	BB	IBB	SO	WP	BK	AVG	WHIP	BF
Zack Britton	0-0	3.86	2	0	0	0	0	0	2.1	1	1	1	1	0	1	0	1	1	0	.125	0.86	9
A. Chapman	0-0	0.00	2	0	0	0	1	1	2.2	1	0	0	0	0	2	0	4	0	0	.111	1.13	11
Chad Green	1-0	0.00	2	0	0	0	0	0	2.0	1	0	0	0	0	0	0	1	0	0	.250	0.50	8
J.A. Happ	0-0	0.00	1	0	0	0	0	0	1.0	1	0	0	0	0	1	0	2	0	0	.250	2.00	5
Tommy Kahnle	1-0	3.86	3	0	0	0	0	0	2.1	2	1	1	1	0	1	0	3	0	0	.222	1.29	10
J. Loaisiga	0-0	9.00	1	0	0	0	0	0	1.0	2	1	1	0	0	0	0	2	0	0	.400	2.00	5
Tyler Lyons	0-0	0.00	1	0	0	0	0	0	1.0	0	0	0	0	0	0	0	2	0	0	.000	0.00	3
Adam Ottavino	0-0	0.00	3	0	0	0	0	0	1.0	1	0	0	0	0	2	0	1	0	0	.250	3.00	6
James Paxton	0-0	5.79	1	1	0	0	0	0	4.2	5	3	3	2	0	1	0	8	0	0	.263	1.29	20
Luis Severino	0-0	0.00	1	1	0	0	0	0	4.0	4	0	0	0	0	2	0	4	0	0	.267	1.50	17
M. Tanaka	1-0	1.80	1	1	0	0	0	0	5.0	3	1	1	0	1	1	0	7	0	0	.176	0.80	19
ALDS Totals	3-0	2.33	3	3	0	0	1	1	27.0	22	7	7	4	1	11	0	35	1	0	.218	1.22	113

ALCS	W-L	ERA	G	GS	CG	SHO	SV	SVO	IP	H	R	ER	HR	HP	BB	IBB	SO	WP	BK	AVG	WHIP	BF
Zack Britton	0-0	0.00	5	0	0	0	0	0	5.2	1	0	0	0	0	5	1	5	1	0	.059	1.06	23
Luis Cessa	0-0	0.00	2	0	0	0	0	0	4.0	2	0	0	0	1	0	0	4	0	0	.154	0.50	14
A. Chapman	0-1	6.75	3	0	0	0	1	1	2.2	1	2	2	1	0	2	0	5	0	0	.111	1.13	11
Chad Green	0-0	9.64	4	1	0	0	0	0	4.2	4	5	5	2	0	1	0	5	0	0	.222	1.07	19
J.A. Happ	0-1	3.38	2	0	0	0	0	0	2.2	1	1	1	1	0	1	0	1	0	0	.111	0.75	10
Tommy Kahnle	0-0	1.59	5	0	0	0	0	0	5.2	2	1	1	0	0	2	0	5	0	0	.100	0.71	22
J. Loaisiga	0-0	0.00	3	0	0	0	0	0	1.2	1	1	0	0	0	3	0	1	2	0	.143	2.40	10
Tyler Lyons	0-0	0.00	1	0	0	0	0	0	0.2	0	0	0	0	0	0	0	2	0	0	.000	0.00	2
Adam Ottavino	0-0	11.57	5	0	0	0	0	1	2.1	6	4	3	1	0	1	0	3	1	0	.429	3.00	15
James Paxton	1-0	2.16	2	2	0	0	0	0	8.1	8	2	2	0	0	6	0	12	1	0	.250	1.68	38
CC Sabathia	0-0	0.00	2	0	0	0	0	0	1.0	0	0	0	0	1	0	0	0	0	0	.000	0.00	5
Luis Severino	0-1	4.15	1	1	0	0	0	0	4.1	5	2	2	2	0	3	0	6	0	0	.263	1.85	22
M. Tanaka	1-1	2.45	2	2	0	0	0	0	11.0	5	4	3	1	0	3	0	5	0	0	.135	0.73	40
ALCS Totals	2-4	3.13	6	6	0	0	1	2	54.2	36	22	19	8	2	27	1	54	5	0	.179	1.15	231

2019 Individual Batting

Batter	AVG	G	PA	AB	R	H	2B	3B	HR	RBI	TB	BB	IBB	SO	SB	CS	SF	SH	HP	GIDP	OBP	SLG	OPS
Miguel Andújar	.128	12	49	47	1	6	0	0	0	1	6	1	0	11	0	0	1	0	0	4	.143	.128	.271
Greg Bird	.171	10	41	35	6	6	0	0	1	1	9	6	0	16	0	0	0	0	0	1	.293	.257	.550
Edwin Encarnacion	.249	44	197	177	33	44	11	0	13	37	94	17	1	48	0	0	0	0	3	1	.325	.531	.856
Thairo Estrada	.250	35	69	64	12	16	3	0	3	12	28	3	0	15	4	0	0	1	1	1	.294	.438	.732
Mike Ford	.259	50	163	143	30	37	7	0	12	25	80	17	2	28	0	0	0	0	3	0	.350	.559	.909
Clint Frazier	.267	69	246	225	31	60	14	0	12	38	110	16	1	70	1	2	3	0	2	2	.317	.489	.806
Brett Gardner	.251	141	550	491	86	123	26	7	28	74	247	52	0	108	10	2	3	0	4	6	.325	.503	.829
Didi Gregorius	.238	82	344	324	47	77	14	2	16	61	143	17	1	53	2	1	2	0	1	5	.276	.441	.718
Aaron Hicks	.235	59	255	221	41	52	10	0	12	36	98	31	0	72	1	2	3	0	0	2	.325	.443	.769
Kyle Higashioka	.214	18	57	56	8	12	5	0	3	11	26	0	0	26	0	0	1	0	0	1	.211	.464	.675
Aaron Judge	.272	102	447	378	75	103	18	1	27	55	204	64	4	141	3	2	1	0	3	11	.381	.540	.921
DJ LeMahieu	.327	145	655	602	109	197	33	2	26	102	312	46	0	90	5	2	4	1	2	14	.375	.518	.893
Cameron Maybin	.285	82	269	239	48	68	17	0	11	32	118	30	0	72	9	6	0	0	5	3	.364	.494	.858
Kendrys Morales	.177	19	75	62	9	11	1	0	1	5	15	12	0	6	0	0	0	0	1	3	.320	.242	.562
Austin Romine	.281	73	240	228	29	64	12	0	8	35	100	10	0	50	1	1	1	0	0	7	.310	.439	.748
Gary Sánchez	.232	106	446	396	62	92	12	1	34	77	208	40	3	125	0	1	1	0	9	3	.316	.525	.841
Giancarlo Stanton	.288	18	72	59	8	17	3	0	3	13	29	12	0	24	0	0	1	0	0	1	.403	.492	.894
Mike Tauchman	.277	87	296	260	46	72	18	1	13	47	131	34	0	71	6	0	1	0	1	9	.361	.504	.865
Gleyber Torres	.278	144	604	546	96	152	26	0	38	90	292	48	3	129	5	2	6	1	3	10	.337	.535	.871
Troy Tulowitzki	.182	5	13	11	1	2	1	0	1	1	6	2	0	4	0	0	0	0	0	1	.308	.545	.853
Gio Urshela	.314	132	476	442	73	139	34	0	21	74	236	25	1	87	1	1	4	0	5	13	.355	.534	.889
Breyvic Valera	.219	12	37	32	5	7	1	0	3	10	4	0	5	0	0	0	1	0	.324	.313	.637
Luke Voit	.263	118	510	429	72	113	21	1	21	62	199	71	2	142	0	0	1	0	9	12	.378	.464	.842
Tyler Wade	.245	43	108	94	16	23	3	1	2	11	34	11	0	28	7	0	0	2	1	0	.330	.362	.692
Luis Cessa	.000	43	1	1	0	0	0	0	0	0	0	0	0	1	0	0	0	0	0	0	.000	.000	.000
Domingo Germán	.000	27	8	8	0	0	0	0	0	0	0	0	0	7	0	0	0	0	0	1	.000	.000	.000
Chad Green	.000	54	1	1	0	0	0	0	0	0	0	0	0	1	0	0	0	0	0	0	.000	.000	.000
J.A. Happ	.000	32	4	3	1	0	0	0	0	0	0	0	0	2	0	0	0	1	0	0	.000	.000	.000
James Paxton	.000	29	8	5	0	0	0	0	0	1	0	0	0	5	0	0	0	3	0	0	.000	.000	.000
CC Sabathia	.000	23	3	3	0	0	0	0	0	0	0	0	0	2	0	0	0	0	0	0	.000	.000	.000
Masahiro Tanaka	.000	32	1	1	0	0	0	0	0	0	0	0	0	1	0	0	0	0	0	0	.000	.000	.000
NYY Totals	.267	162	6245	5583	943	1493	290	17	306	904	2735	569	18	1437	55	22	33	10	49	113	.339	.490	.829
Opponents	.248	162	6133	5535	739	1374	277	18	248	711	2131	507	12	1534	71	24	36	7	44	119	.314	.439	.754
NYY Pitchers	.000		26	22	1	0	0	0	0	1	0	0	0	16	0	0	0	4	0	1	.000	.000	.000

2019 Batting vs./at Opponents

Opponent	AVG	G	AB	R	R/G	H	2B	3B	HR	RBI	BB	IBB	SO	HP	LOB	SB	CS	OBP	SLG	OPS
vs. Arizona	.198	4	126	12	3.00	25	8	0	4	12	12	0	31	1	22	0	1	.273	.357	.631
vs. Baltimore	.303	19	673	151	7.95	204	34	2	61	147	88	2	134	5	126	4	2	.386	.632	1.018
vs. Boston	.290	19	665	125	6.58	193	53	0	29	119	70	2	174	5	132	5	4	.360	.501	.860
vs. Cleveland	.244	7	238	31	4.43	58	15	0	11	29	20	1	61	2	45	1	1	.305	.445	.751
vs. Colorado	.286	3	105	23	7.67	30	4	0	5	22	12	0	25	1	20	2	0	.364	.467	.831
vs. Chicago-AL	.251	7	223	36	5.14	56	8	0	7	35	27	1	56	2	43	1	2	.333	.381	.714
vs. Detroit	.236	6	203	32	5.33	48	9	2	12	30	22	2	64	1	36	6	2	.313	.478	.791
vs. Houston	.243	7	230	37	5.29	56	8	1	13	37	20	0	75	0	36	2	0	.302	.457	.758
vs. Kansas City	.280	7	246	43	6.14	69	12	1	9	40	29	0	53	3	52	3	0	.359	.447	.807
vs. L.A.-AL	.233	7	253	41	5.86	59	9	1	11	39	33	3	74	1	51	11	0	.321	.407	.728
vs. L.A.-NL	.266	3	109	16	5.33	29	5	0	9	16	5	1	33	1	18	1	0	.304	.560	.864
vs. Minnesota	.327	6	211	43	7.17	69	15	2	12	39	25	0	57	2	41	1	0	.402	.588	.989
vs. N.Y. Mets	.280	4	143	23	5.75	40	9	1	6	23	12	0	36	0	29	2	0	.335	.483	.818
vs. Oakland	.236	6	203	20	3.33	48	5	0	11	19	14	0	60	1	38	0	0	.286	.424	.710
vs. San Diego	.253	3	99	16	5.33	25	2	1	8	14	8	0	28	2	19	2	0	.318	.535	.854
vs. Seattle	.265	7	238	35	5.00	63	13	2	13	34	16	1	43	2	40	4	0	.315	.500	.815
vs. San Francisco	.339	3	109	24	8.00	37	7	0	4	23	11	0	26	2	20	2	0	.410	.514	.924
vs. Tampa Bay	.234	19	646	96	5.05	151	26	1	33	90	66	4	198	5	109	6	4	.309	.430	.739
vs. Texas	.258	6	198	33	5.50	51	8	1	14	33	16	0	55	2	28	0	0	.318	.520	.838
vs. Toronto	.274	19	665	106	5.58	182	40	2	34	103	63	1	154	11	134	2	6	.345	.493	.838
Ballpark	AVG	G	AB	R	R/G	H	2B	3B	HR	RBI	BB	IBB	SO	HP	LOB	SB	CS	OBP	SLG	OPS
Angel Stadium	.226	4	155	22	5.50	35	4	1	5	20	21	2	45	1	35	10	0	.317	.361	.678
Camden Yards	.320	10	375	95	9.50	120	21	1	43	93	46	1	66	3	68	4	1	.398	.725	1.123
Chase Field	.194	2	62	3	1.50	12	4	0	1	3	6	0	12	0	11	0	1	.265	.306	.571
Citi Field	.239	2	67	7	3.50	16	4	0	2	7	6	0	21	0	14	1	0	.301	.388	.689
Comerica Park	.286	3	112	27	9.00	32	6	2	10	26	13	1	30	0	17	3	1	.360	.643	1.003
Dodger Stadium	.266	3	109	16	5.33	29	5	0	9	16	5	1	33	1	18	1	0	.304	.560	.864
Fenway Park	.265	8	287	43	5.38	76	26	0	11	39	28	1	76	1	59	2	1	.330	.470	.801
Globe Life Park	.275	3	102	19	6.33	28	5	1	7	19	8	0	31	1	12	0	0	.330	.549	.879
Guaranteed Rate Field	.273	4	139	24	6.00	38	6	0	5	23	20	1	35	1	29	1	2	.366	.424	.791
Kauffman Stadium	.279	3	111	20	6.67	31	4	1	2	20	14	0	24	1	23	2	0	.362	.387	.750
London Stadium	.376	2	85	29	14.50	32	10	0	4	28	15	1	21	0	18	0	0	.465	.635	1.101
Minute Maid Park	.228	3	101	12	4.00	23	4	0	4	12	9	0	30	0	19	1	0	.286	.386	.672
Oakland Coliseum	.280	3	107	9	3.00	30	5	0	5	9	5	0	32	0	23	0	0	.310	.467	.777
Oracle Park	.339	3	109	24	8.00	37	7	0	4	23	11	0	26	2	20	2	0	.410	.514	.924
Progressive Field	.218	3	101	13	4.33	22	8	0	3	13	12	1	26	0	18	0	1	.296	.386	.682
Rogers Centre	.251	10	362	57	5.70	91	23	0	19	55	37	0	81	6	70	1	3	.330	.472	.802
T-Mobile Park	.279	4	111	19	6.33	31	7	1	9	19	10	0	24	1	22	2	0	.344	.604	.948
Target Field	.387	3	124	30	10.00	48	2	8	29	13	0	28	0	24	1	0	.442	.726	1.168
Tropicana Field	.204	9	313	34	3.78	64	13	0	12	32	26	1	109	4	50	3	4	.273	.361	.634
Yankee Stadium	.263	81	2651	440	5.43	698	114	8	143	418	264	8	687	27	497	21	8	.334	.474	.809

2019 Batting Splits

General	AVG	G	AB	R	R/G	H	2B	3B	HR	RBI	BB	IBB	SO	HP	LOB	SB	CS	OBP	SLG	OPS
Total	.267	162	5583	943	5.82	1493	290	17	306	904	569	18	1437	49	1039	55	22	.339	.490	.829
vs. Left	.273	-	1509	-	-	412	90	2	86	244	157	8	384	13	-	15	5	.346	.506	.852
vs. Right	.265	-	4074	-	-	1081	200	15	220	660	412	10	1053	36	-	40	17	.336	.484	.820
Home	.263	81	2651	440	5.43	698	114	8	143	418	264	8	687	27	497	21	8	.334	.474	.809
Away	.271	81	2932	503	6.21	795	176	9	163	486	305	10	750	22	542	34	14	.342	.504	.846
Day	.262	64	2180	378	5.91	571	112	6	116	361	252	5	596	24	425	22	10	.343	.478	.821
Night	.271	98	3403	565	5.77	922	178	11	190	543	317	13	841	25	614	33	12	.336	.497	.833
Grass	.272	139	4761	820	5.90	1294	240	17	270	786	485	16	1214	39	890	51	14	.342	.499	.842
Turf	.242	23	822	123	5.35	199	50	0	36	118	84	2	223	10	149	4	8	.319	.434	.753
Pre-All Star	.265	88	3004	503	5.72	795	136	8	149	480	327	11	785	26	573	35	13	.340	.464	.804
Post-All Star	.271	74	2579	440	5.95	698	154	9	157	424	242	7	652	23	466	20	9	.338	.520	.858
None on	.249	-	3254	-	-	810	161	10	178	178	311	0	867	27	-	0	0	.320	.469	.788
None on/out	.252	-	1391	-	-	350	70	3	78	78	123	0	362	12	-	0	0	.318	.474	.792
Runners on	.293	-	2329	-	-	683	129	7	128	726	258	18	570	22	-	55	22	.364	.520	.884
Scoring Posn	.294	-	1271	-	-	374	69	6	68	587	162	18	302	14	-	17	2	.372	.518	.890
ScPos/2 Out	.265	-	577	-	-	153	24	2	29	231	77	9	160	6	-	9	1	.358	.464	.822
Bases Loaded	.361	-	133	-	-	48	10	1	7	141	11	0	20	3	-	0	0	.390	.609	.999
With 0 Outs	.261	162	1934	-	-	504	103	4	102	209	188	0	486	15	-	8	1	.330	.476	.806
With 1 Out	.275	162	1839	-	-	506	93	7	103	351	189	9	456	19	-	21	11	.345	.501	.846
With 2 Outs	.267	162	1810	-	-	483	94	6	101	344	192	9	495	15	-	26	10	.342	.493	.835
Inning 1-6	.272	-	3857	667	-	1048	199	12	222	644	380	4	957	32	-	37	13	.341	.502	.843
Inning 7+	.258	-	1726	276	-	445	91	5	84	260	189	14	480	17	-	18	9	.334	.462	.797
In Wins	.296	103	3613	756	7.34	1069	221	14	240	725	390	16	878	34	658	42	14	.368	.564	.932
In Losses	.215	59	1970	187	3.17	424	69	3	66	179	179	2	559	15	381	13	8	.284	.354	.638
Interleague	.269	20	691	114	5.70	186	35	2	36	110	60	1	179	7	128	9	1	.333	.482	.815
vs. AL	.267	142	4892	829	5.84	1307	255	15	270	794	509	17	1258	42	911	46	21	.339	.491	.830
vs. AL East	.276	76	2649	478	6.29	730	153	5	157	459	287	9	660	26	501	17	16	.351	.515	.865
vs. AL Central	.268	33	1121	185	5.61	300	59	5	51	173	123	4	291	10	217	12	5	.343	.466	.808
vs. AL West	.247	33	1122	166	5.03	277	43	5	62	162	99	4	307	6	193	17	0	.309	.460	.769
March	.277	3	101	15	5.00	28	3	0	4	14	22	0	31	2	33	0	0	.413	.426	.838
April	.257	26	881	141	5.42	226	42	1	42	134	93	3	228	11	169	18	3	.332	.449	.781
May	.255	27	901	144	5.33	230	35	4	45	132	88	4	228	9	158	10	3	.326	.453	.779
June	.286	26	908	176	6.77	260	46	3	47	173	106	4	232	4	178	4	4	.361	.499	.860
July	.275	25	875	143	5.72	241	57	3	42	135	86	2	232	5	164	6	6	.343	.491	.834
August	.278	30	1050	178	5.93	292	59	3	74	172	86	3	244	10	188	9	2	.338	.551	.889
September	.249	25	867	146	5.84	216	48	3	52	144	88	2	242	8	149	8	4	.323	.491	.814

	AVG	G	AB	R	R/G	H	2B	3B	HR	RBI	BB	IBB	SO	HP	LOB	SB	CS	OBP	SLG	OPS
As ph for dh	.333	-	3	1	-	1	0	0	1	1	0	0	1	0	-	0	0	.333	1.333	1.667
As p	.000	-	22	1	-	0	0	0	0	1	0	0	16	0	-	0	0	.000	.000	.000
As c	.246	-	614	87	-	151	27	1	38	107	43	3	181	8	-	1	2	.302	.479	.781
As 1b	.270	-	619	104	-	167	31	0	27	80	82	2	152	7	-	0	0	.361	.451	.812
As 2b	.287	-	627	106	-	180	29	2	22	92	53	0	131	6	-	9	2	.346	.445	.791
As 3b	.312	-	629	102	-	196	43	1	32	108	45	1	113	5	-	3	2	.359	.536	.894
As ss	.257	-	641	105	-	165	32	2	43	120	47	4	130	3	-	7	2	.308	.515	.823
As lf	.286	-	553	104	-	158	33	4	29	96	75	0	140	1	-	18	5	.371	.517	.888
As cf	.259	-	621	109	-	161	38	4	34	103	70	0	161	4	-	9	2	.335	.498	.832
As rf	.260	-	608	111	-	158	29	2	37	89	86	5	217	5	-	6	3	.356	.497	.852
All OF	.268	-	1782	324	-	477	100	10	100	288	231	5	518	10	-	33	10	.353	.503	.857
All DH	.243	-	600	102	-	146	26	1	41	99	64	3	180	10	-	0	3	.325	.495	.820
All PH	.231	-	52	8	-	12	2	0	4	10	4	0	17	0	-	1	1	.286	.500	.786
As dh (not ph)	.243	-	597	101	-	145	26	1	40	98	64	3	179	10	-	0	2	.325	.491	.816
As ph (not dh)	.224	-	49	7	-	11	2	0	3	9	4	0	16	0	-	1	1	.283	.449	.732
As pr	-	-	0	5	-	0	0	0	0	0	0	0	0	0	-	1	1	-	-	-
Batting #1	.290	-	693	121	-	201	33	2	32	106	63	0	121	3	-	9	2	.351	.482	.833
Batting #2	.285	-	625	126	-	178	29	2	46	103	106	5	210	7	-	4	2	.393	.558	.951
Batting #3	.250	-	647	104	-	162	32	2	37	105	73	0	187	5	-	2	2	.328	.478	.805
Batting #4	.240	-	658	94	-	158	28	1	36	117	52	5	186	8	-	1	2	.302	.450	.752
Batting #5	.258	-	629	103	-	162	30	3	40	121	61	4	151	8	-	4	3	.329	.506	.835
Batting #6	.261	-	616	101	-	161	44	2	32	81	50	2	142	4	-	6	5	.319	.495	.814
Batting #7	.275	-	589	99	-	162	27	0	34	96	57	1	142	6	-	7	1	.342	.494	.836
Batting #8	.276	-	583	94	-	161	38	1	25	90	50	1	149	3	-	13	3	.335	.473	.809
Batting #9	.273	-	543	101	-	148	29	4	24	85	57	0	149	5	-	9	2	.347	.473	.820
As LHB	.243	-	1575	-	-	383	77	12	83	255	177	3	368	10	-	-	-	.322	.465	.787
As RHB	.277	-	4008	-	-	1110	213	5	223	649	392	15	1069	39	-	-	-	.345	.500	.845

	AVG	G	AB	R	R/G	H	2B	3B	HR	RBI	BB	IBB	SO	HP	LOB	SB	CS	OBP	SLG	OPS
Leading Off Inn.	.252	-	1304	-	-	329	64	3	72	72	113	0	342	9	-	-	-	.316	.472	.788
vs P, 1st time in G	.257	-	3593	-	-	923	175	10	182	544	393	15	994	36	-	37	16	.334	.463	.797
vs P, 2nd time in G	.294	-	1352	-	-	397	82	4	92	252	109	1	299	8	-	9	5	.348	.564	.913
vs P, 3rd time in G	.268	-	630	-	-	169	31	3	32	108	67	2	142	5	-	3	0	.341	.479	.820
vs P, 4th+ time in G	.500	-	8	-	-	4	2	0	0	0	0	0	2	0	-	0	0	.500	.750	1.250
0-0 Count	.394	-	592	-	-	233	39	3	56	140	0	0	0	13	-	12	5	.403	.753	1.157
0-1 Count	.337	-	460	-	-	155	32	2	25	83	0	0	0	6	-	5	1	.343	.578	.922
0-2 Count	.138	-	564	-	-	78	14	0	15	41	0	0	303	6	-	7	4	.147	.243	.390
1-0 Count	.384	-	341	-	-	131	30	2	30	98	0	0	0	2	-	9	1	.384	.748	1.132
1-1 Count	.346	-	451	-	-	156	26	1	35	90	0	0	0	3	-	2	1	.349	.641	.990
1-2 Count	.189	-	937	-	-	177	36	1	33	94	0	0	425	11	-	5	4	.198	.335	.533
2-0 Count	.385	-	156	-	-	60	13	0	18	46	0	0	0	0	-	4	0	.375	.814	1.189
2-1 Count	.379	-	298	-	-	113	16	2	26	80	0	0	0	1	-	3	2	.377	.718	1.086
2-2 Count	.193	-	948	-	-	183	35	4	27	91	0	0	442	5	-	5	0	.197	.324	.521
3-0 Count	.429	-	14	-	-	6	2	0	6	99	16	0	0	0	-	0	0	.929	1.571	1.501
3-1 Count	.409	-	154	-	-	63	12	0	17	55	151	2	0	0	-	2	0	.699	.818	1.518
3-2 Count	.207	-	668	-	-	138	35	2	24	80	319	0	267	2	-	1	7	.462	.373	.835

2019 Pinch Hitters

Player	AVG	PA	AB	H	2B	3B	HR	RBI	TB	BB	IBB	SO	SF	SH	HP	GIDP	OBP	SLG	OPS
Thairo Estrada	.500	3	2	1	1	0	0	3	2	0	0	0	0	1	0	0	.500	1.000	1.500
Mike Ford	.455	12	11	5	1	0	2	3	12	1	0	3	0	0	0	0	.500	1.091	1.591
Clint Frazier	.000	4	4	0	0	0	0	0	0	0	0	3	0	0	0	0	.000	.000	.000
Brett Gardner	.000	3	3	0	0	0	0	0	0	0	0	1	0	0	0	0	.000	.000	.000
J.A. Happ	.000	1	1	0	0	0	0	0	0	0	0	0	0	0	0	0	.000	.000	.000
Aaron Hicks	1.000	1	1	1	0	0	1	1	4	0	0	0	0	0	0	1	1.000	4.000	5.000
Aaron Judge	.000	2	1	0	0	0	0	0	0	1	0	1	0	0	0	0	.500	.000	.500
DJ LeMahieu	.000	1	1	0	0	0	0	0	0	0	0	0	0	0	0	0	.000	.000	.000
Cameron Maybin	.250	4	4	1	0	0	0	1	1	0	0	2	0	0	0	0	.250	.250	.500
Kendrys Morales	.000	2	1	0	0	0	0	0	0	1	0	0	0	0	0	0	.500	.000	.500
Austin Romine	.000	2	2	0	0	0	0	0	0	0	0	0	0	0	0	1	.000	.000	.000
Gary Sánchez	.200	5	5	1	0	0	0	1	1	0	0	2	0	0	0	0	.200	.200	.400
Mike Tauchman	.000	1	1	0	0	0	0	0	0	0	0	1	0	0	0	0	.000	.000	.000
Gleyber Torres	.000	2	1	0	0	0	0	0	0	1	0	1	0	0	0	0	.500	.000	.500
Troy Tulowitzki	.000	1	1	0	0	0	0	0	0	0	0	1	0	0	0	0	.000	.000	.000
Gio Urshela	.222	9	9	2	0	0	1	2	5	0	0	2	0	0	0	0	.222	.556	.778
Luke Voit	.500	2	2	1	0	0	1	1	4	0	0	0	0	0	0	0	.500	.500	1.000
Tyler Wade	.000	2	2	0	0	0	0	0	0	0	0	0	0	0	0	0	.000	.000	.000
TOTALS	.231	57	52	12	2	0	4	10	26	4	0	17	0	1	0	1	.286	.500	.786

2019 Batting with Runners in Scoring Position

Player	AVG	PA	AB	H	2B	3B	HR	RBI	TB	BB	IBB	SO	SH	SF	HP	GDP	OBP	SLG	OPS
Miguel Andújar	.077	14	13	1	0	0	0	1	1	0	0	4	1	0	0	3	.071	.077	.148
Greg Bird	.167	6	6	1	0	0	0	1	1	0	0	3	0	0	0	0	.167	.167	.333
Edwin Encarnacion	.275	48	40	11	4	0	2	18	21	7	1	10	0	0	1	0	.396	.525	.921
Thairo Estrada	.400	17	15	6	2	0	1	9	11	1	0	3	0	1	0	0	.438	.733	1.171
Mike Ford	.241	35	29	7	1	0	1	10	11	5	2	3	0	0	1	0	.371	.379	.751
Clint Frazier	.362	56	47	17	5	0	5	28	37	5	1	15	3	0	1	0	.411	.787	1.198
Brett Gardner	.198	122	101	20	5	1	6	44	45	17	0	21	3	0	1	1	.311	.446	.757
Didi Gregorius	.308	86	78	24	7	2	5	48	50	6	1	14	2	0	0	3	.349	.641	.990
Aaron Hicks	.255	59	47	12	3	0	3	24	24	9	0	15	3	0	0	0	.356	.511	.867
Kyle Higashioka	.294	18	17	5	0	0	2	10	11	0	0	6	1	0	0	0	.278	.647	.925
Aaron Judge	.242	92	66	16	4	0	2	22	26	22	4	26	1	0	2	2	.440	.394	.833
DJ LeMahieu	.389	145	126	49	6	0	6	73	73	13	0	15	4	1	1	5	.438	.579	1.017
Cameron Maybin	.295	66	61	18	7	0	0	21	25	5	0	18	0	0	1	0	.348	.410	.758
Kendrys Morales	.125	19	16	2	0	0	0	4	2	3	0	3	0	0	0	1	.263	.125	.388
Austin Romine	.314	57	51	16	2	0	1	24	21	4	0	9	1	1	0	0	.357	.412	.769
Gary Sánchez	.231	118	104	24	5	0	9	46	56	11	3	27	1	0	2	2	.314	.538	.852
Giancarlo Stanton	.429	19	14	6	1	0	1	11	10	4	0	5	1	0	0	1	.526	.714	1.241
Mike Tauchman	.324	85	74	24	4	1	5	36	45	9	0	20	1	0	1	5	.400	.608	1.008
Gleyber Torres	.344	145	128	44	5	0	11	60	82	11	3	21	6	0	0	5	.379	.641	1.020
Troy Tulowitzki	.000	3	2	0	0	0	0	0	0	1	0	1	0	0	0	0	.333	.000	.333
Gio Urshela	.333	120	108	36	4	0	3	46	49	7	1	20	4	0	1	8	.367	.454	.820
Breyvic Valera	.429	8	7	3	0	1	0	3	5	1	0	0	0	0	0	0	.500	.714	1.214
Luke Voit	.308	114	91	28	4	0	5	40	47	19	2	30	1	0	3	1	.439	.516	.955
Tyler Wade	.167	28	24	4	0	1	0	8	6	2	0	9	0	2	0	0	.231	.250	.481
Domingo Germán	.000	2	2	0	0	0	0	0	0	0	0	1	0	0	0	1	.000	.000	.000
J.A. Happ	.000	1	1	0	0	0	0	0	0	0	0	0	0	0	0	0	.000	.000	.000
James Paxton	.000	5	3	0	0	0	1	0	0	0	3	0	2	0	0	.000	.000	.000
TOTALS	.294	1488	1271	374	69	6	68	587	659	162	18	302	7	33	14	39	.372	.518	.890

2019 Home Runs

2019 YANKEES HOME RUNS

1st-INNING LEADOFF HRs
7x in 2019 / 6x in 2018

Player	Date/Opp. (Pitcher)
LeMahieu	8/25 at LAD (Kershaw)
LeMahieu	8/13 vs. BAL (Means)
LeMahieu	8/3 vs. BOS-G1 (Sale)
LeMahieu	7/21 vs. COL (Márquez)
LeMahieu	6/25 vs. TOR (Richard)
LeMahieu	5/29 vs. SD (Paddack)
Gardner	4/10 at HOU (McHugh)

PINCH-HIT HRs
4x in 2019 / 1x in 2018

Player	Date/Opp. (Pitcher)
Ford	9/14 at TOR (Shafer)
Urshela	9/12 at DET-G2 (Schreiber)
Ford	9/1 vs. OAK (Hendriks)
Hicks	7/5 at TB (Pagán)

GRAND SLAMS
7x in 2019 / 8x in 2018

Player	Date/Opp. (Pitcher)
Gregorius	8/23 at LAD (Ryu)
Torres	8/2 vs. BOS (Rodríguez)
Encarnación	7/19 vs. COL (Freeland)
Gregorius	7/16 vs. TB (Poche)
Torres	6/19 vs. TB (Drake)
Sánchez	4/27 at SF (Holland)
Gardner	4/17 vs. BOS (Brasier)

"WALK-OFF" HRs
2x in 2019 / 4x in 2018

Player	Date/Opp. (Pitcher)
Ford	9/1 vs. OAK (Hendriks)
LeMahieu	8/31 vs. OAK (Trivino)

INSIDE-THE-PARK HRs
0x in 2019 / 2x in 2018

Player	Date/Opp. (Pitcher)
None in 2019	

Last: Hicks, 5/19/18 at KC (off Duffy)

MULTI-HR INNING (TEAM) / BACK-TO-BACK HRs
34x/11x in 2019 / 27x/10x in 2018

Back-to-Back HRs	Date/Opp. (Inning)
Torres/Voit	9/14 at TOR (6th inn.)
Encarnación/Gregorius	9/10 at DET (7th inn.)
Gregorius/Sánchez	9/3 vs. OAK (3rd inn.)
Gardner/Ford	9/1 vs. OAK (9th inn.)
Gregorius/Torres	8/17 vs. CLE (4th inn.)
Gardner/Maybin	8/6 at BAL (9th inn.)
Tauchman/LeMahieu	8/6 at BAL (3rd inn.)
Gregorius/Urshela	7/3 at NYM (6th inn.)
LeMahieu/Judge	6/25 vs. TOR (1st inn.)
LeMahieu/Voit	5/29 vs. SD (1st inn.)
Tauchman/LeMahieu	4/20 vs. KC (4th inn.)

Last b2b2b: Holliday/Castro/Gregorius, 6/3/17 at TOR (8th inn.)
Last multi-HR inn., indiv.: A. Rodriguez, 10/4/09 at TB (2HR in 6th)

MULTI-HR GAMES
28x in 2019 / 24x in 2018

Player	Date/Opp. (Pitcher)
Gardner	2HR, 9/14 at TOR (Waguespack/Stewart)
Gregorius	2HR, 9/10 at DET (Alexander/Stumpf)
Gardner	2HR, 9/10 at DET (Jackson, 2x)
Sánchez	2HR, 9/3 vs. TEX (Vólquez/Jurado)
Sánchez	2HR, 8/31 vs. OAK (Bailey, 2x)
Ford	2HR, 8/26 at SEA (Milone, 2x)
Gregorius	2HR, 8/23 at LAD (Ryu/Sadler)
Torres	2HR, 8/22 at OAK (Roark/Soria)
Torres	2HR, 8/17 vs. CLE (Plesac/Wittgren)
Torres	2HR, 8/12 vs. BAL-G2 (Phillips/Eshelman)
Urshela	2HR, 8/8 at TOR (Pannone, 2x)
Higashioka	2HR, 8/7 at BAL (Means/Hess)
Urshela	2HR, 8/7 at BAL (Castro/Scott)
Tauchman	2HR, 8/5 at BAL (Kline/Fry)
Torres	2HR, 8/3 vs. BOS-G2 (Johnson/Taylor)
LeMahieu	2HR, 8/3 vs. BOS-G1 (Sale, 2x)
Encarnación	2HR, 7/15 vs. TB (Snell/Kittredge)
Judge	2HR, 7/5 at TB (McKay/Stanek)
Torres	2HR, 5/22 at BAL (Straily/Ynoa)
Frazier	2HR, 5/21 at BAL (Hess, 2x)
Torres	2HR, 5/20 at BAL (Cashner/Givens)
Torres	2HR, 5/15 vs. BAL-G1 (Hess, 2x)
Sánchez	2HR, 5/3 vs. MIN (Gibson/Morin)
Voit	2HR, 4/23 at LAA (Stratton/Freeman)
Sánchez	3HR, 4/7 at BAL (Hess/Wright/Straily)
Frazier	2HR, 4/7 at BAL (Hess/Straily)
Judge	2HR, 4/6 at BAL (Bundy, 2x)
Torres	2HR, 4/4 at BAL (Cobb/Wright)

RUNS VIA HR / RUNNERS ON BASE
HRs: 306 / **Runs:** 943 / **Runs via HR:** 482 (51.1%)

Solo (178): Bird-1, Encarnación-6, Estrada-1, Ford-8, Frazier-5, Gardner-15, Gregorius-9, Hicks-6, Higashioka-1, Judge-18, LeMahieu-15, Maybin-11, Morales-1, Romine-5, Sánchez-19, Stanton-2, Tauchman-6, Torres-24, Tulowitzki-1, Urshela-10, Voit-13, Wade-1

2-Run (87): Encarnación-6, Estrada-2, Ford-4, Frazier-4, Gardner-8, Gregorius-5, Hicks-4, Higashioka-1, Judge-9, LeMahieu-7, Romine-3, Sánchez-9, Tauchman-5, Torres-6, Urshela-11, Voit-5, Wade-1

3-Run (34): Frazier-3, Gardner-4, Gregorius-3, Hicks-2, Higashioka-1, LeMahieu-4, Sánchez-5, Stanton-1, Tauchman-2, Torres-6, Voit-3

Grand Slams (7): Encarnación-1, Gardner-1, Gregorius-2, Sánchez-1, Torres-2

2018: HRs: 267 / Runs: 851 / Runs via HR: 432 (50.8%)
2018: Solo (147) / 2R (83) / 3R (29) / GS (8)

MOST RECENT HOME RUNS BY PLAYERS ON 40-MAN ROSTER AT SEASON'S END

Player	Date/Opp. (Pitcher)
Andújar	9/27/18 at TB (Schultz)
Bird	3/29/19 vs. BAL (Fry)
Encarnación	9/12/19 at DET-G1 (Boyd)
Ellsbury	8/26/17 vs. SEA (Gallardo)
Estrada	5/22/19 at BAL (Straily)
Ford	9/27/19 at TEX (Sampson)
Frazier	9/19/19 vs. LAA (Del Pozo)
Gardner	9/27/19 at TEX (Palumbo)
Gregorius	2HR, 9/10 at DET (Alexander/Stumpf)
Hicks	7/24/19 at MIN (Odorizzi)
Higashioka	2HR, 8/7/19 at BAL (Means/Hess)
Judge	9/29/19 at TEX (Lynn)
LeMahieu	9/22/19 vs. TOR (Thornton)
Maybin	9/27/19 at TEX (Palumbo)
Romine	9/27/19 at TEX (Kelley)
Sánchez	2HR, 9/3/19 vs. TEX (Vólquez/Jurado)
Stanton	9/27/19 at TEX (Palumbo)
Tauchman	9/8/19 at BOS (Porcello)
Torres	9/17/19 vs. LAA (Suarez)
Voit	9/14/19 at TOR (Stewart)
Urshela	9/27/19 at TEX (Sampson)
Wade	9/20/19 vs. TOR (Waguespack)

2019 Individual Pitching

Pitcher	W-L	ERA	G	GS	CG	SHO	SV	SVO	IP	H	R	ER	HR	HP	BB	IBB	SO	WP	BK	AVG	WHIP	BF
Chance Adams	1-1	8.53	13	0	0	0	1	1	25.1	39	25	24	7	2	11	0	23	1	1	.351	1.97	124
Jake Barrett	0-0	14.73	2	0	0	0	0	0	3.2	6	6	6	2	0	2	0	4	0	0	.353	2.18	19
Dellin Betances	0-0	0.00	1	0	0	0	0	0	0.2	0	0	0	0	0	0	0	2	0	0	.000	0.00	2
Zack Britton	3-1	1.91	66	0	0	0	3	7	61.1	38	13	13	3	1	32	1	53	3	0	.182	1.14	245
Luis Cessa	2-1	4.11	43	0	0	0	1	1	81.0	75	42	37	14	3	31	1	75	1	0	.246	1.31	343
Aroldis Chapman	3-2	2.21	60	0	0	0	37	42	57.0	38	18	14	3	1	25	0	85	6	0	.185	1.11	235
Nestor Cortes	5-1	5.67	33	1	0	0	0	1	66.2	75	44	42	16	1	28	1	69	1	0	.281	1.55	298
Ryan Dull	0-0	19.29	3	0	0	0	0	0	2.1	5	5	5	0	0	3	0	4	0	0	.417	3.43	15
Mike Ford	0-0	22.50	1	0	0	0	0	0	2.0	6	5	5	2	0	0	0	1	0	0	.500	3.00	12
Cory Gearrin	1-1	4.50	18	0	0	0	0	0	14.0	17	7	7	2	0	4	0	8	0	1	.298	1.50	61
Domingo Germán	18-4	4.03	27	24	0	0	0	0	143.0	125	69	64	30	5	39	0	153	5	0	.228	1.15	594
Chad Green	4-4	4.17	54	15	0	0	2	2	69.0	66	35	32	10	6	19	0	98	2	0	.247	1.23	295
David Hale	3-0	3.11	20	0	0	0	2	2	37.2	39	13	13	2	1	7	1	23	2	0	.264	1.22	157
J.A. Happ	12-8	4.91	31	30	0	0	0	0	161.1	160	88	88	34	5	49	1	140	3	0	.258	1.30	678
Joe Harvey	1-0	4.50	9	0	0	0	0	0	10.0	11	6	5	1	1	7	0	11	0	0	.282	1.80	48
Ben Heller	0-0	1.23	6	0	0	0	0	0	7.1	6	1	1	1	0	3	1	9	0	0	.250	1.23	28
Jonathan Holder	5-2	6.31	34	1	0	0	0	2	41.1	43	32	29	8	2	11	1	46	0	0	.256	1.31	181
Tommy Kahnle	3-2	3.67	72	0	0	0	0	5	61.1	45	27	25	9	2	20	0	88	8	0	.200	1.06	248
Michael King	0-0	0.00	1	0	0	0	0	0	2.0	2	1	0	0	0	0	0	1	0	0	.222	1.00	9
Brady Lail	0-0	10.13	1	0	0	0	0	0	2.2	2	3	3	1	0	1	0	2	0	0	.222	1.13	10
Jonathan Loaisiga	2-2	4.55	15	4	0	0	0	1	31.2	31	16	16	6	1	16	0	37	1	0	.263	1.48	139
Tyler Lyons	0-1	4.15	11	0	0	0	0	0	8.2	7	4	4	3	1	2	1	12	0	0	.226	1.04	34
Joe Mantiply	1-0	9.00	1	0	0	0	0	0	3.0	3	3	3	1	0	2	0	2	0	0	.250	1.67	14
Jordan Montgomery	0-0	6.75	2	1	0	0	0	0	4.0	7	3	3	1	0	0	0	5	0	0	.368	1.75	19
Adam Ottavino	6-5	1.90	73	0	0	0	2	9	66.1	47	17	14	5	2	40	3	88	3	1	.198	1.31	283
James Paxton	15-6	3.82	29	29	0	0	0	0	150.2	138	71	64	23	2	55	0	186	7	1	.242	1.28	633
Austin Romine	0-0	27.00	1	0	0	0	0	0	1.0	4	3	3	2	0	0	0	0	0	0	.571	4.00	7
Adonis Rosa	0-0	4.50	1	0	0	0	0	0	2.0	1	1	1	1	0	0	0	2	0	0	.143	0.50	7
CC Sabathia	5-8	4.95	23	22	0	0	0	0	107.1	112	64	59	27	3	39	0	107	0	0	.265	1.41	468
Luis Severino	1-1	1.50	3	3	0	0	0	0	12.0	6	2	2	0	1	6	0	17	0	0	.146	1.00	48
Masahiro Tanaka	11-9	4.45	32	31	0	0	0	0	182.0	186	95	90	28	2	40	0	149	7	0	.261	1.24	759
Stephen Tarpley	0-0	6.93	21	1	0	0	0	0	24.2	34	20	19	6	2	15	1	34	5	1	.330	1.99	120
Team Totals	**103-59**	**4.31**	**162**	**162**	**1**	**9**	**50**	**75**	**1443.0**	**1374**	**739**	**691**	**248**	**44**	**507**	**12**	**1534**	**55**	**5**	**.248**	**1.30**	**6133**

2019 Starting Pitchers & Relief Pitchers

AS STARTER	W-L	ERA	G	GS	CG	SHO	SV	SVO	IP	H	R	ER	HR	HP	BB	IBB	SO	WP	BK	AVG	WHIP	BF
Nestor Cortes Jr.	0-0	7.71	1	1	0	0	0	0	2.1	4	4	2	0	1	0	1	0	2	0	0	.500	3.00	13
Domingo Germán	16-4	4.28	24	24	0	0	0	0	134.2	122	69	64	30	4	37	0	142	5	0	.235	1.18	562
Chad Green	0-1	3.72	15	15	0	0	0	0	19.1	18	9	8	4	2	8	0	32	1	0	.243	1.34	84
J.A. Happ	12-8	5.01	30	30	0	0	0	0	156.1	156	87	87	34	5	48	1	134	2	0	.259	1.30	659
Jonathan Holder	0-0	6.75	1	1	0	0	0	0	2.2	3	2	2	0	0	0	0	2	0	0	.273	1.13	11
Jonathan Loaisiga	0-2	6.75	4	4	0	0	0	0	12.0	15	9	9	3	0	7	0	14	1	0	.313	1.83	58
Jordan Montgomery	0-0	0.00	1	1	0	0	0	0	2.0	3	0	0	0	0	0	0	3	0	0	.333	1.50	9
James Paxton	15-6	3.82	29	29	0	0	0	0	150.2	138	71	64	23	2	55	0	186	7	1	.242	1.28	633
CC Sabathia	5-8	4.99	22	22	0	0	0	0	106.1	112	64	59	27	3	39	0	105	0	0	.267	1.42	465
Luis Severino	1-1	1.50	3	3	0	0	0	0	12.0	6	2	2	0	1	6	0	17	0	0	.146	1.00	48
Masahiro Tanaka	11-8	4.47	31	31	0	0	0	0	179.0	181	93	89	28	2	39	0	147	7	0	.259	1.23	744
Stephen Tarpley	0-0	36.00	1	1	0	0	0	0	1.0	4	4	4	3	0	0	0	0	0	0	.571	4.00	7
Totals	**60-38**	**4.51**	**162**	**162**	**1**	**1**	**-**	**-**	**778.1**	**764**	**414**	**390**	**152**	**19**	**240**	**1**	**784**	**23**	**1**	**.254**	**1.29**	**3293**

AS RELIEVER	W-L	ERA	G	GS	CG	SHO	SV	SVO	IP	H	R	ER	HR	HP	BB	IBB	SO	WP	BK	AVG	WHIP	BF
Chance Adams	1-1	8.53	13	-	0	0	1	1	25.1	39	25	24	7	2	11	0	23	1	1	.351	1.97	124
Jake Barrett	0-0	14.73	2	-	0	0	0	0	3.2	6	6	6	2	0	2	0	4	0	0	.353	2.18	19
Dellin Betances	0-0	0.00	1	-	0	0	0	0	0.2	0	0	0	0	0	0	0	2	0	0	.000	0.00	2
Zack Britton	3-1	1.91	66	-	0	0	3	7	61.1	38	13	13	3	1	32	1	53	3	0	.182	1.14	245
Luis Cessa	2-1	4.11	43	-	0	0	1	1	81.0	75	42	37	14	3	31	1	75	1	0	.246	1.31	343
Aroldis Chapman	3-2	2.21	60	-	0	0	37	42	57.0	38	18	14	3	1	25	0	85	6	0	.185	1.11	235
Nestor Cortes Jr.	5-1	5.60	32	-	0	0	0	1	64.1	69	40	40	16	1	27	1	67	1	0	.271	1.49	285
Ryan Dull	0-0	19.29	3	-	0	0	0	0	2.1	5	5	5	0	0	3	0	4	0	0	.417	3.43	15
Mike Ford	0-0	22.50	1	-	0	0	0	0	2.0	6	5	5	2	0	0	0	1	0	0	.500	3.00	12
Cory Gearrin	1-1	4.50	18	-	0	0	0	0	14.0	17	7	7	2	0	4	0	8	0	1	.298	1.50	61
Domingo Germán	2-0	0.00	3	-	0	0	0	0	8.1	3	0	0	0	1	2	0	11	0	0	.103	0.60	32
Chad Green	4-3	4.35	39	-	0	0	2	2	49.2	48	26	24	6	4	11	0	66	1	0	.249	1.19	211
David Hale	3-0	3.11	20	-	0	0	2	2	37.2	39	13	13	2	1	7	1	23	2	0	.264	1.22	157
J.A. Happ	0-0	1.80	1	-	0	0	0	0	5.0	4	1	1	0	0	1	0	6	1	0	.222	1.00	19
Joe Harvey	1-0	4.50	9	-	0	0	0	0	10.0	11	6	5	1	1	7	0	11	0	0	.282	1.80	48
Ben Heller	0-0	1.23	6	-	0	0	0	0	7.1	6	1	1	1	0	3	1	9	0	0	.250	1.23	28
Jonathan Holder	5-2	6.28	33	-	0	0	0	2	38.2	40	30	27	8	2	11	1	44	0	0	.255	1.32	170
Tommy Kahnle	3-2	3.67	72	-	0	0	0	5	61.1	45	27	25	9	2	20	0	88	8	0	.200	1.06	248
Michael King	0-0	0.00	1	-	0	0	0	0	2.0	2	1	0	0	0	0	0	1	0	0	.222	1.00	9
Brady Lail	0-0	10.13	1	-	0	0	0	0	2.2	2	3	3	1	0	1	0	2	0	0	.222	1.13	10
Jonathan Loaisiga	2-0	3.20	11	-	0	0	0	1	19.2	16	7	7	3	1	9	0	23	0	0	.229	1.27	81
Tyler Lyons	0-1	4.15	11	-	0	0	0	0	8.2	7	4	4	3	1	2	1	12	0	0	.226	1.04	34
Joe Mantiply	1-0	9.00	1	-	0	0	0	0	3.0	3	3	3	1	0	2	0	2	0	0	.250	1.67	14
Jordan Montgomery	0-0	13.50	1	-	0	0	0	0	2.0	4	3	3	1	0	0	0	2	0	0	.400	2.00	10
Adam Ottavino	6-5	1.90	73	-	0	0	2	9	66.1	47	17	14	5	2	40	3	88	3	1	.198	1.31	283
Austin Romine	0-0	27.00	1	-	0	0	0	0	1.0	4	3	3	2	0	0	0	0	0	0	.571	4.00	7
Adonis Rosa	0-0	4.50	1	-	0	0	0	0	2.0	1	1	1	1	0	0	0	2	0	0	.143	0.50	7
CC Sabathia	0-0	0.00	1	-	0	0	0	0	1.0	0	0	0	0	0	0	0	2	0	0	.000	0.00	3
Masahiro Tanaka	0-1	3.00	1	-	0	0	0	0	3.0	5	2	1	0	0	1	0	2	0	0	.357	2.00	15
Stephen Tarpley	1-0	5.70	20	-	0	0	2	2	23.2	30	16	15	3	2	15	1	34	5	1	.313	1.90	113
Totals	**43-21**	**4.08**	**162**	**-**	**-**	**-**	**50**	**78**	**664.2**	**610**	**325**	**301**	**96**	**25**	**267**	**11**	**750**	**32**	**4**	**.242**	**1.32**	**2523**

2019 Team Pitching General Splits

	W-L	ERA	SV	SVO	G	CG	IP	H	R	ER	HR	BB	SO	AVG	OBP	SLG	OPS
Total	103-59	4.31	50	75	162	1	1443.0	1374	739	691	248	507	1534	.248	.314	.439	.754
Home	57-24	3.62	28	35	81	1	730.1	644	316	294	114	246	804	.234	.301	.407	.708
Away	46-35	5.01	22	40	81	0	712.2	730	423	397	134	261	730	.262	.328	.471	.799
Day	43-21	3.72	15	22	64	0	573.1	496	252	237	84	184	636	.230	.293	.396	.689
Night	60-38	4.70	35	53	98	1	869.2	878	487	454	164	323	898	.260	.328	.467	.795
Starter	60-38	4.51	0	0	162	1	778.1	764	414	390	152	240	784	.254	.311	.463	.774
Reliever	43-21	4.08	50	75	161	0	664.2	610	325	301	96	267	750	.242	.318	.411	.729
Grass	93-46	4.26	44	64	139	1	1239.1	1169	630	587	207	436	1322	.247	.313	.435	.748
Turf	10-13	4.60	6	11	23	0	203.2	205	109	104	41	71	212	.258	.322	.467	.789
Pre-All Star	57-31	4.14	31	46	88	1	785.2	748	390	361	130	267	815	.248	.312	.429	.741
Post-All Star	46-28	4.52	19	29	74	0	657.1	626	349	330	118	240	719	.249	.317	.452	.769
vs. AL	91-51	4.45	46	70	142	1	1267.0	1221	665	626	228	453	1341	.251	.318	.448	.766
vs. NL	12-8	3.32	4	5	20	0	176.0	153	74	65	20	54	193	.229	.290	.373	.664
vs. AL East	54-22	4.10	29	41	76	1	680.2	646	325	310	114	207	735	.247	.305	.436	.742
vs. AL Central	18-15	5.28	10	17	33	0	291.1	300	185	171	63	111	312	.264	.329	.486	.816
vs. AL West	19-14	4.42	7	12	33	0	295.0	275	155	145	51	135	294	.247	.334	.438	.771
March	1-2	3.33	0	0	3	0	270.0	25	14	10	3	9	29	.240	.301	.365	.666
April	16-10	3.95	6	11	26	0	232.1	197	107	102	32	92	248	.227	.301	.397	.698
May	20-7	3.45	14	16	27	0	242.2	211	102	93	39	74	259	.229	.294	.405	.699
June	17-9	5.46	9	14	26	1	229.0	262	148	139	50	75	224	.285	.340	.498	.838
July	14-11	4.85	7	13	25	0	222.2	243	129	120	44	75	233	.275	.333	.493	.825
August	21-9	4.60	13	16	30	0	266.0	231	138	136	50	104	270	.232	.309	.447	.756
September	14-11	3.67	1	5	25	0	223.1	206	101	91	30	78	271	.243	.311	.400	.712
REST	W-L	ERA	SV	SVO	G	CG	IP	H	R	ER	HR	BB	SO	AVG	OBP	SLG	OPS
GS 0-3 Days Rest	0-2	7.59	0	0	16	0	21.1	32	20	18	8	8	27	.344	.408	.656	1.064
GS 4 Days Rest	32-9	5.00	0	0	59	0	315.0	336	182	175	70	85	321	.268	.318	.504	.822
GS 5 Days Rest	20-17	4.02	0	0	54	1	279.2	259	132	125	48	94	279	.245	.307	.433	.740
GS 6+ Days Rest	8-10	3.99	0	0	33	0	162.1	137	80	72	26	53	157	.226	.290	.400	.691
GS 0-3 Days Since Last GS	0-1	16.88	0	0	3	0	2.2	4	5	5	2	1	5	.333	.385	.833	1.218
GS 4 Days Since Last GS	31-8	5.05	0	0	57	0	303.0	325	176	170	66	84	306	.270	.321	.503	.825
GS 5 Days Since Last GS	20-17	4.04	0	0	55	1	280.2	262	133	126	48	94	279	.246	.308	.435	.743
GS 6+ Days Since Last GS	9-12	4.17	0	0	47	0	192.0	173	100	89	36	61	194	.236	.299	.430	.729
Relief 0 Days Rest	7-4	2.63	15	20	45	0	75.1	61	24	22	8	30	92	.223	.304	.332	.636
Relief 1 Day Rest	7-4	3.13	14	22	77	0	120.2	100	47	42	15	57	142	.223	.315	.376	.692
Relief 2 Days Rest	11-2	3.73	5	9	76	0	132.2	107	59	55	18	56	139	.218	.306	.371	.677
Relief 3-5 Days Rest	15-9	4.65	12	20	94	0	224.2	224	124	116	30	83	257	.259	.323	.435	.758
Relief 6+ Days Rest	3-2	5.34	4	4	47	0	111.1	118	71	66	25	41	120	.265	.334	.492	.826
VS. TEAM	W-L	ERA	SV	SVO	G	CG	IP	H	R	ER	HR	BB	SO	AVG	OBP	SLG	OPS
vs. Arizona	1-3	3.71	1	1	4	0	34.0	32	15	14	5	12	28	.248	.306	.419	.724
vs. Baltimore	17-2	4.05	12	15	19	0	171.0	159	83	77	24	54	172	.243	.306	.420	.726
vs. Boston	14-5	5.55	6	6	19	0	167.0	185	104	103	33	53	171	.279	.332	.498	.830
vs. Cleveland	3-4	7.55	3	5	7	0	62.0	74	53	52	20	22	55	.297	.353	.606	.959
vs. Colorado	2-1	3.67	1	1	3	0	27.0	26	15	11	3	9	35	.250	.316	.423	.739
vs. Chicago-AL	3-4	5.25	0	0	7	0	58.1	63	36	34	12	22	69	.274	.339	.478	.817
vs. Detroit	3-3	3.38	2	4	6	0	53.1	50	26	20	4	22	58	.243	.315	.379	.693
vs. Houston	3-4	5.85	3	6	7	0	60.0	78	39	39	15	31	54	.317	.393	.569	.962
vs. Kansas City	5-2	4.18	1	2	7	0	64.2	61	32	30	11	19	82	.247	.297	.441	.739
vs. Los Angeles-AL	5-2	3.22	2	3	7	0	67.0	53	28	24	8	27	62	.216	.302	.343	.645
vs. Los Angeles-NL	2-1	1.73	0	0	3	0	26.0	17	5	5	2	6	39	.183	.240	.312	.552
vs. Minnesota	4-2	5.94	4	6	6	0	53.0	52	38	35	16	26	48	.254	.343	.512	.855
vs. N.Y. Mets	2-2	4.37	0	1	4	0	35.0	38	20	17	6	8	30	.268	.311	.437	.748
vs. Oakland	2-4	5.26	0	1	6	0	53.0	49	32	31	9	28	50	.247	.355	.470	.825
vs. San Diego	2-1	2.00	1	1	3	0	27.0	20	7	6	1	9	32	.204	.284	.286	.570
vs. Seattle	6-1	3.29	2	2	7	0	63.0	43	25	23	10	26	68	.191	.278	.369	.647
vs. San Francisco	3-0	4.00	1	1	3	0	27.0	20	12	12	3	10	29	.198	.268	.317	.585
vs. Tampa Bay	12-7	2.78	5	9	19	1	174.2	143	56	54	27	56	200	.220	.287	.390	.677
vs. Texas	3-3	4.85	0	0	6	0	52.0	52	31	28	9	23	60	.261	.341	.437	.778
vs. Toronto	11-8	4.07	6	11	19	0	168.0	159	82	76	30	44	192	.245	.296	.435	.732
AT STADIUM	W-L	ERA	SV	SVO	G	CG	IP	H	R	ER	HR	BB	SO	AVG	OBP	SLG	OPS
Angel Stadium	3-1	4.73	2	3	4	0	40.0	32	24	21	7	18	27	.219	.309	.404	.713
Camden Yards	10-0	4.20	7	10	10	0	90.0	88	44	42	12	30	85	.251	.321	.437	.758
Chase Field	0-2	3.38	0	0	2	0	16.0	12	6	6	2	5	17	.207	.266	.379	.645
Citi Field	1-1	2.12	0	1	2	0	17.0	18	5	4	2	3	15	.273	.304	.409	.713
Comerica Park	2-1	5.13	1	3	3	0	26.1	34	20	15	3	11	29	.306	.368	.468	.836
Dodger Stadium	2-1	1.73	0	0	3	0	26.0	17	5	5	2	6	39	.183	.240	.312	.552
Fenway Park	4-4	7.28	0	0	8	0	68.0	89	56	55	15	21	74	.313	.357	.585	.942
Globe Life Park	1-2	6.84	0	0	3	0	25.0	30	22	19	4	16	25	.297	.400	.485	.885
Guaranteed Rate Field	2-2	5.29	0	0	4	0	34.0	41	22	20	7	13	38	.297	.362	.486	.847
Kauffman Stadium	2-1	4.88	1	1	3	0	27.2	29	16	15	5	5	29	.264	.293	.445	.739
London Stadium	2-0	10.50	0	0	2	0	18.0	33	21	21	6	7	13	.398	.460	.687	1.126
Minute Maid Park	0-3	6.75	0	2	3	0	20.0	34	18	15	7	14	26	.343	.417	.596	1.013
Oakland Coliseum	0-3	6.00	0	1	3	0	24.0	25	17	16	5	8	22	.272	.337	.522	.858
Oracle Park	3-0	4.00	1	1	3	0	27.0	20	12	12	3	10	29	.198	.268	.317	.585
Progressive Field	1-2	6.23	1	3	3	0	26.0	26	19	18	8	7	25	.263	.303	.566	.868
Rogers Centre	4-6	4.86	3	6	10	0	87.0	83	51	47	19	31	86	.246	.315	.472	.786
T-Mobile Park	3-0	2.33	1	1	3	0	27.0	10	7	7	3	12	30	.112	.218	.247	.465
Target Field	2-1	8.67	2	4	3	0	27.0	32	27	26	12	16	25	.296	.388	.657	1.045
Tropicana Field	4-5	3.27	3	5	9	0	02.2	77	31	30	14	28	96	.244	.309	.421	.730
Yankee Stadium	57-24	3.62	28	35	81	1	730.1	644	316	294	114	246	804	.234	.301	.407	.708
BY INNING	W-L	ERA	SV	SVO	G	CG	IP	H	R	ER	HR	BB	SO	AVG	OBP	SLG	OPS
In 1st inning	---	5.61	-	-	162	-	162.0	167	103	101	40	58	192	.264	.325	.508	.833
In 2nd inning	---	2.94	-	-	162	-	162.0	125	54	53	22	44	186	.210	.267	.366	.633
In 3rd inning	---	3.11	-	-	162	-	162.0	141	69	56	20	48	153	.232	.292	.395	.687
In 4th inning	---	5.33	-	-	162	-	162.0	171	101	96	35	58	142	.267	.330	.495	.826
In 5th inning	---	5.00	-	-	162	-	162.0	178	96	90	43	51	143	.276	.336	.525	.861
In 6th inning	---	4.78	-	-	162	-	162.0	172	91	86	23	57	174	.273	.334	.452	.786
In 7th inning	---	3.79	-	-	162	-	161.1	134	72	68	14	58	197	.221	.299	.367	.666
In 8th inning	---	4.70	-	-	161	-	161.0	155	90	84	29	71	158	.248	.329	.432	.761
In 9th inning	---	3.63	-	-	130	-	129.0	121	57	52	19	52	163	.244	.316	.409	.725
In Extra Innings	---	2.29	-	-	11	-	19.2	12	6	5	3	10	26	.171	.284	.300	.584

2019 Team Pitching Situational Splits

	G	AB	R	H	2B	3B	HR	RBI	SB	CS	BB	IBB	HBP	SO	GDP	AVG	OBP	SLG	OPS
Total	162	5535	739	1374	277	18	248	711	71	24	507	12	44	1534	119	.248	.313	.439	.754
vs. Left	-	2100	-	529	103	9	88	266	28	10	185	6	20	599	28	.252	.317	.435	.752
vs. Right	-	3435	-	845	174	9	160	445	43	14	322	6	24	935	91	.246	.313	.442	.755
With 0 Outs	162	1914	-	472	89	5	94	182	14	3	160	0	14	549	44	.247	.308	.446	.754
With 1 Out	162	1826	-	456	95	8	81	273	24	10	169	4	13	479	75	.250	.314	.444	.757
With 2 Outs	162	1795	-	446	93	5	73	256	33	11	178	8	17	506	0	.248	.322	.428	.750
By Runners On	G	AB	R	H	2B	3B	HR	RBI	SB	CS	BB	IBB	HBP	SO	GIDP	AVG	OBP	SLG	OPS
None on	-	3290	-	811	163	9	147	147	0	0	287	2	24	920	0	.247	.312	.436	.747
None on/out	-	1418	-	348	65	5	69	69	0	0	110	0	10	405	0	.245	.304	.444	.749
Runners on	-	2245	-	563	114	9	101	564	71	24	220	10	20	614	119	.251	.319	.445	.763
Scoring Posn	-	1197	-	296	64	7	57	450	24	2	139	10	13	341	40	.247	.323	.455	.779
ScPos/2 Out	-	574	-	131	29	2	20	175	13	2	65	6	6	163	0	.228	.313	.390	.703
Bases Loaded	-	102	-	19	6	1	6	66	0	0	2	0	0	26	7	.186	.186	.441	.627
By Inning/Lineup	G	AB	R	H	2B	3B	HR	RBI	SB	CS	BB	IBB	HBP	SO	GIDP	AVG	OBP	SLG	OPS
1st IP	-	2433	-	580	114	6	106	345	45	10	271	7	21	766	58	.238	.317	.421	.738
Inning 1-6	-	3748	514	954	194	11	183	499	48	21	316	3	26	990	73	.255	.315	.459	.774
Inning 7+	-	1787	225	420	83	7	65	212	23	3	191	9	18	544	46	.235	.313	.398	.712
Close and Late	-	750	-	154	35	1	21	85	11	2	101	7	11	240	0	.205	.307	.339	.645
vs 1st Batr	-	495	-	105	21	0	17	51	2	0	40	0	5	177	7	.212	.276	.358	.633
1st time thru LnUp	-	3589	-	851	160	13	150	452	51	14	357	11	29	1100	77	.237	.309	.414	.723
2nd time thru LnUp	-	1324	-	333	66	5	64	160	14	6	105	0	11	305	24	.252	.311	.454	.764
3rd time thru LnUp	-	614	-	188	51	0	34	98	6	4	45	1	4	128	17	.306	.356	.555	.912
4th+ time thru LnUp	-	8	-	2	0	0	0	1	0	0	0	0	0	1	1	.250	.250	.250	.500
By Batting Count	G	AB	R	H	2B	3B	HR	RBI	SB	CS	BB	IBB	HBP	SO	GIDP	AVG	OBP	SLG	OPS
0-0 Count	-	566	-	205	42	4	45	118	20	7	0	0	10	0	16	.362	.370	.689	1.059
0-1 Count	-	500	-	161	27	0	25	65	6	2	0	0	8	0	18	.322	.331	.526	.857
0-2 Count	-	573	-	83	18	1	7	31	2	0	0	0	4	299	13	.145	.150	.216	.366
1-0 Count	-	374	-	138	25	1	27	71	7	3	0	0	3	0	13	.369	.371	.658	1.029
1-1 Count	-	480	-	167	33	3	32	95	11	1	0	0	6	0	18	.348	.352	.629	.981
1-2 Count	-	939	-	144	32	3	17	62	10	4	0	0	8	512	14	.153	.160	.248	.408
2-0 Count	-	134	-	42	11	1	13	27	4	0	0	0	0	0	3	.313	.311	.701	1.013
2-1 Count	-	284	-	109	23	1	18	59	5	0	1	0	1	0	5	.384	.385	.662	1.047
2-2 Count	-	972	-	169	38	2	29	97	5	1	0	0	3	448	10	.174	.176	.307	.482
3-0 Count	-	8	-	3	1	0	2	4	0	0	87	12	0	0	0	.375	.947	1.250	2.197
3-1 Count	-	102	-	28	3	1	8	20	0	0	136	0	0	0	3	.275	.686	.559	1.245
3-2 Count	-	603	-	125	24	1	25	62	1	6	283	0	1	275	0	.207	.460	.375	.835
After (0-1)	-	2987	-	627	132	7	95	298	22	8	176	0	21	1065	63	.210	.258	.354	.612
After (0-2)	-	1317	-	199	46	4	24	87	6	2	45	0	8	680	23	.151	.183	.247	.430
After (1-0)	-	1982	-	542	103	7	108	295	29	9	321	2	13	469	40	.273	.375	.496	.871
After (1-1)	-	2212	-	516	106	5	85	276	25	9	244	0	13	724	42	.233	.312	.401	.713
After (1-2)	-	1787	-	301	68	5	44	143	14	9	119	0	9	889	23	.168	.223	.286	.509
After (2-0)	-	566	-	155	31	4	42	94	7	1	206	0	2	130	7	.274	.465	.565	1.031
After (2-1)	-	1038	-	253	50	2	47	147	7	1	244	0	4	327	14	.244	.387	.432	.819
After (2-2)	-	1399	-	258	58	3	45	144	5	5	191	0	4	647	15	.184	.283	.327	.610
After (3-0)	-	83	-	24	3	1	8	14	0	1	144	12	0	19	1	.289	.737	.639	1.375
After (3-1)	-	278	-	64	7	1	17	35	1	2	228	0	0	76	4	.230	.575	.446	1.021
After (3-2)	-	603	-	125	24	1	25	62	1	6	283	0	1	275	6	.207	.460	.375	.835
Two strikes	-	3087	-	521	112	7	78	252	18	11	283	0	16	1534	43	.169	.241	.285	.526
By Pitch Count	G	AB	R	H	2B	3B	HR	RBI	SB	CS	BB	IBB	HBP	SO	GIDP	AVG	OBP	SLG	OPS
Pitch 1-15	-	1940	-	464	87	3	85	205	33	8	200	7	16	585	45	.239	.314	.419	.732
Pitch 16-30	-	1246	-	302	58	8	53	202	15	3	125	4	10	381	26	.242	.313	.429	.742
Pitch 31-45	-	758	-	179	35	5	31	90	5	4	46	0	3	202	13	.236	.281	.418	.700
Pitch 46-60	-	575	-	139	23	1	27	72	7	4	54	0	7	118	15	.242	.313	.426	.739
Pitch 61-75	-	508	-	145	37	1	26	64	5	3	42	0	6	123	9	.285	.346	.516	.862
Pitch 76-90	-	370	-	109	26	0	22	65	5	2	29	1	2	87	6	.295	.347	.543	.891
Pitch 91-105	-	125	-	33	11	0	4	12	1	0	9	0	0	35	5	.264	.311	.448	.759
Pitch 106-120	-	13	-	3	0	0	1	0	0	0	2	0	0	3	0	.231	.333	.231	.564
By Batting Slot	G	AB	R	H	2B	3B	HR	RBI	SB	CS	BB	IBB	HBP	SO	GIDP	AVG	OBP	SLG	OPS
Batting #1	-	678	-	164	33	3	43	93	13	9	64	1	4	174	15	.242	.309	.490	.799
Batting #2	-	659	-	171	37	3	21	66	18	5	67	2	1	162	7	.259	.327	.420	.747
Batting #3	-	641	-	175	36	1	34	88	8	1	61	2	6	157	18	.273	.340	.491	.831
Batting #4	-	630	-	173	36	3	39	111	6	3	56	3	6	163	16	.275	.336	.527	.863
Batting #5	-	612	-	147	25	1	28	77	5	2	69	1	2	191	13	.240	.318	.422	.740
Batting #6	-	608	-	134	30	1	25	75	6	0	53	1	5	192	11	.220	.286	.396	.682
Batting #7	-	592	-	128	20	3	16	62	6	0	45	2	7	163	14	.216	.279	.341	.620
Batting #8	-	572	-	145	33	1	20	79	4	0	42	0	6	165	15	.253	.309	.420	.728
Batting #9	-	543	-	137	27	2	22	60	5	4	50	0	7	167	10	.252	.323	.431	.754
By Inning	G	AB	R	H	2B	3B	HR	RBI	SB	CS	BB	IBB	HBP	SO	GIDP	AVG	OBP	SLG	OPS
In 1st inning	162	632	103	167	32	1	40	100	11	4	58	0	2	192	11	.264	.325	.508	.833
In 2nd inning	162	595	54	125	25	1	22	53	4	1	44	0	3	186	14	.210	.267	.366	.633
In 3rd inning	162	607	69	141	25	7	20	68	5	6	48	0	4	153	10	.232	.292	.395	.687
In 4th inning	162	640	101	171	41	0	35	98	4	3	58	1	4	142	11	.267	.330	.495	.826
In 5th inning	162	644	96	178	31	0	43	93	11	3	51	2	9	143	12	.276	.336	.525	.861
In 6th inning	162	630	91	172	40	2	23	87	13	4	57	0	4	174	15	.273	.334	.452	.786
In 7th inning	162	605	72	134	38	4	14	66	10	1	58	2	10	197	13	.221	.299	.367	.666
In 8th inning	161	616	90	153	22	2	29	86	4	0	71	3	5	158	20	.248	.329	.432	.761
In 9th inning	130	496	57	121	23	1	19	54	6	1	52	2	2	163	12	.244	.316	.409	.725
In Extra Innings	11	70	6	12	0	0	3	6	3	1	10	2	1	26	1	.171	.284	.300	.584

2019 Fielding Statistics

PITCHER	PCT	G	GS	INN	TC	PO	A	E	DP
Adams	1.000	13	0	25.1	2	0	2	0	0
Barrett	-	2	0	3.2	0	0	0	0	0
Betances	-	1	0	0.2	0	0	0	0	0
Britton	1.000	66	0	61.1	11	1	10	0	0
Cessa	1.000	43	0	81.0	11	2	9	0	1
Chapman	.667	60	0	57.0	6	1	3	2	0
Cortes	.857	33	1	66.2	7	1	5	1	2
Dull	1.000	3	0	2.1	1	1	0	0	0
Ford	1.000	1	0	2.0	1	0	1	0	0
Gearrin	-	18	0	14.0	0	0	0	0	0
Germán	.889	27	24	143.0	18	4	12	2	0
Green	1.000	54	15	69.0	1	0	1	0	0
Hale	1.000	20	0	37.2	13	5	8	0	0
Happ	.933	31	30	161.1	15	2	12	1	0
Harvey	1.000	9	0	10.0	1	0	1	0	0
Heller	-	6	0	7.1	0	0	0	0	0
Holder	1.000	34	1	41.1	5	2	3	0	1
Kahnle	1.000	72	0	61.1	11	4	7	0	1
King	.000	1	0	2.0	1	0	0	1	0
Lail	1.000	2	0	2.2	1	0	1	0	0
Loaisiga	1.000	15	4	31.2	3	1	2	0	1
Lyons	1.000	11	0	8.2	3	2	1	0	1
Mantiply	1.000	1	0	3.0	3	2	1	0	0
Montgomery	-	2	1	4.0	0	0	0	0	0
Ottavino	.857	73	0	66.1	7	3	3	1	1
Paxton	1.000	29	29	150.2	12	2	10	0	0
Romine	-	1	0	1.0	0	0	0	0	0
Rosa	1.000	2	0	2.0	1	1	0	0	0
Sabathia	.600	23	22	107.1	5	0	3	2	1
Severino	.667	3	3	12.0	3	0	2	1	0
Tanaka	.931	32	31	182.0	29	9	18	2	3
Tarpley	1.000	21	1	24.2	4	2	2	0	1
TOTALS	.926	162	162	1443.0	175	45	117	13	13

FIRST BASE	PCT	G	GS	INN	TC	PO	A	E	DP
Bird	1.000	10	10	85.1	85	83	2	0	6
Encarnación	1.000	12	12	104.2	90	88	2	0	6
Ford	.985	29	24	217.0	203	191	9	3	22
LeMahieu	.992	40	28	262.0	236	215	19	2	24
Morales	.983	7	7	62.2	58	56	1	1	4
Urshela	1.000	1	0	5.0	8	8	0	0	1
Voit	.989	83	81	706.1	610	575	28	7	60
TOTALS	.990	162	162	1443.0	1290	1216	61	13	123

SECOND BASE	PCT	G	GS	INN	TC	PO	A	E	DP
Estrada	1.000	17	10	105.0	42	24	18	0	6
LeMahieu	.993	75	66	579.2	275	118	155	2	32
Torres	.967	65	64	547.1	269	113	147	9	48
Valera	1.000	12	9	89.0	35	7	28	0	5
Wade	.985	18	13	122.0	65	24	40	1	10
TOTALS	.983	162	162	1443.0	686	286	388	12	101

SHORTSTOP	PCT	G	GS	INN	TC	PO	A	E	DP
Estrada	.950	9	4	45.0	20	7	12	1	1
Gregorius	.979	80	78	688.1	280	93	181	6	48
Torres	.961	77	73	659.2	282	91	180	11	40
Tulowitzki	1.000	4	4	30.0	10	3	7	0	0
Wade	1.000	4	3	20.0	2	0	2	0	0
TOTALS	.970	162	162	1443.0	594	194	382	18	89

THIRD BASE	PCT	G	GS	INN	TC	PO	A	E	DP
Andújar	.700	4	4	33.0	10	0	7	3	0
LeMahieu	.963	52	47	400.0	109	18	87	4	7
Urshela	.954	123	109	978.1	284	59	212	13	20
Wade	1.000	5	2	31.2	10	5	5	0	0
TOTALS	.952	162	162	1443.0	413	82	311	20	27

LEFT FIELD	PCT	G	GS	INN	TC	PO	A	E	DP
Estrada	1.000	2	2	10.0	1	1	0	0	0
Frazier	1.000	17	14	131.2	23	22	1	0	0
Gardner	1.000	45	37	348.1	66	65	1	0	0
Maybin	.969	46	35	326.1	65	62	1	2	0
Stanton	1.000	10	10	69.0	9	9	0	0	0
Tauchman	1.000	59	55	472.2	101	98	3	0	1
Urshela	1.000	1	0	1.0	2	2	0	0	0
Wade	1.000	14	9	84.0	15	14	1	0	0
TOTALS	.993	162	162	1443.0	282	273	7	2	1

CENTER FIELD	PCT	G	GS	INN	TC	PO	A	E	DP
Gardner	.995	98	94	820.0	218	215	2	1	0
Hicks	.991	58	55	499.1	116	115	0	1	0
Tauchman	1.000	14	11	99.2	26	26	0	0	0
Maybin	1.000	3	2	20.0	5	5	0	0	0
Wade	1.000	2	0	4.0	1	1	0	0	0
TOTALS	.995	162	162	1443.0	366	362	2	2	0

RIGHT FIELD	PCT	G	GS	INN	TC	PO	A	E	DP
Estrada	1.000	2	0	4.0	1	1	0	0	0
Frazier	.947	36	31	263.2	57	49	5	3	1
Judge	1.000	92	90	775.1	184	177	7	0	0
Maybin	1.000	36	26	242.0	55	54	1	0	0
Stanton	.857	3	3	26.0	7	6	0	1	0
Tauchman	.970	19	11	122.0	33	32	0	1	0
Wade	1.000	2	1	10.0	3	3	0	0	0
TOTALS	.985	162	162	1443.0	340	322	13	5	1

ALL OUTFIELD	PCT	G	GS	INN	TC	PO	A	E	DP
Estrada	1.000	4	2	14.0	2	2	0	0	0
Frazier	.963	53	45	395.1	80	71	6	3	1
Gardner	.996	140	131	1168.1	284	280	3	1	0
Hicks	.991	58	55	499.1	116	115	0	1	0
Judge	1.000	92	90	775.1	184	177	7	0	0
Maybin	.984	77	63	588.1	125	121	2	2	0
Stanton	.938	13	13	95.0	16	15	0	1	0
Tauchman	.994	86	77	694.1	160	156	3	1	1
Urshela	1.000	1	0	1.0	2	2	0	0	0
Wade	1.000	18	10	98.0	19	18	1	0	0
TOTALS	.991	486	486	4329.0	988	957	22	9	2

CATCHER	G	GS	INN	TC	PO	A	E	DP	PCT	SB	CCS	SB%	CERA	PB	CPKO	PPKO	PCS
Higashioka	18	14	137.0	154	146	8	0	2	1.000	12	3	80.0	4.14	0	1	0	0
Romine	70	62	563.1	638	610	26	2	4	.997	23	6	79.3	4.35	6	0	4	4
Sánchez	90	86	742.2	840	793	32	15	5	.982	36	11	76.6	4.31	7	3	1	0
TOTALS	162	162	1443.0	1632	1549	66	17	11	.990	71	20	78.0	4.31	13	4	5	4

TEAM	PCT	G	PO	A	E	TC	DP
NYY	.982	162	4329	1347	102	5778	135

2019 Replay Statistics

REPLAY CHALLENGES (70x in 2019)

NYY Challenges: 23 (16 overturned, 0 confirmed, 7 stand)
Opp. Challenges: 35 (17 overturned, 10 confirmed, 8 stand)
Umpires: 12 (3 overturned, 9 confirmed, 0 stand, 0 record keeping)
2018 (80): NYY (26-5-6) / Opp. (19-6-11) / Umps (3-2-1-1)

2019 Highs and Lows

CLUB GENERAL
Longest Winning Streak	9 (7/31-8/8)
Longest Winning Streak, Home / Road	9 (7/31-8/14) / 7 (5/12-25)
Longest Losing Streak	4, 2x (last: 8/18-22)
Longest Losing Streak, Home / Road	3 (4/2-12) / 3, 6x (last: 9/15-9/25)
Longest Game, Time, 9 inn. / All Games	4:42 (6/29 at BOS in London) / 5:03 (7/23 at MIN, 10 inn.)
Longest Game, Innings	14 inn. (4/22 at LAA)
Shortest Game, Time, All Games	2:12 (5/15 vs. BAL-G1)
Largest Margin of Victory	12, 2x (last: 8/7 at BAL)
Largest Margin of Defeat	16 (7/25 at BOS)
Largest Deficit Overcome in a Win	6 (7/23 at MIN)
Highest Paid Attendance, Home / Road	48,101 (8/3 vs. BOS-G2) / 59,659 (6/29 at BOS in London)

TEAM BATTING
Most Runs, Game / Inning	17 (6/29 at BOS in London) / 9 (6/30 at BOS in London, 7th inn.)
Most Hits, 9 inn. / All Games	19, 2x (last: 9/14 at TOR) / 20 (7/23 at MIN)
Most Home Runs, All Games	7 (4/7 at BAL)
Shut Out	2 (9/2 vs. TEX, 9/25 at TB)
Fewest Hits, All Games	1 (9/25 at TB)
Most Strikeouts, 9 inn. / All Games	18 (4/3 vs. DET) / Same
Hitting Streak, Season	LeMahieu (14G, 6/14-30)
Walk-off Wins	6 (4/21 vs. KC, 5/7 vs. SEA, 5/17 vs. TB, 6/26 vs. TOR, 8/31 vs. OAK, 9/1 vs. OAK)

TEAM PITCHING
Most Runs Allowed, Game / Inning	19, 2x (last: 8/15 vs. CLE) / 7, 2x (last: 8/15 vs. CLE, 1st inn.)
Most Hits Allowed, 9 inn. / All Games	24 (8/15 vs. CLE) / Same
Fewest Hits Allowed, Game	1 (4/13 vs. CWS)
Most Strikeouts, 9 inn. / All Games	17 (7/19 vs. COL) / 20 (4/21 vs. KC, 10 inn.)
Shutouts	9 (last: 9/17 vs. LAA)
Complete Games	1 (Tanaka, 6/17 vs. TB)
Walk-Off Losses	5 (5/26 at KC, 7/6 at TB, 9/10 at DET, 9/13 at TOR, 9/24 at TB)

2019 INDIVIDUAL

BATTING: Runs- 4, 2x (Maybin, 9/27 vs. TEX; Judge, 9/12 at DET); Hits- 5 (Gregorius, 7/23 at MIN); Doubles- 3, 2x (Voit, 6/29 at BOS-London; Gardner, 5/22 at BAL); Triples- 1, 17x (many); HR- 3 (Sánchez, 4/7 at BAL); RBI- 7 (Gregorius, 7/23 at MIN); BB- 4, (Urshela, 6/9 at CLE); SB- 2, 4x (last: Maybin, 9/12 at DET).

PITCHING: IP in Start- 9.0, (Tanaka, 6/17 vs. TB); IP in Relief- 5.0, 2x (Happ, 9/25 at TB; Cortes Jr. 6/15 at CWS); Hits- 12 (Tanaka, 7/25 at BOS); Runs- 12 (Tanaka, 7/25 at BOS); ER- 12 (Tanaka, 7/25 at BOS); BB- 5, 2x (Paxton, 8/28 at SEA; Germán, 4/1 vs. DET); K- 12, 3x (All by Paxton, 9/3 vs. TEX, 4/21 vs. KC, 4/16 vs. BOS); HR- 4, 3x (Paxton, 7/26 vs. BOS; Sabathia, 7/22 vs. MIN; Germán, 5/26 at KC); Pitches- 111 (Tanaka, 6/17 vs. TB).

FIELDING: Errors- 2, 4x (Torres, 7/14 vs. TOR; Urshela 6/14 at CWS; Urshela 6/5 at TOR; Andújar, 5/4 vs. MIN).

RHP Masahiro Tanaka tossed the Yankees' only complete game in 2019 — a two-hit shutout on 6/17 vs. Tampa Bay, allowing just 1BB with 10K while tallying a Yankees single-game season-high 111 pitches. It marked his seventh career Major League complete game and fourth career shutout.

SS Didi Gregorius scored the winning run in the Yankees' 14-12 win on 7/23 at Minnesota. He reached base safely in all six plate appearances in the contest, going 5-for-5 with 2 doubles, 1HR and 7RBI, setting Yankees single-game season highs in hits and runs batted in.

2019 MLB Award Winners

AL Player of the Month
INF DJ LeMahieu (June): .395 (45-for-114), 26R, 8 doubles, 2 triples, 6HR, 29RBI, 8BB, .434 OBP, .658 SLG, 1.092 OPS

AL Player of the Week
1B Luke Voit (4/22-28): .433 (13-for-30), 10R, 1 doubles, 4HR, 10RBI, 5BB, .528 OBP, .867 SLG, 1.394 OPS

INF DJ LeMahieu (6/24-30): .625 (15-for-24), 8R, 3 doubles, 1 triples, 2HR, 10RBI, 2BB, .654 OBP, 1.083 SLG, 1.737 OPS

AL Reliever of the Month
LHP Aroldis Chapman (May): 0-0, 11SV, 0.79 ERA, 12G, 11.1IP, 5H, 2R/1ER, 3BB, 18K, 1HR, .128 OBA

RHP Tommy Kahnle (July): 0-0, 0SV, 0.77 ERA, 12G, 11.2IP, 5H, 1R/1ER, 2BB, 17K, 0HR, .128 OBA

LHP Aroldis Chapman (August): 0-0, 9SV, 0.00 ERA, 11G, 11.0IP, 3H, 0R, 5BB, 20K, 0HR, .083 OBA

Opening Day Lineup and Roster

Just four of the Yankees in the 2019 Opening Day starting lineup were also in the 2018 Opening Day starting lineup (Gardner, Judge, Sánchez and Stanton)…Gardner, Judge and Sánchez are the only Yankees to be in each of the last three Opening Day lineups…of the 24* players on the 2019 Opening Day active roster, 14 were not on the club's 2018 Opening Day active roster…the 24* players on the Yankees' 2019 Opening Day active roster had combined to make just 18 Opening Day starts for the club prior to 2019: Gardner (9), Tanaka (3), Judge (2), Sánchez (2), Bird (1), Stanton (1).

2019 Lineup: March 28 vs. Baltimore, 7-2 win: 1. Gardner-CF, 2. Judge-RF, 3. Stanton-LF, 4. Voit-DH, 5. Andújar-3B, 6. Sánchez-C, 7. Bird-1B, 8. Torres-2B, 9. Tulowitzki-SS and Tanaka-SP

2018 Lineup: March 29 at Toronto, 6-1 win: 1. Gardner-LF, 2. Judge-RF, 3. Stanton-DH, 4. Sánchez-C, 5. Hicks-CF, 6. Gregorius-SS, 7. Drury-3B, 8. Walker-2B, 9. Austin-1B and Severino-SP

2019 Opening Day Roster: P (12): LHP Zack Britton, RHP Luis Cessa, LHP Aroldis Chapman, RHP Domingo Germán, RHP Chad Green, LHP J.A. Happ, RHP Jonathan Holder, RHP Tommy Kahnle, RHP Adam Ottavino, RHP James Paxton, RHP Masahiro Tanaka, LHP Stephen Tarpley; **C (2):** Austin Romine, Gary Sánchez; **INF (6):** Miguel Andújar, Greg Bird, DJ LeMahieu, Gleyber Torres, Troy Tulowitzki, Luke Voit; **OF (4):** Brett Gardner, Aaron Judge, Giancarlo Stanton, Mike Tauchman.

Injured List (7): RHP Dellin Betances (right shoulder impingement), OF Jacoby Ellsbury (left hip surgery recovery), SS Didi Gregorius (right elbow UCL surgery recovery), RHP Ben Heller (right elbow UCL surgery recovery), OF Aaron Hicks (left lower back strain), LHP Jordan Montgomery (left elbow UCL surgery recovery) and RHP Luis Severino (right shoulder rotator cuff inflammation)

*****Suspended** (1): LHP CC Sabathia

Yankees on the Injured List

In 2019: 30 players made a total of 39 appearances on the injured list in 2019 (Based on the best available research on this topic, this marks the most different players and most overall stints by any team in a single season in MLB history).

In 2018: 20 players made a total of 23 appearances on the disabled list.

PLAYER	INJURY	ON I.L.	OFF I.L.	TYPE	GAMES LOST
LHP CC Sabathia	Rehab from cardiac surgery	4/3	4/13	10-day	8
C Gary Sánchez	Left calf strain	4/12 (retro to 4/11)	4/24	10-day	11
INF Miguel Andújar	Right shoulder strain	4/1	5/4	10-day	28
OF Clint Frazier	Left ankle sprain	4/25 (retro to 4/23)	5/6	10-day	11
OF Aaron Hicks	Left lower back strain	3/28 (retro to 3/25)	5/13	10-day	40
LHP James Paxton	Left knee inflammation	5/4	5/29	10-day	23
LHP CC Sabathia	Right knee inflammation	5/23	6/2	10-day	9
INF Didi Gregorius	Right elbow UCL surgery recovery	3/28 (retro to 3/25)	6/7	60-day	61
OF Giancarlo Stanton	Left biceps strain	4/1	6/18	10-day	68
OF Aaron Judge	Left oblique strain	4/21	6/21	10-day	54
INF Kendrys Morales	Left calf strain	6/13 (retro 6/12)	6/25	10-day	12
RHP Domingo Germán	Left hip flexor strain	6/9 (retro 6/8)	7/3	10-day	21
INF Luke Voit	Abdominal strain	7/2 (retro 6/30)	7/13	10-day	8
INF Troy Tulowitzki	Left calf strain	4/4	7/25	60-day	95
OF Cameron Maybin	Left calf strain	6/23 (retro 6/22)	7/26	10-day	27
OF Brett Gardner	Left knee inflammation	7/25 (retro 7/22)	8/2	10-day	9
C Gary Sánchez	Left groin strain	7/24	8/10	10-day	16
RHP Jonathan Loaisiga	Right shoulder strain	5/13 (retro 5/10)	8/13	60-day	83
LHP CC Sabathia	Right knee inflammation	7/28	8/18	10-day	21
INF Luke Voit	Sports hernia	7/31	8/30	10-day	29
INF Edwin Encarnación	Right wrist fracture	8/3	9/3	10-day	30
INF Thairo Estrada	Right hamstring strain	8/18	9/8	10-day	18
INF Gio Urshela	Left groin injury	8/30 (retro 8/29)	9/8	10-day	8
RHP Ben Heller	Right elbow UCL surgery recovery	3/28 (retro 3/25)	9/10	60-day	145
LHP CC Sabathia	Right knee inflammation	8/31	9/11	10-day	10
LHP Stephen Tarpley	Left elbow impingement	8/11	9/12	10-day	29
LHP Jordan Montgomery	Left elbow UCL surgery recovery	3/23	9/15	60-day	150
RHP Dellin Betances	Right shoulder impingement	3/28 (retro 3/25)	9/15	60-day	150
RHP Luis Severino	Right shoulder rotator cuff inflammation	3/28 (retro 3/25)	9/17	60-day	151
OF Giancarlo Stanton	Right knee sprain	6/26	9/18	60-day	72
RHP David Hale	Lumbar spine strain	7/31 (retro 7/28)	9/28	60-day	56
OF Jacoby Ellsbury	Left hip surgery recovery	3/28 (retro 3/25)		60-day	162
INF Greg Bird	Left plantar fascia tear	4/16 (retro 4/14)		60-day	148
INF Miguel Andújar	Right labrum tear	5/13		60-day	122
RHP Jake Barrett	Right elbow inflammation	5/26 (retro 5/23)		60-day	114
OF Aaron Hicks	Right flexor strain	8/4		60-day	52
RHP Jonathan Holder	Right shoulder inflammation	8/10 (retro 8/7)		60-day	49
OF Mike Tauchman	Left calf strain	9/10 (retro 9/9)		10-day	18
RHP Dellin Betances	Partial tear of left Achilles' tendon	9/18		60-day	10

Ejections

Manager (5x)   **Date/Opp. (Umpire)**
Aaron Boone . . . . . 9/21 vs. TOR (West)
                     8/17 vs. CLE (May)
                     7/18-G1 vs. TB (Miller)
                     5/1 at ARI (Emmel)
                     4/20 vs. KC (Meals)

Coaches (1x)   **Date/Opp. (Umpire)**
Marcus Thames . . 9/21 vs. TOR (Rehak)

Players (3x)   **Date/Opp. (Umpire)**
CC Sabathia . . . . 8/17 vs. CLE (Cuzzi)
Brett Gardner . . . . . 8/17 vs. CLE (Cuzzi)
                     8/9 at TOR (Segal)

Players Used

The Yankees used 54 players in 2019 (P-30, C-3, INF-14, OF-7)…were one of only two teams in 2019 to use as many as 54 players and finish with a winning record (also Tampa Bay-57)…used 13 rookies (italicized below), including six who made their Major League debuts, marking their second straight season with exactly six MLB debuts…a total of 22 players made their Yankees debuts…10 players remained on the active roster for the entire season: position players LeMahieu, Romine, Torres, and pitchers Britton, Chapman, Cessa, Happ*, Kahnle, Ottavino and Tanaka* (* = Happ and Tanaka each spent three days on the paternity list).

CATCHERS (3)
Kyle Higashioka
Austin Romine
Gary Sánchez

INFIELDERS (14)
Miguel Andújar
Greg Bird
Edwin Encarnación
Thairo Estrada
Mike Ford
Didi Gregorius
DJ LeMahieu
Kendrys Morales
Gleyber Torres
Troy Tulowitzki
Gio Urshela
Breyvic Valera
Luke Voit
Tyler Wade

OUTFIELDERS (7)
Clint Frazier
Brett Gardner
Aaron Hicks
Aaron Judge
Cameron Maybin
Giancarlo Stanton
Mike Tauchman

LHPs (10)
Zack Britton
Aroldis Chapman
Nestor Cortes Jr.
J.A. Happ
Tyler Lyons
Joe Mantiply
Jordan Montgomery
James Paxton
CC Sabathia
Stephen Tarpley

RHPs (20)
Chance Adams
Jake Barrett
Dellin Betances
Luis Cessa
Ryan Dull
Cory Gearrin
Domingo Germán
Chad Green
David Hale
Joseph Harvey
Ben Heller
Jonathan Holder
Tommy Kahnle
Michael King
Brady Lail
Jonathan Loaisiga
Adam Ottavino
Adonis Rosa
Luis Severino
Masahiro Tanaka

*Italics indicates rookie status / * Indicates made Major League debut.*

Starts by Position/Batting Order

The Yankees used 140 different starting defensive alignments (158 including pitchers) in 2019. Their most frequent combination (C-Sánchez, 1B-Voit, 2B-Torres, 3B-LeMahieu, SS-Gregorius, LF-Gardner, CF-Hicks, RF-Judge, DH-Encarnación) was used just five times. Additionally, the club used 155 different batting orders (also 155 including pitchers) in 2019 with no combination being used more than three times.

2019 STARTS BY POSITION

PLAYER	C	1B	2B	3B	SS	LF	CF	RF	DH
Andújar	-	-	-	4	-	-	-	-	8
Bird	-	10	-	-	-	-	-	-	-
Encarnación	-	12	-	-	-	-	-	-	32
Estrada	-	-	10	4	2	-	-	-	-
Ford	-	24	-	-	-	-	-	-	12
Frazier	-	-	-	-	-	14	-	31	14
Gardner	-	-	-	-	-	37	94	-	-
Gregorius	-	-	-	-	78	-	-	-	1
Higashioka	14	-	-	-	-	-	-	-	-
Hicks	-	-	-	-	-	-	55	-	1
Judge	-	-	-	-	-	-	-	90	9
LeMahieu	-	28	66	47	-	-	-	-	1
Maybin	-	-	-	-	-	35	2	26	2
Morales	-	7	-	-	-	-	-	-	10
Romine	62	-	-	-	-	-	-	-	-
Sánchez	86	-	-	-	-	-	-	-	15
Stanton	-	-	-	-	-	10	-	3	5
Tauchman	-	-	-	-	-	55	11	11	-
Torres	-	-	64	-	73	-	-	-	5
Tulowitzki	-	-	-	-	4	-	-	-	-
Urshela	-	-	-	109	-	-	-	-	3
Valera	-	-	9	-	-	-	-	-	-
Voit	-	81	-	-	-	-	-	-	34
Wade	-	-	13	2	3	9	-	1	-

Games with no DH: 10

2019 STARTS BY BATTING ORDER

PLAYER	1	2	3	4	5	6	7	8	9
Andújar	-	-	-	4	5	2	1	-	-
Bird	-	-	-	2	4	2	2	-	-
Encarnación	-	-	12	10	17	5	-	-	-
Estrada	-	-	-	-	-	-	2	9	5
Ford	-	-	-	-	-	5	4	10	9
Frazier	-	-	1	7	7	14	20	9	1
Gardner	27	2	12	-	11	28	15	5	31
Gregorius	-	-	24	15	20	16	4	-	-
Hicks	7	10	22	6	4	1	5	1	-
Higashioka	-	-	-	-	-	-	2	7	5
Judge	1	98	-	-	-	-	-	-	-
LeMahieu	125	2	1	-	4	5	3	-	2
Maybin	-	-	-	-	4	10	17	22	12
Morales	-	-	1	3	6	6	1	-	-
Romine	-	-	-	-	-	1	5	35	21
Sánchez	-	2	29	50	15	5	-	-	-
Stanton	-	-	2	4	9	3	-	-	-
Tauchman	-	-	-	-	5	7	16	16	33
Torres	2	1	16	32	35	28	19	9	-
Tulowitzki	-	-	-	-	-	-	-	2	2
Urshela	-	1	9	9	9	20	33	28	3
Valera	-	-	-	-	-	-	-	2	7
Voit	-	44	31	15	8	8	6	3	-
Wade	-	-	-	-	-	-	1	5	22
Pitchers	-	-	-	-	-	-	-	-	10

Yankees Games by the Numbers

NOTE	2019 (2018)
Standing in AL East:	1st, +7.0G
Final Streak:	Lost 2
Final Road Trip:	1-4
Final Homestand:	4-2
Home Record:	57-24 (53-28)
Road Record:	46-35 (47-34)
Day Record:	43-21 (32-20)
Night Record:	60-38 (68-42)
Pre-All-Star:	57-31 (62-33)
Post-All-Star:	46-28 (38-29)
vs. AL East:	54-22 (44-32)
vs. AL Central:	18-15 (23-11)
vs. AL West:	19-14 (22-10)
vs. National League:	12-8 (11-9)
vs. RH starters:	70-41 (70-47)
vs. LH starters:	33-18 (30-15)
Yankees Score First:	74-25 (72-18)
Opp. Score First:	29-34 (28-45)
Leading After 6:	87-7 (76-5)
Trailing After 6:	8-46 (8-51)
Tied After 6:	8-6 (16-6)
Leading After 7:	90-2 (77-4)
Trailing After 7:	8-47 (9-51)
Tied After 7:	5-9 (13-7)
Leading After 8:	90-1 (84-2)
Trailing After 8:	5-52 (5-55)
Tied After 8:	7-5 (10-5)
Extra-Inning Games:	7-4 (9-5)
One-run Games:	18-19 (23-17)
Two (or fewer)-run Games:	36-30 (37-29)
NYY Scores 5 or more:	84-13 (69-20)
NYY Scores 4 or more:	97-25 (89-27)
NYY Scores 3 or fewer:	6-34 (11-35)
NYY Scores 2 or fewer:	1-25 (5-27)
Opp. Scores 5 or more:	30-42 (20-47)
Opp. Scores 4 or fewer:	73-17 (80-15)
Opp. Scores 3 or fewer:	58-10 (72-10)
Opp. Scores 2 or fewer:	38-6 (54-3)
Yankees No Errors:	57-30 (62-33)
Yankees Make Error(s):	46-29 (38-29)
NYY Starter Goes 6:	46-15 (62-9)
Comeback Wins:	43 (37)
Yankees hit 0HR:	8-15 (10-21)
Yankees hit at least 1HR:	95-44 (90-41)
Yankees hit 2+ HRs:	71-14 (63-15)
Walk-off Wins-Losses:	6-5 (8-3)
Series Record:	33-12-7 (32-13-10)
Series Record, home:	20-3-3 (17-5-5)
Series Record, road:	13-9-4 (15-8-5)
Sweeps by NYY / by Opp.:	12 (12) / 4 (4)
Run Differential	+204
Runs Scored (per gm.)	943 (5.82)
Runs Allowed (per gm.)	739 (4.86)

It's a Home Run

Get into the swing of the season with The Westin New York at Times Square. We invite you to sleep well and wake up feeling energized and invigorated. Refresh in our Heavenly® Bed and Heavenly® Bath and revitalize in our 24-hour WestinWORKOUT® Fitness Studio.

If you need an energy boost, join us in Foundry Kitchen & Bar for healthy meal options and a lively atmosphere. When you book our "It's a Home Run" package, you will also enjoy complimentary drinks for two in Foundry Bar.

Rates from $279.

Conveniently located amid the brilliance of Broadway, Westin offers unparalleled access to top New York City attractions. Catch the train straight to the stadium and experience "the city that never sleeps" from the heart of Manhattan — Times Square.

To make a reservation, call 866-716-8108 and mention YX1 or visit marriott.com/nycsw.

THE WESTIN NEW YORK AT TIMES SQUARE
270 West 43rd Street
New York, New York 10036
United States

T   212-201-2700
F   212-201-2799

marriott.com/nycsw

THE WESTIN
NEW YORK
AT TIMES SQUARE

*Offer cannot be combined with another offer. Offer does not apply to any existing bookings. Offer based on availability at the time of the request. Limited to two (2) complimentary drinks at the Foundry Bar only.
©2019 Marriott International, Inc. All Rights Reserved. Westin and its logos are the trademarks of Marriott International, Inc., or its affiliates. For full terms & conditions, visit marriott.com/nycsw.

Opponents

Mickey Mantle and Stan Musial pose for a photo during spring training in Fort Lauderdale in the 1960s. The Yankees and Cardinals will meet for a three-game series in St. Louis from July 17-19 immediately following the All-Star break.

BALTIMORE ORIOLES

Oriole Park at Camden Yards (1992)
Capacity: 45,474
Exec. VP/GM: Mike Elias
Manager: Brandon Hyde

2020 Schedule
at New York:	at Baltimore:
April 6-9	March 26, 28-29
June 22-24	June 29-July 1
Aug. 25-26	Sept. 4-7

YANKEES vs. BALTIMORE*

2019 vs. Orioles	17-2
2019 at New York	7-2
2019 at Baltimore	10-0
All-Time vs. Orioles	607-491-3
All-Time at New York	316-236-1
All-Time at Baltimore	291-255-2
at current Yankee Stadium	66-37
at Camden Yards	139-91-1

SERIES RESULTS, LAST 10 YEARS

Year	Home	Road	Total
2019	7-2	10-0	17-2
2018	4-5	8-2	12-7
2017	8-2	4-5	12-7
2016	6-4	3-6	9-10
2015	7-3	2-7	9-10
2014	4-6	2-7	6-13
2013	6-3	4-6	10-9
2012	3-6	6-3	9-9
2011	7-2	6-3	13-5
2010	7-2	6-3	13-5
TOTAL	59-35	51-42	110-77

NYY SINGLE-GAME RECORDS*

MOST RUNS
20 . . . . 8/14/55 at BAL
MOST HITS
24 . . . . 7/30/11 vs. BAL
MOST RUNS ALLOWED
18 . . . . 6/8/86 vs. BAL
MOST HITS ALLOWED
22 . . . . 6/8/86 vs. BAL
LONGEST GAME
17 inn. . . . . . . 9/11/74 at BAL (G1)

LONGEST WINNING STREAKS*

by NYY	16 games
	(4/4/19-present)
by NYY at home	11 games
	(4/21/55-5/11/56)
by NYY on road	15 games
	(7/11/18-present)
by BAL	9 games
	(8/15/67-5/22/68)
by BAL at home	10 games
	(2x, 10/3/81-6/21/83; 4/16/66-5/23/67)
by BAL on road	12 games
	(5/2/65-6/21/66)

since franchise moved to BAL in 1954

SERIES SWEEPS

at New York		at Baltimore	
last by NYY	last by BAL	last by NYY	last by BAL
3-gm . . . 6/9-11/17	3-gm 6/6-8/86	3-gm 8/5-7/19	3-gm* . . . 10/3-4/15
4-gm . 8/12-14/19*	4-gm* . 9/21-23/76	4-gm . . 5/20-23/19	4-gm* 9/5-7/66
			5-gm* . .9/13-16/82

includes one doubleheader

BOSTON RED SOX

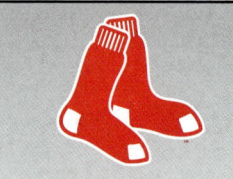

Fenway Park (1912)
Capacity: 37,755 (night); 37,305 (day) — as of 2019
Chief Baseball Officer: Chaim Bloom
Manager: TBD

2020 Schedule
at New York:	at Boston:
May 8-10	June 12-14
July 24-26	July 30-Aug. 2
Sept. 8-10	Aug. 31-Sept. 2

YANKEES vs. BOSTON

2019 vs. Red Sox	*14-5
2019 at New York	8-1
2019 at Boston	*6-4
All-Time vs. Red Sox	*1,203-996-14
All-Time at New York	648-448-7
All-Time at Boston	*555-548-7
at current Yankee Stadium	58-45
at Fenway Park	504-487-4

* inc. 2 road gms in London from 6/29-30/19

SERIES RESULTS, LAST 10 YEARS

Year	Home	Road	Total
2019	8-1	6-4*	14-5*
2018	6-3	3-7	9-10
2017	6-4	5-4	11-8
2016	6-3	2-8	8-11
2015	4-6	7-2	11-8
2014	6-4	6-3	12-7
2013	3-7	3-6	6-13
2012	6-3	7-2	13-5
2011	2-7	4-5	6-12
2010	4-5	5-4	9-9
TOTAL	51-43	48-45*	99-88

* inc. 2 road gms in London from 6/29-30/19

NYY SINGLE-GAME RECORDS

MOST RUNS
24 . . . . 9/28/23 at BOS
MOST HITS*
30 . . . . 9/28/23 at BOS
MOST RUNS ALLOWED
19 . . . . 7/25/2019 at BOS
MOST HITS ALLOWED*
27 . . . . 5/28/2005 vs. BOS
LONGEST GAME
20 inn. . . . . . . 8/29/67 vs. BOS (G2)

LONGEST WINNING STREAKS

by NYY	12 games
	(2x, 8/16/52-4/23/53; 5/27-8/23/36)
by NYY at home	12 games
	(7/8/31-6/5/32)
by NYY on road	10 games
	(5/17/30-4/24/31)
by BOS	17 games
	(10/3/1911-7/1/1912)
by BOS at home	11 games
	(8/1/73-7/29/74)
by BOS on road	18 games
	(10/3/1911-6/2/1913)

in Live Ball Era

SERIES SWEEPS

at New York		at Boston	
last by NYY	last by BOS	last by NYY	last by BOS
3-gm . . 9/27-29/16	3-gm 6/7-9/11	3-gm 5/1-3/15	3-gm . . 4/29-5/1/16
4-gm . . . 8/2-4/19*	4-gm . . . . none	4-gm . . . 10/2-5/86	4-gm 8/2-5/18
5-gm* . . 9/28-30/51	5-gm* 7/7-9/39	5-gm** . 8/18-21/06	5-gm . . . . none

* *includes two doubleheaders*   ** *includes one doubleheader*

CHICAGO WHITE SOX

Guaranteed Rate Field (1991)
Capacity: 40,615 (as of 2019)

Sr. VP/GM: Rick Hahn
Manager: Rick Renteria

2020 Schedule
at New York:	at Chicago:	in Iowa:
Aug. 3-5	Aug. 15-16	Aug. 13*

NYY is the visiting team

YANKEES vs. CHICAGO-AL
2019 vs. White Sox	3-4
2019 at New York	1-2
2019 at Chicago-AL	2-2
All-Time vs. White Sox	1,070-826-13
All-Time at New York	571-374-5
All-Time at Chicago-AL	499-452-8
at current Yankee Stadium	24-12
at Guaranteed Rate Field	63-57

SERIES RESULTS, LAST 10 YEARS
Year	Home	Road	Total
2019	1-2	2-2	3-4
2018	1-2	3-0	4-2
2017	2-1	2-2	4-3
2016	2-1	1-2	3-3
2015	3-1	2-1	5-2
2014	3-0	2-2	5-2
2013	3-0	0-3	3-3
2012	2-2	0-3	2-5
2011	2-2	4-0	6-2
2010	2-1	2-1	4-2
TOTAL	**21-12**	**18-16**	**39-28**

NYY SINGLE-GAME RECORDS
MOST RUNS
22 . . . . 7/26/31 vs. CWS
MOST HITS*
25 . . . . 8/31/74 at CWS
MOST RUNS ALLOWED
17 . . . . 6/18/00 vs. CWS
MOST HITS ALLOWED*
23 . . . . 5/4/50 vs. CWS
LONGEST GAME
18 inn. . . . . 8/21/33 at CWS
6/25/1903 vs. CWS

LONGEST WINNING STREAKS
by NYY . . . . 10 games
(2x, 4/22-6/22/64;
8/14/44-5/26/45)

by NYY at home . . . . 13 games
(2x, 9/19/33-8/27/34;
8/7/27-7/21/28)

by NYY on road . . . . . . 10 games
5/9-8/25/31

by CWS . . . . 8 games
(3x, 9/3/72-7/10/73;
6/10-8/22/67; 7/16-8/22/1906)

by CWS at home . . . . 9 games
6/4/72-7/10/73

by CWS on road . . . . 9 games
7/20/52-6/25/53

in Live Ball Era

SERIES SWEEPS
at New York		at Chicago-AL	
last by NYY	last by CWS	last by NYY	last by CWS
3-gm...8/22-24/14	3-gm... 9/14-16/92	3-gm......8/6-8/18	3-gm.....8/5-7/13
4-gm*...6/6-8/69	4-gm... 6/15-18/00	4-gm...8/1-4/11	4-gm... 8/17-20/64

includes one doubleheader

CLEVELAND INDIANS

Progressive Field (1994)
Capacity: 34,788

Pres., Baseball Ops.: Chris Antonetti
Manager: Terry Francona

2020 Schedule
at New York:	at Cleveland:
April 24-26	Aug. 28-30

YANKEES vs. CLEVELAND
2019 vs. Indians	3-4
2019 at New York	2-2
2019 at Cleveland	1-2
All-Time vs. Indians	1,106-873-12
All-Time at New York	599-391-5
All-Time at Cleveland	507-482-7
at current Yankee Stadium	23-15
at Progressive Field	64-41

SERIES RESULTS, LAST 10 YEARS
Year	Home	Road	Total
2019	2-2	1-2	3-4
2018	3-0	2-2	5-2
2017	0-3	2-2	2-5
2016	2-1	3-1	5-2
2015	1-3	1-2	2-5
2014	1-2	2-2	3-4
2013	3-0	3-1	6-1
2012	3-0	2-1	5-1
2011	3-1	1-2	4-3
2010	3-1	3-1	6-2
TOTAL	**21-13**	**20-16**	**41-29**

NYY SINGLE-GAME RECORDS
MOST RUNS
21 . . . . . 3x, last on 7/24/99 vs. CLE
MOST HITS*
21 . . . . . 3x, last on 7/24/99 vs. CLE
MOST RUNS ALLOWED
24 . . . . 7/29/28 at CLE
MOST HITS ALLOWED*
27 . . . . 7/29/28 at CLE
LONGEST GAME
19 inn. . . . . 5/24/1918 vs. CLE

LONGEST WINNING STREAKS
by NYY . . . . 13 games
(7/2/76-7/7/77)

by NYY at home . . . . 19 games
(6/10/60-4/21/62)

by NYY on road . . . . 8 games
(4x, last from 7/2/76-4/24/77)

by CLE . . . . 13 games
(7/13-9/23/1908)

by CLE at home . . . . 8 games
(2x, 6/8/1912-5/11/1913;
8/8/1904-7/14/1905)

by CLE on road . . . . 9 games
(7/13/1908-6/18/1909)

in Live Ball Era

SERIES SWEEPS
at New York		at Cleveland	
last by NYY	last by CLE	last by NYY	last by CLE
3-gm.....5/4-6/18	3-gm*..8/28-30/17	3-gm..... 8/10-12/07	3-gm.. 9/11-13/70
4-gm... 7/17-20/03	4-gm .... none	4-gm*...6/21-23/96	4-gm*.. 6/15-17/62

* includes one doubleheader*

249

DETROIT TIGERS

Comerica Park (2000)
Capacity: 41,083
Exec. VP of Baseball Ops/GM: Al Avila
Manager: Ron Gardenhire

2020 Schedule
at New York: April 28-30
at Detroit: April 20-23

YANKEES vs. DETROIT

2019 vs. Tigers	3-3
2019 at New York	1-2
2019 at Detroit	2-1
All-Time vs. Tigers	1,054-931-10
All-Time at New York	573-418-4
All-Time at Detroit	481-513-6
at current Yankee Stadium	22-14
at Comerica Park	39-37

SERIES RESULTS, LAST 10 YEARS

Year	Home	Road	Total
2019	1-2	2-1	3-3
2018	2-2	2-1	4-3
2017	1-2	2-1	3-3
2016	1-2	2-1	3-3
2015	2-1	3-1	5-2
2014	3-1	1-2	4-3
2013	2-1	1-2	3-3
2012	2-1	4-3	6-4
2011	2-1	1-3	3-4
2010	3-1	1-3	4-4
TOTAL	19-14	19-18	38-32

NYY SINGLE-GAME RECORDS

MOST RUNS
22 . . . . 5/2/39 at DET
MOST HITS*
23 . . . . 7/22/58 at DET
MOST RUNS ALLOWED
19 . . . . . 2x, last on 9/29/28 at DET
MOST HITS ALLOWED*
27 . . . . 9/29/28 at DET
LONGEST GAME
22 inn. . . . . 6/24/62 at DET

LONGEST WINNING STREAKS

by NYY . . . . 11 games
(7/12-9/17/42)
by NYY at home . . . . 10 games
(2x, 6/29/88-9/30/89; 7/22/31-5/7/32)
by NYY on road . . . . 12 games
(6/9/96-4/18/98)
by DET . . . . 12 games
(6/10-8/18/1908)
by DET at home . . . . 9 games
(2x, 8/9/87-6/28/89; 6/3-9/19/1912)
by DET on road . . . . 7 games
6/10-8/25/46

in Live Ball Era

SERIES SWEEPS

at New York		at Detroit	
last by NYY	last by DET	last by NYY	last by DET
3-gm... 7/17-19/09	3-gm.. 4/29-5/1/08	3-gm... 9/20-22/02	3-gm... 5/12-14/00
4-gm... 9/8-11/88	4-gm*.. 6/13-15/58	4-gm .. 6/8-11/26	4-gm*.. 8/12-13/45
*includes one doubleheader		* includes two doubleheaders	

HOUSTON ASTROS

Minute Maid Park (2000)
Capacity: 41,168
General Manager: James Click
Manager: Dusty Baker

2020 Schedule
at New York: Sept. 21-24
at Houston: May 15-17

YANKEES vs. HOUSTON

2019 vs. Astros	3-4
2019 at New York	3-1
2019 at Houston	0-3
All-Time vs. Astros	32-23
All-Time at New York	17-12
All-Time at Houston	15-11
at current Yankee Stadium	15-11
at Minute Maid Park	15-11

SERIES RESULTS, ALL TIME

Year	Home	Road	Total
2019	3-1	0-3	3-4
2018	2-1	3-1	5-2
2017	1-3	1-2	2-5
2016	2-1	2-1	4-2
2015	1-2	2-2	3-4
2014	1-2	1-2	2-4
2013	2-1	3-0	5-1
2010	3-0	---	3-0
2008	---	3-0	3-0
2003	2-1	---	2-1
TOTAL	17-12	15-11	32-23

NYY SINGLE-GAME RECORDS

MOST RUNS
16 . . . . 4/6/16 vs. HOU
MOST HITS
17 . . . . 4/6/16 vs. HOU
MOST RUNS ALLOWED
15 . . . . 8/25/15 vs. HOU
MOST HITS ALLOWED
17 . . . . 4/29/13 vs. HOU
LONGEST GAME
14 inn. . . . . 9/29/13 at HOU

LONGEST WINNING STREAKS

by NYY . . . . 7 games
(6/12/03-6/13/10)
by NYY at home . . . . 5 games
(5/29/18-6/22/19)
by NYY on road . . . . 6 games
(6/13/08-9/29/13)
by HOU . . . . 3 games
(4x, 4/8-10/19 7/1/17-4/30/18; 7/27/16-5/12/17; 8/25/15-4/5/16)
by HOU at home . . . . 3 games
(2x, 4/8/19-present, 7/1/17-4/30/18)
by HOU on road . . . . 3 games
(8/25/15-4/5/16)

SERIES SWEEPS

at New York		at Houston	
last by NYY	last by HOU	last by NYY	last by HOU
3-gm ..6/11-13/10	3-gm ....none	3-gm .. 9/27-29/13	3-gm ... 4/8-10/19
4-gm . . . . . . none	4-gm . . . . none	4-gm . . . . . . none	4-gm . . . . none

KANSAS CITY ROYALS

Kauffman Stadium (1973)
Capacity: 37,903

Sr. VP/GM: Dayton Moore
Manager: Mike Matheny

2020 Schedule
at New York: June 9-11
at Kansas City: Aug. 10-12

YANKEES vs. KANSAS CITY
2019 vs. Royals	5-2
2019 at New York	3-1
2019 at Kansas City	2-1
All-Time vs. Royals	300-199-1
All-Time at New York	167-85
All-Time at Kansas City	133-114-1
at current Yankee Stadium	26-13
at Kauffman Stadium	120-103

SERIES RESULTS, LAST 10 YEARS
Year	Home	Road	Total
2019	3-1	2-1	5-2
2018	3-1	2-1	5-2
2017	3-1	2-1	5-2
2016	3-1	2-1	5-2
2015	3-0	1-2	4-2
2014	1-2	2-2	3-4
2013	2-2	3-0	5-2
2012	2-1	2-2	4-3
2011	1-2	2-1	3-3
2010	3-1	2-2	5-3
TOTAL	**24-12**	**20-13**	**44-25**

NYY SINGLE-GAME RECORDS
MOST RUNS
18 . . . . 9/5/82 at KC
MOST HITS
26 . . . . 8/27/72 vs. KC
MOST RUNS ALLOWED
17 . . . . 9/13/04 at KC
MOST HITS ALLOWED
22 . . . . 6/6/82 vs. KC
LONGEST GAME
16 inn. . . . . . . 8/27/72 vs. KC (G2)

LONGEST WINNING STREAKS
by NYY . . . . 12 games
(8/13/97-8/18/98)
by NYY at home . . . . 14 games
(8/7/02-4/13/06)
by NYY on road . . . . 8 games
(5/4/97-8/18/98)
by KC . . . . 5 games
(2x, 5/26-7/4/90;
5/14-7/24/78)
by KC at home . . . . 6 games
(5/26/90-4/12/91)
by KC on road . . . . 4 games
(2x, 8/22/93-6/5/94;
4/20-8/14/91)

SERIES SWEEPS
at New York		at Kansas City	
last by NYY	last by KC	last by NYY	last by KC
3-gm . 5/25-27/15	3-gm . . . 6/3-5/94	3-gm.. 5/10-12/13	3-gm . . 5/31-6/2/05
4-gm* .. 8/7-9/98	4-gm . . . . none	4-gm . . . . none	4-gm . . . . none
5-gm* 7/12-15/84			

includes one doubleheader

LOS ANGELES ANGELS

Angel Stadium of Anaheim (1966)
Capacity: 45,517

General Manager: Billy Eppler
Manager: Joe Maddon

2020 Schedule
at New York: July 20-23
at Los Angeles-AL: May 29-31

YANKEES vs. LOS ANGELES-AL
2019 vs. Angels	5-2
2019 at New York	2-1
2019 at Los Angeles-AL	3-1
All-Time vs. Angels	366-298
All-Time at New York	204-125
All-Time at Los Angeles-AL	162-173
at current Yankee Stadium	29-12
at Angel Stadium	138-152

SERIES RESULTS, LAST 10 YEARS
Year	Home	Road	Total
2019	2-1	3-1	5-2
2018	2-1	3-0	5-1
2017	1-2	1-2	2-4
2016	4-0	2-1	6-1
2015	3-0	1-2	4-2
2014	2-1	2-1	4-2
2013	3-1	1-2	4-3
2012	4-2	1-2	5-4
2011	2-1	3-3	5-4
2010	3-2	1-2	4-4
TOTAL	**26-11**	**18-16**	**44-27**

NYY SINGLE-GAME RECORDS
MOST RUNS
17 . . . . 8/20/96 vs. CAL
MOST HITS
19 . . . . . . 4x, last on 8/13/13 vs. LAA
MOST RUNS ALLOWED
18 . . . . 8/21/07 at LAA
MOST HITS ALLOWED
19 . . . . . . 3x, last on 7/29/98 at ANA
LONGEST GAME
15 inn. . . 2x, last on 8/27/76 at CAL

LONGEST WINNING STREAKS
by NYY . . . . 7 games
(2x, 7/1/15-8/20/16;
8/23/80-5/4/81)
by NYY at home . . . . 11 games
(4/20/61-6/29/62)
by NYY on road . . . . 6 games
(4/27/18-4/24/19)
by LAA . . . . 5 games
(4x, last 4/27-7/23/05)
by LAA at home . . . . 6 games
(2x, 7/14/91-7/18/92;
7/9/82-5/25/83)
by LAA on road . . . . 4 games
(4x, last 8/21/96-4/15/97)

SERIES SWEEPS
at New York		at Los Angeles-AL	
last by NYY	last by LAA	last by NYY	last by LAA
3-gm 6/5-7/15	3-gm . . . 5/25-27/07	3-gm . . 4/27-29/18	3-gm . . 7/10-12/09
4-gm 6/6-9/16	4-gm . . . . none	4-gm . . 7/21-24/94	4-gm . . . . none

251

MINNESOTA TWINS

Target Field (2010)
Capacity: 38,544

Pres., Baseball Ops.: Derek Falvey
Manager: Rocco Baldelli

2020 Schedule
at New York: at Minnesota:
May 26-28   June 18-21

YANKEES vs. MINNESOTA*
2019 vs. Twins 4-2
2019 at New York 2-1
2019 at Minnesota 2-1

All-Time vs. Twins 370-261-1
All-Time at New York 193-117-1
All-Time at Minnesota 177-144

at current Yankee Stadium 27-10
at Target Field 23-11

SERIES RESULTS, LAST 10 YEARS
Year	Home	Road	Total
2019	2-1	2-1	4-2
2018	4-0	1-2	5-2
2017	3-0	1-2	4-2
2016	2-1	3-1	5-2
2015	3-0	2-1	5-1
2014	1-2	3-1	4-3
2013	1-2	4-0	5-2
2012	2-2	2-1	4-3
2011	3-1	3-1	6-2
2010	2-1	2-1	4-2
TOTAL	23-10	23-11	46-21

NYY SINGLE-GAME RECORDS*
MOST RUNS
18 . . . . 4/18/88 at MIN
MOST HITS
22 . . . . 8/13/99 vs. MIN
MOST RUNS ALLOWED
13 . . . . . . 2x, last on 5/18/94 at MIN
MOST HITS ALLOWED
20 . . . . 2x, last on 5/17/02 vs. MIN
LONGEST GAME
19 inn. . . . . 8/25/76 vs. MIN

LONGEST WINNING STREAKS*
by NYY . . . . 13 games
(5/10/02-4/21/03)
by NYY at home . . . . 10 games
(2x, 7/5/07-5/15/10; 5/17/02-7/26/05)
by NYY on road . . . . 8 games
(7/19/85-7/12/86)
by MIN . . . . 6 games
(3x, last 5/24-6/4/69)
by MIN at home . . . . 8 games
(9/4/66-9/22/67)
by MIN on road . . . . 5 games
(9/27/63-7/3/64)

*since franchise moved to MIN in 1961

SERIES SWEEPS
at New York		at Minnesota	
last by NYY	last by MIN	last by NYY	last by MIN
3-gm . . . 9/18-20/17	3-gm . . . 8/9-11/68	3-gm . . . 7/7-9/09	3-gm . . . 9/6-8/91
4-gm . . . 4/23-26/18	4-gm . . . . none	4-gm 7/1-4/13	4-gm* . . . 7/3-5/67

*includes one doubleheader

OAKLAND ATHLETICS

Oakland Coliseum (1968)
Capacity: 46,847

Exec. VP, Baseball Ops: Billy Beane
Manager: Bob Melvin

2020 Schedule
at New York: at Oakland:
Aug. 6-9   April 10-12

YANKEES vs. OAKLAND*
2019 vs. Athletics 2-4
2019 at New York 2-1
2019 at Oakland 0-3

All-Time vs. Athletics 283-254
All-Time at New York 155-113
All-Time at Oakland 128-141

at current Yankee Stadium 24-16
at Oakland Coliseum 128-141

SERIES RESULTS, LAST 10 YEARS
Year	Home	Road	Total
2019	2-1	0-3	2-4
2018	2-1	1-2	3-3
2017	2-1	0-4	2-5
2016	0-3	4-0	4-3
2015	2-1	1-3	3-4
2014	1-2	1-2	2-4
2013	1-2	0-3	1-5
2012	2-1	3-4	5-5
2011	3-3	3-0	6-3
2010	4-0	5-1	9-1
TOTAL	19-15	18-22	37-37

NYY SINGLE-GAME RECORDS*
MOST RUNS
22 . . . . 8/25/11 vs. OAK
MOST HITS
22 . . . . 8/26/97 at OAK
MOST RUNS ALLOWED
19 . . . . 8/29/89 vs. OAK
MOST HITS ALLOWED
20 . . . . 6/12/71 at OAK
LONGEST GAME
18 inn. . . . . 6/13/13 at OAK

LONGEST WINNING STREAKS*
by NYY . . . . 11 games
(7/5/10-7/22/11)
by NYY at home . . . . 10 games
(5/6/77-8/27/78)
by NYY on road . . . . 9 games
(7/5/10-5/27/12)
by OAK . . . . 16 games
(9/9/89-5/1/91)
by OAK at home . . . . 10 games
(9/9/89-5/1/91)
by OAK on road . . . . 6 games
(2x, 4/30-9/9/90; 5/31/71-4/25/72)

*since franchise moved to OAK in 1968

According to *Elias*, the Yankees did not lose a season series to the A's over a 40-year stretch (1931-70), marking the most consecutive non-losing season series by one team against another opponent in Major League history.

SERIES SWEEPS
at New York		at Oakland	
last by NYY	last by OAK	last by NYY	last by OAK
3-gm . . 7/18-20/08	3-gm . . 4/19-21/16	3-gm . . . 5/25-27/12	3-gm . . . 8/20-22/19
4-gm . . 8/30-9/2/10	4-gm* . . 7/14-16/72	4-gm . . . 5/19-22/16	4-gm . 6/15-18/17

* includes one doubleheader

SEATTLE MARINERS

T-Mobile Park (July 15, 1999)
Capacity: 47,500

Exec. VP/GM: Jerry Dipoto
Manager: Scott Servais

2020 Schedule
at New York: at Seattle:
May 22-25   June 1-3

YANKEES vs. SEATTLE
2019 vs. Mariners 6-1
2019 at New York 3-1
2019 at Seattle 3-0

All-Time vs. Mariners 245-182
All-Time at New York 121-90
All-Time at Seattle 124-92

at current Yankee Stadium 23-17
at T-Mobile Park 57-30

SERIES RESULTS, LAST 10 YEARS

Year	Home	Road	Total
2019	3-1	3-0	6-1
2018	3-0	2-1	5-1
2017	2-1	3-1	5-2
2016	1-2	2-1	3-3
2015	2-1	3-0	5-1
2014	0-3	3-0	3-3
2013	1-2	3-1	4-3
2012	4-2	2-1	6-3
2011	2-1	3-3	5-4
2010	3-3	3-1	6-4
TOTAL	21-16	27-9	48-25

NYY SINGLE-GAME RECORDS
MOST RUNS
16 . . . . 2x, last on 5/8/03 at SEA
MOST HITS
23 . . . . 8/25/84 at SEA
MOST RUNS ALLOWED
16 . . . . 7/11/79 at SEA
MOST HITS ALLOWED
20 . . . . 5/4/07 vs. SEA
LONGEST GAME
17 inn. . . . . 5/11/84 vs. SEA

LONGEST WINNING STREAKS
by NYY . . . . 8 games
(2x, 9/4/07-5/25/08
5/9-8/29/99)

by NYY at home . . . . 10 games
(2x, 9/4/07-7/1/09;
5/8/79-8/30/80)

by NYY on road . . . . 8 games
(6/8/13-6/3/15)

by SEA . . . . 5 games
(3x, last 5/29-6/10/95)

by SEA at home . . . . 7 games
(8/19/78-7/11/79)

by SEA on road . . . . 6 games
(2x, 8/18/01-4/29/03;
8/5/00-4/26/01)

SERIES SWEEPS

at New York		at Seattle	
last by NYY	last by SEA	last by NYY	last by SEA
3-gm . . 6/19-21/18	3-gm . . . 5/3-5/02	3-gm . 8/26-28/19	3-gm . . 8/26-28/96
4-gm . . . . none	4-gm . . . . none	4-gm . . . 8/5-8/99	4-gm . . . . none

TAMPA BAY RAYS

Tropicana Field (1998)
Capacity: 25,025

SVP, Baseball Ops/GM: Erik Neander
Manager: Kevin Cash

2020 Schedule
at New York: at Tampa Bay:
June 5-7   March 30-April 1
Aug. 17-19   May 11-14
Sept. 25-27   Sept. 14-16

YANKEES vs. TAMPA BAY
2019 vs. Rays 12-7
2019 at New York 8-2
2019 at Tampa Bay 4-5

All-Time vs. Rays . . . . ^*230-159
All-Time at New York 128-66
All-Time at Tampa Bay . . . . . ^*102-93

at current Yankee Stadium 63-40
at Tropicana Field 99-91

*inc. 2 road gms in Tokyo from 3/30-31/04
^inc. 3 road gms at Citi Field from 9/11-13/17

SERIES RESULTS, LAST 10 YEARS

Year	Home	Road	Total
2019	8-2	4-5	12-7
2018	6-3	4-6	10-9
2017	8-2	4-5^	12-7^
2016	7-3	4-5	11-8
2015	6-3	6-4	12-7
2014	3-6	5-5	8-11
2013	3-7	4-5	7-12
2012	6-3	2-7	8-10
2011	6-3	3-6	9-9
2010	4-5	4-5	8-10
TOTAL	57-37	40-53	97-90

^inc. 3 road gms at Citi Field from 9/11-13/17

NYY SINGLE-GAME RECORDS
MOST RUNS
21 . . . . 7/22/07 vs. TB
MOST HITS
25 . . . . 7/22/07 vs. TB
MOST RUNS ALLOWED
19 . . . . 7/29/06 vs. TB
MOST HITS ALLOWED
20 . . . . 5/2/14 vs. TB
LONGEST GAME
14 inn. . . . . 5/2/14 vs. TB

LONGEST WINNING STREAKS
by NYY . . . . 11 games
(9/17/98-9/24/99)

by NYY at home . . . . 11 games
(4/14/04-4/18/05)

by NYY on road . . . . 7 games
(9/13/05-7/8/06)

by TB . . . . 7 games
(9/22/11-4/8/12)

by TB at home . . . . 9 games
(7/21/11-7/3/12)

by TB on road . . . . 5 games
(5/4-9/9/14)

Due to Hurricane Irma, the Yankees-Rays series from 9/11-13/17 was relocated from Tropicana Field to Citi Field.

SERIES SWEEPS

at New York		at Tampa Bay	
last by NYY	last by TB	last by NYY	last by TB
3-gm . . 6/17-19/19	3-gm 6/30-7/2/14	3-gm . . . 4/17-19/15	3-gm . . . 6/22-24/18
4-gm* . . . 9/7-9/09	4-gm . . . . none	4-gm . . . 7/9-12/98	4-gm . . . . none

* includes one doubleheader

253

TEXAS RANGERS

Globe Life Field (2020)
Capacity: 40,300 (Approximately)

Pres., Baseball Ops/GM: Jon Daniels
Manager: Chris Woodward

2020 Schedule
at New York: July 10-12
at Texas: April 13-15

YANKEES vs. TEXAS*

2019 vs. Rangers	3-3
2019 at New York	2-1
2019 at Texas	1-2
All-Time vs. Rangers	269-204
All-Time at New York	154-87
All-Time at Texas	115-117
at current Yankee Stadium	26-17
at Globe Life Field	0-0

SERIES RESULTS, LAST 10 YEARS

Year	Home	Road	Total
2019	2-1	1-2	3-3
2018	3-1	1-2	4-3
2017	1-2	2-1	3-3
2016	2-2	1-2	3-4
2015	0-3	2-2	2-5
2014	3-1	1-2	4-3
2013	1-2	2-2	3-4
2012	3-1	1-2	4-3
2011	5-1	2-1	7-2
2010	3-0	1-4	4-4
TOTAL	23-14	14-20	37-34

NYY SINGLE-GAME RECORDS*

MOST RUNS
21 . . . . 2x, last 7/28/15 at TEX

MOST HITS
23 . . . . 8/23/99 at TEX

MOST RUNS ALLOWED
20 . . . . 7/19/87 at TEX

MOST HITS ALLOWED
22 . . . . 7/19/87 at TEX

LONGEST GAME
15 inn. . . . . 6/16/91 at TEX

LONGEST WINNING STREAKS*

by NYY . . . . 8 games
(2x, 7/24/06-5/9/07; 7/20/05-5/7/06)

by NYY at home . . . . 8 games
(2x, 4/16/11-8/15/12; 4/4/94-4/12/96)

by NYY on road . . . . 10 games
(7/20/05-5/3/07)

by TEX . . . . 7 games
(4/20-9/10/90)

by TEX at home . . . . 15 games
(7/20/89-9/3/91)

by TEX on road . . . . 5 games
(5/22/15-6/28/16)

since franchise moved to TEX in 1972

SERIES SWEEPS

at New York		at Texas	
last by NYY	last by TEX	last by NYY	last by TEX
3-gm…6/14-16/11	3-gm..5/22-24/15	3-gm*…5/1-3/07	3-gm..9/10-12/10
4-gm…8/11-14/05	4-gm…….none	4-gm…….none	4-gm..7/20-23/89

* includes one doubleheader

TORONTO BLUE JAYS

Rogers Centre (June 3, 1989)
Capacity: 49,286

Exec. VP, Baseball Ops/GM: Ross Atkins
Manager: Charlie Montoyo

2020 Schedule
at New York: April 2, 4-5; Aug. 20-23; Sept. 11-13
at Toronto: May 1-3; July 3-5; Sept. 18-20

YANKEES vs. TORONTO

2019 vs. Blue Jays	11-8
2019 at New York	7-2
2019 at Toronto	4-6
All-Time vs. Blue Jays	360-291
All-Time at New York	192-135
All-Time at Toronto	168-156
at current Yankee Stadium	68-35
at Rogers Centre	120-125

SERIES RESULTS, LAST 10 YEARS

Year	Home	Road	Total
2019	7-2	4-6	11-8
2018	7-3	6-3	13-6
2017	5-4	4-6	9-10
2016	5-4	2-8	7-12
2015	2-8	4-5	6-13
2014	7-3	4-5	11-8
2013	10-0	4-5	14-5
2012	7-2	4-5	11-7
2011	7-2	4-5	11-7
2010	5-4	3-6	8-10
TOTAL	62-32	39-54	101-86

NYY SINGLE-GAME RECORDS

MOST RUNS
18 . . . . 8/28/04 at TOR

MOST HITS
22 . . . . 4/8/02 at TOR

MOST RUNS ALLOWED
19 . . . . 9/10/77 vs. TOR

MOST HITS ALLOWED
21 . . . . . . 2x, last on 8/21/08 at TOR

LONGEST GAME
17 inn. . . . . 4/19/01 at TOR

LONGEST WINNING STREAKS

by NYY . . . . 13 games
(5/10/95-6/4/96)

by NYY at home . . . . 17 games
(9/19/12-7/25/14)

by NYY on road . . . . 7 games
(5/10/95-6/11/96)

by TOR . . . . 10 games
(4/14-9/25/92)

by TOR at home . . . . 8 games
(4/13-9/25/16)

by TOR on road . . . . 7 games
(4/9-9/12/15-G2)

SERIES SWEEPS

at New York		at Toronto	
last by NYY	last by TOR	last by NYY	last by TOR
3-gm…6/24-26/19	3-gm….8/7-9/15	3-gm..3/31-4/2/03	3-gm..5/30-6/1/16
4-gm*..8/20-22/13	4-gm…5/22-25/03	4-gm…….none	4-gm…….none

* includes one doubleheader

CHICAGO CUBS

Wrigley Field (1914)
Capacity: TBD

Pres. Baseball Ops: Theo Epstein
Manager: David Ross

2020 Schedule
at New York: June 26-28
at Chicago-NL: N/A

SERIES RESULTS, ALL TIME

Year	Home	Road	Total
2017	---	3-0	3-0
2014	2-0	1-1	3-1
2011	---	2-1	2-1
2005	3-0	---	3-0
2003	---	1-2	1-2
TOTAL	5-0	7-4	12-4

YANKEES vs. CHICAGO-NL

2019 vs. Chicago-NL . . . . N/A
2019 at New York . . . . N/A
2019 at Chicago-NL . . . . N/A

All-Time vs. Chicago-NL 12-4
All-Time at New York 5-0
All-Time at Chicago-NL 7-4

at current Yankee Stadium 2-0
at original Yankee Stadium 3-0
at Wrigley Field 7-4

SERIES SWEEPS
at New York
last by NYY 4/16/14* (2G)
last by CHC . . . . None
at Chicago-NL
last by NYY 5/5-7/17 (3G)
last by CHC . . . . None
*includes one doubleheader

NYY SINGLE-GAME RECORDS
MOST RUNS
11 . . . . 5/6/17 at CHC
MOST HITS
15 . . . . 6/17/05 vs. CHC
MOST RUNS ALLOWED
8 . . . . 6/8/03 at CHC
MOST HITS ALLOWED
13 . . . . 6/8/03 at CHC
LONGEST GAME
18 inn. . . . . 5/7/17 at CHC

CINCINNATI REDS

Great American Ball Park (2003)
Capacity: 42,271

Pres. Baseball Ops: Dick Williams
Manager: David Bell

2020 Schedule
at New York: April 17-19
at Cincinnati: N/A

SERIES RESULTS, ALL TIME

Year	Home	Road	Total
2017	2-0	1-1	3-1
2014	3-0	---	3-0
2012	1-2	---	1-2
2011	---	2-1	2-1
2008	1-2	---	1-2
2003	---	1-2	1-2
TOTAL	7-4	4-4	11-8

YANKEES vs. CINCINNATI

2019 vs. Cincinnati . . . . N/A
2019 at New York . . . . N/A
2019 at Cincinnati . . . . N/A

All-Time vs. Cincinnati 11-8
All-Time at New York 7-4
All-Time at Cincinnati 4-4

at current Yankee Stadium 6-2
at original Yankee Stadium 1-2
at Great American Ball Park 4-4

SERIES SWEEPS
at New York
last by NYY 7/25-26/17 (2G)
last by CIN . . . . None
at Cincinnati
last by NYY . . . . None
last by CIN . . . . None

NYY SINGLE-GAME RECORDS
MOST RUNS
10 . . . . 2x, last: 5/8/17 at CIN
MOST HITS
16 . . . . 6/5/2003 at CIN
MOST RUNS ALLOWED
10 . . . . 6/22/2011 at CIN-G2
MOST HITS ALLOWED
14 . . . . 6/22/2011 at CIN-G2
LONGEST GAME
9 inn. . . . . 19 times

MILWAUKEE BREWERS

Miller Park (2001)
Capacity: 41,700

Pres., Baseball Ops/GM: David Stearns
Manager: Craig Counsell

2020 Schedule
at New York: N/A
at Milwaukee: May 19-21

SERIES RESULTS, SINCE 1998

Year	Home	Road	Total
2017	1-2	---	1-2
2014	---	1-2	1-2
2011	3-0	---	3-0
2005	---	1-2	1-2
TOTAL	4-2	2-4	6-6

YANKEES vs. MILWAUKEE

2019 vs. Milwaukee . . . . N/A
2019 at New York . . . . N/A
2019 at Milwaukee . . . . N/A

All-Time vs. Milwaukee . . . *213-186-1
All-Time at New York 124-74
All-Time at Milwaukee . . . 85-110-1
*includes a 7-5 mark against
Seattle Pilots in 1969

at current Yankee Stadium 4-2
at original Yankee Stadium . . 109-65
at Miller Park 2-4

SERIES SWEEPS
at New York
last by NYY 6/28-30/11 (3G)
last by MIL 10/2-4/72 (3G)
at Milwaukee
last by NYY 9/26-27/95 (2G)
last by MIL 4/16-17/97 (2G)

NYY SINGLE-GAME RECORDS
MOST RUNS
19 . . . . 9/25/1996 vs. MIL-G1
MOST HITS
20 . . . 3x, last 9/25/1996 vs. MIL-G1
MOST RUNS ALLOWED
16 . . . . 7/18/1996 at MIL
MOST HITS ALLOWED
17 . . . . . . 6x, last 6/19/1994 vs. MIL
LONGEST GAME
15 inn. . . . . 9/2/1969 vs. SEA

255

PITTSBURGH PIRATES

PNC Park (2001)
Capacity: 38,747

Gen. Manager: Ben Cherington
Manager: Derek Shelton

2020 Schedule
at New York: May 5-6
at Pittsburgh: June 16-17

SERIES RESULTS, ALL TIME

Year	Home	Road	Total
2017	---	1-2	1-2
2014	2-1	---	2-1
2008	---	1-2	1-2
2007	3-0	---	3-0
2005	3-0	---	3-0
TOTAL	8-1	2-4	10-5

YANKEES vs. PITTSBURGH

2019 vs. Pittsburgh	N/A
2019 at New York	N/A
2019 at Pittsburgh	N/A
All-Time vs. Pittsburgh	10-5
All-Time at New York	8-1
All-Time at Pittsburgh	2-4
at current Yankee Stadium	2-1
at original Yankee Stadium	6-0
at PNC Park	2-4

SERIES SWEEPS

at New York
last by NYY 6/8-10/07 (3G)
last by PIT .... None

at Pittsburgh
last by NYY .... None
last by PIT .... None

NYY SINGLE-GAME RECORDS

MOST RUNS
13 .... 6/10/07 vs. PIT
MOST HITS
16 .... 6/25/08 at PIT
MOST RUNS ALLOWED
12 .... 6/24/08 at PIT
MOST HITS ALLOWED
19 .... 6/24/08 at PIT
LONGEST GAME
10 inn. ...... 6/15/05 & 6/8/07 vs. PIT

ST. LOUIS CARDINALS

Busch Stadium (2006)
Capacity: 44,383

Pres., Baseball Ops: John Mozeliak
Manager: Mike Shildt

2020 Schedule
at New York: N/A
at St. Louis: July 17-19

SERIES RESULTS, ALL TIME

Year	Home	Road	Total
2017	3-0	---	3-0
2014	---	2-1	2-1
2005	---	1-2	1-2
2003	3-0	---	3-0
TOTAL	6-0	3-3	9-3

YANKEES vs. ST. LOUIS

2019 vs. St. Louis	N/A
2019 at New York	N/A
2019 at St. Louis	N/A
All-Time vs. St. Louis	9-3
All-Time at New York	6-0
All-Time at St. Louis	3-3
at current Yankee Stadium	3-0
at original Yankee Stadium	3-0
at Busch Stadium	3-3

SERIES SWEEPS

at New York
last by NYY 4/14-16/17 (3G)
last by STL .... None

at St. Louis
last by NYY .... None
last by STL .... None

NYY SINGLE-GAME RECORDS

MOST RUNS
13 .... 6/14/03 vs. STL
MOST HITS
15 .... 6/14/03 vs. STL
MOST RUNS ALLOWED
8 .... 6/10/05 at STL
MOST HITS ALLOWED
13 .... 5/28/14 at STL
LONGEST GAME
12 inn. .... 5/26/14 at STL

OPPONENTS BATTING RECORDS SINCE 1921

Single Season

MOST HITS vs. NYY
Carl Reynolds, 1930 CWS 43
Charlie Gehringer, 1929 DET 42
Red Kress, 1938 SLB 38
Al Simmons, 1925 PHA 38
4 others tied 37

MOST HR vs. NYY
Hank Greenberg, 1938 DET 11
Jimmie Foxx, 1932 PHA 10
Jimmie Foxx, 1933 PHA 10
Charlie Maxwell, 1959 DET 10
Fred Whitfield, 1965 CLE 10

HIGHEST AVG. vs. NYY (min. 20AB)
David Ortiz, 2012 BOS ...... .619 (13-for-21)
Hank Severeid, 1925 SLB/WAS .. .609 (14-for-23)
Rod Carew, 1975 MIN .... .595 (22-for-37)
Howie Kendrick, 2006 LAA .. .591 (13-for-22)
Manny Ramirez, 2006 BOS ... .556 (25-for-45)

Career

MOST HITS vs. NYY
Charlie Gehringer 420
Al Kaline 380
Luke Appling 380
Goose Goslin 375
Al Simmons 374

MOST HR vs. NYY
Jimmie Foxx 70
Ted Williams 62
Manny Ramirez 55
Hank Greenberg 53
David Ortiz 53

HIGHEST AVG. vs. NYY (min. 300AB)
Harry Heilmann ... .375 (292-for-779)
Dale Alexander ... .356 (128-for-360)
Ty Cobb .... .345 (185-for-536)
Ted Williams .... .345 (357-for-1,035)
Bob Fothergill ..... .343 (150-for-437)

All-Time at Current Yankee Stadium

MOST HITS
Adam Jones 82
Evan Longoria 82
Nick Markakis 76
Edwin Encarnación 68
Dustin Pedroia 65
José Bautista 65

MOST HR
José Bautista 19
Edwin Encarnación 18
Evan Longoria 16
David Ortiz 15
Victor Martinez 13

HIGHEST AVG. (min. 30AB)
José Ramirez .... .455 (30-for-66)
Justin Morneau ..... .433 (26-for-60)
Adam Eaton .... .429 (15-for-35)
Pedro Ciriaco ...... .400 (12-for-30)
Dee Gordon .... .389 (14-for-36)

Source: Baseball-Reference.com

NEW YORK METS

Citi Field (2009)
Capacity: 41,922

Exec. VP/GM: Brodie Van Wagenen
Manager: Luis Rojas

2020 Schedule
at New York-AL: July 7-8
at New York-NL: July 28-29

YANKEES vs. NEW YORK METS	
2019 vs. Mets	2-2
2019 at New York-AL	1-1
2019 at New York-NL	1-1
All-Time vs. Mets	*71-51
All-Time at New York-AL	36-25
All-Time at New York-NL	35-26
at current Yankee Stadium	16-12
at original Yankee Stadium	20-13
at Citi Field (vs. the Mets)	18-10
at Shea Stadium	17-16

*Entering 2020, mark the most wins over one opponent in Interleague history

SERIES RESULTS, ALL TIME

Year	Home	Road	Total
2019	1-1	1-1	2-2
2018	1-2	2-1	3-3
2017	2-0	2-0	4-0
2016	1-1	1-1	2-2
2015	2-1	2-1	4-2
2014	0-2	2-0	2-2
2013	0-2	0-2	0-4
2012	3-0	2-1	5-1
2011	2-1	2-1	4-2
2010	2-1	1-2	3-3
2009	2-1	3-0	5-1
2008	0-3	2-1	2-4
2007	2-1	1-2	3-3
2006	2-1	1-2	3-3
2005	1-2	2-1	3-3
2004	2-1	0-3	2-4
2003	3-0	3-0	6-0
2002	2-1	1-2	3-3
2001	2-1	2-1	4-2
2000	2-1	2-1	4-2
1999	2-1	1-2	3-3
1998	---	2-1	2-1
1997	2-1	---	2-1
TOTAL	**36-25**	**35-26**	**71-51**

SERIES SWEEPS
at New York-AL
last by NYY...... 8/14-15/17 (2G)
last by NYM..... 5/12-13/14 (2G)
at New York-NL
last by NYY...... 8/16-17/17 (2G)
last by NYM..... 5/27-28/13 (2G)

NYY SINGLE-GAME RECORDS
MOST RUNS
16................7/2/06 vs. NYM
MOST HITS
17...... 2x, last on 6/14/09 vs. NYM
MOST RUNS ALLOWED
15........... 6/27/08 vs. NYM-G1
MOST HITS ALLOWED
16....... 2x, last 6/13/09 vs. NYM
LONGEST GAME
11 inn. ..... 2x, last 5/20/06 at NYM

LONGEST WINNING STREAKS
by NYY..................7 games
(6/30/02-6/29/03)
by NYY at home........5 games
(5/21/11-6/10/12)
by NYY on road ....4 games
(2x, 8/16/17-6/9/18; 6/26/09-5/21/10)
by NYM..................6 games
(5/27/13-5/13/14)
by NYM at home ....3 games
(3x, last 5/21/06-5/19/07)
by NYM on road..........4 games
(5/29/13-5/13/14)

Due to Hurricane Irma, the Yankees-Rays series from 9/11-13/17 was relocated from Tropicana Field to Citi Field. The Yankees went 2-1.

Yankees-Mets All-Time Transactions

Date	Transaction
11/30/64	Yankees selected **OF Duke Carmel** off Triple-A Buffalo roster in the Rule 5 Draft.
6/15/66	Yankees acquired cash considerations from the Mets in exchange for **RHP Bob Friend**.
6/29/67	Yankees acquired cash considerations from the Mets in exchange for **RHP Hal Reniff**.
12/9/77	Yankees acquired **INF Roy Staiger** from the Mets for **INF Sergio Ferrer**.
8/20/79	Yankees acquired cash considerations from the Mets in exchange for **RHP Ray Burris**.
4/1/80	Yankees acquired **1B Marshall Brant** from the Mets in exchange for cash considerations.
4/18/83	Yankees acquired **LHP Steve Ray** and **INF Felix Perdomo** from the Mets in exchange for **INF Tucker Ashford**.
12/11/87	Yankees acquired **INF Rafael Santana** and **LHP Victor Garcia** from the Mets in exchange for **LHP Steve Frey, C Phil Lombardi** and **OF Darren Reed**.
7/10/89	Yankees acquired **OF Marcus Lawton** from the Mets in exchange for **RHP Scott Nielsen**.
6/9/92	Yankees acquired **RHP Tim Burke** from the Mets in exchange for **LHP Lee Guetterman**.
12/7/92	Mets selected **RHP Mike Draper** off Triple-A Columbus roster in the Rule 5 Draft.
9/17/93	Yankees acquired **LHP Frank Tanana** from the Mets in exchange for **RHP Kenny Greer**.
12/7/01	Yankees acquired **INF Robin Ventura** from the Mets in exchange for **OF/DH David Justice**.
7/16/03	Yankees acquired **RHP Armando Benitez** from the Mets **for RHP Jason Anderson, RHP Anderson Garcia** and **RHP Ryan Bicondoa**.
12/3/04	Yankees acquired **LHP Mike Stanton** from the Mets for **LHP Felix Heredia**.
12/19/14	Yankees acquired **RHP Gonzalez Germen** from the Mets for cash considerations.
4/10/18	Yankees acquired **INF/OF L.J. Mazzilli** from the Mets for **OF Kendall Coleman**.

Two-Stadium Doubleheaders

On three occasions, the Yankees and Mets have played two-stadium day-night doubleheaders. Each instance was precipitated by a rainout. According to the *Elias Sports Bureau*, the first occurrence in 2000 marked the first dual-venue doubleheader in the Majors since September 7, 1903, when the New York Giants and the Brooklyn Superbas (later called the Dodgers) faced off in Game 1 (Giants 6 - Brooklyn 4) at Washington Park in Brooklyn and Game 2 (Brooklyn 3 - Giants 0) at the Polo Grounds in Manhattan.

Date	Game	Stadium	Score	WP	LP	SV	Att.
7/8/00	Game 1	Shea Stadium	Yankees 4 - Mets 2	Gooden	Jones	Rivera	54,165
	Game 2	Orig. Yankee Stadium	Yankees 4 - Mets 2	Clemens	Rusch	Rivera	55,821
6/28/03	Game 1	Orig. Yankee Stadium	Yankees 7 - Mets 1	Clemens	Griffiths	None	55,343
	Game 2	Shea Stadium	Yankees 9 - Mets 8	Claussen	Glavine	Rivera	36,372
6/27/08	Game 1	Orig. Yankee Stadium	Mets 15 - Yankees 6	Pelfrey	Giese	None	54,978
	Game 2	Shea Stadium	Yankees 9 - Mets 0	Ponson	P. Martinez	None	56,308

Played for or Managed Yankees and Mets

Through the 2019 season, there have been 135 players to appear in at least one game for both the Yankees and Mets. The first was "Marvelous" Marv Throneberry, who broke in with the Yankees (1955, '58-59) before joining the Mets via a May 9, 1962, trade with Baltimore. The only other Yankee to play on the Mets in their inaugural 1962 season was Gene Woodling, who played six seasons in the Bronx from 1949-54, winning World Series championships in each of his first five seasons with the club. He was purchased by the Mets from Washington on June 15, 1962. There have been 34 players who have played on World Series-winning Yankees teams who have also appeared in at least one game for the Mets. Conversely, there have been nine World Series-winning Mets (1969-Swoboda; 1986-Elster, Gooden, Jefferson, Mazzilli, Ojeda, Orosco, Santana and Strawberry) to play for the Yankees at some point in their careers.

*Indicates played for Yankees and Mets in same season (16 players).

Dwight Gooden [L] and Darryl Strawberry [R] are the only players to be part of World Series-winning teams for both the Yankees and Mets. While each player won rings with the Mets in 1986, Gooden played on championship Yankees clubs in 1996 and 2000, and Strawberry was a member of Yankees World Series winners in 1996, '98 and '99.

Player	w/Yankees	w/Mets
David Aardsma	2012	2013
Bobby Abreu	2006-08	2014
Juan Acevedo	2003	1997
Jack Aker	1969-72	1974
Neil Allen	1985, '87-88	1979-83
Sandy Alomar	1974-76	1967
*Jason Anderson	2003, '05	2003
Tucker Ashford	1981	1983
Luis Ayala	2011	2008
Carlos Beltran	2014-16	2005-11
*Armando Benitez	2003	1999-2003
Yogi Berra	1946-63	1965
*Angel Berroa	2009	2009
Daryl Boston	1994	1990-92
*Darren Bragg	2001	2001
*Tim Burke	1992	1991-92
*Ray Burris	1979	1979-80
Miguel Cairo	2004, '06-07	2005
John Candelaria	1988-89	1987
Robinson Canó	2005-13	2019
Chris Capuano	2014-15	2011
Buddy Carlyle	2011	2014-15
Duke Carmel	1965	1963
Alberto Castillo	2002	1995-98
Rick Cerone	1980-84, '87, '90	1991
Tony Clark	2004	2003
Tyler Clippard	2007, '16-17	2015
Bartolo Colon	2011	2014-16
David Cone	1995-2000	1987-92, 2003
Billy Cowan	1969	1965
Ike Davis	2016	2010-14
Wilson Delgado	2000	2004
Octavio Dotel	2006	1999
Dock Ellis	1976-77	1979
Kevin Elster	1994-95	1986-92
Scott Erickson	2006	2004
Alvaro Espinoza	1988-91	1996
Kyle Farnsworth	2006-08	2014
Tony Fernandez	1995	1993
Tim Foli	1984	1970-71, '78-79
Todd Frazier	2017	2018-19
*Bob Friend	1966	1966
Karim Garcia	2002-03	2004
Rob Gardner	1970-72	1965-66
*Paul Gibson	1993-94, '96	1992-93
Jesse Gonder	1960-61	1963-65
Dwight Gooden	1996-97, 2000	1984-94
Curtis Granderson	2010-13	2014-17
*Lee Guetterman	1988-92	1992
Greg A. Harris	1994	1981
LaTroy Hawkins	2008	2013
Adeiny Hechavarria	2018	2019
Rickey Henderson	1985-89	1999-2000
Sean Henn	2005-07	2013
Felix Heredia	2003-04	2005
Orlando Hernandez	1998-2002, '04	2006-07
Keith Hughes	1987	1990
Ryota Igarashi	2012	2010-11

Player	w/Yankees	w/Mets
Stan Jefferson	1989	1986
Kelly Johnson	2014	2015-16
Lance Johnson	2000	1996-97
*Dave Kingman	1977	1975-77, '81-83
Brandon Knight	2001-02	2008
Aaron Laffey	2011	2013
Matt Lawton	2005	2001
Tim Leary	1990-92	1981, '83-84
Ricky Ledee	1998-2000	2006-07
Al Leiter	1987-89, 2005	1998-2004
Cory Lidle	2006	1997
Phil Linz	1962-65	1967-68
Graeme Lloyd	1996-98	2003
Phil Lombardi	1986-87	1989
Terrence Long	2006	1999
Bob MacDonald	1995	1996
Elliott Maddox	1974-76	1978-80
*Josias Manzanillo	1995	1993-95, '99
Lee Mazzilli	1982	1976-81, '86-89
Doc Medich	1972-75	1977
Doug Mientkiewicz	2007	2005
Gustavo Molina	2011	2008
Dale Murray	1983-85	1978-79
Xavier Nady	2008-09	2006
C.J. Nitkowski	2004	2001
Bob Ojeda	1994	1986-90
John Olerud	2004	1997-99
Jesse Orosco	2003	1979, 81-87
John Pacella	1982	1977, '79-80
Juan Padilla	2004	2005
Chan Ho Park	2010	2007
Andy Phillips	2004-07	2008
Lenny Randle	1979	1977-78
Willie Randolph	1976-88	1992
Jeff Reardon	1994	1979-81
Tim Redding	2005	2009
*Hal Reniff	1961-67	1967
Royce Ring	2010	2005-06
Kenny Rogers	1996-97	1999
Rey Sanchez	1997, 2005	2003
Rafael Santana	1988	1984-87
Don Schulze	1989	1987
Gary Sheffield	2004-06	2009
Bill Short	1960	1968
Charley Smith	1967-68	1964-65
Shane Spencer	1998-2002	2004
Roy Staiger	1979	1975-77
Mike Stanton	1997-2002, 2005	2003-04
*Kelly Stinnett	2006	1994-95, 2006
Darryl Strawberry	1995-99	1983-90
Tom Sturdivant	1955-59	1964
Bill Sudakis	1974	1972
Anthony Swarzak	2016	2018
Ron Swoboda	1971-73	1965-70
*Frank Tanana	1993	1993
Tony Tarasco	1999	2002
Walt Terrell	1989	1982-84
Ralph Terry	1956-57, '59-64	1966-67
Ryan Thompson	2000	1992-95
Marv Throneberry	1955, '58-59	1962-63
Dick Tidrow	1974-79	1984
Mike Torrez	1977	1983-84
Bubba Trammell	2003	2000
Raul Valdes	2011	2010
Robin Ventura	2002-03	1999-2001
Jose Vizcaino	2000	1994-96
Neil Walker	2018	2016-17
Claudell Washington	1986-88, '90	1980
*Allen Watson	1999-2000	1999
David Weathers	1996-97	2002-04
Wally Whitehurst	1996	1989-92
Gerald Williams	1992-96, 2001-02	2004-05
Justin Wilson	2015	2019
Gene Woodling	1949-54	1962
*Chris Young	2014-15	2014
Eric Young Jr.	2016	2013-15
Todd Zeile	2003	2000-01, '04

Manager	w/Yankees	w/Mets
Yogi Berra	1964, '84-85	1972-75
Dallas Green	1989	1993-96
Casey Stengel	1949-60	1962-65
Joe Torre	1996-2007	1977-81

Players to Play for the Dodgers, Giants, Mets and Yankees

Three players have played for the four original New York clubs. They are listed below in order of accomplishing the feat.

Name	Dodgers	Giants	Mets	Yankees
Darryl Strawberry	1991-93	1994	1983-90	1995-99
Jose Vizcaino	1989-90, '98-00	1997, 2006	1994-96	2000
Ricky Ledee	2005-06	2004	2006-07	1998-2000

Most Recent Trades with Each Team

AMERICAN LEAGUE EAST
Baltimore (July 24, 2018): Yankees acquire LHP Zack Britton for RHP Dillon Tate, RHP Cody Carroll and LHP Josh Rogers.
Boston (July 31, 2014): Yankees acquire INF Stephen Drew and cash considerations for INF Kelly Johnson.
Tampa Bay (Feb. 20, 2018): Yankees trade INF Nick Solak to Tampa Bay as part of a three-team trade. The Yankees also acquire INF Brandon Drury from Arizona and send RHP Taylor Widener to Arizona. Tampa Bay sends OF Steven Souza, Jr. to Arizona, and Arizona sends LHP Anthony Banda and two players to be named later to Tampa Bay.
Toronto (Aug. 4, 2018): Yankees acquire INF Gio Urshela for cash considerations.

AMERICAN LEAGUE CENTRAL
Chicago (July 29, 2018): Yankees acquire international signing bonus pool money for LHP Caleb Frare.
Cleveland (April 25, 2019): Yankees acquire OF Cameron Maybin for cash considerations.
Detroit (Dec. 13, 2018): Yankees acquire OF Tyler Hill for cash considerations.
Kansas City (Dec. 23, 2019): Yankees acquire minor league infielder Cristian Perez from the Kansas City Royals in exchange for right-handed pitcher Chance Adams.
Minnesota (July 30, 2018): Yankees acquire RHP Lance Lynn and cash considerations for INF Tyler Austin and RHP Luis Rijo.

AMERICAN LEAGUE WEST
Houston (Nov. 17, 2016): Yankees acquire RHPs Albert Abreu and Jorge Guzman for C Brian McCann and cash considerations.
Los Angeles (Feb. 21, 2018): Yankees acquire a player to be named later or cash considerations for OF Jabari Blash.
Oakland (May 14, 2019): Yankees acquire 1B/DH Kendrys Morales and cash considerations for a player to be named later or cash considerations.
Seattle (Nov. 25, 2019): Yankees acquire international signing bonus pool money in exchange for Nestor Cortes Jr.
Texas (Feb. 7, 2018): Yankees acquire INF Russell Wilson for future considerations.

NATIONAL LEAGUE EAST
Atlanta (Jan. 1, 2015): Yankees acquire RHP David Carpenter and LHP Chasen Shreve for LHP Manny Banuelos.
Miami (Jan. 15, 2020): Yankees acquire 3B James Nelson and cash considerations in exchange for LHP Stephen Tarpley.
New York (April 10, 2018): Yankees acquire INF/OF L.J. Mazzilli for OF Kendall Coleman.
Philadelphia (July 1, 2012): Yankees acquire RHP Chad Qualls for cash considerations.
Washington (April 23, 2018): Yankees acquire RHP A.J. Cole for cash considerations.

NATIONAL LEAGUE CENTRAL
Chicago (Nov. 28, 2018): Yankees acquire a player to be named later or cash consideration for INF Ronald Torreyes.
Cincinnati (Jan. 21, 2019): Yankees acquire 2B Shed Long and a Competitive Balance Round A pick in the 2019 First-Year Player Draft for RHP Sonny Gray and LHP Reiver Sanmartin.
Milwaukee (Sept. 1, 2019): Yankees acquire INF Brenny Escanio and international signing bonus pool money for RHP J.P. Feyereisen.
Pittsburgh (Aug. 31, 2018): Yankees acquire SS Adeiny Hechavarria and cash considerations for a player to be named later or cash considerations.
St. Louis (July 28, 2018): Yankees acquire 1B Luke Voit and international signing bonus pool money for LHP Chasen Shreve and RHP Giovanny Gallegos.

NATIONAL LEAGUE WEST
Arizona (Jan. 16, 2019): Yankees acquire LHP Ronald Roman and cash considerations for OF Tim Locastro.
Colorado (July 31, 2019): Yankees acquire LHP Alfredo Garcia for RHP Joseph Harvey.
Los Angeles (Nov. 21, 2018): Yankees acquire OF Tim Locastro for RHP Drew Finley and cash considerations.
San Diego (Dec. 12, 2017): Yankees acquire OF Jabari Blash for INF Chase Headley, RHP Bryan Mitchell and cash considerations.
San Francisco (Aug. 31, 2018): Yankees acquire OF Andrew McCutchen and cash considerations for INF Abiatal Avelino and RHP Juan De Paula.

as of 2/1/20

Most Strikeouts by a Pitcher in a Single Game vs. Yankees

17	Pedro Martinez, Boston Red Sox, Sept. 10, 1999
16	Curt Schilling, Philadelphia Phillies, Sept. 1, 1997
16	Mike Moore, Seattle Mariners, Aug. 19, 1988 (G2)
16	Rube Waddell, Philadelphia A's, April 21, 1904 (12 inn.)
15	Chuck Finley, California Angels, May 23, 1995
15	Sandy Koufax, LA Dodgers, Oct. 2, 1963 (WS, G1)
15	Ed Cicotte, Chicago White Sox, Aug. 26, 1914

30 Career Wins vs. Yankees

Walter Johnson	60
Lefty Grove	35
Eddie Cicotte	35
Early Wynn	33
Hal Newhouser	33
Red Faber	32
Stan Coveleski	32
Bob Feller	30
Chief Bender	30
George Mullin	30
George Dauss	30
Jim Palmer	30

All-Time Results by Year vs. AL

YEAR	BAL	BOS	CWS	CLE	DET	HOU	KC	LAA	MIL	MIN	OAK	SEA	TB	TEX	TOR
2019	17-2	14-5	3-4	3-4	3-3	3-4	5-2	5-2	–	4-2	2-4	6-1	12-7	3-3	11-8
2018	12-7	9-10	4-2	5-2	4-3	5-2	5-2	5-1	–	5-2	3-3	5-1	10-9	4-3	13-6
2017	12-7	11-8	4-3	2-5	3-3	2-5	5-2	2-4	*1-2	4-2	2-5	5-2	12-7	3-3	9-10
2016	9-10	8-11	3-3	5-2	3-3	4-2	5-2	6-1	–	5-2	4-3	3-3	11-8	3-4	7-12
2015	9-10	11-8	5-2	2-5	5-2	3-4	4-2	4-2	–	5-1	3-4	5-1	12-7	2-5	6-13
2014	6-13	12-7	5-2	3-4	4-3	2-4	3-4	4-2	*1-2	4-3	2-4	3-3	8-11	4-3	11-8
2013	10-9	6-13	3-3	6-1	3-3	5-1	5-2	4-3	–	5-2	1-5	4-3	7-12	3-4	14-5
2012	9-9	13-5	2-5	5-1	6-4	–	4-3	5-4	–	4-3	5-5	6-3	8-10	4-3	11-7
2011	13-5	6-12	6-2	4-3	3-4	–	3-3	5-4	*3-0	6-2	6-3	5-4	9-9	7-2	11-7
2010	13-5	9-9	4-2	6-2	4-4	*3-0	5-3	4-4	–	4-2	9-1	6-4	8-10	4-4	8-10
2009	13-5	9-9	4-3	5-3	5-1	–	4-2	5-5	–	7-0	7-2	6-4	11-7	5-4	12-6
2008	11-7	9-9	5-2	3-4	2-4	*3-0	5-5	3-7	–	6-4	5-1	7-2	11-7	3-4	9-9
2007	9-9	10-8	6-4	6-0	4-4	–	9-1	5-4	–	5-2	2-4	5-5	10-8	5-1	10-8
2006	12-7	11-8	4-2	4-3	5-2	–	7-2	4-6	–	3-3	3-6	3-3	13-5	8-2	10-8
2005	11-7	10-9	3-3	4-3	5-1	–	3-3	4-6	*1-2	3-3	7-2	7-3	8-11	7-3	12-6
2004	14-5	8-11	4-3	4-2	3-4	–	5-1	4-5	–	4-2	7-2	6-3	15-4	5-4	12-7
2003	13-6	10-9	2-4	5-2	5-1	*2-1	4-2	6-3	–	7-0	3-6	5-4	14-5	4-5	10-9
2002	13-6	10-9	4-2	6-3	8-1	–	5-1	4-3	–	6-0	5-4	4-5	13-5	4-3	10-9
2001	13-5	13-5	5-1	5-4	5-4	–	6-0	3-4	–	2-4	3-6	3-6	13-6	3-4	11-8
2000	7-5	7-6	4-8	5-5	4-8	–	8-2	5-5	–	5-5	6-3	4-6	6-6	10-2	5-7
1999	9-4	8-4	7-5	7-3	7-5	–	4-5	4-6	–	6-4	6-4	9-1	8-4	8-4	10-2
1998	9-3	7-5	7-4	7-4	8-3	–	10-0	5-6	–	7-4	8-3	8-3	11-1	8-3	6-6
1997	4-8	8-4	9-2	6-5	10-2	–	8-3	7-4	7-4	8-3	6-5	4-7	–	7-4	7-5
1996	10-3	6-7	7-6	9-3	8-5	–	8-4	6-7	6-6	7-5	9-3	3-9	–	5-7	8-5
1995	7-6	8-5	2-3	6-6	8-5	–	7-3	5-7	6-5	4-3	4-9	4-9	–	6-3	12-1
1994	6-4	7-3	2-4	9-0	3-3	–	2-4	8-4	7-2	5-4	7-5	8-4	–	3-2	3-4
1993	7-6	7-6	8-4	7-6	9-4	–	6-6	6-6	9-4	8-4	6-6	7-5	–	3-9	5-8
1992	8-5	6-7	4-8	6-7	8-5	–	7-5	5-7	7-6	5-7	6-6	6-6	–	6-6	2-11
1991	8-5	7-6	4-8	7-6	5-8	–	5-7	6-6	7-6	2-10	6-6	3-9	–	5-7	6-7
1990	7-6	4-9	2-10	8-5	6-7	–	4-8	6-6	7-6	6-6	0-12	9-3	–	3-9	5-8
1989	5-8	6-7	6-5	4-9	7-6	–	6-6	6-6	5-8	6-6	3-9	8-4	–	5-7	7-6
1988	10-3	4-9	9-3	7-6	5-8	–	6-6	6-6	7-6	9-3	6-6	5-7	–	5-6	6-7
1987	10-3	6-7	7-5	7-6	8-5	–	7-5	9-3	6-7	6-6	5-7	7-5	–	5-7	6-7
1986	8-5	8-5	6-6	8-5	7-6	–	8-4	5-7	5-8	8-4	5-7	8-4	–	7-5	7-6
1985	12-1	8-5	6-6	7-6	3-9	–	7-5	9-3	6-7	9-3	7-5	9-3	–	8-4	6-7
1984	8-5	6-7	5-7	11-2	6-7	–	7-5	4-8	7-6	4-8	8-4	7-5	–	6-6	8-5
1983	7-6	6-7	4-8	7-6	8-5	–	6-6	7-5	9-4	8-4	8-4	7-5	–	7-5	7-6
1982	2-11	6-7	4-8	9-4	5-8	–	7-5	5-7	5-8	10-2	7-5	6-6	–	7-5	6-7
1981	6-7	3-3	7-5	5-7	7-3	–	10-2	2-2	3-3	3-3	4-3	2-3	–	5-4	2-3
1980	6-7	10-3	7-5	8-5	8-5	–	4-8	10-2	8-5	8-4	8-4	9-3	–	7-5	10-3
1979	6-5	8-5	8-4	8-5	6-7	–	7-5	5-7	4-9	5-7	9-3	6-6	–	8-4	9-4
1978	9-6	9-7	9-1	9-6	11-4	–	5-6	5-5	5-10	7-3	8-2	6-5	–	6-4	11-4
1977	7-8	7-8	7-3	12-3	9-6	–	5-5	7-4	7-8	8-2	9-2	6-4	–	7-3	9-6
1976	5-13	11-7	11-1	12-4	8-9	–	5-7	7-5	13-5	10-2	6-6	–	–	9-3	–
1975	10-8	5-11	6-6	9-9	12-6	–	5-7	5-7	9-9	8-4	6-6	–	–	8-4	–
1974	7-11	7-11	8-4	11-7	11-7	–	8-4	9-3	9-9	8-4	7-5	–	–	8-4	–
1973	9-9	4-14	4-8	11-7	11-7	–	6-6	6-6	8-10	9-3	4-8	–	–	8-4	–
1972	6-7	9-9	5-7	11-7	9-7	–	5-7	8-4	9-9	6-6	3-9	–	–	8-4	–
1971	7-11	11-7	7-5	10-8	8-10	–	7-5	6-6	10-2	4-8	5-7	–	–	7-11	–
1970	7-11	8-10	7-5	10-8	11-7	–	11-1	7-5	9-3	7-5	6-6	–	–	10-8	–
1969	7-11	7-11	9-3	8-9	8-10	–	7-5	9-3	7-5	2-10	6-6	–	–	10-8	–
1968	5-13	8-10	12-6	8-10	8-10	–	–	12-6	–	6-12	10-8	–	–	14-4	–
1967	5-13	6-12	6-12	9-9	8-10	–	–	9-9	–	6-12	11-7	–	–	12-6	–
1966	3-15	10-8	9-9	6-12	7-11	–	7-11	–	–	10-8	13-5	–	–	5-10	–
1965	5-13	9-9	10-8	6-12	8-10	–	12-6	–	–	5-13	11-7	–	–	11-7	–
1964	8-10	9-9	12-6	15-3	10-8	–	–	11-7	–	10-8	12-6	–	–	12-6	–
1963	11-7	12-6	10-8	11-7	10-8	–	–	13-5	–	11-6	12-6	–	–	14-4	–
1962	7-11	12-6	10-8	7-11	11-7	–	–	10-8	–	11-7	13-5	–	–	15-3	–
1961	9-9	13-5	12-6	14-4	10-8	–	–	12-6	–	14-4	14-4	–	–	11-7	–
1960	13-9	15-7	12-10	16-6	14-8	–	–	–	–	12-10	15-7	–	–	–	–
1959	10-12	9-13	9-13	11-11	8-14	–	–	–	–	15-7	17-5	–	–	–	–
1958	14-8	13-9	15-7	15-7	10-12	–	–	–	–	12-10	13-9	–	–	–	–
1957	13-9	14-8	13-9	13-9	12-10	–	–	–	–	13-9	19-3	–	–	–	–
1956	13-9	14-8	13-9	12-10	10-12	–	–	–	–	17-5	18-4	–	–	–	–
1955	19-3	14-8	11-11	9-13	12-10	–	–	–	–	16-6	15-7	–	–	–	–
1954	17-5	13-9	15-7	11-11	16-6	–	–	–	–	13-9	18-4	–	–	–	–
1953	17-5	11-10	13-9	11-11	16-6	–	–	–	–	14-6	17-5	–	–	–	–
1952	14-8	14-8	14-8	12-10	13-9	–	–	–	–	15-7	13-9	–	–	–	–
1951	17-5	11-11	14-8	15-7	12-10	–	–	–	–	16-6	13-9	–	–	–	–
1950	17-5	13-9	14-8	14-8	11-11	–	–	–	–	14-8	15-7	–	–	–	–
1949	17-5	13-9	15-7	12-10	11-11	–	–	–	–	15-7	14-8	–	–	–	–
1948	16-6	8-14	16-6	12-10	13-9	–	–	–	–	17-5	12-10	–	–	–	–
1947	15-7	13-9	12-10	15-7	14-8	–	–	–	–	15-7	13-9	–	–	–	–
1946	14-8	8-14	14-8	12-10	9-13	–	–	–	–	14-8	16-6	–	–	–	–
1945	7-15	16-6	12-9	9-12	7-15	–	–	–	–	14-8	16-6	–	–	–	–
1944	10-12	11-11	12-10	14-8	8-14	–	–	–	–	15-7	13-9	–	–	–	–
1943	17-5	17-5	12-10	13-9	12-10	–	–	–	–	11-11	16-6	–	–	–	–
1942	15-7	10-12	15-7	15-7	15-7	–	–	–	–	17-5	16-6	–	–	–	–
1941	18-4	13-9	14-8	15-7	11-11	–	–	–	–	16-6	14-8	–	–	–	–
1940	14-8	13-9	11-11	12-10	8-14	–	–	–	–	17-5	13-9	–	–	–	–

All-Time Results by Year vs. AL

YEAR	BAL	BOS	CWS	CLE	DET	HOU	KC	LAA	MIL	MIN	OAK	SEA	TB	TEX	TOR
1939	19-3	8-11	18-4	15-7	13-9	–	–	–	–	15-7	18-4	–	–	–	–
1938	15-7	11-11	14-8	13-8	14-8	–	–	–	–	16-6	16-5	–	–	–	–
1937	16-6	15-7	13-9	15-7	13-9	–	–	–	–	16-6	14-8	–	–	–	–
1936	14-8	15-7	14-7	16-6	14-8	–	–	–	–	13-9	16-6	–	–	–	–
1935	12-10	12-9	11-9	14-8	11-11	–	–	–	–	15-7	14-6	–	–	–	–
1934	17-5	12-10	17-5	11-11	10-12	–	–	–	–	12-10	15-7	–	–	–	–
1933	14-7	14-8	15-7	13-7	15-7	–	–	–	–	8-14	12-9	–	–	–	–
1932	16-6	17-5	17-5	15-7	17-5	–	–	–	–	11-11	14-8	–	–	–	–
1931	16-6	16-6	15-6	9-13	14-8	–	–	–	–	13-9	11-11	–	–	–	–
1930	16-6	16-6	14-8	12-10	13-9	–	–	–	–	5-17	10-12	–	–	–	–
1929	14-8	17-5	16-6	8-14	13-9	–	–	–	–	12-10	8-14	–	–	–	–
1928	12-10	16-6	13-9	16-6	15-7	–	–	–	–	13-9	16-6	–	–	–	–
1927	21-1	18-4	17-5	12-10	14-8	–	–	–	–	14-8	14-8	–	–	–	–
1926	16-6	17-5	14-8	11-11	12-10	–	–	–	–	12-10	9-13	–	–	–	–
1925	11-11	13-9	9-13	12-10	8-14	–	–	–	–	7-15	9-13	–	–	–	–
1924	12-10	17-5	16-6	14-8	9-13	–	–	–	–	9-13	12-8	–	–	–	–
1923	15-5	14-8	15-7	10-12	12-10	–	–	–	–	16-6	16-6	–	–	–	–
1922	14-8	9-13	13-9	15-7	11-11	–	–	–	–	15-7	17-5	–	–	–	–
1921	13-9	15-7	9-13	14-8	17-5	–	–	–	–	13-8	17-5	–	–	–	–
1920	12-10	13-9	12-10	13-9	15-7	–	–	–	–	11-11	19-3	–	–	–	–
1919	12-8	9-10	8-12	7-13	12-8	–	–	–	–	14-6	18-2	–	–	–	–
1918	10-10	11-6	6-12	7-11	10-9	–	–	–	–	8-11	8-4	–	–	–	–
1917	13-9	9-13	10-12	7-15	9-13	–	–	–	–	8-13	15-7	–	–	–	–
1916	9-13	11-11	12-10	10-12	8-14	–	–	–	–	15-7	15-7	–	–	–	–
1915	12-10	12-10	7-15	13-9	5-17	–	–	–	–	9-13	11-9	–	–	–	–
1914	11-11	11-11	10-12	14-8	9-13	–	–	–	–	7-15	8-14	–	–	–	–
1913	11-11	6-14	10-11	8-14	11-11	–	–	–	–	6-16	5-17	–	–	–	–
1912	13-9	2-19	9-13	8-13	6-16	–	–	–	–	7-15	5-17	–	–	–	–
1911	16-5	10-12	9-13	8-14	15-7	–	–	–	–	12-10	6-15	–	–	–	–
1910	16-6	13-9	13-8	13-8	9-13	–	–	–	–	15-7	9-12	–	–	–	–
1909	13-8	9-13	8-14	14-8	8-14	–	–	–	–	14-6	8-14	–	–	–	–
1908	5-17	10-12	6-16	6-16	7-15	–	–	–	–	9-13	8-14	–	–	–	–
1907	8-14	12-8	10-12	7-15	8-13	–	–	–	–	15-7	10-9	–	–	–	–
1906	13-8	17-5	10-12	11-10	11-11	–	–	–	–	15-7	13-8	–	–	–	–
1905	15-7	8-13	7-15	10-12	8-13	–	–	–	–	15-7	8-11	–	–	–	–
1904	16-6	10-12	10-12	11-9	15-7	–	–	–	–	18-4	12-9	–	–	–	–
1903	15-5	7-13	11-7	6-14	9-10	–	–	–	–	14-5	10-8	–	–	–	–
TOTALS	1318-890	1203-996	1070-826	1106-873	1054-931	32-23	300-199	366-298	213-186-	1125-768	1131-774	245-182	230-159	390-278	360-291

*Interleague Play; Houston joined the AL in 2013 and Milwaukee played its last season in the AL in 1997.

Orioles include St. Louis Browns, 1903-1953 (711-399). Brewers include Seattle Pilots, 1969 (7-5). Twins include original Washington Senators, 1903-1960 (755-507). A's include Philadelphia A's, 1903-1954 (665-445) and Kansas City A's, 1955-1967 (183-75). Rangers include Washington Senators, 1961-1971 (121-74).

All-Time Results in Interleague Play

YEAR	ARI	ATL	CHC	CIN	COL	HOU	LAD	MIA	MIL	NYM	PHI	PIT	SD	SF	STL	WAS	TOTAL
2019	1-3	–	–	–	2-1	–	2-1	–	–	2-2	–	–	2-1	3-0	–	–	12-8
2018	–	2-1	–	–	–	–	–	2-2	–	3-3	2-1	–	–	–	–	2-2	11-9
2017	–	–	3-0	3-1	–	–	–	–	1-2	4-0	–	1-2	–	–	3-0	–	15-5
2016	1-2	–	–	–	1-3	–	1-2	–	–	2-2	–	–	1-2	2-1	–	–	8-12
2015	–	3-0	–	–	–	–	–	2-2	–	4-2	1-2	–	–	–	–	1-3	11-9
2014	–	–	3-1	3-0	–	–	1-2	2-2	–	2-1	–	–	2-1	–	–	13-7
2013	2-1	–	–	–	2-1	2-2	–	–	–	0-4	–	–	1-2	2-1	–	–	9-11
2012	–	4-2	–	1-2	–	–	–	–	–	5-1	–	–	–	–	3-0	–	13-5
2011	–	–	2-1	2-1	2-1	–	3-0	–	4-2	–	–	–	–	–	–	13-5
2010	2-1	–	–	–	–	3-0	2-1	–	–	3-3	1-2	–	–	–	–	–	11-7
2009	–	2-1	–	–	–	1-2	–	–	–	5-1	1-2	–	–	–	–	1-2	10-8
2008	–	–	–	1-2	–	3-0	–	–	–	2-4	–	–	1-2	3-0	–	–	10-8
2007	3-0	–	–	–	0-3	–	–	–	–	3-3	–	–	3-0	–	1-2	–	10-8
2006	–	2-1	–	–	–	–	2-1	–	–	3-3	2-1	–	–	–	–	1-2	10-8
2005	–	–	3-0	–	–	–	1-2	–	3-3	–	3-0	–	1-2	–	11-7
2004	2-1	–	–	–	3-0	1-2	–	–	2-4	–	–	–	2-1	–	–	10-8
2003	–	–	1-2	1-2	–	2-1	–	–	–	6-0	–	–	–	–	3-0	–	13-5
2002	2-1	–	–	–	2-1	–	–	–	–	3-3	–	–	2-1	2-1	–	–	11-7
2001	–	1-2	–	–	–	1-2	–	–	4-2	2-1	–	–	–	2-1	–	10-8
2000	–	2-1	–	–	–	1-1	–	–	4-2	2-1	–	–	–	2-1	–	11-6
1999	–	1-2	–	–	–	2-1	–	–	3-3	1-2	–	–	–	2-1	–	9-9
1998	–	3-1	–	–	–	3-0	–	–	2-1	3-0	–	–	–	2-1	–	13-3
1997	–	1-2	–	–	–	1-2	–	–	2-1	0-3	–	–	–	1-2	–	5-10
TOTALS	13-9	21-13	12-4	11-8	12-10	8-1	8-8	15-13	6-6	71-51	15-15	10-5	11-7	10-5	9-3	17-15	249-173

Milwaukee joined the National League in 1998 and Houston left the National League following the 2012 season.

Nationals include Montreal Expos, 1997-2004 (9-6).

Home Record vs. AL Opponents, 1981-2019

YEAR	BAL	BOS	CWS	CLE	DET	HOU	KC	LAA	MIL	MIN	OAK	SEA	TB	TEX	TOR	TOTAL
2019	7-2	8-1	1-2	2-2	1-2	3-1	3-1	2-1	–	2-1	2-1	3-1	8-2	2-1	7-2	51-20
2018	4-5	6-3	1-2	3-0	2-2	2-1	3-1	2-1	–	4-0	2-1	3-0	6-3	3-1	7-3	48-23
2017	8-2	6-4	2-1	0-3	1-2	1-3	3-1	1-2	1-2*	3-0	2-1	2-1	8-2	1-2	5-4	43-28
2016	6-4	6-3	2-1	2-1	1-2	2-1	3-1	4-0	–	2-1	0-3	1-2	7-3	2-2	5-4	43-28
2015	7-3	4-6	3-1	1-3	2-1	1-2	3-0	3-0	–	3-0	2-1	2-1	6-3	0-3	2-8	39-32
2014	4-6	6-4	3-0	1-2	3-1	1-2	1-2	2-1	–	1-2	1-2	0-3	3-6	3-1	7-3	36-35
2013	6-3	3-7	3-0	3-0	2-1	2-1	2-2	3-1	–	1-2	1-2	1-2	3-7	1-2	10-0	41-30
2012	3-6	6-3	2-2	3-0	2-1	–	2-1	4-2	–	2-2	2-1	4-2	6-3	3-1	7-2	46-26
2011	7-2	2-7	2-2	3-1	2-1	–	1-2	2-1	*3-0	3-1	3-3	2-1	6-3	5-1	7-2	45-27
2010	7-2	4-5	2-1	3-1	3-1	*3-0	3-1	3-2	–	2-1	4-0	3-3	4-5	3-0	5-4	46-26
2009	7-2	7-2	3-0	2-2	3-0	–	2-1	3-1	–	4-0	5-1	2-1	6-3	3-3	6-3	53-19
2008	6-3	4-5	3-1	1-2	0-3	–	4-3	2-2	–	3-0	3-0	6-0	6-3	1-2	5-4	44-28
2007	5-4	6-3	2-1	3-0	3-1	–	3-0	2-4	–	3-1	1-2	4-3	5-4	2-1	5-4	44-28
2006	5-4	4-6	3-0	2-1	2-1	–	5-1	2-2	–	2-1	2-4	2-1	7-2	2-2	6-3	44-28
2005	7-2	5-4	1-2	3-1	3-0	–	3-0	3-3	–	2-1	2-1	3-0	3-6	5-2	6-4	46-26
2004	7-3	5-4	2-2	2-1	1-2	–	3-0	2-4	–	3-0	5-1	2-1	10-0	2-1	6-3	50-22
2003	6-4	5-5	1-2	4-0	3-0	*2-1	3-0	1-2	–	3-0	1-2	3-3	6-3	2-4	4-6	42-31
2002	7-3	5-4	1-2	3-0	5-1	–	2-1	2-1	–	3-0	3-3	0-3	7-2	2-2	6-3	46-25
2001	5-3-1	8-1	3-0	3-3	3-0	–	3-0	2-2	–	1-2	3-0	1-5	8-1	1-2	5-5	46-24-1
2000	4-2	2-4	1-5	1-3	3-3	–	5-1	2-2	–	3-3	4-2	1-3	4-2	5-1	4-2	39-33
1999	4-3	2-4	4-2	4-2	5-1	–	1-2	2-4	–	2-2	2-2	5-1	3-3	4-2	5-1	43-29
1998	6-0	3-3	4-1	4-1	5-1	–	5-0	3-3	–	5-1	4-1	4-1	6-0	4-2	2-4	55-18
1997	1-5	4-2	4-1	3-2	4-2	–	4-2	2-2	5-0	3-2	4-2	3-2	–	4-1	3-3	43-28
1996	4-3	4-2	3-3	4-3	5-1	–	5-1	3-3	5-1	3-2	4-2	2-4	–	4-2	3-3	49-31
1995	4-2	6-1	0-2-1	2-4	4-2	–	3-1	4-2	3-3	2-2	3-4	3-3	–	5-0	7-0	46-26-1
1994	3-3	4-2	1-2	7-0	1-2	–	0-3	3-3	1-2	3-0	3-3	3-3	–	2-0	2-1	33-24
1993	4-3	4-3	4-2	4-2	5-1	–	4-2	4-3	4-2	4-2	4-2	4-2	–	2-4	3-4	50-31
1992	3-3	4-2	1-5	3-4	4-3	–	4-2	4-2	5-2	2-4	4-2	3-3	–	3-3	1-5	41-40
1991	5-2	3-4	3-3	4-2	3-3	–	2-4	2-4	3-3	2-4	3-3	2-4	–	4-2	3-4	39-42
1990	3-3	4-2	1-5	4-3	3-4	–	3-3	3-3	3-4	3-3	0-6	4-2	–	3-3	3-3	37-44
1989	2-5	4-3	4-2	1-5	5-1	–	3-3	5-1	3-3	3-3	1-5	3-3	–	4-2	3-4	41-40
1988	5-1	2-4	5-1	4-3	5-2	–	2-4	3-3	6-1	4-2	4-2	2-4	–	3-2	1-5	46-34
1987	6-1	4-3	4-2	4-2	5-1	–	6-0	4-2	3-3	4-2	3-3	3-3	–	3-3	2-5	51-30
1986	2-4	2-4	2-4	5-2	4-3	–	4-2	3-3	4-3	3-3	3-2	–	–	4-2	2-4	41-39
1985	7-0	5-2	4-2	3-3	2-3	–	5-1	5-1	3-3	6-0	5-1	5-1	–	6-0	2-5	58-22
1984	4-2	2-4	3-3	7-0	4-3	–	6-0	2-4	5-2	3-3	5-1	2-4	–	3-3	5-1	51-30
1983	4-3	4-3	2-4	4-2	3-3	–	3-3	5-1	6-0	5-1	4-2	3-3	–	3-3	5-2	51-30
1982	2-4	3-3	1-5	3-4	3-4	–	4-3	4-3	5-1	4-2	3-3	4-2	–	4-2	4-2	42-39
1981	5-2	2-1	4-2	2-4	3-0	–	5-1	0-0	2-1	1-2	2-1	1-1	–	4-2	1-2	32-19

Road Record vs. AL Opponents, 1981-2019

YEAR	BAL	BOS	CWS	CLE	DET	HOU	KC	LAA	MIL	MIN	OAK	SEA	TB	TEX	TOR	TOTAL
2019	10-0	6-4+	2-2	1-2	2-1	0-3	2-1	3-1	–	2-1	0-3	2-1	4-5	1-2	4-6	40-31
2018	8-2	3-7	3-0	2-2	2-1	3-1	2-1	3-0	–	1-2	1-2	2-1	4-6	1-2	6-3	41-30
2017	4-5	5-4	2-2	2-2	2-1	1-2	2-1	1-2	–	1-2	0-4	3-1	#4-5	2-1	4-6	33-38
2016	3-6	2-8	1-2	3-1	2-1	2-1	2-1	–	–	3-1	4-0	2-1	4-5	1-2	2-8	33-38
2015	2-7	7-2	2-1	3-1	3-1	2-2	1-2	1-2	–	2-1	1-3	3-0	6-4	2-2	4-5	37-34
2014	2-7	6-3	2-2	2-2	1-2	1-2	2-2	2-1	*1-2	3-1	1-2	3-0	5-5	1-2	4-5	35-36
2013	4-6	3-6	0-3	3-1	1-2	3-0	3-0	1-2	–	4-0	0-3	3-1	4-5	2-2	4-5	35-36
2012	6-3	7-2	0-3	2-1	4-3	–	2-2	1-2	–	2-1	3-4	2-1	2-7	1-2	4-5	36-36
2011	6-3	4-5	4-0	1-2	1-3	–	5-1	3-3	–	3-1	3-0	3-3	3-6	2-1	4-5	39-33
2010	6-3	5-4	2-1	3-1	1-3	–	2-2	1-2	–	2-1	5-1	3-1	4-5	1-4	3-6	38-34
2009	6-3	2-7	1-3	3-1	2-1	–	2-2	2-4	–	3-0	2-1	4-3	5-4	2-1	6-3	40-32
2008	5-4	5-4	2-1	2-2	2-1	*3-0	1-2	1-5	–	3-4	2-1	1-2	5-4	2-2	4-5	35-37
2007	4-5	4-5	4-3	3-0	1-3	–	6-1	1-2	–	2-1	1-2	1-2	5-4	3-0	5-4	40-32
2006	7-3	7-2	1-2	2-2	3-1	–	2-1	2-4	–	1-2	1-2	1-2	6-3	6-0	4-5	43-29
2005	4-5	5-5	2-1	1-2	2-1	–	0-3	1-3	*1-2	1-2	5-1	4-3	5-5	2-1	6-2	38-34
2004	7-2	3-7	2-1	2-1	2-2	–	2-1	2-1	–	1-2	4-0	2-4	^5-4	3-3	6-4	41-31
2003	7-2-1	5-4	1-2	1-2	2-1	–	1-2	5-1	–	4-0	2-4	2-1	8-2	2-1	6-3	46-25-1
2002	6-3	5-5	3-0	3-3	3-0	–	3-0	2-2	–	3-0	2-1	4-2	6-3	2-1	4-6	46-26
2001	8-2	5-4	2-1	2-1	2-4	–	3-0	1-2	–	1-2	0-6	2-1	5-5	2-2	6-3	39-33
2000	3-3	5-2	3-3	4-2	1-5	–	3-1	3-3	–	2-2	2-1	3-3	2-4	5-1	1-5	37-35
1999	5-1	2-4	3-3	3-1	2-4	–	3-3	2-2	–	4-2	4-2	4-0	5-1	4-2	5-1	46-26
1998	3-3	4-2	3-3	3-3	3-2	–	5-0	2-3	–	2-3	4-2	4-2	5-1	4-1	4-2	46-27
1997	3-3	4-2	5-1	3-3	6-0	–	4-1	5-2	2-4	5-1	2-3	–	–	3-3	4-2	48-28
1996	6-0	2-5	2-4	6-0	4-2	–	3-3	3-4	1-5	4-3	5-1	1-5	–	1-5	5-2	43-39
1995	3-4	2-4	2-1	4-2	4-3	–	1-5	3-2	2-1	1-5	1-6	–	–	1-3	5-1	33-39
1994	3-1	3-1	1-2	2-0	2-1	–	2-1	5-1	6-0	2-4	4-2	5-1	–	1-2	1-3	37-19
1993	3-3	3-3	4-2	3-4	4-3	–	2-4	2-4	5-2	4-2	2-4	3-3	–	1-5	2-4	38-43
1992	5-2	2-5	3-3	2-4	3-3	–	3-3	1-5	2-4	3-3	2-4	3-3	–	1-5	1-6	35-46
1991	3-3	4-2	1-5	3-4	2-5	–	3-3	4-2	4-3	0-6	3-3	1-5	–	1-5	3-3	32-49
1990	4-3	0-7	1-5	4-2	3-3	–	1-5	3-3	4-2	3-3	0-6	1-5	–	0-6	2-5	30-51
1989	3-3	2-4	2-3	3-4	2-5	–	3-3	1-5	2-5	3-3	2-4	5-1	–	1-5	4-2	33-47
1988	5-2	2-5	4-2	3-3	0-6	–	2-4	4-3	1-5	5-1	2-4	3-3	–	2-4	5-2	39-42
1987	4-2	2-4	2-3	3-3	3-4	–	1-5	5-1	3-4	2-4	4-2	–	–	2-4	3-3	38-43
1986	6-1	6-1	4-2	3-3	3-3	–	4-2	2-4	1-5	5-4	5-2	–	–	3-3	5-2	49-33
1985	5-1	3-3	2-4	4-3	1-6	–	2-4	4-2	3-4	3-3	2-4	4-2	–	2-4	4-2	39-42
1984	4-3	4-3	2-4	4-2	2-4	–	1-5	2-4	2-4	1-5	3-3	5-1	–	3-3	3-4	36-45
1983	3-3	2-4	2-4	3-4	5-2	–	3-3	2-4	3-4	3-3	4-2	2-4	–	4-2	2-5	40-41
1982	0-7	3-4	3-3	6-0	2-4	–	4-2	2-4	1-5	3-3	4-2	3-3	–	2-4	2-5	37-44
1981	1-5	1-2	3-3	3-3	4-3	–	5-1	2-2	2-1	2-2	1-2	–	–	1-2	1-1	27-29

*Took place in Interleague play, not counted in totals at right | ^ inc. 2 road gms in Tokyo from 3/30-31/04 | # inc. 3 road gms at Citi Field from 9/11-13/17
+incl. 2 road gms in London from 6/29-30

Swig for the Fences!

DRINK FROM A BAT
DUGOUT Mugs®
SWIG FOR THE FENCES

© 2020 MLB

Officially Licensed ~ Solid Wood ~ Made in N. America

From the stadium seats to backyard BBQ's in the Bronx, Dugout Mugs® are giving Yankees fans a NEW WAY to enjoy the game they love so much!

www.DugoutMugs.com

KEEP YOUR OPTIONS OPEN.

At MINI, we've got a family of models to fit your lifestyle. Certified Pre-Owned options have plenty of unique design combinations to choose from. With choices like that, your perfect MINI is out there. All Certified Pre-Owned MINI vehicles come with a MINI CPO Limited Warranty. No matter which MINI you choose, legendary handling, stylish design and pure driving fun come standard. To test drive a Certified Pre-Owned MINI that's perfect for you, stop by your local MINI dealer today.

CERTIFIED PRE-OWNED | MINI

All model year 2018 MINI vehicles and newer sold or leased by an authorized MINI dealer come standard with Complimentary Scheduled MINI Maintenance for the first 3 years or 36,000 miles whichever comes first. Only the following maintenance items are included with Complimentary Scheduled MINI Maintenance when they are performed as outlined in the vehicle's Maintenance booklet: Engine oil filter, Brake fluid, Cabin microfilter, Engine air filter, Spark plugs and Remote control key battery. For important details, see the MINI Service and Warranty Information booklet or visit an authorized MINI Dealer for terms, conditions & limitations. © 2019 MINI USA, a division of BMW of North America, LLC. The MINI name, model names and logo are registered trademarks.

History & Records

This year marks the 100th anniversary of Babe Ruth joining the Yankees, as the club completed the purchase of his contract from the Boston Red Sox on January 5, 1920, in exchange for $100,000 plus interest and a $300,000 loan against the mortgage of Fenway Park.

History of the New York Yankees

The Yankees are baseball's most storied franchise. With 27 World Championships and 40 American League pennants, the club stands alone in both categories.

The team's glorious history has surprisingly humble origins at the start of the previous century, when the upstart American League declared itself a Major League following the 1900 season. At that time, the league sought to place a team in New York for the 1901 campaign. But due to the political strength of the National League's New York Giants, the American League instead put a team in Baltimore, calling it the Orioles, with the hope of establishing a team in New York as soon as possible.

Managed by John McGraw, the 1901 Orioles finished 68-65 and failed to draw substantial crowds. The following season, McGraw, uncertain about the club's future, precipitated a midseason release from his contract. He immediately teamed with Giants owner Andrew Freedman and Cincinnati Reds owner John T. Brush, helping them acquire a majority interest in the Orioles. With control of Baltimore's players, the pair of owners decimated the squad, divvying up the players between them. On July 17, 1902, the Baltimore Orioles were left with five players on their roster and were forced to forfeit their game against the St. Louis Browns. The American League quickly stepped in and lent Baltimore players from other teams so they could finish the season.

Prior to the start of the 1903 campaign, the two leagues reached a truce, part of which involved the National League agreeing to allow an American League team in New York City. With the Orioles having been dissolved, saloon owner Frank Farrell and ex-New York chief of police Bill Devery were awarded the right to establish a new franchise in New York for $18,000.

New York's American League entry was the city's third Major League team, joining the Giants and Brooklyn Dodgers of the National League. The new club played its home games at American League Park, a hastily constructed all-wooden structure at 168th Street and Broadway in Manhattan. Because the site was one of the highest spots in the borough, the team was commonly called the "Hilltoppers" or "Highlanders" and their home field "Hilltop Park." The club played its inaugural game on April 22, 1903, at Washington, losing, 3-1, to the Senators. The next day, they defeated the Senators, 7-2, recording the very first win in franchise history.

Led by future Hall of Famers Jack Chesbro, Clark Griffith and Wee Willie Keeler, the 1903 Highlanders finished with a 72-62 record, 17.0 games out of first place. The club nearly captured the American League pennant in 1904—finishing 1.5 games behind the Boston Americans (later known as the Red Sox)—as Chesbro went 41-12 with a 1.82 ERA in 454.2 innings pitched, setting a modern era (since 1900) record with his win total. That season marked the first of three second-place finishes for the club between 1904 and 1910.

After a devastating fire severely damaged the Polo Grounds in 1911, the Highlanders' owners invited the Giants to share Hilltop Park until their home could be rebuilt. Two years later, the Giants returned the favor and allowed the Highlanders to become tenants in their new, vastly superior facility.

Following the move in 1913, newspapers and the public increasingly referred to the club as the "Yankees," which first appeared in the press in 1904. While no official announcement was ever made to formally establish the team's nickname, 1913 is considered the year that "Yankees" became the team's principal moniker.

Manager Miller Huggins [L] led the Yankees to three World Series championships and six American League pennants after being hired by owner Jacob Ruppert [R] in 1918.

From 1911 to 1919, the Yankees won as many as 80 games in a season only twice. However, three key moves—the January 1915 purchase of the ballclub by Colonel Jacob Ruppert and Colonel Tillinghast L'Hommedieu Huston, the 1918 hiring of Manager Miller Huggins by Ruppert (without Huston's blessing) and the 1919 midseason trade for right-handed pitcher Carl Mays (26 wins in 1920 and 27 wins in 1921)—set the stage for the greatest course-altering transaction in baseball history, when on January 5, 1920, the Yankees completed the purchase of the contract of George Herman "Babe" Ruth from the Boston Red Sox for $100,000 plus interest along with a reported $300,000 personal loan against the mortgage on Fenway Park.

Ruth's impact was immediate. The Yankees won 95 games in 1920, their highest victory total up to that point, then captured their first AL pennant a year later. With the Babe hitting 54 home runs in 1920—more than any other *team* in the American League—Yankees attendance at the Polo Grounds doubled to 1,289,422. In 1921, the Giants, being outdrawn in their own park, asked the Yankees to vacate the Polo Grounds as soon as possible. Now bitter rivals, the two teams squared off in the World Series in 1921 and 1922 with the Giants winning on both occasions.

Though he came up on the wrong end in both Series, Yankees pitcher (and 1969 Hall of Fame inductee) Waite Hoyt allowed just one earned run over 35.0 combined innings over the two Fall Classics. Remarkably, he went 2-2 in his five appearances (four starts), including a 1-0, Series-clinching loss (on an unearned run) in Game 8 of the 1921 best-of-nine championship.

With their departure from the Polo Grounds inevitable, the Yankees' owners set out to build a ballpark of their own. Designed to be baseball's first triple-decked structure with an advertised capacity of 70,000, it would be the first baseball facility to be called a "stadium" at its inaugural opening.

The team's upcoming success was masterminded by business manager and future Hall of Famer Ed Barrow, whose responsibilities from 1921 through 1945 included both player personnel and the club's finances. He developed a fantastic relationship with Huggins from the outset and brought in Paul Krichell, who not only developed the Yankees scouting department but personally signed Lou Gehrig, Phil Rizzuto and Whitey Ford to their first Yankees contracts.

Construction on the original Yankee Stadium began on May 5, 1922, and in only 284 working days, it was ready for its inaugural game on April 18, 1923, against the Boston Red Sox. An announced crowd of 74,200 fans packed the Stadium for a glimpse of Baseball's grandest facility while thousands milled around outside after the fire department finally ordered the gates closed. Appropriately, Ruth christened the Stadium with a three-run homer to cap a four-run third inning as the Yankees, behind starter Bob Shawkey, won, 4-1.

Playing in their new stadium, dubbed "The House that Ruth Built" by *New York Telegram* sportswriter Fred Lieb, the Yankees won the American League by 16.0 games in 1923, using just eight pitchers all season. Each of their five starting pitchers—Shawkey, Hoyt, Joe Bush, Sam Jones and Herb Pennock—won at least 16 games. In October, the Stadium hosted the first of 37 World Series at the structure, and the Yankees won the first World Championship in franchise history, defeating their former landlord, the Giants, in six games.

Less than two seasons later, one of the greatest players in franchise history was given his chance to crack the lineup. On June 1, 1925, in a 5-3 loss vs. Washington, Huggins called upon Gehrig, a 21-year-old first baseman with 34 career games to his name, to pinch-hit for light-hitting shortstop Paul "Pee Wee" Wanninger. It would mark the first of 2,130 consecutive games played by the "Iron Horse," who replaced Wally Pipp as the Yankees' starting first baseman the very next day. The story of Gehrig replacing Pipp because of a headache is a myth. Pipp, who led the AL in homers in 1916 and 1917 and was an integral part of the Yankees' World Series clubs from 1921-23, had a poor start to the season, and Manager Miller Huggins wanted to see what the younger, much-heralded Gehrig could do.

After the Yankees suffered a tough loss to the St. Louis Cardinals in the 1926 World Series (which famously ended with Babe Ruth making the final out in Game 7 while trying to steal second base), the Yankees rolled to World Championships in both 1927 and 1928, sweeping the Pittsburgh Pirates and St. Louis Cardinals, respectively. The 1927 club, known as "Murderers' Row," is often the yardstick by which team greatness is measured. During that season, Ruth broke his own single-season home run record (previously 59 in 1921) with his 60th on September 30, 1927, off Washington's Tom Zachary. Gehrig also added 47 homers and 173 RBI.

Lou Gehrig

267

In his 15 seasons in pinstripes from 1920-34, Ruth helped establish a winning tradition with seven American League pennants and four World Championships. He finished his unparalleled career with 714 home runs (including 49 with the Red Sox from 1914-19 and six with the Boston Braves in 1935). He also tallied 12 American League home run titles and six RBI crowns, including five seasons with more than 150 RBI. A charter member of Baseball's Hall of Fame, he remains widely regarded as the greatest player of all time.

Throughout Ruth's time in pinstripes, he often overshadowed the soft-spoken, Manhattan-born Gehrig, who posted incredible numbers in his own right. From 1926 through 1938, Gehrig drove in at least 112 runs each season. A player on seven World Championship clubs (1927-28, 1932, 1936-39) and a major contributor to the first six, he finished with a .340 lifetime batting average and 493 career home runs in just 8,001 at-bats. He was the AL's starting first baseman in each of the first five Major League Baseball All-Star Games, and in 1934, became the first of two Yankees in franchise history (also Mickey Mantle in 1956) to win the Triple Crown, hitting .363 with a career-high-tying 49 homers and 166 RBI. He also still holds the American League record for RBI in a single season with 184 in 1931.

After the 1934 season, Ruth's last in New York, the Yankees purchased the contract of a budding star named Joe DiMaggio from the San Francisco Seals of the Pacific Coast League. Two years later, DiMaggio made his debut in pinstripes and helped the Yankees to an incredible string of four consecutive World Championships under Manager Joe McCarthy from 1936 through 1939. The 1930s also produced one of the game's greatest lefty-righty pitching combinations in future Hall of Famers Lefty Gomez and Red Ruffing. A four-time 20-game winner—including 24-7 in 1932 and 26-5 in 1934—Gomez posted a 6-0 record in five World Series. Ruffing, who was acquired on May 6, 1930, from Boston for outfielder Cedric Durst and $50,000, had been 39-96 with the Red Sox since his 1924 rookie season. After coming to the Yankees, however, he built his Cooperstown credentials, going 231-124 in pinstripes while posting 20, 20, 21 and 21 wins on the four World Championship clubs from 1936 through 1939. He was also an exceptionally good hitter for a pitcher, totaling 36 career home runs and a .269 lifetime batting average.

From 1931 through part of the 1946 season, the Yankees were led by McCarthy, who compiled a Yankees-record 1,460 wins in his time at the helm. Having also spent time leading the Chicago Cubs (1926-30) and Boston Red Sox (1948-50), he is eighth on the all-time managerial wins list with 2,125 victories. With the Yankees, he reached eight World Series (1932, 1936-39, 1941-43), winning a World Championship in all but one—the 1942 Fall Classic against St. Louis.

Sadly, in 1939, Gehrig was diagnosed with a crippling disease, eventually determined to be amyotrophic lateral sclerosis (ALS), and his streak of playing in 2,130 consecutive games came to an end. On May 2, he took himself out of the lineup prior to the Yankees' 22-2 win at Detroit. He never played in a Major League game again.

On July 4 of the same season, the Yankees honored their captain with an emotional Lou Gehrig Appreciation Day at Yankee Stadium, and on Jan. 6, 1940, team president Ed Barrow announced that his No. 4 would become the first-ever retired number in baseball. Gehrig passed away from the effects of ALS on June 2, 1941.

Joe DiMaggio

DiMaggio became the pillar of the next generation of Yankees champions. In his 13 seasons in pinstripes (1936-42 and '46-51), DiMaggio made the AL All-Star team every year, and his club played in the World Series in all but three years (1940, '46, '48), winning nine World Series titles. Along the way, he tallied three AL MVP Awards (1939, '41, '47) and batted .325 over his career, marking the third-highest average in franchise history. The legendary "Yankee Clipper" compiled one of the game's most remarkable records in 1941, when he hit safely in an all-time-best 56 consecutive games.

DiMaggio's retirement after the 1951 season at the age of 37 was made easier by the emergence of Mickey Mantle, who played side-by-side with DiMaggio in the outfield in the Yankee Clipper's final campaign. With contributions from future Hall of Famers Yogi Berra, Whitey Ford and Phil Rizzuto, the Yankees were nearly unstoppable from the late 1940s through the early 1960s. Manager Casey Stengel sublimely handled the Yankees juggernaut following his surprising appointment prior to the 1949 season, as the club marched to an all-time record five consecutive World Series titles from 1949 through 1953.

His emphasis on platooning players (often to their chagrin) allowed him to exploit matchups in a way not emphasized at that time. Nicknamed "The Old Perfessor," with a vernacular called "Stengelese," he remains one of the most colorful personalities in the game's history. In 12 seasons as manager of the Yankees, Stengel brought his club to the World Series 10 times, winning on seven occasions (also 1956 and 1958).

His staff during the remarkable five-year run of championships was anchored by a trio of starters who each pitched eight seasons with the Yankees and combined for 10 All-Star appearances while with the club. Allie Reynolds, known as "Superchief," went 131-60 with a 3.31 ERA in 295 games (209 starts) from 1947-54, after being acquired from Cleveland in exchange for fellow Hall of Famer Joe Gordon. Reynolds also finished 70 regular season games for the Yankees in an era

Lefty Gomez

Mickey Mantle [L] and Roger Maris

before the save was an official statistic. The No. 2 starter, Vic Raschi, broke into the Majors at age 27 and didn't become a full member of the Yankees rotation until the second half of the 1947 season. He won exactly 21 games in each of three consecutive years from 1949-51 and tallied a .706 winning percentage (120-50) and 3.47 ERA with the club from 1946-1953. The least-heralded of the three, "Steady" Eddie Lopat, went 113-59 with a 3.19 ERA with the Yankees from 1948-1955, including an AL-leading 2.43 ERA in 1953.

For all of the great players of the 1950s and early 60s, Mantle overshadowed everyone. He would achieve greatness despite suffering from osteomyelitis (a painful inflammatory bone disease) and numerous other injuries. A powerful switch-hitter, he belted 536 home runs, collected 2,415 hits and batted .300 or higher 10 times in an 18-year career. In his first 14 seasons in pinstripes (1951-64), the Yankees missed the World Series only twice (1954 and 1959) and won the Fall Classic seven times. With his .353 batting average, 52 homers and 130 RBI in 1956, he remains the last Yankees player to win the Triple Crown.

Ford, who played his whole career in pinstripes, is the Yankees' all-time wins leader. His lifetime record of 236-106 gives him the second-best career winning pct. (.690) of any pitcher with 100 or more decisions who began his career in the modern era (since 1900), trailing only career-Yankee Spud Chandler (.717, 109-43, from 1937-47). Ford paced the AL in victories three times and in ERA and shutouts twice. He still holds many World Series records, including those for wins (10), consecutive scoreless innings (33.0) and strikeouts (94).

The heart of the Yankees for 18 seasons, Berra played on 14 pennant winners and 10 World Championship teams—a record number for any individual player in MLB history. He is one of only 10 players in Major League history to win three MVP Awards and was selected to the All-Star team in every season from 1948 through 1962. Incredibly, he led the Yankees in RBI every season from 1949-55, had more career 100-RBI seasons (five) than Mantle (four), and hit at least 20 homers in 11 different seasons. Known as much for his quotes ("It ain't over 'til it's over" and "I really didn't say everything I said," etc.) as he is for his accomplishments on the field, he remains one of the most beloved players to ever play the game.

Elected to the Baseball Hall of Fame in 1994, Rizzuto was a defensive-minded shortstop who played on 10 pennant winners and eight World Series championship teams from 1941 through 1956, capturing the league's MVP award in 1950 with a .324 batting average and 125 runs scored. Following his playing career, he became a longtime Yankees broadcaster, known for punctuating big moments with his signature phrase, "Holy cow!"

However, not every notable Yankee was a future Hall of Famer. In Game 5 of the 1956 World Series vs. Brooklyn, right-hander Don Larsen authored baseball's greatest pitching performance, retiring all 27 Dodgers batters for the only perfect game in World Series history.

The Yankees opened the 1960s winning pennants in the first five seasons (1960-64) and World Series titles in 1961 and 1962. Incredibly, in the 29 seasons from 1936 to 1964, the Yankees won 22 pennants and 16 World Championships. The 1961 club is still regarded as one of the best teams in baseball history. With Mantle and Roger Maris embroiled in a season-long race to break Ruth's single-season home run record, the Yankees rolled to 109 wins en route to a World Championship. Maris broke Ruth's record when he belted his 61st home run on October 1 off Boston's Tracy Stallard at Yankee Stadium in the last game of the season.

Age finally caught up with the ballclub after a seven-game Series loss to the St. Louis Cardinals in 1964. The Yankees finished above fourth place just once in the next nine seasons, bottoming out in 1966 with the club's first last-place finish since 1912.

The team's fall from grace ended on January 3, 1973, when it was sold by CBS to a group headed by George M. Steinbrenner III. With the addition of Catfish Hunter (baseball's first marquee free agent), shrewd trades that brought Ed Figueroa, Mickey Rivers, Chris Chambliss and Willie Randolph to the club, and a strong nucleus that included Thurman Munson, Graig Nettles, Roy White and Sparky Lyle, the Yankees returned to the postseason in 1976, ending an 11-year drought (1965-1975) by winning their first American League East title. Then on October 14, 1976, in the deciding Game 5 of the American League Championship Series vs. Kansas City, Chambliss launched a ninth-inning, pennant-winning home run to put the Yankees back in the World Series.

Reggie Jackson hit three home runs in Game 6 of the 1977 World Series.

This newfound success took place in a remodeled Yankee Stadium after the club played the 1974 and 1975 seasons in Shea Stadium while vast improvements were made to the original facility (for more details, see "History of Original Yankee Stadium").

After a disheartening four-game sweep by the Cincinnati Reds in the 1976 World Series, the Yankees introduced Reggie Jackson—the most prolific slugger of his era—as the club's newest free-agent acquisition. Jackson capped an exciting 1977 season with one of baseball's greatest individual batting performances. In the World Series-clinching win vs. Los Angeles in Game 6 at Yankee Stadium, "Mr. October" belted three home runs on three swings of the bat to join Babe Ruth (and now Albert Pujols and Pablo Sandoval) as the only players to hit three home runs in a single World Series game.

In 1978, the Yankees overcame a 14.0-game deficit in the American League East to force a one-game playoff with Boston at Fenway Park to decide the division. Shortstop Bucky Dent erased a 2-0, seventh-inning Red Sox lead with a dramatic three-run homer, and the Yankees went on to win, 5-4. The Yankees then defeated Kansas City for the third straight year in the ALCS, and took care of the Dodgers in six games for their first back-to-back World Series titles since 1961-62.

The 1978 season also saw Ron Guidry compile one of the most dominating pitching seasons in baseball history. On the way to earning his nickname of "Louisiana Lightning," Guidry went 25-3 with a 1.74 ERA, winning the AL Cy Young Award in unanimous fashion and setting franchise records with 248 strikeouts and nine shutouts. On June 17 that season, Guidry set the single-game club record for strikeouts, fanning 18 California Angels at Yankee Stadium in a game that established the Stadium tradition of fans applauding for a strikeout once a Yankees pitcher reaches two strikes. A five-time Gold Glove Award winner and four-time American League All-Star, Guidry also racked up 20-win seasons in 1983 (21-9) and 1985 (22-6).

Sadly, the 1970s ended with tragedy. Thurman Munson, the 1976 AL MVP and the Yankees' first captain since Gehrig, was killed when the private jet he was piloting crashed on August 2, 1979, at Akron-Canton Airport in Ohio. Only 32 years old at the time of his death, Munson was the undisputed leader of the Yankees teams that won three consecutive pennants and two World Championships. After the captain's death, the Yankees would make only one World Series appearance (1981) over the 16-year stretch from 1979-95 despite compiling the best record in the Majors during the 1980s.

During this period, Don Mattingly became one of the most popular players in franchise history, batting .307 in a 14-year career (1982-95) played entirely in pinstripes. He compiled an incredible six-year stretch from 1984 through 1989, in which he batted .327 and topped 100 RBI five times, including a career-high 145 in 1985, when he captured the AL MVP Award. A year earlier, he outdueled teammate Dave Winfield for the 1984 AL batting crown (.343 to .340), going 4-for-5 on the final day of the season. Mattingly's performance and loyalty were recognized when he was named Yankees captain from 1991-95.

Winfield, who came to the Yankees as the game's most sought-after free agent in 1981, compiled Hall of Fame credentials in his nine seasons in pinstripes (1981-88, '90). With the Yankees, he belted 205 home runs with 818 RBI and won five Gold Glove Awards.

After a 13-year absence (1982-94), the Yankees returned to postseason play in 1995 as the American League's first-ever "Wild Card" entry. A heart-wrenching five-game loss to the Seattle Mariners in the Division Series marked the start of a 13-year run of postseason appearances (1995-2007) — a record topped only by the Atlanta Braves' 14-season streak (1991-93, 1995-2005).

In 1996 under new skipper Joe Torre, the Yankees returned to the World Series against Atlanta, coming back from an 0-2 deficit to win four straight games, including Games 3, 4 and 5 on the road. Following a Division Series exit in 1997, the Yankees won three straight World titles from 1998 through 2000, giving them four championships in five years. Their 114 regular season victories in 1998 shattered the 44-year-

Mayor Rudolph Giuliani, owner George Steinbrenner and manager Joe Torre celebrate the 1996 World Series win.

old AL mark of 111 wins set by the 1954 Cleveland Indians (since broken by Seattle in 2001) and their 125 total victories, including 11 postseason wins, remains the highest single-season total in baseball history.

Beginning in the early 90s, the Yankees made a concerted effort to draft and cultivate homegrown talent such as Bernie Williams, Derek Jeter, Andy Pettitte, Jorge Posada and Mariano Rivera. In addition, trades and free-agent acquisitions brought All-Stars such as Wade Boggs, Scott Brosius, David Cone, Jimmy Key and Tino Martinez to the Bronx. Another of those players, Paul O'Neill, acquired in a November 3, 1992, trade with Cincinnati, became adored by Yankees fans for his intense and gritty approach and was given the nickname "warrior." Winner of the 1994 batting title (.359), he was a key part of the club's turn-of-the-century success.

Bucky Dent hits his famous three-run home run in the one-game AL East playoff contest on Oct. 2, 1978 at Fenway Park.

In 2001, the Yankees fell just shy of becoming the second team in history to win four consecutive World Series titles, but they nevertheless captured the hearts of the nation in the aftermath of the terrorist attacks of September 11. The Yankees dropped the first two games of the Series at the Arizona Diamondbacks' Bank One Ballpark but rallied to win the next three at Yankee Stadium behind dramatic ninth-inning comebacks in Games 4 and 5. On consecutive nights, Martinez and Brosius erased two-run, ninth-inning Diamondbacks leads with home runs, and the Yankees won both games in extra innings. It was in Game 4 that Jeter earned his "Mr. November" nickname with a 10th-inning "walk-off" home run. The victories marked the first time in World Series history that a team won two games in the same Series when trailing by at least two runs in the ninth inning.

No one embodies the Yankees' success since 1996 more than Jeter, who was a rookie on that squad. He played his franchise-record 20th and final season with the Yankees in 2014, retiring with a personal career winning percentage of .593 (1,628-1,117-2) and five World Series rings. He is sixth in baseball history with 3,465 career hits and tops the Yankees' all-time list in hits, games played (2,747), doubles (544), stolen bases (358), at-bats (11,195), singles (2,595) and hit-by-pitches (170). Jeter also recorded eight 200-hit seasons and is one of two players in franchise history along with Gehrig (eight) with as many as four. In fact, according to the *Elias Sports Bureau*, no other player in Baseball history has had as many as four 200-hit seasons while playing at least 100 games at shortstop per year. Jeter capped his farewell season with a dramatic "walk-off" RBI-single in his final career game at Yankee Stadium and another RBI-single in his final career at-bat three days later at Boston's Fenway Park.

Derek Jeter

Posada and Rivera also crafted special places for themselves in the annals of the franchise. Posada, a 24th-round selection in the 1990 First-Year Player Draft, hit at least 20 home runs in eight different seasons. Known for his toughness and durability, the Puerto Rico-born backstop started at least 120 games in eight consecutive seasons from 2000-07, and retired after the 2011 season having never worn another uniform.

Rivera, who retired at the conclusion of the 2013 season with 652 career saves, became Baseball's all-time saves leader in 2011, surpassing Trevor Hoffman (601). His reputation was cemented by postseason excellence, which included an 8-1 record and 0.70 ERA in 96 career postseason games (141.0 innings pitched) and an all-time record 33.1 consecutive scoreless postseason innings. His Major League-leading 42 career postseason saves are more than the second and third place totals combined (34). Additionally, his 2.21 career ERA is the second-lowest all time among pitchers with at least 1,000.0IP since ERA was made an official statistic in 1912 in the NL and 1913 in the AL (Eddie Cicotte-2.20).

In 2004, the organization acquired Alex Rodriguez in a trade with Texas. After his arrival in the Bronx, the 14-time All-Star transitioned to a new position at third base and was named AL MVP in 2005 and 2007, while becoming the seventh—and youngest—player in Baseball history to reach the 600-home run plateau in 2010.

The original Yankee Stadium took its curtain call in 2008, which was also the first of 10 seasons under manager Joe Girardi. Full of nostalgia and notable events, 2008 featured the third Papal Mass in Stadium history on April 20 and a 15-inning, 4-3 American League victory in the All-Star Game on July 15. Though the Yankees played their last-ever home game in the original Stadium on September 21, 2008, defeating the Baltimore Orioles, 7-3, the drama of the season didn't end until its final day as Mike Mussina earned a win in the first game of a doubleheader over Boston at Fenway Park to become the oldest first-time 20-game winner in Baseball history.

The following season was storybook material as the club finished the inaugural season in the newly-constructed Yankee Stadium with the best regular season record in the Majors (103-59) and a 2009 World Series win over the Phillies in six games. Free-agent acquisitions CC Sabathia (19 wins) and Mark Teixeira (second in AL MVP voting, 39HR, 122RBI) each played major roles in the club's success.

The joy, however, was shortlived as the franchise mourned the losses of Principal Owner George M. Steinbrenner III and longtime public address announcer Bob Sheppard in the summer of 2010.

While the Yankees have been regular participants in the postseason since the mid-90s (having made the playoffs in 21-of-25 seasons from 1995-2019), the organization is committed to complementing player development with shrewd acquisitions to bring a 28th championship to the Bronx.

Going forward, the future of the franchise looks extremely bright as the club looks to build on recent postseason appearances. Manager Aaron Boone has won 100 and 103 games in his first two years at the helm in 2018 and 2019, and he has a roster infused with young talent, including 2017 AL Rookie of the Year Aaron Judge, Gary Sánchez, Luis Severino, Gleyber Torres and 2020 free agent signing Gerrit Cole, among many others.

Aaron Judge won the 2017 AL Rookie of the Year Award, setting the then-MLB rookie record with 52 home runs.

271

History of the Yankees Uniform & NY Logo

When the Yankees (then "Highlanders") first took the field for their inaugural season in 1903, their uniforms did not resemble the iconic style for which they are known today. A large ornate "N" decorated one breast and a large ornate "Y" the other. Two years later for the 1905 season, the "N" and "Y" were merged side by side into a monogram on the left breast, creating a forerunner of the now legendary emblem.

It wasn't until 1909 that the most recognizable insignia in sports—the interlocking "NY"—made its first appearance on the caps and left sleeves of Highlanders uniforms. It is thought that the design was inspired by a similar one created in 1877 by Tiffany & Co. for a medal to be given by the New York City Police Department to Officer John McDowell, a policeman shot in the line of duty. Perhaps because one of the club's owners, Bill Devery, was a former New York City police chief, the design was adopted by the organization. The familiar "NY" eventually migrated from the left sleeve to the left breast of home uniforms from 1912-15, albeit in a larger version than is currently worn today.

In 1912, their final season at Hilltop Park, the Yankees (as they were frequently called by then) made a fashionable debut at their April 11 home opener by wearing pinstripes for the first time in their history. The club was not the first team to wear pinstripes (eight of baseball's other 15 teams had already worn them at some point), and they would actually abandon the look in the following two seasons (1913-14). By 1915, though, home pinstripes were back for good.

In 1916, the Yankees removed the "NY" monogram from the jersey and went with a plain, pinstripes-only look. The "NY" remained off the uniform—except for the cap—for the next 20 years until it was reinstated in 1936. Babe Ruth, whose Yankees career spanned 1920-34, played his entire Yankees career without ever wearing the club's now-legendary insignia on his jersey.

The Yankees utilized numerous cap designs from 1903 until 1921—including pinstripes in 1915, '16, '19 and '21—until they finally settled on a solid navy cap with the interlocking "NY" insignia in 1922.

The club's road uniforms have remained relatively unchanged since 1918—solid grey with "NEW YORK" in block letters across the chest. The notable exception was from 1927-30, when "NEW YORK" was replaced by "YANKEES." In 1973, with the introduction of more breathable double-knit uniforms, Yankees road jerseys added navy-and-white banded trim to the cuffs of the sleeves as well as white shadowing behind the jersey lettering.

The home uniform remains the Yankees' signature look. With the exception of minor alterations—including bolder pinstripes in the 1940s—it has remained mostly unchanged for more than 70 years. The most-recent team-specific tweak to either Yankees uniform set was the switch from glossy to matte road helmets prior to the 2016 season.

In keeping with the team's reverence of tradition, the Yankees have worn "alternate" uniforms just twice in their history. On April 8, 1996, at Detroit, the team wore replica uniforms of the Negro National League's New York Black Yankees, and on April 20, 2012, in Boston (on the 100th anniversary of the first game at Fenway Park), the Yankees wore polyester reproductions of their 1912 ensemble. Additionally, on three occasions, the Yankees have worn their batting practice caps during regular season games (Aug. 9, 2013, and May 12 and 14, 2014).

In recent years, the Yankees have also participated in other MLB-wide initiatives relating to various holidays, including camouflage and American-flag inspired elements on Memorial Day and Independence Day, and pink and baby blue elements on Mother's Day (to recognize breast cancer awareness) and Father's Day (for prostate cancer awareness).

Most recently, the Yankees have joined all MLB clubs in wearing special "Players Weekend" jerseys in each season since 2017. These jerseys have included individualized nicknames on the back, marking the only times the Yankees have had last names or nicknames on the backs of their jerseys.

Additionally in 2017, the Yankees joined all MLB clubs in adding a New Era logo on the left side of their caps. For 2020, the club has joined all other Major League teams with a Nike logo on the front of their jerseys.

Pitcher Jack Chesbro dons the 1908 uniform.

Babe Ruth wears the pinstriped cap of 1921.

Lou Gehrig and Tony Lazzeri pose at Yankee Stadium in 1927. Yankees jerseys did not feature the "NY" insignia from 1916 through 1935.

Derek Jeter sports the 1912 throwback uniform worn by the club on the 100th anniversary of Fenway Park on April 20, 2012, in Boston.

Origin of Numbered Uniforms

Numbers first appeared on Major League uniforms on June 26, 1916, when the Cleveland Indians wore large numerals on their left sleeves in an experiment that lasted just a few weeks. Another brief trial by Cleveland the next season and a similar sleeve trial by the St. Louis Cardinals in 1923 both proved temporary. It wasn't until the 1929 season that another attempt was made, as both Cleveland and the Yankees began their seasons with numbers as a permanent part of their respective uniforms. Though the Yankees are typically credited as being the team with the longest-standing such policy, it should be noted that the Indians began their season two days earlier than the Bombers, as the Yankees' April 16 Opening Day contest was rained out.

The initial distribution of numbers to the Yankees roster was made according to the player's respective position in the batting order. Therefore, in 1929, leadoff hitter Earle Combs wore No. 1, Mark Koenig No. 2, Babe Ruth No. 3, Lou Gehrig No. 4, Bob Meusel No. 5, Tony Lazzeri No. 6, Leo Durocher No. 7, Johnny Grabowski No. 8, Benny Bengough No. 9 and Bill Dickey No. 10 (Grabowski, Bengough and Dickey shared the catching duties). By the mid-1930s, other teams adopted the idea, and uniform numbers became standard for all teams.

Babe Ruth wore No. 3 with the Yankees from 1929-34.

Top Hat Logo Design

Though not appearing on the uniform, the Yankees "top hat" logo is one of the most identifiable in sports. It was created by well-known, longtime graphic artist Henry Alonzo "Lon" Keller after a commission from then-Yankees co-owner Larry MacPhail. An initial version consisting solely of the Yankees script with a top hat above the "k" first appeared on the cover of the 1946 spring training roster. MacPhail, however, asked Keller to further develop his work. The designer's more elaborate design debuted during the 1946 season and remains largely unchanged to the present day. (Information regarding Keller's contribution was taken from articles in the 1976 Yankees scorecard and the Aug. 22, 1995, edition of *Yankees Magazine*.)

Origin of the Names "Highlanders" and "Yankees"

In the early 1900s, fans, the media and front office personnel did not see club nicknames as the defining elements they are today. People thought of clubs by the city they represented and the league in which they played. Anything beyond that was the work of clever newspapermen trying to freshen up the references to teams in their stories.

Much of the logo- and nickname-oriented merchandise items we have today, such as caps, T-shirts or jerseys simply didn't exist a century ago when games weren't televised and men uniformly wore jackets and ties to the park.

When the Yankees franchise was launched in New York prior to the 1903 season, the enmity between the upstart American League (about to enter its third season) and the long-established National League was just beginning to ebb. It was commonplace for clubs and the media to refer to AL teams as "Americans" and NL clubs as "Nationals," especially as half of the cities with Major League Baseball at the time had teams in both leagues (Boston, Chicago, New York, Philadelphia and St. Louis). This terminology frequently served to differentiate the New York AL team from the two longstanding NL clubs—the Brooklyn Superbas (as the Dodgers were then known) and the New York Giants—with whom they were now battling for fans.

The club's first home in New York was a rickety wooden structure often referred to as "American League Park." It was located on 168th St. and Broadway, one of the highest spots in Manhattan. As a result, the team became known as the "Hilltoppers" and their field "Hilltop Park."

The name "Highlanders," as the team of that era is most-popularly remembered today, also started in the club's formative years. It originated not only as a nod to their elevated Manhattan perch, but also as a reference to club president Joseph W. Gordon, whose last name conjured up thoughts of the famous Scottish army unit, the Gordon Highlanders.

Other nicknames for the team were the "Greater New Yorks" and "Griffiths," the latter of which was a reference to Clark Griffith, who managed the club from 1903-08.

As early as 1904, however, the name "Yankees" became common in the press. The earliest known use was in an April 7, 1904, article in the *New York Evening Journal* that bore the headline "YANKEES WILL START HOME FROM SOUTH TODAY," which was published following a successful spring training. A week later, the same newspaper's coverage of Opening Day was headlined "YANKEES BEAT BOSTON," and the term also appeared in the article's lead sentence.

The name "Yankees" likely owes its success to newspaper typesetters and editors grateful for a team nickname with fewer letters than "Highlanders" or "Hilltoppers."

When the franchise moved from Hilltop Park to the low-lying Polo Grounds in 1913, the media and public dropped the other nicknames (which were no longer fitting) in favor of "Yankees."

Patches & Armbands on the Yankees Uniform

Over the Yankees' history, temporary patches and armbands have been worn to commemorate special occasions and mourn losses in the Yankees family. The list below represents the most thorough compilation of such additions. Annual alterations such as Major League Baseball's Mothers' Day and Fathers' Day ribbons, or permanent additions such as MLB logo patches on the backs of caps and jerseys are not included in the list below.

*Please note that all sleeve notations reflect game jerseys (GJ) unless otherwise noted to be batting practice jerseys (BPJ).
Additional Key: LS=Left Sleeve; RS=Right Sleeve; LC=Left Side of Cap; RC=Right Side of Cap; BC=Back of Cap; LH=Left Side of Helmet

YEAR(S)	DATE(S)	ITEM	LOCATION*	COMMEMORATION
1918	Regular Season	Armband	Left Sleeve	Red, white and blue armband for U.S. involvement in World War I
1920	Aug. 18 - End Season	Armband	Left Sleeve	Death of Indians shortstop Ray Chapman on Aug. 17, 1920
1929	Sept. 26 - End Season	Armband	Left Sleeve	Death of Miller Huggins on Sept. 25, 1929
1938	Regular Season	Patch	Left Sleeve	1939 New York World's Fair; also worn by Giants and Dodgers
1939	Regular Season	Patch	Left Sleeve	Baseball's "Centennial Season"; worn by all MLB teams
1942	Regular Season	Patch	Left Sleeve	"Health" Shield for U.S. in WWII; worn by all MLB teams
1943-45	Regular Season	Patch	Left Sleeve	U.S. flag shield for WW II; worn by most MLB teams
1945	July 26 - End Season	Patch	Left Sleeve	"Ruptured Duck" patch for honorably discharged former servicemen; worn only by Red Ruffing and Aaron Robinson
1948	Aug. 18 - End Season	Armband	Left Sleeve	Death of Babe Ruth on Aug. 16, 1948
1951	Regular Season	Patch	Left Sleeve	50th anniv. of the American League; worn by all AL teams
1952	Regular Season	Patch	Left Sleeve	Yankees' 50th Season (1903-52)
1955	Postseason Tour	Patch	Left Sleeve	"U.S.-Japan Good Will Tour 1955" during exhibition in Japan
1969	Regular Season	Patch	Left Sleeve	Centennial Patch for Baseball's 100th season; worn by all teams
1973	Regular Season	Patch	Left Sleeve	50th anniversary of Yankee Stadium (1923-73)
1976	Reg. and Postseason	Armband	Left Sleeve	Death of Casey Stengel on Sept. 29, 1975; worn by Billy Martin
1979-80	Aug. 3, 1979 - 1980 Season	Armband	Left Sleeve	Death of Thurman Munson on Aug. 2, 1979
1981	Reg. and Postseason	Armband	Left Sleeve	Death of Elston Howard on Dec. 14, 1980
1985	Aug. 16 - End season	Armband	Left Sleeve	Death of clubhouse manager Pete Sheehy on Aug. 14, 1985
1986	Regular Season	Armband	Left Sleeve	Death of Roger Maris on Dec. 14, 1985
1990	Regular Season	Number	Left Sleeve	Number "1" for death of Billy Martin on Dec. 25, 1989
1994	Regular Season	Patch	Left Sleeve	125th anniversary of Major League Baseball
1995	Aug. 13 - Postseason	Armband	Left Sleeve	Death of Mickey Mantle on Aug. 13, 1995
	Aug. 28 - Postseason	Number	Left Sleeve	Number "7" added for death of Mickey Mantle
1996	June 17 - Postseason	Armband	Left Sleeve	Death of former broadcaster Mel Allen on June 16, 1996
	World Series	Patch	RS / LC	1996 World Series logo
1997	Reg. and Postseason	Patch	Right Sleeve	50th anniversary of Jackie Robinson breaking color barrier
1998	Reg. and Postseason	Patch	Left Sleeve BPJ	75th anniversary of Yankee Stadium
	World Series	Patch	RS / LC	1998 World Series logo
1999	Spring Training	Patch	Left Sleeve BPJ	Number "5" patch for death of Joe DiMaggio on Mar. 8, 1999
	Reg. and Postseason	Number	Left Sleeve	Number "5" for death of Joe DiMaggio
	Sept. 10 - Postseason	Armband	Left Sleeve	Death of Catfish Hunter on Sept. 9, 1999
	World Series	Patch	RS / LC	1999 World Series logo
2000	Spr. Training - Postseason	Armband	Left Sleeve BPJ	Death of Bob Lemon on Jan. 11, 2000
	Reg. and Postseason	Armband	Left Sleeve GJ	Death of Bob Lemon
	World Series	Patch	RS / LC	2000 World Series logo
2001	Reg. and Postseason	Patch	Right Sleeve	100th anniversary of American League
	Sept. 18 - End Season	Patch	LC / Back GJ	American flag patch for Sept. 11th terrorist attacks
	Sept. 25 - End Season	Armband	Left Sleeve	Sept. 11th terrorist attacks
	World Series	Patch	Left Sleeve	2001 World Series logo
2002	Sept. 11	Armband	Left Sleeve	First anniversary of the Sept. 11 attacks
2003	Reg. and Postseason	Patch	Left Sleeve	100th anniversary of the New York Yankees (1903-2002)
	World Series	Patch	RS / LC	2003 World Series logo
2004	Opening Series of Reg. Season in Japan (vs. TB)	Patch	RS of BPJ & GJ / Helmet	"Ricoh" logo patches on B.P. and game jersey; "Ricoh" sticker on helmet (Right side for RH hitters; Left side for LH hitters)
		Patch	Left Cap	"Opening Series Japan 2004" logo
2005	Sept. 8-10	Patch	Right Sleeve	Salvation Army relief logo for Hurricane Katrina relief
2007	Reg. and Postseason	Armband	Left Sleeve	Death of Cory Lidle on Oct. 11, 2006
	May 23	Patch	Left Cap	Virginia Tech shooting on Apr. 16, 2007
	Aug. 14 - Postseason	Number	Left Sleeve	Number "10" for death of Phil Rizzuto on Aug. 13, 2007
2008	Regular Season	Patch	Left Sleeve	Stadium logo with "1923-2008" for closing of Yankee Stadium
	Regular Season	Patch	Right Sleeve	2008 MLB All-Star Game logo (played at Yankee Stadium)
	July 13 - End Season	Armband	Left Sleeve	Death of Bobby Murcer on July 12, 2008
2009	Reg. and Postseason	Patch	LS / BC	Inaugural season of Yankee Stadium
	World Series	Patch	RS / LC	2009 World Series logo
2010	All-Star Game	Armband	Left Sleeve	Worn by NYY players and coaches for GMS & Sheppard passings
	July 16 - Postseason	Patch	Left Sleeve	Death of Bob Sheppard on July 11, 2010
	July 16 - Postseason	Patch	Left Front Jersey	Death of George M. Steinbrenner III on July 13, 2010
	July 22 - Postseason	Armband	Left Sleeve	Death of Ralph Houk on July 21, 2010
2013	Mar. 29 (Spring Exhibition)	Patch	LS / LC	West Point visit
	April 1	Patch	Above NY Logo	Patch with black ribbon to remember Sandy Hook Elem. tragedy
	Sept. 22, 24-26	Patch	LS / LC	Final Season of Mariano Rivera's career
2014	July 2	Patch	Right Breast	75th Anniv. Gehrig "Luckiest Man" speech (worn by all MLB teams)
	Sept. 7 - End Season	Patch	LS / LC	Final Season of Derek Jeter's career
2015	May 17	Patch	Left Sleeve	No. 28 patch for Ernie Banks as part of Negro Leagues salute
	May 24, Aug. 22-23	Patch	Left Sleeve	Mon. Park Ceremony patches for B. Williams, Posada, Pettitte
	Sept. 23 - End Season	Number	Left Sleeve	No. 8 worn for Yogi Berra, who passed away on Sept. 22, 2015
2016	Regular Season	Number	Left Sleeve	No. 8 worn for Yogi Berra, who passed away on Sept. 22, 2015
2017	Sept. 7 - End Postseason	Armband	Left Sleeve	Death of Gene "Stick" Michael on Sept. 7, 2017
2019	Reg. and Postseason	Armband	Left Sleeve	Death of Mel Stottlemyre, who passed away on Jan. 13, 2019
	June 29-30 (London Series)	Patch	RS/RC	London Series logo
	June 29-30 (London Series)	Patch	Helmet	Mitel (Sponsorship) — (Right side for RH hitters; Left side for LH hitters)
	June 29-30 (London Series)	Patch	Left Sleeve	Biofreeze (Sponsorship)

Important Dates in Yankees History

Jan. 9, 1903 - Frank Farrell and Bill Devery purchase the right to establish a new AL franchise in New York City for $18,000.

March 12, 1903 - The New York franchise is approved as a member of the American League. The team will play in a hastily constructed, wooden ballpark at 168th Street and Broadway. Because the site is one of the highest spots in Manhattan, their home field is referred to as "Hilltop Park."

Apr. 22, 1903 - The Highlanders (as the Yankees were commonly known then) play their first game, a 3-1 loss at Washington.

Apr. 23, 1903 - Pitcher Harry Howell records the first victory in franchise history, a 7-2 win at Washington.

Apr. 30, 1903 - The Highlanders notch a 6-2 win vs. Washington in their inaugural home opener at Hilltop Park.

May 11, 1903 - John Ganzel hits the first home run in franchise history - an inside-the-park homer at Detroit's Bennett Park off George Mullin in an 8-2 Highlanders victory.

Apr. 29, 1906 - At Hilltop Park, the Highlanders and A's raise $5,600 to benefit victims of the San Francisco earthquake and fire.

Apr. 11, 1912 - Pinstripes first appear on Highlanders uniforms.

Apr. 21, 1912 - At the Polo Grounds, the Highlanders and Giants stage a benefit game for survivors of the Titanic. The Giants win, 11-2, as $9,425.25 is raised.

May 3, 1912 - The Highlanders lose at Philadelphia, 18-15. The 33 combined runs tie for the highest total in franchise history (also 5/22/30-G2 and 6/3/32, each in 20-13 Yankees wins at the A's).

Apr. 1913 - The name "Yankees" becomes the predominant nickname of the club after the team moves to the Polo Grounds, home of the National League's New York Giants.

Apr. 5, 1913 - The Yankees play an exhibition game against the Dodgers, losing, 3-2, in the first-ever game at Ebbets Field.

Apr. 17, 1913 - The Yankees play their first home game at the Polo Grounds, losing to Washington, 9-3. It marks the beginning of 10 seasons as tenants of the National League's New York Giants.

Jan. 11, 1915 - Col. Jacob Ruppert and Col. Tillinghast L'Hommedieu Huston agree to purchase the Yankees for $460,000. The deal is formally completed on Jan. 30.

Apr. 24, 1917 - Lefthander George Mogridge becomes the first Yankee to throw a no-hitter in a 2-1 win at Fenway Park.

Apr. 3, 1919 - In a spaghetti-eating contest during spring training in Jacksonville, Fla., Yankees outfielder Ping Bodie defeats an ostrich named Percy, after Percy passes out following his 10th plate of pasta (credit: SABR Biography Project).

Jan. 5, 1920 - After being announced two days earlier, the Yankees complete the purchase of the contract of Babe Ruth from the Boston Red Sox for $100,000 plus interest and a $300,000 loan against the mortgage on Fenway Park.

May 1, 1920 - Babe Ruth hits his first homer as a Yankee in a 6-0 win over the Red Sox at the Polo Grounds.

Feb. 5, 1921 - The Yankees issue a press release announcing the purchase of 10 acres of land in the West Bronx that will eventually become the site of the original Yankee Stadium. The land was purchased from the estate of William Waldorf Astor for $675,000.

Oct. 5, 1921 - The Yankees play the first postseason game in franchise history, as Carl Mays tosses a complete game shutout to defeat the Giants at the Polo Grounds in World Series Game 1.

May 5, 1922 - The construction contract for Yankee Stadium is awarded to White Construction Company with the edict that the job is to be completed "at a definite price" of $2.5 million by Opening Day 1923.

Apr. 18, 1923 - Yankee Stadium hosts its first regular season game as the Yankees defeat Boston Red Sox, 4-1, before an announced crowd of 74,200. Thousands more fans are turned away when fire marshalls order the gates closed. Babe Ruth hits the Stadium's first home run — a three-run shot in the third inning — and starter Bob Shawkey records a complete-game win.

Yankee Stadium on its first Opening Day in 1923

Apr. 30, 1923 - The Yankees sign 19-year-old Columbia pitcher and position player Lou Gehrig to a professional contract.

May 21, 1923 - Yankees announce that Col. Ruppert buys out Col. Huston for $1.5 million to become sole owner of the Yankees.

Sept. 28, 1923 - The Yankees record 30 hits in a 24-4 win over Boston at Fenway Park. The hit total remains the most in a nine-inning game in franchise history.

Oct. 15, 1923 - The Yankees defeat the New York Giants, 6-4, at the Polo Grounds in Game 6 of the World Series, clinching the first World Championship in franchise history.

June 1, 1925 - Lou Gehrig begins his record streak of 2,130 consecutive games played, pinch-hitting for "Pee Wee" Wanninger in a 5-3 loss to Washington at Yankee Stadium.

Oct. 6, 1926 - Babe Ruth becomes the first player to hit three home runs in a single World Series game in Game 4 at St. Louis.

June 23, 1927 - In an 11-4 Yankees win at Fenway Park, Lou Gehrig become the first (of two) players in franchise history to hit 3HR in a single game against the Red Sox (also see May 8, 2010).

Sept. 30, 1927 - Babe Ruth breaks his own single-season Major League record by hitting his 60th home run (off Tom Zachary) in a 4-2 win over Washington at Yankee Stadium.

Apr. 20, 1928 - Yankee Stadium's LF stands are enlarged to three decks.

Oct. 9, 1928 - In Game 4 of the World Series vs. the Cardinals at St. Louis' Sportsman's Park, Babe Ruth hits three home runs, marking his second three-homer World Series game.

Apr. 18, 1929 - The Yankees wear numbered uniforms for the first time, two days after the Indians permanently adopt them as well (Numbers would become standard for all teams by 1932).

Sept. 24, 1929 - The Yankees celebrate Babe Ruth Day at Fenway Park defeating Boston, 5-3. Ruth goes 2-for-3 with a double, and Tom Zachary (pitching for the Yankees) records his final decision of the season, improving to 12-0, still a Major League record for most wins in a season without a loss.

June 4, 1933 - Starter Johnny Allen allows a first-inning single to Philadelphia's Ed Coleman, then holds the A's hitless the rest of the way, notching a one-hit shutout in a 6-0 home victory in the second game of a doubleheader.

Hilltop Park was home to the Yankees from 1903 through 1912.

275

July 6, 1933 - In the very first MLB All-Star Game, Babe Ruth hits the game's first HR — a two-run shot off the Cardinals' Bill Hallahan — leading the AL to a 4-2 victory at Comiskey Park. Lefty Gomez starts for the AL, tossing 3.0 scoreless IP to earn the win. He also records the first All-Star RBI with a second-inning single.

June 6, 1934 - Myril Hoag goes 6-for-6 in a 15-3, nine-inning win in Game 1 of a doubleheader at Boston, becoming the first of only two Yankees to go 6-for-6 in a single game (see June 7, 2008- Johnny Damon).

Nov. 21, 1934 - The Yankees purchase Joe DiMaggio from the San Francisco Seals of the Pacific Coast League for $25,000 and five players.

May 24, 1936 - The Yankees tally their single-game franchise-high in runs in a 25-2 win at Philadelphia. Tony Lazzeri is the star with three home runs (including two grand slams) and a triple. His 11 RBI set a still-standing AL single-game record.

Apr. 20, 1937 - The Yankees' 15th season at Yankee Stadium opens with the right-field stands enlarged to three decks. Wooden bleachers are replaced by a concrete structure, and the distance to center field drops from 490 feet to 461 feet.

May 30, 1938 - A franchise-record crowd of 81,841 attends a doubleheader sweep of Boston at Yankee Stadium.

June 22, 1938 - In a rematch of their 1936 bout, Joe Louis KOs Max Schmeling in 124 seconds to avenge his prior loss to the German and retain the heavyweight title in front of 70,043 fans at Yankee Stadium and an estimated 70 million people listening on the radio.

Aug. 27, 1938 - Monte Pearson authors the first Yankee Stadium no-hitter by a Yankee, defeating Cleveland, 13-0, in Game 2 of a doubleheader.

Jan. 13, 1939 - Col. Ruppert passes away, and his estate takes ownership of the ballclub.

Lou Gehrig bats at Comiskey Park during the 1938 season.

Apr. 30, 1939 - Lou Gehrig plays in the last of his 2,130 consecutive games, going 0-for-4 in a 3-2 loss vs. Washington at the Stadium.

May 2, 1939 - Lou Gehrig's playing streak of 2,130 consecutive games ends when he does not make an appearance in a 22-2 Yankees win at Detroit. Babe Dahlgren plays first base for the Yankees and contributes a double and a home run.

June 26, 1939 - At Philadelphia's Shibe Park, the Yankees play their first-ever night game, losing to the Athletics, 3-2.

July 4, 1939 - "Lou Gehrig Appreciation Day" is held at Yankee Stadium in between games of a doubleheader vs. Washington. Gehrig makes his famous "luckiest man on the face of the earth" speech.

May 15, 1941 - Joe DiMaggio's 56-game hitting streak begins with a single off Edgar Smith in a 13-1 loss at Chicago.

June 2, 1941 - Lou Gehrig dies of amyotrophic lateral sclerosis at the age of 37 in the Riverdale section of the Bronx.

July 2, 1941 - In an 8-4 win vs. Boston, Joe DiMaggio goes 1-for-5 with a three-run home run, extending his hitting streak to 45 games and surpassing Wee Willie Keeler's single-season Major League record 44-game streak set in 1897.

July 17, 1941 - Joe DiMaggio's consecutive-game hitting streak ends at 56 when he goes 0-for-3 in a 4-3 win at Cleveland. Indians 3B Ken Keltner twice robs DiMaggio with great fielding plays. DiMaggio hits safely in his next 16 games, giving him hits in 72 of 73 games.

Aug. 14, 1942 - The Yankees set a still-standing MLB fielding mark with 7DP in an 11-2 win at Philadelphia (since tied three times).

June 26, 1944 - The Yankees, Dodgers and Giants play a three-way exhibition game at the Polo Grounds to promote the purchase of war bonds. Each team batted six times and played the field six times while a crowd of 50,000 fans bought $5.5 million in war bonds. Brooklyn wins by a score of 5 to 1 (Yankees) to 0 (Giants).

Jan. 25, 1945 - Dan Topping, Del Webb and Larry MacPhail purchase the Yankees for $2.8 million from the estate of the late Col. Jacob Ruppert. MacPhail replaces Ed Barrow as President and General Manager.

May 28, 1946 - The first night game is played at Yankee Stadium, a 2-1 loss vs. Washington before 49,917 fans.

Apr. 27, 1947 - "Babe Ruth Day" is celebrated at Yankee Stadium and throughout Major League Baseball.

June 29 - July 17, 1947 - The Yankees reel off a franchise-record 19 consecutive wins, outscoring their opposition 119-41.

Oct. 3, 1947 - Yankees pitcher Bill Bevens loses his no-hitter and the game with two outs in the bottom of the ninth as pinch-hitter Cookie Lavagetto doubles home two runs in a 3-2 Dodgers win in Game 4 of the World Series at Ebbets Field.

June 13, 1948 - Babe Ruth's uniform No. 3 is retired at Yankee Stadium's 25th Anniversary celebration. The visit marks the Babe's final Stadium appearance.

Aug. 16, 1948 - Babe Ruth dies of throat cancer in New York at age 53.

Oct. 12, 1948 - The Yankees announce that Casey Stengel will replace Bucky Harris as manager.

Oct. 1-2, 1949 - The Yankees come back from a one-game deficit with two games to play, defeating Boston in the final two games of the season at Yankee Stadium, 5-4 and 5-3, respectively, marking the first of five consecutive American League pennants.

Oct. 5, 1949 - In Game 1 of the World Series at Yankee Stadium, Tommy Henrich breaks up a scoreless pitchers' duel between the Yankees' Allie Reynolds and the Dodgers' Don Newcombe, hitting a game-winning solo HR in the bottom of the ninth.

Apr. 17, 1951 - Mickey Mantle makes his Major League debut, going 1-for-4 in a 5-0 win vs. Boston at Yankee Stadium. The game also marks Bob Sheppard's first as Yankees public-address announcer. Boston's Dom DiMaggio is the first hitter announced.

Sept. 28, 1951 - In an 8-0 Game 1 win in a doubleheader vs. Boston at Yankee Stadium, Allie Reynolds becomes the second of five players in Baseball history to toss two no-hitters in the same season (also Johnny Vander Meer in 1938, Virgil Trucks in 1952, Nolan Ryan in 1973 and Max Scherzer on 2015). Reynolds had previously no-hit the Indians at Cleveland's Municipal Stadium on July 12 in a 1-0 win.

Dec. 11, 1951 - Joe DiMaggio officially announces his retirement.

Oct. 7, 1952 - Second baseman Billy Martin makes a running catch on a two-out, seventh-inning, bases-loaded pop-up off the bat of Jackie Robinson to preserve the Yankees' lead in a 4-2 World Series-clinching Game 7 win at Brooklyn's Ebbets Field.

Apr. 17, 1953 - Mickey Mantle clears the LF wall at Washington's Griffith Stadium with a 565-foot home run off Chuck Stobbs in the fifth inning of a 7-3 Yankees win. Yankees PR representative Red Patterson retrieves the ball and reportedly measures off the distance, giving birth to the phrase "tape-measure home run."

Oct. 5, 1953 - Billy Martin singles home the winning run in the ninth inning of a 4-3, Game 6 victory over the Brooklyn Dodgers at Yankee Stadium. The win clinches the Yankees' all-time record fifth-consecutive World Championship.

Apr. 14, 1955 - Elston Howard becomes the first black player in Yankees history, making his Major League debut in an 8-4 loss at Boston. He records an RBI single in his only plate appearance.

Oct. 4, 1955 - Brooklyn's Johnny Podres outduels Yankees starter Tommy Byrne and two relievers, 2-0, clinching the Dodgers' first World Championship. The World Series loss snaps the Yankees' string of seven consecutive appearances in the Fall Classic without losing a Series (1943, '47, '49-53). It also marks the Yankees' first World Series loss to Brooklyn after wins in 1941, '47, '49, '52 and '53.

Elston Howard became the Yankees' first African-American player on Apr. 14, 1955.

May 30, 1956 - Batting against Pedro Ramos in Game 1 of a doubleheader vs. Washington, Mickey Mantle nearly hits a home run out of Yankee Stadium, with the ball striking the upper deck frieze in right field.

Oct. 8, 1956 - Don Larsen hurls the only perfect game in World Series history, a 2-0, Game 5 win over Brooklyn at Yankee Stadium.

Oct. 10, 1956 - In World Series Game 7, Johnny Kucks pitches a 9-0 complete game shutout over Brooklyn at Ebbets Field.

June 15, 1957 - Following the "Copacabana incident," the Yankees trade Billy Martin to Kansas City with Woodie Held, Bob Martyn and Ralph Terry for Ryne Duren, Jim Pisoni and Harry Simpson.

Apr. 22, 1959 - Whitey Ford pitches a 1-0, 14-inning complete game shutout at Washington, allowing seven hits with 15 strikeouts.

May 7, 1959 - The Yankees and Dodgers play an exhibition game before 93,103 fans at the L.A. Coliseum. The game is played to honor paralyzed Dodgers catcher Roy Campanella.

Oct. 8, 1960 - Second baseman Bobby Richardson sets an all-time World Series record (since tied by Hideki Matsui on 11/4/09 vs. Philadelphia, Albert Pujols on 10/22/11 w/ St. Louis at Texas and Addison Russell on 11/1/16 w/ Chicago-NL at Cleveland) with 6RBI in Game 3 of the World Series vs. Pittsburgh, hitting a grand slam in the first inning and two-run single in the fourth inning of a 10-0 Yankees win.

Sept. 26, 1961 - Roger Maris hits his 60th home run of the season off Baltimore's Jack Fisher in a 3-2 Yankees win at Yankee Stadium, tying Babe Ruth's Major League record.

Oct. 1, 1961 - Roger Maris hits his 61st home run in the season's final game off Boston's Tracy Stallard at Yankee Stadium, establishing a then-Major League record and still-standing AL record. It was the only run in a 1-0 Yankees victory. The ball was caught in right field by local teenager Sal Durante.

June 24, 1962 - Jack Reed's two-run, 22nd-inning home run ends the longest game in Yankees history, a 9-7 win at Detroit.

Oct. 16, 1962 - In Game 7 of the World Series, superb fielding from RF Roger Maris holds Matty Alou at third base after a two-out, ninth-inning Willie Mays double. Bobby Richardson then snares a screaming line drive off the bat of Willie McCovey for the game's final out, securing a 1-0, Series-clinching victory over the Giants at Candlestick Park. New York scores the game's only run when Tony Kubek grounds into a fifth-inning double play. It would be the last championship for the Yankees until 1977.

May 22, 1963 - In an 8-7, 11-inning win vs. the Kansas City A's, Mickey Mantle hits the upper deck frieze in right field for the second time in his career, this time off righthander Bill Fischer.

June 20, 1963 - The Yankees lose to the Mets at Yankee Stadium, 6-2, in the first Mayor's Trophy game between the crosstown rivals.

Nov. 2, 1964 - CBS purchases 80 percent of the Yankees for $11.2 million. The network later buys the remaining 20 percent.

May 14, 1967 - Mickey Mantle becomes only the sixth player—and second Yankee—to reach the 500 home run plateau, when he connects off Baltimore's Stu Miller in a 6-5 win at Yankee Stadium.

Aug. 23, 1968 - The Yankees play the longest tied game in franchise history, matching Detroit, 3-3, in Game 2 of a doubleheader at Yankee Stadium. Yankees pitcher Lindy McDaniel tosses seven perfect innings in relief in the 19-inning affair.

June 8, 1969 - "Mickey Mantle Day" is celebrated at Yankee Stadium and his uniform No. 7 is retired.

June 24, 1970 - Bobby Murcer hits HRs in four consecutive ABs over two games of a doubleheader vs. Cleveland at Yankee Stadium.

Aug. 8, 1972 - The Yankees sign a 30-year lease to play in a remodeled Yankee Stadium with completion scheduled for 1976.

Jan. 3, 1973 - A limited partnership, headed by George M. Steinbrenner III as its managing general partner, purchases the Yankees for a net price of $8.7 million from CBS.

Apr. 6, 1973 - At Fenway Park in Boston, the Yankees' Ron Blomberg becomes MLB's first designated hitter. Batting in the top of the first inning, he walks with the bases loaded off Luis Tiant. He goes 1-for-3 with 1RBI as the Yankees lose to the Red Sox, 15-5.

Sept. 30, 1973 - The Yankees play their final game in Yankee Stadium before gets remodeled, losing 8-5 vs. Detroit. Tigers pitcher John Hiller gets Yankees first baseman Mike Hegan to fly out to centerfield for the game's final out.

Apr. 6, 1974 - The Yankees begin the first of two seasons at Shea Stadium as Yankee Stadium is remodeled. The Yankees will go 90-69 at Shea over the two seasons (1974-75).

Dec. 31, 1974 - Free agent Catfish Hunter signs a then-record five-year contract with the Yankees.

Aug. 1, 1975 - Billy Martin replaces Bill Virdon for his first of five stints as manager.

Jim "Catfish" Hunter

Apr. 15, 1976 - Remodeled Yankee Stadium opens with an 11-4 win over Minnesota. The Twins' Dan Ford hits the first home run.

Apr. 17, 1976 - In a 10-0 win, catcher Thurman Munson homers off the Minnesota Twins' Jim Hughes, marking the first home run hit by a Yankee in remodeled Yankee Stadium.

Oct. 14, 1976 - Chris Chambliss' ninth-inning home run off Mark Littell in Game 5 of the ALCS vs. Kansas City at Yankee Stadium gives the Yankees their 30th AL pennant and first trip to the World Series since 1964.

Nov. 29, 1976 - Free agent Reggie Jackson signs a five-year contract.

June 30, 1977 - The Yankees set a franchise record (since tied on 6/21/05 vs. Tampa Bay and 10/1/12 vs. Boston) with four home runs in a single inning in an 11-5 win at Toronto. Cliff Johnson hits three homers in the game, including two of the Yankees' four in the eighth inning.

Oct. 9, 1977 - The Yankees rally for one run in the eighth and three runs in the ninth for a 5-3, series-clinching win in the decisive Game 5 of the 1977 ALCS at Kansas City. Sparky Lyle earns the win for the second consecutive night, finishing the game with 1.1 scoreless innings on no rest following his scoreless 5.1-inning relief appearance at Kauffman Stadium in Game 4.

Oct. 18, 1977 - Reggie Jackson hits three home runs (on three consecutive pitches) in Game 6 of the World Series vs. the Los Angeles Dodgers at Yankee Stadium. Jackson, Babe Ruth, Albert Pujols and Pablo Sandoval are the only players to hit at least three homers in a single World Series game.

Sparky Lyle

Apr. 13, 1978 - The Yankees defeat the White Sox, 4-2, in the Yankee Stadium opener on "Reggie!" Candy Bar Day. When Jackson slugs a three-run HR in the first inning, the field is showered with the chocolate and peanut candy bars, which were given out free to fans at the game.

June 17, 1978 - Ron Guidry establishes a franchise record by striking out 18 batters in the Yankees' 4-0 win vs. California.

July 24, 1978 - Billy Martin resigns as manager.

July 25, 1978 - Bob Lemon is named manager, replacing Billy Martin.

July 29, 1978 - On Old-Timers' Day, the Yankees announce that Billy Martin will return as Yankees manager in 1980 and Bob Lemon will become general manager (also see June 18, 1979).

Oct. 2, 1978 - The Yankees, 14.0 games behind Boston as late as July 19, defeat the Red Sox, 5-4, at Fenway Park in only the second one-game playoff in AL history. Bucky Dent's three-run, seventh-inning home run becomes one of the most memorable in Baseball history.

June 18, 1979 - Billy Martin is rehired as Yankees manager, replacing Bob Lemon.

Aug. 2, 1979 - Yankees Captain Thurman Munson dies in a plane crash in Canton, Ohio, at age 32. His No. 15 is immediately retired.

Aug. 6, 1979 - After delivering a eulogy at Thurman Munson's funeral earlier that morning in Canton, Ohio, Bobby Murcer hits a three-run seventh inning homer and a two-run ninth-inning single, accounting for all five of the Yankees' runs in an emotional 5-4 comeback win vs. Baltimore at Yankee Stadium.

Oct. 28, 1979 - Dick Howser replaces Billy Martin as manager.

Dec. 15, 1980 - Free agent Dave Winfield signs a then-record 10-year contract.

Nov. 21, 1980 - Gene Michael replaces Dick Howser as manager.

May 4, 1981 - Yankees reliever Ron Davis enters in the bottom of the seventh of a 4-2 Yankees win at California. After getting Don Baylor to pop out, he strikes out eight consecutive Angels to record the save. The performance ties the AL record for consecutive strikeouts in a single game, previously set by Nolan Ryan (twice) and later tied by Roger Clemens and Blake Stein. Davis remains the all-time MLB leader in consecutive strikeouts in a relief appearance.

Sept. 6, 1981 - Bob Lemon is named manager for a second time, replacing Gene Michael.

Apr. 26, 1982 - Gene Michael becomes manager for a second time, replacing Bob Lemon.

Aug. 3, 1982 - Clyde King replaces Gene Michael as manager.

Jan. 11, 1983 - Billy Martin is named Yankees manager for the third time, replacing Clyde King.

July 4, 1983 - Dave Righetti pitches the sixth regular season no-hitter in franchise history and the first since 1951 in a 4-0 win vs. Boston at Yankee Stadium. Righetti strikes out Wade Boggs for the final out.

July 24, 1983 - The Yankees and Kansas City play the infamous "Pine Tar" game at Yankee Stadium. George Brett hits a two-out, ninth-inning home run off Goose Gossage to give the Royals an apparent 5-4 lead. Manager Billy Martin points out that the pine tar on Brett's bat is above the allowable 18 inches and Brett is subsequently called out for using an illegal bat. The Yankees (temporarily) win 4-3 (see Aug. 18, 1983).

Aug. 18, 1983 - Kansas City's protest is upheld and play is resumed at Yankee Stadium from the point immediately after Brett's home run. Yankees pitcher Ron Guidry plays CF while lefthanded first baseman Don Mattingly plays second base. Royals' reliever Dan Quisenberry retires the Yankees in order in the bottom of the ninth for a 5-4 Royals win.

"The Pine Tar Game"

Dec. 16, 1983 - Yogi Berra is named manager for the second time, replacing Billy Martin.

Apr. 8, 1985 - At 46 yrs., 7 days old, Phil Niekro becomes the oldest Opening Day starter in Yankees franchise history (and third-oldest all time), allowing 5ER in 4.0IP while picking up the loss in a 9-2 Yankees defeat at Boston.

Apr. 28, 1985 - Billy Martin is named manager for a fourth time, replacing Yogi Berra.

Aug. 4, 1985 - The Yankees celebrate "Phil Rizzuto Day" at Yankee Stadium, dedicating a plaque in his honor and retiring his No. 10. The Yankees lose their scheduled game to the Chicago White Sox, 4-1, as Tom Seaver wins his 300th career game.

Oct. 6, 1985 - Phil Niekro tosses a four-hit complete game shutout in an 8-0 victory at Toronto's Exhibition Stadium for his 300th career win.

Oct. 17, 1985 - Lou Piniella is named manager for the first time, replacing Billy Martin.

June 29, 1987 - At Toronto's Exhibition Stadium, the Yankees defeat the Blue Jays, 15-14, behind a pair of grand slams from Don Mattingly and Dave Winfield.

July 18, 1987 - Don Mattingly homers off Texas' Jose Guzman to tie Dale Long's Major League record of hitting a home run in eight consecutive games (Mattingly hits 10 HR during the streak).

Sept. 29, 1987 - Don Mattingly hits a grand slam off Boston's Bruce Hurst, setting a Major League record (tied by Travis Hafner in 2008) with six grand slams in a season.

Oct. 19, 1987 - Billy Martin is named manager for the fifth time, replacing Lou Piniella.

June 23, 1988 - Lou Piniella is named manager for the second time as Billy Martin is replaced as Yankees manager for the fifth and final time.

July 27, 1988 - Tommy John commits three errors on one play during the fourth inning of a 16-3 Yankees victory vs. Milwaukee. John becomes the first pitcher in the Modern Era to commit three miscues in the same inning.

Oct. 7, 1988 - Dallas Green is named manager, replacing Lou Piniella.

Dec. 9, 1988 - The Yankees sign a 12-year television contract with the Madison Square Garden Network.

Aug. 18, 1989 - Bucky Dent is named manager, replacing Dallas Green.

Dec. 25, 1989 - Billy Martin dies in an automobile accident near Binghamton, N.Y., at age 61.

June 6, 1990 - Stump Merrill is named manager, replacing Bucky Dent.

July 1, 1990 - With a no-hitter intact with two out in the bottom of the eighth at Comiskey Park, the Yankees make three errors behind starter Andy Hawkins, leading to four unearned runs as the Yankees go on to lose, 4-0. While initially ruled a "no-hitter," MLB removes the designation in 1991 after redefining a "no-hitter" as requiring a pitcher(s) to complete at least 9.0IP.

Oct. 29, 1991 - Buck Showalter replaces Stump Merrill as manager.

Sept. 4, 1993 - Jim Abbott tosses a no-hitter in a 4-0 win vs. Cleveland at Yankee Stadium.

Aug. 13, 1995 - Mickey Mantle dies of cancer at age 63 in Dallas, Tex.

Sept. 6, 1995 - Lou Gehrig's record of 2,130 consecutive games played is broken when Baltimore's Cal Ripken, Jr. plays in his 2,131st.

Oct. 4, 1995 - The Yankees play the longest postseason game in their history, a 15-inning, 7-5 win over Seattle at Yankee Stadium won on a two-run homer by Jim Leyritz. The contest was the final Yankee Stadium game for Don Mattingly.

Nov. 2, 1995 - Joe Torre is named the Yankees' 31st manager, replacing Buck Showalter.

Mar. 1, 1996 - The Yankees defeat the Cleveland Indians, 5-2, in the first ever game at Legends Field (renamed George M. Steinbrenner Field in 2008), the club's new spring training home.

Apr. 9, 1996 - The Yankees defeat the Kansas City Royals, 7-3, in a snowy Bronx home opener. Starter Andy Pettitte earns the win as newcomers Joe Girardi (replacing Mike Stanley) and Tino Martinez (replacing Don Mattingly) get booed during pregame introductions. Hitting in the ninth spot, rookie shortstop Derek Jeter goes 1-for-3 with a single.

May 1, 1996 - Outfielder Gerald Williams goes 6-for-8 with 1HR and 3RBI in a 15-inning, 11-6 win at Baltimore. With Myril Hoag (6/6/1934 at Boston) and Johnny Damon (6/7/2008 vs. Kansas City), he is one of three Yankees in franchise history with six hits in a single game.

May 14, 1996 - Dwight Gooden hurls the eighth regular season no-hitter in Yankees history, a 2-0 blanking of the Seattle Mariners at Yankee Stadium.

June 16, 1996 - Mel Allen, the legendary "Voice of the Yankees" from 1939-64, passes away at age 83.

Aug. 25, 1996 - A monument in honor of Mickey Mantle is unveiled in Yankee Stadium's Monument Park.

Oct. 23, 1996 - In Game 4 of the World Series at Atlanta, Jim Leyritz hits a three-run, eighth-inning homer off the Braves' Mark Wohlers, tying the game, 6-6. The Yankees go on to win, 8-6, in 10 innings.

Oct 24, 1996 - The Yankees' Andy Pettitte (8.1IP) outduels Atlanta's John Smoltz (8.0IP), 1-0, in Game 5 in Atlanta.

Oct. 26, 1996 - In Game 6 of the World Series at Yankee Stadium, John Wetteland closes out a 3-2 win vs. Atlanta, giving the Yankees their first World Championship in 18 years.

June 23, 1997 - With 16K in a 5-2 Yankees win at Detroit, David Cone establishes the Yankees' all-time single-game high for an RHP (since tied by Michael Pineda in 2015).

May 17, 1998 - David Wells tosses the first regular-season perfect game by a Yankee (and 14th in Baseball history), defeating Minnesota 4-0 at Yankee Stadium.

Sept. 25, 1998 - The Yankees set a then-American League record with their 112th win of the season (a 6-1 win vs. Tampa Bay at Yankee Stadium), breaking the mark of 111 by the 1954 Indians.

Sept. 27, 1998 - The Yankees finish their regular season with a 114-48 (.704) mark, becoming the first team since the 1954 Indians (111-43, .721) with a winning percentage above .700.

Oct. 21, 1998 - The Yankees complete an incredible season with a four-game World Series sweep of the San Diego Padres to capture the franchise's 24th World Championship. The 3-0 win gives the club a 125-50 record over the entire season (114-48 in the regular season, 11-2 in postseason).

1998 World Series MVP Scott Brosius celebrates after the Yankees' clinch the title at San Diego.

Mar. 8, 1999 - Joe DiMaggio dies at age 84 in Hollywood, Fla.

Apr. 25, 1999 - A monument in honor of Joe DiMaggio is unveiled in Yankee Stadium's Monument Park in front of a sold out Stadium and many of DiMaggio's former teammates. Paul Simon sings "Mrs. Robinson" while standing in center field.

July 18, 1999 - On "Yogi Berra Day," David Cone tosses the 15th regular season perfect game in Baseball history, one season after David Wells accomplishes the feat. Coincidentally, Don Larsen — who tossed a perfect game in the 1956 World Series — throws out the ceremonial first pitch.

Oct. 27, 1999 - The Yankees play Baseball's last game of the century and complete a four-game sweep of the Atlanta Braves, capturing their 25th World Championship.

Apr. 23, 2000 - In a 10-7 Yankees win at Toronto, Jorge Posada and Bernie Williams become the first pair of teammates in MLB history to each homer from both sides of the plate in the same game.

July 8, 2000 - The Yankees and Mets play the first two-stadium, split doubleheader in nearly 100 years with the Yankees sweeping both games by the score of 4-2. Game 1 took place at Shea Stadium followed by Game 2 that night at Yankee Stadium. It marked the first day-night doubleheader to take place in different venues since the New York Giants and Brooklyn Superbas faced off on 9/7/1903.

Oct. 21, 2000 - The Yankees' World Series Game 1 win vs. the Mets at Yankee Stadium marks their 13th consecutive victory in World Series play, breaking the 12-game record-streak of the 1927, 1928 and 1932 Yankees.

Oct. 26, 2000 - The Yankees win World Series Game 5 over the Mets at Shea Stadium, clinching their third consecutive World Championship in the first "Subway Series" since 1956. It marks the first time a club has won three consecutive World Series titles since the 1972-74 Oakland Athletics.

Sept. 2, 2001 - Mike Mussina comes within one out of a perfect game at Fenway Park, before Carl Everett singles with two outs in the ninth.

Sept. 23, 2001 - Yankee Stadium hosts "A Prayer for America" service for those lost on September 11. It was the first large-scale, formally staged program offered in memory of those killed or missing and presumed dead in World Trade Center attacks.

Oct. 13, 2001 - With a 1-0 lead and two out in the bottom of the seventh of Game 3 of the ALDS in Oakland, Derek Jeter picks up Shane Spencer's errant throw from the outfield and "flips" the ball in a backhand motion to Jorge Posada, who tags Jeremy Giambi for the final out of the inning. The Yankees go on to win the game, 1-0, and the series 3 games to 2. The play will be known as "The Flip Play."

Oct. 30, 2001 - President George W. Bush throws out the first pitch prior to the Yankees' 2-1 World Series Game 3 win vs. Arizona at Yankee Stadium.

Oct. 31, 2001 - In Game 4 of the World Series vs. Arizona at Yankee Stadium, Tino Martinez's two-out, bottom-of-the-ninth, two-run home run off Byung-Hyun Kim sends the game into extra innings. Shortly after the stroke of midnight, Derek Jeter wins the game with a "walk-off" solo home run in the 10th, earning him the nickname "Mr. November."

Nov. 1, 2001 - In the late innings of Game 5 of the World Series vs. Arizona at Yankee Stadium, fans serenade Paul O'Neill, who is playing in his last game at Yankee Stadium. Scott Brosius' two-out, bottom-of-the-ninth, two-run home run off Byung-Hyun Kim sends the game into extra innings, and Alfonso Soriano singles in the winning run in the 12th.

May 17, 2002 - Jason Giambi becomes only the 21st player — and second Yankee — to hit a "walk-off" grand slam with his team trailing by three runs (Babe Ruth did it on 9/24/25). His 14th-inning slam off Minnesota's Mike Trombley erases a 12-9 Twins lead, giving the Yankees a 13-12 win.

Apr. 8, 2003 - Hideki Matsui hits a grand slam in his Yankee Stadium debut, leading the Yankees to a 7-3 win over Minnesota.

June 3, 2003 - Derek Jeter is named team captain.

June 13, 2003 - In a 5-2 win vs. St. Louis at Yankee Stadium, Roger Clemens records his 300th career win and 4,000th strikeout.

Oct. 16, 2003 - In Game 7 of the ALCS vs. Boston at Yankee Stadium, Aaron Boone becomes the fifth player—and second Yankee (also Chris Chambliss, 1976 ALCS vs. Kansas City)—to end a postseason series with a "walk-off" HR, when his 11th-inning leadoff solo shot off Tim Wakefield clinches the Yankees' 39th pennant.

Mar. 30-31, 2004 - The Yankees play their first-ever regular season games outside of North America, splitting a pair against Tampa Bay at the Tokyo Dome, losing 8-3 and winning 12-1, respectively.

July 1, 2004 - Derek Jeter makes his most famous catch, diving into Yankee Stadium's third base stands to nab a 12th-inning popup off the bat of Boston's Trot Nixon. John Flaherty wins the game with a 13th-inning RBI single.

Apr. 26, 2005 - Alex Rodriguez hits three home runs (all off Bartolo Colon) and becomes just the second Yankee in franchise history to record at least 10 RBI in a game (also Tony Lazzeri, 11 on 5/24/36) in a 12-4 win vs. the Angels at Yankee Stadium.

June 15, 2005 - The Yankees announce plans for a new Yankee Stadium to be constructed in Macombs Dam and John Mullaly Parks, located on the north side of 161st Street (adjacent to the site of the original Stadium).

Apr. 29, 2006 - For the second time in franchise history, the Yankees score in each inning of a game during a 17-6 win vs. Toronto (also 7/26/39 vs. St. Louis).

May 11, 2006 - Hideki Matsui is removed from the game in the top of the first vs. Boston after fracturing his left wrist. According to Rule 10.24 (c), his 1,768 consecutive-games-played streak (1,250 with the Yomiuri Giants and 518 with the Yankees) comes to an end as he did not play one half-inning in the field or complete a time at-bat by reaching base or making an out. His streak as a Yankee is the longest since Lou Gehrig's (2,130 games).

May 16, 2006 - The Yankees tie a franchise record by overcoming a nine-run deficit vs. Texas to win, 14-13, in nine innings. Jorge Posada hits a two-run "walk-off" home run off Akinori Otsuka.

Aug. 16, 2006 - The Yankees break ground for a new Yankee Stadium, scheduled to be ready for Opening Day 2009.

George Steinbrenner [C] breaks ground for the current Yankee Stadium on Aug. 16, 2006.

Aug. 4, 2007 - In a 16-8 win vs. Kansas City, Alex Rodriguez becomes the 22nd and youngest (32y, 8d) player in MLB history to reach the 500-HR mark. He is the third player to hit his 500th career homer as a Yankee, joining Babe Ruth and Mickey Mantle.

Sept. 5, 2007 - Bob Sheppard works his final game as Yankees Public Address Announcer, a 3-2 win over Seattle.

Oct. 30, 2007 - Joe Girardi is named the 32nd manager in Yankees franchise history.

Mar. 18, 2008 - The Yankees visited Blacksburg, Va., to play an exhibition game vs. Virginia Tech to honor the victims and aid in the healing process following the tragic events on the college's campus on Apr. 16, 2007. Prior to the game at English Field, Yankees players and staff visited the campus' memorial site.

March 27, 2008 - Prior to the Yankees' final home spring training game, Legends Field is renamed George M. Steinbrenner Field.

June 7, 2008 - Johnny Damon goes 6-for-6 in the Yankees' 12-11 win vs. Kansas City, matching the franchise record for hits in a nine-inning game (see June 6, 1934 - Myril Hoag) and becoming the only Yankee in original Yankee Stadium history to record six hits in a game of any length. His final hit is a "walk-off" single.

Sept. 16, 2008 - Derek Jeter singles off Chicago's Gavin Floyd in the first inning for his 1,270th career hit at Yankee Stadium, surpassing Lou Gehrig for the most all-time hits at the ballpark.

Sept. 21, 2008 - The Yankees play their last ever game in the original Yankee Stadium. Julia Ruth Stevens, daughter of Babe Ruth, throws out the first pitch, and Jose Molina hits the park's final home run in the fourth inning. Following the Yankees' 7-3 win over Baltimore, Derek Jeter thanks the fans over the Stadium PA system.

Sept. 28, 2008 - On the season's final day at Boston's Fenway Park, Mike Mussina records his 20th win of the year, becoming the oldest pitcher in MLB history to win 20 games for the first time.

Nov. 8, 2008 - Local Bronx high school youth groups are joined by former players Scott Brosius, David Cone, Jeff Nelson and Paul O'Neill and Yankees General Partner Jennifer Steinbrenner Swindal in removing home plate, the pitcher's rubber and pails of dirt from the original Stadium, then installing them in the current Stadium.

Apr. 3-4, 2009 - The Yankees play their first exhibition games in Yankee Stadium, defeating the Cubs, 7-4 and 10-1, respectively. Chien-Ming Wang tosses the first pitch in the Apr. 3 contest.

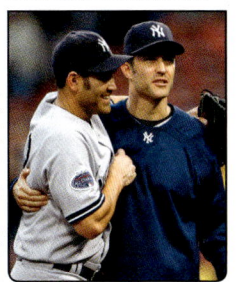

Mike Mussina [R] smiles with Johnny Damon on Sept. 28, 2008, after becoming the oldest pitcher to win 20 games for the first time.

Apr. 16, 2009 - The Yankees play the first regular season game in Yankee Stadium history, falling to Cleveland, 10-2. CC Sabathia tosses the Stadium's first official pitch, Johnny Damon records the first hit (first-inning single off Cliff Lee) and Jorge Posada hits the first HR (fifth-inning off Lee).

May 14 – June 1, 2009 - The Yankees set an all-time MLB mark with 18 consecutive errorless games (safely handling 660 chances).

Sept. 11, 2009 - Derek Jeter breaks Lou Gehrig's all-time franchise mark of 2,721 hits with a single off Baltimore's Chris Tillman at Yankee Stadium. Gehrig had held the mark since 9/6/37.

Oct. 4, 2009 - Alex Rodriguez hits a three-run HR and a grand slam in the sixth inning of the season finale at Tampa Bay in a 10-2 Yankees win, setting an all-time AL mark with 7RBI in an inning.

Nov. 4, 2009 - The Yankees win their 27th World Series, defeating Philadelphia in Game 6, 7-3. Hideki Matsui ties Bobby Richardson's World Series mark (1960 Game 3 vs. Pittsburgh) with 6RBI (since tied by Albert Pujols in 2011 and Addison Russell in 2016). Andy Pettitte records the win, becoming the first pitcher to start and record the win in the clinching game in all three rounds of a single postseason. Manager Joe Girardi joins Billy Martin and Ralph Houk as the only Yankees to win a World Series with the club as a player and manager.

June 12-13, 2010 - Jorge Posada becomes the first Yankee since Bill Dickey (June 3, G2 - June 4, 1937) to hit grand slams in back-to-back games. He accomplishes the feat in 9-3 and 9-5 wins vs. Houston.

July 11 and 13, 2010 - Longtime Yankees P.A. announcer Bob Sheppard passes away at his home in Baldwin, Long Island, at age 99 and Yankees Principal Owner George M. Steinbrenner III passes away in Tampa, Fla. at age 80.

Aug. 4, 2010 - Alex Rodriguez becomes the seventh (and youngest) player in MLB history to hit his 600th HR, accomplishing the feat at 35 years, 8 days old in a 5-1 win vs. Toronto.

Sept. 20, 2010 - The Yankees dedicate a monument to Principal Owner George M. Steinbrenner III in Monument Park.

July 9, 2011 - Derek Jeter becomes the 28th player all time to record 3,000 hits, accomplishing the feat with a third-inning solo home run off David Price in a 5-4 win vs. Tampa Bay. He goes 5-for-5 on the day, matching his personal career high in hits.

July 30, 2011 - In Game 2 of a doubleheader vs. Baltimore, the Yankees score 12 first-inning runs in a 17-3 win, sending 16 men to the plate with 13 reaching base (seven singles, two doubles, 1HR, 2BB and 1E). All nine batters had at least 1H and 1R. The club sets a franchise record for most runs scored in the first inning in any game.

Aug. 25, 2011 - In a 22-9 win vs. Oakland, Robinson Cano, Russell Martin and Curtis Granderson each hit grand slams. The Yankees become the first MLB team to hit three grand slams in a single game.

Sept. 19, 2011 - Mariano Rivera records his 602nd career save, closing out a 6-4 win vs. Minnesota at Yankee Stadium to surpass Trevor Hoffman and become the all-time Major League leader.

Aug. 13-14, 2013 - Alfonso Soriano records 2HR and 6RBI then 2HR and 7RBI in consecutive games vs. Los Angeles-AL. He becomes just the third player all time since RBIs became official statistic in 1920 to record at least 6RBI in consecutive games.

Sept. 22 and 26, 2013 - The Yankees celebrate the career of Mariano Rivera with a 50-minute pregame ceremony, including the unveiling of his No. 42 in Monument Park and a live performance of "Enter Sandman" by Metallica. Four days later at Yankee Stadium, Rivera makes his final career appearance. He is removed from the game by longtime teammates Derek Jeter and Andy Pettitte, who come out of the dugout to make the pitching change.

Aug. 23, 2014 - The Yankees retire Joe Torre's No. 6.

Sept. 7, 2014 - The Yankees hold "Derek Jeter Day" in front of a sellout crowd of 48,110.

Sept. 25, 2014 - Derek Jeter plays his final game at Yankee Stadium, hitting a "walk-off" single to defeat Baltimore, 6-5, after closer David Robertson allows three runs in the top of the ninth to allow the Orioles to tie the score.

May 10, 2015 - Michael Pineda records 16K vs. Baltimore in just 7.0IP, becoming just the third pitcher in franchise history with at least 16K in a single game (LHP Guidry-18K and RHP Cone-16K).

May 24, 2015 - The Yankees retire Bernie Williams' No. 51.

Derek Jeter celebrates after hitting a walk-off single in his final career home game on Sept. 25, 2014.

June 19, 2015 - Alex Rodriguez records his 3,000th career hit with a solo HR off Detroit's Justin Verlander at Yankee Stadium.

Aug. 8-9, 2015 - The Yankees are shut out in consecutive games for the first time since 5/12-13/99, having played 2,665 games in between, ending the longest streak of not being shut out in consecutive games in MLB history.

Aug. 22-23, 2015 - The Yankees retire Jorge Posada's No. 20 and Andy Pettitte's No. 46 on consecutive days.

Oct. 1, 2015 - The Yankees record the 10,000th regular season win in franchise history, defeating Boston, 4-1, to clinch a postseason berth and the club's first-ever appearance in the AL Wild Card Game. They are the first AL club to reach the 10,000-win plateau, and — according to the *Elias Sports Bureau* — own the best winning pct. (.569) of any franchise at the time of its 10,000th win.

Aug. 13, 2016 - After the 1996 team was honored for its 20 anniversary in a pregame ceremony, Tyler Austin and Aaron Judge make their MLB debuts and hit back-to-back HRs in the second inning in their first career plate appearances. It marks the first time in MLB history that debuting teammates homered in the same game. There had been just one prior game in MLB history in which two players each hit HRs in their first career at-bats, but they were on opposing teams (on 4/19/38 at Shibe Park, the Phillies' Emmett "Heinie" Mueller and the Dodgers' Ernie Koy — both in the first inn.).

Aaron Judge [R] congratulates Tyler Austin after hitting the first of back-to-back HRs, each coming in their first career plate appearances on Aug. 13, 2016.

Aug. 14, 2016 - Mariano Rivera's Monument Park plaque is unveiled in a pregame ceremony.

Sept. 28, 2016 - Mark Teixeira hits his 409th and final career home run — a "walk-off" grand slam vs. Boston in a 5-3 Yankees win.

May 7, 2017 - The Yankees outlast the Cubs, 5-4, in 18 innings at Wrigley Field, as the teams combine for an all-time MLB high 48 strikeouts. Yankees pitchers tie the all-time single-game mark with 26K (third time in MLB history).

May 14, 2017 - In between games of a Mother's Day doubleheader vs. Houston, Derek Jeter's No. 2 is retired and his Monument Park plaque is unveiled.

Sept. 25, 2017 - In an 11-3 win vs. Kansas City, Aaron Judge hits his 49th and 50th home runs of the season, tying and breaking Mark McGwire's all-time MLB rookie home run mark (49HR in 1987).

Oct. 8, 2017 - In ALDS Game 3 vs. Cleveland, Greg Bird hits a solo HR to lead off the seventh, joining Jorge Posada (2001 ALDS G3 at Oakland, fifth inn.) and Tommy Henrich (1949 WS G1 vs. Brooklyn, ninth inn.) as the only Yankees to homer in 1-0 postseason wins.

Oct. 11, 2017 - The Yankees win ALDS Game 5 at Cleveland, 5-2, overturning a two-games-to-none deficit to win the series over the AL's winningest regular season team. Didi Gregorius drives in three runs with a first-inning solo HR and a third-inning HR in the third, both off AL Cy Young Award winner Corey Kluber.

Mar. 29, 2018 - Giancarlo Stanton makes his Yankees debut, going 3-for-5 with 1 double, 2HR and 4RBI at Toronto. He becomes just the second Yankee to homer twice in his first game with the club, joining Roger Maris (2HR on 4/19/60 at Boston). He also becomes the seventh Yankee to hit 2HR on Opening Day, the first since Joe Pepitone on 4/9/63 at the K.C. A's.

Apr. 3, 2018 - Didi Gregorius goes 4-for-4 with 1 double, 2HR, 1BB and 8BBI in Yankees' 11-4 home opener win vs. Tampa Bay, setting single-game franchise records for RBI by a shortstop, RBI by a Yankee in a home opener and RBI in the current Yankee Stadium.

May 6, 2018 - At 21 years, 144 days old, Gleyber Torres becomes the youngest Yankee in franchise history to hit a "walk-off" HR with a three-run shot in the ninth inning of a 7-4 win vs. Cleveland.

April 30, 2019: At Arizona's Chase Field, CC Sabathia fans former batterymate John Ryan Murphy for career strikeout No. 3,000 to become the 17th pitcher and third LHP to reach the milestone.

June 29-30, 2019 - The Yankees sweep Boston in a two-game series at England's London Stadium, the site of the 2012 Olympic Games, in the first two Major League games ever played in Europe. The Yankees emerge victorious in 17-13 and 12-8 slugfests.

September 27, 2019 - A day after the Minnesota Twins become the first team to hit 300HR in a season, the Yankees join them, as Giancarlo Stanton takes Texas' Joe Palumbo deep in the first inning of a 14-7 win at Globe Life Park. It is the first of six Yankees longballs that night, as the club finishes the season with a franchise-record 306 home runs, one shy of the Twins' Major League-record 307.

Lou Gehrig Appreciation Day - July 4, 1939

Prior to the Yankees' May 2, 1939, game at Detroit's Briggs Stadium, captain Lou Gehrig gave the umpires his team's lineup card — which did not have his name on it. He watched the entire game from the bench, marking the end of his 2,130-consecutive-games-played streak. "The Iron Horse" was suffering the effects of amyotrophic lateral sclerosis (ALS), a disease known since as Lou Gehrig's disease. He would never play again.

Just over two months later, on July 4, 1939, Lou Gehrig Appreciation Day was held in front of approximately 62,000 fans at Yankee Stadium. Ceremonies took place between games of a doubleheader against the Washington Senators. Gehrig and his teammates were joined by members of the 1927 Yankees. After speeches by Mayor Fiorello La Guardia and Postmaster James A. Farley, Manager Joe McCarthy said his public goodbye to Gehrig: "Lou, what can I say except that it was a sad day in the life of everybody who knew you when you came to my hotel room that day in Detroit and told me you were quitting as a ballplayer because you felt yourself a hindrance to the team. My God, man, you were never that."

Various gifts were presented to Gehrig from club employees and the rival New York Giants. His teammates gave him a trophy, which was inscribed with a poem by *New York Times* writer John Kieran. As the crowd chanted, "We want Lou; We want Lou…," Gehrig stepped to the microphone to deliver one of the most oft-quoted speeches in American history.

"For the past two weeks you've been reading about a bad break. Today I consider myself the luckiest man on the face of the Earth. I have been in ballparks for 17 years and have never received anything but kindness and encouragement from you fans.

"When you look around, wouldn't you consider it a privilege to associate yourself with such fine-looking men as are standing in uniform in this ballpark today? Sure, I'm lucky. Who wouldn't consider it an honor to have known Jacob Ruppert? Also, the builder of baseball's greatest empire, Ed Barrow? To have spent six years with such a grand little fellow as Miller Huggins? To have spent the next nine years with that smart student of psychology, the best manager in baseball today, Joe McCarthy? Who wouldn't feel honored to room with such a grand guy as Bill Dickey?

"When the New York Giants, a team you would give your right arm to beat, and vice versa, sends you a gift—that's something. When the groundskeepers and office staff and writers and old-timers and players and concessionaires all remember you with trophies—that's something. When you have a wonderful mother-in-law who takes sides with you in squabbles against her own daughter—that's something. When you have a father and a mother who work all their lives so that you can have an education and build your body—it's a blessing. When you have a wife who has been a tower of strength and shown more courage than you ever dreamed existed—that's the finest I know.

"So I close in saying that I might have been given a bad break, but I've got an awful lot to live for. Thank you."

On January 6, 1940, Yankees team president Ed Barrow announced that No. 4 would be retired from use. To this day, Gehrig remains the only Yankee ever to wear the number.

Gehrig died on June 2, 1941, at his home in the Riverdale section of the Bronx. He was 37.

Babe Ruth Day - April 27, 1947

On April 27, 1947, Babe Ruth Day was celebrated throughout Major League Baseball, as the Babe said goodbye in an on-field ceremony at Yankee Stadium. Dressed in a topcoat, Ruth, weakened by throat cancer, made the following remarks:

"Thank you very much, ladies and gentlemen. You know how bad my voice sounds—well it feels just as bad.

"You know this baseball game of ours comes up from the youth. That means the boys. And after you're a boy and grow up to know how to play ball, then you come to the boys you see representing themselves today in your national pastime. The only real game—I think—in the world is baseball.

"As a rule, some people think if you give them a football, or a baseball, or something like that—naturally they're athletes right away. But you can't do that in baseball. You've gotta start from way down [at] the bottom, when you're 6 or 7 years of age. You can't wait until you're 15 or 16. You gotta let it grow up with you. And if you're successful, and you try hard enough, you're bound to come out on top—just like these boys have come to the top now.

"There's been so many lovely things said about me, and I'm glad that I've had the opportunity to thank everybody. Thank you."

Ruth memorably returned to Yankee Stadium on June 13, 1948, to celebrate the 25th anniversary of Yankee Stadium and have his uniform No. 3 retired.

He died on August 16, 1948, at Memorial Hospital in New York at age 53. His body laid in state at the entrance of Yankee Stadium on Aug. 17 and 18, before his funeral on Aug. 19 at New York's St. Patrick's Cathedral.

George M. Steinbrenner III (1930-2010)

From 1973 until his passing on July 13, 2010, George M. Steinbrenner III created a legacy of winning unmatched by his peers. His foresight, drive and commitment permanently transformed not only the Yankees organization, but the game of Baseball.

On January 3, 1973, a group of businessmen formed and led by Mr. Steinbrenner purchased the New York Yankees from CBS for a net price of $8.7 million. It took just five years for his aggressive leadership to turn the organization back into World Champions. In his time as Principal Owner of the club (1973-2010), the Yankees won more pennants (11) and World Series (7) than any other team in baseball, while posting a Major League-best .566 winning percentage (3,364-2,583-3 record) over the stretch.

In addition to the team's on-field success under the direction of Mr. Steinbrenner, the New York Yankees consistently shattered franchise and league attendance records at home and on the road. In 2009, they drew 3,719,358 fans in their first season of play in the current Yankee Stadium, topping the American League in attendance for the seventh straight season (2003-09). The Yankees remain the only franchise in Baseball history to draw more than 4 million fans at home in four consecutive seasons (2005-08).

Mr. Steinbrenner's foresight in both sports and business continued to build the value and prominence of the franchise, positioning it for the future. In 2002, *Sporting News* named him the No. 1 "Most Powerful Man in Sports," and *Forbes* magazine has continued to list the Yankees as the most valuable franchise in all of Baseball.

Mr. Steinbrenner's vision led to the creation of YankeeNets, which owned the New Jersey Nets and New Jersey Devils and ultimately led to the launch of the YES Network, a trailblazing enterprise that has been the nation's most watched regional sports network since 2003. Additionally, Mr. Steinbrenner teamed with long-time friend and Dallas Cowboys owner Jerry Jones, creating Legends Hospitality, LLC, a concession and merchandising company which currently operates at the Yankees' and Cowboys' new stadiums.

In 2006, his participation in the groundbreaking ceremony for the new Yankee Stadium underscored his role as the principal impetus in moving the much-anticipated facility towards its opening in 2009.

Mr. Steinbrenner's tenure of over 37 years exceeded that of any other New York Yankees owner by 13 years (Colonel Jacob Ruppert purchased the Yankees with Tillinghast L'Hommedieu Huston in January 1915, bought out Huston in 1923, and maintained sole ownership in the club until his death in January 1939—a total of 24 years). During Mr. Steinbrenner's time as the sole Principal Owner of the Yankees, the other 29 Major League clubs had over 100 owners or ownership groups.

Mr. Steinbrenner's success in the sports world began at an early age. He was a multi-sport athlete at Culver Military Academy (where he is in the Athletic Hall of Fame) and at Williams College. He began his successful coaching career as an assistant football coach at two Big Ten universities, Northwestern and Purdue. Then he assembled championship basketball teams in the National Industrial and American Basketball Leagues. In 2002, he was honored with the prestigious Gold Medal Award from the National Football Foundation and College Hall of Fame for a lifetime of "outstanding commitment, dedication and dynamic leadership in his business, as well as his personal life."

Mr. Steinbrenner devoted as much time and effort to the U.S. Olympic Committee (USOC) as he did to his many other sporting endeavors. He was on the U.S. Olympic Foundation Board from 1986-2002 and served as Chairman over the last six years of his tenure. He also was Chairman of the 1989 Olympic Overview Commission, which was created to evaluate the structure and efforts of the U.S. Olympic program, and served as Vice President of the USOC from 1989 to 1992. As a result of his distinguished service, he was presented with the General Douglas MacArthur USOC Foremost Award and the F. Don Miller United States Olympic Award. In 2005, the U.S. Olympic Foundation created the George M. Steinbrenner Sports Leadership Award in his honor, which celebrates a member of the U.S. Olympic family who has made outstanding contributions to sport.

Additionally, Mr. Steinbrenner was a member of the Baseball Hall of Fame's Board of Directors and served on the NCAA Foundation Board of Trustees beginning in 1990.

Most of Mr. Steinbrenner's philanthropic endeavors were performed without fanfare. However, he was repeatedly recognized by the communities in which he immersed himself. In 1993, he earned the Tampa Civitan Club's "Outstanding Citizen" Award, and in 1998, Tampa Law Enforcement named him "Citizen of the Year" for founding a scholarship fund for the children of slain law enforcement officers. Mr. Steinbrenner was also honored as an "Outstanding New Yorker" by the N.Y. Society of Association Executives in 1997 and credited in 2009 by the Museum of the City of New York as one of the "New York City 400," recognizing "people who have helped create the world's greatest city since its founding in 1609."

In February 2008, the Tampa City Council and the Board of the Hillsborough County Commissioner's Office both passed resolutions endorsing the renaming of Legends Field in Tampa after Mr. Steinbrenner to pay tribute to his numerous contributions to the area. On March 27, 2008, Mr. Steinbrenner—joined by his family—pulled down a curtain draped above the outfield scoreboard to unveil the new name for the Yankees' spring training home: George M. Steinbrenner Field.

In the fall of 2009, George M. Steinbrenner High School opened in Lutz, Fla. The school was named after Mr. Steinbrenner by the Hillsborough County School Board in recognition of his philanthropic involvement in the community, particularly with the school system.

Mr. Steinbrenner was dually honored in January 2011, winning the Joan Payson Community Service Award from the New York chapter of the BBWAA and having his legacy of charitable work recognized at the 22nd annual Baseball Assistance Team (B.A.T.) Dinner.

At the time of his passing, he was survived by his wife, Joan; sisters, Susan Norpell and Judy Kamm; children, Hank, Hal, Jennifer and Jessica; and his grandchildren.

On September 20, 2010, prior to the team's game vs. Tampa Bay, the Yankees unveiled a monument in Mr. Steinbrenner's honor in Monument Park, reflecting the special connection, appreciation and responsibility that he felt toward Yankees fans.

GEORGE M. STEINBRENNER III
JULY 4, 1930 – JULY 13, 2010

New York Yankees Principal Owner
"The Boss"
1973 - 2010

Purchased the New York Yankees on January 3, 1973. A true visionary who changed the game of baseball forever, he was considered the most influential owner in all of sports. In his 37 years as Principal Owner, the Yankees posted a Major League-best .566 winning percentage, while winning 11 American League pennants and seven World Series titles, becoming the most recognizable sports brand in the world.

A devoted sportsman, he was Vice President of the United States Olympic Committee, a member of the Baseball Hall of Fame's Board of Directors and a member of the NCAA Foundation Board of Trustees.

A great philanthropist whose charitable efforts were mostly performed without fanfare, he followed a personal motto of the greatest form of charity is anonymity.

Dedicated by the New York Yankees
September 20, 2010

Chronology of Yankees Ownership

Jan. 9, 1903:	Frank Farrell and Bill Devery purchase the rights to establish a new American League franchise in New York for $18,000.
Jan. 11, 1915:	Col. Jacob Ruppert and Col. Tillinghast L'Hommedieu Huston agree to purchase the Yankees for $460,000. The transfer is formally completed on January 30.
May 21, 1923:	Col. Ruppert buys out Col. Huston for $1.5 million (transfer is completed on June 1).
Jan. 13, 1939:	Col. Ruppert passes away and his estate takes over ownership of the club.
Jan. 25, 1945:	Dan Topping, Del Webb and Larry MacPhail purchase the Yankees for $2.8 million from the estate of the late Col. Ruppert (Topping and Webb later buy out MacPhail's share following the 1947 season).
Nov. 2, 1964:	CBS purchases 80 pct. of the Yankees for $11.2 million and later buys the remaining 20 percent (Webb sells his 10 pct. share in March 1965 and Topping sells his 10 pct. share in September 1966).
Jan. 3, 1973:	A limited partnership, headed by George M. Steinbrenner as its Managing General Partner, purchases the Yankees from CBS for a net price of $8.7 million.
Nov. 20, 2008:	Hal Steinbrenner named Managing General Partner.

Bob Sheppard - "The Voice of Yankee Stadium"

Bob Sheppard will forever be the "The Voice of Yankee Stadium." With his instantly recognizable elocution — in which each syllable was given meticulous attention — Sheppard provided a soundtrack of irreproachable dignity to Yankee Stadium for 57 years.

Sadly, he passed away on July 11, 2010, at his home in Baldwin, N.Y., with his wife, Mary, by his side. He was 99 years old.

Born in Ridgewood, Queens, Sheppard began his tenure as Yankees public address announcer on April 17, 1951—Opening Day of Joe DiMaggio's final season and the day of Mickey Mantle's Major League debut. Among the approximately 4,500 baseball games he worked over his tenure with the Yankees were 121 consecutive postseason contests from 1951 to 2006, including 62 games in 22 World Series.

Sheppard's incredible career behind the microphone started when he volunteered his services for a charity football game in Freeport, Long Island, in the late 1940s. An executive from the Brooklyn Dodgers football team of the All-America Conference was at the game. He liked Sheppard's style ("clear, concise and correct") and hired him. The football Dodgers folded after just one season at Ebbets Field (1948), but one of their opponents—the New York football Yankees—heard Sheppard's booming voice and offered him their PA job at Yankee Stadium. Baseball's Yankees discovered him as a result and offered him their PA role for the 1950 season. Though he turned down their offer due to conflicts with his teaching schedule, he changed his mind the following year.

In addition to his baseball duties, Sheppard was the public address voice for the New York football Giants for 50 seasons—from their move to Yankee Stadium in 1956 until his retirement after the 2005 season. Sheppard also served the New York Titans of the American Football League at the Polo Grounds, the New York Stars of the World Football League at Downing Stadium, the New York Cosmos soccer team, and St. John's University's basketball and football teams. Sheppard also handled PA duties for five Army-Navy football games in Philadelphia.

Some of the events he listed as the most memorable of his incredible career were: Don Larsen's perfect game in Game 5 of the 1956 World Series on October 8, 1956; Roger Maris' 61st home run on October 1, 1961; Reggie Jackson's three home runs in Game 6 of the World Series on October 18, 1977; and the Giants-Colts overtime NFL Championship Game on December 28, 1958.

Sheppard attended St. John's College, which eventually became St. John's University. Always a talented athlete, he received a full athletic scholarship to the school, playing quarterback on the football team all four years. He later enrolled at Columbia University, where he received his master's degree in speech and worked his way up from teacher-in-training to substitute teacher to permanent teacher to department chairman. In order to supplement his teaching salary, Sheppard played semiprofessional football on Sundays in Long Island with the Valley Stream Red Riders and the Hempstead Monitors, earning $25 a game.

In 1998, Sheppard was presented with the prestigious William J. Slocum "Long and Meritorious Service" Award by the New York chapter of the BBWAA as well as the "Pride of the Yankees" award by the ballclub.

On May 7, 2000, a plaque was dedicated to Sheppard in Monument Park of the original Yankee Stadium to commemorate his 50th anniversary season. Additionally, the Yankee Stadium media dining room was named "Sheppard's Place" prior to the 2009 season to commemorate his legacy.

The native New Yorker was elected to the St. John's University Sports Hall of Fame, the Long Island Sports Hall of Fame and the New York Sports Hall of Fame.

He was awarded honorary doctorates from St. John's University (Pedagogy) and Fordham University (Rhetoric), and in 2007, received St. John's' Medal of Honor, the highest award that the university can confer on a graduate.

Sheppard also made cameo appearances in numerous motion pictures and television shows, including 61*, It's My Turn, It Could Happen to You, For Love of the Game, Anger Management, Seinfeld and Mad About You.

Sheppard announced his final game at Yankee Stadium on September 5, 2007, a 3-2 Yankees victory over the Seattle Mariners.

On Sept. 21, 2008, Sheppard provided a valedictory in the bottom of the seventh inning of the final game at the original Yankee Stadium. Unable to say goodbye in person as he continued to recover from an illness that had kept him away from the Stadium since the final weeks of the 2007 season, Sheppard gave his tribute through a taped segment which played on the video board. He recited, "Farewell, old Yankee Stadium, farewell / What a wonderful story you can tell / DiMaggio, Mantle, Gehrig and Ruth / A baseball cathedral in truth."

BOB SHEPPARD'S FIRST LINEUP CARD April 17, 1951	
Boston Red Sox	**New York Yankees**
Dom DiMaggio, CF	Jackie Jensen, LF
Billy Goodman, RF	*Phil Rizzuto, SS
*Ted Williams, LF	*Mickey Mantle, RF
Vern Stephens, 3B	*Joe DiMaggio, CF
Walt Dropo, 1B	*Yogi Berra, C
*Bobby Doerr, 2B	*Johnny Mize, 1B
*Lou Boudreau, SS	Billy Johnson, 3B
Buddy Rosar, C	Jerry Coleman, 2B
Billy Wight, P	Vic Raschi, P
*Member of Baseball Hall of Fame	

Voices Before Sheppard

Not even Bob Sheppard himself could remember who preceded him as Yankee Stadium's public address announcer. Surprisingly, the history of Sheppard's predecessors at the microphone — or, earlier, the megaphone — spanned four decades and three ballparks before Sheppard's first game on April 17, 1951. The lineage extends to Hilltop Park in 1910, when the Yankees were commonly called the "Highlanders." On June 11, *Sporting Life* noted a new method of announcing the starting batteries. Writer E.H. Simmons described an unnamed scorecard vendor with a "deep, carrying voice" shouting the names through a megaphone at the start of each game.

In 1913, the Yankees began playing their home games at the Polo Grounds, which was also home to the New York Giants. Jack Lenz and George Levy debuted as announcers for both teams two years later. When Yankee Stadium opened in 1923, Levy continued working with the Giants while Lenz carried his megaphone to the Bronx. "I grabbed the offer," Lenz recalled in 1935. "Who wouldn't, with the old Bambino holding forth at the Stadium?"

Lenz's game-day duties began with receiving the starting lineups from the managers of both teams 15 minutes before the first pitch. After delivering a copy of each lineup to the umpire, Lenz relayed the "necessary dope" to writers in the press box via telephone. He then raised his megaphone and announced the batting orders and batteries — first toward the bleachers, then to the upper tiers of the grandstand, and finally to the lower stands. During games, Lenz occupied Field Box 133 adjacent to the Yankees dugout. He broadcasted each batter's name only once, prior to the first plate appearance by each respective player. Lenz also announced lineup changes made throughout the game.

Lenz became a fixture at Yankee Stadium. Fans chuckled at his occasional malapropisms, such as advertising a doubleheader as "two games for the price of one omission." The *New York Evening Journal* praised Lenz as "the mild-mannered megaphone man" upon announcing his 2,000th game in 1933. Lenz set aside his megaphone to inaugurate Yankee Stadium's public address system during Game 3 of the 1936 World Series.

George Levy occasionally joined Lenz at the Stadium. In 1927, Lenz and Levy announced the Opening Day lineups to the 72,000 fans as part of a "two-ply announcer system." Levy replaced Lenz as Yankee Stadium's official announcer by 1939 and was likely responsible for a famous gaffe made on May 31, 1946.

"Will the spectators in the front row boxes please remove their clothing…," Levy began, only to have the second half of the request ("from the front railing") obscured by the crowd's laughter.

Al Frazin served as Yankee Stadium's public address announcer from 1947 through 1950. Frazin, a longtime announcer at Madison Square Garden, handled P.A. duties in the 1930s for the pro football Brooklyn Dodgers, who were owned by future Yankees co-owner Dan Topping. Frazin served in the U.S. Army during World War II and was recalled into active military service in August 1950.

Research indicates that Yankees public relations director Arthur "Red" Patterson handled public address duties immediately prior to Bob Sheppard's debut in 1951. Patterson likely filled Al Frazin's vacated position through the 1950 World Series.

Jack Lenz

Current Yankees Public Address Announcer Paul Olden

On April 15, 2009, the Yankees announced that Paul Olden would assume full-time duties as Yankee Stadium public address announcer, replacing the iconic Bob Sheppard. Olden, a 12-time Super Bowl public address announcer (1994-2005), first manned the Yankees booth during the team's workout day on April 2. He also worked the team's first-ever Stadium exhibition games vs. Chicago-NL on April 3-4.

Sheppard, the Yankees PA announcer since 1951, had been suffering from a bronchial infection and was last able to perform his role on September 5, 2007. His longtime backup, Jim Hall, handled PA responsibilities in 2008.

Olden had a long broadcasting career prior to taking the Yankees PA position, including three seasons in the Yankees television broadcast booth from 1994-96 alongside Phil Rizzuto and Bobby Murcer. He also called games on the radio for the Tampa Bay Devil Rays (1998-2004), California Angels (1991), and Cleveland Indians (1988-89), as well as for the NFL's New York Jets (1993-96) and Los Angeles Rams (1991-92).

Previously, Olden did fill-in radio work with the NBA's New Jersey Nets (1995-96) and MLB's Angels (1989-90, '92). He was also a full-time radio broadcaster for UCLA's basketball and football teams (1989-1992) and worked for The Football Network (2003), FOX SportsNet LA (1997) and ESPN (1991-92), calling Major League Baseball and college football.

Olden's other prior PA work included the NCAA's Outback Bowl from 2002-05 and USC Trojans baseball from 1972-76. He also did on-air radio work for KPMC and KNX in Los Angeles.

Born in Chicago and raised in L.A., Olden attended Los Angeles City College and Los Angeles Valley College (2006-08). He was presented with a New York Emmy Award for best local sports coverage in 1994 for his work on Yankees telecasts.

The 1927 Yankees - "Murderers' Row"

Many baseball writers and historians consider the 1927 Yankees the greatest baseball team of all time. With a lineup known as Murderers' Row, the Yankees marched to a 110-44 regular season record, leading the AL from wire-to-wire and finishing ahead of the second-place Philadelphia A's by 19.0 games. The club featured seven Hall of Famers in uniform (outfielders Babe Ruth and Earle Combs, first baseman Lou Gehrig, second baseman Tony Lazzeri, pitchers Waite Hoyt and Herb Pennock, and manager Miller Huggins). Additionally, the team was constructed by an eighth Hall-of-Famer (general manager Ed Barrow) and owned by a ninth (Jacob Ruppert).

Ruth had his signature season, hitting 60 home runs, including 17 in September. With his final blast of the year off the Washington Senators' Tom Zachary, he surpassed his own single-season record of 59 set in 1921. Ruth also led the Majors in on-base pct. (.486), slugging pct. (.772), runs (158), walks (137) and strikeouts (89).

Hitting behind Ruth in the clean-up spot, Gehrig won the AL MVP Award, batting .373 with 173 RBI, 117 extra-base hits and 447 total bases. While this marked Gehrig's breakout season, his winning the award had a lot to do with the rules of the time, which prohibited a repeat winner (Ruth had won in 1923). Nevertheless Gehrig's totals for extra-base hits, total bases and RBI are the second-highest, third-highest and tied for the fourth-highest, respectively, in a single season in Baseball history.

As a club, the Yankees led the Majors in almost every offensive category, including runs (975), triples (103), home runs (158), walks (642), batting avg. (.307), on-base pct. (.384) and slugging pct. (.488). Ruth and Gehrig alone tallied 107 combined homers, just two shy of the New York Giants, who had the second-most as a team in the Majors.

For all the attention that the hitters received, the pitchers were every bit as good. They led the Majors with a 3.20 combined ERA and allowed the third-fewest walks (409) and homers (42) among the Majors' 16 teams. They tossed 82 complete games (second in the AL) and led their league with 11 shutouts.

The group was paced by Hoyt, who had the best overall season of his career, going 22-7 with a 2.64 ERA and tying for the AL lead in wins. Urban Shocker, a four-time former 20-game winner with the St. Louis Browns, went 18-6 with a 2.84 ERA, while dealing with a mitral valve disorder that forced him to sleep sitting up and contributed to his death the following year.

Even though most people use the term "Murderers' Row" to refer to the 1927 Yankees [pictured above], the nickname was first applied to the club by pundits in 1918.

The biggest surprise on the staff was Wilcy Moore—a player recommended to Barrow in 1926 by "bird dog" scout Jack Walsh (popular legend holds that Barrow discovered Moore while reading minor league statistics in *The Sporting News*). Moore became a spot starter as well as the Yankees' principal all-purpose relief pitcher, tossing 213.0 innings (93.0 as a starter, 120.0 as a reliever), going 19-7 with a Major League-leading 2.28 ERA.

The Yankees capped off their season with a four-game World Series sweep of Pittsburgh, outscoring the Pirates 23-10. Ruth hit the only two homers of the Series and Moore tossed a complete game in the clincher.

Lineup	(Typical Batting Order)	BA	G	AB	R	H	2B	3B	HR	RBI	BB
CF	Earle Combs (L)	.356	152	648	137	231	36	23	6	65	63
SS	Mark Koenig (S)	.285	123	526	99	150	20	11	3	62	25
RF/LF	Babe Ruth (L)	.356	151	540	158	192	29	8	60	164	137
1B	Lou Gehrig (L)	.373	155	584	149	218	52	18	47	175	109
LF/RF	Bob Meusel	.337	135	516	75	174	47	9	8	103	45
2B	Tony Lazzeri	.309	153	570	92	176	29	8	18	102	69
3B	Joe Dugan	.269	112	387	44	104	24	3	2	43	27
C	Pat Collins	.275	92	251	38	69	9	3	7	36	54
Reserves		BA	G	AB	R	H	2B	3B	HR	RBI	BB
2B	Ray Morehart (L)	.256	73	194	45	50	7	2	1	20	29
C	Johnny Grabowski	.277	70	195	29	54	6	4	0	25	20
OF	Cedric Durst (L)	.248	65	129	18	32	4	3	0	25	6
SS-3B	Mike Gazella	.278	54	115	17	32	6	4	0	9	23
OF	Ben Paschal	.317	50	82	16	26	9	2	2	16	4
3B	Julie Wera	.238	38	42	7	10	3	0	1	8	1
C	Benny Bengough	.247	31	85	6	21	3	3	0	10	4
Team Totals		.307	155	5354	975	1644	291	103	158	907	642

Pitchers		W-L	ERA	G	GS	CG	IP	H	R	ER	BB	SO
SP	Waite Hoyt	22-7	2.64	36	32	23	256.0	242	90	75	54	86
SP	Herb Pennock (L)	19-8	3.00	34	26	18	210.0	222	89	70	49	51
SP	Urban Shocker	18-6	2.84	31	27	13	200.0	207	86	63	38	35
SP	Dutch Ruether (L)	13-6	3.38	27	26	12	184.0	202	86	69	52	45
SP	George Pipgras	10-3	4.12	29	21	9	166.0	148	81	76	77	80
SP/RP	Wilcy Moore	19-7	2.28	50	12	6	213.0	185	68	54	61	75
SP/RP	Myles Thomas	7-4	4.85	21	9	1	89.0	109	54	48	43	25
RP	Bob Shawkey	2-3	2.86	19	2	0	44.0	44	19	14	16	23
RP	Joe Giard (L)	0-0	8.00	16	0	0	27.0	38	25	24	19	10
RP	Walter Beall	0-0	9.00	1	0	0	1.0	1	1	1	0	0
Team Totals		110-44	3.20	155	155	82	1390.0	1398	599	494	409	431

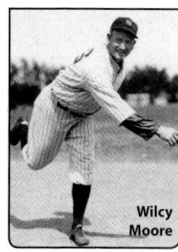

Babe Ruth

Wilcy Moore

"Culmination of a Dynasty" - The 1939 Yankees

In a year that the American and National Leagues celebrated the 100th anniversary of the mythologized creation of baseball, the 1939 Yankees overwhelmed opponents with flawless execution and a balanced attack of pitching, defense and clutch hitting. The club tallied 106 regular season victories before taking four straight from Cincinnati to win the last of four consecutive World Series championships.

Discipline and intensity formed the bedrock of the club's success. Talented young stars—harvested from baseball's most fertile farm system—adopted their veteran teammates' no-nonsense attitude. Manager Joe McCarthy even banned card playing, smoking and radio playing from the team's clubhouse.

The season began with concern over Lou Gehrig's declining on-field performance. His severely diminished skills mystified teammates and sportswriters. The ailing first baseman batted just .143 through the first eight regular season games before benching himself on May 2 to end his streak of 2,130 consecutive games played.

Babe Dahlgren assumed first base duties, and the Yankees hit their stride in May. The team soon made a mockery of the American League pennant race, winning 28-of-32 games through June 4, including a 12-game winning streak. On June 26, the Yankees played the first night game in franchise history at Philadelphia's Shibe Park. Two days later they launched 13 home runs in a doubleheader sweep of the A's (by scores of 23-2 and 10-0).

"It hardly seems necessary to say that the Yankees appear headed for their fourth straight pennant," wrote Richards Vidmer in the *Herald Tribune*. "They have everything that a championship club needs, from pitching to power, defensive skill, leadership and a fine balance of youth and experience."

Indeed, the team's success stemmed from this potent blend. The Yankees scored 967 runs and surrendered 556. The 411 run differential remains a modern era (since 1900) record.

On July 4, a reported 61,808 spectators packed Yankee Stadium for ceremonies honoring Lou Gehrig. The team captain had been diagnosed with Amyotrophic Lateral Sclerosis (ALS), a terminal illness now commonly called "Lou Gehrig's Disease." The honoree stood silently, with head bowed, through speeches and gift presentations. When he finally addressed the crowd, Gehrig uttered one of the most famous declarations ever made on a baseball field, calling himself "the luckiest man on the face of the Earth." He concluded by offering that "I might have been given a bad break, but I've got an awful lot to live for."

Just one week later, Yankee Stadium hosted the seventh annual All-Star Game on July 11. McCarthy managed an AL starting lineup that included six Yankees—Red Ruffing (P), Bill Dickey (C), Joe Gordon (2B), Red Rolfe (3B), George Selkirk (LF) and Joe DiMaggio (CF). Gehrig served as honorary captain in the AL's 3-1 victory.

Standout performances powered McCarthy's winning machine in 1939. Dickey (.302, 24HR, 105RBI) had a .403 on-base percentage, and Rolfe (.329, 14HR, 80RBI) paced the AL in runs scored (139), hits (213), and doubles (46), while fielding every inning of every game at third base. Gordon (.284, 28HR, 111RBI) was an All-Star in his second big league season, and rookie outfielder Charlie Keller (.334, 11HR, 83RBI) posted what would be his highest career single-season average. Selkirk (.306, 21HR, 101RBI) scored 103 runs in just 128 games.

Red Ruffing led the staff with a 21-7 mark and posted a 2.93 ERA despite an ailing arm. Six other pitchers each won between 10 and 13 games on an evenly-worked staff that led the AL with a 3.31 ERA and had only two pitchers start more than 20 games or toss more than 154 innings (Ruffing-28GS/233.1IP and Lefty Gomez-26GS/198.0IP).

Of all the 1939 Yankees, Joe DiMaggio's star shone the brightest. Despite a torn leg muscle early in the season, the graceful center fielder batted an AL-best .381 (176-for-462) with 30 home runs and 126 RBI in 120 games, earning his "Yankee Clipper" nickname from radio broadcaster Arch McDonald along the way. With 53 RBI in August, he is one of just two players in MLB history to reach the total in any single calendar month (also the Cubs' Hack Wilson, Aug. 1930). Though DiMaggio's batting average hovered above the .400 mark into early September, a late-season eye infection triggered a September dip. Nonetheless, he went on to earn the first of three career AL MVP Awards (also 1941 and '47).

The Yankees clinched the AL pennant on Sept. 16 and completed the regular season with a 106-45 record. In the World Series, they dispensed with the Reds in Games 1 and 2 at Yankee Stadium in contests timed at 93 and 87 minutes, respectively. On the road at Crosley Field in Game 3, the Bronx Bombers launched four homers, and in Game 4, the Yankees won on "Lombardi's Snooze," with Charlie Keller crashing into Reds catcher Ernie Lombardi and rendering him temporarily immobile. This allowed three runs to cross the plate in the 10th inning in a 7-4 win, giving the Yankees their eighth Series title.

"One can write of these powerful, amazing Yankees only in superlatives," penned veteran sportswriter Fred Lieb at the end of the season. "They have accomplished feats which only a year ago would have been considered unbelievable.... They have come closer to perfection than any other club in the first 100 years of baseball. Perhaps in another 100 years the feats of this team will have become legendary. Fans still unborn, thumbing through the records of this decade, will ask: 'Could a team have been that good?'"

Lou Gehrig holds court in the Yankees home dugout on June 21, 1939, approximately one month after his final game. [From L to R]: Gehrig, second baseman Joe Gordon, pitcher Lefty Gomez, catcher Bill Dickey and coach Johnny Schulte.

Top Row: Bill Dickey, Red Ruffing, Joe DiMaggio, Oral Hildebrand, Steve Sundra, Paul Schreiber, Johnny Murphy, Lefty Gomez, Atley Donald, Tommy Henrich, Art Jorgens. **Middle Row:** Joe Gordon, Bump Hadley, Monte Pearson, Marius Russo, Lou Gehrig (Capt.), George Selkirk, Bill Knickerbocker, Erle "Doc" Painter (Trainer). **Front Row:** Buddy Rosar, Charlie Keller, Spud Chandler, Jake Powell, Art Fletcher (Coach), Joe McCarthy (Mgr.), Earle Combs (Coach), Johnny Schulte (Coach), Red Rolfe, Babe Dahlgren, Frank Crosetti. **Seated on Ground:** Tim Sullivan (batboy).

The 1961 Yankees and Roger Maris' 61-Home Run Season

The 1961 Yankees are considered to be among the greatest teams of all time. Led by Roger Maris, who broke Babe Ruth's all-time single-season home run mark, the club powered their way to the 19th World Series championship in franchise history.

The Yankees finished the regular season with a 109-53 (.673) record, eight games ahead of the 101-61 (.623) Detroit Tigers. The clubs were just 1.5 games apart in the standings heading into the final full month of the season before the Yankees reeled off a 13-game winning streak from Sept. 1-12 to vault an insurmountable 11.5 games in front. Their massive win total was fueled by a 65-16 mark at Yankee Stadium, the best single-season home record in Major League history.

The Yankees had sluggers up and down the lineup, including Moose Skowron (28 HR), Yogi Berra (22 HR), Elston Howard (21 HR) and "Super-sub" Johnny Blanchard, who hit 21 homers in just 243 at-bats. Of the 240 home runs the Yankees hit, 10 were pinch-hit homers, setting a still-standing single-season franchise mark.

The pitching staff was paced by Whitey Ford, who had a career year, going 25-4 with a 3.21 ERA. Under first-year manager Ralph Houk, Ford took the ball every fourth day for the first time in his career and set career highs in wins, winning percentage (.862), starts (39) and innings pitched (283.0), earning the Cy Young Award as the best pitcher in both leagues. Bill Stafford (14-9, 2.68 ERA), Ralph Terry (16-3, 3.15 ERA) and Rollie Sheldon (11-5, 3.60 ERA) were the Yankees' other top starters, and Luis Arroyo picked up 15 wins in relief, the highest total by a reliever in franchise history.

In the World Series, the Yankees triumphed over Cincinnati, 4-games-to-1, as Ford tossed 14.0 combined scoreless innings, earning wins in Game 1 and 4. With the Series knotted at one game apiece, Game 3 proved pivotal. Down, 2-1, heading into the eighth, Blanchard tied the game with a solo homer before Maris hit a game-winning solo shot in the ninth. The Yankees then outscored the Reds 20-5 over the final two contests to win the first of two consecutive World Series titles.

Much of the season's drama centered on the chase by the M&M Boys — Roger Maris and Mickey Mantle — to break Ruth's seemingly untouchable single-season record of 60 home runs, which he set with the 1927 Yankees. Maris, the American League MVP in 1960 and 1961, was joined in his pursuit by Mantle, who topped out at 54 home runs after sitting out seven of the club's final 10 games with an abscess in his right hip.

Maris tied Ruth's mark on Sept. 26 at Yankee Stadium with a home run off Baltimore's Jack Fisher in the team's 159th game of the season. Needing one homer to break the record with four games to go (the Yankees had played a tie earlier in the year), Maris was given a full game off prior to going homerless in the first two games of a three-game series against Boston at Yankee Stadium.

In the season's final game on Oct. 1, Maris connected in the fourth inning off Tracy Stallard, hitting a line-drive into the right-field stands for his 61st home run, which turned out to be the only run in a 1-0 Yankees victory. The quiet and humble Maris had to be pushed back onto the field by his teammates for his curtain call.

The chase was not without controversy as writers and fans loyal to Ruth clamored that the record should receive a special notation given that the American League was playing a 162-game schedule in 1961 due to the addition of two expansion teams. With the exceptions of 1901-03 and 1918-19, the AL had always played a 154-game format.

Ford Frick, a former sportswriter and New York City sportscaster who had previously ghostwritten Ruth's 1928 autobiography *Babe Ruth's Own Book of Baseball*, was the commissioner of baseball at the time. In the middle of the season, he issued the directive that baseball's official record book, *The Little Red Book of Major League Baseball*, compiled by the *Elias Sports Bureau*, should show two records — one for a 154-game schedule and another for a 162-game schedule. Contrary to popular lore, an asterisk was never used for the notation, and separate designations remained in the official record book until 1991, when Major League Baseball finally rescinded the distinction.

Maris' 61 in 1961 remains the highest single-season home run total in American League history and the seventh-highest single-season total all time, behind those of Barry Bonds (73), Mark McGwire (70, 65) and Sammy Sosa (66, 64 and 63).

Roger Maris hits his 61st home run of the season on Oct. 1, 1961 at Yankee Stadium.

Top Row: Bobby Richardson, Al Downing, Luis Arroyo, John Blanchard, Bill Stafford, Rollie Sheldon, Jim Coates, Spud Murray (Batting Practice Pitcher), Bud Daley, Bruce Henry (Traveling Secretary). **Middle Row:** Gus Mauch (Trainer), Billy Gardner, Bob Hale, Joe DeMaestri, Tony Kubek, Tex Clevenger, Ralph Terry, Hector Lopez, Bob Cerv, Elston Howard, Roger Maris, Bob Turley, Joe Soares (Trainer). **Front Row:** Whitey Ford, Bill Skowron, Hal Reniff, Jim Hegan, Frank Crosetti, Ralph Houk, John Sain, Wally Moses, Earl Torgeson, Clete Boyer, Yogi Berra, Mickey Mantle. **Seated on Ground:** Batboys Frank Prudenti, Fred Bengis.

The 1998 Yankees - "Most Wins in a Single Season"

The 1998 Yankees were one of the most dominant teams in Major League baseball history. Despite starting the season with a three-game losing streak and dropping four of their first five, they proceeded to go 64-16 dating from their sixth game of the year, marking the best single-season 80-game run in franchise history.

Ultimately, the Yankees finished the regular season 114-48 (.704) and won the AL East by 22.0 games, marking the third-largest margin of any league or division winner in Major League history, behind only Cleveland in 1995 (+30.0) and Pittsburgh in 1902 (+27.5). Their regular season winning percentage trailed only the 1927 Murderers' Row team (.714) for the best in franchise history, and their 125-50 overall record, including the postseason, marks the most single-season wins by any team all time.

The 1998 club excelled at every facet of the game, leading the American League in runs scored (965), runs per game (5.96), on-base percentage (.364), fewest runs per game allowed (4.05) and ERA (3.82). They ranked second in stolen bases (153) and tallied the league's third-fewest errors (98). Five members of the club (Scott Brosius, Derek Jeter, Paul O'Neill, David Wells and Bernie Williams) were named to the AL All-Star team.

The club fielded a remarkably balanced lineup as 10 different batters hit at least 10 home runs, with no player hitting more than 28. Additionally, the 1998 club became the first team all time to have eight players hit at least 17 home runs in a single season.

Second baseman Chuck Knoblauch was the team's leadoff hitter (.265 BA, 117R, 17HR, 64RBI), after being acquired from Minnesota for four players just before the start of spring training. He was followed in the second spot by Jeter, who batted .324 (203-for-626) in posting the first of his eight career 200-hit seasons. The future captain led the AL with 127 runs scored while making his first All-Star team.

O'Neill, Williams and Tino Martinez were the Yankees principal 3-4-5 hitters, though Martinez batted cleanup for stretches, including when Williams was on the disabled list with a sprained right knee from June 11 - July 18. O'Neill, in his sixth year with the club after parts of eight seasons with Cincinnati, batted .317 (191-for-602) with 40 doubles, 24HR and 116RBI, setting career highs in hits and runs scored (95). Williams won his only career batting title, posting a .339 (169-for-499) mark with 26HR, 97RBI and a .422 on-base percentage. He also won a Gold Glove for his play in centerfield.

Martinez led the club with 123RBI and solidified the defense at first base. On the opposite corner, Scott Brosius had a career year, batting .300 (159-for-530) with 19HR and 98RBI, making his only All-Star team. The catching duties were split between Jorge Posada (.268 BA, 17HR and 63RBI in 111 games) in his first year as the first-string backstop and Joe Girardi (.276 BA in 78 games).

One of the hallmarks of the club was its depth. Darryl Strawberry hit 24 home runs in just 295 at-bats and Tim Raines put up a .395 on-base percentage in 109 games. Rookie Shane Spencer lit up the Bronx with 10 homers in 67 at-bats, including eight after being called up in September and seven in the Yankees' last 11 games of the season. The bench was so strong that over the course of the season, the substitutes (.370) had a better on-base percentage than the starters (.364).

The pitching staff was anchored by David Cone (20-7, 3.55 ERA in 31GS), who tied for the AL and Major League lead in wins. Lefthander David Wells (18-4, 3.49 ERA in 30GS) led the AL with five shutouts and a 1.05 WHIP. Along with tossing a perfect game on May 17 vs. Minnesota, Wells also had eight complete games during the season, a total that no Yankee has equaled since.

Orlando Hernandez added a boost to the rotation following his June call-up. Signed in March as a free agent from Cuba, "El Duque" went 12-4 with a 3.13 ERA in 21 starts. Andy Pettitte (16-11, 4.24 ERA) and Hideki Irabu (13-9, 4.06 ERA) rounded out the rotation, which often got bailed out by utility pitcher Ramiro Mendoza, who went 10-2 with a 3.25 ERA in 41 appearances, including 14 starts. Mike Stanton (4-1, 5.47 ERA in 67G), Jeff Nelson (5-3, 3.79 ERA in 45G) and lefthanded specialist Graeme Lloyd (3-0, 1.67 ERA in 50G in his best career season) provided the bridge to Mariano Rivera (3-0, 1.91 ERA), who notched 36 saves and allowed just four of 24 inherited runners to score.

In the postseason, the Yankees swept Texas in three games in the ALDS, outscoring them 9-1 and outhitting them 23-13. The ALCS was trickier as Cleveland took a 2-games-to-1 series lead before the Yankees won in six games. David Wells earned MVP honors, winning both of his starts in Game 1 and Game 5.

The Yankees met San Diego in the World Series, and the turning point came early. Down 5-2 in the seventh inning of Game 1 at Yankee Stadium, Knoblauch tied the score with a three-run homer. Five batters later, Tino Martinez hit a two-out, full-count grand slam off Mark Langston into the upper deck in right field to cap a seven-run inning in a 9-6 Yankees win.

The Yankees never looked back. They won Game 2, 9-3, and they took Game 3 due to the heroics of World Series MVP Scott Brosius (.471 BA, 8-for-17, 2HR, 6RBI), who got the Yankees on the board in the seventh with a solo home run and then provided the margin of victory with a three-run homer in the eighth, propelling the Yankees to a 5-4 win.

Andy Pettitte held the Padres scoreless over 7.1 innings in Game 4, which was closed out by Mariano Rivera, who recorded his third save of the series and sixth of the postseason. Rivera tossed 13.1 scoreless innings in 10 appearances during the 1998 postseason, allowing just six hits.

The championship was the Yankees' second in three years (also 1996) and the first of three consecutive (1998-2000). It marked the highpoint of one of the greatest eras in club history, establishing the yardstick by which all of baseball's post-integration teams are measured.

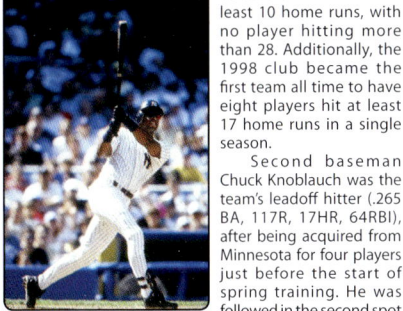

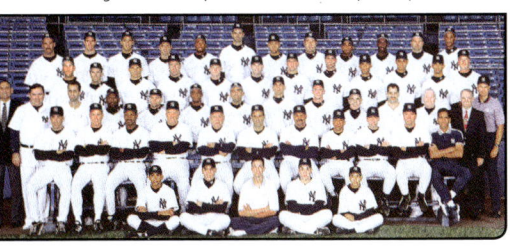

Bernie Williams led the AL with a .339 batting average in 1998.

Tino Martinez celebrates his World Series Game 1 grand slam with Derek Jeter.

Official Scoring at Yankee Stadium

The Yankees-Tigers contest at the Polo Grounds on May 15, 1922, might be the most significant game in the history of official scoring. In the second inning that wet day, Yankees shortstop Everett Scott failed to come up with a ground ball off the bat of Ty Cobb. Official scorer John Kieran (the first *Sports of the Times* columnist and founding editor of the *Information Please Almanac*) charged an error on Scott. Glancing over his shoulder as he fled the rain that was blowing into the press box, Fred Lieb (national president of the Baseball Writers Association of America and New York chapter chairman) scored it a hit. It was so reported by the Associated Press, for whom Lieb was compiling the box score. As was the custom, Kieran did not announce his call and Lieb, who was probably more interested at that moment in staying dry, did not ask.

The hit/error mattered — a lot. When official American League statistics were compiled (at the end of the season), the one-hit discrepancy was discovered. Cobb's season average was either .401 or .399. A predictable brouhaha ensued. Despite Lieb's willingness to cede to Kieran's official capacity, and despite the BBWAA's December vote that no hit be awarded, AL president Ban Johnson ordered the record to reflect that Cobb earned a hit and thus a .401 average. So it remains, officially, for all time.

As a result of "The Case of the Two-Point Base Hit" (as it was known), official scorers were instructed to contemporaneously communicate their calls to the press box, and the leagues assured the BBWAA that, in the future, a scorer's judgment would not be questioned.

Scorers' calls on close plays have also had a hand in Yankee Stadium no-hitters (and near misses). Had Lieb scored Whitey Witt's leadoff grounder to third on Sept. 11, 1923, an error and not a hit, Boston's Howard Ehmke would be remembered with Johnny

Babe Ruth and Ty Cobb at the Polo Grounds, which was the site of the "Two-Point Base Hit."

Vander Meer as hurlers of consecutive no-hitters. And had John Drebinger of *The Times* not changed a hit (originally scored an error) back to an error after consulting during the game with Detroit's Johnny Pesky regarding Phil Rizzuto's fourth-inning grounder to short, Virgil Trucks would have thrown only one no-hitter in 1952.

Dan Daniel of the *World-Telegram* scored many Yankees home games during Joe DiMaggio's 56-game hitting streak in 1941, and according to Jerome Holtzman (later the official historian of Major League Baseball), he awarded at least two arguable hits to help keep the streak alive. Four years later, a reversed call on the last day of the season by Bert Gumpert of the *Bronx Home News* gave Yankees second baseman Snuffy Stirnweiss the hit he needed to edge the White Sox's Tony Cuccinello for the AL batting title by .000087.

The cavalcade of scorers who have worked at Yankee Stadium includes some of the giants of the baseball writers industry: Lieb, Daniel, Sid Mercer (an original BBWAA member in 1908), Frank Graham (Lou Gehrig's first biographer), John Drebinger (who covered 203 consecutive World Series games over 34 years), Dick Young (who covered New York baseball for the *Daily News* and *New York Post* for 44 years), Leonard Koppett (author of *The Thinking Fan's Guide to Baseball*), Jack Lang (BBWAA secretary-treasurer for 22 years), Maury Allen (author of over 30 sports books), Red Foley (senior scorer in New York for 15 years) and Bill Shannon (senior scorer in New York for nine seasons and author of *Official Scoring in the Big Leagues*).

Bill Shannon (pictured here in 1983) was the official scorer for approximately 800 games at Yankee Stadium from 1979 until his passing in 2010.

-Authored by Major League Baseball official scorer Jordan Sprechman.

Yankees in Cooperstown

Including 2020 inductee Derek Jeter, there are 57 members of the Baseball Hall of Fame who have played, managed, coached, owned or been a general manager for the New York Yankees at one time or another. The Yankees' first inductee was Babe Ruth, who entered the Hall in its inaugural 1936 class along with Ty Cobb, Walter Johnson, Christy Mathewson and Honus Wagner. Of recent note, 2019 inductee Mariano Rivera became the first ever individual to be inducted unanimously via the writer's ballot, receiving a vote on 425-of-425 submissions.

In addition to the 57 individuals below, at least three Hall of Famers worked for the Yankees in other capacities, including Joe Kelley (HOF in 1971 — Yankees scout from 1915-25), Dick Williams (HOF in 2008 — NYY adviser from 1995-2001) and Pat Gillick (HOF in 2011 — NYY scouting director from 1974-76).

The *Elias Sports Bureau* notes that there have been nine HOFers who spent their entire playing careers with the Yankees: Earle Combs, Lou Gehrig, Bill Dickey, Joe DiMaggio, Derek Jeter, Phil Rizzuto, Whitey Ford, Mickey Mantle and Mariano Rivera.

Currently, the choice of which insignia appears on the cap of each Hall of Famer's plaque belongs to the Hall of Fame itself. The decision is based on the "historical accomplishments" of the player and "where that player makes his most indelible mark," though the wishes of the inductee are always considered. It is important to remember that caps have not always had insignias and some players' images are cast as profiles without visible insignias.

YANKEES HALL OF FAMERS LISTED IN ORDER OF INDUCTION YEAR

Below each photo includes the name of the Hall of Famer, primary career position, year inducted, years with the Yankees, number of games played or managed with the Yankees and the insignia on his Hall of Fame cap.

Babe Ruth
OF (1936)
1920-34, 2,084 games
Cap: New York Yankees

Lou Gehrig
1B (1939)
1923-39, 2,164 games
Cap: New York Yankees

Willie Keeler
RF (1939)
1903-09, 873 games
Cap: Brooklyn Superbas

Frank Chance
1B/Manager (1946)
1913-14 (1B), 12 games
1913-14 (Mgr), 290 games
Cap: Chicago Cubs

Jack Chesbro
RHP (1946)
1903-09, 269 games
Cap: Insignia unseen

Clark Griffith
Player, Mgr., Exec. (1946)
903-07 (RHP), 87 games
1903-08 (Mgr), 807 games
Cap: No insignia

Herb Pennock
LHP (1948)
1923-33, 346 games
Cap: No insignia

Paul Waner
RF (1952)
1944-45, 10 games
Cap: Pittsburgh Pirates

Ed Barrow
Executive (1953)
1920-45
No Cap

Bill Dickey
C (1954)
1928-46 (Player), 1,789 gms.
1946 (Mgr), 105 games
Cap: New York Yankees

Joe DiMaggio
CF (1955)
1936-51, 1,736 games
Cap: New York Yankees

Frank "Home Run" Baker
3B (1955)
1916-19, '21-22, 676 games
Cap: No insignia (A's style)

Dazzy Vance
RHP (1955)
1915, '18, 10 games
Cap: Brooklyn Dodgers

Joe McCarthy
Manager (1957)
1931-46, 2,348 games
Cap: New York Yankees

Bill McKechnie
Manager (1962)
1913 (INF), 44 games
Cap: Cincinnati Reds

291

Burleigh Grimes
RHP (1964)
1934, 10 games
Cap: Brooklyn Dodgers

Miller Huggins
Manager (1964)
1918-29, 1,796 games
Cap: New York Yankees

Casey Stengel
Manager (1966)
1949-60, 1,851 games
Cap: New York Yankees

Branch Rickey
Executive (1967)
1907 (OF, C, 1B), 52 gms.
No Cap

Red Ruffing
RHP (1967)
1930-42, '45-46, 426 games
Cap: New York Yankees

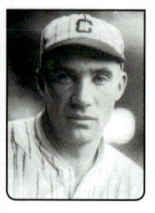

Stan Coveleski
RHP (1969)
1928, 12 games
Cap: Cleveland Indians

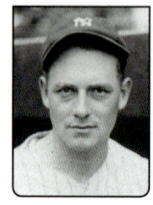

Waite Hoyt
RHP (1969)
1921-30, 365 games
Cap: New York Yankees

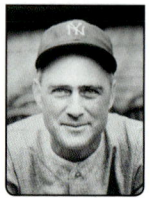

Earle Combs
CF (1970)
1924-35, 1,454 games
Cap: New York Yankees

George Weiss
Executive (1971)
1932-60
No Cap

Yogi Berra
C (1972)
1946-63 (Player), 2,116G
1964, 1984-85 (Mgr), 342G
Cap turned, insignia unseen

Lefty Gomez
LHP (1972)
1930-42, 367 games
Cap: New York Yankees

Whitey Ford
LHP (1974)
1950, '53-67, 498 games
Cap: New York Yankees

Mickey Mantle
CF (1974)
1951-68, 2,401 games
Cap: New York Yankees

Bucky Harris
Manager (1975)
1947-48, 309 games
Cap: Wash. Senators

Bob Lemon
RHP (1976)
1978-79, '81-82 (Mgr), 172G
Cap: Cleveland Indians

Joe Sewell
SS (1977)
1931-33, 389 games
Cap: Cleveland Indians

Larry MacPhail
Executive (1978)
1945-47
No Cap

Johnny Mize
1B (1981)
1949-53, 375 games
No Cap

Enos Slaughter
OF (1985)
1954-55, '56-59, 350 games
Cap: St. Louis Cardinals

Jim "Catfish" Hunter
RHP (1987)
1975-79, 137 games
Cap: No insignia

Tony Lazzeri
2B (1991)
1926-37, 1,658 games
Cap: New York Yankees

Gaylord Perry
RHP (1991)
1980, 10 games
Cap: San Francisco Giants

Reggie Jackson
RF (1993)
1977-81, 653 games
Cap: New York Yankees

Leo Durocher
Manager (1994)
1925, '28-29 (INF), 210 gms.
Cap: Brooklyn Dodgers

Phil Rizzuto
SS (1994)
1941-42, '46-56, 1,661 gms.
Cap: New York Yankees

Phil Niekro
RHP (1997)
1984-85, 65 games
Cap: Atlanta Braves

Lee MacPhail
Executive (1998)
1949-58, '66-73
No Cap

Dave Winfield
RF (2001)
1981-88, '90, 1,172 games
Cap: San Diego Padres

Wade Boggs
3B (2005)
1993-97, 602 games
Cap: Boston Red Sox

Rich "Goose" Gossage
RHP (2008)
1978-83, '89, 319 games
Cap: New York Yankees

Joe Gordon
2B (2009)
1938-43, '46, 1,000 games
Cap: New York Yankees

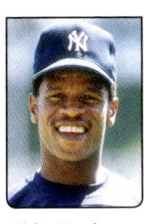

Rickey Henderson
CF/LF (2009)
1985-89, 596 games
Cap: Oakland A's

Bobby Cox
3B/Coach (2014)
1968-69 (Player), 220 gms.
1977 (Coach), 162 gms.
Cap: Atlanta Braves

Col. Jacob Ruppert
Owner (2013)
1915-39
No Cap

Joe Torre
Manager (2014)
1996-2007, 1,942 games
Cap: New York Yankees

Randy Johnson
LHP (2015)
2005-06, 67 games
Cap: Arizona Diamondbacks

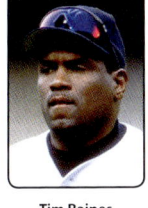

Tim Raines
LF (2017)
1996-98, 242 games
Cap: Montreal Expos

Ivan Rodriguez
C (2017)
2008, 33 games
Cap: Texas Rangers

Mike Mussina
RHP (2019)
2001-08, 249 games
Cap: No insignia

Mariano Rivera
RHP (2019)
1995-2013, 1,115 games
Cap: New York Yankees

Lee Smith
RHP (2019)
1993, 8 games
Cap: Chicago Cubs

Derek Jeter
SS (2020)
1995-2014, 2,747 games
Cap: New York Yankees

NATIONAL BASEBALL HALL OF FAME AND MUSEUM
25 Main Street, Cooperstown, New York 13326
Phone: (607) 547-7200 • **Fax:** (607) 547-2044 • **PR Dept.:** (607) 547-0215
E-mail Address: info@baseballhall.org • **Website:** baseballhall.org
Summer Hours: Memorial Day Weekend - Labor Day: 9 a.m. to 9 p.m. • **Other Hours:** 9 a.m. to 5 p.m.
Holiday Closings: Thanksgiving Day, Christmas Day and New Year's Day.
PR CONTACTS: V.P. Jon Shestakofsky (jshesta@baseballhall.org) / Director Craig Muder (cmuder@baseballhall.org)

HALL OF FAME WEEKEND 2020: July 24-27
Awards Presentation: Sat., July 25, 4:30 p.m. ET, Doubleday Field
  (Spink Award to Nick Cafardo and Frick Award to Ken Harrelson)
Induction: Sun., July 26, 1:30 p.m. ET, Clark Sports Center
Inductees: Derek Jeter, Marvin Miller, Ted Simmons, Larry Walker

Yankees Retired Uniform Numbers

The Yankees have retired 21 uniform numbers to honor 22 Yankees players and managers, including Lou Gehrig's No. 4, which was the first retired number in MLB history. Contrary to popular belief, the number was not retired on July 4, 1939 (when the Iron Horse gave his famous "Luckiest Man" speech), but on Jan. 6, 1940, via announcement by team president Ed Barrow.

On April 15, 1997, Major League Baseball retired No. 42 throughout the game to honor the Dodgers' Jackie Robinson. While the number could never again be issued by an MLB team, players already assigned No. 42 could continue to wear it. Mariano Rivera was grandfathered into that decision and was the last active player to use the number. During a pregame celebration on Sept. 22, 2013 (one week prior to his last day in uniform), the Yankees organization also retired the number for him, placing a Yankees-style "42" within the Yankees Retired Number Display in Monument Park. As part of that ceremony, the Yankees also recognized Robinson by unveiling a new bronze plaque to replace the Dodgers-style "42" which had previously been on display.

1 Billy Martin (Number retired: August 10, 1986)
Born: May 16, 1928 in Berkeley, Calif. • **Died:** Dec. 25, 1989 in Binghamton, N.Y. • **HT:** 5-11 • **WT:** 165 • **B/T:** R/R

Martin had as much "Yankees Pride" as any player or manager to wear pinstripes, and he implanted his own fierce desire to win in his teams. He played an integral part in four World Series in the 1950s as a player, and added another ring managing the Yankees in 1977. His .333 lifetime World Series batting average is sixth all time among players with at least 75 at-bats. Martin had five separate stints managing the club.

2 Derek Jeter (Number retired: May 14, 2017)
Born: June 26, 1974 in Pequannock, N.J. • **HT:** 6-3 • **WT:** 195 • **B/T:** R/R

The face of baseball for a a generation of fans, Jeter played a franchise-record 20 seasons with the Yankees from 1995-2014, retiring with a personal career winning percentage of .593 (1,628-1,117-2) and five World Series championships (1996, 1998-2000, '09). A 14-time All-Star and 2020 Hall of Fame inductee, Jeter retired with the sixth-most hits in baseball history (3,465) and played in 16 different postseasons. He tops the Yankees' all-time list in hits, games played (2,747), doubles (544), steals (358), at-bats (11,195), singles (2,595) and hit-by-pitches (170).

3 Babe Ruth (Number retired: June 13, 1948)
Born: Feb. 6, 1895 in Baltimore, Md. • **Died:** Aug. 16, 1948 in New York, N.Y. • **HT:** 6-2 • **WT:** 215 • **B/T:** L/L

Most consider Ruth the most colorful figure in the game's history. He started his career as a pitcher for the Boston Red Sox, winning 89 games over six seasons before converting to a full-time outfielder because of his tremendous power. He was sold to the Yankees in 1920 and his 54 home runs that year were more than any other American League team. En route to 714 career home runs, he won 12 home run titles, including 60HR in 1927. A member of the inaugural class of Hall of Fame inductees in 1936, the Bambino also added 15HR in World Series competition, leading the Yankees to seven Series appearances and four World Championships.

4 Lou Gehrig (Number retired by announcement on Jan. 6, 1940. No ceremony)
Born: June 19, 1903 in New York, N.Y. • **Died:** June 2, 1941 in Riverdale, N.Y. • **HT:** 6-1 • **WT:** 212 • **B/T:** L/L

Gehrig was a uniquely durable, powerhitting first baseman who played in 2,130 consecutive games from 1925 to 1939. He drove in at least 100 runs in 13 straight seasons (1926-38) and holds the AL record with 184 RBI in 1931. In a career shortened by terminal illness, he compiled a .340 batting avg. with 493 HRs, two AL MVP Awards (1927, '36) and the 1934 Triple Crown. He was honored at Yankee Stadium on July 4, 1939, when he made his memorable "Luckiest Man" speech. That offseason, the Yankees announced that his No. 4 was being retired. He was inducted into the Hall of Fame in 1939, and was immortalized in the 1942 film, *The Pride of the Yankees*, starring Gary Cooper.

5 Joe DiMaggio (Number retired: April 18, 1952 at the home opener)
Born: Nov. 25, 1914 in Martinez, Calif. • **Died:** March 8, 1999 in Hollywood, Fla. • **HT:** 6-2 • **WT:** 193 • **B/T:** R/R

The "Yankee Clipper" is considered by many experts as the best all-around baseball player in history. The California native was a sensational hitter for both average and power, and a splendid, graceful, ball-hawking center fielder with a powerful and accurate arm. A two-time batting champion and three-time MVP, he compiled a .325 lifetime batting average from 1936 to 1951 and powered the Yankees to nine World Series titles despite losing three complete seasons (1943-45) to military service. Many rate his 56-game hitting streak in 1941 as the top baseball feat of all time. He was inducted into the Hall of Fame in 1955.

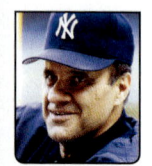

6 Joe Torre (Number retired: August 23, 2014)
Born: July 18, 1940 in Brooklyn, N.Y. • **HT:** 6-2 • **WT:** 212 • **B/T:** R/R

With a calming influence in the clubhouse and a stoic outward expression in the dugout, Torre piloted the Yankees to six World Series appearances (1996, '98-2001, '03) and four championships (1996, '98-2000) during his tenure from 1996-2007. The 2014 Hall of Famer led the club to the playoffs in all 12 seasons at the helm, going 1,173-767-2 (.605) in the regular season and 76-47 (.618) in the postseason, including a 21-11 mark in the World Series. His regular season wins total is second in club history to Joe McCarthy, who went 1,460-867-21 over 16 seasons.

7 Mickey Mantle (Number retired: June 8, 1969)
Born: Oct. 20, 1931 in Spavinaw, Okla. • **Died:** Aug. 13, 1995 in Dallas, Tex. • **HT:** 6-0 • **WT:** 201 • **B/T:** S/R

"The Mick" was the most feared hitter on some of the most successful teams in history. Fast and powerful, his reported 565-foot home run in Washington in 1953 brought about the term "tape-measure home run." In the 14 seasons between 1951 and 1964, he led the Yanks to 12 Fall Classics and seven World Championships. He still owns records for most homers, RBI, runs and walks in World Series play. In 1956, Mantle had one of the greatest seasons ever at the plate, hitting 52 homers with 130 RBI and a .353 average to win the Triple Crown. A three-time AL MVP (1956-57, '62), he was inducted into the Hall of Fame in 1974.

8 Yogi Berra (Number retired: July 22, 1972 on Old-Timers' Day)
Born: May 12, 1925 in St. Louis, Mo. • **Died:** Sept. 22, 2015 in West Caldwell, N.J.
Height: 5-8 • **Weight:** 191 • **B/T:** L/R

Beloved by generations of baseball fans, Berra was part of the foundation of the dominant Yankees teams from the end of World War II through the early 1960s. Although he never led the league in a single major offensive category, he is one of just 10 players all time to win at least three Most Valuable Player Awards. Selected to play in the All-Star Game in 15 successive seasons from 1948-62, he played on 14 pennant winners and an all-time record 10 World Champions. He led the Yankees to the 1964 pennant as manager and was inducted into the Hall of Fame in 1972.

8 Bill Dickey (Number retired: July 22, 1972 on Old-Timers' Day)
Born: June 6, 1907 in Bastrop, La. • **Died:** Nov. 12, 1993 in Little Rock, Ark.
Height: 6-1 • **Weight:** 185 • **B/T:** L/R

Regarded as one of the greatest catchers of all time, Dickey was a durable and tireless worker, catching more than 100 games in an AL-record 13 consecutive seasons (1929-41). In 1931, he did not allow a single passed ball in 125 games behind the plate, another AL record. Dickey also excelled as a hitter, batting over .300 in 10 of his first 11 full seasons, while hitting 202 homers during his career. He handled Yankees pitching staffs on eight World Series teams, winning seven championships. He was inducted into the Hall of Fame in 1954.

9 Roger Maris (Number retired: July 21, 1984 on Old-Timers' Day)
Born: Sept. 10, 1934 in Hibbing, Minn. • **Died:** Dec. 14, 1985 in Houston, Tex.
Height: 6-0 • **Weight:** 197 • **B/T:** L/R

In one of the most dramatic assaults on a baseball record, Maris surpassed Babe Ruth's single-season record of 60 home runs on the final day of the 1961 season. Maris' 61 homers that season was a Major League record until 1998 and still remains the American League mark. A two-time American League MVP (1960-61), he is considered one of the best defensive right fielders in Yankees history.

10 Phil Rizzuto (Number retired: Aug. 4, 1985)
Born: Sept. 25, 1917 in New York, N.Y. • **Died:** Aug. 13, 2007 in West Orange, N.J.
Height: 5-6 • **Weight:** 150 • **B/T:** R/R

Playing 13 years for the Yankees, the "Scooter" went to nine World Series, winning seven. Diminutive yet tough, he was a skilled bunter and baserunner with a .273 career batting average. In 1950, Rizzuto earned the AL MVP Award, batting .324 with 200 hits, 92 walks and 125 runs. In the 1951 World Series, he batted .320 and was named Series MVP. He also spent 40 years as a Yankees broadcaster (1957-96) tossing around his signature phrase, "Holy cow!" and calling his partners "Huckleberry." He was inducted into the Hall of Fame in 1994.

15 Thurman Munson (Number retired by announcement on Aug. 3, 1979)
Born: June 7, 1947 in Akron, Ohio • **Died:** Aug. 2, 1979 in Canton, Ohio
Height: 5-11 • **Weight:** 190 • **B/T:** R/R

Munson was the undisputed leader and most respected man on Yankees teams that won three consecutive AL pennants from 1976-78 and two World Championships in '77 and '78. He was a tremendous defensive catcher, winning three straight Gold Glove Awards (1973-75) and the AL MVP in 1976. In each season from 1975-77, Thurman drove in more than 100 runs and hit better than .300. There is no more tragic date in Yankees history than August 2, 1979, when Munson passed away in a plane crash at age 32.

16 Whitey Ford (Number retired: Aug. 3, 1974 on Old-Timers' Day)
Born: Oct. 21, 1928 in New York, N.Y.
Height: 5-10 • **Weight:** 181 • **B/T:** L/L

"The Chairman of the Board" was the ace pitcher on the great Yankees teams of the 1950s and early '60s. His lifetime record of 236-106 gives him the best winning percentage (.690) of any pitcher with 200-or-more decisions whose career began in the modern era (since 1900). He paced the AL in victories three times, and in ERA and shutouts twice. The 1961 Cy Young Award winner still holds many World Series records, including 10 wins, 33.0 consecutive scoreless innings and 94 strikeouts. He was inducted into the Hall of Fame in 1974.

20 Jorge Posada (Number retired: Aug. 22, 2015)
Born: Aug. 17, 1971 in Santurce, P.R.
Height: 6-2 • **Weight:** 215 • **B/T:** S/R

One of the best-hitting catchers of his era, Posada spent each of his 17 Major League seasons with the Yankees, batting .273 with 379 doubles, 275 homers, 1,065 RBI, a .374 OBP and .848 OPS in 1,829 games from 1995-2011. A player on five World Series winners (1996, '98, '99, 2000, '09), Posada was also a five-time All-Star and five-time Silver Slugger winner. He is one of just seven catchers all time to have at least 11 seasons of 17-or-more home runs.

23 Don Mattingly (Number retired: Aug. 31, 1997)
Born: April 20, 1961 in Evansville, Ill.
Height: 6-0 • **Weight:** 185 • **B/T:** L/L

Respected for his talent, professionalism and humility, "Donnie Baseball" was the premier first baseman of the mid-1980s before back problems robbed him of much of his power at age 29. Nevertheless, he remained the most loved Yankee of his era and a defensive star, tallying nine Gold Gloves in his 14 years in pinstripes (1982-95). The "Hit Man" won the 1984 AL batting title (.343) and the 1985 American League MVP (.324, 35HR, 145RBI), setting the (since-tied) all-time record with six grand slams in a single season.

32 Elston Howard (Number retired: July 21, 1984 on Old-Timers' Day)
Born: Feb. 23, 1929 in St. Louis, Mo. • **Died:** Dec. 14, 1980 in New York, N.Y.
Height: 6-2 • **Weight:** 196 • **B/T:** R/R

Howard became the first black player in Yankees history when he made the club in the spring of 1955. The versatile, two-time Gold Glove Award-winning catcher contributed to nine AL pennant-winning teams in his first 10 seasons with the club. Winner of the 1963 American League MVP (.287, 28HR, 85RBI), Howard was elected to the All-Star Game in nine different seasons (1957-65). A clubhouse leader as a player from 1955-67 and as a Yankees coach from 1969-79, his dignified manner and competitive spirit set a powerful example.

37 Casey Stengel (Number retired: Aug. 8, 1970 on Old-Timers' Day)
Born: July 30, 1890 in Kansas City, Mo. • **Died:** Sept. 29, 1975 in Glendale, Calif.
Height: 5-11 • **Weight:** 175 • **B/T:** L/L

In a distinguished 54-year professional career, "The Old Perfessor" became one of the game's greatest managers. His feat of guiding the Yankees to 10 pennants and seven world titles in a 12-year span from 1949-60 ranks as one of the top managerial accomplishments of all time. Simply put, Casey Stengel was one of the best things to ever happen to the game of Baseball. He was an authentic baseball ambassador, making the game fun for millions of Americans. He was inducted into the Hall of Fame in 1966.

42 Mariano Rivera
(Number retired by MLB on Apr. 15, 1997. Rivera recognized by NYY on Sept. 22, 2013)
Born: Nov. 29, 1969 in Panama City, Panama • **Height:** 6-2 • **Weight:** 195 • **B/T:** R/R

Rivera is the Majors' all-time leader with 652 career saves. Even more impressive is his 2.21 career ERA, which is the second-lowest mark among pitchers with at least 1,000.0IP since ERA became an official MLB statistic (1912-NL/1913-AL). The "Sandman" pitched 19 seasons, racking up an all-time best 15 seasons of at least 30 saves in 1,115 career games. His postseason dominance is legendary, including MLB record marks with 42 postseason saves, a 0.70 ERA (min: 30.0IP) and 96 appearances. In 141.0 career postseason IP, he allowed just 86H, 11ER, 21BB and 2HR with 110K. He won five World Series (1996, '98-2000, '09) and appeared in two others (2001, '03).

44 Reggie Jackson (Number retired: August 14, 1993)
Born: May 18, 1946 in Wyncote, Pa.
Height: 5-10 • **Weight:** 181 • **B/T:** L/L

"Mr. October" blasted 563 career home runs, including 144 as a Yankee from 1977-81. In Game 6 of the 1977 World Series, Jackson hit 3HR, all on the first pitch, as the Yankees beat the Dodgers to wrap up the club's first World Championship since 1962. He was an All-Star in each of his five years in pinstripes and had his best year with the club in 1980 (.300, 41HR, 111RBI), finishing second in AL MVP voting. Jackson said, "Some people call October a time of pressure. I call it a time of character." He was inducted into the Hall of Fame in 1993.

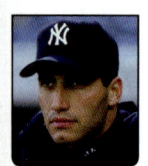

46 Andy Pettitte (Number retired: August 23, 2015)
Born: June 15, 1972 in Baton Rouge, La.
Height: 6-5 • **Weight:** 225 • **B/T:** L/L

Reliable and consistent throughout his career, Pettitte pitched 15 seasons with the club (1995-2003, '07-10, '12-13), going 219-127 with a 3.94 ERA (447G/438GS, 2,796.1IP, 2,020K). The left-hander is the franchise leader in strikeouts and is tied with Whitey Ford for the most starts. He trails only Ford (236 wins, 3,171.0IP) and Red Ruffing (231 wins, 3,168.0IP) in wins and innings pitched. A three-time AL All-Star (1996, 2001 and '10), Pettitte is the only pitcher drafted by the Yankees to win 200 games in the Majors. As a Yankee, Pettitte went 18-10 with a 3.76 ERA (251.1IP, 105ER) in 40 career postseason starts, winning five World Series titles (1996, '98-2000, '09). He famously started and won all three series-clinching games in the 2009 postseason.

49 Ron Guidry (Number retired: August 23, 2003)
Born: Aug. 28, 1950 in Lafayette, La.
Height: 5-11 • **Weight:** 165 • **B/T:** L/L

Known as "Louisiana Lightning," Ron Guidry was a four-time All-Star and three-time 20-game winner whose 1978 season was one of the most dominant by a pitcher in Major League history. He went 25-3 with a 1.74 ERA in leading the Yankees back from a 14.0-game AL East deficit and winning the AL Cy Young Award in unanimous fashion. He also set still-standing franchise records with nine shutouts, 248 total strikeouts and 18 strikeouts in a single game (June 17 vs. California). From 1986 through his retirement in 1989, "Gator" also served as a co-captain with Willie Randolph. He remains in the Yankees' all-time top 10 in games pitched (368), innings pitched (2,392.0), wins (170), winning percentage (.651), strikeouts (1,778) and shutouts (26).

51 Bernie Williams (Number retired: May 24, 2015)
Born: Sept. 13, 1968 in San Juan, P.R.
Height: 6-2 • **Weight:** 205 • **B/T:** S/R

Williams played his entire 16-year Major League career with the Yankees (1991-2006), batting .297 (2,336-for-7,869) with 449 doubles, 278 home runs and 1,257RBI in 2,076 games. A five-time AL All-Star (1997-2001), four-time Gold Glove winner (1997-2000) and one-time Silver Slugger Award recipient (2002), Williams won the 1998 AL batting title with a .339 average. A four-time World Series champion (1996, '98, '99, 2000), he is the Yankees' all-time postseason leader in HR (22) and RBI (80) and ranks third in games played (121). He was named the 1996 ALCS MVP after batting .474 (9-for-19) with 2HR and 6RBI in the Yankees' five-game victory over the Orioles. In Game 1 of the 1999 ALCS vs. Boston, he hit a memorable 10th-inning, "walk-off" home run.

All-Time Roster

In the Yankees' 117 seasons since being established in New York in 1903, 1,683 players have appeared in at least one game.

Asterisks (*) note players who are deceased.

A (50)

David Aardsma 2012
Jim Abbott............... 1993-94
Harry Ables*.................1911
Bobby Abreu............. 2006-08
Juan Acevedo..................2003
Alfredo Aceves........2008-10,'14
Dustin Ackley............ 2015-16
Chance Adams........... 2018-19
David Adams 2013
Spencer Adams*............1926
Doc Adkins*.................1903
Steve Adkins.................1990
Luis Aguayo..................1988
Jack Aker 1969-72
Jonathan Albaladejo 2008-10
Mike Aldrete.................1996
Doyle Alexander ......1976,'82-83
Walt Alexander* 1915-17
Bernie Allen.............. 1972-73
Johnny Allen*............ 1932-35
Neil Allen ....1985,'87-88
Carlos Almanzar 2001
Erick Almonte............2001,'03
Zoilo Almonte 2013-14
Sandy Alomar............ 1974-76
Felipe Alou 1971-73
Matty Alou*..................1973
Dell Alston............... 1977-78
Ruben Amaro*........... 1966-68
Jason Anderson..........2003,'05
John Anderson*.......... 1904-05
Rick Anderson* 1979
Ivy Andrews* ..... 1931-32,'37-38
Miguel Andújar 2017-19
Dean Anna.......................2014
Pete Appleton* (aka Jablonowski)...1933
Angel Aragon*..... 1914, 1916-17
Alex Arias....................2002
Rugger Ardizoia*.............1947
Mike Armstrong.......... 1984-86
Brad Arnsberg 1986-87
Luis Arroyo* 1960-63
Tucker Ashford...............1981
Paul Assenmacher 1993
Joe Ausanio.............. 1994-95
Jimmy Austin* 1909-10
Tyler Austin.............. 2016-18
Chick Autry* 1924
Luis Ayala....................2011
Oscar Azocar*................1990

B (152)

Loren Babe* 1952-53
Stan Bahnsen ....1966,'68-71
Andrew Bailey 2015
Bill Bailey* 1911
Frank Baker* ...... 1916-19,'21-22
Frank Baker.............. 1970-71
Steve Balboni ..... 1981-83,'89-90
Neal Ball*................ 1907-09
Scott Bankhead..............1995
Willie Banks.............. 1997-98
Johnny Barbato 2016
Steve Barber*............ 1967-68
Jesse Barfield 1989-92
Cy Barger*............... 1906-07
Ray Barker*.............. 1965-67
Frank Barnes*................1930
Honey Barnes*...............1926
Ed Barney*...................1915
Jake Barrett..................2019
Chris Basak 2007
George Batten* 1912
Hank Bauer*............. 1948-59
Paddy Baumann* 1915-17
Don Baylor*.............. 1983-85
Walter Beall*............. 1924-27
T.J. Beam.....................2006
Colter Bean 2005-07
Jim Beattie............... 1978-79
Rich Beck 1965
Zinn Beck*...................1918
Fred Beene 1972-74
Joe Beggs*...................1938
Jack Bell* 1907
Zeke Bella* 1957
Mark Bellhorn................2005
Clay Bellinger 1999-2001
Carlos Beltrán............ 2014-16
Benny Bengough* 1923-30
Juan Beniquez 1979
Armando Benitez 2003
Lou Berberet*........... 1954-55
Dave Bergman*.........1975,'77
Lance Berkman 2010
Juan Bernhardt 1976
Walter Bernhardt*...........1918
Dale Berra 1985-86
Yogi Berra*.............. 1946-63
Angel Berroa................2009
Dellin Betances ....2011,'13-19
Wilson Betemit........... 2007-08
Bill Bevens*.............. 1944-47
Monte Beville*........... 1903-04
Harry Billiard*...............1908
Bruce Billings 2014
Doug Bird............... 1980-81
Greg Bird ....2015,'17-19
Ewell Blackwell*.......... 1952-53
Rick Bladt...................1975
Paul Blair* 1977-80
Walter Blair* 1907-11
Johnny Blanchard*. 1955, 1959-65
Gil Blanco...................1965
Wade Blasingame...........1972
Steve Blateric 1972
Gary Blaylock 1959
Curt Blefary*............ 1970-71
Richard Bleier...............2016
Elmer Bliss*.................1903
Ron Blomberg 1969, 1971-76
Mike Blowers 1989-91
Eddie Bockman* 1946
Ping Bodie*............. 1918-21
Len Boehmer ....1969,'71
Brian Boehringer... 1995-97, 2001
Brennan Boesch.............2013
Wade Boggs 1993-97
Don Bollweg*................1953
Bobby Bonds* 1975
Ricky Bones.................1996
Ernie "Tiny" Bonham*..... 1940-46

Ernie "Tiny" Bonham

Juan Bonilla.............1985,'87
Aaron Boone.................2003
Lute Boone* 1913-16
Chris Bootcheck.............2013
Frenchy Bordagaray*.........1941
Rich Bordi...............1985,'87
Joe Borowski............ 1997-98
Hank Borowy* 1942-45
Babe Borton* 1913
Daryl Boston.................1994
Jim Bouton* 1962-68
Clete Boyer* 1959-66
Andrew Brackman 2011
Ryan Bradley.................1998
Scott Bradley 1984-85
Neal Brady*.............1915,'17
Darren Bragg 2001
Ralph Branca*...............1954
Norm Branch* 1941-42
Marshall Brant 1980
Garland Braxton* 1925-26
Don Brennan* 1933
Jim Brenneman*.............1965
Ken Brett* 1976
Marv Breuer* 1939-43
Billy Brewer..................1996
Fritzie Brickell*.......... 1958-59
Jim Bridewe ser*.......... 1951-53
Marshall Bridges* 1962-63
Harry Bright*............ 1963-64
Reid Brignac 2013
Ed Brinkman* 1975
Chris Britton 2007-08
Zack Britton............. 2018-19
Johnny Broaca*.......... 1934-37
Lew Brockett*........1907,'09,'11
Jim Bronstad.................1959
Tom Brookens 1989
Scott Brosius.......... 1998-2001
Bob Brower 1989
Jim Brower...................2007
Boardwalk Brown* 1914-15
Dr. Bobby Brown......1946-52,'54
Bobby Brown 1979-81
Curt Brown 1984
Hal Brown* 1962
Jumbo Brown*.... 1932-33,'35-36
Kevin Brown 2004-05
Brian Bruney............ 2006-09
Jim Bruske 1998
Billy Bryan 1966-67
Jess Buckles*................1916
Mike Buddie 1998-99
Jay Buhner.............. 1987-88
Danny Burawa 2015
Bill Burbach............. 1969-71
Lew Burdette* 1950
Tim Burke....................1992
A.J. Burnett 2009-11
George Burns*........... 1928-29
Alex Burr*....................1914
Ray Burris....................1979
Homer Bush 1997-98, 2004
Joe Bush*................ 1922-24
Tom Buskey*............ 1973-74
Billy Butler 2016
Ralph Buxton* 1949
Joe Buzas*...................1945
Harry Byrd* 1954
Sammy Byrd* 1929-34
Tommy Byrne*.. 1943,'46-51,'54-57
Marty Bystrom 1984-85

C (136)

Cesar Cabral 2013-14
Melky Cabrera 2005-09
Greg Cadaret 1989-92
Miguel Cairo ....2004,'06-07
Charlie Caldwell*............1925
Ray Caldwell*........... 1910-18
Johnny Callison*........ 1972-73
Howie Camp*................1917
Bert Campaneris 1983
Archie Campbell* 1928
John Candelaria.......... 1988-89
Andy Cannizaro.............2006
Robinson Canó 2005-13
Jose Canseco 2000
Mike Cantwell*...............1916
Chris Capuano 2014-15
Andy Carey* 1952-60
Buddy Carlyle................2011
Roy Carlyle*.................1926
Duke Carmel.................1965
David Carpenter 2015
Dick Carroll* 1909
Ownie Carroll* 1930
Tommy Carroll 1955-56
Chris Carter..................2017
Chuck Cary 1989-91
Hugh Casey*.................1949
Kevin Cash...................2009
Alberto Castillo 2002
Roy Castleton*...............1907
Bill Castro....................1981
Starlin Castro 2016-17
Danny Cater 1970-71
Rick Cerone.......1980-84,'87,'90
Bob Cerv*......... 1951-56,'60-62
Francisco Cervelli 2008-14
Luis Cessa.............. 2016-19
Shawn Chacon........... 2005-06
Joba Chamberlain........ 2007-13
Chris Chambliss.......1974-79,'88

Chris Chambliss

Frank Chance* 1913-14
Spud Chandler*.......... 1937-47
Les Channell*............1910,'14
Darrin Chapin................1991
Aroldis Chapman 2016-19
Ben Chapman*........... 1930-36
Mike Chartak* ....1940,'42
Hal Chase*.............. 1905-13
Eric Chavez 2011-12
Jack Chesbro*........... 1903-09
Randy Choate........... 2000-03
Ji-Man Choi..................2017
Justin Christian 2008
Clay Christiansen............1984
Al Cicotte* 1957
Anthony Claggett............2009
Preston Claiborne........ 2013-14
Allie Clark*...................1947
George Clark*................1913
Jack Clark....................1988
Tony Clark 2004
Horace Clarke........... 1965-74
Walter Clarkson* 1904-07
Brandon Claussen............2003
Ken Clay 1977-79
Roger Clemens..... 1999-2003,'07
Pat Clements............ 1987-88
Tex Clevenger*.......... 1961-62
Lou Clinton* 1966-67
Tyler Clippard.........2007,'16-17
Al Closter 1971-72
Andy Coakley* 1911
Jim Coates* ....1956,'59-62
Jim Cockman* 1905
Rich Coggins............ 1975-76
Phil Coke ....2008-09,'16
Rocky Colavito...............1968
A.J. Cole 2018
King Cole* 1914-15
Curt Coleman*...............1912
Jerry Coleman* 1949-57
Michael Coleman 2001
Rip Coleman*............ 1955-56
Bob Collins* 1944
Dave Collins 1982
Joe Collins* 1948-57
Orth Collins*.................1904
Pat Collins* 1926-28
Rip Collins* 1920-21
Frank Colman*........... 1946-47
Bartolo Colon................2011
Loyd Colson 1970
Earle Combs* 1924-35
David Cone 1995-2000
Tom Connelly* 1920-21
Joe Connor* 1905
Wid Conroy* 1903-08
Jose Contreras 2003-04
Andy Cook...................1993
Doc Cook*............... 1913-16
Dusty Cooke*............ 1930-32
Ron Coomer 2002
Johnny Cooney* 1944
Phil Cooney*.................1905
Don Cooper 1985
Garrett Cooper...............2017
Guy Cooper*.................1914
Nestor Cortes Jr..............2019
Dan Costello* 1913
Caleb Cotham 2015
Henry Cotto 1985-87
Ensign Cottrell* 1915
Clint Courtney* 1951
Ernie Courtney*..............1903
Stan Coveleski* 1928
Billy Cowan 1969
Joe Cowley 1984-85
Bobby Cox.............. 1968-69
Casey Cox.............. 1972-73
Birdie Cree*............. 1908-15
Lou Criger* 1910
Herb Crompton* 1945
Bubba Crosby........... 2004-06
Frank Crosetti* 1932-48
Ivan Cruz 1997
Jose Cruz 1988
Luis Cruz.....................2013
Jack Cullen...........1962,'65-66
Roy Cullenbine*..............1942
Nick A. Cullop*.......... 1916-17
Nick Cullop * 1926
John Cumberland........ 1968-70
Jim Curry* 1911
Chad Curtis 1997-99
Colin Curtis 2010
Fred Curtis*..................1905

D (74)

Babe Dahlgren* 1937-40
Bud Daley 1961-64
Matt Daley 2013-14
Tom Daley* 1914-15
Johnny Damon 2006-09
Bert Daniels* 1910-13
Bobby Davidson 1989
Kyle Davies 2015
Chili Davis 1998-99
George Davis* 1912
Ike Davis 2016
Kiddo Davis* 1926
Lefty Davis* 1903
Ron Davis 1978-81
Russ Davis 1994-95
Brian Dayett 1983-84
John Deering* 1903
Jim Deidel 1974
Ivan De Jesus 1986
Frank Delahanty* ..... 1905-06, '08
Wilson Delgado 2000
Bobby Del Greco* 1957-58
David Dellucci 2003
Jim Delsing* 1949-50
Joe DeMaestri* 1960-61
Ray Demmitt* 1909
Rick Dempsey 1973-76
Bucky Dent 1977-82
Jorge De Paula 2003-05
Jose De Paula 2015
Claud Derrick* 1913
Russ Derry* 1944-45
Matt DeSalvo 2007
Jim Deshaies 1984
Jimmie Deshong* 1934-35
Orestes Destrade* 1987
Charlie Devens* 1932-34
Al DeVormer* 1921-22
Chris Dickerson 2011-12
Bill Dickey* .... 1928-43, '46
Murry Dickson* 1958
Joe DiMaggio* .... 1936-42, '46-51
Kerry Dineen* 1975-76
Craig Dingman* 2000
Art Ditmar 1957-61
Sonny Dixon* 1956
Pat Dobson* 1973-75
Cozy Dolan* 1911-12
Atley Donald* 1938-45
Mike Donovan* 1908
Wild Bill Donovan* 1915-16
Brian Dorsett 1989-90
Octavio Dotel 2006
Richard Dotson 1988-89
Patsy Dougherty* 1904-06
John Dowd* 1912
Al Downing 1961-69
Brian Doyle 1978-80
Jack Doyle* 1905
Slow Joe Doyle* 1906-10
Doug Drabek 1986
Bill Drescher* 1944-46
Stephen Drew 2014-15
Karl Drews* 1946-48
Brandon Drury 2018
Monk Dubiel* 1944-45
Joe Dugan* 1922-28
Ryan Dull 2019
Mariano Duncan 1996-97
Shelley Duncan 2007-09
Michael Dunn 2009
Ryne Duren 1958-61
Leo Durocher* .... 1925, '28-29
Cedric Durst* .... '27-30

E (31)

Mike Easler 1986-87
Rawly Eastwick 1978
Doc Edwards* 1965
Foster Edwards* 1930
Robert Eenhoorn 1994-96
Dave Eiland .... 1988-91, '95
Darrell Einertson 2000
Norman "Kid" Elberfeld* .. 1903-09
Gene Elliott* 1911
Dock Ellis 1976-77
John Ellis 1969-72
Jacoby Ellsbury 2014-17
Kevin Elster 1994-95
Alan Embree 2005
Red Embree* 1948
Edwin Encarnación 2019
Clyde Engle* 1909-10
Jack Enright* 1917
Morgan Ensberg 2008
Nathan Eovaldi 2015-16
Cody Eppley 2012-13
Todd Erdos 1998-2000
Roger Erickson 1982-83
Scott Erickson 2004
Felix Escalona 2004-05
Juan Espino .... 1982-83, '85-86
Alvaro Espinoza 1988-91
Bobby Estalella 2001
Thairo Estrada 2019
Nick Etten* 1943-46
Barry Evans 1982

F (52)

Charles Fallon* 1905
Kyle Farnsworth 2006-08
Steve Farr 1991-93
Doc Farrell* 1932-33
Sal Fasano 2006
Alex Ferguson* ...... 1918, '21, '25
Frank Fernandez 1967-69
Tony Fernandez 1995
Mike Ferraro .... 1966, '68
Wes Ferrell* 1938-39
Tom Ferrick* 1950-51
Chick Fewster* 1917-22
Cecil Fielder 1996-97
Mike Figga 1997-99
Cole Figueroa 2015
Ed Figueroa 1976-80
Pete Filson 1987
Happy Finneran* 1918
Mike Fischlin 1986
Brian Fisher 1985-86
Gus Fisher* 1912
Ray Fisher* 1910-17
Mike Fitzgerald* 1911
John Flaherty 2003-05
Ramon Flores 2015
Tim Foli 1984
Ray Fontenot 1983-84
Barry Foote 1981-82
Ben Ford 2000
Mike Ford 2019
Russ Ford* 1909-13
Whitey Ford .... 1950, '53-67
Tony Fossas 1999
Eddie Foster* 1910
Jack Fournier* 1918
Dustin Fowler 2017
Andy Fox 1996-97
Jeff Francis 2014
Ray Francis* 1925
Ben Francisco 2013
Wayne Franklin 2005
Clint Frazier 2017-19
George Frazier 1981-83
Todd Frazier 2017
Mark Freeman* 1959
Ray French* 1920
Lonny Frey* 1947-48
Bob Friend 1966
John Frill* 1910
Bill Fulton 1987
Dave Fultz* 1903-05
Liz Funk* 1929

G (88)

John Gabler* 1959-60
Joe Gallagher* 1939
Mike Gallego 1992-94
Giovanny Gallegos 2017-18
Oscar Gamble .... 1976, '79-84
Ben Gamel 2016
John Ganzel* 1903-04
Mike Garbark* 1944-45
Damaso Garcia 1978-79

Freddy Garcia 2011-12
Jaime García 2017
Karim Garcia 2002-03
Billy Gardner 1961-62
Brett Gardner 2008-19
Earle Gardner* 1908-12
Rob Gardner 1970-72
Steve Garrison 2011
Ned Garvin* 1904
Milt Gaston* 1924
Chad Gaudin 2009-10
Mike Gazella* ...... 1923, '26-28
Cory Gearrin 2019
Joe Gedeon* 1916-17
Lou Gehrig* 1923-39
Bob Geren 1988-91
Domingo Germán 2017-19
Al Gettel* 1945-46
Jason Giambi 2002-08
Joe Giard* 1927
Jake Gibbs 1962-71
Paul Gibson .... 1993-94, '96
Sam Gibson* 1930
Dan Giese 2008
Frank Gilhooley* 1913-18
Charles Gipson 2003
Joe Girardi 1996-99
Fred Glade* 1908
Frank Gleich* 1919-20
Joe Glenn* .... 1932-33, '35-38
Greg Golson 2010-11
Lefty Gomez* 1930-42
Jessie Gonder* 1960-61
Alberto Gonzalez ..... 2007-08, '13
Fernando Gonzalez 1974
Pedro Gonzalez 1963-65
Wilbur Good* 1905
Dwight Gooden 1996-97, 2000
Nick Goody 2015-16
Art Goodwin* 1905
Brian Gordon 2011
Joe Gordon* .... 1938-43, '46
Tom Gordon 2004-05
Tom Gorman* 1952-54
Rich Gossage .... 1978-83, '89
Dick Gossett* 1913-14
Larry Gowell 1972
Johnny Grabowski* 1927-29
Alex Graman 2004-05
Curtis Granderson 2010-13
Wayne Granger 1973
Sonny Gray 2017-18
Ted Gray* 1955
Eli Grba* 1959-60
Chad Green 2016-19
Nick Green 2006
Paddy Greene* 1903
Shane Greene 2014
Todd Greene 2001
Didi Gregorius 2015-19
Ken Griffey, Sr. 1982-86
Mike Griffin 1979-81
Clark Griffith* 1903-07
Bob Grim* 1954-58
Burleigh Grimes* 1934
Oscar Grimes* 1943-46
Jason Grimsley 1999-2000
Lee Grissom* 1940
Buddy Groom 2005
Cecilio Guante 1987-88
Lee Guetterman 1988-92
Ron Guidry 1975-88
Aaron Guiel 2006
Brad Gulden 1979-80
Don Gullett 1977-78
Bill Gullickson 1987
Randy Gumpert* 1946-48
Larry Gura 1974-75
Freddy Guzman 2009

H (127)

John Habyan 1990-93
Bump Hadley* 1936-40
Kent Hadley* 1960
Travis Hafner 2013
Ed Hahn* 1905-06
Noodles Hahn* 1906
Hinkey Haines* 1923
Jerry Hairston, Jr. 2009
George Halas* 1919
Bob Hale* 1961
David Hale 2018-19
Jimmie Hall 1969
Mel Hall 1989-92
Brad Halsey* 2004
Roger Hambright 1971
Steve Hamilton 1963-70
Chris Hammond 2003

Mike Handiboe* 1911
Jim Hanley* 1913
Truck Hannah* 1918-20
Ron Hansen 1970-71
Harry Hanson* 1913
J.A. Happ 2018-19
Jim Hardin* 1971
Bubbles Hargrave* 1930
Harry Harper* 1921
Toby Harrah* 1984
Greg Harris 1994
Joe Harris* 1914
Jim Ray Hart* 1973-74
Roy Hartzell* 1911-16
Joseph Harvey 2019
Buddy Hassett* 1942
Ron Hassey 1985-86
Andy Hawkins 1989-91
LaTroy Hawkins 2008
Chicken Hawks* 1921
Charlie Hayes .... 1992, '96-97
Chase Headley 2014-17
Fran Healy 1976-78
Mike Heath 1978
Slade Heathcott 2015
Neal Heaton 1993
Adeiny Hechavarria 2018
Don Heffner* 1934-37
Mike Hegan* ..... 1964, '66-67, '73-74
Fred Heimach* 1928-29
Woodie Held* .... 1954, '57
Ben Heller .... 2016-17, '19
Charlie Hemphill* 1908-11
Rollie Hemsley* 1942-44
Bill Henderson* 1930
Rickey Henderson 1985-89

Rickey Henderson

Harvey Hendrick* 1923-24
Elrod Hendricks* 1976-77
Tim Hendryx* 1915-17
Sean Henn 2005-07
Tommy Henrich* ..... 1937-42, '46-50
Bill Henry 1966
Drew Henson 2002-03
Felix Heredia 2003-04
Adrian Hernandez 2001-02
Leo Hernandez 1986
Michel Hernandez 2003
Orlando Hernandez ... 1998-2002, '04
Xavier Hernandez 1994
Ronald Herrera 2017
Ed Herrmann* 1975
Aaron Hicks 2016-19
Hugh High* 1915-18
Oral Hildebrand* 1939-40
Kyle Higashioka 2017-19
Glenallen Hill 2000
Jesse Hill* 1935
Rich Hill 2014
Shawn Hillegas 1999
Frank Hiller .... 1946, '48-49
Mack Hillis* 1924
Eric Hinske 2009
Rich Hinton 1972
Sterling Hitchcock ... 1992-95, '01-03
Myril Hoag* .... 1931-32, '34-38
Butch Hobson 1982
Chester Hoff* 1911-13
Danny Hoffman* 1906-07
Solly Hofman* 1916
Fred Hofmann* 1919-25
Bill Hogg* 1905-08
Bobby Hogue* 1951-52
Ken Holcombe* 1945
Bill Holden* 1913-14
Jonathan Holder 2016-19
Al Holland 1986-87
Matt Holliday 2017
Ken Holloway* 1930
Darren Holmes 1998

Fred Holmes* 1903
Roger Holt 1980
Ken Holtzman 1976-78
Rick Honeycutt 1995
Don Hood 1979
Wally Hood* 1949
Johnny Hopp* 1950-52
Shags Horan* 1924
Ralph Houk* 1947-54
Elston Howard* 1955-67
Matt Howard 1996
Steve Howe* 1991-96
Harry Howell* 1903
Jay Howell 1982-84
Dick Howser* 1967-68
Waite Hoyt* 1921-30

Waite Hoyt

Rex Hudler 1984-85
Charles Hudson 1987-88
David Huff 2013-14
Chad Huffman 2010
Keith Hughes 1987
Phil Hughes 2007-13
Long Tom Hughes* 1904
Tom Hughes* .... 1906-07, '09-10
John Hummel* 1918
Mike Humphreys 1991-93
Ken Hunt* 1959-60
Billy Hunter 1955-56
Catfish Hunter* 1975-79
Mark Hutton .... 1993-94, '96
Ham Hyatt* 1918

I (6)

Raul Ibañez 2012
Ryota Igarashi 2012
Pete Incaviglia 1997
Kei Igawa 2007-08
Hideki Irabu* 1997-99
Travis Ishikawa 2013

J (49)

Fred Jacklitsch* 1905
Grant Jackson 1976
Reggie Jackson 1977-81
Dion James .... 1992-93, '95-96
Johnny James .... 1958, '60-61
Stan Javier 1984
Domingo Jean 1993
Stanley Jefferson 1989
Jackie Jensen* 1950-52
Mike Jerzembeck 1998
Derek Jeter 1995-2014
D'Angelo Jimenez 1999
Elvio Jimenez 1964
Brett Jodie 2001
Tommy John .... 1979-82, '86-89
Alex Johnson* 1974-75
Billy Johnson* .... 1943, '46-51
Cliff Johnson 1977-79
Darrell Johnson* 1957-58
Deron Johnson* 1960-61
Don Johnson* .... 1947, '50
Ernie Johnson* 1923-25
Hank Johnson* .... 1925-26, '28-32
Jeff Johnson 1991-93
Johnny Johnson* 1944
Kelly Johnson 2014
Ken Johnson* 1969
Lance Johnson 2000
Nick Johnson .... 2001-03, '10
Otis Johnson* 1911
Randy Johnson 2005-06
Roy Johnson* 1936-37
Russ Johnson 2005
Jay Johnstone 1978-79
Andruw Jones 2011-12
Darryl Jones 1979
Garrett Jones 2015
Gary Jones 1970-71
Jimmy Jones 1989-90
Ruppert Jones 1980
Sad Sam Jones* 1922-26
Tim Jordan* 1903
Art Jorgens* 1929-39
Felix Jose 2000
Corban Joseph 2013
Jeff Juden 1999
Aaron Judge 2016-19
Mike Jurewicz 1965
David Justice 2000-01

K (60)

Jim Kaat 1979-80
Tommy Kahnle 2017-19
Scott Kamieniecki 1991-96
Bob Kammeyer* 1978-79
Frank Kane* 1919
Bill Karlon* 1930
Herb Karpel* 1946
Steve Karsay 2002-05
Jeff Karstens 2006-07
Benny Kauff* 1912
Curt Kaufman 1982-83
Austin Kearns 2010
Eddie Kearse* 1942
Ray Keating* .... 1912-16, '18
Bob Keefe* 1907
Willie Keeler* 1903-09
Randy Keisler 2000-01
Mike Kekich 1969-73
Charlie Keller* .... 1939-43, '45-49, '52
Shawn Kelley 2013-14
Pat Kelly 1991-97
Roberto Kelly 1987-92, 2000
Steve Kemp 1983-84
Ian Kennedy 2007-09
John Kennedy* 1967
Jerry Kenney .... 1967, '69-72
Matt Keough 1983
Jimmy Key 1993-96
Steve Kiefer 1989
Michael King 2019
Dave Kingman 1977
Harry Kingman* 1914
Fred Kipp 1960
Frank Kitson* 1907
Ron Kittle 1986-87
Ted Kleinhans* 1936
Red Kleinow* 1904-10
Ed Klepfer* .... 1911, '13
Ron Klimkowski* .... 1969-70, '72
Steve Kline* 1970-74
Mickey Klutts 1976-78
Bill Knickerbocker* 1938-40
Brandon Knight 2001-02
John Knight* .... 1909-11, '13
Chuck Knoblauch 1998-2001
Mark Koenig* 1925-30
Jim Konstanty* 1954-56
George Kontos .... 2011, '18
Andy Kosco 1968
Pete Kozma 2017
Steve Kraly* 1953
Jack Kramer* 1951
Erik Kratz 2017
Ernie Krueger* 1915
Dick Kryhoski* 1949
Tony Kubek 1957-65
Johnny Kucks* 1955-59
Bill Kunkel* 1963
Hiroki Kuroda 2012-14
Bob Kuzava* 1951-54

L (77)

Aaron Laffey 2011
Brady Lail 2019
Joe Lake* 1908-09
Brandon Laird 2011
Bill Lamar* 1917-19
Hal Lanier 1972-73
Dave Lapoint 1989-90
Frank LaPorte* 1905-10
Dave LaRoche 1981-83
Don Larsen* 1955-59
Lyn Lary* 1929-34
Chris Latham 2003
Marcus Lawton 1989
Matt Lawton 2005
Gene Layden* 1915
Tommy Layne 2016-17
Tony Lazzeri* 1926-37
Tim Leary 1990-92
Wade LeBlanc 2014
Ricky Ledee 1998-00
Travis Lee 2004
Joe Lefebvre 1980
Al Leiter 1987-89, 2005
Mark Leiter 1990
Frank Leja* 1954-55
Jack Lelivelt* 1912-13
DJ LeMahieu 2019
Eddie Leon 1975
Chris Leroux 2014
Louis LeRoy* 1905-06
Ed Levy* .... 1942, '44
Duffy Lewis* 1919-20
Jim Lewis 1982
Terry Ley 1971
Jim Leyritz .... 1990-96, '99-2000
Cory Lidle* 2006
Jon Lieber 2004
Brent Lillibridge 2013
Ted Lilly 2000-02
Paul Lindblad* 1978
Johnny Lindell* 1941 50
Jacob Lindgren 2015
Phil Linz 1962-65
Bryan Little 1986
Jack Little* 1912
Clem Llewellyn* 1922
Graeme Lloyd 1996-98
Jonathan Loaisiga 2018-19
Esteban Loaiza 2004
Gene Locklear 1976-77
Kenny Lofton 2004
Boone Logan 2010-13
Sherm Lollar* 1947-48
Tim Lollar 1980
Phil Lombardi 1986-87
Dale Long* .... 1960, '62-63
Herman Long* 1903
Terrence Long 2006
Ed Lopat* 1948-55
Arturo Lopez 1965
Hector Lopez 1959-66
Baldy Louden* 1907
Slim Love* 1916-18
Torey Lovullo 1991
Derek Lowe 2012
Mike Lowell 1998
Johnny Lucadello* 1947
Joe Lucey* 1920
Roy Luebbe* 1925
Matt Luke 1996
Jerry Lumpe* 1956-59
Scott Lusader 1991
Sparky Lyle 1972-78
Lance Lynn 2018
Al Lyons* .... 1944, '46-47
Tyler Lyons 2019
Jim Lyttle 1969-71

M (176)

Duke Maas* 1958-61
Kevin Maas 1990-93
Bob MacDonald 1995
Danny MacFayden* 1932-34
Ray Mack* 1947
Tommy Madden* 1910
Elliott Maddox 1974-76
Dave Madison* 1950
Lee Magee* 1916-17
Sal Maglie* 1957-58
Stubby Magner* 1911
Jim Magnuson* 1973
Fritz Maisel* 1913-17
Hank Majeski* 1946
Frank Makosky* 1937
Pat Malone* 1935-37
Pat Maloney* 1912
Al Mamaux* 1924
Rube Manning* 1907-10
Joe Mantiply 2019
Mickey Mantle* 1951-68
Jeff Manto 1999
Josias Manzanillo 1995
Cliff Mapes* 1948-51
Roger Maris* 1960-66
Cliff Markle* .... 1915-16, '24
Jeff Marquez 2011
Jim Marquis* 1925
Armando Marsans* 1917-18
Brett Marshall 2013
Cuddles Marshall* .... 1946, '48-49
Sam Marsonek 2004
Damaso Marte 2008-10
Billy Martin* .... 1950-53, '55-57
Chris Martin 2015
Hersh Martin* 1944-45
Jack Martin* 1912
Russell Martin 2011-12
Tino Martinez .... 1996-2001, '05
Tippy Martinez 1974-76
Jim Mason 1974-76
Victor Mata 1984-85
Hideki Matsui 2003-09
Don Mattingly 1982-95
Carlos May 1976-77
Darrell May 2005
Rudy May .... 1974-76, '80-83
John Mayberry 1982
Cameron Maybin 2019
Carl Mays* 1919-23
Lee Mazzilli 1982
Larry McCall 1977-78
Brian McCann 2014-16
Brandon McCarthy 2014
Joe McCarthy* 1905
Pat McCauley* 1903
Larry McClure* 1910
George McConnell* .... 1909, '12-13
Mike McCormick 1970
Lance McCullers 1989-90
Andrew McCutchen 2018
Lindy McDaniel 1968-73
Mickey McDermott* 1956
Danny McDevitt* 1961
Darnell McDonald 2012
Dave McDonald* 1969
Donzell McDonald 2001
Jim McDonald* 1952-54
Gil McDougald* 1951-60
Jack McDowell 1995
Sam McDowell 1973-74
Lou McEvoy* 1930-31
Herm McFarland* 1903
Andy McGaffigan 1981
Casey McGehee 2012
Lynn McGlothen* 1982
Bob McGraw* 1917-20
Deacon McGuire* 1904-07
Marty McHale* 1913-15
Irish McIlveen* 1908-09
Tim McIntosh 1996
Bill McKechnie* 1913
Billy McKinney 2018
Rich McKinney 1972
Frank McManus* 1904
Norm McMillan* 1922
Tommy McMillan* 1912
Mike McNally* 1921-24
Herb McQuaid* 1926
George McQuinn* 1947-48
Bobby Meacham 1983-88
Charlie Meara* 1914
Jim Mecir 1996-97
George "Doc" Medich 1972-75
Mark Melancon 2009-10
Bob Melvin 1994
Ramiro Mendoza .... 1996-2002, '05
Fred Merkle* 1925-26
Melky Mesa 2012-13
Andy Messersmith 1978
Tom Metcalf 1963
Bud Metheny* 1943-46
Hensley Meulens 1989-93
Bob Meusel* 1920-29
Bob Meyer 1964
Danny Miceli 2003
Gene Michael* 1968-74
Ezra Midkiff* 1912-13
Doug Mientkiewicz 2007
Pete Mikkelsen* 1964-65
Larry Milbourne 1981-83
Sam Militello 1992-93
Andrew Miller 2015-16
Bill Miller* 1952-54
Elmer Miller* .... 1915-18, '21-22
Jim Miller 2013-14
John Miller 1966
Alan Mills 1990-91
Buster Mills* 1940
Mike Milosevich* 1944-45
Paul Mirabella 1979
Juan Miranda 2008-10
Willy Miranda* 1953-54
Bobby Mitchell* 1970
Bryan Mitchell 2014-17
D.J. Mitchell 2012
Fred Mitchell* 1910
Johnny Mitchell* 1921-22
Sergio Mitre 2009-11
Johnny Mize* 1949-53
Kevin Mmahat 1989
Chad Moeller .... 2008, '10
George Mogridge* 1915-20
Dale Mohorcic 1988-89
Fenton Mole* 1949
Gustavo Molina 2011
Jose Molina 2007-09

Bill Monbouquette* 1967-68
Raul Mondesi 2002-03
Ed Monroe* 1917-18
Zack Monroe 1958-59
John Montefusco 1983-86
Rich Monteleone 1990-93
Jesus Montero 2011
Jordan Montgomery 2017-19
Archie Moore 1964-65
Earl Moore* 1907
Wilcy Moore* ..... 1927-29, '32-33
Kendrys Morales 2019
Ray Morehart* 1927
Diego Moreno 2015
Omar Moreno 1983-85
Mike Morgan 1982
Tom Morgan* ..... 1951-52, '54-56
George Moriarty* 1906-08
Jeff Moronko 1987
Hal Morris 1988-89
Ross Moschitto ....1965, '67
Dustin Moseley 2010
Jerry Moses* 1973
Terry Mulholland 1994
Conor Mullee 2016
Charlie Mullen* 1914-16
Jerry Mumphrey 1981-83
Bob Muncrief* 1951
Bobby Munoz 1993
Thurman Munson* 1969-79
Bobby Murcer* 1965-66, '69-74, '79-83

Bobby Murcer

Johnny Murphy* ...1932, '34-43, '46
John Ryan Murphy 2013-15
Rob Murphy 1994
Dale Murray 1983-85
George Murray* 1922
Larry Murray 1974-76
Mike Mussina 2001-08
Mike Myers 2006-07

N (36)

Xavier Nady 2008-09
Jerry Narron 1979
Dan Naulty 1999
Dioner Navarro 2004
Denny Neagle 2000
Thomas Neal 2013
Bots Nekola* 1929
Chris Nelson 2013
Gene Nelson 1981
Jeff Nelson .... 1996-2000, '03
Luke Nelson* 1919
Graig Nettles 1973-83
Tex Neuer* 1907
Ernie Nevel* 1950-51
Floyd Newkirk* 1934
Bobo Newsom* 1947
Doc Newton* 1905-09
Gus Niarhos* ....1946, '48-50
Joe Niekro* 1985-87
Phil Niekro 1984-85
Jerry Nielsen 1992
Scott Nielsen ....1986, '88-89
Wil Nieves 2005-07
Harry Niles* 1908
C. J. Nitkowski 2004
Jayson Nix 2012-13
Otis Nixon 1983
Rico Noel 2015
Hector Noesi 2011
Matt Nokes 1990-94
Irv Noren* 1952-56
Don Nottebart* 1969
Ivan Nova 2010-16
Les Nunamaker* 1914-17
Eduardo Nunez 2010-13
Vidal Nuno 2013-14

O (31)

Johnny Oates* 1980-81
Mike O'Berry 1984
Andy O'Connor* 1908
Jack O'Connor* 1903
Paddy O'Connor* 1918
Heinie Odom* 1925
Lefty O'Doul* ....1919-20, '22
Rowland Office 1983
Ross Ohlendorf 2007-08
Bob Ojeda 1994
Rube Oldring* ....1905, '16
John Olerud 2004
Bob Oliver 1975
Joe Oliver 2001
Nate Oliver 1969
Tyler Olson 2016
Paul O'Neill 1993-2001
Steve O'Neill* 1925
Jesse Orosco 2003
Queenie O'Rourke* 1908
Al Orth* 1904-09
Donovan Osborne 2004
Champ Osteen* 1904
Joe Ostrowski* 1950-52
Antonio Osuna 2003
Bill Otis* 1912
Adam Ottavino 2019
Josh Outman 2014
Lyle Overbay 2013
Stubby Overmire* 1951
Spike Owen 1993

P (78)

John Pacella 1982
Del Paddock* 1912
Juan Padilla 2004
Dave Pagan 1973-76
Joe Page* 1944-50
Mike Pagliarulo 1984-89
Donn Pall 1994
Chan Ho Park 2010
Blake Parker 2016
Christian Parker 2001
Clay Parker 1989-90
Chris Parmelee 2016
Ben Paschal* 1924-29
Dan Pasqua 1985-87
Gil Patterson 1977
Jeff Patterson 1995
Mike Patterson 1981-82
Scott Patterson 2008
Carl Pavano ....2005, '07-08
Dave Pavlas 1995-96
James Paxton 2019
James Pazos 2015-16
Steve Pearce 2012
Monte Pearson* 1936-40
Roger Peckinpaugh* 1913-21
Steve Peek* 1941
Hipolito Pena 1988
Ramiro Pena 2009-12
Lance Pendleton 2011
Herb Pennock* 1923-33
Joe Pepitone 1962-69
Eury Perez 2014
Marty Perez 1977
Melido Perez 1992-95
Pascual Perez* 1990-91
Robert Perez 2001
Cecil Perkins 1967
Cy Perkins* 1931
Gaylord Perry 1980
Fritz Peterson 1966-74
Jace Peterson 2018
Gregorio Petit 2015
Andy Pettitte .. 1995-2003, '07-10, '12-13
David Phelps 2012-14
Josh Phelps 2007
Ken Phelps 1988-89
Andy Phillips 2004-07
Eddie Phillips* 1932
Jack Phillips* 1947-49
Cy Pieh* 1913-15
Bill Piercy* ....1917, '21
Duane Pillette* 1949-50
Branden Pinder 2015-16
Michael Pineda 2014-17
Lou Piniella 1974-84
George Pipgras* .. 1923-24, '27-33
Wally Pipp* 1915-25
Jose Pirela 2014-15
Jim Pisoni* 1959-60
Eric Plunk 1989-91
Dale Polley 1996
Luis Polonia ....1989-90, '94-95, '00
Sidney Ponson ....2006, '08

Bob Porterfield* 1948-51
Jorge Posada 1995-2011
Scott Pose 1997
Jack Powell* 1904-05
Jake Powell* 1936-40
Mike "Doc" Powers* 1905
Martin Prado 2014
Del Pratt* 1918-20
Jerry Priddy* 1941-42
Curtis Pride 2003
Johnny Priest* 1911-12
Bret Prinz 2003-04
Scott Proctor ....2004-07, '11
Alfonso Pulido 1986
Ambrose Puttmann* 1903-05

Q (6)

Chad Qualls 2012
Paul Quantrill 2004-05
Mel Queen* ....1942, '44, '46-47
Ed Quick* 1903
Jack Quinn* .... 1909-12, '19-21
Jamie Quirk 1989

R (96)

Tim Raines 1996-98
Dave Rajsich 1978
Edwar Ramirez 2007-09
Jose Ramirez 2014-15
Bobby Ramos 1982
Domingo Ramos 1978
John Ramos 1991
Pedro Ramos 1964-66
Lenny Randle 1979
Willie Randolph 1976-88

Willie Randolph

Cody Ransom 2008-09
Clay Rapada 2012
Vic Raschi* 1946-53
Dennis Rasmussen 1984-87
Darrell Rasner 2006-08
Shane Rawley 1982-84
Jeff Reardon 1994
Tim Redding 2005
Jack Reed 1961-63
Kevin Reese 2005-06
Jimmie Reese* 1930-31
Rob Refsnyder 2015-17
Hal Reniff* 1961-67
Bill Renna* 1953
Tony Rensa* 1933
Roger Repoz 1964-66
Rick Reuschel 1981
Dave Revering 1981-82
Al Reyes 2003
Allie Reynolds* 1947-54
Bill Reynolds* 1913-14
Mark Reynolds 2013
Rick Rhoden 1987-88
Gordon Rhodes* 1929-32
Harry Rice* 1930
Antoan Richardson 2014
Bobby Richardson 1955-66
Nolen Richardson* 1935
Branch Rickey* 1907
Dave Righetti ....1979, '81-90
Jose Rijo 1984
Royce Ring 2010
Danny Rios 1997
Juan Rivera 2001-03
Mariano Rivera 1995-2013
Ruben Rivera 1995-96
Mickey Rivers 1976-79
Phil Rizzuto* ...... 1941-42, '46-56
Roxey Roach* 1910-11
Brian Roberts 2014
Dale Roberts* 1967
Andre Robertson 1981-85
David Robertson .. 2008-14, '17-18
Gene Robertson* 1928-29
Aaron Robinson* ......1943, '45-47

Bill Robinson* 1967-69
Bruce Robinson 1979-80
Eddie Robinson 1954-56
Hank Robinson* 1918
Jeff Robinson 1990
Shane Robinson 2018
Alex Rodriguez ..... 2004-13, '15-16
Aurelio Rodriguez* 1980-81
Carlos Rodriguez 1991
Edwin Rodriguez 1982
Ellie Rodriguez 1968
Felix Rodriguez 2005
Henry Rodriguez 2001
Ivan Rodriguez 2008
Chaz Roe 2014
Gary Roenicke 1986
Oscar Roettger* 1923-24
Esmil Rogers 2014-15
Jay Rogers* 1914
Kenny Rogers 1996-97
Tom Rogers* 1921
Jim Roland* 1972
Austin Romine ....2011, '13-19
Red Rolfe* ....1931, '34-42
Adonis Rosa 2019
Buddy Rosar* 1939-42
Larry Rosenthal* 1944
Steve Roser* 1944-46
Braggo Roth* 1921
Jerry Royster 1987
Muddy Ruel* 1917-20
Dutch Ruether* 1926-27
Red Ruffing* ...... 1930-42, '45-46
Nick Rumbelow 2015
Allan Russell* 1915-19
Kevin Russo 2010
Marius Russo* ....1939-43, '46
Babe Ruth* 1920-34
Blondy Ryan* 1935
Brendan Ryan 2013-15
Rosy Ryan* 1928

S (157)

CC Sabathia 2009-19
Johnny Sain* 1951-55
Lenn Sakata 1987
Mark Salas 1987
Jack Saltzgaver* ....1932, '34-37
Billy Sample 1985
Celerino Sanchez* 1972-73
Gary Sánchez 2015-19
Humberto Sanchez 2008
Rey Sanchez 1997, 2005
Romulo Sanchez 2010
Deion Sanders 1989-90
Roy Sanders* 1918
Scott Sanderson* 1991-92
Charlie Sands* 1967
Fred Sanford* 1949-51
Amauri Sanit 2011
Rafael Santana 1988
Sergio Santos 2015
Bronson Sardinha 2007
Don Savage* 1944-45
Rick Sawyer 1974-75
Steve Sax 1989-91
Ray Scarborough* 1952-53
Germany Schaefer* 1916
Harry Schaeffer* 1952
Roy Schalk* 1932
Art Schallock 1951-55
Wally Schang* 1921-25
Bob Schmidt* 1965
Butch Schmidt* 1909
Johnny Schmitz* 1952-53
Pete Schneider* 1919
Dick Schofield 1966
Paul Schreiber* 1945
Art Schult* 1953
Al Schulz* 1912-14
Don Schulze 1989
Pius Schwert* 1914-15
Everett Scott* 1922-25
George Scott* 1979
Rodney Scott 1982
Rod Scurry* 1985-86
Scott Seabol 2001
Ken Sears* 1943
Bob Seeds* 1936
Kal Segrist* 1952
Fernando Seguignol 2003
George Selkirk* 1934-42
Ted Sepkowski* 1947
Hank Severeid* 1926
Luis Severino 2015-19
Joe Sewell* 1931-33
Richie Sexson 2008
Howard Shanks* 1925

Billy Shantz* 1960
Bobby Shantz 1957-60
Bob Shawkey* 1915-27
Spec Shea* .... 1947-49, '51
Al Shealy* 1928
George Shears* 1912
Tom Sheehan* 1921
Gary Sheffield 2004-06
Justus Sheffield 2018
Rollie Sheldon .... 1961-62, '64-65
Skeeter Shelton* 1915
Roy Sherid* 1929-31
Pat Sheridan 1991
Dennis Sherrill .... 1978, '80
Ben Shields* 1924-25
Steve Shields 1988
Bob Shirley 1983-87
Urban Shocker* ..... 1916-17, '25-28
Tom Shopay .... 1967, '69
Ernie Shore* 1919-20
Bill Short 1960
Chasen Shreve 2015-18
Norm Siebern* ...... 1956, '58-59
Ruben Sierra 1995-96, 2003-05
Charlie Silvera* 1948-56
Dave Silvestri 1992-95
Ken Silvestri* .... 1941, '46-47
Hack Simmons* 1912
Dick Simpson 1969
Harry Simpson* 1957-58
Duke Sims 1973-74
Scott Sizemore 2014
Bill Skiff* 1926
Camp Skinner* 1922
Joel Skinner 1986-88
Lou Skizas 1956
Bill "Moose" Skowron* ... 1954-62
Roger Slagle 1979
Don Slaught 1988-89
Enos Slaughter* .... 1954-55, '56-59
Aaron Small 2005-06
Roy Smalley 1982-84
Walt Smallwood* .... 1917, '19
Caleb Smith 2017
Charley Smith 1967-68
Elmer Smith* 1922-23
Joe Smith* 1913
Keith Smith 1984-85
Klondike Smith* 1912
Lee Smith 1993
Matt Smith 2006
Harry Smythe* 1934
J.T. Snow 1992
Eric Soderholm 1980
Luis Sojo .... 1996-99, 2000-01, '03
Tony Solaita* 1968
Donovan Solano 2016
Yangervis Solarte 2014
Alfonso Soriano .. 1999-2003, '13-14
Rafael Soriano 2011-12
Steve Souchock* .... 1946, '48
Jim Spencer* 1978-81
Shane Spencer 1998-2002
Charlie Spikes* 1972
Russ Springer 1992
Bill Stafford* 1960-65
Jake Stahl* 1908
Roy Staiger 1979
Tuck Stainback* 1942-45
Gerry Staley* 1955-56
Charley Stanceu* .... 1941, '46
Andy Stankiewicz 1992-93
Fred Stanley 1973-80
Mike Stanley .... 1992-95, '97
Giancarlo Stanton 2018-19
Mike Stanton ...... 1997-2002, '05
Dick Starr* 1947-48
Dave Stegman 1982
Dutch Sterrett* 1912-13
Bud Stewart* 1948
Chris Stewart .... 2008, '12-13
Lee Stine* 1938
Kelly Stinnett 2006
Snuffy Stirnweiss* 1943-50
Tim Stoddard 1986-88
Mel Stottlemyre* 1964-74
Hal Stowe 1960
Darryl Strawberry 1995-99
Gabby Street* 1912
Marlin Stuart* 1954
Bill Stumpf* 1912-13
Tom Sturdivant* 1955-59
Johnny Sturm* 1941
Tanyon Sturtze 2004-06
Bill Sudakis 1974
Steve Swindal* ...... 1936, '38-40
Ichiro Suzuki 2012-14
Dale Sveum 1998
Anthony Swarzak 2016
Jeff Sweeney* 1908-15
Nick Swisher 2009-12
Ron Swoboda 1971-73

T (63)
Fred Talbot* 1966-69
Vito Tamulis* 1934-35
Masahiro Tanaka 2014-19
Frank Tanana 1993
Jesse Tannehill* 1903
Tony Tarasco 1999
Stephen Tarpley 2018-19
Danny Tartabull 1992-95
Mike Tauchman 2019
Wade Taylor 1991
Zack Taylor* 1934
Mark Teixeira 2009-16
Frank Tepedino ..... 1967, '69-72
Walt Terrell 1989
Ralph Terry .... 1956-57, '59-64
Jay Tessmer .... 1998-2000, '02
Dick Tettelbach* 1955
Bob Tewksbury 1986-87
Marcus Thames .... 2002, '10
Ira Thomas* 1906-07
Justin Thomas 2012
Lee Thomas 1961
Myles Thomas* 1926-29
Stan Thomas 1977
Gary Thomasson 1978
Homer Thompson* 1912
Kevin Thompson 2006-07
Ryan Thompson 2000
Tommy Thompson* 1912
Jack Thoney* 1904
Hank Thormahlen* 1917-20
Matt Thornton 2014
Marv Throneberry* .... 1955, '58-59

Yankees Serving Their Country

The following Yankees lost Major League service time for military service in World War II, the Korean War or Vietnam.

Bobby Murcer	1967-68
Steve Peck	1942-45
Mel Queen	1945-46
Phil Rizzuto	1943-45
Aaron Robinson	1944
Red Ruffing	1943-44
Marius Russo	1944-45
Ken Sears	1944-45
George Selkirk	1943-45
Ken Silvestri	1942-45
Charley Stanceu	1943-44
Johnny Sturm	1942-45
Jake Wade	1945
Roy Weatherly	1944-45
Bob Wiesler	1951-52
Butch Wensloff	1945-46

World War I Service

Phil Rizzuto is one of 41 Yankees that lost Major League service time between 1941 and 1968.

Rich Beck	1967
Norm Branch	1943-45
Bobby Brown	1952-54
Tommy Byrne	1944-45
Tommy Carroll	1958
Spud Chandler	1944-45
Jerry Coleman	1952-53
Bill Dickey	1944-45
Joe DiMaggio	1943-45
Frank Fernandez	1967
Whitey Ford	1951-52
Joe Gordon	1944-45
Randy Gumpert	1943-45
Buddy Hassett	1943-45
Mike Hegan	1967
Rollie Hemsley	1945
Tommy Henrich	1943-45
Billy Johnson	1944-46
Jerry Kenney	1968
Tony Kubek	1962
Al Lyons	1945
Hank Majeski	1943-45
Billy Martin	1954-55
Tom Morgan	1952-53
Ross Moschitto	1966

According to Marty Appel's book *Pinstripe Empire*, the following Yankees went into the armed forces in WWI: Walter Bernhardt, Neil Brady, Alex Ferguson, Ray Fisher, Frank Kane, Bill Lamar, Bob McGraw, Ed Monroe, Wally Pipp, Muddy Ruel, Bob Shawkey, Walt Smallwood, Sammy Vick and Aaron Ward.

Future Yankees who served in WWI included Carl Mays, Mike McNally, Herb Pennock, Urban Shocker, Ernie Shore and Casey Stengel. Former Yankees Les Nunamaker and Fritz Maisel also served in the "Great War."

Additional research shows that Tom Burr, a Chicago native who attended Choate Prep in Connecticut and Williams College, is the only Yankee to have been killed in military service. He was a defensive replacement for the Yankees in one game on April 21, 1914 vs. Washington in his only Major League appearance. He was killed in an air training accident on Oct. 12, 1918, in Cazaux, France at age 24.

Mike Thurman	2002
Luis Tiant	1979-80
Dick Tidrow	1974-79
Bobby Tiefenauer*	1965
Eddie Tiemeyer*	1909
Ray Tift*	1907
Bob Tillman*	1967
Thad Tillotson*	1967-68
Dan Tipple*	1915
Wayne Tolleson	1986-90
Brett Tomko	2009
Earl Torgeson*	1961
Gleyber Torres	2018-19
Rusty Torres	1971-72
Ronald Torreyes	2016-18
Mike Torrez	1977
Cesar Tovar*	1976
Josh Towers	2009
Billy Traber	2008
Matt Tracy	2015
Bubba Trammell	2003
Tom Tresh*	1961-69
Gus Triandos*	1953-54
Steve Trout	1987
Virgil Trucks*	1958
Frank Truesdale*	1914
Troy Tulowitzki	2019
Bob Turley*	1955-62
Chris Turner	2000
Jim Turner*	1942-45

U (5)
George Uhle*	1933-34
Tom Underwood*	1980-81
Bob Unglaub*	1904
Cecil Upshaw*	1974
Gio Urshela	2019

V (23)
Raul Valdes	2011
Breyvic Valera	2019
Elmer Valo*	1960
Russ Van Atta*	1933-35
Dazzy Vance*	1915, '18
Joe Vance*	1937-38
John Vander Wal	2002
Bobby Vaughn*	1909
Hippo Vaughn*	1908, '10-12
Javier Vazquez	2004, '10
Bobby Veach*	1925
Randy Velarde	1987-1995, 2001
Otto Velez	1973-76
Mike Vento	2005
Robin Ventura	2002-03
Jose Veras	2006-09
Joe Verbanic*	1967-68, '70
Frank Verdi*	1953
Sammy Vick*	1917-20
Ron Villone	2006-07
Jose Vizcaino	2000
Luis Vizcaino	2007
Luke Voit	2018-19

W (108)
Cory Wade	2011-12
Jake Wade*	1946
Tyler Wade	2017-19
Dick Wakefield*	1950
Jim Walewander	1990
Curt Walker*	1919
Dixie Walker*	1931, '33-36
Neil Walker	2018
Mike Wallace	1974-75
Jimmy Walsh*	1914
Joe Walsh*	1910-11
Roxy Walters*	1915-18
Danny Walton*	1971
Paul Waner*	1944-45
Chien-Ming Wang	2005-09
Jack Wanner*	1909
Pee Wee Wanninger*	1925
Aaron Ward*	1917-26
Gary Ward	1987-89
Joe Ward*	1909
Pete Ward	1970
Jack Warhop*	1908-15
Adam Warren	2011, '13-18
George Washburn*	1941
Claudell Washington	1986-88, '90
Gary Waslewski	1970-71
Allen Watson	1999-2000
Bob Watson	1980-82
Roy Weatherly*	1943, '46
David Weathers	1996-97
Jeff Weaver	2002-03
Jim Weaver*	1931
Tyler Webb	2017
Dave Wehrmeister	1981
Lefty Weinert*	1931
David Wells	1997-98, '02-03
Ed Wells*	1929-32
Vernon Wells	2013
Butch Wensloff*	1943, '47
Julie Wera*	1927, '29
Billy Werber*	1930, '33
Dennis Werth	1979-81
Jake Westbrook	2000
John Wetteland	1995-96
Stefan Wever	1982
Zelous Wheeler	2014
Kevin Whelan	2011
Steve Whitaker	1966-68
Gabe White	2003-04
Rondell White	2002
Roy White	1965-79
Wally Whitehurst	1996
George Whiteman*	1913
Mark Whiten	1997
Terry Whitfield	1974-76
Chase Whitley	2014-15
Ed Whitson	1985-86
Kemp Wicker*	1936-38
Al Wickland*	1919
Bob Wickman	1992-96
Chris Widger	2002
Bob Wiesler*	1951, '54-55
Bill Wight*	1946-47
Ted Wilborn	1980
Ed Wilkinson*	1911
Bernie Williams	1991-2006
Bob Williams	1911-13
Gerald Williams	1992-96, 2001-02
Harry Williams*	1913-14
Jimmy Williams*	1903-07
Mason Williams	2015-17
Stan Williams	1963-64

Todd Williams ... 2001
Walt Williams* ... 1974-75
Archie Wilson* ... 1951-52
Enrique Wilson ... 2001-04
George Wilson* ... 1956
Craig Wilson ... 2006
Justin Wilson ... 2015
Kris Wilson ... 2006
Pete Wilson* ... 1908-09
Snake Wiltse* ... 1903
Gordie Windhorn ... 1959
Dave Winfield ... 1981-90
Randy Winn ... 2010
Dewayne Wise ... 2012
Jay Witasick ... 2001
Mickey Witek* ... 1949
Mike Witt ... 1990-91, '93
Whitey Witt* ... 1922-25
Mark Wohlers ... 2001
Wilbert "Barney" Wolfe* ... 1903-04
Harry Wolter* ... 1910-13
Harry Wolverton* ... 1912
Dooley Womack ... 1966-68
Tony Womack ... 2005
Kerry Wood ... 2010
Gene Woodling* ... 1949-54
Ron Woods ... 1969-71
Dick Woodson ... 1974
Hank Workman ... 1950
Chase Wright ... 2007
Jaret Wright ... 2005-06
Ken Wright* ... 1974
Yats Wuestling* ... 1930
John Wyatt* ... 1968
Butch Wynegar ... 1982-86
Jimmy Wynn ... 1977

X (0)

Y (9)

Ed Yarnall ... 1999-2000
Kirby Yates ... 2016
Joe Yeager* ... 1905-06
Jim York ... 1976
Kevin Youkilis ... 2013
Chris Young ... 2014-15
Curt Young ... 1992
Eric Young Jr. ... 2016
Ralph Young* ... 1913

Z (9)

Tom Zachary* ... 1928-30
Mike Zagurski ... 2013
Jack Zalusky* ... 1903
George Zeber ... 1977-78
Rollie Zeider* ... 1913
Todd Zeile ... 2003
Guy Zinn* ... 1911-12
Bill Zuber* ... 1943-46
Paul Zuvella ... 1986-87

Managers Roster

Through the 2019 season, there have been 33 managers in franchise history. (* = Deceased)

Yogi Berra* ... 1964, '84-85
Aaron Boone ... 2018-19
Frank Chance* ... 1913-14
Hal Chase* ... 1910-11
Bucky Dent ... 1989-90
Bill Dickey* ... 1946
"Wild" Bill Donovan* ... 1915-17
Norman "Kid" Elberfeld* ... 1908
Art Fletcher* ... 1929
Clark Griffith* ... 1903-08
Joe Girardi ... 2008-17
Dallas Green* ... 1989
Bucky Harris* ... 1947-48
Ralph Houk* ... 1961-63, '66-73
Dick Howser* ... 1980
Miller Huggins* ... 1918-29
Johnny Keane* ... 1965-66
Clyde King* ... 1982
Bob Lemon* ... 1978-79, '81-82
Billy Martin* ... 1975-78, '79, '83, '85, '88
Joe McCarthy* ... 1931-46
Stump Merrill ... 1990-91
Gene Michael* ... 1981, '82
Johnny Neun* ... 1946
Roger Peckinpaugh* ... 1914
Lou Piniella ... 1986-87, '88
Bob Shawkey* ... 1930
Buck Showalter ... 1992-95
George Stallings* ... 1909-10
Casey Stengel* ... 1949-60
Joe Torre ... 1996-2007
Bill Virdon ... 1974-75
Harry Wolverton* ... 1912

OLDEST LIVING YANKEES

As of February 1, 2020, available records indicate that the oldest living former Yankees players are:

Player	Date of Birth
Eddie Robinson	12/15/1920
Art Schallock	4/25/1924
Bobby Brown	10/25/1924
Bobby Shantz	9/26/1925
Hank Workman	2/5/1926
Billy Gardner	7/19/1928
Billy Hunter	6/4/1928
Whitey Ford	10/21/1928

Coaches Roster

Available records show that 126 individuals have served as a coach for the Yankees at the Major League level. (* = Deceased)

Neil Allen ... 2005
Joe Altobelli ... 1981-82, 1986
Loren Babe* ... 1967
Josh Bard ... 2018-19
Vern Benson* ... 1965-66
Yogi Berra* ... 1963, '76-83
Larry Bowa ... 2006-07
Clete Boyer* ... 1988, '92-94
Cloyd Boyer ... 1975, 1977
Jason Brown ... 2018-19
Jimmy Burke* ... 1931-33
Brian Butterfield ... 1994-95
Jose Cardenal ... 1996-99
Chris Chambliss ... 1988, '96-2000
Tony Cloninger* ... 1992-2001
Alan Cockrell ... 2015-17
Earle Combs* ... 1936-44
Mark Connor ... 1984-85, '86-87, '90-93
Billy Connors* ... 1989-90, '94-95, 2000
Nardi Contreras ... 1995
Pat Corrales ... 1989
John Corriden* ... 1947-48
Bobby Cox ... 1977
Frank Crosetti* ... 1946-68
Tom Daly* ... 1914
Ellis "Cot" Deal* ... 1965
Gary Denbo ... 2001
Bill Dickey* ... 1949-57, '60
Rick Down* ... 1993-95, 2002-03
Chuck Dressen* ... 1947-48
Dave Eiland ... 2008-10
Lee Elia ... 1989
Sammy Ellis* ... 1982-84, '86
Joe Espada ... 2015-17
Darrell Evans ... 1990
Duke Farrell* ... 1909, '11, '15-17
Mike Ferraro ... 1979-82, '87-91
Art Fletcher* ... 1927-45
Whitey Ford ... 1964, '68, '74-75
Art Fowler* ... 1977-79, '83, '88
Charlie Fox* ... 1989
Joe Girardi ... 2005
Jimmy Gleeson* ... 1964
Ron Guidry ... 2006-07
Randy Gumpert* ... 1957
Mike Harkey ... 2008-13, '16-19
Jim Hegan* ... 1960-73, '79-80
Tommy Henrich* ... 1951
Marc Hill ... 1991
Doug Holmquist* ... 1984-85
Willie Horton ... 1985
Ralph Houk* ... 1953-54, '58-60
Elston Howard* ... 1969-79
Frank Howard ... 1989, '91-93
Dick Howser* ... 1969-78
Mick Kelleher ... 2009-14
Charlie Keller* ... 1957, 1959
Joe Kerrigan ... 2006-07
Clyde King* ... 1978, '81-82, '88
Charlie Lau* ... 1979-81
Bob Lemon* ... 1976
Dale Long* ... 1963
Kevin Long ... 2007-14
Eddie Lopat* ... 1960
Mickey Mantle* ... 1970
Harry Mathews* ... 1929
Don Mattingly ... 2004-07
Lee Mazzilli ... 2000-03, '06
Jerry McNertney ... 1984
Bobby Meacham ... 2008
Carlos Mendoza ... 2018-19
Fred Merkle* ... 1925-26
Stump Merrill ... 1985, '87
Russ "Monk" Meyer* ... 1992
Gene Michael* ... 1976, '78, '84-86, '88-89
George Mitterwald ... 1988
Bill Monbouquette* ... 1985-86
Rich Monteleone ... 2002-04
Tom Morgan* ... 1979
Wally Moses* ... 1961-62, '66
Ed Napoleon ... 1992-93
Graig Nettles ... 1991
Johnny Neun* ... 1944-46
Phil Nevin ... 2018-19
Tom Nieto ... 2000-02
Paddy O'Connor* ... 1918-19
Charley O'Leary* ... 1920-30
Tony Peña ... 2006-17
Jeff Pentland ... 2015
Joe Pepitone ... 1982
Cy Perkins* ... 1932-33
P.J. Pilittere ... 2018-19
Lou Piniella ... 1984-85
Willie Randolph ... 1994-2004
Red Rolfe* ... 1946
Frank Roth* ... 1921-22
Larry Rothschild ... 2011-19
Johnny Sain* ... 1961-63
Germany Schaefer* ... 1916
Paul Schreiber* ... 1942, '45
John Schulte* ... 1934-48
Joe Sewell* ... 1934-35
Bob Shawkey* ... 1929
Glenn Sherlock ... 1995
Buck Showalter ... 1990-91
Luis Sojo ... 2004-05
Joe Sparks ... 1990
John Stearns ... 1989
Mel Stottlemyre* ... 1996-2005
Champ Summers* ... 1989-90
Marcus Thames ... 2016-19
Rob Thomson ... 2008-17
Jeff Torborg ... 1979-88
Earl Torgeson* ... 1961
Gary Tuck ... 1997-99, 2003-04, '14-15
Jim Turner* ... 1949-59, '66-73
Mickey Vernon* ... 1982
Jerry Walker ... 1981-82
Lee Walls* ... 1983
Jay Ward* ... 1987
Roy White ... 1983-84, '86, 2004-05
Stan Williams ... 1980-82, '87-88
Reggie Willits ... 2018-19
George Wiltse* ... 1925
Mel Wright* ... 1974-75
Don Zimmer* ... 1983, '86, '96-03

PASSINGS SINCE LAST PUBLICATION

NYY PLAYERS & COACHES

Jim Bouton
Tex Clevenger
Jim Coates
Bobby Del Greco
Don Larsen
Bobby Mitchell
Irv Noren
Scott Sanderson
Charlie Silvera

EXECUTIVES, FAMILY AND FRIENDS

Howard Cassidy
Harding Peterson
Chace Numata
Julia Ruth Stevens

Yankees Captains

The function of a team captain in baseball has changed over time. Early 20th century baseball rules required teams to designate an active, uniformed player as captain to do many things a modern-day manager typically would take care of, such as changing pitchers, positioning fielders and arguing with umpires. Non-playing managers at that time were limited to directing players from within the confines of the dugout. By the mid-1910s, however, managers assumed the modern responsibilities they have today, and the designation of captain became largely ceremonial. (Please note that extensive research efforts have not uncovered if the Yankees had a captain in 1912. Additionally, Everett Scott filled the role of captain during the 1922 and 1923 World Series).

1. Clark Griffith ... 1903-05
2. Norman "Kid" Elberfeld ... 1906-08
3. Willie Keeler ... 1909
4. Hal Chase ... 1910-11
5. Frank Chance ... start 1913 - midseason
6. Rollie Zeider ... midseason 1913 - end of season
7. Roger Peckinpaugh ... 1914-21
8. Babe Ruth ... 3/13/22-5/25/22*
9. Lou Gehrig ... 4/12/35-1939
10. Thurman Munson ... 4/17/76-8/2/79
11. Graig Nettles ... 1/29/82-3/30/84
12. Willie Randolph ... 3/4/86-10/2/88
13. Ron Guidry ... 3/4/86-7/12/89
14. Don Mattingly ... 2/28/91-1995
15. Derek Jeter ... 6/3/03-2014

*Did not play in the team's first 33 games of the season. Was an active captain for just six total games from 5/20-25/22.

Roger Peckinpaugh, who also managed the club in 1914, was the second-longest serving captain in team history.

All-Time Numerical Roster

In 1929, the New York Yankees and Cleveland Indians became the first teams to make numbers a permanent part of the uniform. Other teams quickly adopted the idea and, by 1932, uniform numbers became standard for all teams. The Yankees' initial distribution of numbers was made according to the player's spot in the batting order. Therefore, in 1929, leadoff hitter Earle Combs wore No. 1; Mark Koenig No. 2; Babe Ruth No. 3; Lou Gehrig No. 4; Bob Meusel No. 5; Tony Lazzeri No. 6; Leo Durocher No. 7; Johnny Grabowski No. 8; Benny Bengough No. 9; and Bill Dickey No. 10 (Grabowski, Bengough and Dickey shared catching duties). After some exhaustive research, the Yankees' Media Relations staff compiled the following list of Yankees uniform numbers.

The list represents uniform numbers worn by coaches (c), managers (m) and players who officially appeared in a regular season game. Yankees retired numbers are denoted in boldface text.

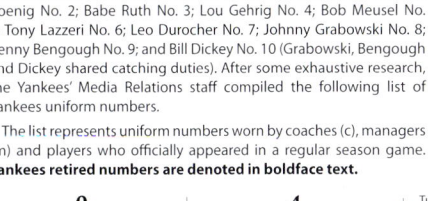

Yogi Berra (No. 8) congratulates Roger Maris on hitting his 61st home run on Oct. 1, 1961.

0
Adam Ottavino 2019

1
Earle Combs 1929-35
George Selkirk 1934
Roy Johnson 1936
Frank Crosetti 1937-44
Tuck Stainback................1944
Snuffy Stirnweiss......... 1945-50
Billy Martin 1951-57
Bobby Richardson....... 1958-66
Bobby Murcer.............. 1969-74
Billy Martin (m).......1975-79, '83, '85, '88

2
Mark Koenig 1929-30
Yats Wuestling 1930
Joe Sewell 1931
Lyn Lary 1931-34
Red Rolfe 1934-42
Snuffy Stirnweiss......... 1943-44
Frank Crosetti 1945-46
Frank Crosetti (c)......... 1947-68
Jerry Kenney............... 1969-72
Matty Alou.......................1973
Sandy Alomar.............. 1974-76
Paul Blair 1977-79
Darryl Jones 1979
Bobby Murcer.............. 1979-83
Tim Foli.........................1984
Dale Berra 1985-86
Wayne Tolleson 1986-90
Graig Nettles (c)...............1991
Mike Gallego............... 1992-94
Derek Jeter.......... 1995-2014

Derek Jeter wore No. 2.

3
Babe Ruth............. 1929-34
George Selkirk 1935-42
Bud Metheny.............. 1943-46
Eddie Bockman 1946
Roy Weatherly 1946
Allie Clark......................1947
Frank Colman..................1947
Cliff Mapes.....................1948

4
Lou Gehrig 1929-39

5
Bob Meusel....................1929
Tony Lazzeri 1930-31
Frank Crosetti 1932-36
Nolen Richardson 1935
Joe DiMaggio ... 1937-42, '46-51
Nick Etten 1943-45

6
Tony Lazzeri 1929, 1934-37
Dusty Cooke 1930-31
Ben Chapman............. 1932-33
Joe Gordon .... 1938-43, '46
Don Savage.............. 1944-45
Bobby Brown 1947-52
Mickey Mantle.................1951
Andy Carey 1952-60
Deron Johnson 1961
Clete Boyer 1961-66
Charley Smith............. 1967-68
Roy White.................. 1969-79
Ken Griffey, Sr. 1982
Roy White (c)........ 1983-84, '86
Mike Pagliarulo................1985
Rick Cerone 1987
Jack Clark......................1988
Clete Boyer (c) 1988, 1992-94
Steve Sax 1989-91
Tony Fernandez................1995
Joe Torre (m) 1996-2007

7
Leo Durocher 1929
Ben Chapman... 1930-31, '34-36
Jack Saltzgaver 1932
Tony Lazzeri 1933
Jake Powell 1936-38
Tommy Henrich 1939-42
Mke Chartak 1940
Roy Cullenbine................1942
Billy Johnson...................1943
Oscar Grimes 1944-46
Bobby Brown 1946
Chuck Dressen (c) 1947-48
Cliff Mapes.................. 1949-51
Bob Cerv.......................1951
Mickey Mantle....... 1951-68
Mickey Mantle (c)............. 1970

8
Johnny Grabowski.............1929
Bill Dickey............. 1930-43
Johnny Lindell............. 1944-45
Aaron Robinson........... 1945, '47
Frank Colman..................1946
Bill Dickey (m)............ 1946
Yogi Berra........... 1948-63
Yogi Berra (c) ..... 1963, '76-83
Yogi Berra (m) ..... 1964, '84-85

9
Benny Bengough 1929
Bubbles Hargrave 1930
Cy Perkins 1931
Art Jorgens 1932-35
Joe Glenn......................1933
Joe DiMaggio..................1936
Myril Hoag................. 1937-38
Charlie Keller .... 1939-43, '45, '49
Ed Levy 1944

Tuck Stainback................1944
Hersh Martin.............. 1944-45
Nick Etten 1946
George McQuinn.......... 1947-48
Dick Wakefield 1950
Hank Workman 1950
Jim Brideweser.................1951
Bobby Brown 1951
Hank Bauer 1952-59
Roger Maris 1960-66
Steve Whitaker.................1968
Dick Simpson..................1969
Ron Woods................. 1969-71
Graig Nettles 1973-82

10
Bill Dickey 1929
Benny Bengough 1930
Art Jorgens 1931
Tony Rensa 1933
George Pipgras............ 1932-33
Don Heffner 1934-37
Bill Knickerbocker.......... 1938-40
Phil Rizzuto .... 1941-42, '46-56
Roy Weatherly 1943
Mike Garbark 1944-45
Tony Kubek................. 1958-65
Dick Howser 1967-68
Frank Fernandez 1969
Danny Cater 1970-71
Celerino Sanchez 1972-73
Chris Chambliss 1974-79
Rick Cerone 1980-84

11
Herb Pennock..................1929
Ownie Carroll..................1930
Waite Hoyt.....................1930
Lefty Gomez............... 1932-42
Tommy Byrne 1943
Bob Collins 1944
Joe Page 1945-50
Johnny Sain................ 1951-55
Jerry Lumpe 1956-59
Hector Lopez 1959-66
Bill Robinson............... 1967-69
Danny Walton..................1971
Bernie Allen 1972-73
Fred Stanley 1973-80
Sandy Alomar..................1974
Gene Michael (m) 1981-82
Jeff Torborg (c) 1983
Toby Harrah 1984
Billy Sample 1985
Gary Roenicke 1986
Lenn Sakata...................1987
Don Slaught 1988-89
Rick Cerone 1990
Buck Showalter (c) 1991
Buck Showalter (m) 1992-95
Dwight Gooden............ 1996-97
Chuck Knoblauch 1998-2001
Chris Widger...................2002
Erick Almonte..................2003
Curtis Pride 2003
Gary Sheffield............. 2004-06
Doug Mientkiewicz 2007
Morgan Ensberg 2008
Brett Gardner.............. 2008-19

12
Waite Hoyt.....................1929
George Pipgras 1930-31
Herb Pennock.............. 1932-33
Jack Saltzgaver........... 1934-37
Babe Dahlgren 1938-40
Buddy Rosar 1941-42
Oscar Grimes 1943
Mike Milosevich................1944
Joe Buzas......................1945
Charlie Keller 1945-49
Ralph Buxton 1949
Billy Martin 1950
Gil McDougald............. 1951-60
Billy Gardner 1961-62
Mike Hegan....................1964
Phil Linz 1965
Ruben Amaro, Sr. 1966-68
Billy Cowan 1969
Ron Blomberg .... 1969, '71-77
Jim Spencer................ 1978-81
Dave Revering............. 1981-82
Roy Smalley................ 1983-84
Ron Hassey................. 1985-86
Joel Skinner................ 1986-88
Tom Brookens 1989
Alvaro Espinoza...............1990
Jim Leyritz .... 1990-92, '99
Torey Lovullo 1991
Carlos Rodriguez..............1991
Wade Boggs................ 1993-97
Roger Clemens.................1999
Denny Neagle 2000
Clay Bellinger..................2001
Alfonso Soriano........ 2002-03, '13-14
Kenny Lofton 2004
Tony Womack..................2005
Andy Phillips 2006-07
Kevin Thompson...............2007
Alberto Gonzalez 2008
Ivan Rodriguez.................2008
Cody Ransom 2009
Josh Towers...................2009
Eduardo Nunez 2010
Eric Chavez 2011-12
Vernon Wells...................2013
Chase Headley 2014-17
Tyler Wade....................2018
Troy Tulowitzki.................2019

13
Cliff Mapes....................1948
Curt Blefary................ 1970-71
Walt Williams 1974-75
Bobby Brown 1980-81
Keith Smith 1985
Mike Pagliarulo............ 1986-89
Mike Blowers 1989
Alvaro Espinoza...............1990
Torey Lovullo 1991
Gerald Williams 1992
Jim Leyritz .... 1993-96, '99-2000
Charlie Hayes 1997
Willie Banks 1998
Mike Figga................. 1998-99
Jeff Manto 1999
Jose Vizcaino..................2000
Michael Coleman 2001
Lee Mazzilli (c) 2002
Antonio Osuna................2003
Alex Rodriguez.... 2004-13, '15-16

14

George Pipgras	1929
Hank Johnson	1930-31
Ed Wells	1932
Russ Van Atta	1933-35
Bump Hadley	1936-40
Jerry Priddy	1941-42
Butch Wensloff	1943
Monk Dubiel	1944-45
Cuddles Marshall	1946
Rugger Ardizoia	1947
Ted Sepkowski	1947
Lonny Frey	1947-48
Gene Woodling	1949-54
Bill "Moose" Skowron	1955-62
Harry Bright	1963-64
Pedro Ramos	1964-66
Jerry Kenney	1967
Bobby Cox	1968-69
Ron Swoboda	1971-73
Lou Piniella	1974-84
Lou Piniella (c)	1984-85
Lou Piniella (m)	1986-88
Mike Blowers	1991
Pat Kelly	1991-97
Hideki Irabu	1998-99
Wilson Delgado	2000
Luis Sojo	2000
Joe Oliver	2001
Enrique Wilson	2001-04
Robinson Cano	2005
Russ Johnson	2005
Andy Phillips	2005
Miguel Cairo	2006
Kevin Thompson	2007
Matt DeSalvo	2007
Wilson Betemit	2007-08
Angel Berroa	2009
Eric Hinske	2009
Curtis Granderson	2010-13
Brian Roberts	2014
Martin Prado	2014
Stephen Drew	2015
Starlin Castro	2016-17
Neil Walker	2018
Tyler Wade	2019

15

Hank Johnson	1929
Art Jorgens	1929
Roy Sherid	1930-31
Red Ruffing	1932-42, '46
Hank Borowy	1943-45
Tommy Henrich	1946-50
Tommy Henrich (c)	1951
Archie Wilson	1952
Joe Collins	1953-57
Jim Pisoni	1959-60
Jack Reed	1961
Tom Tresh	1961-69
Thurman Munson	**1969-79**

Thurman Munson's No. 15 was retired in 1979.

16

Tom Zachary	1929-30
Herb Pennock	1930-31
Gordon Rhodes	1932
Wilcy Moore	1932-33
Jimmie DeShong	1934-35
Monte Pearson	1936-40
Johnny Lindell	1941
Tuck Stainback	1942-43
Joe Page	1944
Mel Queen	1944
Herb Crompton	1945
Bill Bevens	1946-47
Ernie Nevel	1950
Whitey Ford	**1953-67**
Whitey Ford (c)	1964, '68, '74-75

17

Fred Heimach	1929
Ed Wells	1930-31
Hank Johnson	1932
Danny MacFayden	1932-34
Jumbo Brown	1935-36
Tommy Henrich	1938-39
Jake Powell	1939-40
Buster Mills	1940
Charley Stanceu	1941
Ed Levy	1942
Bill Zuber	1943-46
Mel Queen	1946-47
Vic Raschi	1947-53
Enos Slaughter	1954-59
Bobby Richardson	1955-56
Elmer Valo	1960
Bob Cerv	1960-62
Lee Thomas	1961
Bobby Murcer	1965-66
Tom Shopay	1967
Gene Michael	1968-74
Mickey Rivers	1976-79
Oscar Gamble	1979-84
Victor Mata	1985
Mike Easler	1986-87
Paul Zuvella	1987
Rafael Santana	1988
Bucky Dent (m)	1989
Claudell Washington	1990
Scott Lusader	1991
Pat Sheridan	1991
Andy Stankiewicz	1992
Spike Owen	1993
Luis Polonia	1994-95
Ruben Rivera	1995
Kenny Rogers	1996-97
Dale Sveum	1998
Ricky Ledee	1999-2000
Dwight Gooden	2000
Darren Bragg	2001
Gerald Williams	2001-02
Alex Arias	2002
John Flaherty	2003-05
Nick Green	2006

Oscar Gamble wore No. 17 from 1979-84.

Chris Basak	2007
Jeff Karstens	2007
Shelley Duncan	2007-08
Justin Christian	2008
Steven Jackson	2009
Kevin Cash	2009
Jerry Hairston, Jr.	2009
Chad Moeller	2010
Lance Berkman	2010
Francisco Cervelli	2011
Jayson Nix	2012-13
Brendan Ryan	2014-15
Ronald Torreyes	2016
Matt Holliday	2017
Aaron Boone (m)	2018-19

18

Wilcy Moore	1929
Bill Werber	1930
Lou McEvoy	1930
Tom Zachary	1930
Red Ruffing	1931
Johnny Allen	1932-35
Art Jorgens	1936-39
Steve Peek	1941
Johnny Lindell	1942-43
Johnny Johnson	1944
Tuck Stainback	1945
Randy Gumpert	1946-48
Bob Porterfield	1948-50
Jack Kramer	1951
Bob Muncrief	1951
Jim McDonald	1952-54
Don Larsen	1955-59
Eli Grba	1960
Fred Kipp	1960
Hal Reniff	1961-67
Steve Barber	1967-68
Mike Kekich	1969-73
Dave Pagan	1973
Mike Hegan	1973-74
Larry Murray	1974
Dave Bergman	1975
Tippy Martinez	1976
Elrod Hendricks	1976-77
Dennis Sherrill	1978
Brian Doyle	1979-80
Larry Milbourne	1981-82
Mike Patterson	1982
Rodney Scott	1982
Andre Robertson	1982-85
Claudell Washington	1986-88
Jamie Quirk	1989
Deion Sanders	1989
Randy Velarde	1989-95
Mariano Duncan	1996-97
Andy Fox	1997
Mike Stanley	1997
Scott Brosius	1998-2001
Marcus Thames	2002
Jeff Weaver	2002-03
Homer Bush	2004
John Olerud	2004
Bubba Crosby	2005
Andy Phillips	2005
Johnny Damon	2006-09
Chad Moeller	2010
Andruw Jones	2011
Hiroki Kuroda	2012-14
Didi Gregorius	2015-19

19

Ed Wells	1929
Harry Rice	1930
Gordon Rhodes	1930-31
Lefty Weinert	1931
Jumbo Brown	1932-33
Johnny Murphy	1934-41, '43, '46
Hersh Martin	1944

Larry Rosenthal	1944
Ken Holcombe	1945
Karl Drews	1947-48
Dick Starr	1948
Cuddles Marshall	1949
Whitey Ford	1950
Bob Porterfield	1951
Spec Shea	1951
Ray Scarborough	1953
Harry Byrd	1954
Bob Turley	1955-62
Stan Williams	1963-64
Bob Friend	1966
Fritz Peterson	1967-74
Dick Tidrow	1974-79
Rick Anderson	1979
Brad Gulden	1980
Dave Righetti	1981-90
Dion James	1992-93
Kevin Elster	1994
Bobby Ojeda	1994
Jack McDowell	1995
Luis Sojo	1996-2001
Luis Polonia	2000
Roberto Kelly	2000
Robin Ventura	2002-03
Aaron Boone	2003
Al Leiter	2005
Bubba Crosby	2004-06
Chris Basak	2007
Kevin Thompson	2007
Tyler Clippard	2007
Chad Moeller	2008
Ramiro Pena	2009-11
Chris Stewart	2012-13
Masahiro Tanaka	2014-19

20

Myles Thomas	1929
Julie Wera	1929
Lefty Gomez	1931
Charlie Devens	1932-33
Johnny Murphy	1932
Don Brennan	1933
Burleigh Grimes	1934
Floyd Newkirk	1934
Harry Smythe	1934
Johnny Broaca	1935-37
Kemp Wicker	1937-38
Oral Hildebrand	1939-40
Ernie "Tiny" Bonham	1940-46
Spec Shea	1947-49, '51
Art Schallock	1951-52
Willy Miranda	1953-54
Billy Hunter	1955-56
Marv Throneberry	1958-59
Joe DeMaestri	1960-61
Bill Kunkel	1963
Horace Clarke	1965-74
Ed Brinkman	1975
Eddie Leon	1975
Mickey Klutts	1976
Bucky Dent	1977-82
Edwin Rodriguez	1982
Rowland Office	1983
Bobby Meacham	1983-88
Keith Smith	1984
Alvaro Espinoza	1989-91
Bucky Dent (m)	1990
Mike Stanley	1992-95, '97
Mike Aldrete	1996
Robert Eenhoorn	1996
Jorge Posada	**1997-2011**

21

George Burns	1929
Gordon Rhodes	1929, '31
Red Ruffing	1930
Joe Sewell	1932-33
John Schulte (c)	1934
Pat Malone	1935-37
Spud Chandler	1938-44, '46, '47
Johnny Cooney	1944
Bill Bevens	1944-45
Cuddles Marshall	1948
Fred Sanford	1949-50
Bob Kuzava	1951-54
Jim Konstanty	1954-56
Sonny Dixon	1956
Ralph Terry	1956-57
Sal Maglie	1957-58
Virgil Trucks	1958
Tex Clevenger	1962
Johnny Keane (m)	1965-66
Roy White	1968
Jim Lyttle	1969
Nate Oliver	1969
Frank Tepedino	1970-71
Rusty Torres	1971-72
Bill Virdon (m)	1974-75

Spud Chandler wore No. 21 from 1938-44 and '46-47.

Cloyd Boyer (c) .... 1975, '77
Bob Lemon (c) 1976
Jay Johnstone 1978
Bob Lemon (m) ... 1978-79, '81-82
Eric Soderholm 1980
Steve Kemp 1983-84
Dan Pasqua 1985-87
Jose Cruz 1988
Ken Phelps 1988-89
Hal Morris 1989
Mike Blowers 1990
Kevin Maas 1990
Deion Sanders 1990
Scott Sanderson 1991-92
Paul O'Neill 1993-2001
LaTroy Hawkins 2008

22

Gene Robertson 1929
Lefty Gomez 1930
Ivy Andrews 1931
Doc Farrell 1932-33
Vito Tamulis 1934-35
Bob Seeds 1936
Tommy Henrich 1937
Roy Johnson 1937
Joe Beggs 1938
Mel Queen 1942
Marius Russo 1939-43
Russ Derry 1944
Bill Drescher 1944
Paul Waner 1945
Red Ruffing 1945-46
Allie Reynolds 1947-54
Mickey McDermott 1956
Darrell Johnson 1958
Gary Blaylock 1959
Jim Bronstad 1959
Billy Short 1960
Bill Stafford 1960-65
Fred Talbot 1966-69
Jack Aker 1969-72
Ron Klimkowski 1972
Hal Lanier 1973
Jim Mason 1974-76
Gil Patterson 1977
Bobby Brown 1979
Ruppert Jones 1980
Jerry Mumphrey 1981-83
Omar Moreno 1983-85
Mike Fischlin 1986
Gary Ward 1987-89
Hal Morris 1989
Luis Polonia 1989-90
Mike Witt 1990
Stump Merrill (m) 1991
Scott Kamieniecki 1992
Jimmy Key 1993-96
Jorge Posada 1997
Mark Whiten 1997
Homer Bush 1998
Tony Tarasco 1999
Roger Clemens ..... 1999-2003, '07
Jon Lieber 2004
Robinson Cano 2005-06
LaTroy Hawkins 2008
Xavier Nady 2008-09
Randy Winn 2010
Chad Huffman 2010
Colin Curtis 2010
Brian Gordon 2011
Aaron Laffey 2011
Greg Golson 2011
Andruw Jones 2012
Brennan Boesch 2013
Thomas Neal 2013
Travis Ishikawa 2013
Vernon Wells 2013
Jacoby Ellsbury 2014-17

23

Tony Lazzeri 1932
Dick Kryhoski 1949
Fenton Mole 1949
Archie Wilson 1951
Bill Miller 1952-54
Tommy Byrne 1954-57
Murry Dickson 1958
Ralph Terry 1959-64
Rich Beck 1965
Jim Brenneman 1965
Billy Bryan 1966-67
Bob Tillman 1967
Ellie Rodriguez 1968
Don Nottebart 1969
John Ellis 1969-72
Jerry Moses 1973
Alex Johnson 1974-75
Oscar Gamble 1976
Damaso Garcia 1978
Luis Tiant 1979-80
Barry Foote 1981-82
Don Zimmer (c) 1983
Don Mattingly 1984-95
Don Mattingly (c) 2004-07

24

Lyn Lary 1929-30
Jim Weaver 1931
Sammy Byrd 1932
Billy Werber 1933
Charlie Devens 1934
Steve Sundra 1936
Ivy Andrews 1937-38
Marv Breuer 1939-43
Al Lyons 1944
Paul Waner 1944
Steve Roser 1945
Billy Johnson 1946-51
Stubby Overmire 1951
Tom Gorman 1952-54
Ralph Branca 1954
Gerry Staley 1955-56
Al Cicotte 1957
Duke Maas 1958-60
Danny McDevitt 1961
Al Downing 1961-69
Ron Klimkowski 1970
Felipe Alou 1971-73
Otto Velez .... 1973-74, '76
Rick Bladt 1975
Mike Torrez 1977
Jimmy Wynn 1977
Mickey Klutts 1978
Gary Thomasson 1978
Dennis Werth 1979-81
Butch Hobson 1982
Lee Mazzilli 1982
John Montefusco 1983-84
Rickey Henderson 1985-89
Marcus Lawton 1989
Deion Sanders 1989
Mike Blowers 1990
Kevin Maas 1990-93
Russ Davis 1994-95
Tino Martinez ...... 1996-2001, '05
Ruben Sierra 2003-04
Sidney Ponson 2006
Robinson Cano 2007-13
Scott Sizemore 2014
Zoilo Almonte 2014
Chris Young 2014-15
Ike Davis 2016
Gary Sánchez 2017-19

25

Ben Paschal 1929
Jimmie Reese 1930
Sammy Byrd 1933-34
Jesse Hill 1935
Ted Kleinhans 1936
Kemp Wicker 1936-37
Joe Vance 1937-38
Wes Ferrell 1938-39
Steve Sundra 1940
Eddie Kearse 1942
Aaron Robinson 1943
Al Gettel 1945-46
Ray Mack 1947
Butch Wensloff 1947
Hank Bauer 1948-51
Jackie Jensen 1952
Irv Noren 1952-56
Norm Siebern 1958-59
Kent Hadley 1960
Dale Long 1960
Jesse Gonder 1961
Joe Pepitone 1962-69
Pete Ward 1970
Len Boehmer 1971
Johnny Callison 1972-73
Bobby Bonds 1975
Grant Jackson 1976
Willie Randolph 1976
George Zeber 1977-78
Brian Doyle 1978
Tommy John ...... 1979-82, '86-89
Stefan Wever 1982
Don Baylor 1983-85
Greg Cadaret 1989-92
Jim Abbott 1993-94
Scott Bankhead 1995
Ruben Sierra 1995-96
Cecil Fielder 1996
Joe Girardi 1996-99
Lance Johnson 2000
Chris Turner 2000
Randy Velarde 2001
Jason Giambi 2002-08
Mark Teixeira 2009-16
Shane Robinson 2018
Gleyber Torres 2018-19

26

Cedric Durst 1929
Sammy Byrd 1930
Jimmie Reese 1931
Joe Glenn .... 1932, '35-38
George Uhle 1933-34
Johnny Broaca 1934
Buddy Rosar 1939-40
Ken Silvestri 1941
Ken Sears 1943
Steve Roser .... 1944, '46
Mike Milosevich 1945
Karl Drews 1946
Marius Russo 1946
Don Johnson .... 1947, '50
Hugh Casey 1949
Tom Ferrick 1950-51
Ernie Nevel 1951
Gus Triandos 1953-54
Ryne Duren 1958-61
Tex Clevenger 1961-62
Dale Long 1962-63
Archie Moore 1964-65
John Kennedy 1967
Mike Ferraro 1968
Jimmie Hall 1969
Ron Klimkowski 1969
Frank Baker 1970-71
Fernando Gonzalez 1974
Rich Coggins 1975-76
Juan Bernhardt 1976
Cesar Tovar 1976
Domingo Ramos 1978
Juan Beniquez 1979
Johnny Oates 1980-81
Shane Rawley 1982-84
John Montefusco 1985-86
Joe Niekro 1985-86
Ivan De Jesus 1986
Bryan Little 1986
Paul Zuvella 1986
Rick Rhoden 1987-88
Stan Jefferson 1989
Steve Kiefer 1989
Jimmy Jones 1989-90
Steve Farr 1991-93
Daryl Boston 1994
Kevin Elster 1995
Darryl Strawberry 1995
Andy Fox 1996-97
Homer Bush 1997
Scott Pose 1997
Rey Sanchez 1997, 2005
Shane Spencer 1998
Orlando Hernandez .... 1998-'02, '04
Mark Bellhorn 2005
Sal Fasano 2006
Koyie Hill 2006
Terrence Long 2006
Wil Nieves 2006-07
Jose Molina 2007-09
Nick Johnson 2010
Kevin Russo 2010
Greg Golson 2010
Austin Kearns 2010
Eduardo Nunez 2011-13
Darnell McDonald 2012
Ramiro Pena 2012
Yangervis Solarte 2014
Chris Capuano 2014-15
Johnny Barbato 2016
Chris Parmelee 2016
Tyler Austin 2016-18
Andrew McCutchen 2018
DJ LeMahieu 2019

27

Sammy Byrd 1929
Cedric Durst 1930
Joe Sewell 1931
Myril Hoag 1932
Dixie Walker 1933-36
Zack Taylor 1934
Blondy Ryan 1935
Joe Gallagher 1939
Lee Grissom 1940
Buster Mills 1940
Frenchy Bordagaray 1941
Rollie Hemsley 1943-44
Russ Derry 1945
Johnny Lindell 1946-50
Lew Burdette 1950
Jackie Jensen 1951
Tom Morgan 1951
Jim Brideweser 1952-53
Bobby Brown 1954
Marlin Stuart 1954
Woodie Held .... 1954, '57
Bobby Del Greco 1957-58
Johnny James 1958
Jack Reed 1961-63
Duke Carmel 1965
Dick Schofield 1966
Tom Shopay .... 1967, '69
Jim Lyttle 1970-71
Rich McKinney 1972
Elliott Maddox 1974-76
Marty Perez 1977
Dell Alston 1977-78
Jay Johnstone 1978-79
Brad Gulden 1979
Darryl Jones 1979
Bobby Murcer 1979
Paul Blair 1980
Aurelio Rodriguez 1980-81
Butch Wynegar 1982-86
Keith Hughes 1987
Mark Salas 1987
Neil Allen 1988
Mel Hall 1989-92
Bob Wickman 1993-96
Graeme Lloyd 1996-98
Tony Fossas 1999
Allen Watson 1999-2000
Rondell White 2002
Luis Sojo 2003
Todd Zeile 2003
Kevin Brown 2004-05
Kevin Reese 2006

Tino Martinez wore No. 24 (1996-2001, '05).

Kevin Thompson ... 2006
Darrell Rasner ... 2007
Joe Girardi (m) ... 2008-09
Kevin Russo ... 2010
Colin Curtis ... 2010
Greg Golson ... 2010
Chris Dickerson ... 2011
Raul Ibanez ... 2012
Shawn Kelley ... 2013-14
Ramon Flores ... 2015
Austin Romine ... 2016-17
Giancarlo Stanton ... 2018-19

28

Liz Funk ... 1929
Art Jorgens ... 1930
Myril Hoag ... 1931, '34-36
Babe Dahlgren ... 1937
Frank Makosky ... 1937
Atley Donald ... 1938-45
Spud Chandler ... 1944-45
Hank Majeski ... 1946
Tommy Byrne ... 1946-51, '54
Bill Wight ... 1947
Tom Morgan ... 1951-52, '54-56
Charlie Keller ... 1952
Bill Renna ... 1953
Art Ditmar ... 1957-61
Bud Daley ... 1961-64
Gil Blanco ... 1965
Steve Whitaker ... 1966-67
Andy Kosco ... 1968
Ron Hansen ... 1970-71
Sparky Lyle ... 1972-78
Mike Griffin ... 1979
Bob Watson ... 1980-82
John Mayberry ... 1982
Steve Balboni ... 1983
Bill Monbouquette (c) ... 1985
Rod Scurry ... 1986
Henry Cotto ... 1987
Randy Velarde ... 1987-88
Jerry Royster ... 1987
Al Leiter ... 1988-89
Jesse Barfield ... 1989
Marcus Lawton ... 1989
Hensley Meulens ... 1989
Dale Mohorcic ... 1989
Hal Morris ... 1989
Dave Eiland ... 1989, '91
Brian Dorsett ... 1990
Alan Mills ... 1990
Charlie Hayes ... 1992
Andy Stankiewicz ... 1993
Scott Kamieniecki ... 1993-96
Ruben Rivera ... 1996
Chad Curtis ... 1997-99
David Justice ... 2000-01
John Vander Wal ... 2002
Karim Garcia ... 2003
Charles Gipson ... 2003
Chris Latham ... 2003
Esteban Loaiza ... 2004
Ruben Sierra ... 2005
Melky Cabrera ... 2006-08
Anthony Claggett ... 2009
Brett Tomko ... 2009
Shelley Duncan ... 2009
Joe Girardi (m) ... 2010-17
Austin Romine ... 2018-19

29

Bob Shawkey (c) ... 1929
Lou McEvoy ... 1930
Bob Shawkey (m) ... 1930
Sammy Byrd ... 1931
Art Fletcher (c) ... 1932-39
George Washburn ... 1941
Oscar Grimes ... 1943
Bill Drescher ... 1945-46
Steve Souchock ... 1946
Charley Stanceu ... 1946
Johnny Lucadello ... 1947
Sherm Lollar ... 1947-48
Charlie Silvera ... 1949-56
Bobby Richardson ... 1957
Fritz Brickell ... 1958-59
Hal Stowe ... 1960
Duke Maas ... 1961
Earl Torgeson (c) ... 1961
Hal Brown ... 1962
Harry Bright ... 1963
Tom Metcalf ... 1963
Mike Jurewicz ... 1965
Bobby Tiefenauer ... 1965
Bill Henry ... 1966
Rocky Colavito ... 1968
Mike McCormick ... 1970
Jim Hardin ... 1971
Wade Blasingame ... 1972

Eddie Lopat wore No. 30 as a Yankees player from 1948-55.

Casey Cox ... 1973
Sam McDowell ... 1973
Tom Buskey ... 1973-74
Dick Woodson ... 1974
Catfish Hunter ... 1975-79
Dave Collins ... 1982
Bob Shirley ... 1983-87
Al Holland ... 1987
Paul Zuvella ... 1987
Randy Velarde ... 1987-88
Luis Aguayo ... 1988
Dave LaPoint ... 1989
Jesse Barfield ... 1989-92
Mike Humphreys ... 1993
Andy Stankiewicz ... 1993
Gerald Williams ... 1994-96
Ricky Bones ... 1996
Mike Stanton ... 1997-2002, '05
Bubba Trammell ... 2003
Tony Clark ... 2004
Felix Escalona ... 2005
Tim Redding ... 2005
Octavio Dotel ... 2006
Kei Igawa ... 2007-08
Xavier Nady ... 2008
Cody Ransom ... 2008
Juan Miranda ... 2009
Francisco Cervelli ... 2009-10, '13-14
Rafael Soriano ... 2011-12
David Carpenter ... 2015
Dustin Ackley ... 2016
Tyler Clippard ... 2016-17
Todd Frazier ... 2017
Brandon Drury ... 2018
Adeiny Hechavarria ... 2018
Gio Urshela ... 2019

30

Bots Nekola ... 1929
Gordon Rhodes ... 1929
Art Fletcher (c) ... 1930-31
Jimmy Burke (c) ... 1932
Cy Perkins (c) ... 1933
Joe Sewell (c) ... 1934-35
Earle Combs (c) ... 1936-39
Mike Chartak ... 1940
Norm Branch ... 1941-42
Jim Turner ... 1942-45
Bill Wight ... 1946
Dick Starr ... 1947
Ed Lopat ... 1948-55
Rip Coleman ... 1955-56
Bobby Shantz ... 1957-60
Marshall Bridges ... 1962-63
Mel Stottlemyre ... 1964-74
Willie Randolph ... 1976-88
Bucky Dent (m) ... 1989
Willie Randolph (c) ... 1994-2004
Cory Lidle ... 2006
Matt Smith ... 2006
Scott Patterson ... 2008
Nathan Eovaldi ... 2015-16
Pete Kozma ... 2017
Rob Refsnyder ... 2017
Giovanny Gallegos ... 2017
Ronald Herrera ... 2017
Clint Frazier ... 2017
David Robertson ... 2008-14, '17-18
Edwin Encarnación ... 2019
Thairo Estrada ... 2019

31

Roy Sherid ... 1929
Charles O'Leary (c) ... 1930
Jimmy Burke (c) ... 1931, '33
Cy Perkins (c) ... 1932
John Schulte (c) ... 1935-39
Art Fletcher (c) ... 1940-45
Red Rolfe (c) ... 1946
John Corriden (c) ... 1947-48
Jim Turner (c) ... 1949-59, '66-73
Johnny Sain (c) ... 1961-63
Jim Gleeson (c) ... 1964
Cot Deal (c) ... 1965
Mel Wright (c) ... 1974-75
Ed Figueroa ... 1976-80
Dave Winfield ... 1981-90
Brian Dorsett ... 1990
Hensley Meulens ... 1990-91, '93
Mike Humphreys ... 1992
Bob Wickman ... 1992
Frank Tanana ... 1993
Xavier Hernandez ... 1994
Brian Boehringer ... 1995
Tim Raines ... 1996-98
Dan Naulty ... 1999
Ben Ford ... 2000
Glenallen Hill ... 2000
Lance Johnson ... 2000
Steve Karsay ... 2002-05
Jason Anderson ... 2005
Aaron Small ... 2005
Jose Veras ... 2006
Josh Phelps ... 2007
Edwar Ramirez ... 2007
Ian Kennedy ... 2008
Michael Dunn ... 2009
Javier Vazquez ... 2010
Ichiro Suzuki ... 2012-14
Gregorio Petit ... 2015
Ramon Flores ... 2015
Greg Bird ... 2015
Aaron Hicks ... 2016-19

32

Art Jorgens ... 1929
Frank Barnes ... 1930
Ken Holloway ... 1930
Bill Karlon ... 1930
Dusty Cooke ... 1932
Eddie Phillips ... 1932
Steve Sundra ... 1938-39
Earle Combs (c) ... 1940-44
Johnny Neun (c) ... 1944-46
Johnny Neun (m) ... 1946
Ralph Houk ... 1947-52
Ralph Houk (c) ... 1953-54
Elston Howard ... 1955-67
Elston Howard (c) ... 1969-79

33

Charles O'Leary (c) ... 1929
Jim Weaver ... 1931
Pete Appleton* (aka Jablonowski) ... 1933
Charlie Devens ... 1933
Lee Stine ... 1938
John Schulte (c) ... 1940-48
Bill Dickey (c) ... 1949-57, '60
Randy Gumpert (c) ... 1957
Charlie Keller (c) ... 1957-59
George "Doc" Medich ... 1974-75
Bob Lemon (c) ... 1976
Bobby Cox (c) ... 1977
Gene Michael (c) ... 1978
Mike Ferraro (c) ... 1979-82
Ken Griffey, Sr. ... 1983-86
Tim Stoddard ... 1986
Claudell Washington ... 1986
Ron Kittle ... 1986-87
Jack Clark ... 1988
Steve Shields ... 1988
Bob Brower ... 1989
Scott Nielsen ... 1989
Eric Plunk ... 1989-91
Melido Perez ... 1992-95
Charlie Hayes ... 1996
David Wells ... 1997-98, 2002-03
Jose Canseco ... 2000
Ryan Thompson ... 2000
Alfonso Soriano ... 2000-01
Javier Vazquez ... 2004
Jaret Wright ... 2005
Kelly Stinnett ... 2006
Brian Bruney ... 2006-08
Nick Swisher ... 2009-12
Travis Hafner ... 2013
Kelly Johnson ... 2014
Stephen Drew ... 2014
Garrett Jones ... 2015
Chris Martin ... 2015
Greg Bird ... 2017-19

34

Art Fletcher (m) ... 1929
Foster Edwards ... 1930
Lou McEvoy ... 1931
Ivy Andrews ... 1931-32
Frank Makosky ... 1937
Johnny Sturm ... 1941
Buddy Hassett ... 1942
Ken Silvestri ... 1946-47
Bobo Newsom ... 1947
Bob Cerv ... 1952
Kal Segrist ... 1952
Tony Kubek ... 1957
Clete Boyer ... 1959-61
Bob Hale ... 1961
Phil Linz ... 1962-64
Mike Hegan ... 1966-67
Dick Howser (c) ... 1969-78
Lenny Randle ... 1979
Dick Howser (m) ... 1980
Dave LaRoche ... 1981-82
Roy Smalley ... 1982
Matt Keough ... 1983
Scott Bradley ... 1984-85
Mike Armstrong ... 1986
Doug Drabek ... 1986
Mike Ferraro (c) ... 1987-88
Bob Davidson ... 1989
Rich Dotson ... 1989
Don Schulze ... 1989
Walt Terrell ... 1989
Pascual Perez ... 1990-91
Mike Humphreys ... 1992
Jerry Nielsen ... 1992
Andy Cook ... 1993
Sterling Hitchcock ... 1993
Sam Militello ... 1993
Greg Harris ... 1994
Rob Murphy ... 1994
Bob MacDonald ... 1995
Mel Stottlemyre (c) ... 1996-2005
Jaret Wright ... 2006
Sean Henn ... 2007
Phil Hughes ... 2008
Damaso Marte ... 2008
A.J. Burnett ... 2009-11
Derek Lowe ... 2012
Vidal Nuno ... 2013
Chris Bootcheck ... 2013
Jim Miller ... 2013
Brian McCann ... 2014-16
Dustin Fowler ... 2017
Jaime García ... 2017
Jace Peterson ... 2018
J.A. Happ ... 2018-19

35

Dixie Walker ... 1931
Spud Chandler ... 1937
Paul Schreiber (c) ... 1945
Aaron Robinson ... 1946
Yogi Berra ... 1947
Red Embree ... 1948
Mickey Witek ... 1949
Duane Pillette ... 1949-50
Joe Ostrowski ... 1950-52
Steve Kraly ... 1953
Johnny Schmitz ... 1953

Lou Berberet ... 1955
Ralph Houk (c) ... 1958-60
Ralph Houk (m) ... 1961-63,'66-73
Vern Benson (c) ... 1965-66
Don Gullett ... 1977-78
Bill Castro ... 1981
Roger Erickson ... 1982-83
Phil Niekro ... 1984-85
Bob Tewksbury ... 1986-87
Steve Trout ... 1987
Lee Guetterman ... 1988-92
Curt Young ... 1992
Andy Stankiewicz ... 1993
Paul Gibson ... 1993-1994
John Wetteland ... 1995-96
Hideki Irabu ... 1997
Clay Bellinger ... 1999-2000
Mike Mussina ... 2001-08
David Aardsma ... 2012
Brendan Ryan ... 2013
Michael Pineda ... 2014-17
Phil Nevin (c) ... 2018
Chance Adams ... 2019
Cory Gearrin ... 2019

36

Mel Queen ... 1942
Jake Wade ... 1946
Al Lyons ... 1946-1947
Jack Phillips ... 1947-49
Johnny Mize ... 1949-53
Eddie Robinson ... 1954-56
Norm Siebern ... 1956
Harry Simpson ... 1957-58
Ed Lopat (c) ... 1960
Wally Moses (c) ... 1961-62, '66
Loren Babe (c) ... 1967
Hal Lanier ... 1972
Pat Dobson ... 1973-75
Dock Ellis ... 1976-77
Stan Thomas ... 1977
Rawly Eastwick ... 1978
Paul Lindblad ... 1978
Dave Rajsich ... 1978
Don Hood ... 1979
Paul Mirabella ... 1979
Jim Kaat ... 1979-80
Gaylord Perry ... 1980
Rick Reuschel ... 1981
Steve Balboni ... 1981-82
Mike Armstrong ... 1984-86
Al Holland ... 1986
Phil Lombardi ... 1986
Brad Arnsberg ... 1987
Jeff Moronko ... 1987
Rich Dotson ... 1988
Billy Connors (c) ... 1989-90, '94-95
Mike Humphreys ... 1991
Mike Witt ... 1991
Shawn Hillegas ... 1992
Dave Silvestri ... 1992
Russ Springer ... 1992
Gerald Williams ... 1993
David Cone ... 1995-2000
Bobby Estalella ... 2001
Nick Johnson ... 2002-03, '10
Tom Gordon ... 2004-05
Mike Myers ... 2006-07
Jim Brower ... 2007
Ian Kennedy ... 2007
Edwar Ramirez ... 2008-09
Freddy Garcia ... 2011-12
Kevin Youkilis ... 2013
Carlos Beltran ... 2014-16
Billy Butler ... 2016
Tyler Webb ... 2017
Ji-Man Choi ... 2017
Erik Kratz ... 2017
Lance Lynn ... 2018
Jake Barrett ... 2019
Mike Ford ... 2019
Kendrys Morales ... 2019
Breyvic Valera ... 2019

37

Herb Karpel ... 1946
Gus Niarhos ... 1946
Bucky Harris (m) ... 1947-48
Casey Stengel (m) ... 1949-60

38

Hank Borowy ... 1942
Yogi Berra ... 1946
Frank Hiller ... 1946
Karl Drews ... 1947
Gus Niarhos ... 1948-50
Johnny Hopp ... 1950-52
Loren Babe ... 1952-53
Art Schallock ... 1953-55
Ted Gray ... 1955
Johnny Blanchard ... 1955,'59-65
Doc Edwards ... 1965
Frank Fernandez ... 1967-68
Len Boehmer ... 1969
Steve Kline ... 1970-74
Cecil Upshaw ... 1974
Ken Brett ... 1976
Carlos May ... 1976-77
Jerry Narron ... 1979
Tom Underwood ... 1980-81
Barry Evans ... 1982
Curt Kaufman ... 1982
Dave Stegman ... 1982
Dave LaRoche ... 1983
Jose Rijo ... 1984
Ed Whitson ... 1985-86
Leo Hernandez ... 1986
Pat Clements ... 1987-88
Hal Morris ... 1988
Scott Nielsen ... 1988
Clay Parker ... 1989-90
Matt Nokes ... 1990-94
Josias Manzanillo ... 1995
Jeff Patterson ... 1995
Matt Howard ... 1996
Homer Bush ... 1997
Scott Pose ... 1997
Ricky Ledee ... 1998
Jason Grimsley ... 1999-2000
Randy Choate ... 2001-03
Drew Henson ... 2003
Bret Prinz ... 2003
Travis Lee ... 2004
Buddy Groom ... 2005
Ramiro Mendoza ... 2005
T.J. Beam ... 2006
Kris Wilson ... 2006
Chase Wright ... 2007
Chris Stewart ... 2008
Dan Giese ... 2008
Brian Bruney ... 2009
Ian Kennedy ... 2009
Marcus Thames ... 2010
Luis Ayala ... 2011
Cody Eppley ... 2012-13
Preston Claiborne ... 2013-14
Brandon McCarthy ... 2014
Jose Pirela ... 2015
Andrew Bailey ... 2015
Ben Gamel ... 2016
Chad Green ... 2016
Rob Refsnyder ... 2016-17
Kyle Higashioka ... 2017
Shane Robinson ... 2018
Jonathan Loaisiga ... 2018-19
Cameron Maybin ... 2019

39

Mike Chartak ... 1942
Rollie Hemsley ... 1942
Tommy Byrne ... 1946
Frank Hiller ... 1948-49
Wally Hood Jr. ... 1949
Harry Schaeffer ... 1952
Bob Wiesler ... 1954-55
George Wilson ... 1956
Darrell Johnson ... 1957
Jim Coates ... 1959-62
Steve Hamilton ... 1963-70
Gary Jones ... 1970-71
Rob Gardner ... 1971
Casey Cox ... 1972
Wayne Granger ... 1973
Jim Magnuson ... 1973
Larry Gura ... 1974-75
Gene Michael (c) ... 1976
Mickey Klutts ... 1977
Ron Davis ... 1979-81
Mike Morgan ... 1982
Roy Smalley ... 1982
Bert Campaneris ... 1983
Larry Milbourne ... 1983
Don Cooper ... 1985
Joe Niekro ... 1986-87
Pat Clements ... 1987
Roberto Kelly ... 1987-92
Mike Humphreys ... 1993
Mike Witt ... 1993
Donn Pall ... 1994
Dion James ... 1995-96
Brian Boehringer ... 1996
Paul Gibson ... 1996
Matt Luke ... 1996
Darryl Strawberry ... 1996-99
Mark Wohlers ... 2001
Ron Coomer ... 2002
Chris Hammond ... 2003
Andy Phillips ... 2004
Melky Cabrera ... 2005
Kevin Reese ... 2005
Shawn Chacon ... 2005-06
Craig Wilson ... 2006
Chris Britton ... 2007-08
Ross Ohlendorf ... 2008
Richie Sexson ... 2008
Anthony Claggett ... 2009
Mark Melancon ... 2009-10
Kerry Wood ... 2010
Lance Pendleton ... 2011
Amauri Sanit ... 2011
Aaron Laffey ... 2011
Clay Rapada ... 2012
Chris Nelson ... 2013
David Adams ... 2013
Brent Lillibridge ... 2013
Mark Reynolds ... 2013
Shane Greene ... 2014
Chase Whitley ... 2014-15
Kirby Yates ... 2016
Chad Green ... 2016
Tommy Layne ... 2016-17
Tyler Wade ... 2017
Billy McKinney ... 2018
Mike Tauchman ... 2019

40

Charlie Silvera ... 1948
Jackie Jensen ... 1950-51
Bob Wiesler ... 1951
Bobby Hogue ... 1951-52
Johnny Schmitz ... 1952
Ewell Blackwell ... 1952-53
Tom Carroll ... 1955-56
John Gabler ... 1959-60
Jack Cullen ... 1962
Lou Clinton ... 1966-67
Bill Monbouquette ... 1967-68
Lindy McDaniel ... 1968-73
Rick Sawyer ... 1974
Tippy Martinez ... 1974-76
Fran Healy ... 1976-78
Ron Davis ... 1978
Bob Kammeyer ... 1978
Larry McCall ... 1978
Charlie Lau (c) ... 1979-81
Mickey Vernon (c) ... 1982
Don Zimmer (c) ... 1983, '86
Gene Michael (c) ... 1984-86
Stan Williams (c) ... 1987
Clyde King (c) ... 1988
Steve Shields ... 1988
Andy Hawkins ... 1989-91
Scott Kamieniecki ... 1991
Tony Cloninger (c) ... 1992-2001
Darren Holmes ... 1998
Dan Miceli ... 2003
Gabe White ... 2003-04
C.J. Nitkowski ... 2004
Chien-Ming Wang ... 2005-09
Dustin Moseley ... 2010
Bartolo Colon ... 2011
Chad Qualls ... 2012
Francisco Cervelli ... 2012
Alberto Gonzalez ... 2013
Reid Brignac ... 2013
Matt Daley ... 2013-14
Bruce Billings ... 2014
Eury Perez ... 2014
Matt Tracy ... 2015
Kyle Davies ... 2015
Branden Pinder ... 2015
Sergio Santos ... 2015
Cole Figueroa ... 2015
Luis Severino ... 2015-19

41

Steve Souchock ... 1946, '48
Frank Hiller ... 1946, '49
Joe Collins ... 1949-52
Bob Cerv ... 1953-56
Zeke Bella ... 1957
Ken Hunt ... 1960
Jake Gibbs ... 1962-71
Frank Tepedino ... 1972
Otto Velez ... 1973
Duke Sims ... 1974
Mike Wallace ... 1974-75
Rick Sawyer ... 1975
Cliff Johnson ... 1977-79
George Scott ... 1979
Jeff Torborg (c) ... 1980-83
Shane Rawley ... 1983
Sammy Ellis (c) ... 1983-84, '86
Joe Cowley ... 1984-85
Scott Nielsen ... 1986
Charles Hudson ... 1987-88
Lance McCullers ... 1989-90
Stump Merrill (m) ... 1990
Darrell Evans (c) ... 1990
Wade Taylor ... 1991
Tim Burke ... 1992
Russ Springer ... 1992
Jake Gibbs (c) ... 1993
Sterling Hitchcock ... 1994-95, '01-03
Jorge Posada ... 1996
Brian Boehringer ... 1996-97, 2001
Tony Cloninger (c) ... 1998
Mike Buddie ... 1999
Ed Yarnall ... 2000
Jorge De Paula ... 2003
Miguel Cairo ... 2004
Randy Johnson ... 2005-06
Miguel Cairo ... 2007
Jose Veras ... 2007-09
Chad Gaudin ... 2009-10
Ivan Nova ... 2010
Buddy Carlyle ... 2011
Jeff Marquez ... 2011
Scott Proctor ... 2011
David Phelps ... 2012-14
Justin Wilson ... 2015
Nick Goody ... 2016
Chad Green ... 2016
Anthony Swarzak ... 2016
Ronald Herrera ... 2017
Mason Williams ... 2017
Miguel Andújar ... 2017
Ben Heller ... 2017
Caleb Smith ... 2017
Miguel Andújar ... 2018-19

42

Vic Raschi ... 1946
Butch Wensloff ... 1947
Joe Collins ... 1948
Bud Stewart ... 1948
Jerry Coleman ... 1949-57
Pedro Gonzalez ... 1963-65
Ray Barker ... 1965-67
Charlie Spikes ... 1972
George "Doc" Medich ... 1973
Ken Wright ... 1974
Bob Oliver ... 1975
Art Fowler (c) ... 1977-79, '83, '88
Tom Morgan (c) ... 1979
Stan Williams (c) ... 1980-82, '88
Clyde King (c) ... 1981
Clyde King (m) ... 1982
Jerry Walker (c) ... 1982
Jerry McNertney (c) ... 1984
Doug Holmquist (c) ... 1984-85
Stump Merrill (c) ... 1985-87
Billy Connors (c) ... 1989
Dave LaPoint ... 1989-90
John Habyan ... 1991-93
Domingo Jean ... 1993
Mariano Rivera ... 1995-2013

43

Vic Raschi ... 1947
Art Schult ... 1953
Dick Tettlebach ... 1955
Deron Johnson ... 1960
Roger Repoz ... 1964-66
Mike Ferraro ... 1966
Ross Moschitto ... 1967
Dale Roberts ... 1967
Rob Gardner ... 1970-72
Terry Ley ... 1971
Jim Magnuson ... 1973
Jim Ray Hart ... 1973-74
Jim Deidel ... 1974
Rudy May ... 1974-76
Jim York ... 1976
Ken Clay ... 1978-79
Doug Bird ... 1980-81
George Frazier ... 1981-83
Jeff Torborg (c) ... 1984
Rich Bordi ... 1985
Tim Stoddard ... 1986-88
Lee Elia (c) ... 1989
Gene Michael (c) ... 1989
Jeff Robinson ... 1990
Torey Lovullo ... 1991
Jeff Johnson ... 1991-93
Sam Militello ... 1992
Paul Assenmacher ... 1993
Bob Melvin ... 1994
Nardi Contreras (c) ... 1995
Dave Silvestri ... 1995
Jeff Nelson ... 1996-2000, '03
Todd Greene ... 2001
Christian Parker ... 2001
Ted Lilly ... 2002
Raul Mondesi ... 2002-03
Jorge De Paula ... 2004
Scott Proctor ... 2005-07
Darrell Rasner ... 2008
Damaso Marte ... 2009-10
D.J. Mitchell ... 2012

Ryota Igarashi....2012
Steve Pearce....2012
Phil Coke....2016
Anthony Swarzak....2016
Adam Warren....2012-18
Chance Adams....2018
Jonathan Loaisiga....2019

44

Frank Verdi....1953
Marv Throneberry....1955
Ken Hunt....1959-60
Jim Hegan (c)....1960-73
Bill Sudakis....1974
Terry Whitfield....1975-76
Reggie Jackson....1977-81
Jeff Torborg (c)....1984-88
John Stearns (c)....1989
Mike Ferraro (c)....1990-91

45

Clint Courtney....1951
Don Bollweg....1953
Lou Skizas....1956
Mark Freeman....1959
Rollie Sheldon....1961-62, '64-65
Jack Cullen....1965-66
Stan Bahnsen....1966, '68-71
Steve Barber....1967
Larry Gowell....1972
Rich Hinton....1972
Ed Herrmann....1975
Jim Beattie....1978-79
Rudy May....1980-83
Dennis Rasmussen....1984-87
Bill Gullickson....1987
John Candelaria....1988-89
Kevin Mmahat....1989
Steve Balboni....1990
Alan Mills....1991
Rich Monteleone....1991
Danny Tartabull....1992-95
Andy Fox....1995
Joe Girardi....1996
Cecil Fielder....1996-97
Chili Davis....1998-99
Felix Jose....2000
Ryan Thompson....2000
Henry Rodriguez....2001
Jay Witasick....2001
Alberto Castillo....2002
Jason Anderson....2003
Armando Benitez....2003
Felix Heredia....2003-04
Carl Pavano....2005, '07-08
Kevin Whelan....2011
Sergio Mitre....2009-11
Hector Noesi....2011
Dewayne Wise....2012
Casey McGehee....2012
Ben Francisco....2013
Zoilo Almonte....2013
David Adams....2013
Dean Anna....2014
Scott Sizemore....2014
Zelous Wheeler....2014
Austin Romine....2014
Chasen Shreve....2015-18
Luke Voit....2018-19

Cecil Fielder wore No. 45 with the Yankees.

46

Charlie Silvera....1948
Dave Madison....1950
Bill Short....1960
Frank Tepedino....1969
Bobby Mitchell....1970
Roger Hambright....1971
Otto Velez....1973
Rick Dempsey....1973-76
Gene Locklear....1976-77
Mike Heath....1978
Don Hood....1979
Joe Lefebvre....1980
Gene Nelson....1981
Joe Pepitone (c)....1982
Shane Rawley....1982
Don Mattingly....1982-83
Mike Pagliarulo....1984
Henry Cotto....1985-86
Ivan DeJesus....1986
Rich Bordi....1987
Roberto Kelly....1987
Jerry Royster....1987
Hipolito Pena....1988
Randy Velarde....1988
Ken Phelps`....1988
Dallas Green (m)....1989
Stump Merrill (m)....1990
Joe Sparks (c)....1990
Frank Howard (c)....1991-93
Terry Mulholland....1994
Donovan Osborne....2004
Alan Embree....2005
Darrell May....2005
Scott Erickson....2006
Aaron Guiel....2006
Jose Veras....2006
Andy Pettitte....1995-2003, '07-10, '12-13

47

Frank Colman....1947
Eli Grba....1959
Tom Sturdivant....1955-59
Billy Shantz....1960
Luis Arroyo....1960-63
Bob Schmidt....1965
John Miller....1966
Frank Tepedino....1967
Fred Beene....1972-74
Kerry Dineen....1976
Larry Murray....1976
Bob Lemon (m)....1978
Andy Messersmith....1978
Jim Kaat....1979
Jeff Torborg (c)....1979
Bruce Robinson....1980
Dennis Sherrill....1980
Curt Kaufman....1982
Ray Fontenot....1983-84
Rod Scurry....1985
Al Pulido....1986
Juan Bonilla....1987
Pete Filson....1987
Alvaro Espinoza....1988
Scott Nielsen....1988
Pat Corrales (c)....1989
Champ Summers (c)....1989-90
Marc Hill (c)....1991
Lee Smith....1993
Dave Silvestri....1993-94
Dave Eiland....1995
Rick Honeycutt....1995
Billy Brewer....1996
Dave Pavlas....1996
Ruben Rivera....1996
Ivan Cruz....1997
Shane Spencer....1998-2002
Erick Almonte....2003
Jesse Orosco....2003
Al Reyes....2003
Bret Prinz....2004
Felix Rodriguez....2005
Ron Villone....2006-07
Colter Bean....2007
Chris Britton....2008
Sidney Ponson....2008
Freddy Guzman....2009
Romulo Sanchez....2010
Ivan Nova....2010-16
Blake Parker....2016
Jordan Montgomery....2017-19

48

Frank Colman....1947
Elvio Jimenez....1964
Pedro Ramos....1964
Roy White....1965-68
Cecil Perkins....1967
Sam McDowell....1973-74
Dave Kingman....1977
Mike Torrez....1977
Clyde King (c)....1978
Jim Hegan (c)....1979-80
Joe Altobelli (c)....1981-82, '86
Dale Murray....1983-85
Willie Horton (c)....1985
Neil Allen....1987
Gene Michael (c)....1988
George Mitterwald (c)....1988
Frank Howard (c)....1989
Buck Showalter (c)....1990-91
John Ramos....1991
Russ Meyer (c)....1992
Rick Down (c)....1993-95
Don Zimmer (c)....1996-97
Chris Chambliss (c)....1998-2000
Randy Keisler....2001
Robert Perez....2001
Scott Seabol....2001
Brandon Knight....2002
Jay Tessmer....2002
Fernando Seguignol....2003
Paul Quantrill....2004-05
Wayne Franklin....2005
Kyle Farnsworth....2006-08
Phil Coke....2008-09
Boone Logan....2010-13
Matt Thornton....2014
Josh Outman....2014
Preston Claiborne....2014
Andrew Miller....2015-16
Eric Young Jr.....2016
Chris Carter....2017
Tommy Kahnle....2017-19

49

Lou Berberet....1954
Bob Meyer....1964
Charlie Sands....1967
Loyd Colson....1970
Kerry Dineen....1975
Ron Guidry....1975-88, (c) 2006-07
Jeff Johnson....1992

50

Bill Bryan....1967
Bill Burbach....1969-71
Alan Closter....1971-72
George "Doc" Medich....1972
Dave Pagan....1973
Duke Sims....1973
Ken Clay....1977
Roger Slagle....1979
Clyde King (c)....1981
Lynn McGlothen....1982
John Pacella....1982
Jay Howell....1983-84
Marty Bystrom....1985
Phil Lombardi....1986
Jay Ward (c)....1987
Chris Chambliss....1988
Chris Chambliss (c)....1996-97
Steve Balboni....1989
Oscar Azocar....1990
John Habyan....1990
Alan Mills....1991
Ed Napoleon (c)....1992-93
Robert Eenhoorn....1994-95
Don Zimmer (c)....1998-99
Todd Erdos....2000
Rich Monteleone (c)....2003-04
Matt Lawton....2005
Larry Bowa (c)....2006-07
Bobby Meacham (c)....2008
Mick Kelleher (c)....2009-14
Nick Rumbelow....2015
Tyler Olson....2016
(Note: Despite being issued No. 50, Olson wore No. 42 in his only career NYY appearance which occurred on Jackie Robinson Day.)
Conor Mullee....2016
Richard Bleier....2016
Kirby Yates....2016
Domingo Germán....2017
Ben Heller....2017
Tyler Webb....2017
Giovanny Gallegos....2017
Reggie Willits (c)....2018-19

51

George McQuinn....1947
Frank Leja....1954-55
Gordie Windhorn....1959
Pete Mikkelsen....1964-65
Ralph Houk (m)....1966
Tony Solaita....1968
John Wyatt....1968
Ron Klimkowski....1969
Terry Whitfield....1974
Larry McCall....1977
Dom Scala (c)....1978-86
Cecilio Guante....1987-88
Chuck Cary....1989-91
Bernie Williams....1991-2006

52

Ken Silvestri....1947
Jim Delsing....1949
Jim Coates....1956
Bobby Murcer....1965
Fritz Peterson....1966
Joe Verbanic....1967-70
Larry Murray....1974
Otto Velez....1975
Doyle Alexander....1976, '82-83
Dave Rajsich....1978
Mike Griffin....1979-81
Otis Nixon....1983
Mark Connor (c)....1984-87, '90-93
Juan Espino....1985
Dave Eiland....1988
Bob Geren....1988
Mike Ferraro (c)....1989
Charlie Fox (c)....1989
Mark Hutton....1994, '96
David Weathers....1996-97
Joe Borowski....1997
Pete Incaviglia....1997
Danny Rios....1997
Mike Buddie....1998
Ed Yarnall....1999
Don Zimmer (c)....2000
Gary Denbo (c)....2001
Jose Contreras....2003-04
Joe Girardi....2005
Tony Pena (c)....2006
Luis Vizcaino....2007
Dave Eiland (c)....2008
CC Sabathia....2009-19

53

Bill "Moose" Skowron....1954
Johnny Kucks....1955-59
Johnny James....1960-61
Ross Moschitto....1965, '67
Dave Pagan....1974-76
Ken Holtzman....1976-78
Ron Davis....1978
Larry McCall....1978
Ray Burris....1979
Bob Kammeyer....1979
Tim Lollar....1980
Jerry Walker (c)....1981
Jay Howell....1982-83
Lee Walls (c)....1983
Marty Bystrom....1984
Neil Allen....1985
Orestes Destrade....1987
Bob Geren....1989-91
Glenn Sherlock (c)....1992, '94-95
Neal Heaton....1993
Mark Hutton....1993
Jose Cardenal (c)....1996-99
Alfonso Soriano....2000
Mike Thurman....2002
Don Zimmer (c)....2001
Lee Mazzilli (c)....2003
Luis Sojo (c)....2004-05
Larry Bowa (c)....2006
Bobby Abreu....2006-08
Melky Cabrera....2009
Juan Miranda....2010
Gustavo Molina....2011
Amauri Sanit....2011
Kevin Whelan....2011
Cory Wade....2011-12
Ryota Igarashi....2012
Austin Romine....2013-14
Jim Miller....2014
Jeff Francis....2014
Esmil Rogers....2014-15
Caleb Cotham....2015
Nick Rumbelow....2015
Austin Romine....2015
Joe Espada (c)....2017
Phil Nevin (c)....2018
Zack Britton....2018-19

54

Jim Delsing....1950
Andy Carey....1952
Thad Tillotson....1967-68
Ken Johnson....1969
Gary Waslewski....1970-71
Steve Blateric....1972
Jim Roland....1972
Alex Johnson....1974
Dave Bergman....1977
Cecilio Guante....1987
Rich "Goose" Gossage....1978-83, '89
Brian Fisher....1985-86
Jay Buhner....1987-98
Dale Mohorcic....1988-89
Tim Leary....1990-92
Sterling Hitchcock....1992
Bobby Munoz....1993
Jeff Reardon....1994
Joe Ausanio....1994-95

Jim Mecir ... 1996-97
Todd Erdos ... 1998-99
Lee Mazzilli (c) ... 2000-01, '06
Don Zimmer (c) ... 2002-03
Roy White (c) ... 2004-05
Kevin Long (c) ... 2007-14
Joe Espada (c) ... 2015
Richard Bleier ... 2016
Aroldis Chapman ... 2016-19

Goose Gossage wore No. 54 for all nine teams he played for over a 22-year career.

55

Bob Grim ... 1954-58
Zack Monroe ... 1958-59
Spud Murray (BP pitcher) ... 1961-69
Dave McDonald ... 1969
Paul Mirabella ... 1979
Roger Holt ... 1980
Andre Robertson ... 1981-82
Roy Smalley ... 1982
Stan Javier ... 1984
Victor Mata ... 1984
Juan Bonilla ... 1985
Rich Monteleone ... 1990, '92-93
Brian Butterfield (c) ... 1994-95
Jorge Posada ... 1996
Wally Whitehurst ... 1996
Ramiro Mendoza ... 1997-2002
Hideki Matsui ... 2003-09
Russell Martin ... 2011-12
Lyle Overbay ... 2013
Wade LeBlanc ... 2014
David Huff ... 2014
Jose Ramirez ... 2015
Slade Heathcott ... 2015
Bryan Mitchell ... 2015-17
Sonny Gray ... 2017-18
Domingo Germán ... 2019

56

Jim Bouton ... 1962-68
John Cumberland ... 1968-70
Mike McCormick ... 1970
Gary Jones ... 1970
Dave Righetti ... 1979
Ted Wilborn ... 1980
Mike Patterson ... 1981-82
Andre Robertson ... 1982
Bert Campaneris ... 1983
Curt Brown ... 1984
Rex Hudler ... 1984-85
Al Leiter ... 1987
Brian Dorsett ... 1989
Mark Leiter ... 1990
Dave Silvestri ... 1992
Andy Cook ... 1993
Dave Pavlas ... 1995
Dale Polley ... 1996
Darrell Einertson ... 2000
Ted Lilly ... 2000
Juan Rivera ... 2001
Todd Williams ... 2001
Rick Down (c) ... 2002-03
Scott Proctor ... 2004
Tanyon Sturtze ... 2004-06
Tony Peña (c) ... 2007-17
Jonathan Holder ... 2018-19

57

Arturo Lopez ... 1965
Roy Staiger ... 1979
Clyde King (c) ... 1980
Tucker Ashford ... 1981
Bobby Ramos ... 1982
Juan Bonilla ... 1987
Bob Geren ... 1988
Hensley Meulens ... 1989
Steve Howe ... 1991-96
Ramiro Mendoza ... 1996
Joe Borowski ... 1998
Jeff Juden ... 1999
Jay Tessmer ... 1999-2000
Jake Westbrook ... 2000
Billy Connors (c) ... 2000
Carlos Almanzar ... 2001
Erick Almonte ... 2001
Mark Wohlers ... 2001
Karim Garcia ... 2002
Drew Henson ... 2002
Juan Acevedo ... 2003
Michel Hernandez ... 2003
Alex Graman ... 2004
Brad Halsey ... 2004
Scott Proctor ... 2004
Neil Allen (c) ... 2005
Joe Kerrigan (c) ... 2006-07
Mike Harkey (c) ... 2008-13
Vidal Nuno ... 2014
Rich Hill ... 2014
Chris Martin ... 2015
Branden Pinder ... 2015-16
Gary Sanchez ... 2016
Conor Mullee ... 2016
Nick Goody ... 2016
Donovan Solano ... 2016
Chad Green ... 2016-19

58

Dooley Womack ... 1966-68
Bobby Brown ... 1979
Bruce Robinson ... 1979
Andy McGaffigan ... 1981
Dave Wehrmeister ... 1981
Sammy Ellis (c) ... 1982
Juan Espino ... 1982, '85-86
Mike O'Berry ... 1984
Bob Geren ... 1988
Hensley Meulens ... 1989
Dave Eiland ... 1990
Mike Jerzembeck ... 1998
Alfonso Soriano ... 1999
Randy Choate ... 2000
Randy Keisler ... 2001
Jorge De Paula ... 2005
Alex Graman ... 2005
Sean Henn ... 2005
Mike Vento ... 2005
Colter Bean ... 2005-06
T.J. Beam ... 2006
Jeff Karstens ... 2006-07
Darrell Rasner ... 2006
Dave Eiland (c) ... 2009-10
Larry Rothschild (c) ... 2011-19

59

Damaso Garcia ... 1979
Steve Adkins ... 1990
Hensley Meulens ... 1992
Billy Brewer ... 1996
Ryan Bradley ... 1998
D'Angelo Jimenez ... 1999
Donzell McDonald ... 2001
Juan Rivera ... 2002-03
Rob Thomson (c) ... 2007-17
Josh Bard (c) ... 2018-19

60

Hipolito Pena ... 1988
John Habyan ... 1990
Darrin Chapin ... 1991
J.T. Snow ... 1992
Tim McIntosh ... 1996
Homer Bush ... 1997
Mike Lowell ... 1998
Craig Dingman ... 2000
Brett Jodie ... 2001
Nick Johnson ... 2001
Brandon Knight ... 2002
Erick Almonte ... 2003
Brandon Claussen ... 2003
Felix Escalona ... 2004
Sam Marsonek ... 2004
Wil Nieves ... 2005-06
Ross Ohlendorf ... 2007
Kevin Russo ... 2010
Brandon Laird ... 2011
Chris Dickerson ... 2012
Melky Mesa ... 2013
David Huff ... 2013
Gary Tuck (c) ... 2014-15
Mike Harkey (c) ... 2016-19

61

Marshall Brant ... 1980
Jim Lewis ... 1982
Phil Lombardi ... 1987
John Habyan ... 1990
Jim Bruske ... 1998
Ted Lilly ... 2001
Brad Halsey ... 2004
Juan Padilla ... 2004
Jorge De Paula ... 2005
Darrell Rasner ... 2006
Matt DeSalvo ... 2007
Billy Traber ... 2008
Chan Ho Park ... 2010
Royce Ring ... 2010
Steve Garrison ... 2011
Raul Valdes ... 2011
Corban Joseph ... 2013
David Huff ... 2013
Luis Cruz ... 2013
Dellin Betances ... 2013
Shane Greene ... 2014
Jeff Pentland (c) ... 2015
David Hale ... 2018
Giovanny Gallegos ... 2018
Justus Sheffield ... 2018
Ben Heller ... 2016-17, '19

62

Cloyd Boyer (c) ... 1975
Brian Dayett ... 1983-84
Brad Arnsberg ... 1986
Hal Morris ... 1988
Jorge Posada ... 1995
Willie Banks ... 1997
Jay Tessmer ... 1998, 2000
Brandon Knight ... 2001
Bubba Crosby ... 2004
Sean Henn ... 2006
Joba Chamberlain ... 2007-13
Austin Romine ... 2014
Alan Cockrell (c) ... 2015-17
Marcus Thames (c) ... 2018-19

63

Mike Morgan ... 1982
Jim Walewander ... 1990
Mike Figga ... 1997
Danny Rios ... 1997
Randy Keisler ... 2000
Andy Cannizaro ... 2006
Alberto Gonzalez ... 2007
Jonathan Albaladejo ... 2008-10
Chris Britton ... 2008
Jesus Montero ... 2011
Justin Thomas ... 2012
Chris Leroux ... 2014
Jose Ramirez ... 2014
Antoan Richardson ... 2014
Mason Williams ... 2015
Jose Pirela ... 2015
Marcus Thames (c) ... 2016-17
P.J. Pilitere (c) ... 2018-19

64

Bill Fulton ... 1987
Steve Kiefer ... 1989
Bronson Sardinha ... 2007
Francisco Cervelli ... 2008
Romulo Sanchez ... 2010
Hector Noesi ... 2011
Cesar Cabral ... 2013-14
Chaz Roe ... 2014
Jacob Lindgren ... 2015
Jose De Paula ... 2015
Nick Rumbelow ... 2015
Rob Refsnyder ... 2015
Diego Moreno ... 2015
Ben Gamel ... 2016
Nick Goody ... 2016
Garrett Cooper ... 2017
Domingo Germán ... 2017
Carlos Mendoza (c) ... 2018-19

65

Clyde King (c) ... 1981-82
Juan Espino ... 1983
Adrian Hernandez ... 2001-02
Phil Hughes ... 2007-13
Bryan Mitchell ... 2014-15
Jose Ramirez ... 2015
Danny Burawa ... 2015
Diego Moreno ... 2015
Caleb Cotham ... 2015
Jonathan Holder ... 2016-17
Domingo Germán ... 2018
James Paxton ... 2019

66

Bob Lemon (m) ... 1981
Steve Balboni ... 1981-83
Jim Deshaies ... 1984
Juan Miranda ... 2008
Andrew Brackman ... 2011
John Ryan Murphy ... 2013-15
Mason Williams ... 2016
Bryan Mitchell ... 2017
Kyle Higashioka ... 2018-19

67

Clay Christiansen ... 1984
Dale Mohorcic ... 1988
Greg Golson ... 2011
Melky Mesa ... 2012
Mike Zagurski ... 2013
Jose Pirela ... 2014
James Pazos ... 2015-16
Miguel Andújar ... 2017
A.J. Cole ... 2018
Nestor Cortes Jr. ... 2019

68

Dioner Navarro ... 2004
Dellin Betances ... 2011, '14-19

69

Alan Mills ... 1990

70

George Kontos ... 2011, '18
Brett Marshall ... 2013
Rico Noel ... 2015
Tyler Lyons ... 2019
Breyvic Valera ... 2019

71

Austin Romine ... 2011
Stephen Tarpley ... 2018-19

72

Juan Miranda ... 2009
Slade Heathcott ... 2015
Chance Adams ... 2019
Brady Lail ... 2019

73

Gary Sánchez ... 2015
Ryan Dull ... 2019
Michael King ... 2019
Adonis Rosa ... 2019

74

Nick Goody ... 2015
Ronald Torreyes ... 2017-18
Mike Ford ... 2019
Joseph Harvey ... 2019
Joe Mantiply ... 2019
Breyvic Valera ... 2019

75

David Hale ... 2019

77

Humberto Sanchez ... 2008
Clint Frazier ... 2017-19

85

Luis Cessa ... 2016-19

88

Josh Outman ... 2014
Phil Nevin (c) ... 2019

90

Thairo Estrada ... 2019

91

Alfredo Aceves ... 2008-10, '14

99

Brian Bruney ... 2009
Aaron Judge ... 2016-19

Unknown: Sam Gibson (1930), Roy Schalk (1932)

(c) denotes coach
(m) denotes manager

Brian Bruney was the first Yankee to wear No. 99 in a Major League game.

Home Opener Ceremonial First Pitches

2019 Mariano Rivera
2018 Bucky Dent and Mickey Rivers
2017 Joe Torre, Tino Martinez and Willie Randolph (from WBC-winning Team USA)
2016 Hideki Matsui
2015 Joe Torre
2014 Andy Pettitte and Mariano Rivera caught by Derek Jeter and Jorge Posada
2013 Lou Piniella
2012 Jorge Posada
2011 Mike Mussina
2010 Bernie Williams
2009 Yogi Berra
2008 Reggie Jackson
2007 Melanie Lidle and Christopher Lidle, widow and son of Cory Lidle
2006 Yogi Berra
2005 Yogi Berra
2004 Yogi Berra, Whitey Ford and Phil Rizzuto
2003 Yogi Berra and Whitey Ford
2002 Michael Bloomberg, NYC Mayor
2001 Mel Stottlemyre
2000 Yogi Berra
1999 Yogi Berra
1998 Joe DiMaggio
1997 Joe DiMaggio
1996 Joe DiMaggio
1995 Joe DiMaggio
1994 Joe DiMaggio
1993 Dean Smith, U. of North Carolina Head Basketball Coach (representing N.C. State University Head Basketball Coach Jim Valvano, who was too ill to attend)
1992 Joe DiMaggio
1991 General Colin Powell, Chairman, Joint Chiefs of Staff
1990 Bill Martin Jr.
1989 P.J. Carlesimo, Seton Hall University Head Basketball Coach
1988 Diana Munson, widow of Thurman Munson; and Arlene Howard, widow of Elston Howard
1987 Rachel Robinson, widow of Jackie Robinson
1986 Robert Merrill, Met. Opera
1985 Mickey Mantle
1984 Scott Hamilton, U.S. Olympic Skater
1983 Joe DiMaggio
1982 Jimmy Esposito, Head Groundskeeper whose crew got the field in shape after a heavy snow storm
1981 Elston Howard Jr.
1980 Eric Heiden, Mike Eruzione, and Herb Brooks; 1980 U.S. Olympic Heroes
1979 Lucielle James, widow of WWII hero
1978 No first-pitch ceremony (Mantle and Maris raised 1977 championship flag)
1977 Vince Polito, randomly selected fan
1976 Bob Shawkey, Yankees starting pitcher at opener of Yankee Stadium on 4/18/23
1975 Five children of slain "Good Samaritan" Frank J. Walker
1974 Ted Kennedy Jr., son of United States Senator Ted Kennedy
1973 Herb Bluestone, who attended opening of Yankee Stadium in 1923
1972 Jim Farley, former Postmaster General of the United States
1971 John Lindsay, NYC Mayor
1970 Whitney Young Jr., President of the National Urban League
1969 Paul Simon, singer/songwriter
1968 Marianne Moore, 81-year-old poet and baseball fan
1967 John Lindsay, NYC Mayor
1966 John Lindsay, NYC Mayor
1965 Rick O'Keefe, 7-year-old fan (he would later be a first-round draft pick of the Milwaukee Brewers in 1975)
1964 William Braccidieta, Columbia University student and baseball player (second winner of Yogi Berra Scholarship Award)
1963 Joe DiMaggio
1962 Claire Ruth, widow of Babe Ruth
1961 James Lyons, Bx. Borough Pres. (replacing Mayor Robert Wagner, who was ill)
1960 Joe Cronin, Hall of Famer and AL President

1959 Will Harridge, recently-retired AL President
1958 James Lyons, Bronx Borough President
1957 Robert Wagner Jr., NYC Mayor
1956 Robert Wagner Jr., NYC Mayor
1955 Robert Wagner Jr., NYC Mayor
1954 James Lyons, Bronx Borough Pres.
1953 Vincent Impellitteri, NYC Mayor
1952 Joe DiMaggio (retired after 1951 season)
1951 Whitey Ford (in military service)
1950 Ed Barrow, former Yankees President
1949 Gary Simpson, student at St. Mary's Industrial School in Baltimore, Md. (which was attended by Babe Ruth, who passed away in 1948). Ruth monument unveiled.
1948 Thomas Dewey, New York Governor
1947 Sgt. Anthony Guzzetta, wounded WWII veteran
1946 Sgt. Hulon B. Whittington, Medal of Honor recipient
1945 Fiorello LaGuardia, NYC Mayor
1944 Fiorello LaGuardia, NYC Mayor
1943 Fiorello LaGuardia, NYC Mayor
1942 Fiorello LaGuardia, NYC Mayor
1941 Fiorello LaGuardia, NYC Mayor
1940 Fiorello LaGuardia, NYC Mayor
1939 Fiorello LaGuardia, NYC Mayor
1938 Newbold Morris, NYC Council Pres.
1937 Fiorello LaGuardia, NYC Mayor
1936 Fiorello LaGuardia, NYC Mayor
1935 Fiorello LaGuardia, NYC Mayor
1934 Fiorello LaGuardia, NYC Mayor
1933 John O'Brien, NYC Mayor
1932 Jimmy Walker, NYC Mayor
1931 Jimmy Walker, NYC Mayor
1930 Jimmy Walker, NYC Mayor
1929 Joseph V. McKee, Pres. of the N.Y.C. Board of Aldermen (substituting for Mayor Walker)
1928 Jimmy Walker, NYC Mayor
1927 Jimmy Walker, NYC Mayor
1926 Jimmy Walker, NYC Mayor
1925 Rear Admiral Charles P. Plunkett
1924 John F. Hylan, NYC Mayor
1923 Al Smith, New York Governor
1922 John F. Hylan, NYC Mayor
1921 John F. Hylan, NYC Mayor

New York Governor Al Smith throws out the ceremonial first pitch at Yankee Stadium's inaugural game on April 18, 1923.

1920 Lt. General Robert Bullard
1919 Robert Moran, President of the NYC Board of Aldermen
1918 Brigadier General William Mann
1917 Major General Leonard Wood
1916 Al Smith, Sheriff of New York
1915 John Mitchell, NYC Mayor
1914 Robert Wagner, New York Lieutenant Governor
1913 Bill Devery, co-owner
1912 Edward B. McCall, judge
1911 City Chamberlain Hyde
1910 Bill Devery, co-owner
1909 Tim Foley, Sheriff of New York
1908 George McClellan, NYC Mayor
1907 Diamond Jim Brady
1906 John M. Ward, former player
1905 Game was rained out (Congressman Tim Sullivan had thrown the first pitch)
1904 William Olcott, judge
1903 Ban Johnson, AL President

OPENING DAY RESULTS
The Yankees are 65-51-1 all time on Opening Day (Home: 36-17-1; Road 29-34).

OPENING DAY HOME RUNS
The Yankees have hit 106 Opening Day home runs in franchise history by 65 different players, most recently in 2019, when Luke Voit and Greg Bird each homered vs. Baltimore. Giancarlo Stanton was the last Yankee to homer *twice* on Opening Day, hitting two at Toronto in 2018 (including one in his first PA as a Yankee). Prior to Stanton, **Joe Pepitone** (pictured) was the last Yankee to homer twice on Opening Day (1963).

Babe Ruth hit a franchise-high five OD-HRs, and he is followed by Yogi Berra, Mickey Mantle and Jorge Posada (4HR each). Jorge Posada and Curtis Granderson (2010 at Boston) are the most recent pair of Yankees to hit back-to-back homers in an opener, and they marked the first Yankees to accomplish the feat since Dave Winfield and Steve Kemp in 1983 at Seattle.

MULTI-HOME RUN GAMES ON OPENING DAY (7x, all 2HR games)
Giancarlo Stanton . . . . 3/29/2018 at TOR
Joe Pepitone. . . . . 4/9/1963 at KCA
Roger Maris. . . . . 4/19/1960 at BOS
Mickey Mantle. . . . . 4/17/1956 at WAS
Russ Derry . . . . 4/17/1945 vs. BOS
Babe Ruth & Sammy Byrd . . . . . . 4/12/1932 at PHA

GRAND SLAMS ON OPENING DAY (4)
Alex Rodriguez . . . . 4/3/06 at OAK (2nd inn. off Barry Zito)
Alfonso Soriano . . . . 3/31/03 at TOR (6th inn. off Roy Halladay)
Bobby Murcer . . . . 4/9/81 vs. TEX (as PH - 7th inn. off Steve Comer)
Russ Derry. . . . . .4/17/45 vs. BOS (7th inn. off Rex Cecil)

New York Yankees Managers

MANAGER	YEARS	WON	LOST	TIED	PCT	AL TITLES	WS TITLES
Joe McCarthy	1931-46	1,460	867	21	.627	8	7
Joe Torre	1996-2007	1,173	767	2	.605	6	4
Casey Stengel	1949-60	1,149	696	6	.623	10	7
Miller Huggins	1918-29	1,067	719	10	.597	6	3
Ralph Houk	1961-63, '66-73	944	806	7	.539	3	2
Joe Girardi	2008-17	910	710	0	.562	1	1
Billy Martin	1975-78, '79, '83, '85, '88	556	385	0	.591	2	1
Clark Griffith	1903-08	419	370	18	.531	0	0
Buck Showalter	1992-95	313	268	1	.539	0	0
Lou Piniella	1986-87, '88	224	193	0	.537	0	0
Bill Donovan	1915-17	220	239	6	.479	0	0
AARON BOONE	**2018-19**	**203**	**121**	**0**	**.627**	**0**	**0**
Yogi Berra	1964, '84-85	192	148	2	.565	1	0
Bucky Harris	1947-48	191	117	1	.620	1	1
George Stallings	1909-10	153	138	7	.526	0	0
Bill Virdon	1974-75	142	124	0	.534	0	0
Stump Merrill	1990-91	120	155	0	.436	0	0
Frank Chance	1913-14	117	168	5	.411	0	0
Dick Howser	1978 (1 game),1980	103	60	0	.632	0	0
Bob Lemon	1978-79, '81-82	99	73	0	.576	2	1
Gene Michael	1981, '82	92	76	0	.548	0	0
Bob Shawkey	1930	86	68	0	.558	0	0
Hal Chase	1910-11	85	78	1	.521	0	0
Johnny Keane	1965-66	81	101	0	.445	0	0
Bill Dickey	1946	57	48	0	.543	0	0
Dallas Green	1989	56	65	0	.463	0	0
Harry Wolverton	1912	50	102	1	.329	0	0
Bucky Dent	1989-90	36	53	0	.404	0	0
Clyde King	1982	29	33	0	.468	0	0
Norman "Kid" Elberfeld	1908	27	71	0	.276	0	0
Roger Peckinpaugh	1914	10	10	0	.500	0	0
Johnny Neun	1946	8	6	0	.571	0	0
Art Fletcher	1929	6	5	0	.545	0	0
TOTALS	**1903-2019**	**10,378**	**7,840**	**88**	**.570**	**40**	**27**

Joe McCarthy [C] is the winningest manager in Yankees history, having compiled a 1,460-867 (.627) regular season record over 16 seasons. He won seven World Series (1932, '36-39, '41, '43) in eight appearances with the club and owns the best career winning percentage of any Yankees skipper who piloted the club for at least two full seasons. In the photo above, he stands between sluggers Lou Gehrig [L] and Babe Ruth [R].

New York Yankees General Managers

Joseph Gavin (1)	1903
Abe Nahon (1)	1904-2/27/1909
Thomas Davis (2)	2/27/1909-12/5/1912
Arthur Irwin (3)	12/6/1912-1914
Harry Sparrow (3)	1/11/1915-5/7/1920
Ed Barrow (4)	10/28/1920-2/20/1945
Larry MacPhail	2/21/1945-10/7/1947
George Weiss	10/7/1947-11/2/1960
Roy Hamey	11/3/1960-10/22/1963
Ralph Houk	10/22/1963-5/7/1966
Dan Topping, Jr. (5)	5/7/1966-10/12/1966
Lee MacPhail	12/3/1966-10/23/1973
Gabe Paul (6)	11/1/1973-12/31/1977
Cedric Tallis (7)	1/1/1978-10/31/1979
Gene Michael	11/1/1979-11/20/1980
Cedric Tallis and Bill Bergesch (8)	11/21/1980-7/1/1983
Murray Cook	7/1/1983-4/9/1984
Clyde King	4/9/1984-10/9/1986
Woody Woodward	10/10/1986-10/18/1987
Lou Piniella	10/19/1987-5/29/1988
Bob Quinn	6/8/1988-3/20/1989
Syd Thrift (9)	3/21/1989-8/29/1989
Bob Quinn	8/29/1989-10/13/1989
Harding Peterson	10/18/1989-8/19/1990
Gene Michael	8/20/1990-10/22/1995
Bob Watson	10/23/1995-2/2/1998
Brian Cashman	2/3/1998-present

(1) Held title of Secretary and handled all business affairs.
(2) Served as Secretary through the end of 1914, however ceased control over all business matters after the arrival of Arthur Irwin on 12/6/1912.
(3) Held title of Business Manager.
(4) Held titles of Yankees Business Manager and Secretary until 1/17/1939 when he was named president, but performed GM duties throughout.
(5) Served as acting GM and frequently consulted Ralph Houk.
(6) Did not have title of general manager during points of his tenure but performed GM duties.
(7) Al Rosen, who was team president from 3/27/1978-7/19/1979, also performed baseball operations duties typical of a GM during parts of his tenure.
(8) Did not have title of general manager but together performed GM duties.
(9) Formally held title of "Senior Vice President of Baseball Operations" but performed the duties of a GM. Bob Quinn served as his assistant while maintaining the General Manager title he held previous to Thrift's arrival.

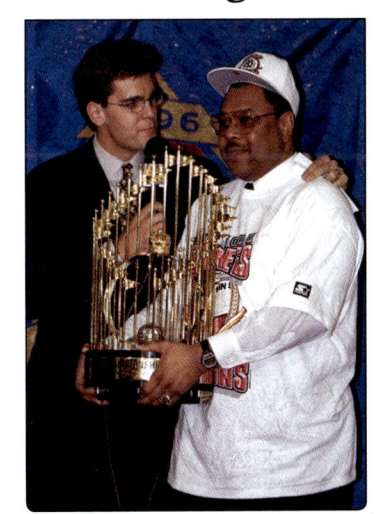

General Manger Bob Watson [R] celebrates with the 1996 World Series trophy after the Yankees defeated Atlanta in Game 6 at Yankee Stadium.

Year-by-Year Results

Franchise History: 117 seasons, 55 playoff apps. (Won 27 WS, Lost 13 WS, Lost 6 ALCS, Lost 8 ALDS, Lost 1 WC Game)
AL East Winner (since start of Div. play in 1969): 19 times (incl. first-half win in 1981); **Wild Card:** 7 times (1995, '97, 2007, '10, '15, '17-18)

Year	Postseason	Position	GA/GB	Won	Lost	Tied	Pct.	Manager	Attendance	Stadium
1903		Fourth	-17.0	72	62	2	.537	Clark Griffith	211,808	Hilltop Park
1904		Second	-1.5	92	59	4	.609	Clark Griffith	438,919	Hilltop Park
1905		Sixth	-21.5	71	78	3	.477	Clark Griffith	309,100	Hilltop Park
1906		Second	-3.0	90	61	4	.596	Clark Griffith	434,700	Hilltop Park
1907		Fifth	-21.0	70	78	4	.473	Clark Griffith	350,020	Hilltop Park
1908		Eighth	-39.5	51	103	1	.331	Griffith-Kid Elberfeld	305,500	Hilltop Park
1909		Fifth	-23.5	74	77	2	.490	George Stallings	501,000	Hilltop Park
1910		Second	-14.5	88	63	5	.583	Stallings-Hal Chase	355,857	Hilltop Park
1911		Sixth	-25.5	76	76	1	.500	Hal Chase	302,444	Hilltop Park
1912		Eighth	-55.0	50	102	1	.329	Harry Wolverton	242,194	Hilltop Park
1913		Seventh	-38.0	57	94	2	.377	Frank Chance	357,551	Polo Grounds
1914		T-Sixth	-30.0	70	84	3	.455	Chance-Peckinpaugh	359,477	Polo Grounds
1915		Fifth	-32.5	69	83	2	.454	Bill Donovan	256,035	Polo Grounds
1916		Fourth	-11.0	80	74	2	.519	Bill Donovan	469,211	Polo Grounds
1917		Sixth	-28.5	71	82	2	.464	Bill Donovan	330,294	Polo Grounds
1918		Fourth	-13.5	60	63	3	.488	Miller Huggins	282,047	Polo Grounds
1919		Third	-7.5	80	59	2	.576	Miller Huggins	619,164	Polo Grounds
1920		Third	-3.0	95	59	0	.617	Miller Huggins	1,289,422	Polo Grounds
1921	Lost WS	First	+4.5	98	55	0	.641	Miller Huggins	1,230,696	Polo Grounds
1922	Lost WS	First	+1.0	94	60	0	.610	Miller Huggins	1,026,134	Polo Grounds
1923	Won WS	First	+16.0	98	54	0	.645	Miller Huggins	1,007,066	Orig. Yankee Stadium
1924		Second	-2.0	89	63	1	.586	Miller Huggins	1,053,533	Orig. Yankee Stadium
1925		Seventh	-28.5	69	85	2	.448	Miller Huggins	697,267	Orig. Yankee Stadium
1926	Lost WS	First	+3.0	91	63	1	.591	Miller Huggins	1,027,095	Orig. Yankee Stadium
1927	Won WS	First	+19.0	110	44	1	.714	Miller Huggins	1,164,015	Orig. Yankee Stadium
1928	Won WS	First	+2.5	101	53	0	.656	Miller Huggins	1,072,132	Orig. Yankee Stadium
1929		Second	-18.0	88	66	0	.571	Huggins-Art Fletcher	960,148	Orig. Yankee Stadium
1930		Third	-16.0	86	68	0	.558	Bob Shawkey	1,169,230	Orig. Yankee Stadium
1931		Second	-13.5	94	59	2	.614	Joe McCarthy	912,437	Orig. Yankee Stadium
1932	Won WS	First	+13.0	107	47	2	.695	Joe McCarthy	962,320	Orig. Yankee Stadium
1933		Second	-7.0	91	59	2	.607	Joe McCarthy	728,014	Orig. Yankee Stadium
1934		Second	-7.0	94	60	0	.610	Joe McCarthy	854,682	Orig. Yankee Stadium
1935		Second	-3.0	89	60	1	.597	Joe McCarthy	657,508	Orig. Yankee Stadium
1936	Won WS	First	+19.5	102	51	2	.667	Joe McCarthy	976,913	Orig. Yankee Stadium
1937	Won WS	First	+13.0	102	52	3	.662	Joe McCarthy	998,148	Orig. Yankee Stadium
1938	Won WS	First	+9.5	99	53	5	.651	Joe McCarthy	970,916	Orig. Yankee Stadium
1939	Won WS	First	+17.0	106	45	1	.702	Joe McCarthy	859,785	Orig. Yankee Stadium
1940		Third	-2.0	88	66	1	.571	Joe McCarthy	988,975	Orig. Yankee Stadium
1941	Won WS	First	+17.0	101	53	2	.656	Joe McCarthy	964,722	Orig. Yankee Stadium
1942	Lost WS	First	+9.0	103	51	0	.669	Joe McCarthy	988,251	Orig. Yankee Stadium
1943	Won WS	First	+13.5	98	56	1	.636	Joe McCarthy	645,006	Orig. Yankee Stadium
1944		Third	-6.0	83	71	0	.539	Joe McCarthy	789,995	Orig. Yankee Stadium
1945		Fourth	-6.5	81	71	0	.533	Joe McCarthy	881,846	Orig. Yankee Stadium
1946		Third	-17.0	87	67	0	.565	McCarthy-Dickey-Neun	2,265,512	Orig. Yankee Stadium
1947	Won WS	First	+12.0	97	57	1	.630	Bucky Harris	2,178,937	Orig. Yankee Stadium
1948		Third	-2.5	94	60	0	.610	Bucky Harris	2,373,901	Orig. Yankee Stadium
1949	Won WS	First	+1.0	97	57	0	.630	Casey Stengel	2,281,676	Orig. Yankee Stadium
1950	Won WS	First	+3.0	98	56	1	.636	Casey Stengel	2,081,380	Orig. Yankee Stadium
1951	Won WS	First	+5.0	98	56	0	.636	Casey Stengel	1,950,107	Orig. Yankee Stadium
1952	Won WS	First	+2.0	95	59	0	.617	Casey Stengel	1,629,665	Orig. Yankee Stadium
1953	Won WS	First	+8.5	99	52	0	.656	Casey Stengel	1,537,811	Orig. Yankee Stadium
1954		Second	-8.0	103	51	1	.669	Casey Stengel	1,475,171	Orig. Yankee Stadium
1955	Lost WS	First	+3.0	96	58	0	.623	Casey Stengel	1,490,138	Orig. Yankee Stadium
1956	Won WS	First	+9.0	97	57	0	.680	Casey Stengel	1,491,138	Orig. Yankee Stadium
1957	Lost WS	First	+8.0	98	56	0	.636	Casey Stengel	1,497,134	Orig. Yankee Stadium
1958	Won WS	First	+10.0	92	62	1	.597	Casey Stengel	1,428,438	Orig. Yankee Stadium
1959		Third	-15.0	79	75	1	.513	Casey Stengel	1,552,030	Orig. Yankee Stadium
1960	Lost WS	First	+8.0	97	57	1	.630	Casey Stengel	1,627,349	Orig. Yankee Stadium
1961	Won WS	First	+8.0	109	53	0	.673	Ralph Houk	1,747,725	Orig. Yankee Stadium
1962	Won WS	First	+5.0	96	66	0	.593	Ralph Houk	1,493,574	Orig. Yankee Stadium
1963	Lost WS	First	+10.5	104	57	0	.646	Ralph Houk	1,308,920	Orig. Yankee Stadium
1964	Lost WS	First	+1.0	99	63	2	.611	Yogi Berra	1,305,638	Orig. Yankee Stadium
1965		Sixth	-25.0	77	85	0	.475	Johnny Keane	1,213,552	Orig. Yankee Stadium
1966		Tenth	-26.5	70	89	1	.440	Keane-Houk	1,124,648	Orig. Yankee Stadium
1967		Ninth	-20.0	72	90	1	.444	Ralph Houk	1,259,514	Orig. Yankee Stadium
1968		Fifth	-20.0	83	79	2	.512	Ralph Houk	1,185,666	Orig. Yankee Stadium
1969		Fifth	-28.5	80	81	1	.497	Ralph Houk	1,067,996	Orig. Yankee Stadium
1970		Second	-15.0	93	69	1	.574	Ralph Houk	1,136,879	Orig. Yankee Stadium
1971		Fourth	-21.0	82	80	0	.506	Ralph Houk	1,070,771	Orig. Yankee Stadium
1972		Fourth	-6.5	79	76	0	.510	Ralph Houk	966,328	Orig. Yankee Stadium
1973		Fourth	-17.0	80	82	0	.494	Ralph Houk	1,262,103	Orig. Yankee Stadium
1974		Second	-2.0	89	73	0	.549	Bill Virdon	1,273,075	Shea Stadium
1975		Third	-12.0	83	77	0	.519	Virdon-Billy Martin	1,288,048	Shea Stadium

Year	Postseason	Position	GA/GB	Won	Lost	Tied	Pct.	Manager	Attendance	Stadium
1976	Lost WS	First	+10.5	97	62	0	.610	Billy Martin	2,012,434	Orig. Yankee Stad. (R)
1977	Won WS	First	+2.5	100	62	0	.617	Billy Martin	2,103,092	Orig. Yankee Stad. (R)
1978	Won WS	First	+1.0	100	63	0	.613	Martin-Bob Lemon	2,335,871	Orig. Yankee Stad. (R)
1979		Fourth	-13.5	89	71	0	.556	Lemon-Martin	2,537,765	Orig. Yankee Stad. (R)
1980	Lost ALCS	First	+3.0	103	59	0	.636	Dick Howser	2,627,417	Orig. Yankee Stad. (R)
1981	Lost WS	First	+2.0	34	22	0	.607	Gene Michael		
		Sixth	-5.0	25	26	0	.490	Michael-Lemon	1,614,353	Orig. Yankee Stad. (R)
1982		Fifth	-16.0	79	83	0	.488	Lemon-Michael-C. King	2,041,219	Orig. Yankee Stad. (R)
1983		Third	-7.0	91	71	0	.562	Billy Martin	2,257,976	Orig. Yankee Stad. (R)
1984		Third	-17.0	87	75	0	.537	Yogi Berra	1,821,815	Orig. Yankee Stad. (R)
1985		Second	-2.0	97	64	0	.602	Berra-Martin	2,214,587	Orig. Yankee Stad. (R)
1986		Second	-5.5	90	72	0	.556	Lou Piniella	2,268,030	Orig. Yankee Stad. (R)
1987		Fourth	-9.0	89	73	0	.549	Lou Piniella	2,427,672	Orig. Yankee Stad. (R)
1988		Fifth	-3.5	85	76	0	.528	Martin-Piniella	2,633,701	Orig. Yankee Stad. (R)
1989		Fifth	-14.5	74	87	0	.460	Dallas Green-B. Dent	2,170,485	Orig. Yankee Stad. (R)
1990		Seventh	-21.0	67	95	0	.414	Dent-Stump Merrill	2,006,436	Orig. Yankee Stad. (R)
1991		Fifth	-21.0	71	91	0	.438	Stump Merrill	1,863,733	Orig. Yankee Stad. (R)
1992		T-Fourth	-20.0	76	86	0	.469	Buck Showalter	1,748,773	Orig. Yankee Stad. (R)
1993		Second	-7.0	88	74	0	.543	Buck Showalter	2,416,965	Orig. Yankee Stad. (R)
1994		First	+6.5	70	43	0	.619	Buck Showalter	1,675,556	Orig. Yankee Stad. (R)
1995	Lost ALDS	Second (WC)	-7.0	79	65	1	.549	Buck Showalter	1,705,263	Orig. Yankee Stad. (R)
1996	Won WS	First	+4.0	92	70	0	.568	Joe Torre	2,250,877	Orig. Yankee Stad. (R)
1997	Lost ALDS	Second (WC)	-2.0	96	66	0	593	Joe Torre	2,580,445	Orig. Yankee Stad. (R)
1998	Won WS	First	+22.0	114	48	0	.704	Joe Torre	2,919,046	Orig. Yankee Stad. (R)
1999	Won WS	First	+4.0	98	64	0	.605	Joe Torre	3,292,736	Orig. Yankee Stad. (R)
2000	Won WS	First	+2.5	87	74	0	.540	Joe Torre	3,227,657	Orig. Yankee Stad. (R)
2001	Lost WS	First	+13.5	95	65	1	.594	Joe Torre	3,264,777	Orig. Yankee Stad. (R)
2002	Lost ALDS	First	+10.5	103	58	0	.640	Joe Torre	3,461,644	Orig. Yankee Stad. (R)
2003	Lost WS	First	+6.0	101	61	1	.623	Joe Torre	3,465,585	Orig. Yankee Stad. (R)
2004	Lost ALCS	First	+3.0	101	61	0	.623	Joe Torre	3,775,292	Orig. Yankee Stad. (R)
2005	Lost ALDS	T-First	0.0	95	67	0	.586	Joe Torre	4,090,692	Orig. Yankee Stad. (R)
2006	Lost ALDS	First	+10.0	97	65	0	.599	Joe Torre	4,243,780	Orig. Yankee Stad. (R)
2007	Lost ALDS	Second (WC)	-2.0	94	68	0	.580	Joe Torre	4,271,083	Orig. Yankee Stad. (R)
2008		Third	-8.0	89	73	0	.549	Joe Girardi	4,298,543	Orig. Yankee Stad. (R)
2009	Won WS	First	+8.0	103	59	0	.636	Joe Girardi	3,719,358	Yankee Stadium
2010	Lost ALCS	Second (WC)	-1.0	95	67	0	.586	Joe Girardi	3,765,807	Yankee Stadium
2011	Lost ALDS	First	+6.0	97	65	0	.599	Joe Girardi	3,653,700	Yankee Stadium
2012	Lost ALCS	First	+2.0	95	67	0	.586	Joe Girardi	3,542,406	Yankee Stadium
2013		T-Third	-12.0	85	77	0	.525	Joe Girardi	3,279,589	Yankee Stadium
2014		Second	-12.0	84	78	0	.519	Joe Girardi	3,401,624	Yankee Stadium
2015	Lost WC	Second (WC)	-6.0	87	75	0	.537	Joe Girardi	3,193,795	Yankee Stadium
2016		Fourth	-9.0	84	78	0	.519	Joe Girardi	3,063,405	Yankee Stadium
2017	Lost ALCS	Second (WC)	-2.0	91	71	0	.562	Joe Girardi	3,146,966	Yankee Stadium
2018	Lost ALDS	Second (WC)	-8.0	100	62	0	.617	Aaron Boone	3,482,865	Yankee Stadium
2019	Lost ALCS	First	+7.0	103	59	0	.636	Aaron Boone	3,304,404	Yankee Stadium
Totals				10,378	7,840	88	.570			

T=Tied / R=Remodeled Orig. Yankee Stad.

The 1923 Yankees — The first World Series-winning team in franchise history

Led by Manager Miller Huggins, the 1923 Yankees went 98-54 during the regular season before winning the first World Series in franchise history, 4-games-to-2 over the New York Giants. The season was a turning point for the Yankees in many ways, most notably because it marked the inaugural season of the original Yankee Stadium. The victory also established the Yankees as New York City's dominant team after losses to John McGraw's Giants in the prior two Fall Classics, 5-games-to-3 in 1921 and 4-games-to-0 (with one tie) in 1922.

Top Row: Doc Woods (trainer), Joe Bush, Bob Meusel, Fred Hofmann, Herb Pennock, Waite Hoyt, Bob Shawkey, Elmer Smith, Carl Mays, Oscar Roettger, Babe Ruth, Wally Pipp. **Middle Row:** Sam Jones, Whitey Witt, Everett Scott, Wally Schang, Miller Huggins (manager), Charlie O'Leary (coach), Mike McNally, Aaron Ward, Joe Dugan. **Seated:** Benny Bengough, Hinkey Haines, Lou Gehrig, George Pipgras, Ernie Johnson, Mike Gazella, Harvey Hendrick.

Year-by-Year Team Hitting Statistics

YEAR	AVG	AB	R	H	HR	RBI	SB	BB	SO	E
1903	.249	4565	579	1136	18	474	160	332	465	264
1904	.259	5220	598	1354	27	499	163	312	548	275
1905	.248	4957	587	1228	23	480	200	360	537	293
1906	.264	5095	641	1345	17	528	192	331	--	272
1907	.249	5042	604	1257	15	497	206	304	--	334
1908	.236	5036	456	1187	13	372	230	288	--	337
1909	.248	4981	591	1234	16	473	187	407	--	330
1910	.248	5050	629	1252	20	492	289	464	--	285
1911	.272	5056	686	1375	25	577	270	493	--	328
1912	.259	5095	632	1320	18	502	247	463	--	382
1913	.237	4880	529	1157	8	430	203	534	617	293
1914	.229	4992	536	1144	12	416	251	577	711	238
1915	.233	4982	583	1162	31	459	198	570	668	217
1916	.246	5200	575	1277	35	492	179	516	632	225
1917	.239	5136	524	1226	27	445	136	496	535	219
1918	.257	4224	491	1085	20	406	88	367	370	161
1919	.267	4775	582	1275	45	499	101	386	479	193
1920	.280	5176	838	1448	115	747	64	539	626	194
1921	.300	5249	948	1576	134	861	89	588	567	222
1922	.287	5245	758	1504	95	674	62	497	532	157
1923	.291	5347	823	1554	105	770	69	521	516	144
1924	.289	5340	798	1516	98	734	69	478	420	156
1925	.275	5353	706	1471	110	638	67	470	482	160
1926	.289	5221	847	1508	121	794	79	642	580	210
1927	.307	5347	975	1644	158	908	90	635	605	195
1928	.296	5337	894	1578	133	817	51	562	544	194
1929	.295	5379	899	1587	142	828	51	554	518	178
1930	.309	5448	1062	1683	152	986	91	644	569	207
1931	.297	5608	1067	1667	155	990	139	748	554	169
1932	.286	5477	1002	1564	160	955	77	766	527	188
1933	.283	5274	927	1495	144	849	74	700	506	165
1934	.278	5368	842	1494	135	791	71	700	597	157
1935	.280	5214	818	1462	104	755	68	604	469	151
1936	.300	5591	1065	1676	182	995	76	700	594	163
1937	.283	5487	979	1554	174	922	60	709	607	170
1938	.274	5410	966	1480	174	917	91	749	616	169
1939	.287	5300	967	1521	166	903	72	701	543	126
1940	.259	5286	817	1371	155	757	59	648	606	152
1941	.269	5444	830	1464	151	774	51	616	565	165
1942	.269	5305	801	1429	108	744	69	591	556	142
1943	.256	5282	669	1350	100	635	46	624	562	160
1944	.264	5331	674	1410	96	631	91	523	627	156
1945	.259	5176	676	1343	93	639	64	618	567	175
1946	.248	5139	684	1275	136	649	48	627	706	150
1947	.271	5308	794	1439	115	746	27	610	581	109
1948	.278	5324	857	1480	139	806	24	623	478	120
1949	.269	5196	829	1396	115	759	58	731	539	138
1950	.282	5361	914	1511	159	863	41	687	463	119
1951	.269	5194	798	1395	140	741	78	605	547	144
1952	.267	5294	727	1411	129	672	52	566	652	127
1953	.273	5194	801	1420	139	762	34	656	644	126
1954	.268	5226	805	1400	133	747	34	650	632	126
1955	.260	5161	762	1342	175	722	55	609	658	128
1956	.270	5312	857	1433	190	788	51	615	755	136
1957	.268	5271	723	1412	145	682	49	562	709	123
1958	.268	5294	759	1418	164	715	48	537	822	128
1959	.260	5379	687	1397	153	651	45	457	828	131
1960	.260	5290	746	1377	193	699	37	537	818	129
1961	.263	5559	827	1461	240	781	28	543	785	124
1962	.267	5644	817	1509	199	791	42	584	842	131
1963	.252	5506	714	1387	188	666	42	434	808	110
1964	.253	5705	730	1442	162	688	54	520	976	109
1965	.235	5470	611	1286	149	576	35	489	951	137
1966	.235	5330	611	1254	162	569	49	485	817	142
1967	.225	5443	522	1225	100	473	63	532	1043	154
1968	.214	5310	536	1137	109	501	90	566	958	139
1969	.235	5308	562	1247	94	521	119	565	840	131
1970	.251	5492	680	1381	111	627	105	588	808	130
1971	.254	5413	648	1377	97	607	75	581	717	125
1972	.249	5168	557	1288	103	526	71	491	689	134
1973	.261	5492	641	1435	131	616	47	489	680	156
1974	.263	5524	671	1451	101	637	53	515	690	142
1975	.264	5415	681	1430	110	642	102	486	710	135
1976	.269	5555	730	1496	120	682	163	470	616	126
1977	.281	5605	831	1576	184	784	93	533	681	132
1978	.267	5583	735	1489	125	693	98	505	695	113
1979	.266	5421	734	1443	150	594	64	509	590	122
1980	.267	5553	820	1484	189	772	86	643	739	138
1981	.252	3529	421	889	100	403	46	391	434	72
1982	.256	5526	709	1417	161	666	69	590	719	128
1983	.273	5631	770	1535	153	728	84	533	686	139
1984	.276	5661	758	1560	130	725	62	534	673	142
1985	.267	5458	839	1458	176	793	155	620	771	126
1986	.271	5570	797	1512	188	745	139	645	911	127
1987	.262	5511	788	1445	196	749	105	604	949	102
1988	.263	5592	772	1469	148	713	146	588	935	134
1989	.269	5458	698	1470	130	657	137	502	831	122
1990	.241	5483	603	1322	147	561	119	427	1027	126
1991	.256	5541	674	1418	147	630	109	473	861	133
1992	.261	5593	733	1462	163	703	78	536	903	114
1993	.279	5615	821	1568	178	793	39	629	910	105
1994	.290	3986	670	1155	139	632	55	530	660	80
1995	.276	4947	749	1365	122	709	50	625	851	74
1996	.288	5628	871	1621	162	830	96	632	909	91
1997	.287	5710	891	1636	161	846	99	676	954	104
1998	.288	5643	965	1625	207	907	153	653	1025	98
1999	.282	5568	900	1568	193	855	104	718	978	111
2000	.277	5556	871	1541	205	833	99	631	1007	109
2001	.267	5577	804	1488	203	774	161	519	1035	109
2002	.275	5601	897	1540	223	857	100	640	1171	127
2003	.271	5605	877	1518	230	845	98	684	1042	114
2004	.268	5527	897	1483	242	863	84	670	982	99
2005	.276	5624	886	1552	229	847	84	637	989	95
2006	.285	5651	930	1608	210	902	139	649	1053	104
2007	.290	5717	968	1656	201	929	123	637	991	88
2008	.271	5572	789	1512	180	758	118	535	1015	83
2009	.283	5660	915	1604	244	881	111	663	1014	86
2010	.267	5567	859	1485	201	823	103	662	1136	69
2011	.263	5518	867	1452	222	836	147	627	1138	102
2012	.265	5524	804	1462	245	774	93	565	1176	75
2013	.242	5449	650	1321	144	614	115	466	1214	63
2014	.245	5497	633	1349	147	591	112	452	1133	92
2015	.251	5567	764	1397	212	737	63	554	1227	93
2016	.252	5458	680	1378	183	647	72	475	1188	86
2017	.262	5594	858	1463	241	821	90	616	1386	95
2018	.249	5515	851	1374	267	821	63	625	1421	94
2019	.267	5583	943	1493	306	904	55	569	1437	102

The 1930 Yankees finished with the highest single-season batting average (.309) and more hits (1,683) than any other team in franchise history. The club was led by Lou Gehrig [L] and Babe Ruth [R], who hit .379 and .359, respectively.

Year-by-Year Team Pitching Statistics

YEAR	W-L	ERA	CG	SHO	SV	SO	BB
1903	72-62	3.08	111	7	2	463	245
1904	92-59	2.57	123	15	1	684	311
1905	71-78	2.93	88	10	9	642	396
1906	90-61	2.78	99	18	5	605	351
1907	70-78	3.03	93	9	7	511	428
1908	51-103	3.16	91	11	6	584	457
1909	74-77	2.68	94	16	14	597	442
1910	88-63	2.59	110	14	10	654	364
1911	76-76	3.54	91	5	9	667	406
1912	50-102	4.13	109	3	3	637	436
1913	57-94	3.27	78	7	6	530	455
1914	70-84	2.81	97	5	7	563	390
1915	69-83	3.09	100	11	2	577	389
1916	80-74	2.77	83	10	18	616	476
1917	71-82	2.66	87	9	7	571	427
1918	60-63	3.03	59	9	11	369	463
1919	80-59	2.78	85	14	7	500	433
1920	95-59	3.31	88	16	11	400	420
1921	98-55	3.79	92	7	15	481	470
1922	94-60	3.39	98	7	14	458	423
1923	98-54	3.66	102	9	10	506	491
1924	89-63	3.86	76	13	13	487	522
1925	69-85	4.33	80	8	13	492	505
1926	91-63	3.86	64	4	20	486	478
1927	110-44	3.20	82	11	20	431	409
1928	101-53	3.74	82	13	21	487	452
1929	88-66	4.17	64	12	18	484	485
1930	86-68	4.88	65	7	15	572	524
1931	94-59	4.20	78	4	17	686	543
1932	107-47	3.98	95	11	15	780	561
1933	91-59	4.36	70	8	22	711	612
1934	94-60	3.76	83	13	10	656	542
1935	89-60	3.60	76	12	13	594	516
1936	102-51	4.17	77	6	21	624	663
1937	102-52	3.65	82	15	21	612	560
1938	99-53	3.91	91	11	13	567	566
1939	106-45	3.31	87	13	26	565	567
1940	88-66	3.89	76	10	14	599	571
1941	101-53	3.53	75	13	26	589	598
1942	103-51	2.91	88	18	17	553	541
1943	98-56	2.93	83	14	13	653	489
1944	83-71	3.39	78	9	13	529	532
1945	81-71	3.45	78	9	14	474	485
1946	87-67	3.13	68	17	17	653	552
1947	97-57	3.39	73	14	21	691	628
1948	94-60	3.75	62	16	24	654	641
1949	97-57	3.69	59	12	36	671	812
1950	98-56	4.15	66	12	31	712	708
1951	98-56	3.56	66	24	22	664	562
1952	95-59	3.14	72	17	27	666	581
1953	99-52	3.20	50	16	39	604	500
1954	103-51	3.26	51	16	37	655	552
1955	96-58	3.23	52	19	33	732	688
1956	97-57	3.63	50	10	35	732	652
1957	98-56	3.00	41	13	42	810	580
1958	92-62	3.22	53	21	33	796	557
1959	79-75	3.60	38	15	28	836	594
1960	97-57	3.52	38	16	42	712	609
1961	109-53	3.46	47	14	39	866	542
1962	96-66	3.70	33	10	42	838	499
1963	104-57	3.07	59	19	31	965	476
1964	99-63	3.15	46	18	45	989	504
1965	77-85	3.28	41	11	31	1001	511
1966	70-89	3.42	29	7	32	842	443
1967	72-90	3.24	37	16	27	898	480
1968	83-79	2.79	45	14	27	831	424
1969	80-81	3.23	53	13	20	801	522
1970	93-69	3.25	36	6	49	777	451
1971	81-80	3.45	67	15	12	707	423
1972	79-76	3.05	35	19	39	625	419
1973	80-82	3.34	47	16	39	708	457
1974	89-73	3.31	53	13	24	829	528
1975	83-77	3.29	70	11	20	809	502
1976	97-62	3.19	62	15	37	448	674
1977	100-62	3.61	52	16	34	758	486
1978	100-63	3.18	39	16	36	817	478
1979	89-71	3.83	43	10	37	731	455
1980	103-59	3.58	29	15	50	845	463
1981	59-48	2.90	16	13	30	606	287
1982	79-83	3.99	24	8	39	939	491
1983	91-71	3.86	47	12	32	892	455
1984	87-75	3.78	15	12	43	992	518
1985	97-64	3.69	25	9	49	907	518
1986	90-72	4.11	13	8	58	878	492
1987	89-73	4.36	19	10	47	900	542
1988	85-76	4.25	16	4	43	861	487
1989	74-87	4.50	15	9	44	787	521
1990	67-95	4.21	15	6	41	909	618
1991	71-91	4.42	3	11	37	936	506
1992	76-86	4.21	20	9	44	851	612
1993	88-74	4.35	11	13	38	899	552
1994	70-43	4.34	8	2	31	656	398
1995	79-65	4.56	18	5	35	908	535
1996	92-70	4.65	6	9	52	1139	610
1997	96-66	3.84	11	10	51	1165	532
1998	114-48	3.82	22	16	48	1080	466
1999	98-64	4.13	6	10	50	1111	581
2000	87-74	4.76	9	6	40	1040	577
2001	95-65	4.02	7	9	57	1266	465
2002	103-58	3.87	9	11	53	1135	403
2003	101-61	4.02	8	12	49	1119	375
2004	101-61	4.69	1	5	59	1058	445
2005	95-67	4.52	8	14	46	985	463
2006	97-65	4.41	5	8	43	1019	496
2007	94-68	4.49	1	5	34	1009	578
2008	89-73	4.28	1	11	42	1141	489
2009	103-59	4.26	3	8	51	1260	574
2010	95-67	4.06	3	8	39	1154	540
2011	97-65	3.73	5	8	47	1222	507
2012	95-67	3.84	6	9	51	1318	431
2013	85-77	3.94	7	10	49	1233	437
2014	84-78	3.75	5	10	48	1370	398
2015	87-75	4.03	3	4	48	1370	474
2016	84-78	4.16	0	10	48	1393	444
2017	91-71	3.72	2	7	36	1560	504
2018	100-62	3.78	2	11	49	1634	494
2019	103-59	4.31	1	9	50	1534	507

Urban Shocker went 61-37 as a Yankee (1916-17, '26-28), including an 18-6 mark with a 2.84 ERA in his final full season in the Majors in 1927.

Yankees Year-by-Year Save Leaders

Year	Pitcher	W	SV	Year	Pitcher	W	SV	Year	Pitcher	W	SV
1969	Aker	8	11	1988	Righetti	5	25	2008	Rivera	6	39
1970	McDaniel	9	29	1989	Righetti	2	25	2009	Rivera	3	44
1971	McDaniel	5	4	1990	Righetti	1	36	2010	Rivera	3	33
	Aker	4	4	1991	Farr	5	23	2011	Rivera	1	44
1972	Lyle	9	AL35	1992	Farr	2	30	2012	Soriano	2	42
1973	Lyle	5	27	1993	Farr	2	25	2013	Rivera	6	44
1974	Lyle	9	15	1994	Howe	3	15	2014	Robertson	4	39
1975	Martinez	1	8	1995	Wetteland	1	31	2015	Miller	3	36
1976	Lyle	7	AL23	1996	Wetteland	2	AL43	2016	CHAPMAN	3	20
1977	Lyle	13	26	1997	Rivera	6	43	2017	CHAPMAN	4	22
1978	Gossage	10	AL27	1998	Rivera	3	36	2018	CHAPMAN	3	32
1979	Gossage	5	18	1999	Rivera	4	MLB45	2019	CHAPMAN	3	37
1980	Gossage	6	TM/TL33	2000	Rivera	7	36				
1981	Gossage	3	20	2001	Rivera	4	MLB50				
1982	Gossage	4	30	2002	Rivera	1	28				
1983	Gossage	13	22	2003	Rivera	5	40				
1984	Righetti	5	31	2004	Rivera	4	MLB53				
1985	Righetti	12	29	2005	Rivera	7	43				
1986	Righetti	8	MLB46	2006	Rivera	5	34				
1987	Righetti	8	31	2007	Rivera	3	30				

Official statistic since 1969
AL=Led AL; MLB=Led MLB;
T=tied for AL or MLB lead

Dave Righetti is one of three pitchers in MLB history (along with Dennis Eckersley and Derek Lowe), who has led a league in saves and thrown a no-hitter. The photo above is from his 4-0, no-hitter on July 4, 1983 vs. Boston.

Year-by-Year Hitting Leaders

BATTING AVERAGE

Year	Player	AVG	Year	Player	AVG	Year	Player	AVG	Year	Player	AVG
1903	Keeler	.318	1927	Gehrig	.373	1951	McDougald	.306	1975	Munson	.318	1999	Jeter	.349
1904	Keeler	.343	1928	Gehrig	.374	1952	Mantle	.311	1976	Rivers	.312	2000	Jeter	.339
1905	Keeler	.302	1929	Lazzeri	.353	1953	Bauer	.304	1977	Rivers	.326	2001	Jeter	.311
1906	Chase	.323	1930	Gehrig	.379	1954	Noren	.319	1978	Piniella	.314	2002	B. Williams	.333
1907	Chase	.287	1931	Ruth	.373	1955	Mantle	.306	1979	Piniella, Jackson	.297	2003	Jeter	.324
1908	Hemphill	.297	1932	Gehrig	.349	1956	Mantle*	.353	1980	Watson	.307	2004	Matsui	.298
1909	LaPorte	.298	1933	Gehrig	.334	1957	Mantle	.365	1981	Mumphrey	.307	2005	Rodriguez	.321
1910	Knight	.312	1934	Gehrig*	.363	1958	Mantle	.304	1982	Mumphrey	.300	2006	Jeter	.343
1911	Cree	.348	1935	Gehrig	.329	1959	Richardson	.301	1983	Baylor	.303	2007	Posada	.338
1912	Paddock	.288	1936	Dickey	.362	1960	Skowron	.309	1984	Mattingly*	.343	2008	Damon	.303
1913	Cree	.272	1937	Gehrig	.351	1961	Howard	.348	1985	Mattingly	.324	2009	Jeter	.334
1914	Cook	.282	1938	DiMaggio	.324	1962	Mantle	.321	1986	Mattingly	.352	2010	Canó	.319
1915	Maisel	.281	1939	DiMaggio*	.381	1963	Howard	.287	1987	Mattingly	.327	2011	Canó	.302
1916	Pipp	.263	1940	DiMaggio	.352	1964	Howard	.313	1988	Winfield	.322	2012	Jeter	.316
1917	Baker	.282	1941	DiMaggio	.357	1965	Tresh	.279	1989	Sax	.315	2013	Canó	.314
1918	Baker	.306	1942	Gordon	.322	1966	Mantle	.288	1990	R. Kelly	.285	2014	Ellsbury	.271
1919	Peckinpaugh	.305	1943	Johnson	.280	1967	Clarke	.272	1991	Sax	.304	2015	Beltrán	.276
1920	Ruth	.376	1944	Stirnweiss	.319	1968	White	.267	1992	Mattingly	.288	2016	Gregorius	.276
1921	Ruth	.377	1945	Stirnweiss*	.309	1969	White	.290	1993	O'Neill	.311	2017	Gregorius	.287
1922	Pipp	.329	1946	DiMaggio	.290	1970	Munson	.302	1994	O'Neill*	.359	2018	ANDÚJAR	.297
1923	Ruth	.394	1947	DiMaggio	.315	1971	Murcer	.331	1995	Boggs	.324	2019	LEMAHIEU	.327
1924	Ruth*	.378	1948	DiMaggio	.320	1972	Murcer	.292	1996	Jeter	.314			
1925	Combs	.342	1949	Henrich	.287	1973	Murcer	.304	1997	B. Williams	.328			
1926	Ruth	.372	1950	Rizzuto	.324	1974	Piniella	.305	1998	B. Williams*	.339			

HITS

Year	Player	H	Year	Player	H	Year	Player	H	Year	Player	H	Year	Player	H
1903	Keeler	164	1927	Combs*	231	1951	Berra	161	1975	Munson	190	1999	Jeter*	219
1904	Keeler	185	1928	Gehrig	210	1952	Mantle	171	1976	Chambliss	188	2000	Jeter	201
1905	Keeler	169	1929	Combs	202	1953	McDougald	154	1977	Rivers	184	2001	Jeter	191
1906	Chase	193	1930	Gehrig	220	1954	Berra	179	1978	Munson	183	2002	Soriano*	209
1907	Chase	143	1931	Gehrig	211	1955	Mantle	158	1979	Randolph, Chambliss	155	2003	Soriano	198
1908	Hemphill	150	1932	Gehrig	208	1956	Mantle	188	1980	Jackson	154	2004	Jeter	188
1909	Engle	137	1933	Gehrig	198	1957	Mantle	173	1981	Winfield	114	2005	Jeter	202
1910	Chase	151	1934	Gehrig	210	1958	Mantle	158	1982	Randolph	155	2006	Jeter	214
1911	Cree	181	1935	Rolfe	192	1959	Mantle	154	1983	Winfield	169	2007	Jeter	206
1912	Chase	143	1936	DiMaggio	206	1960	Skowron	166	1984	Mattingly*	207	2008	Abreu	180
1913	Cree	145	1937	DiMaggio	215	1961	Richardson	173	1985	Mattingly	211	2009	Jeter	212
1914	Cook	133	1938	Rolfe	196	1962	Richardson*	209	1986	Mattingly*	238	2010	Canó	200
1915	Maisel	149	1939	Rolfe*	213	1963	Richardson	167	1987	Mattingly	186	2011	Canó	188
1916	Pipp	143	1940	DiMaggio	179	1964	Richardson	181	1988	Mattingly	186	2012	Jeter*	216
1917	Pipp*	156	1941	DiMaggio	193	1965	Tresh	168	1989	Sax	205	2013	Canó	190
1918	Baker	154	1942	DiMaggio	186	1966	Richardson	153	1990	R. Kelly	183	2014	Ellsbury	156
1919	Baker	166	1943	Johnson	166	1967	Clarke	160	1991	Sax	198	2015	Headley	150
1920	Pratt	180	1944	Stirnweiss*	205	1968	White	154	1992	Mattingly	184	2016	Castro	156
1921	Ruth	204	1945	Stirnweiss*	195	1969	Clarke	183	1993	Boggs	169	2017	GARDNER	157
1922	Pipp	190	1946	Keller	148	1970	White	180	1994	O'Neill	132	2018	ANDÚJAR	170
1923	Ruth	205	1947	DiMaggio	190	1971	Murcer	175	1995	B. Williams	173	2019	LEMAHIEU	197
1924	Ruth	200	1948	DiMaggio	190	1972	Murcer	171	1996	Jeter	183			
1925	Combs	203	1949	Rizzuto	169	1973	Murcer	187	1997	Jeter	190			
1926	Ruth	184	1950	Rizzuto	200	1974	Murcer	166	1998	Jeter	203			

HOME RUNS

Year	Player	HR	Year	Player	HR	Year	Player	HR	Year	Player	HR	Year	Player	HR
1903	McFarland	5	1927	Ruth*	60	1951	Berra	27	1975	Bonds	32	1999	Martinez	28
1904	Dougherty, Ganzel	6	1928	Ruth*	54	1952	Berra	30	1976	Nettles*	32	2000	B. Williams	30
1905	Williams	6	1929	Ruth*	46	1953	Berra	27	1977	Nettles	37	2001	Martinez	34
1906	Conroy	4	1930	Ruth*	49	1954	Mantle	27	1978	Jackson, Nettles	27	2002	Giambi	41
1907	Hoffman	5	1931	Ruth*, Gehrig*	46	1955	Mantle*	37	1979	Jackson	29	2003	Giambi	41
1908	Niles	4	1932	Ruth	41	1956	Mantle*	52	1980	Jackson*	41	2004	Rodriguez, Sheffield	36
1909	Chase, Demmitt	4	1933	Ruth	34	1957	Mantle	34	1981	Jackson, Nettles	15	2005	Rodriguez*	48
1910	Wolter, Cree	4	1934	Gehrig	49	1958	Mantle*	42	1982	Winfield	37	2006	Giambi	37
1911	Wolter, Cree	4	1935	Gehrig	30	1959	Mantle	31	1983	Winfield	32	2007	Rodriguez*	54
1912	Zinn	6	1936	Gehrig*	49	1960	Mantle*	40	1984	Baylor	27	2008	Rodriguez	35
1913	Wolter, Sweeney	2	1937	DiMaggio*	46	1961	Maris*	61	1985	Mattingly	35	2009	Teixeira*	39
1914	Peckinpaugh	3	1938	DiMaggio	32	1962	Maris	33	1986	Mattingly	31	2010	Teixeira	33
1915	L. Boone, Peckinpaugh	5	1939	DiMaggio	30	1963	Howard	28	1987	Pagliarulo	32	2011	Granderson	41
1916	Pipp*	12	1940	DiMaggio	31	1964	Mantle	35	1988	Clark	27	2012	Granderson	43
1917	Pipp*	9	1941	Keller	33	1965	Tresh	26	1989	Mattingly	23	2013	Canó	27
1918	Baker	6	1942	Keller	26	1966	Pepitone	31	1990	Barfield	25	2014	McCann	23
1919	Baker	10	1943	Keller	31	1967	Mantle	22	1991	Nokes	24	2015	Rodriguez	33
1920	Ruth*	54	1944	Etten*	22	1968	Mantle	18	1992	Tartabull	25	2016	Beltrán	22
1921	Ruth*	59	1945	Etten	18	1969	Pepitone	27	1993	Tartabull	31	2017	JUDGE*	52
1922	Ruth*	35	1946	Keller	30	1970	Murcer	23	1994	O'Neill	21	2018	STANTON	38
1923	Ruth*	41	1947	DiMaggio	20	1971	Murcer	25	1995	O'Neill	22	2019	TORRES	38
1924	Ruth*	46	1948	DiMaggio*	39	1972	Murcer	33	1996	B. Williams	29			
1925	Meusel*	33	1949	Henrich	24	1973	Murcer, Nettles	22	1997	Martinez	44			
1926	Ruth*	47	1950	DiMaggio	32	1974	Nettles	22	1998	Martinez	28			

RBI (official statistic since 1920)

Year	Player	RBI	Year	Player	RBI	Year	Player	RBI	Year	Player	RBI	Year	Player	RBI
1903	Williams	82	1927	Gehrig*	173	1951	Berra	88	1975	Munson	102	1999	B. Williams	115
1904	Anderson	82	1928	Gehrig*	147	1952	Berra	98	1976	Munson	105	2000	B. Williams	121
1905	Williams	60	1929	Ruth	154	1953	Berra	108	1977	Jackson	110	2001	Martinez	113
1906	Williams	77	1930	Gehrig*	173	1954	Berra	125	1978	Jackson	97	2002	Giambi	122
1907	Chase	68	1931	Gehrig*	184	1955	Berra	108	1979	Jackson	89	2003	Giambi	107
1908	Hemphill	44	1932	Gehrig	151	1956	Mantle*	130	1980	Jackson	111	2004	Sheffield	121
1909	Engle	71	1933	Gehrig	139	1957	Mantle	94	1981	Winfield	68	2005	Rodriguez	130
1910	Chase	73	1934	Gehrig*	166	1958	Mantle	97	1982	Winfield	106	2006	Rodriguez	121
1911	Hartzell	91	1935	Gehrig	119	1959	Mantle	75	1983	Winfield	116	2007	Rodriguez*	156
1912	Chase	58	1936	Gehrig	152	1960	Maris*	112	1984	Mattingly	110	2008	Rodriguez	103
1913	Cree	63	1937	DiMaggio	167	1961	Maris*	141	1985	Mattingly*	145	2009	Teixeira*	122
1914	Peckinpaugh	51	1938	DiMaggio	140	1962	Maris	100	1986	Mattingly	113	2010	Rodriguez	125
1915	Pipp	58	1939	DiMaggio	126	1963	Pepitone	89	1987	Mattingly	115	2011	Granderson*	119
1916	Pipp	99	1940	DiMaggio	133	1964	Mantle	111	1988	Winfield	107	2012	Granderson	106
1917	Pipp	72	1941	DiMaggio	125	1965	Tresh	74	1989	Mattingly	113	2013	Canó	107
1918	Baker	68	1942	DiMaggio	114	1966	Pepitone	64	1990	Barfield	78	2014	McCann	75
1919	Baker	78	1943	Etten	107	1967	Pepitone	64	1991	Hall	80	2015	McCann	94
1920	Ruth*	136	1944	Lindell	103	1968	White	62	1992	Mattingly	86	2016	Castro, Gregorius	70
1921	Ruth*	168	1945	Etten*	111	1969	Murcer	82	1993	Tartabull	102	2017	JUDGE	114
1922	Ruth	99	1946	Keller	100	1970	White	94	1994	O'Neill	83	2018	STANTON	100
1923	Ruth*	130	1947	Henrich	98	1971	Murcer	94	1995	O'Neill	96	2019	LEMAHIEU	102
1924	Ruth	121	1948	DiMaggio*	155	1972	Murcer	96	1996	Martinez	117			
1925	Meusel*	136	1949	Berra	91	1973	Murcer	95	1997	Martinez	141			
1926	Ruth*	153	1950	Berra	124	1974	Murcer	88	1998	Martinez	123			

*Tied or Led League

RUNS

Year	Player		Year	Player		Year	Player		Year	Player	
1903	Keeler	98	1927	Ruth*	158	1951	Berra	92	1975	Bonds	93	1999	Jeter	134
1904	Dougherty*	80	1928	Ruth*	163	1952	Berra	97	1976	White*	104	2000	Jeter	119
1905	Keeler	81	1929	Gehrig	127	1953	Mantle	105	1977	Nettles	99	2001	Jeter	110
1906	Keeler	96	1930	Ruth	150	1954	Mantle*	129	1978	Randolph	87	2002	Soriano*	128
1907	Hoffman	81	1931	Gehrig*	163	1955	Mantle	121	1979	Randolph	98	2003	Soriano	114
1908	Hemphill	62	1932	Combs	143	1956	Mantle*	132	1980	Randolph	99	2004	Sheffield	117
1909	Demmitt	68	1933	Gehrig*	138	1957	Mantle*	121	1981	Randolph	59	2005	Rodriguez*	124
1910	Daniels	68	1934	Gehrig	128	1958	Mantle*	127	1982	Randolph	85	2006	Jeter	118
1911	Cree	90	1935	Gehrig*	125	1959	Mantle	104	1983	Winfield	99	2007	Rodriguez*	143
1912	Daniels	72	1936	Gehrig*	167	1960	Mantle*	119	1984	Winfield	106	2008	Rodriguez	104
1913	Hartzell	60	1937	DiMaggio*	151	1961	Maris*	132	1985	Henderson*	146	2009	Damon, Jeter	107
1914	Maisel	78	1938	Rolfe	132	1962	Richardson	99	1986	Henderson*	130	2010	Teixeira*	113
1915	Maisel	77	1939	Rolfe*	139	1963	Tresh	91	1987	Randolph	96	2011	Granderson*	136
1916	Pipp	70	1940	Gordon	112	1964	Mantle	91	1988	Henderson	118	2012	Canó	105
1917	Pipp	82	1941	DiMaggio	122	1965	Tresh	94	1989	Sax	88	2013	Canó, GARDNER	81
1918	Baker, Pratt	65	1942	DiMaggio*	123	1966	Pepitone	85	1990	R. Kelly	85	2014	GARDNER	87
1919	Peckinpaugh	89	1943	Keller	97	1967	Clarke	74	1991	Sax	85	2015	GARDNER	94
1920	Ruth*	158	1944	Stirnweiss*	125	1968	White	89	1992	Mattingly	89	2016	GARDNER	80
1921	Ruth*	177	1945	Stirnweiss*	107	1969	Clarke, Murcer	82	1993	Tartabull	87	2017	JUDGE*	128
1922	Witt	98	1946	Keller	98	1970	White	109	1994	B. Williams	80	2018	STANTON	102
1923	Ruth*	151	1947	Henrich	109	1971	Murcer	94	1995	B. Williams	93	2019	LEMAHIEU	109
1924	Ruth*	143	1948	Henrich*	138	1972	Murcer*	102	1996	B. Williams	108			
1925	Combs	117	1949	Rizzuto	110	1973	White	88	1997	Jeter	116			
1926	Ruth*	139	1950	Rizzuto	125	1974	Maddox	75	1998	Jeter*	127			

DOUBLES

Year	Player		Year	Player		Year	Player		Year	Player		Year	Player	
1903	Williams	30	1927	Gehrig*	52	1951	McDougald	23	1975	Chambliss	38	1999	O'Neill	39
1904	Williams	31	1928	Gehrig*	47	1952	Mantle	37	1976	Chambliss	32	2000	B. Williams, Martinez	37
1905	Williams	20	1929	Lazzeri	37	1953	McDougald	27	1977	Jackson	39	2001	B. Williams	38
1906	Williams	25	1930	Gehrig	42	1954	Berra	28	1978	Piniella	34	2002	Soriano	51
1907	Chase	23	1931	Lary	36	1955	Mantle	25	1979	Chambliss	27	2003	Matsui	42
1908	Conroy	22	1932	Gehrig	42	1956	Berra	29	1980	Cerone	30	2004	Jeter	44
1909	Engle	20	1933	Gehrig	41	1957	Mantle	28	1981	Winfield	25	2005	Matsui	45
1910	Knight	25	1934	Gehrig	40	1958	Bauer, Skowron	24	1982	Mumphrey, Winfield	24	2006	Canó	41
1911	Chase	33	1935	Chapman	38	1959	Berra, Kubek	25	1983	Baylor	33	2007	Posada	42
1912	Daniels	25	1936	DiMaggio	44	1960	Skowron	34	1984	Mattingly*	44	2008	Abreu	39
1913	Cree	25	1937	Gehrig	37	1961	Kubek	38	1985	Mattingly*	48	2009	Canó	48
1914	Maisel	23	1938	Rolfe	36	1962	Richardson	38	1986	Mattingly*	53	2010	Canó	41
1915	Pipp	20	1939	Rolfe*	46	1963	Tresh	28	1987	Mattingly*	38	2011	Canó	46
1916	Baker	23	1940	Gordon	32	1964	Howard	27	1988	Mattingly, Winfield	37	2012	Canó	48
1917	Pipp	29	1941	DiMaggio	43	1965	Tresh	29	1989	Mattingly	37	2013	Canó	41
1918	Baker	25	1942	Henrich	30	1966	Boyer	22	1990	R. Kelly	32	2014	Beltrán	34
1919	Pratt, Bodie	27	1943	Etten	35	1967	Tresh	23	1991	Sax	38	2015	Gregorius	32
1920	Meusel	40	1944	Stirnweiss	35	1968	White	20	1992	Mattingly	40	2016	Headley	30
1921	Ruth	44	1945	Stirnweiss	32	1969	White	30	1993	O'Neill	34	2017	ANDUJAR	47
1922	Pipp	32	1946	Keller	29	1970	White	30	1994	B. Williams	29	2019	URSHELA	34
1923	Ruth	45	1947	Henrich	35	1971	Murcer	25	1995	Mattingly	32			
1924	Meusel	40	1948	Henrich	42	1972	Murcer	30	1996	O'Neill	35			
1925	Combs	36	1949	Rizzuto	22	1973	Murcer, Munson	26	1997	O'Neill	42			
1926	Gehrig	47	1950	Rizzuto	36	1974	Maddox, Piniella	26	1998	O'Neill	40			

TRIPLES

Year	Player		Year	Player		Year	Player		Year	Player		Year	Player	
1903	Williams, Conroy	12	1927	Combs*	23	1951	Woodling	8	1975	White	5	1999	Jeter	9
1904	Anderson, Conroy	12	1928	Combs*	21	1952	Rizzuto	10	1976	Rivers	8	2000	B. Williams	6
1905	Conroy	11	1929	Combs	15	1953	McDougald	7	1977	Randolph	11	2001	Jeter, Soriano, Knoblauch	3
1906	Chase, Conroy	10	1930	Combs*	22	1954	Mantle	12	1978	Rivers	8	2002	Soriano, Spencer, Williams, Wilson	2
1907	Conroy, LaPorte, Williams	11	1931	Gehrig	15	1955	Mantle*, Carey*	11	1979	Randolph	13	2003	Soriano	5
1908	Hemphill	9	1932	Lazzeri	16	1956	Bauer	7	1980	Randolph	7	2004	Lofton	5
1909	Demmitt	12	1933	Combs	16	1957	Bauer*, McDougald*	9	1981	Mumphrey	5	2005	Jeter	5
1910	Cree	16	1934	Chapman*	13	1958	Bauer	6	1982	Mumphrey	10	2006	Damon	5
1911	Cree	22	1935	Selkirk	12	1959	McDougald	8	1983	Winfield	8	2007	Cabrera	8
1912	Hartzell, Daniels	11	1936	DiMaggio*, Rolfe*	15	1960	Maris	7	1984	Moreno	6	2008	Damon	5
1913	Peckinpaugh	7	1937	DiMaggio	15	1961	Mantle, Kubek	6	1985	Winfield	6	2009	GARDNER	8
1914	Maisel, Hartzell	9	1938	DiMaggio	13	1962	Maris	7	1986	Henderson, Winfield	5	2010	GARDNER, Granderson	7
1915	Pipp	13	1939	Rolfe	10	1963	Howard, Richardson	6	1987	Henderson, Pagliarulo	3	2011	Granderson	10
1916	Pipp	14	1940	Keller	15	1964	Tresh, Boyer	5	1988	Washington	3	2012	Granderson	4
1917	Pipp	12	1941	DiMaggio	11	1965	Tresh, Boyer	6	1989	R. Kelly, Sax, Slaught	3	2013	GARDNER*	10
1918	Pipp	9	1942	DiMaggio	13	1966	Boyer, Clarke, Tresh, Pepitone	4	1990	R. Kelly	4	2014	GARDNER	8
1919	Pipp	10	1943	Lindell*	12	1967	Pepitone, Smith, Tresh, Whitaker	3	1991	B. Williams, P. Kelly	4	2015	GARDNER	6
1920	Pipp	14	1944	Stirnweiss*, Lindell*	16	1968	White, Robinson	7	1992	Hall	3	2016	GARDNER	6
1921	Ruth, Meusel	16	1945	Stirnweiss*	22	1969	Clarke	7	1993	B. Williams	4	2017	Ellsbury, FRAZIER, GARDNER	4
1922	Meusel	11	1946	Keller	10	1970	Kenney	7	1994	Polonia	6	2018	GARDNER	7
1923	Ruth	13	1947	Henrich*	13	1971	Clarke, White	7	1995	B. Williams	9	2019	GARDNER	7
1924	Pipp*	19	1948	Henrich*	14	1972	Kenney	7	1996	B. Williams	7			
1925	Combs	13	1949	Rizzuto, Woodling	7	1973	Munson	4	1997	Jeter	7			
1926	Gehrig*	20	1950	Bauer, DiMaggio	10	1974	White	8	1998	Jeter	8			

STOLEN BASES

Year	Player		Year	Player		Year	Player		Year	Player		Year	Player	
1903	Conroy	33	1927	Meusel	24	1951	Rizzuto	18	1975	Bonds	30	1999	Knoblauch	28
1904	Conroy	30	1928	Lazzeri	15	1952	Rizzuto	17	1976	Rivers	43	2000	Jeter	22
1905	Fultz	44	1929	Combs, Lazzeri	11	1953	Mantle	8	1977	Rivers	22	2001	Soriano	43
1906	Hoffman	33	1930	Combs	16	1954	Mantle, Carey	5	1978	Randolph	36	2002	Soriano*	41
1907	Conroy	41	1931	Chapman*	61	1955	Hunter	9	1979	Randolph	33	2003	Soriano	35
1908	Hemphill	42	1932	Chapman*	38	1956	Mantle	10	1980	Randolph	30	2004	Rodriguez	28
1909	Austin	30	1933	Chapman	27	1957	Mantle	16	1981	Randolph	14	2005	Womack	27
1910	Daniels	41	1934	Chapman	26	1958	Mantle	18	1982	Randolph	16	2006	Jeter	34
1911	Cree	48	1935	Chapman	17	1959	Mantle	21	1983	Randolph, Mumphrey	14	2007	Damon	27
1912	Daniels	37	1936	Crosetti	18	1960	Mantle	14	1984	Moreno	20	2008	Damon	29
1913	Daniels	28	1937	Crosetti	13	1961	Mantle	12	1985	Henderson*	80	2009	Jeter	30
1914	Maisel*	74	1938	Crosetti*	27	1962	Richardson	11	1986	Henderson*	87	2010	GARDNER	47
1915	Maisel	51	1939	Selkirk	12	1963	Richardson	15	1987	Henderson	41	2011	GARDNER*	49
1916	Magee	29	1940	Gordon	18	1964	Tresh	13	1988	Henderson*	93	2012	Suzuki	14
1917	Maisel	19	1941	Rizzuto	14	1965	Richardson	7	1989	Sax	43	2013	GARDNER	24
1918	Bodie	16	1942	Rizzuto	22	1966	White	14	1990	Sax	43	2014	Ellsbury	39
1919	Pratt	22	1943	Stirnweiss	11	1967	Clarke	21	1991	R. Kelly	32	2015	Ellsbury	21
1920	Ruth	14	1944	Stirnweiss*	55	1968	Clarke, White	20	1992	R. Kelly	28	2016	Ellsbury	20
1921	Meusel, Pipp, Ruth	17	1945	Stirnweiss*	33	1969	Clarke	33	1993	P. Kelly	14	2017	GARDNER	23
1922	Meusel	13	1946	Stirnweiss	18	1970	Clarke, White	23	1995	Polonia	20	2018	GARDNER	16
1923	Ruth	17	1947	Henrich	11	1971	Clarke	17	1995	Polonia	10	2019	GARDNER	10
1924	Meusel	26	1948	Henrich	6	1972	White	23	1996	B. Williams	17			
1925	Paschal	14	1949	Rizzuto	18	1973	White	16	1997	Jeter	23			
1926	Meusel	16	1950	Rizzuto	12	1974	White	15	1998	Knoblauch	31			

*Tied or Led League

Year-by-Year Pitching Leaders

WINS

Year	Pitcher	W-L
1903	Chesbro	21-15
1904	Chesbro*	41-12
1905	Chesbro	19-15
1906	Orth*	27-17
1907	Orth	14-21
1908	Chesbro	14-20
1909	Lake	14-11
1910	Ford	26-6
1911	Ford	22-11
1912	Ford	13-21
1913	Fisher, Ford	12-16, 12-18
1914	Caldwell	17-9
1915	Caldwell	19-16
1916	Shawkey	24-14
1917	Caldwell, Shawkey	13-16, 13-15
1918	Mogridge	16-13
1919	Shawkey	20-11
1920	Mays	26-11
1921	Mays*	27-9
1922	Bush	26-7
1923	Jones	21-8
1924	Pennock	21-9
1925	Pennock	16-17
1926	Pennock	23-11
1927	Hoyt*	22-7
1928	Pipgras*	24-13
1929	Pipgras	18-12
1930	Pipgras, Ruffing	15-15, 15-5
1931	Gomez	21-9
1932	Gomez	24-7
1933	Gomez	16-10
1934	Gomez*	26-5
1935	Ruffing	16-11
1936	Ruffing	20-12
1937	Gomez*	21-11
1938	Ruffing*	21-7
1939	Ruffing	21-7
1940	Ruffing	15-12
1941	Ruffing, Gomez	15-6, 15-5
1942	Bonham	21-5
1943	Chandler*	20-4
1944	Borowy	17-12
1945	Bevens	13-9
1946	Chandler	20-8
1947	Reynolds	19-8
1948	Raschi	19-8
1949	Raschi	21-10
1950	Raschi	21-8
1951	Raschi, Lopat	21-10, 21-9
1952	Reynolds	20-8
1953	Ford	18-6
1954	Grim	20-6
1955	Ford*	18-7
1956	Ford	19-6
1957	Sturdivant	16-6
1958	Turley*	21-7
1959	Ford	16-10
1960	Ditmar	15-9
1961	Ford*	25-4
1962	Terry*	23-12
1963	Ford*	24-7
1964	Bouton	18-13
1965	Stottlemyre	20-9
1966	St'myre, Peterson	12-20, 12-11
1967	Stottlemyre	15-15
1968	Stottlemyre	21-12
1969	Stottlemyre	20-14
1970	Peterson	20-11
1971	Stottlemyre	16-12
1972	Peterson	17-15
1973	Stottlemyre	16-16
1974	Dobson, Medich	19-15, 19-15
1975	Hunter*	23-14
1976	Figueroa	19-10
1977	Guidry, Figueroa	16-7, 16-11
1978	Guidry*	25-3
1979	John	21-9
1980	John	22-9
1981	Guidry	11-5
1982	Guidry	14-8
1983	Guidry	21-9
1984	Niekro	16-8
1985	Guidry*	22-6
1986	Rasmussen	18-6
1987	Rhoden	16-10
1988	Candelaria	13-7
1989	Hawkins	15-15
1990	Guetterman	11-7
1991	Sanderson	16-10
1992	M. Perez	13-16
1993	Key	18-6
1994	Key*	17-4
1995	McDowell	15-10
1996	Pettitte*	21-8
1997	Pettitte	18-7
1998	Cone*	20-7
1999	O. Hernandez	17-9
2000	Pettitte	19-9
2001	Clemens	20-3
2002	Wells	19-7
2003	Pettitte	21-8
2004	Lieber, Vazquez	14-8, 14-10
2005	Johnson	17-8
2006	Wang*	19-6
2007	Wang	19-7
2008	Mussina	20-9
2009	Sabathia*	19-8
2010	Sabathia*	21-7
2011	Sabathia	19-8
2012	Hughes, Kuroda	16-13, 16-11
2013	Sabathia	14-13
2014	TANAKA	13-5
2015	Eovaldi	14-3
2016	TANAKA	14-4
2017	Sabathia, SEVERINO	14-5, 14-6
2018	SEVERINO	19-8
2019	GERMÁN	18-4

INNINGS PITCHED

Year	Pitcher	IP
1903	Chesbro	323.0
1904	Chesbro*	455.0
1905	Orth	305.0
1906	Orth*	339.0
1907	Orth	249.0
1908	Chesbro	289.0
1909	Warhop	243.0
1910	Ford	300.0
1911	Ford	281.0
1912	Ford	292.0
1913	Fisher	246.0
1914	Warhop	217.0
1915	Caldwell	303.0
1916	Shawkey	278.0
1917	Shawkey	236.0
1918	Mogridge	239.0
1919	Quinn	266.0
1920	Mays	312.0
1921	Mays*	336.0
1922	Shawkey	300.0
1923	Bush	275.0
1924	Pennock	286.0
1925	Pennock*	276.0
1926	Pennock	266.0
1927	Hoyt	256.0
1928	Pipgras	302.0
1929	Pipgras*	225.0
1930	Pipgras	221.0
1931	Gomez	242.0
1932	Gomez	265.0
1933	Gomez, Ruffing	235.0
1934	Gomez*	282.0
1935	Gomez	246.0
1936	Ruffing	271.0
1937	Gomez	278.0
1938	Ruffing	247.0
1939	Ruffing	233.0
1940	Ruffing	226.0
1941	Russo	210.0
1942	Bonham	226.0
1943	Chandler	253.0
1944	Borowy	253.0
1945	Bevens	184.0
1946	Chandler	257.0
1947	Reynolds	242.0
1948	Reynolds	236.0
1949	Raschi	275.0
1950	Raschi	257.0
1951	Raschi	258.0
1952	Reynolds	244.0
1953	Ford	207.0
1954	Ford	211.0
1955	Ford	254.0
1956	Ford	226.0
1957	Sturdivant	202.0
1958	Turley	245.0
1959	Ford	204.0
1960	Ditmar	200.0
1961	Ford*	283.0
1962	Terry*	299.0
1963	Ford*	269.0
1964	Bouton	271.0
1965	Stottlemyre*	291.0
1966	Stottlemyre	251.0
1967	Stottlemyre	255.0
1968	Stottlemyre	279.0
1969	Stottlemyre	303.0
1970	Stottlemyre	271.0
1971	Peterson	274.0
1972	Stottlemyre	260.0
1973	Stottlemyre	273.0
1974	Dobson	281.0
1975	Hunter*	328.0
1976	Hunter	299.0
1977	Figueroa	239.0
1978	Guidry	274.0
1979	John	276.0
1980	John	265.0
1981	May	148.0
1982	Guidry	222.0
1983	Guidry	250.1
1984	Niekro	215.2
1985	Guidry	259.0
1986	Rasmussen	202.0
1987	John	187.2
1988	Rhoden	197.0
1989	Hawkins	208.1
1990	Leary	208.0
1991	Sanderson	208.0
1992	M. Perez	247.2
1993	Key	236.2
1994	Key	168.0
1995	McDowell	217.2
1996	Pettitte	221.0
1997	Pettitte	240.1
1998	Pettitte	216.1
1999	O. Hernandez	214.1
2000	Pettitte	204.2
2001	Mussina	228.2
2002	Mussina	215.2
2003	Mussina	214.2
2004	Vazquez	198.0
2005	Johnson	225.2
2006	Wang	218.0
2007	Pettitte	215.1
2008	Pettitte	204.0
2009	Sabathia	230.0
2010	Sabathia	237.2
2011	Sabathia	237.1
2012	Kuroda	219.2
2013	Sabathia	211.0
2014	Kuroda	199.0
2015	Sabathia	167.1
2016	TANAKA	199.2
2017	SEVERINO	193.1
2018	SEVERINO	191.1
2019	TANAKA	182.0

ERA (Qualifiers only/ Official statistic in AL since 1913)

Year	Pitcher	ERA
1903	Griffith	2.70
1904	Chesbro	1.82
1905	Chesbro	2.20
1906	Clarkson	2.32
1907	Chesbro	2.53
1908	Chesbro	2.93
1909	Lake	1.88
1910	Ford	1.65
1911	Ford	2.28
1912	McConnell	2.75
1913	Caldwell	2.43
1914	Caldwell	1.94
1915	Fisher	2.10
1916	Cullop	2.05
1917	Shawkey	2.44
1918	Mogridge	2.27
1919	Mogridge	2.50
1920	Shawkey*	2.45
1921	Mays	3.04
1922	Shawkey	2.91
1923	Hoyt	3.01
1924	Pennock	2.83
1925	Pennock	2.96
1926	Shocker	3.38
1927	W. Moore*	2.28
1928	Pennock	2.56
1929	Sherid	3.49
1930	Pipgras	4.11
1931	Gomez	2.63
1932	Ruffing	3.09
1933	Gomez	3.18
1934	Gomez*	2.33
1935	Ruffing	3.12
1936	Pearson	3.71
1937	Gomez*	2.33
1938	Ruffing	3.32
1939	Ruffing	2.94
1940	Russo	3.29
1941	Russo	3.09
1942	Bonham	2.27
1943	Chandler*	1.64
1944	Borowy	2.63
1945	Bonham	3.28
1946	Chandler	2.10
1947	Shea	3.07
1948	Shea	3.41
1949	Lopat	3.27
1950	Lopat	3.47
1951	Lopat	2.91
1952	Reynolds*	2.07
1953	Lopat*	2.43
1954	Ford	2.82
1955	Ford	2.62
1956	Ford*	2.47
1957	Shantz*	2.45
1958	Ford*	2.01
1959	Ditmar	2.90
1960	Ditmar	3.06
1961	Stafford	2.68
1962	Ford	2.90
1963	Bouton	2.53
1964	Ford	2.13
1965	Stottlemyre	2.63
1966	Peterson	3.31
1967	Downing	2.63
1968	Bahnsen	2.06
1969	Peterson	2.55
1970	Peterson	2.91
1971	Stottlemyre	2.87
1972	Kline	2.40
1973	Medich	2.95
1974	Dobson	3.07
1975	Hunter	2.58
1976	Figueroa	3.01
1977	Guidry	2.82
1978	Guidry*	1.74
1979	Guidry*	2.78
1980	May*	2.46
1981	Righetti	2.05
1982	John	3.69
1983	Guidry	3.42
1984	Niekro	3.09
1985	Guidry	3.27
1986	Rasmussen	3.88
1987	Rhoden	3.86
1988	Rhoden	4.29
1989	Hawkins	4.80
1990	Leary	4.11
1991	Sanderson	3.81
1992	M. Perez	2.87
1993	Key	3.00
1994	Key	3.27
1995	Cone	3.82
1996	Pettitte	3.87
1997	Cone	2.82
1998	Wells	3.49
1999	Cone	3.44
2000	Clemens	3.70
2001	Mussina	3.15
2002	Wells	3.75
2003	Mussina	3.40
2004	Lieber	4.33
2005	Johnson	3.79
2006	Mussina	3.51
2007	Wang	3.70
2008	Mussina	3.37
2009	Sabathia	3.37
2010	Sabathia	3.18
2011	Sabathia	3.00
2012	Kuroda	3.32
2013	Kuroda	3.31
2014	Kuroda	3.71
2015	Sabathia	4.73
2016	TANAKA	3.07
2017	SEVERINO	2.98
2018	SEVERINO	3.39
2019	TANAKA	4.45

STRIKEOUTS

Year	Pitcher	SO
1903	Chesbro	147
1904	Chesbro	239
1905	Chesbro	156
1906	Chesbro	152
1907	Doyle	94
1908	Chesbro	124
1909	Lake	117
1910	Ford	209
1911	Ford	158
1912	Ford	112
1913	Fisher	92
1914	Keating	109
1915	Caldwell	130
1916	Shawkey	122
1917	Caldwell	102
1918	Love	95
1919	Shawkey	123
1920	Shawkey	126
1921	Shawkey	126
1922	Shawkey	133
1923	Bush, Shawkey	125
1924	Shawkey	114
1925	Jones	92
1926	Pennock	78
1927	Hoyt	86
1928	Pipgras	138
1929	Pipgras	125
1930	Ruffing	117
1931	Gomez	150
1932	Ruffing*	190
1933	Gomez*	164
1934	Gomez*	158
1935	Gomez	138
1936	Pearson	118
1937	Gomez*	194
1938	Gomez	129
1939	Gomez	102
1940	Ruffing	97
1941	Russo	105
1942	Borowy	85
1943	Chandler	134
1944	Borowy	107
1945	Bevens	76
1946	Chandler	138
1947	Reynolds	129
1948	Raschi	124
1949	Byrne	129
1950	Reynolds	160
1951	Raschi*	164
1952	Reynolds*	160
1953	Ford	110
1954	Ford	126
1955	Turley	210
1956	Ford	141
1957	Turley	152
1958	Turley	168
1959	Ford	114
1960	Terry	92
1961	Ford	209
1962	Terry	176
1963	Ford	189
1964	Downing*	217
1965	Downing	179
1966	Downing	152
1967	Downing	171
1968	Bahnsen	162
1969	Peterson	150
1970	Stottlemyre	127
1971	Peterson	139
1972	Stottlemyre	110
1973	Medich	145
1974	Dobson	157
1975	Hunter	177
1976	Hunter	173
1977	Guidry	176
1978	Guidry	248
1979	Guidry	201
1980	Guidry	166
1981	Guidry	104
1982	Righetti	163
1983	Righetti	169
1984	Niekro	136
1985	Niekro	149
1986	Guidry	140
1987	Rhoden	107
1988	Candelaria	121
1989	Hawkins	98
1990	Leary	138
1991	Sanderson	130
1992	M. Perez	218
1993	Key	173
1994	M. Perez	109
1995	McDowell	157
1996	Pettitte	162
1997	Cone	222
1998	Cone	209
1999	Cone	177
2000	Clemens	188
2001	Mussina	214
2002	Clemens	192
2003	Mussina	195
2004	Vazquez	150
2005	Johnson	211
2006	Johnson, Mussina	172
2007	Pettitte	141
2008	Pettitte	158
2009	Sabathia	197
2010	Sabathia	197
2011	Sabathia	230
2012	Sabathia	197
2013	Sabathia	175
2014	Kuroda	146
2015	Pineda	156
2016	Pineda	207
2017	SEVERINO	230
2018	SEVERINO	220
2019	PAXTON	186

*** Tied or Led League**

Top 10 Single-Season Leaders

Special thanks to the *Elias Sports Bureau*

BATTING

At-Bats
1. Soriano . . . . . 696 . . . 2002
2. Richardson 692 . . . 1962
3. Clarke . . . . . 686 . . . 1970
4. Jeter . . . . . . 683 . . . 2012
5. Soriano . . . . . 682 . . . 2003
6. Richardson . . 679 . . . 1964
7. Mattingly . . . 677 . . . 1986
8. Richardson . . 664 . . . 1965
9. Jeter . . . . . . 663 . . . 2010
10. Richardson . . 662 . . . 1961

Runs Scored
1. Ruth . . . . 177 . . . 1921
2. Gehrig . . . . . 167 . . . 1936
3. Ruth . . . . 163 . . . 1928
   Gehrig . . . . . 163 . . . 1931
5. Ruth . . . . 158 . . . 1920
   Ruth . . . . 158 . . . 1927
7. Ruth . . . . 151 . . . 1923
   DiMaggio . 151 . . . 1937
9. Ruth . . . . 150 . . . 1930
10. Gehrig . . . . . 149 . . . 1927
    Ruth . . . . 149 . . . 1931

Hits
1. Mattingly . . 238 . . . 1986
2. Combs . . . . . 231 . . . 1927
3. Gehrig . . . . . 220 . . . 1930
4. Jeter . . . . . . 219 . . . 1999
5. Gehrig . . . . . 218 . . . 1927
6. Jeter . . . . . . 216 . . . 2012
7. DiMaggio . . 215 . . . 1937
8. Jeter . . . . . . 214 . . . 2006
9. Rolfe . . . . . . 213 . . . 1939
10. Jeter . . . . . . 212 . . . 2009

Doubles
1. Mattingly . . . 53 . . . 1986
2. Gehrig . . . . . . 52 . . . 1927
3. Soriano . . . . . 51 . . . 2002
4. Mattingly . . . 48 . . . 1985
   Canó . . . . . . 48 . . . 2009
   Canó . . . . . . 48 . . . 2012
7. Gehrig . . . . . . 47 . . . 1926
   Meusel . . . . . 47 . . . 1927
   Gehrig . . . . . . 47 . . . 1928
   ANDÚJAR . . 47 . . 2018

Triples
1. Combs . . . . . 23 . . . 1927
2. Cree . . . . 22 . . . 1911
   Combs . . . . . 22 . . . 1930
   Stirnweiss . . 22 . . . 1945
5. Combs . . . . . 21 . . . 1928
6. Gehrig . . . . . 20 . . . 1926
7. Pipp . . . . 19 . . . 1924
8. Gehrig . . . . . 18 . . . 1927
9. Gehrig . . . . . 17 . . . 1930
10. 7 tied 16

Home Runs
1. Maris . . . . 61 . . . 1961
2. Ruth . . . . 60 . . . 1927
3. Ruth . . . . 59 . . . 1921
4. Ruth . . . . 54 . . . 1920
   Ruth . . . . 54 . . . 1928
   Mantle . . . . . 54 . . . 1961
   Rodriguez . . 54 . . . 2007
8. JUDGE . . . . 52 . . 2017
   Mantle . . . . . 52 . . . 1956
10. Ruth . . . . 49 . . . 1930
    Gehrig . . . . . 49 . . . 1934
    Gehrig . . . . . 49 . . . 1936

Runs Batted In
1. Gehrig . . . . . 184 . . . 1931
2. Gehrig . . . . . 173 . . . 1930
   Gehrig . . . . . 173 . . . 1927
4. Ruth . . . . 168 . . . 1921
5. DiMaggio . . 167 . . . 1937
6. Gehrig . . . . . 166 . . . 1934
7. Ruth . . . . 165 . . . 1927
8. Ruth . . . . 162 . . . 1931
9. Gehrig . . . . . 158 . . . 1937
10. Rodriguez . . 156 . . . 2007

Total Bases
1. Ruth . . . . 457 . . . 1921
2. Gehrig . . . . . 447 . . . 1927
3. Gehrig . . . . . 419 . . . 1930
4. DiMaggio . . 418 . . . 1937
5. Ruth . . . . 417 . . . 1927
6. Gehrig . . . . . 410 . . . 1931
7. Gehrig . . . . . 409 . . . 1934
8. Gehrig . . . . . 403 . . . 1936
9. Ruth . . . . 399 . . . 1923
10. Ruth . . . . 391 . . . 1924

Stolen Bases
1. Henderson . . 93 . . . 1988
2. Henderson . . 87 . . . 1986
3. Henderson . . 80 . . . 1985
4. Maisel . . . . . . 74 . . . 1914
5. Chapman . . . 61 . . . 1931
6. Stirnweiss . . 55 . . . 1944
7. Maisel . . . . . . 51 . . . 1915
8. GARDNER . . 49 . . 2011
9. Cree . . . . 48 . . . 1911
10. GARDNER . . 47 . . 2010

Walks
1. Ruth . . . . 170 . . . 1923
2. Ruth . . . . 150 . . . 1920
3. Mantle . . . . . 146 . . . 1957
4. Ruth . . . . 144 . . . 1921
   Ruth . . . . 144 . . . 1926
6. Ruth . . . . 142 . . . 1924
7. Ruth . . . . 137 . . . 1927
   Ruth . . . . 137 . . . 1928
9. Ruth . . . . 136 . . . 1930
10. Gehrig . . . . . 133 . . . 1935

Strikeouts (Batter)
1. STANTON . 211 . . 2018
2. JUDGE . . . 208 . . 2017
3. Granderson . 195 . . . 2012
4. Granderson . 169 . . . 2011
5. Soriano . . . . . 157 . . . 2002
6. Tartabull . . . 156 . . . 1993
7. JUDGE . . . 152 . . 2018
8. Posada . . . . 151 . . . 2000
9. Barfield . . . . 150 . . . 1990
10. R. Kelly . . . . 148 . . . 1990

Batting Avg. (min. 500 PA)
1. Ruth . . . . .394 . . . 1923
2. DiMaggio . . .381 . . . 1939
3. Gehrig . . . . . .379 . . . 1930
4. Ruth . . . . .378 . . . 1924
5. Ruth . . . . .377 . . . 1921
6. Ruth . . . . .376 . . . 1920
7. Gehrig . . . . . .374 . . . 1928
8. Gehrig . . . . . .373 . . . 1927
9. Ruth . . . . .373 . . . 1931
10. Ruth . . . . .372 . . . 1926

Hitting Streaks
1. DiMaggio . . 56 . . . 1941
2. Chase . . . . . . 33 . . . 1907
3. Peckinpaugh . 29 . . . 1919
   Combs . . . . . 29 . . . 1931
   Gordon . . . . . 29 . . . 1942
6. Ruth . . . . 26 . . . 1921
7. Jeter . . . . 25 . . . 2006
8. Mattingly . . . 24 . . . 1986
9. DiMaggio . . . 23 . . . 1940
   Canó . . . . 23 . . . 2012

PITCHING

Games Pitched
1. Quantrill . . . . 86 . . . 2004
2. Proctor . . . . . 83 . . . 2006
3. Gordon . . . . . 80 . . . 2004
   Logan . . . . . . 80 . . . 2012
5. Stanton . . . . . 79 . . . 2002
   Gordon . . . . . 79 . . . 2005
7. Karsay . . . . . . 78 . . . 2002
8. Nelson . . . . . 77 . . . 1997
   Vizcaino . . . . 77 . . . 2007
10. Stanton . . . . . 76 . . . 2001

Complete Games
1. Chesbro . . . . 48 . . . 1904
2. Powell . . . . . . 38 . . . 1904
3. Orth . . . . 36 . . . 1906
4. Chesbro . . . . 33 . . . 1903
5. Caldwell . . . . 31 . . . 1915
6. R. Ford . . . . . 30 . . . 1912
   Mays . . . . 30 . . . 1921
   Hunter . . . . . 30 . . . 1975
9. R. Ford . . . . . 29 . . . 1910
10. Orth . . . . 26 . . . 1905
    R. Ford . . . . . 26 . . . 1911
    Mays . . . . . . 26 . . . 1920

Wins
1. Chesbro . . . . 41 . . . 1904
2. Orth . . . . 27 . . . 1906
   Mays . . . . 27 . . . 1921
4. R. Ford . . . . . 26 . . . 1910
   Mays . . . . 26 . . . 1920
   Bush . . . . 26 . . . 1922
   Gomez . . . . . 26 . . . 1934
8. W. Ford . . . . 25 . . . 1961
   Guidry . . . . . 25 . . . 1978
10. 4 tied 24

Shutouts
1. Guidry . . . . 9 . . . 1978
2. R. Ford . . . . . . 8 . . . 1910
   W. Ford . . . . . . 8 . . . 1964
4. Reynolds . . . . 7 . . . 1951
   W. Ford . . . . . . 7 . . . 1958
   Stottlemyre . . . 7 . . . 1971
   Stottlemyre . . . 7 . . . 1972
   Hunter . . . . . . 7 . . . 1975
9. 14 tied 6

Strikeouts (Pitcher)
1. Guidry . . . . . 248 . . . 1978
2. Chesbro . . . 239 . . . 1904
3. SEVERINO . . 230 . . 2017
   Sabathia . . . 230 . . . 2011
5. Cone . . . . . . 222 . . . 1997
6. SEVERINO . 220 . . 2018
7. M. Perez . . . 218 . . . 1992
8. Downing . . . 217 . . . 1964
9. Mussina . . . 214 . . . 2001
10. Clemens . . . 213 . . . 2001

ERA (min. 1.0 IP per team game)
1. Chandler . . 1.64 . . . 1943
2. Guidry . . . . 1.74 . . . 1978
3. Caldwell . . . 1.95 . . . 1914
4. W. Ford . . . 2.01 . . . 1958
5. Cullop . . . . 2.05 . . . 1916
6. Bahnsen . . 2.06 . . . 1968
7. Reynolds . . 2.07 . . . 1952
8. Chandler . . 2.10 . . . 1946
9. R. Fisher . . 2.11 . . . 1915
10. W. Ford . . . 2.13 . . . 1964

Since earned runs became an official AL statistic in 1913.

Saves
1. Rivera . . . . . 53 . . . 2004
2. Rivera . . . . . 50 . . . 2001
3. Righetti . . . . 46 . . . 1986
4. Rivera . . . . . 45 . . . 1999
5. Rivera . . . . . 44 . . . 2013
   Rivera . . . . . 44 . . . 2011
   Rivera . . . . . 44 . . . 2009
8. Wetteland . 43 . . . 1996
   Rivera . . . . . 43 . . . 1997
   Rivera . . . . . 43 . . . 2005

Top 20 Career Batting Leaders
Special thanks to the *Elias Sports Bureau*

Games
1. Jeter............2747
2. Mantle...........2401
3. Gehrig...........2164
4. Berra............2116
5. Ruth.............2084
6. B. Williams......2076
7. White............1881
8. Posada...........1829
9. Dickey...........1789
10. Mattingly.......1785
11. DiMaggio........1736
12. Randolph........1694
13. Crosetti........1683
14. Rizzuto.........1661
15. Lazzeri.........1659
16. Nettles.........1535
17. Rodriguez.......1509
18. **GARDNER**....**1499**
19. Howard..........1492
20. Pipp............1488

At-Bats
1. Jeter...........11195
2. Mantle...........8101
3. Gehrig...........8001
4. B. Williams......7869
5. Berra............7545
6. Ruth.............7215
7. Mattingly........7003
8. DiMaggio.........6821
9. White............6650
10. Dickey..........6305
11. Randolph........6303
12. Crosetti........6276
13. Lazzeri.........6096
14. Posada..........6092
15. Rizzuto.........5818
16. Combs...........5752
17. Pipp............5594
18. Rodriguez.......5577
19. Nettles.........5519
20. Richardson......5386

Runs
1. Ruth.............1958
2. Jeter............1923
3. Gehrig...........1889
4. Mantle...........1675
5. DiMaggio.........1389
6. B. Williams......1366
7. Combs............1186
8. Berra............1176
9. Randolph.........1027
10. Rodriguez.......1012
11. Crosetti........1007
    Mattingly.......1007
13. White............964
14. Lazzeri..........952
15. Rolfe............940
16. Dickey...........930
17. Henrich..........902
18. Posada...........900
19. Rizzuto..........878
20. **GARDNER**.....**876**

Hits
1. Jeter............3465
2. Gehrig...........2721
3. Ruth.............2518
4. Mantle...........2415
5. B. Williams......2336
6. DiMaggio.........2215
7. Mattingly........2153
8. Berra............2148
9. Dickey...........1969
10. Combs...........1866
11. White...........1803
12. Lazzeri.........1785
13. Randolph........1731
14. Posada..........1664
15. Canó............1649
16. Rizzuto.........1588
17. Rodriguez.......1580
18. Pipp............1577
19. Meusel..........1565
20. Munson..........1558

Doubles
1. Jeter.............544
2. Gehrig............534
3. B. Williams......449
4. Mattingly.........442
5. Ruth..............424
6. DiMaggio..........390
7. Posada............379
8. Canó..............375
9. Mantle............344
10. Dickey...........343
11. Meusel...........339
12. Lazzeri..........327
13. Berra............321
14. Combs............309
15. O'Neill..........304
16. White............300
17. Henrich..........269
18. Rodriguez........263
19. Crosetti.........261
20. Pipp, Randolph...259

Triples
1. Gehrig............163
2. Combs.............154
3. DiMaggio..........131
4. Pipp..............121
5. Lazzeri...........115
6. Ruth..............106
7. Meusel............86
8. Henrich...........73
9. Dickey............72
   Mantle............72
11. Keller...........69
12. **GARDNER**.....**68**
13. Rolfe............67
14. Jeter............66
    Stirnweiss.......66
16. Crosetti.........65
17. Chapman..........64
18. Cree.............62
    Rizzuto..........62
20. Conroy...........60

Home Runs
1. Ruth..............659
2. Mantle............536
3. Gehrig............493
4. DiMaggio..........361
5. Berra.............358
6. Rodriguez.........351
7. B. Williams.......287
8. Posada............275
9. Jeter.............260
10. Nettles..........250
11. Mattingly........222
12. Giambi...........209
13. Teixeira.........206
14. Winfield.........205
15. Canó.............204
16. Maris............203
17. Dickey...........202
18. Martinez.........192
19. O'Neill..........185
20. Keller...........184

RBI (since 1920)
1. Gehrig...........1994
2. Ruth.............1980
3. DiMaggio.........1535
4. Mantle...........1509
5. Berra............1430
6. Jeter............1311
7. B. Williams......1257
8. Dickey...........1210
9. Lazzeri..........1164
10. Mattingly.......1099
11. Rodriguez.......1096
12. Posada..........1065
13. Meusel..........1012
14. O'Neill..........858
15. Nettles..........834
16. Canó.............822
17. Winfield.........818
18. Henrich..........797
19. White............758
20. Martinez.........739

Batting Avg. (min. 2500PA)
1. Ruth..............349
2. Gehrig............340
3. DiMaggio..........325
4. Combs.............324
5. Boggs.............313
6. Dickey............312
7. Meusel............311
8. Jeter.............310
9. Canó..............309
10. Mattingly........307
11. Chapman..........305
12. O'Neill..........303
13. Mantle...........298
14. B. Williams......297
15. Piniella.........295
16. Skowron..........294
17. Keller...........294
18. Lazzeri..........293
19. Cree.............292
20. Matsui...........292

On-Base Pct. (min. 2500PA)
1. Ruth.............484
2. Gehrig...........448
3. Mantle...........420
4. Keller...........410
5. Giambi...........404
6. Selkirk..........400
7. DiMaggio.........398
8. Combs............397
9. Boggs............396
10. Henderson.......395
11. Woodling........389
12. Henrich.........382
13. Dickey..........382
14. B. Williams.....381
15. Lazzeri.........380
16. Chapman.........379
17. Rodriguez.......378
18. O'Neill.........377
19. Jeter...........377
20. Posada..........374

Walks
1. Ruth.............1853
2. Mantle...........1733
3. Gehrig...........1512
4. Jeter............1082
5. B. Williams......1069
6. Randolph.........1005
7. Posada............936
8. R. White..........933
9. Lazzeri...........837
10. DiMaggio.........790
11. Crosetti.........789
12. Rodriguez........779
13. Keller...........760
14. Henrich..........713
15. Berra............700
16. Dickey...........679
17. Combs............673
18. Rizzuto..........658
19. Nettles..........627
20. Giambi...........619

Stolen Bases
1. Jeter.............358
2. Henderson........326
3. **GARDNER**.....**267**
4. Randolph.........251
5. Chase............249
6. White............232
7. Conroy...........185
8. Chapman..........184
9. Maisel...........183
10. Mantle..........153
11. Rodriguez.......152
12. Clarke..........151
    R. Kelly........151
14. Rizzuto.........150
15. Lazzeri.........147
    B. Williams.....147
17. Daniels.........146
18. Peckinpaugh.....143
19. Meusel..........133
20. Cree............132

Seasons (includes pitchers)
1. Jeter...............20
2. Rivera..............19
3. Mantle..............18
   Berra...............18
5. Posada..............17
   Crosetti............17
   Dickey..............17
   Gehrig..............17
9. B. Williams.........16
   W. Ford.............16
11. Pettitte...........15
    R. White...........15
    Ruffing............15
    Ruth...............15
15. Mattingly..........14
    Guidry.............14
17. Randolph, Murcer, Howard....13
    Rizzuto, DiMaggio,
    Gomez, Shawkey

Consec. Games (Top 10 only)
1. Gehrig............2130
2. A. Ward...........565
3. Matsui............518
4. E. Scott..........475
5. Gordon............471
6. Crosetti..........418
7. R. White..........388
8. Stirnweiss........368
9. Etten.............360
10. Mattingly........335

Single-Season Leaders by Position

P	No.	Player	Year
BA	.374	Ruffing	1930
H	49	Mays	1921
HR	5	Ruffing	1936
RBI	22	Mays	1921
	22	Ruffing	1936, '41

C	No.	Player	Year
BA	.362	Dickey	1936
H	192	Berra	1950
HR	34	**SÁNCHEZ**	**2019**
RBI	133	Dickey	1937

1B	No.	Player	Year
BA	.379	Gehrig	1930
H	238	Mattingly	1986
HR	49	Gehrig	1934, '36
RBI	184	Gehrig	1931

2B	No.	Player	Year
BA	.354	Lazzeri	1929
H	209	Soriano	2002
HR	39	Soriano	2002
RBI	118	Canó	2011

3B	No.	Player	Year
BA	.342	Boggs	1994
H	213	Rolfe	1939
HR	54	Rodriguez	2007
RBI	156	Rodriguez	2007

SS	No.	Player	Year
BA	.349	Jeter	1999
H	219	Jeter	1999
HR	27	Gregorius	2018
RBI	107	Lary	1931

OF	No.	Player	Year
BA	.394	Ruth	1923
H	231	Combs	1927
HR	61	Maris	1961
RBI	168	Ruth	1921

*Played at least 75% of games at the position (min. 100PA for BA; pitchers - 50% at P)

Top 20 Career Pitching Leaders

Special thanks to the Elias Sports Bureau

Games Pitched
1. Rivera 1115
2. Righetti 522
3. Robertson 501
4. Ford, W. 498
5. Stanton 456
6. Pettitte 447
7. Ruffing 426
8. Lyle 420
9. Shawkey 415
10. Murphy 383
11. Guidry 368
12. Gomez 367
13. Hoyt 365
14. Stottlemyre 360
15. Betances 358
16. Pennock 346
17. Nelson 331
18. Gossage 319
19. Hamilton 311
20. Sabathia 307

Wins
1. Ford, W. 236
2. Ruffing 231
3. Pettitte 219
4. Gomez 189
5. Guidry 170
6. Shawkey 168
7. Stottlemyre 164
8. Pennock 162
9. Hoyt 157
10. Sabathia 134
11. Reynolds 131
12. Chesbro 128
13. Mussina 123
    Raschi 120
15. Lopat 113
16. Chandler 109
    Peterson 109
18. Caldwell 95
19. Murphy 93
    Pipgras 93

Strikeouts
1. Pettitte 2020
2. Ford, W. 1958
3. Guidry 1778
4. Sabathia 1700
5. Ruffing 1529
6. Gomez 1470
7. Mussina 1278
8. Stottlemyre 1259
9. Rivera 1173
10. Shawkey 1167
11. Downing 1028
12. Clemens 1014
13. Reynolds 967
14. TANAKA 947
15. Righetti 940
16. Chesbro 913
17. Turley 909
18. Peterson 891
19. Cone 888
20. Raschi 832

Complete Games
1. Ruffing 261
2. Gomez 173
3. Chesbro 168
4. Pennock 165
5. Shawkey 164
6. Ford, W. 156
   Hoyt 156
8. Stottlemyre 152
9. Caldwell 150
10. Chandler 109
11. Warhop 105
12. Orth 102
13. Ford, R. 100
14. Raschi 99
15. Reynolds 96
16. Guidry 95
17. Bonham 91
    Lopat 91
    Mays 91
20. Fisher 88

Games Started
1. Ford, W. 438
   Pettitte 438
3. Ruffing 391
4. Stottlemyre 356
5. Guidry 323
6. Gomez 319
7. Sabathia 306
8. Hoyt 276
9. Shawkey 274
10. Pennock 268
11. Peterson 265
12. Mussina 248
13. Chesbro 227
14. Reynolds 209
15. Raschi 207
16. John 203
17. Lopat 202
18. Caldwell 196
19. Chandler 184
20. Downing 175
    Turley 175

Win Pct. (min. 100 decisions)
1. Chandler .... .717
2. Raschi .... .706
3. Ford, W. .... .690
4. Reynolds .... .686
5. Mays .... .669
6. Clemens .... .664
7. Lopat .... .657
8. Gomez .... .652
9. Guidry .... .651
10. Ruffing .... .651
11. Byrne .... .643
    Pennock .... .643
13. Murphy .... .637
14. TANAKA .... .636
15. Pettitte .... .633
16. Mussina .... .631
17. Bush .... .620
18. Hoyt .... .616
19. Cone .... .615
20. Figueroa .... .614

Walks
1. Gomez 1089
2. Ford, W 1086
3. Ruffing 1066
4. Pettitte 889
5. Shawkey 859
6. Reynolds 819
7. Stottlemyre 809
8. Byrne 763
9. Turley 761
10. Guidry 633
11. Hoyt 632
12. Raschi 620
13. Caldwell 578
14. Sabathia 576
15. Pipgras 548
16. Downing 526
17. Pennock 474
18. Righetti 473
19. Chandler 463
20. Chesbro 434

ERA (Since 1913, min. 800.0 IP)
1. Rivera 2.21
2. Fisher 2.60
3. Caldwell 2.71
4. Mogridge 2.74
5. Ford, W. 2.75
6. Bonham 2.75
7. Chandler 2.84
8. Stottlemyre 2.97
9. Peterson 3.10
10. Bahnsen 3.11
11. Righetti 3.11
12. Shawkey 3.12
13. May, R 3.12
14. Shocker 3.16
15. Lopat 3.19
16. Downing 3.22
17. Mays 3.25
18. Guidry 3.29
19. Reynolds 3.31
20. Gomez 3.34

Earned runs became an official AL statistic in 1913.

Innings
1. Ford, W. 3171.0
2. Ruffing 3168.0
3. Pettitte 2796.1
4. Stottlemyre .. 2662.0
5. Gomez 2497.0
6. Shawkey 2494.0
7. Guidry 2393.0
8. Hoyt 2274.0
9. Pennock 2201.0
10. Chesbro 1951.0
11. Sabathia 1918.0
12. Peterson ... 1856.0
13. Caldwell 1713.0
14. Reynolds ... 1699.0
15. Mussina 1553.0
16. Raschi 1538.0
17. Lopat 1497.0
18. Chandler ... 1485.0
19. Warhop 1413.0
20. Fisher 1386.0

Losses
1. Stottlemyre 139
2. Shawkey 131
3. Pettitte 127
4. Ruffing 124
5. Ford, W 106
   Peterson 106
7. Gomez 101
8. Caldwell 99
9. Hoyt 98
10. Chesbro 93
    Warhop 93
12. Guidry 91
13. Pennock 90
14. Sabathia 88
15. R. Fisher 78
16. Orth 73
17. Mussina 72
18. Quinn 65
19. Pipgras 64
20. Righetti 61

Shutouts
1. Ford, W. 45
2. Stottlemyre 40
   Ruffing 40
4. Gomez 28
5. Reynolds 27
6. Chandler 26
   Guidry 26
   Shawkey 26
9. Raschi 24
10. Turley 21
11. Lopat 20
12. Pennock 19
13. Chesbro 18
    Peterson 18
15. Bonham 17
    Caldwell 17
17. Hoyt 15
18. Orth 14
    Pipgras 14
    Terry 14

Saves (Official stat since 1969)
1. Rivera 652
2. Righetti 224
3. Gossage 151
4. Lyle 141
5. CHAPMAN 111
6. Farr 78
7. Wetteland 74
8. Robertson 53
9. McDaniel 48
10. Miller 45
11. Soriano 44
12. Betances 36
13. Aker 31
    Howe 31
15. Tidrow 23
16. Davis 22
17. Guetterman 21
    B. Fisher 20
19. Mendoza 16
20. Stanton 15

All-Time Club Records

KEY: ^–ML record (since 1900)   **–tied for ML record   +–AL record   #–tied for AL record

Note: Records in "fewest" categories are based on full seasons and do not include 1918, 1981 and 1994.

TEAM GENERAL

Season

Most Wins
Season 114 1998
Home .... 65^ 1961
Road 54 1939
Month .... 28 .... Aug. 1938
Consecutive 19 1947
Consecutive, home 18 1942
Consecutive, road 15 1953
Shutout 24 1951
1-0 .... 6 .... 1908, 1968

Fewest Wins
Season 50 1912
Home 27 1913
Road 19 1912

Most Losses
Season 103 1908
Home .... 47 .... 1908, 1913
Road 58 1912
Month .... 24 .... July 1908
Consecutive 13 1913
Consecutive, home 17 1913
Consecutive, road 12 1908
Shutout 27 1914
1-0 .... 9 1914

Fewest Losses
Season 44 1927
Home .... 15^ 1932
Road .... 20+ 1939

Miscellaneous
Most games .... 164** 1964, 1968
Fewest games 107 1981
Consecutive extra-inning games ...... 4 .... 1992 (5/19-23)
Longest 1-0 game won .... 15 inn. ..... 7/4/1925 G1 vs. PHA
Longest 1-0 game lost .... 14 inn. ..... 9/24/1969 at BOS
Most players used 58 2014
Fewest players used .... 25 .... 1923, 1927
Most pitchers used .... 33 (2x) 2014, 2015
Fewest pitchers used .... 8 .... 1922, 1923
Most position players used ... 33 2013

Game

Margin of victory, home ...... 20 .. 7/4/1927 vs. WAS (21-1)
                                                7/24/1999 vs. CLE (21-1)
Margin of victory, road .... 23 . 5/24/1936 at PHA (25-2)
Margin of defeat, home .... 22 . 8/31/2004 vs. CLE (22-0)
Margin of defeat, road .... 18 (2x) ... 7/4/2006 at CLE (19-1)
                                                7/29/1928 at CLE (24-6)
Longest game, time .... 7:00 .. 6/24/1962 at DET (22 inn.)
Longest game, time, 9 inn. ... 4:45^ .... 8/18/2006 at BOS
Largest deficit overcome ..... 9 (5x) .... 4/21/2012 at BOS
                                                5/16/2006 vs. TEX
                                                6/26/1987 vs. BOS
                                                7/25/1953 at DET
                                                4/18/1950 at BOS
Largest lead blown .... 9 (2x) .... 7/28/1931 vs. CWS
                                                9/26/1912 at BOS

TEAM PITCHING

Season

Lowest ERA (since 1913) 2.66 1917
Highest ERA (since 1913) 4.88 1930
Innings pitched 1506.2 1964
Complete games 123 1904
Fewest complete games 0 2016
Most shutouts 24 1951
Consecutive shutouts 4 1932
Consecutive shutout innings . 40 .... 5/10-16/1932
Fewest shutouts .... 2 .... 1994 (113G)
Fewest shutouts, non-strike season ... 4 1926
Most saves (since 1969) 59 2004
Lowest opp. BA .... .228 2017
Highest opp. BA .... .289 1925
Lowest opp. OBP .... .293 1981
Lowest opp. OBP, non-strike season .. .282 1904
Highest opp. OBP .... .354 1930
Fewest hits, non-interrupted season .. 1163 1955
Most hits allowed 1566 1930
Fewest home runs allowed ... 13 1907
Most home runs allowed 248 2019
Fewest runs allowed 507 1942
Most runs allowed 898 1930
Fewest earned runs allowed . 394 1904
Most earned runs allowed ... 753 2000
Fewest bases on balls (min: 150G) .245 1904
Most bases on balls 812 1949
Fewest strikeouts 431 1927
Most strikeouts 1634 2018

Game or Inning

Most runs allowed
Game, home .... 22 (2x) .... 4/18/2009 vs. CLE (22-4)
                                                8/31/2004 vs. CLE (22-0)
Game, road .... 24 .... 7/29/1928 at CLE (24-6)
Shutout loss .... 22-0 .... 8/31/2004 vs. CLE (22-0)
Inning .... 14 .... 4/18/2009 vs. CLE (2nd)
Two consecutive games .... 33 .... 9R on 7/28/1928 at CLE
                                            and 24R on 7/29/1928 at CLE

Most hits allowed
Game, home .... 27 .... 5/28/2005 vs. BOS
Game, road .... 28 .... 9/29/1928 at DET
Inning .... 12 ... (last) 6/21/2005 vs. TB (8th inn.)

Most home runs allowed
Game .... 7 (2x) .... 8/15/2019 vs. CLE
                                                7/4/2003 vs. BOS
Inning .... 4 (6x) .... 9/21/2016 at TB (3rd inn.)
                                                4/22/2007 at BOS (3rd inn.)
                                                8/21/2005 at CWS (4th inn.)
                                                5/2/1992 vs. MIN (5th inn.)
                                                6/17/1977 at BOS (1st inn.)
                                                6/23/1950 at DET (4th inn.)

Most strikeouts
Game, 9 inn. .... 18 (4x) .... 9/29/2017 vs. TOR
                                                5/10/2015 vs. BAL
                                                7/26/2011 vs. SEA
                                                6/17/1978 vs. CAL (all Ron Guidry)
Game, extra inn. ...... 26 **# ..... 5/7/2017 at CHC (18 inn.)

Most walks
Game .... 17 ..... 9/11/1949 G1 vs. WAS (9 inn.)
Inning .... 11 .. 9/11/1949 G1 vs. WAS (3rd inn.)

Most wild pitches
Game .... 5 (2x) .... 4/10/2012 at BAL
                                                6/24/1994 vs. CLE

KEY: ^–ML record (since 1900)   **–tied for ML record   +–AL record   #–tied for AL record

TEAM BATTING

Season

Most at-bats	5717		2007
Most runs	1067^		1931
Fewest runs	459		1908
Run Differential	411^		1939
Most hits	1683		1930
Fewest hits	1136		1903
Highest batting average	.309		1930
Lowest batting average	.214		1968
Most singles	1237		1988
Most doubles	327		2006
Most triples	110		1930
Most home runs	306		2019
Most home runs (home)	144		2018
Most home runs (road)	163		2019
Most home runs (month)	74		Aug. 2019
Most inside-the-park HR	22		1904, 1923
Consecutive games with a HR	31^ (57 total)		2019
Grand slams	10		1987, 2010-12
Pinch hit home runs	10		1961
Total bases	2735		2019
Runs batted in	995^		1936
Most bases on balls	766		1932
Most hit by pitch	81		2003
Fewest hit by pitch	14		1969
Most stolen bases	289		1910
Fewest stolen bases	24		1948
Most caught stealing	82		1920
Fewest caught stealing	18		1961, 1964
Most strikeouts	1437		2019
Fewest strikeouts	420		1924
Highest on-base pct.	.384		1930
Lowest on-base pct.	.282		1908
Highest slugging pct.	.490		2019
Lowest slugging pct.	.287		1914
Most GIDP	153		1996
Fewest GIDP	91		1963
Most left on base	1258		1996
Fewest left on base	1010		1920
Double-digit HR hitters	14		2019
Most .300 hitters	6		1930,'31,'36 (min. 300AB)
Most "walk-off" wins	17		1943

Game or Inning

Most runs
Game, 9 innings, home ... 22 (2x) ... 8/25/2011 vs. OAK
  7/26/1931-G2 vs. CWS
Game, 9 innings, road ... 25 ... 5/24/1936 at PHA
Game, both teams, home ... 31 (2x) ... 8/25/2011 vs. OAK
  6/21/2005 vs. TB
Game, both teams, road ... 33 (3x) ... 6/3/1932 at PHA
  5/22/1930-G2 at PHA
  5/3/1912 at PHA
Shutout win ... 21-0 ... 8/13/1939 at PHA
Two consecutive games ... 40 ... 15 on 5/23/1936-G2 at PHA
  and 25 on 5/24/1936 at CLE
Three consecutive games ... 52 ... 12 in 5/23/1936-G1 at PHA
  15 in 5/23/1936-G2 at PHA
  and 25 on 5/24/1936 at PHA
Consecutive games scoring 10 or more .. 5 ... 6/12-17/1930
Inning (any) ... 14 ... 7/6/1920 at WAS (5th)
First inning ... 12 ... 7/30/2011-G2 vs. BAL
Extra inning ... 11 ... 7/26/1928-G1 vs. DET (12th inn.)
Start of game, no outs ... 8 (2x) ... 9/25/1990 vs. BAL
  4/24/1960 vs. DET
Scored every inn. (all official games) ... 2x ... 4/29/2006 vs. TOR (9 inn.)
  7/26/1939 vs. SLB (9 inn.)

Most walks
Game ... 17 ... 9/11/1949-G1 vs. WAS
Game, vs. one pitcher ... 9 (11x) ... last: Josh Beckett, 8/19/2006 at BOS

Most strikeouts
Game ... 22 ... 5/7/2017 at CHC (18 inn.)
Game, 9 inn. ... 18 ... 4/3/2019 vs. DET

Most Hit by Pitch
Game ... 6 ... 6/20/1913-G2 at WAS

Most hits
Game, 9 innings ... 30 ... 9/28/1923 at BOS
Game, 9 innings, both teams ... 45# ... 9/29/1928 at DET
Consecutive, start of game ... 8** ... 9/25/1990 vs. BAL
Most singles ... 22 ... 8/12/1953 at WAS
Most doubles ... 10 ... 4/12/1988 at TOR
  and 6/5/2003 at CIN
Most triples ... 5 ... 5/1/1934 at WAS
Most extra-base hits, game ... 12 (3x) ... 6/5/2003 at CIN
  5/24/1936 at PHA
  7/17/1920 vs. CWS
Most extra-base hits, inning ... 7 ... 5/3/1951 vs. SLB

Most home runs
Game ... 8 (2x) ... 7/31/2007 vs. CWS
  6/28/1939 at PHA (G1)
Game, both teams ... 11 ... 6/23/1950 at DET
  (NYY-6 HR, DET-5 HR)
Game, off one pitcher ... 6 ... 6/27/1936 at SLB off Tommy Thomas
Inning ... 4 (4x) ... 6/3/2017 at TOR (8th inn.)
  10/1/2012 vs. BOS (2nd inn.)
  6/21/2005 vs. TB (8th inn.)
  6/30/1977 at TOR (8th inn.)
Inning, w/ 2 outs ... 3 (4x) ... 6/3/2017 at TOR (8th inn.)
  6/8/2012 vs. NYM (3rd inn.)
  6/21/2005 vs. TB (8th inn.)
  6/28/1939 at PHA (3rd inn.)
Consecutive ... 3 (14x) ... last 6/3/2017 at TOR (8th inn.)
  (Holliday, Castro, Gregorius)
Start of game ... 2 (11x) .. last 6/25/2019 vs TOR, LEMAHIEU/JUDGE
  5/29/2019 vs. SD, LEMAHIEU/VOIT
  7/7/2018 at TOR, GARDNER/JUDGE
  5/26/2018 vs. LAA, GARDNER/JUDGE
  9/28/2017 vs. TB, GARDNER/JUDGE
  4/16/2012 vs. MIN, Jeter/Granderson
  9/23/2005 vs. TOR, Jeter/Canó
  6/28/2003-G2 at NYM, Soriano/Jeter
  4/6/2003 at TB, Soriano/Johnson
  7/30/1999 at BOS, Knoblauch/Jeter
  4/27/1955 vs. CWS, Bauer/Carey
"Walk-off," season ... 7 ... 2009

Most grand slams
Game ... 3^ ... 8/25/2011 vs. OAK
Inning ... 1 ... (Many times)

Most stolen bases
Game ... 15^ ... 9/28/1911 vs. SLB
Game, both clubs ... 15# .. NY 15, SLB 0, 9/28/1911
Game, steals of home ... 3** ... 4/17/1915 vs. PHA

Most GIDP
Game ... 6 ... 4/15/2011 vs. TEX

Most LOB
Game, 9 innings ... 20^ ... 9/21/1956 at BOS
Game, extra innings ... 23 ... 9/5/1927-G1 at BOS

TEAM FIELDING

Season

Highest fielding pct.	.988		2013
Lowest fielding pct.	.939		1912
Fewest errors (min. 150G)	69		2010, 2013
Most errors	386		1912
Most errorless games	108		2013
Consecutive errorless games	18^		5/14-6/1/2009
Most putouts	4520^		1964
Fewest putouts (min. 150G)	3958		1907
Most assists	2086		1904
Fewest assists (min. 150G)	1344		2018
Most double plays	214		1956
Fewest double plays	81		1912
Consecutive games, DP turned	19 (27 DPs)		1992
Most passed balls	32		1913
Fewest passed balls	0^		1931
Most chances	6584		1916
Fewest chances	5551		1935

Game or Inning

Most errors, game ... 10 ... 6/12/1907 vs. DET
Most errors, inning (since 1969) ... 5 ... 5/9/1969 at OAK
  (5th inn. - Stottlemyre, Clarke, Pepitone, Murcer-2)
Most double plays turned ... 7** ... 8/14/1942 at PHA

KEY: ^–ML record (since 1900) **–tied for ML record
+–AL record #–tied for AL record

INDIVIDUAL BATTING

Season

Batting Average
- LHH .... .394 .... Babe Ruth, 1923
- RHH .... .381 ..... Joe DiMaggio, 1939
- SH .... .365^ .... Mickey Mantle, 1957

Hits
- LHH .... 238 ..... Don Mattingly, 1986
- RHH .... 219 ..... Derek Jeter, 1999
- SH .... 204 ... Bernie Williams, 2002
- Hitting Streak .... 56^ ..... Joe DiMaggio, 1941
- Singles .... 171 ...... Steve Sax, 1989
- Doubles .... 53 ..... Don Mattingly, 1986
- Triples .... 23 ...... Earle Combs, 1927
- Extra-base hits .... 119^ ...... Babe Ruth, 1921

Home Runs
- LHH .... 61^ ...... Roger Maris, 1961
- RHH .... 54 ..... Alex Rodriguez, 2007
- SH .... 54^ .... Mickey Mantle, 1961
- Current Yankee Stad., LHH .... 26 .... C. Granderson, 2012
- Current Yankee Stad., RHH .... 33 .... AARON JUDGE, 2017
- Current Yankee Stad., SH ..... 24 ..... Mark Teixeira, 2009
- Original Yankee Stad., LHH ... 30 ..... Roger Maris, 1961
  Lou Gehrig, 1934
- Original Yankee Stad., RHH ... 26 . Alex Rodriguez, 2005,'07
- Original Yankee Stad., SH .... 27 ... Mickey Mantle, 1956
- Polo Grounds, LHH .... 32 ...... Babe Ruth, 1921
- Polo Grounds, RHH .... 14 ..... Bob Meusel, 1921
- Road, LHH .... 32# ..... Babe Ruth, 1927
- Road, RHH .... 28 .... Alex Rodriguez, 2007
- Road, SH .... 30 .... Mickey Mantle, 1961
- Rookie, LHH .... 21 ..... Kevin Maas, 1990
- Rookie, RHH .... 52^ .... AARON JUDGE, 2017
- Rookie, SH .... 20 ...... Tom Tresh, 1962
- Month .... 17 ... Babe Ruth, Sept. 1927
- In consecutive games .... 8** ... Don Mattingly, 1987
- Grand slams .... 6** ... Don Mattingly, 1987
- Longest (since Statcast est. 2015) ...... 495 ft ... AARON JUDGE, 6/11/17 vs. BAL

RBI
- LHH .... 184+ .... Lou Gehrig, 1931
- RHH .... 167 ..... Joe DiMaggio, 1937
- SH .... 130 .... Mickey Mantle, 1956
- Home .... 98 ...... Lou Gehrig, 1934
- Road .... 117^ ...... Lou Gehrig, 1930
- Rookie .... 125 ..... Joe DiMaggio, 1936
- Current Yankee Stadium .. 71 ..... Mark Teixeira, 2009
- Total in back-to-back games .. 15 ... T. Lazzeri, 5/23G2-24/1936
- Consec. games with RBI ...... 11 (3x). Don Mattingly, 8/5-14/1940 (23RBI)
  Joe DiMaggio, 8/25G1-9/3G2/1939 (28RBI)
  B. Ruth, 6/24-7/2/1931 (18RBI)

Runs
- All games .... 177^ .... Babe Ruth, 1921
- Home .... 94+ .... Babe Ruth, 1921
- Road .... 87^ .... Babe Ruth, 1928
- Rookie .... 132+ ..... Joe DiMaggio, 1936
- Current Yankee Stadium .. 73 ..... AARON JUDGE, 2017
- In consecutive games .... 18** ... Red Rolfe, 8/9-25/1939 (30R)

Strikeouts
- LHH .... 195 ... Curtis Granderson, 2012
- RHH .... 211 .. GIANCARLO STANTON, 2018
- SH .... 151 ...... Jorge Posada, 2000

Walks
- LHH .... 170+ .... Babe Ruth, 1921
- RHH .... 127 ..... AARON JUDGE, 2017
- SH .... 146 .... Mickey Mantle, 1957

Other
- At-bats .... .696 .... Alfonso Soriano, 2002
- Caught stealing .... 23 ..... Ben Chapman, 1931
- Games .... 163 .... Hideki Matsui, 2003
- GIDP (most since 1933)... 30 .... Dave Winfield, 1983
- GIDP (fewest since 1933). 1 ..... AARON HICKS, 2018
- Hit by pitch .... 24 ...... Don Baylor, 1985
- OBP .... .546 .... Babe Ruth, 1923
- OPS .... 1.383 .... Babe Ruth, 1920
- Sacrifice flies .... 17# ...... Roy White, 1971
- Sacrifice hits .... 42 ..... Willie Keeler, 1905
- Slugging pct. .... .847+ .... Babe Ruth, 1920
- Stolen bases .... 93 .... Rickey Henderson, 1988
- Total bases .... 457^ .... Babe Ruth, 1921

Game or Inning

- At-bats .... 11** ... B. Richardson, 6/24/1962 at DET (22 inn.)
- Caught stealing 3 (2x). .... Lee Magee, 6/29/1918 at PHA
  Fritz Maisel, 4/26/1916 vs. BOS
- GIDPs .... 3 (3x). .... Matt Nokes, 5/3/1992 vs. MIN
  Jim Leyritz, 7/4/1990 at KC
  Eddie Robinson, 5/30/1955 at WAS
- Grand slams ..... 2** .... Tony Lazzeri, 5/24/1936 at PHA
- Hits .... 6 (3x)# ..... Johnny Damon (6-for-6), 6/7/2008 vs. KC
  G. Williams (6-for-8), 5/1/1996 at BAL (15 inn.)
  Myril Hoag (6-for-6), 6/6/1934 at BOS
- Singles .... 6** .... Myril Hoag, 6/6/1934 at BOS
- Doubles .... 4 (2x)** .... Jim Mason, 7/8/1974 at TEX
  Johnny Lindell, 8/17/1944 vs. CLE
- Triples ..... 3 (3x)** ..... Joe DiMaggio, 8/27/1938 vs. CLE (G1)
  Earle Combs, 9/22/1927 vs. DET
  Hal Chase, 8/30/1906 vs. WAS
- Hit by pitch .... 3 .... Wally Schang, 5/15/1923 at DET
  Bert Daniels, 6/20/1913 at WAS (G2)
- Home runs ...... 4** . Lou Gehrig (consecutive), 6/3/1932 at PHA
  T. Lazzeri 5/24/1936 at PHA (2GS, solo HR, 2R-triple)
- RBI (game) ..... 11+ .. T. Lazzeri 5/24/1936 at PHA (2GS, solo HR, 2R-triple)
- RBI (Game by Pitcher). 7+ .... Vic Raschi, 8/4/1953 vs. DET
- RBI (inning) ..... 7+ ... A. Rodriguez 10/4/2009 at TB (GS, 3R-HR)
- Reaching safely (9 inn.) . 7+** ..... Ben Chapman, 5/24/1936 at PHA
- Runs .... 5 (18x) ... last by BRETT GARDNER, 7/28/2015 at TEX
- Sac. flies .... 3 (2x)** .... Don Mattingly, 5/3/1986 vs. TEX
  Bob Meusel, 9/15/1926 at CLE
- Stolen bases . 4 (19x) ..... last by Ichiro Suzuki, 9/19/2012 vs. TOR (G2)
- Strikeouts .... 5 (11x) .. last by E. Encarnación, 6/29/2019 at BOS (London)
- Total bases ..... 16 .... Lou Gehrig, 6/3/1932 at PHA
- Walks .... 5 (10x) ..... last by Matt Holliday, 4/9/2017 at BAL

Youngest/Oldest Yankees to Play in a Regular Season Game

Youngest Position Player: Harry Hanson, 17 years-178 days on 7/14/1913 at St. Louis-AL (Did not start. Went 0-for-2 at catcher.)
Youngest Pitcher: Neal Brady, 18 years-205 days on 9/25/1915 vs. Cleveland (Entered in relief, ND, 5.2IP, 3H, 0R, 5BB, 4K)
Oldest Position Player: Deacon McGuire, 43 years-193 days on 5/30/1907 Game 2 at Wash. (Did not start. Went hitless at catcher.)
Oldest Pitcher: Phil Niekro, 46 years-188 days on 10/6/1985 at Toronto (Was his 300th career win. CG, SHO, 9.0IP, 4H, 3BB, 5K)

KEY: ^–ML record (since 1900)   **–tied for ML record   +–AL record   #–tied for AL record

INDIVIDUAL PITCHING

Season

Wins, RHP	41+	Jack Chesbro, 1904
Wins, LHP	26	Lefty Gomez, 1934
Wins, in relief	15	Luis Arroyo, 1961
Consecutive wins, RHP	16#	Roger Clemens, 2001
Consecutive wins, LHP	14	Whitey Ford, 1961
Shutouts won	9	Ron Guidry, 1978
Shutouts lost	7	Bill Zuber, 1945
ERA (low), LHP	1.74	Ron Guidry, 1978
ERA (low), RHP	1.64	Spud Chandler, 1943
ERA (high), LHP	5.00	Randy Johnson, 2006
ERA (high), RHP	5.30	Bump Hadley, 1937
Winning pct.	.893	Ron Guidry, 1978
Losses, RHP	22	Joe Lake, 1908
Losses, LHP	17	Herb Pennock, 1921
Consec. losses, RHP	9 (4x)	Thad Tillotson, 1967
		Johnny Murphy, 1942
		Ray Keating, 1914
		Bill Hogg, 1908
Consecutive losses, LHP	11	George Mogridge, 1916
Innings pitched, RHP	454.0	Jack Chesbro, 1904
Innings pitched, LHP	286.0	Herb Pennock, 1924
Consecutive scoreless IP	39.0	Al Orth, 6/29-7/21/1905
Saves, RHP	53	Mariano Rivera, 2004
Saves, LHP	46	Dave Righetti, 1986
Games, RHP	86	Paul Quantrill, 2004
Games, LHP	80	Boone Logan, 2013
Starts	51^	Jack Chesbro, 1904
Complete games	48^	Jack Chesbro, 1904
Strikeouts, RHP	239	Jack Chesbro, 1904
Strikeouts, LHP	248	Ron Guidry, 1978
Strikeouts, in relief	135	Dellin Betances, 2014
Walks, RHP	177	Bob Turley, 1955
Walks, LHP	179	Tommy Byrne, 1949
Hits allowed	337	Jack Chesbro, 1904
Runs allowed	165	Russ Ford, 1912
Earned runs allowed	127	Sam Jones, 1925
Home runs allowed, RHP	40	Ralph Terry, 1962
Home runs allowed, LHP	34	J.A. HAPP, 2019
Home runs allowed, reliever	16	Nestor Cortes Jr., 2019
Hit-by-pitch	26	Jack Warhop, 1909
Wild pitches	25	A.J. Burnett, 2011

Game or Inning

Runs, game	13 (3x)	Carl Mays, 7/17/1923 at CLE
		Ray Caldwell, 10/3/1913 at PHA
		Jack Warhop, 7/31/1911 vs. CWS
Earned runs, game	13	Carl Mays, 7/17/1923 at CLE
Hits, game	21	Jack Quinn, 6/29/1912 at BOS
HR, game	5 (6x)	CC Sabathia, 8/12/2011 vs. TB

David Wells, 7/4/2003 vs. BOS; Jeff Weaver, 7/21/2002 vs. BOS
Ron Guidry, 9/17/1985 at DET; John Cumberland, 5/24/1970 at CLE
Joe Ostrowski, 6/22/1950 at CLE

HR, inning	4 (5x)	M. TANAKA, 9/21/2016 at TB (3rd)
		Chase Wright, 4/22/2007 at BOS (3rd)
		(for Wright, all consecutive, tying MLB record)
		Randy Johnson, 8/21/2005 at CWS (4th)
		Scott Sanderson, 5/2/1992 vs. MIN (5th)
		Catfish Hunter, 6/17/1977 at BOS (1st)
Strikeouts, game, LH	18	Ron Guidry, 6/17/1978 vs. CAL
Strikeouts, game, RH	16 (2x)	Michael Pineda, 5/10/2015 vs. BAL
		David Cone, 6/23/1997 at DET
Strikeouts, inning	4** (2x)	Phil Hughes 9/20/2012 vs. TOR
		A.J. Burnett, 6/24/2011 vs. COL
Strikeouts, relief	12	Jumbo Brown, 6/3/1933 vs. PHA
Consecutive strikeouts, game	8	Ron Davis, 5/4/1981 at CAL
Consecutive Ks over mult. games	9	Ron Davis, 5/4-9/1981
Walks, game	13	Tommy Byrne, 6/8/1949 at DET
Balks, game	#4	Vic Raschi, 5/3/1950 vs. CWS
Hit by pitch, game	4	Tommy Byrne, 7/5/1950 vs. PHA

Longest Games in Club History
(Innings)

Inn.	Date/Opponent, Result
22	6/24/1962 at Detroit, 9-7 win
20	8/29/1967 (G2) vs. Boston, 4-3 win
19 (4x)	4/10/2015 vs. Boston, 6-5 loss
	8/25/1976 vs. Minnesota, 5-4 win
	8/23/1968 (G2) vs. Detroit, 3-3 tie
	5/24/1918 vs. Cleveland, 3-2 loss
18 (8x)	5/7/2017 at Chicago-NL, 5-4 win
	6/13/2013 at Oakland, 3-2 loss
	9/11/1988 vs. Detroit, 5-4 win
	4/22/1970 at Washington, 2-1 loss
	4/16/1967 vs. Boston, 7-6 win
	8/21/1933 at Chicago, 3-3 tie
	9/5/1927 at Boston, 12-11 loss
	6/25/1903 vs. Chicago, 6-6 tie
17 (11x)	6/1/2003 at Detroit, 10-9 win
	4/19/2001 at Toronto, 6-5 win
	7/20/1998 (G1) vs. Detroit, 4-3 loss
	5/11/1984 vs. Seattle, 4-3 loss
	6/26/1982 vs. Cleveland, 4-3 win
	8/2/1978 vs. Boston, 7-5 loss
	9/11/1974 (G1) at Baltimore, 3-2 loss
	6/21/1964 (G2) at Chicago-AL, 2-1 win
	7/20/1941 at Detroit, 12-6 win
	7/17/1919 at St. Louis, 7-6 win
	7/10/1917 at St. Louis, 7-5 win

MOST RECENT

Inn.	Date/Opponent, Result
at least 14 at home:	4/6/2018 vs. Baltimore (14 inn.), 7-3 loss
at least 12 at home:	4/8/2018 vs. Baltimore (12 inn.), 8-7 loss
more than 13 on road:	4/22/2019 at Los Angeles-AL (14 inn.), 4-3 loss

Hitting for the Cycle

YANKEES TO HIT FOR THE CYCLE (15x by 11 players)

**Melky Cabrera (CF)	8/2/2009	at Chicago-AL
**Tony Fernandez (SS)	9/3/1995	vs. Oakland
Bobby Murcer (CF)	8/29/1972-G1	vs. Texas
**Mickey Mantle (CF)	7/23/1957	vs. Chicago
Joe DiMaggio (CF)	5/20/1948	at Chicago
Joe Gordon (2B)	9/8/1940	at Boston
Buddy Rosar (C)	7/19/1940	vs. Cleveland
Lou Gehrig (1B)	8/1/1937	vs. St. Louis
Joe DiMaggio (CF)	7/9/1937	vs. Washington
Lou Gehrig (1B)	6/25/1934	vs. Chicago
*Tony Lazzeri (2B)	6/3/1932	at Philadelphia
Bob Meusel (RF)	7/26/1928	at Detroit
Bob Meusel (RF)	7/3/1922	at Philadelphia
Bob Meusel (RF)	5/7/1921	at Washington
Bert Daniels (LF)	7/25/1912	vs. Chicago

OPPONENTS TO HIT FOR THE CYCLE AGAINST THE YANKEES (11x by 11 players - incl. once in postseason)

**Jonathan Villar	8/5/2019	at Baltimore
***Brock Holt (2B/1B)	ALDS G3 10/8/2018	vs. Boston
B.J. Upton (CF)	8/2/2009	vs. Tampa Bay
Travis Fryman (3B)	7/28/1993	at Detroit
Jim Fregosi (SS)	7/28/1964	at Los Angeles
Doc Cramer (OF)	6/10/1934	vs. Philadelphia
Mickey Cochrane (C)	8/2/1933	vs. Philadelphia
Goose Goslin (LF)	8/28/1924	vs. Washington
Frank Baker (3B)	7/3/1911	vs. Philadelphia (G2)
**Otis Clymer (RF)	10/2/1908	vs. Washington
Patsy Dougherty (LF)	7/29/1903	at Boston

* Natural Cycle (single, then double, then triple, then HR)
Switch-hitter   * First cycle by any player in postseason history.

KEY: ^–ML record (since 1900)   **–tied for ML record   +–AL record   #–tied for AL record

Award Winners

AL MVP (Chalmers Award 1911-14 / League Award 1922-29 / BBWAA voting since 1931. Won 22 times by 13 players.)

YEAR	PLAYER	AGE	POS	G	AB	R	H	2B	3B	HR	RBI	BA	E
1923	Babe Ruth	28	OF	152	520	151*	205	45	13	41*†	130*	.394	11
1927	Lou Gehrig	23	1B	155*†	584	149	218	52*	18	47	175*	.373	15
1936	Lou Gehrig	32	1B	155†	579	167*	205	37	7	49*	152	.354	9
1939	Joe DiMaggio	24	OF	120	462	108	176	32	6	30	126	.381*	5
1941	Joe DiMaggio	26	OF	139	541	122	193	43	11	30	125*	.357	9
1942	Joe Gordon	27	2B	147	538	88	173	29	4	18	103	.322	28
1947	Joe DiMaggio	32	OF	141	534	97	168	31	10	20	97	.315	1
1950	Phil Rizzuto	32	SS	155	617	125	200	36	7	7	66	.324	14
1951	Yogi Berra	25	C	141	547	92	161	19	4	27	88	.294	13
1954	Yogi Berra	28	C	151	584	88	179	28	6	22	125	.307	8
1955	Yogi Berra	29	C	147	541	84	147	20	3	27	108	.272	13
1956	Mickey Mantle	24	OF	150	533	132*	188	22	5	52*	130*	.353*	4
1957	Mickey Mantle	25	OF	144	474	121*	173	28	6	34	94	.365	7
1960	Roger Maris	25	OF	136	499	98	141	18	7	39	112	.283	4
1961	Roger Maris	26	OF	161	590	132*	159	16	4	61*	141†	.269	9
1962	Mickey Mantle	30	OF	123	377	96	121	15	1	30	89	.321	5
1963	Elston Howard	34	C	135	487	75	140	21	6	28	85	.287	5
1976	Thurman Munson	28	C	152	616	79	186	27	1	17	105	.302	14
1985	Don Mattingly	23	1B	159	652	107	211	48*	3	35	145*	.324	7
2005	Alex Rodriguez	29	3B	162*†	605	124	194	29	1	48	130	.321	12
2007	Alex Rodriguez	31	3B	158	583	143*	183	31	0	54*	156*	.314	13

YEAR	PITCHER	AGE	POS	G	GS	IP	W	L	PCT.	SV	H	R	ER	SO	BB	ERA
1943	Spud Chandler	35	RHP	30	30	253.0	20†	4	.833*	0	197	62	46	134	54	1.64*

AL Cy Young Award (One winner for all of MLB from 1956-66 / Winners for each league since 1967)

YEAR	PITCHER	AGE	POS	G	GS	IP	W	L	PCT.	SV	H	R	ER	SO	BB	ERA
1958	Bob Turley	27	RHP	33	31	245.1	21	7	.750*	1	178	82	81	168	128*	2.97
1961	Whitey Ford	32	LHP	39	39*	283.0*	25*	4	.862*	0	242	108	101	209	92	3.21
1977	Sparky Lyle	32	LHP	72	0	137.0	13	5	.722	26	131	41	33	68	33	2.17
1978	Ron Guidry	27	LHP	35	35	273.2	25*	3	.893*	0	187	61	53	248	72	1.74*
2001	Roger Clemens	38	RHP	33	33	220.1	20	3	.870*	0	205	94	86	213	72	3.51

AL Rookie of the Year (One winner for all of MLB from 1948-49 / Winners for each league since 1950)

YEAR	PLAYER	AGE	POS	G	AB	R	H	2B	3B	HR	RBI	BA	E
1951	Gil McDougald	22	INF	131	402	72	123	23	4	14	63	.306	14
1957	Tony Kubek	21	INF-OF	127	431	56	128	21	3	3	39	.297	20
1962	Tom Tresh	24	INF-OF	157	622	94	178	26	5	20	93	.286	20
1970	Thurman Munson	22	C	132	453	59	137	25	4	6	53	.302	8
1996	Derek Jeter	21	SS	157	582	104	183	25	6	10	78	.314	22
2017	AARON JUDGE	25	OF	155	542	128	154	24	3	52	114	.284	5

YEAR	PITCHER	AGE	POS	G	GS	IP	W	L	PCT.	SV	H	R	ER	SO	BB	ERA
1954	Bob Grim	24	RHP	37	20	199.0	20	6	.769	0	175	78	72	108	85	3.26
1968	Stan Bahnsen	23	RHP	37	34	267.1	17	12	.586	0	216	72	61	162	68	2.05
1981	Dave Righetti	22	LHP	15	15	105.1	8	4	.667	0	75	25	24	89	38	2.05

Other Awards (Postseason awards are listed at the end of the Yankees Postseason Summaries section.)

Please note in brackets: [Number of Yankees award winners, year the award was established, description of award if necessary]

AL Comeback Player of the Year Award [2x, since 2005]: Jason Giambi (2005) and Mariano Rivera (2013)
AL Hank Aaron Award [3x, since 1999, given to the best offensive performer in AL]: Derek Jeter (2006 and '09) and Alex Rodriguez (2007)
AL Manager of the Year Award [3x, since 1983]: Buck Showalter (1994) and Joe Torre (1996 tie with Texas' Johnny Oates and 1998)
AL Outstanding Designated Hitter Award [1x, since 1973]: Don Baylor (1985)
AL Rolaids Relief Man of the Year Award [8x, 1976-2012, awarded on a points system based on saves, "tough saves," relief wins, relief losses & blown saves]: Dave Righetti (1986-87), John Wetteland (1996), Mariano Rivera (1999, 2001, '04-05, & '09 tie with Joe Nathan)
Baseball America Executive of the Year [1x, since 1998]: Brian Cashman (2017)
Baseball America Organization of the Year [1x, since 1982]: Yankees (1998)
MLB Delivery Man of the Year Award [3x, 2005-13, given to MLB's outstanding reliever as voted by fans]: Mariano Rivera (2005-06, '09)
MLBPAA Heart and Hustle Award [1x, since 2005, given to the active MLB player who embodies the values, spirit and traditions of the game]: Brett Gardner (2017). Yearly Yankees nominees have been Derek Jeter (2005-06, '08), Mariano Rivera (2007), Nick Swisher (2009), Brett Gardner (2010, '13-15, '17), Curtis Granderson (2011-12), Didi Gregorius (2016), Austin Romine (2018) and DJ LeMahieu (2019).
Mariano Rivera AL Reliever of the Year Award [2x, since 2014, rebranding of MLB Delivery Man of the Year noted above]: Andrew Miller (2015) and Aroldis Chapman (2019)
MLB Hutch Award [2x, since 1965, given to the player who best exemplifies the fighting spirit and competitive desire of former player and manager Fred Hutchinson by persevering through adversity]: Mickey Mantle (1965) and David Cone (1998)
MLB Roberto Clemente Award [3x, since 1971, given for commitment to community and helping others]: Ron Guidry (1984), Don Baylor (1985) and Derek Jeter (2009)
Wilson Defensive Player of the Year [4x, from 2012-13, best at position in league; and from 2014-present, best at position in all MLB]: Robinson Canó-2B (2012-13), Brett Gardner-LF (2016) and Aaron Judge-RF (2019)

KEY: *Italics* – league leader   *–Major League leader   †–Tied for AL or ML lead

Gold Glove Award (Award since 1957. AL-only since 1958. Won 65 times by 23 players.)

By Year

- 1957: *Bobby Shantz (P)
- 1958: Bobby Shantz (P)
  - Norm Siebern (OF)
- 1959: Bobby Shantz (P)
- 1960: Bobby Shantz (P)
  - Roger Maris (OF)
- 1961: Bobby Richardson (2B)
- 1962: Bobby Richardson (2B)
  - Mickey Mantle (OF)
- 1963: Elston Howard (C)
  - Bobby Richardson (2B)
- 1964: Elston Howard (C)
  - Bobby Richardson (2B)
- 1965: Joe Pepitone (1B)
  - Bobby Richardson (2B)
  - Tom Tresh (OF)
- 1966: Joe Pepitone (1B)
- 1969: Joe Pepitone (1B)
- 1972: Bobby Murcer (OF)
- 1973: Thurman Munson (C)
- 1974: Thurman Munson (C)
- 1975: Thurman Munson (C)
- 1977: Graig Nettles (3B)
- 1978: Chris Chambliss (1B)
  - Graig Nettles (3B)
- 1982: Ron Guidry (P)
  - Dave Winfield (OF)
- 1983: Ron Guidry (P)
  - Dave Winfield (OF)
- 1984: Ron Guidry (P)
  - Dave Winfield (OF)
- 1985: Ron Guidry (P)
  - Don Mattingly (1B)
  - Dave Winfield (OF)
- 1986: Dave Winfield (OF)
  - Ron Guidry (P)
  - Don Mattingly (1B)
- 1987: Don Mattingly (1B)
  - Dave Winfield (OF)
- 1988: Don Mattingly (1B)
- 1989: Don Mattingly (1B)
- 1991: Don Mattingly (1B)
- 1992: Don Mattingly (1B)
- 1993: Don Mattingly (1B)
- 1994: Don Mattingly (1B)
  - Wade Boggs (3B)
- 1995: Wade Boggs (3B)
- 1997: Bernie Williams (OF)
- 1998: Bernie Williams (OF)
- 1999: Scott Brosius (3B)
  - Bernie Williams (OF)
- 2000: Bernie Williams (OF)
- 2001: Mike Mussina (P)
- 2003: Mike Mussina (P)
- 2004: Derek Jeter (SS)
- 2005: Derek Jeter (SS)
- 2006: Derek Jeter (SS)
- 2008: Mike Mussina (P)
- 2009: Mark Teixeira (1B)
  - Derek Jeter (SS)
- 2010: Mark Teixeira (1B)
  - Robinson Canó (2B)
  - Derek Jeter (SS)
- 2012: Mark Teixeira (1B)
  - Robinson Canó (2B)
- 2016: BRETT GARDNER (LF)

*In 1957 only, one award was given at each position encompassing both AL & NL players.

By Position

- P: Bobby Shantz (4: 1957-60)
  - Ron Guidry (5: 1982-86)
  - Mike Mussina (3: 2001; '03, '08)
- C: Elston Howard (2: 1963-64)
  - Thurman Munson (3: 1973-75)
- 1B: Joe Pepitone (3: 1965-66, '69)
  - Chris Chambliss (1: 1978)
  - Don Mattingly (9: 1985-89; '91-94)
  - Mark Teixeira (3: 2009-10, '12)
- 2B: Bobby Richardson (5: 1961-65)
  - Robinson Canó (2: 2010, '12)
- 3B: Graig Nettles (2: 1977-78)
  - Wade Boggs (2: 1994-95)
  - Scott Brosius (1: 1999)
- SS: Derek Jeter (5: 2004-06; '09-10)
- OF: Norm Siebern (1: 1958)
  - Roger Maris (1: 1960)
  - Mickey Mantle (1: 1962)
  - Tom Tresh (1: 1965)
  - Bobby Murcer (1: 1972)
  - Dave Winfield (5: 1982-85, '87)
  - Bernie Williams (4: 1997-2000)
  - BRETT GARDNER (1: 2016)

Silver Slugger Award (Award since 1980. Won 46 times by 22 players.)

By Year

- 1980: Willie Randolph (2B)
  - Reggie Jackson (DH)
- 1981: Dave Winfield (OF)
- 1982: Dave Winfield (OF)
- 1983: Dave Winfield (OF)
  - Don Baylor (DH)
- 1984: Dave Winfield (OF)
- 1985: Don Mattingly (1B)
  - Rickey Henderson (OF)
  - Dave Winfield (OF)
  - Don Baylor (DH)
- 1986: Don Mattingly (1B)
- 1987: Don Mattingly (1B)
- 1993: Mike Stanley (C)
  - Wade Boggs (3B)
- 1994: Wade Boggs (3B)
- 1997: Tino Martinez (1B)
- 2000: Jorge Posada (C)
- 2001: Jorge Posada (C)
- 2002: Jorge Posada (C)
  - Jason Giambi (1B)
  - Alfonso Soriano (2B)
  - Bernie Williams (OF)
- 2003: Jorge Posada (C)
- 2004: Gary Sheffield (OF)
- 2005: Alex Rodriguez (3B)
  - Gary Sheffield (OF)
- 2006: Robinson Canó (2B)
  - Derek Jeter (SS)
- 2007: Jorge Posada (C)
  - Alex Rodriguez (3B)
  - Derek Jeter (SS)
- 2008: Alex Rodriguez (3B)
  - Derek Jeter (SS)
- 2009: Mark Teixeira (1B)
  - Derek Jeter (SS)
- 2010: Robinson Canó (2B)
- 2011: Robinson Canó (2B)
  - Curtis Granderson (OF)
- 2012: Robinson Canó (2B)
  - Derek Jeter (SS)
- 2013: Robinson Canó (2B)
- 2015: Brian McCann (C)
- 2017: GARY SÁNCHEZ (C)
  - AARON JUDGE (OF)
- 2019: DJ LEMAHIEU (2B)

By Position

- C: Mike Stanley (1: 1993)
  - Jorge Posada (5: 2000-03, '07)
  - Brian McCann (1: 2015)
  - GARY SÁNCHEZ (1: 2017)
- 1B: Don Mattingly (3: 1985-87)
  - Tino Martinez (1: 1997)
  - Jason Giambi (1: 2002)
  - Mark Teixeira (1: 2009)
- 2B: Willie Randolph (1: 1980)
  - Alfonso Soriano (1: 2002)
  - Robinson Canó (5: 2006, '10-13)
  - DJ LEMAHIEU (1: 2019)
- 3B: Wade Boggs (2: 1993-94)
  - Alex Rodriguez (3: 2005, '07-08)
- SS: Derek Jeter (5: 2006-09, '12)
- OF: Dave Winfield (5: 1981-85)
  - Rickey Henderson (1: 1985)
  - Bernie Williams (1: 2002)
  - Gary Sheffield (2: 2004-05)
  - Curtis Granderson (1: 2011)
  - AARON JUDGE (1: 2017)
- DH: Don Baylor (2: 1983, '85)

All-MLB Team (Award since 2019)

By Year ("Team")

- 2019: DJ LEMAHIEU-2B (1st)
  - AROLDIS CHAPMAN-RP (2nd)

By "Team"

- 1st: DJ LEMAHIEU-2B (1: 2019)
- 2nd: AROLDIS CHAPMAN-RP (1: 2019)

AL Player of the Month Award (Award since 1974. Included pitchers through 1978.)

By Month – 38 times by 20 players

1974 Apr.: Graig Nettles (3B)	2003 Sept.: Alfonso Soriano (2B)
1974 July: Doc Medich (RHP)	2005 May: Alex Rodriguez (3B)
1977 Aug.: Graig Nettles (3B)	2005 July: Jason Giambi (1B)
1978 June: Ron Guidry (LHP)	2005 Aug.: Alex Rodriguez (3B)
1978 Sept.: Ron Guidry (LHP)	2006 Apr.: Jason Giambi (1B)
1980 July: Reggie Jackson (OF), co-winner w/ George Brett	2006 May: Alex Rodriguez (3B)
	2006 Sept.: Robinson Canó (2B)
1982 Sept.: Dave Winfield (OF)	2007 Apr.: Alex Rodriguez (3B)
1985 June: Rickey Henderson (OF)	2007 June: Alex Rodriguez (3B)
1985 Aug.: Don Mattingly (1B)	2007 July: Hideki Matsui (OF)
1985 Sept.: Don Mattingly (1B)	2010 Apr.: Robinson Canó (2B)
1986 Sept.: Don Mattingly (1B)	2010 Sept.: Alex Rodriguez (3B)
1987 July: Don Mattingly (1B)	2011 Aug.: Curtis Granderson (OF)
1988 Apr.: Dave Winfield (OF)	2016 Aug.: GARY SÁNCHEZ (C)
1997 Aug.: Bernie Williams (OF)	2017 June: AARON JUDGE (OF)
1998 May: Bernie Williams (OF)	2017 Sept.: AARON JUDGE (OF)
1998 Aug.: Derek Jeter (SS)	2018 Apr.: Didi Gregorius (SS)
2000 July: Glenallen Hill (DH)	2019 June: DJ LEMAHIEU (2B)
2002 May: Jason Giambi (1B)	
2003 Apr.: Alfonso Soriano (2B)	
2003 June: Jason Giambi (1B)	

By Position

P:	Ron Guidry (2)
	Doc Medich (1)
C:	GARY SÁNCHEZ (1)
1B:	Jason Giambi (4)
	Don Mattingly (4)
2B:	Robinson Canó (2)
	Alfonso Soriano (2)
	DJ LEMAHIEU (1)
3B:	Alex Rodriguez (6)
	Graig Nettles (2)
SS:	Derek Jeter (1)
	Didi Gregorius (1)
OF:	AARON JUDGE (2)
	Bernie Williams (2)
	Dave Winfield (2)
	Curtis Granderson (1)
	Rickey Henderson (1)
	Reggie Jackson (1)
	Hideki Matsui (1)
DH:	Glenallen Hill (1)

AL Pitcher of the Month Award
(Award since 1979. From 1974-78, pitchers were eligible for the Player of the Month Award)

By Month – 19 times by 14 pitchers*

1979 Apr.: Tommy John (L)	1998 July: David Cone (R)	2007 Aug.: Andy Pettitte (R)
1979 Sept.: Rich Gossage (R)	1999 July: Hideki Irabu (R)	2009 Aug.: CC Sabathia (L)
1981 Aug.: *Ron Guidry (L)	1999 Aug.: Mariano Rivera (R)	2011 July: CC Sabathia (L)
1985 Aug.: Dave Righetti (L)	2000 July: Roger Clemens (R)	2013 Aug.: Ivan Nova (R)
1993 Apr.: Jimmy Key (L)	2001 June: Roger Clemens (R)	2014 May: MASAHIRO TANAKA (R)
1997 Apr.: Andy Pettitte (L)	2002 Sept.: Andy Pettitte (L)	
1998 May: Hideki Irabu (R)	2004 Apr.: Kevin Brown (R)	

*Note: Ron Guidry twice won AL Player of the Month (June & Sept. 1978) before the creation of a separate AL Pitcher of the Month Award.

AL Reliever of the Month Award (Award since 2017)

By Month – 4 times by 2 players

2017 Sept.: AROLDIS CHAPMAN (LHP)	2019 July: TOMMY KAHNLE (RHP)
2019 May: AROLDIS CHAPMAN (LHP)	2019 Aug.: AROLDIS CHAPMAN (LHP)

AL Rookie of the Month Award (Award since 2001)

By Month – 10 times by 6 players

2003 June: Hideki Matsui (OF)	2017 Apr.: AARON JUDGE (OF)	2018 May: GLEYBER TORRES (2B)
2005 Sept.: Robinson Canó (2B)	2017 May: AARON JUDGE (OF)	2018 June: MIGUEL ANDÚJAR (3B)
2016 Aug.: GARY SÁNCHEZ (C)*	2017 June: AARON JUDGE (OF)*	2018 Aug.: MIGUEL ANDÚJAR (3B)
	2017 Sept.: AARON JUDGE (OF)*	

*Note: Sánchez & Judge also won AL Player of the Month, becoming the ninth and 10th players in either league to notch both in the same calendar month.

AL Player of the Week Award (Award since 1974)

By Week Ending Date – 123 times by 62 players (including 42 position players, 7-LHP, 13-RHP)

4/16/1974.........Graig Nettles	8/7/1983..........Dave Winfield	5/6/2001....Mike Mussina-RHP	5/11/2009.......Johnny Damon
4/23/1974.........Graig Nettles	8/14/1983.........Dave Winfield	6/10/2001....Bernie Williams	6/29/2009...Mariano Rivera-RHP
8/27/1974............Roy White	6/3/1984...........Steve Kemp	7/29/2001..........Paul O'Neill	5/30/2010......Robinson Canó
4/27/1975............Roy White	7/29/1984......Don Mattingly	8/5/2001...........Derek Jeter	8/22/2010......Robinson Canó
5/4/1975.....Thurman Munson	6/16/1985......Bob Shirley-LHP	9/2/2001...Mike Mussina-RHP	9/5/2010.........Mark Teixeira
9/7/1975....Catfish Hunter-RHP	6/23/1985....Rickey Henderson	5/19/2002...Roger Clemens-RHP	7/10/2011..........Derek Jeter
9/21/1975.........Bobby Bonds	6/23/1985.....Ron Guidry-LHP	6/23/2002.......Alfonso Soriano	9/25/2011...Mariano Rivera-RHP
6/20/1976......Sparky Lyle-LHP	8/11/1985......Don Mattingly	8/18/2002.....Bernie Williams	7/1/2012........Robinson Canó
7/25/1976.....Thurman Munson	10/6/1985.......Phil Niekro-RHP	4/6/2003........Alfonso Soriano	9/23/2012..........Ichiro Suzuki
10/4/1976.........Graig Nettles	10/5/1986.....Dave Righetti-LHP	6/15/2003..Roger Clemens-RHP	6/9/2013......BRETT GARDNER
5/9/1977...........Roy White	7/13/1987......Don Mattingly	6/29/2003.......Hideki Matsui	8/18/2013......Alfonso Soriano
8/15/1977......Chris Chambliss	7/20/1987......Don Mattingly	8/17/2003...Mike Mussina-RHP	4/13/2014.........Carlos Beltrán
8/22/1977.........Graig Nettles	7/17/1988......Don Mattingly	9/21/2003.......Alfonso Soriano	8/3/2014......BRETT GARDNER
9/18/1977......Reggie Jackson	8/26/1990........Roberto Kelly	5/2/2004..........Ruben Sierra	8/31/2014.......Jacoby Ellsbury
6/18/1978.....Ron Guidry-LHP	6/21/1992..............Mel Hall	5/30/2004........Hideki Matsui	4/26/2015.........Mark Teixeira
8/6/1978....Catfish Hunter-RHP	7/18/1993......Don Mattingly	6/6/2004........Gary Sheffield	5/10/2015...Michael Pineda-RHP
8/27/1978.........Graig Nettles	9/5/1993.........Jim Abbott-LHP	9/12/2004..........Derek Jeter	6/28/2015....BRETT GARDNER
9/3/1978.....Rich Gossage-RHP	8/13/1995....Jack McDowell-RHP	5/2/2005........Alex Rodriguez	8/21/2016......GARY SÁNCHEZ
9/10/1978......Ron Guidry-LHP	5/19/1996....Dwight Gooden-RHP	5/16/2005.......Tino Martinez	8/28/2016......GARY SÁNCHEZ
10/1/1978.....Ed Figueroa-RHP	7/14/1996....John Wetteland-RHP	6/20/2005........Hideki Matsui	6/11/2017........AARON JUDGE
5/13/1979......Reggie Jackson	5/4/1997........Tino Martinez	7/18/2005........Gary Sheffield	9/24/2017........AARON JUDGE
5/20/1979.....Tommy John-LHP	6/29/1997........Tino Martinez	9/19/2005.......Robinson Canó	4/29/2018........Didi Gregorius
9/30/1979........Oscar Gamble	8/31/1997......Bernie Williams	4/17/2006........Jason Giambi	5/27/2018......GLEYBER TORRES
5/4/1980.......Reggie Jackson	9/14/1997........Wade Boggs	8/21/2006........Johnny Damon	9/2/2018......GLEYBER TORRES
5/11/1980.....Tommy John-LHP	4/12/1998...Darryl Strawberry	9/4/2006........Alex Rodriguez	9/30/2018............LUKE VOIT
6/1/1980..........Bobby Brown	5/17/1998....David Wells-LHP	4/9/2007........Alex Rodriguez	4/28/2019............LUKE VOIT
6/15/1980......Reggie Jackson	5/31/1998......Bernie Williams	6/11/2007.......Alex Rodriguez	6/30/2019.........DJ LEMAHIEU
9/9/1980........Oscar Gamble	7/5/1998.......David Cone-RHP	7/23/2007........Robinson Canó	
9/14/1980........Ron Davis-RHP	9/27/1998......Shane Spencer	8/6/2007........Robinson Canó	Note: Most by pos. players–Canó/
10/5/1980......Reggie Jackson	4/11/1999...........Chili Davis	9/10/2007.......Alex Rodriguez	Mattingly-6, R. Jackson/Nettles/A.
5/30/1982........Oscar Gamble	6/27/1999.......Tino Martinez	6/2/2008....Mariano Rivera-RHP	Rodriguez-5; Most by pitchers-
7/10/1983.....Dave Righetti-LHP	7/18/1999........David Cone-RHP	8/4/2008............Xavier Nady	Guidry/Mussina/Rivera-3.

complete your collection at | **YANKEES BOOKSHELF**

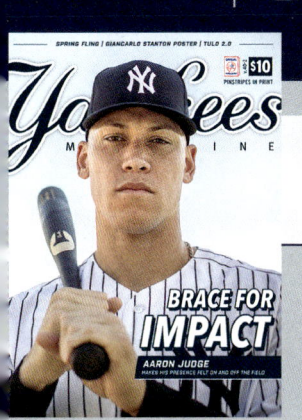

YANKEES MAGAZINE
1-year subscription
Eight issues
$34.⁹⁹
special offer

YEARBOOKS
2020 **$20.⁰⁰** '05–'19 **$15.⁰⁰**

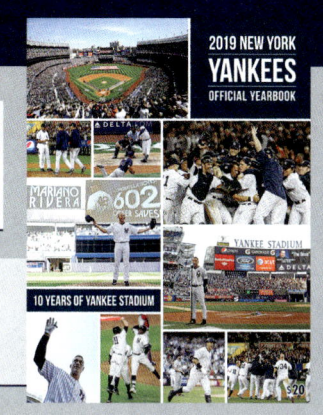

$20.⁰⁰ | **YANKEES MAGAZINE: DEREK JETER COMMEMORATIVE EDITION** (EXPANDED EDITION)

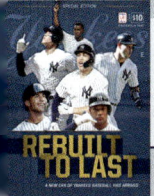

YANKEES MAGAZINE: 2018 SPECIAL EDITION
ALSO AVAILABLE: YANKEES MAGAZINE: MONUMENT PARK EDITION
YANKEES MAGAZINE: HOME RUN EDITION
$10.⁰⁰

$19.⁹⁵ | **2020 MEDIA GUIDE & RECORD BOOK**

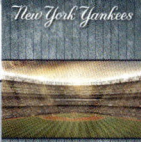

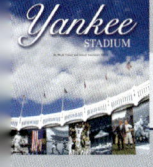

YANKEE STADIUM: THE OFFICIAL RETROSPECTIVE | **$50.⁰⁰**

Call (800) GO-YANKS
or visit www.yankees.com/publications
Follow Yankees Magazine on Twitter @YanksMagazine

AL Batting Leaders

Batting Average

Year	Player	Age	Pos.	Avg.	G	AB	R	H	2B	3B	HR	RBI	E
1924	Babe Ruth	29	OF	.378	153	529	*143**	200	39	7	*46**	124	14
1934	Lou Gehrig	31	1B	*.363*	154*†	579	128	210	40	6	*49**	*166**	7
1939	Joe DiMaggio	24	OF	.381	120	462	108	176	32	6	30	126	5
1940	Joe DiMaggio	25	OF	.352	132	508	93	179	28	9	31	133	8
1945	Snuffy Stirnweiss	26	2B	.309	152	632	107	195	32	22*	10	64	29
1956	Mickey Mantle	24	OF	.353	150	533	*132**	188	22	5	*52**	*130**	4
1984	Don Mattingly	23	1B	.343	153	603	91	207	*44**	2	23	110	6
1994	Paul O'Neill	31	OF	.359	103	368	68	132	25	1	21	83	1
1998	Bernie Williams	29	OF	.339	128	499	101	169	30	5	26	97	3

Home Runs

Year	Player	G	AB	HR
1916	Wally Pipp	151	545	12*†
1917	Wally Pipp	155	587	9
1920	Babe Ruth	142	458	54*
1921	Babe Ruth	152	541	59*
1923	Babe Ruth	152	520	41*†
1924	Babe Ruth	153	529	46*
1925	Bob Meusel	156	624	33
1926	Babe Ruth	152	495	47*
1927	Babe Ruth	151	540	60*
1928	Babe Ruth	154	536	54*
1929	Babe Ruth	135	499	46*
1930	Babe Ruth	145	518	49
1931	Babe Ruth	145	534	46*
	Lou Gehrig	155	619	46*
1934	Lou Gehrig	154	579	49*
1936	Lou Gehrig	155	579	49*
1937	Joe DiMaggio	151	621	46*
1944	Nick Etten	154	573	22
1948	Joe DiMaggio	153	594	39
1955	Mickey Mantle	147	517	37
1956	Mickey Mantle	150	533	52*
1958	Mickey Mantle	150	519	42
1960	Mickey Mantle	153	527	40
1961	Roger Maris (All-time AL record)	161	590	61*
1976	Graig Nettles	158	583	32
1980	Reggie Jackson	143	514	41†
2005	Alex Rodriguez	162	605	48
2007	Alex Rodriguez	158	583	54*
2009	Mark Teixeira	156	609	39†
2017	AARON JUDGE	155	542	52

RBI

Year	Yankee	G	AB	RBI
1920	Babe Ruth	142	458	136*
1921	Babe Ruth	152	541	168*
1923	Babe Ruth	152	520	130†
1925	Bob Meusel	156	624	136
1926	Babe Ruth	152	495	153*
1927	Lou Gehrig	155	584	173*
1928	Lou Gehrig	154	562	147*
1930	Lou Gehrig	154	581	173
1931	Lou Gehrig (All-time AL record)	155	619	184*
1934	Lou Gehrig	154	579	166*
1941	Joe DiMaggio	139	541	125*
1945	Nick Etten	152	565	111
1948	Joe DiMaggio	153	594	155*
1956	Mickey Mantle	150	533	130*
1960	Roger Maris	136	499	112
1961	Roger Maris	161	590	141†
1985	Don Mattingly	159	652	145*
2007	Alex Rodriguez	158	583	156*
2009	Mark Teixeira	156	609	122
2011	Curtis Granderson	156	583	119

200-Hit Seasons

Year	Yankee	AVG	AB	H
1921	Babe Ruth	.377	541	204
1923	Babe Ruth	.394	520	205
1924	Babe Ruth	.378	529	200
1925	Earle Combs	.342	593	203
1927	Earle Combs	.356	648*	231
	Lou Gehrig	.373	584	218
1928	Lou Gehrig	.374	562	210
1929	Earle Combs	.345	586	202
1930	Lou Gehrig	.379	581	220
1931	Lou Gehrig	.341	619	211
1932	Lou Gehrig	.349	596	208
1934	Lou Gehrig	*.363**	579	210
1936	Joe DiMaggio	.323	637	206
	Lou Gehrig	.354	579	205
1937	Joe DiMaggio	.346	621	215
	Lou Gehrig	.351	569	200
1939	Red Rolfe	.329	648	*213**
1944	Snuffy Stirnweiss	.319	643	*205**
1950	Phil Rizzuto	.324	617	200
1962	Bobby Richardson	.302	692	209
1984	Don Mattingly	*.343*	603	207
1985	Don Mattingly	.324	652	211
1986	Don Mattingly	.352	677	238*
1989	Steve Sax	.315	651	205
1998	Derek Jeter	.324	626	203
1999	Derek Jeter	.349	627	*219**
	Bernie Williams	.342	591	202
2000	Derek Jeter	.339	593	201
2002	Alfonso Soriano	.300	696*	*209**
	Bernie Williams	.333	612	204
2005	Derek Jeter	.309	654	202
2006	Derek Jeter	.343	623	214
2007	Derek Jeter	.322	639	206
2009	Derek Jeter	.334	634	212
	Robinson Canó	.320	637	204
2010	Robinson Canó	.319	626	200
2012	Derek Jeter	.316	683*	216*

Don Mattingly led the AL in hits twice, including a single-season franchise record 238 hits in 1984.

KEY: *Italics* indicates AL leader, * indicates Major League leader, † indicates tied for AL or ML lead

Hits

Year	Player	Total
1927	Earl Combs	231
1931	Lou Gehrig	211
1939	Red Rolfe	213*
1944	Snuffy Stirnweiss	205*
1962	Bobby Richardson	209
1984	Don Mattingly	207
1986	Don Mattingly	238
1999	Derek Jeter	219
2002	Alfonso Soriano	209
2012	Derek Jeter	216*

Singles

Year	Player	Total
1904	Willie Keeler	162*
1905	Willie Keeler	151
1906	Willie Keeler	166*
1927	Earle Combs	166
1929	Earle Combs	151
1944	Snuffy Stirnweiss	146*
1950	Phil Rizzuto	150*
1961	Bobby Richardson	148
1962	Bobby Richardson	158
1964	Bobby Richardson	148
1967	Horace Clarke	140
1969	Horace Clarke	147
1975	Thurman Munson	151
1989	Steve Sax	171*
1997	Derek Jeter	.142†
1998	Derek Jeter	151*
2012	Derek Jeter	169*

Doubles

Year	Player	Total
1927	Lou Gehrig	52*
1928	Lou Gehrig	47
1939	Red Rolfe	46
1984	Don Mattingly	44*
1985	Don Mattingly	48*
1986	Don Mattingly	53*

Triples

Year	Player	Total
1924	Wally Pipp	19
1926	Lou Gehrig	20
1927	Earl Combs	23*
1928	Earl Combs	21*
1930	Earl Combs	22
1934	Ben Chapman	13
1936	Joe DiMaggio	15*†
	Red Rolfe	15*†
1943	Johnny Lindell	12†
1944	Johnny Lindell	16†
	Snuffy Stirnweiss	16†
1945	Snuffy Stirnweiss	22*
1947	Tommy Henrich	13
1948	Tommy Henrich	14
1955	Andy Carey	11†
	Mickey Mantle	11†
1957	Hank Bauer	9†
	Gil McDougald	9†
2013	BRETT GARDNER	10

On-Base Pct.

Year	Player	Pct.
1920	Babe Ruth	.532*
1921	Babe Ruth	.512*
1923	Babe Ruth	.545*
1924	Babe Ruth	.513*
1926	Babe Ruth	.516*
1927	Babe Ruth	.486*
1928	Lou Gehrig	.467
1930	Babe Ruth	.493*
1931	Babe Ruth	.495*
1932	Babe Ruth	.489*
1934	Lou Gehrig	.465*
1935	Lou Gehrig	.466
1936	Lou Gehrig	.478*
1937	Lou Gehrig	.473*
1953	Gene Woodling	.429
1955	Mickey Mantle	.431
1962	Mickey Mantle	.486*
1964	Mickey Mantle	.423*
1971	Bobby Murcer	.427*
2005	Jason Giambi	.440

Runs

Year	Player	Total
1920	Babe Ruth	158*
1921	Babe Ruth (Modern Era Record)	177*
1923	Babe Ruth	151*
1924	Babe Ruth	143*
1926	Babe Ruth	139*
1927	Babe Ruth	158*
1928	Babe Ruth	163*
1931	Lou Gehrig	163*
1933	Lou Gehrig	138*
1935	Lou Gehrig	125
1936	Lou Gehrig	167*
1937	Joe DiMaggio	151*
1939	Red Rolfe	139*
1944	Snuffy Stirnweiss	125*
1945	Snuffy Stirnweiss	107
1948	Tommy Henrich	138*
1954	Mickey Mantle	128*
1956	Mickey Mantle	132*
1957	Mickey Mantle	121*
1958	Mickey Mantle	129*
1960	Mickey Mantle	119*
1961	Roger Maris	132*
1972	Bobby Murcer	102
1976	Roy White	104
1985	Rickey Henderson	146*
1986	Rickey Henderson	130*
1998	Derek Jeter	127
2002	Alfonso Soriano	128*
2005	Alex Rodriguez	124
2007	Alex Rodriguez	143*
2010	Mark Teixeira	113
2011	Curtis Granderson	136*
2017	AARON JUDGE	128

Slugging Pct.

Year	Player	Pct.
1920	Babe Ruth (All-time AL record)	.847*
1921	Babe Ruth	.846*
1922	Babe Ruth	.672
1923	Babe Ruth	.764*
1924	Babe Ruth	.739*
1926	Babe Ruth	.737*
1927	Babe Ruth	.772*
1928	Babe Ruth	.709*
1929	Babe Ruth	.697*
1930	Babe Ruth	.732*
1931	Babe Ruth	.700*
1934	Lou Gehrig	.706*
1936	Lou Gehrig	.696*
1937	Lou Gehrig	.673*
1945	Snuffy Stirnweiss	.476
1950	Joe DiMaggio	.585
1955	Mickey Mantle	.611
1956	Mickey Mantle	.705*
1960	Roger Maris	.581
1961	Mickey Mantle	.687*
1962	Mickey Mantle	.605
1986	Don Mattingly	.573*
2005	Alex Rodriguez	.610
2007	Alex Rodriguez	.645*
2008	Alex Rodriguez	.573

Strikeouts

Year	Player	Total
1916	Wally Pipp	82
1920	Aaron Ward	84
1921	Bob Meusel	88*
1923	Babe Ruth	94*
1924	Babe Ruth	81*
1926	Tony Lazzeri	97*
1927	Babe Ruth	89*
1928	Babe Ruth	88
1929	Lou Gehrig	71
1937	Frank Crosetti	107
1938	Frank Crosetti	97
1942	Joe Gordon	95*
1946	Charlie Keller	102
1952	Mickey Mantle	111†
1954	Mickey Mantle	107*
1958	Mickey Mantle	123*
1959	Mickey Mantle	126*
1960	Mickey Mantle	124
2003	Jason Giambi	140
2017	AARON JUDGE	208*

Stolen Bases

Year	Player	Total
1914	Fritz Maisel	74*
1931	Ben Chapman	61*
1932	Ben Chapman	38*
1933	Ben Chapman	27*
1938	Frank Crosetti	27*
1944	Snuffy Stirnweiss	44*
1945	Snuffy Stirnweiss	33*
1985	Rickey Henderson	80
1986	Rickey Henderson	87
1988	Rickey Henderson	93*
2002	Alfonso Soriano	41
2011	BRETT GARDNER	49†

Total Bases

Year	Player	Total
1921	Babe Ruth (All-time MLB record)	457*
1923	Babe Ruth	399*
1924	Babe Ruth	391*
1926	Babe Ruth	365*
1927	Lou Gehrig	447*
1928	Babe Ruth	380*
1930	Lou Gehrig	419
1931	Lou Gehrig	410*
1934	Lou Gehrig	409*
1937	Joe DiMaggio	418*
1941	Joe DiMaggio	348*
1944	Johnny Lindell	297
1945	Snuffy Stirnweiss	301
1948	Joe DiMaggio	355
1956	Mickey Mantle	376*
1958	Mickey Mantle	307
1960	Mickey Mantle	294
1961	Roger Maris	366*
1972	Bobby Murcer	314
1985	Don Mattingly	370*
1986	Don Mattingly	388*
2007	Alex Rodriguez	376
2009	Mark Teixeira	344

Walks

Year	Player	Total
1920	Babe Ruth	150*
1921	Babe Ruth	144*
1922	Whitey Witt	89*
1923	Babe Ruth (All-time AL record)	170*
1924	Babe Ruth	142*
1926	Babe Ruth	144*
1927	Babe Ruth	137*
1928	Babe Ruth	144*
1930	Babe Ruth	136*
1931	Babe Ruth	128*
1932	Babe Ruth	130*
1933	Babe Ruth	115*
1935	Lou Gehrig	133*
1936	Lou Gehrig	130*
1937	Lou Gehrig	127*
1940	Charlie Keller	106
1943	Charlie Keller	106*
1944	Nick Etten	97
1955	Mickey Mantle	113*
1957	Mickey Mantle	146*
1958	Mickey Mantle	129*
1961	Mickey Mantle	126*
1962	Mickey Mantle	122*
1972	Roy White	92†
1980	Willie Randolph	119*
2003	Jason Giambi	129
2005	Jason Giambi	108
2017	AARON JUDGE	127

Lou Gehrig paced the AL in RBI a franchise-record five times, including a league-record 184 RBI in 1931.

KEY: * indicates Major League leader, † indicates tied for AL or ML lead

AL Pitching Leaders

Wins

Year	Player	W
1904	Jack Chesbro (Modern Era Record)	41*
1906	Al Orth	27*†
1921	Carl Mays	27*†
1927	Waite Hoyt	22†
1928	George Pipgras	24†
1934	Lefty Gomez	26
1937	Lefty Gomez	21
1938	Red Ruffing	21
1943	Spud Chandler	20†
1955	Whitey Ford	18†
1958	Bob Turley	21
1961	Whitey Ford	25*
1962	Ralph Terry	23
1963	Whitey Ford	24
1975	Catfish Hunter	23*†
1978	Ron Guidry	25*
1985	Ron Guidry	22
1994	Jimmy Key	17*
1996	Andy Pettitte	21
1998	David Cone	20*†
2006	Chien-Ming Wang	19*†
2009	CC Sabathia	19*†
2010	CC Sabathia	21*†

Losses

Year	Player	L
1907	Al Orth	21†
1908	Joe Lake	22
1912	Russ Ford	21
1925	Sam Jones	21*
1966	Mel Stottlemyre	20
1972	Mel Stottlemyre	18†
1990	Tim Leary	19†

Winning Pct. (min: 15 dec.)

Year	Player	Pct.
1904	Jack Chesbro	.774 (41-12)
1916	Nick Cullop	.684 (13-6)
1921	Carl Mays	.750 (27-9)*
1922	Joe Bush	.788 (26-7)*
1923	Herb Pennock	.760 (19-6)
1932	Johnny Allen	.810 (17-4)*
1933	Russ Van Atta	.750 (12-4)†
1934	Lefty Gomez	.839 (26-5)*
1936	Bump Hadley	.778 (14-4)
1939	Atley Donald	.813 (13-3)*
1941	Lefty Gomez	.750 (15-5)
1942	Tiny Bonham	.808 (21-5)
1943	Spud Chandler	.833 (20-4)*
1947	Spec Shea	.737 (14-5)
1950	Vic Raschi	.724 (21-8)
1953	Eddie Lopat	.800 (16-4)*
1955	Tommy Byrne	.762 (16-5)
1956	Whitey Ford	.760 (19-6)
1957	Tom Sturdivant	.727 (16-6)*†/ALt
1958	Bob Turley	.750 (21-7)*
1960	Jim Coates	.813 (13-3)*
1961	Whitey Ford	.862 (25-4)*
1963	Whitey Ford	.774 (24-7)
1977	Don Gullett	.778 (14-4)
1978	Ron Guidry	.893 (25-3)*
1979	Ron Davis	.875 (14-2)*
1985	Ron Guidry	.786 (22-6)
1994	Jimmy Key	.810 (17-4)*
1998	David Wells	.818 (18-4)
2001	Roger Clemens	.870 (20-3)*
2015	Nathan Eovaldi	.824 (14-3)
2019	DOMINGO GERMÁN	.818 (18-4)*

ERA

Year	Player	ERA
1927	Wilcy Moore	2.28
1934	Lefty Gomez	2.33*
1937	Lefty Gomez	2.33
1943	Spud Chandler	1.64*
1947	Spud Chandler	2.46
1952	Allie Reynolds	2.07*
1953	Ed Lopat	2.43*
1956	Whitey Ford	2.47*
1957	Bobby Shantz	2.45*
1958	Whitey Ford	2.01*
1978	Ron Guidry	1.74*
1979	Ron Guidry	2.78*
1980	Rudy May	2.47*

Games

Year	Player	G
1904	Jack Chesbro	55*
1906	Jack Chesbro	49*
1918	George Mogridge	45*†/ALt
1921	Carl Mays	49*
1948	Joe Page	55
1949	Joe Page	60*
1961	Luis Arroyo	65*†
1977	Sparky Lyle	72
1994	Bob Wickman	53
2004	Paul Quantrill	86
2006	Scott Proctor	83
2012	Boone Logan	80*†

Games Started

Year	Player	GS
1904	Jack Chesbro (Modern Era Record)	51*
1906	Jack Chesbro	42*
1928	George Pipgras	38*
1949	Vic Raschi	37
1951	Vic Raschi	34*
1961	Whitey Ford	39*
1962	Ralphy Terry	39
1963	Whitey Ford / Ralph Terry	37†
1964	Jim Bouton	37
1994	Jimmy Key	25*
1997	Andy Pettitte	35†
2007	Andy Pettitte	34†
2008	Mike Mussina	34*†/ALt
2010	CC Sabathia	34*†/ALt

Complete Games

Year	Player	CG
1904	Jack Chesbro (Modern Era Record)	48*
1906	Al Orth	36
1934	Lefty Gomez	25*†
1942	Tiny Bonham	22†
1943	Spud Chandler	20†
1955	Whitey Ford	18
1958	Bob Turley	19†
1963	Ralph Terry	18†
1965	Mel Stottlemyre	18
1969	Mel Stottlemyre	24
1975	Catfish Hunter	30
1983	Ron Guidry	21*
1995	Jack McDowell	8

Shutouts

Year	Player	SHO
1920	Carl Mays	6
1928	Herb Pennock	5
1930	George Pipgras	3†
1934	Lefty Gomez	6†
1937	Lefty Gomez	6*
1938	Lefty Gomez	4
1939	Red Ruffing	5
1942	Tiny Bonham	6
1943	Spud Chandler	5†
1951	Allie Reynolds	7*†
1952	Allie Reynolds	6*†/ALt
1958	Whitey Ford	7*†
1960	Whitey Ford	4†
1978	Ron Guidry	9*
1980	Tommy John	6*†
1998	David Wells	5*†
2018	LUIS SEVERINO	1*†/ALt

Innings Pitched

Year	Player	IP
1904	Jack Chesbro	455.0*
1906	Al Orth	339.0
1921	Carl Mays	336.0
1925	Herb Pennock	276.0
1928	George Pipgras	302.0
1934	Lefty Gomez	282.0
1961	Whitey Ford	283.0*
1962	Ralph Terry	299.0
1963	Whitey Ford	269.0
1965	Mel Stottlemyre	291.0
1975	Catfish Hunter	328.0*

David Cone, pictured here on Opening Day 2000, went 20-7 in 1998, tying for the Major League lead in wins.

KEY: * indicates Major League leader, † indicates tied for AL or ML lead

Hits

1906	Al Orth	317
1928	George Pipgras	314
1968	Mel Stottlemyre	243

Walks

1918	Slim Love	116
1924	Joe Bush	109*
1928	Hank Johnson	104
1949	Tommy Byrne	179*
1950	Tommy Byrne	160*
1955	Bob Turley	177
1958	Bob Turley	128*
1964	Al Downing	120
1982	Dave Righetti	108
1985	Phil Niekro	120*
2009	A.J. Burnett	97

Strikeouts

1932	Red Ruffing	190
1933	Lefty Gomez	163
1934	Lefty Gomez	158
1937	Lefty Gomez	194*
1951	Vic Raschi	164*t
1952	Allie Reynolds	160
1964	Al Downing	217

Runs

1908	Joe Lake	157*
1912	Russ Ford	165*
1976	Catfish Hunter	117*t/ALt
1989	Andy Hawkins	111*

Earned Runs

1976	Catfish Hunter	117*
1989	Andy Hawkins	111*t/ALt
2013	CC Sabathia	112*

Home Runs

1904	Jack Powell	15*
1912	Russ Ford	11*t/ALt
1913	Russ Ford	9t
1914	Jack Warhop	8
1915	Ray Fisher / Jack Warhop	7
1916	Allen Russell	8
1917	Ray Caldwell	8
1923	Bob Shawkey	17*t/ALt
1926	Urban Shocker	16
1940	Red Ruffing	24*t/ALt
1947	Allie Reynolds	23*t/ALt
1962	Ralph Terry	40*
1976	Catfish Hunter	28*t/ALt

Saves

1972	Sparky Lyle	35
1976	Sparky Lyle	23
1978	Goose Gossage	27
1980	Goose Gossage	33*t/ALt
1986	Dave Righetti	46*
1996	John Wettleland	43
1999	Mariano Rivera	45*
2001	Mariano Rivera	50*
2004	Mariano Rivera	53*

Red Ruffing won 231 games as a Yankee, including an AL-best 21 victories in 1938 and a league-leading five shutouts in 1939.

Yankees 20-Game Winners

Year	Pitcher	Record
1903	Jack Chesbro	21-15
1904	Jack Chesbro	41-12
	Jack Powell	23-19
1906	Al Orth	27-17
	Jack Chesbro	24-16
1910	Russ Ford	26-6
1911	Russ Ford	22-11
1916	Bob Shawkey	24-14
1919	Bob Shawkey	20-11
1920	Carl Mays	26-11
	Bob Shawkey	20-13
1921	Carl Mays	27-9
1922	Joe Bush	26-7
	Bob Shawkey	20-12
1923	Sad Sam Jones	21-8
1924	Herb Pennock	21-9
1926	Herb Pennock	23-11
1927	Waite Hoyt	22-7
1928	George Pipgras	24-13
	Waite Hoyt	23-7
1931	Lefty Gomez	21-9
1932	Lefty Gomez	24-7
1934	Lefty Gomez	26-5
1936	Red Ruffing	20-12
1937	Lefty Gomez	21-11
	Red Ruffing	20-7
1938	Red Ruffing	21-7
1939	Red Ruffing	21-7
1942	Ernie Bonham	21-5
1943	Spud Chandler	20-4
1946	Spud Chandler	20-8
1949	Vic Raschi	21-10
1950	Vic Raschi	21-8
1951	Eddie Lopat	21-9
	Vic Raschi	21-10
1952	Allie Reynolds	20-8
1954	Bob Grim	20-6
1958	Bob Turley	21-7
1961	Whitey Ford	25-4
1962	Ralph Terry	23-12
1963	Whitey Ford	24-7
	Jim Bouton	21-7
1965	Mel Stottlemyre	20-9
1968	Mel Stottlemyre	21-12
1969	Mel Stottlemyre	20-14
1970	Fritz Peterson	20-11
1975	Catfish Hunter	23-14
1978	Ron Guidry	25-3
	Ed Figueroa	20-9
1979	Tommy John	21-9
1980	Tommy John	22-9
1983	Ron Guidry	21-9
1985	Ron Guidry	22-6
1996	Andy Pettitte	21-8
1998	David Cone	20-7
2001	Roger Clemens	20-3
2003	Andy Pettitte	21-8
2008	Mike Mussina	20-9
2010	CC Sabathia	21-7

Hall of Famer Waite Hoyt was a 20-game winner in each of the Yankees' back-to-back championship seasons of 1927 and 1928.

KEY: * indicates Major League leader, † indicates tied for AL or ML lead

Home Run Feats by Yankees (Regular Season Only)

Four HRs, One Game
(1 time by 1 player)
Lou Gehrig . . . . 6/3/32 at PHA

Three-or-more HRs, One Game
(31x by 22 players in reg. season. 3HR hit 30x and 4HR hit once, all noted below)*
GARY SÁNCHEZ . . . . 4/7/2019 at BAL
AARON HICKS. . . . . .7/1/2018 vs. BOS
Alex Rodriguez (3rd) . . . 7/25/2015 at MIN
Curtis Granderson . . . 4/19/2012 vs. MIN
Mark Teixeira . . . . 5/8/2010 at BOS
Alex Rodriguez (2nd) . . . . 8/14/2010 at KC
Alex Rodriguez (1st) . . . 4/26/2005 vs. LAA
Tony Clark . . . . 8/28/2004 at TOR
Tino Martinez . . . . 4/2/1997 at SEA
Darryl Strawberry . . . . 8/6/1996 vs. CWS
Paul O'Neill . . . . 8/31/1995 vs. CAL
Mike Stanley . . . . .8/10/1995 vs. CLE
Cliff Johnson . . . . 6/30/1977 at TOR
Bobby Murcer (2nd) . . . . .7/13/1973 vs. KC
Bobby Murcer (1st) . . . 6/24/1970 vs. CLE
Tom Tresh. . . . . 6/6/1965 vs. CWS
Mickey Mantle . . . . 5/13/1955 vs. DET
Johnny Mize . . . . 9/15/1950 at DET
Joe DiMaggio (3rd) . . .9/10/1950 at WAS
Joe DiMaggio (2nd) . . . 5/23/1948 at CLE
Charlie Keller . . . . 7/28/1940 at CWS
Bill Dickey . . . . 7/26/1939 vs. STL
Joe DiMaggio (1st). . . . . .6/13/1937 at STL
Tony Lazzeri (2nd). . . . . 5/24/1936 at PHA
Ben Chapman. . . . . . . .7/9/1932 vs. DET (G2)
Lou Gehrig (4th) . . . . . **(4HR)** 6/3/1932 at PHA
Lou Gehrig (3rd) . . . . . . 5/22/1930 at PHA
Babe Ruth* . . . . 5/21/1930 at PHA
Lou Gehrig (2nd) . . . . . . 5/4/1929 at CWS
Lou Gehrig (1st) . . . . 6/23/1927 at BOS
Tony Lazzeri (1st) . . . . . 6/8/1927 vs. CWS

*Also accomplished three times in World Series play by Babe Ruth twice, (6/26 G4 at STL and 10/9/28 G4 at STL; and by Reggie Jackson, 10/18/77 G6 vs. LAD)

Multi-HR Games - Top 20 (Reg. Season Only)
1. Ruth 68   12. B. Williams . . . 18
2. Mantle 46   13. Posada 17
3. Gehrig 43   14. T. Martinez . . . 15
4. DiMaggio 35   Dickey 15
5. Rodriguez . . . 29   16. Murcer 14
6. Giambi 22   17. Canó 13
7. Teixeira 21   Mattingly . . . 13
8. Winfield, Nettles,   Henrich. 13
   Maris, Berra . . . 19   Gordon 13

Consecutive Games with at least 1HR
Don Mattingly 8G (7/8-18/87, 10HR)
*Tied with Dale Long (PIT 5/19-28/56, 8HR) and Ken Griffey Jr. (SEA 7/20-28/93, 8HR) for the all-time MLB record.

HR, First MLB Plate App. and AB (5x)
*also first MLB game
#AARON JUDGE*. . . . . . .8/13/2016 vs. TB
#Tyler Austin*. . . . . .8/13/2016 vs. TB
Andy Phillips. . . . . .9/26/2004 at BOS
Marcus Thames* . . . . . 6/10/2002 vs. ARI
John Miller*. . . . . .9/11/1966 at BOS
#Hit in consecutive PAs in the second inn. (Austin, then Judge). It marked the first time in MLB history that teammates each homered in their MLB debuts in the same game (not just their first PAs or consecutive PAs). There had been just one other game in MLB history in which two players each hit HRs in their first career ABs, on 4/19/38 - BRO at PHI, the Phillies' Emmett "Heinie" Mueller and the Dodgers' Ernie Koy – both in the first inn.).

HR, First Two PAs or ABs w/ Yankees (1x)
Cody Ransom. . . . . 8/17/2008 vs. KC
  and 8/22/2008 at BAL

HR in First Two Major League Games (2x)
AARON JUDGE. 8/13-14/2016
Joe Lefebvre 5/22-23/1980

Two HR, One Inning (5x)
Alex Rodriguez. . . . 10/4/2009 at TB (6th)
Alex Rodriguez. . . 9/5/2007 vs. SEA (7th)
Cliff Johnson. . . . . . 6/30/1977 at TOR (8th)
Joe Pepitone . . . . .5/23/1962 vs. KCA (8th)
Joe DiMaggio . . . . . 6/24/1936 vs. CWS (5th)

HR in Four Consecutive ABs (4x)
Bobby Murcer*. . . . 6/24/1970 vs. CLE (DH)
Mickey Mantle 7/4-7/6/1962
John Blanchard 7/21-7/26/1961
Lou Gehrig. . . . . .6/3/1932 at PHA
* All but Murcer were consecutive PAs

Pinch-Hit HR in Consecutive ABs (4x)
Ray Barker 1965
John Blanchard 1961
Charlie Keller 1948
Ray Caldwell 1915

Most "Walk-off" HR, Career
1. Mickey Mantle 12
2. Babe Ruth. 11
3. Yogi Berra .7
T4. Graig Nettles, A. Rodriguez 6
T6. Joe DiMaggio, Reggie Jackson 4
T8. Gehrig, Dickey, Gordon, Keller, Henrich,
    J. Collins, Tresh, Gamble, Chambliss, Baylor,
    Hall, B. Williams, Giambi, GARDNER 3

HR Both Sides of Plate, Single Game (57x)
1. Mickey Mantle 10x
2. Mark Teixeira. 9x
T3. Posada, B.Williams* 8x
5. Nick Swisher, Roy White 5x
7. Tom Tresh 3x
8. AARON HICKS. 2x
T9. Beltran, Cabrera, T. Clark, Sierra, Smalley, Walker. . . . 1x
*Also twice in postseason play - on 10/6/95 at SEA; and 10/5/96 at TEX.

HR Both Sides of Plate, in a Season
Nick Swisher (2009), Mark Teixeira (2009), . . . 3*
*Tied for all-time AL record with T. Clark (DET 1998), Swisher (OAK 2007) and J. Ramirez (CLE 2017).

HR Both Sides of Plate, Teammates in Season
In 2009, three Yankees homered from both sides of the plate (M. Cabrera-1x, Swisher-3x; Teixeira-3x), marking the only MLB team all time with three such players in a single season.

HR Both Sides of Plate, One Game
Bernie Williams & Jorge Posada each hit HRs from both sides of the plate in a 10-7 win on 4/23/2000 at Toronto, marking the first time in MLB history that teammates accomplished the feat in the same game. (Since matched by Arizona's Felipe Lopez/Tony Clark on 4/6/09 vs. Colorado).

Most Back-to-Back HR by Yankees Teammates in a Single Season
1. Johnny Damon/Mark Teixeira 6 (2009)
T2. Gary Sheffield/Alex Rodriguez . . 5 (2005)
    Joe DiMaggio/Lou Gehrig 5 (1941)
    Babe Ruth/Lou Gehrig 5 (1927)

Back-to-Back HR to Start Game (11x)
LEMAHIEU/JUDGE . . . . 6/25/2019 vs. TOR
LEMAHIEU/VOIT. . . . . 5/29/2019 vs. SD
GARDNER/JUDGE (3x). . . . . . . .7/7/2018 at TOR,
             5/26/2018 vs. LAA & 9/28/2017 vs. TB
Jeter/Granderson . . . . 4/16/2012 vs. MIN
Jeter/Canó. . . . . 9/23/2005 vs. TOR
Soriano/Jeter . . . 6/28/2003-G2 at NYM
Soriano/N. Johnson . . . . .4/6/2003 at TB
Knoblauch/Jeter . . . . . .7/30/1999 at BOS
Bauer/Carey . . . . 4/27/1955 at CWS

"Walk-off" HR followed by leadoff HR in next team game
BRETT GARDNER. . . . . . . .7/27-28/2017 vs. TB
Roberto Kelly . . . . .8/5-6/1990 vs. CLE
Joe Gordon . . . . 8/11/1940 vs. PHA,
                  8/13/1940 vs. BOS

Most Yankees With At Least 25HR in the Same Season
5 . .2019 (Gardner, Judge, LeMahieu, Sánchez, Torres)
5 . . . 2018 (Andújar, Gregorius, Hicks, Judge, Stanton)
5 . . . 2009 (Canó, Matsui, Rodriguez, Swisher, Teixeira)
4 . . . . .2010 (Canó, Rodriguez, Swisher, Teixeira)
4 . . . . .1938 (Dickey, DiMaggio, Gehrig, Gordon)

Extra Innings HR, Team in One Season
8 . . . . .1941, '62, 88
7 1957
6 . . . . 1955, '60, '80, '83, 2006, '18
5 . . . . 1922, '59, '61, '84, '97, 2009

Extra Innings HR, Player in Career
Mickey Mantle, Babe Ruth 14
Yogi Berra. 9
Graig Nettles. 8
Tommy Henrich 7
Jason Giambi 6
Gordon, Posada, Rodriguez, Winfield 5

Extra Innings HR, Player in Season
Gehrig (1935), Mantle (1959) 3
Many Players. 2

Most Leadoff HR
Career
1. Derek Jeter 29
2. Rickey Henderson. 24
3. Alfonso Soriano 21
4. Hank Bauer 18
5. BRETT GARDNER. 15
   Chuck Knoblauch 15
Season
1. Alfonso Soriano. 13 (2003)
2. Rickey Henderson. 9 (1986)
3. Chuck Knoblauch 8 (1999)
   Alfonso Soriano. 8 (2002)
5. Rickey Henderson. 7 (1985)

Most Inside-the-Park HR
Career   Earle Combs 23
Season   Patsy Dougherty (1904) 6

Youngest to hit HR
Bobby Murcer. . . . . . . .9/14/1965 at WSH (19y, 117d)

Oldest to hit HR
Enos Slaughter . . . . . 7/19/1959-G1 vs. CWS (43y, 83d)

Yankees to Win MLB's All-Star Week Home Run Derby (4x)
AARON JUDGE (2017), Robinson Cáno (2011), Jason Giambi (2002) and Tino Martinez (1997)

LAST TIME IT HAPPENED

Pitcher to Homer
Lindy McDaniel . . . . .9/28/1972 at DET

Multi-HR Game, MultipleYankees, in Same Game
GARDNER-2; Gregorius-2 . . . .9/10/2019 at TOR

HR in First At-Bat as a Yankee
GIANCARLO STANTON . . . 3/29/2018 at TOR

HR in First Plate App. as a Yankee
GIANCARLO STANTON . . . 3/29/2018 at TOR

Multi-HR Game, First game as a Yankee
G. STANTON (2HR) . . . . . . 3/29/2018 at TOR

Inside-the-Park HR
Road: AARON HICKS. . . . .5/19/2018 at KC
Home: Derek Jeter. . . . . . 7/22/2010 vs. KC

Cody Ransom is the only player in franchise history to hit a HR in each of his first two plate appearances as a Yankee.

Grand Slams

Recent grand slam notes: Yankees batters hit seven grand slams in 2019 (two by Gregorius and Torres and one each by Encarnación, Gardner and Sánchez) after hitting eight in 2018, four in 2017, four in 2016, seven in 2015, two in 2014, four in 2013 and exactly 10 grand slams in each year from 2010-12…the 10GS in each year of that stretch (2010-12) tied the all-time single-season franchise high (also 1987)…the Yankees' total of 66GS over the last ten seasons (2010-19) leads the Majors and is 17 more than the next-closest team (Boston-49)…**Yankees pitchers** allowed 6GS in 2019, 7GS in 2018 and 5GS in 2017 after allowing just 1GS in each of the previous three seasons (2014-16).

Career Leaders
1. Gehrig 23
2. Rodriguez* 15
3. DiMaggio 13
4. Ruth 12
5. B. Williams 11
6. Posada 10
T7. Berra, Canó, Mantle 9
T10. Dickey, Lazzeri, Teixeira 8
T13. Keller, T. Martinez 7
T15. Giambi, Mattingly, Stanley .. 6
*Rodriguez is MLB's all-time career leader with 25 grand slams.

Single-Season Leaders
*Don Mattingly 6 1987
Tommy Henrich 4 1948
Lou Gehrig 4 1934
Nick Swisher 3 2012
Robinson Canó 3 2011
Alex Rodriguez .... 3 ... 2007, '10
Ruben Sierra 3 2004
Jorge Posada 3 2001
^Shane Spencer 3 1998
Mike Stanley 3 1993
Joe DiMaggio 3 1937
Lou Gehrig 3 1931
Babe Ruth 3 1931
*Tied with Travis Hafner (CLE 2006) for the all-time MLB single-season record.
^Most in single season by a NYY rookie

Most by Club, Season
10 .... 1987, 2010-12
9 .... 1998, 2003, '04
8 2018
7 .... 1940, '48, '80, '99, 2005, '08, '15, '19
6 ... 1927, '29, '30-32, '35, '37, '62, 2000-02
5 ...... 1934, '36, '41, '42, '56, '65-66, '78, '82, '93-94

Most Allowed by Club, Season
9 2000
8 1995
7 .... 2007, '08, '18
6 ..... 1935, '59, '84, '90, '91, '98, 2013, '19

Three Grand Slams in Same Game (only time in MLB history)
Canó/Martin/Granderson …8/25/2011 vs. OAK

Multiple Grand Slams in Same Game (4x)
Canó/Martin/Granderson …8/25/2011 vs. OAK
B. Williams/O'Neill .... 9/14/1999 at TOR
Winfield/Mattingly .... 6/29/1987 at TOR
*Tony Lazzeri (2nd & 5th inn.)... 5/24/1936 at PHA
*Was the first MLB player to hit 2GS in the same game and remains the only Yankee to accomplish the feat.

Grand Slams in Consecutive Games (4x)
Jorge Posada .... 6/12-13/2010 vs. HOU
Bill Dickey ...... 8/3(G2)-4/1937 vs. CWS
Babe Ruth ... 8/6/1929 (G2) vs. WAS and 8/7/1929 (G1) at PHA
Babe Ruth ...... 9/27/1927 vs. WAS and 9/29/1927 vs. PHA

"Walk-off" Grand Slams (9x)
Mark Teixeira....... 9/28/2016 vs. BOS (9th)
Alex Rodriguez ..... 4/7/2007 vs. BAL (9th)
*Jason Giambi ... 5/17/2002 vs. MIN (14th)
Mike Pagliarulo ..... 5/8/1987 vs. MIN (9th)
Ruppert Jones ...8/12/1980 vs. CWS (10th)
Joe Pepitone..... 4/17/1969 (G1) vs. WAS (10th)
Charlie Keller....... 8/12/1942 vs. BOS (9th)
Red Ruffing ..... 4/14/1933 vs. BOS (9th)
*Babe Ruth ...... 9/24/1925 vs. CWS (10th)
*Hit when trailing by three runs.

Pinch-Hit Grand Slams (22x)
Murcer, Skowron, Strawberry* 2
18 others 1
*Strawberry is the only Yankee with two PH-GS in one season (1998).

Pitchers to Hit Grand Slam (4x)
Mel Stottlemyre...... 7/20/1965 vs. BOS
Don Larsen .... 4/22/1956 vs. BOS
Spud Chandler....... 7/26/1940 at CWS
Red Ruffing .... 4/14/1933 at PHA

Grand Slam Hit on Birthday (1x)
*Hideki Matsui .... 6/12/2008 at OAK
*Accounted for all four runs in a 4-1 win.

On June 12, 2008 at Oakland, Hideki Matsui became the only Yankee in franchise history to hit a grand slam on his birthday.

LAST TIME IT HAPPENED

Pinch-Hit Grand Slam
Stephen Drew .... 4/13/2015 at BAL

Inside-the-Park Grand Slam
Mel Stottlemyre ...... 7/20/1965 vs. BOS

Extra-inning Grand Slam
Bobby Abreu ... 9/24/2008 at TOR (10th)

First HR as a Yankee is Grand Slam
Road: Richie Sexson..... 8/5/2008 at TEX
Home: Hideki Matsui ... 4/8/2003 vs. MIN

Pinch-Hit Home Runs

2019 Notes: The Yankees hit four pinch-hit HR in 2019 after hitting just one during the 2018 season.

Other Pinch-hit HR Notes: The Yankees have hit 282 pinch-hit home runs in franchise history, including 22 pinch-hit grand slams…in 1998, the Yankees hit two pinch-hit home runs, both ninth-inning grand slams by Darryl Strawberry (on 5/2 at KC and 8/4-G2 at OAK).

Last Yankee with more than one pinch-hit HR in a single season: Mike Ford in 2019 (2HR - 9/14 at TOR and 9/1 vs. OAK).

NYY Career Leaders
1. Yogi Berra 9
2. Bob Cerv 8
T3. Mickey Mantle, Bobby Murcer 7
5. Johnny Blanchard 6
T6. Mize, Posada, Skowron 5

Most by Club in a Single Season
1961 10
1953, '54, '60, '86 7
1959, '66, '79, '80, '87, '90, 2012 ... 6
1955, '56, '62, '70, '85, 88, 94, 2004 .. 5

Most by Player in a Single Season
Johnny Blanchard 4 1961
Ken Phelps 3 1989
Dan Pasqua 3 1987
Bobby Murcer 3 1981
Ray Barker 3 1965
Bob Cerv 3 1961
Johnny Mize 3 1953
Tommy Henrich 3 1950

Johnny Blanchard [L] is the Yankees' single-season leader in pinch-hit home runs, hitting four in 1961. Yogi Berra [R] holds the Yankees' career mark with nine.

Yankees AL Triple Crown Winners

Batters

YEAR	PLAYER	AGE	POS	G	AB	R	H	2B	3B	HR	RBI	BA
1934	Lou Gehrig	30	1B	154*†	579	128	210	40	6	49*	165*	.363*
1956	Mickey Mantle	24	OF	150	533	132*	188	22	5	52*	130*	.353*

Pitchers

YEAR	PITCHER	AGE	POS	W	L	PCT.	ERA	G	GS	CG	SHO	SV	IP	H	R	ER	HR	BB	SO
1934	Lefty Gomez	25	LHP	26	5	*.839	2.33	38	33	*25	6	-	281.2	223	86	73	12	96	158
1937	Lefty Gomez	28	LHP	21	11	.656	*2.33	34	34	25	6	-	278.1	233	88	72	10	93	*194

KEY: *Italics – league leader*   *–Major League leader   †–Tied for AL or ML lead

30HR/30SB Seasons in Franchise History

Year	Player	AVG	G	AB	R	H	2B	3B	HR	RBI	SH	SF	HP	BB	SO	SB	CS	E	OBP	SLG
1975	Bobby Bonds	.270	145	529	93	143	26	3	32	85	0	5	3	89	137	30	17	4	.375	.512
2002	Alfonso Soriano	.300	156	*696	*128	*209	51	2	39	102	1	7	14	23	157	41	13	23	.332	.547
2003	Alfonso Soriano	.290	156	*682	114	198	36	5	38	91	0	2	12	38	130	35	8	19	.338	.525

KEY: *Italics – league leader*   *–Major League leader   †–Tied for AL or ML lead

First Home Runs in Franchise History
Courtesy of the Elias Sports Bureau

The first home run in franchise history was hit by John Ganzel on May 11, 1903. It was a fifth-inning, inside-the-park, solo homer at the Detroit Tigers' Bennett Park off George Mullin in an 8-2 Highlanders victory.

The first home run hit at home in franchise history was by Ernie Courtney on June 1, 1903, at Hilltop Park off Boston's Tom Hughes. The two-run, one-out homer in the bottom of the ninth accounted for the Highlanders' only runs in an 8-2 loss.

1921 American League Champion Yankees
The first pennant-winning team in franchise history

The Yankees won their first American League pennant in 1921, finishing 98-55, 4.5 games ahead of Cleveland. The club was led by Babe Ruth, who batted .378 (204-for-540) with 59HR and a career-high 171RBI. Carl Mays (27-5), Waite Hoyt (19-13) and Bob Shawkey (18-12) fronted a pitching staff that allowed the fewest earned runs in the American League (579). In the World Series, the last of Baseball's three-year experiment with a nine-game format, the Yankees were defeated 5-games-to-3 by the Giants, with whom they shared the Polo Grounds. Hoyt, who lost Game 8, 1-0, on an unearned run in the first inning, went 2-1 (27.0IP) in three complete games. Injuries suffered by Ruth in Game 2 (cut arm while sliding, which later became infected) and Game 5 (wrenched knee) limited him to just one pinch-hitting plate appearance in the final three games of the Series.

Top Row: Jack Quinn, Tom Rodgers, Alex Ferguson, Elmer Miller, Mike McNally, Harry "Rip" Collins, Bill Piercy, Frank "Home Run" Baker, Harry Harper, Al DeVormer, Fred Hofmann, Bob Meusel, Bob "Braggo" Roth, Roger Peckinpaugh. **Middle Row:** Aaron Ward, Bill "Chick" Fewster, Wally Pipp, Bob Shawkey, Wally Schang, Babe Ruth, Carl Mays, Waite Hoyt, Nelson "Chicken" Hawks. **Seated:** Johnny Mitchell, Bennet (Mascot), Miller Huggins (manager), Charles O'Leary (coach), Frank Roth (coach).

No-Hitters and Perfect Games

Regular Season No-Hitters

Thrown by Yankees (10, including two perfect games)

Pitcher	Date/Opp/Score	IP	H	R	ER	BB	SO	HR	Pit/Str	Catcher	Opp. Starter
David Cone (R)-Perfect Game	7/18/1999 vs. MON (6-0)	9.0	0	0	0	0	10	0	88/68	Joe Girardi	J. Vazquez
David Wells (L)-Perfect Game	5/17/1998 vs. MIN (4-0)	9.0	0	0	0	0	11	0	120/79	Jorge Posada	L. Hawkins
Dwight Gooden (R)	5/14/1996 vs. SEA (2-0)	9.0	0	0	0	6	5	0	134/74	Joe Girardi	S. Hitchcock
Jim Abbott (L)	9/4/1993 vs. CLE (4-0)	9.0	0	0	0	5	3	0	119/66	Matt Nokes	Bob Milacki
Dave Righetti (L)	7/4/1983 vs. BOS (4-0)	9.0	0	0	0	4	9	0	132/NA	B. Wynegar	John Tudor
Allie Reynolds (R)	9/28/1951 (G1) vs. BOS (8-0)	9.0	0	0	0	4	9	0	NA	Yogi Berra	Mel Parnell
Allie Reynolds (R)	7/12/1951 at CLE (1-0)	9.0	0	0	0	3	4	0	NA	Yogi Berra	Bob Feller
Monte Pearson (R)	8/27/1938 (G2) vs. CLE (13-0)	9.0	0	0	0	2	7	0	NA	Joe Glenn	J. Humphries
"Sad" Sam Jones (R)	9/4/1923 at PHA (2-0)	9.0	0	0	0	1	0	0	NA	F. Hofmann	Bob Hasty
George Mogridge (L)	4/24/1917 at BOS (2-1)	9.0	0	1	0	3	3	0	NA	L. Nunamaker	D. Leonard

No-hitter notes: The only Yankees no-hitters thrown in a night game were Allie Reynolds' on 7/12/51 and Dwight Gooden's on 5/14/1996. Reynolds also is one of only five pitchers all time to throw two 9.0-inning no-hitters in the same season (also Johnny Vander Meer-1938 w/ CIN; Virgil Trucks-1952 w/ DET; Nolan Ryan-1973 w/CAL; and Max Scherzer-2015 w/WSH).

Thrown by Opponents (7, no perfect games)

Pitcher	Date/Opp/Score	IP	H	R	ER	BB	SO	HR	Pit/Str	Catcher	Opp. Starter
*Six Houston Pitchers	6/11/2003 HOU at NYY (8-0)	9.0	0	0	0	3	13	0	151/93	Brad Ausmus	Jeff Weaver
Hoyt Wilhelm (R)	9/20/1958 BAL vs. NYY (1-0)	9.0	0	0	0	2	8	0	NA	Gus Tirandos	Don Larsen
**Virgil Trucks (R)	8/25/1952 DET at NYY (1-0)	9.0	0	0	0	1	8	0	NA	Matt Batts	Bill Miller
Bob Feller (R)	4/30/1946 CLE at NYY (1-0)	9.0	0	0	0	5	11	0	NA	Frankie Hayes	Bill Bevens
Ray Caldwell (R)	9/10/1919 (G1) CLE at NYY (3-0)	9.0	0	0	0	1	5	0	NA	Steve O'Neill	Carl Mays
Rube Foster (R)	6/21/1916 BOS vs. NYY (2-0)	9.0	0	0	0	3	3	0	NA	Bill Carrigan	Bob Shawkey
Cy Young (R)	6/30/1908 BOS at NYY (8-0)	9.0	0	0	0	1	2	0	NA	Lou Criger	Rube Manning

*Houston pitchers in order were: Oswalt (1.0), Munro (2.2), Saarloos (1.1), Lidge (2.0), Dotel (1.0), Wagner (1.0). Their team performance is tied for the most pitchers in MLB history to combine on a no-hitter (also Seattle on 6/8/2012 vs. Los Angeles-NL).
** Was the second of his two no-hitters during the 1952 season (also 5/15/52 vs. Washington, 1-0 win).

Postseason No-Hitters

Thrown by Yankees (1, was also a perfect game)

Pitcher	Date/Opp/Score	IP	H	R	ER	BB	SO	HR	Pit/Str	Catcher	Opp. Starter
Don Larsen (R)-Perfect Game	WS-G5 10/8/1956 vs. BRO (2-0)	9.0	0	0	0	0	7	0	97/71	Yogi Berra	Sal Maglie

Don Larsen's perfect game in Game 5 of the 1956 World Series vs. Brooklyn remains the only no-hitter in World Series history and the only perfect game in any round of postseason play. The only other pitcher to throw a no-hitter in postseason play was Roy Halladay on 10/6/2010 in NLDS Game 1 with Philadelphia vs. Cincinnati.

No Hits Allowed in Official Games Less than 9.0 Innings

Thrown by Yankees (1)

Pitcher	Date/Opp/Score	IP	H	R	ER	BB	SO	HR	Pit/Str	Catcher	Opp. Starter
Andy Hawkins	7/1/1990 at CWS (0-4, loss)	8.0	0	4	0	5	3	0	131/79	Bob Geren	Greg Hibbard

Hawkins allowed all four unearned runs in the bottom of the eighth inning. The White Sox' Sammy Sosa reached first base on a two-out fielding error by 3B Mike Blowers, then stole second. Hawkins then walked Ozzie Guillen and Lance Johnson, loading the bases. The next batter, Robin Ventura, hit a fly ball that LF Jim Leyritz dropped for an error, allowing all three runners to score and Ventura to reach second. RF Jesse Barfield then dropped a fly ball hit by Ivan Calderon, allowing Ventura to score and Calderon to reach second. Hawkins got out of the inning by getting Dan Pasqua to pop out to short. The total for the bottom of the eighth was four unearned runs on two walks and three errors. Also of note in this game, White Sox starter Greg Hibbard began the game perfect through his first 16 batters.

Thrown by Opponents (2)

Pitcher	Date/Opp/Score	IP	H	R	ER	BB	SO	HR	Pit/Str	Catcher	Opp. Starter
*Melido Perez	7/12/1990 CWS at NYY (8-0, rain)	6.0	0	0	0	4	9	0	NA	Carlton Fisk	A. Hawkins
**Ed Walsh	5/26/1907 CWS vs. NYY (8-1, rain)	5.0	0	1	-	2	1	0	NA	Billy Sullivan	Al Orth

* The Yankees starter vs. Perez was Andy Hawkins, who tossed an 8.0-inning unofficial no-hitter vs. the White Sox 11 days earlier.
** Allowed the Highlanders' Kid Elberfeld to score in the first after a walk, stolen base and two pitches that eluded the catcher.

No-Hit Opponent through 9.0 Innings and Allowed Hit in Extra-Innings

Thrown by Yankees (1) / Thrown against the Yankees (0)

Pitcher	Date/Opp/Score	IP	H	R	ER	BB	SO	HR	Pit/Str	Catcher	Opp. Starter
"Long" Tom Hughes	8/30/1910 (G2) vs. CLE (0-5, loss)	11.0	7	5	-	1	7	0	NA	Lou Criger	George Kahler

Over the first 9.0 innings of the game, Hughes allowed just one baserunner to reach (on a throwing error by 3B Jimmy Austin in the seventh). The no-hitter was broken up by a single by Harry Niles with one out in the 10th. Nap Lajoie also singled in the 10th, but Hughes did not allow any runs. However with two out in the 11th, Hughes allowed five runs on five hits and a walk to take the loss. Cleveland's George Kahler allowed just 3H and 2BB in tossing a complete-game shutout.

337

Perfect Games

Don Larsen - Oct. 8, 1956
World Series Game 5 vs. Brooklyn at Yankee Stadium

With the 1956 World Series knotted at two games apiece, Don Larsen authored what many consider the greatest game ever pitched, a 2-0 perfect game over the Brooklyn Dodgers in front of 64,519 at Yankee Stadium.

Amazingly, Larsen didn't even know he was going to be pitching that day until he got to the Stadium. As was the Yankees' tradition at the time, he arrived in the clubhouse to find a brand new baseball placed in one of his shoes by coach Frank Crosetti, which was manager Casey Stengel's way of letting a pitcher know he was being tabbed to start.

Larsen's date with history came on the heels of a disastrous start in Game 2 in which he was pulled with a 6-1 lead with two out in the second inning. He faced just 10 batters in the outing, allowing four unearned runs on four walks and a single in a game that the Yankees ultimately lost, 13-8.

After realizing he was getting the Game 5 start, Larsen went into the training room and took a nap, only to be awakened less than an hour before the first pitch.

According to the 6-foot-4-inch righthander, he had the best control of his career on that October day, reaching three balls once in the entire game with a full count on Pee Wee Reese in the first inning.

The perfect game was preserved by three notable fielding plays. In the second inning, Jackie Robinson was retired on a groundout that ricocheted off 3B Andy Carey's glove to SS Gil McDougald, who threw out the speedy infielder at first. Additionally, Brooklyn's Gil Hodges was robbed twice, first on a fly to deep left center that was tracked down by CF Mickey Mantle and again in the eighth by Carey on a low liner.

Brooklyn starter Sal Maglie held the first 11 Yankees batters off the bases until Mantle's fourth-inning solo homer into the right-field stands. The balance of the scoring came on Hank Bauer's sixth-inning RBI single which brought in Carey, who had been advanced to second on a sac bunt by Larsen.

In the ninth, Larsen set down Carl Furillo on a fly to right before getting Roy Campanella on a grounder to 2B Billy Martin. As his last gasp, Dodgers manager Walter Alston sent pinch-hitter Dale Mitchell to bat but he was famously called out on strikes by National League umpire Babe Pinelli, who was calling his final game behind the plate after a distinguished career.

The momentum from the win did not carry over to Game 6 at Ebbets Field as Yankees starter Bob Turley lost a 10-inning duel with Brooklyn's Clem Labine, 1-0. Game 7, however, was a romp as sophomore pitcher Johnny Kucks tossed the game of his life, shutting out the Dodgers, 9-0, on three hits and three walks to give the Yankees their 17th World Championship and avenge their seven-game Series loss to Brooklyn in 1955.

Larsen's performance was the sixth perfect game all time, fourth in the modern era and first since the White Sox's Charlie Robertson blanked Detroit, 2-0, on April 30, 1922, at Navin Field. It remains the only perfect game in postseason history.

Larsen played with seven franchises over his 14-year Major League career, finishing with an 81-91 record. He tallied a 45-24 mark in five seasons with the Yankees before being part of the Dec. 11, 1959, trade that brought Roger Maris to New York from the Kansas City Athletics.

Don Larsen delivers the final pitch of the game — a called strike to Dodgers pinch-hitter Dale Mitchell.

Don Larsen [R] and Yogi Berra celebrate the perfect game after the final pitch.

	1 2 3	4 5 6	7 8 9	R H E
Brooklyn	0 0 0	0 0 0	0 0 0	0 0 0
Yankees	0 0 0	1 0 1	0 0 x	2 5 0

Brooklyn	AB	R	H	RBI	BB	SO
Jim Gilliam 2B	3	0	0	0	0	1
Pee Wee Reese SS	3	0	0	0	0	1
Duke Snider CF	3	0	0	0	0	1
Jackie Robinson 3B	3	0	0	0	0	0
Gil Hodges 1B	3	0	0	0	0	1
Sandy Amoros LF	3	0	0	0	0	0
Carl Furillo RF	3	0	0	0	0	0
Roy Campanella C	3	0	0	0	0	1
Sal Maglie P	2	0	0	0	0	1
Dale Mitchell PH	1	0	0	0	0	1
Totals	27	0	0	0	0	7

Team LOB: 0. RISP: 0-for-0. DP: 2. Hodges-Campanella-Robinson; Campanella-Robinson; Reese-Hodges.

Yankees	AB	R	H	RBI	BB	SO
Hank Bauer RF	4	0	1	1	0	1
Joe Collins 1B	4	0	1	0	0	2
Mickey Mantle CF	3	1	1	1	0	0
Yogi Berra C	3	0	0	0	0	0
Enos Slaughter LF	2	0	0	0	1	0
Billy Martin 2B	3	0	1	0	0	1
Gil McDougald SS	2	0	0	0	1	0
Andy Carey 3B	3	1	1	0	0	0
Don Larsen P	2	0	0	0	0	1
Totals	26	2	5	2	2	5

HR: Mantle (3, off Maglie; 4th inn., 0 on, 2 outs to deep RF line). SH: Larsen (1, off Maglie). RBI: Bauer (3); Mantle (4). Team LOB: 3. RISP: 1-for-3.

Brooklyn	IP	H	R	ER	BB	SO	HR
Sal Maglie, L (1-1)	8	5	2	2	2	5	1
Totals	8	5	2	2	2	5	1

Yankees	IP	H	R	ER	BB	SO	HR
Don Larsen, W (1-0)	9	0	0	0	0	7	0
Totals	9	0	0	0	0	7	0

Pitches-Strikes: Maglie NA, Larsen 97-71. Balks: None. WP: None. HBP: None. IBB: None. Pickoffs: None.

Umpires: HP-Babe Pinelli, 1B-Hank Soar, 2B-Dusty Boggess, 3B-Larry Napp, LF-Tom Gorman, RF-Ed Runge. Time of Game: 2:06. Attendance: 64,519.

David Wells — May 17, 1998
vs. Minnesota at Yankee Stadium

The 1998 season was full of highlights for the Yankees, a team that went 114-48 on the way to a World Series title. But one of the season's signature moments came on "Beanie Baby Day" in front of 49,820 fans at Yankee Stadium when David Wells pitched the second perfect game in franchise history, matching the feat of Don Larsen, who, like Wells, attended Point Loma H.S. in San Diego.

By the time the game rolled around to the seventh, Wells and his teammates were well aware of what was taking place. The only player willing to talk to him was pitcher David Cone, who tried to ease the tension by saying, "I think it's time…to break out the knuckleball."

The 34-year-old lefthander struck out nine of his first 17 hitters and 11 over the game, including Twins catcher Javier Valentin three times. He reached three balls on just four batters.

The Yankees gave Wells an early lead, scoring runs on a wild pitch in the second and a Bernie Williams solo-HR in the fourth. They tacked on two more in the seventh on an RBI triple by Darryl Strawberry and an RBI single from Chad Curtis.

In the ninth, Wells got leadoff hitter Jon Shave to pop to Paul O'Neill in right and Valentin to strike out swinging. Pat Mears made the final out, flying out to O'Neill. Delirious fans cheered Wells being carried off the field on his teammates' shoulders. Then they filed out too, clutching their Beanie Babies.

David Wells at work during his perfect game.

Beanie Baby "Valentino" was given away to children at Yankee Stadium on the day of Wells' perfect game.

	1 2 3	4 5 6	7 8 9	R H E
Minnesota	0 0 0	0 0 0	0 0 0	0 0 0
Yankees	0 1 0	1 0 0	2 0 x	4 6 0

Minnesota	AB	R	H	RBI	BB	SO
Matt Lawton CF	3	0	0	0	0	0
Brent Gates 2B	3	0	0	0	0	1
Paul Molitor DH	3	0	0	0	0	1
Marty Cordova LF	3	0	0	0	0	1
Ron Coomer 1B	3	0	0	0	0	2
Alex Ochoa RF	3	0	0	0	0	0
Jon Shave 3B	3	0	0	0	0	2
Javier Valentin C	3	0	0	0	0	3
Pat Meares SS	3	0	0	0	0	1
Totals	27	0	0	0	0	11

Team LOB: 0. RISP: 0 for 0. PB: Valentin (4).

Yankees	AB	R	H	RBI	BB	SO
Chuck Knoblauch 2B	4	0	0	0	0	0
Derek Jeter SS	3	0	1	0	1	2
Paul O'Neill RF	4	0	0	0	0	2
Tino Martinez 1B	4	0	0	0	0	0
Bernie Williams CF	3	3	3	1	0	0
Darryl Strawberry DH	3	1	1	1	0	0
Chad Curtis LF	3	0	1	1	0	0
Jorge Posada C	3	0	0	0	0	1
Scott Brosius 3B	3	0	0	0	0	1
Totals	30	4	6	3	1	6

2B: Williams 2 (11, 2 off Hawkins). 3B: Strawberry (2, off Hawkins). HR: Williams (3, off Hawkins; 4th inn, 0 on, 2 outs to deep RF). RBI: Curtis (24); Strawberry (19); Williams (19). Team LOB: 3. RISP: 2-for-8.

Minnesota	IP	H	R	ER	BB	SO	HR
LaTroy Hawkins, L (2-4)	7	6	4	4	0	5	1
Dan Naulty	0.1	0	0	0	1	0	0
Greg Swindell	0.2	0	0	0	0	1	0
Totals	8	6	4	4	1	6	1

Yankees	IP	H	R	ER	BB	SO	HR
David Wells, W (5-1)	9	0	0	0	0	11	0
Totals	9	0	0	0	0	11	0

Pitches-Strikes: Hawkins 123-84, Naulty 7-3, Swindell 12-8, Wells 120-79. Balks: None. WP: Hawkins (2). HBP: None. IBB: None. Pickoffs: None.

Umpires: HP-Tim McClelland, 1B-John Hirschbeck, 2B-Mike Reilly, 3B-Rich Garcia. Time of Game: 2:40. Attendance: 49,820.

David Cone — July 18, 1999
vs. Montreal at Yankee Stadium

Fans arrived at Yankee Stadium on July 18, 1999, to celebrate Yogi Berra Day, but they left saluting David Cone. The righthander needed just 88 pitches to throw the third perfect game in Yankees history in front of 41,930 fans and a host of legendary Yankees, including Don Larsen, who threw out the game's ceremonial first pitch.

On a day in which the temperature hovered in the 90s, the Yankees gave Cone a 5-0 second-inning lead via a pair of two-run homers from Ricky Ledee and Derek Jeter sandwiched around an RBI-double by Joe Girardi.

Cone's masterpiece, just one season removed from David Wells' perfect game at Yankee Stadium, was a picture of economy. Of the last 20 regular season and postseason perfect games thrown since 1922, Cone required the fewest pitches. It also gave the Yankees a record three perfect games in their history, a mark since tied by the White Sox (Charlie Robertson, Mark Buehrle and Philip Humber). It was the third perfect game at the original Yankee Stadium—the most for any single venue.

Over the course of the game, Cone got 13 outs in the air, four on the ground and 10 via strikeout. The closest he came to allowing a baserunner was with one out in the eighth, when second baseman Chuck Knoblauch made a nice play ranging far to his right throwing out Jose Vidro at first. The final out was a foul pop to third off the bat of Orlando Cabrera, which was snagged by the sure-handed Scott Brosius. Cone's gem remains the only perfect game in the history of regular season Interleague Play.

David Cone is carried off the field by his teammates after his perfect game.

	1 2 3	4 5 6	7 8 9	R H E
Montreal	0 0 0	0 0 0	0 0 0	0 0 0
Yankees	0 5 0	0 0 0	0 1 x	6 8 0

Montreal	AB	R	H	RBI	BB	SO
Wilton Guerrero DH	3	0	0	0	0	1
Terry Jones CF	2	0	0	0	0	1
James Mouton CF	1	0	0	0	0	1
Rondell White LF	3	0	0	0	0	1
Vladimir Guerrero RF	3	0	0	0	0	1
Jose Vidro 2B	3	0	0	0	0	0
Brad Fullmer 1B	3	0	0	0	0	1
Chris Widger C	3	0	0	0	0	2
Shane Andrews 3B	2	0	0	0	0	1
Ryan McGuire PH	1	0	0	0	0	0
Orlando Cabrera SS	3	0	0	0	0	1
Totals	27	0	0	0	0	10

Team LOB: 0. RISP: 0 for 0. DP: 1 Vidro-Cabrera-B Fullmer.

Yankees	AB	R	H	RBI	BB	SO
Chuck Knoblauch 2B	2	1	1	0	1	1
Derek Jeter SS	4	1	1	2	0	0
Paul O'Neill RF	4	1	0	0	0	0
Bernie Williams CF	4	0	1	0	0	0
Tino Martinez 1B	4	0	1	0	0	0
Chili Davis DH	3	1	1	0	1	0
Ricky Ledee LF	4	1	2	2	0	1
Scott Brosius 3B	2	1	0	0	0	1
Joe Girardi C	3	0	1	1	0	0
Totals	30	6	8	6	2	3

2B: O'Neill (20, off Vazquez); Girardi (9, off Vazquez). HR: Ledee (3, off Vazquez; 2nd inn, 1 on, 1 out to deep RF); Jeter (16, off Vazquez; 2nd inn, 1 on, 2 outs). HBP: Knoblauch (16, by Vazquez); Brosius (2, by Vazquez). GIDP: Davis (9). RBI: Ledee 2 (13); Jeter 2 (64); Girardi (10); Williams (55). Team LOB: 4. RISP: 1-for-4.

Montreal	IP	H	R	ER	BB	SO	HR
Javier Vazquez, L (2-5)	7	7	6	6	2	3	2
Bobby Ayala	1	1	0	0	0	0	0
Team Totals	8	8	6	6	2	3	2

Yankees	IP	H	R	ER	BB	SO	HR
David Cone, W (10-4)	9	0	0	0	0	10	0
Team Totals	9	0	0	0	0	10	0

Pitches-Strikes: Vazquez 118-76, Ayala 14-8, Cone 88-68. Balks: None. WP: None. HBP: Vazquez 2 (4; Knoblauch, S Brosius). IBB: None. Pickoffs: None.

Umpires: HP-Ted Barrett, 1B-Larry McCoy, 2B-Jim Evans, 3B-Chuck Meriwether. Time of Game: 2:16. Attendance: 41,930.

Yankees All-Star Selections by Year

Please note that the All-Star Game was first played in 1933, and two All-Star Games were played in each year from 1959-62.

For All Listings: *=Selected as starter, †=Started, but not elected, (R)=Rookie, #=Selected via MLB.com Final Vote, (MVP)=ASG MVP
For 1959-62: **G1**=On team for first game only, **G2**=On team for second game only, **Both**=On team for both games

- 1933: Chapman*-lf, Dickey-c, Gehrig*-1b, Gomez†-p, Lazzeri-2b , Ruth*-rf
- 1934: Chapman-of, Dickey*-c, Gehrig*-1b, Gomez†-p, Ruffing-p, Ruth*-rf
- 1935: Chapman-of, Gehrig*-1b, Gomez†-p
- 1936: Crosetti-ss, Dickey-c, DiMaggio*(R)-rf, Gehrig*-1b, Gomez-p, Pearson-p, Selkirk-of, McCarthy-mgr
- 1937: Dickey*-c, DiMaggio*-rf, Gehrig-1b, Gomez†-p, Murphy-p, Rolfe*-3b, McCarthy-mgr
- 1938: Dickey*-c, DiMaggio*-rf, Gehrig-1b, Gomez†-p, Rolfe-3b, Ruffing-p, McCarthy-mgr
- 1939: Crosetti-ss, Dickey*-c, DiMaggio*-cf, Gehrig-1b (honorary), Gomez-p, Gordon*-2b, Murphy-p, Rolfe-*3b, Ruffing†-p, Selkirk*-lf, McCarthy-mgr
- 1940: Dickey*-c, DiMaggio*-cf, Gordon*-2b, Keller*-rf, Pearson-p, Rolfe-3b, Ruffing†-p, McCarthy-mgr
- 1941: Dickey*-c, DiMaggio*-cf, Gordon-2b, Keller-of, Ruffing-p, Russo-p
- 1942: Bonham-p , Chandler†-p, Dickey-c, DiMaggio*-cf, Gordon*-2b, Henrich*-rf, Rizzuto-ss, Rosar-c, Ruffing-p, McCarthy-mgr
- 1943: Bonham-p, Chandler-p, Dickey-c, Gordon-2b, Keller-of, Lindell-of, McCarthy-mgr
- 1944: Borowy†-p, Hemsley-c, Page (R)-p, McCarthy-mgr
- 1945: No game due to WWII travel restrictions. Formal balloting not conducted.
- 1946: Chandler-p, Dickey-c, DiMaggio*-cf, Gordon-2b, Keller*-rf, Stirnweiss-3b
- 1947: Chandler-p, DiMaggio*-cf, Henrich-of, Johnson-3b, McQuinn*-1b, Page-p, Robinson-c, Shea (R)-p, Keller-of
- 1948: Berra-c, DiMaggio*-of, Henrich†-rf, McQuinn-1b, Page-p, Raschi-p, Harris-mgr
- 1949: Berra-c, DiMaggio*-of, Henrich-of, Raschi-p, Reynolds-p
- 1950: Berra*-c, Byrne-p, Coleman-2b, DiMaggio-of, Henrich-1b, Raschi†-p, Reynolds-p, Rizzuto*-ss, Stengel-mgr
- 1951: Berra*-c, DiMaggio-of, Lopat-p, Rizzuto-ss, Stengel-mgr
- 1952: Bauer*-rf, Berra*-c, Mantle-of, Raschi†-p, Reynolds-p, Rizzuto-ss, McDougald-2b, Stengel-mgr
- 1953: Bauer*-rf, Berra*-c, Mantle*-cf, Mize-1b, Reynolds-p, Rizzuto-ss, Sain-p, Stengel-mgr
- 1954: Bauer-of, Berra*-c, Ford†-p, Mantle*-cf, Noren-of, Reynolds-p, Stengel-mgr
- 1955: Berra*-c, Ford-p, Mantle-cf, Turley-p
- 1956: Berra*-c, Ford-p, Kucks-p, Mantle*-cf, Martin-2b, McDougald-ss, Stengel-mgr
- 1957: Berra*-c, Grim-p, Howard-c, Mantle*-cf, McDougald-ss, Richardson (R)-2b, Shantz-p, Skowron-1b, Stengel-mgr
- 1958: Berra-c, Duren (R)-p, Ford-p, Howard-c, Kubek-inf, Mantle*-cf, McDougald-2b, Skowron-1b, Turley†-p, Stengel-mgr
- 1959: Berra-c (both), Duren-p (both), Ford-p (G1), Mantle-of (both), McDougald-ss (both), Richardson-2b (G2), Skowron*-1b (both), Howard-c (G2), Kubek-ss (both), Stengel-mgr (both)
- 1960: Berra*-c (both), Coates-p (both), Ford†-p (both), Howard-c (both), Mantle*-cf (both), Maris*-rf (both), Skowron*-1b (both)
- 1961: Arroyo-p (G2), Berra-of (both), Ford-p (both), Howard-c (both), Kubek-ss (both), Mantle*-cf (both), Maris*-rf (both), Skowron-1b (G2)
- 1962: Berra (G2), Howard-c (both), Mantle*-rf (both), Maris*-of (both), Richardson-2b (both), Terry-p (both), Tresh (R)-ss (both), Houk-mgr (both)
- 1963: Bouton-p, Howard-c, Mantle-of, Pepitone*-1b, Richardson-2b, Tresh-of
- 1964: Ford-p, Howard*-c, Mantle*-cf, Pepitone-1b, Richardson-2b
- 1965: Howard-c, Mantle-of, Pepitone-1b, Richardson-2b, Stottlemyre-p
- 1966: Richardson-2b, Stottlemyre-p
- 1967: Downing-p, Mantle-1b
- 1968: Mantle-1b, Stottlemyre-p
- 1969: Stottlemyre†-p
- 1970: Peterson-p, Stottlemyre-p, White-of
- 1971: Munson-c, Murcer*-cf
- 1972: Murcer*-cf
- 1973: Lyle-p, Munson-c, Murcer*-lf
- 1974: Munson*-c, Murcer*-cf
- 1975: Bonds*-cf, Hunter-p, Munson*-c, Nettles*-3b
- 1976: Chambliss-1b, Hunter-p, Lyle-p, Munson*-c, Randolph (R)-2b, Rivers-of
- 1977: Jackson*-rf, Lyle-p, Munson-c, Nettles-3b, Randolph*-2b, Martin-mgr
- 1978: Gossage-p, Guidry-p, Jackson*-rf, Nettles-3b, Martin-mgr
- 1979: Guidry-p, Jackson-of, John-p, Nettles-3b, Lemon-mgr
- 1980: Dent*-ss, Gossage-p, Jackson*-rf, John-p, Nettles*-3b, Randolph*-2b
- 1981: Davis-p, Dent*-ss, Gossage-p, Jackson*-rf, Randolph*-2b, Winfield*-cf
- 1982: Gossage-p, Guidry-p, Winfield-of
- 1983: Guidry-p, Winfield*-rf
- 1984: P. Niekro-p, Mattingly-1b, Winfield*-lf
- 1985: Henderson*-cf, Mattingly-1b, Winfield*-rf
- 1986: Henderson*-lf, Mattingly-1b, Righetti-p, Winfield*-rf
- 1987: Henderson*-cf, Mattingly*-1b, Randolph*-2b, Righetti-p, Winfield*-rf
- 1988: Henderson*-cf, Mattingly-1b, Winfield*-rf
- 1989: Mattingly-1b, Sax-2b
- 1990: Sax-2b
- 1991: Sanderson-p
- 1992: R. Kelly-of
- 1993: Boggs*-3b, Key-p
- 1994: Boggs*-3b, Key*-p, O'Neill-of
- 1995: Boggs*-3b, O'Neill-of, Stanley-c, Showalter-mgr
- 1996: Boggs*-3b, Pettitte-P, Wetteland-p
- 1997: Cone-p, Martinez*-1b, O'Neill†-of, Rivera-p, B. Williams-of, Torre-mgr
- 1998: Brosius-3b, Jeter-ss, O'Neill-of, Wells*-p, B. Williams-of
- 1999: Cone-p, Jeter-ss, Rivera-p, B. Williams-of, Torre-mgr
- 2000: Jeter† (MVP)-ss, Posada-c, Rivera-p, B. Williams*-of, Torre-mgr
- 2001: Clemens†-p, Jeter-ss, Pettitte-P, Posada-c, Rivera-p, Stanton-p, B. Williams-of, Torre-mgr
- 2002: Giambi*-1b, Jeter-ss, Posada*-c, Rivera-p, Soriano*-2b, Ventura-3b, Torre-mgr
- 2003: Clemens-p, Giambi-1b, Matsui*(R)-cf, Posada*-c, Soriano*-2b
- 2004: Giambi*-1b, Gordon-p, Jeter*-ss, Matsui-of, Rivera-p, Rodriguez*-3b, Sheffield-of, Vazquez-p, Torre-mgr
- 2005: Rodriguez*-3b, Rivera-p, Sheffield-of
- 2006: Rodriguez*-3b, Jeter*-ss, Canó-2b, Rivera-p
- 2007: Jeter*-ss, Posada-c, Rodriguez*-3b
- 2008: Jeter*-ss, Posada-c, Rodriguez*-3b
- 2009: Jeter*-ss, Rivera-p, Teixeira*-1b
- 2010: Canó*-2b, Girardi-mgr, Hughes-p, Jeter*-ss, Pettitte-p, Rivera-p, Rodriguez-3b, Sabathia-p, Swisher#-of
- 2011: Canó*-2b, Granderson*-of, Jeter*-ss, Martin-c, Rivera-p, Robertson-p, Rodriguez*-3b, Sabathia-p
- 2012: Canó*-2b, Granderson*-of, Jeter*-ss, Sabathia-p
- 2013: Canó*-2b, Rivera (MVP) -p
- 2014: Betances (R)-p, Jeter*-ss, TANAKA (R)-p
- 2015: Betances-p, GARDNER-of, Teixeira-1b
- 2016: Beltrán-of, Betances-p, Miller-p
- 2017: Betances-p, Castro-2b, JUDGE*(R)-rf, SÁNCHEZ-c, SEVERINO-p
- 2018: CHAPMAN-p, JUDGE*-lf, SEVERINO-p, TORRES (R)-2b
- 2019: CHAPMAN-p, LEMAHIEU-2b, SÁNCHEZ-c, TANAKA-p, TORRES-2b

Yankees in the All-Star Home Run Derby (est. 1985)

Year	Player	Ballpark (Team Stad.)	Result	Year	Player	Ballpark (Team Stad.)	Result
1997	Tino Martinez	Jacobs Field (CLE)	Won	2012	Robinson Canó	Kauffman Stadium (KC)	1st Rd.
2002	Jason Giambi	Miller Park (MIL)	Won	2013	Robinson Canó	Citi Field (NYM)	1st Rd.
2003	Jason Giambi	U.S. Cellular Field (CWS)	Semis	2017	AARON JUDGE	Marlins Park (MIA)	Won
2010	Nick Swisher	Angel Stadium (LAA)	1st Rd.	2017	GARY SÁNCHEZ	Marlins Park (MIA)	Semis
2011	Robinson Canó	Chase Field (ARI)	Won				

All-Star Selections and Starts

The Yankees have had 430 all-time All-Star selections (55 pitchers with 136 selections; and 76 position players with 294 selections). Additionally, the AL team has been skippered by nine different Yankees managers on 32 total occasions.

According to Major League Baseball, on three occasions Yankees elected to start the game were ultimately replaced in the starting lineup (OF Reggie Jackson by Fred Lynn in 1978, SS Derek Jeter by Asdrubal Cabrera in 2011, and 3B Alex Rodriguez by Adrian Beltre in 2011). Conversely, there have been five Yankees who have started the game after replacing the originally elected starters (Bobby Murcer replacing Tony Oliva in the OF in 1971, Thurman Munson replacing Carlton Fisk at C in 1974, Willie Randolph replacing Paul Molitor at 2B in 1980, Graig Nettles replacing George Brett at 3B in 1980, and Derek Jeter replacing Alex Rodriguez at SS in 2000).

There have been 12 Yankees rookies selected to the ASG (Joe DiMaggio-1936, Joe Page-1944, Spec Shea-1947, Bobby Richardson-1957, Ryne Duren-1958, Tom Tresh-1962, Willie Randolph-1976, Hideki Matsui-2003, Dellin Betances-2014, Masahiro Tanaka-2014, Aaron Judge-2017 and Gleyber Torres-2018).

In 1939, Lou Gehrig (who retired earlier that season) was named an honorary AL team member. That selection is not included in the totals below.

Formal balloting was not conducted by Major League Baseball in 1945, when the All-Star Game was canceled due to WWII travel restrictions. The AP polled 13 of 16 AL managers who unofficially voted RHP Hank Borowy, 1B Nick Etten, 2B Snuffy Stirnweiss and 3B Oscar Grimes as All-Stars, with the former three as starters. However, the 1945 voting was unofficial and is not included in the totals below.

Please note that two All-Star Games were played in each year from 1959-62. Games participated in are noted below with a "G1" and/or a "G2".

Players — Selections (Starts)

Mickey Mantle (1952-58, '59 '62 G1&G2, '63-65, '67-68).....20 (13)
Yogi Berra (1948-58, 1959-61 G1&G2, 1962 G2).........18 (11)
Derek Jeter (1998-2002, '04, '06-12, '14)....14 (9)
Joe DiMaggio (1936-42, '46-51) 13 (9)
Mariano Rivera (1997, '99-2002, '04-06, '08-11, '13).............13 (0)
Elston Howard (1957-58, '59 G2, 1960-62 G1&G2, '63-65)........12 (1)
Bill Dickey (1933-34, '36-43, '46) 11 (6)
Whitey Ford (1954-56, '58, '59 G1, 1960-61 G1&G2, '64)....10 (3)
Bobby Richardson (1957, '59 G2, '62 G1&G2, '63-66).......8 (1)
Dave Winfield (1981-88) 8 (7)
Lefty Gomez (1933-39) 7 (5)
Thurman Munson (1971, '73-78) 7 (3)
Alex Rodriguez (2004-08, '10-11) 7 (5)
Bill Skowron (1957-58, '59-60G1&G2, '61G2)..7 (4)
Lou Gehrig (1933-38) - see note above....6 (5)
Joe Gordon (1939-43, '46) 6 (3)
Roger Maris (1960-62 G1&G2) 6 (5)
Don Mattingly (1984-89) 6 (1)
Gil McDougald (1952, '56-58, '59 G1&G2)... 6 (0)
Red Ruffing (1934, '38-42) 6 (2)
Robinson Canó (2006, 2010-13)....5 (4)
Tommy Henrich (1942, '47-50) 5 (2)
Reggie Jackson (1977-81) 5 (3)
Charlie Keller (1940-41, '43, '46-47) 5 (2)
Graig Nettles (1975, '77-80) 5 (2)
Jorge Posada (2000-03, '07).......5 (2)
Willie Randolph (1976-77, '80-81, '87) 5 (3)
Allie Reynolds (1949-50, '52-54)....5 (0)
Phil Rizzuto (1942, '50-53) 5 (2)
Mel Stottlemyre (1965-66, '68-70) ...5 (1)
Bernie Williams (1997-2001) 5 (1)
Dellin Betances (2014-17) 4 (0)
Wade Boggs (1993-96) 4 (4)
Spud Chandler (1942-43, '46-47) 4 (1)
Goose Gossage (1978, '80-82).......4 (0)
Ron Guidry (1978-79, '82-83)......4 (0)
Rickey Henderson (1985-88).......4 (4)
Tony Kubek (1958, '59 G2, '61 G1&G2) 4 (1)
Bobby Murcer (1971-74)............4 (4)
Paul O'Neill (1994-95, '97-98) 4 (1)
Vic Raschi (1948-50, '52) 4 (2)
Red Rolfe (1937-40) 4 (2)
Hank Bauer (1952-54) 3 (1)
Ben Chapman (1933-35).............3 (1)
Ryne Duren (1958, 1959 G1&G2)....3 (0)
Jason Giambi (2002-04) 3 (2)
Sparky Lyle (1973, '76-77).........3 (0)
Johnny Murphy (1937-39) 3 (0)
Joe Page (1944, '47-48) 3 (0)
Joe Pepitone (1963-65)............3 (1)
Andy Pettitte (1996, 2001, '10) 3 (0)
CC Sabathia (2010-12).............3 (0)
Tom Tresh (1962 G1&G2, '63)......3 (0)
Ernie Bonham (1942-43)...........2 (0)
AROLDIS CHAPMAN (2018-19).....2 (0)
Roger Clemens (2001, '03) 2 (1)
Jim Coates (1960 G1&G2)..........2 (0)
David Cone (1997, '99).............2 (0)
Frank Crosetti (1936, '39) 2 (0)
Bucky Dent (1980-81) 2 (2)
Curtis Granderson (2011-12).......2 (2)
Catfish Hunter (1975-76) 2 (0)
Tommy John (1979-80)............2 (0)
AARON JUDGE (2017-18)..........2 (2)
Jimmy Key (1993-94) 2 (1)
Hideki Matsui (2003-04) 2 (1)
George McQuinn (1947-48).........2 (2)
Monte Pearson (1936, '40) 2 (0)
Dave Righetti (1986-87) 2 (0)
Babe Ruth (1933-34) 2 (2)
GARY SÁNCHEZ (2017, '19) 2 (1)
Steve Sax (1989-90) 2 (1)
George Selkirk (1936, '39)..........2 (0)
LUIS SEVERINO (2017-18).........2 (0)
Gary Sheffield (2004-05)...........2 (0)
Alfonso Soriano (2002-03)..........2 (2)
MASAHIRO TANAKA (2014, '19) 2 (0)
Ralph Terry (1962 G1&G2) 2 (0)
Mark Teixeira (2009, '15) 2 (1)
GLEYBER TORRES (2018-19)......2 (2)
Bob Turley (1955, '58)..............2 (0)
Roy White (1969-70)...............2 (0)
Luis Arroyo (1961 G2) 1 (0)
Carlos Beltran (2016) 1 (0)
Bobby Bonds (1975)................1 (1)
Hank Borowy (1944)...............1 (0)
Jim Bouton (1963)..................1 (0)
Scott Brosius (1998) 1 (0)
Tommy Byrne (1950)...............1 (0)
Starlin Castro (2017)...............1 (0)
Chris Chambliss (1976) 1 (0)
Jerry Coleman (1950)..............1 (0)
Ron Davis (1981) 1 (0)
Al Downing (1967) 1 (0)
BRETT GARDNER (2015) 1 (0)
Tom Gordon (2004) 1 (0)
Bob Grim (1957) 1 (0)
Rollie Hemsley (1944) 1 (1)
Phil Hughes (2010) 1 (0)
Billy Johnson (1947)...............1 (0)
Roberto Kelly (1992) 1 (0)
Johnny Kucks (1956) 1 (0)
Tony Lazzeri (1933)................1 (0)
DJ LEMAHIEU (2019)..............1 (1)
Johnny Lindell (1943) 1 (0)
Eddie Lopat (1951) 1 (0)
Billy Martin (1956).................1 (0)
Russell Martin (2011)..............1 (0)
Tino Martinez (1997) 1 (1)
Andrew Miller (2016)..............1 (0)
Johnny Mize (1953) 1 (0)
Phil Niekro (1984) 1 (0)
Irv Noren (1954)...................1 (0)
Fritz Peterson (1970) 1 (0)
Mickey Rivers (1976) 1 (0)
David Robertson (2011) 1 (0)
Aaron Robinson (1947)............1 (0)
Buddy Rosar (1942) 1 (0)
Marius Russo (1941)...............1 (0)
Johnny Sain (1953).................1 (0)
Scott Sanderson (1991)............1 (0)
Bobby Shantz (1957) 1 (0)
Spec Shea (1947)..................1 (0)
Mike Stanley (1995) 1 (0)
Mike Stanton (2001)...............1 (0)
Snuffy Stirnweiss (1946) 1 (0)
Nick Swisher (2010) 1 (0)
Javier Vazquez (2004) 1 (0)
Robin Ventura (2002)..............1 (0)
David Wells (1998) 1 (1)
John Wetteland (1996) 1 (0)

As AL Manager (32 times)

Casey Stengel (1950-54, '56-58, '59 G1&G2) ... 10
Joe McCarthy (1936-39, '42-44) 7
Joe Torre (1997, '99-2002, '04).........6
Ralph Houk (1962 G1&G2, '63) 3
Billy Martin (1977-78) 2
Joe Girardi (2010) 1
Bucky Harris (1948)..................1
Bob Lemon (1979) 1
Buck Showalter (1995) 1

Starts by Position
(ASG starters are listed below. See text above for additional explanation and details.)

C (25): Berra-11 (1950-57, '59G2, '60G1&G2)
Dickey-6 (1934, '37-41)
Munson-3 (1974-76)
Posada-2 (2002-03)
Hemsley-1 (1944)
Howard-1 (1964)
SÁNCHEZ-1 (2019)

1B (17): Gehrig-5 (1933-37)
Skowron-4 (1958, '59G1, '60G1&G2)
Giambi-2 (2002, '04)
McQuinn-2 (1947-48)
Martinez-1 (1997)
Mattingly-1 (1987)
Pepitone-1 (1963)
Teixeira-1 (2009)

2B (16): Gordon-3 (1939-40, '42)
Richardson-1 (1964)
Randolph-4 (1977, '80-81, '87)
Sax-1 (1990)
Soriano-2 (2002-03)
Canó-4 (2010-13)
LEMAHIEU-1 (2019)

SS (14): Jeter-9 (2000, '04, '06-10, '12, '14)
Dent-2 (1980-81)
Rizzuto-2 (1950, '52)
Kubek-1 (1961G1)

3B (13): Rodriguez-5 (2004-08)
Boggs-4 (1993-96)
Nettles-2 (1975, '80)
Rolfe-2 (1937, '39)

LF (7): Chapman-1 (1933)
Henderson-1 (1986)
Henrich-1 (1948)
JUDGE-1 (2018)
Murcer-1 (1973)
Selkirk-1 (1939)
Winfield-1 (1984)

CF (32): Mantle-12 (1953-58, '59G2, '60G1&G2, '61G1&G2, '64)
DiMaggio-6 (1939-42, '47, '49)
Henderson-3 (1985, '87-88)
Murcer-3 (1971-72, '74) Granderson-2 (2011-12)
Maris-2 (1962G1&G2)
Bonds-1 (1975)
Matsui-1 (2003)
Williams-1 (2000)
Winfield-1 (1981)

RF (25): Winfield-5 (1983, '85-88)
Bauer-3 (1952-54)
DiMaggio-3 (1936-38)
Jackson-3 (1977, '80-81)
Maris-3 (1960G1&G2, '61G1)
Keller-2 (1940, '46)
Ruth-2 (1933-34)
Henrich-1 (1942)
JUDGE-1 (2017)
Mantle-1 (1962G1)
O'Neill-1 (1997)

SP (19): Gomez-5 (1933-35, '37-38)
Ford-3 (1954, '60G2, '61G1)
Raschi-2 (1950, '52)
Ruffing-2 (1939-40)
Borowy-1 (1944)
Chandler-1 (1942)
Clemens-1 (2001)
Key-1 (1994)
Stottlemyre-1 (1969)
Turley-1 (1958)
Wells-1 (1998)

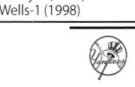

341

Yankees All-Time All-Star Batting Statistics

Data below includes all Yankees position players who have been selected for an All-Star Game along with the batting records of all pitchers who have made at least one plate appearance in the game. 3B Billy Johnson (1947) and OF Irv Noren (1954) made their only Yankees All-Star Game appearances as defensive replacements without ever receiving a PA. Additionally, there have been six Yankees position players named to an All-Star team who never entered the game at all in their only ASG as a Yankee (2B Tony Lazzeri-1933; C Buddy Rosar-1942; OF Johnny Lindell-1943; C Aaron Robinson-1947; C Russell Martin-2011; Starlin Castro-2017).

Player	AVG	SEL	G	GS	PA	AB	R	H	2B	3B	HR	RBI	SH	SF	HP	SB	CS	BB	SO	OBP	SLG
Hank Bauer	.286	3	3	3	8	7	0	2	0	0	0	0	0	0	0	0	1	1	3	.375	.286
Carlos Beltran	.000	1	1	0	1	1	0	0	0	0	0	0	0	0	0	0	0	0	0	.000	.000
Yogi Berra	.195	18	15	11	43	41	5	8	0	0	1	3	0	0	0	0	0	2	3	.233	.268
Wade Boggs	.222	4	4	4	10	9	1	2	0	0	0	0	0	0	0	0	0	1	2	.300	.222
Bobby Bonds	.000	1	1	1	3	3	0	0	0	0	0	0	0	0	0	0	0	0	1	.000	.000
Hank Borowy	1.000	1	1	1	1	1	0	1	0	0	0	1	0	0	0	0	0	0	0	1.000	1.000
Scott Brosius	.500	1	1	0	2	2	1	1	0	0	0	0	0	0	0	1	0	0	1	.500	.500
Robinson Canó	.200	5	4	4	7	5	0	1	0	0	0	1	0	1	1	0	0	0	0	.286	.200
Chris Chambliss	.000	1	1	0	1	1	0	0	0	0	0	0	0	0	0	0	0	0	0	.000	.000
Spud Chandler	.000	4	1	1	1	1	0	0	0	0	0	0	0	0	0	0	0	0	0	.000	.000
Ben Chapman	.286	3	3	1	7	7	0	2	0	1	0	0	0	0	0	0	0	0	1	.286	.571
Jerry Coleman	.000	1	1	0	2	2	0	0	0	0	0	0	0	0	0	0	0	0	2	.000	.000
Frank Crosetti	.000	2	1	0	1	1	0	0	0	0	0	0	0	0	0	0	0	0	1	.000	.000
Bucky Dent	.750	2	2	2	4	4	0	3	1	0	0	0	0	0	0	0	0	0	1	.750	1.000
Bill Dickey	.263	11	8	6	23	19	3	5	2	0	0	1	0	0	0	0	0	4	2	.391	.368
Joe DiMaggio	.225	13	11	9	43	40	7	9	2	0	1	6	0	0	0	0	1	3	3	.279	.350
Ryne Duren	.000	3	1	0	1	1	0	0	0	0	0	0	0	0	0	0	0	0	0	.000	.000
Whitey Ford	.000	10	6	3	3	3	0	0	0	0	0	0	0	0	0	0	0	0	2	.000	.000
BRETT GARDNER	.000	1	1	0	2	2	0	0	0	0	0	0	0	0	0	0	0	0	1	.000	.000
Lou Gehrig	.222	6	6	5	24	18	4	4	1	0	2	5	0	0	0	0	0	6	6	.417	.611
Jason Giambi	.600	3	3	2	5	5	3	3	0	0	1	1	0	0	0	0	0	0	1	.600	1.200
Lefty Gomez	.167	7	5	5	6	6	0	1	0	0	0	0	0	0	0	0	0	0	3	.167	.167
Joe Gordon	.143	6	5	3	14	14	1	2	1	0	0	2	0	0	0	0	0	0	6	.143	.214
Curtis Granderson	.000	2	2	2	4	4	0	0	0	0	0	0	0	0	0	0	0	0	0	.000	.000
Rollie Hemsley	.000	1	1	1	2	2	0	0	0	0	0	0	0	0	0	0	0	0	0	.000	.000
Rickey Henderson	.273	4	4	4	12	11	1	3	0	0	0	0	0	0	0	1	0	1	2	.333	.273
Tommy Henrich	.111	5	4	2	10	9	1	1	1	0	0	0	0	0	0	0	0	1	4	.200	.222
Elston Howard	.000	12	6	1	11	9	0	0	0	0	0	0	0	0	1	0	0	1	7	.182	.000
Player	AVG	SEL	G	GS	PA	AB	R	H	2B	3B	HR	RBI	SH	SF	HP	SB	CS	BB	SO	OBP	SLG
Reggie Jackson	.333	5	4	3	8	6	0	2	0	0	0	0	0	0	0	0	0	2	2	.500	.333
Billy Johnson	---	1	1	0	0	0	0	0	0	0	0	0	0	0	0	0	0	0	0	---	---
Derek Jeter	.481	14	13	9	29	27	6	13	2	0	1	3	0	0	1	1	0	1	6	.517	.667
Tommy John	.000	2	1	0	1	1	0	0	0	0	0	0	0	0	0	0	0	0	1	.000	.000
AARON JUDGE	.200	2	2	2	6	5	1	1	0	0	1	1	0	0	0	0	0	1	1	.333	.800
Charlie Keller	.143	5	3	2	8	7	2	1	0	0	1	2	0	0	0	0	0	1	3	.250	.571
Roberto Kelly	.500	1	1	0	2	2	0	1	1	0	0	0	0	0	0	0	0	0	1	.500	1.000
Tony Kubek	.000	4	2	1	6	5	1	0	0	0	0	0	0	0	0	0	0	1	2	.167	.000
DJ LEMAHIEU	.000	1	1	1	2	2	0	0	0	0	0	0	0	0	0	0	0	0	0	.000	.000
Mickey Mantle	.233	20	16	13	52	43	5	10	0	0	2	4	0	0	0	0	1	9	17	.365	.372
Roger Maris	.118	6	6	5	21	17	2	2	1	0	0	2	0	1	0	0	0	3	4	.238	.176
Billy Martin	.000	1	1	0	1	1	0	0	0	0	0	0	0	0	0	0	0	0	0	.000	.000
Tino Martinez	.000	1	1	1	2	2	0	0	0	0	0	0	0	0	0	0	0	0	0	.000	.000
Hideki Matsui	.333	2	2	1	3	3	0	1	0	0	0	0	0	0	0	0	0	0	0	.333	.333
Don Mattingly	.111	6	6	1	11	9	0	1	1	0	0	0	0	0	0	0	0	2	2	.273	.222
Gil McDougald	.250	6	4	0	4	4	1	1	0	0	0	1	0	0	0	0	0	0	1	.250	.250
George McQuinn	.250	2	2	2	8	8	1	2	0	0	0	0	0	0	0	0	1	0	1	.250	.250
Johnny Mize	1.000	1	1	0	1	1	0	1	0	0	0	0	0	0	0	0	0	0	0	1.000	1.000
Thurman Munson	.200	7	6	3	12	10	1	2	1	0	0	0	0	0	0	0	0	1	2	.333	.300
Bobby Murcer	.091	4	4	4	12	11	0	1	0	0	0	0	0	0	0	0	1	1	1	.167	.091
Graig Nettles	.222	5	5	2	9	9	2	2	0	0	0	0	0	0	0	1	0	0	2	.222	.222
Irv Noren	---	1	1	0	0	0	0	0	0	0	0	0	0	0	0	0	0	0	0	---	---
Paul O'Neill	.000	4	4	1	6	6	0	0	0	0	0	0	0	0	0	0	0	0	1	.000	.000
Joe Pepitone	.000	3	3	1	5	5	0	0	0	0	0	0	0	0	0	0	0	0	3	.000	.000
Jorge Posada	.182	5	5	2	11	11	0	2	2	0	0	0	0	0	0	0	0	0	5	.182	.364
Willie Randolph	.308	5	4	4	13	13	0	4	0	0	0	1	0	0	0	0	0	0	3	.308	.308
Vic Raschi	.500	4	4	2	2	2	0	1	0	0	0	2	0	0	0	0	0	0	0	.500	.500
Player	AVG	SEL	G	GS	PA	AB	R	H	2B	3B	HR	RBI	SH	SF	HP	SB	CS	BB	SO	OBP	SLG
Allie Reynolds	.000	5	2	0	1	1	0	0	0	0	0	0	0	0	0	0	0	0	0	.000	.000
Bobby Richardson	.091	8	6	1	11	11	1	1	0	0	0	0	0	0	0	0	0	0	1	.091	.091
Mickey Rivers	.500	1	1	0	2	2	0	1	0	0	0	0	0	0	0	0	0	0	0	.500	.500
Phil Rizzuto	.222	5	4	2	9	9	2	2	0	0	0	1	0	0	0	0	0	0	1	.222	.222
Alex Rodriguez	.250	7	5	5	13	12	1	3	0	1	0	1	0	0	0	1	0	1	2	.308	.417
Red Rolfe	.375	4	2	2	8	8	2	3	0	1	0	2	0	0	0	0	0	0	1	.444	.625
Red Ruffing	.500	6	3	2	2	2	0	1	0	0	0	2	0	0	0	0	0	0	0	.500	.500
Babe Ruth	.333	2	2	2	8	6	2	2	0	0	1	2	0	0	0	0	0	2	3	.500	.833
GARY SÁNCHEZ	.250	2	2	1	4	4	1	1	1	0	0	0	0	0	0	0	0	0	1	.250	.500
Steve Sax	.000	2	2	1	3	2	0	0	0	0	0	0	0	0	0	0	0	1	0	.333	.000
George Selkirk	.500	2	2	1	5	2	0	1	0	0	0	0	0	0	0	0	0	3	0	.800	.500
Spec Shea	.000	1	1	0	1	1	0	0	0	0	0	0	0	0	0	0	0	0	0	.000	.000
Gary Sheffield	.000	2	2	0	2	2	0	0	0	0	0	0	0	0	0	0	0	0	0	.000	.000
Bill Skowron	.429	7	5	4	15	14	1	6	1	0	0	0	0	0	0	0	0	1	3	.467	.500
Alfonso Soriano	.200	2	2	2	5	5	1	1	0	0	1	0	0	0	0	0	0	0	2	.200	.800
Mike Stanley	.000	1	1	0	1	1	0	0	0	0	0	0	0	0	0	0	0	0	0	.000	.000
Snuffy Stirnweiss	.333	1	1	1	0	3	3	1	0	0	0	0	0	0	0	0	0	0	0	.333	.333
Nick Swisher	.000	1	1	1	1	1	0	0	0	0	0	0	0	0	0	0	0	0	1	.000	.000
Mark Teixeira	.000	2	2	1	5	5	0	0	0	0	0	0	0	0	0	0	0	0	0	.000	.000
GLEYBER TORRES	.500	2	1	0	2	2	1	1	0	0	0	1	0	0	0	0	0	0	0	.500	.500
Tom Tresh	.500	3	2	0	2	2	1	1	0	0	1	0	0	0	0	0	0	0	1	.500	1.000
Robin Ventura	.000	1	1	1	1	1	0	0	0	0	0	0	0	0	0	0	0	0	0	.000	.000
David Wells	.000	1	1	1	1	1	0	0	0	0	0	0	0	0	0	0	0	0	0	.000	.000
Roy White	.000	2	1	0	1	1	0	0	0	0	0	0	0	0	0	0	0	0	0	.000	.000
Bernie Williams	.000	5	4	1	6	5	1	0	0	0	0	0	0	0	0	0	0	1	1	.167	.000
Dave Winfield	.360	8	8	7	27	25	4	9	5	0	0	0	0	0	0	0	2	1	.407	.560
ALL-TIME TOTALS	**.230**				**626**	**566**	**63**	**130**	**24**	**3**	**12**	**50**	**0**	**4**	**9**	**2**	**54**	**134**	**.300**	**.346**	

Yankees All-Time All-Star Pitching Statistics

Data below includes all Yankees with at least one All-Star pitching appearance. Additionally, there have been 14 pitchers named to at least one All-Star team as a Yankee without ever making an All-Star appearance with the club: (Luis Arroyo-1; Tiny Bonham-2; Tommy Byrne-1; Johnny Kucks-1; Johnny Murphy-3; Phil Niekro-1; Monte Pearson-1; Marius Russo-1; CC Sabathia-3; Johnny Sain-1; Scott Sanderson-1; Bobby Shantz-1; Ralph Terry-2; and John Wetteland-1).

Pitcher	SEL	G	GS	W-L	ERA	GF	CG	SHO	SV	IP	H	R	ER	HR	HP	BB	IBB	SO	WP	BK	BF
Dellin Betances	4	3	0	0-0	0.00	0	0	0	0	3.0	2	0	0	0	0	3	0	5	3	0	14
Hank Borowy	1	1	1	0-0	0.00	0	0	0	0	3.0	3	0	0	0	0	1	0	0	0	0	12
Jim Bouton	1	1	0	0-0	0.00	0	0	0	0	1.0	0	0	0	0	0	0	0	0	0	0	3
Spud Chandler	4	1	1	1-0	0.00	0	0	0	0	4.0	2	0	0	0	0	1	0	2	0	0	14
AROLDIS CHAPMAN	2	1	0	0-0	0.00	1	0	0	1	1.0	0	0	0	0	0	0	0	3	0	0	3
Roger Clemens	2	2	1	0-0	0.00	0	0	0	0	3.0	0	0	0	0	0	0	0	3	0	0	9
Jim Coates	2	1	0	0-0	0.00	0	0	0	0	2.0	2	0	0	0	0	1	0	0	0	0	8
David Cone	2	2	0	0-0	3.00	0	0	0	0	3.0	4	1	1	0	0	3	0	3	0	0	15
Ron Davis	1	1	0	0-0	9.00	0	0	0	0	1.0	1	1	1	0	0	0	0	1	0	0	4
Al Downing	1	1	0	0-0	0.00	0	0	0	0	2.0	2	0	0	0	0	0	0	2	0	0	8
Ryne Duren	3	1	0	0-0	0.00	0	0	0	0	3.0	1	0	0	0	0	1	0	4	0	0	10
Whitey Ford	10	6	3	0-0	8.25	0	0	0	0	12.0	19	13	11	3	0	3	0	5	0	0	57
Lefty Gomez	7	5	5	3-1	2.50	0	0	0	0	18.0	11	6	5	2	0	3	0	9	0	0	68
Tom Gordon	1	1	0	0-0	0.00	0	0	0	0	0.1	0	0	0	0	0	0	0	0	0	0	1
Rich Gossage	4	2	0	0-1	18.00	2	0	0	0	2.0	5	4	4	0	0	1	0	1	1	0	11
Bob Grim	1	1	0	0-0	0.00	1	0	0	0	0.1	0	0	0	0	0	0	0	0	0	0	1
Ron Guidry	4	2	0	0-0	0.00	1	0	0	0	0.2	0	0	0	0	0	1	0	0	0	0	3
Phil Hughes	1	1	0	0-1	54.00	0	0	0	0	0.1	2	2	2	0	0	0	0	0	0	0	3
Catfish Hunter	2	2	0	0-1	9.00	0	0	0	0	4.0	5	4	4	1	0	0	0	5	0	0	17
Tommy John	2	1	0	0-1	11.57	0	0	0	0	2.1	4	3	3	1	0	0	0	1	0	0	11
Jimmy Key	2	2	1	0-0	6.00	0	0	0	0	3.0	3	2	2	0	0	0	0	0	0	0	12
Eddie Lopat	1	1	0	0-1	27.00	0	0	0	0	1.0	3	3	3	2	0	0	0	0	0	0	6
Sparky Lyle	3	2	0	0-0	6.00	1	0	0	0	3.0	4	2	2	0	1	0	0	2	1	0	13
Andrew Miller	1	1	0	0-0	0.00	0	0	0	0	0.2	2	0	0	0	0	1	0	1	0	0	5
Joe Page	3	1	0	0-0	0.00	1	0	0	0	1.1	1	0	0	0	0	1	0	0	0	0	6
Fritz Peterson	1	1	0	0-0	0.00	0	0	0	0	0.0	1	0	0	0	0	0	0	0	0	0	1
Andy Pettitte	3	2	0	0-0	0.00	0	0	0	0	2.0	2	0	0	0	0	0	0	3	0	0	8
Vic Raschi	4	4	2	1-0	2.45	1	0	0	0	11.0	7	3	3	1	0	4	0	8	0	0	44
Allie Reynolds	5	2	0	0-1	3.60	0	0	0	0	5.0	3	2	2	0	1	2	1	2	0	0	22
Dave Righetti	2	2	0	0-0	0.00	1	0	0	0	1.0	3	0	0	0	0	0	0	0	0	0	6
Mariano Rivera	13	9	0	0-0	0.00	6	0	0	4	9.0	5	1	0	0	0	0	0	5	0	0	30
David Robertson	1	1	0	0-0	0.00	0	0	0	0	1.0	1	0	0	0	0	0	0	1	0	0	3
Red Ruffing	6	3	2	0-1	9.00	0	0	0	0	7.0	13	7	7	1	0	2	1	6	0	0	36
LUIS SEVERINO	2	1	0	0-0	0.00	0	0	0	0	1.0	1	0	0	0	0	0	0	2	0	0	4
Spec Shea	1	1	0	1-0	3.00	0	0	0	0	3.0	3	1	1	1	0	2	0	2	0	0	14
Mike Stanton	1	1	0	0-0	0.00	0	0	0	0	0.2	0	0	0	0	0	0	0	0	0	0	2
Mel Stottlemyre	5	4	1	0-1	3.00	0	0	0	0	6.0	5	3	2	1	0	1	1	4	1	0	25
MASAHIRO TANAKA	2	1	0	1-0	0.00	0	0	0	0	1.0	1	0	0	0	0	0	0	1	0	0	4
Bob Turley	2	1	1	0-0	16.20	0	0	0	0	1.2	3	3	3	0	1	2	0	0	1	0	11
Javier Vazquez	1	1	0	0-0	0.00	0	0	0	0	1.0	0	0	0	0	0	0	0	2	0	0	3
David Wells	1	1	1	0-0	0.00	0	0	0	0	2.0	0	0	0	0	0	1	0	1	0	0	6
ALL-TIME TOTALS		77	19	7-11	3.99	14	0	0	5	126.1	124	61	56	14	5	31	3	85	7	0	533

Yankees Single-Game All-Star Highs

MLB All-time MLB All-Star Game high / AL All-time American League All-Star Game high / † tied for high

BATTING

Most AB: 6, 3x – Berra & Mantle-1955 (12 inn.) and Rizzuto-1950 (14 inn.); In 9 inn. game – 5, 4x Randolph-1977; Mantle-1956; DiMaggio-1936; B. Chapman-1933
Most R: 3, 1x – DiMaggio-1941
Most H: 3, 3x – Jeter-2004 & '00; Winfield-1983
Most 2B: 1, 24x – last by SÁNCHEZ-2019
Most 3B: 1, 3x – A. Rodriguez-2004; Rolfe-1937; B. Chapman-1934
Most HR: 1, 12x – Judge-2018; Giambi-2003; Soriano-2002; Jeter-2001; Berra-1959 (G2); Mantle-1956 & '55; Keller-1946; DiMaggio-1939; Gehrig-1937 & '36; Ruth-1933
Most RBI: 4, 1x – Gehrig-1937
Most SB: 1, 9x – last by Jeter-2008
Most BB: 2, 8x – last by Mattingly-1987
Most K: MLB 3, 1x – Gordon-1942; Gehrig-1934 (tied w/ many for most in 9 inn. game)

PITCHING

Wins: 7x – TANAKA-2019; Raschi-1948; Shea-1947, Chandler-1942; Gomez-1937, '35, '33
Losses: 11x – Hughes-2010; John-1980; Gossage-1978; Hunter-1975; Stottlemyre-1969; Ford-1960 (G2) & '59 (G1); Reynolds-1953; Lopat-1951; Ruffing-1940; Gomez-1938
Saves: 5x – CHAPMAN-2019; Rivera-2009, '06, '05, 1997
Most IP: MLB 6.0, 1x – Gomez-1935
Most H: 5, 3x – Ford-1960 (G2) & '55; Ruffing-1940
Most K: MLB 5, 1x – Ford-1955
Most ER: 4, 2x – Gossage-1978; Gomez-1934
Most BB: 3, 1x – Raschi-1949
Most K: 4, 3x – Duren-1959 (G1); Ruffing-1939; Gomez-1935
Most HR: 2, 3x – Ford-1960 (G2); Lopat-1951; Gomez-1934

Yankees All-Star Game Notes and Highlights

Since the game originated in 1933, the Yankees have had the most All-Star players (131) and most total All-Star selections (430) of any Major League franchise…the Yankees have had two ASG MVPs — Derek Jeter (2000) and Mariano Rivera (2013)…Yankees pitcher Lefty Gomez is the only pitcher in All-Star Game history to earn three wins (1933, '35, '37), having made five career All-Star starts…Babe Ruth hit the first-ever All-Star homer in 1933 off the Cardinals' Bill Hallahan…Joe DiMaggio-1936, Hideki Matsui-2003 and Aaron Judge-2017 own the distinction of being the only Yankees rookies to start for the American League…Judge totaled 4,488,702 fan votes in 2017 to become the first Yankee since Derek Jeter (2009) to lead the AL in balloting…Jeter's .481 (13-for-27) career All-Star average is second all time among batters with at least 15 All-Star ABs, trailing only Detroit's Charlie Gehringer (.500, 10-for-20).

Yankees All-Star Career Top 10 Leaders

^{MLB} All-time Major League All-Star Game high / ^{AL} All-time American League All-Star Game high / ^t tied for high

BATTING

Games Played
1. Mickey Mantle 16
2. Yogi Berra 15
3. Derek Jeter 13
4. Joe DiMaggio 11
5. Dave Winfield 8
   Bill Dickey 8
7. Gehrig, Ford, Howard, Maris, Mattingly, Munson, Richardson 6

Games Started
1. Mickey Mantle (CF-12; RF-1) 13
2. Yogi Berra (C-11) 11
3. Derek Jeter (SS-9) 9
   Joe DiMaggio (CF-6; RF-3) 9
5. Dave Winfield (RF-5; CF-1; LF-1) 7
6. Bill Dickey (C-6) 6
7. Lou Gehrig (1B-5) 5
   Lefty Gomez (P-5) 5
   Roger Maris (RF-3; CF-2) 5
   Alex Rodriguez (3B-5) 5

Plate Appearances
1. Mickey Mantle 52
2. Yogi Berra 43
   Joe DiMaggio 43
4. Derek Jeter 29
5. Dave Winfield 27
6. Lou Gehrig 24
7. Bill Dickey 23
8. Roger Maris 21
9. Bill Skowron 15
10. Joe Gordon 14

At-Bats
1. Mickey Mantle 43
2. Yogi Berra 41
3. Joe DiMaggio 40
4. Derek Jeter 27
5. Dave Winfield 25
6. Bill Dickey 19
7. Lou Gehrig 18
8. Roger Maris 17
9. Bill Skowron 14
   Joe Gordon 14

Runs
1. Joe DiMaggio 7
2. Derek Jeter 6
3. Mickey Mantle 5
   Yogi Berra 5
5. Dave Winfield 4
   Lou Gehrig 4
7. Bill Dickey 3
   Jason Giambi 3
9. Maris, Rolfe, Keller, Ruth 2

Hits
1. Derek Jeter 13
2. Mickey Mantle 10
3. Joe DiMaggio 9
   Dave Winfield 9
5. Yogi Berra 8
6. Bill Skowron 6
7. Bill Dickey 5
8. Lou Gehrig 4
   Willie Randolph 4
10. Dent, Giambi, Henderson, A. Rodriguez, Rolfe 3

Doubles
1. Dave Winfield .... ^{AL} 5
2. Dickey, DiMaggio, Jeter, Posada 2
6. Dent, Gehrig, Gordon, Henrich, R. Kelly, Maris, Mattingly, Munson, SÁNCHEZ, Skowron, Tresh 1

Triples
1. Ben Chapman 1
   Alex Rodriguez 1
   Red Rolfe 1

Home Runs
1. Lou Gehrig 2
   Mickey Mantle 2
3. Berra, DiMaggio, Giambi, Jeter, JUDGE, Keller, Ruth, Soriano 1

RBI
1. Joe DiMaggio 6
2. Lou Gehrig 5
3. Mickey Mantle 4
4. Yogi Berra 3
   Derek Jeter 3
6. Gordon, Keller, R. Kelly, Maris, Raschi, Rolfe, Ruffing, Ruth 2

Batting Average (min. 10AB)
1. Derek Jeter .... .481
2. Bill Skowron .... .429
3. Dave Winfield .... .360
4. Willie Randolph .... .308
5. Rickey Henderson .... .273
6. Bill Dickey .... .263
7. Alex Rodriguez .... .250
8. Mickey Mantle .... .233
9. Joe DiMaggio .... .225
10. Lou Gehrig .... .222

Slugging Percentage (min. 10AB)
1. Derek Jeter .... .667
2. Lou Gehrig .... .600
3. Dave Winfield .... .560
4. Bill Skowron .... .500
5. Alex Rodriguez .... .417
6. Mickey Mantle .... .372
7. Bill Dickey .... .368
8. Jorge Posada .... .364
9. Joe DiMaggio .... .350
10. Willie Randolph .... .308

Other Career Records
^{MLB} Mickey Mantle is the all-time ASG leader in strikeouts (17).

PITCHING

Appearances
1. Mariano Rivera 9
2. Whitey Ford 6
3. Lefty Gomez 5
4. Vic Raschi 4
   Mel Stottlemyre 4
6. Dellin Betances, Red Ruffing 3
7. Clemens, Cone, Gossage, Guidry, Hunter, Key, Lyle, Pettitte, Reynolds, Righetti 2

Games Started
1. Lefty Gomez .... ^{MLBt/ALt} 5
2. Whitey Ford 3
3. Vic Raschi 2
   Red Ruffing 2
5. Borowy, Chandler, Clemens, Key, Stottlemyre, Turley, Wells 1

Innings Pitched
1. Lefty Gomez .... ^{AL} 18.0
2. Whitey Ford 12.0
3. Vic Raschi 11.0
4. Mariano Rivera 9.0
5. Red Ruffing 7.0
6. Mel Stottlemyre 6.0
7. Allie Reynolds 5.0
8. Spud Chandler 4.0
   Catfish Hunter 4.0
10. Betances, Borowy, Clemens, Cone, Duren, Key, Lyle, Shea 3.0

Wins
1. Lefty Gomez .... ^{MLB} 3
2. Spud Chandler 1
   Vic Raschi 1
   Spec Shea 1
   MASAHIRO TANAKA 1

Losses
1. Whitey Ford .... ^{MLBt/ALt} 2
2. Gomez, Gossage, Hughes, Hunter, John, Lopat, Reynolds, Ruffing, Stottlemyre 1

Strikeouts
1. Lefty Gomez 9
2. Vic Raschi 8
3. Red Ruffing 6
4. Dellin Betances 5
   Whitey Ford 5
   Catfish Hunter 5
   Mariano Rivera 5
8. Ryne Duren 4
   Mel Stottlemyre 4
10. CHAPMAN, Clemens, Cone, Pettitte .. 3

ERA (min. 3.0IP)
1. Dellin Betances 0.00
   Hank Borowy 0.00
   Spud Chandler 0.00
   Roger Clemens 0.00
   Ryne Duren 0.00
   Mariano Rivera 0.00
7. Vic Raschi 2.45
8. Lefty Gomez 2.50
9. David Cone 3.00
   Spec Shea 3.00
   Mel Stottlemyre 3.00

Saves (official stat since 1969)
1. Mariano Rivera .... ^{MLB} 4
2. Aroldis Chapman 1

Other Career Records
^{MLB} Whitey Ford is the all-time ASG leader in runs (13), ER (11) and hits (18) allowed.

All-Star MVPs
(Award given since 1962)

Derek Jeter and **Mariano Rivera** are the only Yankees to be named All-Star MVP. Jeter took home the honor at the 2000 All-Star Game at Turner Field in Atlanta with a 3-for-3 performance with 1R, 1 double and 2RBI. He doubled in the first inning off Randy Johnson, singled and scored in the third off Kevin Brown and had a two-run single in the fourth off Al Leiter in the American League's 6-3 win. Rivera received the honor at the 2013 Midsummer Classic at Citi Field, tossing a scoreless eighth inning (Jean Segura groundout to 2B, Allen Craig lineout to LF, Carlos Gomez groundout to SS) in the AL's 3-0 win.

All-Star Games at the Original Yankee Stadium

The Yankees have hosted four All-Star Games, including the 2008 Midsummer Classic in the original Yankee Stadium's final season. The Stadium also hosted the All-Star Game in 1977 (48th), 1960 (29th) and 1939 (seventh). Only Cleveland's old Municipal Stadium hosted as many All-Star Games as Yankee Stadium. Overall, New York City has hosted nine MLB All-Star Games, the highest total in Major League history, with the Polo Grounds (1934 and 1942), Ebbets Field (1949), Shea Stadium (1964) and Citi Field (2013) also serving as host sites. The 2008 game marked the first time the Midsummer Classic was held in the host team's final season at its ballpark.

Seventh All-Star Game
American League 3, National League 1
July 11, 1939, Yankee Stadium

Yankee Stadium was chosen to host the 1939 All-Star Game due to the World's Fair which was being held at Flushing Meadows in Queens during the 1939 season. The Cubs' Gabby Hartnett managed the National League squad while Yankees skipper Joe McCarthy led the American League team, which featured nine Yankees All-Stars (Crosetti, Dickey, Dimaggio, Gomez, Gordon, Murphy, Rolfe, Ruffing, Selkirk), six of whom started. Additionally, Lou Gehrig (who retired earlier that season) was named an honorary member of the AL squad. Yankees centerfielder Joe DiMaggio went 1-for-4 in the game, hitting a solo home run.

All-Star Team	1	2	3	4	5	6	7	8	9	R	H	E
National League	0	0	1	0	0	0	0	0	0	1	7	1
American League	0	0	0	2	1	0	0	0	x	3	6	1

Winning Pitcher: Tommy Bridges (DET)
Losing Pitcher: Bill Lee (CHC)
MVP: None Selected

29th All-Star Game
National League 6, American League 0
July 13, 1960 (Game #2), Yankee Stadium

Yankee Stadium was the host site for baseball's second All-Star Game in three days in 1960. The National League completed the All-Star sweep with a 6-0 win, having won Game 1 on July 11 in Kansas City, marking the only year that both All-Star games were won by the same team. Yankees hurler Whitey Ford was the starting pitcher for the AL squad, while fellow Yankees Yogi Berra (catcher), Mickey Mantle (left field), Roger Maris (center field) and Bill Skowron (first base) all appeared in the starting lineup. The National League used six different pitchers to combine on the shutout effort and hit an All-Star record-tying four home runs, including one by Willie Mays. The 38,000 fans who attended the game witnessed Ted Williams in his final All-Star appearance.

All-Star Team	1	2	3	4	5	6	7	8	9	R	H	E
National League	0	2	1	0	0	0	1	0	2	6	10	0
American League	0	0	0	0	0	0	0	0	0	0	8	0

Winning Pitcher: Vern Law (PIT)
Losing Pitcher: Whitey Ford (NYY)
MVP: None Selected

48th All-Star Game
National League 7, American League 5
July 19, 1977, Yankee Stadium

Showcasing its renovation, Yankee Stadium hosted the All-Star Game on July 19, 1977, in a game dedicated to Jackie Robinson. With the Yankees defending their 1976 pennant, Billy Martin managed the AL team on his home field. The National League won its sixth consecutive All-Star Game, part of the Senior Circuit's 11-game win streak. Joe Morgan opened the game with a home run off Jim Palmer as the NL squad scored four first-inning runs. Yankees outfielder Reggie Jackson and second baseman Willie Randolph were AL starters. National League Manager Sparky Anderson described the game's final score by saying, "the only reason we're here is to kick the living hell out of those guys."

All-Star Team	1	2	3	4	5	6	7	8	9	R	H	E
National League	4	0	1	0	0	0	0	2	0	7	9	1
American League	0	0	0	0	2	1	0	2	0	5	8	0

Winning Pitcher: Don Sutton (LAD)
Losing Pitcher: Jim Palmer (BAL)
MVP: Don Sutton (LAD)

79th All-Star Game
American League 4, National League 3
July 15, 2008, Yankee Stadium

In the final Midsummer Classic at the original Yankee Stadium, the American League emerged with a 4-3 win in 15 innings as Texas' Michael Young brought home Minnesota's Justin Morneau with a "walk-off" sacrifice fly. The 4-hour, 50-minute contest was the longest All-Star Game time-wise and tied for the longest ASG in innings (also 1967 at Anaheim, 2-1 NL win). It was the AL's 12th straight All-Star Game victory and ensured American League home-field advantage in the World Series. SS Derek Jeter started and recorded the game's first hit in the first inning. RHP Mariano Rivera pitched 1.2 scoreless innings. Yankees Manager Joe Girardi joined the AL coaching staff as did Yankees Head Athletic Trainer Gene Monahan, who made his fourth All-Star Game appearance (also 1977, '86 and '92). Pregame ceremonies included 49 Hall of Famers, marking one of the largest gatherings of living baseball HOFers ever. The festivities were highlighted by Yankees Principal Owner/Chairperson George Steinbrenner, who delivered baseballs to the ceremonial first pitch participants (Reggie Jackson, Whitey Ford, Yogi Berra and Goose Gossage).

All-Star Team	1	2	3	4	5	6	7	8	9	10	11	12	13	14	15	R	H	E
National League	0	0	0	0	1	1	0	1	0	0	0	0	0	0	0	3	13	4
American League	0	0	0	0	0	0	2	1	0	0	0	0	0	0	1	4	14	1

Winning Pitcher: Scott Kazmir (TB)
Losing Pitcher: Brad Lidge (PHI)
MVP: J.D. Drew (BOS)

Exhibition Games vs. Mets/Dodgers/Giants

Notable Exhibitions between the Yankees, Dodgers and Giants

The Yankees, Dodgers and Giants played a number of preseason games against each other over the years in Florida and on the East Coast (while heading north from spring training). The clubs also played games in New York just prior to the start of the season. Additionally, many in-season exhibitions were arranged, including the Mayor's Trophy Games (noted in left column) and other charitable endeavors. Some of the most notable games are listed below.

July 4, 1909 - At Washington Park in Brooklyn, the Yankees dropped a benefit game for newsboys, 7-3. Due to a rule banning exhibition games between teams of the AL and NL, the catchers and pitchers switched teams for the contest.

Sept. 4, 1910 - The Yankees defeated the Giants, 4-2, in a newsboys benefit at Washington Park in Brooklyn, with various Dodgers (then known as the Superbas) playing for both teams.

October 1910 - The Yankees and Giants faced each other for the first time in a series of exhibition games following the 1910 regular season (while the World Series was contested elsewhere). Pitcher Christy Mathewson won three of the games as the Giants won the series, 4 games to 2. In a similar exhibition rematch after the 1914 regular season, the Giants again defeated the Yankees, 4 games to 1.

Apr. 21, 1912 - At the Polo Grounds, the Yankees and Giants staged a benefit game for survivors of the Titanic. The Giants won, 11-2, as $9,425.25 was raised before a crowd of 14,083.

Apr. 5 and 7, 1913 - The Yankees helped the Dodgers (known then as the "Superbas") open Ebbets Field with an exhibition game won by Brooklyn, 3-2, in front of approximately 30,000 fans. Dodgers rookie outfielder Casey Stengel hits the park's first unofficial home run. Two days later, in icy conditions before approximately 1,000 fans at Ebbets field, the Yankees came out on top, 8-4.

Sept. 30, 1917 - On a tiny field at Fort Hamilton in Brooklyn, the Yankees defeated the Dodgers (then known as the Robins), 11-8. Seven "home runs" were hit in a game played for soldiers soon to be sent off to fight in World War I.

Sept. 9 and 24, 1931- The three local clubs played a two-day, round-robin with proceeds going to the Mayor's Unemployment Fund. In the first game in front of 60,549 fans at Yankee Stadium, the Yankees defeated the Giants, 7-3, netting $59,642 as Babe Ruth hit the game's only home run. On Sept. 24, the teams played a doubleheader at the Polo Grounds, bringing in $48,135 for the fund with 44,119 fans on hand. The Giants defeated Brooklyn, 3-1, in Game 1 and the Yankees defeated the Dodgers (then known as the "Robins"), 5-1, in Game 2 behind homers from Lyn Lary, Bill Dickey and Lou Gehrig. Contests among the players were held in between games, including Babe Ruth hitting the longest fungo (421 ft., 8 in.) and Ben Chapman making the longest throw (392 ft., 10 in.).

June 26, 1944 - The Yankees, Giants and Dodgers played a mid-season "three-cornered" exhibition game at the Polo Grounds, which generated over $6.5 million worth of war bond sales. Each team batted in six innings and played defense for six innings with Brooklyn coming out on top (Dodgers 5 - Yankees 1 - Giants 0). The clubs reprised the format for the sake of charity five years later (see entry for July 11, 1949).

July 9, 1945 - The Yankees defeated the Giants, 7-1, in a rain-shortened 7-inn. game in front of 41,267 at the Polo Grounds. The contest was one of seven interleague games in the Majors to benefit the war effort and serve as a substitute for the All-Star Game, which had been canceled.

July 11, 1949 - In a reprise of their June 26, 1944, exhibition game at the Polo Grounds (see above), the Yankees, Giants and Dodgers played a three-cornered "Night of Champions" benefit game for the N.Y. Heart Fund, Babe Ruth Foundation and Lou Gehrig Memorial Fund. Approximately $32,000 was raised as 26,120 Yankee Stadium spectators saw Brooklyn win on total runs, 6 to 3 to 3.

Oct. 12, 1958 - In a rare postseason exhibition at Yankee Stadium, a team of AL All-Stars led by Mickey Mantle lost to a team of NL All-Stars led by Willie Mays, 6-2, in front of 21,129.

May 7, 1959 - At the L.A. Coliseum in front of a record baseball crowd of 93,103, the Yankees defeated the Dodgers, 6-2, with net proceeds going to benefit recently paralyzed catcher Roy Campanella.

June 27, 1960 - The Dodgers defeated the Yankees, 4-3, in front of 53,492 in their first game at Yankee Stadium since Don Larsen's perfect game in the 1956 World Series.

July 24, 1961 - The Giants defeated the Yankees, 4-1, in front of 47,346 at Yankee Stadium. Mickey Mantle's solo HR accounts for the Yankees' only run.

Mayor's Trophy Game

In the majority of seasons from 1944-83, the Yankees played the Giants, Dodgers or Mets in an annual mid-season exhibition game. The Mayor's office began sponsoring the contests beginning in 1946 and awarded a trophy to the game's winner. The proceeds from each game supported sandlot baseball programs and other New York charities. The Yankees won 20 of the 32 Mayor's Trophy Games played, going 7-1 vs. the Giants, 3-2 vs. the Dodgers and 10-8-1 vs. the Mets.

Date	Score	Location	Att.
7/1/46	Yankees 3 - Giants 0	Polo Grounds	27,486
8/5/46	Yankees 3 - Giants 2	Yankee Stadium	25,067
6/12/47	Yankees 7 - Giants 0	Polo Grounds	39,970
8/18/47	Giants 4 - Yankees 1	Yankee Stadium	22,184
8/16/48	Yankees 4 - Giants 2 (11)	Polo Grounds	17,091
6/27/49	Yankees 5 - Giants 3	Yankee Stadium	37,537
6/26/50	Yankees 9 - Giants 4	Polo Grounds	12,864
6/25/51	Yankees 4 - Dodgers 3 (10)	Yankee Stadium	71,289
7/21/52	Yankees 5 - Dodgers 3 (8)	Yankee Stadium	48,263
6/29/53	Dodgers 9 - Yankees 0	Yankee Stadium	56,136
6/14/54	Dodgers 2 - Yankees 1	Yankee Stadium	28,084
6/27/55	Yankees 4 - Giants 1	Yankee Stadium	19,193
1956	NO GAMES PLAYED		
5/23/57	Yankees 10 - Dodgers 7	Ebbets Field	30,000
1958-62	NO GAMES PLAYED		
6/20/63	Mets 6 - Yankees 2	Yankee Stadium	50,742
8/24/64	Yankees 6 - Mets 4	Shea Stadium	55,396
5/3/65	Mets 2 - Yankees 1 (10)	Yankee Stadium	22,881
6/27/66	Yankees 5 - Mets 2	Shea Stadium	56,367
7/12/67	Mets 4 - Yankees 0	Yankee Stadium	31,852
5/27/68	Mets 4 - Yankees 3	Shea Stadium	35,198
9/29/69	Mets 7 - Yankees 6	Shea Stadium	32,720
8/17/70	Yankees 9 - Mets 4	Shea Stadium	43,987
9/9/71	Yankees 2 - Mets 1	Shea Stadium	48,872
8/24/72	Yankees 2 - Mets 1	Yankee Stadium	53,949
5/10/73	Mets 8 - Yankees 4	Shea Stadium	36,915
5/30/74	Yankees 8 - Mets 4	Shea Stadium	35,894
5/15/75	Yankees 9 - Mets 4	Shea Stadium	26,427
6/14/76	Yankees 8 - Mets 4	Yankee Stadium	36,361
6/23/77	Mets 6 - Yankees 4	Shea Stadium	15,510
4/27/78	Yankees 4 - Mets 3 (13)	Yankee Stadium	9,792
4/16/79	Yankees 1 - Mets 1 (5)	Shea Stadium	13,719
1980-81	NO GAMES PLAYED		
5/27/82	Mets 4 - Yankees 1	Yankee Stadium	41,614
4/21/83	Yankees 4 - Mets 1	Shea Stadium	20,471

Big Apple Series (1989-90) and Mayor's Challenge (1992-93)

The Yankees and Mets also played a series of exhibition games at their respective home stadiums prior to the start of the season.

Date	Score	Location	Att.
4/1/89	Yankees 4 - Mets 3	Yankee Stadium	52,119
4/2/89	Yankees 4 - Mets 0	Shea Stadium	54,128
4/8/90	Mets 2 - Yankees 1	Yankee Stadium	32,843
4/4/92	Yankees 6 - Mets 4	Shea Stadium	26,038
4/5/92	Yankees 6 - Mets 5	Shea Stadium	38,579
4/3/93	Mets 5 - Yankees 1	Shea Stadium	14,425
4/4/93	Mets 7 - Yankees 2	Yankee Stadium	24,782

Spring Training Games vs. the Mets

The Yankees and Mets used to meet on a regular basis in spring training, dating back to the Mets' inaugural season in 1962. The very first game between the clubs was a 4-3 Mets victory on March 22, 1962, at their spring facility in St. Petersburg. The clubs met twice during the spring last year, with the Yankees winning both games (3/7/18 at Port St. Lucie, 11-4; and 3/10/18 at GMS Field, 10-3). The clubs are not scheduled to meet during 2020 spring training.

Year	Record	Year	Record	Year	Record	Year	Record
1962	1-1	1972	0-1	1982	0-1	1992	3-1
1963	1-1	1973	3-3	1983	1-0	1993	2-0
1964	1-1	1974	3-2	1984	2-0	1994	2-2
1965	1-1	1975	3-2	1985	1-1	1995	4-3
1966	1-0	1976	4-1	1986	0-0	1996	1-1
1967	2-0	1977	1-2	1987	0-0	2012	1-1
1968	2-0	1978	2-0	1988	0-0	2015	0-2
1969	1-0	1979	1-1	1989	2-2	2016	1-0-1
1970	1-1	1980	0-0	1990	0-1	2018	2-0
1971	1-1	1981	1-1	1991	0-0	Tot.	50-36-1

Head Athletic Trainers

Unknown/Unavailable (1)	1903
Mike Martin	1904–08
James Burke (2)	start 1909–8/22/1909
Jack McCormick	8/23/1909–end 1909
Harry Lee	1910–11
Daniel Mulcahey (3)	start 1912–mid 1912
Charles Barrett (4)	mid 1912–1914
Jimmy Duggan	1915–17
Al "Doc" Woods	1918–29
Erle "Doc" Painter	1930–42
Eddie Froelich	1943–47
Gus Mauch (5)	1948–61
Joe Soares	1962–72
Gene Monahan	1973–2011
Steve Donohue	2012–19

(1) Research has been unable to determine if the club had a trainer in 1903.
(2) Burke suffered health problems during the season and was replaced by McCormick.
(3) Alternately spelled "Mulcahy." Was released from duties midseason. Exact date unknown.
(4) Was also a trainer at Williams College and reportedly worked with the team during the summers of 1910 and 1911.
(5) Handled spring training operations in 1947.

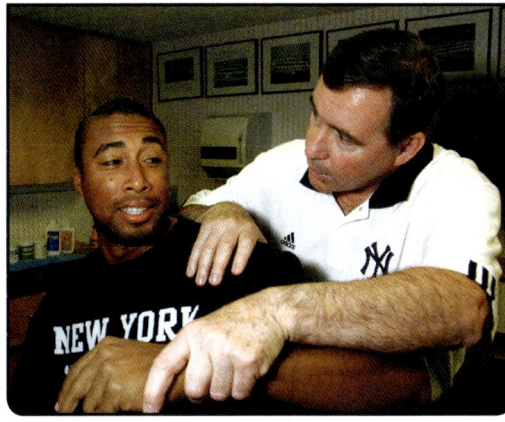

Gene Monahan [R] tends to Bernie Williams in the Yankees training room at the original Yankee Stadium. "Geno" is the longest-serving head trainer in club history, having manned the post for 29 years from 1973-2011.

Yankees assistant trainers have included: Gus Mauch (1946), Joe Soares (1960-61), Don Seger (1962-68), Herman Schneider (1977-78), Barry Weinberg (1979-81), Mark Letendre (1982-85), Steve Donohue (1986-2011), Mark Littlefield (2012-15), Michael Schuk (2015-19) and Tim Lentych (2016-19).

Forfeited Games

The Yankees have played in four forfeited games in their history (described below), winning them all. Player statistics from forfeited games count in the historical record, however the final score of each game is officially recorded as 9-0. Interestingly, a forfeited game precipitated the creation of the Yankees franchise.

The Baltimore Orioles were a charter member of the American League in 1901. Prior to their game vs. St. Louis on July 17, 1902, New York Giants owner Andrew Freedman and Cincinnati Reds owner John T. Brush gained a controlling interest in Baltimore with the help of its former manager John McGraw. The two owners then sent almost all of the Orioles players to their respective NL teams, leaving the Orioles unable to field a squad. Though the they were forced to forfeit that day, the American League soon stepped in by providing players from other teams so they could finish the season. At the end of the season, the Orioles were dissolved and a new franchise filling its AL spot was established in New York in 1903.

In their short time in Baltimore, the Orioles also participated in three other forfeits, all of which were losses (May 31, 1901 at Detroit; August 21, 1901 vs. Detroit; and June 28, 1902 vs. Boston).

July 2, 1906 at Philadelphia (Game 2): With two outs in the bottom of the ninth inning and the Highlanders leading, 5-1, Columbia Park spectators started swarming the field. According to *The New York Times*, "the three or four policemen on hand to handle the crowd of 11,000 spectators were powerless." After waiting 15 minutes, umpire Timothy C. Hurst forfeited the game to the Highlanders.

September 3, 1906 vs. Philadelphia (Game 2): With two outs in the bottom of the ninth and the Highlanders trailing, 3-1, with runners on second (Willie Keeler) and third (Wid Conroy), Jimmy Williams hit a grounder to A's shortstop Monte Cross. Keeler ran into Cross just as he was about to handle the ball, allowing the ball to roll into outfield and Conroy and Keeler to score, tying the game. After a heated argument from A's first baseman and captain Harry Davis, umpire Frank O'Loughlin awarded the game to New York.

June 13, 1924 at Detroit: At the start of the ninth inning at Navin Field with the Yankees leading, 10-6, Tigers pitcher Bert Cole threw a pitch that narrowly missed hitting Babe Ruth in the head. Cole immediately hit the next batter, Bob Meusel, with a pitch in the ribs. Meusel's protest incited a riot, leading to both benches becoming involved and the storming of the field by incensed fans. Umpire William G. Evans was forced to forfeit the game to the Yankees when the field could not be cleared. Ultimately, Meusel was fined $100 and suspended 10 days, Cole was fined $50 and suspended 10 days, and Ruth received a $50 fine but no suspension. AL President Ban Johnson said of the fights that day, "They must be staged in a vacant lot, far removed from the ball parks."

September 30, 1971 at Washington: At Robert F. Kennedy Stadium, unruly fans cascaded onto the field with two outs in the top of the ninth inning and the Senators winning, 7-5, in the last game before the Senators' relocation to Texas for the 1972 season. After three minutes of on-field chaos, including the bases literally being stolen, the umpires awarded the Yankees the victory.

Yankees Postseason Series-by-Series

YEAR	SERIES	OPP.	W	L
1921	WS	Giants	3	5
1922*	WS	Giants (1 tie)	0	4
1923	WS	Giants	4	2
1926	WS	Cardinals	3	4
1927	WS	Pirates	4	0
1928	WS	Cardinals	4	0
1932	WS	Cubs	4	0
1936	WS	Giants	4	2
1937	WS	Giants	4	1
1938	WS	Cubs	4	0
1939	WS	Reds	4	0
1941	WS	Dodgers	4	1
1942	WS	Cardinals	1	4
1943	WS	Cardinals	4	1
1947	WS	Dodgers	4	3
1949	WS	Dodgers	4	1
1950	WS	Phillies	4	0
1951	WS	Giants	4	2
1952	WS	Dodgers	4	3
1953	WS	Dodgers	4	2
1955	WS	Dodgers	3	4
1956	WS	Dodgers	4	3
1957	WS	Braves	3	4
1958	WS	Braves	4	3
1960	WS	Pirates	3	4
1961	WS	Reds	4	1
1962	WS	Giants	4	3
1963	WS	Dodgers	0	4
1964	WS	Cardinals	3	4
1976	LCS	Royals	3	2
	WS	Reds	0	4
1977	LCS	Royals	3	2
	WS	Dodgers	4	2
1978	LCS	Royals	3	1
	WS	Dodgers	4	2
1980	LCS	Royals	0	3
1981	DS	Brewers	3	2
	LCS	Athletics	3	0
	WS	Dodgers	2	4
1995	DS	Mariners	2	3
1996	DS	Rangers	3	1
	LCS	Orioles	4	1
	WS	Braves	4	2
1997	DS	Indians	2	3
1998	DS	Rangers	3	0
	LCS	Indians	4	2
	WS	Padres	4	0
1999	DS	Rangers	3	0
	LCS	Red Sox	4	1
	WS	Braves	4	0
2000	DS	Athletics	3	2
	LCS	Mariners	4	2
	WS	Mets	4	1
2001	DS	Athletics	3	2
	LCS	Mariners	4	1
	WS	D-backs	3	4
2002	DS	Angels	1	3
2003	DS	Twins	3	1
	LCS	Red Sox	4	3
	WS	Marlins	2	4
2004	DS	Twins	3	1
	LCS	Red Sox	3	4
2005	DS	Angels	2	3
2006	DS	Tigers	1	3
2007	DS	Indians	1	3
2009	DS	Twins	3	0
	LCS	Angels	4	2
	WS	Phillies	4	2
2010	DS	Twins	3	0
	LCS	Rangers	2	4
2011	DS	Tigers	2	3
2012	DS	Orioles	3	2
	LCS	Tigers	0	4
2015	WC	Astros	0	1
2017	WC	Twins	1	0
	DS	Indians	3	2
	LCS	Astros	3	4
2018	WC	Athletics	1	0
	DS	Red Sox	1	3
2019	DS	Twins	3	0
	LCS	Astros	2	4

ALL POSTSEASON ROUNDS	W	L	T
AL Wild Card Game (2-1 in series, 3 games)	2	1	0
ALDS (13-8 in series, 88 games)	51	37	0
ALCS (11-6 in series, 90 games)	50	40	0
World Series (27-13 in series, 225 games)	134	90	1*
All Postseason (53-28 in series, 406 games)	237	168	1*

*1922 WS Game 2 vs. Giants was a 3-3, 10-inn. tie called due to darkness.

Yankees Postseason Record by Opponent

For all teams below, all games played while representing former home cities are included.
Numbers in chart note: Record in games (Record in series)

Franchise	WC	DS	LCS	WS	Total
Arizona	--	--	--	3-4 (0-1)	3-4 (0-1)
Atlanta	--	--	--	15-9 (3-1)	15-9 (3-1)
Baltimore	--	3-2 (1-0)	4-1 (1-0)	--	7-3 (2-0)
Boston	--	1-3 (0-1)	11-8 (2-1)	--	12-11 (2-2)
Chicago-AL	--	--	--	--	--
Chicago-NL	--	--	--	8-0 (2-0)	8-0 (2-0)
Cincinnati	--	--	--	8-5 (2-1)	8-5 (2-1)
Cleveland	--	6-8 (1-2)	4-2 (1-0)	--	10-10 (2-2)
Colorado	--	--	--	--	--
Detroit	--	3-6 (0-2)	0-4 (0-1)	--	3-10 (0-3)
Kansas City	--	--	9-8 (3-1)	--	9-8 (3-1)
Houston	0-1 (0-1)	--	5-8 (0-2)	--	5-9 (0-3)
L.A. Angels	--	3-6 (0-2)	4-2 (1-0)	--	7-8 (1-2)
L.A. Dodgers	--	--	--	37-29 (8-3)	37-29 (8-3)
Miami	--	--	--	2-4 (0-1)	2-4 (0-1)
Milwaukee	--	3-2 (1-0)	--	--	3-2 (1-0)
Minnesota	1-0 (1-0)	15-2 (5-0)	--	--	16-2 (6-0)
New York-NL	--	--	--	4-1 (1-0)	4-1 (1-0)
Oakland	1-0 (1-0)	6-4 (2-0)	3-0 (1-0)	--	10-4 (4-0)
Philadelphia	--	--	--	8-2 (2-0)	8-2 (2-0)
Pittsburgh	--	--	--	7-4 (1-1)	7-4 (1-1)
San Diego	--	--	--	4-0 (1-0)	4-0 (1-0)
San Francisco	--	--	--	23-19-1 (5-2)	23-19-1 (5-2)
St. Louis	--	--	--	15-13 (2-3)	15-13 (2-3)
Seattle	--	2-3 (0-1)	8-3 (2-0)	--	10-6 (2-1)
Tampa Bay	--	--	--	--	--
Texas	--	9-1 (3-0)	2-4 (0-1)	--	11-5 (3-1)
Toronto	--	--	--	--	--
Washington	--	--	--	--	--
Total Games	2-1	51-37	50-40	134-90-1	237-168-1
Postseason Rds.	(2-1)	(13-8)	(11-6)	(27-13)	(53-28)

1962 World Series MVP Ralph Terry is carried off the field following his complete-game, 1-0 win in Game 7 at Candlestick Park over the S.F. Giants. During the Series he went 2-1 in three starts, allowing just 5ER in 25.0IP with two walks and 16 strikeouts. The title was the Yankees' second in a row and their 10th in a 16-year span dating to 1947. For Terry, his clutch Game 7 performance was a measure of redemption. Two years earlier he allowed Bill Mazeroski's Game 7, World Series-winning, "walk-off" home run, which gave Pittsburgh the 1960 championship even though the Pirates had been outscored by the Yankees, 55-27, over the course of the Series.

Yankees Postseason Summaries

1921 WORLD SERIES
Marked the Yankees' first ever World Series appearance in Baseball's last nine-game Fall Classic…Waite Hoyt went 2-1 despite not allowing an earned run in 27.0IP (18H, 11BB) over three starts…is tied with Christy Mathewson (1905) for the most IP without allowing an ER in a single World Series…lost, 1-0, in the Game 8 clincher, tossing a complete game and allowing an unearned run in the first inning…Carl Mays went 1-2 with a 1.73 ERA (26.0IP, 5ER) in his three starts, setting a still-standing record for most innings pitched in a single postseason without allowing a walk…Babe Ruth hit the first of his 15 career World Series home runs in a losing effort in Game 4.

New York Yankees (AL)	3
New York Giants (NL)	5

Babe Ruth hit the first of his 15 career World Series home runs in Game 4 of the 1921 World Series.

1922 WORLD SERIES
The Yankees went 0-4-1 against the Giants, marking just one of three times in 40 World Series appearances that the Yankees have been held without a win (were swept in 1963 vs. Los Angeles and 1976 vs. Cincinnati)…hit just .203 as a team…Game 2 marked the Yankees' only tie in 225 overall World Series games (134-90-1).

New York Yankees (AL)	0
New York Giants (NL)	4

1923 WORLD SERIES
Won the first World Series in franchise history in the inaugural season of the original Yankee Stadium…their Game 2 win snapped a nine-game World Series winless streak dating to 1921 (0-8-1)…scored five runs in the eighth inning of the Game 6 clincher to win, 6-4…Babe Ruth and Bob Meusel led the Yankees in HR (3) and RBI (8), respectively.

New York Giants (NL)	2
New York Yankees (AL)	4

1926 WORLD SERIES
The Series is most remembered for Game 7, which featured Pete Alexander's bases-loaded, seventh-inning strikeout of Tony Lazzeri, and Babe Ruth making the final out of the series attempting to steal second base with the Yankees down, 3-2, in the ninth…Ruth became the first player to hit 3HR in a single World Series game (Game 4 at St. Louis) and the first to hit 4HR over an entire World Series.

St. Louis Cardinals (NL)	4
New York Yankees (AL)	3

1927 WORLD SERIES
The Murderers' Row Yankees became the first AL team to sweep a World Series…Babe Ruth had a Series-high 7RBI and his 2HR were the only homers of the Series…Herb Pennock was perfect through his first 22 batters of Game 3 before a Pie Traynor single…the Yankees completed the sweep on a ninth-inning wild pitch from Pirates pitcher Johnny Miljus in Game 4…marked the first of eight consecutive winning World Series appearances for the franchise (1927-28, 32, '36-39, '41).

New York Yankees (AL)	4
Pittsburgh Pirates (NL)	0

1928 WORLD SERIES
The Yankees' win marked their first back-to-back titles…was the sixth and last Series for manager Miller Huggins, who died during the 1929 season…used only three pitchers in the entire Series as each earned complete-game wins (Waite Hoyt in Games 1 and 4; George Pipgras in Game 2 and Tom Zachary in Game 3)…Lou Gehrig led the Yankees with 4HR and 9RBI…Babe Ruth tied his own record with 3HR in Game 4 at St. Louis.

St. Louis Cardinals (NL)	0
New York Yankees (AL)	4

1932 WORLD SERIES
The Yankees swept the Cubs to run their World Series winning streak to 12 games…was the first of Manager Joe McCarthy's eight Series appearances and seven titles with the club…Babe Ruth had his "called shot" off Cubs pitcher Charlie Root in the fifth inning of Game 3…he and Gehrig each hit 2HR in the game…the Yankees outscored the Cubs, 37-19, in the Series…Gehrig batted .529 (9-for-17) with 9R, 3HR and 8RBI…was Ruth's last World Series with the Yankees.

Chicago Cubs (NL)	0
New York Yankees (AL)	4

1936 WORLD SERIES
The Yankees' victory was the first of four consecutive titles…had their 12-game World Series winning streak snapped with a Game 1 loss…the Yankees' 18-4 Game 2 win still marks the most runs scored by one team in a World Series game…Bill Dickey and Tony Lazzeri (grand slam) each had 5RBI in the game…rookie Joe DiMaggio batted .346 (9-for-26) with 3RBI in the Series.

New York Yankees (AL)	4
New York Giants (NL)	2

1937 WORLD SERIES
The Yankees defeated the Giants for the second year in a row…Yankees pitchers posted a 2.45 ERA (44.0IP, 12ER) in the Series…Lefty Gomez recorded complete-game wins in Game 1 and in the Game 5 clincher…George Selkirk led the Yankees with 5R and 6RBI.

| New York Giants (NL) | 1 |
| New York Yankees (AL) | 4 |

1938 WORLD SERIES
The Yankees ran their all-time World Series mark vs. the Cubs to 8-0…became the first team to win three consecutive Series…middle infielders Joe Gordon and Frank Crosetti each drove in a team-high 6R in the series…used just four pitchers, who sported a 1.75 combined ERA (36.0IP, 7ER)…Red Ruffing recorded complete-game wins in Game 1 and 4, compiling a 1.50 ERA in the Series (18.0IP, 3ER).

| New York Yankees (AL) | 4 |
| Chicago Cubs (NL) | 0 |

Fans leave Yankee Stadium following the team's 5-2 win in Game 3 of the 1938 World Series vs. Chicago.

1939 WORLD SERIES
The Yankees won the last of four consecutive World Series with their second straight sweep…were led by Charlie Keller, who batted .438 (7-for-16) with 8R, 3HR and 6RBI…the Yankees hit just .206 (27-for-131) as a team…Yankees pitching compiled a 1.22 ERA, holding the Reds to just four extra-base hits (0HR) in the Series…Game 4 was won in the 10th inning on Joe DiMaggio's single with Charlie Keller on first and Frank Crosetti on third…after the Cincinnati RF misplayed the ball, Keller successfully scored from first, crashing into Reds catcher Ernie Lombardi and dazing him long enough for DiMaggio to score in a play since known as "Lombardi's Snooze."

| Cincinnati Reds (NL) | 0 |
| New York Yankees (AL) | 4 |

1941 WORLD SERIES
Marked the first World Series meeting between the Yankees and Dodgers…Game 4 featured the famous passed ball by Dodgers catcher Mickey Owen, which would have been the final out of the game and evened the Series at 2-2…the Yankees went on to score 4R with two out in the ninth to win, 7-4, at Ebbets Field…in the Game 5 clincher, Tiny Bonham tossed a complete game (1ER, 5H) and Tommy Henrich hit a solo homer…Joe Gordon (.500, 1HR, 5RBI) and Charlie Keller (.389, 5RBI) paced Yankees hitters…capped a run of 32 wins in 36 World Series games dating to 1927.

| Brooklyn Dodgers (NL) | 1 |
| New York Yankees (AL) | 4 |

1942 WORLD SERIES
The Yankees won Game 1 behind Red Ruffing but lost the next four games…marked the Yankees' first losing World Series since falling in seven games to the Cardinals in 1926…Joe DiMaggio went 7-for-21 (.333) and Phil Rizzuto went 8-for-21 (.381), while Charlie Keller led the Yankees with 2HR and 5RBI.

| New York Yankees (AL) | 1 |
| St. Louis Cardinals (NL) | 4 |

1943 WORLD SERIES
The Yankees reversed the prior year's result, winning in five games…Spud Chandler was dominant, allowing just 1ER over 18.0IP for complete-game wins in Games 1 and 5…Bill Dickey's two-run homer in the Game 5 clincher marked the only runs of the game…Yankees Joe DiMaggio, Tommy Henrich, Phil Rizzuto, George Selkirk, Red Ruffing and Buddy Hassett were all serving in the military and did not appear in the Series…marked the seventh and final World Series title in eight appearances under manager Joe McCarthy.

| St. Louis Cardinals (NL) | 1 |
| New York Yankees (AL) | 4 |

1947 WORLD SERIES
The Yankees were piloted by Bucky Harris in his only World Series managing the team…in Game 4, Yankees pitcher Bill Bevens lost both his no-hit bid and the game with two outs in the bottom of the ninth as pinch-hitter Cookie Lavagetto doubled home two runs for a 3-2 Brooklyn win…Spec Shea recorded two wins and Johnny Lindell batted .500 (9-for-18) with 7RBI.

| Brooklyn Dodgers (NL) | 3 |
| New York Yankees (AL) | 4 |

1949 WORLD SERIES
Marked the first of five straight World Series championships…was the first of 10 World Series appearances in a 12-year stretch under manager Casey Stengel (won seven)…Allie Reynolds allowed just 2H, winning Game 1, 1-0, over Don Newcombe on Tommy Henrich's leadoff homer in the bottom of the ninth…also pitched 3.1 scoreless innings to close out Game 4…Commissioner Happy Chandler ordered lights turned on during Game 5, marking the first time a World Series game was finished under electric light.

| Brooklyn Dodgers (NL) | 1 |
| New York Yankees (AL) | 4 |

Manager Casey Stengel led the Yankees to a record five consecutive World Series titles from 1949-53.

1950 WORLD SERIES
Yankees pitchers allowed just 5R (3ER) all Series, tallying a 0.73 combined ERA in 37.0IP…each of the first three games was decided by one run, including a 1-0 victory behind Vic Raschi in Game 1 and a 2-1, 10-inning win behind Allie Reynolds in Game 2…Whitey Ford earned the first of his record 10 career World Series wins in the Game 4 clincher as Reynolds came out of the bullpen to strike out the final batter of the game with two runners on base.

New York Yankees (AL)	4
Philadelphia Phillies (NL)	0

1951 WORLD SERIES
The Yankees defeated the Giants in Joe DiMaggio's final World Series…Willie Mays and Mickey Mantle made their Series debuts, both in their rookie seasons…in Game 2, Mantle seriously injured his right knee after getting his cleat caught in a drainpipe, ending his Series…Ed Lopat allowed just 1ER in 18.0IP, notching wins in Games 2 and 5.

New York Giants (NL)	2
New York Yankees (AL)	4

1952 WORLD SERIES
Led by Mickey Mantle (.345, 5R, 2HR), Johnny Mize (.400, 3HR, 6RBI) and Gene Woodling (.348), the Yankees won in seven games…Allie Reynolds and Vic Raschi each recorded a pair of victories…the Yankees slugged 10HR in the Series…in Game 7, second baseman Billy Martin made a running catch on a two-out, seventh-inning, based-loaded pop-up from Jackie Robinson to preserve the Yankees' lead.

New York Yankees (AL)	4
Brooklyn Dodgers (NL)	3

Billy Martin makes a game-saving catch on a two-out, seventh-inning, based-loaded pop-up from Jackie Robinson to preserve the win in Game 7 of the 1952 World Series.

1953 WORLD SERIES
The Yankees won their all-time record fifth consecutive title…Billy Martin batted .500 (12-for-24) with 2HR and 8RBI…still shares the all-time mark for hits in a six-game World Series…Mickey Mantle won Game 2 with a two-run homer in the eighth inning…added a grand slam in the Game 5 win…Martin drove in the winning run in the Game 6 clincher with a single in the bottom of the ninth.

Brooklyn Dodgers (NL)	2
New York Yankees (AL)	4

1955 WORLD SERIES
Marked the Yankees' first Series loss to the Dodgers after five successive wins (1941, '47, '49, '52, '53)…is the only time the Dodgers triumphed over the Yankees before relocating to Los Angeles in 1958…Brooklyn's Johnny Podres tossed an eight-hit, 2-0, shutout in the Game 7 clincher at Yankee Stadium…with two on and no outs in the sixth, Yogi Berra's slicing line drive was famously caught by Brooklyn's Sandy Amoros, who then threw the ball back to the infield to double off Gil McDougald, preventing a potential rally.

Brooklyn Dodgers (NL)	4
New York Yankees (AL)	3

1956 WORLD SERIES
The Yankees lost the first two games in Brooklyn, then came back to win in seven…was highlighted by Don Larsen's Game 5 perfect game caught by Yogi Berra, the only no-hitter in World Series history…Larsen didn't know he was pitching until he got to the park that day…had lasted only 1.2 innings in his Game 2 start, (4R, 0ER, 1H, 4BB)…Berra led the Yankees with a .360 (9-for-25) batting average, 3HR and a then-record 10 RBI…the Yankees hit 12HR, the second-highest total in Series history (San Francisco 14HR in 2002).

New York Yankees (AL)	4
Brooklyn Dodgers (NL)	3

1957 WORLD SERIES
The Yankees dropped their second seven-game World Series in three years in their first-ever meeting against Milwaukee…the Braves' Lew Burdette won Games 2, 5 and 7, the latter two on seven-hit shutouts…second baseman Jerry Coleman batted .364 (8-for-22) with 2 doubles and 2RBI in a losing effort.

Milwaukee Braves (NL)	4
New York Yankees (AL)	3

1958 WORLD SERIES
The Yankees came back from two-games-to-none and three-games-to-one deficits to win in seven…after getting bombed for 4ER in just 0.1IP in his Game 2 start, Yankees pitcher Bob Turley tossed a five-hit shutout in Game 5 and also got the final out in Game 6 after entering the contest with two on and a one-run lead in the 10th…Turley also earned the victory in Game 7 with 6.2 innings (1ER) in relief of Don Larsen…winning the title gave the Yankees a World Series championship over each of the eight modern NL teams (since 1900)…Hank Bauer batted .323 (10-for-31) with 4HR, making him just one of four Yankees in franchise history to hit four-or-more homers in a single Series (also Ruth 4HR in 1926; Gehrig 4HR in 1928; and Reggie Jackson 5HR in 1977)…was held hitless in Game 4, snapping an all-time Major League-best 17-game World Series hitting streak.

New York Yankees (AL)	4
Milwaukee Braves (NL)	3

1960 WORLD SERIES

Despite outscoring Pittsburgh, 55-27, and setting still-standing World Series marks for runs scored and team batting average (.338), the Yankees lost the decisive Game 7, 10-9, on Bill Mazeroski's ninth-inning "walk-off" homer off Ralph Terry…marked Casey Stengel's final game as Yankees manager…Bobby Richardson batted .367 (11-for-30) and recorded a still-standing record 12RBI, becoming the only player in Baseball history to win the World Series MVP Award on a losing team…Whitey Ford tossed complete game shutouts in Games 3 and 6, allowing just 11H and 2BB in 18.0 Series IP.

New York Yankees (AL)	3
Pittsburgh Pirates (NL)	4

Bobby Richardson [crossing home plate] drove in an all-time record 12 runs in the 1960 Fall Classic, becoming the only player to win World Series MVP honors on a losing team.

1961 WORLD SERIES

With the Series tied 1-1, the Yankees won Game 3 on a game-tying solo homer by Johnny Blanchard in the eighth and Roger Maris' game-winning solo shot in the ninth…outscored Cincinnati 20-5 in the final two games…Manager Ralph Houk became the third Yankees skipper to win the World Series in his first season managing the club…Hector Lopez led the Yankees with 7RBI in just 9AB…Whitey Ford pitched 14.0 scoreless innings, notching wins in Games 1 and 4.

Cincinnati Reds (NL)	1
New York Yankees (AL)	4

1962 WORLD SERIES

The Yankees clinched a tight seven-game Series on a 1-0, four-hit, Game 7 shutout from Ralph Terry…scored their only run on Tony Kubek's fifth-inning double-play ground out…the Giants' Willie McCovey lined out to second baseman Bobby Richardson for the final out of the Series…Terry allowed just 17H and 5ER in 25.0 Series IP, earning the MVP Award…the teams combined for just 41 total runs in a Series that stretched over 13 days due to rainouts.

New York Yankees (AL)	4
San Francisco Giants (NL)	3

1963 WORLD SERIES

The Yankees were swept despite allowing just 12 overall runs, marking just one of two four-game Series exits in franchise history (also 1976 vs. Cincinnati)…scored just four runs and batted .171 over the four games, marking the third and fifth-lowest all-time totals, respectively, by any team in a World Series.

Los Angeles Dodgers (NL)	4
New York Yankees (AL)	0

1964 WORLD SERIES

The Yankees' seven-game loss marked Mickey Mantle's final World Series…batted .333 (8-for-24) with 3HR, giving him a record 18 World Series HR for his career…Jim Bouton won both of his starts, allowing just 3ER in 17.1IP…Bobby Richardson batted .406 (13-for-32), setting an all-time record for hits in a Series (since tied by Lou Brock in 1968 and Marty Barrett in 1986).

New York Yankees (AL)	3
St. Louis Cardinals (NL)	4

1976 CHAMPIONSHIP SERIES

Chris Chambliss batted .524 (11-for-21) with 2HR and 8RBI, including the Series-winning "walk-off" home run off the Royals' Mark Littell in Game 5.

Kansas City Royals (AL)	2
New York Yankees (AL)	3

1976 WORLD SERIES

Marked the Yankees' first World Series appearance after an 11-year drought…was the first Series appearance under the majority ownership of George M. Steinbrenner…also was the club's first Series following the 1974-75 remodeling of the original Yankee Stadium…was the second and last time the Yankees have been swept in a Series…Thurman Munson led the Yankees, batting .529 (9-for-17) with 2R and 2RBI.

New York Yankees (AL)	0
Cincinnati Reds (NL)	4

1977 CHAMPIONSHIP SERIES

Sparky Lyle appeared in four of the five games and recorded wins in relief in Game 4 (5.1IP, 2H, 0R, 0BB, 1K) and Game 5 (1.1IP, 1H, 0R, 1K)…the Yankees scored 1R in the eighth and 3R in the ninth to win the Game 5 clincher, 5-3.

New York Yankees (AL)	3
Kansas City Royals (AL)	2

1977 WORLD SERIES

The Yankees snapped a 14-season championship drought, defeating the Dodgers in six games…in the Game 6 clincher, Reggie Jackson joined Babe Ruth (twice, 1926 Game 4 and 1928 Game 4) as the only players to hit 3HR in a single World Series game (since matched by Albert Pujols-2011 Game 3; and Pablo Sandoval-2012 Game 1)…batted .450 (9-for-20) with 10R (tied for most all time), 5HR (tied for most all time) and 8RBI, taking home the Series MVP…Mike Torrez won both of his starts, tossing complete-game wins in Games 3 and 6.

Los Angeles Dodgers (NL)	2
New York Yankees (AL)	4

1978 CHAMPIONSHIP SERIES
Reggie Jackson led the Yankees in batting .462 (6-for-13), HR (2) and RBI (6)…Ron Guidry (8.0IP, 1ER) and Goose Gossage (1.0IP, 0ER) pitched the Yankees to a Game 4 win.

Kansas City Royals (AL)	1
New York Yankees (AL)	3

1978 WORLD SERIES
The Yankees defeated the Dodgers for the second consecutive year, 4-games-to-2…Series cemented Graig Nettles' reputation for defensive excellence…Bucky Dent won the MVP, batting .417 (10-for-24) with 7RBI…second baseman Brian Doyle, filling in for the injured Willie Randolph, batted .438 (7-for-16) with 4R…Catfish Hunter allowed just 2ER in 7.0IP in recording the win in the Game 6 clincher at Los Angeles.

New York Yankees (AL)	4
Los Angeles Dodgers (NL)	2

1980 CHAMPIONSHIP SERIES
The Yankees scored just two runs in each game, marking the first time in franchise history the Yankees had been swept in the ALCS.

Kansas City Royals (AL)	3
New York Yankees (AL)	0

1981 DIVISION SERIES
The Yankees almost squandered a two-games-to-none lead…Dave Righetti recorded two wins (one as a starter in Game 2 and one as a reliever in Game 5)…Oscar Gamble went 6-for-10 with 2HR and 4RBI in the series.

Milwaukee Brewers (AL)	2
New York Yankees (AL)	3

1981 CHAMPIONSHIP SERIES
The Yankees outscored Oakland, 20-4, in their only ALCS sweep in franchise history…Graig Nettles drove in three runs in each game, batting .500 (6-for-12) with 1HR.

New York Yankees (AL)	3
Oakland Athletics (AL)	0

1981 WORLD SERIES
After winning the first two games of the Series, the Yankees dropped the next four, falling to 8-3 in their World Series appearances vs. the Dodgers…pitcher George Frazier became the first pitcher to lose three games in a best-of-seven World Series…future general manager Bob Watson led the club with 7RBI.

Los Angeles Dodgers (NL)	4
New York Yankees (AL)	2

1995 DIVISION SERIES
The Yankees snapped a 13-year playoff drought…Don Mattingly batted .417 (10-for-24) with 1HR and 6RBI in his only career postseason series…won the first two games at home before dropping three straight in Seattle…won Game 2, 7-5, on Jim Leyritz's 15th-inning "walk-off" homer in the longest postseason game in franchise history…after throwing 135 pitches in a Game 1 win, David Cone threw 147 pitches in a Game 5 no-decision.

New York Yankees (AL)	2
Seattle Mariners (AL)	3

1996 DIVISION SERIES
The Yankees bullpen recorded wins in Games 2, 3 and 4, allowing just 1ER in 19.2IP over the series.

New York Yankees (AL)	3
Texas Rangers (AL)	1

1996 CHAMPIONSHIP SERIES
Down, 4-3, going into the bottom of the eighth inning of Game 1, the Yankees tied the score on Derek Jeter's disputed home run to right field…Bernie Williams (9-for-19) batted .474 with 6R, 2HR and 6RBI, earning ALCS MVP honors.

Baltimore Orioles (AL)	1
New York Yankees (AL)	4

1996 WORLD SERIES
The Yankees snapped a 17-year World Championship drought, coming back from a two-games-to-none deficit…Manager Joe Torre won in his first year at the helm…club came back from a 6-0 deficit in Game 4, with Jim Leyritz knotting the score at 6-6 with a three-run, eighth-inning homer…Andy Pettitte (8.1IP) outdueled John Smoltz, 1-0, in Game 5…Jimmy Key defeated Greg Maddux in the Game 6 clincher…John Wetteland saved each of the Yankees' victories, earning MVP honors.

Atlanta Braves (NL)	2
New York Yankees (AL)	4

Third baseman Charlie Hayes catches the final out of the 1996 World Series.

1997 DIVISION SERIES
The Yankees' Game 1 win featured the first-ever back-to-back-to-back postseason homers (Tim Raines, Derek Jeter and Paul O'Neill)…O'Neill finished the series with a .421 batting average (8-for-19), 2HR and 7RBI, including a grand slam in Game 3…Mariano Rivera suffered a blown save in Game 4, on Sandy Alomar, Jr.'s eighth-inning solo home run…would not allow another run in his next 23 postseason appearances, spanning an all-time postseason best 33.1IP.

New York Yankees (AL)	2
Cleveland Indians (AL)	3

1998 DIVISION SERIES
The Yankees outscored Texas, 9-1, in the series, behind wins from David Wells, Andy Pettitte and David Cone…outfielder Shane Spencer had 4RBI in the series, including a three-run homer in Game 3.

New York Yankees (AL)	3
Texas Rangers (AL)	0

1998 CHAMPIONSHIP SERIES
The Yankees won the final three games of the series, taking the series in six…their Game 4 win featured 7.0 scoreless IP from starter Orlando Hernandez…David Wells earned series MVP honors with wins in Games 1 and 5.

Cleveland Indians (AL)	2
New York Yankees (AL)	4

Orlando Hernandez recorded the first of nine career post-season wins with the Yankees in Game 4 of the 1998 ALCS vs. Cleveland.

1998 WORLD SERIES
The Yankees swept the Padres to finish with a 125-50 overall record (including the postseason), setting the all-time mark for most wins in a season…trailing, 5-2, in Game 1 at Yankee Stadium, Chuck Knoblauch's three-run HR tied the game and Tino Martinez's grand slam put the Yankees ahead in the seventh…also came back from a 3-0 deficit after six innings in Game 3 with Series MVP Scott Brosius hitting a leadoff HR in the seventh and a three-run HR in the eighth…Mariano Rivera notched three saves, marking his highest total in a single World Series.

San Diego Padres (NL)	0
New York Yankees (AL)	4

1999 DIVISION SERIES
The Yankees defeated the Rangers in the ALDS for the third time in three attempts over a four-year stretch…outscored them 14-1 in the series…in Game 1, Orlando Hernandez limited Texas to 2H over 8.0 scoreless IP and Bernie Williams drove in six runs, which tied Bobby Richardson (1960 WS, Game 3), Hideki Matsui (2009 WS, Game 6) and Robinson Canó (2011 ALDS Game 1) for the most in a single postseason game in franchise history.

Texas Rangers (AL)	0
New York Yankees (AL)	3

1999 CHAMPIONSHIP SERIES
The Yankees won their first-ever postseason meeting vs. Boston…Bernie Williams won Game 1 with a 10th-inning walk-off home run…the club had a 12-game postseason winning streak snapped in a Game 3 loss…Derek Jeter led the Yankees with a .350 (7-for-20) batting average.

Boston Red Sox (AL)	1
New York Yankees (AL)	4

1999 WORLD SERIES
The Yankees recorded their second straight World Series sweep…in recording a Game 1 win, Orlando Hernandez allowed just 1R on 1H in 7.0IP (10K) in Game 1…David Cone followed with 7.0 scoreless innings on 1H in Game 2…Chad Curtis hit a 10th-inning walk-off homer in Game 3…the Game 4 win extended the Yankees' World Series winning streak to 12 games.

Atlanta Braves (NL)	0
New York Yankees (AL)	4

2000 DIVISION SERIES
The Yankees dropped Game 1 of a postseason series for the first time since the 1996 World Series, snapping a winning streak of seven such games…also lost Game 4 at Yankee Stadium, snapping their home postseason winning streak at 10 games…Andy Pettitte and Mariano Rivera shut out the A's, 4-0, in Game 2…the Yankees scored 6R in the first inning of the deciding Game 5 in Oakland to provide the margin of victory in a 7-5 win.

New York Yankees (AL)	3
Oakland Athletics (AL)	2

2000 CHAMPIONSHIP SERIES
The Yankees scored 19 of their 31 total runs in the series in the seventh-inning-or-later, including three come-from-behind victories…MVP David Justice hit 2HR and had a series-best 8RBI…Bernie Williams hit .435 (10-for-23)…Roger Clemens struck out 15 batters while tossing a 1H, 2BB complete-game shutout in Game 4 at Seattle.

Seattle Mariners (AL)	2
New York Yankees (AL)	4

2000 WORLD SERIES
Marked the first "Subway Series" since the Yankees-Dodgers matchup in 1956…the Yankees were victorious in Games 1 and 5 in their last at-bat, winning on a 12th-inning single from Jose Vizcaino and a ninth-inning Luis Sojo single, respectively…Derek Jeter was named Series MVP, batting .409 (9-for-22) with 6R and 2 solo HR, including one on the first pitch of Game 4.

New York Mets (NL)	1
New York Yankees (AL)	4

2001 DIVISION SERIES
The postseason began less than a month after the attacks of 9/11…after losing Games 1 and 2, the Yankees won three straight…were held to just two hits in Game 3 at Oakland but won, 1-0, behind Mike Mussina (7.0IP), Mariano Rivera (2.0IP) and Jorge Posada's fifth-inning solo home run…the game also featured Derek Jeter's famous "Flip Play," which nailed Jeremy Giambi at the plate in the seventh.

Oakland Athletics (AL)	2
New York Yankees (AL)	3

Derek Jeter [R] makes his famous "Flip Play" relay throw to Jorge Posada in Game 3 of the 2001 ALDS at Oakland.

2001 CHAMPIONSHIP SERIES
The Yankees defeated a Seattle club that won an AL-record 116 games during the regular season…Andy Pettitte was named Series MVP, going 2-0 with a 2.51 ERA…Game 4 ended on Alfonso Soriano's two-run "walk-off" homer in the ninth…Bernie Williams homered in three consecutive games (Games 3-5).

New York Yankees (AL)	4
Seattle Mariners (AL)	1

2001 WORLD SERIES
All games were won by the home team in one of the most thrilling World Series of all time…President George W. Bush threw out the ceremonial first pitch prior Game 3 at Yankee Stadium…the Yankees came back from two-run deficits with two outs in the ninth vs. Arizona's Byung-Hyun Kim in both Games 4 and 5…Tino Martinez tied Game 4 with a two-run home run and Derek Jeter earned the nickname, "Mr. November," with a solo HR to win it in the 10th…Scott Brosius hit a two-run homer to tie Game 5 before Alfonso Soriano won the game with an RBI-single in the 12th…despite taking a 2-1 lead on a Soriano solo homer in the eighth inning of Game 7, the Yankees lost the Series in the ninth on a bloop single by Luis Gonzalez off Mariano Rivera.

New York Yankees (AL)	3
Arizona Diamondbacks (NL)	4

2002 DIVISION SERIES
The Yankees had their DS winning streak snapped at four, losing their first DS since 1997 vs. Cleveland…Derek Jeter batted .500 (8-for-16) with 2HR and 3RBI.

Anaheim Angels (AL)	3
New York Yankees (AL)	1

2003 DIVISION SERIES
The Yankees held Minnesota to just six runs in four games, including one run in each of Games 2, 3 and 4…Derek Jeter batted .429 (6-for-14) with 1HR.

Minnesota Twins (AL)	1
New York Yankees (AL)	3

2003 CHAMPIONSHIP SERIES
Defined by the final game, the Series was won on Aaron Boone's first pitch leadoff home run off Tim Wakefield in the bottom of the 11th inning of Game 7…in the contest, the Yankees came back from a 5-2 deficit heading into the bottom of the eighth…Mike Mussina made his first-ever relief appearance, getting a strikeout and double play with two on and no outs in the fourth to keep the Yankees in the game…tossed 3.0 scoreless IP on two days' rest…Jason Giambi hit solo homers in the fifth and seventh…the Yankees scored three runs in the eighth off Pedro Martinez to tie the game, 5-5…Mariano Rivera tossed 3.0 scoreless innings, pitching the ninth, 10th and 11th, to earn the win.

Boston Red Sox (AL)	3
New York Yankees (AL)	4

2003 WORLD SERIES
The Yankees outscored Florida, 21-17, in defeat…Andy Pettitte allowed just 3R (1ER) in 15.2IP over two starts, including a win in Game 2 and a loss in the decisive Game 6…Bernie Williams batted .400 (10-for-25) with 5R, 2HR and 5RBI.

Florida Marlins (NL)	4
New York Yankees (AL)	2

Aaron Boone wins Game 7 of the 2003 ALCS with his 11th-inning home run off Boston's Tim Wakefield.

2004 DIVISION SERIES
The Yankees defeated Minnesota in the ALDS for the second straight season…won Game 2 scoring twice in the 12th inning and Game 4 with one run in the 11th…Alex Rodriguez batted .421 (8-for-19) with 1HR and 3RBI.

Minnesota Twins (AL)	1
New York Yankees (AL)	3

2004 CHAMPIONSHIP SERIES
The Yankees became the first team in MLB postseason history to drop a series after leading 3-games-to-0…scored 19 runs in their Game 3 win, marking the most ever by one team in an ALCS game…Hideki Matsui batted .412 (14-for-34) with 6 doubles, 1 triple, 2HR and 10RBI in the series, establishing the all-time mark for extra-base hits in a postseason series.

Boston Red Sox (AL)	4
New York Yankees (AL)	3

2005 DIVISION SERIES
Mariano Rivera saved both of the Yankees' victories…Derek Jeter tied for the team lead in both RBI (5) and runs scored (4).

New York Yankees (AL)	2
Los Angeles Angels of Anaheim (AL)	3

2006 DIVISION SERIES
Chien-Ming Wang recorded his first career postseason win in Game 1…Derek Jeter (8-for-16) and Jorge Posada (7-for-14) combined for 15 of the team's 33 overall hits.

Detroit Tigers (AL)	3
New York Yankees (AL)	1

2007 DIVISION SERIES
The Yankees were outhit, .315 to .228, in the series…the Yankees' 2-1, 11-inning loss in Game 2 featured the unusual postseason debut of Joba Chamberlain, who allowed the go-ahead run in the eighth on 2BB, 2WP and 1HP while "midges" descended on the pitcher's mound.

New York Yankees (AL)	1
Cleveland Indians (AL)	3

2009 DIVISION SERIES
The Yankees recorded their third all-time ALDS sweep (also 1998-99 vs. Texas), and fourth "best-of-five" series sweep (also 1981 ALCS vs. Oakland)…came back from deficits in all three games…out-homered the Twins, 6-0…Yankees starters allowed just 3ER and three extra-base hits in 19.0IP with a 1.42 ERA…Alex Rodriguez batted a team-high .455 (5-for-11) with 2HR and 6RBI.

Minnesota Twins (AL)	0
New York Yankees (AL)	3

2009 CHAMPIONSHIP SERIES
The Yankees won their 40th AL pennant…hit 8HR and drew 38BB over the six games, while holding the Majors' second-highest scoring team to an average of 3.2R/G…won Game 2 in 13 innings on a throwing error by Maicer Izturis…CC Sabathia earned ALCS MVP honors, going 2-0 with a 1.13 ERA (16.0IP, 2ER) in two starts…Alex Rodriguez batted a team-high .429 (9-for-21) with 6R, 3HR, 6RBI and 8BB.

Los Angeles Angels (AL)	2
New York Yankees (AL)	4

2009 WORLD SERIES
The Yankees won their 27th World Championship and first since 2000…Hideki Matsui (.615 BA., 3HR, 8RBI) was the unanimous World Series MVP, marking the first time a Japanese player earned the honor…had 6RBI (single, double, HR) in the Game 6 clincher, tying Bobby Richardson's (1960 Game 3) single-game World Series record, since matched by the Cardinals' Albert Pujols (2011 Game 3 at Texas) and the Cubs' Addison Russell (2016 Game 6 at Cleveland)…Andy Pettitte became the third-oldest pitcher to win a World Series clinching game (behind Burleigh Grimes-1931 and Eddie Plank-1913) and the first pitcher in baseball history to start and win all three clinching games of a single postseason (DS, CS, WS).

Philadelphia Phillies (NL)	2
New York Yankees (AL)	4

2010 DIVISION SERIES
The Yankees swept Minnesota for the second straight year in the ALDS…marked their first ALDS series win after qualifying for the postseason as a Wild Card…outscored the Twins, 17-7, in the series…10 different Yankees drove in at least one run…Yankees relievers combined to allow just 1ER in 7.0IP…Phil Hughes won Game 3 with 7.0 shutout IP (4H, 1BB) in his first career postseason start.

New York Yankees (AL)	3
Minnesota Twins (AL)	0

2010 CHAMPIONSHIP SERIES
The Yankees lost a postseason series to Texas for the first time after wins in the ALDS in 1996, '98 and '99…were outscored 38-19 in the series and outhit 63-38…their 8-0 loss in Game 3 marked the worst postseason shutout loss in franchise history…Robinson Canó batted .348 (8-for-23) with 4HR and 5RBI…Curtis Granderson reached base safely in 13 of his 25PA (.520 OBP).

New York Yankees (AL)	2
Texas Rangers (AL)	4

2011 DIVISION SERIES
The Yankees dropped to 10-7 all time in Division Series, losing an ALDS for the first time since 2007…Robinson Canó set a Yankees ALDS record with 9RBI…marked the most RBI by a Yankee in a postseason series of five-or-fewer games since Graig Nettles had 9RBI in the 1981 ALCS vs. Oakland…also had four extra-base hits (2 doubles, 2HR)…Jorge Posada posted a .579 OBP with 5 singles, 1 triple, 4BB and 1HP in 19PA…Brett Gardner batted .412 (7-for-17) with 5RBI.

Detroit Tigers (AL)	3
New York Yankees (AL)	2

2012 DIVISION SERIES
The Yankees improved to 12-11 all time in winner-take-all postseason games, snapping a three-game losing streak in such contests with their 3-1 win in Game 5…Yankees starters went 2-1 with a 2.04 ERA (39.2IP, 9ER) over the five games and Yankees relievers allowed just 1ER in 11.1IP (0.79 ERA)…did not have a multi-run inning over the last four games…in Game 3 at Yankee Stadium, Raul Ibanez became the first player in MLB history to hit 2HR in a postseason game he didn't start, tying the game with a solo HR in the ninth and winning it with a solo HR in the 12th…CC Sabathia tossed a complete game in Game 5 (4H, 1R, 2BB, 9K).

Baltimore Orioles (AL)	2
New York Yankees (AL)	3

The Yankees are presented the 2009 World Series trophy following their 4-games-to-2 victory over Philadelphia.

2012 CHAMPIONSHIP SERIES
The Yankees were swept by Detroit, falling to 0-3 all time in postseason series vs. the Tigers…did not lead at any point, marking the second such postseason series in franchise history (also 1963 WS vs. Los Angeles)…Yankees batters hit just .157 (22-for-140) and scored six runs over the four games…lost Derek Jeter to injury for the series (fractured ankle) while fielding a grounder in the 12th inning of Game 1 loss…Ichiro Suzuki collected four hits in Game 1, marking the most by a Yankee in the postseason since Derek Jeter had 5H in 2006 ALDS Game 1 vs. Detroit.

Detroit Tigers (AL)	4
New York Yankees (AL)	0

2015 WILD CARD GAME
The Yankees played in their first-ever Wild Card Game and first-ever postseason game against Houston, falling, 3-0, at home…Masahiro Tanaka made his first career postseason start and took the loss, allowing 2ER on two solo HRs in 5.0IP…Yankees batters tallied just three hits.

Houston Astros (AL)	3
New York Yankees (AL)	0

2017 WILD CARD GAME
The Yankees advanced to the ALDS with an 8-4 win vs. Minnesota…trailed, 3-0, four batters into the game, then scored in each of the first four innings for the second time in franchise postseason history (also 1977 ALCS Game 4 at Kansas City) – credit: *Elias Sports Bureau*…Didi Gregorius hit a three-run HR in the first to tie the game at 3-3…Brett Gardner hit a solo HR in the second to give the Yankees a 4-3 lead…Aaron Judge hit a two-run HR in the fourth…Luis Severino (0.1IP, 4H, 3ER, 1BB, 0K, 2HR) made his postseason debut and matched the shortest start by a Yankees pitcher in postseason history…Yankees relievers tossed 8.2IP, allowing just 1ER (5H, 3BB, 13K) to tie the MLB mark for strikeouts by a bullpen in a postseason game.

Minesota Twins (AL)	0
New York Yankees (AL)	1

2017 DIVISION SERIES
The Yankees came back from a two-games-to-none deficit to win in the decisive Game 5 at Cleveland, 5-2…was the 10th time in postseason history that a team won a best-of-five series after losing the first two games (second time by the Yankees, also 2001 ALDS vs. Oakland)…Didi Gregorius (3-for-4, 3RBI) homered twice off 2017 AL Cy Young Award winner Corey Kluber in the Game 5 clincher…won Game 3 at Yankee Stadium with 7.0 scoreless IP (3H, 1BB, 7K) from Masahiro Tanaka and a seventh-inning solo HR from Greg Bird, who joined Jorge Posada (2001 ALDS Game 3 at Oakland, fifth inn.) and Tommy Henrich (1949 WS Game 1 vs. Brooklyn, ninth inn.) as the only Yankees to homer in a 1-0 postseason win…Aroldis Champan tossed 5.2 scoreless IP (4H, 2BB, 10K) over three appearances, notching saves in Games 3 and 5…Yankees pitchers held Cleveland hitters to a .171 BA with 61K over the five games.

New York Yankees (AL)	3
Cleveland Indians (AL)	2

2017 CHAMPIONSHIP SERIES
The Yankees fell in a seven-game ALCS in which every game was won by the home team…outscored Houston 22-20 over the series but tallied just three total runs in their four losses at Minute Maid Park…prior to their Game 7 loss, had won four elimination games in the 2017 postseason…Aaron Judge led both clubs with 3HR and 7RBI…Chase Headley had a series-best .389 (7-for-18) batting average and Greg Bird led both clubs with a .464 OBP, reaching base safely 13 times (2 singles, 2 doubles, 1HR, 8BB)…Yankees starting pitchers tallied a 2.00 ERA (8ER, 36.0IP) in the series, marking the second-best starters' ERA for a club in a seven-game postseason series since 1992 (Arizona, 1.43 starters ERA in the 2001 WS).

New York Yankees (AL)	3
Houston Astros (AL)	4

2018 WILD CARD GAME
The Yankees won the AL Wild Card Game for the second straight year, defeating Oakland, 7-2…became the first team to win consecutive Wild Card Games…Luis Severino (4.0IP, 2H, 0R, 4BB, 7K) took a no-decision in his fifth career postseason start…did not allow a hit until the fifth…Aaron Judge (2-for-3, double, BB) hit a two-run HR in the first…Giancarlo Stanton (1-for-3, 1BB, 1SB) homered to lead off the eighth…Luke Voit (1-for-4, 1R) hit a two-run triple in the sixth inning of his postseason debut…Dellin Betances (2.0IP, 3K) retired all 6BF to earn the win.

Oakland Athletics (AL)	0
New York Yankees (AL)	1

2018 DIVISION SERIES
The Yankees lost the ALDS in four games, falling to 2-2 in all-time postseason series against Boston…Aaron Judge led the Yankees with 4R scored, 6H and a .375/.444/.750 slash line…also tied for the team lead with 2HR…Masahiro Tanaka allowed 1ER in 5.0IP in earning the Yankees' lone victory in Game 2 at Boston…Gary Sánchez had 2HR and 4RBI in Game 2, becoming the second catcher in franchise history with a multi-HR postseason game and joining Yogi Berra (1956 Game 7 win at Brooklyn)…in their 16-1 Game 3 loss at Yankee Stadium, set a franchise record for runs allowed and margin of defeat in a postseason game.

New York Yankees (AL)	1
Boston Red Sox (AL)	3

2019 DIVISION SERIES
The Yankees swept Minnesota in the ALDS, becoming the first team in baseball history to sweep a 100-win team in the DS… outscored the Twins, 23-7, after the Twins averaged 5.8R/G in the regular season and hit an all-time record 307HR….in Game 1, DJ LeMahieu joined Bobby Abreu (2006 ALDS Game 1 vs. Detroit) as the second player in franchise history to record at least 4RBI in his first postseason game with the club… Didi Gregorius led both clubs with 6RBI, including a third-inning grand slam in Game 2, becoming the first shortstop in franchise history to hit a postseason slam… Gleyber Torres batted .417 (5-for-12) with 3 doubles, 1HR and 4RBI in the series.

Minnesota Twins (AL)	0
New York Yankees (AL)	3

2019 CHAMPIONSHIP SERIES
The Yankees lost the ALCS in six games, falling to 0-3 in all-time postseason series against the Astros (also lost the 2017 ALCS and 2015 WC)…Gleyber Torres recorded 5RBI in a 7-0 Game 1 road win…DJ LeMahieu led the Yankees with a .346 (9-for-26) BA and .414 OBP, hitting a leadoff home run in Game 5 off Justin Verlander…Aaron Hicks provided the margin of victory in Game 5 with a three-run, first-inning HR in a 4-1 win to stave off elimination…in Game 6 at Houston, DJ LeMahieu hit a game-tying, two-run HR off Roberto Osuna with one out in the ninth…the Yankees lost the series in the bottom half of the inning on a two-out, two-run "walk-off" HR by Jose Altuve off Aroldis Chapman.

New York Yankees (AL)	2
Houston Astros (AL)	4

Postseason Awards

ALCS and World Series MVP Awards are issued by Major League Baseball in a voting process involving MLB officials and select reporters. Yankees winners are listed below.

Additionally, the New York Baseball Writers Association established its own award—the **Babe Ruth Award**—in 1949, one year after the slugger's death. From 1949 through 2006 it was given to the top player in the World Series. Since 2007, it has been awarded to the best player in the postseason (including all rounds). Former Yankees winners of the Babe Ruth Award are: Joe Page (1949), Jerry Coleman (1950), Phil Rizzuto (1951), Johnny Mize (1952), Billy Martin (1953), Don Larsen (1956), Elston Howard (1958), Whitey Ford (1961), Ralph Terry (1962), Reggie Jackson (1977), Bucky Dent (1978), Cecil Fielder (1996), Scott Brosius (1998), Mariano Rivera (1999), Derek Jeter (2000) and Alex Rodriguez (2009).

ALCS MVP (awarded in AL since 1980)

YEAR	PLAYER	AGE	POS	G	AB	R	H	2B	3B	HR	RBI	BA
1981	Graig Nettles	37	3B	3	12	2	6	2	0	1	9	.500
1996	Bernie Williams	28	CF	5	19	6	9	3	0	2	6	.474
2000	David Justice	34	LF	6	26	4	6	2	0	2	8	.231

YEAR	PITCHER	AGE	POS	G	GS	IP	W	L	SV	H	R	ER	SO	BB	ERA
1998	David Wells	35	LHP	2	2	15.2	2	0	0	12	5	5	18	2	2.87
1999	Orlando Hernandez	30	RHP	2	2	15.0	1	0	0	12	4	3	13	6	1.80
2001	Andy Pettitte	29	LHP	2	2	14.1	2	0	0	11	4	4	8	2	2.51
2003	Mariano Rivera	33	RHP	4	0	8.0	1	0	2	5	1	1	6	0	1.13
2009	CC Sabathia	29	LHP	2	2	16.0	2	0	0	9	2	2	12	3	1.13

WORLD SERIES MVP (awarded since 1955)

YEAR	PLAYER	AGE	POS	G	AB	R	H	2B	3B	HR	RBI	BA
1960	Bobby Richardson	25	2B	7	30	8	11	2	2	1	12	.367
1977	Reggie Jackson	31	RF	6	20	10	9	1	0	5	8	.450
1978	Bucky Dent	26	SS	6	24	3	10	1	0	0	7	.417
1998	Scott Brosius	32	3B	4	17	3	8	0	0	2	6	.471
2000	Derek Jeter	26	SS	5	22	6	9	2	1	2	2	.409
2009	Hideki Matsui	35	DH	6	13	3	8	1	0	3	8	.615

YEAR	PITCHER	AGE	POS	G	GS	IP	W	L	SV	H	R	ER	SO	BB	ERA
1956	Don Larsen	27	RHP	2	2	10.2	1	0	0	1	4	0	7	4	0.00
1958	Bob Turley	28	RHP	4	2	16.1	2	1	1	10	5	5	13	7	2.76
1961	Whitey Ford	32	LHP	2	2	14.0	2	0	0	6	0	0	7	1	0.00
1962	Ralph Terry	26	RHP	3	3	25.0	2	1	0	17	5	5	16	2	1.80
1996	John Wetteland	30	RHP	5	0	4.1	0	0	4	4	1	1	6	1	2.08
1999	Mariano Rivera	29	RHP	3	0	4.2	1	0	2	3	0	0	3	1	0.00

Prior to Game 5 of the 1958 World Series, Bob Turley [L] poses with future 1961 World Series MVP Whitey Ford. Turley earned MVP honors in the 1958 Fall Classic, going 2-1 with a 2.76 ERA in four games (two starts) against the Braves. After surrendering 4ER and lasting just 0.1IP in his Game 2 start, Turley tossed a five-hit shutout in Game 5 and also got the final out in Game 6 after entering the contest with two on and a one-run lead in the 10th. Turley also earned the win in the Yankees' Game 7 win at Milwaukee, finishing the 6-2 victory with 6.2 innings of one-run relief.

Yankees All-Time Postseason Leaders

Please note that the players' totals listed below are as a Yankee only and do not include statistics accumulated while playing for other teams. **KEY:** MLB = All-time Major League leader with the total listed; AL = All-time American League leader with the total listed; T= Tied for lead.

BATTING

Games Played
1. Derek Jeter............... MLB 158
2. Jorge Posada............... 125
3. Bernie Williams............ 121
4. Mariano Rivera............. 96
5. Tino Martinez.............. 81

At-Bats
1. Derek Jeter............... MLB 650
2. Bernie Williams............ 465
3. Jorge Posada............... 416
4. Tino Martinez.............. 287
5. Paul O'Neill............... 270

Runs
1. Derek Jeter............... MLB 111
2. Bernie Williams............ 83
3. Jorge Posada............... 53
4. Mickey Mantle.............. 42
5. Yogi Berra................. 41

Hits
1. Derek Jeter............... MLB 200
2. Bernie Williams............ 128
3. Jorge Posada............... 103
4. Paul O'Neill............... 76
5. Yogi Berra................. 71

Doubles
1. Derek Jeter............... MLB 32
2. Bernie Williams............ 29
3. Jorge Posada............... 23
4. Hideki Matsui.............. 15
T5. Tino Martinez............. 14
    Paul O'Neill.............. 14

Triples
1. Derek Jeter............... MLBT 5
2. Bill Johnson............... 4
T3. Bauer, B. Brown, Canó,
    Gehrig, Martin, Meusel.... 3

Home Runs
1. Bernie Williams............ 22
2. Derek Jeter................ 20
3. Mickey Mantle.............. 18
4. Babe Ruth.................. 15
T5. Yogi Berra................ 12
    Reggie Jackson............ 12

RBI
1. Bernie Williams............ MLB 80
2. Derek Jeter................ 61
3. Jorge Posada............... 42
4. Mickey Mantle.............. 40
T5. Yogi Berra, Hideki Matsui.. 39

Walks
1. Bernie Williams............ AL 71
2. Jorge Posada............... 70
3. Derek Jeter................ 66
4. Mickey Mantle.............. 43
5. Alex Rodriguez............. 36

Batting Average (min. 75PA)
1. Lou Gehrig ..... .361 (43-for-119)
2. Thurman Munson .357 (46-for-129)
3. Babe Ruth ..... .347 (41-for-118)
4. Billy Martin ... .333 (33-for-99)
5. Reggie Jackson .. .328 (39-for-119)

On-Base Percentage (min. 75PA)
1. Babe Ruth.................. .497
2. Lou Gehrig................. MLB .483
3. Gene Woodling.............. .442
4. Reggie Jackson............. .417
5. Jason Giambi............... .409

Slugging Percentage (min. 75PA)
1. Babe Ruth.................. .788
2. Lou Gehrig................. .731
3. Reggie Jackson............. .672
4. Charlie Keller............. .611
5. Billy Martin............... .566

Stolen Bases
1. Derek Jeter................ 18
T2. Phil Rizzuto............... 10
    Alfonso Soriano........... 10
4. Bernie Williams............ 8
5. Alex Rodriguez............. 7

Hitting Streak
T1. Jeter (10/13/98-10/27/99) ..... MLBT 17
    Bauer (10/3/56-10/4/58) .... MLBT 17
3. B. Williams (10/16/03-10/12/04).. 12
4. Jeter (10/11/00-10/11/01)........ 12
5. Seven players 11

PITCHING

Games
1. Mariano Rivera............. MLB 96
2. Jeff Nelson................ 44
3. Andy Pettitte.............. 40
4. Mike Stanton............... 31
5. David Robertson............ 30

Games Started
1. Andy Pettitte.............. AL 40
2. Whitey Ford................ 22
T3. CC Sabathia............... 18
    Roger Clemens............. 18
5. Mike Mussina............... 15

Innings Pitched
1. Andy Pettitte.............. AL 251.1
2. Whitey Ford................ 146.0
3. Mariano Rivera............. 141.0
4. CC Sabathia................ 105.1
5. Roger Clemens.............. 102.1

Wins
1. Andy Pettitte.............. AL 18
2. Whitey Ford................ 10
3. Orlando Hernandez.......... 9
T4. Mariano Rivera............ 8
    CC Sabathia............... 8

Losses
1. Andy Pettitte.............. 10
2. Whitey Ford................ 8
3. Mike Mussina............... 7
T4. Roger Clemens, Ed Figueroa,
    Phil Hughes, Catfish Hunter,
    CC Sabathia, Ralph Terry....... 4

Strikeouts
1. Andy Pettitte.............. 167
2. Mariano Rivera............. 110
3. Orlando Hernandez.......... 101
4. Roger Clemens.............. 99
5. CC Sabathia................ 97

ERA (min. 40.0IP)
1. Mariano Rivera............. MLB 0.70
2. Waite Hoyt................. 1.62
3. MASAHIRO TANAKA............ 1.76
4. Herb Pennock............... 2.06
5. Vic Raschi................. 2.24

Saves (official stat since 1969)
1. Mariano Rivera............. MLB 42
T2. Goose Gossage.............. 7
    John Wetteland............ 7
4. AROLDIS CHAPMAN............ 5
T5. Ken Clay, TOMMY KAHNLE,
    Sparky Lyle, Ramiro Mendoza.... 1

Shutouts
1. Whitey Ford................ AL 3
2. Allie Reynolds............. 2
T3. Chandler, Clemens, Hoyt,
    Kucks, Larsen, Mays, Pearson,
    Raschi, Terry, Turley 1

Complete Games
1. Red Ruffing................ 8
2. Whitey Ford................ 7
3. Waite Hoyt................. 6
4. Allie Reynolds............. 5
T5. Lefty Gomez................ 4
    Herb Pennock.............. 4

Scoreless Innings Streak
Mariano Rivera holds the all-time MLB record, 33.1IP (9/29/98-10/17/00).

Yankees All-Time World Series Leaders

Please note that the players' totals listed below are as a Yankee only and do not include statistics accumulated while playing for other teams. **KEY:** MLB = All-time Major League leader with the total listed; AL = All-time American League leader with the total listed; T= Tied for lead.

BATTING

Games Played
1. Yogi Berra .... MLB 75
2. Mickey Mantle 65
T3. Hank Bauer 53
    Gil McDougald 53
5. Phil Rizzuto 52

At-Bats
1. Yogi Berra .... MLB 259
2. Mickey Mantle 230
3. Joe DiMaggio 199
4. Gil McDougald 190
5. Hank Bauer 188

Runs
1. Mickey Mantle .... MLB 42
2. Yogi Berra 41
3. Babe Ruth 37
4. Derek Jeter 32
5. Lou Gehrig 30

Hits
1. Yogi Berra .... MLB 71
2. Mickey Mantle 59
3. Joe DiMaggio 54
4. Derek Jeter 50
5. Hank Bauer 46

Doubles
1. Yogi Berra .... MLBT 10
2. Derek Jeter 9
3. Lou Gehrig 8
4. Elston Howard 7
T5. Seven players tied 6

Triples
1. Bill Johnson .... MLBT 4
T2. Bauer, B. Brown, Gehrig,
    Martin, Meusel 3

Home Runs
1. Mickey Mantle .... MLB 18
2. Babe Ruth 15
3. Yogi Berra 12
4. Lou Gehrig 10
T5. Joe DiMaggio 8
    Reggie Jackson 8

RBI (official stat since 1920)
1. Mickey Mantle .... MLB 40
2. Yogi Berra 39
3. Lou Gehrig 35
T4. Joe DiMaggio 30
    Babe Ruth 30

Walks
1. Mickey Mantle .... MLB 43
2. Babe Ruth 33
3. Yogi Berra 32
4. Phil Rizzuto 30
5. Lou Gehrig 26

Batting Average (min. 40PA)
1. B. Brown .... .439 (18-for-41)
2. R. Jackson .... .400 (22-for-55)
3. Hideki Matsui ... .389 (14-for-36)
4. T. Munson .... .373 (25-for-67)
5. Lou Gehrig ..... .361 (43-for-119)

On-Base Percentage (min. 40PA)
T1. Bobby Brown .... .500
    Reggie Jackson .... .500
3. Babe Ruth .... .497
4. Lou Gehrig .... .483
5. Hideki Matsui .... .463

Slugging Percentage (min. 40PA)
1. Reggie Jackson .... .891
2. Babe Ruth .... .788
3. Hideki Matsui .... .750
4. Lou Gehrig .... .731
5. Bobby Brown .... .707

Stolen Bases
1. Phil Rizzuto 10
2. Bob Meusel 5
T3. Derek Jeter 4
    Babe Ruth 4
T5. Damon, Mantle, Rivers 3

Hitting Streak
1. H. Bauer (10/3/56-10/4/58) 17
2. D. Jeter (10/26/96-10/26/00) 14
3. R. Jackson (10/14/77-10/25/81) ... 12
T4. B. Martin (10/1/55-10/10/56) 11
    Y. Berra (10/2/53-10/4/55) 11

PITCHING

Games
1. Mariano Rivera .... MLB 24
2. Whitey Ford 22
3. Jeff Nelson 16
T4. Allie Reynolds 15
    Bob Turley 15

Games Started
1. Whitey Ford .... MLB 22
2. Andy Pettitte 12
T3. Waite Hoyt 10
    Red Ruffing 10
5. Allie Reynolds 9

Innings Pitched
1. Whitey Ford .... MLB 146.0
2. Red Ruffing 85.2
3. Waite Hoyt 77.2
4. Allie Reynolds 77.1
5. Andy Pettitte 71.2

Wins
1. Whitey Ford .... MLB 10
T2. Allie Reynolds 7
    Red Ruffing 7
T4. Lefty Gomez 6
    Waite Hoyt 6

Losses
1. Whitey Ford .... MLB 8
T2. Andy Pettitte 4
    Ralph Terry 4
T4. Bush, Frazier, Hoyt, Hunter,
    Mays, Raschi, Turley 3

Strikeouts
1. Whitey Ford .... MLB 94
2. Allie Reynolds 62
3. Red Ruffing 61
4. Andy Pettitte 52
5. Waite Hoyt 48

ERA (min. 25.0IP)
1. Mariano Rivera 0.99
2. Monte Pearson 1.01
3. Roger Clemens 1.50
4. Spud Chandler 1.62
5. Waite Hoyt 1.62

Saves (official stat since 1969)
1. Mariano Rivera .... MLB 11
2. John Wetteland 4
3. Goose Gossage 2

Shutouts
1. Whitey Ford .... AL 3
2. Allie Reynolds 2
T3. Chandler, Hoyt, Kucks,
    Larsen, Mays, Pearson,
    Raschi, Terry, Turley 1

Complete Games
1. Red Ruffing 8
2. Whitey Ford 7
3. Waite Hoyt 6
4. Allie Reynolds 5
T5. Lefty Gomez 4
    Herb Pennock 4

Scoreless Innings Streak
Whitey Ford holds the all-time MLB record, 33.0IP (10/8/60-10/04/62).

Yankees All-Time League Championship Series Leaders

Please note that the players' totals listed below are as a Yankee only and do not include statistics accumulated while playing for other teams. KEY: MLB = All-time Major League leader with the total listed; AL = All-time American League leader with the total listed; T= Tied for lead. The Divisional Play and the LCS began in 1969.

BATTING

Games Played (incl. pitchers)
1. Derek Jeter .... MLB 54
2. Jorge Posada 45
3. Bernie Williams 41
4. Mariano Rivera 33
5. BRETT GARDNER 28

At-Bats
1. Derek Jeter .... MLB 226
2. Bernie Williams 162
3. Jorge Posada 147
4. Tino Martinez 105
5. Paul O'Neill 89

Runs
1. Derek Jeter .... MLB 32
2. Bernie Williams 31
3. Jorge Posada 21
4. Alex Rodriguez 18
5. Tino Martinez 15

Hits
1. Derek Jeter .... AL 58
2. Bernie Williams 52
3. Jorge Posada 33
4. Hideki Matsui 27
5. Paul O'Neill 26

Doubles
T1. Derek Jeter .... MLBT 10
    Hideki Matsui .... MLBT 10
    Jorge Posada .... MLBT 10
    Bernie Williams ...... MLBT 10
T5. Martinez, Rodriguez, White 6

Triples
T1. Robinson Canó 2
    Derek Jeter 2
T3. Berkman, Brosius, Chambliss, Girardi, Gregorius, Matsui, Nettles, Nuñez, Rivers, Sierra, Watson 1

Home Runs
1. Bernie Williams 9
2. Derek Jeter 7
3. Graig Nettles 5
    Alex Rodriguez 5
T5. Canó, JUDGE, O'Neill, Posada, Strawberry 4

RBI
1. Bernie Williams .... MLB 33
2. Derek Jeter 24
T3. Hideki Matsui 17
    Graig Nettles 17
    Jorge Posada 17

Walks
1. Jorge Posada .... AL 32
2. Derek Jeter 29
3. Bernie Williams 25
4. Alex Rodriguez 15
5. Chuck Knoblauch 12

Batting Average (min. 40PA)
1. Rivers .... .386 (22-for-57)
2. Chambliss ... .340 (18-for-53)
3. Munson ...... .339 (21-for-62)
4. Matsui ...... .333 (27-for-81)
5. B. Williams.. .321 (52-for-162)

On-Base Percentage (min. 40PA)
1. Roy White .... .422
2. Mickey Rivers .... .417
3. Bernie Williams .... .413
4. Alex Rodriguez .... .396
5. Hideki Matsui .... .389

Slugging Percentage (min. 40PA)
1. Graig Nettles .... .557
2. Hideki Matsui .... .556
3. Roy White .... .553
4. Bernie Williams .... .549
5. AARON JUDGE .... .531

Stolen Bases
1. Derek Jeter 8
T2. Alfonso Soriano 4
    Bernie Williams 4
4. BRETT GARDNER 3
T5. Chambliss, R. Jackson, JUDGE, Martinez, O'Neill, Rodriguez, Vizcaino 2

Hitting Streak
1. Jeter (10/16/04-10/22/09) 10
T2. A. Rodriguez (10/16/09-10/16/10) ... 8
    Matsui (10/14/03-10/18/04) 8
    B.Williams (10/9/96-10/9/98) 8
T5. Canó, Martinez, Jeter, Munson 7

PITCHING

Games
1. Mariano Rivera .... MLB 33
2. Jeff Nelson 14
3. Andy Pettitte 13
4. David Robertson 12
5. Joba Chamberlain 10

Games Started
1. Andy Pettitte .... AL 13
T2. Orlando Hernandez 7
    CC Sabathia 7
T4. Roger Clemens 5
    Mike Mussina 5

Innings Pitched
1. Andy Pettitte .... AL 86.0
2. Mariano Rivera 48.2
3. Orlando Hernandez 47.0
4. CC Sabathia 40.0
5. Mike Mussina 34.0

Wins
1. Andy Pettitte 7
T2. Orlando Hernandez 4
    Mariano Rivera 4
    CC Sabathia 4
5. David Wells 3

Losses
1. Phil Hughes .... ALT 4
T2. Ed Figueroa 2
    Mike Mussina 2
    Denny Neagle 2
    Jeff Nelson 2
    Andy Pettitte 2
    CC Sabathia 2
    AROLDIS CHAPMAN 2
    LUIS SEVERINO 2
    MASAHIRO TANAKA 2

Strikeouts
1. Andy Pettitte 51
2. Orlando Hernandez 46
3. Mike Mussina 35
4. Mariano Rivera 34
5. Roger Clemens 32

ERA (min. 20.0IP)
1. Mariano Rivera 0.92
2. MASAHIRO TANAKA 1.88
3. David Wells 2.70
4. Orlando Hernandez 3.26
5. David Cone 3.33

Saves (official stat since 1969)
1. Mariano Rivera .... MLB 13
T2. AROLDIS CHAPMAN 2
    Goose Gossage 2
T4 Clay, Lyle, Mendoza, Wetteland . 1

Shutouts
1. Roger Clemens .... MLBT 1

Complete Games
T1. Roger Clemens 1
    Ron Guidry 1
    Catfish Hunter 1
    Rudy May 1

Yankees All-Time Division Series Leaders

Please note that the players' totals listed below are as a Yankee only and do not include statistics accumulated while playing for other teams. **KEY:** MLB = All-time Major League leader with the total listed; AL = All-time American League leader with the total listed; T= Tied for lead. The Division series was played in the strike-shortened 1981 season and every year since 1995.

BATTING

Games Played (incl. pitchers)
1. Derek Jeter .... MLB 66
2. Jorge Posada 51
3. Bernie Williams 48
4. Mariano Rivera............. 39
5. Alex Rodriguez 32

At-Bats
1. Derek Jeter .... MLB 268
2. Bernie Williams 183
3. Jorge Posada 173
4. Alex Rodriguez 119
5. Robinson Canó 117

Runs
1. Derek Jeter .... MLB 47
2. Bernie Williams 36
3. Jorge Posada 25
4. Paul O'Neill 18
5. Hideki Matsui 15

Hits
1. Derek Jeter .... MLB 92
2. Bernie Williams 51
3. Jorge Posada 49
T4. Robinson Canó 27
    Paul O'Neill 27
    Alex Rodriguez 27

Doubles
1. Bernie Williams .... MLB 16
2. Derek Jeter 13
T3. Robinson Canó 8
    Jorge Posada 8
5. Tino Martinez..............7

Triples
T1. Curtis Granderson 2
    Derek Jeter 2
T3. Robinson Canó 1
    David Justice..............1
    Jorge Posada 1

Home Runs
1. Derek Jeter .... ALT 10
2. Bernie Williams 8
3. Paul O'Neill 6
4. Jorge Posada 5
T5. Canó, Matsui,
    Rodriguez, SÁNCHEZ 4

RBI
1. Bernie Williams .... MLB 33
2. Derek Jeter 28
3. Robinson Canó 23
T4. Paul O'Neill 14
    Jorge Posada 14
    Alex Rodriguez 14

Walks
1. Bernie Williams .... AL 26
2. Derek Jeter 24
3. Jorge Posada 21
4. Alex Rodriguez 18
5. Hideki Matsui 15

Batting Average (min. 30PA)
1. Jeter .... .343 (92-for-268)
2. Giambi........ .311 (19-for-61)
3. Abreu........... .300 (9-for-30)
4. Posada....... .283 (49-for-173)
5. B. Williams ... .279 (51-for-183)

On-Base Percentage (min. 30PA)
1. Jason Giambi................440
2. Derek Jeter.................397
3. Didi Gregorius..............388
4. Bobby Abreu.................382
5. Randy Velarde...............379

Slugging Pct. (min. 30PA)
1. Derek Jeter 519
2. Didi Gregorius 512
3. Paul O'Neill 505
4. Curtis Granderson 500
5. Bernie Williams 497

Stolen Bases
1. Derek Jeter 6
2. Alfonso Soriano............. 5
3. Alex Rodriguez 4
4. BRETT GARDNER...............3
T5. Granderson, Knoblauch,
    Maybin, Raines,
    TORRES, B. Williams 2

Hitting Streak
1. Jeter (10/14/01-10/4/05) ...... MLB 15
2. B. Williams (10/4/02-10/7/05) 13
3. O'Neill (10/5/96-10/7/99) 11
4. Matsui (10/4/03-10/7/05)..........9
T5. Granderson (10/6/10-10/6/11) 8
    Jeter (10/8/07-9/30/11) 8
    A. Rodriguez (10/7/07-10/9/10) 8

PITCHING

Games
1. Mariano Rivera.......... MLB 39
2. Andy Pettitte 15
T3. Jeff Nelson 14
    David Robertson........... 14
5. Mike Stanton............... 12

Games Started
1. Andy Pettitte .... AL 15
2. CC Sabathia..................9
3. Roger Clemens 8
4. Mike Mussina 7
5. David Cone 5

Innings Pitched
1. Andy Pettitte .... AL 93.2
2. Mariano Rivera........... 56.0
3. CC Sabathia...............51.2
4. Mike Mussina 45.0
5. Roger Clemens 41.1

Wins
1. Andy Pettitte 6
2. CC Sabathia..................4
T3. Orlando Hernandez..........3
    David Robertson............3
    David Wells................3
    MASAHIRO TANAKA 3

Losses
T1. Mike Mussina................4
    Andy Pettitte 4
T3. Roger Clemens 3
    Chien-Ming Wang 3
5. Jack McDowell...............2

Strikeouts
1. Andy Pettitte 64
2. CC Sabathia................. 55
3. Mariano Rivera............. 44
4. Mike Mussina 34
T5. Roger Clemens 30
    David Cone 30

ERA (min. 20.0IP)
1. Mariano Rivera........ MLB 0.32
2. Phil Hughes................1.52
3. Orlando Hernandez.......1.98
4. David Wells 3.07
5. CC Sabathia................ 3.48

Saves (official stat since 1969)
1. Mariano Rivera......... MLB 18
T2. AROLDIS CHAPMAN 2
    Goose Gossage 3
4. John Wetteland.............2
5. TOMMY KAHNLE...............1

Shutouts
Yankees pitchers have never thrown a shutout in the ALDS.

Complete Games
T1. CC Sabathia..................1
    David Wells 1

Yankee Stadium

The New York Yankees began a new chapter in their storied history with the opening of Yankee Stadium in 2009. Located directly across the street from the site of the original, the new Stadium's architecture is a celebration of the spirit and tradition of the franchise. While firmly rooted in the past, the Stadium has a vision toward the future, incorporating the best in technology and state-of-the-art guest services.

All of the Stadium's modern amenities exist within the framework of classic elements of the original, most notably the instantly recognizable frieze that again circles the grandstand. Among the countless fan-friendly elements, massive video boards give Yankees fans more information than ever before, and concessions have been placed on concourses that allow for continuous viewing of the game.

Yankee Stadium, as a living museum, has been designed to set the standard—much like the team has done with its 27 World Championships.

The current Yankee Stadium [L] and the original in 2008.

HOMAGE TO THE ORIGINAL

The current Yankee Stadium evokes the spirit of the original, while restoring many of the lost treasures from before the renovations of 1974-75.

The signature frieze once again outlines the top of the Stadium bowl. As in the past, it is attached to a roof that extends into the Stadium, covering the top rows of the Grandstand.

Monument Park has been relocated to its original position in center field, albeit behind the fence, unlike before the renovation when the monuments were on the playing field. All plaques, monuments and tribute displays for the 22 Yankees who have had their numbers retired are on display for fans, who may visit Monument Park prior to all home games.

On the Main Level, near Section 210, the **New York Yankees Museum presented by Bank of America**—a museum within the living museum that is Yankee Stadium—presents Yankees history through displays of artifacts and memorabilia. Items include a "Ball Wall" with hundreds of signed baseballs from Yankees greats, Thurman Munson's locker from the original Yankee Stadium and a replica of a locker from the Yankees clubhouse in the current Stadium. On game days, fans are welcome in the museum beginning 90 minutes prior to the scheduled first pitch until the end of the eighth inning. On non-game days, visitors can enjoy the museum as part of Yankee Stadium tours.

Babe Ruth Plaza, located on the south side of the Stadium in between Gates 4 and 6, honors the man proverbially credited with building the original House that Ruth Built. Through a series of storyboards displayed on light posts, the Babe's life story is recounted throughout the plaza.

Gate 4 at Yankee Stadium

THE STADIUM SITE

The Yankees are proud to play in the Bronx, which is home to approximately 1.5 million residents and is one of the five boroughs that make up New York City.

The Stadium sits on former parkland from Macombs Dam Park and Mullaly Park, with the Stadium grounds bounded by Jerome Avenue to the west, River Avenue to the east, and 161st Street to the south. The northern edge of the site is located between 162nd Street and 164th Street. In a nod to tradition, the footprint of the original Stadium has been replicated in the new Stadium.

Yankee Stadium is the fourth permanent home of the New York Yankees, following Hilltop Park (1903-12), the Polo Grounds (1913-22), and the original Yankee Stadium (1923-73, '76-2008). The Yankees also played two full seasons at Shea Stadium (1974-75) in Queens when the original Stadium underwent remodeling.

INNOVATIVE ARCHITECTURE AND MODERN AMENITIES

One of the goals in building Yankee Stadium was to bring fans closer to the action in a facility more attuned to modern needs and expectations. The new building is 63 percent larger than the original Stadium with about 500,000 square feet of additional space.

Improved sight lines, wider concourses and the installation of nearly 1,400 high-definition video monitors throughout the Stadium all ensure guests won't miss a minute of on-field action while in their seats or at concession stands. In addition to the live game broadcast, these centrally controlled Internet protocol monitors can also provide up-to-the-moment news, scores, weather, traffic information and safety updates.

The **Great Hall** is a 31,000-square-foot space located between the Stadium's exterior wall and the interior of the Stadium. Spanning from Gate 4 to Gate 6, it is covered overhead but has massive open-air archways, which help support the Yankees' green initiatives. It is home to large banners bearing the images of past Yankees greats from Babe Ruth and Lou Gehrig to more modern stars such as Don Mattingly and Paul O'Neill. A 24-foot-high-by-36-foot-wide 10mm true high-definition video board and a 5-foot-by-386-foot LED ribbon board immediately greet guests who enter through this portion of the Stadium.

The audio/visual experience at Yankee Stadium is highlighted by a 59-foot-high-by-101-foot-long 16mm true high-definition centerfield video board, which is flanked by two smaller video boards that display day-of-game lineups, game-in-progress information, statistics and out-of-town scores. Additionally, the entire length of the Terrace Level is spanned by a 3-foot-high, 1,278-foot long full-color LED ribbon board. A distributed sound system optimizes speaker placement for audio quality vastly superior to that in the original Stadium. The entire Stadium is built with a future-proof infrastructure designed by Cisco Systems that is easily adaptable to new technologies. A 7,000-square-foot state-of-the-art **FedEx Banquet and Conference Center** is designed to meet the needs of guests who wish to host business functions in the ballpark.

URBAN PLANNING

The site for Yankee Stadium was in part selected for its proximity to mass transit. Like the original Stadium, it is served at the 161st Street/Yankee Stadium subway stop by the No. 4, B and D trains.

Metro-North offers train service to Yankee Stadium from anywhere in its service territory, and Yankee Stadium is accessible by New York City Transit bus lines. For more information, call the MTA at 511 or visit www.mta.info.

Pedestrian access points are located at Yankee Stadium's four gates: **Gate 2** on Jerome Ave. and 164th St.; **Gate 4** at Jerome Ave. and 161st St.; **Gate 6** at River Ave. and 161st St.; and **Gate 8** at River Ave., south of 164th St.

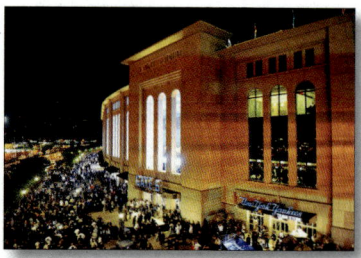

RETAIL & FOOD OPTIONS

There are many distinct retail stores in Yankee Stadium, including the **Yankees Team Store behind home plate on the Field Level** (which houses the largest selection of Yankees merchandise) and the **Yankees Team Store at Gate 6**, which is open year-round (Please call 646-977-8777 for store hours). Additionally, **Yankees-Steiner** authenticated memorabilia can be found a store located on the Field Level near Section 114A.

Yankee Stadium is also home to two premier dining establishments. The iconic **Hard Rock Cafe Yankee Stadium** at Gate 6 is open year-round and houses music memorabilia and Yankees-related pieces. The **Yankees Steakhouse at Yankee Stadium**, located above the Hard Rock Cafe, offers an upscale dining experience, including dry aged USDA prime steaks, fresh seafood and an impressive collection of premium wines.

More casual fare can be found at the Pepsi Food Court on the third-base side of the Field Level concourse and in other locations throughout the Stadium. For more information, please visit "Social Areas Open to All Fans at Yankee Stadium" in this section of the book.

The Yankees Steakhouse is located at Gate 6.

DISABLED SERVICES

The Yankees strive to provide an accessible environment for all their Guests at Yankee Stadium. Wheelchair accessible and designated aisle seats are available at various price points and locations and include Yankees Premium seat locations. The Stadium also offers enhanced accessibility for Guests with hearing loss or low vision and for Guests who are deaf or blind. For more information, please e-mail disabledservices@yankees.com or call (718) 579-4510 (voice) or (718) 579-4595 (TTY).

There are two dedicated open-caption video boards for Guests who are deaf or have hearing loss: one in left field, just below Section 233B, and one in right field, just below Section 206. Captioning is also provided on the right-center field video board, the high-definition video board in the Great Hall, high-definition televisions throughout Yankee Stadium and on the video board in the New York Yankees Museum presented by Bank of America.

COMMITMENT TO SAFETY

In 2012, Yankee Stadium became the first sports venue in the United States to be covered with a federal SAFETY Act designation and certification from the U.S. Department of Homeland Security. In 2017, Yankee Stadium became the first sports venue in the United States to be renewed under the SAFETY Act designation and certification by the U.S. Department of Homeland Security.

As part of Major League Baseball's initiative to standardize security procedures at all 30 Major League parks, all Guests are required to be screened via metal detectors before entering Yankee Stadium. These procedures, which result from MLB's continuing work with the Department of Homeland Security, are in addition to bag checks that are now uniform throughout MLB.

Due to the enhanced security measures, the Yankees strongly urge all fans to budget extra time for entry into the ballpark when planning their trip to the Stadium.

"Nothing is more important to us at Yankee Stadium than the safety of the fans we serve," said Yankees Chief Operating Officer Lonn Trost. "To that end, we are committed to the procedures that Major League Baseball and the Department of Homeland Security have asked us to implement. We want our fans to feel safe in Yankee Stadium, and our staff is dedicated to maintaining the highest security standards possible."

BRONX INCENTIVES

Yankee Stadium is one of the premier building projects to take place in the Bronx in the last 60 years. The hard work and dedication of engineers, architects and construction professionals in building and designing the Stadium made the facility one of the most impressive and fan-friendly venues in the Majors. Equally important was the project's dedication to support local community groups, institutions and residents as the Yankees remain devoted to the long-term development of the Bronx.

Building a new state-of-the-art facility required an army of talented and experienced professionals. As part of the Yankees' commitment to ensure the Stadium project created economic opportunities in the Bronx, the Yankees made a concerted effort to recruit a wide range of vendors and employees from the local community. Of the 190 contracts awarded, 63 were allotted to Bronx-based businesses (accounting for over 33 percent of the contracts and resulting in $133 million in contracts to Bronx-based businesses). The Yankees also stayed committed to hiring at least 25 percent of the total workforce from Bronx residents, again providing incentive to the surrounding community.

In conjunction with the construction of the Stadium, the Yankees also established a $1 million grant for professional skills training for Bronx residents. Among the supported initiatives was Project H.I.R.E. (Help In Re-entering Employment), which taught Bronx residents functional construction skills for practical use in local building projects.

SUSTAINABILITY INITIATIVES
at Yankee Stadium

YANKEES BECOME FIRST MAJOR NORTH AMERICAN SPORTS TEAM TO JOIN THE UN SPORTS FOR CLIMATE ACTION FRAMEWORK

On April 3, 2019, the New York Yankees became the first major North American sports team to sign on to the UN Sports for Climate Action Framework, the aim of which is to bring greenhouse emissions in line with the Paris Climate Change Agreement and inspire others to take ambitious climate action. The team joins numerous prominent international organizations committed to the Framework, including the International Olympic Committee, FIFA, the French Tennis Federation-Roland Garros, Paris 2024 Summer Olympics, Rugby League World Cup 2021, Tokyo 2020 Summer Olympics, UEFA, World Surf League, Formula E, and others.

"The New York Yankees are proud to support the United Nations Sports for Climate Action Framework," said Yankees Managing General Partner Hal Steinbrenner. "For many years the Yankees have been implementing the type of climate action now enshrined in the Sports for Climate Action principles, and with this pledge the Yankees commit to continue to work collaboratively with our sponsors, fans and other relevant stakeholders to implement the UN's climate action agenda in sports."

United Nations
Framework Convention on Climate Change

On Earth Day 2019, the Yankees were joined by Satya S. Tripathi [second from L], the UN Assistant Secretary-General and Head of New York Office at UN Environment, who took part in a pregame ceremony recognizing the Yankees' support of the UNFCCC.

Listed below are some of the ecologically intelligent measures being taken at Yankee Stadium to help promote sustainability.

High Efficiency LED Lighting: Prior to the 2016 Major League Baseball season, the Yankees installed the newest, most efficient lighting in the world, known as light-emitting diodes (LED). At the time we installed LED field lighting, Yankee Stadium became only the second MLB stadium to use the most state-of-the-art energy-efficient lighting system available. The LED lights used at Yankee Stadium are 40% more efficient and 50% brighter than the previous field lighting used at the Stadium, which were also the most efficient lights available for use at the time. Increased Color Temperature of the light produced results in higher contrast, improving player reaction time, alertness and visual acuity. Improved Color Rendering provides the truest colors the human eye can see. Reduced Flicker Rate means the lighting can now support UHD Ultra Slow Motion filming. Improved optical design with twice the aiming points reduces glare and light pollution, and the energy saved from the new field lighting is enough to power about 45 homes every day.

Energy Efficient Technologies and Design: The Great Hall at Yankee Stadium, through which the majority of guests arrive, is the largest open air public entry at any sports venue in the world, a 31,000 square-foot inspirational space spanning from Gate 4 to Gate 6. By building this area with massive open-air archways that allow for natural cooling and ventilation, the space requires no air conditioning. Through the use of natural air-cooling, the energy savings per game is approximately the same as 125 New York City apartments shutting off their air-conditioning on a hot summer day. The Stadium's interior is controlled by automation technologies designed to identify and eliminate wasted or inefficient energy use. The Stadium's high tech energy management program ensures that energy use is reduced and the efficiency of all equipment used is optimized. The diverse systems used to operate Yankee Stadium are carefully calibrated to specific usage patterns, reducing the power consumption of lighting and ventilation systems when they're not needed.

Offsetting Unavoidable GHG Emissions: Even the most efficient operations engender unavoidable greenhouse gas (GHG) emissions. Stadium energy use, team and employee travel, motors that require fossil fuel use, non-recyclable waste generation, and occasional leaks of refrigerants are all examples of GHG impacts that the Yankees carefully measure and offset through a collaboration with The South Pole Group. The high quality, third party verified GHG offsets that the Yankees invests in are carefully chosen to advance the United Nations Sustainable Development Goals, benefitting communities in need in Africa by promoting new employment opportunities, protecting biodiversity, and improving health and safety, including the distribution of thousands of life-saving high-efficiency cookstoves. As a result, the Yankees are leading the way towards a low-carbon, more sustainable future.

The majority of Yankee Stadium guests enter the building via the 31,000-sq.-foot Great Hall. By building this area with massive open-air archways that allow for natural cooling and ventilation, it does not require air conditioning.

Mass Transit: Yankee Stadium benefits from one of the greatest mass transit systems of any city in the world. Located within close proximity of the subway, Metro-North, buses and other mass transportation systems, visitors to Yankee Stadium have better access to mass transit than at any other stadium in Major League Baseball. Yankee Stadium owns no public parking garages, and guests and employees are encouraged to use public transportation in order to reduce the number of cars on the road and their GHG emissions.

Composting and Recycling: The Yankees are committed to achieving zero waste and promoting a circular economy based on composting, recycling, and the recovery and use of waste oil. Compostable cutlery and food-service packaging, trays, boxes, plates and cups, are used instead of non-compostable petroleum-based plastics. Food waste is composted and not landfilled, and cardboard, glass, metal, plastics and paper are recycled. Through the overall efforts of fans and Stadium staff, approximately 85 percent of the Stadium's total trash is diverted away from landfills, making Yankee Stadium one of the most successful recycling venues in all of sports. The use of trash compactors for the small percentage of non-recovered waste at Yankee Stadium improves air quality by reducing the number of trash packer trucks needed. The trucks that are required use Ultra Low Sulfur diesel which produces fewer emissions into the air, and these emissions are offset by the Yankees.

The Yankees installed new LED lighting prior to the 2016 season, reducing Yankee Stadium's carbon footprint.

Recovery of Waste Cooking Oil: During the course of a typical season, more than 20,000 gallons of cooking oil from the Stadium are recovered and recycled. This oil is used to produce more than 18,600 gallons of biodiesel fuel which, when used in vehicles, results in a carbon reduction of more than 30,000 pounds—the equivalent of removing approximately 27 cars from the road for a year.

Water Conservation: Yankee Stadium is a responsible steward when it comes protecting New York City's precious and irreplaceable water system. Through careful monitoring and high efficiency plumbing fixtures, Yankee Stadium saves more than 3 million gallons of water each year, a reduction of 22 percent from water use prior to 2009.

Healthy Air Quality: Yankee Stadium uses high-performance filters and a regular replacement program to ensure particle removal effectiveness of MERV 13 or greater, for better air quality and energy efficiency in our HVAC system.

Smart Construction: The structural steel used in the construction of Yankee Stadium was fabricated from recycled material, and the concrete forms were reusable. Used recycled concrete aggregate was incorporated into the concrete design mix. All construction vehicles and equipment were required to use low-sulfur fuel. During construction, 75 percent of construction waste was diverted from landfills.

YANKEES ESTABLISH FIRST ENVIRONMENTAL SCIENCE APPOINTEE POSITION IN PROFESSIONAL SPORTS

On Jan. 29, 2019, the New York Yankees announced the creation of an environmental science advisor position, appointing recognized industry leader Dr. Allen Hershkowitz to the new role, the first of its kind in professional sports. The appointment represents a defining moment in the team's decades-long commitment to sustainability, and serves to deepen an existing dedication to environmentally-friendly practices and community-wide awareness. Recognized as one of the most environmentally intelligent and healthiest sports venues in the world, with Hershkowitz as Environmental Science Advisor, the Yankees will look to further advance their efforts and invest in the development of best practices that can be adopted by organizations across the sport sector. Specifically, Hershkowitz will seek to guide a number of new and existing environmental initiatives for the Yankees and at Yankee Stadium, with a primary focus on the areas of energy use, waste management, water conservation, and food services.

YANKEES RECOGNIZED BY NEW YORK STATE AS LEADER IN INNOVATION AND SUSTAINABILITY

At the 13th Annual New York State Environmental Excellence Awards on Nov. 15, 2016, the N.Y. State Department of Environmental Conservation recognized the Yankees among eight New York-based organizations for their state-of-the-art programs and commitment to environmental sustainability, social responsibility and economic viability.

"DEC is proud to present Environmental Excellence Awards to these eight businesses and organizations that have demonstrated outstanding leadership in adopting innovative solutions to protect our environment and enhance our economy," said DEC Commissioner Basil Seggos. "These projects set a high bar for others to follow in addressing critical environmental and public health issues such as increasing energy efficiency, cleaning up our waters, keeping materials out of landfills, and making our healthcare sector more sustainable."

"It is vitally important that we help promote sustainability and reduce our impact on the environment," said Yankees Vice President of Stadium Operations Doug Behar. "We have implemented an array of green initiatives at Yankee Stadium and continue to look for new and better ways to conserve natural resources, educate our guests and Yankees Team Members, and support and partner with programs that promote sustainability. We are humbled to receive this award from the State and will continue to work hard to further our efforts in sustainability."

YANKEES WIN ENVIRONMENTAL LEADERSHIP AWARD FROM GREEN SPORTS ALLIANCE

On June 4, 2015, with former MLB Commissioner Bud Selig, in attendance, the Yankees received the 2015 Environmental Leadership Award, presented by the Green Sports Alliance. The award recognizes a sports team and venue that best exemplifies the practices of promoting a sustainable environment. Green Sports Alliance members represent nearly 300 sports teams and venues from 20 different sports leagues and 14 countries across the world. Yankees President Randy Levine (third from L) and V.P. of Stadium Operations Doug Behar (second from R) accepted the award on behalf of the organization.

Cool Swing

ANTIGUA AND BARBUDA
The beach is just the beginnin

VisitAntiguaBarbuda.com

Yankee Stadium Firsts

First Regular Season Game: 4/16/09 (Cleveland 10 - Yankees 2)
All "firsts" from this game unless otherwise noted.

STARTING LINEUPS
Yankees: Derek Jeter-SS, Johnny Damon-LF, Mark Teixeira-1B, Nick Swisher-RF, Jorge Posada-C, Robinson Cano-2B, Hideki Matsui-DH, Cody Ransom-3B, Brett Gardner-CF, CC Sabathia-P; **Indians:** Grady Sizemore-CF, Mark DeRosa-3B, Victor Martinez-1B, Jhonny Peralta-SS, Shin-Soo Choo-DH, Ben Francisco-RF, Kelly Shoppach-C, Tony Graffanino-2B, Trevor Crowe-LF, Cliff Lee-P

BATTING
Out: Sizemore (Clev.), first-inn., ground out to 1B
Hit: Damon, first-inning single to CF
HR: Posada, solo, fifth-inn., to CF off C. Lee (Clev.)
Run Scored: Francisco (Clev.), fourth inn.
RBI: Shoppach (Clev.), fourth inn.
Stolen Base: Damon, first inn. (4/17/09 vs. Clev.)

PITCHING
Pitch: Sabathia to Sizemore (Clev.), first inn. (ball)
Win: Lee (Clev.)
Save: Rivera, 4/17/09 vs. Cleveland
Strikeout: Sabathia (V. Martinez, swinging, first inn.)

GAMES
Exhibition Game: 4/3/09, Yankees 7 - Chicago-NL 4
Reg. Season Game: 4/16/09, Cleveland 10 - Yankees 2
NYY Reg. Season Win: 4/17/09 vs. Cleveland (6-5, WP-Bruney, SV-Rivera)

OTHER
Star-Spangled Banner Performer: Kelly Clarkson
God Bless America Singer: Ronan Tynan
Ceremonial First Pitch: Yogi Berra

Newly-acquired free-agent CC Sabathia tosses the first regular season pitch in Yankee Stadium history to Cleveland's Grady Sizemore on April 16, 2009.

Yankee Stadium Construction Timeline

JUNE 15, 2005 – The Yankees announce plans for a new Yankee Stadium to be constructed on parkland north of 161st Street – adjacent to the original Stadium's longtime site.

AUG. 16, 2006 – The Yankees break ground for Yankee Stadium at a ceremony featuring George M. Steinbrenner, N.Y. Governor George Pataki, N.Y.C. Mayor Michael Bloomberg, Bx. Borough Pres. Adolfo Carrion & MLB Commissioner Bud Selig.

OCT. 2006 – The first concrete is poured.

DEC. 2007 – The first piece of frieze is put in place.

DEC. 2007 – The Stadium is considered 50% completed.

JAN. 14-15, 2008 – Limestone Panels containing "YANKEE STADIUM" gold lettering are installed above Gate 4.

MAR. 29, 2008 – Eagle medallions inspired by those on the 1923 Stadium are lifted into place above Gate 4.

APRIL 2008 – Frieze installation is completed.

MAY 1, 2008 – A "topping off" ceremony is held to commemorate the completion of the steel structure.

MAY 2008 – The foul poles and first seats are installed.

JUNE 18, 2008 – The Yankees hold their first press conference at the new Yankee Stadium, announcing a long-term agreement with Seminole Hard Rock Entertainment to open a Hard Rock Cafe near Gate 6. In addition, the Yankees introduce the newly-branded NYY Steak, a prime steakhouse to be located in Yankee Stadium.

SEPT. 19, 2008 – The massive, blue, backlit "YANKEE STADIUM" lettering above Gate 4 is hoisted and installed.

OCTOBER 2008 – Lighting in the interior bowl is tested.

OCT. 15, 2008 – The first sections of sod are laid.

NOV. 8, 2008 – Yankees executives and former players, including Scott Brosius, David Cone, Paul O' Neill and Jeff Nelson, along with 60 local Bronx high school youth groups remove home plate, the pitcher's rubber and pails of dirt from the original Stadium and install them in the new Yankee Stadium. The participating Bronx youth groups—Youth Force 2020, led by Turner Construction Company, and the ACE Mentor Program at Yankee Stadium, guided by Tishman Speyer—took part in Yankees-sponsored after-school programs relating to the construction and engineering of the new Yankee Stadium.

JAN. 23, 2009 – The front office moves in, bringing World Series trophies from 1977 and 2000 to the new building.

FEBRUARY 2009 – Plaques and monuments are placed in the new Monument Park.

APR. 3-4, 2009 – The first exhibition games vs. the Cubs are played.

APR. 16, 2009 – The first regular season game is played vs. Cleveland (CLE 10 - NYY 2).

Social Areas Open to All Fans at Yankee Stadium

On Oct. 24, 2016, the New York Yankees announced that Yankee Stadium would undergo its first series of major design enhancements which are intended to improve the Guest experience for fans of all ages. Enhancements prior to the 2017 season included numerous new social gathering spaces and additional dynamic food and beverage areas.

"We have listened to our fans and ticketholders and their top requests were for more family-friendly and socially-oriented spaces at Yankee Stadium," said Yankees Managing General Partner Hal Steinbrenner. "Yankees fans will now have many more dedicated areas for spending time with Guests who have tickets in other sections of the Stadium, allowing all Guests to be able to enjoy the game from multiple vantage points while having unique food and drink options available to them. We are also especially excited to provide an engaging children's play area for families to utilize prior to and throughout the game. Having these types of spaces in Yankee Stadium is fundamental to the expectations of our fans, and we look forward to making them a huge part of the Yankee Stadium experience today and beyond."

The following Yankee Stadium food and drink locations are accessible to all Yankee Stadium Guests, regardless of their ticketed seats. Highlights include:

PLYMOUTH ROCK KIDS CLUBHOUSE: The Plymouth Rock Kids Clubhouse is Yankee Stadium's first-ever children's zone. Shaped like a mini-baseball field with a soft artificial surface, the 2,850-square-foot area is located on the 300 Level in right field and outfitted with Yankees-themed playground equipment, including oversized baseballs, bases and baseball cards. The Kids Clubhouse is accessible to all Yankee Stadium Guests.

Children may play among the colorful fixtures, including a 6-foot-high replica World Series trophy. Parents can join their children on the play area or choose to oversee them from a nearby dugout. Television monitors ensure that no one misses any game action. There is also a shaded section of the play area with interactive exhibits, and the Clubhouse includes two family restrooms equipped with changing tables. Nursing mothers will have an additional private space, which includes lounge chairs, a television and power outlets for those using electric breast pumps.

"We want our youngest fans to feel as if Yankee Stadium is an extension of their local park or backyard," Steinbrenner said. "The Kids Clubhouse is designed to nurture their love for experiencing games in person, while providing parents the resources they need to keep their children entertained prior to and during the game."

MASTERCARD BATTER'S EYE DECK: Located on the 200 level in center field with a clear, sweeping view of the entire Stadium, the Mastercard Batter's Eye Deck was expanded to 3,500 square feet with drink-rails overlooking the field. This outdoor gathering space features craft beers, cocktails and a large selection of food options.

BULLPEN TERRACES: Frank's RedHot Terrace in left field and the Toyota Terrace in right field (on the 100 Level in the former Sections 239 and 201, respectively) are open-air social gathering areas overlooking the visitors and Yankees bullpens. Both terraces feature their own specialty food and drink options. Drink-rail locations at the landings have power/USB outlets. As a result of the 2017 reconfiguration, all obstructed-view seats in the Bleachers have been removed.

BUDWEISER PARTY DECKS: The 300 Level of the Stadium includes Budweiser Party Decks at Sections 311 and 328, featuring shaded stand-alone bar areas serving beer, cocktails and food. Drink-rail and barstool seating provides fans a relaxed and casual setting from which to enjoy sweeping views of the field and game action.

FIELD LEVEL SPORTS LOUNGE: The Field Level Sports Lounge at Section 134 on the Field Level includes a full bar with craft beers and cocktails. Tables, stools and large-screen televisions tuned to the Yankees broadcast and other live sporting events provide a sports-bar atmosphere on the Stadium's main outdoor concourse in left field. Additionally, power/USB outlets are available for charging phones or tablets.

PEPSI FOOD COURT: Located between sections 125 and 127B on the Field Level, the Pepsi Food Court contains a wide variety food and drink options for all fans. Centered around a bar with large-screen televisions, fans may enjoy the wide-ranging fare at shaded tabletop seating.

(NEW IN 2020) STELLA ARTOIS LANDING and MICHELOB ULTRA CLUBHOUSE: The Stella Artois Landing, spanning Sections 232A and 232B in left field, and the Michelob ULTRA Clubhouse, spanning Sections 207 and 208 in right field, will be accessible to fans with game day tickets anywhere in the Stadium. Both locations are covered overhead and are available as pregame party spaces for groups of 20 or more people.

Yankee Stadium by the Numbers

MATERIALS IN ORIGINAL CONSTRUCTION
Concrete: approximately 45,000 cubic yards
Excavation: approximately 363,000 cubic yards
Rebar: approximately 4,000 tons
Structural steel: approx. 11,800 tons in over 30,000 pieces
Piles driven: 1,675 piles averaging 80 feet long
Stone: Indiana Limestone and Deer Isle Granite
Frieze: approx. 1,400 feet long with 300 tons of structural steel
Doors: approximately 1,300
Gallons of paint: 15,000
Length of electrical wire: *Currently exceeds distance from Yankee Stadium to Steinbrenner Field in Tampa (approx. 1,012 miles)*
Length of Ethernet cable (CAT 6A): 227 miles

THE STRUCTURE
Location: In the Bronx, bounded by 164th St. (north); 161st St. (south); Jerome Ave. (west); River Ave. (east)
Mailing address: Yankee Stadium, One East 161st Street, Bronx, NY 10451
Switchboard phone number: (718) 293-4300
Architect: Populous (formerly HOK Sport)
Construction: Turner Construction
Developer: Tishman Speyer
Square footage: approximately 1.3 million square feet
Distance around the building: 4,755 linear feet
Size of entire site: 634,335 square feet or 14.56 acres
Height at highest point: The top of the frieze is 134 feet, 7 inches above Field Level.
Internet bandwidth: approx. 35 gigabits
Light bulbs (number of): approximately 20,000
Main centerfield video board size: 59-feet-by-101-feet
Ribbon board ringing the Terrace Level: 3-feet-by-1,278-feet
Great Hall size: 31,000 square feet
Great Hall LED ribbon board: 5-feet-by-386-feet
Great Hall high-definition video board: 24-feet-by-36-feet
Number of player flags in the Great Hall: 10 double-sided
Seating Capacity: 46,537

FIELD
Surface: Kentucky bluegrass grown at DeLea Sod Farms in New Jersey
Acreage: 3.14 acres, including the bullpens
Dimensions: LF 318'; LC 399'; CF 408'; RC 385'; RF 314'
Outfield walls height: From left-field foul pole, wall is 8-feet, 6-inches high until the Yankees bullpen, where it gradually descends to 8 feet at the right-field foul pole.
Distance from the plate to the backstop: 52 feet, 4 inches
Yankees bullpen size: averages approximately 82 feet wide by 32 feet deep
Opponents bullpen size: averages approximately 85 feet wide by 30 feet deep
Distance of batter's eye glass to home plate: 432 feet away and 19 feet off the ground
Height of Mastercard Deck above the field: 37 feet
Infield foundation: Sand-based
Feet below street level: approximately 17 feet on average
Drainage pipe length: 14,000 linear feet
Irrigation pipe: 17,100 linear feet
Irrigation heads: 116
Distance from first or third base to the nearest spectator: 43 feet
Concourse (average width): 32 feet
Foul poles height: 90 feet

IN THE BUILDING
Ticket windows: 25 (including 19 outside the Stadium and six inside the Stadium)
Concessions (fixed): 27
Concessions (moveable): more than 100
Total concessions points of sale: approximately 465
Retail locations (fixed): 10
Retail locations (moveable): approximately 30
Total retail points of sale: approximately 70
Width of seats: 19 inches to 24 inches
Width of aisles: 4 feet
Legroom in front of seats: 33 inches to 39 inches
Number of elevators: 21 (16 public elevators and five service elevators.)
Stairways: 30
Pedestrian ramps: 2 (at Gates 2 and 6)
Video monitors: approximately 1,500 flat-panel, high-definition monitors
Cup holders: approximately 40,000
Toilet fixtures: approximately 878
Men's fixtures ratio in non-premium seating: approx. 1 fixture per 78 men (based on 50% male / 50% female attendance)
Women's fixtures ratio in non-premium seating: approx. 1 fixture per 75 women (based on 50% male / 50% female attendance)
Family bathrooms: 12
Yankees clubhouse dressing area: 3,344 square feet
Visitors clubhouse dressing area: 1,496 square feet

371

Other Events at the Current Yankee Stadium

NEW ERA PINSTRIPE BOWL

Michigan State 27 – Wake Forest 21   12/27/19
MVP: QB Brian Lewerke   Att: 36,895

Michigan State edged Wake Forest, 27-21, in the 10th annual Pinstripe Bowl. Down 7-3 in the first quarter, Spartans senior DT Mike Panasiuk returned a 14-yard interception for a touchdown to put the them up 10-7. Despite a 21-20 Wake Forest lead at the half, Michigan State captain and Pinstripe Bowl MVP QB Brian Lewerke (passing: 26-for-37, 320 yards, 1 TD; rushing: 46 yards, 1 TD) put the Spartans on top for good with a 10-yard touchdown pass to WR Cody White. In the second half, the Demon Deacons were limited to 101 yards and shut out despite recovering two fumbles.

Wisconsin 35 – Miami 3   12/27/18
MVP: RB Jonathan Taylor   Att: 37,821

Led by sophomore running back and Pinstripe Bowl MVP Jonathan Taylor (205 yards and 1 TD), Wisconsin routed Miami, 35-3, in both schools' first appearances in the Pinstripe Bowl. Carrying the Badgers to a wire-to-wire victory, the defense forced five turnovers that led to 21 points. UW controlled the clock, possessing the ball for nearly 40 minutes, while collecting 406 yards of total offense.

Wisconsin RB Jonathan Taylor led the offense with 205 yards rushing and 1 TD in the school's 2018 Pinstripe Bowl win.

Iowa 27 – Boston College 20   12/27/17
MVP: RB Akrum Wadley   Att: 37,667

Despite being outgained in total yards, 383-200, Iowa defeated Boston College, 27-20. The Hawkeyes forced three turnovers while not committing any themselves. New Jersey native Akrum Wadley, who had 283 all-purpose yards (22 carries, 88 yards; 2 receptions, 24 yards; and 171 return yards) earned MVP honors for Iowa in his final college game. Eagles' running back AJ Dillon carried 32 times for 157 yards and one touchdown, and tight end Tommy Sweeney had seven catches for 137 yards and one touchdown.

Northwestern 31 – Pittsburgh 24   12/28/16
MVP: RB Justin Jackson   Att: 37,918

Northwestern RB Justin Jackson earned MVP honors as the Wildcats defeated Pitt, 31-24. Northwestern running back Justin Jackson ran for three touchdowns and gained 224 yards, falling three yards shy of tying the NEPB's all-time, single-game rushing record. Despite losing QB Nathan Peterman and RB James Conner to injury, the Panthers led 24-21 early in the fourth quarter before Northwestern answered with a touchdown and field goal. Safety Kyle Queiro sealed the Wildcats' win with an interception on Pitt's final drive.

Duke 44 – Indiana 41 (OT)   12/26/15
Co-MVPs: QB Thomas Sirk/RB Shaun Wilson   Att: 37,218

Co-MVPs Thomas Sirk and Shaun Wilson led Duke to its first bowl game victory since 1961, after Indiana kicker Griffin Oakes missed a game-tying, 38-yard field goal attempt in OT. Wilson scored twice, on an 85-yard touchdown run and a 98-yard kickoff return. Indiana's Devine Redding scored a touchdown and had a game-high 35 carries in a losing effort, establishing the all-time NEPB mark with 227 yards rushing. Indiana totaled 667 total yards in the loss, including 389 passing yards by QB Nate Sudfeld. The contest was the first-ever matchup under Yankee Stadium's new LED lights.

Penn State 31 – Boston College 30 (OT)   12/27/14
MVP: QB Christian Hackenberg   Att: 49,012

A NEPB record-setting sold out crowd saw the first OT contest in the bowl game's history. After a BC touchdown and subsequent missed PAT on the opening possession of OT, Penn State QB Christian Hackenberg tossed a 10-yard TD pass to WR Kyle Carter to tie the game, 30-30. Kicker Sam Ficken, who tied the game with a 45-yard field goal with 20 seconds remaining in the fourth quarter, clinched the Nittany Lions' victory with a "walk-off" PAT.

Notre Dame 29 – Rutgers 16   12/28/13
MVP: OT Zack Martin   Att: 47,122

Notre Dame broke a 13-13 halftime tie by outscoring Rutgers, 16-3, in the second half. Fighting Irish QB Tommy Rees went 27-for-47 for 319 yards and K Kyle Brindza went 5-for-6 in field goal attempts. Notre Dame had possession for 38:23.

Syracuse 38 – West Virginia 14   12/29/12
MVP: RB Prince-Tyson Gulley   Att: 39,098

In a snow-filled contest, Syracuse junior RB Prince-Tyson Gulley had 213 rushing yards (26 carries, 2TDs) and 56 rec. yards (5 catches, 1TD) to win MVP honors. Syracuse's defense held the Mountaineers to 285 total yards and 0-for-14 on third and fourth downs.

Syracuse RB Prince-Tyson Gulley was named the Most Valuable Player of the 2012 Pinstripe Bowl.

Rutgers 27 – Iowa State 13   12/30/11
MVP: RB Jawan Jamison   Att: 38,328

The Scarlet Knights led, 17-6, at halftime and put the game away with an 86-yard touchdown pass from QB Chas Dodd to WR Brandon Coleman in the fourth quarter. MVP Jawan Jamison rushed for 131 yards on 27 carries with two TDs.

Syracuse 36 – Kansas State 34   12/30/10
MVP: RB Delone Carter   Att: 38,274

The inaugural New Era Pinstripe Bowl was decided by one play – a failed Wildcats two-point conversion with just over one minute left in regulation. Syracuse's Delone Carter rushed for 198 yards on 27 carries with two TDs and QB Ryan Nassib threw for 239 yards (13-for-21) with three TDs. Kansas State RB Daniel Thomas ran for 90 yards on 22 carries with three TDs.

The inaugural 2010 Pinstripe Bowl featured Kansas State and Syracuse, with the Orange winning, 36-34.

OTHER COLLEGE FOOTBALL

Dartmouth 27 – Princeton 10 Att: 21,506 11/9/19
In a matchup that featured two unbeaten Ivy League rivals, Dartmouth was victorious in a thrilling 27-10 win over Princeton. After forcing three first-half turnovers, including a pick-six from senior DE Niko Lalos in the first quarter, the Big Green took a commanding 17-7 lead at half and never looked back. Dartmouth's run-heavy offense was led by New York native QB Jared Gerbino (3-for-6, 36 passing yards, 16 carries, 97 rushing yards, 2TD). The Big Green never trailed in the game and outgained Princeton in total yards, 293-246.

Notre Dame 36 – Syracuse 3 Att: 48,104 11/17/18
No. 3 Notre Dame dispatched of No. 12 Syracuse, 36-3, as a sold-out crowd watched the highest-ranked matchup in New York City since 1947. The game – played as the ninth installment of Notre Dame's famed Shamrock Series – also marked the first time a top-20 ranked Notre Dame team played in New York City since 1946 (at the original Yankee Stadium). Quarterback Ian Book (23-for-37, 292 yards, 2 TD) led the undefeated Irish on offense, while the defense held Syracuse scoreless until the final minute of the game.

Notre Dame WR (No. 83) Chase Claypool celebrates his third-quarter touchdown in the team's 36-3 win over Syracuse.

Fordham 54 – Holy Cross 14 Att: 21,375 11/12/16
The 31st Ram-Crusader Cup was the first to take place at the current Yankee Stadium. Fordham's offense was led by QB Kevin Anderson (28-of-33, 426 yards, 3TD) and RB Chase Edmonds (23 carries, 121 rushing yards, 4TD). Edmonds' third rushing score of the day set the Patriot League record for career rushing touchdowns. Fordham outgained Holy Cross in yards, 608-302.

Lafayette 27 – Lehigh 7 Att: 48,256 11/22/14
In the 150th meeting of college football's most-played rivalry, Lafayette RB Ross Scheuerman led his team to victory with a record-setting day on the ground. His 304 rushing yards (45 carries, 3TD) established a school and Patriot League record.

Army 35 – UConn 21 Att: 27,453 11/8/14
With Army holding on to a 28-21 lead late in the fourth quarter, DB Chris Carnegie sealed the victory for the Black Knights with a 99-yard interception return for a touchdown. Army's victory was their first at the current Yankee Stadium and their first in the Bronx since 1960.

Rutgers 27 – Army 12 Att: 30,028 11/12/11
The Scarlet Knights scored 14 unanswered points at the end of the fourth quarter, including a 32-yard return of a blocked punt with 6:36 left. Rutgers WR Mohamed Sanu caught a game-high 13 passes for 129 yards.

Notre Dame 27 – Army 3 Att: 54,251 11/20/10
The first football game at the current Yankee Stadium marked the 50th all-time meeting between the two teams. Heisman Trophy winners Johnny Lujack and Pete Dawkins served as honorary captains, joining Hal Steinbrenner for the coin toss. ND outgained Army in yards, 369-to-174, as Fighting Irish QB Tommy Rees threw for 214 yards (13-for-20) with one TD.

SOCCER

Liverpool 2 – Sporting CP 2 Att: 31,112 7/24/19
Reigning UEFA Champions League winners Liverpool played to a 2-2 draw against Sporting CP of Lisbon.
Goals: Liverpool-Origi (20), Wijnaldum (44); Sporting-Fernandes (4), Wendel (53). Shots (On Goal): Liverpool-16 (5); Sporting-11 (5). Yellow: Liverpool-Fabinho (68); Sporting-Neto (30). Red: None. Half: Liverpool 2 – Sporting 1.

Man. City 2 (1) – Liverpool 2 (3) Att: 49,653 7/30/14
As part of the International Champions Cup tournament, Liverpool defeated Manchester City on penalty kicks after playing to a 2-2 draw during regulation. The match drew the largest soccer crowd in the history of the current Yankee Stadium.
Goals: Manchester City-Jovetic (53, 67); Liverpool-Henderson (59), Sterling (85). Shots (On Goal): MC-28 (8); Liverpool-15 (7). Yellow: Manchester City-None; Liverpool-Coates (73). Red: None. Half: Manchester City 0 – Liverpool 0.

Spain 2 – Ireland 0 Att: 39,368 6/11/13
Spain, the defending World Cup and European Champion, defeated Ireland in the first match between national teams at the current Yankee Stadium.
Goals: Spain-Soldado (69), Mata (88); Ireland-None. Shots (On Goal): Spain-22 (12); Ireland-5 (3). Yellow: Spain-Pedro (11); Ireland-Cox (72), Quinn (82). Red: None. Half: Spain 0 – Ireland 0.

Manchester City defender Vincent Kompany plays the ball during his club's 5-3 win over Chelsea on May 25, 2013.

Manchester City 5 – Chelsea 3 Att: 39,462 5/25/13
The Manchester City victory took place just three days after a May 22 press conference announced the club's partnership with the Yankees on new MLS team New York City Football Club (NYCFC).
Goals: Manchester City-Barry (5), Nasri (29, 74), Milner (55), Dzeko (84); Chelsea-Ramires (46, 69), Mata (82). Shots (On Goal): MC-13 (11); Chelsea-25 (13). Yellow: Manchester City-Tevez (22); Chelsea-None. Red: None. Half: Manchester City 2 – Chelsea 0.

Real Madrid 5 – AC Milan 1 Att: 49,407 8/8/12
Yankees reliever Mariano Rivera took part in the ceremonial coin toss before Cristiano Ronaldo led Real Madrid to victory.
Goals: Real Madrid-Di Maria (24), Ronaldo (49, 66), Ramos (81), Callejon (89); AC Milan-Robinho (33). Shots (On Goal): Real Madrid-27 (12); AC Milan-8 (2). Yellow: Real Madrid-None; AC Milan-Nocerino (27), Prince-Boateng (55). Red: None. Half: Real Madrid 1 – AC Milan 1.

Cristiano Ronaldo [C] scored two goals in leading Real Madrid to a 5-1 victory over A.C. Milan on Aug. 8, 2012.

Chelsea 1 – PSG 1 Att: 38,202 7/22/12
Chelsea, the reigning Champions League champions, and PSG, eventual winners of the 2012-13 French Ligue 1 title, played to a 1-1 draw in the first soccer match at the current Yankee Stadium.
Goals: Chelsea-Piazon (82); PSG-Nene (50). Shots (On Goal): Chelsea-12 (3); PSG-14 (5). Yellow: Chelsea-Mikel (58); PSG-Lavezzi (8), Sakho (41), Verratti (60). Red: None. Half: Chelsea 0 – PSG 1.

CONCERTS

Garth Brooks — 7/8-9/16
Joined by Trisha Yearwood, Garth Brooks played his first major New York City concerts in 20 years. The two shows marked the first country music events held at the current Yankee Stadium.

Romeo Santos — Att: 36,572 / 39,744 — 7/11-12/14
The "King of Bachata" became the first Latin artist to headline at the current Yankee Stadium with shows on consecutive nights.

JAY-Z/Justin Timberlake — Att: 43,609 / 42,561 — 7/19-20/13
The Legends of Summer tour made two stops at Yankee Stadium.

Madonna — Att: 37,775 / 37,767 — 9/6&8/12
The pop icon and best-selling female rock artist of the 20th century played two nights at Yankee Stadium on her MDNA Tour.

Roger Waters — Att: 31,752 / 28,392 — 6/6-7/12
The co-founder and principal songwriter of Pink Floyd brought his production of *The Wall*, including a 20,000-square-foot screen.

The Big 4 — Att: 41,451 — 9/14/11
Metallica, Slayer, Megadeth and Anthrax performed a combined 9 hours of music in front of a headbanging crowd.

Paul McCartney — Att: 44,037 / 43,966 — 7/15-16/11
The legendary Beatle performed hits spanning his entire career.

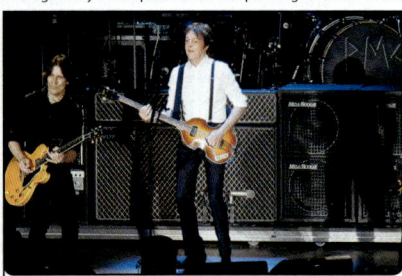

Paul McCartney performs on July 15, 2011, in the first of two consecutive nights of shows at Yankee Stadium.

JAY-Z/Eminem — Att: 45,434 / 46,272 — 9/13-14/10
This double-bill of Grammy winners performed in Yankee Stadium's first-ever concerts.

BOXING

Cotto def. Foreman (TKO-9) — Att: 20,372 — 6/5/10
Boxing returned to the home of the Yankees for the first time since 1976 with "Stadium Slugfest," as Miguel Cotto recorded a ninth-round TKO of Yuri Foreman in the main event, securing the WBA Super Welterweight title.

Yuri Foreman [L] lands a right hand during his main event fight with Miguel Cotto at Yankee Stadium.

Press Conference to Announce Manny Pacquiao-Miguel Cotto Fight — 9/10/09
Yankee Stadium played host to a press conference announcing the Nov. 14, 2009, bout between Miguel Cotto and Manny Pacquiao, which took place at the MGM Grand Garden in Las Vegas.

HOCKEY

Yankee Stadium was proud to host the NHL Stadium Series, marking the first hockey games played in the venue.

N.Y. Rangers 2 – N.Y. Islanders 1 — Att: 50,027 — 1/29/14
Goals: First Period—None. Second Period—NYI-Nelson, 18:33 (Donovan, Clutterbuck); NYR-Pouliot, 19:13 (Brassard, Zuccarello). Third Period—NYR-Carcillo, 4:36 (Moore, Boyle). Shots on Goal: NYR 6-14-14–34; NYI 10-15-6–31. Goalies: NYR-Lundqvist (31 shots, 30 saves), NYI-Nabakov (34 shots, 32 saves).

N.Y. Rangers 7 – N.J. Devils 3 — Att: 50,105 — 1/26/14
Goals: First Period—NJD-Elias, 5:36 (Clowe); NYR-Moore, 9:07 (Stralman, Boyle); NJD-Elias PPG, 11:00 (Jagr, Zidlicky); NJD-Zajac, 16:07 (Jagr, Fayne); NYR-Staal, 16:59 (Moore). Second Period—NYR-Zuccarello, 2:48 (Moore, Brassard); NYR-Zuccarello, 12:44 (Brassard, Pouliot); NYR-Hagelin, 13:53 (Callahan, Stralman); NYR-Nash, 19:31 (Stepan, Staal); Third Period—NYR-Stepan PS, 10:06 (None). Shots on Goal: NYR 10-11-5–26; NJD 10-7-5–22. Goalies: NYR-Lundqvist (22 shots, 19 saves), NJD-Brodeur (21 shots, 15 saves); Schneider (5 shots, 4 saves).

The Rangers and Devils skated in the first-ever hockey game at Yankee Stadium on Jan. 26, 2014.

DAMON RUNYON 5K RUN/WALK

Since the current Yankee Stadium opened in 2009, the Damon Runyon 5K Charity Run/Walk has been an annual event. Thousands of participants, including cancer patients, survivors, family, friends and scientists have run or walked the Yankee Stadium concourses, warning track and playing field to raise money for charity. Proceeds support young scientists funded by the Damon Runyon Cancer Research Foundation. Dates of the events have been: 5/11/19, 4/15/18, 7/15/17, 8/21/16, 11/15/15, 8/3/14, 8/18/13, 8/12/12, 8/7/11, 8/15/10 and 11/15/09.

WINTER WONDERLAND

Beginning in 2010, Yankee Stadium has been transformed into the North Pole for the Bronx Winter Wonderland event. Each year, approximately 5,000 children from the Bronx are treated to a holiday festival in the Great Hall, complete with Christmas decorations, holiday music and food and beverages. Santa also hands out a toy to each child in attendance. Dates of the events have been: 12/13/19, 12/14/18, 12/15/17, 12/9/16, 12/11/15, 12/12/14, 12/13/13, 12/7/12, 12/16/11 and 12/17/10.

The Great Hall is transformed into a Winter Wonderland annually for local Bronx youth during the holiday season.

PSAL CHAMPIONSHIP BASEBALL

2019 Championship Games 6/12/19
Game 1 "AA-Division": Lafayette Edu. Complex 2 – Inwood Campus 0
Game 2 "AAA-Division": Gregorio Luperon 5 – Beacon 4
2018 Championship Games 6/11/18
Game 1 "AA-Division": Bathgate Edu. 6 – Henry Van Arsdale 1
Game 2 "AAA-Division": James Monroe 3 – Grand Street 0
2017 Championship Games 6/12/17
Game 1 "AA-Division": Petrides 2 – HS of American Studies 1
Game 2 "AAA-Division": James Monroe 13 – Tottenville 2
2016 Championship Games 6/13/16
Game 1 "AA-Division": Bayside 3 – Eleanor Roosevelt 2
Game 2 "AAA-Division": Midwood 3 – Tottenville 0
2015 Championship Games 6/3/15
Game 1 "AA-Div.": East Side Community 7 – HS of American Studies 0
Game 2 "AAA-Division": George Washington 1 – Tottenville 0
2014 Championship Games 6/12/14
Game 1 "B-Division": Beach Channel/Channel View 7 – Bx. Science 5
Game 2 "A-Division": Benjamin N. Cardozo 3 – Tottenville 1
2009 Championship Games 6/9/09
Game 1 "B-Division": Health Profession/Human Services 4 – Taft 2
Game 2 "A-Division": Norman Thomas 5 – Monroe 2

PSAL FOOTBALL CHAMPIONSHIP

Erasmus 27 - Tottenville 0	Att: 2,625	12/4/19
Erasmus 34 - South Shore 7	Att: 2,497	12/4/18
Curtis 36 - Erasmus 35	Att: 3,242	12/5/17
Curtis 24 - Erasmus 21	Att: 3,429	12/2/16
Grand Street 28 – Erasmus 26	Att: 3,856	12/6/15
Lincoln 13 – Erasmus 6	Att: 2,802	12/10/14
Lincoln 28 – Tottenville 27	Att: 3,354	12/4/13
Erasmus 15 – Tottenville 14	Att: 4,077	12/4/12
Lincoln 20 – Erasmus 12	Att: 3,955	12/7/11
Ft. Hamilton 8 – Lincoln 6	Att: NA	12/6/10

NYU COMMENCEMENT

On May 14, 2008, NYU held its commencement at the original Yankee Stadium. Since then, the school has continued the tradition in the current Yankee Stadium. Commencement speakers have been: Poet Elizabeth Alexander (5/22/19); Canadian Prime Minster Justin Trudeau (5/16/18); Pharrell Williams (5/17/17); Ford Foundation President Darren Walker (5/18/16); Sherrilyn A. Ifill, President and Director/Counsel of the NAACP's Legal Defense and Educational Fund (5/20/15), Janet Yellen, Chair of the Board of Governors of the Federal Reserve System, (5/21/14); lawyer David Boies (5/22/13); Supreme Court Justice Sonia Sotomayor (5/16/12); former President Bill Clinton (5/18/11); actor Alec Baldwin (5/12/10); and then-Secretary of State Hillary Clinton (5/13/09).

Supreme Court Justice Sonia Sotomayor addresses students at the 2012 NYU Commencement.

BEYOND SPORT

This unique one-day event is designed to serve as a forum for discussion of the best community initiatives of sports teams and organizations from around the world. Dates of the events have been: 6/10-11/14, 11/13/12 and 9/27/11.

OTHER PERFORMERS/EVENTS

Babe Ruth Auction 6/15/19
Hunts Auction, Inc. hosted a historic live auction at Yankee Stadium that featured the personal collection of Babe Ruth. With over 400 items sold, the highlight of the auction was a Babe Ruth New York Yankees professional model road jersey dating to the 1928-30 period that sold for a record-breaking $5,640,000. The jersey is the most expensive piece of sports memorabilia to have ever been sold.

PitCCh In Foundation Charity Softball Game 5/16/19, 6/28/18
The New York Yankees Foundation and CC Sabathia's charitable nonprofit – the PitCCh In Foundation – joined together to host the second annual CC Sabathia Charity Softball Game on May 16, 2019, at Yankee Stadium. The star-studded event has featured many celebrities and athletes, including Michael Strahan, The Kid Mero, Tiki Barber, Johnny Damon, Fat Joe, Giancarlo Stanton, Leslie Jones and Victor Cruz, among others. The group walked the red carpet, attended a VIP reception and played in the softball game itself. All proceeds from the event benefitted the PitCCh In Foundation, helping to enrich the lives of inner city children through education and athletics, and the New York Yankees Foundation.

***Megan Leavey* Movie Premiere** 6/5/17
Yankee Stadium hosted its first-ever movie premiere, debuting *Megan Leavey*, which tells the story of a young Marine injured in combat in Iraq and her unbreakable bond with her combat dog Rex. Stars Kate Mara and Edie Falco attended with rapper/actor Common, who performed a concert for those in attendance.

Green Sports Alliance Leadership Awards 6/4/15
The Green Sports Alliance leverages the cultural and market influence of sports to promote healthy, sustainable communities where we live and play. They do so by inspiring sports leagues, teams, venues, their partners and millions of fans to embrace renewable energy, healthy food, recycling, water efficiency, species preservation, safer chemicals and other environmentally preferable practices. During the ceremony, the Yankees were honored with the 2015 Environmental Leadership Award.

"True Blue" Celebrity Charity Softball Game 6/3/15
The Yankees, WFAN and its Boomer and Carton Morning Show hosted "True Blue" – a celebrity softball game that honored the memories of NYPD officers Brian Moore, Wenjian Liu and Rafael Ramos, who were lost in the line of duty. All net ticket proceeds benefited the Silver Shield Foundation, N.Y. PBA Widows' and Children's Fund and the families of officers Moore, Liu and Ramos.

Joel and Victoria Osteen – "A Night of Hope" 6/7/14, 4/25/09
Joel and Victoria Osteen have brought their celebration of faith to Yankee Stadium on two different occasions. Their service in 2009 was the first non-baseball event at the current Yankee Stadium.

MLB Diversity Summit 4/14-15/14
The Yankees and Major League Baseball co-hosted the 2014 MLB Diversity Summit, a unique sports career and trade fair that provided job seekers and entrepreneurs with opportunities to connect directly with decision-makers from various MLB entities.

H.S. Baseball All-Star Game: NYC vs. Chicago 7/1/13
A team of Chicago all-star high school baseball players defeated a team of New York City PSAL All-Stars, 9-0.

Ascend Foundation Conference 4/20/13
Ascend is a non-profit professional association that helps to realize the leadership potential of Pan-Asians in global corporations. Hideki Matsui was the guest speaker.

Victoria's Secret Model Search 10/3/09
Yankee Stadium hosted an open casting call to select Runway Angels to walk in the 2009 Victoria's Secret Fashion Show. Five finalists were selected from nearly 3,000 entrants.

New York City FC

New York City Football Club is an American professional soccer team based in New York City that competes in Major League Soccer (MLS) in the Eastern Conference of the league. It was announced as the League's 20th franchise on May 21, 2013 and is the first and only MLS Club located within the five boroughs of New York City. Majority owned by City Football Group (CFG), New York City FC plays its home games at Yankee Stadium, which is also home to minority owner, the New York Yankees.

NYCFC made its MLS debut on March 8, 2015, in a 1-1 draw at Orlando City SC. One week later, in its home opener at Yankee Stadium on March 15, 2015, the club earned its first win, defeating the New England Revolution, 2-0.

Though the club did not qualify for the postseason in its inaugural season, NYCFC has made the playoffs in each of the last four years (2016-19).

The YES Network is the exclusive local television home for the club.

Main Office
600 Third Avenue, 30th Floor
New York, NY 10016
Phone: (212) 738-5900
E-mail: nycfc@nycfc.com

Website: www.nycfc.com

Twitter: @nycfc, @nycfcespanol

Ticketing & Fan Services
855.77.NYCFC (855.776.9232)
FanServices@nycfc.com, @NYCFCHelp

Administration/Staff
CEO: Brad Sims
Sporting Director: David Lee
Head Coach: Ronny Deila
Asst. Coaches: Nick Cushing, Javier Perez, Robert Vartughian

Media Relations
Press Inquiries: press@nycfc.com
Vice President: Sam Cooke
Director, Communications: Amanda Marston
Director, Media Relations: Nicole Chayet
Manager, Media Relations: Woody Wilder
Mgr., Communications: Modupeh Jahamaliah

2020 NYCFC REGULAR SEASON HOME SCHEDULE
(Start times subject to change.)

Sat., 3/14 vs. FC Dallas - 12:30 p.m.
Sat., 3/21 vs. Vancouver - 12:30 p.m.
Sun., 4/12 vs. Chicago - 12:30 p.m.
Sun., 4/26 vs. Nashville SC - 5:00 p.m. (CF)
Wed., 5/13 vs. Toronto - 7:00 p.m.
Sat., 5/16 vs. Colorado - 7:00 p.m.
Sun., 5/31 vs. N.Y. Red Bulls - 3:00 p.m.
Sun., 6/14 vs. New England - 5:00 p.m.
Wed., 6/17 vs. Atlanta - 7:00 p.m.
Wed., 7/1 vs. Orlando City - 7:00 p.m.
Wed., 7/15 vs. FC Cincinnati - 7:00 p.m.
Sat., 7/25 vs. Montreal - 5:00 p.m. (CF)
Sat., 8/8 vs. Philadelphia - 7:00 p.m. (CF)
Wed., 8/12 vs. Columbus - 7:00 p.m.
Sun., 8/30 vs. L.A. Galaxy - 4:00 p.m.
Wed., 9/16 vs. Inter Miami - 7:00 p.m.
Sat., 9/26 vs. D.C. United - 7:00 p.m. (CF)

CF= Game to played at Citi Field in Flushing, New York

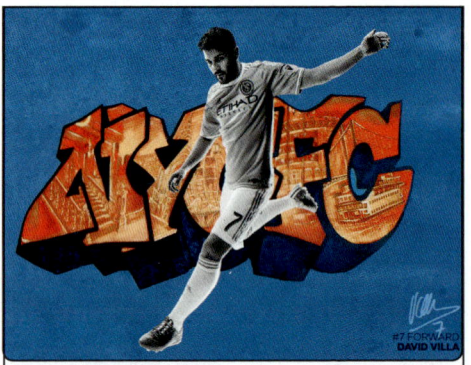

David Villa, who left the club following the 2018 season, is NYCFC's all-time regular season leader in games played (117), starts (109), goals (77) and assists (26). He also won the 2016 MLS MVP Award.

NYCFC — ALL-TIME REGULAR SEASON RECORD

Year	W-L-T	Total PTS	GF	GA	Home W-L-T	Away W-L-T	Leading Scorer	Head Coach	Conf. Finish/ Playoffs Result
2015	10-17-7	37	49	58	6-7-4	4-10-3	Villa (18)	Jason Kreis	8th-DNQ
2016	15-10-9	54	62	57	8-3-6	7-7-3	Villa (23)	Patrick Vieira	2nd-Conf. Semis
2017	16-9-9	57	56	43	*10-2-5	6-7-4	Villa (22)	Patrick Vieira	2nd-Conf. Semis
2018	16-10-8	56	59	45	12-1-4	4-9-4	Villa (14)	Vieira/Torrent	3rd-Conf. Semis
2019	18-6-10	64	63	42	11-1-5	7-5-5	Heber (15)	Domenec Torrent	**1st-Conf. Semis
ALL-TIME	75-52-43	268	289	245	*47-14-24	28-38-19	Villa (77)		

*Includes two games in 2017 (0-0-2) played at substitute venues due to Yankee Stadium scheduling conflicts.
**Played 2019 Eastern Conference Semifinal vs. Toronto at Citi Field.

Attendance Records

Yankees All-Time Attendance Records (Regular Season)
Largest Single-Season Home Attendance (2008) 4,298,543
Largest Single-Season Road Attendance (2004) 3,308,666
Largest Single-Season Combined Home-Road Attendance (2006) 7,325,051
Largest Crowd in Baseball History (Exhibition Game for Roy Campanella - 5/7/1959, NYY vs. LAD at the L.A. Coliseum).... 93,103
Most Consecutive Seasons with 4 Million Attendance in Baseball History: 4 (2005-2008)
Most Consecutive Seasons with 3 Million Attendance in Baseball History: 21 (1999-2019)

2019 Regular Season Attendance

HOME
Largest Day Game (8/17 vs. CLE) 47,347
Largest Night Game (8/3 vs. BOS-G2) 48,101
Straight Doubleheader 2
Sellouts 12

ROAD
Largest Day Game (6/30 at BOS-London) . 59,059
Largest Night Game (6/29 at BOS-London) 59,659
Straight Doubleheader 1
Sellouts 19

OVERALL
Home (79 dates/81G) .... 3,304,404 (40,795 avg.)
Road (80 dates/81G) ...... 2,460,744 (30,379 avg.)
Total (159 dates/162G) 5,765,148

Current Yankee Stadium Attendance Records 2009-19
Largest Single-Game Regular Season Attendance (8/7/10 vs. Boston) 49,716
Largest Single-Game Postseason Attendance (10/6/11 ALDS Game 5 vs. Detroit) 50,960
Largest Home Opening Day Attendance (4/1/13 vs. Boston) 49,514
Largest Three-Game Series Attendance (9/24-26/10 vs. Boston) 148,244
Largest Four-Game Series Attendance (8/6-9/10 vs. Boston) 197,843
Most Single-Season Home Sellouts (2018) 23
Largest Single-Season Home Attendance (2010) .... 3,765,807 (46,491 avg.)

Top 5 Postseason Crowds at Current Yankee Stadium (2009-19)
1. 10/6/11 vs. Detroit, ALDS Game 5 50,960
2. 9/30/11 vs. Detroit, ALDS Game 1 50,940
3. 10/9/10 vs. Minnesota, ALDS Game 3 50,840
4. 10/2/11 vs. Detroit, ALDS Game 2 50,596
5. 10/10/12 vs. Baltimore, ALDS Game 3 50,497

Top 5 Regular Season Crowds at Current Yankee Stadium (2009-19)
1. 8/7/10 vs. Boston 49,716
2. 7/28/12 vs. Boston 49,573
3. 7/27/12 vs. Boston 49,571
4. 9/25/10 vs. Boston 49,558
5. 9/24/11 vs. Boston 49,556

Remodeled Original Yankee Stadium 1976-2008 (Regular Season)
Largest Single-Game Home Attendance, Day (4/10/1998 vs. Oakland - Opening Day) 56,717
Largest Single-Game Home Attendance, Night (6/17/1997 vs. N.Y. Mets) 56,253
Largest Day Doubleheader Home Attendance (10/4/1980 vs. Detroit) 55,410
Largest Twi-Night Doubleheader Attendance (9/10/1983 vs. Baltimore) 55,605
Largest Weekday/Day/Non-Opening Day Crowd (Wed. 6/18/1997 vs. N.Y. Mets) 56,278
Largest Opening Day Home Attendance (4/10/1998 vs. Oakland) 56,717
Largest Old-Timers' Day Attendance (7/25/1998 vs. Chicago-AL) 55,642
Largest Home Series Attendance, three-game series (6/4-6/1999 vs. N.Y. Mets) 168,404
Largest Home Series Attendance, all series (9/16-17/2006 vs. Boston, 4 games, 2 day-night DH) 220,481
Largest Single-Season Home Attendance (2008) 4,298,543

Top 10 Postseason Crowds at Remodeled Yankee Stadium (1976-2008)
1. 10/7/99 vs. Texas, ALDS Game 2 57,485
2. 9/30/97 vs. Cleveland, ALDS Game 1 57,398
3. 9/29/98 vs. Texas, ALDS Game 1 57,362
4. 9/30/98 vs. Texas, ALDS Game 2 57,360
   10/2/97 vs. Cleveland, ALDS Game 2 57,360
6. 10/1/96 vs. Texas, ALDS Game 1 57,205
7. 10/13/99 vs. Boston, ALCS Game 1 57,181
8. 10/14/99 vs. Boston, ALCS Game 2 57,180
9. 10/3/95 vs. Seattle, ALDS Game 1 57,178
10. 10/2/96 vs. Texas, ALDS Game 2 57,156

Top 10 Regular Season Crowds at Remodeled Yankee Stadium (1976-2008)
1. 4/10/98 vs. Oakland, Opening Day 56,717
2. 4/11/97 vs. Oakland, Opening Day 56,710
3. 4/4/94 vs. Texas, Opening Day 56,706
4. 4/12/93 vs. Kansas City, Opening Day 56,704
5. 4/9/99 vs. Detroit, Opening Day 56,583
6. 4/7/92 vs. Boston, Opening Day 56,572
7. 4/9/96 vs. Kansas City, Opening Day 56,329
8. 6/6/99 vs. N.Y. Mets 56,294
9. 6/18/97 vs. N.Y. Mets 56,278
10. 6/17/97 vs. N.Y. Mets 56,253

Pre-Remodeled Original Yankee Stadium, 1923-73 (Regular Season)
Please note: Official Attendance Records are not available prior to 1938.
Largest Single-Game Home Attendance, Day (9/26/1948 vs. Boston) 69,755*
Largest Single-Game Home Attendance, Night (5/26/1947 vs. Boston) 74,747
Largest Doubleheader Home Attendance (5/30/1938 vs. Boston) 81,841
Largest Opening Day Home Attendance (4/19/1946 vs. Washington) 54,826*
Largest Old-Timers' Day Attendance (8/9/1958 vs. Boston) 67,916
Largest Home Series Attendance, all series (6/11-13/1948 vs. Cleveland, 4 games including DH on 6/12) 186,151
Largest Single-Season Total Attendance (1948) 2,373,901
According to published reports, the Stadium's first Opening Day (vs. Boston, 4/18/23) had an estimated attendance of 74,200.

All Home Ballparks
TOTAL ATTENDANCE
Hilltop Park (1903-12, 10 seasons, 168th St. & Broadway, Manhattan) 3,451,542
Polo Grounds (1913-22, 10 seasons, 157th St. & 8th Avenue, Manhattan) 6,220,031
Pre-Remodeled Original Yankee Stadium (1923-73, 51 seasons, 161st St. & River Avenue, Bronx) 64,333,705
Shea Stadium (1974-75, two seasons, 126th St. & Roosevelt Avenue, Queens) 2,561,123
Remodeled Original Yankee Stadium (1976-2008, 33 seasons, 161st St. & River Avenue, Bronx) 87,625,300*
Yankee Stadium (2009-19, 11 seasons, One East 161st St., Bronx) 37,553,919
TOTAL **201,745,620**

In 2019, the Yankees became the first North American team to reach 200 million in attendance while maintaining their franchise home in one city (Research by David Kronheim of numbertamer.com)

Game on 4/15/1998 vs. Anaheim was played at Shea Stadium when Yankee Stadium was closed by the City of New York after an expansion joint fell on 4/13/1998.

History of the Original Yankee Stadium

One year after changing the course of Baseball history with the purchase of Babe Ruth from the Boston Red Sox, the Yankees made another acquisition that would forever alter the way the game was watched.

On February 5, 1921, the Yankees issued a press release announcing the purchase of 10 acres of property in the west Bronx. The land, purchased from the estate of William Waldorf Astor for $675,000, sat directly across the Harlem River from the Manhattan-situated Polo Grounds, which the Yankees had been unhappily sharing with their landlord, the New York Giants of the National League, since 1913.

The relationship between the clubs crumbled after the 1920 season when the Yankees' attendance—boosted by their new slugging sensation—doubled to almost 1.3 million, approximately 25 percent more than that of the Giants. In 1921, the Giants asked the Yankees to vacate the Polo Grounds as soon as possible. With their departure from the Polo Grounds now inevitable, Yankees co-owners Jacob Ruppert and Tillinghast l'Hommedieu Huston set out to build a spectacular ballpark of their own, Baseball's first triple-decked structure. With an advertised capacity of 70,000, it would also be the first to be labeled a "stadium."

Original plans by the architect—the Osborn Engineering Company of Cleveland, Ohio—had the Stadium triple-decked and roofed all the way around. An early press release, in fact, described the Yankees' new home as a field enclosed with towering embattlements rendering the events inside "impenetrable to all human eyes, save those of aviators." But the initial grand design was quickly scaled back with the triple-decked grandstand not reaching either foul pole. Contrary to the owners' wishes, the action would be visible from the elevated trains that passed by the outfield, as well as from the buildings that would spring up across River Avenue. Fortunately, a purely decorative element survived the project's early downsizing and would become the park's most recognizable feature. A 15-foot-high copper frieze adorned the front of the roof, which covered much of the Stadium's third deck. It would give Yankee Stadium a stately dignity that became its signature.

The new stadium would favor left-handed power hitters with the right-field foul pole only 295 feet from home plate (though the right-field fence would shoot out to 429 feet in right-center). The left-field pole measured only 281 feet from the plate, but right-handed hitters would be neutralized by a 395-foot left field and a whopping 460 feet to left-center. The new stadium would also be patron-friendly, boasting an unheard of "eight toilet rooms for men and as many for women scattered throughout the stands and bleachers." (After the Stadium was remodeled 50 years later, it included more than 50 restrooms.) The club's executive offices would be moved from Midtown Manhattan and relocated between the main and mezzanine decks with an electric elevator connecting them with the main entrance.

The construction contract was awarded to New York's White Construction Company on May 5, 1922, with the edict that the job be completed "at a definite price" of $2.5 million by Opening Day 1923. Incredibly, it was. In only 284 working days, Yankee Stadium was ready for its inaugural game on April 18, 1923 vs. the Boston Red Sox.

An announced crowd of 74,200 fans packed Yankee Stadium while thousands more milled around outside after the fire department finally ordered the gates closed. Before the game began, John Philip Sousa and the Seventh Regiment Band led both clubs to the flagpole in deep center field, where the American flag and the Yankees' 1922 pennant were raised. Appropriately, Ruth christened his new home with a three-run homer to cap a four-run third inning as the Yankees coasted to a 4-1 win over the Boston Red Sox.

Because it was widely recognized that Ruth's tremendous drawing power made the new stadium possible, *New York Evening Telegram* sportswriter Fred Lieb dubbed it "The House That Ruth Built." Later that season, the Stadium hosted the first of 37 World Series, as the Yankees won their first World Championship by defeating their former landlord, the Giants. Of course, as the original Stadium became the stage for a staggering 26 world titles, it would also become known as "The Home of Champions."

In its early years, when wooden bleachers surrounded the outfield, a grass slope rose toward the outfield walls from foul pole to foul pole. Outfielders, especially Ruth in right, routinely backed up the small hill to pull down fly balls. Advertising signs lined the tops of the bleachers except in right-center, where a lone manually operated wooden scoreboard was large enough to record 12 innings for games played by every club in the two major leagues. Over the years, the board would be replaced by more modern models. The Yankees, in fact, would unveil Baseball's first electronic message board in 1959.

By 1928, the Stadium was ready for its first major face-lift. The triple-decked grandstand in left field was extended beyond the foul pole and several rows of box seats were removed in order to extend the left-field foul pole distance to 301 feet. The right-field grandstand was extended in 1937, allowing for "upper-deck" home runs in both directions. With the grandstand expansion, the remaining wooden bleachers were replaced with a concrete structure, and the distance to center field dropped from 490 feet to a still-distant 461 feet.

In 1932, the Yankees began their tradition of commemorating their heroes with monuments and plaques when they dedicated a monument to Manager Miller Huggins, who had died suddenly during the 1929 season. Five more monuments were added (one each for Lou Gehrig, Ruth, Mickey Mantle

Yankee Stadium in the 1920s

The original manual scoreboard

and Joe DiMaggio and one to honor the victims and heroes of the terrorist attacks of September 11, 2001) along with numerous plaques. For years, existing monuments were in the field of play in deep center field, and outfielders occasionally had to work around them to retrieve baseballs hit to that part of the park.

Except for the addition of lights in 1946, the look of Yankee Stadium remained relatively unchanged until the winter of 1966-67. Then, under the direction of the Yankees' new owner, CBS, the 44-year-old facility received a $1.5 million modernization, most of which was spent on 90 tons of paint. The brown concrete exterior was painted white as was the timeworn greenish copper frieze. Also, all of the grandstand seats went from green to blue, a color scheme that would be retained when the Stadium was completely remodeled after the 1973 season.

On August 8, 1972, after years of debate about the future of the aging ballpark, the Yankees signed a 30-year lease with the City of New York, which called for Yankee Stadium to be completely modernized in time for the 1976 season. After completing the Stadium's 50th-anniversary in 1973, the Yankees moved to Shea Stadium for two seasons while the majority of Yankee Stadium was torn down and rebuilt.

The most striking change of the modernization was the removal of the numerous obstructive steel columns that supported the second and third decks, as well as the roof. By "cantilevering" the upper decks and lowering the playing field while increasing the slope of the lower stands, sight lines for fans were dramatically improved. Capacity was reduced from 65,010 in 1973 to 54,028 upon reopening as wider plastic seats replaced wooden seats.

Of course, with the removal of the original roof, the Stadium almost lost its most-recognizable feature: the copper frieze. However, an innovative design concept included an exact replica of the frieze atop the new 560-foot-long scoreboard wall, which stretched across the rear of the bleachers. The board also included Baseball's first "telescreen," which could provide instant replays of the action by employing a then-incredible "nine shades of gray."

Yankee Stadium's exterior changed dramatically, as three escalator towers were added, one at each of the Stadium's three entrances. With seven additional

The original Yankee Stadium, shown during construction, was completed in only 284 working days.

379

rows of seats added to the upper deck, the already grand Stadium received an even more majestic look. A 138-foot Louisville Slugger-shaped smokestack, commonly called "The Bat," was added outside the Stadium near the home-plate entrance.

The renovated Stadium also saw the mammoth fence distances in left and center field greatly reduced as "Death Valley" in left-center was brought in from 457 feet to 430 feet, and straightaway center field was slimmed from 463 feet to 417 feet. Subsequent alterations prior to the 1985 and 1988 seasons brought fences in to the configuration that is now replicated in the current Yankee Stadium.

The remodeled original Yankee Stadium reopened on April 15, 1976—with the Yankees topping Minnesota, 11-4. Like its predecessor and successor, it hosted the World Series in its inaugural season. In fact, the remodeled Stadium hosted the Fall Classic in its first three seasons, as the Yankees followed their 1976 Series loss to Cincinnati by winning back-to-back World Series titles in 1977 and 1978 over the Dodgers.

As one of the world's most prestigious addresses, the original Yankee Stadium was also the home for scores of other sports, entertainment and cultural events. While the Yankees were on the road or in the offseason, the Stadium opened its gates to college and pro football, soccer, political assemblies, religious conventions, concerts and even the circus.

Boxing immediately found a home at Yankee Stadium with Benny Leonard winning a 15-round decision over Lou Tendler for the lightweight title just three months after the gates opened on July 23, 1923. When Muhammad Ali stopped Ken Norton on September 28, 1976, it marked the 30th championship fight at the Stadium. All previous Stadium title bouts had taken place between 1923 and 1959–perhaps none more memorable than the June 22, 1938, heavyweight championship rematch between Joe Louis and Germany's Max Schmeling. After suffering a knockout loss in the initial non-title encounter at the Stadium two years earlier, Louis—now the heavyweight champ—avenged his defeat with a stunning first-round KO.

Football also became an immediate fixture at Yankee Stadium with Syracuse and Pittsburgh inaugurating a rich history of collegiate and professional matchups on October 20, 1923. Five years later at Yankee Stadium, on November 12, 1928, during halftime of a scoreless Army-Notre Dame contest, legendary coach Knute Rockne made his famous "Win One for the Gipper" speech, spurring the Fighting Irish to a 12-6 victory.

The New York Football Giants also called Yankee Stadium home from 1956 through 1973 and on December 28, 1958, took part in what has since been dubbed "The Greatest Game Ever Played." With the NFL championship at stake, a crowd of 64,185 watched the Baltimore Colts tie the game, 17-17, on a Steve Myrha field goal with seven seconds left. Eight minutes into professional football's first-ever "sudden-death" overtime period, the Colts' Alan Ameche crashed into the end zone from the 1-yard line, ending a contest that would help establish pro football as a major sport.

The Stadium was also an important stop for religious conventions, especially those of the Jehovah's Witnesses. In 1950, the group began holding conventions at the Stadium, including one that drew 123,707 people on August 3, 1958—the largest single-day event in Stadium history. On October 4, 1965—with the Yankees out of the World Series for only the third time in 17 years—the Stadium held the first-ever Papal Mass in the United States as Pope Paul VI celebrated Mass before a crowd in excess of 80,000. Pope John Paul II also celebrated Mass at the original Yankee Stadium on October 2, 1979, during his tour of the United States.

On August 16, 2006, a groundbreaking ceremony was held for a new Yankee Stadium to be ready for the 2009 season. The location chosen for the new building was the north side of 161st Street and River Avenue in the Bronx, directly across the street from the site of the original.

As part of its final season in 2008, Yankee Stadium hosted a third papal visit on April 20 from Pope Benedict XVI, NYU's commencement ceremony on May 14 (believed to be the first-ever college commencement in Stadium history) and a 15-inning, 4-3, AL victory in the All-Star Game on July 15 (the fourth at Yankee Stadium, joining Midsummer Classics in 1939, 1960-Game 2 and 1977).

The building took its final bow on Sept. 21, 2008, when the Yankees played the last game in Stadium history. Gates opened at 1:00 p.m., allowing approximately 13,000 fans the opportunity to visit Monument Park and walk around the warning track. With a national Sunday night audience watching on television, all-time Yankees greats, along with the evening's starting lineup, took their positions in the field before Julia Ruth Stevens, daughter of Babe Ruth, tossed out the ceremonial first pitch. Fittingly, the game ended in a Yankees victory, this one over the Baltimore Orioles, 7-3. After the final out, the club assembled by the pitcher's mound at the side of captain Derek Jeter. Over the PA, he thanked the crowd for their years of support, while reminding everyone of the new memories soon to be made.

> In the bottom of the seventh inning of the Yankees' final home game on September 21, 2008, a taped valedictory was given on the Yankee Stadium video board by longtime public address announcer Bob Sheppard, who was unable to say goodbye in person as he continued to recover at home from an illness that had kept him away from the Stadium for the entire season. His appearance on screen brought a reverential hush to the crowd as everyone recognized they were about to hear the most perfect of all couplings perhaps for the last time—Bob Sheppard's voice reverberating in the original Yankee Stadium. He said the following:
>
> *"Farewell, old Yankee Stadium, farewell. What a wonderful story you can tell. DiMaggio, Mantle, Gehrig and Ruth, A baseball cathedral in truth."*

Original Yankee Stadium Information

Original Yankee Stadium Dimensions

Field	Distances/Dates	Distances/Dates	Distances/Dates	Distances/Dates	Distances/Dates
Left-Field Foul Pole:	281 ft. (1923-27)	301 ft. (1928-73)	312 ft. (1976-84)	312 ft. (1985-87)	318 ft. (1988-2008)
Left Field:	395 ft. (1923-27)	402 ft. (1928-73)	387 ft. (1976-84)	379 ft. (1985-87)	N/A
Left-center Field:	460 ft. (1923-36)	457 ft. (1937-73)	430 ft. (1976-84)	411 ft. (1985-87)	399 ft. (1988-2008)
Center Field:*	461 ft. (1937-66)	463 ft. (1967-73)	417 ft. (1976-84)	410 ft. (1985-87)	408 ft. (1988-2008)
Right-center Field:	429 ft. (1923-36)	407 ft. (1937-73)	385 ft. (1976-84)	385 ft. (1985-87)	385 ft. (1988-2008)
Right Field:	370 ft. (1923-36)	344 ft. (1937-73)	353 ft. (1976-84)	353 ft. (1985-87)	N/A
Right-field Foul Pole:	295 ft. (1923-38)	296 ft. (1939-73)	310 ft. (1976-84)	310 ft. (1985-87)	314 ft. (1988-2008)

*(490 ft. from 1923-27 and 475 ft. from 1928-36)

Original Yankee Stadium Firsts and Lasts

FIRSTS
- **Game:** April 18, 1923 (4-1 win vs. Boston Red Sox)
- **Ceremonial First Pitch:** N.Y. Governor Al Smith
- **Pitch:** Bob Shawkey (ball)
- **Victory:** April 18, 1923 (4-1 vs. Boston)
- **Loss:** April 22, 1923 (4-3 vs. Washington)
- **Batter:** Boston's Chick Fewster (grounded to short)
- **Yankees Batter:** Whitey Witt
- **Hit:** Boston's George Burns (April 18, 2nd-inning single)
- **Yankees Hit:** Aaron Ward (April 18, 3rd-inning single)
- **Run:** Bob Shawkey (April 18, on Joe Dugan's single in 3rd)
- **Home Run:** Babe Ruth (April 18, three-run HR in 3rd)
- **Error:** Babe Ruth (April 18, dropped fly ball in 5th)

PRE-REMODELING LASTS
- **Game:** Sept. 30, 1973 (8-5 loss vs. Detroit Tigers)
- **Attendance:** 32,969
- **Batter:** Mike Hegan (flied out to CF)
- **Home Run:** Duke Sims (Sept. 30 off Detroit's Fred Holdsworth)
- **Pitch:** Detroit's John Hiller
- **Victory:** Sept. 29, 1973 (3-0 vs. Detroit Tigers)
- **Yankees Winning Pitcher:** Doc Medich (Sept. 29, 3-0 CG vs. Detroit)

REMODELED YANKEE STADIUM LASTS
- **Game:** Sept. 21, 2008 (7-3 win vs. Baltimore)
- **Ceremonial First Pitch:** Julia Ruth Stevens (daughter of Babe Ruth)
- **Pitch:** Mariano Rivera to Baltimore's Brian Roberts
- **Batter:** Baltimore's Brian Roberts (9th-inning ground out to first base)
- **Yankees Batter:** Derek Jeter (8th-inning ground out to third base)
- **Hit:** Jason Giambi (7th-inning single to left)
- **Run:** Brett Gardner (7th inning)
- **Home Run:** Jose Molina (4th-inning, two-run homer to left off Baltimore's Chris Waters on Sept. 21, 2008)
- **Error:** Baltimore's Brandon Fahey (misplayed grounder in 7th inning on Sept. 21, 2008)
- **Winning Pitcher:** Andy Pettitte on Sept. 21, 2008 vs. Baltimore
- **Star-Spangled Banner Performer:** United States Army Field Band
- **God Bless America Singer:** Ronan Tynan
- **Final Two Songs Played over PA:** "Good Night Sweetheart" played by organist Ed Alstrom in memory of Eddie Layton, followed by "New York, New York" sung by Frank Sinatra

ORIGINAL YANKEE STADIUM LEADERS (1923-2008)

Most Career Games
1. Mickey Mantle 1,213
2. Lou Gehrig 1,080
3. Yogi Berra 1,068
4. Bernie Williams 1,039
5. Derek Jeter 1,004

Most Career Hits
1. Derek Jeter 1,274
2. Lou Gehrig 1,269
3. Mickey Mantle 1,211
4. Bernie Williams 1,123
5. Joe DiMaggio 1,060

Most Career Home Runs
1. Mickey Mantle 266
2. Babe Ruth 259
3. Lou Gehrig 251
4. Yogi Berra 210
5. Joe DiMaggio 148

Most Career RBI
1. Lou Gehrig 949
2. Babe Ruth 777
3. Mickey Mantle 744
4. Yogi Berra 727
5. Joe DiMaggio 720

Most Career Wins
1. Red Ruffing 126
2. Whitey Ford 120
3. Lefty Gomez 112
4. Ron Guidry 99
5. Andy Pettitte 94

Best Career ERA (min: 500.0 IP)
1. Fritz Peterson 2.52
2. Whitey Ford 2.57
3. Mariano Rivera 2.61
4. Spud Chandler 2.62
5. Stan Bahnsen 2.65

Most Career Strikeouts
1. Ron Guidry 969
2. Andy Pettitte 816
3. Whitey Ford 748
4. Roger Clemens 710
5. Mike Mussina 701

Most Career Saves (since 1969)
1. Mariano Rivera 230
2. Dave Righetti 111
3. Goose Gossage 70
4. Sparky Lyle 63
5. Steve Farr 45

Most Career Managerial Wins
1. Joe McCarthy 809
2. Joe Torre 614
3. Casey Stengel 604
4. Ralph Houk 550
5. Miller Huggins 339

The Yankees posted an all-time regular season record of 4,133-2,430-17 at the original Yankee Stadium, and went 101-60 there in postseason play.

Negro Leagues at the Original Yankee Stadium

Satchel Paige warming up at Yankee Stadium on August 2, 1942.

For almost 20 years in the 1930s and '40s, Yankee Stadium was a regular home to Negro Leagues baseball. During that time the greatest black stars of the day drew thousands of fans to watch players prohibited from playing in the Major Leagues at the time. Almost every Negro Leagues player of note over that two-decade stretch played at Yankee Stadium, including Hall of Famers Leroy "Satchel" Paige, John Henry "Pop" Lloyd, "Cool Papa" Bell, Oscar Charleston, Buck Leonard, Hilton Smith and Josh Gibson, who hit some of the longest home runs in the Stadium's history.

Yankee Stadium opened to black baseball on July 5, 1930, when Yankees owner Jacob Ruppert donated the free use of the facility to the New York Lincoln Giants and Baltimore Black Sox for a benefit doubleheader to raise money for the Brotherhood of Sleeping Car Porters, one of America's most prominent black unions. The games raised approximately $3,500 and included the appearance of Bill "Bojangles" Robinson who entertained the crowd along with the 369th Hell Fighters marching band.

Black baseball games at Yankee Stadium usually took place on Sundays when the Yankees played on the road. Sometimes a pair of teams would play a doubleheader, while at other times four-team doubleheaders were scheduled in order to maximize attendance and profits. Bands often performed and celebrities such as Joe Louis and New York City Mayor Fiorello LaGuardia were common. Track races and other pregame contests also delighted fans.

In 1931, Lloyd organized an All-Star team of black players named the "Harlem Stars," which played several games at Yankee Stadium. Eventually, that team became the New York Black Yankees of the Negro National League. The club went on to use Yankee Stadium for a portion of their home schedule between 1936 and 1947, often wearing the used uniforms of the Major League Yankees. In the spring of 1941, Paige, black baseball's greatest pitcher, briefly joined the Black Yankees, pitching and winning his only game in a New York uniform at Yankee Stadium.

Yankee Stadium also served as the venue for black baseball All-Star games and championship contests. One of the most memorable Negro Leagues All-Star games took place on August 27, 1939, when the Negro National League defeated the Negro American League, 10-2, with the help of Gibson's bases-clearing triple.

Ruppert's death in 1939 did not put a stop to black baseball at the Stadium. In fact, the Yankees sponsored a Jacob Ruppert Memorial Cup tournament among Negro National League teams. Ten doubleheaders were held at Yankee Stadium that summer to determine a winner, and on September 24, 1939, the Baltimore Elite Giants were crowned champs in Ruppert's name.

In October 1946, Yankee Stadium was home to two noteworthy exhibition games between an African-American All-Star team managed by Paige and an American League All-Star team led by future Hall of Famer Bob Feller. Cleveland Indians pitcher Bob Lemon hit a home run to win the first game for the AL but Paige out-pitched Feller in the second game to earn a split.

When Jackie Robinson finally broke the color barrier with the Brooklyn Dodgers in 1947 (after having played at the Stadium as a member of the Kansas City Monarchs in 1945), it was a watershed moment in the history of civil rights in the United States. But it also precipitated the decline and eventual extinction of the Negro Leagues.

Black baseball's relationship with the New York Yankees came to a close on August 20, 1961, as stars of the Negro American League gathered for its All-Star Game at Yankee Stadium. Paige, reportedly 55 years old at the time, pitched three scoreless innings and claimed the game's Most Valuable Player honors.

Dressed in their Homestead Grays uniforms, Hall of Famers Josh Gibson [L] and Buck Leonard [R] join Sam Bankhead [C] at Yankee Stadium in 1939.

Other Events at the Original Yankee Stadium

Boxing

Prizefighting was a regular staple of the original Yankee Stadium. Notable championship fights are listed below, while other cards (including the first-ever $1 million non-title bout with Jack Dempsey knocking out Jack Sharkey on 7/21/27) also took place.

DATE	WINNER/LOSER	DATE	WINNER/LOSER
7/23/23	Leonard dec Tendler	6/19/46	Louis KO Conn
6/26/24	Greb dec Moore	9/18/46	Louis KO Mauriello
5/30/25	Berlenbach dec McTigue	9/27/46	Zale KO Graziano
9/11/25	Berlenbach KO Slattery	6/25/48	Louis KO Walcott
9/21/25	Walker dec Shade	9/23/48	Williams KO Flores
6/10/26	Berlenbach dec Stribling	8/10/49	Charles KO Lesnevich
7/26/28	Tunney KO Heeney	9/8/50	Saddler KO Pep
7/18/29	Loughran dec Braddock	9/27/50	Charles dec Louis
6/12/30	Schmeling DQ (foul) Sharkey	6/25/52	Maxim KO Robinson
7/17/30	Singer KO Mandell	6/17/54	Marciano dec Charles
8/30/37	Louis dec Farr	9/17/54	Marciano KO Charles
6/22/38	Louis KO Schmeling	9/21/55	Marciano KO Moore
6/28/39	Louis KO Galento	9/23/57	Basilio dec Robinson
8/22/39	Ambers dec Armstrong	6/26/59	Johansson KO Patterson
6/20/40	Louis KO Godoy	9/28/76	Ali dec Norton

The boxing ring was located just above second base at the original Yankee Stadium.

Professional Football

1926	New York Yankees (AFL)
1927-28	New York Yankees (NFL)
1936-37	New York Yankees (AFL)
1940	New York Yankees (AFL)
1946-49	New York Yankees (AAFC)
1950-51	New York Yanks (NFL)
1956-73	New York Giants (NFL); all-time regular season record at Yankee Stadium, 66-49-6. All-time postseason record at Yankee Stadium, 2-2.
1976	New York Jets (NFL) exhibition games

Notable Games:

11/3/23	Third Army Corps (Md.) 55 - Toronto Argonauts 7 (First professional game at Yankee Stadium)
10/21/36	N.Y. Yankees 7 - Pittsburgh Americans 6 (AFL) (First night football game at Yankee Stadium)
12/30/56	New York Giants 47 - Chicago Bears 7; NFL Championship Game, Giants win third title in team history.
12/28/58	Baltimore Colts 23 - New York Giants 17 (OT); "The Greatest Game Ever Played," NFL Championship Game, first OT game in NFL history.
12/30/62	Green Bay Packers 16 - New York Giants 7; NFL Championship Game
12/10/72	Miami Dolphins 23 - New York Giants 13; Dolphins improve to 13-0 in perfect 17-0 season.

College Football

1923-46	Fordham vs. NYU series
1923-46	NYU uses Stadium as a secondary home field
1925-46	Army vs. Notre Dame at the Stadium (also played in 1969)
1930-31	Army vs. Navy played at the Stadium
1968-'73; '76-87	Grambling played 18 times

Notable Games:

11/12/28	Notre Dame 12 - Army 6, scoreless at halftime, Knute Rockne gives his famous "win one for the Gipper" speech in the locker room
11/9/46	Notre Dame 0 - Army 0 in battle featuring four Heisman Trophy winners (Doc Blanchard-1945, Glenn Davis-1946, Johnny Lujack-1947 and Leon Hart-1949)
12/15/62	Gotham Bowl, Nebraska 36 - Miami 34

Notable Team Records in Yankee Stadium Games:

Army	17-17-4 in 38 games
Fordham	13-5-1 in 19 games
Notre Dame	15-6-3 in 24 games
NYU	52-40-4 in 96 games

Soccer

6/28/31	Exhibition: Glasgow Celtic 4, New York Yankees 1 (of the American Soccer League)
9/16/34	Charity match: Jewish All-Stars 3 - Irish All-Stars 0
9/27/36	Macabees of Palestine 6 - NY State All-Stars 0
11/8/36	ASL All-Stars 4 - Macabees of Palestine 1
5/4/47	Hapoel of Palestine 2 - U.S. All-Stars 0 (61,000 tickets sold)
1952	American Soccer League games
6/15/52	Tottenham Hotspur 7 - Manchester United 1
6/8/53	International Friendly: England 6 - U.S.A. 3
6/14/53	Liverpool 1 - Young Boys Club of Switzerland 1
4/29/56	Israel Olympic Team 2 - ASL All-Stars 1
9/5/66	Santos 4 - Inter Milan 1
1967	New York Skyliners a.k.a. Cerro of Uruguay (United Soccer Association)
1967-68	New York Generals (NPSL)
8/26/67	Inter Milan 1 - Santos 0
10/15/67	Israel National Team 3 - ASL All-Stars 1
6/21/68	Santos 4 - Napoli 2 (Att: 43,702)
7/12/68	New York Generals 5 - Santos 3
8/21/68	Real Madrid 4 - New York Generals 1
9/1/68	Santos 3 - Benfica 3 (including Eusebio)
5/30/69	Barcelona 3 - Juventus 2
6/27/69	Inter Milan 2 (PK win) - Sparta Prague 2 A.C. Milan 4 - Panathinaikos 0
6/29/69	A.C. Milan 6 - Inter Milan 4
1971, 1976	New York Cosmos (NASL), including Pele
5/28/76	USA Bicentennial Cup, England 3 - Italy 2, Att: 40,650

Notable Performers and Events

8/15-26/23	Tex Austin's Championship Rodeo
5/26/25	Finnish-American A.C. Track Meet feat. Paavo Nurmi
6/27/25	Aida performed by the Manhattan Opera Company.
5/22/27	Holy Name Society incl. address from Cardinal Hayes
8/2/28	Polyphonic Symphony Orchestra
4/30/31	Cinder Track Motorcycle Racing
5/17/31-5/30/39	20 Gaelic football games, Total Att.: 424,000
9/20/34	United Jewish Appeal benefit for German Jews, incl. George Burns/Gracie Allen, Kate Smith & Jack Benny
6/20/35	"June Night Frolic" benefit for Jewish National Fund
5/30-6/7/47	World's Greatest Rodeo and Thrill Circus
9/10/48	Rally for presidential candidate Henry A. Wallace
8/11/50	Chicago 3 - Springfield 1 of AAGPBL (3 inn.)
7/20/57	Rev. Billy Graham preaches.
9/7/57	Cardinal Spellman celebrates Mass.
8/3/58	Jehovah's Witnesses convention draws a single-day Stadium record 123,707 people.
10/4/65	Pope Paul VI celebrates Mass.
6/10/66	"Soundblast '66" featuring Ray Charles, The Byrds, The Beach Boys and Stevie Wonder
6/22/68	James Brown concert
6/21/69	The Isley Brothers perform, along with other acts.
7/7-8/72	Newport Jazz Festival, incl. Dizzy Gillespe, B.B. King Thelonius Monk, Roberta Flack and Ray Charles
8/24/73	Fania All-Stars perform, including Willie Colon.
6/1/76	Rev. Sun Myung Moon's - "God Bless America Festival"
10/2/79	Pope John Paul II celebrates Mass.
5/1/86	Cardinal O'Connor officiates World Youth Assembly.
6/26/88 & 7/4/89	Beach Boys perform postgame concerts.
8/27/89	Charlie Daniels Band performs.
6/21/90	Nelson Mandela welcomed with a huge celebration.
6/22-23/90	Billy Joel - "Storm Front" Tour
8/29-30/92	U2 - "Zoo TV" Tour
6/10-11/94	Pink Floyd performs on back-to-back nights.
6/25/94	Closing ceremonies for the 1994 Unity Games.
4/25/99	Paul Simon sings "Mrs. Robinson" in centerfield on the day Joe DiMaggio's Monument is dedicated.
9/23/01	"A Prayer for America" service held for those lost on September 11, 2001.
3/10/06	Baseball reporter Ed Lucas marries Allison Pheifle in the first on-field wedding in Stadium history.
4/20/08	Pope Benedict XVI celebrates Mass.
5/14/08	New York University holds commencement.

Previous Homes of the Yankees

Hilltop Park

American League Park (commonly known as Hilltop Park) was the Yankees' first home. Hastily constructed in just six weeks on one of the highest points in Upper Manhattan, the all-wooden ballpark sat on a block bounded by Broadway, 165th Street, Fort Washington Avenue and 168th Street, in close proximity to the New York Giants' 157th Street home, the Polo Grounds. The first game at Hilltop Park was played on April 30, 1903—a 6-2 win over Washington, started by Hall of Famer Jack Chesbro.

The ballpark had a covered grandstand ringing the infield from first base to third base and uncovered bleachers running up the foul lines. There was seating for approximately 15,000 people, but as was the case in many ballparks of that time, it could accommodate overflow crowds both in the outfield and along foul ground in the infield, occasionally bringing capacity up toward 25,000.

When a fire ravaged the Polo Grounds on April 14, 1911, the Yankees allowed the Giants to play their home games at Hilltop Park until the Polo Grounds could be rebuilt. From April 15 through May 30, the Giants put together a 20-8 record at their temporary home.

The Yankees were successful in their 10 years at Hilltop Park, compiling a 398-342-8 all-time record there. The club's final game at the structure came on October 5, 1912—an 8-6 win vs. Washington. After the Yankees' lease at Hilltop Park expired at the end of the season, they decided to leave the rickety ballpark to become renters at the Polo Grounds, where the Giants became their landlords. The move, unthinkable years earlier, was facilitated by the Yankees' post-fire hospitality.

In 1914, Hilltop Park was torn down. Currently, its former location is the site of NewYork-Presbyterian Medical Center.

Hilltop Park (above/below) served as the Yankees' first home. It was built in just six weeks and was located near Broadway and 168th Street in Upper Manhattan.

Polo Grounds

The Yankees called the Polo Grounds home from 1913 through 1922, sharing the park with the New York Giants. Located on West 157th Street and Eighth Avenue in Upper Manhattan, the Polo Grounds was overlooked by a promontory called Coogan's Bluff to the west. To the east was the Harlem River—on the other side of which Yankee Stadium was built in 1923.

The Polo Grounds was constructed with straight sides, and the outfield fences by the foul poles ran parallel to each other and away from home plate. The foul poles in left and right were approximately 277 and 258 feet away from the plate, respectively, while left-center, center and right fields were all in the range of 445-483 feet away from home.

The Yankees compiled a 416-338-10 all-time regular season record at the uniquely-shaped facility, winning the first two pennants in franchise history while tenants in 1921 and 1922. The club lost both of those World Series to the NL Champion Giants—5 games to 3 in 1921 and 4 games to none with one tie in 1922—in Fall Classics played entirely at the Polo Grounds.

The Polo Grounds, located on West 157th Street and Eighth Avenue in Upper Manhattan, served as the home of the Yankees from 1913-22.

The American Leaguers were welcome tenants as long as they remained less popular than the Giants. But with Babe Ruth's arrival in 1920 and the team's subsequent success, the dynamic quickly changed. After the Yankees started outdrawing the Giants in their own park in 1920 and 1921, the National Leaguers asked the Yankees to vacate to a new facility as soon as possible. The 1922 season marked their final season in Manhattan before their April 18, 1923, Yankee Stadium debut in the Bronx.

The Polo Grounds remained home to the Giants until they moved to San Francisco in 1958. It stood empty until 1962 when the Mets arrived to play two seasons there before moving into Shea Stadium. In 1964, the Polo Grounds was demolished. Apartment buildings called the Polo Grounds Towers occupy the site today.

College Football at the Original Yankee Stadium

YEAR	DATE	TEAM	SCORE	TEAM	SCORE	ATT.	YEAR	DATE	TEAM	SCORE	TEAM	SCORE	ATT.
1923	Oct. 20	Syracuse	3	Pittsburgh	0	25,000	1930	Oct. 4	NYU	41	W. Va. Wesleyan	6	20,000
	Oct. 27	West Virginia	13	Penn State	13	25,000		Oct. 11	NYU	20	Villanova	6	40,000
	Nov. 6	NYU	20	Fordham	0	10,000		Oct. 18	NYU	38	Missouri	0	27,000
	Nov. 10	Holy Cross	23	Fordham	7	8,000		Oct. 25	Fordham	7	NYU	0	78,500
	Nov. 17	Haskell Indian Sch.	14	Quantico Marines	14	10,000		Nov. 1	Hampton Instit.	0	Lincoln University	0	9,000
	Nov. 24	NYU	7	Boston Univ.	0	2,500		Nov. 8	Army	13	Illinois	0	74,000
	Dec. 1	Georgetown	6	Fordham	0	5,000		Nov. 15	NYU	2	Georgetown	0	20,000
	Dec. 8	U.S.S. Wright	6	U.S.S. Wyoming	6	8,000		Nov. 22	NYU	33	Rutgers	0	25,000
								Nov. 29	Fordham Fresh.	27	NYU Fresh.	0	5,000
1924	Oct. 25	Lafayette	20	Wash. & Jeff.	6	15,000		Dec. 6	Colgate	7	NYU	6	20,000
	Oct. 27	Navy Scout. Fleet	7	Quantico Marines	6	4,000		Dec. 13	Army	6	Navy	0	70,000
	Nov. 1	Fordham	27	NYU	0	15,000							
							1931	Oct. 3	NYU	54	W. Va. Wesleyan	0	16,000
1925	Oct. 10	Georgia Tech	16	Penn State	7	8,000		Oct. 10	NYU	34	Georgetown	0	35,000
	Oct. 17	Army	27	Notre Dame	0	80,000		Oct. 17	NYU	27	Rutgers	7	15,000
	Oct. 31	Fordham	26	NYU	6	15,000		Oct. 24	NYU	13	Colgate	0	45,000
								Oct. 31	Oregon	14	NYU	6	20,000
1926	Oct. 16	NYU	21	Tulane	0	25,000		Nov. 7	Georgia	7	NYU	6	65,000
	Oct. 23	NYU	30	Rutgers	0	20,000		Nov. 14	NYU	0	Fordham	0	78,000
	Oct. 30	NYU	27	Fordham	3	35,000		Nov. 26	NYU	7	Carnegie Tech	6	25,000
	Nov. 6	NYU	6	Carnegie Tech	0	35,000		Nov. 28	Army	12	Notre Dame	0	78,000
	Nov. 13	Notre Dame	7	Army	0	72,000		Dec. 5	Tennessee	13	NYU	0	40,684
								Dec. 9	Columbia	13	Princeton	0	8,000
1927	Oct. 15	NYU	32	Fordham	0	45,000		Dec. 9	Cornell	0	Penn	0	8,000
	Oct. 22	NYU	60	Rutgers	6	20,000		Dec. 12	Army	17	Navy	7	75,000
	Oct. 29	NYU	0	Colgate	0	45,000							
	Oct. 30	Princeton Alumni	7	Harvard Alumni	4	4,000	1932	Oct. 8	NYU	21	Rutgers	0	12,000
	Nov. 5	NYU	20	Carnegie Tech	6	30,000		Oct. 15	NYU	39	Georgetown	0	30,000
	Nov. 12	Army	18	Notre Dame	0	80,000		Oct. 22	Colgate	14	NYU	0	35,000
	Nov. 19	NYU Freshmen	6	Dean Academy	0	25,000		Oct. 29	Purdue	34	NYU	9	25,000
	Nov. 19	NYU	81	Allegheny	0	25,000		Nov. 5	NYU	13	Georgia	7	15,000
								Nov. 12	Fordham	7	NYU	0	40,000
								Nov. 19	Manhattan Col.	0	Holy Cross	0	5,000
								Nov. 24	NYU	13	Carnegie Tech	6	18,000
								Nov. 26	Notre Dame	21	Army	0	80,000
							1933	Oct. 7	W. Va. Wesleyan	3	NYU	0	12,000
								Oct. 14	NYU	13	Lafayette	12	12,000
								Oct. 21	Colgate	7	NYU	0	25,000
								Nov. 4	Tulane	7	Colgate	0	18,000
								Nov. 11	Fordham	20	NYU	12	30,000
								Nov. 18	NYU	6	Rutgers	6	12,000
								Nov. 25	NYU	7	Carnegie Tech	6	15,000
								Dec. 2	Notre Dame	13	Army	12	78,000
							1934	Oct. 6	Fordham	57	Westminster	0	6,000
								Oct. 20	NYU	12	Lafayette	7	10,000
								Oct. 27	NYU	0	Georgetown	0	15,000
								Nov. 3	Carnegie Tech	6	NYU	0	15,000
								Nov. 10	Colgate	20	Tulane	6	45,000
								Nov. 24	Notre Dame	12	Army	6	80,000
								Nov. 29	Fordham	39	NYU	13	25,000
1928	Oct. 20	NYU	48	Rutgers	0	25,000	1935	Oct. 5	NYU	34	Bates College	7	10,000
	Oct. 27	NYU	47	Colgate	6	52,000		Oct. 12	NYU	25	Carnegie Tech	6	20,000
	Nov. 3	Georgetown	7	NYU	2	50,000		Oct. 19	NYU	33	Penn. Military Col.	7	10,000
	Nov. 6	West Virginia	18	Fordham	0	30,000		Oct. 26	NYU	7	Georgetown	6	20,000
	Nov. 10	Notre Dame	12	Army	6	85,000		Nov. 2	NYU	14	Bucknell	0	15,000
	Nov. 17	NYU	27	Missouri	6	45,000		Nov. 9	NYU	45	City College of NY	0	6,000
	Nov. 29	Oregon State	25	NYU	13	40,000		Nov. 16	Army	6	Notre Dame	0	80,000
	Dec. 1	Stanford	26	Army	0	88,000		Nov. 28	Fordham	21	NYU	0	75,000
1929	Oct. 19	NYU	7	Penn State	0	30,000	1936	Oct. 10	Army	27	Columbia	16	38,000
	Oct. 26	NYU Freshmen	20	Dean Academy	0	25,000		Oct. 17	North Carolina	14	NYU	13	8,000
	Oct. 26	NYU	13	Butler	6	25,000		Oct. 24	NYU	7	Georgetown	7	16,000
	Nov. 2	Georgetown	14	NYU	0	50,000		Oct. 31	NYU	46	Lafayette	0	10,000
	Nov. 9	NYU	27	Georgia	19	42,000		Nov. 7	Carnegie Tech	14	NYU	9	9,000
	Nov. 16	NYU	14	Missouri	0	35,000		Nov. 14	Notre Dame	20	Army	6	80,000
	Nov. 23	NYU Freshmen	12	Rutgers Freshmen	0	20,000		Nov. 21	NYU	25	City College of NY	7	7,000
	Nov. 23	NYU	20	Rutgers	7	20,000		Nov. 26	NYU	7	Fordham	6	50,000
	Nov. 28	Carnegie Tech	20	NYU	0	55,000	1937	Oct. 23	Lafayette	13	NYU	0	7,500
	Nov. 30	Notre Dame	7	Army	0	85,000		Oct. 30	NYU	14	Colgate	7	25,000
								Nov. 6	NYU	13	Lehigh	0	11,000
								Nov. 13	Notre Dame	7	Army	0	65,000
								Nov. 27	Fordham	20	NYU	7	65,000

The football field ran along the third base line at the original Yankee Stadium, as seen in the above photo.

YEAR	DATE	TEAM	SCORE	TEAM	SCORE	ATT.	YEAR	DATE	TEAM	SCORE	TEAM	SCORE	ATT.
1938	Oct. 15	North Carolina	7	NYU	0	15,000	1948	Nov. 6	Army	43	Stanford	0	46,695
	Oct. 22	Georgetown	14	Manhattan Col.	13	12,000		Nov. 13	Rutgers	40	NYU	0	4,000
	Oct. 29	Notre Dame	19	Army	7	79,000	1949	Nov. 12	Notre Dame	42	North Carolina	6	67,000
	Nov. 5	Manhattan Col.	3	N.C. State	0	8,000	1950	Oct. 14	Army	27	Michigan	6	67,076
	Nov. 11	NYU	13	Colgate	7	25,000	1951	Nov. 3	USC	28	Army	6	16,508
	Nov. 19	Manhattan Col.	13	West Virginia	0	5,000	1959	Oct. 31	Army	13	Air Force	13	67,000
	Nov. 26	Fordham	25	NYU	0	50,000	1960	Nov. 5	Army	9	Syracuse	6	66,000
1939	Oct. 21	NYU	6	Carnegie Tech	0	25,000	1961	Nov. 18	Oklahoma	14	Army	8	37,200
	Oct. 28	NYU	14	Georgia	13	15,000	1962	Nov. 17	Pittsburgh	7	Army	6	23,917
	Nov. 4	Notre Dame	14	Army	0	75,600		Dec. 15	Nebraska	36	Miami	34	6,166
	Nov. 11	Missouri	20	NYU	7	30,000	1963	Nov. 28	Syracuse	14	Notre Dame	7	56,972
	Nov. 18	Georgetown	14	NYU	0	17,000	1964	Nov. 7	Syracuse	27	Army	15	37,552
	Dec. 2	Fordham	18	NYU	7	57,000	1968	Sept. 28	Morgan State	9	Grambling	7	60,811
1940	Oct. 12	Syracuse	47	NYU	13	8,000	1969	Sept. 20	Grambling	30	Morgan State	12	60,118
	Oct. 19	Holy Cross	13	NYU	7	12,000		Oct. 11	Notre Dame	45	Army	0	63,786
	Oct. 26	Georgetown	26	NYU	0	11,000	1970	Sept. 11	Southern Univ.	21	N.C. A&T	6	25,000
	Nov. 2	Notre Dame	7	Army	0	76,000	1971	Sept. 11	Grambling	31	Morgan State	13	65,055
	Nov. 9	Manhattan Col.	45	Marquette	41	6,000	1972	Sept. 9	Grambling	6	Morgan State	0	63,917
	Nov. 30	Fordham	26	NYU	0	35,000	1973	Sept. 22	Grambling	31	Morgan State	14	64,243
1941	Oct. 11	Texas A&M	49	NYU	7	18,000	1976	Oct. 30	Norfolk State	23	Bethune-Cookman	14	23,518
	Oct. 18	Syracuse	31	NYU	0	10,000	1977	Sept. 17	Grambling	35	Morgan State	19	34,403
	Nov. 1	Army	0	Notre Dame	0	76,000	1978	Sept. 23	Grambling	21	Morgan State	0	39,118
	Nov. 8	Missouri	26	NYU	0	6,700	1979	Sept. 8	Grambling	28	Morgan State	18	N/A
	Nov. 15	Tulane	45	NYU	0	8,100	1980	Sept. 13	Grambling	34	Morgan State	13	36,631
	Nov. 29	Fordham	30	NYU	9	31,000	1981	Sept. 5	Grambling	21	Florida A&M	10	40,661
1942	Oct. 10	Princeton	10	Navy	0	20,000	1982	Sept. 4	Grambling	42	Morgan State	13	33,142
	Nov. 7	Notre Dame	13	Army	0	75,142	1983	Sept. 17	Grambling	33	Morgan State	0	34,098
	Nov. 21	Army	40	Princeton	7	18,000	1984	Sept. 8	Boston Univ.	16	Grambling	9	31,979
	Nov. 28	Fordham	6	N.C. Pre-Flight	0	24,500	1985	Sept. 21	Grambling	45	N.C. Central	14	37,192
1943	Nov. 6	Notre Dame	26	Army	0	76,000	1986	Sept. 20	Grambling	32	N.C. Central	24	31,968
1944	Nov. 11	Army	59	Notre Dame	0	74,430	1987	Sept. 12	Central State	37	Grambling	21	29,411
1945	Oct. 13	Army	28	Michigan	7	70,000							
	Nov. 10	Army	48	Notre Dame	0	75,000							
1946	Nov. 9	Army	0	Notre Dame	0	74,000							
	Nov. 16	NYU	33	Fordham	28	28,000							
	Nov. 23	Georgetown	19	NYU	12	10,000							
1947	Oct. 11	Army	0	Illinois	0	65,000							
	Oct. 18	West Virginia	40	NYU	0	8,000							
	Nov. 11	NYU	19	Bucknell	6	5,000							

Picture Perfect

The grandeur of the original Yankee Stadium was a much sought-out location for filming during its existence. Though no official list of which movies were shot at the House That Ruth Built exists, below is a list of films culled through research in which the Stadium was either prominently featured or used as a primary location for filming. The Stadium also appeared briefly in numerous other projects, as well as several episodes of the television series Seinfeld (1990-98).

Life's Greatest Game (1924)
Slide, Kelly, Slide (1927)
The Cameraman (1928)
Fast Company (1929)
Pride of the Yankees (1942)
Woman of the Year (1942)
The Babe Ruth Story (1948)
It Happens Every Spring (1949)
The Stratton Story (1949)
Angels in the Outfield (1951)
The Winning Team (1952)
The Kid from Left Field (1953)
Beau James (1957)
Damn Yankees (1958)
The F.B.I. Story (1959)

Safe at Home! (1962)
Bang the Drum Slowly (1973)
Manhattan (1979)
It's My Turn (1980)
Big (1988)
Major League (1989)
It Could Happen to You (1994)
Little Big League (1994)
The Scout (1994)
Die Hard with a Vengance (1995)
For Love of the Game (1999)
Life (1999)
Anger Management (2003)
P.S. I Love You (2007)

The current Yankee Stadium has been featured in film, appearing in *The Adjustment Bureau* (2011), *Megan Leavey* (2016) and *Set It Up* (2018), as well as episodes of television's *Extreme Makeover: Home Edition* (2010), *Entourage* (2011), *White Collar* (2012) and *God Friended Me* (2019). The Stadium was also the site of Mariah Carey's 2009 music video for "I Want to Know What Love Is," and it featured in a widely regarded Facebook Groups commercial in 2019. It has been additionally featured on talk shows such as the *Tonight Show Starring Jimmy Fallon* and *Late Night with Seth Myers* as well as in a segment in ESPN's *Peyton's Place* series.

Monument Park

Since 1932, the New York Yankees have honored their all-time greats with the dedication of monuments and plaques in Yankee Stadium. The tradition continues in the current Stadium in Monument Park, located behind the outfield fence in center field.

The first monument was dedicated on May 30, 1932, to the memory of Miller Huggins, who died suddenly in 1929. The diminutive manager guided the Yankees to six American League pennants and three World Championships in his 11-plus seasons.

The first plaque was placed on the center-field wall in April 1940, a tribute to Jacob Ruppert, the former owner who built Yankee Stadium and brought the tradition of winning to the Yankees.

Two additional monuments followed: in 1941 for Lou Gehrig and in 1949 for Babe Ruth. Later plaques were placed in center field for General Manager Ed Barrow (1954) and two great Yankees center fielders, Joe DiMaggio and Mickey Mantle (1969). After his death, Mantle's plaque was removed and replaced by a fourth monument on August 25, 1996. On April 25, 1999, DiMaggio—who passed away less than two months earlier—was honored with the Stadium's fifth monument. (The two plaques which previously honored DiMaggio and Mantle were donated by the Yankees to the Yogi Berra Museum and Learning Center in Montclair, N.J.).

Originally, the monuments, plaques and Stadium flagpole were located in the field of play on the warning track in straight-away center field, approximately 10 feet in front of the wall. On many occassions, long hits and fly balls forced fielders to go behind the monuments to retrieve the baseball.

One tradition of Yankee Stadium before it was remodeled was to allow fans to exit through the center-field gates via the warning track, where they could pause and reflect on the achievements of these honored legends. After the Stadium was remodeled in 1974 and 1975, the monuments and plaques were relocated to an area off the field between the Yankees' and visitors' bullpens.

In 1976, two more plaques were added to memorialize managers Joe McCarthy and Casey Stengel. In the 1980s, plaques were dedicated to Yankees greats Thurman Munson (1980), Elston Howard and Roger Maris (1984), Phil Rizzuto (1985), Billy Martin (1986), Whitey Ford and Lefty Gomez (1987), Yogi Berra and Bill Dickey (1988), and Allie Reynolds (1989). The team also dedicated two plaques to non-uniformed Yankees legends — the "Voice of the Yankees," Mel Allen (1998), and the "Voice of Yankee Stadium," public address announcer Bob Sheppard (2000). Yankees greats Don Mattingly (1997), Reggie Jackson (2002), Ron Guidry (2003) and Red Ruffing (2004) had their plaques added prior to the closing of the original Yankee Stadium. At the current Stadium, Tino Martinez, Goose Gossage, Paul O'Neill and Joe Torre (all 2014), Bernie Williams, Willie Randolph, Mel Stottlemyre, Jorge Posada and Andy Pettitte (2015), Mariano Rivera (2016) and Derek Jeter (2017) have had their plaques added as well.

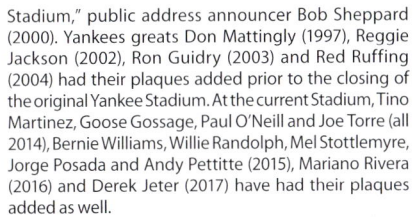

Plaques commemorating the visits of Pope Paul VI in 1965 and Pope John Paul II in 1979 were dedicated by the Knights of Columbus, and a plaque commemorating the Yankees' interlocking "NY" insignia was added to the park in 2001. A plaque was also dedicated in 2008 following the visit of Pope Benedict XVI, and another was added in 2014 to commemorate the 1990 visit of Nelson Mandela.

In 1985, after the left-center-field fence of the original Stadium was moved in, the Yankees were able to open Monument Park for up-close fan viewing. By 1988, long lines and increased fan interest caused the Yankees to move the fence in further and expand the area. A special walkway was added with an exhibit honoring those Yankees who have had their uniform numbers retired.

Monument Park is located just behind the centerfield fence and is accessible to all fans.

In a pregame ceremony on Sept. 11, 2002, the Yankees dedicated a monument in remembrance of the victims and heroes of the 9/11 tragedy. It was the sixth monument dedicated in Yankee Stadium and the first to non-Yankees personnel.

During a special pregame ceremony on Sept. 20, 2010, the entire Yankees team joined the Steinbrenner family and Yankees alumni in unveiling a monument for longtime Principal Owner George M. Steinbrenner III, who passed away on July 13 of that season.

Additionally, in the current Yankee Stadium, plaques were added to commemorate the achievements of Jackie Robinson (dedicated on Sept. 22, 2013 — the same day the Yankees honored the career of Mariano Rivera), the life of Nelson Mandela and his June 21, 1990, visit to Yankee Stadium (dedicated on April 15, 2014) and the 50th anniversary of the Stonewall Inn uprising (dedicated on June 25, 2019).

In all, there are seven monuments (for four Yankees players, one manager, one owner and one to commemorate the tragedy of 9/11) and 38 plaques (for 24 Yankees players, three managers, one owner, one executive, one PA announcer, one broadcaster, three Papal visit commemorations, ones recognizing Jackie Robinson, Nelson Mandela, the Stonewall Inn, and one noting the history of the NY logo).

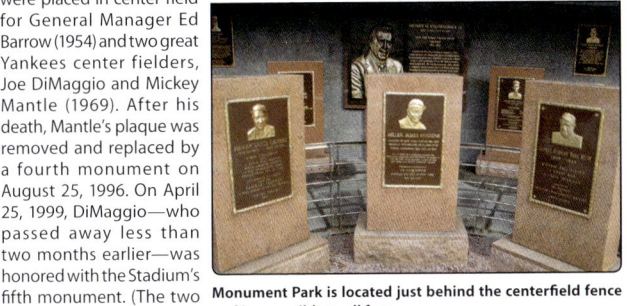

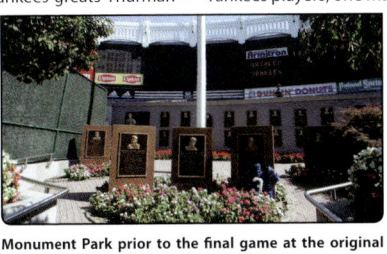

Monument Park prior to the final game at the original Yankee Stadium on September 21, 2008.

Monument Park Monuments
(In order of dedication)

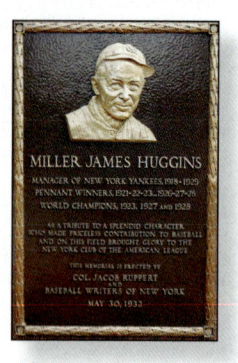

MILLER JAMES HUGGINS
MANAGER OF NEW YORK YANKEES, 1918-1929
PENNANT WINNERS, 1921-22-23...1926-27-28
WORLD CHAMPIONS, 1923, 1927 AND 1928

AS A TRIBUTE TO A SPLENDID CHARACTER
WHO MADE PRICELESS CONTRIBUTION TO BASEBALL
AND ON THIS FIELD BROUGHT GLORY TO THE
NEW YORK CLUB OF THE AMERICAN LEAGUE

THIS MEMORIAL IS ERECTED BY
COL. JACOB RUPPERT
AND
BASEBALL WRITERS OF NEW YORK

MAY 30, 1932

HENRY LOUIS GEHRIG
JUNE 19TH 1903 - JUNE 2ND 1941
A MAN, A GENTLEMAN
AND
A GREAT BALL PLAYER
WHOSE AMAZING RECORD
OF 2130 CONSECUTIVE GAMES
SHOULD STAND FOR ALL TIME.

THIS MEMORIAL IS A TRIBUTE
FROM THE
YANKEE PLAYERS
TO THEIR BELOVED CAPTAIN AND TEAM MATE

JULY THE FOURTH
1941

(Dedication ceremony held July 6, 1941)

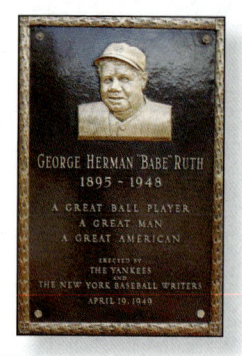

GEORGE HERMAN "BABE" RUTH
1895 - 1948
A GREAT BALL PLAYER
A GREAT MAN
A GREAT AMERICAN

ERECTED BY
THE YANKEES
AND
THE NEW YORK BASEBALL WRITERS

APRIL 19, 1949

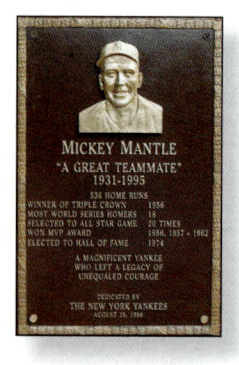

MICKEY MANTLE
"A GREAT TEAMMATE"
1931-1995

536 HOME RUNS	
WINNER OF TRIPLE CROWN	1956
MOST WORLD SERIES HOMERS	18
SELECTED TO THE ALL STAR GAME	20 TIMES
WON MVP AWARD	1956, 1957 + 1962
ELECTED TO HALL OF FAME	1974

A MAGNIFICENT YANKEE
WHO LEFT A LEGACY OF
UNEQUALED COURAGE

DEDICATED BY
THE NEW YORK YANKEES
AUGUST 25, 1996

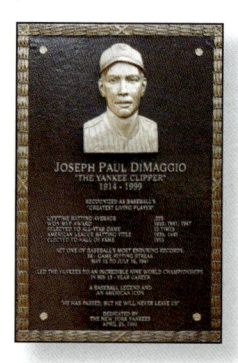

JOSEPH PAUL DiMAGGIO
"THE YANKEE CLIPPER"
1914 - 1999
RECOGNIZED AS BASEBALL'S
"GREATEST LIVING PLAYER"

LIFETIME BATTING AVERAGE	.325
WON MVP AWARD	1939, 1941, 1947
SELECTED TO ALL-STAR GAME	13 TIMES
AMERICAN LEAGUE BATTING TITLE	1939, 1940
ELECTED TO HALL OF FAME	1955

SET ONE OF BASEBALL'S MOST ENDURING RECORDS,
56-GAME HITTING STREAK
MAY 15 TO JULY 16, 1941

LED THE YANKEES TO AN INCREDIBLE NINE WORLD
CHAMPIONSHIPS
IN HIS 13-YEAR CAREER

A BASEBALL LEGEND AND
AN AMERICAN ICON
"HE HAS PASSED, BUT HE WILL NEVER LEAVE US"

DEDICATED BY
THE NEW YORK YANKEES,
APRIL 25, 1999

SEPTEMBER 11, 2001 TRIBUTE

We Remember
On September 11, 2001, despicable acts of terrorism were perpetrated on our country.

In tribute to the eternal spirit of the innocent victims of these crimes and to the selfless courage shown by both public servants and private citizens, we dedicate this plaque.

These valiant souls, with unfettered resolve, exemplify the true character of this great nation. Their unity and resilience during this time of distress defined American heroism for future generations.

Dedicated by the New York Yankees
September 11, 2002

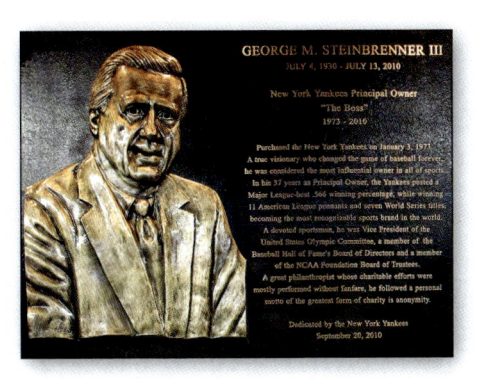

GEORGE M. STEINBRENNER III
July 4, 1930 – July 13, 2010

New York Yankees Principal Owner
"The Boss"
1973 - 2010

Purchased the New York Yankees on January 3, 1973.
A true visionary who changed the game of baseball forever,
he was considered the most influential owner in all of sports.
In his 37 years as Principal Owner, the Yankees posted a
Major League-best .566 winning percentage, while winning
11 American League pennants and seven World Series titles,
becoming the most recognizable sports brand in the world.
A devoted sportsman, he was Vice President of the
United States Olympic Committee, a member of the
Baseball Hall of Fame's Board of Directors and a member
of the NCAA Foundation Board of Trustees.
A great philanthropist whose charitable efforts were
mostly performed without fanfare, he followed a personal
motto of the greatest form of charity is anonymity.

Dedicated by the New York Yankees
September 20, 2010

Monument Park Plaques (In order of dedication)

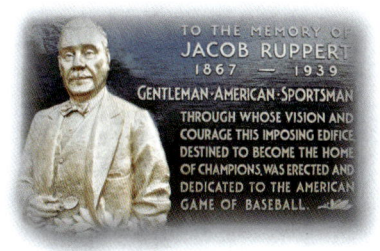

TO THE MEMORY OF
JACOB RUPPERT
1867-1939

GENTLEMAN - AMERICAN - SPORTSMAN
THROUGH WHOSE VISION AND
COURAGE THIS IMPOSING EDIFICE,
DESTINED TO BECOME THE HOME
OF CHAMPIONS, WAS ERECTED AND
DEDICATED TO THE AMERICAN
GAME OF BASEBALL.

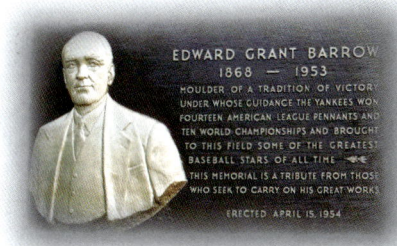

EDWARD GRANT BARROW
1868-1953
MOULDER OF A TRADITION OF VICTORY
UNDER WHOSE GUIDANCE THE YANKEES WON
FOURTEEN AMERICAN LEAGUE PENNANTS AND
TEN WORLD CHAMPIONSHIPS AND BROUGHT
TO THIS FIELD SOME OF THE GREATEST
BASEBALL STARS OF ALL TIME
THIS MEMORIAL IS A TRIBUTE FROM THOSE
WHO SEEK TO CARRY ON HIS GREAT WORKS
ERECTED APRIL 15, 1954

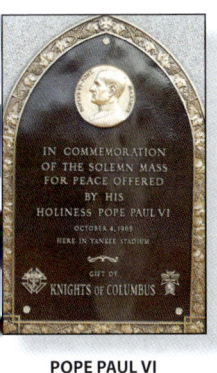

POPE PAUL VI
IN COMMEMORATION
OF THE SOLEMN MASS
FOR PEACE OFFERED
BY HIS
HOLINESS POPE PAUL VI
OCTOBER 4, 1965
HERE IN YANKEE STADIUM
GIFT OF
KNIGHTS OF COLUMBUS

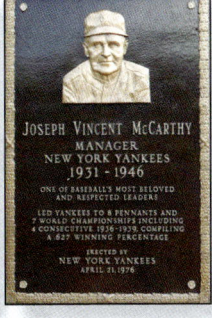

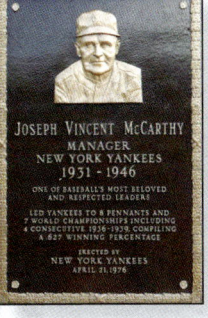

JOSEPH VINCENT McCARTHY
MANAGER
NEW YORK YANKEES
1931-1946

ONE OF BASEBALL'S MOST BELOVED
AND RESPECTED LEADERS
LED YANKEES TO 8 PENNANTS AND
7 WORLD CHAMPIONSHIPS INCLUDING
4 CONSECUTIVE 1936-1939, COMPILING
A .627 WINNING PERCENTAGE

ERECTED BY
NEW YORK YANKEES
APRIL 21, 1976

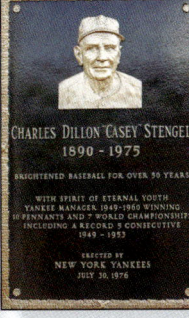

CHARLES DILLON
"CASEY" STENGEL
1890-1975

BRIGHTENED BASEBALL FOR OVER 50 YEARS

WITH SPIRIT OF ETERNAL YOUTH
YANKEE MANAGER 1949-1960 WINNING
10 PENNANTS AND 7 WORLD CHAMPIONSHIPS
INCLUDING A RECORD 5 CONSECUTIVE
1949 - 1953

ERECTED BY
NEW YORK YANKEES
JULY 30, 1976

POPE JOHN PAUL II
IN COMMEMORATION
OF THE MASS FOR
WORLD JUSTICE AND PEACE
OFFERED BY
HIS HOLINESS
POPE JOHN PAUL II
OCTOBER 2, 1979
HERE IN YANKEE STADIUM
GIFT OF
KNIGHTS OF COLUMBUS

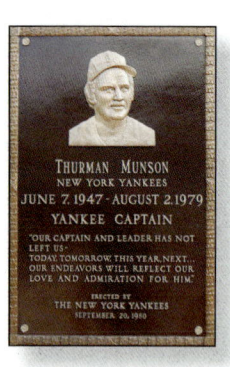

THURMAN MUNSON
NEW YORK YANKEES
JUNE 7, 1947-AUGUST 2, 1979
YANKEE CAPTAIN

"OUR CAPTAIN AND LEADER HAS NOT
LEFT US—
TODAY, TOMORROW, THIS YEAR, NEXT...
OUR ENDEAVORS WILL REFLECT OUR
LOVE AND ADMIRATION FOR HIM."

ERECTED BY
THE NEW YORK YANKEES
SEPTEMBER 20, 1980

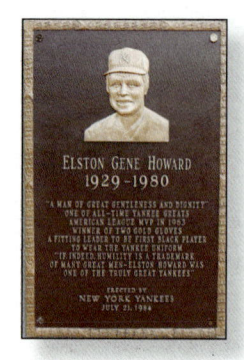

ELSTON GENE HOWARD
1929-1980

"A MAN OF GREAT GENTLENESS AND DIGNITY"
ONE OF ALL-TIME YANKEE GREATS
AMERICAN LEAGUE MVP IN 1963
WINNER OF TWO GOLD GLOVES
A FITTING LEADER TO BE FIRST BLACK PLAYER
TO WEAR THE YANKEE UNIFORM
"IF INDEED, HUMILITY IS A TRADEMARK
OF MANY GREAT MEN—ELSTON HOWARD WAS
ONE OF THE TRULY GREAT YANKEES"

ERECTED BY
NEW YORK YANKEES
JULY 21, 1984

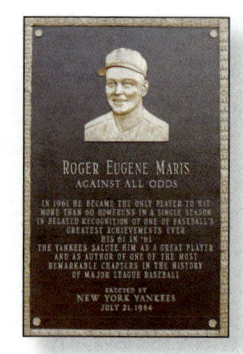

ROGER EUGENE MARIS
AGAINST ALL ODDS

IN 1961 HE BECAME THE ONLY PLAYER TO HIT
MORE THAN 60 HOMERUNS IN A SINGLE SEASON
IN BELATED RECOGNITION OF ONE OF BASEBALL'S
GREATEST ACHIEVEMENTS EVER
HIS 61 IN '61
THE YANKEES SALUTE HIM AS A GREAT PLAYER
AND AS AUTHOR OF ONE OF THE MOST
REMARKABLE CHAPTERS IN THE HISTORY
OF MAJOR LEAGUE BASEBALL

ERECTED BY
NEW YORK YANKEES
JULY 21, 1984

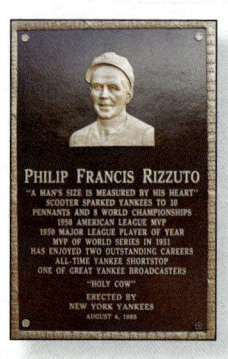

PHILIP FRANCIS RIZZUTO

"A MAN'S SIZE IS MEASURED BY HIS HEART"
SCOOTER SPARKED YANKEES TO 10
PENNANTS AND 8 WORLD CHAMPIONSHIPS
1950 AMERICAN LEAGUE MVP
1950 MAJOR LEAGUE PLAYER OF THE YEAR
MVP OF WORLD SERIES IN 1951
HAS ENJOYED TWO OUTSTANDING CAREERS
ALL-TIME YANKEE SHORTSTOP
ONE OF GREAT YANKEE BROADCASTERS
"HOLY COW"

ERECTED BY
NEW YORK YANKEES
AUGUST 4, 1985

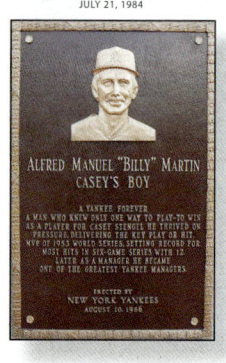

ALFRED MANUEL "BILLY" MARTIN
CASEY'S BOY

A YANKEE FOREVER
A MAN WHO KNEW ONLY ONE WAY TO PLAY-TO WIN
AS A PLAYER FOR CASEY STENGEL HE THRIVED ON
PRESSURE, DELIVERING THE KEY PLAY OR HIT.
MVP OF 1953 WORLD SERIES, SETTING RECORD FOR
MOST HITS IN SIX-GAME SERIES WITH 12.
LATER AS A MANAGER HE BECAME
ONE OF THE GREATEST YANKEE MANAGERS.

ERECTED BY
NEW YORK YANKEES
AUGUST 10, 1986

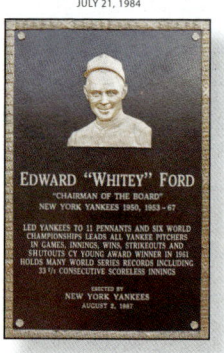

EDWARD "WHITEY" FORD
"CHAIRMAN OF THE BOARD"
NEW YORK YANKEES 1950, 1953-67

LED YANKEES TO 11 PENNANTS AND SIX WORLD
CHAMPIONSHIPS LEADS ALL YANKEE PITCHERS
IN GAMES, INNINGS, WINS, STRIKEOUTS AND
SHUTOUTS CY YOUNG AWARD WINNER IN 1961
HOLDS MANY WORLD SERIES RECORDS INCLUDING
33 2/3 CONSECUTIVE SCORELESS INNINGS

ERECTED BY
NEW YORK YANKEES
AUGUST 2, 1987

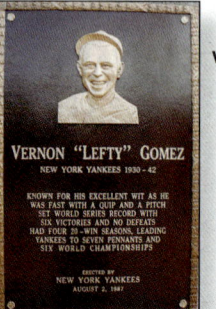

VERNON "LEFTY" GOMEZ
NEW YORK YANKEES 1930-42

KNOWN FOR HIS EXCELLENT WIT AS HE
WAS FAST WITH A QUIP AND A PITCH
SET WORLD SERIES RECORD WITH
SIX VICTORIES AND NO DEFEATS
HAD FOUR 20-WIN SEASONS, LEADING
YANKEES TO SEVEN PENNANTS AND
SIX WORLD CHAMPIONSHIPS

ERECTED BY
NEW YORK YANKEES
AUGUST 2, 1987

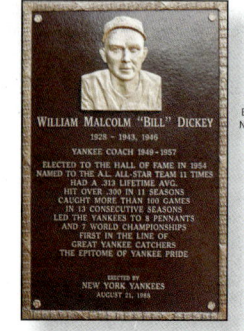

WILLIAM MALCOLM "BILL" DICKEY
1928-1943, 1946
YANKEE COACH 1949-1957

ELECTED TO THE HALL OF FAME IN 1954
NAMED TO THE A.L. ALL-STAR TEAM 11 TIME
HAD A .313 LIFETIME AVG.
HIT OVER .300 IN 11 SEASONS
CAUGHT MORE THAN 100 GAMES
IN 13 CONSECUTIVE SEASONS
LED THE YANKEES TO 8 PENNANTS
AND 7 WORLD CHAMPIONSHIPS
FIRST IN THE LINE OF
GREAT YANKEE CATCHERS
THE EPITOME OF YANKEE PRIDE

ERECTED BY
NEW YORK YANKEES
AUGUST 21, 1988

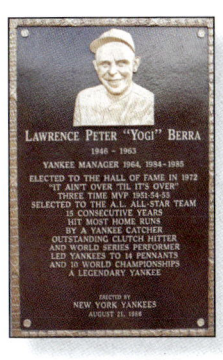

LAWRENCE PETER "YOGI" BERRA
1946-1963
YANKEE MANAGER 1964, 1984-1985

ELECTED TO THE HALL OF FAME IN 1972
"IT AIN'T OVER 'TIL IT'S OVER"
THREE TIME MVP 1951-54-55
SELECTED TO THE A.L. ALL-STAR TEAM
15 CONSECUTIVE YEARS
HIT MOST HOME RUNS
BY A YANKEE CATCHER
OUTSTANDING CLUTCH HITTER
AND WORLD SERIES PERFORMER
LED YANKEES TO 14 PENNANTS
AND 10 WORLD CHAMPIONSHIPS
A LEGENDARY YANKEE

ERECTED BY
NEW YORK YANKEES
AUGUST 21, 1988

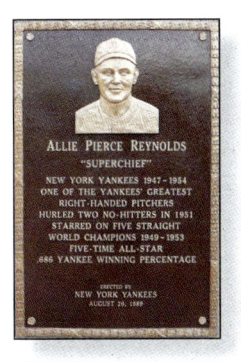

ALLIE PIERCE REYNOLDS
"SUPERCHIEF"

NEW YORK YANKEES 1947-1954
ONE OF THE YANKEES' GREATEST
RIGHT-HANDED PITCHERS
HURLED TWO NO-HITTERS IN 1951
STARRED ON FIVE STRAIGHT
WORLD CHAMPIONS 1949-1953
FIVE-TIME ALL-STAR
.686 YANKEE WINNING PERCENTAGE

ERECTED BY
NEW YORK YANKEES
AUGUST 26, 1989

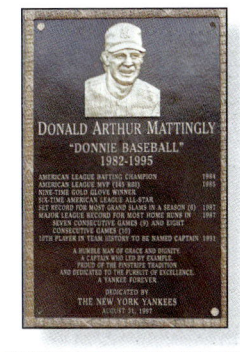

DONALD ARTHUR MATTINGLY
"DONNIE BASEBALL"
1982-1995

AMERICAN LEAGUE BATTING CHAMPION	1984
AMERICAN LEAGUE MVP (145 RBI)	1985
NINE-TIME GOLD GLOVE WINNER	
SIX-TIME AMERICAN LEAGUE ALL-STAR	
SET RECORD FOR MOST GRAND SLAMS IN A SEASON (6)	1987
MAJOR LEAGUE RECORD FOR MOST HOME RUNS IN SEVEN CONSECUTIVE GAMES (9) AND EIGHT CONSECUTIVE GAMES (10)	1987
10TH PLAYER IN TEAM HISTORY TO BE NAMED CAPTAIN	1991

A HUMBLE MAN OF GRACE AND DIGNITY.
A CAPTAIN WHO LED BY EXAMPLE.
PROUD OF THE PINSTRIPE TRADITION
AND DEDICATED TO THE PURSUIT OF EXCELLENCE,
A YANKEE FOREVER.

DEDICATED BY
THE NEW YORK YANKEES
AUGUST 31, 1997

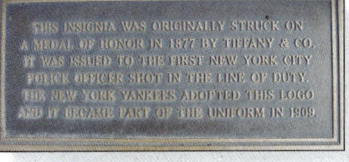

NEW YORK YANKEES INSIGNIA

THIS INSIGNIA WAS ORIGINALLY STRUCK ON
A MEDAL OF HONOR IN 1877 BY TIFFANY & CO.
IT WAS ISSUED TO THE FIRST NEW YORK CITY
POLICE OFFICER SHOT IN THE LINE OF DUTY.
THE NEW YORK YANKEES ADOPTED THIS LOGO
AND IT BECAME PART OF THE UNIFORM IN 1909.

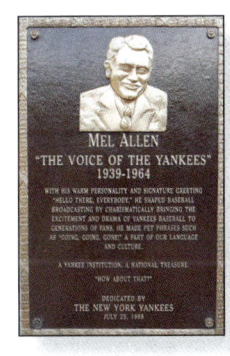

MEL ALLEN
"THE VOICE OF THE YANKEES"
1939-1964

WITH HIS WARM PERSONALITY AND SIGNATURE GREETING
"HELLO THERE, EVERYBODY," HE SHAPED BASEBALL
BROADCASTING BY CHARISMATICALLY BRINGING THE
EXCITEMENT AND DRAMA OF YANKEES BASEBALL TO
GENERATIONS OF FANS. HE MADE PET PHRASES SUCH
AS "GOING, GOING, GONE!" A PART OF OUR LANGUAGE
AND CULTURE.

A YANKEE INSTITUTION, A NATIONAL TREASURE.

"HOW ABOUT THAT?"

DEDICATED BY
THE NEW YORK YANKEES
JULY 25, 1998

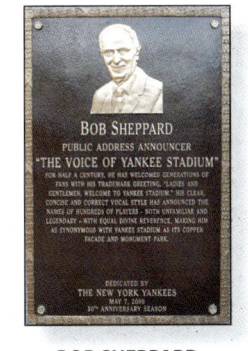

BOB SHEPPARD
PUBLIC ADDRESS ANNOUNCER
"THE VOICE OF YANKEE STADIUM"

FOR HALF A CENTURY, HE HAS WELCOMED GENERATIONS OF
FANS WITH HIS TRADEMARK GREETING, "LADIES AND
GENTLEMEN, WELCOME TO YANKEE STADIUM." HIS CLEAR,
CONCISE AND CORRECT VOCAL STYLE HAS ANNOUNCED THE
NAMES OF HUNDREDS OF PLAYERS - BOTH UNFAMILIAR AND
LEGENDARY - WITH EQUAL DIVINE REVERENCE, MAKING HIM
AS SYNONYMOUS WITH YANKEE STADIUM AS ITS COPPER
FACADE AND MONUMENT PARK.

DEDICATED BY
THE NEW YORK YANKEES
MAY 7, 2000
50TH ANNIVERSARY SEASON

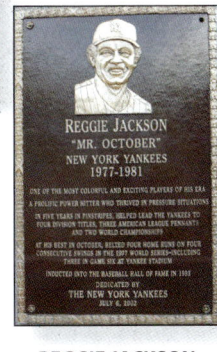

REGGIE JACKSON
"MR. OCTOBER"
NEW YORK YANKEES
1977-1981

ONE OF THE MOST COLORFUL AND EXCITING PLAYERS OF HIS ERA

A PROLIFIC POWER HITTER WHO THRIVED IN PRESSURE SITUATIONS

IN FIVE YEARS IN PINSTRIPES, HELPED LEAD THE YANKEES TO
FOUR DIVISION TITLES, THREE AMERICAN LEAGUE PENNANTS
AND TWO WORLD CHAMPIONSHIPS

AT HIS BEST IN OCTOBER, BELTED FOUR HOME RUNS ON FOUR
CONSECUTIVE SWINGS IN THE 1977 WORLD SERIES–INCLUDING
THREE IN GAME SIX AT YANKEE STADIUM

INDUCTED INTO THE BASEBALL HALL OF FAME IN 1993

DEDICATED BY
THE NEW YORK YANKEES
JULY 6, 2002

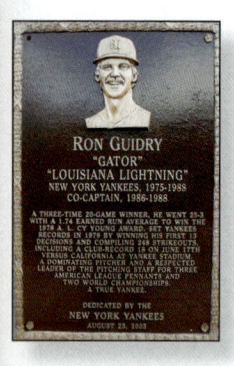

RON GUIDRY
"GATOR"
"LOUISIANA LIGHTNING"
NEW YORK YANKEES, 1975-1988
CO-CAPTAIN, 1986-1988

A THREE-TIME 20-GAME WINNER, HE WENT 25-3
WITH A 1.74 EARNED RUN AVERAGE TO WIN THE
1978 A.L. CY YOUNG AWARD. SET YANKEES
RECORDS IN 1978 BY WINNING HIS FIRST 13
DECISIONS AND COMPILING 248 STRIKEOUTS,
INCLUDING A CLUB-RECORD 18 ON JUNE 17TH
VERSUS CALIFORNIA AT YANKEE STADIUM.
A DOMINATING PITCHER AND A RESPECTED
LEADER OF THE PITCHING STAFF FOR THREE
AMERICAN LEAGUE PENNANTS AND
TWO WORLD CHAMPIONSHIPS.
A TRUE YANKEE.

DEDICATED BY THE
NEW YORK YANKEES
AUGUST 23, 2003

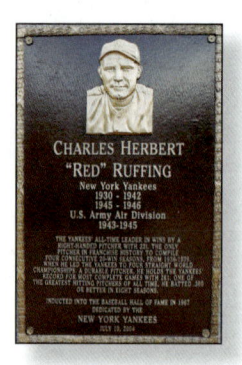

CHARLES HERBERT "RED" RUFFING
New York Yankees
1930-1942
1945-1946
U.S. ARMY AIR DIVISION

THE YANKEES' ALL-TIME LEADER IN WINS BY A
RIGHT-HANDED PITCHER WITH 231. THE ONLY
PITCHER IN FRANCHISE HISTORY TO COMPILE
FOUR CONSECUTIVE 20-WIN SEASONS, FROM 1936-1939,
WHEN HE LED THE YANKEES TO FOUR STRAIGHT WORLD
CHAMPIONSHIPS. A DURABLE PITCHER, HE HOLDS THE YANKEES'
RECORD FOR MOST COMPLETE GAMES WITH 261. ONE OF
THE GREATEST HITTING PITCHERS OF ALL TIME, HE BATTED .300
OR BETTER IN EIGHT SEASONS.

INDUCTED INTO THE BASEBALL HALL OF FAME IN 1967
DEDICATED BY THE
NEW YORK YANKEES
JULY 10, 2004

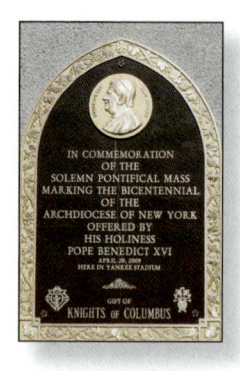

POPE BENEDICT XVI

IN COMMEMORATION
OF THE
SOLEMN PONTIFICAL MASS
MARKING THE BICENTENNIAL
OF THE
ARCHDIOCESE OF NEW YORK
OFFERED BY
HIS HOLINESS
POPE BENEDICT XVI
APRIL 20, 2008
HERE IN YANKEE STADIUM

GIFT OF
KNIGHTS OF COLUMBUS

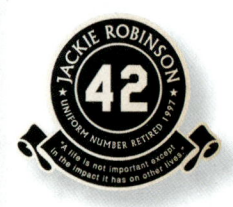

JACKIE ROBINSON
42
UNIFORM NUMBER RETIRED 1997

"A LIFE IS NOT IMPORTANT EXCEPT
IN THE IMPACT IT HAS ON OTHER LIVES."

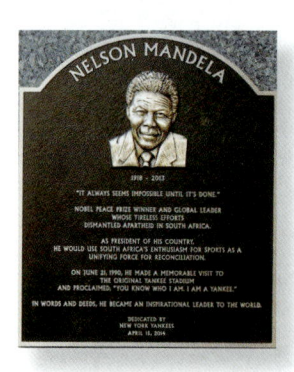

NELSON MANDELA
NELSON MANDELA
1918 – 2013

"IT ALWAYS SEEMS IMPOSSIBLE UNTIL IT'S DONE."
NOBEL PEACE PRIZE WINNER AND GLOBAL LEADER
WHOSE TIRELESS EFFORTS
DISMANTLED APARTHEID IN SOUTH AFRICA.
AS PRESIDENT OF HIS COUNTRY,
HE WOULD USE SOUTH AFRICA'S ENTHUSIASM FOR SPORTS AS A
UNIFYING FORCE FOR RECONCILIATION.
ON JUNE 21, 1990, HE MADE A MEMORABLE VISIT TO
THE ORIGINAL YANKEE STADIUM
AND PROCLAIMED, "YOU KNOW WHO I AM. I AM A YANKEE."
IN WORDS AND DEEDS, HE BECAME AN INSPIRATIONAL LEADER TO THE WORLD.

DEDICATED BY
NEW YORK YANKEES
APRIL 15, 2014

CONSTANTINO "TINO" MARTINEZ
NEW YORK YANKEES
1996 - 2001, 2005

KNOWN FOR HIS POWERFUL BAT AND
SUPERLATIVE DEFENSE AT FIRST BASE,
MARTINEZ WAS A FAN FAVORITE ON FOUR
YANKEES WORLD CHAMPIONSHIP TEAMS.
HIT TWO OF THE MOST MEMORABLE HOME
RUNS IN YANKEES POSTSEASON HISTORY –
A GRAND SLAM IN GAME 1 OF THE 1998 WORLD
SERIES AND A GAME-TYING, NINTH-INNING
HOMER IN GAME 4 OF THE 2001 FALL CLASSIC.
AMASSED 192 HOME RUNS AND 739 RBI
IN SEVEN SEASONS WITH THE CLUB.

DEDICATED BY THE
NEW YORK YANKEES
JUNE 21, 2014

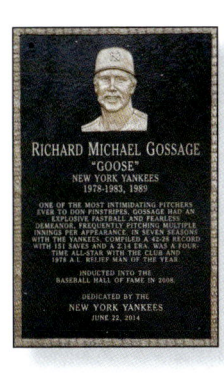

RICHARD MICHAEL GOSSAGE
"GOOSE"
NEW YORK YANKEES
1978-1983, 1989

ONE OF THE MOST INTIMIDATING PITCHERS EVER TO DON PINSTRIPES, GOSSAGE HAD AN EXPLOSIVE FASTBALL AND FEARLESS DEMEANOR, FREQUENTLY PITCHING MULTIPLE INNINGS PER APPEARANCE. IN SEVEN SEASONS WITH THE YANKEES, COMPILED A 42-28 RECORD WITH 151 SAVES AND A 2.14 ERA. WAS A FOUR-TIME ALL-STAR WITH THE CLUB AND 1978 A.L. RELIEF MAN OF THE YEAR

INDUCTED INTO
BASEBALL HALL OF FAME IN 2008.

DEDICATED BY THE
NEW YORK YANKEES
JUNE 22, 2014

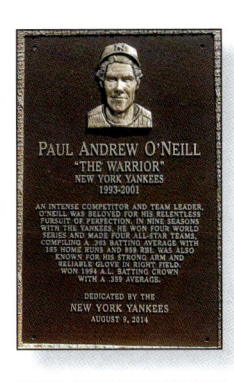

PAUL ANDREW O'NEILL
"THE WARRIOR"
NEW YORK YANKEES
1993 - 2001

AN INTENSE COMPETITOR AND TEAM LEADER, O'NEILL WAS BELOVED FOR HIS RELENTLESS PURSUIT OF PERFECTION. IN NINE SEASONS WITH THE YANKEES, HE WON FOUR WORLD SERIES AND MADE FOUR ALL-STAR TEAMS, COMPILING A .303 BATTING AVERAGE WITH 185 HOME RUNS AND 858 RBI. WAS ALSO KNOWN FOR HIS STRONG ARM AND RELIABLE GLOVE IN RIGHT FIELD. WON 1994 A.L. BATTING CROWN WITH A .359 AVERAGE.

DEDICATED BY THE
NEW YORK YANKEES
AUGUST 9, 2014

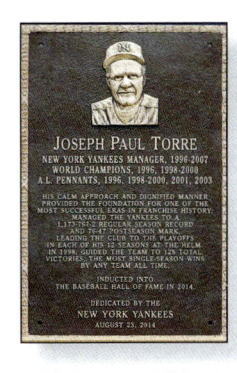

JOSEPH PAUL TORRE
NEW YORK YANKEES MANAGER, 1996-2007
WORLD CHAMPIONS, 1996, 1998-2000
A.L. PENNANTS, 1996, 1998-2000, 2001, 2003

HIS CALM APPROACH AND DIGNIFIED MANNER PROVIDED THE FOUNDATION FOR ONE OF THE MOST SUCCESSFUL ERAS IN FRANCHISE HISTORY. MANAGED THE YANKEES TO A 1,173-767-2 REGULAR SEASON RECORD AND 76-47 POSTSEASON MARK, LEADING THE CLUB TO THE PLAYOFFS IN EACH OF HIS 12 SEASONS AT THE HELM. IN 1998, GUIDED THE TEAM TO 125 TOTAL VICTORIES, THE MOST SINGLE-SEASON WINS BY ANY TEAM ALL TIME.

INDUCTED INTO
THE BASEBALL HALL OF FAME IN 2014.

DEDICATED BY THE
NEW YORK YANKEES
AUGUST 23, 2014

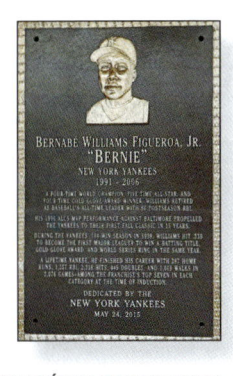

BERNABÉ WILLIAMS FIGUEROA, JR.
"BERNIE"
NEW YORK YANKEES
1991-2006

A FOUR-TIME WORLD CHAMPION, FIVE-TIME ALL-STAR, AND FOUR-TIME GOLD GLOVE AWARD WINNER, WILLIAMS RETIRED AS BASEBALL'S ALL-TIME LEADER WITH 80 POSTSEASON RBI.

HIS 1996 ALCS MVP PERFORMANCE AGAINST BALTIMORE PROPELLED THE YANKEES TO THEIR FIRST FALL CLASSIC IN 15 YEARS.

DURING THE YANKEES' 114-WIN SEASON IN 1998, WILLIAMS HIT .339 TO BECOME THE FIRST MAJOR LEAGUER TO WIN A BATTING TITLE, GOLD GLOVE AWARD AND WORLD SERIES RING IN THE SAME YEAR.

A LIFETIME YANKEE, HE FINISHED WITH 287 HOME RUNS, 1,257 RBI, 2,336 HITS, 449 DOUBLES AND 1,069 WALKS IN 2,076 GAMES—AMONG THE FRANCHISE'S TOP SEVEN IN EACH CATEGORY AT THE TIME OF INDUCTION.

DEDICATED BY THE
NEW YORK YANKEES
MAY 24, 2015

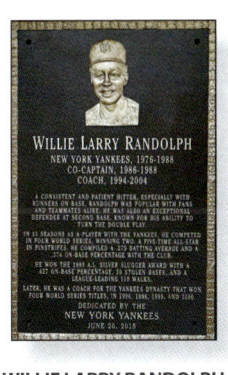

WILLIE LARRY RANDOLPH
NEW YORK YANKEES, 1976-1988
CO-CAPTAIN, 1986-1988
COACH, 1994-2004

A CONSISTENT AND PATIENT HITTER, ESPECIALLY WITH RUNNERS ON BASE, RANDOLPH WAS POPULAR WITH FANS AND TEAMMATES ALIKE. HE WAS ALSO AN EXCEPTIONAL DEFENDER AT SECOND BASE, KNOWN FOR HIS ABILITY TO TURN THE DOUBLE PLAY.

IN 13 SEASONS AS A PLAYER WITH THE YANKEES, HE COMPETED IN FOUR WORLD SERIES, WINNING TWO. A FIVE-TIME ALL-STAR IN PINSTRIPES, HE COMPILED A .275 BATTING AVERAGE AND A .374 ON-BASE PERCENTAGE WITH THE CLUB.

HE WON THE 1980 A.L. SILVER SLUGGER AWARD WITH A .427 ON-BASE PERCENTAGE, 30 STOLEN BASES AND A LEAGUE-LEADING 119 WALKS.

LATER, HE WAS A COACH FOR THE YANKEES DYNASTY THAT WON FOUR WORLD SERIES TITLES IN 1996, 1998, 1999 AND 2000.

DEDICATED BY THE
NEW YORK YANKEES
JUNE 20, 2015

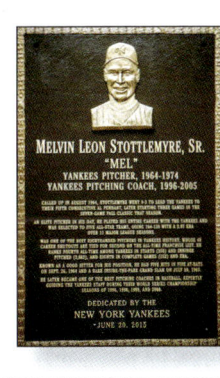

MELVIN LEON STOTTLEMYRE, SR.
"MEL"
YANKEES PITCHER, 1964-1974
YANKEES PITCHING COACH, 1996-2005

CALLED UP IN AUGUST 1964, STOTTLEMYRE WENT 9-3 TO LEAD THE YANKEES TO THEIR FIFTH CONSECUTIVE AL PENNANT, LATER STARTING THREE GAMES IN THE SEVEN-GAME FALL CLASSIC THAT SEASON.

AN ELITE PITCHER IN HIS DAY, HE PLAYED HIS ENTIRE CAREER WITH THE YANKEES, AND WAS SELECTED TO FIVE ALL-STAR TEAMS, GOING 164-139 WITH A 2.97 ERA OVER 11 MAJOR LEAGUE SEASONS.

WAS ONE OF THE BEST RIGHTHANDED PITCHERS IN YANKEES HISTORY, WHOSE 40 CAREER SHUTOUTS ARE TIED FOR SECOND ON THE ALL-TIME FRANCHISE LIST. HE RANKS FOURTH ALL-TIME AMONG YANKEES IN STARTS (356) AND INNINGS PITCHED (2,662), AND EIGHTH IN COMPLETE GAMES (152) AND ERA.

KNOWN AS A GOOD HITTER FOR HIS POSITION, HE HAD FIVE HITS IN FIVE AT-BATS ON SEPT. 26, 1964 AND A RARE INSIDE-THE-PARK GRAND SLAM ON JULY 20, 1965.

HE LATER BECAME ONE OF THE BEST PITCHING COACHES IN BASEBALL, EXPERTLY GUIDING THE YANKEES STAFF DURING THEIR WORLD SERIES CHAMPIONSHIP SEASONS OF 1996, 1998, 1999, AND 2000.

DEDICATED BY THE
NEW YORK YANKEES
JUNE 20, 2015

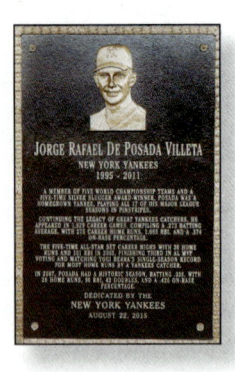

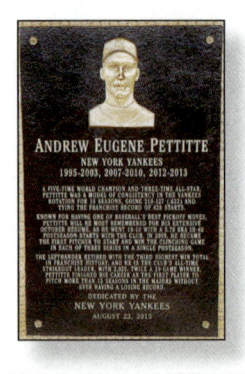

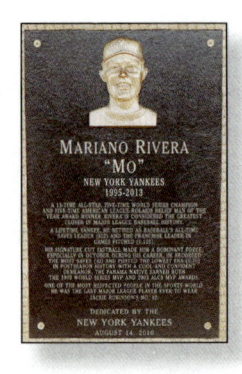

JORGE RAFAEL DE POSADA VILLETA
NEW YORK YANKEES
1995 - 2011

A MEMBER OF FIVE WORLD CHAMPIONSHIP TEAMS AND A FIVE-TIME SILVER SLUGGER AWARD-WINNER, POSADA WAS A HOMEGROWN YANKEE, PLAYING ALL 17 OF HIS MAJOR LEAGUE SEASONS IN PINSTRIPES.

CONTINUING THE LEGACY OF GREAT YANKEES CATCHERS, HE APPEARED IN 1,829 CAREER GAMES, COMPILING A .273 BATTING AVERAGE, WITH 275 CAREER HOME RUNS, 1,065 RBI, AND A .374 ON-BASE PERCENTAGE.

THE FIVE-TIME ALL-STAR SET CAREER HIGHS WITH 30 HOME RUNS AND 101 RBI IN 2003, FINISHING THIRD IN AL MVP VOTING AND MATCHING YOGI BERRA'S SINGLE-SEASON RECORD FOR MOST HOME RUNS BY A YANKEES CATCHER.

IN 2007, POSADA HAD A HISTORIC SEASON, BATTING .338, WITH 20 HOME RUNS, 90 RBI, 42 DOUBLES, AND A .426 ON-BASE PERCENTAGE.

DEDICATED BY THE
NEW YORK YANKEES
AUGUST 22, 2015

ANDREW EUGENE PETTITTE
NEW YORK YANKEES
1995-2003, 2007-2010, 2012-2013

A FIVE-TIME WORLD CHAMPION AND THREE-TIME ALL-STAR, PETTITTE WAS A MODEL OF CONSISTENCY IN THE YANKEES ROTATION FOR 15 SEASONS, GOING 219-127 (.633) AND TYING THE FRANCHISE RECORD OF 438 STARTS.

KNOWN FOR HAVING ONE OF BASEBALL'S BEST PICKOFF MOVES, PETTITTE WILL BE MOST REMEMBERED FOR HIS EXTENSIVE OCTOBER RÉSUMÉ, AS HE WENT 18-10 WITH A 3.76 ERA IN 40 POSTSEASON STARTS WITH THE CLUB. IN 2009, HE BECAME THE FIRST PITCHER TO START AND WIN THE CLINCHING GAME IN EACH OF THREE SERIES IN A SINGLE POSTSEASON.

THE LEFTHANDER RETIRED WITH THE THIRD HIGHEST WIN TOTAL IN FRANCHISE HISTORY, AND HE IS THE CLUB'S ALL-TIME STRIKEOUT LEADER, WITH 2,020. TWICE A 20-GAME WINNER, PETTITTE FINISHED HIS CAREER AS THE FIRST PLAYER TO PITCH MORE THAN 15 SEASONS IN THE MAJORS WITHOUT EVER HAVING A LOSING RECORD.

DEDICATED BY THE
NEW YORK YANKEES
AUGUST 23, 2015

MARIANO RIVERA
"MO"
NEW YORK YANKEES
1995 - 2013

A 13-TIME ALL-STAR, FIVE-TIME WORLD SERIES CHAMPION AND FIVE-TIME AMERICAN LEAGUE ROLAIDS RELIEF MAN OF THE YEAR AWARD WINNER, RIVERA IS CONSIDERED THE GREATEST CLOSER IN MAJOR LEAGUE BASEBALL HISTORY.

A LIFETIME YANKEE, HE RETIRED AS BASEBALL'S ALL-TIME SAVES LEADER (652) AND THE FRANCHISE LEADER IN GAMES PITCHED (1,115).

HIS SIGNATURE CUT FASTBALL MADE HIM A DOMINANT FORCE, ESPECIALLY IN OCTOBER. DURING HIS CAREER, HE RECORDED THE MOST SAVES (42) AND POSTED THE LOWEST ERA (0.70) IN POSTSEASON HISTORY. WITH A COOL AND CONFIDENT DEMEANOR, THE PANAMA NATIVE EARNED BOTH THE 1999 WORLD SERIES MVP AND 2003 ALCS MVP AWARDS.

ONE OF THE MOST RESPECTED PEOPLE IN THE SPORTS WORLD, HE WAS THE LAST MAJOR LEAGUE PLAYER EVER TO WEAR JACKIE ROBINSON'S NO. 42.

DEDICATED BY THE
NEW YORK YANKEES
AUGUST 14, 2016

DEREK SANDERSON JETER
"THE CAPTAIN"
"MR. NOVEMBER"
NEW YORK YANKEES
1995-2014

AS THE CORNERSTONE OF FIVE WORLD CHAMPIONSHIP TEAMS, JETER WAS A LEADER ON THE FIELD AND IN THE CLUBHOUSE, SETTING AN EXAMPLE FOR HIS TEAMMATES WITH HIS UNCOMPROMISING DESIRE FOR TEAM SUCCESS.

HE RETIRED WITH A FRANCHISE-BEST 3,465 HITS – SIXTH ON BASEBALL'S ALL-TIME LIST – HAVING PLAYED MORE SEASONS (20) AND GAMES (2,747) THAN ANY OTHER YANKEE. A LIFETIME .310 HITTER WITH A .377 ON-BASE PERCENTAGE, JETER WAS THE LONGEST-TENURED CAPTAIN IN TEAM HISTORY, HOLDING THE ROLE FROM JUNE 3, 2003 THROUGH THE END OF HIS CAREER IN 2014.

JETER GARNERED 14 ALL-STAR NOMINATIONS, FIVE GOLD GLOVES, AND FIVE SILVER SLUGGER AWARDS. IN 2000, THE SHORTSTOP BECAME THE FIRST PLAYER IN MAJOR LEAGUE HISTORY TO BE NAMED ALL-STAR GAME MVP AND WORLD SERIES MVP IN THE SAME SEASON.

A CONSISTENT WINNER, HE COMPILED AN INCREDIBLE .593 REGULAR SEASON WINNING PERCENTAGE (1,628-1,117-2) IN GAMES PLAYED, AND HE RETIRED AS BASEBALL'S ALL-TIME POSTSEASON LEADER IN GAMES (158), HITS (200), RUNS (111), AND DOUBLES (32).

DEDICATED BY THE
NEW YORK YANKEES
MAY 14, 2017

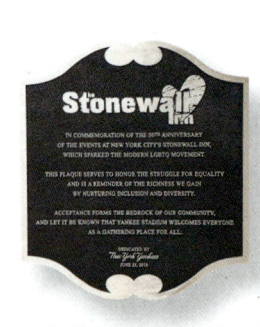

THE STONEWALL INN

IN COMMEMORATION OF THE 50TH ANNIVERSARY OF THE EVENTS AT NEW YORK CITY'S STONEWALL INN, WHICH SPARKED THE MODERN LGBTQ MOVEMENT.

THIS PLAQUE SERVES TO HONOR THE STRUGGLE FOR EQUALITY AND IS A REMINDER OF THE RICHNESS WE GAIN BY NURTURING INCLUSION AND DIVERSITY.

ACCEPTANCE FORMS THE BEDROCK OF OUR COMMUNITY, AND LET IT BE KNOWN THAT YANKEE STADIUM WELCOMES EVERYONE AS A GATHERING PLACE FOR ALL.

DEDICATED BY
NEW YORK YANKEES
JUNE 25, 2019

Fellow Monument Park inductees join Derek Jeter during his May 14, 2017, induction ceremony. From L to R: Paul O'Neill, Tino Martinez, Andy Pettitte, Mariano Rivera, Jorge Posada, Derek Jeter, Bernie Williams, Willie Randolph and Joe Torre.

Player Development

RHP Deivi García, 20, was a 2019 Eastern League Mid-Season All-Star and started for the AL team at the SiriusXM All-Star Futures Game in Cleveland.

2020 Player Development & Scouting Directory

EXECUTIVE
Damon Oppenheimer .................V.P., Domestic Amateur Scouting
Tim Naehring .... Vice President, Baseball Operations

PLAYER DEVELOPMENT
Kevin Reese...............................Senior Director, Player Development
Eric Schmitt ....Director, Player Development
Stephen Swindal Jr. ....Assistant Director, Player Development
Victor Roldan........................Manager, International Operations
Nick Avanzato ....Manager, Minor League Operations
Rob Owens..Engineer, Baseball Solutions
Brad Smith, Dan Walco .... Analysts, Player Development
Giuliano Montanez .... Assistant, International Operations
Nick Leon ....Assistant, Minor League Operations
Tino Martinez, Marc Bombard .......................P.D. Consultants

PLAYER DEVELOPMENT COORDINATORS
Mario Garza ....Coordinator, Baseball Development
Pat McMahon........................ Coord. of Instruction/Outfield Coord.
David Adams .... Complex Coordinator/Tampa Manager
Dillon Lawson ....Hitting Coordinator
Sam Briend..Director of Pitching
John Kremer..................Pitching Coord./Perf. Science Consultant
Desi Druschel .... Manager, Pitch Development
Miguel Cairo ....Infield Coordinator
Travis Chapman............... Asst. Infield Coordinator/GCL East Manager
Aaron Gershenfeld...Catching Coordinator
Matt Talarico ....Baserunning Coord./Roving Hitting Coach
Rachel Balkovec, Trevor Amicone ....Complex Hitting Coaches

PLAYER HEALTH & PERFORMANCE
Donovan Santas........ Asst. Director, Player Health & Performance
Mark Littlefield ....Medical Coordinator
Greg Spratt..Assistant Head Athletic Trainer
David Colvin .... Physical Therapist, Player Development
Joe Bello........... Assistant Physical Therapist, Player Development
Rigo Febles......................Strength and Conditioning Coordinator
Ty Hill ....Rehab Strength Coach
Greg Pavlick ....Rehab Pitching Coach

MENTAL CONDITIONING
Chris Passarella................. Associate Director, Mental Conditioning
Hector Gonzalez .... Coordinator, Cultural Development
Lauren Johnson................................ Coordinator, Mental Conditioning
David Schnabel ....Video Coordinator, Mental Conditioning
Noel Garcia...Mental Conditioning Coach

PERFORMANCE SCIENCE
David Whiteside ....Director, Performance Science
Joe Siara ....Manager, Peak Performance Programs
Mike Wickland ....Coordinator, Preventative Programs
Patrick Hipes..Junior Sports Scientist
Sydney Boehnlein ....Minor League Nutrition Coordinator
Christina Williamson.......................Analyst, Performance Science
Chandler Falcon ....Minor League Dietitian

PLAYER DEVELOPMENT VIDEO
Chris Whiting... Video Coordinator, P.D.
Joe Wielbruda .... Minor League Video Coordinator
Zach Iannarelli .... Assistant Video Coordinator, P.D.
Dan O'Connor .... Video Coordinator, International P.D.
Eliezer Beard, Javier Deyan,
Kevin Valera .... Trackman Assistants, International P.D.
Paul Henshaw, Kurt Bathelt, Mike Triller,
Nick Horning, Luke Morris, Davy Vartanian,
Brian Sheffler, Dylan Elber...........................Affiliate Video Managers

INTERNATIONAL PLAYER DEVELOPMENT
Andrew Wright ....Director, D.R. Baseball Operations
Joel Lithgow.............................Director, Latin Baseball Academy
Luis Sojo.................................D.R./U.S. Transition Infield Coach
Josias Cabrera ....Supervisor, Dominican Academy
Manuel Castillo, J.T. Hernandez ....Assistants, Int'l Baseball Ops.

EDUCATION
Joe Perez.. Education Coordinator
Melissa Hernandez....................Lead Teacher/Player Dev. Assistant
Greta Martinez .... Teacher
Carolina Crespo ....Lead Teacher, International P.D.
Joel Alvarez, Karla Lister,
Guillermo Matos .... Teachers, International P.D.

PROFESSIONAL SCOUTING
Dan Giese .... Director, Pro Scouting
Matt Daley .... Director, Pro Scouting
Jim Hendry ....Special Assignment Scout
Adam Charnin-Aker .... Coordinator, Pro Scouting

PROFESSIONAL SCOUTS
Scott Atchison, Kendall Carter, Jay Darnell, Marc DelPiano, Jonathan Diaz, Brandon Duckworth, Tyler Greene, Kevin Hart, Shawn Hill, Dave Jauss, Cory Melvin, Pat Murtaugh, James Stokes, JT Stotts, Alex Sunderland, Dennis Twombley, Donnie Veal, Aron Weston, Tom Wilson.

AMATEUR SCOUTING
Mitch Colahan........ Asst. Dir., Dom. Amateur Scouting, Operations
Scott Benecke .... Asst. Dir., Dom. Amateur Scouting, Analytics
Sam Hughes, Tim Kelly, Steve Kmetko,
Jeff Patterson, Mike Wagner .... National Crosscheckers
Scott Lovekamp .... Am. Scouting & Affiliate Pitching Analyst
Jeff Deardorff..Hitting Analyst
Justin Sharpe..Draft Medical Coordinator
Tristam Osgood......... Amateur Scouting Asst., Operations/Analytics
Ricky Castle ....Video Coordinator, Amateur Scouting

AMATEUR SCOUTS
Troy Afenir..Arizona, Southern California
Tim Alexander.....................Delaware, Maryland, New York (state), Pennsylvania, West Virginia
Chuck Bartlett................Alabama, Florida, Mississippi, Tennessee
Denis Boucher ....Canada
Bobby DeJardin ....Southern California
Mike Gibbons..........................Indiana, Kentucky, Michigan, Ohio
Matt Hyde...................Connecticut, Maine, Massachusetts, New Hampshire, New Jersey, New York (state), Rhode Island, Vermont
Brian Jeroloman ....South Florida
David Keith ....California, Hawaii, Las Vegas
Steve Lemke ....Illinois, Iowa, Minnesota, Missouri, Wisconsin
Mike Leuzinger..Louisiana, Northern Texas
Ronnie Merrill ....North Florida
Darryl Monroe ....Georgia, South Carolina, Chattanooga
Bill Pintard ....Southern California
Cesar Presbott...New York City
Matt Ranson ....Arkansas, Colorado, Kansas, Missouri, Nebraska, North Dakota, Oklahoma, South Dakota
Brian Rhees ....New Mexico, Southern Texas
Tyler Robertson .... Northern California, Northern Nevada
Kelly Rodman ....Northeast
Stewart Smothers.......... North Carolina, Virginia, Washington D.C.
Mike Thurman............... Alaska, British Columbia, Idaho, Montana, Oregon, Utah, Washington, Wyoming

2020 Player Development & Scouting Directory

INTERNATIONAL SCOUTING

Donny Rowland	Director, International Scouting
Brady LaRuffa	Assistant Director, International Scouting
Edgar Mateo	Assistant to Director, Latin America
Steve Wilson, Dennis Woody,	
Ricardo Finol	Crosscheckers, International Scouting
Juan Rosario	Supervisor, Dominican Republic
Miguel Benitez, Victor Mata	Crosscheckers, Latin America
Jose Gavidia	Supervisor, Venezuela
Raymon Sanchez	Coordinator, Latin America
Ethan Sander	Video Coordinator, International Scouting
Luis Rodriguez	Video Assistant, Dominican Republic
Vianco Martinez	Technology/Data Analyst, Int'l Scouting
Victor Deyan	Technology/Data Analyst, Venezuela
Cary Broder	Amateur Research and Data Analysis

INTERNATIONAL SCOUTS

Doug Skiles	ABC Islands (Aruba, Bonaire, Curaçao)/Bahamas
John Wadsworth	Australia
Alvaro Noriega, Luis Sierra	Colombia
Esdras Abreu, Luis Brito, R. Arturo Peña,	
Juan Piron, Jose Ravelo, Jose Sabino	Dominican Republic
Troy Williams	Europe
Rudy Gomez	International
Raul Gonzalez, Lee Sigman	México
Edgard Rodriguez	Nicaragua
Carlos Levy	Panamá
Chi Lee	South Korea
Peng Pu Lee	Taiwan
Alan Atacho, Darwin Bracho, Roney Calderon,	
Cesar Suarez, Jesus Taico, Luis Tinoco	Venezuela

Player Development & Scouting Staff

ERIC SCHMITT – DIRECTOR, PLAYER DEVELOPMENT
BORN: 7/23/78 in Falls Church, Va. • **RESIDES:** Tampa, Fla.
Enters his 14th season in the Yankees organization, his third as the director of player development…spent three seasons as the director of minor league operations (2015-17)…has also served as assistant director of amateur scouting (2013-14) and assistant director of baseball operations for player development (2008-12)…joined the Yankees player development staff in 2007 as the assistant director of international operations…**PLAYING CAREER:** Was selected by the Yankees in the 25th round of the 2000 First-Year Player Draft…went 26-23 with a 4.35 ERA (521.1IP, 252ER) in 167 games (68 starts) over seven minor league seasons with the Yankees (2000-05) and Braves (2006)…**PERSONAL:** Married to wife, Jaclyn, with three sons, Owen, Ryan and Austin…graduated from Wake Forest University with a bachelor's degree in communications and went 23-3 over four seasons (1997-2000), including an ACC-best 2.57 ERA in his senior year…graduated from Woodson H.S. (Va.) in 1996…was selected by the Mets in the 18th round of the 1996 First-Year Player Draft but did not sign.

DAN GIESE – DIRECTOR, PRO SCOUTING
BORN: 5/19/77 in Anaheim, Calif. • **RESIDES:** San Clemente, Calif.
Enters his third season as director of pro scouting after two years as the assistant scouting director (2015-17)…**PLAYING CAREER:** Was selected by Boston in the 34th round of the 1999 First-Year Player Draft…made 35 appearances (four starts) across three Major League seasons with San Francisco (2007), the Yankees (2008) and Oakland (2009), going 1-8 with a 4.22 ERA (74.2IP, 35ER)…also pitched in 396 games over 12 minor league seasons (1999-2010), going 48-28 with a 2.86 ERA…**PERSONAL:** He and his wife, Shannon, have three daughters, Avery, Payton and Camdyn, and a son, Gavin…pitched for the University of San Diego, where he graduated with a B.S. in business administration in 2006…completed his Master's Degree in Special Education at National University in 2011…graduated from Rubidoux (Calif.) H.S.…following his retirement as a player, was a police officer for the San Diego Harbor Police from 2011-14.

MATT DALEY – DIRECTOR, PRO SCOUTING
BORN: 6/23/82 in Flushing, N.Y. • **RESIDES:** Hoboken, N.J.
Enters his sixth season with the Yankees…was promoted to director of pro scouting in 2019 after one year as assistant director of pro scouting…was a pro scout for the club for three years (2015-17)…**PLAYING CAREER:** The right-handed pitcher appeared in 112 games over parts of five Major League seasons with Colorado (2009-11) and the Yankees (2013-14), going 2-3 with a 4.47 ERA (100.2IP, 92H, 53R/50ER, 36BB, 98K, 13HR)…was originally signed by the Rockies as a non-drafted free agent on 6/11/04…was signed by the Yankees as a minor league free agent on 12/19/13 and went 1-1 with a 3.54 ERA (20.1IP, 14H, 11R/8ER, 6BB, 18K, 4HR) in 20 appearances over two seasons in the Bronx…famously was the Yankees reliever when entered the game following Hall of Famer Mariano Rivera's final Major League appearance on 9/26/13 vs. Tampa Bay…**PERSONAL:** He and his wife, Clare, have two children: CJ and Quinn…pitched three seasons at Bucknell (Pa.) University, earning his degree in accounting with a minor in economics…is a 2000 graduate of Garden City (N.Y.) H.S.

JIM HENDRY – SPECIAL ASSIGNMENT SCOUT
BORN: 7/27/55 in Dunedin, Fla. • **RESIDES:** Lafayette, La.
Enters his ninth season as a special assignment scout for the Yankees…during his 10-year stint as Chicago Cubs General Manager (2002-11), he became the first GM to take the Cubs to the postseason three times (2002, '07-08)…spent a total of 18 years with the Cubs (1994-2011) after three seasons with the Florida Marlins organization (1992-94)…was named the 1991 National Coach of the Year by *Baseball America* after leading Creighton University (Neb.) to a third-place finish at the College World Series…spent seven years at Creighton (1984-91) after beginning his career as the head coach at Miami's Columbus H.S. (1978-83)…**PERSONAL:** Has two children, Lauren and John…received a bachelor's degree in communications and journalism from Spring Hill College (Ala.) in 1977, and a master's degree in Athletic Administration from Biscayne College (now St. Thomas University) in Miami in 1980…received the 2019 Legends in Scouting Award from the PBSA at a ceremony in Beverly Hills, Calif., in January 2019.

MARIO GARZA – COORDINATOR, BASEBALL DEVELOPMENT
BORN: 5/26/81 in Shreveport, La. • **RESIDES:** Titusville, Fla.
COACHING CAREER: Enters his 10th season with the Yankees and first as coordinator of baseball development…spent the last three seasons (2017-19) as the Director of Latin American Operations…spent two seasons (2015-16) as the assistant director of international player development after managing short-season Single-A Staten Island in 2014…made his managerial debut in 2013 with the GCL Yankees 2, leading the club to a first-place finish in the Northeast Division with a 36-24 (.600) record…served as a coach with Single-A Tampa from 2011-12…prior to that, assisted hitters and catchers at his alma mater, Melbourne Central Catholic H.S. (Fla.)…**PLAYING CAREER:** Was selected by the Astros in the 25th round of the 2003 First-Year Player Draft…played four seasons in Houston's minor league system (2003-06), batting .253 with 41HR in 285 minor league games…finished his career in the independent Frontier League in 2007…**PERSONAL:** After graduating from Melbourne Central Catholic, played two seasons at Stanford University (2000-01) before transferring to the University of Florida (2002-03)…played for the U.S. in the 1997 World Youth Championship.

PAT McMAHON – COORDINATOR OF INSTRUCTION/OUTFIELD COORDINATOR
BORN: 5/28/53 in Lackawanna, N.Y. • **RESIDES:** Gainesville, Fla.

COACHING CAREER: Enters his 13th season with the Yankees organization, his third as the coordinator of instruction…was an outfield and base running coordinator in 2017…served as the Director of International Player Development for five seasons (2012-16)…was inducted into the American Baseball Coaches Association (ABCA) Hall of Fame in January 2018…received the ABCA's Lefty Gomez Award in 2015, which recognizes individuals who make significant contributions to the game of baseball locally, nationally and internationally…joined the Yankees in 2008 as the manager for short-season Single-A Staten Island, leading the team to a league-best 49-26 record…was the head coach of the University of Florida for seven seasons (2001-07) and earned the Collegiate Baseball Foundation's "National Coach of the Year" and SEC "Coach of the Year" Awards in 2005 after guiding the Gators to a national runner-up finish at the College World Series…owns a career college coaching record of 555-287-1 in 16 seasons with Old Dominion (1990-94), Mississippi State (1997-2000) and Florida…served three stints with the USA National Team: was the pitching coach for the team that won bronze at the 1991 Pan-American Games in Cuba; was an assistant in 1997; and managed the 2001 USA team that played in tournaments in the U.S., Japan and Taiwan…was inducted into the Old Dominion Sports Hall of Fame in Oct. 2015…the pitching lab at Mississippi State was named after McMahon in Nov. 2019…**PLAYING CAREER:** Was selected by the Mets in the 18th round of the 1971 First-Year Player Draft but chose to play collegiately at St. John's River College (1972-73) and Stetson University (1974-75)…**PERSONAL:** Is married to wife, Cheri, with daughter, Logan, and son, J. Wells…is one of eight siblings.

DAVID ADAMS – COMPLEX COORDINATOR/MANAGER, SINGLE-A TAMPA
BIO ON PAGE 410

DILLON LAWSON – HITTING COORDINATOR
BORN: 5/23/85 in Louisville, Ky. • **RESIDES:** Tampa, Fla.

COACHING CAREER: Enters his second season as the Yankees' minor league hitting coordinator…was the hitting coach at Houston's Single-A Quad Cities affiliate in 2018…served as the hitting coach at the University of Missouri in 2017 to split up his two stints with the Astros organization, which began in 2016 as the hitting coach at short-season Single-A Tri-City…began his coaching career on the collegiate side, serving as an assistant coach at Lindenwood University (Mo.) from 2007-09, at Morehead State University (Ky.) from 2009-12 and at Southeast Missouri State University from 2013-15…**PERSONAL:** He and his wife, Amanda, have a son, Asa "Ace"…graduated from Transylvania University (Ky.) in 2007 and earned his Master's in Education from Lindenwood University in 2009.

SAM BRIEND – DIRECTOR OF PITCHING
BORN: 3/29/88 in Utica, N.Y. • **RESIDES:** Tampa, Fla.

COACHING CAREER: Joins the Yankees organization after three seasons as the director of player development at Driveline Baseball in Seattle, Wash.…spent one season as pitching coach for the St. Cloud Rox of the summer collegiate Northwoods League…returned to his alma mater, serving as the pitching coach and head strength coach for five years…**PLAYING CAREER:** The right-handed pitcher played two seasons of independent baseball, for the NYSL Federals of the Canadian-American Association in 2011, and in the Pecos League in 2013 for the Taos Blizzard and Trinidad Triggers…**PERSONAL:** Played four years at Oglethorpe (Ga.) University, where he graduated in 2011 with a degree in psychology while receiving All-SCAC First Team honors…earned his Master's degree in Strength and Conditioning at LaGrange (Ga.) College.

JOHN KREMER – PITCHING COORDINATOR/PERFORMANCE SCIENCE CONSULTANT
BORN: 11/19/76 in Indianapolis, Ind. • **RESIDES:** Lutz, Fla.

Enters his 17th season with the Yankees organization, his first as a pitching coordinator…will again contribute to the organizations' performance science efforts, having previously spent five seasons as the director of performance science (2015-19) after serving as the director of player personnel from 2013-14…was the assistant director of amateur scouting from 2005-12 after joining the player development department in 2004 as a baseball operations assistant…**PLAYING CAREER:** Was selected by the Yankees in the 19th round of the 1999 First-Year Player Draft…spent five years in the Yankees minor league system (1999-2003), compiling a 15-15 record with a 3.91 ERA (292.0IP, 127ER) in 175 games (one start)…**PERSONAL:** Married to wife, Julie, with two children, McKenzie and John Cannon…pitched for the University of Evansville (Ind.), where he graduated with a B.S. in mathematics…received an MBA from the University of South Florida in 2011 and a professional certificate in strategic decision and risk management from Stanford in 2012.

DESI DRUSCHEL – MANAGER, PITCH DEVELOPMENT
BORN: 6/19/75 in Vinton, Iowa • **RESIDES:** Cedar Rapids, Iowa

COACHING CAREER: Enters his second season with the Yankees organization…spent four years at the University of Iowa, where he was the team's pitching coach for one season (2018) after three seasons as the director of baseball operations (2015-17)…began his coaching career as an assistant coach at Vinton-Shellsburg H.S. (Iowa) in 1998, before joining the collegiate ranks at Indiana University in 1999…was an assistant (2000-01) before taking over as head coach (2001-04) at Franciscan University (Iowa), née Mount St. Clare College, and now known as Ashford University…**PERSONAL:** He and his wife, Jessica, have two children, Jace and Halle…played baseball and basketball at Upper Iowa University and Mount Mercy (Iowa) University from 1994-98…earned his master's degree in athletic administration from Indiana University in 2001.

MIGUEL CAIRO – INFIELD COORDINATOR
BORN: 5/4/74 in Anaco, Venezuela • **RESIDES:** Clearwater, Fla.

COACHING CAREER: Enters his third season as the Yankees' infield coordinator…was a special assistant to Reds General Managers Walt Jocketty and Dick Williams for five seasons (2013-17)…served as an extra coach for the Reds at the Major League level in 2013…**PLAYING CAREER:** The infielder played in 1,490 Major League games over 17 seasons with the Blue Jays (1996), Cubs (1997, 2001), Devil Rays (1998-2000), Cardinals (2001-03, '07), Yankees (2004, '06-07), Mets (2005), Mariners (2008), Phillies (2009) and Reds (2010-12)…hit .264 with 504R, 41HR, 394RBI and 139SB…reached the postseason with four different clubs: St. Louis (2001-02), Yankees (2004), Philadelphia (2009) and Cincinnati (2010, '12)…**PERSONAL:** He and his wife, Nicole, have one son, Christian, and one daughter, Lauren…graduated from Escuela Anaco H.S. (Ven.).

TRAVIS CHAPMAN – ASST. INFIELD COORDINATOR/MANAGER, GCL YANKEES WEST
BIO ON PAGE 415

AARON GERSHENFELD – CATCHING COORDINATOR
BORN: 5/15/92 in Lansing, Mich. • **RESIDES:** Tampa, Fla.

COACHING CAREER: Joins the Yankees organization after six years as a collegiate assistant…spent the last three seasons (2017-19) as the hitting coach and recruiting coordinator for The Citadel (S.C.)…was the hitting coach for one year at East Tennessee State University after beginning his career as an assistant coach at Vanderbilt (Tenn.) University…**PERSONAL:** Played two seasons at the University of Louisville, reaching the College World Series twice…graduated *cum laude* in sport administration from Louisville…attended Butler (Ind.) University for one year before transferring…is a graduate of Cushing (Mass.) Academy.

MATT TALARICO – BASERUNNING COORDINATOR/ROVING HITTING COACH
BORN: 3/30/84 in Fort Wayne, Ind. • **RESIDES:** Springfield, Ohio
COACHING CAREER: Joins the Yankees organization after 13 years coaching collegiate baseball…was an assistant coach at four Ohio schools: Wright State University (2015-19), University of Dayton (2010-15), University of Toledo (2009-10) and Heidelberg University (2007-09)…**PERSONAL:** He and his wife, Jasa, have two daughters, Callie and Lia…played four seasons at Manchester (Ind.) College before earning his master's degree in education from Heidelberg (Ohio) University…is a graduate of Bishop Dwenger (Ind.) H.S.

DAVID WHITESIDE – DIRECTOR, PERFORMANCE SCIENCE
BORN: 6/9/87 in Perth, Australia • **RESIDES:** Tampa, Fla.
Enters his fourth season with the Yankees, his second as the director of performance science…was the organization's first principal sports scientist (2017-18)…prior to joining the Yankees, was a sports performance scientist with Tennis Australia (2015-16), Australia's governing tennis body…completed a research fellowship at the University of Michigan, where he worked with a number of varsity sports (2013-14)…serves on the editorial board of the Journal of Sports Engineering and Technology, and has previously authored peer-reviewed journals and book chapters…graduated from the University of Western Australia in 2012 with a PhD in sport biomechanics, completed in partnership with Tennis Australia…is married to Ishani.

MARK LITTLEFIELD – MEDICAL COORDINATOR
BORN: 11/27/67 in Portland, Maine • **RESIDES:** Tampa, Fla.
Enters the fifth season of his second stint as the medical coordinator for Yankees player development operations, his 24th season overall in the role (1993-2011, 2016-present)…also served as the Yankees assistant athletic trainer at the Major League level for four seasons (2012-15)…marks his 30th season in the Yankees organization…began his training career with short-season Single-A Oneonta from 1991-92…graduated from Portland H.S. (Maine) in 1986 and earned his bachelor of science degree from the University of South Carolina in physical education/athletic training…is married to Cara and has a son, R.J., and a daughter, Alexis.

GREG SPRATT – ASSISTANT HEAD ATHLETIC TRAINER
BORN: 7/8/65 in Lexington, Ky. • **RESIDES:** Plant City, Fla.
Enters his 29th season with the Yankees and his ninth as assistant head athletic trainer in player development…previously served as an athletic trainer for short-season Single-A Oneonta (1990), Single-A Greensboro (1991-92), Double-A Albany-Colonie (1993-94), Double-A Norwich (1995-97, 2001-02), GCL Yankees (1998-2000, 2007-11) and Double-A Trenton (2003-04)…was named PBATS "Athletic Trainer of the Year" in his league three times (1992, '96, 2003)…has served as an athletic trainer in three league All-Star games (1992, 1994, 2002)…was also the athletic trainer for the Peoria Javelinas in the AFL in 1994 and the Tigres de Aragua in the Venezuelan Winter League in 1992 and 1996…served as Head Athletic Trainer for the NBA's Toronto Raptors for two seasons (2004-06)…he and his wife, Vicky, have two sons, David and Jarrett.

MIKE WICKLAND – COORDINATOR, PREVENTATIVE & PERFORMANCE PROGRAMS
BORN: 7/24/77 in Bridgeport, W.Va. • **RESIDES:** Tampa, Fla.
Enters his sixth season as the Yankees' coordinator of preventative and performance programs after serving as the organization's medical coordinator from 2013-14…marks his 21st season with the organization…was the strength and conditioning coordinator for player development from 2008-12…served as the athletic trainer at Single-A Tampa (2002-07) and Single-A Greensboro (2000-01)…graduated in 1999 with a bachelor's degree in exercise and sports science from the University of North Carolina at Greensboro, where he was an athletic trainer in his four years there…is married to Bonnie, and the couple has four sons: Graham, Grayson, Griffin, and Gunnar.

DAVID COLVIN – PHYSICAL THERAPIST, PLAYER DEVELOPMENT
BORN: 7/3/88 in Hatfield, Pa. • **RESIDES:** Tampa, Fla.
Enters his fifth season in the Yankees organization as the physical therapist in player development…served as the 2015 training camp intern for the Miami Dolphins…was previously a physical therapist at Pittsburgh's UPMC Rooney Sports Complex…received his doctor of physical therapy degree from the University of Pittsburgh in 2015…was a graduate assistant athletic trainer at the University of Tennessee from 2010-12 while earning his M.S. in kinesiology with a concentration in biomechanics…also earned his B.S. in athletic training from Pittsburgh in 2010…is a 2006 graduate from North Penn H.S. in Lansdale, Pa.

RIGO FEBLES – STRENGTH AND CONDITIONING COORDINATOR
BORN: 9/12/86 in Tampa, Fla. • **RESIDES:** Tampa, Fla.
Enters his fifth season with the Yankees organization as the player development strength and conditioning coordinator…began his career with six seasons in the Reds organization (2010-15), the final two as minor league assistant strength and conditioning coordinator (2014-15)…spent three seasons (2011-13) as the Reds' strength and conditioning supervisor for Latin America…was named the Pioneer League "Strength and Conditioning Coach of the Year" in all three of his seasons at Rookie-level Billings (2010, '12-13)…earned a bachelor's degree in applied physiology and kinesiology from the University of Florida…graduated from Sickles H.S. (Fla.)…has his CSCS and RSCC certifications…he and his wife, Louise, have two sons, Maximo and Rocco.

TY HILL – REHAB STRENGTH COACH
BORN: 5/25/74 in Pittsburgh, Pa. • **RESIDES:** Miami, Fla.
Enters his second season with the Yankees organization…was the GCL Yankees East strength and conditioning coach in 2019…spent seven seasons as the Marlins' Major League strength and conditioning coach (2012-18)…was the Royals' Major League strength and conditioning coordinator for five years (2007-11) and their minor league strength and conditioning coordinator for two years (2005-06)…spent eight years in the Pirates organization, including seven as a minor league conditioning coach (1998-2004), also serving as an assistant to the Major League strength coach in 2003-04…also worked as a consultant for the Roberto Clemente Foundation in 1998…played baseball at Penn State University, graduating in 1997 with a B.S. in exercise and sports science.

GREG PAVLICK – REHAB PITCHING COACH
BORN: 3/10/50 in Washington, D.C. • **RESIDES:** Tierra Verde, Fla.
COACHING CAREER: Enters his 10th season as rehab pitching coach and his 24th overall in the Yankees organization…previously served as the pitching coach for Single-A Tampa (2002-10) and Triple-A Columbus (2001)…helped lead Tampa to the 2004 FSL Championship…spent four years as the Yankees' roving pitching instructor (1997-2000)…also spent 26 seasons in the Mets organization…began his coaching career in 1977 as a pitching instructor for Triple-A Tidewater and was a player/coach for the club from 1977-79…coached the Mets at the Major League level for parts of nine seasons (1985-86, '88-91, '94-96)…**PLAYING CAREER:** Pitched seven seasons in the Mets organization (1971-77), going 38-30 with a 3.86 ERA…**PERSONAL:** Graduated from Thomas Edison H.S. in Alexandria, Va.…played at the University of North Carolina at Chapel Hill.

TINO MARTINEZ – PLAYER DEVELOPMENT CONSULTANT
BORN: 12/7/67 in Tampa, Fla. • **RESIDES:** Tampa, Fla.
COACHING CAREER: Enters his sixth season as a player development consultant with the Yankees…in 2013, served as the hitting coach for the Marlins…previously spent five seasons (2008-12) as a special assistant to Yankees GM Brian Cashman, serving as a special instructor during spring training and working with first basemen on defensive skills…**PLAYING CAREER:** Played 16 seasons with the Mariners (1990-95), Yankees (1996-2001, '05), Cardinals (2002-03) and Devil Rays (2004), compiling a .271 (1,925-for-7,111) career average with 1,009R, 365 doubles, 339HR and 1,271RBI in 2,023 games…the first baseman was acquired by the Yankees from Seattle prior to the 1996 season, helped New York to four World Series titles (1996, '98-2000) while totaling 192HR and 739RBI in 1,054 games as a Yankee…won the "Good Guy" Award presented by the Tampa Bay BBWAA in 2004…was originally selected in the first round (14th overall) of the 1988 First-Year Player Draft…**PERSONAL:** He and his wife Marie have three children: Olivia, Tino Jr. and Victoria…graduated from the University of Tampa, where he was a three-time Division-II All-American, as well as an Academic All-American…was inducted into the Sunshine State Conference Hall of Fame in 1998…graduated from Jefferson H.S. (Fla.)…won an Olympic Gold medal with Team U.S.A. at the 1988 Seoul Olympics.

MARC BOMBARD – PLAYER DEVELOPMENT CONSULTANT
BORN: 11/15/49 in Baltimore, Md. • **RESIDES:** Tampa, Fla.
COACHING CAREER: Enters his fifth season as a player development consultant for the Yankees and his sixth year in the organization overall…served as the manager of the GCL Yankees 2 in 2015…has 27 seasons of minor league managing experience…prior to joining the Yankees, managed Triple-A Round Rock from 2009-10 and Triple-A Charlotte from 2007-08…served as the Phillies first base coach from 2005-06 in his second stint as a Major League coach, having also been the third base coach for the Cincinnati Reds in 1996…has also coached or managed in farm systems for the Reds (1977-87, '93-95), Milwaukee (1989), Pittsburgh (1990-92) and Philadelphia (1997-2004)…began his coaching career as a player/coach for Single-A Tampa from 1974-77…was named "Minor League Manager of the Year" by *USA Today* in 2002 after leading Triple-A Scranton/Wilkes-Barre to 91 wins…was also named the "Minor League Manager of the Year" by *Baseball America* and "Triple-A Manager of the Year" by *USA Today* "Baseball Weekly" in 1995…**PLAYING CAREER:** Spent seven years (1971-77) in the Reds organization, going 39-29 with a 2.72 ERA in 152 games…**PERSONAL:** Attended the University of Texas at El Paso and graduated from Eastwood H.S. (Tex.)…he and his wife, Gemma, have two daughters, Janet and Amy.

MLB All-Star Futures Game History

Major League Baseball, in conjunction with the 30 Major League Clubs, MLB.com and *Baseball America*, select the 25-man rosters for the U.S. Team and the World Team in the annual All-Star Futures Game. Players from all full-season minor leagues are eligible to participate. Five members of the Yankees' 40-man roster as of 2/1/20 (**bolded below**) were named to at least one Futures Game roster while in the Yankees' minor league system.

YEAR	PLAYER, POS. (TEAM)	YEAR	PLAYER, POS. (TEAM)
2019	**RHP Deivi García (AL)**	2007	RHP Joba Chamberlain (U.S.)
2018	RHP Domingo Acevedo (World)	2006	RHP Phil Hughes (U.S.)
	OF Estevan Florial (World)		OF Jose Tabata (World)
2017	RHP Domingo Acevedo (World)	2005	OF Melky Cabrera (World)
	OF Estevan Florial (World)	2004	INF Robinson Canó (World)
2016	INF Jorge Mateo (World)		C Dioner Navarro (World)
	C Gary Sánchez (World)	2003	INF Robinson Canó (World)
2015	**OF Aaron Judge (U.S.)**		RHP Chien-Ming Wang (World)
	C Gary Sánchez (World)	2002	INF Drew Henson (U.S.)
2014	RHP Luis Severino (World)	2001	INF Nick Johnson (U.S.)
	INF Peter O'Brien (U.S.)		OF Juan Rivera (World)
2013	RHP Rafael De Paula (World)	2000	INF Drew Henson (U.S.)
2012	OF Tyler Austin (U.S.)		OF Jackson Melian (World)
2011	C Austin Romine (U.S.)	1999	INF Nick Johnson (U.S.)
2010	C Austin Romine (U.S.)		*INF Alfonso Soriano (World)
	RHP Hector Noesi (World)		
2009	LHP Manny Banuelos (World)		
2008	C Jesus Montero (World)		*Most Valuable Player
	INF Ramiro Peña (World)		

Yankees Around the Globe

As the game of Baseball continues to grow on a global scale, "America's Pastime" has become infused with talent from every corner of the world.

The New York Yankees, as one of the most recognized brands in the world, are dedicated to making meaningful and lasting footprints throughout the international Baseball community.

The Yankees began the 2019 season with 10 foreign-born players, hailing from seven nations outside of the United States (Canada, Cuba, Dominican Republic, Japan, Mexico, the Netherlands, Venezuela). Shortstop Didi Gregorius of the Netherlands was one of only three European-born players to appear on a Major League Opening Day roster in 2019 (German-born Max Kepler of Minnesota, Lithuanian-born Dovydas Neverauskas of Pittsburgh).

Signing and developing exceptional talent from around the globe has become a trademark of the Yankees organization. Some of the club's acquisitions include 2019 Hall of Fame inductee and Panamá native Mariano Rivera, five-time All-Star Jorge Posada of Puerto Rico, seven-time All-Star Alfonso Soriano out of the Dominican Republic, two-time All-Star Hideki Matsui from Japan, and 2006 Cy Young Award runner-up Chien-Ming Wang from Taiwan. Japanese pitcher Masahiro Tanaka has been a stalwart in the Yankees starting rotation after signing via the posting system in 2014.

The organization has developed top minor league talent from around the world, placing three foreign-born players in the top-three of AL "Rookie of the Year" balloting since 2016 (Gary Sánchez, Miguel Andújar, Gleyber Torres). The Yankees have filled their minor league ranks in recent years by signing players from Australia, Brazil, Canada, China, Colombia, Cuba, the Czech Republic, Israel, Mexico, Nicaragua, Panamá, Poland, South Korea, Taiwan and Venezuela. In addition, the Yankees field a Dominican Summer League team and operate a state-of-the-art Latin Baseball Academy in the Dominican Republic.

The Latin Béisbol Academy

For the vast majority of the Yankees' Latin American prospects, the Latin Béisbol Academy is the starting point for their professional careers.

Located in Boca Chica, Dominican Republic, the academy was constructed from scratch, allowing player development personnel to manage every detail of the project, from the trainer's room to the clubhouses to the classrooms. The finished product is a four-building, four-field complex with the capacity to house up to 110 players. There is also a small apartment building for coaches and instructors. Officially opening in June 2005 and finally completed in the spring of 2006, the academy has a campus-like feel to it that is not lost on the ballplayers, many of whom are spending time away from their families for the very first time.

Previously, the Yankees had leased a variety of facilities in Latin America for scouting and player development use, but it became apparent that it was necessary to develop their own facility.

As a dedicated investor in Latin American talent, the Yankees make every effort to provide their players with a well-rounded education off the field. The complex is staffed with educators who teach players academic disciplines such as Spanish and English, along with broad-based life skills such as conflict resolution, financial literacy and American customs. Players are also given guidance on how to deal with the heavy travel inherent to a baseball lifestyle. Throughout their time at the academy, the young Yankees hopefuls participate in clinics with local children, reminding them to always be mindful of their community.

The Yankees also arrange for past and present Major League stars, such as Mariano Rivera and Reggie Jackson, to be guest lecturers for the prospects. The players received a special visitor in January 2011 when professional boxing champion Miguel Cotto paid a visit. In January 2020, Yankees Manager Aaron Boone visited the Béisbol Academy.

The players and staff are also active in local community events, hosting annual instructional clinics in the Dominican Republic, Nicaragua and Venezuela. In addition, the Yankees' Latin complex has hosted R.B.I. (Reviving Baseball in the Inner City) tournament games, joined the Yankees organization in 2007 to donate $65,000 in food and cash to hurricane-damaged areas in the D.R. and Nicaragua, and adopted an orphanage in La Romana, D.R., supplying it with food, money and clothing. In 2013, the Yankees donated a fire truck and an ambulance—along with firefighting and medical equipment—to the city of Boca Chica.

In July 2010, Dominican Summer League players delivered gifts to ailing children at a local hospital in Santo Domingo. The Latin Béisbol Academy also played host to a fundraiser game in 2010 against the Dominican National Police Department to raise money for local charities throughout the D.R. And in 2011, select Yankees draft picks held a clinic in San Pedro de Macorís for more than 100 kids, handing out shoes, equipment and uniforms to participants.

The Yankees field a DSL team annually and won back-to-back titles in 2005-06. With the hard work and dedication of the Yankees Player Development staff, the organization looks forward to the future, when these young players will lead the way to a 28th World Championship in the Bronx.

Yankees Sweep London

In June 2019, the Yankees flew across the pond to London, England, to play a two-game series against the rival Boston Red Sox at London Stadium, the first-ever Major League games played in Europe.

While there, the Yankees continued to do their part to grow the game globally through numerous community initiatives.

The day before the London Series opened, the Yankees hosted a baseball clinic at Finsbury Park for approximately 100 youth in the London community, in conjunction with the London Meteorites Baseball and Softball Club. Manager Aaron Boone, as well as former Yankees Carlos Beltrán, Reggie Jackson, Hideki Matsui, Andy Pettitte, Mariano Rivera, Alex Rodriguez and Nick Swisher, served as clinic coaches before a BBQ reception. At the close of the event, the Yankees presented the London Meteorites with a legacy gift that included baseball and softball equipment (bats, baseballs, helmets, gloves, catcher's gear, etc.).

Yankees Travel to Panamá

In conjunction with Major League Baseball and the Major League Baseball Players Association, the Yankees traveled to Panamá prior to the 2014 season for the "Legend Series," a set of two exhibition games against the Miami Marlins at Panamá City's Rod Carew Stadium. The trip served as a tribute to the career of former Yankees reliever and Panamá native Mariano Rivera, who had capped off his Hall of Fame career by retiring as MLB's all-time saves leader at the conclusion of the 2013 season.

Rivera played host for the weekend, which featured a number of charitable events away from the field. Chief among them was a gala benefitting the Mariano Rivera Foundation, the proceeds of which supported the Children's Hospital in Panamá City, the largest pediatric hospital in the country. Yankees players also visited the hospital, bringing with them a large donation of toys and spending time with the children.

Rivera also took a Yankees contingent – including General Partner/Vice Chairperson Jennifer Steinbrenner Swindal, President Randy Levine, COO Lonn Trost, Manager Joe Girardi, hitting coach Kevin Long, bench coach Tony Peña, spring training instructor Willie Randolph, outfielder Brett Gardner and reliever David Robertson – on a behind-the-scenes tour of the Panamá Canal.

The Yankees' brand transcends international borders as fans show their pride in Panamá.

The visit marked the first appearance by Major League Baseball in the Central American country since 1947, when the Yankees faced the Brooklyn Dodgers in several exhibition games on a trip that also included stops in Cuba, Puerto Rico and Venezuela.

Yankees Teach in Taiwan

In January 2009, the Yankees joined the Chinese Taipei Baseball Association under the auspices of Major League Baseball in holding a clinic for high school pitchers, catchers and coaches at the National Taiwan Sport University's Taoyuan Campus in Taipei, Taiwan. It marked the Yankees' first-ever large-scale outreach in Taiwan and represented the club's initiative in cultivating baseball talent and increasing brand recognition in Asia and the greater international community. The five-day clinic focused on pitching and catching fundamentals and philosophy.

Yankees and Chinese Baseball Association Reach Memorandum of Understanding

The New York Yankees and the Chinese Baseball Association (CBA) held a press conference in Beijing, China, on Jan. 29, 2007, to announce a Memorandum of Understanding that for the first time formalized a strategic alliance between a Major League Baseball club and the CBA. During the Yankees' 2009 World Series trophy tour, club officials met with the CBA in Beijing to further the cooperation agreement between the two entities.

The agreement, subject to Major League Baseball's rules, regulations and agreements pertaining to the People's Republic of China, states that the Yankees will provide the CBA with guidance in training baseball players, including sending coaches, player development staff, scouting and training personnel to China to assist the CBA. The partnership also allows the CBA to send staff to the Yankees' facilities in the United States in furtherance of those goals.

During their 2007 trip, the Yankees were represented in Beijing by team President Randy Levine, Senior Vice President and General Manager Brian Cashman, Vice President and Assistant General Manager Jean Afterman, and Vice President of Corporate Sales and Sponsorship Michael Tusiani. Beijing Womei Advertising Company Limited and Sportscorp China, headed by President and Managing Director Marc Ganis and Managing Director Kenneth Huang, coordinated the meetings and were instrumental in the Yankees' involvement in China.

The CBA was represented by Chairman Hu Jianguo, Secretary General Shen Wei and Deputy Secretary General Tian Yuan.

On June 16, 2007, the Yankees announced the signings of catcher Zhenwang Zhang and left-handed pitcher Kai Liu to minor league contracts, marking the first-ever acquisition by a Major League organization of Chinese baseball players. Both players were members of the Chinese National team that competed in the 2008 Olympics in Beijing.

Yankees Team President Randy Levine and GM Brian Cashman established a working agreement with the Chinese Baseball Association on Jan. 29, 2007.

Partners in Japan

During the 2002 season, the Yankees entered into a working agreement with the Yomiuri Giants, winners of 22 Japan Series Championships. Pursuant to the agreement, the teams consented to share baseball information, ideas and strategies. Also in 2002, the Yankees pursued and signed three-time Central League MVP Hideki Matsui. A nine-time Japanese League All-Star and three-time home run champion, Matsui became the first bona fide power hitter to make the transition from Japan to the Major Leagues.

In 2004, the Yankees traveled to Tokyo to open the regular season against the Tampa Bay Devil Rays. The historic trip marked the 70th anniversary of Babe Ruth and Lou Gehrig's 1934 All-Star tour of Japan. It also recognized the anniversary of the founding of the Yomiuri Giants franchise, Japan's oldest professional baseball team. The two-game series was just the second-ever Major League season opener to take place in Japan. At the time, the two games were the highest-rated televised Major League games in Japan's history.

Yankees Championship Trophy Tour of the Dominican Republic, Japan and China

Following their 2009 championship season, the Yankees embarked on a world tour with their 2009 World Series Trophy, traveling to the Dominican Republic and Asia.

A Yankees contingent took the championship trophy to the Dominican Republic for a three-day tour from Jan. 7-9, 2010. The D.R. leg of the trophy tour included stops at the National Palace for a ceremony with President Dr. Leonel Fernández, who was joined by bench coach Tony Peña, and players Robinson Canó, Damaso Marte, Francisco Cervelli and Edwar Ramírez as well as by several Yankees minor leaguers. The next day, the Yankees visited the U.S. Embassy and the National Police Headquarters. That evening, the Yankees displayed the trophy for fans at the Dominican Winter League playoff game between los Tigres del Licey and los Leones del Escogido at Estadio Quisqueya Juan Marichal in Santo Domingo. On their final day in the D.R., the Yankees placed the trophy on display for residents of the town of Casa de Campo.

The Yankees' 2009 World Series trophy visited the MLB Café in Tokyo, where it was displayed alongside the Yomiuri Giants' 2009 Championship trophy.

Three weeks later, a Yankees delegation consisting of team President Randy Levine, Senior Vice President and General Manager Brian Cashman, Vice President and Assistant General Manager Jean Afterman and Senior Vice President of Corporate Sales and Sponsorships Michael Tusiani took the trophy on a six-day tour to Tokyo, Beijing and Hong Kong from Jan. 31 through Feb. 5, 2010.

The contingent was met by fans and media at Tokyo's Narita Airport, marking this first-ever occasion of a Yankees World Series Trophy being brought to Asia. The next day, another historic moment took place at the MLB Café in Tokyo as the trophy was displayed alongside the Yomiuri Giants' 2009 Japan Series championship trophy.

From there, the trophy traveled to China, where fans in Beijing and Hong Kong had their first opportunity to gaze at Major League Baseball's grandest prize. The trophy tour in China was organized by QSL Sports, which has been active in the promotion of Baseball in the People's Republic of China and operates the China Youth Baseball League together with the Chinese Baseball Association. The events in China were hosted by QSL Sports, New World Department Stores (one of the largest owners and operators of department stores in China), and K11, the "World's First Art Mall," which integrates elements of art, culture and nature, while elevating the shopping experience.

On Feb. 3, 2010, Yankees officials met with the CBA in Beijing to further the cooperation agreement between the two entities, after which the groups held a joint press conference at the Kunlun Hotel. Later that evening, the championship trophy made its first public appearance in China at the New World Department Store, which included traditional Chinese performances and ceremonies. Joining the Yankees delegation were CBA officials, New World representatives and the Beijing Yankees youth baseball team, which is part of MLB's "Play Ball" youth baseball program in China.

Chinese youth were on hand with the trophy during a press event with the Chinese Baseball Association.

Hong Kong marked the final stop on the Asian tour, with a Feb. 5, 2010, event at the Hyatt Regency hotel adjacent to the recently-opened K11 Mall. The next morning, the trophy was introduced to players and fans during the opening ceremony for the 2010 Phoenix Cup, Hong Kong's International Women's Baseball Tournament.

The Yankees thank their partner Delta Air Lines for ensuring the safe transportation of the World Series trophy and appreciate the efforts of Sportscorp China, led by president Marc Ganis.

The 2012 Little League World Series championship team from Japan visited Yankee Stadium as the Yankees' guests on Aug. 28, 2012, after capturing the country's second LLWS title in three years and eighth overall. They are pictured above with Yankees outfielder Ichiro Suzuki.

Mariano Rivera poses with Uganda's 2012 Little League World Series team, which became the first team from Africa to participate in the LLWS, and was the Yankees' guest on Aug. 29, 2012. The team also received a clubhouse tour from Manager Joe Girardi and participated in "roll call" with the Bleacher Creatures.

New York Yankees 2019 First-Year Player Draft

RD (SEL)	PLAYER	POS	SCHOOL (STATE)	B/T	HT/WT	DOB
1 (#30)	Anthony Volpe	SS	Delbarton School (N.J.)	R/R	5'11"/180	4/28/01
CB A (#38)	TJ Sikkema	LHP	University of Missouri	L/L	6'0"/220	7/25/98
2 (#67)	Josh Smith	INF	LSU	L/R	5'10"/175	8/7/97
3 (#105)	Jacob Sanford	CF	Western Kentucky University	L/R	6'2"/215	10/24/97
4 (#135)	Jake Agnos	LHP	East Carolina University (N.C.)	L/L	5'11"/210	5/23/98
5 (#165)	Ken Waldichuk	LHP	Saint Mary's College (Calif.)	L/L	6'4"/220	1/8/98
6 (#195)	Hayden Wesneski	RHP	Sam Houston State (Texas)	R/R	6'3"/210	12/5/97
7 (#225)	Nick Paciorek	RHP	Northwestern University (Ill.)	R/R	6'2"/195	6/1/98
8 (#255)	Zach Greene	RHP	University of South Alabama	R/R	6'1"/215	8/29/96
9 (#285)	Spencer Henson	1B	Oral Roberts University (Okla.)	R/R	6'2"/235	11/3/97
10 (#315)	Mitch Spence	RHP	USC Aiken (S.C.)	R/R	6'1"/185	5/6/98
11 (#345)	Oliver Dunn	2B	University of Utah	L/R	5'10"/185	9/2/97
12 (#375)	Ryan Anderson	LHP	University of Nevada	L/L	6'6"/205	9/9/98
13 (#405)	Nelson Alvarez	RHP	University of South Florida	R/R	6'4"/220	6/11/98
14 (#435)	Kevin Milam	RHP	Saint Mary's College (Calif.)	R/R	6'0"/200	2/13/98
15 (#465)	Edgar Barclay	LHP	Cal State University, Bakersfield	L/L	5'10"/200	5/25/98
16 (#495)	Shaine McNeely	RHP	Hope International University (Calif.)	L/R	6'4"/210	5/10/98
17 (#525)	Pat DeMarco	OF	Vanderbilt University (Tenn.)	R/R	5'9"/195	3/10/98
18 (#555)	Evan Voliva	RHP	East Carolina University (N.C.)	R/R	5'10"/205	6/10/96
19 (#585)	Chad Bell	3B	University of Louisiana-Monroe	L/R	6'3"/210	3/4/97
20 (#615)	*Jack Leiter	RHP	Delbarton School (N.J.)	R/R	6'1"/195	4/21/00
21 (#645)	Zach Kohn	RHP	Central Michigan University	R/R	6'4"/190	9/30/97
22 (#675)	Gerrit van Zijll	LHP	Alvin Community College (Texas)	L/L	6'4"/210	8/2/96
23 (#705)	Matt Minnick	LHP	Mercyhurst College (Pa.)	R/L	6'2"/210	3/11/96
24 (#735)	Jake Pries	OF	UCLA	R/R	6'4"/225	10/11/96
25 (#765)	*Luke Brown	OF	John A. Logan College (Ill.)	L/R	5'11"/190	3/12/99
26 (#795)	*Ryan Brown	RHP	South Salem H.S. (Ore.)	R/R	6'2"/200	11/2/00
27 (#825)	Kyle MacDonald	1B	Arkansas State University	L/R	6'3"/240	6/17/96
28 (#855)	Michael Giacone	LHP	North Greenville University (S.C.)	L/L	6'0"/165	10/23/96
29 (#885)	Chase Illig	C	West Virginia University	S/R	6'0"/210	9/14/96
30 (#915)	*Zachary Maxwell	RHP	North Paulding H.S. (Ga.)	R/R	6'6"/245	1/26/01
31 (#945)	*Chad Knight	C	Staples H.S. (Conn.)	R/R	6'0"/205	12/16/00
32 (#975)	*Ethan Hoopingarner	RHP	Aliso Niguel H.S. (Calif.)	R/R	6'3"/200	8/29/00
33 (#1005)	Javier Reynoso	3B	Colegio Angel David H.S. (P.R.)	R/R	6'2"/190	7/27/00
34 (#1035)	*Joey Lancellotti	RHP	University of North Carolina	R/R	5'11"/205	1/15/98
35 (#1065)	*Nathaniel Espelin	LHP	The Winchendon School (Mass.)	R/L	5'11"/185	9/3/99
36 (#1095)	Montana Semmel	RHP	Westhill H.S. (Conn.)	R/R	6'4"/225	1/1/02
37 (#1125)	*Bryce Jarvis	RHP	Duke University (N.C.)	L/R	6'2"/185	12/26/97
38 (#1155)	*Dontae Mitchell	OF	Lakewood H.S. (Fla.)	R/R	6'0"/185	2/2/01
39 (#1185)	Jake Farrell	1B	Northeastern University (Mass.)	L/R	6'4"/215	5/10/96
40 (#1215)	*Alex Garbrick	RHP	Morehead State University (Ky.)	R/R	6'1"/200	6/4/98

*Did not sign

New York Yankees No. 1 Draft Choices

YEAR	RD	SEL	PLAYER	POS	SCHOOL (STATE)	w/NYY in Majors
2019	1	30	Anthony Volpe	SS	Delbarton HS (N.J.)	-
2018	1	23	Anthony Seigler	C	Cartersville HS (Ga.)	-
2017	1	16	Clarke Schmidt	RHP	University of South Carolina	-
2016	1	18	Blake Rutherford	OF	Chaminade College Prep HS (Calif.)	-
2015	1	16	James Kaprielian	RHP	UCLA	-
	1	30	Kyle Holder	SS	University of San Diego	-
2014	2	55	Jacob Lindgren	LHP	Mississippi State University	2015
2013	1	26	Eric Jagielo	3B	University of Notre Dame	-
	1	32	Aaron Judge	CF	Fresno State University	2016-19
	1	33	Ian Clarkin	LHP	James Madison HS (Calif.)	-
2012	1	30	Ty Hensley	RHP	Edmond Sante Fe HS (Okla.)	-
2011	Comp A	51	Dante Bichette, Jr.	3B	Orangewood Christian HS (Fla.)	-
2010	1	32	Cito Culver	SS	Irondequoit HS (N.Y.)	-
2009	1	29	Slade Heathcott	OF	Texas HS (Tex.)	2015
2008	1	28	Gerrit Cole	RHP	Orange Lutheran HS (Calif.)	Did not sign
2007	1	30	Andrew Brackman	RHP	North Carolina State University	2011
2006	1	21	Ian Kennedy	RHP	University of Southern California	2007-09
2005	1	17	Carl (C.J.) Henry	SS	Putnam City HS (Okla.)	-
2004	1	23	Phil Hughes	RHP	Foothill HS (Calif.)	2007-13
2003	1	27	Eric Duncan	3B	Seton Hall Prep (N.J.)	-
2002	2	71	Brandon Weeden	RHP	Santa Fe HS (N.M.)	-
2001	1	23	John-Ford Griffin	OF	Florida State University	-
	1	34	Bronson Sardinha	INF	Kamehameha HS (Hawaii)	2007
	1	42	Jon Skaggs	RHP	Rice University	-
2000	1	28	David Parrish	C	University of Michigan	-
1999	1	27	David Walling	RHP	University of Arkansas	-
1998	1	24	Andrew Brown	OF	Richmond HS (Ind.)	-
	1	43	Mark Prior	RHP	University HS (Calif.)	Did not sign
1997	1	24	Tyrell Godwin	OF	East Bladen HS (N.C.)	-
	1	40	Ryan Bradley	RHP	Arizona State University	1998
1996	1	20	Eric Milton	LHP	University of Maryland	-
1995	1	27	Shea Morenz	RF	University of Texas	-
1994	1	24	Brian Buchanan	OF	University of Virginia	-
1993	1	13	Matt Drews	RHP	Sarasota HS (Fla.)	-
1992	1	6	Derek Jeter	SS	Kalamazoo Central HS (Mich.)	1995-2014
1991	1	1	Brien Taylor	LHP	East Carteret HS (N.C.)	-
1990	1	10	Carl Everett	OF	Hillsborough HS (Fla.)	-
1989	2	45	Andy Fox	3B	Christian Brothers HS (Calif.)	1995-97
1988	4	105	Todd Malone	LHP	Casa Robles HS (Calif.)	-
1987	3	81	Bill Dacosta	RHP	New York Tech	-
1986	2	53	Rich Scheid	LHP	Seton Hall University	-
1985	1	28	Rick Balabon	RHP	Conestoga HS (Pa.)	-
1984	1	22	Jeff Pries	RHP	UCLA	-
1983	4	93	Mitch Lyden	C	Beaverton HS (Ore.)	-
1982	2	36	Tim Birtsas	LHP	Michigan State University	-
	2	50	Bo Jackson	SS	McAdory HS (Ala.)	Did not sign
1981	2	52	John Elway	OF	Stanford University	-
1980	3	74	Billy Cannon, Jr.	SS	Broadmoor HS (La.)	Did not sign
1979	2	51	Todd Demeter	INF	Grant HS (Okla.)	-
1978	1	18	Rex Hudler	SS	Bullard HS (Calif.)	1984-85
	1	24	Matt Winters	OF	Williamsville HS (N.Y.)	-
	1	26	Brian Ryder	RHP	Shrewsbury HS (Mass.)	-
1977	1	23	Steve Taylor	RHP	University of Delaware	-
1976	1	16	Pat Tabler	OF	McNicholas HS (Ohio)	-
1975	1	19	Jim McDonald	1B	Verbum Dei HS (Calif.)	-
1974	1	12	Dennis Sherrill	SS	South HS (Fla.)	1978, '80
1973	1	13	Doug Heinold	RHP	Stroman HS (Tex.)	-
1972	1	14	Scott McGregor	LHP	El Segundo HS (Calif.)	-
1971	1	19	Terry Whitfield	OF	Palo Verde HS (Calif.)	1974-76
1970	1	12	Dave Cheadle	LHP	Asheville HS (N.C.)	-
1969	1	11	Charlie Spikes	OF	Central Memorial HS (La.)	1972
1968	1	4	Thurman Munson	C	Kent State University	1969-79
1967	1	1	Ron Blomberg	1B	Druid Hills HS (Ga.)	1969, '71-76
1966	1	10	Jim Lyttle	OF	Florida State University	1969-71
1965	1	19	Bill Burbach	RHP	Wahlert HS (Wisc.)	1969-71

2019 Organizational Summary

AAA	Scranton/Wilkes-Barre RailRiders	International League	76-65 (.539)
AA	Trenton Thunder	Eastern League	76-62 (.551)
A	Tampa Tarpons	Florida State League	64-71 (.474)
A	Charleston RiverDogs	South Atlantic League	73-66 (.525)
Short-Season A	Staten Island Yankees	New York-Penn League	40-36 (.526)
R	Pulaski Yankees	Appalachian League	42-26 (.618)
R	GCL Yankees East	Gulf Coast League	18-29 (.383)
R	GCL Yankees West	Gulf Coast League	22-27 (.449)
DSL	DSL Yankees	Dominican Summer League	33-31 (.516)

2019 Draft Recap

The Yankees signed 29 of their 41 draft picks from the 2019 First-Year Player Draft, selecting 26 pitchers (RHP-17, LHP-9) and 15 position players (C-2, INF-8, OF-5) with a split of 31 college players and 10 high schoolers…selected **SS Anthony Volpe** from Delbarton School (New Jersey) with their first pick (1st round, No. 30)…batted .215 (26-for-121) with 19R, 7 doubles, 2 triples, 2HR, 11RBI and 23BB in 34G with Pulaski…second-round selection (No. 67) **2B Josh Smith** hit .324 (36-for-111) with 17R, 6 doubles, 1 triple, 3HR, 15RBI and 25BB in 33G with Staten Island…**LHP Ken Waldichuk** (5th round, No. 165) went 0-2 with a 3.68 ERA (29.1IP, 19H, 12R/12ER, 7BB, 49K) in 10 starts with Pulaski…eighth-round selection (No. 255) **RHP Zach Greene** went 1-1 with a 1.50 ERA (18.0 IP, 11H, 5R/3ER, 4BB, 24K) and 5 saves in 14 appearances with the GCL Yankees East and Staten Island…**RHP Kevin Milam** (14th round, No. 435) led the Gulf Coast League with eight saves.

2018 Draft Review

C Josh Breaux batted .271 (54-for-199) with 28R, 10 doubles, 13HR, 49RBI and 15BB in 51G with Charleston…was named an SAL Mid-season All-Star…**OF Ryder Green** hit .262 (59-for-225) with 45R, 15 doubles, 8HR, 28RBI and 10SB in 61G with Pulaski…**OF Brandon Lockridge** was named a SAL Mid-season All-Star with Charleston after tying for third in the league with 33 doubles and hitting .251 (125-for-498) with 69R, 12HR, 56RBI and 22SB in 121G…**RHP Daniel Bies** went 3-3 with a 3.33 ERA (92.0IP, 82H, 43R/34ER, 33BB, 105K) in 24 games (eight starts) between Charleston, Tampa and Scranton/Wilkes-Barre.

Up-and-Comers

RHP Miguel Yajure led all of minor league baseball in ERA, going 9-6 with a 2.14 ERA (138.2IP, 119H, 48R/33ER, 30BB, 133K, 5HR) with Tampa and Trenton…**RHP Luis Gil** posted an 11.53 K/9.0IP while going 5-5 with a 2.72 ERA (96.0IP, 71H, 36R/29ER, 47BB, 123K, 1HR) in 20 starts between Charleston and Tampa…**1B Chris Gittens** was named Eastern League Most Valuable Player at Trenton and led all Yankees minor leaguers with 77RBI…also finished second with 23HR…**OF Canaan Smith** hit .307/.405/.465 (138-for-449) with 67R, 32 doubles, 11HR, 74RBI, 74BB and 16SB in 124G at Charleston…**RHP Clarke Schmidt** went 6-5 with a 3.47 ERA (90.2IP, 79H, 43R/35ER, 28BB, 102K) in 19 games (18 starts) at three stops in his first full season since returning from "Tommy John" surgery…**RHP Brian Keller** pitched a seven-inning no-hitter for Trenton on 8/1, defeating the Altoona Curve, 2-0.

2019 ORGANIZATIONAL LEADERS

Batting Average
Maikol Escotto	DSL	.315
Ryan McBroom	SWB	.315
Breyvic Valera	SWB	.315
Canaan Smith	CHA	.307
Chris Gittens	TRE	.281

Home Runs
Ryan McBroom	SWB	26
Mike Ford	SWB	23
Chris Gittens	TRE	23
Trey Amburgey	SWB	22
Kyle Higashioka	SWB	20

RBI
Chris Gittens	TRE	77
Mandy Alvarez	SWB/TRE	76
Canaan Smith	CHA	74
Ryan McBroom	SWB	66
Trey Amburgey	SWB	62

Stolen Bases
Josh Stowers	CHA	35
Ben Ruta	TRE	25
Oswald Peraza	SI/CHA	23
Brandon Lockridge	CHA	22
Two tied at		21

Earned Run Average
Miguel Yajure	TAM/TRE	2.14
Luis Gil	CHA/TAM	2.72
Nick Nelson	TAM/TRE/SWB	2.81
Jio Orozco	CHA/TAM	3.10
Daniel Bies	TAM/CHA/SWB	3.33

Wins
Roansy Contreras	CHA	12
J.P. Feyereisen	SWB	10
Miguel Yajure	TAM/TRE	9
Adonis Rosa	SWB/TRE	9
Three tied at		8

Strikeouts
Deivi Garcia	TAM/TRE/SWB	165
Miguel Yajure	TAM/TRE	133
Rony Garcia	TAM/TRE	129
Alexander Vizcaino	CHA/TAM	128
Luis Medina	CHA/TAM	127

Saves
Daniel Alvarez	TRE/SWB	21
Brooks Kriske	TAM/TRE	12
Joe Harvey	SWB	9
Matthew Wivinis	TRE/TAM	9
Two tied at		8

Kevin Lawn Award Winners

Each year, the Yankees present the Kevin Lawn Award to the organization's minor league "Pitcher of the Year" and "Player of the Year." The annual awards are dedicated to Kevin O'Brien Lawn—the son of longtime Yankees Vice President and Chief of Operations Jack Lawn—who passed away in 1999. The winners of the 2019 awards will be announced during 2020 spring training.

2018: INF Brandon Wagner / RHP Michael King
2017: 3B Miguel Andújar / RHP Domingo Acevedo
2016: OF Aaron Judge / RHP Chance Adams
2015: C Gary Sánchez / RHP Luis Severino
2014: INF Rob Refsnyder / RHP Luis Severino
2013: 1B Greg Bird / RHP Shane Greene
2012: OF Tyler Austin / RHP Mark Montgomery
2011: C Austin Romine / RHP D.J. Mitchell
2010: SS Eduardo Nuñez / RHP David Phelps
2009: C Austin Romine / RHP Zach McAllister
2008: OF Brett Gardner / LHP Phil Coke
2007: OF Austin Jackson / RHP Ian Kennedy
2006: 1B Cody Ehlers / RHP Phil Hughes
2005: OF Kevin Thompson / RHP Matt DeSalvo
2004: 1B Andy Phillips / RHP Chien-Ming Wang
2003: C Dioner Navarro / RHP Jorge DePaula
2002: 2B Andy Phillips / LHP Danny Borrell, RHP Jorge DePaula
2001: OF Juan Rivera, OF Marcus Thames / LHP Brandon Claussen
2000: 3B Scott Seabol / LHP Randy Keisler
1999: 2B D'Angelo Jimenez, 1B Nick Johnson / LHP Ed Yarnall
1998: 1B Nick Johnson / RHP Ryan Bradley
1997: 3B Mike Lowell / LHP Eric Milton
1996: OF Ricky Ledee / RHP Jay Tessmer
1995: SS Derek Jeter / RHP Matt Drews
1994: SS Derek Jeter / LHP Andy Pettitte
1993: OF Billy Masse / LHP Ryan Karp
1992: 1B J.T. Snow / RHP Sam Militello
1991: C Kiki Hernandez, SS Dave Silvestri / RHP Ed Martel, RHP Sam Militello
1990: OF Hensley Meulens / RHP Dave Eiland
1989: 1B Hal Morris / LHP Steve Adkins
1988: 1B Kevin Maas / RHP Todd Malone
1987: OF Darren Reed / RHP Dana Ridenour
1986: 3B Chris Alvarez / RHP Logan Easley
1985: OF Dan Pasqua / RHP Brad Arnsberg
1984: C/OF Scott Bradley / LHP Jim Deshaies
1983: OF Brian Dayett / RHP Jose Rijo
1982: OF Matt Winters / RHP Bob Tewksbury
1981: 1B Don Mattingly / LHP Pete Filson
1980: 1B Steve Balboni / RHP Gene Nelson

Yankees 2020 Top Prospects

Baseball America
1. OF Jasson Domínguez
2. RHP Clarke Schmidt
3. RHP Deivi García
4. RHP Luis Gil
5. INF Oswald Peraza
6. INF Anthony Volpe
7. RHP Luis Medina
8. RHP Roansy Contreras
9. RHP Alexander Vizcaíno
10. RHP Albert Abreu

MLB Pipeline
1. RHP Deivi García
2. OF Jasson Domínguez
3. OF Estevan Florial
4. RHP Luis Gil
5. RHP Clarke Schmidt
6. RHP Albert Abreu
7. RHP Yoendrys Gomez
8. C Anthony Seigler
9. OF Everson Pereira
10. INF Anthony Volpe

The **Pulaski Yankees** won the 2019 John H. Johnson's President's Award, which is Minor League Baseball's top award and recognizes "the complete baseball franchise."

Scranton/Wilkes-Barre RailRiders (AAA)

Affiliate Since 2007 • International League
2019 RECORD: 76-65, 1st in North Division (Lost in IL Semifinals)
PNC Field • 235 Montage Mountain Road, Moosic, PA 18507
Phone: (570) 969-2255 • **Website:** www.swbrailriders.com
Team President: John Adams • **Director of Communications/Broadcaster:** Adam Marco

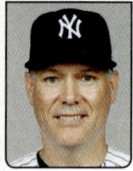

DOUG DAVIS – MANAGER
BORN: 9/24/62 in Bloomsburg, Pa. • **RESIDES:** Bloomsburg, Pa.
COACHING CAREER: Takes over as RailRiders manager after three seasons as the club's bullpen coach…is his first managerial role since 2008, and has won league championships twice in eight seasons at the helm…managed Triple-A Syracuse (2007-08) and Double-A New Hampshire (2006) in the Blue Jays system…also managed in the Mets system at short-season Single-A Pittsfield (1996-97), Single-A Capital City (1998) and Double-A Binghamton (1999-2000), winning the NYPL Championship in 1997 and South Atlantic League Championship in 1998…prior to joining the Yankees in 2017, spent the previous 11 seasons with the Blue Jays, including seven (2010-16) as minor league field coordinator…also served as minor league catching coordinator (2009)…was a minor league field coordinator for the Expos in 2001 and spent three seasons (2003-05) with the Marlins organization, including two as the Major League bench coach (2003-04)…won the 2003 World Series with Florida…began his coaching career in 1996 with Single-A Lake Elsinore in the Angels organization…**PLAYING CAREER:** Was originally selected by California in the ninth round of the 1984 First-Year Player Draft…the catcher played in seven Major League games with the Angels (1988) and Rangers (1992), going 1-for-13 (.077)…played 12 minor league seasons in the Angels, Royals and Rangers systems…**PERSONAL:** Is married to Maryjane, and the couple has three children: Austin, Rachel and Cade…played three seasons at North Carolina State University (1982-84)…graduated from Central Columbia H.S. (Pa.).

TOMMY PHELPS – PITCHING COACH
BORN: 3/4/74 in Seoul, South Korea • **RESIDES:** Valrico, Fla.
COACHING CAREER: Enters his 13th season as a coach in the Yankees organization and his fifth as RailRiders pitching coach…in 2019, Scranton/WB pitchers ranked second in the IL in strikeouts for the second time in three years (also 2017)…Scranton/WB pitchers posted a 2.98 ERA in 2016, the IL's lowest team ERA and the first sub-3.00 ERA since the 1980 Columbus Clippers (2.92), as well as the only full-season minor league team with an ERA under 3.00 that year…served as pitching coach for Single-A Tampa in 2015 after six seasons as the pitching coach for Double-A Trenton (2009-14)…was the Yankees' rehab pitching coach in 2008…**PLAYING CAREER:** Was selected by Montreal in the eighth round of the 1992 First-Year Player Draft…appeared in 75 Major League games (11 starts) with Florida (2003-04) and Milwaukee (2005)…won the 2003 World Series with Florida…pitched 14 seasons in the Expos (1993-99), Tigers (2000-01), Marlins (2002-04), Brewers (2005) and Yankees (2006) organizations…**PERSONAL:** Is a 1992 graduate of Robinson H.S. (Fla.).

PHIL PLANTIER – HITTING COACH
BORN: 1/27/69 in Manchester, N.H. • **RESIDES:** San Diego, Calif.
COACHING CAREER: Begins his third season in the Yankees organization, each as RailRiders hitting coach…in 2019, the RailRiders ranked second in the IL in BA (.277) and HRs (212)…served as the Padres' Major League hitting coach from 2012-14…served as the hitting coach and interim manager at Single-A Lake Elsinore in 2011…helped lead the Storm to their first California League championship since 2001…prior to joining the Padres, spent three seasons in the Mariners organization, serving as a hitting coordinator (2010), Double-A West Tennessee's Manager (2009) and coach (2009)…**PLAYING CAREER:** Was originally selected by Boston in the 11th round of the 1987 First-Year Player Draft…appeared in 610 games over parts of eight Major League seasons, hitting .243 (610-for-1883) with 260R, 90 doubles, 91HR and 292RBI with the Red Sox (1990-92), Padres (1993-95, '97), Astros (1995), Athletics (1996) and Cardinals (1997)…his 91 home runs are the record for any New Hampshire-born player…**PERSONAL:** He and his wife, Jennifer, have three children: Ryan, Tyler and Emily…earned a B.A. in social science from California State University San Marco.

RAÚL DOMÍNGUEZ – DEFENSIVE COACH
BORN: 7/25/80 in Panamá City, Panamá • **RESIDES:** Panamá City, Panamá
COACHING CAREER: Joins the Scranton/WB staff after two seasons as Double-A Trenton's defensive coach…enters his 14th season with the organization…served in the same role for Tampa in 2017…was also a manager for the GCL Yankees East (2016), DSL Yankees 1 (2011-15) and DSL Yankees 2 (2009-10)…reached the DSL semifinals in 2015…finished at least 10 games over .500 in four consecutive seasons from 2012-15…began his coaching career in 2008 with the DSL Yankees 2 after spending 2007 as the Yankees' tryout scout in the Dominican Republic…**PLAYING CAREER:** Signed by the Yankees as a non-drafted free agent in 2001…played four minor league seasons as an outfielder with the DSL and GCL Yankees…**PERSONAL:** He and his wife, Aracely, have a son, Raul Jr., and a daughter, Nathaly.

AARON BOSSI – DEFENSIVE COACH
BORN: 10/22/93 in St. Louis, Mo. • **RESIDES:** Tampa, Fla.
COACHING CAREER: Makes his professional coaching debut in 2020…spent the last three years (2017-19) assisting rehabbing players at the minor league complex…**PLAYING CAREER:** The catcher/infielder was signed by the Yankees as a non-drafted free agent on 6/24/16 and played one season with the GCL Yankees East, hitting .333 (19-for-57) in 22 games in 2016…**PERSONAL:** Played four seasons (2013-16) at Marshall University (W. Va.), where he was named to the ABCA Mideast All-Region First Team as a senior…earned his B.S. at Marshall and a masters degree in business administration from Columbia (Mo.) College…graduated in 2012 from St. John Vianney H.S. (Mo.).

DARREN LONDON – ATHLETIC TRAINER
BORN: 12/26/66 in Sherman Station, Maine • **RESIDES:** Grove City, Ohio
Enters his 28th season with the Yankees' Triple-A affiliate, his 32nd in the organization…was honored in 2006 and '12 as the IL "Athletic Trainer of the Year"…began his career in 1989 with Single-A Prince William, where he worked for two seasons…**PERSONAL:** He and his wife, Lee Ann, have twin sons, Lance and Layne…graduated from the University of Maine-Orono, earning a B.S. in physical education with a coaching minor.

BRAD HYDE – STRENGTH AND CONDITIONING COACH
BORN: 5/26/85 in Rogers, Ark. • **RESIDES:** Bentonville, Ark.
Enters his fifth season as the strength and conditioning coach at Scranton/WB and his seventh season in the Yankees organization…served as the Yankees' assistant director of strength and conditioning from 2014-15…previously spent two seasons in the Reds organization, serving as the assistant strength and conditioning coach for Cincinnati in 2013 and the strength and conditioning coach for Single-A Dayton in 2012…was the strength and conditioning coach for the AZL Giants in 2010…graduated from the University of Arkansas in 2009 with a B.S. in exercise science.

Trenton Thunder (Double-A)

Affiliate Since 2003 • Eastern League
2019 RECORD: 76-62, 2nd in Eastern Division (Won EL Championship)
ARM & HAMMER Park • One Thunder Rd., Trenton, NJ 08611
Phone: (609) 394-3300 • **Website:** www.trentonthunder.com
General Manager/COO: Jeff Hurley • **Dir., Broadcast & Media Relations:** Jon Mozes

JULIO MOSQUERA – MANAGER
BORN: 1/29/72 in Panamá City, Panamá • **RESIDES:** Tarpon Springs, Fla.
COACHING CAREER: Enters his first season as manager for Trenton and his 15th in the Yankees organization…was the Single-A Charleston manager for two seasons (2018-19)…managed short-season Single-A Staten Island in 2017, guiding the club to a first-place finish in the NYPL McNamara Division with a 46-29 record, the club's highest win total since 2009 (47-27)…spent two seasons (2015-16) as a skipper for the GCL Yankees 1 and GCL Yankees West…spent nine seasons (2006-14) as the catching coordinator with the Yankees after wrapping up a 15-year playing career…**PLAYING CAREER:** Was signed by the Blue Jays as a non-drafted free agent in 1991 and played parts of 15 seasons in the minor league systems of Toronto, Tampa Bay, the Yankees, Texas, Seattle and Milwaukee…the catcher made his Major League debut on 8/17/96 with Toronto and appeared in 12 Major League games across three seasons (1996-97, 2005)…**PERSONAL:** Is married to Jennifer, with two children, Dayana and Julio, Jr.

TRAVIS PHELPS – PITCHING COACH
BORN: 7/25/77 in Rocky Comfort, Mo. • **RESIDES:** Seminole, Fla.
COACHING CAREER: Joins the Trenton staff in 2020, his fifth season with the Yankees organization…spent his first four seasons as the pitching coach at short-season Single-A Staten Island…Staten Island pitchers ranked second in the New York-Penn League with 713K in 2019…in 2018, Staten Island pitchers posted a 2.60 ERA, the team's best since 2009 (2.53)…in 2017, Staten Island pitchers led the NYPL with a 2.64 ERA, which led all U.S.-based minor league teams…led the league in shutouts (11), the most in the NYPL since 2010…prior to joining the Yankees, served as the head coach for St. Petersburg H.S. (Fla.) for three seasons (2011-14) and operated a baseball training facility in the Tampa Bay area…**PLAYING CAREER:** Was selected by Tampa Bay in the 89th round of the 1996 First-Year Player Draft…is the latest-round draft pick to reach the Majors, surpassing former Pulaski hitting coach Scott Seabol, selected three picks before him by the Yankees in the 88th round of the same draft…in three Major League seasons with the Devil Rays (2001-02) and Brewers (2004), was 3-5 with a 4.34 ERA and five saves over 79 relief appearances…pitched 11 minor league seasons in the Devil Rays, Braves, Brewers, Rockies, Cubs, Reds and Astros organizations, before rounding out his career with two years (2008-09) with York of the independent Atlantic League…**PERSONAL:** He and his wife, Erin, have two children: Emerson and Anderson…pitched for two seasons at Crowder College (Mo.)…graduated from Wheaton H.S. (Mo.).

KEN JOYCE – HITTING COACH
BORN: 10/28/64 in Portland, Maine • **RESIDES:** Portland, Maine
COACHING CAREER: Enters his fourth season as a hitting coach in the Yankees organization and his first in Trenton…served in the same role for Staten Island (2018-19) and Charleston (2017)…Staten Island hitters led the NYPL with 52HR in 2019…joined the Yankees after seven seasons with the Giants organization (2010-16)…was the hitting coach at Double-A Richmond for six seasons (2011-16) after one year with Triple-A Fresno (2010)…was the hitting coach for Scottsdale of the Arizona Fall League in 2011…worked in the Blue Jays system for eight seasons (2002-09), managing Single-A Charleston (W. Va.) in 2004 and Single-A Lansing from 2005-06…was a hitting coach at Rookie-level Medicine Hat (2002), Double-A New Haven (2003), Double-A New Hampshire (2007-08) and Triple-A Las Vegas (2009)…began his coaching career with six seasons in the Marlins organization, starting as the bullpen coach at Double-A Portland (1994-95) and continuing as Portland's hitting coach in 1996…spent three seasons at short-season Single-A Utica as the hitting coach (1997) and the manager (1998-99)…also coached in the independent leagues with Catskill (2000) and Adirondack (2001)…**PERSONAL:** He and his wife, Janet, have two children, Tommy and Jill…graduated from the University of Southern Maine, where he played in the 1985 NAIA College World Series and later served as an assistant coach for four seasons, including a trip to the 1989 Division-III College World Series…set an NCAA record with seven hits in a game…was inducted into the USM Hall of Fame in 1998 and the State of Maine Baseball Hall of Fame in 2001.

CAONABO COSME – DEFENSIVE COACH
BORN: 3/18/79 in La Vega, D.R. • **RESIDES:** La Vega, D.R.
COACHING CAREER: Enters his ninth season in the Yankees organization, his first as Trenton's defensive coach…was the manager of the DSL Yankees for the last two seasons…spent two years as a scout for the Braves (2016-17)…spent six seasons with the Yankees from 2010-15…was the hitting coach for the GCL Yankees 1 for two seasons, helping them lead the GCL in all three triple slash categories in 2015 (.267/.351/.372)…spent the previous three seasons (2011-13) as the hitting coach for the DSL Yankees 2…**PLAYING CAREER:** Was signed by the Athletics as a minor league free agent in 1995…played in parts of 13 minor league seasons (1996-2008) in the A's, Cardinals, Yankees, Reds and Tigers organizations, batting a combined .257 with 231 doubles, 57HR and 447RBI in 1,127 career games.

JOSÉ JAVIER – DEFENSIVE COACH
BORN: 9/16/92 in Puerto Plata, D.R. • **RESIDES:** Puerto Plata, D.R.
COACHING CAREER: Begins his fourth season as a coach in the Yankees organization and his first at Trenton…was the lower level base running and outfield coordinator in 2019…served as a defensive coach for Single-A Tampa in 2018 and Single-A Charleston in 2017…**PLAYING CAREER:** Was signed by the Yankees as a non-drafted free agent on 4/1/10…played six minor league seasons with the Yankees (2010-15), hitting .250 in 277 games while playing all four infield positions…**PERSONAL:** He and his wife, Edilenia, have one daughter, Abigail.

JIMMY DOWNAM – ATHLETIC TRAINER
BORN: 1/29/87 in Somers Point, N.J. • **RESIDES:** Tampa, Fla.
Enters his fourth season as Trenton's trainer and his eighth overall with the Yankees…also spent three seasons with Charleston (2014-16)…joined the organization in 2013 as the trainer for short-season Single-A Staten Island…previously worked with the Phillies organization in 2012 as an intern at the team's rehabilitation facilities in Clearwater, Fla.…attended Liberty University (Va.), where he received his B.S. in athletic training in 2009 and his M.S. in sports administration in 2012.

DANNY RUSSO – STRENGTH AND CONDITIONING COACH
BORN: 10/12/87 in Worcester, Mass. • **RESIDES:** Tampa, Fla.
Enters his first season as the strength and conditioning coach for Trenton and his eighth with the Yankees organization…has also served in the same role for Charleston (2018-19), Staten Island (2016-17), Pulaski (2015) and the GCL Yankees 2 (2014)…also interned for the GCL Yankees 2 in 2013…graduated from the University of South Florida in 2013 with a bachelor's degree in exercise science.

Tampa Tarpons (A)

Affiliate Since 1994 • Florida State League
2019 RECORD (First Half): 28-38, 5th in North Division
2019 RECORD (Second Half): 36-33, 2nd in North Division
George M. Steinbrenner Field • One Steinbrenner Dr., Tampa, FL 33614
Phone: (813) 673-3055 • **Website:** www.tarponsbaseball.com
General Manager: Matt Gess • **Media Contact:** Matt Gess

DAVID ADAMS – MANAGER
BORN: 5/15/87 in Margate, Fla. • **RESIDES:** Odessa, Fla.
COACHING CAREER: Takes over as the manager at Tampa after managing short-season Single-A Staten Island in 2019 and the GCL Yankees West in 2018…will also serve as the Yankees' complex coordinator…is his fourth season with the Yankees organization…made his debut in 2017 as the defensive coach for the GCL Yankees East…**PLAYING CAREER:** Was selected by the Yankees in the third round of the 2008 First-Year Player Draft…appeared in 43 Major League games for the Yankees in 2013…made his Major League debut on 5/15/13, becoming the first Yankee to debut on his birthday…over nine minor league seasons with the Yankees (2008-13), Orioles (2014), Marlins (2015) and Blue Jays (2016), batted .282 (707-for-2507) with 347R, 167 doubles, 22 triples, 45HR and 341RBI in 701 games…**PERSONAL:** He and his wife, Camille, have two sons, Jethro and Brooks…attended the University of Virginia, where he was named to the *Baseball America* Freshman All-America Second Team and a Louisville Slugger Freshman All-American.

JOSÉ ROSADO – PITCHING COACH
BORN: 11/9/74 in Jersey City, N.J. • **RESIDES:** Dorado, P.R.
COACHING CAREER: Enters his 10th season as a coach in the Yankees organization and his third with Tampa…Tarpons pitchers ranked second from the Florida State League in strikeouts (1,186) after leading the FSL in 2018 (1,257)…previously served as Trenton's pitching coach from 2015-17…Trenton pitchers led the Eastern League in 2017 with a 2.83 ERA, the lowest in franchise history and fourth-lowest among full-season clubs in 2017…the pitching staff also led the league in strikeouts (1,160K) and set a franchise record with 20 shutouts…also served as the pitching coach for Puerto Rico for the second consecutive World Baseball Classic in 2017…in 2016, his Thunder pitching staff led the Eastern League in ERA (3.12) and strikeouts (1,239)…filled the same role for the World Team in the 2015 All-Star Futures Game and for the Surprise Saguaros in the 2015 Arizona Fall League…spent 2011-14 as a pitching coach in the GCL…**PLAYING CAREER:** Was selected by Kansas City in the 12th round of the 1994 First-Year Player Draft…in five seasons with the Royals (1996-2000), went 37-45 with a 4.27 ERA in 125 games (112 starts)…the two-time AL All-Star earned the win in the 1997 game in Cleveland and was the only left-handed pitcher selected to the AL team for the 1999 game at Fenway Park…**PERSONAL:** He and his wife, Adalyz, have a daughter, Genesis, and a son, Jose III…attended Galveston Junior College (Tex.)…was named MVP of the National Junior College World Series in 1994, recording two wins and one save.

JOE MIGLIACCIO – HITTING COACH
BORN: 1/18/91 in Mount Holly, N.J. • **RESIDES:** Land O'Lakes, Fla.
COACHING CAREER: Enters his second season with Tampa and the Yankees organization…Tarpons hitters ranked second in the Florida State League with 93HR in 2019…started his career in the college ranks, coaching at the University of Iowa, Murray State University, University of Missouri, Southeast Missouri State and Siena College…**PERSONAL:** Played baseball at Florida International (2009-10), Parkland College (2010-12), and Oral Roberts (2012-14)…graduated cum laude from Oral Roberts in 2014 with a degree in recreation administration with a minor in humanities…earned his master's degree in education from Missouri in 2018.

KEVIN MAHONEY – DEFENSIVE COACH
BORN: 5/11/87 in Miller Place, N.Y. • **RESIDES:** Wesley Chapel, Fla.
COACHING CAREER: Enters his sixth season in the Yankees organization and his second as the defensive coach for Tampa…served in the same role for the GCL Yankees East in 2018…spent 2017 as the hitting coach at short-season Single-A Staten Island…was also Pulaski's hitting coach in 2016, when his hitters tied for the league lead with 60HR…made his coaching debut with the GCL Yankees East in 2015…**PLAYING CAREER:** Was selected by the Yankees in the 23rd round of the 2009 First-Year Player Draft…in five minor league seasons, the infielder batted .252 with 183R, 34HR and 160RBI in 381 games, reaching Triple-A…retired in 2014 after one season with Amarillo in the independent American Association…**PERSONAL:** He and his wife, Kimberly, have a son, Kaiden, and a daughter, Kensington…played four seasons (2006-09) at Canisius College (N.Y.), setting school records in games played (216), runs scored (202), hits (254), doubles (52), home runs (47), RBI (187) and walks (116)…was named MAAC Player of the Year in 2009…is a 2005 graduate of Miller Place H.S. (N.Y.), where he earned All-State honors as a senior.

JASON PHILLIPS – DEFENSIVE COACH
BORN: 9/27/76 in La Mesa, Calif. • **RESIDES:** Glendale, Ariz.
COACHING CAREER: Enters his second season in the Yankees organization, his first with Tampa…was the bullpen coach at Double-A Trenton in 2019…prior to joining the organization, served as the bullpen catcher for the Toronto Blue Jays (2016-18) and Seattle Mariners (2009-15)…**PLAYING CAREER:** Was selected by the New York Mets in the fourth round of the 1997 First-Year Player Draft…spent parts of seven Major League seasons as a catcher and first baseman with the Mets (2001-04), Los Angeles Dodgers (2005) and Toronto Blue Jays (2006-07)…in 465 Major League games, batted .249 (344-for-1,382) with 138R, 77 doubles, 30HR and 168RBI…**PERSONAL:** Graduated from El Capitan H.S. (Calif.) and attended San Diego State University.

MICHAEL BECKER – ATHLETIC TRAINER
BORN: 12/16/88 in Bennington, Vt. • **RESIDES:** Bennington, Vt.
Begins his ninth season as a trainer in the Yankees organization, his seventh with Tampa…worked with Single-A Charleston in 2013 and short-season Single-A Staten Island in 2012…worked as an athletic training student intern at Triple-A Scranton/Wilkes-Barre during the 2010 season…graduated from Ithaca College in 2011 with a B.S. in athletic training…previously served as an athletic training intern with Cornell University, Ithaca College and Siena College.

JAKE DUNNING – STRENGTH AND CONDITIONING COACH
BORN: 3/3/86 in Flagstaff, Ariz. • **RESIDES:** Tampa, Fla.
Begins his eighth season in the Yankees organization and his fourth as Tampa's strength and conditioning coach…also served in the same role with Double-A Trenton (2016) and short-season Single-A Staten Island (2014-15)…joined the Yankees organization in March 2013 as a member of the GCL staff…graduated from the University of South Florida in 2012 with a B.S. in exercise science…was a member of the U.S. Army from 2004-08 and served in Afghanistan.

Charleston RiverDogs (A)

Affiliate Since 2005 • South Atlantic League
2019 RECORD (First Half): 37-33, 3rd in Southern Division
2019 RECORD (Second Half): 36-33, 3rd in Southern Division
Joseph P. Riley, Jr. Ballpark • 360 Fishburne Street, Charleston, SC 29403
Phone: (843) 723-7241 • **Website:** www.riverdogs.com
President/General Manager: Dave Echols • **Dir., Media Relations:** Jason Kempf

LUIS DORANTE – MANAGER
BORN: 10/25/68 in Coro, Venezuela • **RESIDES:** Weston, Fla.
COACHING CAREER: Enters his ninth season in the Yankees organization…begins his second stint as the Charleston manager, also guiding the club from 2014-16…managed Rookie-level Pulaski in 2017 and 2019, winning the Appalachian League "Manager of the Year" Award in both years…in 2017, guided Pulaski to a 41-26 mark and a berth in the Appalachian League championship…spent 2018 as the Double-A Trenton bullpen coach…served as a coach at Double-A Trenton for two seasons (2012-13), helping win the 2013 Eastern League Championship…spent four seasons with the Pirates as the Latin American Field Coordinator (2011) and Major League bullpen coach (2008-10)…was a minor league coach and manager for 13 seasons in the Marlins (2002-07) and Expos (1995-2001) organizations…spent three seasons managing Single-A Jupiter (2002-04)…shared "Manager of the Year" honors in 2002 and 2003…led the GCL Expos to a league-best 41-18 record in 1996…was a scout for the Expos in 1994…**PLAYING CAREER:** Was originally signed as a non-drafted free agent in 1986 by Boston…played in 221 games over six minor league seasons in the Red Sox organization, primarily as a catcher…**PERSONAL:** Is married to Solange and has two children, Luis and Valeria.

DANIEL MOSKOS – PITCHING COACH
BORN: 4/28/86 in Greenville, S.C. • **RESIDES:** Charleston, S.C.
COACHING CAREER: Joins the Yankees organization in 2020 after one year at Driveline Baseball in Seattle, Wash.…**PLAYING CAREER:** The left-handed pitcher was selected by Pittsburgh with the fourth overall pick in the 2007 First-Year Player Draft and made 31 relief appearances for the Pirates in 2011, going 1-1 with a 2.96 ERA (24.1IP, 8ER)…also spent time in the minors with the White Sox, Dodgers, Padres and Cubs organizations before pitching in the Mexican League in 2018…**PERSONAL:** He and his wife, Cameron, have a daughter, McKenna…pitched three seasons at Clemson (S.C.) University (2005-07), where he was named to the Roger Clemens Award Watch List and was a semifinalist for the Golden Spikes Award in 2007…graduated from Damien (Calif.) H.S.…pitched the U.S. Collegiate National Team to a gold medal at the 2006 World Championships in Cuba.

CASEY DYKES – HITTING COACH
BORN: 1/27/90 in Franklin, Tenn. • **RESIDES:** Wesley Chapel, Fla.
COACHING CAREER: Joins the Yankees organization after one season (2019) as the hitting coach at Indiana University, where his Hoosiers won the Big Ten regular season championship and led all of Division I in home runs during the regular season…served as hitting coach and recruiting coordinator at Virginia Military Institute from 2015-18…began his coaching career with two seasons (2013-14) as an assistant at his alma mater, Western Kentucky University…**PERSONAL:** He and his wife, Chaney, have two sons, Jett and Kash…played four seasons at Western Kentucky (2009-12), graduating with a bachelor's degree in sport management before completing his master's in athletic administration in 2014…graduated from Franklin (Tenn.) H.S.

FRANCISCO LEANDRO – DEFENSIVE COACH
BORN: 7/19/80 in Caracas, Venezuela • **RESIDES:** Miami, Fla.
COACHING CAREER: Returns for a second season as a Charleston defensive coach, his fifth in the Yankees organization…served as the hitting coach for Rookie-level Pulaski in 2018 and for the GCL Yankees East in 2017…helped the GCL East squad capture the 2017 GCL Championship…made his professional coaching debut in the GCL in 2016…**PLAYING CAREER:** Was selected by Tampa Bay in the 24th round of the 2004 First-Year Player Draft…spent 2004-06 in the minors with Tampa Bay, batting .289 (292-for-1,010) with 168R, 75 doubles, 15HR and 131RBI in 291 games…also spent time playing the independent Canadian-American League (2007-08), Venezuelan Winter League (2007-11) and independent American Association (2008-11)…**PERSONAL:** Attended the University of Central Missouri…he and his wife, Xoana Garcia, have two children, Shanti and Santiago.

RYAN HUNT – DEFENSIVE COACH
BORN: 12/6/95 in Glen Burnie, Md. • **RESIDES:** Millersville, Md.
COACHING CAREER: Enters his second season in the Yankees organization, his first as Charleston's defensive coach…served in the same role with Rookie-level Pulaski in 2019…began his coaching career as an assistant at his alma mater, University of Charleston (W.Va.), in 2019…**PERSONAL:** Played infield for three seasons at Division II Charleston (2016-18) after his freshman season (2015) at the University of South Carolina-Aiken…earned his bachelor's degree in accounting from Charleston…graduated in 2014 from Archbishop Spalding (Md.) H.S.

MICHAEL SOLE – ATHLETIC TRAINER
BORN: 3/5/92 in Morristown, N.J. • **RESIDES:** Parsippany, N.J.
Begins his fourth season as Charleston's trainer after serving in the same role with short-season Single-A Staten Island in 2016…in 2017, received the South Atlantic League Athletic Trainer of the Year Award…also earned his Strength and Conditioning Specialist certification (CSCS) in 2017…interned with Staten Island in 2013…previously worked as an athletic trainer for Florida Atlantic University while he pursued his master's in exercise science and health promotion…at FAU, primarily worked with men's soccer, men's and women's tennis and beach volleyball…graduated from Rowan (N.J.) University with a B.S. in athletic training in 2014…interned in Rowan's athletic training department, assisting with men's soccer, swimming and diving, and football…also completed an athletic training internship for the Florida Launch of Major League Lacrosse.

LARRY ADEGOKE – STRENGTH AND CONDITIONING COACH
BORN: 4/3/93 in Gainesville, Fla. • **RESIDES:** Atlanta, Ga.
Enters his third season with the Yankees organization, his first with Charleston…spent the last two seasons with Rookie-level Pulaski…joined the Yankees organization full-time in 2018 after serving as the team's performance science assistant in spring 2017…was a strength and conditioning intern for the Kennesaw State football team…graduated with a B.S. in exercise science from Kennesaw State University (Ga.), where he played club hockey…earned his M.S. in exercise and nutrition science from the University of Tampa…played junior hockey in Atlanta, Philadelphia and Washington, D.C.…full name is Lawrence Adegoke ("add-uh-GOH-kay").

Staten Island Yankees (Short-Season A)

Affiliate Since 1999 • New York-Penn League
2019 RECORD: 40-36, 4th in McNamara Division
Richmond County Bank Ballpark at St. George • 75 Richmond Terrace, Staten Island, NY 10301
Phone: (718) 720-9265 • **Website:** www.siyanks.com
General Manager: Jane M. Rogers • **Media Contact:** Michael Galayda

DAN FIORITO – MANAGER
BORN: 8/20/90 in Yonkers, N.Y. • **RESIDES:** Yonkers, N.Y.
COACHING CAREER: Enters his fourth season with the Yankees organization, his first as the Staten Island manager…made his managerial debut in 2019 with the GCL Yankees East…served as the defensive coach at Single-A Charleston in 2018…made his professional coaching debut as defensive coach with Rookie-level Pulaski in 2017…**PLAYING CAREER:** Was signed by the Yankees as a non-drafted free agent in 2012…over four seasons in the Yankees system, the infielder batted .240 (264-for-1102) with 107R, 52 doubles, 6 triples, 7HR and 98RBI in 322 career minor league games…**PERSONAL:** Is married to Elizabeth…played three years at Manhattanville College in Purchase, N.Y., where he was named to the 2012 ABCA All-America Third Team, making him the first male two-time All-American in school history…was also a D3Baseball.com honorable mention All-American in 2010…was named 2012 NCBWA Mid-Atlantic Region Player of the Year…is a 2008 graduate of Fordham Prep in the Bronx.

DUSTIN GLANT – PITCHING COACH
BORN: 7/20/81 in Decatur, Ind. • **RESIDES:** Tampa, Fla.
COACHING CAREER: Joins the Yankees organization in 2020…has coached at the high school and college level since 2013, most recently serving as the pitching coach at Ball State (Ind.) University from 2017-19…his Cardinals staff led NCAA Division I with an 11.1 K/9.0IP ratio in 2019 and set a school strikeout record for the third straight season with 628K…was the head coach at Division III Anderson (Ind.) University in 2016…was the head coach at Lapel (Ind.) H.S. in 2015 and Mt. Vernon (Ind.) H.S. in 2014…began his coaching career as a volunteer assistant at Ball State in 2013…**PLAYING CAREER:** Was originally selected by Arizona in the seventh round of the 2003 First-Year Player Draft…pitched in 264 games over six seasons in the Dbacks organization (2003-08), reaching Triple-A in his final two seasons…finished his career with stints in the Mexican League (2009-10) and independent Northern League (2009-10) and American Association (2011)…**PERSONAL:** He and his wife, Ashley, have a daughter, Evelyn, and a son, David…pitched three seasons (2001-03) at Purdue (Ind.) University…graduated from Wayne (Ind.) H.S. in 2000.

RYAN CHIPKA – HITTING COACH
BORN: 1/26/90 in Waterville, Ohio • **RESIDES:** New Hudson, Mich.
COACHING CAREER: Enters his first season in the Yankees organization…served as the director of program development for University of Michigan baseball in 2019, handling travel logistics, analytics and other non-coaching responsibilities as the Wolverines reached their first College World Series since 1984 and finished as national runners-up…was an assistant coach at the University of Toledo (Ohio) in 2018 and 2016…spent 2017 as the director of program development and scouting at Norfolk State (Va.) University…from 2014-15, was the head coach of his alma mater, NAIA-level Rochester (Mich.) College, reaching the USCAA Small College World Series both years…while at Rochester, was also the school's sports information director…served as an associate scout for the Dbacks before entering the coaching ranks…**PERSONAL:** Is married to wife, Audrey…was a four-year captain and a first-team All-American at Rochester College (2009-12)…also helped the Warriors reach back-to-back USCAA Small College World Series and set the school's all-time hits record…graduated in 2008 from Anthony Wayne (Ohio) H.S., where he also played football and basketball.

TEURIS OLIVARES – DEFENSIVE COACH
BORN: 12/15/78 in San Francisco de Macoris, D.R. • **RESIDES:** San Francisco de Macoris, D.R.
COACHING CAREER: Enters his 10th season as a coach in the Yankees organization and his fourth with Staten Island (also 2016-17, '19)…previously coached at Rookie-level Pulaski in 2018…spent five seasons in the DSL, with the DSL Yankees 1 (2011-12, '14-15) and the DSL Yankees 2 (2013)…helped lead the DSL Yankees 1 to a 52-20 record in 2015, a 41-28 mark in 2014 and a 49-21 mark in 2012…**PLAYING CAREER:** Was signed by the Yankees as a non-drafted free agent in 1995…over nine seasons in the Yankees system (1996-2004), the infielder batted .250 with 101 doubles, 27 triples, 40HR and 270RBI in 669 career minor league games…finished his career with six seasons in the independent Atlantic League (2005-10).

JON BECKER – ATHLETIC TRAINER
BORN: 3/16/91 in Baton Rouge, La. • **RESIDES:** Strasburg, Ill.
Enters his fourth season in the Yankees organization, all as the trainer for Staten Island…previously served as an athletic trainer for HSHS St. Joseph's Hospital (Ill.) and Nashville Community High School (Ill.)…also interned with the Puget Sound Collegiate League in 2014…graduated from McKendree University in 2013 with a B.S. in athletic training.

DANIEL SMITH – STRENGTH AND CONDITIONING COACH
BORN: 6/3/92 in Bradford, Pa. • **RESIDES:** Tampa, Fla.
Begins his fourth season in the Yankees organization and his third as the strength and conditioning coach for Staten Island…served in the same role for Rookie-level Pulaski in 2017…prior to joining the Yankees, served as the assistant strength and conditioning coach for Western Kentucky University (2016-17) and the University of South Florida (2015-16)…also interned at Penn State (2015) and Gannon University (2014-15)…graduated from the University of Pittsburgh at Bradford with a B.S. in Sports Medicine in 2014 and earned his M.S. in Sport and Exercise Science from Gannon University in 2015.

Pulaski Yankees (Rookie)

Affiliate Since 2015 • Appalachian League
2019 RECORD: 42-26, 1st in East Division (Lost in AL Semifinals)
Calfee Park • 700 South Washington Ave., Pulaski, VA 24301
Phone: (540) 980-1070 • **Website:** www.pulaskiyankees.net
General Manager: Betsy Haugh • **Media Contact:** Betsy Haugh

In 2019, the Pulaski Yankees won the John H. Johnson's President's Award, which is Minor League Baseball's top award and recognizes "the complete baseball franchise"

The Pulaski manager was TBD as of the printing date of this book.

GERARDO CASADIEGO – PITCHING COACH
BORN: 12/19/80 in Barquisimeto, Venezuela • **RESIDES:** Cabudare, Venezuela
COACHING CAREER: Continues with his fourth season as the Pulaski pitching coach and his eighth season in the Yankees organization…served as the pitching coach for the DSL Yankees 1 (2014-15) and the DSL Yankees 2 (2016)…the 2017 Pulaski team led the Appalachian League with 654K and a 10.21 K/9.0IP ratio…in 2016, the DSL 2 squad led the 42-team league with a 8.65 K/9.0IP ratio (568K, 590.2IP)…made his professional coaching debut in 2014, leading the DSL 1 staff to a league-high 632K…**PLAYING CAREER:** Played 10 minor league seasons in the Expos, Yankees, Rockies and Orioles organizations (1999-2004, '06-09)…went 30-42 with 33 saves and a 4.15 ERA in 72 appearances (30 starts)…was a 2006 FSL Mid-Season All-Star with Single-A Tampa…**PERSONAL:** He and his wife, Raquel, have two sons, Abraham and Isaac.

KEVIN MARTIR – HITTING COACH
BORN: 2/11/94 in Brooklyn, N.Y. • **RESIDES:** Dallas, N.C.
COACHING CAREER: Joins the Yankees organization in 2020…made his coaching debut in 2019 as a development coach for the GCL Phillies East, serving on the same staff as former Yankees 3B Charlie Hayes…**PLAYING CAREER:** The catcher was originally selected by Houston in the 18th round of the 2015 First-Year Player Draft…played two seasons in the Astros organization, and also saw time with the Brewers and Phillies organizations…**PERSONAL:** Played three seasons at the University of Maryland (2013-15)…as a junior in 2015, was a D1baseball.com Third-Team All-American and was named a semifinalist for the Johnny Bench Award, given annually to the nation's top catcher…graduated in 2012 from the Grand Street Campus in Brooklyn after transferring from Xaverian H.S. in Brooklyn prior to his senior year…is the first player ever to win PSAL and CHSAA championships in consecutive years, helping Grand Street Campus win the 2012 PSAL Class A title after leading Xaverian to the 2011 CHSAA title…was named to the *New York Post*'s 2012 All-Brooklyn first team…was a 2011 Perfect Game Preseason High School All-America honorable mention.

TYSON BLASER – DEFENSIVE COACH
BORN: 12/8/87 in Rock Island, Ill. • **RESIDES:** Bettendorf, Iowa
COACHING CAREER: Enters his fourth season with the Yankees organization, his first with Pulaski…was with Staten Island in 2019 and the GCL Yankees East in 2018 after joining the organization in 2017 as a coaching assistant with Triple-A Scranton/Wilkes-Barre…was the head coach at United Township H.S. (Iowa) from 2015-17…**PLAYING CAREER:** Was signed by the Yankees as a non-drafted free agent on 6/18/11…played four seasons in the organization, batting .263/.347/.333 with 50R, 21 doubles, 1HR and 48RBI in 135 games…**PERSONAL:** He and his wife, Holley, have a son, Bryce, and daughter, Brooklyn…played four seasons at the University of Iowa, where he was a four-time Academic All-Big Ten honoree…was named the 2006 "Quad City Male Athlete of the Year" as a senior at Rockridge H.S. (Iowa)…used his history degree and teaching certificate to teach U.S. History while coaching at United Township.

MANNY OZOA – ATHLETIC TRAINER
BORN: 11/22/90 in Orland Park, Ill. • **RESIDES:** Tampa, Fla.
Enters his fifth season as Pulaski's athletic trainer…was named the 2019 Appalachian League "Athletic Trainer of the Year" by the Professional Baseball Athletic Trainers Society (PBATS)…since 2014, has spent his offseasons as a seasonal athletic trainer for the Tampa Bay Buccaneers…also spent time as an athletic training intern for the Blue Jays in 2014…was an athletic training student with Illinois Wesleyan University in 2013, working with the football, women's basketball, softball and men's and women's track and field teams…served in the same role for Illinois State University in 2012, working with the women's gymnastics team…interned with the athletic training staff of the San Francisco 49ers in 2012…received his bachelor's degree in athletic training from Illinois State University…received his master's degree in medical sciences with a concentration in athletic training and adolescent athletes from the University of South Florida.

The Pulaski strength & conditioning coach was TBD as of the printing date of this book.

GCL Yankees West (Rookie)

Affiliate Since 1990 · Gulf Coast League
2019 RECORD: 22-27, 4th in North Division
Yankees Player Development Complex · 3102 N. Himes Ave, Tampa, FL 33607
Phone: (813) 875-7569

The GCL Yankees West manager was TBD as of the printing date of this book.

PRESTON CLAIBORNE – PITCHING COACH
BORN: 1/21/88 in Dallas, Tex. · **RESIDES:** Rockport, Tex.
COACHING CAREER: Makes his coaching debut in 2020…**PLAYING CAREER:** The right-handed pitcher was selected by the Yankees in the 17th round of the 2010 First-Year Player Draft and spent five seasons in the organization…made 62 Major League relief appearances with the Yankees from 2013-14, going 3-2 with a 3.79 ERA (71.1IP, 75H, 32R/30ER, 24BB, 58K, 8HR)…tied the Major League record for the Modern Era (since 1900) by issuing zero walks over his first 14 career appearances; did not walk a batter over his first 19.1IP, the second-longest such streak by any Yankees pitcher to begin his Major League career (John Frill-20.2IP in 1910)…also made one appearance with Texas in 2017…spent time in the Giants and Indians organizations before retiring following the 2018 season…**PERSONAL:** Pitched four seasons (2007-10) at Tulane (La.) University…graduated from Newman Smith (Tex.) H.S.…was tabbed by *Baseball America* as the No. 35 prospect in the 2006 high school class nationwide…was selected by Pittsburgh in the 23rd round of the 2006 First-Year Player Draft but did not sign.

JAKE HIRST – HITTING COACH
BORN: 2/22/95 in Davenport, Iowa · **RESIDES:** Tampa, Fla.
COACHING CAREER: Enters his second season with the GCL Yankees West and second in the Yankees organization…served as an assistant coach at Augustana College (Ill.) for two seasons (2017-18)…**PERSONAL:** Played four seasons (2013-17) at Central College (Iowa), where he graduated with a B.A. in exercise science…earned a Master's in exercise physiology from St. Ambrose University (Iowa).

LINO DÍAZ – DEFENSIVE COACH
BORN: 7/22/70 in Panamá City, Panamá · **RESIDES:** Parrish, Fla.
COACHING CAREER: Enters his sixth season with the Yankees, his fourth as a GCL defensive coach (2015-16, '19-present)…managed short-season Single-A Staten Island in 2018…served as defensive coach for Double-A Trenton in 2017…was the manager of cultural development for the White Sox from 2013-14, traveling with the Major League club as part of the dugout staff…spent 11 seasons (2002-12) in various roles with the Indians, including stints as the cultural development coordinator (2002-04, '10-12), director of Latin American operations (2007-09) and assistant farm director (2005-06)…managed the GCL Royals in 2001 and was a member of the GCL Reds staff from 1999-2001…began his coaching career in 1998 with Triple-A Indianapolis in the Reds system…**PLAYING CAREER:** Was originally drafted by Kansas City in the 30th round of the 1993 First-Year Player Draft…batted .294 with 21HR in 504 games over five seasons in the Royals minor league system…**PERSONAL:** Graduated from University of Nevada-Las Vegas with a degree in international relations…married to wife, Stacey, with four children: Chase, Tristan, Nicholas and Patrick.

MICHEL HERNÁNDEZ – DEFENSIVE COACH
BORN: 8/12/78 in Havana, Cuba · **RESIDES:** Lutz, Fla.
COACHING CAREER: Enters his eighth season as a coach in the Yankees organization…returns to the GCL, where he made his professional coaching debut (2013-14 w/ GCL Yankees 1)…spent the last four seasons with Single-A Tampa, two as catching coach (2018-19) and two as bullpen coach (2016-17)…served as defensive coach for Double-A Trenton in 2015…**PLAYING CAREER:** Was originally signed by the Yankees as a non-drafted free agent in 1998…played in 45 games in parts of three seasons in the Majors with the Yankees (2003) and Tampa Bay (2008-09), combining to hit .237 with 1HR and 12RBI…in 15 minor league seasons with the Yankees, Philadelphia, San Diego, St. Louis, Tampa Bay, Pittsburgh, Baltimore and Cleveland organizations, hit a combined .257 with 35HR and 340RBI in 997 games…also played for the Havana Industriales in Cuba…**PERSONAL:** He and his wife, Marta, have one son, Michael…attended one year of college in Cuba after graduating from high school in 1995.

A.J. CANO – ATHLETIC TRAINER
BORN: 4/3/89 in Perryton, Tex. · **RESIDES:** Perryton, Tex.
Enters his fourth season as the trainer for the GCL Yankees West and fifth in the Yankees organization…spent 2016 as the trainer for the GCL Yankees East…previously served as the trainer for the DSL Dodgers in 2015 after interning with the DSL Red Sox in 2014…graduated from West Texas A&M University in 2013 with a B.S. in Athletic Training and a B.S. in Sport and Exercise Sciences.

JAMES GONZALEZ – STRENGTH AND CONDITIONING COACH
BORN: 5/4/82 in Brooklyn, N.Y. · **RESIDES:** Tampa, Fla.
Begins his sixth season as a strength and conditioning coach in the Yankees organization, all in the GCL…helped the GCL East squad capture the 2017 GCL Championship…served as the strength and conditioning coach for the Dominican Republic team in the 2017 World Baseball Classic…prior to joining the Yankees, spent three seasons in the Braves organization…spent two seasons (2010-11) in the Pirates organization and was named the 2010 and 2016 "GCL Strength and Conditioning Coach of the Year" by the Professional Baseball Strength and Conditioning Society…began his career in professional baseball as an assistant strength and conditioning coach in the Indians system from 2007-2009…graduated from the University of South Florida, where he worked with the Bulls' baseball and football team and earned a degree in physical education with a specialization in exercise science and a minor in leadership skills…he and his wife, Donna, have two daughters, Khloe and Liliana.

GCL Yankees East (Rookie)

Affiliate Since 2013 • Gulf Coast League
2019 RECORD: 18-29, 7th in North Division
Yankees Player Development Complex • 3102 N. Himes Ave, Tampa, FL 33607
Phone: (813) 875-7569

TRAVIS CHAPMAN – MANAGER
BORN: 6/5/78 in Jacksonville, Fla. • **RESIDES:** St. Johns, Fla.
COACHING CAREER: Enters his eighth season in the Yankees organization, starting a second stint as a GCL manager in 2020…made his managerial debut in 2014, leading the GCL Yankees 1 to the Northwest Division title (38-22)…spent 2017 as the manager of the DSL Yankees…will also serve as the assistant infield coordinator in 2020…was a defensive coach for Single-A Charleston for three seasons (2015-16, '19)…served as the defensive coach for Triple-A Scranton/Wilkes-Barre in 2018…made his professional coaching debut in 2013 as a coach for the GCL Yankees 2, helping lead the club to a 36-24 record and a first-place finish in the Northeast Division…was an assistant coach for the 18U USA National team that won a gold medal in Seoul, South Korea…**PLAYING CAREER:** The infielder was originally selected by the Phillies in the 17th round of the 2000 First-Year Player Draft and made his Major League debut with the club in 2003…played in 506 combined minor league games over seven seasons with the Philadelphia (2000-03), Kansas City (2004), Cincinnati (2005) and Pittsburgh (2006) organizations…**PERSONAL:** Played four seasons Mississippi State University (1997-2000), and left as the school's all-time doubles (71) leader.

BEN BUCK – PITCHING COACH
BORN: 11/19/82 in Denver, Colo. • **RESIDES:** Tampa, Fla.
COACHING CAREER: Joins the Yankees organization after guiding his alma mater Lamar (Colo.) Community College to the NJCAA Region 9 Championship in his only season as head coach (2019)…brings 12 years of college coaching experience, including stints as assistant coach/recruiting coordinator at Tarleton State (Texas) University (2015-17) and pitching coach/recruiting coordinator at West Texas A&M (2013-14), Regis (Colo.) University (2011-12) and Lamar Community College (2008-10)…**PLAYING CAREER:** Pitched one season (2004) for the Mid-Missouri Mavericks of the independent Frontier League…**PERSONAL:** He and his wife, Candice, have a daughter, Cameron, and a son, Clayton…pitched two seasons at the University of Utah (2003-04) after two seasons at Lamar Community College (2001-02), where he helped lead the Lopes to the JUCO World Series…is a graduate of Skyview (Colo.) H.S.

AARON LEANHARDT – HITTING COACH
BORN: 1/5/77 in Plymouth, Mich. • **RESIDES:** Las Vegas, Nev.
COACHING CAREER: Enters his third season in the Yankees organization…returns to the GCL Yankees East, where he began his professional coaching debut as the hitting coach in 2018…served as the DSL Yankees hitting coach in 2019…joined the Yankees after spending the 2017-18 season as the hitting coach and recruiting coordinator at Dawson Community College in Glendive, Mont.…**PERSONAL:** Graduated from Plymouth-Salem H.S. (Mich.)…earned his bachelor's degree in electrical engineering from the University of Michigan and a Ph.D. in physics from the Massachusetts Institute of Technology.

ANTONIO PACHECO – DEFENSIVE COACH
BORN: 6/4/64 in Santiago, Cuba • **RESIDES:** Tampa, Fla.
COACHING CAREER: Enters his sixth season with the Yankees and his fifth in the GCL (2015, '17-present)…spent the 2016 season as a coach with Single-A Tampa…managed Santiago de Cuba from 2004-11, winning three National titles…managed the 2008 Cuban National Team to a silver medal at the 2008 Summer Olympics in Beijing…**PLAYING CAREER:** Played in the Cuban National League from 1983-2001, batting .334 (2,356-for-7,045) with 1,258R, 366 doubles, 63 triples, 284HR and 1,304RBI in 1,853 games…was a five-time Cuban National Series Champion…from 2002-04 played in the Japanese Industrial Leagues with Shidax…is a three-time Olympic medalist, winning the gold in Barcelona in 1992 and Atlanta in 1996, and the silver in Sydney in 2000…**PERSONAL:** Is married with three children.

JULIO BORBÓN – DEFENSIVE COACH
BORN: 2/20/86 in Starkville, Miss. • **RESIDES:** Nashville, Tenn.
COACHING CAREER: Enters his second season with the Yankees, his first in the GCL…began his coaching career as the baserunning/outfield/bunting coach at Triple-A Scranton/Wilkes-Barre in 2019…**PLAYING CAREER:** Was selected by Texas in the supplemental round (35th overall) of the 2007 First-Year Player Draft…the outfielder played parts of five Major League seasons with the Rangers (2009-11, '13), Cubs (2013) and Orioles (2016), hitting .273 with 112R, 19 doubles, 8 triples, 8HR, 76RBI and 47SB in 294 games…helped Texas reach the franchise's first World Series in 2010…finished his career in the Mexican League (2017-18) and independent Atlantic League (2018)…**PERSONAL:** He and his wife, Amber, have two daughters, Bellamy and Annelise…played three seasons at the University of Tennessee (2005-07), where he was named Louisville Slugger Freshman All-America after helping the Vols reach the 2005 College World Series…graduated in 2004 from De La Salle H.S. in Santo Domingo, D.R.…helped the U.S. win gold at the 2006 World University Championships.

JORDAN GOSZTOLA – ATHLETIC TRAINER
BORN: 12/10/93 in South Bend, Ind. • **RESIDES:** Osceola, Ind.
Enters his third season as a full-time trainer, all with the GCL Yankees East…spent 2017 as an intern with the GCL Yankees and extended spring training…earned his B.S. in athletic training from Ball State University (Ind.) in 2017…was a student athletic trainer for the Cardinals athletic department…also completed a student internship at South Bend Orthopaedics-Physical Therapy.

DSL Yankees/International Player Development
The Latin Béisbol Academy • One Yankee Way • Boca Chica, Dominican Republic

DONNY ROWLAND – DIRECTOR OF INTERNATIONAL SCOUTING
BORN: 12/16/62 in Grosse Pointe, Mich. • **RESIDES:** Tampa, Fla.

Enters his 11th season as the Yankees' Director of International Scouting, his 14th season since rejoining the organization, and his 19th season overall with the Yankees (1995-99, 2007-present)…returned to the Yankees in 2007 as a national crosschecker, a role he held for three seasons (2007-09) before being named to his current position in 2010…also served as a national scout and pro crosschecker with the Yankees for five seasons (1995-99)…worked in the Tigers organization for six years as a minor league instructor (1989), area scout (1990) and East Coast Supervisor (1991-94)…was the Director of Scouting with the Angels for five seasons (1999-2003) and Senior Director, Player Personnel with the Royals for three years (2004-06)…**PLAYING CAREER:** Hit .263 in 371 minor league games over five seasons in the Tigers system (1985-89) after being selected by Detroit in the eighth round of the 1985 First-Year Player Draft…**PERSONAL:** In four seasons (1982-85) as an infielder at the University of Miami (Fla.), won two national championships with the Hurricanes (1982, '85)…earned his bachelor's degree in Management and Finance from Miami in 1987…he and his wife, Annette, have two sons, Shane and Tristan…was inducted into the Professional Baseball Scouts Hall of Fame in 2008.

LUIS SOJO – D.R./U.S. TRANSITION AND INFIELD COACH
BORN: 1/3/65 in Caracas, Venezuela • **RESIDES:** Tampa, Fla.

COACHING CAREER: Begins his 25th season with the Yankees (18th as a coach, seven as a player), his third in the D.R./U.S. transition and infield coaching role…managed the GCL Yankees East to the 2017 GCL Championship…managed the Tijuana Toros of the Mexican League in 2016, his lone job away from the organization since 1996…served as an assistant field coordinator in 2015…spent the 2014 season as a coach for Triple-A Scranton/Wilkes-Barre after spending seven seasons (2006-09, '11-13) as the manager of Single-A Tampa (504-451, .528)…led Tampa to the 2009 Florida State League Championship and was named by *Baseball America* as the "Best Managerial Prospect" in the FSL…served on Joe Torre's Major League staff for two seasons (2004-05)…spent the second half of the 2003 season as a special instructor before returning to action as an active player…made his managerial debut with Double-A Norwich in 2002 and led the team to the EL championship…**PLAYING CAREER:** Played parts of seven seasons with the Yankees (1996-2001, '03) and contributed to four World Championships (1996, '98, '99 and 2000)…was originally signed by Toronto as a non-drafted free agent in 1986 and spent parts of 13 seasons with five Major League clubs (Toronto, 1990, '93; California, 1991-92; Seattle, 1994-96; Pittsburgh, 2000; and the Yankees)…hit a career-high .307 in his first full season with the Yankees in 1997…drove in the 2000 World Series-clinching run with a ninth-inning single in Game 5 vs. the Mets…won four Venezuelan Winter League batting crowns and on 12/18/06, recorded the 1,000th hit in his Venezuelan career…is part of an elite group of players to reach the 1,000-hit plateau in both MLB and the VWL…**PERSONAL:** Married to Zuleima and has two children, LesLuis and Luis.

ANDREW WRIGHT – DIRECTOR, DOMINICAN REPUBLIC BASEBALL OPERATIONS
BORN: 2/27/81 in Woodstock, N.B., Can. • **RESIDES:** Largo, Fla.

COACHING CAREER: Enters his second season with the Yankees…served as the Yankees manager of staff development in 2019…was the head coach at Concord (W.Va.) University (2011-15) and the University of Charleston, W.Va. (2016-19), setting single-season school records in wins at both stops…served assistant coaching roles at Concord (2003-04, '10) and West Virginia University (2006-07) in addition to one year (2005) as director of operations at West Virginia…**PERSONAL:** He and his wife, Stacy, have two daughters, Alex and Kennedy…played at Concord from 2000-02, where he earned his bachelor's degree in sport management…completed his master's degree in athletic coaching education at West Virginia.

JOEL LITHGOW – DIRECTOR, LATIN BASEBALL ACADEMY
BORN: 12/4/78 in Santo Domingo, D.R. • **RESIDES:** Santo Domingo, D.R.

Enters his 11th season as the Director of the Latin Baseball Academy…as director, supervises the Yankees' entire Dominican baseball development program…responsibilities include overseeing scouting, player signings and ensuring proper maintenance of all baseball-related facilities…also aids in coordinating community events, such as skill-building baseball clinics…prior to joining the Yankees organization, worked as an attorney in the Department of Investigations for Major League Baseball in the Dominican Republic…is a graduate of the Pontifica Universidad Catolica Madre y Maestra in the D.R.

RAINIERO COA – MANAGER, DSL YANKEES
BORN: 1/2/93 in Puerto Ordaz, Venezuela • **RESIDES:** Puerto Ordaz, Venezuela

COACHING CAREER: Enters his fifth season in the Yankees organization, his first as a manager…returns for his fourth season with the DSL Yankees…spent one season (2019) as defensive coach with the GCL Yankees East…was the DSL Yankees catching coach in 2017-18 and the defensive coach in 2016…**PLAYING CAREER:** Played six seasons as a catcher in the Yankees organization (2010-15), reaching Single-A in 2015…was signed by the Yankees as a non-drafted free agent on 4/30/10…**PERSONAL:** Is married to Claudia.

GABRIEL TATIS – PITCHING COACH, DSL YANKEES
BORN: 5/18/85 in Santa María, Monte Cristi, D.R. • **RESIDES:** Santiago, D.R.

COACHING CAREER: Enters his seventh season in the Yankees organization…returns to the DSL after spending 2019 with the GCL Yankees West…made his coaching debut and spent his first five seasons as a DSL pitching coach (2014-18)…**PLAYING CAREER:** Played five seasons in the Yankees minor league system (2006-10), going 10-10 with four saves and a 4.04 ERA (164.2IP, 74ER) in 97 appearances (three starts)…reached the Single-A level, making 52 relief appearances for Charleston in 2009 and 2010…**PERSONAL:** He and his wife, Rosa Castillo, have two children, Engel Sabriel and Adrián David.

BRETT DeGAGNE – PITCHING COACH, DSL YANKEES
BORN: 8/17/92 in Willmar, Minn. • **RESIDES:** Richmond, Minn.

COACHING CAREER: Joins the Yankees organization in 2020…was the pitching coach at North Iowa Area Community College from 2018-19…served as the pitching coach for the Bismarck Larks of the collegiate Northwoods League in 2018 after a two-year stint in the same role at St. Cloud State (Minn.)…during his playing career as a coach at Sauk Rapids (Minn.) H.S. in 2012…**PERSONAL:** Last name is pronounced "dee-GAHN-yay"…earned his bachelor's degree from the University of North Dakota in 2016 and a master's in educational and administrative leadership from St. Cloud State in 2018.

EDWAR RAMÍREZ – PITCHING COACH, DSL YANKEES
BORN: 3/28/81 in San Rafael de El Cercado, D.R. • **RESIDES:** Santo Domingo, D.R.
COACHING CAREER: Enters his second season with the Yankees organization…**PLAYING CAREER:** Appeared in 103 Major League games with the Yankees (2007-09) and A's (2010), going 7-2 with two saves and a 5.19 ERA (109.1IP, 102H, 66R/63ER, 66BB, 126K)…pitched in eight minor league seasons with the Angels (2002-05), Yankees (2006-09) and A's (2010), posting a 17-18 record and 3.03 ERA (290.2IP, 98ER) over 152 appearances…was named the 2007 MiLB Reliever of the Year…also played in the Mexican League (2011) and Dominican Winter League (2006-15)…was originally signed by the Angels as a non-drafted free agent on 2/6/01.

EDWIN BEARD – HITTING COACH, DSL YANKEES
BORN: 8/31/89 in Moca, D.R. • **RESIDES:** Moca, D.R.
COACHING CAREER: Enters his seventh season as a hitting coach for the DSL Yankees…**PLAYING CAREER:** Played three seasons with the DSL Yankees 1 (2008-10), batting .270 (100-for-371) with a .372 on-base percentage in 110 games…was originally signed by the Yankees as a non-drafted free agent on 7/2/07.

SELWYN LANGAIGNE – HITTING COACH, DSL YANKEES
BORN: 3/22/76 in Caracas, Venezuela • **RESIDES:** Barquisimeto, Venezuela
COACHING CAREER: Enters his third season as a hitting coach with the DSL Yankees…made his coaching debut as the hitting coach for the DSL Mariners in 2017…**PLAYING CAREER:** Played in 704 games over seven seasons as a first baseman/outfielder in the Blue Jays (1996-2002) and Twins (2005) organizations…continued playing in independent leagues and the Venezuelan Winter League for seven more seasons before retiring in 2009.

ARI ADUT – HITTING COACH, DSL YANKEES
BORN: 10/20/92 in Burbank, Calif. • **RESIDES:** Tampa, Fla.
COACHING CAREER: Joins the Yankees organization in 2020 after five seasons as an assistant coach and strength & conditioning coach at Los Angeles Valley College…**PLAYING CAREER:** The outfielder played in the independent Pecos League with the Garden City Wind (2015) and Alpine Cowboys (2016)…**PERSONAL:** Is married to Denver…earned his bachelor's degree at East Central (Okla.) University and his master's in kinesiology from Fresno Pacific (Calif.) University.

CARLOS MOTA – DEFENSIVE COACH, DSL YANKEES
BORN: 1/10/67 in San Cristobal, D.R. • **RESIDES:** Barrio San Jose, D.R.
COACHING CAREER: Enters his fourth season as a defensive coach in the DSL and his 19th season coaching in the Yankees player development system…spent the 2016 season managing the DSL Yankees 1 after serving as the rehab manager of the Yankees' Latin Béisbol Academy for two seasons (2014-15)…also managed the DSL Yankees 2 squad in 2013…joined the Yankees in 2002 after coaching in the Diamondbacks' system from 2000-01…began his career in player development with St. Paul of the independent Northern League…**PLAYING CAREER:** Played for 12 seasons in the minor leagues as a catcher, reaching as high as Triple-A…was signed by Cleveland as a non-drafted free agent in 1986 and played in the Indians system through 1993…also played five seasons in the independent leagues from 1995-99…**PERSONAL:** Married to wife, Runalina Medina, with two children: Carlos and Dahiana…played baseball at San Marcos H.S. in Haina, D.R.

OSCAR ESCOBAR – DEFENSIVE COACH, DSL YANKEES
BORN: 8/24/66 in La Sabana, Venezuela • **RESIDES:** Cabudare, Venezuela
COACHING CAREER: Enters his fourth season in the Yankees organization, his first as a defensive coach…was the manager for the DSL parallel program from 2018-19…previously served as the field coordinator for the Cardenales de Lara of the Venezuelan Winter League from 2012-16…was also a coach for Team Venezuela in the 2006 and 2009 World Baseball Classic…was a coach for Team Venezuela in the 2009 Baseball World Cup…**PLAYING CAREER:** Appeared in 487 minor league games over six seasons with the Blue Jays (1983-87) and Pirates (1988), batting .257 (442-for-1723) with 245R, 66 doubles, 19HR and 165RBI…**PERSONAL:** He and his wife, María Castañeda de Escobar, have two daughters, Osmary and Oscary…managed the baseball team at Universidad Pedagógica Experimental Libertador, where he was also a professor in Integral Education…has a Master's degree in physical education training.

CARLOS VIDAL – DEFENSIVE COACH, DSL YANKEES
BORN: 11/29/95 in Lorica, Colombia • **RESIDES:** Barranquilla, Colombia
COACHING CAREER: Enters his second season with the Yankees, both as a defensive coach in the DSL…**PLAYING CAREER:** Was originally signed by the Yankees as a non-drafted free agent on 5/5/14…played five seasons with the Yankees (2014-18), spending his final season at Single-A Charleston…recorded 15 outfield assists over his final two seasons…was named an Appalachian League Postseason All-Star by Pulaski in 2015 after leading the league in runs scored (49) and finishing third in hits (74) and RBI (46) and fifth in steals (16)…led the DSL with a .482 OBP in 2014…hit for the cycle on 7/30/14 vs. the DSL Marlins.

VICTOR REY – DEFENSIVE COACH, DSL YANKEES
BORN: 6/29/95 in Santiago, D.R. • **RESIDES:** Santiago, D.R.
COACHING CAREER: Enters his second season as a DSL defensive coach for the Yankees…**PLAYING CAREER:** Was originally signed by the Yankees as a non-drafted free agent on 9/13/11…was a catcher and infielder, hitting .228/.324/.306 (170-for-744) with 89R, 34 doubles, 3 triples, 6HR and 85RBI in 230 games over six seasons (2012-17)…spent his first three seasons in the DSL (2012-14) before one season in the GCL (2015) and two with Rookie-level Pulaski (2016-17).

BRIAN REYES – DEFENSIVE COACH, DSL YANKEES
BORN: 6/28/95 in Santo Domingo Este, D.R. • **RESIDES:** Santo Domingo Este, D.R.
COACHING CAREER: Enters his third season as a defensive coach for the DSL Yankees after making his professional coaching debut in 2018…**PLAYING CAREER:** Was originally signed by the Yankees as a non-drafted free agent on 1/4/13 and played five seasons as a catcher in the organization (2013-17)…reached short-season Single-A Staten Island in 2017…in his lone season in the DSL (2013), threw out 40-of-100 (40.0%) attempted base stealers.

ADDITIONAL DOMINICAN SUMMER LEAGUE STAFF
Athletic Trainers, DSL: Yessnar Barela, Logan Eck, Joan Fernandez, Luis Morillo
Latin American Strength & Conditioning Coordinator: Jhoan Perez
Strength & Conditioning Coaches, DSL: Rafael Alvarez, Robinson Palacios
Teachers, Dominican Academy: Carolina Crespo, Joel Alvarez-Barega, Chantal Tejada

Yankees Arizona Fall League Participants

1992 PHOENIX
RHP Andy Cook
INF Bobby De Jardin
OF Carl Everett
LHP Jerry Nielsen
OF Jason Robertson
RHP Russ Springer
Darren London (T)

1993 SCOTTSDALE
RHP Andy Croghan
INF Russ Davis
INF Robert Eenhoorn
RHP Ron Frazier
LHP Keith Garagozzo
LHP Sterling Hitchcock
OF Lyle Mouton
RHP Rich Polak
Billy Evers (M)

1994 PEORIA (J)
LHP Matt Dunbar
INF Andy Fox
INF Rob Hinds
INF Derek Jeter
OF Matt Luke
OF Lyle Mouton
OF Ruben Rivera
Greg Spratt (T)

1995 SCOTTSDALE
LHP Chris Cumberland
RHP Mike DeJean
OF Nick Delvecchio
INF Robert Eenhoorn
INF Andy Fox
INF Rob Hinds
INF Eric Knowles
INF Tate Seefried
Tom Filer (PC)
Darren London (T)

1996 MESA
OF Kurt Bierek
RHP Mike Buddie
INF Matt Howard
OF Matt Luke
RHP Katsuhiro Maeda
OF Shane Spencer
RHP Jay Tessmer
Jimmy Johnson (HC)

1997 PHOENIX
OF Brian Buchanan
INF Homer Bush
RHP Darrell Einertson
RHP Ben Ford
RHP Larry Mitchell
RHP Ray Ricken
Carlos Acosta (PC)

1998 GRAND CANYON
RHP Jason Beverlin
C Mike Figga
INF Rudy Gomez
RHP Mike Jerzembeck
OF Chris Singleton
INF Alfonso Soriano
Trey Hillman (HC)

1999 GRAND CANYON
OF Kurt Bierek
RHP Ryan Bradley
LHP Randy Choate
RHP Craig Dingman
RHP Darrell Einertson
RHP Mark Johnson
OF Donzell McDonald
Tom Nieto (M)

2000 MARYVALE
INF Erick Almonte
RHP Jeremy Blevins
RHP Ryan Bradley
OF Rich Brown
OF Donzell McDonald
RHP Jake Robbins
Carl Randolph (T)

2001 PEORIA (J)
RHP Jeremy Blevins
RHP Ryan Bradley
INF Drew Henson
INF Nick Johnson
RHP Adam Roller
OF Marcus Thames

2002 MARYVALE
RHP Jason Anderson
RHP Bryan Grace
INF Drew Henson
RHP Adrian Hernandez
C Dave Parrish
INF Andy Phillips
OF Marcus Thames
Greg Spratt (T)

2003 GRAND CANYON
RHP Colter Bean
C Michel Hernandez
RHP Sam Marsonek
RHP Ramon Ramirez
INF Ferdin Tejeda
OF Mike Vento
Andy Stankiewicz (M)

2004 GRAND CANYON
INF Yovar Duenas
OF Mitch Jones
LHP Ben Julianel
RHP Sam Marsonek
RHP Eric Schmitt
OF Kevin Thompson
Dave Eiland (PC)

2005 GRAND CANYON
RHP T.J. Beam
INF Eric Duncan*
C Dave Parrish
OF Bronson Sardinha
LHP Matt Smith
RHP Steven White
Darren London (T)

2006 PEORIA (S)
RHP T.J. Beam
INF Eric Duncan
OF Brett Gardner
LHP Sean Henn
RHP Jeff Kennard
C P.J. Pilittere
RHP Darrell Rasner
James Rowson (HC)

2007 PEORIA (J)
INF Reegie Corona
OF Brett Gardner
RHP Steven Jackson
RHP Jeff Karstens^
INF Juan Miranda
RHP Ross Ohlendorf
RHP Kevin Whelan
RHP Steven White
RHP Eric Wordekemper
Tony Franklin (M)

2008 PEORIA (J)
RHP Phil Hughes
OF Austin Jackson
RHP Jeff Marquez
INF Juan Miranda
INF Kevin Russo
RHP Humberto Sanchez
RHP Kevin Whelan
Scott Aldred (PC)
Tim Lentych (T)

2009 SURPRISE
OF Colin Curtis
RHP Grant Duff
LHP Mike Dunn
RHP Ian Kennedy
LHP Zach Kroenke
INF Brandon Laird
C Austin Romine
Tommy Phelps (HC)

2010 PHOENIX
LHP Manny Banuelos
RHP Craig Heyer
RHP George Kontos
INF Brandon Laird
INF Jose Pirela
RHP Ryan Pope
C Austin Romine
Danny Borrell (PC)
Scott DeFrancesco (T)

2011 PHOENIX
RHP Danny Burawa
RHP Preston Claiborne
INF Corban Joseph
INF Ronnier Mustelier
RHP David Phelps
OF Rob Segedin
RHP Chase Whitley
Tom Slater (HC)

2012 SCOTTSDALE
INF David Adams
RHP Dellin Betances
RHP Danny Burawa
OF Slade Heathcott
RHP Mark Montgomery
RHP Zach Nuding
C Austin Romine
Carlos Mendoza (M)

2013 SCOTTSDALE
INF Tyler Austin
RHP Brett Gerritse
LHP Fred Lewis
LHP Vidal Nuño
C Peter O'Brian
LHP James Pazos
OF Mason Williams
Lee Meyer (T)

2014 SCOTTSDALE
OF Tyler Austin
INF Dante Bichette, Jr.
INF Greg Bird*
RHP Caleb Cotham
RHP Kyle Haynes
C Kyle Higashioka
OF Aaron Judge
RHP Alex Smith
P.J. Pilittere (HC)

2015 SURPRISE
RHP Domingo Acevedo
OF Tyler Austin
LHP Ian Clarkin
OF Dustin Fowler
LHP Chaz Hebert
C Gary Sánchez
INF Tyler Wade
LHP Tyler Webb
Jose Rosado (PC)

2016 SCOTTSDALE
INF Miguel Andújar
INF Greg Bird
LHP Nestor Cortes Jr.
RHP J.P. Feyereisen
RHP James Kaprielian
RHP Brady Koerner
RHP Dillon Tate
INF Gleyber Torres*
INF/OF Tyler Wade
Carlos Mendoza (M)

2017 SCOTTSDALE
RHP Albert Abreu
RHP Cody Carroll
INF Thairo Estrada
OF Estevan Florial
INF Kyle Holder
OF Billy McKinney
RHP Andrew Schwaab
LHP Justus Sheffield
Jay Bell (M)

2018 GLENDALE
INF Thairo Estrada
OF Estevan Florial
RHP Jordan Foley
RHP Hobie Harris
INF Steven Sensley
RHP Matt Wivinis
RHP Kyle Zurak
Michael Becker (T)

2019 SURPRISE
RHP Daniel Bies
RHP Derek Craft
RHP Aaron McGarity
RHP Glenn Otto
C Donny Sands
OF Josh Stowers
INF Brandon Wagner
Ken Joyce (HC)

KEY:
(M) - Manager (PC) - Pitching Coach
(T) - Trainer (HC) - Hitting Coach
(J) - Peoria Javelinas / (S) - Peoria Saguaros
^ - Team USA player
* - Arizona Fall League MVP
BOLD - On Yankees 40-man (as of 2/1/20)

Minor League Players and Non-Roster Invitees

ABREGO, Gerardo – RHP
HT: 6-3; **WT:** 190; **B:** R; **T:** R; **BORN:** 4/16/01 in Panamá, Panamá; **RESIDES:** Panamá, Panamá; **OBTAINED:** Signed by the Yankees as a non-drafted free agent on 7/2/19; **M.L. SVC:** 0.000.

ABREU, Joensy – RHP
HT: 6-1; **WT:** 190; **B:** R; **T:** R; **BORN:** 12/29/97 in Santo Domingo Centro, D.R.; **RESIDES:** Santo Domingo Norte, D.R.; **OBTAINED:** Signed by the Yankees as a non-drafted free agent on 3/7/17; **M.L. SVC:** 0.000.

ACEVEDO, Domingo – RHP   NON-ROSTER INVITEE
HT: 6-7; **WT:** 240; **B:** R; **T:** R; **BORN:** 3/6/94 in Villa Los Almácigos, D.R.; **RESIDES:** Villa Los Almácigos, D.R.; **OBTAINED:** Signed by the Yankees as a minor league free agent on 8/26/19; **M.L. SVC:** 0.001; **CAREER NOTES:** Was originally signed by the Yankees as a non-drafted free agent on 10/17/12…**2019:** In his first year as a reliever, went 8-1 with a 4.35 ERA (51.2IP, 42H, 27R/25ER, 14BB, 54K, 11HR) in 32 appearances between Double-A Trenton and Triple-A Scranton/Wilkes-Barre…limited opponents to a .219 BA (42-for-192)…began the season with Trenton before being transferred to Scranton/WB on 6/28…was placed on the Scranton/WB injured list on 8/8 (retro to 8/7) and released on 8/23…was re-signed on 8/26 and immediately placed on the Scranton/WB injured list, missing the remainder of the season…**2018:** Did not appear in a game for the Yankees in his only stint with the club (7/21)…combined with Double-A Trenton and short-season Single-A Staten Island to go 3-3 with a 2.99 ERA (69.1IP, 23ER) in 16 games (12 starts)…missed approximately two-and-a-half months on the minor league disabled list…started the season with Trenton and went 3-3 with a 2.92 ERA (64.2IP, 21ER) in 14 games (10 starts)…allowed 2ER-or-fewer in eight of his 10 starts…made his final two starts of the season with Staten Island, posting a 3.86 ERA (4.2IP, 2ER)…**2017:** Combined with Single-A Tampa, Double-A Trenton and Triple-A Scranton/Wilkes-Barre to go 6-6 with a 3.25 ERA (133.0IP, 48ER) and 142K in 23 starts…ranked among Yankees farmhands in strikeouts (second) and ERA (seventh)…won the Kevin Lawn "Player of the Year" Award, presented annually to the Yankees organization's top hitter and pitcher…began the season with Tampa, going 0-4 with a 4.57 ERA (41.1IP, 21ER) in seven starts before being promoted to Trenton on 5/18…in 14 starts with the Thunder, went 5-1 with a 2.38 ERA (79.1IP, 21ER)…made two starts with the RailRiders in June, going 1-1 with a 4.38 ERA (12.1IP, 6ER)…ended the season on the minor league D.L.…pitched for the World Team in the SiriusXM All-Star Futures Game in Miami…following the season, was tabbed by *Baseball America* as the Yankees' No. 10 prospect and as having the system's "Best Changeup"…was added to the Yankees' 40-man roster on 11/20/17…**2016:** Combined at Single-A Charleston and Single-A Tampa to go 5-4 with 1CG, a 2.61 ERA (93.0IP, 27ER) and 102K in 18 starts…began the season by making eight starts for the RiverDogs, going 3-1 with a 1.90 ERA (42.2IP, 9ER)…was promoted to Tampa on 6/14 and went 2-3 with a 3.22 ERA (50.1IP, 18ER) in 10 starts…tossed a 7.0-inning complete game shutout (5H, 6K, 1HP) on 6/27-G2 vs. Brevard County…following the season, was ranked by *Baseball America* as the No. 10 prospect in the Yankees organization and was labeled as having the "Best Fastball" and "Best Changeup" in the system…**2015:** Began the season with Single-A Charleston, making one start for the RiverDogs (1.2IP, 1ER)…spent the majority of the season with short-season Single-A Staten Island, going 3-0 with a 1.69 ERA (48.0IP, 9ER) in 11 starts…allowed 1ER-or-fewer in nine of his 11 starts with the club, doing so in each of his final seven starts of the season (0.77 ERA, 35.0IP, 3ER in those games)…was named Big Easy's "Pitcher of the Week" for 8/17-23…after the season, made seven relief appearances with the Surprise Saguaros of the Arizona Fall League, going 1-0 with a 2.25 ERA (12.0IP, 9H, 3ER, 3BB, 11K)…following the season, was ranked by *Baseball America* as the No. 3 prospect in the New York-Penn League and the No. 5 prospect in the Yankees organization…was also tabbed by the publication as the "Short-Season Pitcher of the Year" and was named to the Short-Season All-Star Team…**2014:** Made five starts for the GCL Yankees 2, going 0-1 with a 4.11 ERA (15.1IP, 7ER, 21K)…**2013:** Made his professional debut with the DSL Yankees 1, going 1-2 with a 2.63 ERA (41.0IP, 42H, 20R/12ER, 11BB, 43K) in 11 appearances (10 starts)…**PERSONAL:** Full name is Domingo Antonio Acevedo.

Acevedo's Career Pitching Record

Year	Club	W	L	ERA	G	GS	CG	SHO	SV	IP	H	R	ER	HR	HP	BB	SO	WP	BK
2013	DSL Yankees 1	1	2	2.63	11	10	0	0	0	41.0	42	20	12	0	2	11	43	7	0
2014	GCL Yankees 2	0	1	4.11	5	5	0	0	0	15.1	16	8	7	0	1	6	21	2	0
2015	Charleston	0	0	5.40	1	1	0	0	0	1.2	2	1	1	0	0	1	1	1	0
	Staten Island	3	0	1.69	11	11	0	0	0	48.0	37	15	9	2	1	15	53	3	1
2016	Charleston	3	1	1.90	8	8	0	0	0	42.2	34	13	9	1	1	7	48	1	0
	Tampa	2	3	3.22	10	10	1	1	0	50.1	49	19	18	3	2	15	54	1	2
2017	Tampa	0	4	4.57	7	7	0	0	0	41.1	49	29	21	5	2	9	52	0	1
	Trenton	5	1	2.38	14	14	1	0	0	79.1	65	23	21	8	2	17	82	1	1
	Scranton/WB	1	1	4.38	2	2	0	0	0	12.1	12	6	6	0	0	8	8	0	2
2018	Trenton	3	3	2.92	14	10	0	0	0	64.2	51	24	21	3	0	20	52	1	1
	YANKEES	-	-	-	-	-	-	-	-	-	-	-	-	-	-	-	-	-	-
	Staten Island	0	0	3.86	2	2	0	0	0	4.2	5	2	2	0	0	1	3	0	0
2019	Trenton	7	1	3.86	22	0	0	0	0	35.0	23	17	15	7	0	10	33	2	0
	Scranton/WB	1	0	5.40	10	0	0	0	0	16.2	19	10	10	4	1	4	21	2	0
Minor League Totals		**26**	**17**	**3.02**	**117**	**80**	**2**	**1**	**0**	**453.0**	**404**	**187**	**152**	**33**	**12**	**124**	**471**	**21**	**8**

AGNOS, Jake – LHP
HT: 6-0; **WT:** 210; **B:** L; **T:** L; **BORN:** 5/23/98 in Haymarket, Va.; **RESIDES:** Haymarket, Va.; **COLLEGE:** East Carolina University; **OBTAINED:** Selected by the Yankees in the fourth round of the 2019 First-Year Player Draft; **M.L. SVC:** 0.000; **PERSONAL:** Pitched at East Carolina (N.C.), where he set the American Athletic Conference career strikeout record with 295 in just three seasons (2017-19) while compiling an 18-10 record and 3.05 ERA (230.0IP, 78ER) in 55 games (41 starts)…as a junior in 2019, was the AAC Pitcher of the Year was named First-Team All-America by *Collegiate Baseball* and the NCBWA, Second-Team All-America by *Baseball America*, D1Baseball and the ABCA and Third-Team All-America by Perfect Game…set a school and American Athletic Conference record in 2019 with 145 strikeouts and led the league in wins and ERA, going 11-3 with a 2.29 ERA (102.0IP, 26ER) in 17 starts…was also named a 2019 Academic All-American and was the AAC Male and Baseball Scholar-Athlete of the Year as a management information systems major, in which he posted a 3.95 GPA…pitched for the Team USA Collegiate National Team during the summer of 2018…graduated from Battlefield (Va.) H.S. in 2016, where he was named Virginia 6A All-State First Team and Washington Post Player of the Year as a senior.

AGUILAR, Angel – INF
HT: 6-0; **WT:** 170; **B:** R; **T:** R; **BORN:** 6/13/95 in Barinas, Venezuela; **RESIDES:** Barinas, Venezuela; **OBTAINED:** Signed by the Yankees as a non-drafted free agent on 1/17/12; **M.L. SVC:** 0.000; **CAREER NOTES: 2018:** With Single-A Tampa, tied for second in the Florida State League with seven triples…following the season, played for Zulia in the Venezuelan Winter League and hit .287/.320/.447 (27-for-94) with 13R, 6 doubles, 3HR, 17RBI and 5SB in 35 games…**2017:** Was named a South Atlantic League Mid-Season All-Star at Single-A Charleston…**2016:** Was one of three players in 2016 to reach double digits in both homers and steals (13HR/14SB) with Yankees affiliates (Dustin Fowler-12HR/25SB; Mark Payton-10HR/11SB)…following the season, played in a total of 19 games between Magallanes and Zulia in the Venezuelan Winter League (.154, 4-for-26)…**2014:** Was named a GCL Postseason All-Star, batting .311/.373/.576 (47-for-151) with 34R, 11 doubles, 1 triple, 7HR and 31RBI in 39 games with the GCL Yankees 2…ranked second in the GCL in home runs and slugging and 10th in BA…finished second in the Yankees organization in BA.

ALCANTARA, Kevin – OF
HT: 6-5; **WT:** 175; **B:** R; **T:** R; **BORN:** 7/12/02 in Santo Domingo Centro, D.R.; **RESIDES:** Santo Domingo Centro, D.R.; **OBTAINED:** Signed by the Yankees as a non-drafted free agent on 7/12/18; **M.L. SVC:** 0.000; **PERSONAL:** Was ranked by MLB Pipeline as the No. 12 prospect and by *Baseball America* as the No. 15 prospect in the 2018 international signing class.

ALEXANDER, Evan – OF
HT: 6-2; **WT:** 175; **B:** L; **T:** L; **BORN:** 2/26/98 in Plano, Tex.; **RESIDES:** Frisco, Tex.; **OBTAINED:** Selected by the Yankees in the 19th round of the 2016 First-Year Player Draft; **M.L. SVC:** 0.000; **CAREER NOTE: 2018:** Tied for the Appalachian League lead with nine triples at Rookie-level Pulaski…tied with three DSL Yankees players for the most triples by a Yankees minor leaguer…**PERSONAL:** Graduated from Hebron H.S. (Tex.) in 2016…was named a 2016 Rawlings/Perfect Game Preseason All-America honorable mention.

ALFARO, Ricardo – RHP
HT: 6-5; **WT:** 175; **B:** R; **T:** R; **BORN:** 11/27/01 in Panamá, Panamá; **RESIDES:** Panamá, Panamá; **OBTAINED:** Signed by the Yankees as a non-drafted free agent on 8/25/19; **M.L. SVC:** 0.000.

ALONZO, Felix – RHP
HT: 6-2; **WT:** 185; **B:** R; **T:** R; **BORN:** 6/3/99 in Santo Domingo Centro, D.R.; **RESIDES:** Santo Domingo Oeste, D.R.; **OBTAINED:** Signed by the Yankees as a non-drafted free agent on 1/17/18; **M.L. SVC:** 0.000.

ALVAREZ, Asdrubal – INF
HT: 6-0; **WT:** 155; **B:** R; **T:** R; **BORN:** 10/10/99 in Caracas, Venezuela; **RESIDES:** Barlovento, Venezuela; **OBTAINED:** Signed by the Yankees as a non-drafted free agent on 7/2/16; **M.L. SVC:** 0.000.

ALVAREZ, Daniel – RHP
HT: 6-2; **WT:** 190; **B:** R; **T:** R; **BORN:** 6/28/96 in Barquisimeto, Venezuela; **RESIDES:** Barquisimeto, Venezuela; **OBTAINED:** Signed by the Yankees as a non-drafted free agent on 3/14/14; **M.L. SVC:** 0.000; **CAREER NOTES: 2019:** Was an Eastern League Mid-Season All-Star with Double-A Trenton and finished second in the Eastern League with 21 saves while going 7-2 with a 2.31 ERA (58.1IP, 41H, 17R/15ER, 23BB, 76K, 4HR) in 46 relief appearances…recorded the final out of Trenton's Eastern League Championship Series-clinching win…**2018:** Following the season, made 14 appearances for Lara in the Venezuelan Winter League and posted 1-0 record and 3.57 ERA (17.2IP, 7ER)…**2017:** With short-season Single-A Staten Island, his 9.42 K/9.0IP ratio (67K/64.0IP) as a starter was fourth-highest among New York-Penn League starting pitchers…following the season, made 16 relief appearances for the Cardenales de Lara of the Venezuelan Winter League, going 0-1 with a 2.57 ERA (21.0IP, 6ER)…**2016:** At two stops (GCL Yankees East, Rookie-level Pulaski), went 6-1 with a 1.60 ERA (62.0IP, 11ER) in 12 games (10 starts)…led all qualified Yankees minor leaguers in ERA…was 5-1 with a 1.74 ERA (57.0IP, 11ER) in 11 GCL games (nine starts)…finished third in the GCL in ERA, fourth in innings pitched and tied for fourth in wins…prior to the season, appeared in one game for Spain in a WBC qualifier, striking out his only batter in a loss vs. France (3/18/16).

ALVAREZ, Mandy – INF
HT: 6-1; **WT:** 205; **B:** R; **T:** R; **BORN:** 7/14/94 in Miami, Fla.; **RESIDES:** Miami, Fla.; **COLLEGE:** Eastern Kentucky University; **OBTAINED:** Selected by the Yankees in the 17th round of the 2016 First-Year Player Draft; **M.L. SVC:** 0.000; **CAREER NOTES: 2019:** Finished second in the Yankees organization in RBI (76) between Double-A Trenton and Triple-A Scranton/Wilkes-Barre…**2018:** Was an Eastern League Mid-Season All-Star with Double-A Trenton…was also named an MILB.com Organization All-Star…**PERSONAL:** Full name is Armando Francisco Alvarez…played two seasons at Eastern Kentucky (2015-16) after a season apiece at Florida International University (2013) and Miami Dade Community College (2014)…hit .367/.415/.608 (163-for-444) with 28 doubles, 25HR and 105RBI over 105 games at EKU…in 2016, was named Ohio Valley Conference Co-Player of the Year and earned a spot on the ABCA/Rawlings NCAA Division I All-Region Second Team after leading the NCAA in hits during the regular season (97)…graduated in 2012 from Miami Killian H.S. (Fla.).

ALVAREZ, Nelson B. – OF
HT: 6-3; **WT:** 207; **B:** L; **T:** L; **BORN:** 3/10/96 in Santo Domingo Centro, D.R.; **RESIDES:** Santo Domingo Este, D.R.; **OBTAINED:** Signed by the Yankees as a non-drafted free agent on 3/16/15; **M.L. SVC:** 0.000.

ALVAREZ, Nelson L. – RHP
HT: 6-4; **WT:** 220; **B:** R; **T:** R; **BORN:** 6/11/98 in Miami, Fla.; **RESIDES:** Miami, Fla.; **COLLEGE:** University of South Florida; **OBTAINED:** Selected by the Yankees in the 13th round of the 2019 First-Year Player Draft; **M.L. SVC:** 0.000; **PERSONAL:** Pitched one season at USF (2019) after transferring from Miami Dade College (2017-18)…graduated from Braddock (Fla.) H.S. in 2016.

AMBURGEY, Trey – OF NON-ROSTER INVITEE
HT: 6-2; **WT:** 210; **B:** R; **T:** R; **BORN:** 10/24/94 in Lake Worth, Fla.; **RESIDES:** Lake Worth, Fla.; **COLLEGE:** St. Petersburg College; **OBTAINED:** Selected by the Yankees in the 13th round of the 2015 First-Year Player Draft; **M.L. SVC:** 0.000; **CAREER NOTES: 2019:** Spent the entire season with Triple-A Scranton/Wilkes-Barre, slashing .274/.329/.494 (129-for-470) with 73R, 31 doubles, 3 triples, 22HR, 62RBI and 6SB in 124 games…set career highs in runs, hits, doubles and HRs…ranked second in runs, third in hits, tied for third in doubles, fourth in HR and fifth in RBI among Yankees' minor leaguers…tied for fifth in doubles, tied for sixth in XBH (56) and was ninth in hits in the International League…was placed on the minor league injured list on 9/3 and missed the Governors' Cup playoffs…was named an Organization All-Star by MiLB.com. **2018:** Was both an Eastern League Mid-Season and Post-Season All-Star at Double-A Trenton, hitting .258/.300/.418 (124-for-481) with 25 doubles, 2 triples, 16HR, 74RBI and 12SB in 125 games…his 74RBI were tied for the most in the Yankees organization…was also named an Organization All-Star by MiLB.com. **2017:** Batted .236 (109-for-461) with 63R, 19 doubles, 3 triples, 14HR and 57RBI in 121 games with Single-A Tampa. **2016:** Across three levels (Single-A Charleston, GCL Yankees West and East, Single-A Tampa), combined to hit .274 (74-for-270) with 40R, 17 doubles, 3 triples, 2HR, 32RBI and 11SB in 68 games…also appeared in one postseason game for Double-A Trenton (0-for-4)…began the season with Charleston and batted .281 (18-for-64) with 11R, 7 doubles, 2 triples, 1HR, 10RBI and 7SB in 16 games…was promoted to Tampa on 7/3 and hit .279 (53-for-190) with 26R, 9 doubles, 1HR, 22RBI and 4SB in 47 games. **2015:** In his professional debut, combined at the GCL Yankees 1 and short-season Single-A Staten Island to bat .346/.399/.523 (74-for-214) with 46R, 11 doubles, 6 triples, 5HR, 30RBI, 16BB and 21SB in 58 games…led Yankees minor leaguers in BA…was named the New York-Penn League "Player of the Week" in consecutive weeks: 8/17-23 (.500, 7-for-14, 5XBH) and 8/24-30 (.452, 14-for-31, 6R, 7RBI, 5XBH)…was named an Organization All-Star by MiLB.com at the conclusion of the season. **PERSONAL:** Full name is Tommy Wayne Amburgey…hit .368/.409/.522 with 32 stolen bases his final year at St. Petersburg College (Fla.)…graduated from Park Vista Community (Fla.) H.S.

Amburgey's Career Batting Record

Year	Club	AVG	G	AB	R	H	2B	3B	HR	RBI	SH	SF	HP	BB	SO	SB	CS	E	OBP	SLG
2015	GCL Yankees 1	.333	37	135	28	45	5	4	0	12	0	0	4	12	20	14	3	1	.404	.430
	Staten Island	.367	21	79	18	29	6	2	5	18	0	3	1	4	13	7	1	0	.391	.684
2016	Charleston	.281	16	64	11	18	7	2	1	10	0	1	1	6	5	7	0	0	.347	.500
	GCL Yankees West	.231	4	13	3	3	1	0	0	0	0	0	1	1	3	0	0	0	.333	.308
	GCL Yankees East	.000	1	3	0	0	0	0	0	0	0	0	0	0	1	0	0	0	.000	.000
	Tampa	.279	47	190	26	53	9	1	1	22	0	5	3	6	45	4	3	0	.304	.353
2017	Tampa	.236	121	461	63	109	19	3	14	57	0	4	8	33	115	13	3	2	.296	.382
2018	Trenton	.258	125	481	65	124	25	2	16	74	0	5	9	22	108	12	2	1	.300	.418
2019	Scranton/WB	.274	124	470	73	129	31	3	22	62	2	0	6	32	112	6	2	3	.329	.494
Minor League Totals		**.269**	**496**	**1896**	**287**	**510**	**103**	**17**	**59**	**255**	**2**	**18**	**33**	**116**	**422**	**63**	**14**	**7**	**.319**	**.435**

ANDERSON, Reid – RHP
HT: 6-0; **WT:** 205; **B:** R; **T:** R; **BORN:** 9/6/95 in Dallas, Tex.; **RESIDES:** Aledo, Tex.; **COLLEGE:** Brown University; **OBTAINED:** Selected by the Yankees in the 40th round of the 2018 First-Year Player Draft; **M.L. SVC:** 0.000; **CAREER NOTES: 2019:** Tied for second in wins in the Appalachian League, logging a 6-1 record with a 3.09 ERA (46.2IP, 36H, 17R/16ER, 17BB, 51K, 1HR) over 11 games (six starts)…**PERSONAL:** Pitched four seasons (2015-18) at Brown University (R.I.), going 6-15 with one save and a 5.88 ERA (145.1IP, 179H, 114R/95ER, 87BB, 130K, 11HR) in 31 appearances (28 starts)…graduated in 2014 from Aledo H.S. (Tex.), where he won the Texas 4A State Championship in both baseball and football as a senior.

ANDERSON, Ryan – LHP
HT: 6-6; **WT:** 198; **B:** L; **T:** L; **BORN:** 9/9/98 in Reno, Nev.; **RESIDES:** Sparks, Nev.; **COLLEGE:** University of Nevada; **OBTAINED:** Selected by the Yankees in the 12th round of the 2019 First-Year Player Draft; **M.L. SVC:** 0.000; **PERSONAL:** Pitched three seasons at Nevada (2017-19)…graduated from Spanish Springs (Nev.) H.S. in 2016.

ANDRADE, Christian – OF
HT: 6-0; **WT:** 215; **B:** L; **T:** R; **BORN:** 4/14/99 in Caracas, Venezuela; **RESIDES:** Santa Teresa, Venezuela; **OBTAINED:** Signed by the Yankees as a non-drafted free agent on 7/2/16; **M.L. SVC:** 0.000.

ANILLO, Jeison – INF
HT: 5-11; **WT:** 168; **B:** L; **T:** R; **BORN:** 2/16/02 in San Juan Nepomuceno, Colombia; **RESIDES:** San Juan Nepomuceno, Colombia; **OBTAINED:** Signed by the Yankees as a non-drafted free agent on 7/2/19; **M.L. SVC:** 0.000.

ARIAS, Daury – OF
HT: 5-10; **WT:** 170; **B:** L; **T:** L; **BORN:** 8/7/01 in Puerto Plata, D.R.; **RESIDES:** Puerto Plata, D.R.; **OBTAINED:** Signed by the Yankees as a non-drafted free agent on 12/6/19; **M.L. SVC:** 0.000.

ASCANIO, Enyerberth – C
HT: 5-10; **WT:** 170; **B:** R; **T:** R; **BORN:** 12/3/00 in Valencia, Venezuela; **RESIDES:** Valencia, Venezuela; **OBTAINED:** Signed by the Yankees as a non-drafted free agent on 7/2/17; **M.L. SVC:** 0.000.

AVILÁN, Luis – LHP
NON-ROSTER INVITEE

HT: 6-2; **WT:** 220; **B:** L; **T:** L; **BORN:** 7/19/89 in Caracas, Venezuela; **RESIDES:** Doral, Fla.; **OBTAINED:** Signed by the Yankees as a minor league free agent on 1/6/20; **M.L. SVC:** 6.146; **CAREER NOTES:** Was originally signed by Atlanta as a non-drafted free agent on 8/22/05…was acquired by Los Angeles-NL from Atlanta in a three-team, 13-player trade on 7/30/15 that also saw the Dodgers receive LHP Alex Wood, RHP Jim Johnson, INF Jose Peraza, RHP Bronson Arroyo and cash considerations from Atlanta, and RHP Mat Latos and OF Mike Morse from Miami, with Atlanta acquiring INF Hector Olivera, LHP Paco Rodriguez and RHP Zack Bird from the Dodgers and a 2016 Competitive Balance Round A pick from Miami, and Miami acquiring RHP Jeff Brigham, RHP Victor Araujo and RHP Kevin Guzman from the Dodgers…was acquired by Chicago-AL from the Dodgers along with cash considerations in a three-team trade on 1/4/18 that also saw the White Sox receive RHP Joakim Soria from Kansas City, with the Dodgers acquiring LHP Scott Alexander from Kansas City and INF Jake Peter from the White Sox, and Kansas City receiving INF Erick Mejia and RHP Trevor Oaks from the Dodgers…was acquired by Philadelphia from the White Sox in exchange for RHP Felix Paulino on 8/22/18…was signed by New York-NL as a minor league free agent on 1/10/19…has pitched for five clubs over parts of eight Major League seasons, with the Braves (2012-15), Dodgers (2015-17), White Sox (2018), Phillies (2018) and Mets (2019)…has held left-handed batters to a .203 BA (120-for-590) in his career…has pitched for the Cardenales de Lara of the Venezuelan Winter League in six offseasons (following the 2009-12, '14, '16 seasons)…**2019:** Was selected to the Mets' Major League roster on 3/28 and went 4-0 with a 5.06 ERA (33.0IP, 33H, 18ER, 14BB, 30K, 5HR) in 45 relief appearances…held left-handed batters to a .102 BA (5-for-49) with 1HR…did not allow a run over 18 appearances from 5/3-8/20 (13.0IP, 9H, 4BB, 11K)…was on the 10-day I.L. from 5/4-7/2 with left elbow soreness and made four rehab appearances with Triple-A St. Lucie and Triple-A Syracuse (1-0, 2.08 ERA, 4.1IP, 1H, 1ER, 1BB, 6K)…**2018:** Combined to go 2-1 with a 3.77 ERA (45.1IP, 44H, 19ER, 18BB, 51K, 3HR) in 70 games between Chicago-AL and Philadelphia…earned his first Major League save on 8/2 vs. Kansas City…held left-handed batters to a .220 BA (18-for-82)…**2017:** Appeared in 61 games for Los Angeles-NL, going 2-3 with a 2.93 ERA (46.0IP, 15ER)…limited left-handed batters to a .195 BA (15-for-82)…was placed on the D.L. with left triceps soreness from 5/24-6/9…made two rehab appearances with Triple-A Oklahoma City (2.0IP, 1H, 2ER, 1BB, 3K)…was on the Paternity List from 8/8-11…**2016:** Split the season between Los Angeles-NL and Triple-A Oklahoma City, posting a 3-0 record with a 3.20 ERA (19.2IP, 7ER) in 27 appearances across seven different stints with the Dodgers…appeared in five postseason games, tossing 3.2 scoreless innings (4H, 1BB, 3K) in the NLDS and NLCS…**2015:** Combined to go 2-5 with a 4.05 ERA (53.1IP, 24ER) in 73 relief appearances between Atlanta and Los Angeles-NL…was on the Dodgers' NLDS roster, appearing in two games and retiring all 4BF with 2K…**2014:** Went 4-1 with a 4.57 ERA (43.1IP, 22ER) in 62 appearances for Atlanta…suffered his first career loss in his 111th Major League appearance on 4/10 vs. New York-NL…according to *Elias*, his 110 appearances without a loss to start his career was the fifth-longest such streak in Major League history (since 1900)…**2013:** Did not allow a run in 65 of his 75 appearances with Atlanta, going 5-0 with a 1.52 ERA (65.0IP, 11ER)…his career-high 75 games ranked fourth among NL pitchers…finished seventh among Major League relief pitchers in ERA…allowed just 1HR in 65.0IP…limited opposing lefties to a .144 (15-for-104) batting average…made his postseason debut, appearing in all four NLDS games against the Dodgers and tossing 2.2 scoreless innings…**2012:** Was promoted from Double-A Mississippi to Atlanta on 7/5 and made his Major League debut on 7/14 against New York-NL, striking out the only batter he faced (Ike Davis) to end the sixth…made 31 appearances with the Braves, going 1-1 with a 2.00 ERA (36.0IP, 8ER)…recorded his first career win on 10/3 at Pittsburgh…in 16 games (12 starts) at Mississippi, was 3-6 with a 3.23 ERA (61.1IP, 22ER)…**2011:** Spent the entire season with Double-A Mississippi and posted a 4-8 record and 4.57 ERA (106.1IP, 54ER) in 36 games (13 starts)…was added to the Braves' 40-man roster on 11/16…**2010:** Combined to go 6-4 with nine saves and a 3.54 ERA (68.2IP, 27ER) in 41 relief appearances between Single-A Rome and Single-A Myrtle Beach…**2009:** Limited opposing hitters to a .185 average (25-for-135, 1HR) in 14 games (three starts) with Rookie-level Danville, while posting an 0-2 record and 3.05 ERA (38.1IP, 13ER)…was named Appalachian League "Pitcher of the Week" for 7/13-19…**2008:** Pitched in 10 games (four starts) for the GCL Braves, going 0-3 with a 2.58 ERA (38.1IP, 11ER)…**2007:** Spent the entire season with the DSL Braves, posting a 6-3 record and 2.44 ERA (70.0IP, 19ER)…**2006:** Made his professional debut at age 16 with the DSL Braves…**PERSONAL:** His last name is pronounced "ah-vee-LAHN."

Avilán's Career Pitching Record

Year	Club	W	L	ERA	G	GS	CG	SHO	SV	IP	H	R	ER	HR	HP	BB	SO	WP	BK
2006	DSL Braves	2	4	3.29	12	8	0	0	0	41.0	45	17	15	5	4	12	30	2	0
2007	DSL Braves	6	3	2.44	14	13	0	0	0	70.0	54	23	19	4	5	16	71	5	1
2008	GCL Braves	0	3	2.58	10	4	0	0	0	38.1	31	14	11	2	3	15	49	1	0
2009	Danville	0	2	3.05	14	3	0	0	0	38.1	25	14	13	1	4	17	34	0	0
2010	Rome	2	1	2.61	10	0	0	0	0	20.2	15	8	6	1	0	9	21	0	0
	Myrtle Beach	4	3	3.94	31	0	0	0	9	48.0	42	25	21	5	3	18	37	3	1
2011	Mississippi	4	8	4.57	36	13	0	0	1	106.1	113	66	54	10	8	36	78	5	3
2012	Mississippi	3	6	3.23	16	12	0	0	1	61.1	50	27	22	7	1	31	55	5	0
	ATLANTA	1	1	2.00	31	0	0	0	0	36.0	27	9	8	1	1	10	33	3	1
2013	ATLANTA	5	0	1.52	75	0	0	0	0	65.0	40	12	11	1	4	22	38	3	1
2014	ATLANTA	4	1	4.57	62	0	0	0	0	43.1	47	22	22	2	3	21	25	5	0
	Gwinnett	0	1	5.40	9	0	0	0	0	11.2	13	8	7	0	0	11	6	0	0
2015	ATLANTA	2	4	3.58	50	0	0	0	0	37.2	35	15	15	4	0	10	31	1	1
	LOS ANGELES-NL	0	1	5.17	23	0	0	0	0	15.2	13	9	9	2	1	5	18	1	0
2016	Oklahoma City	0	3	4.24	33	0	0	0	4	34.0	35	19	16	3	0	16	37	1	0
	LOS ANGELES-NL	3	0	3.20	27	0	0	0	0	19.2	12	8	7	0	2	10	28	1	0
2017	LOS ANGELES-NL	2	3	2.93	61	0	0	0	0	46.0	42	16	15	2	1	22	52	1	0
	Oklahoma City	0	0	9.00	2	0	0	0	0	2.0	1	2	2	0	1	1	3	0	0
2018	CHICAGO-AL	2	1	3.86	58	0	0	0	2	39.2	40	20	17	2	2	14	46	2	0
	PHILADELPHIA	0	0	3.18	12	0	0	0	0	5.2	4	2	2	1	0	4	5	0	0
2019	NEW YORK-NL	4	0	5.06	45	0	0	0	0	32.0	33	18	18	5	3	14	30	2	0
	St. Lucie	1	0	4.50	2	0	0	0	0	2.0	1	1	1	0	1	1	2	0	0
	Syracuse	0	0	0.00	2	0	0	0	0	2.1	0	0	0	0	0	0	4	0	0
Minor League Totals		22	34	3.54	191	53	0	0	17	476.0	425	224	187	38	34	183	427	22	5
Major League Totals		23	10	3.28	444	0	0	0	2	340.2	293	131	124	20	17	132	306	19	3

BARCLAY, Edgar – LHP

HT: 5-10; **WT:** 200; **B:** L; **T:** L; **BORN:** 5/24/98 in Oklahoma City, Okla.; **RESIDES:** Hilo, Hawaii; **COLLEGE:** Cal State University-Bakersfield; **OBTAINED:** Selected by the Yankees in the 15th round of the 2019 First-Year Player Draft; **M.L. SVC:** 0.000; **PERSONAL:** Pitched one season each at Central Arizona College (2017), GateWay (Ariz.) Community College (2018) and Cal State-Bakersfield (2019)…graduated from St. Joseph (Hawaii) School in 2016.

BARRIOS, Pedro – RHP
HT: 6-1; **WT:** 155; **B:** R; **T:** R; **BORN:** 3/27/99 in Barcelona, Venezuela; **RESIDES:** Barcelona, Venezuela; **OBTAINED:** Signed by the Yankees as a non-drafted free agent on 7/2/15; **M.L. SVC:** 0.000; **CAREER NOTES: 2018:** His 0.70 ERA (25.2IP, 7R/2ER) over five games (four starts) with the GCL Yankees was the lowest ERA in the GCL (min. 25.0IP).

BARRIOS, Wilser – RHP
HT: 6-2; **WT:** 160; **B:** R; **T:** R; **BORN:** 3/21/98 in Valencia, Venezuela; **RESIDES:** Valencia, Venezuela; **OBTAINED:** Signed by the Yankees as a non-drafted free agent on 5/2/17; **M.L. SVC:** 0.000.

BASTIDAS, Jesús – INF
HT: 5-10; **WT:** 145; **B:** R; **T:** R; **BORN:** 9/14/98 in Barquisimeto, Venezuela; **RESIDES:** Cabudare, Venezuela; **OBTAINED:** Signed by the Yankees as a non-drafted free agent on 7/2/15; **M.L. SVC:** 0.000.

BELL, Chad – INF
HT: 6-3; **WT:** 210; **B:** L; **T:** R; **BORN:** 3/4/97 in Fort Collins, Colo.; **RESIDES:** Fort Collins, Colo.; **COLLEGE:** University of Louisiana-Monroe; **OBTAINED:** Selected by the Yankees in the 19th round of the 2019 First-Year Player Draft; **M.L. SVC:** 0.000; **CAREER NOTES: 2019:** Finished fifth in the Appalachian League in HRs (nine) and sixth in RBI (41) with Rookie-level Pulaski…was named App. League "Player of the Week" for 7/8-14 after hitting .429 (9-for-21) with 4R, 1 double, 3HR, 12RBI and 2BB in 6G…**PERSONAL:** Played three seasons at Louisiana-Monroe (2017-19)…as a senior in 2019, was named to the All-Central Region First Team by the ABCA/Rawlings and set a school record with a Sun Belt-high 21 home runs…transferred after his freshman year at Western Nevada College (2016)…graduated from Rocky Mountain (Colo.) H.S. in 2015.

BELTRAN, Lester – LHP
HT: 6-0; **WT:** 190; **B:** L; **T:** L; **BORN:** 1/28/00 in Havana, Cuba; **RESIDES:** Havana, Cuba; **OBTAINED:** Signed by the Yankees as a non-drafted free agent on 7/5/19; **M.L. SVC:** 0.000.

BERNABE, José – RHP
HT: 6-3; **WT:** 160; **B:** R; **T:** R; **BORN:** 1/15/02 in San Francisco de Macoris, D.R.; **RESIDES:** San Francisco de Macoris, D.R.; **OBTAINED:** Signed by the Yankees as a non-drafted free agent on 7/2/19; **M.L. SVC:** 0.000.

BERSING, Jan – C
HT: 6-1; **WT:** 195; **B:** R; **T:** R; **BORN:** 10/17/02 in Maracay, Venezuela; **RESIDES:** Maracay, Venezuela; **OBTAINED:** Signed by the Yankees as a non-drafted free agent on 12/11/19; **M.L. SVC:** 0.000.

BERTSCH, Jackson – RHP
HT: 6-3; **WT:** 225; **B:** L; **T:** R; **BORN:** 2/14/95 in Eugene, Ore.; **RESIDES:** Pleasant Hill, Ore.; **COLLEGE:** Liberty University; **OBTAINED:** Selected by the Yankees in the 29th round of the 2018 First-Year Player Draft; **M.L. SVC:** 0.000; **CAREER NOTES: 2018:** Ranked second in the GCL with seven saves…**PERSONAL:** Pitched two seasons (2017-18) at Liberty University (Va.), going 6-8 with three saves and a 5.08 ERA (127.2IP, 140H, 87R/72ER, 42BB, 134K, 16HR) in 35 games (19 starts)…spent his first two seasons (2014-15) at Lane Community College (Ore.) before transferring and using a medical redshirt in 2016…is a 2013 graduate of Pleasant Hill (Ore.) H.S.

BIES, Daniel – RHP
HT: 6-8; **WT:** 245; **B:** R; **T:** R; **BORN:** 4/9/96 in Redmond, Wash.; **RESIDES:** Woodinville, Wash.; **COLLEGE:** Gonzaga University; **OBTAINED:** Selected by the Yankees in the seventh round of the 2018 First-Year Player Draft; **M.L. SVC:** 0.000; **CAREER NOTES: 2019:** Following the season, played for Surprise in the Arizona Fall League, going 0-1 with a 3.97 ERA (11.1IP, 14H, 6R/5ER, 2BB, 14K) in 10 appearances…**PERSONAL:** Pitched three seasons (2016-18) at Gonzaga University (Wash.), going 12-7 with 3CG, 1 save and a 3.34 ERA (164.1IP, 153H, 67R/61ER, 59BB, 165K) in 35 games (25 starts)…is a 2014 graduate of Redmond (Wash.) H.S., where he also played basketball and golf.

BLANTON, Bryan – RHP
HT: 6-0; **WT:** 190; **B:** R; **T:** R; **BORN:** 12/19/95 in Charlotte, N.C.; **RESIDES:** Albemarle, N.C.; **COLLEGE:** Catawba College; **OBTAINED:** Selected by the Yankees in the 21st round of the 2017 First-Year Player Draft; **M.L. SVC:** 0.000; **PERSONAL:** Spent three seasons at Catawba College (N.C.)…as a junior, went 1-0 with 14 saves, a 2.70 ERA (33.1IP, 10ER) and 50K.

BONIFACIO, Mauro – OF
HT: 6-6; **WT:** 220; **B:** R; **T:** R; **BORN:** 8/31/01 in Villa Mella, D.R.; **RESIDES:** Santo Domingo, D.R.; **OBTAINED:** Signed by the Yankees as a non-drafted free agent on 7/2/18; **M.L. SVC:** 0.000.

BORGES, Ernesto – RHP
HT: 6-2; **WT:** 188; **B:** R; **T:** R; **BORN:** 5/17/01 in San Francisco de Campeche, México; **RESIDES:** San Francisco de Campeche, México; **OBTAINED:** Signed by the Yankees as a non-drafted free agent on 8/24/19; **M.L. SVC:** 0.000.

BOYLE, Sean – RHP
HT: 6-1; **WT:** 205; **B:** R; **T:** R; **BORN:** 10/29/96 in Selden, N.Y.; **RESIDES:** Selden, N.Y.; **COLLEGE:** Dallas Baptist University; **OBTAINED:** Selected by the Yankees in the 25th round of the 2018 First-Year Player Draft; **M.L. SVC:** 0.000; **PERSONAL:** Pitched two seasons (2017-18) at Dallas Baptist University (Tex.) and two (2015-16) at Suffolk County Community College (N.Y.)…in 31 games (three starts) with DBU, went 1-1 with a 4.70 ERA (44.0IP, 53H, 31R/23ER, 14BB, 51K, 4HR)…is a 2014 graduate of Newfield H.S. in Selden, N.Y.

BRAVO, Jesús – C
HT: 5-10; **WT:** 170; **B:** R; **T:** R; **BORN:** 9/16/01 in Cartagena, Colombia; **RESIDES:** Cartagena, Colombia; **OBTAINED:** Signed by the Yankees as a non-drafted free agent on 7/2/19; **M.L. SVC:** 0.000.

BREAUX, Josh – C
HT: 6-1; **WT:** 220; **B:** R; **T:** R; **BORN:** 10/7/97 in Houston, Tex.; **RESIDES:** Tomball, Tex.; **COLLEGE:** McLennan Community College; **OBTAINED:** Selected by the Yankees in the second round of the 2018 First-Year Player Draft; **M.L. SVC:** 0.000; **CAREER NOTES: 2019:** Was named a South Atlantic League Mid-Season All-Star and hit .271 (54-for-199) with 28R, 10 doubles, 13HR and 49RBI in 51 games with Single-A Charleston…**PERSONAL:** Played two seasons (2017-18) at McLennan Community College (Tex.), where he hit .403 (155-for-385) with 121R, 32 doubles, 5 triples, 37HR and 151RBI in 115 games…played for Falmouth in the Cape Cod League and earned the 2017 Silva Sportsmanship Award…was ranked by *Baseball America* as the No. 88 prospect in the 2018 draft…had committed to play his junior season at the University of Arkansas…is a 2016 graduate of Tomball (Tex.) H.S.…was selected by Houston in the 36th round of the 2017 draft but did not sign.

BRISTO, Braden – RHP
HT: 6-0; **WT:** 180; **B:** R; **T:** R; **BORN:** 11/1/94 in Monroe, La.; **RESIDES:** Monroe, La.; **COLLEGE:** Louisiana Tech University; **OBTAINED:** Selected by the Yankees in the 23rd round of the 2016 First-Year Player Draft; **M.L. SVC:** 0.000; **CAREER NOTES: 2019:** Was named a Florida State League Mid-Season All-Star with Single-A Tampa, going 3-1 with one save and a 1.94 ERA (41.2IP, 28H, 11R/9ER, 11BB, 57K, 3HR) in 24 relief appearances prior to his promotion to Double-A Trenton…**PERSONAL:** Graduated from Louisiana Tech after pitching three seasons for the Bulldogs (2014-16)…graduated in 2013 from Ouachita Christian School (La.), where he won five state championships in three sports (two in baseball, two in football, one in track) and was the 2012 Louisiana Class 1A Offensive MVP in football.

BRITO, Jhony – RHP
HT: 6-2; **WT:** 160; **B:** R; **T:** R; **BORN:** 2/17/98 in Puerto Plata, D.R.; **RESIDES:** Puerto Plata, D.R.; **OBTAINED:** Signed by the Yankees as a non-drafted free agent on 11/9/15; **M.L. SVC:** 0.000.

BROWN, Blakely – RHP
HT: 6-0; **WT:** 165; **B:** R; **T:** R; **BORN:** 8/20/96 in Augusta, Ga.; **RESIDES:** Statesboro, Ga.; **COLLEGE:** Georgia Southern University; **OBTAINED:** Selected by the Yankees in the 24th round of the 2018 First-Year Player Draft; **M.L. SVC:** 0.000; **CAREER NOTES: 2019:** Was named New York-Penn League "Pitcher of the Week" for 7/29-8/4 after going 1-0 with a 0.84 ERA (10.2IP, 4H, 2R/1ER, 6BB, 17K) in two starts with short-season Single-A Staten Island…**PERSONAL:** Transferred to Georgia Southern after two seasons at the University of Georgia (2016-17), where he went 2-4 with one save and an 8.45 ERA (43.2IP, 48H, 45R/41ER, 27BB, 53K, 4HR) in 30 games (three starts)…sat out the 2018 season due to NCAA ineligibility…is a 2015 graduate of Statesboro (Ga.) H.S.

BURT, Max – INF
HT: 6-2; **WT:** 185; **B:** R; **T:** R; **BORN:** 8/28/96 in North Andover, Mass.; **RESIDES:** North Andover, Mass.; **COLLEGE:** Northeastern University; **OBTAINED:** Selected by the Yankees in the 28th round of the 2018 First-Year Player Draft; **M.L. SVC:** 0.000; **PERSONAL:** Played four seasons (2015-18) at Northeastern (Mass.) and hit .260 (214-for-824) with 130R, 44 doubles, 12HR, 109RBI and 33SB in 224 games…graduated with Northeastern's school record in games played, starting all of the Huskies' 224 games in his four years…was named Colonial Athletic Association Defender of the Year as a junior in 2017…is a 2014 graduate of St. John's Prep (Mass.), where he also played basketball and golf.

CABELLO, Antonio – OF
HT: 5-10; **WT:** 160; **B:** R; **T:** R; **BORN:** 11/1/00 in Puerto Ordaz, Venezuela; **RESIDES:** Puerto Ordaz, Venezuela; **OBTAINED:** Signed by the Yankees as a non-drafted free agent on 12/22/17; **M.L. SVC:** 0.000; **CAREER NOTES: 2019:** Tied for fourth in the Appalachian League with four triples at Rookie-level Pulaski…**2018:** Was named a GCL Postseason All-Star after hitting .321/.426/.555 (44-for-137) with 21R, 9 doubles, 4 triples, 5HR, 20RBI and 21BB in 40G for the GCL Yankees West…led the Gulf Coast League in slugging and OPS (.981), and finished fourth in OBP and fifth in BA…led Yankees farmhands in BA, hitting a combined .308/.427/.522 (49-for-159) with 26R, 9 doubles, 5 triples, 5HR, 21RBI, 27BB and 10SB in 46G…was named the GCL's "Best Hitter for Average" by *Baseball America*…following the 2018 season, was ranked by *Baseball America* as the No. 8 prospect in the Yankees organization…**PERSONAL:** Was ranked by MLB Pipeline as the No. 8 prospect for the 2017 international signing period.

CABRERA, Marcos – INF
HT: 6-2; **WT:** 190; **B:** R; **T:** R; **BORN:** 10/10/01 in Santo Domingo Oeste, D.R.; **RESIDES:** Santo Domingo Oeste, D.R.; **OBTAINED:** Signed by the Yankees as a non-drafted free agent on 7/2/18; **M.L. SVC:** 0.000.

CABRERA, Oswaldo – INF
HT: 5-10; **WT:** 145; **B:** R; **T:** R; **BORN:** 3/1/99 in Guarenas, Venezuela; **RESIDES:** Guarenas, Venezuela; **OBTAINED:** Signed by the Yankees as a non-drafted free agent on 7/2/15; **M.L. SVC:** 0.000; **CAREER NOTES: 2019:** In 120 games at Single-A Tampa, hit .260 (117-for-450) with 55R, 29 doubles, 8HR, 56RBI and 10SB…had the third-most hits in the Yankees organization…tied for third in the Florida State League in doubles and tied for seventh in hits and total bases (170)…**2017:** Opened the season with Single-A Charleston and at 18 years and 1 month, was the youngest player to make a 2017 Opening Day roster in the South Atlantic League.

CACERES, Wellington – RHP
HT: 5-11; **WT:** 185; **B:** R; **T:** R; **BORN:** 1/29/96 in San Francisco de Macoris, D.R.; **RESIDES:** San Francisco de Macoris, D.R.; **OBTAINED:** Signed by the Yankees as a non-drafted free agent on 1/18/16; **M.L. SVC:** 0.000.

CAIRO, José – OF
HT: 6-2; **WT:** 180; **B:** R; **T:** R; **BORN:** 3/27/01 in Azoategui, Venezuela; **RESIDES:** Azoategui, Venezuela; **OBTAINED:** Signed by the Yankees as a non-drafted free agent on 10/17/18; **M.L. SVC:** 0.000.

CALDERON, Daniel – LHP
HT: 6-1; **WT:** 170; **B:** L; **T:** L; **BORN:** 10/13/97 in Bani, D.R.; **RESIDES:** Bani, D.R.; **OBTAINED:** Signed by the Yankees as a non-drafted free agent on 9/15/16; **M.L. SVC:** 0.000.

CALDERON, Yorlin – RHP
HT: 6-3; **WT:** 155; **B:** R; **T:** R; **BORN:** 8/17/01 in San Francisco de Macoris, D.R.; **RESIDES:** San Francisco de Macoris, D.R.; **OBTAINED:** Signed by the Yankees as a non-drafted free agent on 8/16/18; **M.L. SVC:** 0.000.

CAMACHO, Kevyn – C
HT: 5-9; **WT:** 140; **B:** L; **T:** R; **BORN:** 3/9/02 in Maracay, Venezuela; **RESIDES:** Cagua, Venezuela; **OBTAINED:** Signed by the Yankees as a non-drafted free agent on 7/2/18; **M.L. SVC:** 0.000.

CAMPERO, Gustavo – C
HT: 5-6; **WT:** 180; **B:** S; **T:** R; **BORN:** 9/20/97 in Lorica, Colombia; **RESIDES:** San Antero, Colombia; **OBTAINED:** Signed by the Yankees as a non-drafted free agent on 7/12/16; **M.L. SVC:** 0.000.

CARELA, Juan – RHP
HT: 6-3; **WT:** 185; **B:** R; **T:** R; **BORN:** 12/15/01 in Samaná, D.R.; **RESIDES:** Samaná, D.R.; **OBTAINED:** Signed by the Yankees as a non-drafted free agent on 7/2/18; **M.L. SVC:** 0.000.

CARRIZO, Albert – RHP
HT: 6-4; **WT:** 165; **B:** R; **T:** R; **BORN:** 11/11/99 in Valencia, Venezuela; **RESIDES:** Valencia, Venezuela; **OBTAINED:** Signed by the Yankees as a non-drafted free agent on 2/9/18; **M.L. SVC:** 0.000.

CASTANO, Blas – RHP
HT: 5-11; **WT:** 150; **B:** R; **T:** R; **BORN:** 9/8/98 in Moca, D.R.; **RESIDES:** Moca, D.R.; **OBTAINED:** Signed by the Yankees as a non-drafted free agent on 4/5/18; **M.L. SVC:** 0.000; **CAREER NOTES: 2019:** Led the GCL in innings pitched with GCL Yankees West, going 2-5 with a 4.67 ERA (52.0IP, 67H, 31R/27ER, 11BB, 30K, 6HR) in 11 games (seven starts).

CASTELLANO, Enger – INF
HT: 6-0; **WT:** 190; **B:** R; **T:** R; **BORN:** 12/2/02 in Esperanza, D.R.; **RESIDES:** Esperanza, D.R.; **OBTAINED:** Signed by the Yankees as a non-drafted free agent on 9/4/19; **M.L. SVC:** 0.000.

CASTILLO, Darwin – INF
HT: 5-10; **WT:** 153; **B:** R; **T:** R; **BORN:** 2/26/03 in Barquisimeto, Venezuela; **RESIDES:** Barquisimeto, Venezuela; **OBTAINED:** Signed by the Yankees as a non-drafted free agent on 8/31/19; **M.L. SVC:** 0.000.

CASTILLO, Diego – INF
HT: 6-0; **WT:** 170; **B:** R; **T:** R; **BORN:** 10/28/97 in Barquisimeto, Venezuela; **RESIDES:** Barquisimeto, Venezuela; **OBTAINED:** Signed by the Yankees as a non-drafted free agent on 7/2/14; **M.L. SVC:** 0.000; **CAREER NOTES: 2018:** Was named a Florida State League Mid-Season All-Star and MiLB.com Organization All-Star with Single-A Tampa…earned Most Valuable Player of the FSL All-Star Game…ranked third in the FSL with 122 hits…struck out only 47 times in 514PA with Tampa, the best fifth-best PA/K ratio (10.94) in all of minor league baseball…was tabbed by *Baseball America* as the "Best Defensive Infielder" in the FSL…**2017:** Struck out only 51 times in 510PA with Single-A Charleston, the best second-best PA/K ratio (10.00) in the South Atlantic League…**2016:** Following the season, was tabbed by *Baseball America* as the GCL's No. 19 prospect after spending the season with the GCL Yankees West…**PERSONAL:** Was ranked by MLB.com as the No. 16 prospect for the 2014 international signing period.

CASTILLO, Ruben – RHP
HT: 6-1; **WT:** 160; **B:** R; **T:** R; **BORN:** 6/18/01 in Guasdualito, Venezuela; **RESIDES:** Guasdualito, Venezuela; **OBTAINED:** Signed by the Yankees as a non-drafted free agent on 8/8/19; **M.L. SVC:** 0.000.

CASTRO, Yon – RHP
HT: 6-1; **WT:** 195; **B:** R; **T:** R; **BORN:** 5/23/99 in Cotui, D.R.; **RESIDES:** Cotui, D.R.; **OBTAINED:** Signed by the Yankees as a non-drafted free agent on 1/17/18; **M.L. SVC:** 0.000.

CHAMBUCO, José – RHP
HT: 5-11; **WT:** 160; **B:** R; **T:** R; **BORN:** 6/28/02 in Carora, Venezuela; **RESIDES:** Carora, Venezuela; **OBTAINED:** Signed by the Yankees as a non-drafted free agent on 7/21/18; **M.L. SVC:** 0.000.

CHAPARRO, Andrés – INF
HT: 6-1; **WT:** 200; **B:** R; **T:** R; **BORN:** 5/4/99 in El Vigia, Venezuela; **RESIDES:** El Vigia, Venezuela; **OBTAINED:** Signed by the Yankees as a non-drafted free agent on 7/2/15; **M.L. SVC:** 0.000.

CHIRINOS, Roberto – INF
HT: 5-11; **WT:** 172; **B:** R; **T:** R; **BORN:** 9/8/00 in Pariaguán, Venezuela; **RESIDES:** Pariaguán, Venezuela; **OBTAINED:** Signed by the Yankees as a non-drafted free agent on 7/2/17; **M.L. SVC:** 0.000; **CAREER NOTES: 2018:** Was rated by *Baseball America* as having the "Best Infield Arm" in the GCL…**PERSONAL:** Was ranked by MLB Pipeline as the No. 16 prospect for the 2017 international signing period.

COLMENARES, José – INF
HT: 5-11; **WT:** 155; **B:** R; **T:** R; **BORN:** 4/3/02 in San Cristóbal, Venezuela; **RESIDES:** San Cristóbal, Venezuela; **OBTAINED:** Signed by the Yankees as a non-drafted free agent on 7/2/18; **M.L. SVC:** 0.000.

CONTRERAS, Roansy – RHP
HT: 6-0; **WT:** 175; **B:** R; **T:** R; **BORN:** 11/7/99 in Yamasa, D.R.; **RESIDES:** Yamasa, D.R.; **OBTAINED:** Signed by the Yankees as a non-drafted free agent on 7/2/16; **M.L. SVC:** 0.000; **CAREER NOTES: 2019:** Led the Yankees organization and South Atlantic League in wins, going 12-5 with a 3.33 ERA (132.1IP, 105H, 55R/49ER, 36BB, 113K, 10HR) in 24 starts with Single-A Charleston…also ranked among SAL leaders in ERA (second) and innings (fourth)…ranked fourth in the organization in strikeouts…following the season, was ranked by *Baseball America* as the No. 8 prospect in the Yankees organization and the No. 12 prospect in the South Atlantic League…**2018:** Split the season between short-season Single-A Staten Island and Single-A Charleston, going 0-2 with a 2.42 ERA (63.1IP, 44H, 19R/17ER, 21BB, 60K, 5HR) in 12 starts…began the season by posting a 1.26 ERA (28.2IP, 15H, 5R/4ER, 9BB, 32K, 1HR) in five starts with Staten Island…struck out a career-high 10 batters over 6.0 scoreless innings (2H, 1BB, 1HP) on 6/24 vs. Tri-City…was promoted to the RiverDogs on 7/21 and was 0-2 with a 3.38 ERA (34.2IP, 29H, 14R/13ER, 12BB, 28K, 4HR) in seven starts…following the season, was ranked by *Baseball America* as the No. 7 prospect in the Yankees organization and No. 5 prospect in the New York-Penn League…**2017:** In his professional debut, combined at the DSL Yankees and the GCL Yankees East to go 4-4 with a 4.02 ERA (53.2IP, 60H, 37R/24ER, 17BB, 34K, 4HR) in 14 games (11 starts)…began the season with the DSL Yankees, going 0-3 with a 3.68 ERA (22.0IP, 25H, 15R/9ER, 5BB, 17K, 2HR) in six starts…was transferred to the GCL Yankees East on 7/13 and went 4-1 with a 4.26 ERA (31.2IP, 35H, 22R/15ER, 12BB, 17K, 2HR) in eight games (five starts)…**PERSONAL:** First name is pronounced "roh-AHN-see"…was rated by *Baseball America* as the top Dominican pitching prospect for the 2016 international signing period.

CORDERO, Diego – RHP
HT: 6-0; **WT:** 160; **B:** R; **T:** R; **BORN:** 10/21/99 in Maracay, Venezuela; **RESIDES:** San Francisco de Asis, Venezuela; **OBTAINED:** Signed by the Yankees as a non-drafted free agent on 7/2/16; **M.L. SVC:** 0.000.

CORNIEL, Franklin – RHP
HT: 6-2; **WT:** 165; **B:** R; **T:** R; **BORN:** 10/8/01 in San Francisco De Macoris, D.R.; **RESIDES:** San Francisco De Macoris, D.R.; **OBTAINED:** Signed by the Yankees as a non-drafted free agent on 9/2/19; **M.L. SVC:** 0.000.

CORREA, Nelvin – RHP
HT: 6-1; **WT:** 170; **B:** R; **T:** R; **BORN:** 1/25/97 in San Cristóbal, D.R.; **RESIDES:** San Cristóbal, D.R.; **OBTAINED:** Signed by the Yankees as a non-drafted free agent on 7/2/16; **M.L. SVC:** 0.000; **CAREER NOTES: 2019:** Was named New York-Penn League "Pitcher of the Week" for 8/12-18 after throwing 7.0 shutout innings (3H, 1BB, 5K) in an 8/15 win vs. Lowell with short-season Single-A Staten Island.

CORTIJO, Harold – RHP
HT: 6-2; **WT:** 180; **B:** R; **T:** R; **BORN:** 4/27/98 in San Juan, P.R.; **RESIDES:** Largo, Md.; **OBTAINED:** Selected by the Yankees in the 14th round of the 2017 First-Year Player Draft; **M.L. SVC:** 0.000; **PERSONAL:** Attended Riverdale Baptist H.S. (Md.) where he went 11-0 with a 0.55 ERA and 86K and hit .537 with 33RBI as a senior…had committed to Seminole State Community College (Fla.) prior to being drafted.

COWART, Kaleb – RHP
HT: 6-3; **WT:** 225; **B:** S; **T:** R; **BORN:** 6/2/92 in Adel, Ga.; **RESIDES:** Hahira, Ga.; **OBTAINED:** Signed by the Yankees as a minor league free agent on 12/20/19; **M.L. SVC:** 1.095; **CAREER NOTES:** Was originally drafted by the Los Angeles Angels in the first round (18th overall) of the 2010 First-Year Player Draft…has played in 171 games over parts of five seasons with the Angels (2015-19), hitting .176 (65-for-370) with 42R, 21 doubles, 6HR and 34RBI…has primarily played third base in the Majors (108G/41GS) but has also seen time at 2B (62G/52GS) and 1B (6G/4GS)…has a career .983 fielding percentage (418TC/7E)…converted to a pitcher in 2019…**2019:** Was claimed off waivers by Seattle from Los Angeles-AL on 12/10/18…was claimed off waivers by Detroit from Seattle on 1/24/19…was claimed off waivers by Los Angeles-AL from Detroit on 2/23/19…in 9G with the Angels, hit .160 (4-for-25) with 3 doubles and 1RBI also pitched at Triple-A Salt Lake and Double-A Mobile, going 1-2 with one save and a 10.19 ERA (17.2IP, 26H, 23R/20ER, 15BB, 16K) in 17 appearances…**2018:** Began the season with Triple-A Salt Lake, hitting .287 (74-for-258) with 36R, 20 doubles, 3 triples, 6HR and 45RBI in 62 games…was recalled by the Angels on 6/2 and hit .134 (15-for-112) with 7R, 7 doubles, 1 triple, 1HR and 10RBI in 47 games…did not commit an error in 52 games at 1B (5G), 2B (14G), 3B (24G), SS (5G) and LF (4G)…**2017:** Played a career-high 50 games with the Angels, hitting .225 (23-for-102) with 18R, 5 doubles, 1 triple, 3HR and 11RBI…hit .311 (114-for-367) with 65R, 25 doubles, 1 triple, 12HR and 57RBI in 90G with Triple-A Salt Lake…hit for the cycle on 6/22 at Las Vegas, going 6-for-6 with 5R, 3 doubles, 1 triple, 1HR and 5RBI…**2016:** Was a Pacific Coast League Mid-Season All-Star at Triple-A Salt Lake…hit .280 (116-for-414) with 34 doubles, 5 triples, 9HR and 58RBI in 107 games…recalled by the Angels on 5/25 hitting .176 (15-for-85) with 8R, 4 doubles, 1HR and 8RBI in 31 games…**2015:** Had his contract purchased from Triple-A Salt Lake and made his Major League debut on 8/18 vs. Chicago-AL (0-for-3)…recorded his first Major League hit on 8/22 vs. Toronto (solo HR in the fifth off Marco Estrada)…appeared in 34 games with the Angels, hitting .174 (8-for-46) with 8R, 2 doubles, 1HR and 4RBI…combined with Single-A Inland Empire and Triple-A Salt Lake to bat .285 (118-for-414) with 67R, 27 doubles, 7 triples, 8HR and 68RBI in 113 games…**2014:** Spent the season with Double-A Arkansas, batting .223 (97-for-435) with 48R, 18 doubles, 4 triples, 6HR and 54RBI in 126 games…was named the Texas League "Player of the Week" for 4/28-5/4, batting .419 (13-for-31) with 9R, 3 doubles, 3HR and 12 RBI in 7G…following the season, hit .185 (15-for-81) with 11R, 3 triples, 6RBI and 3SB in 20 games for Mesa in the Arizona Fall League…also appeared in the AFL Rising Stars Game…was ranked by *Baseball America* as the No. 4 prospect for the Angels…**2013:** Hit .221 (110-for-498) with 48R, 20 doubles, 1 triple, 6HR and 42RBI in 132 games for Double-A Arkansas…following the season, was ranked by *Baseball America* as the top prospect in Angels organization…**2012:** Combined with Single-A Inland Empire and Single-A Cedar Rapids to bat .276 (145-for-526) with 90R, 31 doubles, 7 triples, 16HR and 103RBI in 135 games…was named a Midwest League Mid-Season All-Star with Cedar Rapids, batting

.293 (77-for-263) with 42R, 16 doubles, 3 triples, 9HR and 54RBI in 66 games…was named Angels Organization Player of the Year and an MiLB.com organization All-Star…following the season, hit .200 (12-for-60) with 7R, 2 doubles, 1HR, 8RBI and 6BB for Scottsdale in the Arizona Fall League…**PERSONAL:** Full name is Kaleb Bryant Cowart…attended Cook H.S. (Ga.)…won the Gatorade Georgia High School Baseball Player of the Year Award in 2010 after hitting .654/.721/1.206 with 36SB as a senior.

CRAFT, Derek – RHP
HT: 6-8; **WT:** 220; **B:** R; **T:** R; **BORN:** 7/11/96 in Nacogdoches, Tex.; **RESIDES:** Hawkins, Tex.; **COLLEGE:** University of Texas at San Antonio; **OBTAINED:** Selected by the Yankees in the 16th round of the 2018 First-Year Player Draft; **M.L. SVC:** 0.000; **CAREER NOTES: 2019:** Following the season, played for Surprise in the Arizona Fall League (2.1IP, 2ER in 3G)…**PERSONAL:** Pitched three seasons at UTSA (2016-18) and was 3-8 with four saves and a 3.82 ERA (108.1IP, 88H, 50R/46ER, 45BB, 97K, 7HR) in 56 appearances (three starts)…is a 2015 graduate of Hawkins (Tex.) H.S., where he also played basketball.

CRISP, Juan – C
HT: 6-1; **WT:** 170; **B:** R; **T:** R; **BORN:** 5/23/00 in Aguadulce, Panamá; **RESIDES:** Aguadulce, Panamá; **OBTAINED:** Signed by the Yankees as a non-drafted free agent on 2/8/18; **M.L. SVC:** 0.000.

CUEVAS, Frederick – OF
HT: 5-11; **WT:** 185; **B:** L; **T:** L; **BORN:** 10/27/97 in Santo Domingo Centro, D.R.; **RESIDES:** Santo Domingo Oeste, D.R.; **OBTAINED:** Signed by the Yankees as a non-drafted free agent on 7/2/14; **M.L. SVC:** 0.000.

CURTIS, Keegan – RHP
HT: 6-0; **WT:** 175; **B:** R; **T:** R; **BORN:** 9/30/95 in Mobile, Ala.; **RESIDES:** Mobile, Ala.; **COLLEGE:** University of Louisiana at Monroe; **OBTAINED:** Selected by the Yankees in the 22nd round of the 2018 First-Year Player Draft; **M.L. SVC:** 0.000; **PERSONAL:** Pitched four seasons at UL-Monroe (2015-18) and had a 9-11 record with 10 saves and a 5.26 ERA (185.0IP, 206H, 119R/108ER, 72BB, 153K, 14HR) in 72 games (21 starts)…graduated in 2014 from Davidson (Ala.) H.S.

DE LEON, Juan – OF
HT: 6-2; **WT:** 185; **B:** R; **T:** R; **BORN:** 9/13/97 in Santo Domingo Oeste, D.R.; **RESIDES:** Santo Domingo Norte, D.R.; **OBTAINED:** Signed by the Yankees as a non-drafted free agent on 7/2/14; **M.L. SVC:** 0.000; **PERSONAL:** Was ranked the No. 2 prospect by *Baseball America* and the No. 5 prospect by MLB Pipeline for the 2014 international signing period.

DeCARR, Austin – RHP
HT: 6-3; **WT:** 218; **B:** R; **T:** R; **BORN:** 3/14/95 in Foxborough, Mass.; **RESIDES:** Foxborough, Mass.; **OBTAINED:** Selected by the Yankees in the third round of the 2014 First-Year Player Draft; **M.L. SVC:** 0.000; **CAREER NOTES: 2015:** Did not pitch…**PERSONAL:** In one post-graduate season at the Salisbury School (Conn.) in 2014, went 7-0 with a 0.64 ERA (42.0IP, 17H, 3ER, 19BB, 93K)…graduated from Xaverian Brothers H.S. (Mass.) in 2013, where he also played quarterback on the football team…was a 2013 Perfect Game Preseason All-American…had committed to play at Clemson University prior to signing with the Yankees.

DEGLAN, Kellin – C   NON-ROSTER INVITEE
HT: 6-2; **WT:** 205; **B:** L; **T:** R; **BORN:** 5/3/92 in Langley, B.C., Canada; **RESIDES:** Langley, B.C., Canada; **OBTAINED:** Signed by the Yankees as a minor league free agent on 12/12/16 and re-signed on 2/9/18, 9/26/18 and 11/11/19; **M.L. SVC:** 0.000; **CAREER NOTES:** Was originally selected by the Texas Rangers in the first round (22nd overall) of the 2010 First-Year Player Draft…**2019:** Split the season between Double-A Trenton and Triple-A Scranton/Wilkes-Barre, batting .257 (64-for-249) with 33R, 13 doubles, 1 triple, 9HR and 32RBI in 71 games…started the season with Scranton/Wilkes-Barre, where he hit .158 (3-for-19) with 1HR and 2RBI in six games…was transferred to Trenton on 5/1 and batted .265 (61-for-230) with 30R, 13 doubles, 1 triple, 8HR and 30RBI in 65 games…was named Eastern League Postseason MVP after slashing .304/.565/.870 (7-for-23) with 4R, 1 double, 1 triple, 1HR and 4RBI in five games en route to Trenton's Eastern League title…**2018:** Spent most of the season with Single-A Tampa, batting .184 (18-for-98) with 8R, 6 doubles, 2HR and 14RBI in 32 games…also played in 3G with Double-A Trenton (1-for-10) and 1G at Single-A Charleston (1-for-4)…**2017:** Did not play…was invited to Major League Spring Training with the Yankees…**2016:** Spent the year with Double-A Frisco, where he hit .194 (52-for-268) with 24R, 8 doubles, 9HR and 27RBI in 83 games…threw out 26-of-99 (26.3%) attempted base stealers…**2015:** Split the campaign between Single-A High Desert and Double-A Frisco, batting .231 (71-for-307) with 41R, 10 doubles, 13HR and 42RBI in 81 games…began the season with High Desert, where he hit .236 (56-for-237) with 36R, 7 doubles, 12HR and 38RBI in 69 games…was on the temporary inactive list from 7/4-21 to play for gold medal-winning Team Canada in the 2015 Pan Am Games in Toronto…was promoted to Frisco on 8/11 and batted .214 (15-for-70) with 1HR and 4RBI in 19 games…**2014:** Combined at Single-A Hickory and Single-A Myrtle Beach to hit .247/.314/.450 (92-for-373) with 49R, 24 doubles, 1HR and 16RBI in 101 games…set career highs in home runs and RBI…set a career high with 7RBI on 6/24 vs. Kannapolis (3-for-5, 2HR)…following the season, played 42 games for the Melbourne Aces of the Australian Baseball League and hit .287 (45-for-157) with 25R, 6 doubles, 16HR and 36RBI to set a new ABL home run record…**2013:** In 89 games with Single-A Myrtle Beach, hit .231/.331/.393 (71-for-308) with 37R, 10 doubles, 12HR and 49RBI…**2012:** In his second season with Single-A Hickory, batted .234/.310/.438 (75-for-320) with 46R, 23 doubles, 12HR and 41RBI in 92 games…was named an MiLB.com Organization All-Star…threw out 36-of-96 (37.5%) attempted base stealers, the second-highest caught stealing rate in the South Atlantic League…played for Canada in WBC qualifying games in September…following the season, played in 10 games for Surprise of the Arizona Fall League (.171, 6-for-35, 1HR)…**2011:** Spent the full season with Single-A Hickory and hit .227 (66-for-291) with 39R, 15 doubles, 6HR and 39RBI in 89 games…**2010:** Made his professional debut, splitting the season between the AZL Rangers and short-season Single-A Spokane while batting a combined .191 (21-for-110) with 12R, 2 doubles, 1HR and 9RBI in 32 games…was the second-youngest player in the Northwest League at the end of the season…played for Canada in the 2010 18U Baseball World Cup from 7/23-8/1…**PERSONAL:** Graduated from R.E. Mountain Secondary School in Langley, B.C.…played for the Langley Blaze of the amateur British Columbia Premier Baseball League…is one of the highest-drafted Canadian-born players in the history of the First-Year Player Draft…was rated the No. 4 catcher and the top Canadian position player in the 2010 draft class by *Baseball America*…had committed to Florida International University before signing with the Rangers…participated in Team Canada's alumni mentorship program in 2010, where he was paired with Justin Morneau…has represented Team Canada at the 2015 Pan Am Games in Toronto, the 2013 World Baseball Classic qualifiers, and the 2010 18U Baseball World Cup in Thunder Bay, Ontario.

Deglan's Career Batting Record

Year	Club	AVG	G	AB	R	H	2B	3B	HR	RBI	SH	SF	HP	BB	SO	SB	CS	E	OBP	SLG
2010	AZL Rangers	.286	10	28	5	8	0	1	0	5	0	0	1	2	7	0	0	0	.355	.357
	Spokane	.159	22	82	7	13	2	0	1	4	0	1	0	7	21	0	0	1	.222	.220
2011	Hickory	.227	89	291	39	66	15	1	6	39	2	4	8	34	91	2	0	13	.320	.347
2012	Hickory	.234	92	320	46	75	25	2	12	41	1	4	5	32	96	4	4	7	.310	.438
2013	Myrtle Beach	.231	89	308	37	71	10	2	12	49	2	2	14	33	94	0	0	9	.331	.393
2014	Hickory	.251	89	327	46	82	21	2	15	60	3	3	4	34	87	2	0	7	.326	.465
	Myrtle Beach	.217	12	46	3	10	3	0	1	8	0	2	0	1	16	0	0	0	.224	.348
2015	High Desert	.236	62	237	36	56	7	1	12	38	1	1	3	17	76	1	0	4	.295	.426
	Frisco	.214	19	70	5	15	3	0	1	4	0	0	0	3	22	0	0	1	.247	.300
2016	Frisco	.194	83	268	24	52	8	1	9	27	1	2	5	18	108	1	3	10	.256	.332
2017								Did not play												
2018	Tampa	.184	32	98	8	18	6	0	2	14	1	0	3	9	32	0	0	2	.273	.306
	Trenton	.100	3	10	0	1	0	0	0	0	0	0	0	0	3	0	0	0	.100	.100
	Charleston	.250	1	4	0	1	0	0	0	0	0	0	0	0	2	0	0	0	.250	.250
2019	Scranton/WB	.158	6	19	3	3	0	0	1	2	0	0	1	2	6	0	0	0	.273	.316
	Trenton	.265	65	230	30	61	13	1	8	30	0	1	7	17	73	1	0	6	.333	.435
Minor League Totals		**.228**	**674**	**2338**	**289**	**532**	**113**	**11**	**80**	**321**	**11**	**20**	**51**	**209**	**734**	**11**	**7**	**60**	**.303**	**.388**

DeMARCO, Pat – OF
HT: 5-9; **WT:** 205; **B:** R; **T:** R; **BORN:** 3/10/98 in Staten Island, N.Y.; **RESIDES:** Staten Island, N.Y.; **COLLEGE:** Vanderbilt University; **OBTAINED:** Selected by the Yankees in the 17th round of the 2019 First-Year Player Draft; **M.L. SVC:** 0.000; **PERSONAL:** Played two seasons at Vanderbilt (Tenn.) in 2018-19…was a *Collegiate Baseball* Freshman All-American in 2018…attended for two years (2016-17) and graduated from Winder-Barrow (Ga.) H.S., where he was named an All-American and the Georgia Player of the Year as a junior in 2016…also attended Poly Prep in Brooklyn, N.Y., from 2014-15, winning the New York State Championship as a freshman in 2014…was selected by the Yankees in the 24th round of the 2017 First-Year Player Draft but did not sign…father, Paul, played baseball at St. John's University.

DIAZ, Deivi – LHP
HT: 6-0; **WT:** 160; **B:** L; **T:** L; **BORN:** 6/9/99 in Carora, Venezuela; **RESIDES:** Carora, Venezuela; **OBTAINED:** Signed by the Yankees as a non-drafted free agent on 7/2/15; **M.L. SVC:** 0.000; **CAREER NOTES: 2018:** With the GCL Yankees West, tossed 5.0 no-hit innings (1BB, 8K, 1HP) in 8/18 win vs. the GCL Braves.

DÍAZ, Pedro – C
HT: 6-2; **WT:** 202; **B:** R; **T:** R; **BORN:** 11/6/97 in Ponce, P.R.; **RESIDES:** Santa Isabel, P.R.; **COLLEGE:** Carl Albert State College; **OBTAINED:** Signed by the Yankees as a non-drafted free agent on 6/29/17; **M.L. SVC:** 0.000; **PERSONAL:** In one season at Carl Albert State (Okla.), hit .282 (20-for-71) with a .407 OBP.

DÍAZ, Wellington – RHP
HT: 6-4; **WT:** 190; **B:** R; **T:** R; **BORN:** 4/25/97 in Santo Domingo Este, D.R.; **RESIDES:** Cabarete, D.R.; **OBTAINED:** Signed by the Yankees as a non-drafted free agent on 7/2/16; **M.L. SVC:** 0.000.

DÍAZ, Yoljeldriz – RHP
HT: 5-11; **WT:** 165; **B:** R; **T:** R; **BORN:** 7/14/01 in San Felipe, Venezuela; **RESIDES:** San Felipe, Venezuela; **OBTAINED:** Signed by the Yankees as a non-drafted free agent on 12/12/18; **M.L. SVC:** 0.000.

DOMINGUEZ, Jasson – OF
HT: 5-11; **WT:** 195; **B:** S; **T:** R; **BORN:** 2/7/03 in Esperanza, D.R.; **RESIDES:** Esperanza, D.R.; **OBTAINED:** Signed by the Yankees as a non-drafted free agent on 7/2/19; **M.L. SVC:** 0.000; **CAREER NOTES: 2019:** Following the season, was named the Yankees' No. 1 prospect and No. 38 overall prospect by *Baseball America*…was tabbed by MLB Pipeline as the No. 2 Yankees prospect and No. 66 overall prospect…**PERSONAL:** First name is pronounced "JAY-sun"…was the top-ranked prospect by MLB.com for the 2019 international signing period.

DUNN, Oliver – INF
HT: 5-10; **WT:** 190; **B:** L; **T:** R; **BORN:** 9/2/97 in Salt Lake City, Utah; **RESIDES:** Salt Lake City, Utah; **COLLEGE:** University of Utah; **OBTAINED:** Selected by the Yankees in the 11th round of the 2019 First-Year Player Draft; **M.L. SVC:** 0.000; **PERSONAL:** Played three seasons at Utah (2017-19) and was named a Third-Team All-American by *Collegiate Baseball* in 2019…graduated from Cottonwood (Utah) H.S. in 2016.

DURAN, Ezequiel – INF
HT: 5-11; **WT:** 185; **B:** R; **T:** R; **BORN:** 5/22/99 in San Juan De La Maguana, D.R.; **RESIDES:** San Juan De La Maguana, D.R.; **OBTAINED:** Signed by the Yankees as a non-drafted free agent on 7/2/17; **M.L. SVC:** 0.000; **CAREER NOTES: 2019:** Was named a Short-Season All-Star by Baseball America after hitting .256 (63-for-246) with 49R, 12 doubles, 4 triples, 13HR, 37RBI and 11SB in 66 games with short-season Single-A Staten Island…led the New York-Penn League in home runs and ranked second in runs, extra-base hits (29) and total bases (122), third in slugging (.496) and sixth in RBI…was ranked the No. 7 prospect in the NYPL by *Baseball America*…was named NYPL "Player of the Month" for July (.333, 36-for-108, 23R, 7 doubles, 2 triples, 7HR, 20RBI in 26G)…earned NYPL "Player of the Week" honors for 7/15-21 (.462, 12-for-26, 5R, 4 doubles, 2HR, 5RBI in 6G).

ERNST, Nick – RHP
HT: 6-3; **WT:** 195; **B:** R; **T:** R; **BORN:** 8/27/96 in Cincinnati, Ohio; **RESIDES:** Cincinnati, Ohio; **COLLEGE:** Miami University; **OBTAINED:** Selected by the Yankees in the 15th round of the 2018 First-Year Player Draft; **M.L. SVC:** 0.000; **PERSONAL:** Pitched three seasons (2016-18) at Miami (Ohio) University and went 7-3 with six saves and a 2.91 ERA (102.0IP, 80H, 39R/33ER, 45BB, 90K, 4HR) in 46 appearances (three starts)…graduated from La Salle (Ohio) H.S. in 2015, where he also played basketball.

ESCANIO, Brenny – INF
HT: 5-9; **WT:** 145; **B:** S; **T:** R; **BORN:** 12/16/02 in Azua, D.R.; **RESIDES:** Azua, D.R.; **OBTAINED:** Acquired by the Yankees from the Milwaukee Brewers in exchange for RHP J.P. Feyereisen on 9/1/19; **M.L. SVC:** 0.000; **CAREER NOTES:** Was originally signed by the Milwaukee Brewers as a non-drafted free agent on 7/2/19…did not appear in a game in the Brewers organization.

ESCOBAR, Elvis – LHP
HT: 5-10; **WT:** 180; **B:** L; **T:** L; **BORN:** 9/6/94 in La Guaira, Venezuela; **RESIDES:** La Guaira, Venezuela; **OBTAINED:** Signed by the Yankees as a minor league free agent on 12/19/19; **M.L. SVC:** 0.000; **CAREER NOTES:** Was originally signed by the Pittsburgh Pirates on 7/2/11…played the first six years of his career as an outfielder before converting to the mound in 2018…earned Florida State League "Player of the Week" honors from 7/10-16/16 with Single-A Bradenton…was a 2015 South Atlantic League Mid-Season All-Star with Single-A West Virginia.

ESCOTTO, Maikol – INF
HT: 5-11; **WT:** 175; **B:** R; **T:** R; **BORN:** 6/4/02 in Boca Chica, D.R.; **RESIDES:** Santo Domingo, D.R.; **OBTAINED:** Signed by the Yankees as a non-drafted free agent on 7/2/18; **M.L. SVC:** 0.000; **CAREER NOTES: 2019:** Led Yankees farmhands in batting average, hitting .315/.432/.552 (57-for-181) with 47R, 11 doubles, 4 triples, 8HR, 26RBI, 13SB and 32BBfor the DSL Yankees…was fifth in the DSL in HRs while his .981 OPS also ranked fifth (min. 200PA).

ESPANA, Juan – RHP
HT: 5-9; **WT:** 145; **B:** R; **T:** R; **BORN:** 2/19/02 in Sincelejo, Colombia; **RESIDES:** Sincelejo, Colombia; **OBTAINED:** Signed by the Yankees as a non-drafted free agent on 8/15/19; **M.L. SVC:** 0.000.

ESPINAL, Carlos – RHP
HT: 5-11; **WT:** 175; **B:** R; **T:** R; **BORN:** 10/21/96 in Santiago de los Caballeros, D.R.; **RESIDES:** Santiago de los Caballeros, D.R.; **OBTAINED:** Signed by the Yankees as a non-drafted free agent on 2/27/15; **M.L. SVC:** 0.000; **CAREER NOTES: 2018:** Following the season, made seven appearances for Escogido in the Dominican Winter League and posted a 4.66 ERA (9.2IP, 5ER)…**2016:** Did not pitch…**2015:** Made his professional debut with the DSL Yankees 2, and ranked eighth in the DSL (min. 60.0IP) with a 5.90 K/BB ratio (59K/10BB).

ESPINO, Kelvin – OF
HT: 6-2; **WT:** 170; **B:** L; **T:** R; **BORN:** 12/8/01 in Santo Domingo Este, D.R.; **RESIDES:** San Pedro de Macoris, D.R.; **OBTAINED:** Signed by the Yankees as a non-drafted free agent on 10/15/18; **M.L. SVC:** 0.000.

ESTEVEZ, Abel – RHP
HT: 6-1; **WT:** 170; **B:** R; **T:** R; **BORN:** 1/17/00 in Dajabon, D.R.; **RESIDES:** Dajabon, D.R.; **OBTAINED:** Signed by the Yankees as a non-drafted free agent on 7/2/16; **M.L. SVC:** 0.000.

EVEY, Marcus – RHP
HT: 5-10; **WT:** 175; **B:** R; **T:** R; **BORN:** 8/4/97 in Salem, Ore.; **RESIDES:** Old Hickory, Tenn.; **COLLEGE:** Tennessee Tech University; **OBTAINED:** Selected by the Yankees in the 20th round of the 2018 First-Year Player Draft; **M.L. SVC:** 0.000; **PERSONAL:** In three seasons (2016-18) at Tennessee Tech, went 10-0 with a 5.00 ERA (122.1IP, 110H, 81R/68ER, 55BB, 148K, 15HR) over 51 games (15 starts)…graduated from Blackman (Tenn.) H.S. in 2015.

FAMILIA, Christopher – OF
HT: 5-11; **WT:** 170; **B:** L; **T:** L; **BORN:** 6/10/00 in Bani, D.R.; **RESIDES:** Santo Domingo, D.R.; **OBTAINED:** Signed by the Yankees as a non-drafted free agent on 7/2/18; **M.L. SVC:** 0.000.

FARRELL, Jake – INF
HT: 6-4; **WT:** 215; **B:** L; **T:** R; **BORN:** 5/10/96 in Newton, Mass.; **RESIDES:** Boston, Mass.; **COLLEGE:** Northeastern University; **OBTAINED:** Selected by the Yankees in the 39th round of the 2019 First-Year Player Draft; **M.L. SVC:** 0.000; **PERSONAL:** Played four seasons at Northeastern (Mass.) University (2016-19), where he left as the school's all-time triples leader (16)…graduated in 2015 from Xaverian Brothers (Mass.) H.S., where he won a state football championship as a quarterback and was also a league All-Star in hockey.

FAVELO, Wilfre – OF
HT: 6-0; **WT:** 170; **B:** R; **T:** R; **BORN:** 4/1/01 in Puerto La Cruz, Venezuela; **RESIDES:** Puerto La Cruz, Venezuela; **OBTAINED:** Signed by the Yankees as a non-drafted free agent on 12/4/17; **M.L. SVC:** 0.000.

FELIZ, Maiker – RHP
HT: 6-0; **WT:** 226; **B:** R; **T:** R; **BORN:** 8/17/97 in Bani, D.R.; **RESIDES:** Bani, D.R.; **OBTAINED:** Signed by the Yankees as a minor league free agent on 4/9/19; **M.L. SVC:** 0.000; **CAREER NOTES:** Was originally signed by the Chicago White Sox as a non-drafted free agent on 8/28/13…spent all five seasons in the White Sox organization as a third baseman before converting to pitcher upon signing with the Yankees.

FERREIRA, Ricardo – OF
HT: 5-11; **WT:** 175; **B:** S; **T:** R; **BORN:** 2/3/95 in Santo Domingo Norte, D.R.; **RESIDES:** Santo Domingo Norte, D.R.; **OBTAINED:** Signed by the Yankees as a non-drafted free agent on 1/27/14; **M.L. SVC:** 0.000; **CAREER NOTES: 2017:** Did not play…**2016:** Ranked fifth in the organization with 26SB…**2015:** Won the DSL batting title (.382) with the DSL Yankees 1 and led the league in runs scored (76), OBP (.513), OPS (1.005) and walks (59)…ranked second in the DSL in hits and SB…reached base safely in 60-of-62 games and recorded 31 multi-hit games.

FULGENCIO, Steven – RHP
HT: 6-2; **WT:** 175; **B:** R; **T:** R; **BORN:** 10/5/00 in San Pedro de Macoris, D.R.; **RESIDES:** San Pedro de Macoris, D.R.; **OBTAINED:** Signed by the Yankees as a non-drafted free agent on 10/15/18; **M.L. SVC:** 0.000.

GALLARDO, Carlos – C
HT: 5-10; **WT:** 160; **B:** R; **T:** R; **BORN:** 1/26/97 in La Victoria, Venezuela; **RESIDES:** La Victoria, Venezuela; **OBTAINED:** Signed by the Yankees as a non-drafted free agent on 12/16/14; **M.L. SVC:** 0.000.

GARCIA, Alex – INF
HT: 5-10; **WT:** 155; **B:** S; **T:** R; **BORN:** 12/8/01 in San Cristóbal, D.R.; **RESIDES:** San Cristóbal, D.R.; **OBTAINED:** Signed by the Yankees as a non-drafted free agent on 10/15/18; **M.L. SVC:** 0.000.

GARCIA, Alfredo – LHP
HT: 6-1; **WT:** 177; **B:** L; **T:** L; **BORN:** 8/8/98 in Puerto Ordaz, Venezuela; **RESIDES:** Puerto Ordaz, Venezuela; **OBTAINED:** Acquired by the Yankees from the Colorado Rockies in exchange for RHP Joséph Harvey on 7/31/19; **M.L. SVC:** 0.000; **CAREER NOTES:** Was originally signed by the Colorado Rockies as a non-drafted free agent on 7/2/16.

GARCIA, Anthony – OF
HT: 6-5; **WT:** 204; **B:** S; **T:** R; **BORN:** 9/5/00 in Sánchez, D.R.; **RESIDES:** Sánchez, D.R.; **OBTAINED:** Signed by the Yankees as a non-drafted free agent on 7/2/17; **M.L. SVC:** 0.000; **CAREER NOTES: 2018:** Led the GCL with 10HR in 44 games while playing for the GCL Yankees West…was fifth in the league with a .513 SLG…logged his first two multi-HR games, on 6/23 at GCL Phillies West (2HR) and 8/17 at GCL Yankees East (2HR)…**PERSONAL:** Was ranked by *Baseball America* as the No. 28 prospect for the 2017 international signing period.

GARCIA, Dermis – INF
HT: 6-3; **WT:** 200; **B:** R; **T:** R; **BORN:** 1/7/98 in Santo Domingo Centro, D.R.; **RESIDES:** San Pedro de Macoris, D.R.; **OBTAINED:** Signed by the Yankees as a non-drafted free agent on 7/2/14; **M.L. SVC:** 0.000; **CAREER NOTES: 2019:** Led the Florida State League in home runs, batting .247 (67-for-271) with 35R, 15 doubles, 17HR and 54RBI in 75 games with Single-A Tampa…earned FSL Mid-Season and Postseason All-Star honors…**2017:** Ranked third among Yankees minor leaguers with 17HR…homered in five consecutive games from 7/29 (G1)-8/1…**2016:** Finished among Appalachian League leaders in home runs (13, second), walks (32, fifth), extra-base hits (22, tied for eighth) and slugging percentage (.454, ninth)…logged his first career multi-HR game on 7/3 vs. Bristol (2HR)…**PERSONAL:** Was ranked by MLB.com as the top prospect for the 2014 international signing period.

GARCIA, Donys – RHP
HT: 6-2; **WT:** 174; **B:** R; **T:** R; **BORN:** 2/18/01 in Maracay, Venezuela; **RESIDES:** Estado Aragua, Venezuela; **OBTAINED:** Signed by the Yankees as a non-drafted free agent on 7/12/19; **M.L. SVC:** 0.000.

GARCIA, Nicolas – C
HT: 5-11; **WT:** 200; **B:** R; **T:** R; **BORN:** 6/15/01 in Santo Domingo Centro, D.R.; **RESIDES:** Santo Domingo Este, D.R.; **OBTAINED:** Signed by the Yankees as a non-drafted free agent on 7/2/18; **M.L. SVC:** 0.000.

GARCIA, Wilkerman – INF
HT: 6-0; **WT:** 176; **B:** S; **T:** R; **BORN:** 4/1/98 in Maracay, Venezuela; **RESIDES:** Maracay, Venezuela; **OBTAINED:** Signed by the Yankees as a non-drafted free agent on 7/2/14; **M.L. SVC:** 0.000; **CAREER NOTES: 2018:** Following the season, played for Magallanes in the Venezuelan Winter League and hit .262 (11-for-42) with 9R, 2 doubles, 1HR and 8RBI in 14 games…**2015:** Following the season, was ranked by *Baseball America* as the No. 6 prospect in the Gulf Coast League and No. 9 prospect in the Yankees organization…**PERSONAL:** Was ranked by *Baseball America* as the No. 7 prospect for the 2014 international signing period.

GASPER, Mickey – INF
HT: 5-10; **WT:** 205; **B:** S; **T:** R; **BORN:** 10/11/95 in Highland Park, N.J.; **RESIDES:** Merrimack, N.H.; **COLLEGE:** Bryant University; **OBTAINED:** Selected by the Yankees in the 27th round of the 2018 First-Year Player Draft; **M.L. SVC:** 0.000; **CAREER NOTES: 2019:** Was named a South Atlantic League Mid-Season All-Star with Single-A Charleston…**PERSONAL:** In four seasons (2015-18) at Bryant University (R.I.), hit .344 (174-for-506) with 127R, 32 doubles, 4 triples, 17HR, 119RBI and 102BB over 165 games…graduated in 2014 from Merrimack (N.H.) H.S., where he also played basketball.

GERMAN, Frank – RHP
HT: 6-2; **WT:** 195; **B:** R; **T:** R; **BORN:** 9/22/97 in Queens, N.Y.; **RESIDES:** Tampa, Fla.; **COLLEGE:** University of North Florida; **OBTAINED:** Selected by the Yankees in the fourth round of the 2018 First-Year Player Draft; **M.L. SVC:** 0.000; **PERSONAL:** Last name is pronounced "JURR-min"…pitched three seasons (2016-18) at North Florida, going 18-8 with a 2.36 ERA (205.2IP, 169H, 67R/54ER, 52BB, 206K, 12HR) in 42 games (35 starts)…as a junior in 2018, was named a semifinalist for the Golden Spikes Award, given to the nation's top collegiate player, and received All-America honors from D1Baseball (second team) and Perfect Game/Rawlings (third team)…is a 2015 graduate of Bishop McLaughlin H.S. in Spring Hill, Fla.

GIACONE, Michael – LHP
HT: 6-0; **WT:** 175; **B:** L; **T:** L; **BORN:** 10/23/96 in Fountain Valley, Calif.; **RESIDES:** Savannah, Ga.; **COLLEGE:** North Greenville University; **OBTAINED:** Selected by the Yankees in the 28th round of the 2019 First-Year Player Draft; **M.L. SVC:** 0.000. **PERSONAL:** Pitched one season (2019) at North Greenville (S.C.) University after two years (2017-18) at Orange Coast (Calif.) Community College…was named a 2019 ABCA/Rawlings Division II Second-Team All-Southeast Region…graduated from Ocean View (Calif.) H.S. in 2016.

GILLIAM, Isiah – OF
HT: 6-3; **WT:** 220; **B:** S; **T:** R; **BORN:** 7/23/96 in Lilburn, Ga.; **RESIDES:** Marianna, Fla.; **COLLEGE:** Chipola College; **OBTAINED:** Selected by the Yankees in the 20th round of the 2015 First-Year Player Draft; **M.L. SVC:** 0.000; **CAREER NOTES: 2019:** Was named a Florida State League Mid-Season All-Star with Single-A Tampa…**2018:** In 125 games with Single-A Tampa, batted .259 (123-for-474) with 59R, 22 doubles, 2 triples, 13HR and 71RBI…tied for the FSL lead in games played, ranked second in hits, third in RBI and tied for third in total bases (188)…was third in the Yankees organization in RBI…**2017:** Hit .275/.356/.468 (122-for-444) with 80R, 33 doubles, 4 triples, 15HR, 85RBI and 9SB in 125 games with Single-A Charleston…ranked second among Yankees minor leaguers in RBI…finished second in the South Atlantic League in RBI and runs scored, third in doubles, fourth in SLG and extra-base hits (52) and fifth in total bases (208)…was named the SAL "Player of the Week" three times: 5/8-14, 7/31-8/6 and 8/28-9/3…**2016:** With Rookie-level Pulaski, tied for third in the Appalachian League in XBH (24) and tied for fourth in HRs (10)…recorded his first career 2HR game on 8/14 (G1) at Bristol…**PERSONAL:** In his only season with Chipola College (Fla.) in 2015, batted .362 (68-for-188) and led the team with 52RBI in 52 games…was named a NJCAA Third-Team All-American.

GITTENS, Chris – INF   NON-ROSTER INVITEE
HT: 6-4; **WT:** 250; **B:** R; **T:** R; **BORN:** 2/4/94 in Sherman, Tex.; **RESIDES:** Sherman, Tex.; **COLLEGE:** Grayson College; **OBTAINED:** Selected by the Yankees in the 12th round of the 2014 First-Year Player Draft; **M.L. SVC:** 0.000; **CAREER NOTES: 2019:** Became the second player in Double-A Trenton franchise history to win the Eastern League MVP award (Brandon Laird in 2010)…appeared in 115 games and hit .281/.393/.500 (112-for-398) with 58R, 16 doubles, 23HR, 77RBI and 71BB…was named an Eastern League Mid-Season and Postseason All-Star…earned Organization All-Star honors from MiLB.com and was named the "Best Defensive First Baseman" in the Eastern League by *Baseball America*…led Yankees farmhands in RBI and tied for second-most in homers, while finishing second in walks…**2018:** Combined with Double-A Trenton and short-season Single-A Staten Island to hit .193 (38-for-197) with 21R, 9 doubles, 6HR, 27RBI and 28BB…**2017:** Batted .268 (66-for-248) with 35R, 12 doubles, 13HR, 43RBI and 37BB in 73 games with Single-A Tampa…**2016:** With Single-A Charleston, was named to the SAL Postseason All-Star Team after finishing second in the South Atlantic League in HRs (21) and pacing the league with a 18.24 AB/HR ratio (383AB/21HR)…led the SAL and tied for third in the minors with four multi-HR games…tied for the highest HR total among Yankees minor leaguers and ranked fifth in RBI (70) to earn MiLB.com Organization All-Star honors…**2015:** Was named a GCL Postseason All-Star with the GCL Yankees 1, batting .363 (45-for-124) with 25R, 9 doubles, 1 triple, 8HR, 29RBI and 17BB in 41 games…ranked third in the GCL in home runs and extra-base hits (18) and tied for third in RBI…**PERSONAL:** Graduated from Sherman H.S. (Tex.) in 2012…played at Grayson College (Tex.).

Gittens's Career Batting Record

Year	Club	AVG	G	AB	R	H	2B	3B	HR	RBI	SH	SF	HP	BB	SO	SB	CS	E	OBP	SLG
2014	GCL Yankees 2	.286	11	35	6	10	4	0	0	5	0	2	1	7	10	0	0	1	.400	.400
2015	GCL Yankees 1	.363	41	124	25	45	9	1	8	29	0	1	4	17	33	2	2	1	.452	.645
	Tampa	.143	5	14	0	2	0	0	0	1	0	0	0	1	3	0	0	0	.200	.143
2016	Charleston	.253	107	383	57	97	23	0	21	70	0	3	9	56	126	4	2	16	.359	.478
2017	Tampa	.266	73	248	35	66	12	0	13	43	0	0	5	37	79	1	1	6	.372	.472
2018	Trenton	.197	53	183	21	36	8	0	6	26	0	2	1	27	65	0	1	4	.300	.339
	Staten Island	.143	4	14	0	2	1	0	0	1	0	0	0	1	5	0	0	0	.200	.214
2019	Trenton	.281	115	398	58	112	16	1	23	77	0	4	5	71	139	0	0	6	.393	.500
Minor League Totals		**.264**	**409**	**1399**	**202**	**370**	**73**	**2**	**71**	**252**	**0**	**12**	**25**	**217**	**460**	**7**	**6**	**34**	**.370**	**.472**

GOMEZ, Antonio – C
HT: 6-2; **WT:** 211; **B:** R; **T:** R; **BORN:** 11/18/01 in Caracas, Venezuela; **RESIDES:** Caracas, Venezuela; **OBTAINED:** Signed by the Yankees as a non-drafted free agent on 7/2/18; **M.L. SVC:** 0.000; **PERSONAL:** Was ranked by MLB Pipeline as the No. 13 prospect and by Baseball America as the No. 14 prospect in the 2018 international signing class.

GOMEZ, Carlos – RHP
HT: 6-1; **WT:** 175; **B:** R; **T:** R; **BORN:** 6/14/98 in Esperanza, D.R.; **RESIDES:** Esperanza, D.R.; **OBTAINED:** Signed by the Yankees as a non-drafted free agent on 4/12/17; **M.L. SVC:** 0.000.

GOMEZ, Ismael – RHP
HT: 5-10; **WT:** 170; **B:** R; **T:** R; **BORN:** 10/8/99 in Porlamar, Venezuela; **RESIDES:** Porlamar, Venezuela; **OBTAINED:** Signed by the Yankees as a non-drafted free agent on 2/19/18; **M.L. SVC:** 0.000.

GOMEZ, Nelson – INF
HT: 6-1; **WT:** 220; **B:** R; **T:** R; **BORN:** 10/8/97 in Los Hidalgos, D.R.; **RESIDES:** Puerto Plato, D.R.; **OBTAINED:** Signed by the Yankees as a non-drafted free agent on 7/2/14; **M.L. SVC:** 0.000; **CAREER NOTES: 2018:** Tied for fifth in the Appalachian League with 11HR and 25 extra-base hits (14 doubles, 11HR)…also led the league in strikeouts (93)…**2015:** Led the DSL in home runs (11) and ranked second in RBI (55) with the DSL Yankees 1…recorded his first career multi-HR game and a career-high 8RBI on 7/3 vs. the DSL Reds (2HR)…**PERSONAL:** Was ranked by *Baseball America* as the No. 6 prospect for the 2014 international signing period.

GOMEZ, Yoendrys – RHP
HT: 6-3; **WT:** 175; **B:** R; **T:** R; **BORN:** 10/15/99 in Nirgua, Venezuela; **RESIDES:** Chivacoa, Venezuela; **OBTAINED:** Signed by the Yankees as a non-drafted free agent on 7/2/16; **M.L. SVC:** 0.000; **CAREER NOTES: 2019:** Was 4-5 with a 3.99 ERA (56.1IP, 25ER) in 12 starts between Rookie-level Pulaski and Single-A Charleston…following the season, was named the Yankees' No. 7 prospect by MLB Pipeline.

GRANITE, Zack – OF
NON-ROSTER INVITEE

HT: 6-1; **WT:** 175; **B:** L; **T:** L; **BORN:** 9/17/92 in Staten Island, N.Y.; **RESIDES:** Staten Island, N.Y.; **COLLEGE:** Seton Hall; **OBTAINED:** Signed by the Yankees as a minor league free agent on 11/21/19; **M.L. SVC:** 0.070; **CAREER NOTES:** Was originally selected by the Minnesota Twins in the 14th round of the 2013 First-Year Player Draft…was acquired by the Texas Rangers from the Minnesota Twins in exchange for RHP Xavier Moore and cash considerations on March 3, 2019… **2019:** Spent the entire season with Triple-A Nashville and hit .290 (146-for-504) with 66R, 18 doubles, 8 triples, 3HR, 37RBI, 31BB and 25SB…was tied for fourth in the PCL in triples, ranked sixth in hits and seventh in stolen bases…was designated for assignment by the Twins on 2/26…was acquired by the Texas Rangers from the Twins in exchange for RHP Xavier Moore and cash considerations on 3/3… **2018:** Appeared in 68 games for Triple-A Rochester, batting .211 (50-for-237) with 28R, 8 doubles, 4RBI, 22BB and 9SB…played in eight games for the Red Wings before being placed on the 7-day disabled list with a right shoulder contusion on 4/21 (retroactive to 4/19), an injury he originally suffered diving for a ball in spring training…was reinstated on 5/10 and was placed back on the 7-day disabled list 7/18 with the same right shoulder contusion…missed the remainder of the season… **2017:** Saw his first Major League action, batting .237 (22-for-93) with 14R, 2 doubles, 1HR, 13RBI, 12BB and 2SB in 40 games over two stints (7/8-8/4, 8/24-end of season) with the Twins…made his Major League debut on 7/8 vs. Baltimore, pinch hitting for Ehire Adrianza in the eighth (0-for-1)…recorded his first Major League hit on 7/14 at Houston with a third-inning double off Charlie Morton…recorded his first Major League home run on 9/23 at Detroit with a three-run shot off Blaine Hardy in the eighth after pinch-running for Joe Mauer earlier in the inning, becoming the first player in Twins history to pinch-run and homer in the same inning and the first in baseball since Boston's Darren Lewis in 2001…spent the majority of the season with Triple-A Rochester, batting .338 (96-for-284) with 46R, 16 doubles, 4 triples, 5HR, 29RBI, 24BB and 15SB in 71 games…was named the International League "Player of the Month" in June, reaching safely in each of his 29 games and batting .470/.527/.667 (55-for-117) with 23R, 11 doubles, 3 triples, 2HR, 12RBI, 14BB and 8SB during that span…was named an International League Mid-Season and Postseason All-Star…was also tabbed an Organization All-Star by MiLB.com…missed the first month of the season with a left oblique strain and made a rehab appearance with Single-A Fort Myers (.368, 7-for-19, 2R, 1 double, 1 triple, 1RBI, 2BB and 3SB)… **2016:** Spent the season with Double-A Chattanooga and hit .295 (155-for-526) with 86R, 18 doubles, 8 triples, 4HR, 52RBI, 42BB and 56 stolen bases…his 56SB were tied for the most by any minor league player in 2016…led the Southern League in hits and stolen bases, ranked second in runs, third in triples and fourth in batting average…recorded at least one stolen base in 41 of 127 games and multiple stolen bases in 11 games, including a season-high 4SB on 4/20 at Mississippi…was named a Southern League Postseason All-Star…was also tabbed an Organization All-Star by MiLB.com…was named the Sherry Robertson Award winner as the Twins minor league Player of the Year…was added to Twins 40-man roster on 11/18… **2015:** Combined with Single-A Cedar Rapids and Single-A Fort Myers to bat .266 (119-for-448) with 76R, 15 doubles, 5 triples, 1HR, 31RBI, 53BB and 28SB in 124 games…his 28SB were the fourth-most among Twins minor leaguers…played his first 19 games with Cedar Rapids, hitting .358 (24-for-67) with 17R, 5 doubles, 1 triple, 5RBI and 12BB…was promoted to Fort Myers on 5/1 and hit .249 (95-for-381) with 59R, 10 doubles, 4 triples, 1HR, 26RBI and 41BB in 105 games… **2014:** Began the season with Single-A Cedar Rapids, batting .291 (23-for-79) with 9R, 2 doubles, 2 triples and 2RBI in 21 games…made a rehab assignment with the GCL Twins, hitting .214 (3-for-14) with 4R and 2BB in four games… **2013:** Made his professional debut with Rookie-level Elizabethton, batting .285 (69-for-242) with 39R, 4 doubles, 5 triples, 24RBI, 29BB and 14SB in 61 games…ranked among Appalachian League leaders in hits (T-third), stolen bases (T-third), triples (T-fourth) and runs (fifth)…was named an Appalachian League Postseason All-Star… **PERSONAL:** Full name is Zachary Thomas Granite…in three seasons at Seton Hall, owned a career .299 (189-for-633) with 23 doubles, 10 triples, 53RBI and 68SB in 156 games…as a freshman in 2011, helped guide the Pirates to their first BIG EAST Championship in 10 years and an NCAA Regional appearance selection…was named the 2013 All-Big East First Team, 2013 Rawlings/ABCA All-East Region Second Team and 2012 All-Big East Third Team…went back to Seton Hall in winter of 2016-17 to earn degree in Criminal Justice…attended Tottenville High School in Staten Island.

Granite's Career Batting Record

Year	Club	AVG	G	AB	R	H	2B	3B	HR	RBI	SH	SF	HP	BB	SO	SB	CS	E	OBP	SLG
2013	Elizabethton	.285	61	242	39	69	4	5	0	24	2	3	2	29	25	14	7	3	.362	.343
2014	Cedar Rapids	.291	21	79	9	23	2	2	0	2	1	1	0	4	8	1	4	0	.321	.367
	GCL Twins	.214	4	14	4	3	0	0	0	0	0	0	0	2	4	3	0	0	.313	.214
2015	Cedar Rapids	.358	19	67	17	24	5	1	0	5	3	0	1	12	6	7	1	0	.463	.463
	Fort Myers	.249	105	381	59	95	10	4	1	26	11	3	5	41	63	21	12	4	.328	.304
2016	Chattanooga	.295	127	526	86	155	18	8	4	52	8	5	3	42	43	56	14	1	.347	.382
2017	Fort Myers	.368	5	19	2	7	1	1	0	1	0	0	0	2	2	3	0	0	.429	.526
	Rochester	.338	71	284	46	96	16	4	5	29	4	0	1	24	34	15	6	1	.392	.475
	MINNESOTA	.237	40	93	14	22	2	0	1	13	1	1	0	12	9	2	2	1	.321	.290
2018	Rochester	.211	68	237	28	50	8	0	0	4	1	1	2	22	28	9	4	2	.282	.245
2019	Nashville	.290	119	504	66	146	18	8	3	37	0	4	2	31	45	25	13	4	.331	.375
Minor League Totals		**.284**	**600**	**2353**	**356**	**668**	**82**	**33**	**13**	**180**	**30**	**17**	**16**	**209**	**258**	**154**	**61**	**15**	**.344**	**.363**
Major League Totals		**.237**	**40**	**93**	**14**	**22**	**2**	**0**	**1**	**13**	**1**	**1**	**0**	**12**	**9**	**2**	**2**	**1**	**.321**	**.290**

GRAY, Kyle – INF
HT: 5-10; **WT:** 175; **B:** L; **T:** R; **BORN:** 3/25/97 in San Marcos, Tex.; **RESIDES:** Blanco, Tex.; **COLLEGE:** West Virginia University; **OBTAINED:** Selected by the Yankees in the 14th round of the 2018 First-Year Player Draft; **M.L. SVC:** 0.000; **CAREER NOTES: 2019:** Tied for fourth in the South Atlantic League with six triples for Single-A Charleston… **PERSONAL:** Played three seasons (2016-18) at West Virginia, batting .302 (174-for-576) with 112R, 27 doubles, 12 triples, 17HR, 91RBI, 102BB and 29SB in 165 games…was named to the 2018 ABCA/Rawlings All-America Third Team as a junior…graduated from Blanco (Tex.) H.S. in 2015.

GREEN, Nick – RHP
HT: 6-1; **WT:** 175; **B:** R; **T:** R; **BORN:** 3/25/95 in Fountain, Colo.; **RESIDES:** Fountain, Colo.; **COLLEGE:** Indian Hills Community College; **OBTAINED:** Returned from Arizona to the Yankees as a Rule 5 Draft return on 3/24/19; **M.L. SVC:** 0.000; **CAREER NOTES:** Was originally selected by Texas in the seventh round of the 2014 First-Year Player Draft…was acquired by the Yankees from Texas with RHP Dillon Tate and RHP Erik Swanson in exchange for OF Carlos Beltrán and cash considerations on 8/1/16…was selected by Arizona from the Yankees in the Major League phase of the Rule 5 Draft on 12/13/18… **2018:** Was named a Florida State Midseason All-Star at Single-A Tampa… **PERSONAL:** Played one season (2014) at Indian Hills Community College (Iowa), where he was named second-team All-Region after going 3-1 with a 2.97 ERA (36.1IP, 12ER)…graduated in 2013 from Fountain-Fort Carson H.S. (Colo.)…was selected by the Yankees in the 35th round of the 2013 First-Year Player draft but did not sign.

GREEN, Ryder – OF
HT: 6-0; **WT:** 200; **B:** R; **T:** R; **BORN:** 5/5/00 in Knoxville, Tenn.; **RESIDES:** Knoxville, Tenn.; **OBTAINED:** Selected by the Yankees in the third round of the 2018 First-Year Player Draft; **M.L. SVC:** 0.000; **CAREER NOTES: 2019:** Hit .262 (59-for-225) with 45R, 15 doubles, 1 triple, 8HR, 28RBI and 10SB in 61 games for Rookie-level Pulaski…led the Appalachian League in runs, tied for fifth in hits and seventh in total bases (100) and ranked 10th in hits…**PERSONAL:** Graduated from Karns (Tenn.) H.S. in 2018…was committed to play at Vanderbilt before signing with the Yankees.

GREENE, Zach – RHP
HT: 6-2; **WT:** 215; **B:** R; **T:** R; **BORN:** 8/29/96 in Jacksonville, Fla.; **RESIDES:** Jacksonville, Fla.; **COLLEGE:** University of South Alabama; **OBTAINED:** Selected by the Yankees in the eighth round of the 2019 First-Year Player Draft; **M.L. SVC:** 0.000; **CAREER NOTES: 2019:** Tied for second in the GCL with five saves while going 1-1 with a 1.69 ERA (16.0IP, 11H, 5R/4ER, 4BB, 22K) in 12 relief appearances at GCL Yankees East…**PERSONAL:** Played two seasons (2018-19) at South Alabama, one season (2017) at St. Johns River (Fla.) Community College and one season (2016) at UNC-Asheville…as a senior in 2019, was named Second-Team All-America by the NCBWA and Third-Team All-America by D1Baseball.com after going 2-0 with 13 saves and a 1.45 ERA (49.2IP, 35H, 13R/8ER, 8BB, 70K) in 27 relief appearances…graduated in 2015 from Atlantic Coast (Fla.) H.S.…was selected by Miami in the 15th round of the 2018 First-Year Player Draft but did not sign.

GUERRERO, Alex – C
HT: 6-0; **WT:** 185; **B:** L; **T:** R; **BORN:** 3/10/00 in Boise, Idaho; **RESIDES:** Eagle, Idaho; **OBTAINED:** Selected by the Yankees in the 18th round of the 2018 First-Year Player Draft; **M.L. SVC:** 0.000; **PERSONAL:** Graduated from Eagle (Idaho) H.S. in 2018…had committed to play at the University of Washington prior to signing with the Yankees.

GUZMAN, José – RHP
HT: 5-11; **WT:** 185; **B:** R; **T:** R; **BORN:** 12/26/01 in Cumana, Venezuela; **RESIDES:** Cumana, Venezuela; **OBTAINED:** Signed by the Yankees as a non-drafted free agent on 8/31/19; **M.L. SVC:** 0.000.

HALE, David – RHP   NON-ROSTER INVITEE
HT: 6-2; **WT:** 210; **B:** R; **T:** R; **BORN:** 9/27/87 in Atlanta, Ga.; **RESIDES:** Marietta, Ga.; **OBTAINED:** Signed by the Yankees as a minor league free agent on 1/30/18 and re-signed on 5/1/18, 5/19/18, 1/21/19 and 1/23/20; **M.L. SVC:** 2.163; **CAREER NOTES:** Was originally selected by Atlanta in the third round of the 2009 First-Year Player Draft…in parts of six Major League seasons with Atlanta (2013-14), Colorado (2015-16), the Yankees (2018-19) and Minnesota (2018), is 13-10 with a 4.27 ERA (230.0IP, 109ER) over 90 games (20 starts)…**2019:** Pitched to a 3-0 record with two saves and a 3.11 ERA (37.2IP, 39H, 13ER, 7BB, 23K, 2HR) in 20 relief appearances for the Yankees…tossed multiple innings in 13-of-20 appearances, including two 4.0-inning outings…began the season with Triple-A Scranton/Wilkes-Barre and was selected to the Yankees' roster on 5/21…earned his first Major League save in his season debut on 5/21 at Baltimore (4.0IP, 1ER)…earned the win on 5/27 vs. San Diego (4.0IP, 2ER), his first since 9/25/15 vs. Los Angeles-NL w/ Colorado…had a 12.2-inning scoreless streak spanning 10 games from 6/23-7/23 (11H, 2BB, 11K)…was placed on the 10-day injured list on 7/31 (retroactive to 7/28) with a lumbar spine strain…was transferred to the 60-day injured list on 9/1…was reinstated from the injured list on 9/28 after missing 80 games…was designated for assignment on 10/12…posted a 3-2 record with a 4.13 ERA (32.2IP, 36H, 17R/15ER, 10BB, 3HR) in seven starts with Scranton/Wilkes-Barre…**2018:** Made three appearances with the Yankees and one with Minnesota, combining for a 4.61 ERA (13.2IP, 16H, 7ER, 5BB, 8K, 3HR) in four MLB outings…in three stints with New York (4/22-23, 5/2-15, 7/1-7), had a 2.53 ERA (10.2IP, 3ER)…began the season with Triple-A Scranton/Wilkes-Barre and was selected to the Yankees' roster on 4/22…threw 2.0 scoreless innings (3H, 3K) in his Yankees debut on 4/23 vs. Minnesota…was claimed off waivers by Minnesota on 4/26 and allowed 4ER in 3.0IP (4H, 4BB, 2K, 1HR) in a relief appearance on 4/27 vs. Cincinnati…was released on 4/30 and re-signed by the Yankees on 5/1…tossed 5.2IP (5H, 1ER, 1BB, 1K) on 7/6 at Toronto, the longest appearance by a Yankees reliever in 2018…in 11 starts at Scranton/WB, went 3-2 with a 4.20 ERA (55.2IP, 58H, 27R/26ER, 17BB, 44K, 5HR)…was released by the Yankees on 7/9 and signed with the Hanwha Eagles of the Korean Baseball Organization…made 12 starts with Hanwha, going 3-4 with a 4.34 ERA (66.1IP, 68H, 35R/32ER, 17BB, 55K, 8HR) in 12 starts…**2017:** Combined with Double-A Tulsa and Triple-A Oklahoma City to go 5-4 with a 4.08 ERA (81.2IP, 37ER) in 15 games (14 starts)…was signed by Atlanta as a minor league free agent on 3/4 before being released on 3/24…was signed by Los Angeles-NL as a minor league free agent on 4/10…**2016:** Made two relief appearances for Colorado, posting a 13.50 ERA (2.0IP, 3ER)…also saw time with Triple-A Albuquerque, going 0-1 with a 1.50 ERA (6.0IP, 1ER) in two starts…was designated for assignment by Colorado on 4/22 and claimed off waivers by Baltimore on 4/25…made 20 starts with Triple-A Norfolk, going 4-7 with a 5.84 ERA (94.0IP, 61ER) and 56K…**2015:** Made his Rockies debut, going 5-5 with a 6.09 ERA (78.1IP, 53ER) in 17 games (12 starts) over four stints with Colorado (5/23, 6/2, 6/8-8/23 and 9/3-10/4)…began the season on the 15-day D.L. with a strained left oblique…was reinstated from the D.L. on 4/26 and optioned to Triple-A Albuquerque, where he went 0-3 with a 6.66 ERA (50.0IP, 37ER) in 11 starts…was recalled as the 26th Man prior to a doubleheader on 5/23 vs. San Francisco, making his Rockies debut as a starter in Game 2 (6.2IP, 2ER)…was placed on the 15-day D.L. from 7/10-8/18 with a strained groin…made one rehab start with Single-A Modesto (L, 2.1IP, 2R/0ER)…was acquired by Colorado from Atlanta with RHP Gus Schlosser for INF Jose Briceno and C Chris O'Dowd on 1/30/15…**2014:** Made his first Opening Day roster with the Braves and went 4-5 with a 3.30 ERA (87.1IP, 32ER) in 45 games (six starts)…as a starter, was 2-1 with a 2.45 ERA (33.0IP, 9ER)…in 39 relief appearances, was 2-4 with a 3.81 ERA (54.1IP, 23ER)…**2013:** Saw his first Major League action with Atlanta, going 1-0 with a 0.82 ERA (11.0IP, 1ER) and 14K in two starts with the Braves…made his Major League debut on 9/13 vs. San Diego, tossing 5.0 scoreless innings (4H, 1BB, 9K)…according to *Elias*, set a Braves franchise record for strikeouts in a Major League debut…earned his first Major League win on 9/26 vs. Philadelphia…made his postseason debut in NLDS Game 3 at Los Angeles-NL, retiring his only batter faced (Juan Uribe)…spent the majority of the season with Triple-A Gwinnett, going 6-9 with a 3.22 ERA (114.2IP, 41ER) in 22 games (20 starts)…following the season, was selected by the Braves organization as the Gwinnett Braves "Most Valuable Pitcher" and was named by *Baseball America* as the Braves' No. 7 prospect…**2012:** Spent the entire season with Double-A Mississippi, going 8-4 with a 3.77 ERA (145.2IP, 61ER) in 27 starts…was named to the Southern League Mid-Season All-Star Team…following the season, was named by *Baseball America* as the Braves' No. 16 prospect…**2011:** Went 4-6 with a 4.10 ERA (101.0IP, 46ER) in 28 games (13 starts) with Single-A Lynchburg…was named the organization's July "Pitcher of the Month"…following the season, was tabbed by *Baseball America* as the No. 21 prospect in the Braves organization…**2010:** Went 5-8 with a 4.13 ERA (93.2IP, 43ER) in 28 games (seven starts) with Single-A Rome, allowing just 1HR…following the season, was tabbed by *Baseball America* as the Braves' No. 17 prospect…was also named by the publication as having the "Best Slider" in the Braves organization…**2009:** Made his professional debut, going 2-1 with one save and a 1.12 ERA (16.0IP, 2ER) in seven appearances (one start) for Rookie-level Danville…**PERSONAL:** Attended Princeton University (N.J.), where he was both a pitcher and outfielder…was rated by *Baseball America* as the top prospect in the Ivy League prior to his junior season in 2009…attended The Walker School in Marietta, where he was an infielder for three years prior to pitching as a senior.

Hale's Career Pitching Record

Year	Club	W	L	ERA	G	GS	CG	SHO	SV	IP	H	R	ER	HR	HP	BB	SO	WP	BK
2009	Danville	2	1	1.13	7	1	0	0	1	16.0	7	4	2	0	2	5	12	2	0
2010	Rome	5	8	4.13	28	7	0	0	5	93.2	97	52	43	1	4	44	69	11	0
2011	Lynchburg	4	6	4.10	28	13	1	0	0	101.0	106	52	46	9	10	30	86	7	0
2012	Mississippi	8	4	3.77	27	27	0	0	0	145.2	121	66	61	11	8	67	124	9	0
2013	Gwinnett	6	9	3.22	22	20	0	0	0	114.2	123	50	41	8	7	36	77	2	0
	ATLANTA	1	0	0.82	2	2	0	0	0	11.0	11	1	1	0	0	1	14	0	1
2014	ATLANTA	4	5	3.30	45	6	0	0	0	87.1	89	38	32	5	3	39	44	5	0
2015	Modesto	0	1	0.00	1	1	0	0	0	2.1	2	2	0	0	0	1	3	0	0
	Albuquerque	0	3	6.66	11	11	0	0	0	50.0	68	40	37	4	2	21	37	2	0
	COLORADO	5	5	6.09	17	12	0	0	0	78.1	95	56	53	14	2	20	61	11	0
2016	Albuquerque	0	1	1.50	2	2	0	0	0	6.0	1	1	1	0	0	2	7	0	0
	COLORADO	0	0	13.50	2	0	0	0	0	2.0	4	3	3	1	0	2	1	0	0
	Norfolk	4	7	5.84	20	20	0	0	0	94.0	133	65	61	10	2	23	56	2	0
2017	Tulsa	3	0	3.72	6	5	0	0	0	29.0	36	13	12	3	2	7	21	2	1
	Oklahoma City	2	4	4.27	9	9	0	0	0	52.2	64	30	25	4	1	7	39	2	0
2018	Scranton/WB	3	2	4.20	11	11	0	0	0	55.2	58	27	26	5	2	17	44	1	0
	YANKEES	0	0	2.53	3	0	0	0	0	10.2	12	3	3	2	1	1	6	0	0
	MINNESOTA	0	0	12.00	1	0	0	0	0	3.0	4	4	4	1	0	4	2	0	0
2019	Scranton/WB	3	2	4.13	7	7	1	0	0	32.2	36	17	15	3	2	10	30	1	0
	YANKEES	3	3	3.11	20	0	0	0	2	37.2	39	13	13	2	1	7	23	2	0
Minor League Totals		40	48	4.20	180	134	2	0	6	793.2	856	419	370	58	44	271	605	41	2
Major League Totals		13	10	4.27	90	20	0	0	2	230.0	254	118	109	25	7	74	151	18	0

HARDY, Tim – LHP
HT: 6-7; **WT:** 250; **B:** L; **T:** L; **BORN:** 3/1/96 in Waxhaw, N.C.; **RESIDES:** Monroe, N.C.; **COLLEGE:** Tusculum University; **OBTAINED:** Signed by the Yankees as a minor league free agent on 4/4/19; **M.L. SVC:** 0.000; **CAREER NOTES:** Was originally selected by Houston in the 18th round of the 2017 First-Year Player Draft…**PERSONAL:** Pitched two seasons (2016-17) at Tusculum (Tenn.) University…graduated from the Central Academy of Technology & Arts (N.C.) in 2015.

HENRIQUEZ, Nolberto – RHP
HT: 6-4; **WT:** 170; **B:** R; **T:** R; **BORN:** 10/16/99 in Azoategui, Venezuela; **RESIDES:** Azoategui, Venezuela; **OBTAINED:** Signed by the Yankees as a non-drafted free agent on 8/16/18; **M.L. SVC:** 0.000; **CAREER NOTES:** Signed by the Colorado Rockies as a non-drafted free agent on 12/2/17 but the contract was later voided.

HENSON, Spencer – INF
HT: 6-2; **WT:** 230; **B:** R; **T:** R; **BORN:** 11/3/97 in Tulsa, Okla.; **RESIDES:** Locust Grove, Okla.; **COLLEGE:** Oral Roberts University; **OBTAINED:** Selected by the Yankees in the ninth round of the 2019 First-Year Player Draft; **M.L. SVC:** 0.000; **PERSONAL:** Played three seasons (2017-19) at Oral Roberts (Okla.) University, winning the Summit League Triple Crown in each of his final two seasons…was also named the 2019 Summit League "Player of the Year"…graduated from Pryor (Okla.) H.S. in 2016 after earning three Louisville Slugger High School All-America honors…also played football and basketball at Pryor.

HEREDIA, José – C
HT: 5-9; **WT:** 182; **B:** R; **T:** R; **BORN:** 12/4/00 in Valencia, Venezuela; **RESIDES:** Guacara, Venezuela; **OBTAINED:** Signed by the Yankees as a non-drafted free agent on 9/3/19; **M.L. SVC:** 0.000.

HERNANDEZ, Franyer – RHP
HT: 6-0; **WT:** 170; **B:** R; **T:** R; **BORN:** 2/1/01 in Rio Chico, Venezuela; **RESIDES:** Rio Chico, Venezuela; **OBTAINED:** Signed by the Yankees as a non-drafted free agent on 3/26/18; **M.L. SVC:** 0.000.

HERNANDEZ, Leonel – OF
HT: 5-9; **WT:** 163; **B:** L; **T:** L; **BORN:** 2/24/98 in Ciego de Ávila, Cuba; **RESIDES:** Boca Chica, D.R.; **OBTAINED:** Signed by the Yankees as a non-drafted free agent on 10/19/18; **M.L. SVC:** 0.000.

HERRERA, Argelis – LHP
HT: 6-5; **WT:** 165; **B:** L; **T:** L; **BORN:** 10/17/98 in Salcedo, D.R.; **RESIDES:** Tenares, D.R.; **OBTAINED:** Signed by the Yankees as a non-drafted free agent on 7/2/15; **M.L. SVC:** 0.000.

HERRERA, Carlos – C
HT: 5-10; **WT:** 165; **B:** R; **T:** R; **BORN:** 9/1/02 in Barquisimeto, Venezuela; **RESIDES:** Tinaquillo, Venezuela; **OBTAINED:** Signed by the Yankees as a non-drafted free agent on 7/3/19; **M.L. SVC:** 0.000.

HERRERA, Rosell – INF/OF
NON-ROSTER INVITEE

HT: 6-3; **WT:** 180; **B:** S; **T:** R; **BORN:** 10/16/92 in Santo Domingo, D.R.; **RESIDES:** Santo Domingo, D.R.; **OBTAINED:** Signed by the Yankees as a minor league free agent on 12/13/19; **M.L. SVC:** 1.046; **CAREER NOTES:** Was originally signed by Colorado as a non-drafted free agent on 7/2/09…signed by Cincinnati as a minor league free agent on 11/17/17…was claimed off waivers by Kansas City from Cincinnati on 6/2/18…was claimed off waivers by Miami from Kansas City on 1/2/19…**2019:** Began the season with Miami and hit .200 (21-for-105) with 10R, 6 doubles, 2HR, 11RBI and 11BB in 63 games…was designated for assignment on 6/18 and outrighted to Triple-A New Orleans on 6/22, where he hit .309 (51-for-165) with 21R, 11 doubles, 1 triple, 5HR and 24RBI over 48 games…**2018:** Saw his first Major League action with Cincinnati and Kansas City, combining to hit .234 (65-for-278) with 25R, 14 doubles, 3 triples, 1HR, 20RBI, 19BB and 3SB in 86 Major League games…made his Major League debut on 4/26 vs. Atlanta w/ Cincinnati (0-for-1)…recorded his first Major League hit in his only start as a Red on 5/1 vs. Milwaukee, a single off Chase Anderson in the second inning…on 6/22 at Houston, robbed Alex Bregman of a HR in the eighth inning of a scoreless game, then hit a go-ahead RBI triple in the top of the ninth in a 1-0 win…hit his first Major League home run on 7/29 at Yankee Stadium w/ Kansas City, a solo HR off David Robertson in the eighth…**2017:** Played the entire season with Triple-A Albuquerque and tied for ninth in the Pacific Coast League with 20SB…missed 10 games on the disabled list from 7/19-29…**2016:** With Double-A Hartford, ranked among Eastern League leaders in SB (third, 36), OBP (T-sixth, .374) and BB (T-eighth, 56)…**2015:** Spent a second season with Single-A Modesto…**2014:** Played the entire season with Single-A Modesto…played in the SiriusXM All-Star Futures Game in Minnesota…missed 36 games on the disabled list from 4/24-5/31…**2013:** Was named the South Atlantic League Most Valuable Player, hitting .343 (162-for-472) with 83R, 33 doubles, 16HR, 76RBI, 61BB and 21SB in 126 games for Single-A Asheville…led all of minor league baseball in batting average (min. 500PA)…ranked second among all Single-A batters in hits…was named a South Atlantic League Mid-Season All-Star…was named SAL "Player of the Week" for 5/26-6/2 after hitting .423 (11-for-26) with 3HR and 8RBI over six games…was named a MiLB.com Organization All-Star and a Topps Class-A All-Star…following the season, was tabbed as the SAL's Most Outstanding Major League Prospect…**2012:** In 110 games between Single-A Asheville and short-season Single-A Tri-City, hit .241 (98-for-407) with 52R, 14 doubles, 4 triples, 2HR, 56RBI, 35BB and 13SB…**2011:** Spent the entire season with Rookie-level Casper, tying for third in the Pioneer League with eight triples…**2010:** Was a DSL Mid-Season All-Star in his professional debut with the DSL Rockies.

Herrera's Career Batting Record

Year	Club	AVG	G	AB	R	H	2B	3B	HR	RBI	SH	SF	HP	BB	SO	SB	CS	E	OBP	SLG
2010	DSL Rockies	.237	67	232	27	55	6	1	1	26	3	1	6	24	24	17	8	16	.323	.284
2011	Casper	.284	63	243	38	69	6	8	6	34	1	1	3	27	62	5	4	24	.361	.449
2012	Asheville	.202	63	213	22	43	8	2	1	26	1	2	0	21	49	6	3	11	.271	.272
	Tri-City	.284	47	194	30	55	6	2	1	30	0	2	1	14	34	7	3	19	.332	.351
2013	Asheville	.343	126	472	83	162	33	0	16	76	6	4	3	61	96	21	8	28	.419	.515
2014	Modesto	.244	72	275	31	67	11	1	4	23	1	2	0	24	52	9	7	23	.302	.335
2015	Modesto	.260	123	466	55	121	20	6	4	36	6	2	1	37	97	9	8	5	.314	.354
2016	Hartford	.292	126	425	61	124	16	3	5	66	7	4	2	56	79	36	8	6	.374	.379
2017	Albuquerque	.278	103	320	59	89	20	4	3	27	4	2	2	35	69	20	6	4	.351	.394
2018	Louisville	.267	23	90	11	24	8	2	3	11	1	0	1	6	15	2	1	3	.320	.500
	CINCINNATI	.154	11	13	0	2	0	0	0	0	0	0	0	0	5	0	1	0	.154	.154
	Omaha	.278	10	36	8	10	3	2	1	5	0	0	0	5	7	4	1	0	.366	.556
	KANSAS CITY	.238	75	265	25	63	14	3	1	20	1	2	2	19	52	3	4	1	.292	.325
2019	MIAMI	.200	63	105	10	21	6	0	2	11	1	0	2	11	27	4	1	1	.288	.314
	New Orleans	.309	48	165	21	51	11	1	5	24	0	0	1	14	32	2	1	4	.367	.479
Minor League Totals		**.278**	**871**	**3131**	**446**	**870**	**148**	**32**	**50**	**384**	**30**	**20**	**20**	**324**	**616**	**138**	**58**	**144**	**.347**	**.393**
Major League Totals		**.225**	**149**	**383**	**35**	**86**	**20**	**3**	**3**	**31**	**2**	**2**	**4**	**30**	**84**	**7**	**6**	**2**	**.286**	**.316**

HIGGINS, Dalton – RHP

HT: 6-2; **WT:** 200; **B:** R; **T:** R; **BORN:** 8/8/95 in Fort Worth, Tex.; **RESIDES:** Fort Worth, Tex.; **COLLEGE:** Dallas Baptist University; **OBTAINED:** Selected by the Yankees in the seventh round of the 2017 First-Year Player Draft; **M.L. SVC:** 0.000; **PERSONAL:** In three seasons with Dallas Baptist (Tex.) University, went 16-6 with a 3.41 ERA (148.0IP, 56ER) in 70 appearances (eight starts) …was a Louisville Slugger Freshman All-American in 2015…graduated from Calvary Christian Academy (Tex.).

HOLDER, Kyle – INF
NON-ROSTER INVITEE

HT: 6-1; **WT:** 204; **B:** L; **T:** R; **BORN:** 5/25/94 in San Diego, Calif.; **RESIDES:** San Diego, Calif.; **COLLEGE:** University of San Diego; **OBTAINED:** Selected by the Yankees in the compensation round of the 2015 First-Year Player Draft; **M.L. SVC:** 0.000; **CAREER NOTES:** **2019:** Played 112 games at Double-A Trenton, hitting .265 (109-for-412) with 48R, 25 doubles, 3 triples, 9HR and 40RBI…set a career high in doubles, home runs and extra-base hits (37)…was an MiLB.com Organization All-Star…**2018:** Was limited to 48 games between Double-A Trenton, Single-A Tampa and Single-A Charleston, hitting .257 (47-for-183) with 18R, 6 doubles, 1 triple, 3HR, 22RBI and 15BB…began the season on the minor league D.L. and hit .267 (12-for-45) with 7R, 1 double, 2HR and 12RBI in 11 rehab games with Tampa and .286 (6-for-21) with 1R and 1 double in five rehab games with Charleston…at Trenton, batted .248 (29-for-117) with 10R, 4 doubles, 1 triple, 1HR and 10RBI in 32 games…did not commit an error in 132 total chances overall…**2017:** Batted .271 (110-for-406) with 41R, 16 doubles, 2 triples, 4HR and 44RBI in 104 games with Single-A Tampa…struck out only 62 times in 442 plate appearances, the fourth-lowest PA/K ratio (7.13) in the Florida State League…following the season, batted .333 (15-for-45) with 5R, 3 doubles, 1 triple, 1HR and 6RBI in 11 games for the Scottsdale Scorpions of the Arizona Fall League…**2016:** Spent the entire season with Single-A Charleston, batting .290/.323/.347 (102-for-352) with 40R, 13 doubles, 2 triples, 1HR, 18RBI and 8SB in 88 games…made 55 starts at SS and 24 starts at 2B, committing just 9E in 346TC (.974)…was named the "Best Defensive Shortstop" in the South Atlantic League by *Baseball America*…**2015:** Made his professional debut with short-season Single-A Staten Island, batting .213 (48-for-225) with 23R, 7 doubles, 1 triple and 12RBI in 56 games…was ranked by *Baseball America* as the No. 18 prospect in the New York-Penn League following the 2015 season…**PERSONAL:** Was ranked by *Baseball America* as the No. 38 prospect (and No. 8 shortstop) in the 2015 First-Year Player Draft…played one season (2013) at Grossmont College (Calif.) before transferring to the University of San Diego for two seasons (2014-15)…as a junior in 2015, was named West Coast Conference Player of the Year and a Third-Team All-American by D1baseball.com after batting .348 (78-for-224) with 45R, 14 doubles, 2 triples, 4HR, 31RBI and 19BB in 55 games…also appeared on the Golden Spikes Award watch list and was a semifinalist for the Brooks Wallace Award, which honors the best collegiate shortstop…graduated in 2012 from University City H.S. (Calif.), where he lettered in both baseball and basketball.

Holder's Career Batting Record

Year	Club	AVG	G	AB	R	H	2B	3B	HR	RBI	SH	SF	HP	BB	SO	SB	CS	E	OBP	SLG
2015	Staten Island	.213	56	225	23	48	7	1	0	12	5	1	2	17	34	6	2	8	.273	.253
2016	Charleston	.290	88	352	40	102	13	2	1	18	2	2	3	15	53	8	6	9	.323	.347
2017	Tampa	.271	104	406	41	110	16	2	4	44	6	2	2	26	62	4	3	12	.317	.350
2018	Trenton	.248	32	117	10	29	4	1	1	10	4	2	1	8	15	0	1	0	.297	.325
	Charleston	.286	5	21	1	6	1	0	0	0	0	0	0	1	1	0	1	0	.318	.333
	Tampa	.267	11	45	7	12	1	0	2	12	0	0	1	6	5	1	1	0	.365	.422
2019	Trenton	.265	112	412	48	109	25	3	9	40	14	1	4	41	65	7	1	10	.336	.405
Minor League Totals		**.264**	**408**	**1578**	**170**	**416**	**67**	**9**	**17**	**136**	**31**	**8**	**13**	**114**	**235**	**26**	**15**	**39**	**.317**	**.350**

HUTCHISON, Rodney – RHP

HT: 6-5; **WT:** 225; **B:** R; **T:** R; **BORN:** 8/9/96 in Cincinnati, Ohio; **RESIDES:** Mason, Ohio; **COLLEGE:** University of North Carolina; **OBTAINED:** Selected by the Yankees in the sixth round of the 2018 First-Year Player Draft; **M.L. SVC:** 0.000; **PERSONAL:** Pitched three seasons (2016-18) at UNC, posting an 11-9 record with one save and a 4.53 ERA (135.0IP, 143H, 80R/68ER, 41BB, 125K, 8HR) in 62 games (14 starts)…graduated from Mason (Ohio) H.S. in 2015, where he was a four-sport athlete (also basketball, football, hockey).

IANNETTA, Chris – C   NON-ROSTER INVITEE

HT: 6-0; **WT:** 230; **B:** R; **T:** R; **BORN:** 4/8/83 in Providence, R.I.; **RESIDES:** Wrentham, Mass.; **COLLEGE:** University of North Carolina; **OBTAINED:** Signed by the Yankees as a minor league free agent on 1/5/20; **M.L. SVC:** 12.154; **CAREER NOTES:** Was originally drafted by the Rockies in the fourth round of the 2004 First-Year Player Draft…was acquired by Los Angeles-AL from Colorado on 11/30/11 in exchange for Tyler Chatwood…was signed by Seattle as a free agent on 11/23/15…was signed by Arizona as a free agent on 1/13/17…was signed by Colorado as a free agent on 12/8/17…has played in 1,197 games over parts of 14 seasons with the Rockies (2006-11, '18-19), Angels (2012-15), Mariners (2016) and Diamondbacks (2017), hitting .230 (820-for-3,563) with 449R, 181 doubles, 141HR, 502RBI and 576BB…has primarily played catcher in the Majors (1,122G/1,032 starts), but has also seen time at 1B (7G/1GS), DH (6G/5GS) and 3B (4G/0GS)…has caught 195-of-802 potential base stealers (24.3%)…is the Rockies' all-time leader among catchers in games played (528), runs (219), hits (386), home runs (69), RBI (260) and walks (241)…is one of seven active catchers with a least 1,000 games played…**2019:** Hit .222 (32-for-144) with 20R, 10 doubles, 6HR and 21RBI in 52 games with Colorado…was placed on the 10-day injured list with a right lat strain on 4/29-5/3…went 0-for-8 with 1RBI on a three-game rehab assignment with Double-A Hartford from 4/29-5/3…was designated for assignment by the Rockies on 8/13 and released on 8/15…**2018:** In 110 games with Colorado, hit .224 (67-for-299) with 13 doubles, 1 triple, 11HR, 36RBI and 50BB…his 110 games played were the most since his career-high 115 games in 2013…made Colorado's NL Wild Card Game and NLDS rosters, going 0-for-9 in 4G/3GS…**2017:** Slashed .254/.354/.511 (69-for-272) with 38R, 19 doubles, 17HR, 43RBI and 37BB in 89 games with Arizona…made his 10th Opening Day roster…was placed on the 7-day disabled list with a concussion on 5/14 (retroactive to 5/13) and reinstated on 5/20…recorded a career-high 7RBI on 6/8 vs. San Diego, going 3-for-5 with 2 doubles and 1HR…set a new career mark on 9/22 vs. Miami with 8RBI, going 3-for-4 with 2HR…became the 21st player (24th time) since 1913 to have multiple games with seven-or-more RBI in the same season since Jonathan Lucroy (2012)…made Arizona's NL Wild Card Game and NLDS rosters (0-for-5)…**2016:** Batted .210 (62-for-295) with 23R, 14 doubles, 7HR, 24RBI and 38BB in 94 games with Seattle…**2015:** Appeared in 92 games with the Angels, hitting .188 (51-for-272) with 28R, 10 doubles, 10HR, 34RBI and 41BB…recorded his 100th career home run (solo HR) on 9/19-G2 at Minnesota in the seventh inning off Mike Pelfrey…**2014:** Hit .252 (77-for-306) with 41R, 22 doubles, 7HR, 43RBI and 54BB in 108 games with Los Angeles-AL…led AL catchers with a .373 OBP (min. 350PA) while his 54BB as a catcher were second most…**2013:** Played in a career-high 115 games with the Angels…batted .225 (73-for-325) with 40R, 15 doubles, 11HR, 39RBI and 68BB…was named AL "Player of the Week" for 9/9-15…batted .429/.500/.952 (9-for-21) with 7R, 2 doubles, 3HR, 5RBI and 2BB in six games during that span…caught all 19 innings on 4/29 in Oakland in a game that lasted 6 hours, 32 minutes…**2012:** Hit .240 (53-for-221) with 27R, 6 doubles, 1 triple, 9HR and 26RBI in 79 games with Los Angeles-AL…caught Jered Weaver's no-hitter on 5/2 vs. Minnesota…was placed on the 15-day disabled list with a fractured right wrist on 5/11 (retroactive to 5/9)…was sent to Triple-A Salt Lake on a rehab assignment on 7/21, hitting .273 (6-for-22) with 3R, 2 doubles, 2RBI and 3BB in six games…was activated from the disabled list on 7/28 after missing 67 games…signed a three-year contract extension through 2015 on 10/5/12…**2011:** Appeared in 112 games with Colorado, batting .238 (82-for-345) with 51R, 17 doubles, 14HR, 55RBI and 70BB…had the most walks by an NL catcher…recorded a .998 fielding percentage behind the plate (2E/817TC) while throwing out 30.0 percent of attempted base stealers (30-for-100)…his 82 assists led NL catchers while his fielding percentage ranked second…**2010:** Batted .197 (37-for-188) with 20R, 6 doubles, 1 triple, 9HR and 27RBI in 61 games over two stints (4/5-27, 5/25-10/3) with Colorado…appeared in 17 games for Triple-A Colorado Springs, slashing .349/.447/.698 (22-for-63) with 17R, 7 doubles, 5HR, 21RBI and 10BB…**2009:** Hit .228 (66-for-289) with 41R, 15 doubles, 2 triples, 16HR, 52RBI and 43BB in 93 games with Colorado…was placed on the 15-day disabled list with a strained right hamstring on 5/24…sent to Triple-A Colorado Springs on a rehab assignment and hit .333 (5-for-15) with 3R, 2 doubles, 1HR, 3RBI and 2BB in four games…activated from the disabled list on 6/9 after missing 15 games…**2008:** Rated .264 (88-for-333) with 22 doubles, 12 triples, 18HR, 65RBI and 56BB in 104 games with Colorado…recorded career highs in hits, HR, RBI, BA and runs…ranked second in OPS (.895) among MLB catchers to Atlanta's Brian McCann (.896)…made his first career appearance at 3B on 4/29 at San Francisco following an injury to Troy Tulowitzki…**2007:** Began the season with Colorado, hitting .218 (43-for-197) with 22R, 8 doubles, 3 triples, 4HR and 27RBI in 67 games…was optioned to Triple-A Colorado Springs on 8/6 and hit .296 (16-for-54) with 8R, 3 doubles, 1HR, 7RBI and 7BB in 16 games…was recalled by Colorado on 8/26…**2006:** Saw his first Major League action, batting .260 (20-for-77) with 12R, 4 doubles, 2HR, 10RBI and 13BB in 21 games with Colorado…made his Major League debut on 8/27 vs. San Diego (1-for-4, 1RBI)…collected his first Major League hit with a fifth-inning RBI single off Jake Peavy…recorded his first Major League home run on 9/12 at San Francisco with a solo shot off Jonathan Sanchez in the second inning…combined with Double-A Tulsa and Triple-A Colorado Springs to hit .336/.433/.564 (103-for-307) with 61R, 22 doubles, 3 triples, 14HR, 48RBI and 68BB in 91 games…began the season with Double-A Tulsa, batting .321 (50-for-156) with 38R, 10 doubles, 2 triples, 11HR, 26RBI and 24BB in 44 games…was named a Texas League Mid-Season All-Star with Tulsa…was promoted to Colorado Springs on 6/26, and hit .351 (53-for-151) with 23R, 12 doubles, 3HR, 22RBI and 24BB in 47 games…**2005:** Combined with Double-A Modesto and Double-A Tulsa to bat .268 (86-for-321) with 18R, 20 doubles, 4 triples, 13HR, 69RBI and 53BB in 93 games…spent the majority of the season with Modesto, batting .276 (72-for-261) with 51R, 17 doubles, 11HR, 58RBI and 45BB in 74 games…played 19 games with Tulsa and hit .233 (14-for-60) with 7R, 3 doubles, 1 triple, 2HR and 11RBI following the season was selected by *Baseball America* as the Best Defensive Catcher in the California League…played for Team

USA in MLB's All-Star Futures Game in Detroit…**2004:** Made his professional debut with Single-A Asheville…**PERSONAL:** Full name is Christopher Domenic Iannetta…he and his wife Lisa have two daughters, Ashlyn and Kylie…was a four-year catcher at St. Raphael Academy in Providence, R.I.…was a three-year starter at University of North Carolina…was a finalist for the Johnny Bench Award and a Third-Team All-America selection by *Baseball America* as a junior in 2004…was the starting catcher for Team USA in 2009 World Baseball Classic, batting .462 (6-for-13) with 4R, 1 double, 1HR and 6RBI in 4 games…was named the Angels' nominee for the Branch Rickey Award for community service…has teamed up with St. Joseph Health in Orange County to promote fitness and nutritional education at community events that focus on low income families.

Iannetta's Career Batting Record

Year	Club	AVG	G	AB	R	H	2B	3B	HR	RBI	SH	SF	HP	BB	SO	SB	CS	E	OBP	SLG
2004	Asheville	.314	36	121	23	38	5	1	5	17	0	0	4	27	29	0	1	3	.454	.496
2005	Modesto	.276	74	261	51	72	17	3	11	58	0	4	2	45	61	1	2	6	.381	.490
	Tulsa	.233	19	60	7	14	3	1	2	11	0	1	1	8	15	0	0	2	.329	.417
2006	Tulsa	.321	44	156	38	50	10	2	11	26	1	1	3	24	26	1	0	3	.418	.622
	Colorado Springs	.351	47	151	23	53	12	1	3	22	1	1	3	24	29	0	0	2	.447	.503
	COLORADO	.260	21	77	12	20	4	0	2	10	1	1	1	13	17	0	1	0	.370	.390
2007	COLORADO	.218	67	197	22	43	8	3	4	27	1	2	5	29	58	0	0	1	.330	.350
	Colorado Springs	.296	16	54	8	16	3	0	1	7	0	0	2	7	6	0	0	0	.397	.407
2008	COLORADO	.264	104	333	50	88	22	2	18	65	2	2	14	56	92	0	0	0	.390	.505
2009	COLORADO	.228	93	289	41	66	15	2	16	52	1	6	11	43	75	0	1	5	.344	.460
	Colorado Springs	.333	4	15	3	5	2	0	1	3	0	0	0	2	6	0	0	1	.412	.667
2010	COLORADO	.197	61	188	20	37	6	1	9	27	0	1	4	30	48	1	0	6	.318	.383
	Colorado Springs	.349	17	63	14	22	7	0	5	21	0	1	2	10	10	0	0	1	.447	.698
2011	COLORADO	.238	112	345	51	82	17	1	14	55	2	4	5	70	89	6	3	2	.370	.414
2012	LOS ANGELES-AL	.240	79	221	27	53	6	1	9	26	0	1	2	29	60	1	3	2	.332	.398
	Salt Lake	.273	6	22	3	6	2	0	0	2	0	0	0	3	7	0	0	0	.360	.364
2013	LOS ANGELES-AL	.225	115	325	40	73	15	0	11	39	0	4	2	68	100	0	1	5	.358	.372
2014	LOS ANGELES-AL	.252	108	306	41	77	22	0	7	43	0	5	8	54	91	3	0	2	.373	.392
2015	LOS ANGELES-AL	.188	92	272	28	51	10	0	10	34	0	3	1	41	83	0	1	0	.293	.335
2016	SEATTLE	.210	94	295	23	62	14	0	7	24	1	2	2	38	83	0	0	5	.303	.329
2017	ARIZONA	.254	89	272	38	69	19	0	17	43	0	1	6	37	87	0	0	6	.354	.511
2018	COLORADO	.224	110	299	36	67	13	1	11	36	1	3	7	50	87	0	0	4	.345	.385
2019	COLORADO	.222	52	144	20	32	10	0	6	21	0	1	1	18	54	0	0	3	.311	.417
	Hartford	.000	3	8	0	0	0	0	0	1	0	1	0	0	2	0	0	0	.000	.000
Minor League Totals		.303	266	911	173	276	61	8	39	168	2	9	17	150	191	2	3	18	.408	.516
Major League Totals		.230	1197	3563	449	820	181	11	141	502	9	36	69	576	1024	11	10	44	.345	.406

ILLIG, Chase – C
HT: 5-11; **WT:** 200; **B:** S; **T:** R; **BORN:** 9/14/96 in Frederick, Md.; **RESIDES:** Bluefield, W.Va.; **COLLEGE:** West Virginia University; **OBTAINED:** Selected by the Yankees in the 29th round of the 2019 First-Year Player Draft; **M.L. SVC:** 0.000; **PERSONAL:** Played two seasons at West Virginia (2017-18) after transferring from College of Charleston (S.C.)…missed the entire 2019 season due to injury…graduated in 2015 from the IMG Academy (Fla.), where he was named a Perfect Game USA All-America honorable mention as a senior…began his high school career at Tazewell (Va.) H.S.

JAVIER, Robert – OF
HT: 5-11; **WT:** 160; **B:** R; **T:** R; **BORN:** 2/1/99 in San Pedro de Macoris, D.R.; **RESIDES:** San Pedro de Macoris, D.R.; **OBTAINED:** Signed by the Yankees as a non-drafted free agent on 7/2/16; **M.L. SVC:** 0.000.

JIMENEZ, Brayan – INF
HT: 6-0; **WT:** 138; **B:** R; **T:** R; **BORN:** 5/31/99 in La Romana, D.R.; **RESIDES:** La Romana, D.R.; **OBTAINED:** Signed by the Yankees as a non-drafted free agent on 7/2/15; **M.L. SVC:** 0.000.

JOHNSON, Tyler – RHP
HT: 6-0; **WT:** 195; **B:** R; **T:** R; **BORN:** 7/12/96 in Columbus, Ohio; **RESIDES:** Columbus, Ohio; **COLLEGE:** Gardner-Webb University; **OBTAINED:** Selected by the Yankees in the 30th round of the 2018 First-Year Player Draft; **M.L. SVC:** 0.000; **PERSONAL:** In three seasons (2016-18) at Gardner-Webb University (N.C.), was 4-2 with a 6.56 ERA (80.1IP, 99H, 66R/59ER, 44BB, 84K, 4HR) in 58 relief appearances…graduated from Olentangy Orange (Ohio) H.S. in 2015.

JUNIOR, Alex – OF
HT: 5-10; **WT:** 188; **B:** L; **T:** L; **BORN:** 5/28/96 in Hendersonville, Tenn.; **RESIDES:** Hendersonville, Tenn.; **COLLEGE:** Tennessee Tech University; **OBTAINED:** Selected by the Yankees in the 19th round of the 2018 First-Year Player Draft; **M.L. SVC:** 0.000; **PERSONAL:** Played three seasons (2016-18) at Tennessee Tech, batting .301 (208-for-692) with 194R, 26 doubles, 6 triples, 13HR, 86RBI, 116BB and 25SB in 176 games…set a school single-season record with 81R in 2018…is a 2014 graduate of Goodpasture Christian (Tenn.) H.S. and played basketball and football.

JUNK, Janson – RHP
HT: 6-1; **WT:** 177; **B:** R; **T:** R; **BORN:** 1/15/96 in Federal Way, Wash.; **RESIDES:** Seattle, Wash.; **COLLEGE:** Seattle University; **OBTAINED:** Selected by the Yankees in the 22nd round of the 2017 First-Year Player Draft; **M.L. SVC:** 0.000; **CAREER NOTES: 2018:** Was named the South Atlantic League's "Pitcher of the Week" from 8/13-19 after throwing 5.0 hitless innings and earning the win on 8/16 at Delmarva (1R/0ER, 1BB, 6K, 2HP)…**PERSONAL:** Played three seasons at Seattle University (2015-17)…graduated from Decatur H.S. (Ga.).

KELLER, Brian – RHP
HT: 6-3; **WT:** 190; **B:** R; **T:** R; **BORN:** 6/21/94 in Milwaukee, Wisc.; **RESIDES:** Germantown, Wisc.; **COLLEGE:** University of Wisconsin-Milwaukee; **OBTAINED:** Selected by the Yankees in the 39th round of the 2016 First-Year Player Draft; **M.L. SVC:** 0.000; **CAREER NOTES: 2019:** Was named Eastern League "Pitcher of the Week" for 7/29-8/4 with Double-A Trenton…**2018:** Recorded the third-most wins in the organization after going 10-9 with Double-A Trenton…**2017:** Led all Yankees farmhands in strikeouts (157) and ranked sixth in ERA (3.13)…were the most strikeouts by a Yankees minor leaguer since 2007 (Alan Horne-165, Ian Kennedy-163)…tied for the Florida State League lead with two complete games…was named the FSL "Pitcher of the Week" after tossing a complete-game shutout on 7/28 vs. Palm Beach (9.0IP, 2H, 1BB)…**2016:** Allowed just 1R/0ER in 20.0IP (11H, 1BB, 23K) in seven GCL outings…**PERSONAL:** Played four seasons at Wisconsin-Milwaukee (2013-16), setting school records as a senior with 10 wins, 103K and 107.1IP while winning the 2016 Horizon League Pitcher of the Year Award…graduated in 2012 from Germantown H.S. (Wisc.), where he was named the Wisconsin Baseball Coaches Association State Player of the Year after going 11-0 with a 0.42 ERA as a senior.

KNOWLES, D'Vaughn – RHP
HT: 5-10; **WT:** 161; **B:** R; **T:** R; **BORN:** 1/16/01 in Nassau, Bahamas; **RESIDES:** Nassau, Bahamas; **OBTAINED:** Signed by the Yankees as a non-drafted free agent on 7/2/18; **M.L. SVC:** 0.000.

KOERNER, Brody – RHP
HT: 6-2; **WT:** 200; **B:** R; **T:** R; **BORN:** 10/17/93 in Winchester, Va.; **RESIDES:** Concord, N.C.; **COLLEGE:** Clemson University; **OBTAINED:** Selected by the Yankees in the 17th round of the 2015 First-Year Player Draft; **M.L. SVC:** 0.000; **CAREER NOTES: 2017:** Recorded a 24.0-inning scoreless streak from 6/21-7/9 with Single-A Tampa…was promoted to Double-A Trenton on 7/3, and was named the Eastern League "Pitcher of the Week" in his first week (7/3-9) after tossing 13.1 scoreless innings over two starts (13H, 1BB, 7K, 1HP)…**2016:** Following the season, went 0-1 with a 5.85 ERA (20.0IP, 24H, 15R/13ER, 11BB, 13K) in six appearances (four starts) with Scottsdale of the Arizona Fall League…**PERSONAL:** Name is pronounced "KERR-nerr"…graduated from Clemson in 2015 with a degree in accounting and was a two-time ACC Academic Honor Roll member…pitched three seasons for the Tigers (2013-15) and was 5-7 with a 7.00 ERA (97.2IP, 76ER) in 31 appearances (19 starts)…graduated in 2012 from Jay M. Robinson H.S. (N.C.), where he lettered three years in baseball, three in basketball and one in football…was a two-time All-State baseball selection.

KOHN, Zach – RHP
HT: 6-4; **WT:** 205; **B:** R; **T:** R; **BORN:** 9/30/97 in Wyandotte, Mich.; **RESIDES:** Woodhaven, Mich.; **COLLEGE:** Central Michigan University; **OBTAINED:** Selected by the Yankees in the 21st round of the 2019 First-Year Player Draft; **M.L. SVC:** 0.000; **PERSONAL:** Pitched three seasons at Central Michigan (2017-19)…as a junior, tossed 2.1 shutout innings of relief to earn the win vs. Miami (Fla.) in the 2019 Starkville Regional, the Chippewas' first NCAA Tournament win since 1988…graduated in 2016 from O.A. Carlson (Mich.) H.S.

KRATZ, Erik – C   NON-ROSTER INVITEE
HT: 6-4; **WT:** 250; **B:** R; **T:** R; **BORN:** 6/15/80 in Telford, Pa.; **RESIDES:** Harrisonburg, Va.; **COLLEGE:** Eastern Mennonite University; **OBTAINED:** Signed as a free agent to a minor league contract on 12/19/19; **M.L. SVC:** 5.054; **CAREER NOTES:** Was originally selected by the Toronto Blue Jays in the 29th round of the 2002 First-Year Player Draft…has appeared in 316 Major League games over 10 seasons with nine clubs: the Pirates (2010, '16), Phillies (2011-13, '15), Blue Jays (2014), Royals (2014-15), Astros (2016), Yankees (2017), Brewers (2018), Giants (2019) and Rays (2019)…is one of six active players (and the only position player) to have played for nine franchises (Edwin Jackson-14, Fernando Rodney-11, Jesse Chavez/Tyler Clippard/Zach Duke-9)…is the first position player to play for at least nine clubs since OF Marlon Byrd, who played for 10 between 2002-16…is one of five players in Yankees history with a 1.000 BA and more than 1H (2-for-2 in 2017)…among players with at least 1PA for the Yankees, is tied for the club record in BA…according to Baseball-Reference's Draft Index, his 316 Major League games are sixth-most by a player drafted and signed in the 29th round (Ken Griffey Sr.-2,097, Adam LaRoche-1,605, Russ Davis-615, Jeff Hamilton-416, Dave Tomlin-409)…**2019:** Combined with San Francisco and Tampa Bay to hit .102 (5-for-49) with 1R, 2 doubles, 1HR and 3RBI in 25 games…was acquired by San Francisco from Milwaukee in exchange for INF C.J. Hinojosa on 3/24…was placed on the 10-day injured list on 5/3 (retroactive to 5/1) with a left hamstring strain…was designated for assignment by San Francisco on 5/13 and acquired by Tampa Bay on 5/16 for a PTBNL or cash…appeared in six games with the Rays before being designated for assignment on 5/31 and released on 6/7…was signed by the Yankees as a minor league free agent on 6/8 and hit .299/.375/.500 (46-for-154) with 27R, 10 doubles, 7HR and 31RBI in 46 games with Triple-A Scranton/Wilkes-Barre…hit a "walk-off" double in a 14-13 victory vs. Syracuse in the IL North tiebreaker game…following the season, played for the USA Professional National Team and hit .381/.435/.714 (8-for-21) with 5R, 2HR and 3RBI over seven games in the 2019 WBSC Premier12 Tournament in México and Japan…**2018:** In 67 games with Milwaukee, hit .236 (48-for-203) with 18R, 6 doubles, 6HR and 23RBI…began the season in the Yankees organization and batted .269 (14-for-52) with 4HR and 6RBI in 17 games with Triple-A Scranton/Wilkes-Barre…was acquired by Milwaukee from the Yankees on 5/25 in exchange for a PTBNL (INF Wendell Rijo, 6/16)…posted a 3.42 catcher's ERA (491.2IP, 187ER), as the Brewers went 33-21 in his 54 starts behind the plate…batted .292 (7-for-24) with 3RBI in nine postseason games…became the oldest position player (38 years, 112 days) to make his postseason debut since Los Angeles-NL's José Morales (38 years, 278 days) in 1983…went 5-for-8 in two NLDS games vs. Colorado, becoming the first player in Brewers history with multi-hit efforts in each of his first two career postseason games…was the second catcher in Major League history with multiple hits in both of his first two postseason games, joining San Diego's Carlos Hernandez (4-for-8) in the 1998 NLDS…**2017:** In four games with the Yankees, went 2-for-2 with 1 double and 2RBI…started the season with Triple-A Columbus, hitting .270/.359/.472 (76-for-282) with 38R, 16 doubles, 1 triple, 13HR, 37RBI and 32BB in 86 games…was acquired by the Yankees from Cleveland in exchange for cash considerations on 8/31…was signed to a Major League contract and selected to the Yankees' active roster from Triple-A Scranton/Wilkes-Barre on 9/1…made his Yankees debut in 9/10 win at Texas, pinch-hitting for Gary Sánchez in the ninth and hitting a two-run double…**2016:** Combined with Houston and Pittsburgh to hit .094 (8-for-85) with 3R, 2 doubles, 1HR and 4RBI in 32 games…combined

to throw out 8-of-17 (47.1%) attempted base stealers…was acquired by the Astros from the Padres in exchange for RHP Dan Straily on 3/28…made the Astros' Opening Day roster and appeared in 15 games for Houston, hitting .069 (2-for-29) with 1 double…also made one relief appearance for the Astros, allowing 2R/1ER in 1.0IP (3H)…was designated for assignment on 5/16 and released on 5/22…was signed by the Angels as a minor league free agent on 5/26…appeared in 12 games for Triple-A Salt Lake, batting .231 (9-for-39) with 6R, 3 doubles and 7RBI…was acquired by the Pirates from the Angels in exchange for cash considerations on 6/11…batted .107 (6-for-56) with 3R, 1 double, 1HR and 4RBI in 18 games with Pittsburgh…also tossed a scoreless inning of relief for Pittsburgh (2H, 1K) on 6/21 vs. San Francisco, becoming the first player in the Modern Era to catch and pitch for two different teams in a season…was designated for assignment on 7/22 and elected free agency in lieu of accepting an outright assignment on 7/23…was signed by the Blue Jays as a minor league free agent on 7/28…appeared in 19 games for Triple-A Buffalo and hit .155 (9-for-58) with 6R, 1 double and 1RBI…was signed by Cleveland as a minor league free agent on 12/3…**2015:** Combined with Kansas City and Philadelphia to hit .192 (5-for-26) with 3R, 2 doubles and 3RBI in 16 games…made the Royals Opening Day roster and went 0-for-4 in four games before being placed on the 15-day D.L. on 5/6 with plantar fasciitis in his left foot…made a rehab assignment with Triple-A Omaha, hitting .214 (12-for-56) with 7R, 2 doubles, 4HR and 12 RBI…was reinstated from the D.L. and was designated for assignment on 6/11…was claimed off waivers by the Red Sox on 6/21 before being designated for assignment by the Red Sox on 6/25…elected free agency in lieu of accepting an outright assignment on 6/29…was signed by Seattle as a minor league free agent on 7/2…hit .205 (8-for-39) with 3R, 4 doubles and 5RBI in 10 games for Triple-A Tacoma before being released on 7/15…was signed by Philadelphia as a minor league free agent on 7/17…hit .312 (24-for-77) with 14R, 8 doubles, 3HR and 15RBI in 26 games for Triple-A Lehigh Valley before having his contract selected by Philadelphia on 9/1…batted .227 (5-for-22) with 3R, 2 doubles and 2RBI in 12 games with the Phillies…**2014:** Combined with the Blue Jays and Royals to hit .218 (24-for-110) with 12R, 4 doubles, 5HR and 13RBI in 47 games…made the Opening Day roster with Toronto, his second career Opening Day roster…hit .198 (16-for-81) with 8R, 3 doubles, 3HR and 10RBI in 34 games with the Blue Jays…also appeared in 27 games with Triple-A Buffalo and batted .299 (26-for-87) with 13R, 10 doubles, 3HR and 17RBI…was acquired by Kansas City from Toronto along with RHP Liam Hendriks in exchange for INF Danny Valencia on 7/28…appeared in 13 games with the Royals, batting .276 (8-for-29) with 4R, 1 double, 2HR and 3RBI…appeared on the Wild Card, ALDS, ALCS and World Series rosters but did not play…**2013:** Made his first career Opening Day roster with the Phillies and hit .213 (42-for-197) with 21R, 7 doubles, 9HR and 26RBI in a career-high 68 games…threw out 6-of-39 (15.4%) attempted base stealers…was placed on the 15-day disabled list from 6/9-7/13 after undergoing left knee surgery…combined to hit .125 (2-for-16) with 1 double and 1RBI in four rehab games with Triple-A Lehigh Valley and Double-A Reading…was acquired by Toronto from Philadelphia along with RHP Rob Rasmussen in exchange for RHP Brad Lincoln on 12/3…**2012:** In 50 games with the Phillies, hit .248 (35-for-141) with 14R, 9 doubles, 9HR and 26RBI…Philadelphia was 23-15 in his 38 starts…threw out 12-of-30 (40.0%) attempted base stealers…hit his first career home run on 5/22 vs. Washington off Tom Gorzelanny…hit a ninth-inning, game-tying HR off Craig Kimbrel against Atlanta on 8/31, the first home run that Kimbrel had ever allowed on an 0-2 pitch…also appeared in 37 games with Triple-A Lehigh Valley and hit .266 (33-for-124) with 17R, 8HR and 30RBI…**2011:** Appeared in two games with the Phillies as a September call-up, going 2-for-6 (.333) with 1 double…was signed to a Major League contract and selected to the 25-man roster on 9/17…spent the majority of the season with Triple-A Lehigh Valley and hit .288 (103-for-358) with 56R, 19 doubles, 15HR and 53RBI in 103 games…was named an International League Mid-Season All-Star for the third straight season…following the season, was tabbed an Organization All-Star by MiLB.com…**2010:** Saw his first Major League action with the Pirates, hitting .118 (4-for-34) with 2R and 1RBI in nine games…threw out 4-of-7 (57.1%) attempted base stealers…began the season with Triple-A Indianapolis before he signed a Major League contract and was selected to the 25-man roster on 7/16…made his Major League debut in 7/17 win vs. Houston, going 2-for-5 with 1R and 1RBI…collected his first Major League hit on a fifth-inning single off Bud Norris…spent the majority of the season with Indianapolis, hitting .274 (63-for-230) with 30R, 22 doubles, 1 triple, 9HR and 41RBI in 79 games…was named an International League Mid-Season All-Star…was designated for assignment on 9/7 and outrighted on 9/9…was signed by Philadelphia as a minor league free agent on 12/1…**2009:** Spent the season at Triple-A Indianapolis, hitting .273 (87-for-319) with 45R, 30 doubles, 11HR and 43RBI in 93 games…threw out 25-of-83 (30.1%) attempted base stealers…was named an International Mid-Season and Postseason All-Star…received "Top Star" honors at the Triple-A All-Star Game after going 2-for-2 with 1BB, 1 double and a two-run home run in the International League's 6-5 win over the Pacific League in Portland…**2008:** Combined at Double-A New Hampshire and Triple-A Syracuse to hit .239 (59-for-247) with 35R, 16 doubles, 1 triple, 16HR and 59RBI in 73 games…combined to throw out 20-for-58 (34.5%) attempted base stealers…**2007:** Split the season between Double-A New Hampshire and Triple-A Syracuse and hit .235 (64-for-272) with 32R, 17 doubles, 1 triple, 13HR and 49RBI in 84 games…combined to throw out 26-of-73 (35.6%) potential base stealers…**2006:** Combined at Double-A New Hampshire and Triple-A Syracuse to hit .228 (68-for-298) with 46R, 12 doubles, 7HR and 34RBI in 83 games…combined to throw out 19-of-60 (31.7%) attempted base stealers…**2005:** Spent the season with Double-A New Hampshire, batting .205 (60-for-292) with 27R, 10 doubles, 11HR and 34RBI in 91 games…threw out 28-of-71 (39.4%) attempted base stealers…**2004:** Across three levels (Single-A Dunedin, Double-A New Hampshire and short-season Single-A Auburn), combined to hit .299 (29-for-97) with 12R, 11 doubles, 1HR and 16RBI in 29 games…**2003:** Combined at Single-A Charleston, short-season Single-A Auburn and Double-A New Haven to bat .306 (55-for-180) with 25R, 18 doubles, 5HR and 28RBI in 58 games…**2002:** Made his professional debut with Rookie-level Medicine Hat, hitting .275 (39-for-142) with 20R, 5 doubles, 4HR and 11RBI in 44 games…hit a home run in his first professional at-bat on 6/20 vs. Billings…**PERSONAL:** Full name is Erik Floyd Kratz…he and his wife, Sarah, have three children, Brayden, Ethan and Avery Grace…played for the Major League All-Star team in its 2014 Tour of Japan…is a 1998 graduate of Christopher Dock High School (Pa.)…earned a degree in business administration from Eastern Mennonite University (Va.), where he hit .415 with 33HR and 159RBI during his four-year collegiate career.

Kratz's Career Batting Record

Year	Club	AVG	G	AB	R	H	2B	3B	HR	RBI	SH	SF	HP	BB	SO	SB	CS	E	OBP	SLG
2002	Medicine Hat	.275	44	142	20	39	5	0	4	11	0	0	3	6	32	0	1	3	.318	.394
2003	Charleston	.316	8	19	0	6	3	0	0	2	0	0	2	1	7	0	0	0	.409	.474
	Auburn	.312	49	157	25	49	15	0	5	26	0	1	6	21	31	0	1	1	.411	.503
	New Haven	.000	1	4	0	0	0	0	0	0	0	0	0	0	1	0	0	0	.000	.000
2004	Dunedin	.286	15	49	6	14	4	0	0	6	0	0	1	2	16	0	0	1	.327	.429
	New Hampshire	.333	4	9	1	3	1	0	0	0	0	0	1	2	2	0	0	0	.500	.444
	Auburn	.308	10	39	5	12	6	0	0	10	0	1	0	1	8	0	0	0	.317	.462
2005	New Hampshire	.205	91	292	27	60	10	0	11	34	3	4	6	27	86	2	0	6	.283	.353
2006	New Hampshire	.225	71	258	34	58	10	0	6	27	1	1	8	16	54	1	0	3	.290	.333
	Syracuse	.250	12	40	12	10	2	0	1	7	0	2	0	5	4	0	0	0	.319	.375
2007	New Hampshire	.250	49	160	22	40	15	1	8	30	2	3	5	12	33	0	0	1	.317	.506
	Syracuse	.214	35	112	10	24	2	0	5	19	3	0	1	8	28	0	1	3	.273	.366
2008	New Hampshire	.245	33	102	15	25	5	0	7	19	0	2	4	13	26	2	0	2	.347	.500
	Syracuse	.234	40	145	20	34	11	1	9	24	1	1	2	9	33	1	0	4	.287	.510
2009	Indianapolis	.273	93	319	45	87	30	0	11	43	0	2	1	31	72	7	0	6	.337	.470
2010	Indianapolis	.274	70	230	30	63	22	1	9	41	0	3	9	32	54	1	2	7	.380	.496
	PITTSBURGH	.118	9	34	2	4	0	0	0	1	0	0	0	2	9	0	0	1	.167	.118
2011	Lehigh Valley	.288	103	358	56	103	19	0	15	53	0	2	11	38	72	2	0	8	.372	.466
	PHILADELPHIA	.333	2	6	0	2	1	0	0	0	0	0	0	0	1	0	0	0	.333	.500
2012	Lehigh Valley	.266	37	124	17	33	10	0	8	30	0	4	3	10	20	0	0	1	.326	.540
	PHILADELPHIA	.248	50	141	14	35	9	0	9	26	0	3	2	11	34	0	0	1	.306	.504
2013	PHILADELPHIA	.213	68	197	21	42	7	0	9	26	0	2	1	18	45	0	0	1	.280	.386
	Lehigh Valley	.167	3	12	0	2	1	0	0	1	0	0	0	1	0	0	0	0	.167	.250
	Reading	.000	1	4	0	0	0	0	0	0	0	0	0	1	0	0	0	0	.000	.000
2014	TORONTO	.198	34	81	8	16	3	0	3	10	0	0	3	12	0	0	0	0	.226	.346
	Buffalo	.299	27	87	13	26	10	0	3	17	1	3	0	9	18	0	1	2	.354	.517
	KANSAS CITY	.276	13	29	4	8	1	0	2	3	0	1	0	1	10	0	0	0	.290	.517
2015	KANSAS CITY	.000	4	4	0	0	0	0	0	1	0	1	0	0	2	0	0	0	.000	.000
	Omaha	.214	15	56	7	12	2	0	4	12	0	1	0	5	9	0	0	1	.274	.464
	Tacoma	.205	10	39	3	8	4	0	0	5	0	0	1	3	7	0	0	0	.279	.308
	Lehigh Valley	.312	26	77	14	24	8	1	3	15	0	2	0	18	18	1	0	1	.433	.558
	PHILADELPHIA	.227	12	22	3	5	2	0	0	2	0	0	1	3	0	0	0	1	.261	.318
2016	HOUSTON	.069	14	29	0	2	1	0	0	0	0	0	0	1	14	0	0	1	.100	.103
	Salt Lake	.231	12	39	6	9	3	0	0	7	0	0	1	1	12	0	0	3	.268	.308
	PITTSBURGH	.107	18	56	3	6	1	0	4	1	0	0	0	18	0	0	0	1	.107	.179
	Buffalo	.155	19	58	6	9	1	0	0	1	1	0	2	7	11	0	0	0	.269	.172
2017	Columbus	.270	86	282	38	76	16	1	13	37	1	1	8	32	64	5	1	2	.359	.472
	YANKEES	1.000	4	2	0	2	1	0	0	2	0	0	0	0	0	0	0	0	1.000	1.500
2018	Scranton/WB	.269	17	52	10	14	2	0	4	6	1	0	0	7	10	0	0	2	.356	.538
	MILWAUKEE	.236	67	203	18	48	6	0	6	23	1	2	7	6	40	1	0	3	.280	.355
2019	SAN FRANCISCO	.125	15	32	1	4	2	0	1	3	0	0	2	2	6	0	0	4	.222	.281
	TAMPA BAY	.059	6	17	0	1	0	0	0	0	0	0	0	0	8	0	0	0	.059	.059
	Scranton/WB	.299	46	154	27	46	10	0	7	31	0	2	3	17	21	1	0	4	.375	.500
Minor League Totals		**.259**	**1027**	**3419**	**469**	**886**	**227**	**5**	**134**	**514**	**14**	**35**	**78**	**333**	**751**	**23**	**7**	**61**	**.336**	**.446**
Major League Totals		**.205**	**316**	**853**	**74**	**175**	**34**	**0**	**31**	**101**	**2**	**9**	**12**	**45**	**202**	**1**	**0**	**11**	**.252**	**.354**

LANE, Trevor – LHP

HT: 5-11; **WT:** 185; **B:** L; **T:** L; **BORN:** 4/26/94 in Redmond, Wash.; **RESIDES:** North Bend, Wash.; **COLLEGE:** University of Illinois at Chicago; **OBTAINED:** Selected by the Yankees in the 10th round of the 2016 First-Year Player Draft; **M.L. SVC:** 0.000; **CAREER NOTES: 2019:** Earned Eastern League Mid-Season All-Star honors with Double-A Trenton…**2018:** Was named a Florida State League Mid-Season All-Star at Single-A Tampa…**2017:** Started the season with Charleston, going 4-2 with two saves and a 0.79 ERA (45.1IP, 29H, 6R/4ER, 13BB, 49K, 0HR) in 24 games…did not allow a run in 21 of his 24 relief appearances…was named a South Atlantic League Mid-Season All-Star…**PERSONAL:** Played two seasons at UIC (2015-16) after one season apiece at Campbell (N.C.) University (2013) and Lower Columbia (Wash.) College (2014)…was named the 2016 Horizon League Relief Pitcher of the Year after going 8-5 with a Horizon League-best 1.41 ERA (70.1IP, 11ER) and 90K…graduated from Mount Si H.S. (Wash.) and was the 2012 State Gatorade Player of the Year.

LARRONDO, Denny – RHP

HT: 6-0; **WT:** 165; **B:** R; **T:** R; **BORN:** 5/31/02 in Camajuani, Cuba; **RESIDES:** Bonao, D.R.; **OBTAINED:** Signed by the Yankees as a non-drafted free agent on 7/2/18; **M.L. SVC:** 0.000; **CAREER NOTES: 2019:** Tied for third in the GCL with nine starts.

LEHNEN, Dalton – LHP

HT: 6-3; **WT:** 222; **B:** L; **T:** L; **BORN:** 5/16/96 in Burnsville, Minn.; **RESIDES:** Lakeville, Minn.; **COLLEGE:** Augustana University; **OBTAINED:** Selected by the Yankees in the sixth round of the 2017 First-Year Player Draft; **M.L. SVC:** 0.000; **PERSONAL:** In his only season at Augustana University (S.Dak.), went 3-3 with a 2.60 ERA (52.0IP, 15ER) and 61K in 11 games (10 starts)…prior to transferring to Augustana, attended the University of Cincinnati for two years.

LEZCANO, Oliver – RHP

HT: 6-0; **WT:** 175; **B:** R; **T:** R; **BORN:** 10/30/99 in Chitré, Panamá; **RESIDES:** Chitré, Panamá; **OBTAINED:** Signed by the Yankees as a non-drafted free agent on 7/11/17; **M.L. SVC:** 0.000.

LIDGE, Ryan – C
HT: 6-2; **WT:** 216; **B:** S; **T:** R; **BORN:** 10/27/94 in Arlington Heights, Ill.; **RESIDES:** Hawthorn Woods, Ill.; **COLLEGE:** University of Notre Dame; **OBTAINED:** Selected by the Yankees in the 20th round of the 2017 First-Year Player Draft; **M.L. SVC:** 0.000; **PERSONAL:** In four seasons with Notre Dame, hit .239 (150-for-627) with 69R, 36 doubles, 92RBI and 84BB in 189 games…recorded a .990 fielding percentage and threw out 32.6 percent of base stealers with the Irish…was selected by the Red Sox in the 40th round of the 2013 First-Year Player Draft but did not sign…is the cousin of former Major Leaguer Brad Lidge…graduated from Barrington H.S. (Ill.).

LOCKRIDGE, Brandon – OF
HT: 6-1; **WT:** 185; **B:** R; **T:** R; **BORN:** 3/14/97 in Pensacola, Fla.; **RESIDES:** Pensacola, Fla.; **COLLEGE:** Troy University; **OBTAINED:** Selected by the Yankees in the fifth round of the 2018 First-Year Player Draft; **M.L. SVC:** 0.000; **CAREER NOTES: 2019:** Hit .251 (125-for-498) with 69R, 33 doubles, 2 triples, 12HR, 56RBI and 22SB in 121 games with Single-A Charleston…led the South Atlantic League in extra-base hits (47), tied for third in doubles and finished fourth in total bases (204)…led Yankees farmhands in doubles and ranked fourth in hits…**PERSONAL:** Played three seasons (2016-18) at Troy University (Ala.), where he hit .306 (219-for-715) with 135R, 38 doubles, 14 triples, 12HR, 101RBI, 70BB and 37SB in 175 games…earned a 2018 ABCA/Rawlings Gold Glove Award…graduated from Pensacola Catholic (Fla.) H.S. in 2015…played on the 2015 Pensacola Catholic team that was named high school national champions by *USA Today* after completing a 30-0 season.

LOPEZ, Jason – C
HT: 5-10; **WT:** 160; **B:** R; **T:** R; **BORN:** 3/16/98 in Valencia, Venezuela; **RESIDES:** Valencia, Venezuela; **OBTAINED:** Signed by the Yankees as a non-drafted free agent on 7/2/14; **M.L. SVC:** 0.000; **CAREER NOTES: 2019:** Was named a Florida State League Mid-Season All-Star with Single-A Tampa…**2018:** Was named an MiLB.com Organizational All-Star at catcher.

LOSEKE, Barrett – RHP
HT: 6-0; **WT:** 170; **B:** R; **T:** R; **BORN:** 11/12/96 in Tulsa, Okla.; **RESIDES:** Tulsa, Okla.; **COLLEGE:** University of Arkansas; **OBTAINED:** Selected by the Yankees in the 17th round of the 2018 First-Year Player Draft; **M.L. SVC:** 0.000; **PERSONAL:** Pitched at Arkansas for three seasons (2016-18), going 8-5 with four saves and a 3.13 ERA (112.0IP, 84H, 42R/39ER, 64BB, 131K, 7HR) in 59 games (10 starts)…graduated in 2015 from Jenks (Okla.) H.S., where he was class salutatorian…is the second cousin of Royals OF Alex Gordon.

LUNA, Anyelo – RHP
HT: 6-2; **WT:** 175; **B:** R; **T:** R; **BORN:** 12/16/97 in Luperon, D.R.; **RESIDES:** Luperon, D.R.; **OBTAINED:** Signed by the Yankees as a non-drafted free agent on 7/2/16; **M.L. SVC:** 0.000.

LYONS, Tyler – LHP   NON-ROSTER INVITEE
HT: 6-2; **WT:** 210; **B:** L; **T:** L; **BORN:** 2/21/88 in Lubbock, Tex.; **RESIDES:** Prosper, Tex.; **COLLEGE:** Oklahoma State University; **OBTAINED:** Signed by the Yankees as a minor league free agent on 12/24/19; **M.L. SVC:** 4.064; **CAREER NOTES:** Was originally selected by the St. Louis Cardinals in the ninth round of the 2010 First-Year Player Draft…owns a 13-12 career record with three saves and a 4.20 ERA (281.0IP, 252H, 141R/131ER, 89BB, 289K, 40HR) in 161 games (20 starts) over seven Major League seasons with the Cardinals (2013-18), Pirates (2019) and Yankees (2019)…**2019:** Combined with the Yankees and Pirates to go 1-2 with a 6.39 ERA (12.2IP, 13H, 9ER, 5BB, 17K, 4HR) in 14 relief appearances…began the season with Triple-A Indianapolis, going 4-3 with a 3.35 ERA (45.2IP, 17ER) in 35 relief appearances…also made three relief outings with Pittsburgh (1-1, 11.25 ERA, 4.0IP, 5ER)…was released by the Pirates on 8/11…was signed by the Yankees to a minor league contract on 8/15…in three games with Triple-A Scranton/Wilkes-Barre, posted a 1.93 ERA (4.2IP, 1ER)…was signed to a Major League contract and selected to the Yankees' active roster from Triple-A Scranton/Wilkes-Barre on 9/1…went 0-1 with a 4.15 ERA (8.2IP, 7H, 4ER, 2BB, 12K, 3HR) in 11 relief appearances in his only stint with the Yankees (9/1-29)…made his Yankees debut in the ninth inning on 9/2 vs. Texas, allowing 1ER in 1.0IP (2H, 1K, 1HR)…allowed a "walk-off" HR to Bo Bichette in the 12th inning on 9/13 at Toronto…was on both the Yankees' ALDS and ALCS rosters…tossed a perfect eighth inning in ALDS Game 2 vs. Minnesota (1.0IP, 2K)…struck out both batters faced in ALCS Game 4 vs. Houston…**2018:** Made his second career Opening Day roster with the Cardinals and went 1-0 with a 8.64 ERA (16.2IP, 24H, 16ER, 8BB, 19K, 3HR) in 27 relief appearances…was placed on the 10-day disabled list on 5/11 with a midback strain…made two rehab appearances with Double-A Springfield (1.2IP, 2H, 2ER, 1HR) before being reinstated from the D.L. on 5/26…made four outings with St. Louis before being placed on the 10-day D.L. on 6/8 due to a sprained left elbow…made a total of three rehab appearances with Triple-A Memphis and Springfield, combining to toss 3.0 scoreless innings (1H, 1BB, 3K)…was reinstated from the D.L. on 7/12…was designated for assignment on 7/27 and outrighted to Memphis on 8/3…including his rehab, made seven appearance (three starts) with Memphis and went 1-1 with one save and a 2.49 ERA (21.2IP, 11H, 6ER, 6BB, 21K, 2HR)…**2017:** Made a career-high 50 relief appearances with St. Louis, going 4-1 with three saves and a 2.83 ERA (54.0IP, 39H, 17ER, 20BB, 68K, 3HR)…held left-handed batters to a .178 (15-for-73) average…began the season on the 10-day disabled list recovering from right knee surgery…made three rehab starts with Triple-A Memphis, posting a 1.29 ERA (14.0IP, 2ER)…was reinstated from the D.L. on 4/20…was placed on the 10-day D.L. on 5/2 due to a right intercostal strain…made rehab starts with Single-A Peoria (2.2IP, 4H, 2ER, 1K), Memphis (3.2IP, 6H, 3ER, 1BB, 3K, 2HR) and Double-A Springfield (5.0IP, 3H, 2ER, 3K, 1HR) before being reinstated from the D.L. on 5/23…earned his fourth Major League save on 6/13 vs. Milwaukee-Game 1 (3.0IP, 3H, 2K)…did not allow a home run in 33 straight appearances from 6/21-9/14 (32.0IP)…recorded a career-high 18.2 scoreless inning streak from 7/7-9/1, the longest by a Cardinals pitcher in 2017…**2016:** Made his first Opening Day roster with the Cardinals and went 2-0 with a 3.38 ERA (48.0IP, 35H, 18ER, 14BB, 46K, 9HR) in 30 relief appearances…tossed multiple innings in 11 of his 30 appearances, posting a 2.01 ERA (31.1IP, 7ER) in those games…tossed a season-high 4.2 scoreless innings on two occasions: 6/25 at Seattle and 7/22 vs. Los Angeles-NL…recorded 7K in 3.2 relief innings on 5/6 vs. Pittsburgh, matching the most strikeouts by a NL relief pitcher in 2016…was the first reliever to record at least 7K in 4.0IP-or-fewer since Tampa Bay's Roberto Hernandez on 9/3/2013 (3.2IP, 7K)…was placed on the D.L. on 8/3 (retro to 7/31) with a right knee stress reaction and missed the remainder of the season…was transferred to the 60-day D.L. on 8/3…underwent surgery in November, performed by Dr. George Paletta…**2015:** Went 3-1 with a 3.75 ERA (60.0IP, 59H, 29R/25ER, 15BB, 60K, 12HR) in 17 games (eight starts) over five stints (5/5-16, 6/12-24, 7/7, 8/7-22, 9/2-end of season) with St. Louis…went 3-1 with a 4.10 ERA (41.2IP, 19ER) as a starter and posted a 2.95 ERA (18.1IP, 6ER) in nine relief appearances…scored three runs in his start on 6/19 vs. Philadelphia, tying the Cardinals franchise record for runs scored by a pitcher…also tallied his first career RBI on 6/19…tossed a career-high 5.1 innings of relief on 8/13 vs. Pittsburgh…tossed 7.0 scoreless innings on 9/30 at Pittsburgh as the Cardinals clinched the N.L. Central division…was on the Division Series roster, but did not pitch…also made 16 starts for Triple-A Memphis, going 9-5 with 2CG and a 3.14 ERA (94.2IP, 104H,

34R/33ER, 13BB, 96K, 12HR)…was named Pacific Coast League "Pitcher of the Week" for 6/1-7 after going 2-0 over two scoreless starts (13.0IP)…his 2CG were tied for the most in the PCL…**2014:** Pitched in 11 games (four starts) over four stints (4/21-6/18, 7/7-10, 8/25-30, 9/2-end of season) with the Cardinals and went 0-4 with 4.42 ERA (36.2IP, 33H, 23R/18ER, 11BB, 36K, 4HR)…posted a 1.23 ERA (14.2IP, 2ER) in his seven relief appearances with St. Louis…began the season with Triple-A Memphis before being recalled on 4/21…went 0-3 with a 6.12 ERA (25.0IP, 17ER) in six games (four starts) before being placed on the 15-day disabled list on 5/13 with a left shoulder strain…made a rehab start with Double-A Springfield on 6/9 (2.0IP, 3H, 1ER, 3K) and one with Memphis on 6/14 (2.2IP, 4H, 1ER, 2BB, 3K)…was reinstated from the D.L. and optioned to Memphis on 6/18…in 14 starts with Memphis (including his rehab start), went 8-2 with 2CG and a 4.43 ERA (81.1IP, 94H, 41R/40ER, 18BB, 75K, 9HR)…ranked second among Pacific Coast League pitchers in complete games and tied for first in shutouts (one)…was named the PCL "Pitcher of the Week" for 7/28-8/3 after going 2-0 with 2CG and a 0.56 ERA (16.0IP, 1ER)…**2013:** Saw his first Major League action with the Cardinals, going 2-4 with a 4.75 ERA (53.0IP, 49H, 29R/28ER, 16BB, 43K, 5HR) in 12 games (eight starts) over four stints (5/22-6/21, 7/30, 8/17-27, 9/3-end of season)…posted a 0.96 ERA (9.1IP, 1ER) in his four relief appearances with St. Louis and went 2-4 with a 5.56 ERA (43.2IP, 27ER) in eight starts…began season with Triple-A Memphis, where he made eight starts before being signed to a Major League contract and selected to the 25-man roster on 5/22…made his Major League debut on 5/22 at San Diego, starting the game and earning the win (7.0IP, 4H, 1ER, 1BB, 4K, 1HR)…struck out Jesus Guzman in the first for his first Major League strikeout…also went 1-for-3 at the plate, recording a single off Tim Stauffer for his first big league hit…in 17 games (16 starts) with Memphis, went 7-2 with a 3.32 ERA (100.1IP, 85H, 40R/37ER, 19BB, 86K, 9HR)…was named PCL "Pitcher of the Week" for 7/1-7 after going 1-0 with a 1.80 ERA (15.0IP, 3ER) in two starts…went 3-0 with a 1.60 ERA (33.2IP, 6ER) in five starts with Memphis during the month of July…**2012:** Combined with Double-A Springfield and Triple-A Memphis to go 9-13 with 3CG and a 4.13 ERA (152.2IP, 157H, 75R/70ER, 37BB, 143K, 15HR) in 27 starts…ranked second among St. Louis farmhands in strikeouts…led all Cardinals minor leaguers and the Pacific Coast League in complete games (3)…began the season with Springfield and went 5-4 with a 3.92 ERA (64.1IP, 70H, 33R/28ER, 19BB, 54K, 6HR) in 12 starts…was promoted to Memphis on 6/11 and made 15 starts for the Redbirds, going 4-9 with a 4.28 ERA (88.1IP, 87H, 42ER, 18BB, 89K, 9HR)…**2011:** Made his professional debut with Single-A Palm Beach, going 9-4 with one save, one complete game and a 4.50 ERA (94.0IP, 93H, 51R/47ER, 29BB, 79K, 8HR) in 33 games (12 starts)…made his first 21 appearances in relief before joining the starting rotation…tossed the first no-hitter in team history in a 7.0-inning, 10-0 win in Game 2 of a doubleheader on 8/8 vs. Fort Myers (1BB, 8K)…following the season, made seven starts for the Peoria Javelinas in the Arizona Fall League and went 3-0 with a 4.85 ERA (29.2IP, 28H, 16ER, 7BB, 28K, 4HR)…**PERSONAL:** Was selected by the Yankees in the 10th round of the 2009 First-Year Player draft but did not sign…he and his wife, Jennifer, have a daughter, Savannah…played four years at Oklahoma State, where he went 22-14 in 65 career games (41 starts)…attended Frenship High School in Wolfforth, Texas…was also an All-State quarterback as a high school senior.

Lyons's Career Pitching Record

Year	Club	W	L	ERA	G	GS	CG	SHO	SV	IP	H	R	ER	HR	HP	BB	SO	WP	BK
2011	Palm Beach	9	4	4.50	33	12	1	1	1	94.0	93	51	47	8	4	29	79	4	1
2012	Springfield	5	4	3.92	12	12	0	0	0	64.1	70	33	28	6	1	19	54	2	0
	Memphis	4	9	4.28	15	15	3	0	0	88.1	87	42	42	9	2	18	89	0	0
2013	Memphis	7	2	3.32	17	16	0	0	0	100.1	85	40	37	6	6	19	86	0	0
	ST. LOUIS	2	4	4.75	12	8	0	0	0	53.0	49	29	28	5	3	16	43	0	0
2014	Memphis	8	2	4.43	14	14	2	1	0	81.1	94	41	40	9	0	18	75	6	1
	ST. LOUIS	0	4	4.42	11	4	0	0	0	36.2	33	23	18	4	2	11	36	0	0
	Springfield	0	0	4.50	1	1	0	0	0	2.0	3	1	1	0	0	0	3	0	0
2015	Memphis	9	5	3.14	16	16	2	1	0	94.2	104	34	33	12	2	13	96	0	1
	ST. LOUIS	3	1	3.75	17	8	0	0	0	60.0	59	29	25	12	1	15	60	4	0
2016	ST. LOUIS	2	0	3.38	30	0	0	0	0	48.0	35	18	18	9	0	14	46	2	0
2017	Memphis	0	0	2.55	4	4	0	0	0	17.2	17	5	5	2	0	3	17	0	0
	ST. LOUIS	4	1	2.83	50	0	0	0	3	54.0	39	17	17	3	7	20	68	1	0
	Peoria	0	1	6.75	1	1	0	0	0	2.2	4	2	2	0	0	1	1	0	0
	Springfield	1	0	3.60	1	1	0	0	0	5.0	3	2	2	1	0	0	3	0	0
2018	ST. LOUIS	1	0	8.64	27	0	0	0	0	16.2	24	16	16	3	2	8	19	2	0
	Springfield	0	0	6.75	3	0	0	0	1	2.2	3	2	2	1	0	1	1	0	0
	Memphis	1	1	2.49	7	3	0	0	1	21.2	11	6	6	2	0	6	21	0	0
2019	Indianapolis	4	3	3.35	35	0	0	0	2	45.2	34	20	17	4	1	16	55	4	0
	PITTSBURGH	1	1	11.25	3	0	0	0	0	4.0	6	5	5	1	0	3	5	0	0
	Scranton/WB	0	0	1.93	3	0	0	0	0	4.2	5	1	1	0	0	3	5	1	0
	YANKEES	0	1	4.15	11	0	0	0	0	8.2	7	4	4	3	1	2	12	0	0
Minor League Totals		48	31	3.79	162	95	8	3	6	625.0	613	280	263	60	16	145	585	18	3
Major League Totals		13	12	4.20	161	20	0	0	3	281.0	252	141	131	40	16	89	289	9	0

MacDONALD, Kyle – INF

HT: 6-3; **WT:** 240; **B:** L; **T:** R; **BORN:** 6/17/96 in Mississauga, Ont., Can.; **RESIDES:** Mississauga, Ont., Can.; **COLLEGE:** Arkansas State University; **OBTAINED:** Selected by the Yankees in the 27th round of the 2019 First-Year Player Draft; **M.L. SVC:** 0.000; **PERSONAL:** Played two seasons at Arkansas State (2018-19) following a transfer from Crowder (Mo.) College, where he also played two seasons (2016-17)…graduated in 2014 from St. Paul Catholic (Ont.) H.S.…was a seven-sport athlete, also playing hockey, basketball, volleyball, golf, lacrosse and badminton.

MACIEJEWSKI, Josh – LHP

HT: 6-3; **WT:** 175; **B:** R; **T:** L; **BORN:** 8/14/95 in Morrisville, N.C.; **RESIDES:** Morrisville, N.C.; **COLLEGE:** University of North Carolina at Charlotte; **OBTAINED:** Selected by the Yankees in the 10th round of the 2018 First-Year Player Draft; **M.L. SVC:** 0.000; **CAREER NOTES: 2019:** Earned South Atlantic League "Pitcher of the Week" honors for 8/19-25 after tossing 8.0 shutout innings (2H, 1BB, 7K) on 8/21 vs. West Virginia…**2018:** Ranked fourth among relievers in the Gulf Coast League with a 12.12K/9.0IP ratio (35K, 26.0IP)…**PERSONAL:** Pitched four seasons at Charlotte (2015-18), posting a 21-21 record and 4.36 ERA (330.1IP, 340H, 190R/160ER, 108BB, 264K, 22HR) in 63 games (55 starts)…left as the school's record holder in starts…graduated in 2014 from Panther Creek (N.C.) H.S., where he also played basketball.

MARINACCIO, Ron – RHP
HT: 6-2; **WT:** 205; **B:** R; **T:** R; **BORN:** 7/1/95 in Brick, N.J.; **RESIDES:** Toms River, N.J.; **COLLEGE:** University of Delaware; **OBTAINED:** Selected by the Yankees in the 19th round of the 2017 First-Year Player Draft; **M.L. SVC:** 0.000; **PERSONAL:** Last name is pronounced "mair-uh-NAH-chee-oh"…pitched three seasons at Delaware (2015-17), going 15-10 with two complete games, three saves and a 3.90 ERA (207.2IP, 197H, 105R/90ER, 83BB, 184K) in 47 career appearances (32 starts) for the Blue Hens…was named to the CAA Second Team and ABCA/Rawlings All-East Second Team as a redshirt junior in 2017…played baseball and basketball at Toms River North H.S. (N.J.).

MARTE, Deurys – RHP
HT: 6-4; **WT:** 170; **B:** R; **T:** R; **BORN:** 6/25/99 in Santo Domingo, D.R.; **RESIDES:** Santo Domingo, D.R.; **OBTAINED:** Signed by the Yankees as a non-drafted free agent on 10/15/18; **M.L. SVC:** 0.000; **CAREER NOTES:** Will make his professional debut in 2019.

MARTE, Miguel – INF
HT: 5-11; **WT:** 165; **B:** R; **T:** R; **BORN:** 5/26/01 in Mao, D.R.; **RESIDES:** Mao, D.R.; **OBTAINED:** Signed by the Yankees as a non-drafted free agent on 7/2/17; **M.L. SVC:** 0.000.

MARTEN, Daniel – RHP
HT: 6-0; **WT:** 165; **B:** R; **T:** R; **BORN:** 5/7/97 in Luperon, D.R.; **RESIDES:** Puerto Plata, D.R.; **OBTAINED:** Signed by the Yankees as a non-drafted free agent on 11/24/15; **M.L. SVC:** 0.000.

MARTINEZ, José – INF
HT: 6-0; **WT:** 198; **B:** R; **T:** R; **BORN:** 1/28/99 in Santiago, D.R.; **RESIDES:** Santiago, D.R.; **OBTAINED:** Signed by the Yankees as a non-drafted free agent on 7/2/17; **M.L. SVC:** 0.000.

MARTINEZ, Nolan – RHP
HT: 6-2; **WT:** 165; **B:** R; **T:** R; **BORN:** 6/30/98 in Los Angeles, Calif.; **RESIDES:** St. Petersburg, Fla.; **OBTAINED:** Selected by the Yankees in the third round of the 2016 First-Year Player Draft; **M.L. SVC:** 0.000; **CAREER NOTES: 2018:** Was named the N.Y.-Penn League's "Pitcher of the Week" for 7/30-8/5 after throwing 5.0 perfect innings (7K) for Staten Island…**PERSONAL:** Attended Culver City H.S. (Calif.) where he went 8-3 record with a 1.56 ERA, striking out 83 batters over 58.1IP…had committed to play at San Diego State University prior to signing with the Yankees.

MARTINEZ, Omar – C
HT: 5-11; **WT:** 192; **B:** L; **T:** R; **BORN:** 7/5/01 in San Felix, Venezuela; **RESIDES:** Agua, Venezuela; **OBTAINED:** Signed by the Yankees as a non-drafted free agent on 6/15/18; **M.L. SVC:** 0.000.

MARTINEZ, Thowar – RHP
HT: 6-1; **WT:** 160; **B:** R; **T:** R; **BORN:** 3/29/98 in La Victoria, Venezuela; **RESIDES:** Barrio Beisbol, Aragua, Venezuela; **OBTAINED:** Signed by the Yankees as a non-drafted free agent on 2/9/18; **M.L. SVC:** 0.000.

MATEO, Welfrin – INF
HT: 5-10; **WT:** 170; **B:** R; **T:** R; **BORN:** 9/8/95 in Santo Domingo Centro, D.R.; **RESIDES:** Santo Domingo Centro, D.R.; **OBTAINED:** Signed by the Yankees as a non-drafted free agent on 10/12/13; **M.L. SVC:** 0.000.

MAURICIO, Alex – RHP
HT: 6-0; **WT:** 180; **B:** R; **T:** R; **BORN:** 8/24/96 in Beverly Hills, Calif.; **RESIDES:** Midlothian, Va.; **COLLEGE:** Norfolk State University; **OBTAINED:** Selected by the Yankees in the 27th round of the 2017 First-Year Player Draft; **M.L. SVC:** 0.000; **CAREER NOTES: 2018:** Was named the South Atlantic League's "Pitcher of the Week" for 8/20-26 (1GS, 6.1IP, 1H, 0R, 1BB, 5K) with Charleston…**PERSONAL:** Played at Norfolk State (Va.) University, where he pitched and played infield…in three seasons (2015-17), went 7-5 with a 3.79 ERA (92.2IP, 81H, 63R/39ER, 44BB, 79K) in 29 appearances (11 starts), and hit .299 (118-for-394) with 75R, 27 doubles, 3 triples, 6HR, 72RBI and 49BB in 122 games at the plate…was named 2017 MEAC Player of the Year and was one of nine semifinalists for the John Olerud Two-Way Player of the Year Award as a junior…graduated from Manchester H.S. (Va.), where he played both baseball and volleyball.

MAZZA, John – C
HT: 5-11; **WT:** 195; **B:** R; **T:** R; **BORN:** 2/15/95 in Boston, Mass.; **RESIDES:** Lexington, Mass.; **COLLEGE:** Northeastern University; **OBTAINED:** Signed by the Yankees as a non-drafted free agent on 12/19/19; **M.L. SVC:** 0.000; **PERSONAL:** Played two seasons (2017-18) at Northeastern (Mass.) University after two seasons (2014-15), one as a redshirt, at the University of Maryland…graduated in 2013 from the Dexter (Md.) School, where he also played football and hockey.

McGARITY, Aaron – RHP
HT: 6-3; **WT:** 185; **B:** R; **T:** R; **BORN:** 1/31/95 in Allentown, Pa.; **RESIDES:** Richmond, Va.; **COLLEGE:** Virginia Tech; **OBTAINED:** Selected by the Yankees in the 15th round of the 2017 First-Year Player Draft; **M.L. SVC:** 0.000; **CAREER NOTES: 2019:** Following the season, played for Surprise in the Arizona Fall League, going 1-0 with a 0.79 ERA (11.1IP, 6H, 1ER, 1BB, 15K, 1HR) in 10 relief appearances…**PERSONAL:** Pitched four seasons for the Hokies (2014-17), posting a 9-15 record, nine saves and a 4.37 ERA (169.0IP, 186H, 100R/82ER, 59BB, 151K) in 69 appearances (16 starts)…graduated from Godwin H.S. (Va.) in 2013…was selected by Boston in the 34th round of the 2016 First-Year Player Draft but did not sign.

McNEELY, Shaine – RHP
HT: 6-4; **WT:** 210; **B:** L; **T:** R; **BORN:** 5/10/98 in Orange, Calif.; **RESIDES:** Murrieta, Calif.; **COLLEGE:** Hope International University; **OBTAINED:** Selected by the Yankees in the 16th round of the 2019 First-Year Player Draft; **M.L. SVC:** 0.000; **PERSONAL:** Pitched one season (2019) at Hope International (Calif.) …pitched two years (2017-18) at Cypress (Calif.) College…is a 2016 graduate of Vista Murrieta (Calif.) H.S.

MEDINA, Nelson – OF
HT: 6-2; **WT:** 175; **B:** R; **T:** R; **BORN:** 9/14/00 in San Cristóbal, D.R.; **RESIDES:** San Cristóbal, D.R.; **OBTAINED:** Signed by the Yankees as a non-drafted free agent on 7/2/17; **M.L. SVC:** 0.000.

MEJIA, Alan – OF
HT: 6-0; **WT:** 165; **B:** R; **T:** R; **BORN:** 7/20/01 in Bonao, D.R.; **RESIDES:** Bonao, D.R.; **OBTAINED:** Signed by the Yankees as a non-drafted free agent on 6/15/18; **M.L. SVC:** 0.000.

MEJIA, Renso – RHP
HT: 6-0; **WT:** 155; **B:** R; **T:** R; **BORN:** 3/6/00 in Santo Domingo Centro, D.R.; **RESIDES:** Santo Domingo Centro, D.R.; **OBTAINED:** Signed by the Yankees as a non-drafted free agent on 1/4/18; **M.L. SVC:** 0.000.

MEJIAS, Alex – RHP
HT: 6-0; **WT:** 165; **B:** R; **T:** R; **BORN:** 11/26/96 in Cabimas, Venezuela; **RESIDES:** Cabimas, Venezuela; **OBTAINED:** Signed by the Yankees as a non-drafted free agent on 7/2/15; **M.L. SVC:** 0.000; **CAREER NOTES: 2018:** Seeing time with both the Yankees GCL affiliates, posted the league's second-lowest opponents' batting average among relievers (.173, 13-for-75)…following the season played for the Aguilas de Zulia of the Venezuela Winter League, appearing in one game (1.0IP, 1H, 1BB, 1K).

MENDEZ, Borinquen – INF
HT: 5-11; **WT:** 165; **B:** S; **T:** R; **BORN:** 2/1/98 in Mao, D.R.; **RESIDES:** Mao, D.R.; **OBTAINED:** Signed by the Yankees as a non-drafted free agent on 3/9/16; **M.L. SVC:** 0.000; **CAREER NOTES: 2018:** His 19SB with the GCL Yankees East ranked fourth among all Yankees farmhands and third in the GCL…**2016:** Tied for fourth in the DSL with 27SB in stolen bases.

MENDEZ, Erick – RHP
HT: 6-0; **WT:** 185; **B:** R; **T:** R; **BORN:** 4/7/96 in Santo Domingo, D.R.; **RESIDES:** Santo Domingo, D.R.; **OBTAINED:** Re-signed by the Yankees as a minor league free agent on 12/18/18; **M.L. SVC:** 0.000; **CAREER NOTES:** Was originally signed by the Yankees as a non-drafted free agent on 7/2/14; **2018:** Was converted from an outfielder to a pitcher…**2015:** His eight triples tied for third in the DSL.

MENDEZ, Joel – OF
HT: 6-1; **WT:** 180; **B:** R; **T:** R; **BORN:** 1/28/03 in Santo Domingo, D.R.; **RESIDES:** Santo Domingo, D.R.; **OBTAINED:** Signed by the Yankees as a non-drafted free agent on 12/6/19; **M.L. SVC:** 0.000.

METZGAR, David – INF
HT: 5-8; **WT:** 170; **B:** R; **T:** R; **BORN:** 12/10/94 in Lancaster, Calif.; **RESIDES:** Lancaster, Calif.; **COLLEGE:** Cal State University-Bakersfield; **OBTAINED:** Signed by the Yankees as a non-drafted free agent on 7/3/17; **M.L. SVC:** 0.000; **PERSONAL:** Played four seasons at CSU-Bakersfield (2014-17), where he hit .341 (249-for-731) with 130R, 38 doubles, 11 triples, 1HR, 117RBI and 39SB in 198 games for the Roadrunners…was two-time All-WAC First Team and named the 2015 WAC Tournament MVP…is a 2013 graduate of Paraclete H.S. (Calif.).

MILAM, Kevin – RHP
HT: 6-0; **WT:** 200; **B:** R; **T:** R; **BORN:** 2/13/98 in Fremont, Calif.; **RESIDES:** Brentwood, Calif.; **COLLEGE:** Saint Mary's College; **OBTAINED:** Selected by the Yankees in the 14th round of the 2019 First-Year Player Draft; **M.L. SVC:** 0.000; **CAREER NOTES: 2019:** Was named a Gulf Coast League All-Star after going 1-0 with a league-leading eight saves and a 0.66 ERA (13.2IP, 3H, 2R/1ER, 6BB, 18K) in 13 relief appearances with the GCL Yankees West…**PERSONAL:** Played three seasons (2017-19) as a two-way player at Saint Mary's (Calif.) College…as a freshman in 2017, was a Third-Team All-America selection as a utility player by D1Baseball.com and *Collegiate Baseball*…graduated in 2016 from Heritage (Calif.) H.S.

MILONE, Thomas – OF   NON-ROSTER INVITEE
HT: 5-11; **WT:** 220; **B:** L; **T:** L; **BORN:** 1/26/95 in Stamford, Conn.; **RESIDES:** Monroe, Conn.; **OBTAINED:** Signed by the Yankees as a minor league free agent on 12/13/19; **M.L. SVC:** 0.000; **CAREER NOTES:** Was originally selected by the Rays in the third round of the 2013 First-Year Player Draft…in seven minor league seasons in the Rays organization, batted .245 (509-for-2,076) with 272R, 77 doubles, 40 triples, 17HR, 160RBI and 89SB in 594 games…**2019:** Combined with Double-A Montgomery and Single-A Charlotte, batting .281 (81-for-288) with 48R, 10 doubles, 10 triples, 4HR, 33RBI and 18SB in 83 games…led all Rays minor leaguers in triples…hit .214 (18-for-84) with 10R, 3 doubles, 1HR, 7RBI, 12BB and 6SB in 28 games at Montgomery…spent the majority of the season with Charlotte and hit .309 (63-for-204) with 38R, 7 doubles, 10 triples, 3HR, 28RBI, 20BB and 12SB in 55 games…**2018:** Led all Tampa Bay minor leaguers with 11 triples at Double-A Montgomery…**2017:** In 68 games with Single-A Charlotte, hit .242 (52-for-215) with 25R, 14 doubles, 1 triple, 1HR, 17RBI and 21BB…**2016:** Spent the entire season with Single-A Charlotte, batting .206 (73-for-355) with 36R, 11 doubles, 5 triples, 2HR, 22RBI, 36BB and 15SB in 115 games…following the season, played for Brisbane in the Australian Baseball League and hit .246 (28-for-114) with 18R, 7 doubles, 2 triples, 2HR, 15RBI and 14BB in 32 games…**2015:** Batted .248 (117-for-472) with 64R, 17 doubles, 5 triples, 3HR, 28RBI, 39BB and 26SB in 119 games with Single-A Bowling Green…tied for third among Rays minor league leaders in stolen bases…**2014:** Spent the entire season with Rookie-level Princeton, batting .266 (62-for-233) with 30R, 12 doubles, 4 triples, 2HR, 23RBI and 12SB in 61 games…**2013:** In his professional debut, combined with the GCL Rays and short-season Single-A Hudson Valley to bat .209 (31-for-148) with 21R, 2 doubles, 4 triples, 1HR, 6RBI and 6SB in 42 games…**PERSONAL:** Attended Masuk H.S. (Conn.).

Milone's Career Batting Record

Year	Club	AVG	G	AB	R	H	2B	3B	HR	RBI	SH	SF	HP	BB	SO	SB	CS	E	OBP	SLG
2013	GCL Rays	.190	40	142	18	27	2	4	0	4	1	0	3	7	38	5	1	1	.243	.261
	Hudson Valley	.667	2	6	3	4	0	0	1	2	0	0	1	0	1	1	0	0	.714	1.167
2014	Princeton	.266	61	233	30	62	12	4	2	23	2	1	2	28	61	12	5	3	.348	.378
2015	Bowling Green	.248	119	472	64	117	17	5	3	28	5	2	8	39	93	26	14	6	.315	.324
2016	Charlotte	.206	115	355	36	73	11	5	2	22	6	3	8	36	98	15	11	2	.291	.282
2017	Charlotte	.242	68	215	25	52	14	1	1	17	1	2	1	21	45	2	5	0	.310	.330
2018	Montgomery	.255	106	365	48	93	11	11	4	29	3	0	6	25	102	10	9	4	.313	.378
2019	Montgomery	.214	28	84	10	18	3	0	1	7	0	0	0	12	19	6	1	0	.313	.286
	Charlotte	.309	55	204	38	63	7	10	3	28	3	4	2	20	42	12	2	1	.370	.485
Minor League Totals		**.245**	**594**	**2076**	**272**	**509**	**77**	**40**	**17**	**160**	**21**	**12**	**31**	**188**	**499**	**89**	**48**	**17**	**.316**	**.345**

MINNICK, Matt – LHP
HT: 6-2; **WT:** 215; **B:** R; **T:** L; **BORN:** 3/11/96 in Buffalo, N.Y.; **RESIDES:** Collins, N.Y.; **COLLEGE:** Mercyhurst University; **OBTAINED:** Selected by the Yankees in the 23rd round of the 2019 First-Year Player Draft; **M.L. SVC:** 0.000; **PERSONAL:** Pitched five seasons (2015-19) at Mercyhurst (Pa.) University…was named *Baseball America*'s Preseason DII Pitcher of the Year in 2017…in 2019, was selected as a DII All-American by D2CCA (First Team) and ABCA/Rawlings (Third Team)…graduated in 2014 from St. Francis H.S. in Hamburg, N.Y.

MOLINA, Leonardo – OF
HT: 6-2; **WT:** 180; **B:** R; **T:** R; **BORN:** 8/1/97 in San Francisco de Macoris, D.R.; **RESIDES:** San Francisco de Macoris, D.R.; **OBTAINED:** Signed by the Yankees as a non-drafted free agent on 8/1/13; **M.L. SVC:** 0.000; **CAREER NOTES: 2016:** Was named the Appalachian League "Player of the Week" for 8/15-21 after hitting .444/.474/1.000 (8-for-18) with 5R, 2 doubles, 2HR and 5RBI in five games with Pulaski…**PERSONAL:** Was ranked by MLB.com as the No. 5 prospect for the 2013 international signing period.

MONTAS, Kenlly – RHP
HT: 6-0; **WT:** 185; **B:** R; **T:** R; **BORN:** 5/31/96 in Bani, D.R.; **RESIDES:** Bani, D.R.; **OBTAINED:** Signed by the Yankees as a non-drafted free agent on 4/17/15; **M.L. SVC:** 0.000.

MORA, Gabriel – C
HT: 5-11; **WT:** 155; **B:** R; **T:** R; **BORN:** 6/1/00 in Barquisimeto, Venezuela; **RESIDES:** Barquisimeto, Venezuela; **OBTAINED:** Signed by the Yankees as a non-drafted free agent on 9/1/16; **M.L. SVC:** 0.000.

MORAY, Silvio – RHP
HT: 6-1; **WT:** 175; **B:** R; **T:** R; **BORN:** 12/17/97 in San Pedro de Macoris, D.R.; **RESIDES:** San Pedro de Macoris, D.R.; **OBTAINED:** Signed by the Yankees as a non-drafted free agent on 2/9/18; **M.L. SVC:** 0.000.

MORENO, Raymundo – OF
HT: 6-1; **WT:** 185; **B:** R; **T:** R; **BORN:** 3/9/98 in Punto Fijo, Venezuela; **RESIDES:** Punto Fijo, Venezuela; **OBTAINED:** Signed by the Yankees as a non-drafted free agent on 7/2/14; **M.L. SVC:** 0.000.

MOTA, Sandy – INF
HT: 6-0; **WT:** 170; **B:** R; **T:** R; **BORN:** 9/25/96 in San Pedro de Macoris, D.R.; **RESIDES:** San Pedro de Macoris, D.R.; **OBTAINED:** Signed by the Yankees as a non-drafted free agent on 7/2/15; **M.L. SVC:** 0.000.

MUÑOZ, Anderson – RHP
HT: 5-11; **WT:** 170; **B:** R; **T:** R; **BORN:** 8/4/98 in La Cañada, Venezuela; **RESIDES:** La Cañada, Venezuela; **OBTAINED:** Signed by the Yankees as a non-drafted free agent on 10/13/17; **M.L. SVC:** 0.000; **CAREER NOTES:** Was originally signed by Minnesota as a non-drafted free agent on 3/23/17 (contract voided)…**2019:** Posted a 7-2 record and 2.60 ERA (62.1IP, 46H, 21R/18ER, 23BB, 63K) in 13 games (10 starts) with short-season Single-A Staten Island…tied for the New York-Penn League lead in wins and ranked fifth in ERA…began the season at Single-A Charleston (1-1, 6.14 ERA, 22.0IP, 15ER, 6G)…**2018:** Following the season, played in the Venezuelan Winter League for the Aguilas de Zulia, going 2-1 with a 2.37 ERA (19.0IP, 11H, 5ER, 9BB/1IBB, 17K, 1HR, 2WP) in 15 appearances.

MUÑOZ, Deivi – INF
HT: 5-8; **WT:** 153; **B:** S; **T:** R; **BORN:** 11/30/99 in San Cristóbal, D.R.; **RESIDES:** Santo Domingo, D.R.; **OBTAINED:** Signed by the Yankees as a non-drafted free agent on 4/6/18; **M.L. SVC:** 0.000; **CAREER NOTES: 2018:** Tied for the DSL and organizational lead with nine triples.

MUÑOZ, Jhonatan – RHP
HT: 6-0; **WT:** 180; **B:** R; **T:** R; **BORN:** 8/10/99 in Valencia, Venezuela; **RESIDES:** Guacara, Venezuela; **OBTAINED:** Signed by the Yankees as a non-drafted free agent on 8/10/15; **M.L. SVC:** 0.000; **CAREER NOTES: 2019:** Went 5-3 with a 4.13 ERA (56.2IP, 52H, 34R/26ER, 18BB, 68K, 8HR) in 11 starts at Rookie-level Pulaski…ranked second in the Appalachian League in innings pitched, tied for second in strikeouts and tied for fifth in wins…was named App. League "Pitcher of the Week" for 7/29-8/4.

MYATT, Tanner – RHP
HT: 6-7; **WT:** 220; **B:** R; **T:** R; **BORN:** 5/21/98 in Fayetteville, N.C.; **RESIDES:** Spring Lake, N.C.; **COLLEGE:** Florence-Darlington Technical College; **OBTAINED:** Selected by the Yankees in the 11th round of the 2018 First-Year Player Draft; **M.L. SVC:** 0.000; **PERSONAL:** Pitched two seasons (2017-18) at Florence-Darlington Technical College (S.C.)…had committed to play at the College of Charleston (S.C.) before signing with the Yankees…graduated from Overhills (N.C.) H.S. in 2016.

NARANJO, Marco – OF
HT: 5-11; **WT:** 155; **B:** R; **T:** R; **BORN:** 3/26/01 in Maracay, Venezuela; **RESIDES:** Maracay, Venezuela; **OBTAINED:** Signed by the Yankees as a non-drafted free agent on 9/4/17; **M.L. SVC:** 0.000.

NARVÁEZ, Carlos – C
HT: 6-0; **WT:** 190; **B:** R; **T:** R; **BORN:** 11/26/98 in Maracay, Venezuela; **RESIDES:** Maracay, Venezuela; **OBTAINED:** Signed by the Yankees as a non-drafted free agent on 7/2/15; **M.L. SVC:** 0.000.

NAVAS, Eduardo – C
HT: 5-10; **WT:** 180; **B:** S; **T:** R; **BORN:** 4/5/96 in Valencia, Venezuela; **RESIDES:** Valencia, Venezuela; **OBTAINED:** Signed by the Yankees as a non-drafted free agent on 7/20/13; **M.L. SVC:** 0.000; **CAREER NOTES: 2018:** Following the season, played for the Aguilas de Zulia of the Venezuela Winter League, appearing in one game…**2017:** Threw out 27-of-56 attempted base stealers (48.2%), the best rate among South Atlantic League catchers (min. 50 att.).

NEGUEIS, Felix – OF
HT: 6-2; **WT:** 185; **B:** R; **T:** R; **BORN:** 12/29/00 in La Romana, D.R.; **RESIDES:** La Romana, D.R.; **OBTAINED:** Signed by the Yankees as a non-drafted free agent on 8/16/18; **M.L. SVC:** 0.000.

NELSON, James – INF
HT: 6-2; **WT:** 180; **B:** R; **T:** R; **BORN:** 10/18/97 in Marianna, Fla.; **RESIDES:** Rex, Ga.; **COLLEGE:** Cisco College; **OBTAINED:** Acquired by the Yankees from Miami in exchange for LHP Stephen Tarpley on 1/15/20; **M.L. SVC:** 0.000; **CAREER NOTES:** Was originally selected by Miami in the 15th round of the 2016 First-Year Player Draft…**2017:** In 102 games with Single-A Greensboro, hit .309/.354/.456 (122-for-395) with 41R, 31 doubles, 3 triples, 7HR and 59RBI to earn South Atlantic League Mid-Season and Postseason All-Star honors…was named an MiLB.com Organization All-Star…**PERSONAL:** Played one season at Cisco (Tex.) College…graduated from Redan (Ga.) H.S. in 2015…was selected by Boston in the 18th round of the 2015 First-Year Player Draft but did not sign.

NOVA, Luis – RHP
HT: 6-0; **WT:** 174; **B:** R; **T:** R; **BORN:** 9/5/97 in San Pedro de Macoris, D.R.; **RESIDES:** San Pedro de Macoris, D.R.; **OBTAINED:** Signed by the Yankees as a non-drafted free agent on 8/16/18; **M.L. SVC:** 0.000.

O'CONNER, Justin – RHP
HT: 6-0; **WT:** 200; **B:** R; **T:** R; **BORN:** 3/31/92 in Indianapolis, Ind.; **RESIDES:** Muncie, Ind.; **OBTAINED:** Signed by the Yankees as a minor league free agent on 12/13/19; **M.L. SVC:** 0.000; **CAREER NOTES:** Was originally selected by the Tampa Bay Rays in the first round (31st overall) of the 2010 First-Year Player Draft…**2019:** Signed by the Chicago White Sox on 1/22/19 and converted to the mound…**2018:** Played for St. Paul of the independent American Association, his final season as a catcher…**2017:** Was named a Southern League Mid-Season All-Star with Double-A Montgomery…**2014:** Was an MiLB.com Rays Organization All-Star after hitting .278 (111-for-399) with 49R, 35 doubles, 12HR and 47RBI in 101G between Single-A Charlotte and Double-A Montgomery…was named to the Florida State League Mid-Season and Postseason All-Star Teams…was selected to the *Baseball America* High Class A All-Star Team…participated in the All-Star Futures Game in Minnesota…was named FSL "Player of the Week" for 7/21-27…following the season, played for the Peoria Javelinas of the Arizona Fall League, batting .303 (20-for-66) with 7R, 6 doubles, 1HR and 10RBI in 17 games…earned AFL Rising Stars and All-Prospect honors…**2013:** Following the season, played for Brisbane in the Australian Baseball League…**PERSONAL:** Is a 2010 graduate of Cowan (Ind.) H.S.

OJEDA, Luis – RHP
HT: 5-11; **WT:** 180; **B:** R; **T:** R; **BORN:** 1/10/97 in Chirgua, Venezuela; **RESIDES:** Chirgua, Venezuela; **OBTAINED:** Signed by the Yankees as a non-drafted free agent on 7/2/15; **M.L. SVC:** 0.000.

OLIVARES, Pablo – OF
HT: 6-0; **WT:** 160; **B:** R; **T:** R; **BORN:** 1/27/98 in Zulia, Venezuela; **RESIDES:** Zulia, Venezuela; **OBTAINED:** Signed by the Yankees as a non-drafted free agent on 7/2/14; **M.L. SVC:** 0.000; **CAREER NOTES: 2019:** Finished fourth in the Florida State League (min. 400PA) with a .358 on-base percentage…**2018:** Was named the South Atlantic League's "Batter of the Week" for 6/18-24 after hitting .450 (9-for-20) with 4R, 1 double, 3HR, 11RBI and 1SB in 4G with Charleston.

OROPEZA, Riordan – RHP
HT: 6-3; **WT:** 181; **B:** R; **T:** R; **BORN:** 1/12/02 in Guanare, Venezuela; **RESIDES:** Boconoito, Venezuela; **OBTAINED:** Signed by the Yankees as a non-drafted free agent on 7/3/19; **M.L. SVC:** 0.000.

OROZCO, Jio – RHP
HT: 6-1; **WT:** 210; **B:** R; **T:** R; **BORN:** 8/15/97 in Tucson, Ariz.; **RESIDES:** Tucson, Ariz.; **OBTAINED:** Acquired by the Yankees with RHP Juan De Paula from the Seattle Mariners in exchange for OF Ben Gamel on 8/31/16; **M.L. SVC:** 0.000; **CAREER NOTES:** Was originally selected by the Mariners in the 14th round of the 2015 First-Year Player Draft…**2016:** His 12.12 K/9.0IP ratio with the AZL Mariners was fourth-highest among relievers in the Arizona Rookie League…**PERSONAL:** Full name is Jiovanni Nikolas Orozco…graduated from Salpointe Catholic H.S. (Ariz.) in 2015…was a member of the USA Baseball 17U National Team Development Program in 2013.

ORT, Kaleb – RHP
HT: 6-4; **WT:** 230; **B:** R; **T:** R; **BORN:** 2/5/92 in Grand Rapids, Mich.; **RESIDES:** Lowell, Mich.; **COLLEGE:** Aquinas College; **OBTAINED:** Signed by the Yankees as a minor league free agent on 5/16/17; **M.L. SVC:** 0.000; **CAREER NOTES:** Was originally signed by Arizona as a non-drafted free agent on 9/23/16…**2017:** Ranked third in the Appalachian League with eight saves while going 2-0 with a 0.63 ERA (14.1IP, 5H, 1ER, 4BB, 23K) in 12 games…after being released by the Dbacks on 3/21, made one relief appearance with Joliet of the independent Frontier League (2.0IP, 1H, 3K) and was signed by the Yankees…**2016:** Pitched for Joliet, going 3-4 with a 6.05 ERA (61.0IP, 41ER) in 20 games (12 starts)…was signed by the Dbacks on 9/23…**PERSONAL:** Graduated from Aquinas College (Mich.) in 2014…pitched four seasons for the Saints (2011-14)…graduated from Lowell H.S. (Mich.).

OTERO, Dan – RHP   NON-ROSTER INVITEE
HT: 6-3; **WT:** 205; **B:** R; **T:** R; **BORN:** 2/19/85 in Miami, Fla.; **RESIDES:** Bellevue, Wash.; **COLLEGE:** University of South Florida; **OBTAINED:** Signed by the Yankees as a minor league free agent on 1/17/20; **M.L. SVC:** 6.124; **CAREER NOTES:** Was originally selected by the San Francisco Giants in the 21st round of the 2007 First-Year Player Draft…was selected off waivers by the Yankees from San Francisco on 3/26/13, then selected off waivers by Oakland from the Yankees on 3/27/13…was selected off waivers by Philadelphia from the Athletics on 11/3/15…was acquired by Cleveland from the Phillies in exchange for cash considerations on 12/18/15…in parts of eight Major League seasons with the Giants (2012), Athletics (2013-15), and Indians (2016-19), is 22-8 with a 3.39 ERA (403.2IP, 152ER) and three saves over 358 relief appearances…his 4.68 career K/BB ratio (262K/56BB) ranks eighth among active pitchers (min. 400.0IP)…**2019:** Made 25 relief appearances with the Indians without recording a decision and pitched to a 4.85 ERA (29.2IP, 42H, 17R/16ER, 3BB, 16K, 6HR)…was placed on the 10-day injured list on 6/2 (retro to 5/31) with right shoulder inflammation…was transferred to the 60-day injured list on 7/31…made 15 relief appearances for short-season Single-A Mahoning Valley, Double-A Akron and Triple-A Columbus while on rehab assignment, combining for a 2.25 ERA (16.0IP, 10H, 4ER, 2BB, 10K, 4HR)…was reinstated from the I.L. on 9/1 after missing 77 games…**2018:** Was 2-1 with a 5.22 ERA (58.2IP, 69H, 36R/34ER, 5BB, 43K, 12HR) and one save in 61 relief appearances for the Indians…only issued 5BB (3IBB) all season, the fewest among Major League relievers with at least 50.0IP…his 2.0% walk rate (5BB/247BF) was the lowest in the Majors among qualified relievers…allowed one walk in his final 26 appearances of the season (24.0IP)…made one postseason appearance in ALDS Game 1 at Houston (1.0IP, 2H, 1ER)…participated in the 2018 MLB Japan All-Star Series in November…**2017:** Made 52 appearances out of the bullpen for Cleveland, going 3-0 with a 2.85 ERA (60.0IP, 63H, 23R/19ER, 9BB, 38K, 6HR)…recorded a 1.29 ERA (21.0IP, 16H, 3ER, 1BB, 13K, 0HR) in his final 17 appearances of the season…was on the paternity list from 8/30-9/1…did not make Cleveland's ALDS roster…signed a two-year contract with 2020 club option on 12/5/17…**2016:** Was 5-1 with a 1.53 ERA (70.2IP, 54H, 14R/12ER, 10BB, 57K, 2HR) in 62 relief appearances…led the Indians' bullpen in innings…his 70.2IP were tied for 15th among American League relievers…was third among Major League relievers in ERA (min. 50.0IP), behind Baltimore's Zack Britton (0.54) and the Yankees'/Cleveland's Andrew Miller (1.45)…appeared in six postseason games and had a 2.70 ERA (6.2IP, 6H, 2ER, 0BB, 2K, 2HR)…pitched in three World Series games against the Chicago Cubs, posting a 2.70 ERA (3.1IP, 2H, 1ER, 0BB, 1K, 1HR)…**2015:** Spent the majority of the season in Oakland's bullpen and went 2-4 with a 6.75 ERA (46.2IP, 64H, 35ER, 6BB, 28K, 7HR) in 41 relief appearances…in 4/20 win at Los Angeles-AL (4.0IP, 1H, 4K), set career highs in innings and strikeouts…also made 15 appearances (two starts) for Triple-A Nashville, going 2-0 with a 1.95 ERA (27.2IP, 23H, 7R/6ER, 4BB, 19K, 1HR)…was selected off waivers by Philadelphia from Oakland on 11/3/15…was acquired by Cleveland from Philadelphia in exchange for cash considerations on 12/18/15…**2014:** Went 8-2 with a 2.28 ERA (86.2IP, 80H, 24R/22ER, 15BB, 45K, 4HR) and one save in 72 relief appearances with Oakland…set career highs in wins and innings pitched…led AL relievers in batters faced (349), ranked second in Oakland history and eighth in BB/9.0IP ratio (1.56)…recorded his first career save in 6/19 win vs. Boston…was the losing pitcher (1.1IP, 3H, 2ER, 1K) in the A's' 9-8, 12-inning loss at Kansas City in the AL Wild Card Game…**2013:** Was selected off waivers by the Yankees from San Francisco on 3/26…was selected off waivers by Oakland from the Yankees on 3/27…began the season with Triple-A Sacramento and went 1-0 with a 0.99 ERA (27.1IP, 4R/3ER, 1BB, 22K) with 15 saves in 23 games…was recalled by the A's on 6/14 and spent the rest of the season in Oakland's bullpen, going 2-0 with a 1.38 ERA (39.0IP, 42H, 7R/6ER, 6BB, 27K, 0HR)…his 1.38 ERA was the third-lowest mark in Oakland history by a rookie (min. 30.0IP), behind Joey Devine (0.59 in 2008) and Brad Ziegler (1.06 in 2008)…earned his first Major League win on 7/2 vs. Chicago-NL (1.0IP, 2H)…appeared in four ALDS games against Detroit (5.2IP, 4H, 0ER, 1BB, 2K)…**2012:** Saw his first Major League action with San Francisco in three separate stints (4/6-4/26, 8/14-8/15, 9/4-10/3)…did not record a decision and posted a 5.84 ERA (12.1IP, 19H, 11R/8ER, 2BB, 8K, 0HR) in 12 games out of the bullpen…made his first Opening Day roster with the Giants and his Major League debut in 4/7 loss at Arizona (2.0IP, 3H, 1ER, 1BB, 2K)…recorded his first career strikeout (Justin Upton in the fifth)…spent most of the season with Triple-A Fresno, going 5-5 with a 2.90 ERA (62.0IP, 70H, 26R/20ER, 8BB, 45K, 4HR) in 48 relief appearances…was honored with the Harry S. Jordon Award in spring training (in recognition of the player whose performance and dedication best exemplifies the San Francisco Giants spirit)…did not appear on San Francisco's postseason roster…**2011:** Split the season between Double-A Richmond and Triple-A Fresno…in 56 games out of the bullpen, went 4-4 with a 2.31 ERA (74.0IP, 72H, 23R/19ER, 11BB, 76K, 4HR) and 13 saves…**2010:** Began the season on the disabled list, recovering from "Tommy John" surgery on his right elbow…combined with the Rookie-level AZL Giants and Single-A San Jose to go 5-0 with a 2.25 ERA (24.0IP, 18H, 10R/6ER, 2BB, 18K, 2HR) and one save in 19 relief appearances…**2009:** Began the season with Double-A Connecticut and posted an 0-3 record with a 1.15 ERA (39.0IP, 40H, 6R/5ER, 10BB, 31K, 0HR) and 19 saves…was placed on the 7-day disabled list on 7/27 with right arm soreness…underwent "Tommy John" surgery and missed the remainder of the season…was named an Eastern League Mid-Season All-Star with Connecticut…**2008:** Combined with Single-A Augusta and Single-A San Jose to go 1-1 with a 2.00 ERA (54.0IP, 56H, 16R/12ER, 7BB, 49K, 1HR) in 52 appearances…ranked second in all of minor league baseball with 34 saves…was named a South Atlantic League Mid-Season All-Star with Augusta…**2007:** Made his professional debut with short-season Single-A Salem-Keizer and recorded a 1.21 ERA (22.1IP, 12H, 3R, 0BB, 15K, 1HR) and 19 saves in 22 appearances…was named the MiLB Short-Season Relief Pitcher of the Year and a Northwest League Postseason All-Star…contributed to Salem-Keizer's NWL title…**PERSONAL:** Full name is Daniel Anthony Otero…he and his wife, Tiffany, have three daughters: Kinsley, Sable and Macey…attended Duke University for his first three seasons (2004-06)…transferred to South Florida for one season (2007)…is a 2003 graduate of Ransom Everglades (Fla.) School, where he also played basketball and golf.

Otero's Career Pitching Record

Year	Club	W	L	ERA	G	GS	CG	SHO	SV	IP	H	R	ER	HR	HP	BB	SO	WP	BK
2007	Salem-Keizer	0	0	1.21	22	0	0	0	19	22.1	12	3	3	1	0	0	15	1	0
2008	Augusta	0	0	0.33	25	0	0	0	18	27.0	22	2	1	0	0	4	26	3	0
	San Jose	1	1	3.67	27	0	0	0	16	27.0	34	14	11	1	2	3	23	0	0
2009	Connecticut	0	3	1.15	39	0	0	0	19	39.0	40	6	5	0	2	10	31	2	0
2010	AZL Giants	2	0	0.00	9	0	0	0	1	10.2	7	4	0	0	0	1	7	2	0
	San Jose	3	0	4.05	10	0	0	0	0	13.1	11	6	6	2	0	1	11	0	0
2011	Richmond	2	1	1.42	23	0	0	0	1	38.0	34	8	6	0	2	4	40	2	0
	Fresno	2	3	3.25	33	0	0	0	12	36.0	38	15	13	4	0	7	36	1	0
2012	SAN FRANCISCO	0	0	5.84	12	0	0	0	0	12.1	19	11	8	0	2	2	8	1	0
	Fresno	5	5	2.90	48	0	0	0	0	62.0	70	26	20	4	3	8	45	1	0
2013	Sacramento	1	0	0.99	23	0	0	0	15	27.1	14	4	3	0	1	1	22	0	0
	OAKLAND	2	0	1.38	33	0	0	0	0	39.0	42	7	6	0	0	6	27	0	0
2014	OAKLAND	8	2	2.28	72	0	0	0	1	86.2	80	24	22	4	2	15	45	1	0
2015	OAKLAND	2	4	6.75	41	0	0	0	0	46.2	64	35	35	7	2	6	28	1	0
	Nashville	2	0	1.95	15	2	0	0	0	27.2	23	7	6	1	0	4	19	0	0
2016	CLEVELAND	5	1	1.53	62	0	0	0	1	70.2	54	14	12	2	0	10	57	2	0
2017	CLEVELAND	3	0	2.85	52	0	0	0	0	60.0	63	23	19	6	0	9	38	0	0
2018	CLEVELAND	2	1	5.22	61	0	0	0	1	58.2	69	36	34	12	3	5	43	0	1
2019	CLEVELAND	0	0	4.85	25	0	0	0	0	29.2	42	17	16	6	1	3	16	1	0
	Mahoning Valley	0	0	0.00	1	1	0	0	0	0.2	1	0	0	0	0	0	1	0	0
	Akron	0	0	9.00	3	0	0	0	0	3.0	4	3	3	0	0	1	1	0	0
	Columbus	0	0	0.73	11	0	0	0	0	12.1	5	1	1	1	0	1	8	0	0
Minor League Totals		18	13	2.03	289	3	0	0	101	346.1	315	99	78	17	10	45	285	12	0
Major League Totals		22	8	3.39	358	0	0	0	3	403.2	433	167	152	37	10	56	262	6	1

OTTO, Glenn – RHP

HT: 6-5; **WT:** 240; **B:** R; **T:** R; **BORN:** 3/11/96 in Spring, Tex.; **RESIDES:** Houston, Tex.; **COLLEGE:** Rice University; **OBTAINED:** Selected by the Yankees in the fifth round of the 2017 First-Year Player Draft; **M.L. SVC:** 0.000; **CAREER NOTES: 2019:** Following the season, played for Surprise in the Arizona Fall League, going 3-1 with a 1.88 ERA (24.0IP, 10H, 5ER, 13BB, 26K, 2HR) in six starts…tied for the AFL lead in innings and ranked fourth in ERA (min. 20.0IP)…**PERSONAL:** Pitched three seasons at Rice, going 18-6 with 17 saves and a 2.61 ERA (172.1IP, 123H, 68R/50ER, 87BB, 222K) in 82 appearances (four starts)…left school tied for fourth on the Owls' all-time saves list…was the 2017 Conference-USA Tournament MVP and a member of the 2016 All-Conference-USA First Team…pitched for the U.S. Collegiate National Team in 2016…graduated from Concordia Lutheran H.S. (Tex.) in 2014, where he was named to the 5A TAPPS All-State First Team.

PACIOREK, Nick – RHP

HT: 6-3; **WT:** 195; **B:** R; **T:** R; **BORN:** 6/1/98 in Tarzana, Calif.; **RESIDES:** Newbury Park, Calif.; **COLLEGE:** Northwestern University; **OBTAINED:** Selected by the Yankees in the seventh round of the 2019 First-Year Player Draft; **M.L. SVC:** 0.000; **PERSONAL:** Played three seasons (2017-19) at Northwestern (Ill.) University…was a catcher for his freshman and sophomore seasons before fully converting to the mound by his junior season in 2019…graduated in 2016 from Oaks Christian (Calif.) H.S.…uncle, Tom, played 18 Major League seasons and is a member of the National Collegiate Baseball Hall of Fame.

PALENCIA, Manuel – C

HT: 6-0; **WT:** 175; **B:** R; **T:** R; **BORN:** 9/5/02 in Valencia, Venezuela; **RESIDES:** Valencia, Venezuela; **OBTAINED:** Signed by the Yankees as a non-drafted free agent on 8/31/19; **M.L. SVC:** 0.000.

PANACUAL, Josue – RHP

HT: 5-10; **WT:** 158; **B:** R; **T:** R; **BORN:** 1/13/02 in Los Teques, Venezuela; **RESIDES:** Barlovento, Venezuela; **OBTAINED:** Signed by the Yankees as a non-drafted free agent on 10/11/18; **M.L. SVC:** 0.000.

PAREDES, Edward – RHP

HT: 6-0; **WT:** 160; **B:** R; **T:** R; **BORN:** 1/7/99 in Maracay, Venezuela; **RESIDES:** Maracay, Venezuela; **OBTAINED:** Signed by the Yankees as a non-drafted free agent on 7/2/15; **M.L. SVC:** 0.000.

PARK, Hoy Jun – INF

HT: 6-1; **WT:** 175; **B:** L; **T:** R; **BORN:** 4/7/96 in Seoul, South Korea; **RESIDES:** Seoul, South Korea; **OBTAINED:** Signed by the Yankees as a non-drafted free agent on 7/2/14; **M.L. SVC:** 0.000; **CAREER NOTES: 2019:** Among Eastern League hitters, ranked fifth with a .363 OBP (min. 400PA), tied for eighth with 57BB and was ninth with 60R…**2018:** Led the Florida State League with a .387 on-base percentage…tied for fifth among all Yankees farmhands with 18SB…**2017:** His 25SB were the fourth-most among Yankees minor leaguers…drew 13BB against just 14K with Tampa and was 7-for-7 on SB attempts…**2016:** Stole 32 bases in 35 attempts (91.4%), second-most among Yankees minor leaguers…led the South Atlantic League in triples and ranked third in walks…reached base safely in 23 consecutive games from 4/11-5/10, the ninth-longest on-base streak in the SAL…**2015:** Ranked second in the Appalachian League in runs scored and tied for fourth with 34BB…hit safely in 42-of-56 games, reached base safely via H/BB/HP in 50 games and scored at least 1R in 34 games…earned Appalachian League "Player of the Week" honors for 8/10-16 after batting .400 (10-for-25) with 7R, 1 double, 2 triples, 2HR, 7RBI, 2BB and 1SB in 6G…was ranked by *Baseball America* as the No. 12 prospect in the Appalachian League following the season…**PERSONAL:** Was ranked by MLB.com as the No. 13 prospect for the 2014 international signing period.

PASTEUR, Isaiah – OF
HT: 6-2; **WT:** 182; **B:** R; **T:** R; **BORN:** 6/19/96 in Baltimore, Md.; **RESIDES:** Westminster, Md.; **COLLEGE:** George Washington University; **OBTAINED:** Selected by the Yankees in the 13th round of the 2018 First-Year Player Draft; **M.L. SVC:** 0.000; **PERSONAL:** As an infielder in college, hit .263 (132-for-502) with 91R, 20 doubles, 10 triples, 16HR, 83RBI and 45SB in 156 games over one season (2018) at George Washington University (D.C.) and two seasons (2015-16) at Indiana University…also pitched at GWU, going 2-1 with three saves and a 3.45 ERA (28.2IP, 30H, 15R/11ER, 16BB, 18K, 1HR) in 12 games (three starts)…was the 2018 Atlantic-10 Conference Player of the Year and a 2018 ABCA/Rawlings Third Team All-American…redshirted at GWU in 2017…is a 2014 graduate of Winters Mill (Md.) H.S.

PAULINO, Starlin – INF
HT: 6-1; **WT:** 170; **B:** R; **T:** R; **BORN:** 2/24/00 in La Vega, D.R.; **RESIDES:** La Vega, D.R.; **OBTAINED:** Signed by the Yankees as a non-drafted free agent on 5/12/17; **M.L. SVC:** 0.000.

PEGUERO, Elvis – RHP
HT: 6-3; **WT:** 185; **B:** R; **T:** R; **BORN:** 3/20/97 in Cotui, D.R.; **RESIDES:** Fantino, D.R.; **OBTAINED:** Signed by the Yankees as a non-drafted free agent on 7/2/15; **M.L. SVC:** 0.000.

PEGUERO, Geremias – LHP
HT: 6-2; **WT:** 180; **B:** L; **T:** L; **BORN:** 2/7/00 in La Romana, D.R.; **RESIDES:** La Romana, D.R.; **OBTAINED:** Signed by the Yankees as a non-drafted free agent on 10/15/18; **M.L. SVC:** 0.000.

PEGUERO, José – RHP
HT: 6-2; **WT:** 175; **B:** R; **T:** R; **BORN:** 8/8/98 in Higuey, D.R.; **RESIDES:** Higuey, D.R.; **OBTAINED:** Signed by the Yankees as a non-drafted free agent on 8/15/16; **M.L. SVC:** 0.000.

PEÑA, Jan – RHP
HT: 6-4; **WT:** 180; **B:** R; **T:** R; **BORN:** 6/15/00 in Las Matas de Santa Cruz, D.R.; **RESIDES:** Las Matas de Santa Cruz, D.R.; **OBTAINED:** Signed by the Yankees as a non-drafted free agent on 12/6/19; **M.L. SVC:** 0.000.

PERAZA, Oswald – INF
HT: 6-0; **WT:** 165; **B:** R; **T:** R; **BORN:** 6/15/00 in Cabudare, Venezuela; **RESIDES:** Barquisimeto, Venezuela; **OBTAINED:** Signed by the Yankees as a non-drafted free agent on 7/2/16; **M.L. SVC:** 0.000; **CAREER NOTES: 2019:** Ranked third in the Yankees organization in stolen bases, hitting .263 (69-for-262) with 38R, 6 doubles, 1 triple, 4HR, 20RBI and 23SB in 65 games between short-season Single-A Staten Island and Single-A Charleston…following the season, was ranked as the No. 5 prospect in the Yankees organization by *Baseball America*.

PEREIRA, Everson – OF
HT: 6-0; **WT:** 191; **B:** R; **T:** R; **BORN:** 4/10/01 in Cabudare, Venezuela; **RESIDES:** Barquisimeto, Venezuela; **OBTAINED:** Signed by the Yankees as a non-drafted free agent on 7/2/17; **M.L. SVC:** 0.000; **CAREER NOTES: 2019:** Hit .171 (12-for-70) with 9R, 3 doubles, 1HR and 3RBI in 18 games with short-season Single-A Staten Island…following the season, was ranked as the No. 9 prospect in the Yankees organization by MLB Pipeline…**2018:** Made his professional debut in 2018, hit .263 (44-for-167) with 21R, 8 doubles, 2 triples, 3HR, 26RBI and 3SB in 41 games (35 starts in center field)…following the season was ranked as the Yankees' No. 3 prospect by *Baseball America*…**PERSONAL:** Was ranked by both *Baseball America* and MLB Pipeline as the No. 4 prospect for the 2017 international signing period.

PÉREZ, Cristian – INF
HT: 5-10; **WT:** 170; **B:** R; **T:** R; **BORN:** 10/26/98 in Cagua, Venezuela; **RESIDES:** San Francisco de Asis, Venezuela; **OBTAINED:** Acquired by the Yankees from the Kansas City Royals in exchange for RHP Chance Adams on 12/23/19; **M.L. SVC:** 0.000; **CAREER NOTES:** Was originally signed as a non-drafted free agent by Kansas City on 10/13/15.

PÉREZ, Danienger – INF
HT: 5-10; **WT:** 155; **B:** R; **T:** R; **BORN:** 11/6/96 in Ciudad Bolivar, Venezuela; **RESIDES:** Ciudad Bolivar, Venezuela; **OBTAINED:** Signed by the Yankees as a non-drafted free agent on 7/2/14; **M.L. SVC:** 0.000; **CAREER NOTES: 2017:** Committed just 4E in 148TC (.973) while playing 2B (25GS), 3B (7G/6GS) and SS (8G/6GS).

PÉREZ, Dayro – INF
HT: 5-11; **WT:** 158; **B:** R; **T:** R; **BORN:** 1/31/02 in Azua, D.R.; **RESIDES:** Azua, D.R.; **OBTAINED:** Signed by the Yankees as a non-drafted free agent on 7/2/18; **M.L. SVC:** 0.000.

PÉREZ, Freicer – RHP
HT: 6-8; **WT:** 190; **B:** R; **T:** R; **BORN:** 3/14/96 in Santiago de los Caballeros, D.R.; **RESIDES:** Santiago de los Caballeros, D.R.; **OBTAINED:** Signed by the Yankees as a non-drafted free agent on 12/15/14; **M.L. SVC:** 0.000; **CAREER NOTES: 2019:** Did not pitch…**2017:** Ranked fifth in the South Atlantic League in opponents' BA (.213) and sixth in ERA (2.84)…was one of three pitchers in the Yankees organization in 2017 to win at least 10 games and post an ERA under 3.00…compiled a string of 12 straight starts allowing 2R-or-fewer from 5/15-7/27, going 7-1 with a 1.78 ERA (70.2IP, 16R/14ER) in that span…went 9-0 over 12 starts from 6/14-8/19…in his lone playoff start in G1 of the SAL Semifinals vs. Greenville, tossed 6.0 scoreless innings (4H, 0BB, 9K) in a no-decision…**PERSONAL:** First name is pronounced "FRAY-surr".

PÉREZ, Starling – RHP
HT: 6-3; **WT:** 170; **B:** R; **T:** R; **BORN:** 9/2/00 in Santo Domingo, D.R.; **RESIDES:** Santo Domingo, D.R.; **OBTAINED:** Signed by the Yankees as a non-drafted free agent on 7/2/18; **M.L. SVC:** 0.000.

PERRONE, Sebastian – RHP
HT: 5-11; **WT:** 180; **B:** R; **T:** R; **BORN:** 8/8/98 in Valencia, Venezuela; **RESIDES:** Tocuyito, Venezuela; **OBTAINED:** Signed by the Yankees as a non-drafted free agent on 9/2/19; **M.L. SVC:** 0.000.

PESTANA, Leonardo – RHP
HT: 6-4; **WT:** 190; **B:** R; **T:** R; **BORN:** 7/30/98 in Guatire, Venezuela; **RESIDES:** Aragua, Venezuela; **OBTAINED:** Signed by the Yankees as a non-drafted free agent on 2/26/18; **M.L. SVC:** 0.000.

PICHARDO, Yordi – RHP
HT: 6-3; **WT:** 180; **B:** R; **T:** R; **BORN:** 7/12/02 in Santiago , D.R.; **RESIDES:** Santiago, D.R.; **OBTAINED:** Signed by the Yankees as a non-drafted free agent on 7/2/19; **M.L. SVC:** 0.000.

PITA, Matt – INF
HT: 5-10; **WT:** 175; **B:** R; **T:** R; **BORN:** 4/21/97 in Richmond, Va.; **RESIDES:** Richmond, Va.; **COLLEGE:** Virginia Military Institute; **OBTAINED:** Selected by the Yankees in the 12th round of the 2018 First-Year Player Draft; **M.L. SVC:** 0.000; **PERSONAL:** Played three seasons (2016-18) at VMI, batting .359 (211-for-588) with 146R, 47 doubles, 11 triples, 32HR, 116RBI and 40SB in 150 games…was a 2018 ABCA/Rawlings Third Team All-American…is a 2015 graduate of Cosby (Va.) H.S., where he also played football.

POZO, Miguel – RHP
HT: 5-11; **WT:** 155; **B:** L; **T:** L; **BORN:** 9/9/01 in Santo Domingo, D.R.; **RESIDES:** Santo Domingo, D.R.; **OBTAINED:** Signed by the Yankees as a non-drafted free agent on 7/2/19; **M.L. SVC:** 0.000.

PRIES, Jake – OF
HT: 6-4; **WT:** 220; **B:** R; **T:** R; **BORN:** 10/11/96 in Newport Beach, Calif.; **RESIDES:** San Juan Capistrano, Calif.; **COLLEGE:** UCLA; **OBTAINED:** Selected by the Yankees in the 24th round of the 2019 First-Year Player Draft; **M.L. SVC:** 0.000; **PERSONAL:** Played four seasons (2016-19) at UCLA…graduated from Junipero Serra Catholic (Calif.) H.S. in 2015…was a 2015 Perfect Game USA All-America honorable mention…was selected by Baltimore in the 37th round of the 2015 First-Year Player Draft but did not sign…father, Jeff, was the Yankees' first-round selection in 1984 and pitched four seasons in the organization.

RADNEY, Ignacio – RHP
HT: 6-3; **WT:** 165; **B:** R; **T:** R; **BORN:** 10/4/01 in Santo Domingo Este, D.R.; **RESIDES:** Samana, D.R.; **OBTAINED:** Signed by the Yankees as a non-drafted free agent on 7/2/19; **M.L. SVC:** 0.000.

RAMIREZ, Agustin – C
HT: 6-0; **WT:** 194; **B:** R; **T:** R; **BORN:** 9/10/01 in Santo Domingo, D.R.; **RESIDES:** Santo Domingo Oeste, D.R.; **OBTAINED:** Signed by the Yankees as a non-drafted free agent on 7/2/18; **M.L. SVC:** 0.000.

RAMOS, Daniel – RHP
HT: 5-10; **WT:** 169; **B:** R; **T:** R; **BORN:** 3/6/95 in Puerto Plata, D.R.; **RESIDES:** Puerto Plata, D.R.; **OBTAINED:** Signed by the Yankees as a non-drafted free agent on 10/26/13; **M.L. SVC:** 0.000.

REEVES, James – LHP
HT: 6-3; **WT:** 200; **B:** R; **T:** L; **BORN:** 6/7/93 in Summerville, S.C.; **RESIDES:** Summerville, S.C.; **COLLEGE:** The Citadel; **OBTAINED:** Selected by the Yankees in the 10th round of the 2015 First-Year Player Draft; **M.L. SVC:** 0.000; **CAREER NOTES: 2018:** Was named an Eastern League Mid-Season All-Star at Double-A Trenton…**2016:** His .175 (59-for-338) opponents' BA ranked fourth among all minor leaguers (min. 75.0IP)…was named the Florida State League "Pitcher of the Week" for 7/18-24 after allowing only 2H over 7.0 scoreless innings on 7/20 at St. Lucie…**PERSONAL:** Graduated from The Citadel (S.C.) and played four seasons for the Bulldogs…was the 2015 Southern Conference Pitcher of the Year and a Louisville Slugger All-America Third Team selection…recorded 14 strikeouts and threw a no-hitter vs. Mercer on 4/2/15, earning Louisville Slugger/*Collegiate Baseball* National "Player of the Week" honors…graduated in 2011 from Ashley Ridge H.S. (S.C.).

REYNOSO, Javier – INF
HT: 6-2; **WT:** 190; **B:** R; **T:** R; **BORN:** 7/27/00 in Vega Baja, P.R.; **RESIDES:** Vega Baja, P.R.; **OBTAINED:** Selected by the Yankees in the 33rd round of the 2019 First-Year Player Draft; **M.L. SVC:** 0.000; **PERSONAL:** Graduated from Colegio Angel David (P.R.) H.S. in 2019…had signed to play at Florida Southwestern State College.

ROBINETT, Alex – RHP
HT: 6-0; **WT:** 215; **B:** R; **T:** R; **BORN:** 11/25/92 in Dhahran, Saudi Arabia; **RESIDES:** Bend, Ore.; **COLLEGE:** U.S. Military Academy, West Point; **OBTAINED:** Selected by the Yankees in the 32nd round of the 2015 First-Year Player Draft; **M.L. SVC:** 0.000; **CAREER NOTES:** Was placed on military leave on 8/17/15…**PERSONAL:** Full name is Alexander Michael Robinett…the West Point graduate is a second lieutenant in the U.S. Army…in four seasons at the USMA, went 22-13 with a 2.53 ERA (309.0IP, 87ER), 281K and 14 complete games in 51 games (47 starts)…was named the 2015 *ABCA/Rawlings* NCAA Northeast All-Region First Team as a senior…in his final collegiate start on 5/1/15, set a school record by recording 21 strikeouts in a three-hit shutout vs. Air Force, which marked the NCAA's highest single-game strikeout total since San Diego State's Stephen Strasburg had 23K vs. Utah in 2008…threw the fifth no-hitter in the Academy's history on 2/28/15 vs. Longwood…represented Saudi Arabia in the Little League World Series in 2004 and 2005…lettered three years at Mountain View H.S. in Bend, Ore., where he was named first-team All-State.

ROBINSON, Mitchell – INF
HT: 6-3; **WT:** 200; **B:** R; **T:** R; **BORN:** 3/17/96 in Langley, B.C., Canada; **RESIDES:** Surrey, B.C., Canada; **COLLEGE:** University of British Columbia; **OBTAINED:** Selected by the Yankees in the 21st round of the 2018 First-Year Player Draft; **M.L. SVC:** 0.000; **PERSONAL:** Played two seasons (2017-18) at UBC after one (2015) at Central Arizona College…graduated from Clayton Heights (B.C.) Secondary School…was selected by the Miami Marlins in the 22nd round of the 2014 First-Year Player Draft but did not sign.

RODRIGUEZ, Carlos D. – RHP
HT: 6-0; **WT:** 155; **B:** R; **T:** R; **BORN:** 12/13/98 in Panamá City, Panamá; **RESIDES:** Colón, Panamá; **OBTAINED:** Signed by the Yankees as a non-drafted free agent on 3/18/16; **M.L. SVC:** 0.000; **CAREER NOTES: 2018:** His 2.44 ERA with the GCL Yankees West ranked third among Yankees U.S.-based minor leaguers…ranked among GCL League leaders in opp. BA (second, .210), WHIP (third, 1.04) and ERA (fifth).

RODRIGUEZ, Jesús – C
HT: 5-11; **WT:** 165; **B:** R; **T:** R; **BORN:** 4/23/02 in La Victoria, Venezuela; **RESIDES:** Cajima, Venezuela; **OBTAINED:** Signed by the Yankees as a non-drafted free agent on 7/2/18; **M.L. SVC:** 0.000.

RODRIGUEZ, Jhoiner – C
HT: 5-11; **WT:** 180; **B:** R; **T:** R; **BORN:** 9/12/99 in Carora, Venezuela; **RESIDES:** Carora, Venezuela; **OBTAINED:** Signed by the Yankees as a non-drafted free agent on 7/13/17; **M.L. SVC:** 0.000.

RODRIGUEZ, Meure – C
HT: 6-2; **WT:** 200; **B:** R; **T:** R; **BORN:** 5/20/99 in Maracaibo, Venezuela; **RESIDES:** Maracaibo, Venezuela; **OBTAINED:** Signed by the Yankees as a non-drafted free agent on 7/2/15; **M.L. SVC:** 0.000.

RODRIGUEZ, Nicio – RHP
HT: 6-3; **WT:** 175; **B:** R; **T:** R; **BORN:** 9/3/99 in Monte Cristi, D.R.; **RESIDES:** Monte Cristi, D.R.; **OBTAINED:** Signed by the Yankees as a non-drafted free agent on 2/9/18; **M.L. SVC:** 0.000.

RODRIGUEZ, Osiel – RHP
HT: 6-2; **WT:** 210; **B:** R; **T:** R; **BORN:** 11/22/01 in Ciego de Ávila, Cuba; **RESIDES:** Santo Domingo, D.R.; **OBTAINED:** Signed by the Yankees as a non-drafted free agent on 7/29/18; **M.L. SVC:** 0.000; **PERSONAL:** Was named by *Baseball America* as the No. 5 prospect (and No. 1 pitcher) in the 2018 international signing period…was also tabbed No. 7 by FanGraphs and No. 10 by MLB.com.

RODRIGUEZ, Pedro – LHP
HT: 5-10; **WT:** 145; **B:** L; **T:** L; **BORN:** 8/11/02 in Valencia, Venezuela; **RESIDES:** Valencia, Venezuela; **OBTAINED:** Signed by the Yankees as a non-drafted free agent on 7/25/19; **M.L. SVC:** 0.000.

ROJAS, Adonny – RHP
HT: 6-0; **WT:** 170; **B:** R; **T:** R; **BORN:** 1/3/96 in Castillo, D.R.; **RESIDES:** San Francisco de Macoris, D.R.; **OBTAINED:** Signed by the Yankees as a non-drafted free agent on 7/2/15; **M.L. SVC:** 0.000.

ROJAS, Angel – INF
HT: 6-0; **WT:** 160; **B:** R; **T:** R; **BORN:** 11/26/00 in Sabana Grande de Palenque, D.R.; **RESIDES:** Sabana Grande de Palenque, D.R.; **OBTAINED:** Signed by the Yankees as a non-drafted free agent on 1/2/18; **M.L. SVC:** 0.000; **CAREER NOTES:** Was signed by the Atlanta Braves as a non-drafted free agent on 7/2/17 but his contract was voided on 11/21/17…**2018:** His nine triples were tied for the most in the DSL…was named a DSL All-Star by *Baseball America*.

ROJAS, Ronny – INF
HT: 6-1; **WT:** 180; **B:** S; **T:** R; **BORN:** 8/23/01 in Santiago de los Caballeros, D.R.; **RESIDES:** Santiago de los Caballeros, D.R.; **OBTAINED:** Signed by the Yankees as a non-drafted free agent on 9/8/17; **M.L. SVC:** 0.000; **CAREER NOTES: 2019:** Led the GCL with 36BB…drew walks in 21.1% of his 171PA…**PERSONAL:** Was ranked by MLB Pipeline as the No. 11 prospect for the 2017 international signing period.

ROMAN, Ronald – LHP
HT: 6-3; **WT:** 185; **B:** L; **T:** L; **BORN:** 10/10/01 in Puerto Plata, D.R.; **RESIDES:** Puerto Plata, D.R.; **OBTAINED:** Was acquired by the Yankees with cash considerations from the Arizona Diamondbacks in exchange for OF Tim Locastro on 1/16/19; **M.L. SVC:** 0.000; **CAREER NOTES:** Was originally signed by the Diamondbacks as a non-drafted free agent on 7/2/18.

ROSA, Adonis – RHP
HT: 6-1; **WT:** 160; **B:** R; **T:** R; **BORN:** 11/17/94 in Santiago de los Caballeros, D.R.; **RESIDES:** Santiago de los Caballeros, D.R.; **OBTAINED:** Signed by the Yankees as a non-drafted free agent on 12/19/13; **M.L. SVC:** 0.001; **CAREER NOTES:** Has pitched for the Gigantes del Cibao of the Dominican Winter League the past four offseasons…**2019:** Made his Major League debut, pitching the final 2.0IP (1H, 1ER, 2K, 1HR) of the Yankees' 8-1 win on 8/13 vs. Baltimore…struck out his first Major League batter (Rio Ruiz) to begin a 1-2-3 eighth…was signed to a Major League contract and selected from Triple-A Scranton/Wilkes-Barre prior to the game and optioned to Scranton/WB following the game…was designated for assignment on 9/10 and outrighted off the Major League roster on 9/13…combined with Scranton/WB and Double-A Trenton to go 9-1 with a 4.18 ERA (103.1IP, 48ER, 88K) in 25 games (13 starts)…**2018:** Led all Yankees farmhands with 14 wins…his 12 wins with Single-A Tampa were second in the Florida State League…was named a FSL Mid-Season All-Star…following the season, threw to a rehabbing Aaron Judge in a sim game on 9/17 at Yankee Stadium…**2016:** Ended the season with a 19.0-inning scoreless streak (8/16-9/1)…**2015:** His seven wins led the Appalachian League.

ROSARIO, Alexander – RHP
HT: 6-3; **WT:** 185; **B:** R; **T:** R; **BORN:** 1/19/95 in Tamboril, D.R.; **RESIDES:** Tamboril, D.R.; **OBTAINED:** Signed by the Yankees as a non-drafted free agent on 12/15/14; **M.L. SVC:** 0.000.

ROSARIO, Carlos – RHP
HT: 6-2; **WT:** 170; **B:** R; **T:** R; **BORN:** 6/26/00 in Villa Altagracia, D.R.; **RESIDES:** Villa Altagracia, D.R.; **OBTAINED:** Signed by the Yankees as a non-drafted free agent on 10/8/19; **M.L. SVC:** 0.000.

ROSARIO, Hemmanuel – C
HT: 6-2; **WT:** 200; **B:** R; **T:** R; **BORN:** 8/21/00 in Juncos, P.R.; **RESIDES:** Juncos, P.R.; **OBTAINED:** Signed by the Yankees as a non-drafted free agent on 6/26/17; **M.L. SVC:** 0.000.

ROSARIO, Stanley – OF
HT: 6-2; **WT:** 195; **B:** L; **T:** R; **BORN:** 12/1/00 in New York, N.Y.; **RESIDES:** Santiago de los Caballeros, D.R.; **OBTAINED:** Signed by the Yankees as a non-drafted free agent on 7/2/17; **M.L. SVC:** 0.000.

RUEGGER, Charlie – RHP
HT: 6-6; **WT:** 218; **B:** R; **T:** R; **BORN:** 7/14/97 in Morris Plains, N.J.; **RESIDES:** Morris Plains, N.J.; **COLLEGE:** Stevens Institute of Technology; **OBTAINED:** Selected by the Yankees in the 33rd round of the 2018 First-Year Player Draft; **M.L. SVC:** 0.000; **PERSONAL:** Pitched three seasons (2016-18) at Stevens Institute of Technology in Hoboken, N.J., going 11-3 with eight saves and a 3.25 ERA (133.0IP, 134H, 57R/48ER, 38BB, 142K, 6HR)…is a 2015 graduate of Whippany Park (N.J.) H.S., where he also played basketball.

RUTA, Ben – OF
HT: 6-3; **WT:** 195; **B:** R; **T:** L; **BORN:** 6/8/94 in Princeton, N.J.; **RESIDES:** Hoboken, N.J.; **COLLEGE:** Wagner College; **OBTAINED:** Selected by the Yankees in the 30th round of the 2016 First-Year Player Draft; **M.L. SVC:** 0.000; **CAREER NOTES: 2019:** Ranked second in the Yankees organization with 25 stolen bases and fifth with 115 hits…**2018:** Led Yankees minor leaguers with 37SB and ranked third in batting average (.300, 134-for-447)…his 25SB with Single-A Tampa were tied for fourth in the Florida State League…following the season, was named an Organization All-Star by MiLB.com…**PERSONAL:** Attended Wagner College (N.Y.), where he earned All-Northeast Conference First Team honors as both a junior and senior…recorded the fourth-most hits in the conference as a senior…over four seasons at Wagner, batted .333 (172-for-516) with 91R, 33 doubles, 4 triples, 4HR and 88RBI in 146 games…graduated from West Windsor-Plainsboro South H.S. (N.J.).

SALAS, Daniel – RHP
HT: 6-3; **WT:** 189; **B:** R; **T:** R; **BORN:** 2/16/03 in Barquisimeto, Venezuela; **RESIDES:** Barquisimeto, Venezuela; **OBTAINED:** Signed by the Yankees as a non-drafted free agent on 9/12/19; **M.L. SVC:** 0.000.

SALINAS, Raimfer – OF
HT: 6-0; **WT:** 175; **B:** R; **T:** R; **BORN:** 12/31/00 in San Felix, Venezuela; **RESIDES:** San Felix, Venezuela; **OBTAINED:** Signed by the Yankees as a non-drafted free agent on 12/22/17; **M.L. SVC:** 0.000; **PERSONAL:** Was ranked by MLB Pipeline as the No. 6 prospect and by *Baseball America* as the No. 10 prospect for the 2017 international signing period.

SÁNCHEZ, Angel – RHP
HT: 6-2; **WT:** 185; **B:** R; **T:** R; **BORN:** 6/26/01 in Punto Fijo, Venezuela; **RESIDES:** Punto Fijo, Venezuela; **OBTAINED:** Signed by the Yankees as a non-drafted free agent on 7/2/19; **M.L. SVC:** 0.000.

SÁNCHEZ, Brandom – LHP
HT: 6-3; **WT:** 185; **B:** L; **T:** L; **BORN:** 2/17/00 in Santo Domingo Centro, D.R.; **RESIDES:** Bajos De Haina, D.R.; **OBTAINED:** Signed by the Yankees as a non-drafted free agent on 10/15/18; **M.L. SVC:** 0.000.

SÁNCHEZ, Cesar – OF
HT: 5-10; **WT:** 150; **B:** L; **T:** L; **BORN:** 4/5/03 in San Carlos, Venezuela; **RESIDES:** San Carlos, Venezuela; **OBTAINED:** Signed by the Yankees as a non-drafted free agent on 8/8/19; **M.L. SVC:** 0.000.

SANDS, Donny – C
HT: 6-2; **WT:** 190; **B:** R; **T:** R; **BORN:** 5/16/96 in Tucson, Ariz.; **RESIDES:** Tucson, Ariz.; **OBTAINED:** Selected by the Yankees in the eighth round of the 2015 First-Year Player Draft; **M.L. SVC:** 0.000; **CAREER NOTES: 2019:** Following the season, played for Surprise in the Arizona Fall League, hitting .204 (11-for-54) with 5R, 3 doubles, 1HR and 9RBI in 16 games…**2017:** Was named an MiLB.com Organization All-Star…**2016:** Converted to catcher and committed just 2E in 182TC (.989) while throwing out 6-of-33 attempted base stealers (18.2%)…**2015:** Ranked third in the GCL in OBP (.405) and seventh in batting average (.309)…was selected as a GCL Postseason All-Star…**PERSONAL:** Graduated from Salpointe Catholic H.S. (Ariz.) and was named the 2015 *ABCA/Rawlings* All-Region VII Team…was formerly a batboy for the University of New Mexico.

SANFORD, Jake – OF
HT: 6-3; **WT:** 215; **B:** L; **T:** R; **BORN:** 10/24/97 in Halifax, N.S., Can.; **RESIDES:** Dartmouth, N.S., Can.; **COLLEGE:** Western Kentucky University; **OBTAINED:** Selected by the Yankees in the third round of the 2019 First-Year Player Draft; **M.L. SVC:** 0.000; **CAREER NOTES: 2019:** Tied for eighth in the New York-Penn League with 7HR at short-season Single-A Staten Island…**PERSONAL:** Won the 2019 Conference-USA "Player of the Year" Award in his only season at Western Kentucky after two seasons (2017-18) at McCook (Neb.) Community College…became the first player in C-USA history to win the Triple Crown, hitting .398/.483/.805 (88-for-221) with 65R, 20 doubles, 2 triples, 22HR, 66RBI and 33BB in 56 games as a junior…led the NCAA in slugging, ranked third in total bases (178) and tied for 10th in HRs…was a 2019 consensus first-team All-American (ABCA, NCBWA, Perfect Game/Rawlings, *Collegiate Baseball*, D1Baseball.com) while placing on the second team at *Baseball America*…was a Dick Howser Trophy Semifinalist and made the midseason watch list for the Golden Spikes Award…was named the 2018-19 Michael L. Slive Conference-USA Male Athlete of the Year…over a two-game span from 3/24-26/19, went 6-for-11 with 9R, 1 double, 5HR and 15RBI…graduated in 2016 from Auburn Drive (N.S.) H.S., where he played both baseball and volleyball…is the highest-selected Nova Scotian in the history of the First-Year Player Draft…only two Nova Scotians have played in the Majors: LHP Vince Horsman (1991-95) and OF Rick Lisi (1981).

SANTANA, Carlos – RHP
HT: 6-7; **WT:** 195; **B:** R; **T:** R; **BORN:** 1/4/99 in Jima Abajo, D.R.; **RESIDES:** Jima Abajo, D.R.; **OBTAINED:** Signed by the Yankees as a non-drafted free agent on 1/18/18; **M.L. SVC:** 0.000.

SANTANA, Geralmi – RHP
HT: 6-3; **WT:** 173; **B:** R; **T:** R; **BORN:** 12/7/00 in San Pedro de Macoris, D.R.; **RESIDES:** San Pedro de Macoris, D.R.; **OBTAINED:** Signed by the Yankees as a non-drafted free agent on 7/2/19; **M.L. SVC:** 0.000.

SANTANA, Victor – RHP
HT: 6-1; **WT:** 185; **B:** R; **T:** R; **BORN:** 5/6/99 in Galvan, D.R.; **RESIDES:** Neiba, D.R.; **OBTAINED:** Signed by the Yankees as a non-drafted free agent on 1/17/18; **M.L. SVC:** 0.000.

SANTOS, Luis – INF
HT: 5-8; **WT:** 160; **B:** R; **T:** R; **BORN:** 1/4/00 in Paso de la Boca, Mexico; **RESIDES:** Tlalixcoyan, Mexico; **OBTAINED:** Signed by the Yankees as a non-drafted free agent on 5/25/17; **M.L. SVC:** 0.000.

SANTOS, Madison – OF
HT: 5-10; **WT:** 165; **B:** R; **T:** R; **BORN:** 9/6/99 in Monte Cristi, D.R.; **RESIDES:** Monte Cristi, D.R.; **OBTAINED:** Signed by the Yankees as a non-drafted free agent on 1/17/18; **M.L. SVC:** 0.000; **CAREER NOTES: 2019:** Was named Appalachian League "Player of the Week" for 8/19-25 at Rookie-level Pulaski…**2018:** His nine triples were tied for the most in the DSL.

SAUER, Matt – RHP
HT: 6-4; **WT:** 205; **B:** R; **T:** R; **BORN:** 1/21/99 in Santa Maria, Calif.; **RESIDES:** Tampa, Fla.; **OBTAINED:** Selected by the Yankees in the second round of the 2017 First-Year Player Draft; **M.L. SVC:** 0.000; **CAREER NOTES: 2018:** Went 3-6 with a 3.90 ERA (67.0IP, 60H, 31R/29ER, 18BB, 45K, 3HR) in 13 starts for short-season Single-A Staten Island…allowed 1ER-or-fewer in eight of his 13 starts…held lefties to a .188 BA (22-for-117)…following the season, was tabbed the No. 10 prospect in the Yankees organization by *Baseball America*…**2017:** Made his professional debut with the GCL Yankees West, going 0-2 with a 5.40 ERA (11.2IP, 13H, 9R/7ER, 8BB, 12K) over six starts…**PERSONAL:** Graduated from Ernest Righetti H.S. (Calif.)…went 9-1 with a 0.98 ERA (78.1IP, 42H, 18R/11ER, 31BB, 142K) in 14 appearances (13 starts) his senior season while also playing shortstop, to earn the 2017 PAC-8 League Most Valuable Player Award…was a member of the 2015 USA 17U National Team Development Program…prior to signing, was committed to the University of Arizona…was tabbed as the No. 28 overall prospect (and No. 15 pitcher) in the 2017 draft class by *Baseball America*.

SAWYER, Wynston – C   NON-ROSTER INVITEE
HT: 6-3; **WT:** 215; **B:** R; **T:** R; **BORN:** 11/14/91 in San Diego, Calif.; **RESIDES:** San Diego, Calif.; **OBTAINED:** Signed by the Yankees as a minor league free agent on 1/24/20; **M.L. SVC:** 0.000; **CAREER NOTES:** Was originally selected by Baltimore in the eighth round of the 2010 First-Year Player Draft…signed by the Minnesota Twins as a minor league free agent on 12/31/17 and re-signed on 11/1/18…signed by the Los Angeles Dodgers as a minor league free agent on 11/12/16…has played 10 minor league seasons in the Orioles (2010-16), Dodgers (2017) and Twins (2018-19) organizations, batting .248 (538-for-2,166) with 274R, 127 doubles, 6 triples, 41HR, 288RBI and 273BB in 641 games…**2019:** Batted .260 (40-for-154) with 23R, 17 doubles, 2HR, 20RBI and 11BB in 43 games with Triple-A Rochester…reached base safely in 32-of-43 games…was placed on Rochester's injured list on two occasions (4/14-5/29, 8/2-8/13) with left hamstring strains…**2018:** Combined with Double-A Chattanooga and Triple-A Rochester to hit .257 (26-for-101) with 3 doubles, 2HR, 13RBI and 16BB over 36 games…caught 12-of-25 (48.0%) attempted base stealers…began the year with Chattanooga and batted .143 (5-for-35)…was promoted to Rochester on 5/1 and slashed .318/.446/.394 with 13R, 2 doubles, 1HR, 11RBI and 11BB in 23 games…ended the season on the D.L. with a left hamate fracture (6/25-9/25)…**2017:** Batted .281/.341/.453 (54-for-192) with 17R, 16 doubles, 1 triple, 5HR, 20RBI and 15BB over 57 games between Double-A Tulsa and Rookie-level AZL Dodgers…played most of the season with Tulsa, batting .277/.333/.429 (51-for-184) with 16R, 14 doubles, 1 triple, 4HR, 17RBI and 13BB in 54 games…was placed on Tulsa's disabled list from 7/8-9/20…hit .375 (3-for-8) with 1R, 2 doubles, 1HR, 3RBI and 2BB in three rehab games with the AZL Dodgers…**2016:** Hit .286/.422/.474 (88-for-308) with 53R, 20 doubles, 1 triple, 12HR, 54RBI and 64BB in 92 games between Single-A Frederick and Double-A Bowie…caught 10-of-31 (32.3%) attempted base stealers…was named the Carolina League "Player of the Week" for 5/23-29, batting .385/.485/.731 (10-for-26) with 5R, 1 double, 1 triple, 2HR, 5RBI and 6BB in eight games…was on Frederick's disabled list from 8/2-17 with a right hamstring injury…**2015:** Spent the entire season with Single-A Frederick, hitting .238 (58-for-254) with 32R, 14 doubles, 2 triples, 2HR, 33RBI and 9SB in 74 games…was on Frederick's disabled list on two occasions (4/9-5/15, 5/20-6/10)…**2014:** Batted .250 (68-for-272) with 29R, 14 doubles, 4HR and 33RBI in 81 games with Single-A Frederick…was on Frederick's disabled list on two occasions (6/5-27, 8/27-9/17)…**2013:** Appeared in 92 games for Single-A Delmarva, hitting .238 (75-for-315) with 54R, 18 doubles, 2 triples, 8HR, 38RBI and 42BB…was on Delmarva's disabled list from 6/5-7/5…**2012:** Spent the entire season with Single-A Delmarva, batting .221 (64-for-289) with 26R, 14 doubles, 2HR, 49RBI and 39BB in 86 games…was on Delmarva's disabled list from 4/19-5/7…**2011:** Batted .231 (59-for-255) with 22R, 11 doubles, 3HR, 27RBI and 25BB with short-season Single-A Aberdeen…**2010:** Made his professional debut with the GCL Orioles and hit .231 (6-for-26) with 1R, 1HR and 1RBI across nine games…**PERSONAL:** Graduated from Scripps Ranch H.S. (Calif.) in 2010.

Sawyer's Career Batting Record

Year	Club	AVG	G	AB	R	H	2B	3B	HR	RBI	SH	SF	HP	BB	SO	SB	CS	E	OBP	SLG
2010	GCL Orioles	.231	9	26	1	6	0	0	1	1	0	0	1	0	2	0	0	0	.259	.346
2011	Aberdeen	.231	71	255	22	59	11	0	3	27	1	2	4	25	61	0	2	4	.308	.310
2012	Delmarva	.221	86	289	26	64	14	0	2	49	0	5	4	39	52	2	1	8	.318	.291
2013	Delmarva	.238	92	315	54	75	18	2	8	38	0	3	6	42	69	1	0	6	.336	.384
2014	Frederick	.250	81	272	29	68	14	0	4	33	1	8	2	33	40	0	0	5	.327	.346
2015	Frederick	.228	74	254	32	58	14	2	2	33	1	4	3	28	53	9	0	5	.308	.323
2016	Frederick	.281	89	299	51	84	19	1	11	51	1	4	12	63	58	3	4	4	.421	.462
	Bowie	.444	3	9	2	4	1	0	1	3	0	1	0	1	0	0	0	0	.455	.889
2017	Tulsa	.277	54	184	16	51	14	1	4	17	0	1	3	13	42	1	2	4	.333	.429
	AZL Dodgers	.375	3	8	1	3	2	0	1	3	0	0	0	2	1	0	0	0	.500	1.000
2018	Chattanooga	.143	13	35	4	5	1	0	1	2	0	0	1	5	5	0	0	0	.268	.257
	Rochester	.318	23	66	13	21	2	0	1	11	0	1	5	7	16	0	0	1	.446	.394
2019	Rochester	.260	43	154	23	40	17	0	2	20	0	0	6	11	48	0	0	5	.333	.409
Minor League Totals		**.248**	**641**	**2166**	**274**	**538**	**127**	**6**	**41**	**288**	**4**	**29**	**47**	**273**	**447**	**16**	**9**	**42**	**.341**	**.369**

SCHMIDT, Clarke – RHP   NON-ROSTER INVITEE

HT: 6-1; **WT:** 200; **B:** R; **T:** R; **BORN:** 2/20/96 in El Toro, Calif.; **RESIDES:** Atlanta, Ga.; **COLLEGE:** University of South Carolina; **OBTAINED:** Selected by the Yankees in the first round (16th overall) of the 2017 First-Year Player Draft; **M.L. SVC:** 0.000; **CAREER NOTES: 2019:** Combined with Single-A Tampa, GCL Yankees East and Double-A Trenton to go 6-5 with a 3.47 ERA (90.2 IP, 79H, 43R/35ER, 28BB, 102K, 4HR) in 19 games (18 starts)…began the season with Tampa and produced a 4-5 record with a 3.84 ERA (63.1IP, 59H, 35R/27ER, 24BB, 69K, 2HR) in 13 games (12 starts) across two stints…in his first start of the season on 4/4 at Lakeland (ND, 5.0IP, 0H, 0R, 0BB, 9K), opposed Casey Mize (5.0IP, 1H, 0R, 0BB, 8K), the No. 1 overall selection in the 2018 First-Year Player Draft…was placed on Tampa's injured list on two separate occasions (5/6-5/14, 5/29-7/11)…on a rehab assignment with the GCL Yankees East, posted a 3.24 ERA (8.1IP, 6H, 3ER, 3BB, 14K, 1HR) without recording a decision in three starts…tied career highs in innings and strikeouts in 8/5 start at Lakeland (7.0IP, 9K)…was promoted to Trenton on 8/15 and posted a 2-0 record with a 2.37 ERA (19.0IP, 14H, 5ER, 1BB, 19K, 1HR) in three starts…helped Trenton capture their first Eastern League Championship since 2013…went 1-0 with a 0.88 ERA (10.2IP, 4H, 2R/1ER, 3BB, 13K) in two games (one start) in the Eastern League playoffs…following the season, was named by *Baseball America* as the Yankees' No. 2 prospect, No. 12 prospect in the Florida State League and No. 62 overall prospect…also labeled by *Baseball America* as having the "Best Curveball" in the system…was named by MLB Pipeline as the No. 5 Yankees prospect…**2018:** Returned from "Tommy John" surgery and made his professional debut on 6/22 with the GCL Yankees East (1.0IP, 3H, 2ER, 2K)…combined with the GCL Yankees East, Rookie-level GCL Yankees West and short-season Single-A Staten Island to go 0-3 with a 3.09 ERA (23.1IP, 16H, 9R/8ER, 6BB, 30K, 1HR) in eight games (seven starts)…appeared in six games (five starts) for both the GCL Yankees East and GCL Yankees West and posted an 0-2 record with a 4.20 ERA (15.0IP, 12H, 8R/7ER, 4BB, 20K, 1HR) before being promoted to Staten Island on 7/30…went 0-1 with a 1.08 ERA (8.1IP, 4H, 1ER, 2BB, 10K) in two starts with Staten Island…**2017:** Did not pitch while recovering from "Tommy John" surgery on his right elbow…**PERSONAL:** In three seasons at South Carolina (2015-17), produced a 15-9 record and 3.21 ERA (229.2IP, 218H, 102R/82ER, 65BB, 254K, 17HR) in 45 games (36 starts)…as a junior in 2017, went 4-2 and ranked second in the nation with a 1.34 ERA (60.1IP, 41H, 15R/9ER, 18BB, 70K, 3HR) in nine starts, posting a 4.6K/9.0IP ratio and .194 (41-for-211) opponents' BA…was named to USA Baseball's Golden Spikes Award Midseason Watch List in both 2016 and 2017…was named to the 2017 NCBWA Pre-Season All-America First Team…was *Baseball America*'s No. 31 overall prospect (and No. 17 pitcher) in the 2017 draft…was tabbed by *Baseball America* as having the Best Control in the SEC…graduated from Allatoona H.S. (Ga.), where he was the Region 5AAAAA 2014 Pitcher of the Year as a senior…older brother, Clate, pitched in both the Tigers and Reds organizations.

Schmidt's Career Pitching Record

Year	Club	W	L	ERA	G	GS	CG	SHO	SV	IP	H	R	ER	HR	HP	BB	SO	WP	BK
2018	GCL Yankees East	0	2	7.04	3	2	0	0	0	7.2	8	7	6	1	1	2	12	1	0
	GCL Yankees West	0	0	1.23	3	3	0	0	0	7.1	4	1	1	0	0	2	8	1	0
	Staten Island	0	1	1.08	2	2	0	0	0	8.1	4	1	1	0	1	2	10	1	0
2019	Tampa	4	5	3.84	13	12	0	0	0	63.1	59	35	27	2	4	24	69	5	0
	GCL Yankees East	0	0	3.24	3	3	0	0	0	8.1	6	3	3	1	0	3	14	2	1
	Trenton	2	0	2.37	3	3	0	0	0	19.0	14	5	5	1	0	1	19	3	0
Minor League Totals		**6**	**8**	**3.39**	**27**	**25**	**0**	**0**	**0**	**114.0**	**95**	**52**	**43**	**5**	**6**	**34**	**132**	**13**	**1**

SEARS, JP – LHP

HT: 5-11; **WT:** 180; **B:** R; **T:** L; **BORN:** 2/19/96 in Sumter, S.C.; **RESIDES:** Charleston, S.C.; **COLLEGE:** The Citadel; **OBTAINED:** Acquired by the Yankees from the Seattle Mariners along with RHP Juan Then in exchange for RHP Nick Rumbelow on 11/18/17; **M.L. SVC:** 0.000; **CAREER NOTES:** Was originally selected by Seattle in the 11th round of the 2017 First-Year Player Draft…**PERSONAL:** Full name is John Patrick Sears Jr.…in three seasons at The Citadel (S.C.), had a 17-15 record and 3.98 ERA (253.0IP, 232H, 125R/112ER, 87BB, 317K) in 46 career appearances (42 starts)…as a junior in 2017, was named the Southern Conference Pitcher of the Year and a Golden Spikes Award semifinalist after going 7-3 with a 2.64 ERA (95.1IP, 69H, 28ER, 27BB, 142K) in 14 starts…ranked fifth in the nation in strikeouts and third in K/9.0IP ratio (13.41)…earned 2017 All-America honors from *Collegiate Baseball* (second team), *Baseball America* (third team), the ABCA (third team), the NCBWA (third team) and D1Baseball.com (third team)…on 3/24/17 vs. VMI, tied a school record with 20K in a two-hit shutout…graduated from Wilson Hall H.S. (S.C.) in 2014…was named the 2014 SCISA Class 3A Player of the Year…also starred as a defensive back on Wilson Hall's 2013 SCISA Class 3A State Championship football team.

SEIGLER, Anthony – C
HT: 5-11; **WT:** 195; **B:** S; **T:** S; **BORN:** 6/20/99 in Phoenix, Ariz.; **RESIDES:** Panamá City, Fla.; **OBTAINED:** Selected by the Yankees in the first round (23rd overall) of the 2018 First-Year Player Draft; **M.L. SVC:** 0.000; **CAREER NOTES: 2019:** Played in just 30 games for Single-A Charleston, hitting .175 (17-for-97) with 10R, 3 doubles and 6RBI…following the season, was named the No. 8 prospect in the Yankees organization by MLB Pipeline…**2018:** In his professional debut, combined with the GCL Yankees West and Rookie-level Pulaski to bat .266 (21-for-79) with 11R, 3 doubles, 1HR, 9RBI and 14BB in 24 games…batted .391 (9-for-23) vs. left-handed pitching…threw out 4-of-24 attempted base stealers (16.7%)…began the season with the GCL Yankees West, hitting .333/.429/.472 (12-for-36) with 7R, 2 doubles, 1HR, 4RBI and 6BB in 12 games…was transferred to Pulaski on 7/31 and batted .209 (9-for-43) with 4R, 1 double, 5RBI and 8BB in 12 games…following the season, was tabbed the No. 4 prospect in the Yankees organization by *Baseball America*…was also named the Best Defensive Catcher in the organization by the publication…**PERSONAL:** Is a 2018 graduate of Cartersville (Ga.) H.S.…as a senior in 2018, was named the ABCA National High School Position Player of the Year and the *Atlanta Journal-Constitution* State Player of the Year…also earned 2018 First Team All-American and Southeast All-Region First Team honors…helped lead Cartersville to the Georgia 4A State Championship in 2018, where they finished runner-up…was ranked by *Baseball America* as the No. 41 prospect in the 2018 draft class…was the third catcher to be chosen by the Yankees in the first round of the MLB First-Year Player Draft since its inception in 1965, joining David Parrish in 2000 (28th overall, University of Michigan) and Thurman Munson in 1968 (fourth overall, Kent State University)…was also an ambidextrous pitcher and posted a 1.09 ERA in 25.2IP as a senior, striking out 29 batters…played for USA Baseball's 18U National Team, winning the 2017 U-18 World Cup…was committed to play at the University of Florida prior to signing with the Yankees…is of Navajo descent, and would join Jacoby Ellsbury as the second Navajo to play in the Majors…is named after the late Tony Phillips, an 18-year Major League veteran infielder and friend of his father's.

SEMMEL, Montana – RHP
HT: 6-4; **WT:** 225; **B:** R; **T:** R; **BORN:** 1/1/02 in Stamford, Conn.; **RESIDES:** Stamford, Conn.; **OBTAINED:** Selected by the Yankees in the 36th round of the 2019 First-Year Player Draft; **M.L. SVC:** 0.000; **PERSONAL:** Graduated in 2019 from Westhill (Conn.) H.S.…had signed to play at Chipola (Fla.) Junior College.

SEMPLE, Shawn – RHP
HT: 6-1; **WT:** 195; **B:** R; **T:** R; **BORN:** 10/9/95 in Chicago, Ill.; **RESIDES:** Glassboro, N.J.; **COLLEGE:** University of New Orleans; **OBTAINED:** Selected by the Yankees in the 11th round of the 2017 First-Year Player Draft; **M.L. SVC:** 0.000; **CAREER NOTES: 2018:** Was named the South Atlantic League "Pitcher of the Week" for 8/27-9/3 after going 2-0 with a 1.50 ERA over two starts (12.0IP, 7H, 2ER, 1BB, 17K)…**PERSONAL:** Played three seasons at the University of New Orleans (2015-17), going 16-12 with a 3.51 ERA (220.1IP, 218H, 101R/86ER, 69BB, 223K) in 39 career appearances (35 starts)…was named to the 2017 All-Southland Conference First Team…graduated from Paul VI H.S. (N.J.).

SENSLEY, Steven – OF
HT: 6-1; **WT:** 220; **B:** L; **T:** L; **BORN:** 9/6/95 in Baton Rouge, La.; **RESIDES:** Baton Rouge, La.; **COLLEGE:** University of Louisiana-Lafayette; **OBTAINED:** Selected by the Yankees in the 12th round of the 2017 First-Year Player Draft; **M.L. SVC:** 0.000; **CAREER NOTES: 2018:** His 17HR were tied for the third-most among Yankees minor leaguers…was named a South Atlantic League Mid-Season All-Star…following the season, appeared in 21G for Glendale in the Arizona Fall League and hit .197 (15-for-76) with 4R, 3 doubles, 1 triple and 9RBI…**2017:** During his stint with Rookie-level Pulaski (6/28-8/1), led the Appalachian League with 9HR…**PERSONAL:** Played two seasons for the Ragin' Cajuns (2016-17), batting .287 (98-for-342) with 58R, 18 doubles, 17HR and 69RBI in 110 games…was a 2017 All-Sun Belt Second Team selection…transferred from LSU-Eunice, where he set a school record with 21HR and won the 2015 NJCAA Division II National Championship after redshirting in 2014…was named to the 2015 Junior College All-America First Team…graduated from University H.S. (La.) in 2013, where he was a Rawlings Third-Team All-American and a Perfect Game All-Southeast Region First Team selection as a senior…earned all-state honors in 2012-13…was selected by Tampa Bay in the 38th round of the 2015 First-Year Player Draft but did not sign…was selected by Minnesota in the 33rd round of the 2013 First-Year Player Draft but did not sign.

SERNA, Jared – INF
HT: 5-8; **WT:** 168; **B:** R; **T:** R; **BORN:** 6/1/02 in Guaymas, México; **RESIDES:** Guaymas, México; **OBTAINED:** Signed by the Yankees as a non-drafted free agent on 7/15/19; **M.L. SVC:** 0.000.

SEVERINO, Anderson – LHP
HT: 5-10; **WT:** 165; **B:** L; **T:** L; **BORN:** 9/17/94 in Santo Domingo Centro, D.R.; **RESIDES:** Santo Domingo Centro, D.R.; **OBTAINED:** Signed by the Yankees as a non-drafted free agent on 6/1/13; **M.L. SVC:** 0.000; **CAREER NOTES: 2018:** Following the season, made one appearance for the Leones del Escogido of the Dominican Winter League (2H, 1ER, 1BB, 1HP, 1WP).

SEVERINO, Felixander – OF
HT: 6-3; **WT:** 165; **B:** S; **T:** R; **BORN:** 6/28/00 in Santiago, D.R.; **RESIDES:** Santiago, D.R.; **OBTAINED:** Signed by the Yankees as a non-drafted free agent on 7/2/19; **M.L. SVC:** 0.000.

SEVERINO, Jesús – OF
HT: 6-0; **WT:** 175; **B:** R; **T:** R; **BORN:** 6/7/00 in Nirgua, Venezuela; **RESIDES:** Nirgua, Venezuela; **OBTAINED:** Signed by the Yankees as a non-drafted free agent on 7/2/16; **M.L. SVC:** 0.000; **CAREER NOTES: 2018:** His 18SB with the GCL Yankees East ranked fourth in the Gulf Coast League.

SIKKEMA, TJ – LHP
HT: 6-0; **WT:** 215; **B:** L; **T:** L; **BORN:** 7/25/98 in Clinton, Iowa; **RESIDES:** DeWitt, Iowa; **COLLEGE:** University of Missouri; **OBTAINED:** Selected by the Yankees in Competitive Balance Round A of the 2019 First-Year Player Draft; **M.L. SVC:** 0.000; **CAREER NOTES: 2019:** Made his pro debut, allowing 1ER over 10.2IP (0.84 ERA, 6H, 1BB, 13K) in four starts with short-season Single-A Staten Island…**PERSONAL:** Pitched three seasons (2017-19) at Missouri…as a junior in 2019, ranked third in the NCAA in ERA, going 7-4 with two shutouts, two saves and a 1.32 ERA (88.2IP, 54H, 23R/13ER, 31BB, 101K, 4HR) in 17 games (13 starts)…was a consensus All-American, earning second-team honors from *Baseball America* and the NCBWA and third-team honors from Perfect Game/Rawlings and *Collegiate Baseball*…was also a Golden Spikes Award Semifinalist…was a 2017 Freshman All-America selection…graduated in 2016 from Central DeWitt (Iowa) H.S., where he was a four-sport athlete, also playing basketball, football and soccer…last name is pronounced "sick-KEHM-uh."

SILVERIO, Oscar – C
HT: 5-9; **WT:** 170; **B:** L; **T:** R; **BORN:** 10/25/01 in Santo Domingo, D.R.; **RESIDES:** San Cristóbal, D.R.; **OBTAINED:** Signed by the Yankees as a non-drafted free agent on 8/15/19; **M.L. SVC:** 0.000.

SMITH, Canaan – OF
HT: 6-0; **WT:** 215; **B:** L; **T:** R; **BORN:** 4/30/99 in Dallas, Tex.; **RESIDES:** Rockwall, Tex.; **OBTAINED:** Selected by the Yankees in the fourth round of the 2017 First-Year Player Draft; **M.L. SVC:** 0.000; **CAREER NOTES: 2019:** Hit .307/.405/.465 (128-for-449) with 67R, 32 doubles, 3 triples, 11HR, 74RBI, 16SB and 74BB in 124 games with Single-A Charleston…led the South Atlantic League in walks and ranked second in OBP, tied for second in hits, third in BA and total bases (209), tied for third in XBHs (46), tied for fifth in doubles and sixth in RBI and slugging…led Yankees farmhands in hits and walks and ranked second in doubles and third in RBI and fourth in BA…earned SAL Mid-Season and Postseason All-Star honors…was an MiLB.com Organization All-Star…was a *Baseball America* Low Class-A All-Star…was named by *Baseball America* as the SAL's No. 20 prospect, "Best Batting Prospect" and "Most Exciting Player"…**2017:** Was named to the GCL All-Star Team…ranked fourth among all Rookie-level hitters in walks (46)…**PERSONAL:** First name is pronounced "CAY-nan"…graduated in 2017 from Rockwall-Heath H.S. (Tex.), where he played catcher, first base and outfield…was named to the TXSWA All-State First Team as an outfielder in 2017 and as a catcher in 2016…also played quarterback for the Hawks' football team…prior to signing, was committed to the University of Arkansas.

SMITH, Josh – INF
HT: 5-10; **WT:** 175; **B:** L; **T:** R; **BORN:** 8/7/97 in Baton Rouge, La.; **RESIDES:** Greenwell Springs, La.; **COLLEGE:** LSU; **OBTAINED:** Selected by the Yankees in the second round of the 2019 First-Year Player Draft; **M.L. SVC:** 0.000; **PERSONAL:** Played three seasons (2017-19) at LSU, serving as the everyday third baseman as a freshman and regular shortstop as a junior…in 2019, tied for seventh nationally with 72 runs scored…was a 2017 *Collegiate Baseball* Freshman All-American…graduated from Catholic (La.) H.S. in 2016…was selected by Detroit in the 38th round of the 2016 First-Year Player Draft but did not sign.

SMITH, Sincere – INF
HT: 5-11; **WT:** 170; **B:** R; **T:** R; **BORN:** 3/13/00 in Elizabethtown, N.C.; **RESIDES:** Clarkton, N.C.; **OBTAINED:** Selected by the Yankees in the 32nd round of the 2018 First-Year Player Draft; **M.L. SVC:** 0.000; **PERSONAL:** Is a 2018 graduate of East Bladen (N.C.) H.S., also playing football and basketball.

SOSA, Yordanny – RHP
HT: 6-2; **WT:** 139; **B:** R; **T:** R; **BORN:** 10/12/01 in Santiago de los Caballeros, D.R.; **RESIDES:** Santiago, D.R.; **OBTAINED:** Signed by the Yankees as a non-drafted free agent on 10/19/18; **M.L. SVC:** 0.000.

SOSEBEE, David – RHP
HT: 6-2; **WT:** 220; **B:** R; **T:** R; **BORN:** 8/25/93 in Gainesville, Ga.; **RESIDES:** Cleveland, Ga.; **COLLEGE:** University of Georgia; **OBTAINED:** Selected by the Yankees in the 28th round of the 2015 First-Year Player Draft; **M.L. SVC:** 0.000; **CAREER NOTES: 2018:** Was named a Florida State League Mid-Season All-Star…**2017:** His 14 saves were tied for second in the Yankees system…**PERSONAL:** Last name is pronounced "SOH-suh-bee"…played three seasons at Georgia (2013-15)…graduated from White County H.S. (Ga.), where he was named Region 8-AAA Pitcher of the Year as a senior…was selected by Boston in the 48th round of the 2011 First-Year Player Draft but did not sign.

SPENCE, Mitch – RHP
HT: 6-1; **WT:** 205; **B:** R; **T:** R; **BORN:** 5/6/98 in Kirkland, Wash.; **RESIDES:** New Hill, N.C.; **COLLEGE:** University of South Carolina-Aiken; **OBTAINED:** Selected by the Yankees in the 10th round of the 2019 First-Year Player Draft; **M.L. SVC:** 0.000; **CAREER NOTES: 2019:** Tied for third in the Appalachian League with four saves for Rookie-level Pulaski…**PERSONAL:** Played three seasons (2017-19) at USC-Aiken…graduated from Green Hope (N.C.) H.S. in 2016.

STEPHAN, Trevor – RHP
HT: 6-5; **WT:** 225; **B:** R; **T:** R; **BORN:** 11/25/95 in Austin, Tex.; **RESIDES:** Magnolia, Tex.; **COLLEGE:** University of Arkansas; **OBTAINED:** Selected by the Yankees in the third round of the 2017 First-Year Player Draft; **M.L. SVC:** 0.000; **CAREER NOTES: 2019:** Was named Florida State League "Pitcher of the Week" for 7/22-28 with Single-A Tampa…**2018:** His 140K ranked third among all Yankees farmhands…was named a Florida State League Mid-Season All-Star…**PERSONAL:** Last name is pronounced "STEFF-in"…played one season at Arkansas (2017), going 6-3 with a 2.87 ERA (91.0IP, 73H, 35R/29ER, 20BB, 120K) in 16 starts…had the third-highest single-season strikeout total in Razorbacks history…pitched two seasons at Hill College (Tex.), earning NTJCAC All-Conference First Team honors as a sophomore in 2016…graduated from Magnolia West H.S. (Tex.) in 2014…was selected by Boston in the 18th round of the 2016 First-Year Player Draft but did not sign.

STOWERS, Josh – OF
HT: 6-1; **WT:** 200; **B:** R; **T:** R; **BORN:** 2/25/97 in Berwyn, Ill.; **RESIDES:** Westchester, Ill.; **COLLEGE:** University of Louisville; **OBTAINED:** Acquired by the Yankees from the Seattle Mariners in exchange for 2B Shed Long on 1/21/19 ; **M.L. SVC:** 0.000; **CAREER NOTES:** Was originally selected by the Mariners in the second round of the 2018 First-Year Player Draft…**2019:** In his first season in the Yankees organization, hit .273/.386/.400 (105-for-385) with 61R, 24 doubles, 2 triples, 7HR, 40RBI and 35SB in 105 games with Single-A Charleston…led Yankees minor leaguers in stolen bases…ranked fifth in the South Atlantic League in walks and sixth in OBP…following the season, played for Surprise in the Arizona Fall League, hitting .131 (8-for-61) in 20 games…**2018:** His 20SB at short-season Single-A Everett were tied for second in the Mariners system and tied for third-most in the Northwest League…was named a Northwest League Mid-Season All-Star and was tabbed the No. 12 prospect in the Northwest League by *Baseball America*…following the season, was also named by *Baseball America* as the No. 10 prospect in the Mariners organization…**PERSONAL:** Played three seasons at the University of Louisville, hitting .323/.449/.525 (140-for-434) with 126R, 29 doubles, 7 triples, 15HR, 96RBI, 85BB and 60SB…graduated from Mount Carmel High School (Chicago, Ill.).

SUMOZA, Christian – RHP
HT: 5-10; **WT:** 165; **B:** R; **T:** R; **BORN:** 11/18/00 in Villa de Cura, Venezuela; **RESIDES:** Agua Amarillo, Venezuela; **OBTAINED:** Signed by the Yankees as a non-drafted free agent on 12/4/17; **M.L. SVC:** 0.000.

THOLE, Josh – C   NON-ROSTER INVITEE
HT: 6-1; **WT:** 190; **B:** L; **T:** R; **BORN:** 10/28/86 in Breese, Ill.; **RESIDES:** Owego, N.Y.; **OBTAINED:** Signed by the Yankees as a minor league free agent on 1/23/20; **M.L. SVC:** 5.165; **CAREER NOTES:** Was originally selected by the New York Mets in the 13th round of the 2005 First-Year Player Draft…was acquired by Toronto from New York-NL on 12/17/12 along with RHP R.A. Dickey and C Mike Nickeas in exchange for RHP Noah Syndergaard, C Travis d'Arnaud, OF Wuilmer Becerra and C John Buck…was signed by Arizona as a minor league free agent on 1/24/17…was signed by Detroit as a minor league free agent on 6/22/18…was signed by Los Angeles-NL as a minor league free agent on 1/17/19…was acquired by Los Angeles-AL from Los Angeles-NL along with LHP Adam McCreery in exchange for cash considerations on 7/12/19…has played in 478 games over parts of eight Major League seasons between the Mets (2009-12) and Blue Jays (2013-16)…**2019:** Batted .243/.352/.327 (55-for-226) with 10 doubles, 3HR, 26RBI and 37BB in 72 games with Double-A Tulsa, Triple-A Oklahoma City and Triple-A Salt Lake…appeared in 47 games with Double-A Tulsa and Triple-A Oklahoma, hitting .245 (34-for-139) with 15R, 5 doubles, 1HR, 14RBI and 21BB…slashed .241/.359/.368 with 5 doubles, 2HR, 12RBI and 16BB in 25 games with Triple-A Salt Lake…combined to throw out 13-of-68 (19.1%) attempted base stealers…**2018:** Spent spring training with the Arizona Diamondbacks and was released on 3/18…signed with the New Britain Bees of the Atlantic League and slashed .317/.425/.367 (19-for-60) with 3 doubles, 10RBI and 11BB in 17 games…batted .238 (15-for-63) with 11R, 1 double, 1HR, 10RBI and 8BB in 21 games with Double-A Erie…allowed just one passed ball and recorded a .994 fielding percentage (1E, 176TC) in 165.0 innings behind the plate with Erie…**2017:** Missed the entire season after suffering a torn left hamstring in a spring training game with Arizona on 3/15…**2016:** Spent the entire season with Toronto, batting .169 (20-for-118) with 7R, 3 doubles, 1HR, 7RBI and 13BB in 50 games with the Blue Jays…**2015:** Hit .204 (10-for-49) with 5R, 2 doubles and 2RBI in 18 games over three stints with the Blue Jays (4/23-6/2, 8/23-28, 9/2-end of season)…started the season with Triple-A Buffalo and batted .228 (34-for-149) with 12R, 5 doubles, 17RBI and 20BB in 45 games…**2014:** Spent the entire season with Toronto and hit .248 (33-for-133) with 11R, 4 doubles and 7RBI in 57 games…**2013:** Batted .175 (21-for-120) with 11R, 3 doubles, 1 triple, 1HR and 8RBI in 45 games with Toronto…began the season with Triple-A Buffalo and hit .322/.383/.510 (48-for-149) with 18R, 5 doubles, 1 triple, 7HR and 31RBI in 41 games before being recalled by the Blue Jays on 6/7…**2012:** Spent most of the season with the Mets, batting .234 (75-for-321) with 24R, 15 doubles, 1HR and 21RBI in 104 games…was the Mets' Opening Day catcher for the second straight season…missed 21 games on the disabled list from 5/8-6/1 after suffering a concussion from a home plate collision with Philadelphia's Ty Wigginton on 5/8…played in two rehab games with Triple-A Buffalo (5/30 and 5/31)…in his first game back from the concussion, caught Johan Santana on 6/1 vs. St. Louis in the first no-hitter in Mets history…caught 26 of NL Cy Young winner R.A. Dickey's 33 starts…**2011:** Played the entire season with the Mets, batting .268/.345/.344 (91-for-340) with 22R, 17 doubles, 3HR and 40RBI in a career-high 114 games…was the Mets' Opening Day catcher…was on the Paternity Leave List from 7/19-20…**2010:** Slashed .277/.357/.366 (56-for-202) with 17R, 7 doubles, 1 triple, 3HR, 17RBI and 24BB in 73 games across two stints with the Mets…threw out 8-of-22 (36.4%) attempted base stealers…began the season with Triple-A Buffalo and batted .267/.353/.430 (44-for-165) with 20R, 19 doubles, 1 triple, 2HR, 17RBI and 22BB in 48 games…hit his first Major League home run on 7/20 at Arizona, a solo shot off of Barry Enright in the eighth inning…**2009:** Batted .321/.356/.396 (17-for-53) with 2R, 2 doubles, 1 triple and 9RBI in 17 games with the Mets…made his Major League debut on 9/3 at Colorado and went 2-for-5 with a double…collected a hit (single) in his first Major League at-bat off of Jason Marquis in the second inning…began the season with Double-A Binghamton and hit .328/.395/.422 (48-for-384) with 48R, 29 doubles, 2 triples, 1HR, 46RBI, 42BB and 8SB in 103 games…ranked second in the Eastern League in batting average…finished second in the Venezuelan Winter League with a .381 (59-for-155) batting average, while registering 16 doubles, 2 triples, 3HR, 28RBI and 25BB in 44 games with Leones del Caracas…ranked by *Baseball America* as the Mets' No. 8 prospect in the system…labeled by *Baseball America* as being the '"Best Hitter for Average" in the Mets organization…was named an EL Mid-Season All-Star with Binghamton…**2008:** Spent the season with Single-A St. Lucie, batting .300/.382/.427 (104-for-347) with 49R, 25 doubles, 2 triples, 5HR, 56RBI and 45BB in 111 games…appeared in 75 games behind the plate after spending his first three professional seasons primarily at first base…was named a Florida State League Mid-Season and Post-Season All-Star…was honored as an Arizona Fall League Rising Star after batting .319 (22-for-69) with 15R, 1 double, 2HR and 17RBI in 19 games with the Peoria Saguaros…**2007:** Spent the season with Single-A Savannah, hitting .267 (104-for-389) with 46R, 17 doubles, 61BB and 37RBI in 117 games…played in 103 games as a first baseman and 11 games as a catcher…was on Savannah's disabled list from 7/27-8/10…**2006:** Played the entire season with Rookie-level Kingsport…**2005:** Made his professional debut with the GCL Mets…**PERSONAL:** Full name is Joshua Michael Thole ("TOLL-ee")…graduated from Breese Mater Dei (Ill.) H.S. in 2005, where he was All-State in baseball and also played football.

Thole's Career Batting Record

Year	Club	AVG	G	AB	R	H	2B	3B	HR	RBI	SH	SF	HP	BB	SO	SB	CS	E	OBP	SLG
2005	GCL Mets	.269	35	104	14	28	2	1	1	12	2	0	4	20	11	1	1	2	.406	.337
2006	Kingsport	.235	36	98	13	23	4	0	1	12	0	2	3	7	25	1	1	4	.300	.306
2007	Savannah	.267	117	389	46	104	17	0	0	36	4	0	4	61	57	4	4	9	.372	.311
2008	St. Lucie	.300	111	347	49	104	25	2	5	56	1	5	4	45	38	2	1	4	.382	.427
2009	Binghamton	.328	103	384	48	126	29	2	1	46	1	9	6	42	34	8	4	5	.395	.422
	NEW YORK-NL	.321	17	53	2	17	2	1	0	9	0	2	0	4	5	1	0	1	.356	.396
2010	Buffalo	.267	48	165	20	44	19	1	2	17	1	2	1	22	25	0	0	4	.353	.430
	NEW YORK-NL	.277	73	202	17	56	7	1	3	17	0	0	1	24	25	1	0	3	.357	.366
2011	NEW YORK-NL	.268	114	340	22	91	17	0	3	40	1	3	4	38	47	0	2	2	.345	.344
2012	NEW YORK-NL	.234	104	321	24	75	15	0	1	21	4	1	1	27	50	0	0	6	.294	.290
	Buffalo	.200	2	5	0	1	0	0	0	0	0	0	0	0	0	0	0	0	.200	.200
2013	Buffalo	.322	41	149	18	48	5	1	7	31	0	2	2	14	25	0	1	2	.383	.510
	TORONTO	.175	45	120	11	21	3	1	1	8	2	0	1	12	25	0	0	2	.256	.242
2014	TORONTO	.248	57	133	11	33	4	0	0	7	3	0	0	14	25	0	3	1	.320	.278
2015	Buffalo	.228	45	149	12	34	5	0	0	17	1	0	0	20	20	0	0	1	.320	.262
	TORONTO	.204	18	49	5	10	2	0	0	2	0	0	0	3	9	0	0	1	.250	.245
2016	TORONTO	.169	50	118	7	20	3	0	0	1	7	2	2	1	13	28	0	0	1	.254	.220
2017						Did Not Play - Injured														
2018	Erie	.238	21	63	11	15	1	0	1	10	1	3	1	8	14	1	0	1	.320	.302
2019	Tulsa	.292	22	65	7	19	3	0	0	10	0	1	1	7	16	0	0	1	.365	.338
	Oklahoma City	.203	25	74	8	15	2	0	1	4	0	1	1	14	19	0	0	3	.333	.270
	Salt Lake	.241	25	87	10	21	5	0	2	12	0	0	0	16	25	1	0	1	.359	.368
Minor League Totals		**.280**	**631**	**2079**	**256**	**582**	**117**	**7**	**21**	**263**	**11**	**25**	**27**	**276**	**309**	**18**	**12**	**36**	**.368**	**.373**
Major League Totals		**.242**	**478**	**1336**	**99**	**323**	**53**	**3**	**9**	**111**	**12**	**8**	**8**	**135**	**214**	**2**	**5**	**18**	**.313**	**.306**

TORDECILLA, Edwin – C
HT: 5-10; **WT:** 165; **B:** R; **T:** R; **BORN:** 5/24/99 in Lorica, Colombia; **RESIDES:** Lorica, Colombia; **OBTAINED:** Signed by the Yankees as a non-drafted free agent on 10/14/17; **M.L. SVC:** 0.000.

TORREALBA, Eduardo – INF
HT: 5-8; **WT:** 140; **B:** R; **T:** R; **BORN:** 3/26/99 in Barquisimeto, Venezuela; **RESIDES:** Cabudare, Venezuela; **OBTAINED:** Signed by the Yankees as a non-drafted free agent on 7/5/16; **M.L. SVC:** 0.000; **CAREER NOTES:** Signed with the Red Sox as a non-drafted free agent on 7/2/15 but his contract was voided on 6/4/16…**2019:** Was named South Atlantic League "Player of the Week" for 8/26-9/1 with Single-A Charleston.

TORRES, Miguel – C
HT: 6-0; **WT:** 170; **B:** R; **T:** R; **BORN:** 3/3/00 in Maracaibo, Venezuela; **RESIDES:** Bachaquero, Venezuela; **OBTAINED:** Signed by the Yankees as a non-drafted free agent on 7/4/16; **M.L. SVC:** 0.000.

TORRES, Saúl – C
HT: 6-2; **WT:** 190; **B:** R; **T:** R; **BORN:** 2/19/00 in Santo Domingo, D.R.; **RESIDES:** Herrera, D.R.; **OBTAINED:** Signed by the Yankees as a non-drafted free agent on 7/2/16; **M.L. SVC:** 0.000.

TRIEGLAFF, Brian – RHP
HT: 6-1; **WT:** 190; **B:** R; **T:** R; **BORN:** 6/13/94 in Houston, Tex.; **RESIDES:** Fort Worth, Tex.; **COLLEGE:** Texas Christian University; **OBTAINED:** Selected by the Yankees in the 13th round of the 2016 First-Year Player Draft; **M.L. SVC:** 0.000; **PERSONAL:** In three seasons with TCU (2014-16), went 9-1 with four saves and a 3.50 ERA (90.0IP, 96H, 43R/35ER, 30BB, 92K) in 62 relief appearances…graduated from Houston Christian (Tex.) H.S. in 2012.

TROPEANO, Nick – RHP   NON-ROSTER INVITEE
HT: 6-4; **WT:** 205; **B:** R; **T:** R; **BORN:** 8/27/90 in West Islip, N.Y.; **RESIDES:** West Islip, N.Y.; **COLLEGE:** Stony Brook University; **OBTAINED:** Signed by the Yankees as a minor league free agent on 1/7/20; **M.L. SVC:** 3.105; **CAREER NOTES:** Was selected by the Houston Astros in the fifth round of the 2011 First-Year Player Draft…was acquired by Los Angeles-AL from Houston along with C Carlos Pérez in exchange for C Hank Conger on 11/5/14…**2019:** Went 0-1 with a 9.88 ERA (13.2IP, 18H, 15ER, 6BB, 10K, 6HR) in three games (one start) across three stints (5/28, 6/9 and 7/26) with the Angels…spent the majority of the season with Triple-A Salt Lake, appearing in 17 games over four stints (4/28-5/28; 5/29-6/9; 6/10-7/26; 7/27-end of season)…spent the first month of the season on the Angels injured list with a right shoulder injury (3/28-4/28)…went 2-2 with a 2.97 ERA (30.1IP, 10ER) and 28K in his final six starts with Salt Lake…**2018:** Went 5-6 with a 4.74 ERA (76.0IP, 68H, 41R/40ER, 31BB, 64K, 16HR) in 14 starts with the Angels…set career highs in games, starts, wins and innings pitched…missed 87 games across three stints on the disabled list with right shoulder inflammation (5/2-12; 6/15-7/21; 8/7-end of season)…opened the season with Triple-A Salt Lake and made one start before being recalled by Angels…made his first Major League appearance since 7/18/16 on 4/12 at Kansas City, earning the win after tossing 6.2 scoreless innings (6H, 2BB, 6K)…limited right-handed batters to a .213 BA (29-for-136) with five starts (5/29-6/9; 6/10-7/26; 7/27-end of season)…set a career high with 7.1IP on 5/24 at Toronto…**2017:** Missed the entire season while recovering from "Tommy John" surgery performed in August 2016…**2016:** Began the season at Triple-A Salt Lake, but did not appear in a game before being recalled by the Angels on 4/7…went 3-2 with a 3.56 ERA in 13 starts with the Angels (68.1IP, 70H, 27ER, 31BB, 66H, 14HR)…was on the 15-day disabled list from 6/4-24 with right forearm tightness…missed the final 69 games of the season after being placed on the disabled list on 7/19 with a right elbow UCL injury…underwent "Tommy John" surgery in August…**2015:** Saw his first Major League action with the Angels, going 3-2 with a 3.82 ERA (37.2IP, 40H, 18R/6ER, 10BB, 38K, 2HR) in eight games (seven starts)…made his Angels debut on 4/23 vs. Oakland and earned the win after tossing 6.0 shutout innings (5H, 1BB, 5K)…struck out a career-high 11 batters over 6.2IP in his final start on 9/29 vs. Oakland…appeared 16 starts for Triple-A Salt Lake, going

3-6 with a 4.81 ERA (88.0IP, 97H, 51R/47ER, 36BB, 96K, 9HR)…was the Angels' No. 3 prospect according to *Baseball America*…**2014:** Made his Major League debut with Houston on 9/10 at Seattle, earning the win (5.0IP, 4H, 2ER, 2BB, 5K)…was the eighth Astros pitcher to earn a win in his first career start…struck out the first batter he faced in his career (Austin Jackson in 1st inning)…was named a Pacific Coast League Mid-Season All-Star with Triple-A Oklahoma City…was named Astros Minor League "Pitcher of the Month" for June (4-0, 2.02 ERA, 35.2IP, 24H, 8ER, 7BB, 34K in 5GS) and August (3-1, 4.13 ERA, 32.2IP, 26H, 15ER, 9BB, 33K in 6GS)…was a *Baseball America* Triple-A All-Star…**2013:** Spent the entire season with Double-A Corpus Christi, going 7-10 with a 4.11 ERA (133.2IP, 140H, 65R/61ER, 39BB, 130K, 15HR) in 28 games (20 starts)…**2012:** Split the season between Single-A Lexington and Single-A Lancaster, combining to go 12-7 with a 3.02 ERA (158.0IP, 149H, 66R/53ER, 47BB, 166K, 11HR) in 27 games (26 starts)…was honored as a South Atlantic League Mid-Season All-Star…was twice named South Atlantic League "Pitcher of the Week" (4/23 and 5/7)…was honored as California League "Player of the Month" for August after going 4-0 with a 2.15 ERA (37.2IP, 35H, 17R/9ER, 8BB, 35K) over six starts during the month…was named California League "Pitcher of the Week" on 7/2…according to *Baseball America*, had the "Best Changeup" in the South Atlantic League…appeared in 11 games (one start) for the Mesa Solar Sox of the Arizona Fall League, posting a 3.00 ERA (15.0IP, 10H, 5ER, 5BB, 18K, 2HR)…**2011:** Went 3-2 with a 2.36 ERA (53.1IP, 42H, 18ER, 21BB, 63K, 1HR) in 12 starts with short-season Single-A Tri-City…made his professional debut on 6/21 at Connecticut, taking a no-decision after allowing 1H over 5.0 scoreless innings (2BB, 3K)…**PERSONAL:** Full name is Nicholas Paul Tropeano…was named America East Conference Pitcher of the Year during his junior season at Stony Brook (N.Y.) University in 2011 after setting school records with 119 strikeouts and 12 wins…attended West Islip (N.Y.) H.S., leading the school to a Suffolk Class AA Championship in 2008 after going 8-1 with a 1.50 ERA.

Tropeano's Career Pitching Record

Year	Club	W	L	ERA	G	GS	CG	SHO	SV	IP	H	R	ER	HR	HP	BB	SO	WP	BK
2011	Tri-City	3	2	2.36	12	12	0	0	0	53.1	42	18	14	1	1	21	63	6	1
2012	Lancaster	6	3	3.31	12	12	0	0	0	70.2	72	37	26	8	3	21	69	10	0
	Lexington	6	4	2.78	15	14	0	0	0	87.1	77	29	27	3	2	26	97	2	0
2013	Corpus Christi	7	10	4.11	28	20	1	0	5	133.2	140	65	61	15	3	39	130	5	0
2014	Oklahoma City	9	5	3.03	23	20	0	0	0	124.2	90	44	42	11	4	33	120	5	0
	HOUSTON	1	3	4.57	4	4	0	0	0	21.2	19	12	11	0	1	9	13	1	0
2015	Salt Lake	3	6	4.81	16	16	1	0	0	88.0	97	51	47	9	3	36	96	3	0
	LOS ANGELES-AL	3	2	3.82	8	7	0	0	0	37.2	40	18	16	2	0	10	38	0	0
	AZL Angels	0	1	2.57	2	2	0	0	0	7.0	6	2	2	1	0	1	6	0	0
2016	LOS ANGELES-AL	3	2	3.56	13	13	0	0	0	68.1	70	27	27	14	2	31	68	4	0
	Inland Empire	0	1	5.40	1	1	0	0	0	5.0	7	5	3	0	0	0	7	2	0
	Salt Lake	1	0	2.70	1	1	0	0	0	6.2	3	2	2	1	0	1	7	0	0
2017							Did Not Pitch - Injured												
2018	Salt Lake	0	0	0.00	1	1	0	0	0	3.2	3	0	0	0	0	3	7	1	0
	LOS ANGELES-AL	5	6	4.74	14	14	0	0	0	76.0	68	41	40	16	2	31	64	2	0
	Inland Empire	1	1	2.00	2	2	0	0	0	9.0	9	3	2	1	0	1	9	0	0
2019	Salt Lake	4	6	5.87	17	15	0	0	0	79.2	90	55	52	12	2	31	85	3	0
	LOS ANGELES-AL	0	1	9.88	3	1	0	0	0	13.2	18	15	15	6	2	6	10	0	0
Minor League Totals		40	39	3.74	130	116	2	0	5	668.2	636	311	278	62	18	213	696	37	1
Major League Totals		12	14	4.51	42	39	0	0	0	217.1	215	113	109	38	7	87	193	7	0

URBANO, Luis – LHP
HT: 6-2; **WT:** 163; **B:** L; **T:** L; **BORN:** 10/1/02 in Puerto La Cruz, Venezuela; **RESIDES:** Puerto La Cruz, Venezuela; **OBTAINED:** Signed by the Yankees as a non-drafted free agent on 7/2/19; **M.L. SVC:** 0.000.

VALDEZ, Jefry – RHP
HT: 6-1; **WT:** 165; **B:** R; **T:** R; **BORN:** 8/20/95 in Hato Mayor, D.R.; **RESIDES:** Hato Mayor, D.R.; **OBTAINED:** Was acquired by the Yankees from Colorado in exchange for RHP Jordan Foley on 11/20/18; **M.L. SVC:** 0.000; **CAREER NOTES:** Was originally signed by the Rockies as a non-drafted free agent on 5/8/15…**2018:** His 11.91 K/9.0IP (45K/34.0IP) ratio at short-season Single-A Boise ranked fifth among relief pitchers in the Northwest League…**2017:** Ranked second in the Pioneer League with 10 saves at Rookie-level Grand Junction.

VALENZUELA, Anthony – OF
HT: 5-11; **WT:** 180; **B:** R; **T:** R; **BORN:** 6/16/01 in San Cristóbal, D.R.; **RESIDES:** San Cristóbal, D.R.; **OBTAINED:** Signed by the Yankees as a non-drafted free agent on 2/9/18; **M.L. SVC:** 0.000.

VALLEJO, Dionys – INF
HT: 6-1; **WT:** 153; **B:** R; **T:** R; **BORN:** 5/25/00 in Sabana Grande de Palenque, D.R.; **RESIDES:** Sabana Grande de Palenque, D.R.; **OBTAINED:** Signed by the Yankees as a non-drafted free agent on 5/21/18; **M.L. SVC:** 0.000.

VAN ZIJLL, Gerrit – LHP
HT: 6-4; **WT:** 210; **B:** L; **T:** L; **BORN:** 8/2/96 in Houston, Tex.; **RESIDES:** Houston, Tex.; **COLLEGE:** Alvin Community College; **OBTAINED:** Selected by the Yankees in the 22nd round of the 2019 First-Year Player Draft; **M.L. SVC:** 0.000; **PERSONAL:** Pitched one season (2019) at Alvin (Tex.) Community College, where he went 6-3 with a 2.35 ERA (76.2IP, 59H, 29R/20ER, 30BB, 122K) in 15 starts…was out of baseball for three years while battling Lyme disease…the ailment was diagnosed during his first semester at Cameron (Okla.) University in 2015…graduated from Clear Lake H.S. in 2015.

VARGAS, Alexander – INF
HT: 5-10; **WT:** 142; **B:** S; **T:** R; **BORN:** 10/29/01 in Matanzas, Cuba; **RESIDES:** Santo Domingo, D.R.; **OBTAINED:** Signed by the Yankees as a non-drafted free agent on 7/31/18; **M.L. SVC:** 0.000; **CAREER NOTES: 2019:** Tied for the GCL lead with five triples…**PERSONAL:** For the 2018 international signing period, was ranked by MLB.com as the No. 8 prospect and FanGraphs as the No. 14 prospect.

VARGAS, Miguel – LHP
HT: 5-11; **WT:** 158; **B:** L; **T:** L; **BORN:** 2/22/01 in Caucagua, Venezuela; **RESIDES:** Caucagua, Venezuela; **OBTAINED:** Signed by the Yankees as a non-drafted free agent on 7/2/18; **M.L. SVC:** 0.000.

VARGAS, Sergio – INF
HT: 6-1; **WT:** 170; **B:** R; **T:** R; **BORN:** 6/16/02 in Santo Domingo, D.R.; **RESIDES:** Santo Domingo, D.R.; **OBTAINED:** Signed by the Yankees as a non-drafted free agent on 10/31/18; **M.L. SVC:** 0.000.

VASQUEZ, Randy – RHP
HT: 6-0; **WT:** 165; **B:** R; **T:** R; **BORN:** 11/3/98 in Navarette, D.R.; **RESIDES:** Navarette, D.R.; **OBTAINED:** Signed by the Yankees as a non-drafted free agent on 5/21/18; **M.L. SVC:** 0.000; **CAREER NOTES: 2019:** Went 4-1 with a 3.29 ERA (54.2IP, 36H, 23R/20ER, 28BB, 53K, 6HR) in 11 starts with Rookie-level Pulaski…ranked fourth in the Appalachian League in innings…limited opponents to an App. League-low .188 BA (36-for-192).

VEGA, Alfred – RHP
HT: 6-1; **WT:** 165; **B:** R; **T:** R; **BORN:** 1/19/01 in Puerto Plata, D.R.; **RESIDES:** Puerto Plata, D.R.; **OBTAINED:** Signed by the Yankees as a non-drafted free agent on 7/2/17; **M.L. SVC:** 0.000.

VELASQUEZ, Luis – RHP
HT: 5-10; **WT:** 155; **B:** R; **T:** R; **BORN:** 7/1/01 in Fantino, D.R.; **RESIDES:** Fantino, D.R.; **OBTAINED:** Signed by the Yankees as a non-drafted free agent on 4/26/19; **M.L. SVC:** 0.000.

VERDECIA, Carlos – INF
HT: 5-11; **WT:** 170; **B:** S; **T:** R; **BORN:** 3/16/02 in Matanzas, Cuba; **RESIDES:** Bonao, D.R.; **OBTAINED:** Signed by the Yankees as a non-drafted free agent on 10/19/18; **M.L. SVC:** 0.000.

VILLA, José – INF
HT: 6-1; **WT:** 170; **B:** R; **T:** R; **BORN:** 11/16/98 in San Pedro de Macoris, D.R.; **RESIDES:** San Pedro de Macoris, D.R.; **OBTAINED:** Signed by the Yankees as a non-drafted free agent on 7/7/16; **M.L. SVC:** 0.000.

VILLAMAN, Abismael – LHP
HT: 6-2; **WT:** 175; **B:** L; **T:** L; **BORN:** 9/27/95 in Santiago de los Caballeros, D.R.; **RESIDES:** Santiago de los Caballeros, D.R.; **OBTAINED:** Signed by the Yankees as a non-drafted free agent on 4/12/18; **M.L. SVC:** 0.000.

VIZCAÍNO, Alexander – RHP   NON-ROSTER INVITEE
HT: 6-2; **WT:** 160; **B:** R; **T:** R; **BORN:** 5/22/97 in San Cristobal, D.R.; **RESIDES:** San Cristobal, D.R.; **OBTAINED:** Signed by the Yankees as a non-drafted free agent on 5/18/16; **M.L. SVC:** 0.000; **CAREER NOTES: 2019:** Combined with Single-A Charleston and Single-A Tampa to start 21 games, posting a 6-6 record and 4.38 ERA (115.0IP, 113H, 61R/56ER, 38BB, 128K, 8HR)…set career highs in innings pitched and strikeouts, while matching his previous combined career win total…recorded a career-high 10K in consecutive starts on 5/17 vs. Augusta (7.0IP, 6H, 2R, 0BB) and 5/23 at Asheville (4.2IP, 4H, 4R/2ER, 4BB, 1HR)…completed 7.0IP four times (had only two prior games in his career)…was named a South Atlantic League Mid-Season All-Star with Charleston…following the season, was named by *Baseball America* as the No. 9 prospect in the Yankees organization and No. 13 prospect in the SAL…was labeled as having the "Best Changeup" among Yankees farmhands…**2018:** Combined with Rookie-level Pulaski and Single-A Charleston to post a 3-4 record with a 5.12 ERA (58.0IP, 57H, 35R/33ER, 23BB, 57K, 9HR)…was named the Appalachian League "Pitcher of the Week" for 7/16-22 after allowing only two baserunners over 7.0 scoreless innings on 7/18 at Danville (W, 1H, 1BB, 6K)…**2017:** Spent the entire season with Rookie-level Pulaski, going 3-5 with a 5.79 ERA (51.1IP, 69H, 40R/33ER, 23BB, 49K, 9HR) in 12 games (11 starts)…**2016:** Made his professional debut with the DSL Yankees 1, going 0-5 with a 4.89 ERA (35.0IP, 40H, 27R/19ER, 13BB, 27K, 4HR) in 11 games (six starts).

Vizcaíno's Career Pitching Record

Year	Club	W	L	ERA	G	GS	CG	SHO	SV	IP	H	R	ER	HR	HP	BB	SO	WP	BK
2016	DSL Yankees 1	0	5	4.89	11	6	0	0	0	35.0	40	27	19	4	4	13	27	4	0
2017	Pulaski	3	5	5.79	12	11	0	0	0	51.1	69	40	33	9	4	23	49	9	1
2018	Pulaski	3	3	4.50	11	11	0	0	0	54.0	49	29	27	7	3	21	55	6	0
	Charleston	0	1	13.50	1	1	0	0	0	4.0	8	6	6	2	1	2	2	1	0
2019	Charleston	5	5	4.41	16	16	1	0	0	87.2	80	47	43	6	9	27	101	11	1
	Tampa	1	1	4.28	5	5	0	0	0	27.1	33	14	13	2	0	11	27	2	1
Minor League Totals		12	20	4.89	56	50	1	0	0	259.1	279	163	141	30	21	97	261	33	3

VOLIVA, Evan – RHP
HT: 5-11; **WT:** 190; **B:** R; **T:** R; **BORN:** 7/21/96 in Virginia Beach, Va.; **RESIDES:** Currituck, N.C.; **COLLEGE:** East Carolina University; **OBTAINED:** Selected by the Yankees in the 18th round of the 2019 First-Year Player Draft; **M.L. SVC:** 0.000; **PERSONAL:** Pitched four seasons (2015-16, '18-19) at East Carolina (N.C.)…took a medical redshirt in 2017 after season-ending "Tommy John" surgery…graduated from Currituck County (N.C.) H.S. in 2014.

VOLPE, Anthony – INF
HT: 5-11; **WT:** 180; **B:** R; **T:** R; **BORN:** 4/28/01 in Watchung, N.J.; **RESIDES:** Watchung, N.J.; **OBTAINED:** Selected by the Yankees in the first round (30th overall) of the 2019 First-Year Player Draft; **M.L. SVC:** 0.000; **CAREER NOTES: 2019:** Made his pro debut, batting .215/.349/.355 (26-for-121) with 19R, 7 doubles, 2 triples, 2HR, 11RBI and 6SB in 34 games with Rookie-level Pulaski…following the season, was ranked by *Baseball America* as the No. 6 prospect in the Yankees organization and by MLB Pipeline as the No. 10 prospect…**PERSONAL:** Graduated in 2019 from the Delbarton (N.J.) School…led Delbarton to the 2019 NJSIAA Non-Public A State Championship as a senior…helped the USA Baseball 18U National Team win the gold medal at the Pan-American Championships in December 2018, earning all-tournament honors by hitting .459 (17-for-37) with 17R, 14RBI and 6SB in 9G…played in the 2018 Perfect Game All-American Classic at Petco Park in San Diego…was ranked by *Baseball America* as the No. 52 prospect in the 2019 draft, and the No. 25 prep prospect by Perfect Game…had signed to play collegiately at Vanderbilt…was the first player from the tri-state area to be selected in the first round by the Yankees since INF Cito Culver (Irondequoit H.S. in western New York) in 2010, and the first from New Jersey since INF Eric Duncan (Seton Hall Prep) in 2003.

VORHOF, Mick – RHP
HT: 6-1; **WT:** 200; **B:** R, **T:** R; **BORN:** 9/7/95 in Bellevue, Wash.; **RESIDES:** Sammamish, Wash.; **COLLEGE:** Grand Canyon University; **OBTAINED:** Selected by the Yankees in the ninth round of the 2018 First-Year Player Draft; **M.L. SVC:** 0.000; **PERSONAL:** Pitched four seasons at Grand Canyon University (Ariz.), where he was 16-6 with 19 saves and a 3.43 ERA (152.1IP, 161H, 72R/58ER, 41BB, 142K, 12HR) in 93 games (three starts)…left as the school's all-time appearances leader…graduated in 2014 from Eastlake (Wash.) H.S., where he also played basketball.

WAGAMAN, Eric – INF
HT: 6-4; **WT:** 210; **B:** R; **T:** R; **BORN:** 8/14/97 in Mission Viejo, Calif.; **RESIDES:** Aliso Viejo, Calif.; **COLLEGE:** Orange Coast College; **OBTAINED:** Selected by the Yankees in the 13th round of the 2017 First-Year Player Draft; **M.L. SVC:** 0.000; **PERSONAL:** Played two seasons (2016-17) at Orange Coast College (Calif.), hitting .304 (73-for-240) with 53R, 17 doubles, 15HR and 56RBI in 72 games…is a 2015 graduate of Aliso Niguel H.S. (Calif.).

WAGNER, Brandon – INF
HT: 6-0; **WT:** 210; **B:** L; **T:** R; **BORN:** 8/24/95 in Princeton, N.J.; **RESIDES:** Hopewell, N.J.; **COLLEGE:** Howard College; **OBTAINED:** Selected by the Yankees in the sixth round of the 2015 First-Year Player Draft; **M.L. SVC:** 0.000; **CAREER NOTES: 2019:** Following the season, led the Arizona Fall League in RBI, hitting .214 (15-for-70) with 10R, 4 doubles, 2HR, 21BBI and 12BB in 20 games for Surprise…tied for seventh in the AFL in walks…was named to the AFL Fall Stars Game…**2018:** Among Yankees minor leaguers, ranked second in home runs (21), fourth in RBI (67) and eighth in batting average (.267)…his 20HR with Single-A Tampa were tied for the second-most in the Florida State League…was named an FSL Mid-Season All-Star…following the season was tabbed by *Baseball America* as having the "Best Strike-Zone Discipline" in the organization…was also named an Organization All-Star by MiLB.com…**2017:** Finished second in the South Atlantic League in OBP (.380) and fifth in walks (57)…was named SAL "Player of the Week" for 7/10-16 after hitting .381 (8-for-21) with 6R, 2 doubles, 3HR, 5RBI and 3BB in 6G…in 27 games in July, slashed .353/.446/.647 (30-for-85) with 16R, 8 doubles, 1 triple, 5HR, 21RBI and 15BB, leading all Single-A players in OPS (1.093) for the month…**PERSONAL:** Played two seasons at Howard College (Tex.)…was named a 2015 NJCAA First-Team All-American and the WJCAC MVP after hitting .435/.571/.891 (84-for-193) with 86R, 20 doubles, 22HR and 80RBI in 58 games as a sophomore…was selected by Philadelphia in the 39th round of the 2013 First-Year Player Draft but did not sign…played at Immaculata H.S. (N.J.), where he was named to the All-Somerset County First Team.

WALDICHUK, Ken – LHP
HT: 6-3; **WT:** 220; **B:** L; **T:** L; **BORN:** 1/8/98 in San Diego, Calif.; **RESIDES:** San Diego, Calif.; **COLLEGE:** Saint Mary's College; **OBTAINED:** Selected by the Yankees in the fifth round of the 2019 First-Year Player Draft; **M.L. SVC:** 0.000; **PERSONAL:** Pitched three seasons (2017-19) at Saint Mary's (Calif.)…was a 2018 *Collegiate Baseball* Second-Team All-American after winning the West Coast Conference ERA title (2.05) as a sophomore…was named a 2019 Second-Team Preseason All-American by *Collegiate Baseball*…graduated in 2016 from University City (Calif.) H.S.

WARREN, Adam – RHP
HT: 6-1; **WT:** 225; **B:** R; **T:** R; **BORN:** 8/25/87 in Birmingham, Ala.; **RESIDES:** Riverview, Fla.; **COLLEGE:** University of North Carolina; **OBTAINED:** Signed by the Yankees as a minor league free agent on 12/18/19; **M.L. SVC:** 7.036; **CAREER NOTES:** Was originally selected by the Yankees in the fourth round of the 2009 First-Year Player Draft…in eight Major League seasons with the Yankees (2012-15, '16-18), Cubs (2016), Mariners (2018) and Padres (2019), has posted a 30-24 career record with six saves and a 3.53 ERA (492.1IP, 435H, 205R/193ER, 171BB, 428K, 56HR) in 323 games (21 starts)…in seven seasons with the Yankees, compiled a 20-20 record with six saves and a 3.18 ERA (407.0IP, 354H, 154R/144ER, 132BB, 361K, 37HR) in 246 games (20 starts) over two stints with the club…*Elias* confirms that only three players have had three separate Major League stints with the Yankees: C Rick Cerrone, OF Bob Cerv, OF Luis Polonia.…was traded to the Chicago Cubs with a player to be named later (Brendan Ryan) on 12/8/15 for 2B Starlin Castro and was traded back to the Yankees on 7/25/16, along with INF Gleyber Torres and OFs Billy McKinney and Rashad Crawford in exchange for LHP Aroldis Chapman…was traded from the Yankees to the Seattle Mariners in exchange for international signing bonus pool money on 7/30/18…has made seven career Opening Day rosters, five with the Yankees (2013-15, '17-18), one with the Cubs (2016) and one with the Padres (2019)…**2019:** Went 4-1 with a 5.34 ERA (28.2IP, 17ER) in 25 relief appearances with San Diego before being placed on the 10-day I.L. on 6/8 with a strained right forearm…was transferred to the 60-Day I.L. on 7/21 and missed the remainder of the season…on 9/4, underwent "Tommy John" surgery performed by Dr. Keith Meister…**2018:** Combined with the Yankees and Mariners to go 3-2 with a 3.14 ERA (51.2IP, 18ER) in 47 relief appearances…began the season with the Yankees, going 0-1 with a 2.70 ERA (30.0IP, 9ER) with 37K in 24 relief appearances…made his sixth career Opening Day roster (2013-15 '16-18)…made his season debut in 3/31 loss to Toronto, allowing 1ER in 0.2IP (1BB)…was removed from the game after taking a comebacker to the right ankle (x-rays were negative)…tossed 2.2 innings in 4/20 loss vs. Toronto (2H, 1ER, 1BB, 3K, 1HR), his longest appearance since 4/29/17 vs. Baltimore (also 2.2IP)…his 46 pitches thrown were his most since 7/9/16 at Pittsburgh (64 pitches)…was placed on the 10-day disabled list on 4/21 with a right back strain (missed 38 team games)…was returned from rehab and reinstated from the 10-day disabled list prior to Game 2 on 6/4…combined to make two rehab starts with Triple-A Scranton/Wilkes-Barre and Double-A Trenton (0-1, 9.82 ERA, 3.2IP, 4ER)…did not allow a run over his first eight appearances after coming off the D.L. from 6/4-30 (10.2IP, 5H, 5BB, 11K)…had a 13.1-inning scoreless streak from 4/20-6/30…tossed 2.2 scoreless innings in 6/30 loss vs. Boston (2H, 4K), matching his longest appearance of the season and marking his most strikeouts since 4/5/17 at Tampa Bay (4K)…made

his 24th and final appearance of the season with the Yankees in Game 1 of 7/28 doubleheader vs. Kansas City, tossing 2.2 perfect innings…was acquired by Seattle from the Yankees in exchange for international bonus pool money on 7/30…in 23 appearances with Seattle, went 3-1 with a 3.74 ERA (21.2IP, 9ER)…did not allow a run in 17 of his 23 appearances with the Mariners…**2017:** Went 3-2 with one save and a 2.35 ERA (57.1IP, 15ER) with 54K in 46 relief appearances with the Yankees…opponents batted .173 (35-for-202, 4HR); LH .208 (16-for-77, 1HR), RH .152 (19-for-125, 3HR)…retired 36-of-46 first batters faced in relief (78.3%)…allowed 5-of-29 inherited runners to score (17.2%)…had 16 scoreless relief appearances of at least 1.1IP, tied for eighth-most in the Majors…retired his first 22BF to begin the season…had the streak snapped with a seventh-inning walk to the White Sox' Tyler Saladino in 4/17 win vs. Chicago-AL…allowed his first hit of the season to Melky Cabrera in the same game…became the first pitcher in Major League history to not allow a baserunner through his first four appearances of a season while tossing at least 6.0 innings over the stretch…from 5/27-10/1, posted a 1.91 ERA (33.0IP, 7ER) with 32K in 30 relief appearances…held opponents scoreless over a career-best 11 consecutive appearances from 6/3-7/21 (13.0IP, 6H, 2BB, 14K)…was placed on the 10-day disabled list from 6/16-7/4 with right shoulder inflammation, missing 17 team games…was on the 10-day D.L. from 9/6 (retro. to 9/3) to 9/29 with lower back spasms, missing 24 team games…made his postseason debut in ALDS Game 1 loss at Cleveland…in three postseason relief appearances, posted a 2.08 ERA (4.1IP, 1ER)…**2016:** Combined to go 7-4 with a 4.68 ERA (65.1IP, 34ER) in 58 games (one start) with the Cubs and Yankees, matching his single-season career high in wins…went 4-2 with a 3.26 ERA (30.1IP, 11ER) in 29 relief appearances after rejoining the Yankees…was acquired by the Yankees with INF Gleyber Torres, OF Billy McKinney and OF Rashad Crawford from the Cubs in exchange for LHP Aroldis Chapman on 7/25…did not allow a run in 11.0IP (4H, 3BB, 10K) over his first nine appearances with the Yankees (7/27-8/15)…was 3-2 with a 5.91 ERA (35.0IP, 23ER) in 29 games (one start) over two stints with the Cubs (4/4-6/21, 7/6-23)…made his only start on 7/6 vs. Cincinnati, allowing 1ER in 5.0IP (3H, 0BB, 6K, 1HR)…made two starts for Triple-A Iowa, posting a 4.15 ERA (8.2IP, 4ER) without recording a decision…**2015:** Went 7-7 with a 3.29 ERA (131.1IP, 48ER) in 43 appearances (17 starts) with the Yankees…set career highs in wins, starts, innings pitched and strikeouts (104)…recorded a 2.1 WAR (FanGraphs), 3.59 FIP and 3.96 xFIP…was one of two pitchers in the Majors to make at least 15 starts and 25 relief appearances (also the Twins' Trevor May)…according to *Elias*, over the last 85 seasons, the only other Yankees to do so were Allie Reynolds (1953), Shane Rawley (1982) and Chad Green (2019)…was the second Yankees pitcher since 1998 to make at least 15 starts and 15 relief appearances in the same season (also David Phelps in 2014 – 17 starts, 15 relief appearances)…began the season in the starting rotation, winning the fifth starter's spot in spring training after going 2-0 with a 2.70 ERA (16.2IP, 5ER) and 11K in five spring starts…went 5-5 with a 3.59 ERA (82.2IP, 33ER) in 14GS before moving to the bullpen after his 6/25 start to make room for the returning Iván Nova…made his next 25 appearances out of the bullpen (2.51 ERA, 32.1IP, 9ER)…rejoined the rotation on 9/15, taking Nova's spot, and went 1-1 with a 4.05 ERA (13.1IP, 6ER) in three September starts before again returning to the bullpen…in 17 starts, was 6-6 with a 3.66 ERA (96.0IP, 39ER)…held opponents to a .245 (87-for-355) batting average with 8HR as a starter, the second-lowest opp. BA among the six Yankees pitchers who made at least 15 starts (Tanaka-.221)…took shutouts into the sixth inning four times: 4/27 vs. Tampa Bay, 5/3 at Boston, 5/26 vs. Kansas City and 5/31 at Oakland…allowed 3R-or-fewer in each of his final 12 starts (beginning 5/8)…was the AL's longest streak of starts with 3R-or-fewer in 2015 and tied for the third-longest in the Majors (Jake Arrieta-20, Gerrit Cole-14)…was the longest streak by a Yankee starter since Hideki Irabu (12, 9/28/97-6/16/98) and the longest in a single season since Ron Guidry (12, 6/2-9/29/81)…in 26 relief appearances, went 1-1 with one save, a 2.29 ERA (35.1IP, 9ER) and 37K…posted a 0.51 HR/9.0IP ratio (2HR)…went 4-2 with a 2.00 ERA (63.0IP, 14ER, 17BB, 52K) in 22 games (seven starts) at Yankee Stadium…was 4-1 with a 2.11 ERA (42.2IP, 10ER) in seven home starts, allowing 2R-or-fewer in all of them…was tied for the second-longest streak of home starts with 2R-or-fewer in the AL in 2015, behind Lance McCullers (nine)…was 0-1 with a 1.77 ERA (20.1IP, 4ER) in 15 relief appearances at home…went 3-5 with one save and a 4.48 ERA (68.1IP, 34ER) in 21 games (10 starts) on the road…tossed 3.0 perfect innings in 7/2 win at Texas…with Diego Moreno tossing 5.1 hitless innings in the same game (1BB, 5K), became the second duo in Major League history to each throw at least 3.0 hitless relief innings in a 9.0-inning game, joining Washington-AL's Ewald Pyle (4.0IP) and Mickey Haefner (3.0IP) on 7/3/43 at St. Louis-AL…was on the Yankees' AL Wild Card Game roster, but did not pitch in the loss vs. Houston…was acquired by the Chicago Cubs with a player to be named later (INF Brendan Ryan) from the Yankees in exchange for 2B Starlin Castro on 12/8/15…**2014:** Went 3-6 with three saves and a 2.97 ERA (78.2IP, 26ER) in 69 relief appearances with the Yankees…of his 26ER allowed, 18 came in just six appearances…did not allow more than 1ER in any of his other 63 relief appearances in 2014…over his final 15 appearances of the season from 8/19-9/28, went 1-1 with one save and a 1.35 ERA (20.0IP, 3ER) while striking out 21 batters…**2013:** Made his first career Opening Day roster and combined to go 3-2 with one save and a 3.39 ERA (77.0IP, 29ER) in two stints with the Yankees (4/1-6/14, 6/18-9/29)…made two starts, going 1-0 with a 2.25 ERA (8.0IP, 2ER)…in 32 relief appearances, was 2-2 with one save and a 3.52 ERA (69.0IP, 27ER)…recorded his first Major League strikeout on 4/3 vs. Boston (Jarrod Saltalamacchia in the fourth)…earned his first career Major League win on 5/9 at Colorado (1.2IP, 2BB)…recorded his first Major League save in Game 2 of a doubleheader on 5/13 at Cleveland, tossing 4.0 scoreless innings (2H, 4K) in relief of Vidal Nuno, who started and earned the win…the duo became the second pair of Yankees pitchers to earn their first career win and first career save in the same game, joining Alan Closter (win) and Fritz Peterson (save) on 7/25/71 (G2) at Milwaukee (credit: *Elias*)…tossed 6.0 scoreless innings out of the bullpen on 6/13 at Oakland (4H, 2BB, 4K)…was the longest appearance by a Yankees reliever since Hector Noesi also threw 6.0 innings on 6/7/11 vs. Boston and the longest scoreless appearance since Kei Igawa recorded 6.0 scoreless innings on 4/28/07 vs. Boston…was optioned to Triple-A Scranton/Wilkes-Barre on 6/14, but did not appear in a game prior to being recalled on 6/18…**2012:** Made one appearance (2.1IP, 2ER) over two stints with the Yankees (6/28-30, 9/1-10/3) in his first Major League action…was signed to a Major League contract and selected to the Yankees' 25-man roster from Triple-A Scranton/Wilkes-Barre on 6/28…made his Major League debut on 6/29 vs. Chicago-AL and did not record a decision, allowing 6ER in 2.1IP (8H, 2BB, 1K, 2HR)…was the shortest outing by a Yankees starter in his Major League debut since LHP Sean Henn on 5/4/05 at Tampa Bay (also 2.1IP)…was the first Yankee to make his debut as a starter since Ian Kennedy on 9/1/07 vs. Tampa Bay (W, 7.0IP, 5H, 3R, 1ER, 2BB, 6K, 1HR)…became the first Yankee from the organization's 2009 draft class to appear in the Majors…was optioned to Scranton/WB on 6/30…was again recalled on 9/1, but did not appear in a game…spent the majority of the season with Scranton/WB, going 7-8 with a 3.71 ERA (152.2IP, 63ER) in 26 starts…led the team in strikeouts (107)…following the season, earned the Rawlings Minor League Gold Glove Award as the top fielding pitcher in the minors…**2011:** Went 6-8 with a 3.60 ERA (152.1IP, 61ER) in 27 starts with Triple-A Scranton/Wilkes-Barre… ranked 10th in the International League in ERA…was named to the IL's Mid-Season All-Star Team…**2010:** Combined to go 11-7 with a 2.59 ERA (135.1IP, 39ER) in 25 starts with Single-A Tampa and Double-A Trenton…began the season with Tampa, going 7-5 with a 2.22 ERA (81.0IP, 20ER)…was named to the FSL Mid-Season All-Star Team…went 4-2 with a 3.15 ERA (54.1IP, 19ER) with Trenton in 10GS after being promoted on 7/16…had a franchise-record 15K in 7.0 shutout innings (2H, 1BB) on 8/18 vs. Bowie…made two postseason appearances (one start) for the Thunder, going 0-1 with a 3.27 ERA (11.0IP, 4ER) and a team-leading 18K…**2009:** Made his professional debut, going 4-2 with a 1.43 ERA (56.2IP, 9ER) in 12 starts with short-season Single-A Staten Island…was named to the NYPL Mid-Season All-Star Team…among NYPL pitchers with at least 50.0IP, ranked third in ERA…made two starts in the playoffs for the NYPL Champions, going 1-0 with a 1.69 ERA (10.2IP, 2ER)…led all postseason pitchers with 15K and tied for the league lead in innings pitched (10.2)…**PERSONAL:** Is married to Kristen…the couple has a son, Kendall James (born November 2016)…graduated from North Carolina with a degree in business administration…went 32-4 with a 3.42 ERA (276.0IP, 105ER) and 240K in 65 games (49 starts) in his collegiate career… left school with the second-most wins by a Tar Heel and tied with Scott Bankhead for the school's highest winning percentage (.889)… won his first 19 decisions at UNC, marking the longest UNC winning streak since Bankhead won 20 straight from 1983-84…helped the North Carolina Tar Heels to the College World Series in three straight years (2006-08), leading them to the championship series in 2006 and '07…graduated fifth in his class from New Bern High School (N.C.), where he earned all-state honors as a junior in 2004 and was selected as the New Bern Sun Journal "Baseball Player of the Year."…was a member of the ping pong club.

WEISSERT, Greg – RHP
HT: 6-2; **WT:** 215; **B:** R; **T:** R; **BORN:** 2/4/95 in Bay Shore, N.Y.; **RESIDES:** Brooklyn, N.Y.; **COLLEGE:** Fordham University; **OBTAINED:** Selected by the Yankees in the 18th round of the 2016 First-Year Player Draft; **M.L. SVC:** 0.000; **PERSONAL:** Played three seasons (2014-16) at Fordham University…in his final season with the Rams, went 5-4 with a 4.04 ERA (78.0IP, 64H, 44R/35ER, 42BB, 82K) in 14 starts…attended Bay Shore H.S. (N.Y.).

WESNESKI, Hayden – RHP
HT: 6-2; **WT:** 210; **B:** R; **T:** R; **BORN:** 12/5/97 in Houston, Tex.; **RESIDES:** Cypress, Tex.; **COLLEGE:** Sam Houston State University; **OBTAINED:** Selected by the Yankees in the sixth round of the 2019 First-Year Player Draft; **M.L. SVC:** 0.000; **PERSONAL:** Pitched three seasons (2017-19) at Sam Houston State (Tex.)…was a 2017 *Collegiate Baseball* Freshman All-American…is a 2016 graduate of Cy-Fair (Tex.) H.S.…was selected by Tampa Bay in the 33rd round of the 2016 First-Year Player Draft but did not sign.

WHITLOCK, Garrett – RHP
HT: 6-5; **WT:** 190; **B:** R; **T:** R; **BORN:** 6/11/96 in Snellville, Ga.; **RESIDES:** Birmingham, Ala.; **COLLEGE:** University of Alabama-Birmingham; **OBTAINED:** Selected by the Yankees in the 18th round of the 2017 First-Year Player Draft; **M.L. SVC:** 0.000; **CAREER NOTES: 2018:** His 1.86 ERA (120.2IP, 25ER) was the second-lowest among all Yankees farmhands…was named the South Atlantic League "Pitcher of the Week" from 4/30-5/6 after tossing 7.0 scoreless innings on 5/5 vs. Lexington (W, 2H, 1BB, 10K)…**PERSONAL:** Pitched two seasons at UAB (2016-17), going 7-11 with two saves and a 3.56 ERA (111.1IP, 115H, 61R/44ER, 45BB, 90K) in 42 games (eight starts)…graduated from Providence Christian Academy (Ga.), where he was a 2015 Perfect Game Preseason All-America honorable mention.

WILSON, Justin – RHP
HT: 6-0; **WT:** 180; **B:** R; **T:** R; **BORN:** 9/9/96 in Murfreesboro, Tenn.; **RESIDES:** Murfreesboro, Tenn.; **COLLEGE:** Vanderbilt University; **OBTAINED:** Selected by the Yankees in the 23rd round of the 2018 First-Year Player Draft; **M.L. SVC:** 0.000; **PERSONAL:** Pitched one season (2018) at Vanderbilt after transferring from Volunteer State (Tenn.) Community College, where he played both ways as a freshman in 2016…made just seven appearances with Vanderbilt, logging a 2.84 ERA (6.1IP, 2H, 2ER, 4BB, 9K)…missed the 2017 season at Vanderbilt while recovering from elbow surgery…graduated in 2015 from Oakland (Tenn.) H.S.…his father, Craig, is a retired NASCAR driver.

WIVINIS, Matt – RHP
HT: 6-0; **WT:** 170; **B:** R; **T:** R; **BORN:** 7/24/93 in Hinsdale, Ill.; **RESIDES:** Downers Grove, Ill.; **COLLEGE:** Eastern Illinois University; **OBTAINED:** Signed by the Yankees as a non-drafted free agent on 10/21/16; **M.L. SVC:** 0.000; **CAREER NOTES: 2019:** Tied for third in the Florida State League with nine saves…**2018:** Led all Yankees minor leaguers in saves (19)…following the season, made 11 relief appearances for the Glendale Desert Dogs of the Arizona Fall League, going 0-1 with one save and a 1.50 ERA (12.0IP, 6H, 2ER, 6BB, 14K)…**2016:** Made 12 appearances (five starts) for Evansville of the independent Frontier League, going 4-0 with a 1.59 ERA (39.2IP, 27H, 7ER, 19BB, 43K)…went 2-1 with a 3.92 ERA in three postseason starts to help lift Evansville to the Frontier League title…**PERSONAL:** Last name is pronounced "WIVV-inn-niss"…pitched one season at Eastern Illinois (2015), going 3-8 with one save and a 6.44 ERA (72.2IP, 98H, 62R/52ER, 25BB, 49K)…transferred from Kansas State after two seasons (2012-13), where he went 7-5 with a 5.14 ERA (115.2IP, 126H, 74R/66ER, 34BB, 88K) in 42 games (17 starts)…graduated from Downers Grove South H.S. (Ill.).

YOUNG, Paul – RHP
HT: 6-2; **WT:** 205; **B:** R; **T:** R; **BORN:** 3/15/93 in Pensacola, Fla.; **RESIDES:** Milton, Fla.; **COLLEGE:** Mississippi State University; **OBTAINED:** Signed by the Yankees as a minor league free agent on 8/30/17; **M.L. SVC:** 0.000; **CAREER NOTES:** Was originally signed by the Kansas City Royals as a non-drafted free agent on 7/8/16…**2017:** Began the season with Southern Illinois of the independent Frontier League, recording a 2.20 ERA (16.1IP, 9H, 5R/4ER, 12BB, 32K) in 17 relief appearances…**PERSONAL:** Spent three years at Mississippi State (2014-16), including one redshirt season…pitched his freshman season (2013) at Central Alabama Community College, tossing a complete game in the Trojans' 2013 NJCAA National Championship Game win over Palm Beach State (9.0IP, 7H, 3R/2ER, 2BB, 5K)…was selected by Cleveland in the 21st round of the 2013 First-Year Player Draft but did not sign.

YULIE, Tyrone – RHP
HT: 6-4; **WT:** 180; **B:** R; **T:** R; **BORN:** 8/4/01 in La Romana, D.R.; **RESIDES:** La Romana, D.R.; **OBTAINED:** Signed by the Yankees as a non-drafted free agent on 7/5/18; **M.L. SVC:** 0.000.

ZEHNER, Zack – OF
HT: 6-4; **WT:** 215; **B:** R; **T:** R; **BORN:** 8/8/92 in San Diego, Calif.; **RESIDES:** San Diego, Calif.; **COLLEGE:** Cal Poly, San Luis Obispo; **OBTAINED:** Selected by the Yankees in the 18th round of the 2015 First-Year Player Draft; **M.L. SVC:** 0.000; **CAREER NOTES: 2018:** His .270 (113-for-418) BA ranked seventh among Yankees minor leaguers…was named to the Eastern League Mid-Season All-Star Team with Double-A Trenton…was fifth in the EL in walks (64)…ranked fifth among Yankees farmhands in RBI (68)…**2016:** Ranked fourth in the Florida State League in OBP (.384)…was named a FSL Postseason All-Star…**PERSONAL:** Played two seasons at Cal Poly (2014-15), where he was named to the 2015 All-Big West First Team after hitting .304 and leading the Mustangs with 9HR and 45RBI…also played two seasons (2012-13) at Santa Barbara City College (Calif.)…is a 2010 graduate of Torrey Pines H.S. (Calif.)…was selected by Toronto in the seventh round of the 2014 First-Year Player Draft but did not sign.

ZURAK, Kyle – RHP
HT: 6-1; **WT:** 192; **B:** R; **T:** R; **BORN:** 11/28/94 in Buffalo, N.Y.; **RESIDES:** Buffalo, N.Y.; **COLLEGE:** Radford University; **OBTAINED:** Selected by the Yankees in the eighth round of the 2017 First-Year Player Draft; **M.L. SVC:** 0.000; **CAREER NOTES: 2019:** Ranked second in the Florida State League with 41 appearances…**2018:** His 11 saves were tied for the second-most among all Yankees farmhands…following the season, appeared in nine games for the Glendale Desert Dogs of the Arizona Fall League, going 0-1 with an 11.57 ERA (9.1IP, 16H, 15R/12ER, 10BB, 3K)…**PERSONAL:** Pitched four seasons (2014-17) at Radford University (Va.), going 4-6 with 10 saves and a 3.74 ERA (120.1IP, 113H, 62R/50ER, 60BB, 117K) in 77 appearances (four starts)…was named a semifinalist for the 2017 Gregg Olson Award, given to the nation's breakout player of the year…followed up 2017 All-Big South First Team honors by winning the Big South Tournament MVP Award after tossing a complete game in the championship game vs. Presbyterian (9.0IP, 6H, 2ER, 1BB, 9K)…is a 2013 graduate of Williamsville North H.S. in Buffalo, N.Y.

PROUDLY SERVING THE NEEDS OF THE PIPEFITTING & HVAC-R INDUSTRY IN NORTHERN NEW JERSEY FOR OVER 100 YEARS

PIPEFITTERS LOCAL 274
205 Jefferson Rd., Parsippany, NJ 07054
(201) 943-4700

For more info contact: Michael J. Stiles
Business Manager/Financial Secretary/Treasurer

Edward Driscoll & Warren Stella
Business Representatives

Jerry DeCarlo
Organizer

Media Information

On December 18, 2019, free agent signing Gerrit Cole was introduced to media at Yankee Stadium's Legends Club, a location which had been used twice before for introductory press conferences for Curtis Granderson and Masahiro Tanaka.

Yankees Media Relations Staff

Please follow us on Twitter @yankeespr / @losyankeespr

| Jason Zillo | Michael Margolis | Lauren Moran | Rob Morse | Kaitlyn Brennan |

| Marlon Abreu *Habla Español* | Mark Torres *Habla Español* | Jon Butensky | Yoshiki Sato | Germania Dolores Hernandez-Simonetti *Habla Español* |

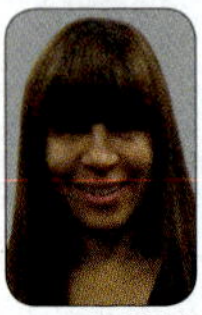

Media Services at Yankee Stadium

Communications and Media Relations Department
Yankee Stadium • One East 161st Street • Bronx, NY 10451
Switchboard: (718) 293-4300
Media Relations: (718) 579-4460
E-mail: media@yankees.com, credentials@yankees.com
Web site: www.yankees.com, www.yankeesbeisbol.com
Twitter: @YankeesPR / @LosYankeesPR

Jason Zillo – Vice President, Comm. & Media Relations
Michael Margolis – Director, Communications & Media Relations
Lauren Moran – Assistant Director, Baseball Information
Rob Morse – Senior Coordinator, Communications & Media Relations
Kaitlyn Brennan – Coordinator, Communications & Media Relations
Mark Torres – Assistant, Media Services
Jon Butensky – Assistant, Communications & Media Relations
Germania Dolores Hernandez-Simonetti – Administrative Asst.
Marlon Abreu – Bilingual Media Relations Coordinator
Yoshiki Sato – Japanese Media Advisor

Media Services for Yankees Games

The New York Yankees Media Relations staff welcomes you to Yankee Stadium. Please see below for helpful information and guidelines for the 2020 season. Contact us with any questions or concerns you may have. We look forward to working with you.

The Yankees Media Relations Department encourages our media to visit **yankeespressbox.com**, a one-stop resource for all Yankees media relations materials. Documents are posted to the site the moment they are available and include: pregame notes, stat packs, the most up-to-date Yankees roster and postgame notes.

All press releases, special packets and a PDF edition of the 2020 Yankees Media Guide & Record Book are also available on the site. Additionally, almost all items available at yankeespressbox.com are archived for access throughout the season.

When accessing the website (which is for media members only), you will be asked to sign in using an mlb.com ID, available only through Major League Baseball.

Servicios para la Prensa en el Yankee Stadium

Departamento de Comunicaciones y Relaciones Públicas
Yankee Stadium • One East 161st Street • Bronx, NY 10451
Central de Teléfonos: (718) 293-4300
Relaciones Públicas: (718) 579-4460
Correo Electrónico: media@yankees.com, credentials@yankees.com
Página de Internet: www.yankees.com, www.yankeesbeisbol.com
Twitter: @YankeesPR / @LosYankeesPR

Jason Zillo – Vice Presidente, Comunicaciones y Relaciones Públicas
Michael Margolis – Director, Comunicaciones y Relaciones Públicas
Lauren Moran – Subdirectora, Información de Beisbol
Rob Morse – Coordinador Superior, Comunicaciones y Relaciones Públicas
Kaitlyn Brennan – Coordinadora, Comunicaciones y Relaciones Públicas
Mark Torres – Asistente, Servicios de Prensa
Jon Butensky – Asistente, Comunicaciones y Relaciones Públicas
Germania Dolores Hernandez-Simonetti – Asistente de Administración
Marlon Abreu – Coordinador Bilingüe y Relaciones Públicas
Yoshiki Sato – Asesor para los Medios de Comunicación Japoneses

Servicios de prensa durante la temporada

El Departamento de Comunicaciones y Relaciones Públicas de los New York Yankees quisiera darle la bienvenida al Yankee Stadium. Por favor vea abajo las pautas para la temporada del 2020. Por favor comuníquese con nuestra oficina para cualquier pregunta o preocupación que usted pueda tener. Deseamos tener el placer de trabajar con ustedes este año.

El Departamento de Relaciones Públicas de los Yankees anima a nuestros medios de comunicación a visitar **yankeespressbox.com**, un recurso integral para todos los materiales dedicados a la prensa departe de los Yankees. Los documentos se publicarán en el momento en que estén disponibles e incluyen: notas previas al juego, los paquetes de estadísticas, rosters, notas después del juego, etc.

Todos los comunicados de prensa, paquetes especiales y una versión PDF del Guía de Medios 2020 de los Yankees también estarán disponibles en el sitio. Además, casi todos los artículos disponibles en yankeespressbox.com se archivan para el acceso durante toda la temporada.

Al acceder a la página web (que es sólo para miembros de la prensa), se le pedirá que inicie la sesión con un ID de mlb.com, disponible sólo a través de la liga mayor de béisbol.

MEDIA INFORMATION, continued

ADMISSION TO STADIUM/CREDENTIAL PICK-UP: All media (except for rightsholders) must enter Yankee Stadium via the Press Gate. Daily credentials may be picked up at the Press Gate. The Press Gate is located on E. 161st Street, in between the ticket windows and Gate 4. The Press Gate opens four-and-a-half hours prior to 1:05 p.m. starts and five hours prior to all other game times. BBWAA cards, MLB-issued passes or credentials issued by the New York Yankees are necessary for admittance. NO OTHER CREDENTIAL WILL BE HONORED. All bags are subject to search upon entry. Photo ID is required.
- Rightsholders should confirm location of their daily credentials with Senior Director of Broadcasting & Technical Operations, Brett Moldoff (bmoldoff@yankees.com).
- Media members are prohibited from posting any photos of credentials at any time, including on any social media platform. Those in violation of this procedure will have credentials revoked and will forfeit any future credentials to Yankees games and Yankee Stadium events.

ADMISSION TO FIELD AND DUGOUTS: All media with BBWAA cards or applicable credentials issued by the New York Yankees or Major League Baseball are permitted on the field in designated areas during pregame. FOR SAFETY PURPOSES, all media MUST leave the field once the batting cage is removed. PLEASE DISPLAY CREDENTIALS AT ALL TIMES. The field and dugouts can be accessed through the tunnel on the Service Level adjacent to the Yankees clubhouse (only during regular clubhouse hours) as well as the Field Access Tunnel on the outfield side of the Visitor's Clubhouse on the Service Level. Take the press elevator or stairs to the Service Level and follow the concourse to the first or third base side. The field is closed to media at the conclusion of the visiting team's batting practice.
- Only media with pre-arranged interviews are permitted inside the home dugout at any time during batting practice.
- Tripods are prohibited in the home dugout during batting practice.
- Media members are prohibited from going on the grass and must remain on the warning track, unless special arrangements have been made in advance with the Yankees Media Relations staff.

CREDENTIAL QUESTIONS: Please direct questions to Mark Torres in the Yankees Media Relations office at credentials@yankees.com or (718) 579-4460.

DAILY CREDENTIALS: All requests for single-game regular season media credentials for games played at Yankee Stadium may be made online at https://credentials.mlb.com. The online application is the only acceptable method for requesting single-game regular season media credentials for games played at Yankee Stadium. Applications must be completed by a Sports Assignment Editor and require at least 24 hours notice.

INTERNET: Wireless internet login and password information is posted in the Press Box. Should you have any questions, a media relations representative can assist you.

INTERVIEW REQUESTS: To schedule interviews requiring special arrangements, please email your request to media@yankees.com.

PARKING: Media are encouraged to park in the Ruppert Plaza Garage, located on the corner of Jerome Ave. and the Macombs Dam Bridge ramp, directly across the street from the Press Gate. The garage will open five hours prior to the start of the game and remain open at least three hours after the last pitch. Please note that media parking is at cost.

PHOTO REQUESTS: Please e-mail media@yankees.com.

PRESS BOX: Take the press elevator or stairs to Main Level. Doors open by the TV and radio booths. The press box, working press room and media dining room will be to your left. Please sit in assigned seats. If no seat is assigned, please ask a Yankees Media Relations representative for assistance.

PRESS CONFERENCE ROOM: Take the press elevator or stairs down to the Service Level. The Press Conference Room is on the first base side, opposite the Yankees clubhouse.

PRESS DINING: Media are invited to dine at Sheppard's Place, located on the Press Box level behind the writing press area. Cost is $13, which includes buffet, salad bar, action station, soda & coffee.
- For 1:05 p.m. games: Open 10:30 a.m. – 3:00 p.m.
- For 7:05 p.m. games: Open 4:30 p.m. – 9:00 p.m.

WORKING PRESS ROOMS: Both Print and Audio Workrooms are located behind the working press box. The Photographers workroom is on the Service Level across from the Visitors' clubhouse on the third base side.

Roving in the stands and concourses is prohibited. Likewise, field access during the game is limited to the first and third base photo boxes.

ADMISIÓN AL ESTADIO/ENTREGA DE CREDENCIALES: Todos los medios (excepto los rightsholders) deben de entrar por la entrada de la prensa (Press Gate), adyacente a la entrada número 4 del estadio (Gate 4). La entrada de la prensa (Press Gate) abre cinco horas antes del inicio de un juego de noche y cuatro horas y media antes del inicio de un juego que se jugará por la tarde. Las tarjetas BBWAA, los pases distribuidos por MLB o las credenciales repartidas por los New York Yankees son necesarios para entrar. NO SE HONRARÁ NINGUNA OTRA CREDENCIAL. Todas las bolsas están sujetas a ser revisadas a la entrada. Identificación de foto será requerida.
- Rightsholders deben confirmar la localización de los credenciales con el Director Superior, Radiodifusión y Operaciones Técnicas, Brett Moldoff (bmoldoff@yankees.com).
- Miembros de la prensa estan prohibidos a subir fotos de sus credenciales a plataformas de redes sociales.

ENTRADA AL TERRENO Y LAS TRINCHERAS: Miembros de la prensa con tarjetas de BBWAA o credenciales emitido por los New York Yankees o Major League Baseball están permitidos en zonas designadas sobre el campo. PARA FINES DE SEGURIDAD, todos los medios DEBEN abandonar el campo una vez que se retire la jaula de bateo. POR FAVOR MOSTRAR CREDENCIALES EN TODO MOMENTO. Se puede acceder al campo y a los refugios a través del túnel en el nivel de servicio adyacente a la casa club de los Yankees (solo durante las horas normales de la casa club), así como el túnel de acceso de campo en el lado del campo exterior de la casa club del visitante en el nivel de servicio. Tome el elevador de prensa o las escaleras hasta el nivel de servicio y siga la explanada hasta el lado de la primera o tercera base. El campo está cerrado a los medios de comunicación al finalizar la práctica de bateo del equipo visitante.
- Solo los medios con entrevistas preestablecidas están permitidos dentro de la caseta en el hogar en cualquier momento durante la práctica de bateo.
- Los trípodes están prohibidos en la caseta casera durante la práctica de bateo.
- Los miembros de los medios tienen prohibido ir al pasto y deben permanecer en la pista de advertencia, a menos que se hayan hecho arreglos especiales con anticipación con el personal de Relaciones Publicas de los Yankees.

PREGUNTAS SOBRE CREDENCIALES: Por favor de dirigir cualquier preguntas a Mark Torres del Departamento de Comunicaciones y Relaciones Públicas, vía correo electrónico a credentials@yankees.com o al número de teléfono (718) 579-4460.

CREDENCIALES POR JUEGO INDIVIDUAL: Solicitudes de credenciales para juegos individuales en el Yankee Stadium deben ser sometidas vía la página web de *Major League Baseball (MLB)* en https://credentials.mlb.com. La solicitud vía el internet es el único método aceptable para el pedido de credenciales para juegos individuales durante la temporada 2020. Dichos pedidos solo pueden ser hechos por un director o editor de deportes y deben ser recibidos con un minimo de 24-horas de aviso.

INTERNET: Para conectarse al internet inalámbrico usar la información en la sala de prensa. Si tiene alguna pregunta por favor contactar a un representante del departamento de prensa.

SOLICITUDES DE ENTREVISTA: Para entrevistas que requieran arreglos especiales, por favor envíe su solicitud por correo electrónico a media@yankees.com

ESTACIONAMIENTO: Los medios de prensa deben de estacionarse en el garaje *Ruppert Plaza*, localizado en la esquina de la avenida Jerome y el *Macombs Dam Bridge*, al otro lado de la entrada número 4 del estadio. El garaje estará abierto cinco horas antes del principio del juego y hasta tres horas después del último lanzamiento. Tenga en cuenta que el estacionamiento para la prensa es a costo normal.

SOLICITUD PARA FOTOGRAFIAS: Por favor envíe un correo electrónico a media@yankees.com.

PALCO PRINCIPAL DE PRENSA: Tome el ascensor de prensa o las escaleras hacia el Main Level. Las puertas del ascensor abren cerca de las salas de televisión y radio. El palco principal de la prensa y el comedor están localizados a la izquierda del ascensor. Por favor tomen los asientos asignados. Si no se le asignó un asiento, por favor pregúntele a un representante del Departamento de Prensa de los New York Yankees.

SALA DE CONFERENCIAS DE PRENSA: Tome el ascensor de prensa o las escaleras hacia abajo para el Service Level. Tome una derecha al salón laborar de prensa que se encuentra al mismo lado de la primera base, al otro lado del clubhouse de los Yankees.

COMEDOR DE PRENSA: La prensa está invitada a comer en Sheppard's Place, localizado en el palco principal de la prensa, atrás de la área de prensa escrita. El costo es $13 y incluye el buffet, ensalada, soda y café.
- Juegos a la 1:05 p.m.: Abierto a las 10:30 a.m. – 3:00 p.m.
- Juegos a las 7:05 p.m.: Abierto a las 4:30 p.m. – 9:00 p.m.

SALA LABORAR DE PRENSA: Las salas laborales de la prensa escritas y de la prensa audiovisual están localizadas detrás de la sesión principal de la prensa. El salón laboral de los fotógrafos está en el Service Level al cruzar el clubhouse de los visitantes en el lado de la tercera base.

Vagando por las gradas y los pasillos públicos es prohibido. El acceso al terreno durante el juego es limitado a las secciones fotográficas de la primera y tercera base.

Yankees Television Broadcasters

Michael Kay

Now in his 19th season as the play-by-play announcer for the YES Network, Kay also serves as the host of YES' *CenterStage* series. In 2008, 2013 and 2016, he handled play-by-play duties for the ESPN Radio Network's coverage of the AL Division Series.

In addition, The Michael Kay Show, a sports talk show heard weekdays on ESPN Radio 98.7 FM in New York which Kay co-hosts with Don LeGreca, has been simulcast live weekday afternoons on YES since February 2014. The Michael Kay Show is the #1-rated afternoon radio show in New York.

A 36-time Emmy Award nominee and 10-time Emmy winner, Kay was named by *Radio Ink* magazine the second-most influential local sports talk show host in America in 2012.

Before joining the YES Network, Kay worked at the MSG Network from 1989-2001 as a Yankees reporter. In 1992, he added the assignment of Knicks locker room reporter to his responsibilities and continued in that role through the 1998-99 season.

In addition to his television work, Kay also worked as a Yankees analyst on WABC Radio from 1992-2002. Kay was a winner with Bob Goldscholl (WBBR) for "Best Sports Reporter" at the 2000 New York Metro Achievement in Radio Awards. After the Yankees' World Series victories in 1996, 1998, 2000 and 2009, Kay and John Sterling were asked by New York City's Mayor to host the post-parade victory celebration at City Hall.

In 1998, Kay also began co-hosting *Sports Talk with John Sterling and Michael Kay*, an MSG-produced nightly sports radio call-in show which aired on WABC Radio during the winter months. During the baseball season, Kay and Sterling hosted *Yankee Talk* which aired 90 minutes prior to all weekend Yankees games.

Shortly after graduating from Fordham University in 1982 with a B.A. in Communications, the Bronx, N.Y., native became one of the hot sports reporters in New York City with a style that combined great reporting skills with quality writing. While at Fordham, he honed his skills working for the school newspaper and radio station, working at Sports Phone and as the public address announcer for the New York Pro Summer Basketball League. In 2018, he was the recipient of the WFUV "Vin Scully Award for Excellence in Sports Broadcasting" and was inducted to the New York State Broadcasters Association Hall of Fame.

In 1982, Kay landed a job as a general assignment writer for the *New York Post*. Two years later he began covering college basketball (1984-85) and then the New Jersey Nets, whom he covered for two seasons before becoming the newspaper's general basketball writer. In 1987, he moved to baseball where he served as his paper's Yankees beat reporter. While he was in that position, he got his first television job with MSG Network as host of the "Hot Stove League" segment of MSG's *Sports Night*. In 1989, Kay moved from the *Post* to the *New York Daily News*, where he covered the Yankees until 1992, when he made the jump to radio. With the move, he became the first newspaper reporter in any sport to make the jump to the broadcast booth full-time, performing both play-by-play and analysis.

Kay was given the "Dick Young Award for Excellence in Sports Media" by the New York Pro Baseball Scouts in 1995. He was also a part of the Yankees/MSG Production team that was nominated for New York Emmy Awards for six consecutive years. In 1998, he was on the MSG team that won for "Outstanding Live Sports Coverage–Series." In 1996 and '97, he was a member of the MSG team that won New York Emmys for "Outstanding Live Sports Coverage–Single Program" for Dwight Gooden's no-hitter and "The Battle for New York: Yankees vs. Mets."

He is active with the Alzheimer's Association in memory of his mother, Rose, who passed away from the disease in 2006. Kay has also joined Joe Girardi for the "Remember When, Remember Now" banquet at the Grand Central Oyster Bar to benefit Girardi's Catch 25 Foundation and Alzheimer's research. He co-hosted the 2013 B.A.T. fundraising dinner in New York, and served as master of ceremonies at the 2013 Thurman Munson Awards fundraising dinner in New York.

In 2016, Kay was inducted into the New York State Baseball Hall of Fame and in 2018 was inducted as part of the inaugural class to the Bronx High School of Science Hall of Fame. In 2005, Kay was honored in his home borough of the Bronx, having an honorary street sign in his name erected on the Grand Concourse. Kay and his wife, Jodi Applegate have a daughter, Caledonia Rose Kay, born in January 2013, and a son, Charles Applegate Kay, born in November 2014.

Ken Singleton

Former Major Leaguer Ken Singleton enters his 19th season as a game analyst and announcer for YES Network broadcasts of the New York Yankees, occasionally handling play-by-play duties as well.

Prior to joining YES, Singleton divided his time calling play-by-play and providing commentary at the MSG Network. In 1998, he was part of MSG's production team that won four New York Emmys for its Yankees coverage.

Singleton joined the MSG Network in 1997 from The Sports Network (TSN), where he served as analyst for the Montreal Expos from 1985-96. From 1991-96, he also called play-by-play and served as analyst for CIQ Radio, the Expos' flagship radio network. In 1996 and '97, FOX Sports named him as a lead analyst for Saturday afternoon baseball broadcasts. In 1997 and '98, he worked as an analyst for Major League Baseball International.

Singleton enjoyed a 15-year Major League career with the New York Mets, Montreal Expos and Baltimore Orioles, batting .282 with 317 doubles and 246HR. He is one of only 16 players in Baseball history to hit 35 or more home runs in a season as a switch-hitter. He also ranks among the all-time leaders in most Baltimore offensive categories, including homers, RBI and total bases. During his career, Singleton was named to the American League All-Star team in 1977, '79, and '81. He was named Most Valuable Oriole in 1975, '77, and '79 and was a member of the Orioles' 1983 World Championship team. In 1982, he was the recipient of Major League Baseball's Roberto Clemente Award, honoring him for his contributions both on and off the field.

Born in Manhattan and raised in nearby Mount Vernon, N.Y., Singleton played both baseball and basketball in high school, and also played baseball in the Bronx Federation League at Macombs Dam Park on the current site of Yankee Stadium. After getting a basketball scholarship to Hofstra University and playing baseball as well for one year, Singleton was drafted by the Mets in 1967. In 2015, he was inducted into the New York State Baseball Hall of Fame.

Singleton serves on the Board of Directors for the Cool Kids Campaign, a nonprofit organization that helps children and their families who are dealing with cancer. He was honored with the "Denzel Lifetime Achievement Award in Sports" at the Boys & Girls Club of Mount Vernon's 100th Anniversary Gala in March 2012.

David Cone

David Cone returns to the YES Network for his 13th season as an analyst. Upon his retirement from the game, Cone joined the YES Network team during its inaugural year in 2002, again for 2008-09 and returned in 2011. Cone has won four New York Emmy Awards while at YES.

Cone compiled a 194-126 record, 3.46 ERA and 2,688 strikeouts in his 17-year Major League career with the Kansas City Royals (1986, 1993-94), New York Mets (1987-1992, 2003), Toronto Blue Jays (1992, '95), New York Yankees (1995-2000) and Boston Red Sox (2001). He was a five-time All-Star (1988, 1992, 1994, 1997 and 1999) and captured the American League Cy Young Award in 1994 after posting a 16-5 record with a 2.94 ERA. With the award, he became the first pitcher to win the Cy Young despite not leading the league in any category or pitching for a first-place club.

While with the Yankees, Cone was 64-40 with a 3.91 ERA and 888 strikeouts, and was part of four World Championship teams (1996, 1998, 1999 and 2000). He had arguably his finest season in pinstripes in 1998, when he was 20-7 with a 3.55 ERA and 209 strikeouts. A year later, on July 18, 1999, he hurled the 14th perfect game in modern Major League history (since 1900, including postseason) in a 6-0 win vs. the Montreal Expos at Yankee Stadium. The performance also marked the third perfect game ever thrown by a Yankees pitcher, following Don Larsen's in Game 5 of the 1956 World Series vs. Brooklyn and David Wells' vs. Minnesota in 1998. The Kansas City, Mo. native was selected by his hometown Kansas City Royals in the third round of the 1981 First-Year Player Draft.

He compiled an 8-3 career postseason record and also won a World Series title with the 1992 Blue Jays.

In 1996, Cone established the David Cone Charitable Gift Fund. He was honored with numerous awards for his community service as a player and still pursues his charitable endeavors, working with the Maria Fareri Children's Hospital at the Westchester Medical Center.

Jack Curry

Jack Curry joined the YES Network in 2010 as a studio analyst, reporter and program contributor, following a 20-year career covering the Yankees for *The New York Times*. In addition, he contributes as a columnist on YESNetwork.com and has the hosted *JCTV: Jack Curry TV*, an innovative YESNetwork.com original series which launched in 2013 and *Yankees Access* specials. Curry earned two Emmy nominations in 2014 for *JCTV: Jack Curry TV* and has four nominations for several Yankees features as well as a nomination in the Writer: Commentary/Editorial category in 2017. He has received four Emmys for his work as part of the YES Yankees broadcast team and has received a total of 10 New York Emmy Award nominations.

In 2019, Curry collaborated on a book with YES colleague David Cone called "Full Count: The Education Of A Pitcher," which was a New York Times best-seller.

During his career with the *Times*, Curry authored more than 4,500 articles, covered 18 World Series, 11 All-Star Games and two World Baseball Classics. The New Jersey native also was nominated for a Pulitzer Prize in 1999, and won multiple Times Publisher Awards.

Curry's television experience extends back to 1991, when he began contributing to Madison Square Garden Network's Yankees pre-game show and weekly baseball magazine show. Since November 2005, Curry has been a regular contributor to YES' *Yankees Hot Stove* show, and for the last six seasons, he has appeared on YES' *Yankees Access* shows. In addition, he was a featured panelist on MSG's *Angles* roundtable show, was a frequent guest on WCBS-TV's *Baseball Insider* weekly studio show, and has also provided expert baseball analysis and commentary on television and radio programs such as ESPN's *Outside the Lines*, MSNBC's *Countdown with Keith Olbermann*, ESPN Radio's *The Michael Kay Show* and various WFAN Radio programs.

Curry also co-wrote a book with Derek Jeter entitled *The Life You Imagine: Life Lessons for Achieving Your Dreams*, which was a *New York Times* best-seller. In January 2013, Curry received the Broadcast Achievement Award from the New Jersey Sports Writers Association and was named "Top Sports Analyst" by the New Jersey-based *201 Magazine*. A 1986 graduate of Fordham University, Curry resides with his wife, Pamela, in New Jersey.

John Flaherty

Former Yankees catcher John Flaherty enters his 15th season as a field reporter, studio analyst and game analyst for YES Network telecasts. He has won six New York Emmy Awards while at YES and earned individual New York Emmy Awards nominations in 2010, 2011, 2013, 2017, and 2019 for his YES work.

Drafted by Boston in 1988, Flaherty progressed through the Red Sox farm system before joining their Major League squad in 1992. He played 14 seasons in the Majors with Boston (1992-93), Detroit (1994-96), San Diego (1996-97), Tampa Bay (1998-2002) and the Yankees (2003-05), compiling a .252 average with 80HR in 1,047 games.

Flaherty brought his knowledge of the game and his veteran style of leadership to the Yankees clubhouse when he signed as a free agent in 2003. He played in 134 games with the Yankees across three seasons, and will be long remembered for his dramatic pinch-hit, "walk-off" single to defeat the Boston Red Sox in the 13th inning on July 1, 2004 — the contest that featured Derek Jeter's famous dive into the third base stands.

Flaherty is a New York City native and a graduate of George Washington University. On May 15, 2009, he was awarded an honorary Doctorate of Humane Letters from St. Thomas Aquinas College in Sparkill, N.Y. In 2015, he was inducted into the New York State Baseball Hall of Fame.

Bob Lorenz

Bob Lorenz returns for his 17th year with the YES Network, serving as the primary studio anchor for Yankees pre- and post-game shows. Lorenz also serves as the host of the Brooklyn Nets pre- and post-game shows, as well as the network's Yankees Hot Stove and Emmy Award-winning *Forbes SportsMoney* programs. Lorenz has won 15 Emmy Awards during his time with the YES Network. In April 2011, he won his third consecutive New York Emmy Award recognizing him as the top sports anchor in New York. He also has play-by-play credits at YES that include Yankees regular season and spring training telecasts, Staten Island Yankees games and Ivy League football.

Prior to joining the YES Network in 2003, Lorenz served as an anchor for CNN/Sports Illustrated, which he joined in April of 1991. He hosted CNN's signature weekly sports programming, including *NFL Preview*, *College Football Preview*, *This Week in the NBA*, *SI Cover to Cover* and *Page One*. He also hosted CNN's weekly baseball show from 1992 to 1996 and, from 1994 to 1996, hosted CNN's *College Basketball Preview* and *College Coaches Corner*. In addition to those duties, Lorenz also worked on a variety of programs for CNN's sister networks, TBS and TNT, hosting Super Bowl specials and serving as back-up host on *Inside the NBA* on TNT.

Before joining CNN, Lorenz was a reporter and anchor at WPTV-TV in West Palm Beach, Fla. Having joined the station in 1988, he wrote, produced and anchored four weekend sportscasts. Lorenz earlier served as sports director at KIEM-TV in Eureka, Calif., and was a writer at CBS Extravision in Los Angeles and an analyst/anchor for Citicable in Torrance, Calif.

Lorenz is on the Honorary Event Committee for the Connecticut chapter of Make-A-Wish and has emceed its annual Make-A-Wish Ball. He has also emceed the Annual Miracle Ball, which raises money and awareness for the Miracle League of Westchester County in New York.

He holds a degree in broadcast journalism from the University of Southern California.

Meredith Marakovits

Meredith Marakovits returns for her ninth season with the YES Network as the New York Yankees clubhouse reporter, reporting on the team within the network's Yankees game telecasts, pre- and post-game shows, *Yankees Batting Practice Today* show and *Yankees Hot Stove*. Marakovits also appears on YES' special Yankees programming and contributes to YESNetwork.com. She has also filled in as YES' Brooklyn Nets reporter and pre-and post-game show host. She has won five Emmy Awards while covering the Yankees at YES and two individual Emmy nominations for her Yankees reporting. She also appears frequently as a guest on MLB Network shows *The Rundown* and *MLB Now* and in 2019 was named to the "Top Women in Sports" list by the trade organization Cynopsis.

Previously, Marakovits served as the Philadelphia 76ers sideline reporter with Comcast SportsNet Philadelphia, also participating in several Comcast SportsNet regional sports network programs. She also covered the Yankees and Mets for 1050 ESPN radio, and contributed to WFAN radio in New York.

Prior to her work in New York, she served as the Phillies reporter for 950 ESPN Radio/97.5 the Fanatic. This came after her stint as the pre- and post-game host and field reporter for the Triple-A Lehigh Valley IronPigs Television Network.

A Northampton, Pa., native, Marakovits is a 2005 graduate of La Salle University in Philadelphia, where she played volleyball and received a degree in communications. She began her career for Service Electric 2's sports division as a sideline reporter for college football, basketball and indoor football broadcasts. In December 2013, Marakovits was honored on the Rockne Wall of Fame at her alma mater — Allentown (Pa.) Central Catholic High School — for her athletic exploits.

Nancy Newman

Nancy Newman returns for her 18th season with the YES Network as a studio host for the New York Yankees and the Brooklyn Nets pre- and post-game shows and lead anchor for YES' Yankees *Batting Practice Today* show, which kicks off YES' Yankees game day coverage by providing the latest news, exclusive looks at teams during batting practice, interaction with YES' on-site announcers, interviews and features.

In addition, Newman is the host of the Network's *Yankees Magazine* program which goes behind the scenes and in the community with the New York Yankees. Newman has served as YES' Yankees reporter as well as sideline reporter for the network's Ivy League college football package and *New York Football Sunday* and is now host for The New Era Pinstripe Bowl college football coverage on YES. Newman has won five New York Emmy Awards while at YES.

Prior to joining the YES Network, Newman held a variety of sports broadcasting positions with the CNN Networks from 1992 to 2002. She hosted *CNN Sports Tonight* and *Latenight* as well as CNN *Sports Sunday* and CNN's *Goodwill Games Preview*. Newman also hosted and worked on programs for CNN's sister networks, including CNN Sports/Illustrated and CNN Headline News for which she anchored sports. She served as occasional reporter for CNN's weekly MLB and NFL preview programs and appeared as a panelist on CNN's *Burden of Proof* discussing the NHL. In 2000, she hosted Turner Sports' Emmy-Award-winning coverage of the NHL Atlanta Thrashers inaugural season.

In 2019, Newman emceed the National Down Syndrome Society's (NDSS) annual gala as it partnered with the Professional Baseball Athletic Trainers Society (PBATS) at Gotham Hall in New York City. In 2015 Newman emceed The Green Sports Alliance Awards at Yankee Stadium honoring the New York Yankees for their dedication to environmental leadership.

Newman earned a Bachelor's degree in English from the University of Toronto. In 2011, U of T awarded Newman with the University's Boundless Voice honors.

Paul O'Neill

Paul O'Neill returns for his 19th season in broadcast television, serving as a game analyst for the YES Network. He has earned three New York Emmy Award for his work at YES.

The five-time All-Star outfielder played 17 years in the Majors, spending his final nine seasons in pinstripes. He appeared in six World Series, winning five titles, including four with the Yankees (1996, '98-2000).

Affectionately known as a "warrior" to most Yankees followers, O'Neill began his Major League career in 1985 with the Cincinnati Reds and earned the first of his five World Series championships in 1990. He joined the Yankees in 1993 after eight seasons with the Reds, and in 1994 claimed the American League batting title with a .359 average. From July 1995 to May 1997, he played in 235 consecutive games in right field without making an error. In 2001, at the age of 38, O'Neill became the oldest player in Major League history to steal 20 bases and hit 20 home runs in the same season.

He lives in his native Cincinnati with his wife, Nevalee, and their three children: Andrew, Aaron and Alexandra. He was named "Father of the Year" in June 2008 by the National Father's Day Council at its 67th Annual Father of the Year dinner in New York. O'Neill was inducted into the New York State Baseball Hall of Fame in November 2017.

Ryan Ruocco

Ryan Ruocco returns for his seventh season as part of the broadcast team, holding a variety of roles within the YES Network's coverage of the New York Yankees. He serves as a backup calling play-by-play and fills in hosting YES' Yankees pre- and post-game shows and periodically handles clubhouse reporting duties. He also shares play-by-play duties with broadcast veteran Ian Eagle on YES' Brooklyn Nets telecasts.

Ruocco has worked at YES since 2007, when he started as a statistician for the network's Yankees telecasts. Ruocco was a member of YES' Nets broadcast team which won a 2014 New York Emmy Award for Best Live Sports Series, and he earned individual New York Emmy nominations in 2015, 2017, 2018 and 2019 for his Nets work on YES.

In addition to his YES work, Ruocco is one of the primary NBA play-by-play voices on ESPN and is the lead play-by-play announcer for the WNBA. He also handles periodic NFL play-by-play on ESPN Radio as well as college football and college basketball play-by-play on ESPN's television networks, and he co-hosted ESPN New York Radio's mid-day show.

Ruocco also currently co-hosts *Uninterrupted's* R2C2 podcast with Yankees' pitcher CC Sabathia.

Prior to joining YES, Ruocco handled basketball and football play-by-play at WFUV, Fordham University's radio station while he was a student there. He also hosted WFUV's One on One, New York's longest-running sports call-in show. In 2008, he received Fordham's prestigious Marty Glickman Award, named for the legendary play-by-play announcer.

Ruocco, who grew up in Fishkill, N.Y., graduated on the Dean's List from Fordham in 2008 with a B.S. in Communications.

Bill Boland
Senior Producer

John Moore
Director

Chris Shearn
Studio Host

THE CHASE FOR... 28

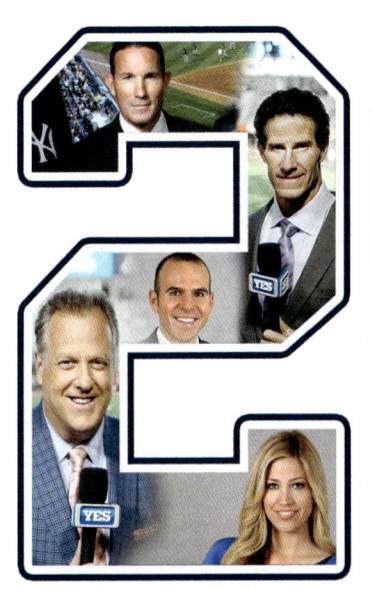

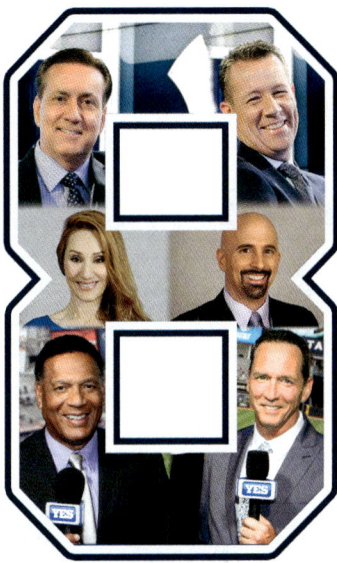

IT'S NOT JUST BASEBALL, IT'S THE *Yankees*™

YES

CONE · CURRY · FLAHERTY · KAY · LORENZ · MARAKOVITS
NEWMAN · O'NEILL · RUOCCO · SHEARN · SINGLETON

Yankees Radio Broadcasters

John Sterling

"Yankees win! Theeeeeee Yankees win!"

If anything has become synonymous with the Yankees' run of success over recent years, it is John Sterling's memorable conclusion to so many Yankees victories. As the radio voice to 162 games a year, plus preseason and postseason, he has called 5,143 official games (4,949 regular season/194 postseason) over the last 31 seasons, missing only four games in his illustrious career, making him one of the most recognized—and imitated voices—in all of New York sports.

Sterling joined the Yankees broadcast team in 1989 from Atlanta's TBS and WSB Radio, where he called Hawks basketball (1981-89) and Braves baseball (1982-87). It marked a return to the town where he first achieved fame, hosting a talk show on WMCA from 1971-78, and calling the Nets (1975-80, and as a fill-in, in 1997) and Islanders (1975-78) for WMCA, WVNJ, WWOR-TV and SportsChannel.

Sterling also previously called Morgan State Football (eight years) and Washington Bullets basketball in 1981. In addition to his seven years at WMCA and a year at WSB in Atlanta, he has also hosted talk shows on WFAN and WABC in New York. Prior to missing the Yankees four-game series in Tampa Bay from 7/4-7/19 due to illness, he had not missed a broadcast of any kind since the fall of 1981. That series snapped a streak of 5,060 consecutive games broadcasted.

As the host of the YES Network's acclaimed *Yankeeography* series, Sterling has won 12 Emmy Awards since 2003. He has also been honored by the N.J. Sportswriters Association with its Radio-TV Excellence Award (1999), and was the winner of the 2001 Whitney Radio Jimmy Cannon Award. In addition, his call of a Jason Giambi home run on WCBS radio in 2002 was voted the "Best Baseball Call of the Year" in a poll conducted by MLB.com. In 2002, Sterling was also honored by the NY Air Awards for being a part of the best play-by-play team on radio.

When he's not in the booth, Sterling serves as a master of on-field ceremonies for major Yankees events, and is well known for his emcee work at City Hall (with his former radio partner Michael Kay) at "Key to the City" ceremonies following Yankees World Series victories.

Sterling enjoys attending Broadway shows and boasts an extensive knowledge of the lyrics to many American pop standards. In 2007, he embarked on his own Broadway venture in a cabaret show titled "Baseball and Broadway" in which he both served as emcee and sang alongside broadway talent.

In 2016, he was inducted, along with Suzyn Waldman, to the New York State Broadcasters Hall of Fame. At the annual BBWAA Awards dinner in January 2020, he received the Casey Stengel "You Could Look It Up" Award. For the past 25 years, he has been a spokesman for the Leukemia Society of America. He enjoys reading, movies and swimming. He is the proud father of four children: daughter Abigail and triplets, Veronica, Bradford and Derek.

Suzyn Waldman

Award-winning journalist Suzyn Waldman begins her 34th season either covering or broadcasting the New York Yankees and her 16th season as the Yankees' radio color commentator, having become the first woman to hold a full-time position as a Major League broadcaster.

Waldman has spent more than three decades overcoming all the obstacles that go along with being a female sports broadcaster and has risen to the top of her profession. In 2006, she became a permanent part of the "Women in Baseball" exhibit at the Hall of Fame in Cooperstown, and in 2009, her World Series Game 6 scorecard was added to the Hall of Fame's collection, commemorating her being the first female broadcaster to call World Series game action.

In 1987, Waldman became the first voice heard on WFAN-AM in New York, the first all-sports radio station in the country. She was a mainstay on that station for almost 15 years, creating the job of the radio beat reporter, covering both the New York Yankees and New York Knicks. Her news-breaking reports, exclusive interviews and always original and controversial opinions won her countless journalism awards. Her accolades include the "International Radio Award" for her live and emotional reporting from the upper deck of Candlestick Park during the 1989 San Francisco earthquake, the 1996 "N.Y. Sportscaster of the Year" Award from the National Sportscasters & Sportswriters and the 1999 "Star Award" for radio from the American Women in Radio and TV. Waldman became a popular talk show host at WFAN and co-hosted the coveted midday slot until leaving WFAN in 2002 to join the YES Network.

The word "first" invariably precedes the name of Suzyn Waldman in every facet of her television and radio career. The first woman to work on a nationally-televised baseball broadcast, Waldman added another first, being the first woman to provide play-by-play for a Major League team, when she started broadcasting New York Yankees games for WPIX, MSG Network and WNYW/FOX5 in the mid 1990s. The first woman ever to host an NBA pre-and post-game show, Suzyn worked in that capacity for the Knicks on WFAN, provided play-by-play for the WNBA on Lifetime TV and was an analyst on St. John's basketball games for MSG and WFAN.

She has been honored by countless organizations, including the Thurman Munson Foundation, the March of Dimes, B'nai B'rith, Jimmy Fund of Boston and the U.S. Federal Women's Program. In 2006, she received the first Women's Global Health Award from the Albert Einstein College of Medicine at the United Nations. She is a tireless motivational speaker at schools and cancer centers around the country, encouraging young women to pursue their dreams despite any pitfalls they may encounter.

Waldman's life and accomplishments have been the subject of hundreds of magazine and newspaper articles, as well as chapters in children's and motivational books. She has been profiled on the *Today Show, CBS Evening News with Dan Rather, ABC's 20/20* and NBC's *Dateline*. In 2013, 2014 and 2015, Waldman was named one of *Radio Ink* magazine's "Most Influential Women in Radio." In 2016, she was inducted, along with John Sterling, to the New York State Broadcasters Hall of Fame. She was also a recipient of the Gracie Award, which acknowledges outstanding team leadership and individual achievement, focusing on women who are making positive change and who further the discussion of what a fulfilling career in media looks like.

A native Bostonian with a degree in Economics from Boston's prestigious Simmons College, Suzyn spent 15 years on the Broadway musical stage and performed in countless night clubs around the world. She is proudest of her two years starring opposite Richard Kiley in *Man of La Mancha*. She lives in Westchester with her German shepherds, Gatsby and Margo.

Sweeny Murti

Sweeny Murti begins his 20th season as the Yankees reporter on the team's flagship radio station WFAN and his seventh year as host of the post-game radio show. Murti provides information and analysis on all of the station's programs and is a featured columnist on WFAN.com. In the 30-plus year history of WFAN, Murti is just the station's second Yankees beat reporter, preceded only by current radio analyst Suzyn Waldman.

Murti has worked in various roles at WFAN since 1993. He has appeared on numerous TV outlets, earning two New York Emmy Awards. Since 2010 he has been a correspondent for MLB Network. Murti has also been seen on YES Network features like "Yankeeography" and Yankees On Demand.

In addition to covering six World Series for WFAN, Murti has worked two Summer Olympics (1996 and 2000) for Westwood One Radio. At the 2000 Sydney Games, Murti called play-by-play of Team USA's Gold Medal game in softball and covered Team USA's gold medal-winning efforts in baseball, as well as men's and women's basketball.

Murti has donated several items to the National Baseball Hall of Fame in Cooperstown, including his scorecard from Derek Jeter's final "walk off" home game in 2014.

Since 2008 Murti has assisted Yankees great Bernie Williams at his annual gala for the Hillside Food Outreach, which helps feed hungry families in the Hudson Valley.

In 2011, the New York Pro Baseball Scouts honored Murti with the Jim Quigley Memorial Award for Baseball Service.

As a fill-in analyst on the radio broadcasts since 2015, Murti is regarded as the first Indian-American to take part in a Major League Baseball broadcast.

Murti began his broadcasting career at age 12 for Middletown, Pa. Area School District's award-winning student radio station WMSS and graduated with a B.A. from Penn State University's School of Communications in 1992. He lives in New York's Hudson Valley with his wife Jessica, daughter, Caroline, and son, Ryan.

Yankees en Español

For the 24th consecutive season, the Yankees – in conjunction with WFAN radio – will provide Spanish radio and SAP (second audio programming) for game broadcasts.

Rickie Ricardo

Rickie Ricardo is in his seventh season as the New York Yankees' Spanish language play-by-play announcer. Prior to joining the Yankees' WADO broadcast team, Ricardo spent seven years in the same role for Philadelphia Phillies, broadcasting their World Series win in 2008 and postseason run in 2009.

Additionally, Ricardo has been the Spanish radio play-by-play voice of the Philadelphia Eagles for the last eight NFL seasons. He also regularly appears on various programs on Philadelphia's 94WIP-FM Sports Radio and New York's WFAN Radio.

Ricardo has spent over 30 years in radio broadcasting, appearing on various stations in New York, Connecticut, Philadelphia, Washington D.C. and Miami. In 2005, he became the daily beat reporter covering the Florida Marlins for Clear Channel radio. His career also includes international radio broadcasting with the 2008 Caribbean Series in the Dominican Republic and the 2009 Caribbean Series in Mexicali, Mexico.

A 1980 graduate from the New York School of Broadcasting, Ricardo currently resides in West New York, N.J. and Orlando, Fla.

Francisco Rivera

Since 1995, Francisco Rivera has been involved in baseball as a color commentator and play-by-play announcer, including 15 years in the Yankees' broadcast booth. A native of Morovis, Puerto Rico, he covered the Philadelphia Phillies for "Radio Tropical" from 1995 to 1998 and worked the American League Championship Series in 2003 and 2004 for WADO.

Rivera received his Bachelor's degree in Spanish literature from Rutgers University and graduated from the Cambridge University-affiliated Miguel Angel Torres School of Communications in Manhattan in 1978. He began his communications career covering NBA basketball for WADO, and was later one of the pioneers of the talk show *WADO Deportivo*, where he worked until 2003. Francisco is married to Ivette Rodriguez and has two daughters, Melissa and Lorraine.

NEW YORK YANKEES SPANISH-LANGUAGE BROADCASTERS

Year	Broadcasters
1997	Beto Villa, Armando Talavera, Roberto Clemente Jr.
1998	Beto Villa, Armando Talavera, Roberto Clemente Jr.
1999	Beto Villa, Armando Talavera, Roberto Clemente Jr.
2000	Beto Villa, Armando Talavera, Roberto Clemente Jr.
2001	Beto Villa, Armando Talavera, Roberto Clemente Jr.
2002	Beto Villa, Armando Talavera
2003	Beto Villa, Armando Talavera
2004	Beto Villa, Armando Talavera
2005	Beto Villa, Francisco Rivera
2006	Beto Villa, Francisco Rivera, Felix DeJesus
2007	Beto Villa, Francisco Rivera, Felix DeJesus
2008	Beto Villa, Francisco Rivera
2009	Beto Villa, Francisco Rivera
2010	Beto Villa, Francisco Rivera
2011	Beto Villa, Francisco Rivera
2012	Beto Villa, Francisco Rivera
2013	Beto Villa, Francisco Rivera, Felix DeJesus
2014	Rickie Ricardo, Francisco Rivera
2015	Rickie Ricardo, Francisco Rivera
2016	Rickie Ricardo, Francisco Rivera
2017	Rickie Ricardo, Francisco Rivera
2018	Rickie Ricardo, Francisco Rivera
2019	Rickie Ricardo, Francisco Rivera

1978 World Series Champion Yankees

The Yankees' memorable 1978 World Championship club came back from a 14.0-game deficit in the AL East standings at the close of play on July 19 to take the division with a dramatic 5-4, one-game playoff victory over the Boston Red Sox at Fenway Park on Oct. 2. The team went on to defeat Kansas City 3-games-to-1 in the ALCS before winning their second straight Fall Classic over Los Angeles, 4-games-to-2. The club was piloted to the title by Bob Lemon, who led the Yankees to a 48-20 record after taking over following Billy Martin's midseason resignation.

Top Row (Standing): Reggie Jackson, Cliff Johnson, Jay Johnstone, Willie Randolph, Catfish Hunter, Chris Chambliss, Paul Lindblad, Paul Blair. **Third Row (Standing):** Gene Monahan (trainer), Dom Scala (bullpen catcher), Brian Doyle, Bucky Dent, Ron Guidry, Ken Clay, Larry McCall, Jim Beattie, Rich Gossage, Dick Tidrow, Lou Piniella, Fred Stanley, Herman Schneider (trainer), Pete Sheehy (clubhouse manager). **Seated (on bench):** Thurman Munson, Elston Howard (coach), Dick Howser (coach), Bob Lemon (manager), Yogi Berra (coach), Art Fowler (coach), Clyde King (coach), Gene Michael (coach), Gary Thomasson, Roy White, Ed Figueroa. **Seated (on ground):** Batboys - Gregg Pinder, Jim Plattner, Sandy Sallandrea.

Yankees Broadcast Teams - Radio & TV

1939	(WABC) Arch McDonald, Garnett Marks, Mel Allen
1940	(WABC) Mel Allen and J. C. Flippen
1941	No games broadcast
1942	(WOR) Mel Allen and Connie Desmond
1943	No games broadcast
1944	(WINS) Don Dunphy and Bill Slater
1945	(WINS) Bill Slater and Al Helfer
1946	(WINS) Mel Allen and Russ Hodges
1947	(WINS) Mel Allen and Russ Hodges
1948	(WINS) Mel Allen and Russ Hodges
1949	(WINS radio, Dumont TV) Mel Allen and Curt Gowdy
1950	(WINS radio, Dumont TV) Mel Allen and Curt Gowdy
1951	(WINS radio, WPIX TV) Mel Allen and Art Gleeson
1952	(WINS radio, WPIX TV) Mel Allen, Art Gleeson, Bill Crowley
1953	(WINS radio, WPIX TV) Mel Allen, Jim Woods, Joe E. Brown
1954	(WINS radio, WPIX TV) Mel Allen, Jim Woods, Red Barber
1955	(WINS radio, WPIX TV) Mel Allen, Jim Woods, Red Barber
1956	(WINS radio, WPIX TV) Mel Allen, Jim Woods, Red Barber
1957	(WINS radio, WPIX TV) Mel Allen, Red Barber, Phil Rizzuto
1958	(WMGM radio, WPIX TV) Mel Allen, Red Barber, Phil Rizzuto
1959	(WMGM radio, WPIX TV) Mel Allen, Red Barber, Phil Rizzuto
1960	(WMGM radio, WPIX TV) Mel Allen, Red Barber, Phil Rizzuto
1961	(WCBS radio, WPIX TV) Mel Allen, Red Barber, Phil Rizzuto
1962	(WCBS radio, WPIX TV) Mel Allen, Red Barber, Phil Rizzuto
1963	(WCBS radio, WPIX TV) Mel Allen, Red Barber, Phil Rizzuto, Jerry Coleman
1964	(WCBS radio, WPIX TV) Mel Allen, Red Barber, Phil Rizzuto, Jerry Coleman
1965	(WCBS radio, WPIX TV) Red Barber, Phil Rizzuto, Jerry Coleman, Joe Garagiola
1966	(WCBS radio, WPIX TV) Red Barber, Phil Rizzuto, Joe Garagiola, Jerry Coleman
1967	(WHN radio, WPIX TV) Phil Rizzuto, Jerry Coleman, Joe Garagiola
1968	(WHN radio, WPIX TV) Phil Rizzuto, Jerry Coleman, Frank Messer
1969	(WHN radio, WPIX TV) Phil Rizzuto, Jerry Coleman, Frank Messer, Whitey Ford
1970	(WHN radio, WPIX TV) Phil Rizzuto, Frank Messer, Whitey Ford, Bob Gamere
1971	(WMCA radio, WPIX TV) Phil Rizzuto, Frank Messer, Bill White, Whitey Ford
1972	(WMCA radio, WPIX TV) Phil Rizzuto, Frank Messer, Bill White
1973	(WMCA radio, WPIX TV) Phil Rizzuto, Frank Messer, Bill White
1974	(WMCA radio, WPIX TV) Phil Rizzuto, Frank Messer, Bill White
1975	(WMCA radio, WPIX TV) Phil Rizzuto, Frank Messer, Bill White, Dom Valentino
1976	(WMCA radio, WPIX TV) Phil Rizzuto, Frank Messer, Bill White
1977	(WMCA radio, WPIX TV) Phil Rizzuto, Frank Messer, Bill White
1978	(WINS radio, WPIX TV) Phil Rizzuto, Frank Messer, Bill White, Mel Allen, Fran Healy
1979	(WINS radio, WPIX TV, Sports Channel) Phil Rizzuto, Frank Messer, Bill White, Mel Allen, Fran Healy
1980	(WINS radio, WPIX TV, Sports Channel) Phil Rizzuto, Frank Messer, Bill White, Mel Allen, Fran Healy
1981	(WABC radio, WPIX TV, Sports Channel) Phil Rizzuto, Frank Messer, Bill White, Mel Allen, Fran Healy
1982	WABC radio, WPIX TV, Sports Channel) Phil Rizzuto, Frank Messer, Bill White, Mel Allen, John Gordon
1983	(WABC radio, WPIX TV, Sports Channel) Mel Allen, Phil Rizzuto, Frank Messer, Bill White, John Gordon
1984	(WABC radio, WPIX TV, Sports Channel) Mel Allen, Phil Rizzuto, Frank Messer, Bill White, John Gordon
1985	(WABC radio, WPIX TV, Sports Channel) Phil Rizzuto, Bill White, Frank Messer, Mel Allen, Mickey Mantle, John Gordon, Spencer Ross
1986	(WABC radio, WPIX TV, Sports Channel) Phil Rizzuto, Bill White, Jim Kaat, Billy Martin, Mel Allen, Mickey Mantle, John Gordon, Spencer Ross, Bobby Murcer
1987	(WABC radio, WPIX TV, Sports Channel) Phil Rizzuto, Bill White, Billy Martin, Ken "Hawk" Harrelson, Bobby Murcer, Mickey Mantle, Spencer Ross, Hank Greenwald, Tommy Hutton
1988	(WABC radio, WPIX TV, Sports Channel) Phil Rizzuto, Bill White, Ken "Hawk" Harrelson, Hank Greenwald, Bobby Murcer, Mickey Mantle, Ed Randall, Tommy Hutton
1989	(WABC radio, WPIX TV, MSG) Phil Rizzuto, George Grande, Tom Seaver, Tommy Hutton, Bobby Murcer, Lou Piniella, Greg Gumbel, Michael Kay, John Sterling, Jay Johnstone
1990	(WABC radio, WPIX TV, MSG) Phil Rizzuto, George Grande, Tom Seaver, Dewayne Staats, Tony Kubek, Al Trautwig, Michael Kay, John Sterling, Jay Johnstone
1991	(WABC radio, WPIX TV, MSG) Phil Rizzuto, Bobby Murcer, Tom Seaver, Dewayne Staats, Tony Kubek, Al Trautwig, Michael Kay, John Sterling, Joe Angel
1992	(WABC radio, WPIX TV, MSG) Phil Rizzuto, Bobby Murcer, Tom Seaver, Dewayne Staats, Tony Kubek, Al Trautwig, John Sterling, Michael Kay
1993	(WABC radio, WPIX TV, MSG) Phil Rizzuto, Bobby Murcer, Tom Seaver, Dewayne Staats, Tony Kubek, Al Trautwig, John Sterling, Michael Kay
1994	(WABC radio, WPIX TV, MSG) Phil Rizzuto, Dewayne Staats, Tony Kubek, Al Trautwig, John Sterling, Michael Kay, Paul Olden
1995	(WABC radio, WPIX TV, MSG) Phil Rizzuto, Bobby Murcer, Paul Olden, Dave Cohen, Jim Kaat, Al Trautwig, Steve Palermo, John Sterling, Michael Kay
1996	(WABC radio, WPIX TV, MSG) Phil Rizzuto, Bobby Murcer, Rick Cerone, Paul Olden, Dave Cohen, Jim Kaat, Al Trautwig, Steve Palermo, John Sterling, Michael Kay
1997	(WABC radio, WPIX TV, MSG) Jim Kaat, Ken Singleton, Bobby Murcer, Al Trautwig, Michael Kay, Rick Cerone, Steve Palermo, Suzyn Waldman, John Sterling, Michael Kay
1998	(WABC radio, WPIX TV, MSG) Bobby Murcer, Jim Kaat, Ken Singleton, Bobby Murcer, Al Trautwig, Tommy John, Suzyn Waldman, John Sterling, Michael Kay
1999	(WABC radio, WNYW TV, MSG) Tim McCarver, Bobby Murcer, Jim Kaat, Ken Singleton, Al Trautwig, Suzyn Waldman, John Sterling, Michael Kay
2000	(WABC radio, WNYW TV, MSG) Tim McCarver, Bobby Murcer, Jim Kaat, Ken Singleton, Al Trautwig, Suzyn Waldman, John Sterling, Michael Kay
2001	(WABC radio, WNYW TV, MSG) Tim McCarver, Bobby Murcer, Jim Kaat, Ken Singleton, Al Trautwig, Suzyn Waldman, John Sterling, Michael Kay
2002	(WCBS radio, WCBS TV, YES) Fred Hickman, Jim Kaat, Michael Kay, Bobby Murcer, Paul O'Neill, Ken Singleton, Suzyn Waldman, Charley Steiner, John Sterling
2003	(WCBS radio, WCBS TV, YES) Fred Hickman, Jim Kaat, Michael Kay, Bobby Murcer, Paul O'Neill, Ken Singleton, Suzyn Waldman, Charley Steiner, John Sterling
2004	(WCBS radio, WCBS TV, YES) Joe Girardi, Fred Hickman, Jim Kaat, Michael Kay, Bobby Murcer, Paul O'Neill, Ken Singleton, Suzyn Waldman, Charley Steiner, John Sterling
2005	WCBS radio, WWOR TV, YES) Jim Kaat, Michael Kay, Bobby Murcer, Paul O'Neill, Ken Singleton, Suzyn Waldman, John Sterling
2006	(WCBS radio, WWOR TV, YES) Kimberly Jones, David Justice, Jim Kaat, Michael Kay, Bobby Murcer, Paul O'Neill, Ken Singleton, Suzyn Waldman, John Sterling
2007	(WCBS radio, WWOR TV, YES) Michael Kay, Ken Singleton, Bobby Murcer, David Justice, Joe Girardi, John Flaherty, Kimberly Jones, Paul O'Neill, Al Leiter, Suzyn Waldman, John Sterling
2008	(WCBS radio, WWOR TV, YES) Michael Kay, Ken Singleton, Bobby Murcer, David Cone, John Flaherty, Kimberly Jones, Paul O'Neill, Al Leiter, Suzyn Waldman, John Sterling
2009	(WCBS radio, WWOR TV, YES) Michael Kay, Ken Singleton, David Cone, John Flaherty, Kimberly Jones, Paul O'Neill, Al Leiter, Suzyn Waldman, John Sterling
2010	(WCBS radio, WWOR TV, YES) Michael Kay, Ken Singleton, John Flaherty, Kimberly Jones, Paul O'Neill, Al Leiter, Suzyn Waldman, John Sterling
2011	(WCBS radio, WWOR TV, YES) Michael Kay, Ken Singleton, David Cone, Jack Curry, John Flaherty, Kimberly Jones, Paul O'Neill, Al Leiter, Suzyn Waldman, John Sterling
2012	(WCBS radio, WWOR TV, YES) Michael Kay, Ken Singleton, David Cone, Jack Curry, John Flaherty, Al Leiter, Meredith Marakovits, Paul O'Neill, Lou Piniella, Suzyn Waldman, John Sterling
2013	(WCBS radio, WWOR TV, YES) Michael Kay, Ken Singleton, David Cone, Jack Curry, John Flaherty, Al Leiter, Meredith Marakovits, Paul O'Neill, Lou Piniella, Bob Lorenz, Suzyn Waldman, John Sterling
2014	(WFAN radio, WWOR TV, YES) Michael Kay, Ken Singleton, David Cone, Jack Curry, John Flaherty, Al Leiter, Bob Lorenz, Meredith Marakovits, Paul O'Neill, Suzyn Waldman, John Sterling
2015	(WFAN radio, WPIX TV, YES) Michael Kay, Ken Singleton, David Cone, Jack Curry, John Flaherty, Al Leiter, Bob Lorenz, Meredith Marakovits, Paul O'Neill, Ryan Ruocco, Suzyn Waldman, John Sterling
2016	(WFAN radio, WPIX TV, YES) Michael Kay, Ken Singleton, David Cone, Jack Curry, John Flaherty, Al Leiter, Bob Lorenz, Meredith Marakovits, Paul O'Neill, Ryan Ruocco, Suzyn Waldman, John Sterling
2017	(WFAN radio, WPIX TV, YES) Michael Kay, Ken Singleton, David Cone, Jack Curry, John Flaherty, Al Leiter, Bob Lorenz, Meredith Marakovits, Paul O'Neill, Ryan Ruocco, Suzyn Waldman, John Sterling
2018	(WFAN radio, WPIX TV, YES) Michael Kay, Ken Singleton, David Cone, Jack Curry, John Flaherty, Al Leiter, Bob Lorenz, Meredith Marakovits, Paul O'Neill, Ryan Ruocco, Suzyn Waldman, John Sterling
2019	(WFAN radio, WPIX TV, YES) Michael Kay, Ken Singleton, David Cone, Jack Curry, John Flaherty, Bob Lorenz, Meredith Marakovits, Paul O'Neill, Ryan Ruocco, Suzyn Waldman, John Sterling

1967 broadcast team [L to R]: Jerry Coleman, Phil Rizzuto and Joe Garagiola

George M. Steinbrenner Field

This year marks the 25th season the Yankees will play their spring training games at George M. Steinbrenner Field in Tampa, Fla. Since opening in 1996, the complex also serves as the home of the Single-A Tampa Tarpons of the Florida State League. The field's dimensions are an exact replica of Yankee Stadium in the Bronx, measuring 318 feet down the left line, 408 feet to center field and 314 feet down the right field line.

Fans will also notice another link to the Bronx with replicas of the Yankees' retired numbers placards from Yankee Stadium greeting them as they enter the complex.

The facility originally opened in 1996 as Legends Field. However on February 14, 2008, Hal and Hank Steinbrenner announced that it would be renamed George M. Steinbrenner Field. The name change followed two unanimous resolutions recommending and supporting the change from the Hillsborough County Commission and the Tampa City Council. In a pregame ceremony prior to the Yankees' March 27, 2008, spring training game against the Pittsburgh Pirates the complex was formally renamed in honor of the late Yankees' Principal Owner and Chairman.

"I am humbled and flattered to have this outstanding and totally unexpected honor conferred on me," said George M. Steinbrenner at the time the resolution was passed. "I extend my thanks to the Tampa City Council and to the Hillsborough County Commissioners for passing resolutions suggesting and recommending the change. I also thank my family for supporting the renaming of the stadium and for everything they have done for so many years that helped bring about this great day."

The resolution passed by the Tampa City Council on February 7, 2008, cited Mr. Steinbrenner's many charitable donations on behalf of youth activities, hospitals and the arts. The resolution passed by the Board of the Hillsborough County Commissioners on February 6, 2008, recognizing Mr. Steinbrenner's numerous extraordinary contributions to the area.

The Yankees Pavilion at George M. Steinbrenner Field [at L] is a half-acre covered party area located next to the Yankees' pregame workout field. It offers fans an exclusive spot to eat, drink and watch warm-ups right before the game.

STADIUM CAPACITY

Total Seating	10,031
Luxury Suites/Seats	13/290
Field Boxes/Seats	19/161
Dugout Club Boxes/Seats	12/104
Loge Boxes/Seats	22/100
Right Field Cabanas	80
Bullpen Rooftop Club	200
3B Rooftop Club	150
Right Field Terrace	471
Left Field Deck	140

FIRST GAME: 3/1/96 vs. Cleveland
LARGEST CROWD: 11,229 – 3/17/11 vs. Tampa Bay

STADIUM DIMENSIONS*

Left Field foul line	318 feet
Center Field	408 feet
Right Field foul line	314 feet

* Identical to Yankee Stadium

SPRING TRAINING RECORDS SINCE 1962

Year	Record	Year	Record	Year	Record
1962	17-10	1982	9-16	2002	20-14
1963	12-17-1	1983	16-8	2003	15-13
1964	12-16	1984	10-16	2004	13-9
1965	12-18	1985	15-12	2005	14-15
1966	17-11	1986	17-11	2006	15-16
1967	13-17	1987	14-15	2007	14-13-3
1968	14-14-1	1988	22-10	2008	14-12-2
1969	16-9	1989	16-15	2009	24-10-1
1970	18-9	1990	5-9	2010	13-15-1
1971	8-23	1991	19-12	2011	13-15-3
1972	11-15-1	1992	17-14	2012	18-12-3
1973	18-11	1993	20-12	2013	14-18-1
1974	14-14-1	1994	12-15-1	2014	17-12-2
1975	14-17	1995	11-18/4-8	2015	17-16-1
1976	10-7	1996	16-15	2016	14-16-2
1977	11-13	1997	20-11	2017	24-9-1
1978	10-13	1998	15-12	2018	18-13-1
1979	7-18	1999	14-19	2019	17-10-4
1980	10-8-1	2000	13-20		
1981	13-13-1	2001	9-20		

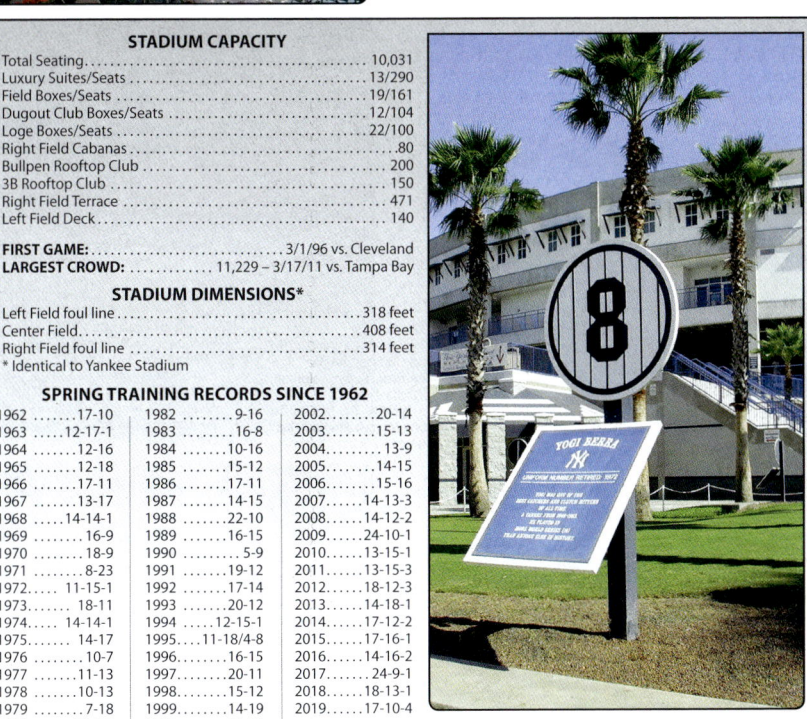

Steinbrenner Field Enhancements

During the winter of 2016-17, George M. Steinbrenner Field underwent significant ballpark enhancements. Some of the highlights include:

Multi-level Bullpen Clubs have been constructed on the first and third base lines. The upper level has a shaded private bar area and is exclusive to Loge Box holders, Club Seat members and private groups. The lower level contains a full-scale bar that is open to all patrons with valid tickets to that day's game.

A newly enhanced Right Field Pavilion allows fans to take in the game with the comfort and shade of a beachside bar. Those with tickets to the Pavilion will have access to a pregame buffet serving traditional ballpark fare and will be provided with two free drink tickets that can be used at the Right Field bar. The Pavilion can comfortably accommodate groups of 20-500 and is available for group purchases and individual game sales.

Loge boxes on the first and third base lines offer semi-private, open-aired, canopied seating for four and access to the exclusive premium lounge, located on the upper level of the first base and third base Bullpen Clubs. Food and beverage (water, soda, beer and wine) are all inclusive in the loge boxes, while premium alcohol is a la carte.

The Left Field Deck is an enclosed and shaded group party area. Those with tickets to the deck will have access to a pregame buffet serving traditional ballpark fare and will be provided with two free drink tickets. The Deck can comfortably accommodate groups of 20-100.

Cabanas are available for groups of 10-or-more on a full season, partial-season or game-day basis. This shaded private area is located in the right field alley in close proximity to the Right Field Pavilion. Food and beverage (water, soda, beer and wine) are all inclusive in the cabanas, while premium alcohol is a la carte.

2020 Yankees Spring Training Schedule

(All times are Eastern and subject to change. ss=Split Squad. Radio and TV listings as of Feb. 1.)

Pitchers and catchers are scheduled to report on Wed., Feb. 12, and hold their first workout on Thurs., Feb. 13. Position players are scheduled to report on Mon., Feb. 17. The club's first full-squad workout is scheduled for Tues., Feb. 18.

Date	Opponent	Site	Time
Sat., Feb. 22	vs. Toronto (WFAN/YES)	GMS Field	1:05 p.m.
Sun., Feb. 23	at Tampa Bay (WFAN)	Port Charlotte	1:05 p.m.
Mon., Feb. 24	vs. Pittsburgh	GMS Field	6:35 p.m.
Tues., Feb. 25	at Toronto	Dunedin	1:07 p.m.
Wed., Feb. 26	vs. Washington (YES)	GMS Field	1:05 p.m.
Thurs., Feb. 27	vs. Tampa Bay (YES)	GMS Field	1:05 p.m.
Fri., Feb. 28	at Atlanta	North Port	1:05 p.m.
Sat., Feb. 29 (ss)	vs. Detroit (WFAN/YES)	GMS Field	1:05 p.m.
	at Boston	Fort Myers	1:05 p.m.
Sun., Mar. 1	at Detroit (WFAN)	Lakeland	1:05 p.m.
Mon., Mar. 2	Off Day	--	--
Tues., Mar. 3	vs. Boston (YES/ESPN)	GMS Field	1:05 p.m.
Wed., Mar. 4	vs. Philadelphia	GMS Field	6:35 p.m.
Thurs., Mar 5	at Detroit	Lakeland	1:05 p.m.
Fri., Mar. 6	vs. Baltimore	GMS Field	6:35 p.m.
Sat., Mar. 7	at Pittsburgh (WFAN/YES)	Bradenton	1:05 p.m.
Sun., Mar. 8 (ss)	vs. Atlanta	GMS Field	1:05 p.m.
	at Baltimore	Sarasota	1:05 p.m
Mon., Mar. 9	at Philadelphia	Clearwater	1:05 p.m.
Tues., Mar. 10	vs. Toronto (YES)	GMS Field	1:05 p.m.
Wed., Mar. 11	at Miami	Jupiter	1:05 p.m.
Thurs., Mar. 12	at Washington	West Palm Beach	1:05 p.m.
Fri., Mar. 13	vs. Detroit (WFAN/YES)	GMS Field	6:35 p.m.
Sat., Mar. 14	vs. Philadelphia (WFAN)	GMS Field	1:05 p.m.
Sun., Mar 15 (ss)	vs. Minnesota (WFAN/YES)	GMS Field	1:05 p.m.
	at Toronto	Dunedin	1:07 p.m.
Mon., Mar. 16	Off Day	--	--
Tues., Mar. 17	at Detroit	Lakeland	1:05 p.m.
Wed., Mar. 18	vs. Pittsburgh	GMS Field	6:35 p.m.
Thurs., Mar. 19	at Philadelphia	Clearwater	1:05 p.m.
Fri., Mar. 20	vs. Miami (YES)	GMS Field	1:05 p.m.
Sat., Mar. 21	at Minnesota (WFAN)	Fort Myers	1:05 p.m.
Sun., Mar. 22	vs. Detroit (WFAN/YES)	GMS Field	1:05 p.m.
Mon., Mar. 23	at Toronto	Montreal	7:07 p.m.
Tues., Mar. 24	at Toronto (WFAN)	Montreal	7:07 p.m.

Time, opponent, date and team rosters and lineups, including the Yankees' roster and lineup, are subject to change.

2019 Spring Training Attendance

Home at GMS Field (15 MLB dates, 9,497 avg.) 142,459
Road (16 dates, 9,020 avg.) 144,325*
Overall Attendance (31 dates, 9,251 avg.) 286,574

*Includes 3/25/19 game at Nationals Park in Washington, D.C.

Yankees All-Time Spring Training Sites

Year	Location
1903-04	Atlanta, GA
1905	Montgomery, AL
1906	Birmingham, AL
1907-08	Atlanta, GA
1909	Macon, GA
1910-11	Athens, GA
1912	Atlanta, GA
1913	Hamilton, Bermuda
1914	Houston, TX
1915	Savannah, GA
1916-18	Macon, GA
1919-20	Jacksonville, FL
1921	Shreveport, LA
1922-24	New Orleans, LA
1925-42	St. Petersburg, FL
1943	Asbury Park, NJ
1944-45	Atlantic City, NJ
1946	Balboa, Panama
1946-50	St. Petersburg, FL
1951	Phoenix, AZ
1952-61	St. Petersburg, FL
1962-93	Ft. Lauderdale, FL
1994-present*	Tampa, FL

(*Of note: From 1994-95 the Single-A Florida State League Yankees played at Red McEwen Field at the University of South Florida in Tampa before moving into Steinbrenner Field — then called Legends Field — in 1996.)

All-Time GMS Field Attendances
(1996-present)

Year	Attendance
1996	173,247
1997	172,092
1998	149,496
1999	164,015
2000	153,385
2001	173,107
2002	172,544
2003	162,890
2004	122,374
2005	152,640
2006	152,024
2007	154,590
2008	139,496
2009	168,905
2010	147,557
2011	163,085
2012	162,832
2013	172,942
2014	159,272
2015	171,712
2016	160,813
2017	149,757
2018	158,106
2019	142,459

The Yankees held spring training at Al Lang Field in St. Petersburg, Fla., from 1925-42, 1946-50 and 1952-61.

ANTICIPATED BATTING PRACTICE SCHEDULE AT YANKEE STADIUM
(Note: Times are subject to change.)

Start Time	1:05 p.m.	4:05 p.m.	6:35 p.m.	7:05 p.m.	8:05p.m
Yankees Hit	10:40-11:30	1:40-2:40	4:10-5:10	4:40-5:40	5:40-6:40
Visitors Hit	11:40-12:20	2:40-3:20	5:10-5:50	5:40-6:20	6:40-7:20
Yankees Infield	12:20-12:30	3:20-3:30	5:50-6:00	6:20-6:30	7:20-7:30
Visitors Infield	12:30-12:40	3:30-3:40	6:00-6:10	6:30-6:40	7:30-7:40

Yankee Stadium Map

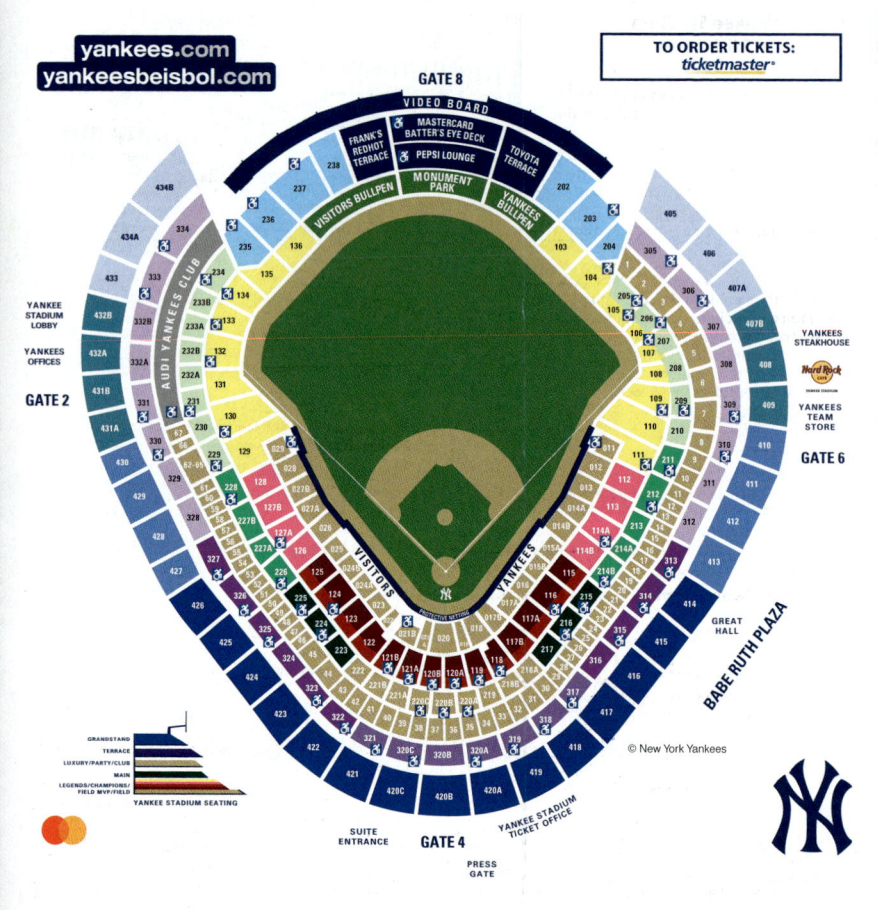

yankees.com
yankeesbeisbol.com

TO ORDER TICKETS:
ticketmaster®

For ticket information, including pricing, please visit yankees.com.

Please note that protective netting of varying heights is used in the Stadium from Section 011 to behind home plate to Section 029

ALCOHOL-FREE SEATING
Sections 407A and 433

ATMs presented by
Bank of America
Great Hall: Adjacent to the Guest Relations & Ticket Sales Booth, near Gate 6
Field Level: Sections 127B-128
Main Level: Section 222
Terrace/Grandstand Level: Sections 330-331

ELEVATORS
Yankee Stadium's 16 public elevators are located in the Great Hall and throughout the Stadium.

ESCALATORS
Escalators are located in the Great Hall.

FAMILY RESTROOMS
Field Level: Sections 106, 124 and 130
Delta SKY360° Suite: Section 221B
Main Level: Sections 219, 227A and 234
Terrace/Grandstand Level: Sections 311, 317, 327 and 333
Bleachers: Section 202

FIRST AID
Field Level: Section 128
Main Level: Section 221
Terrace/Grandstand: Section 320C

GREAT HALL
The Great Hall is located along Babe Ruth Plaza between the exterior wall and the interior of Yankee Stadium between Gates 4 and 6.

GUEST RELATIONS BOOTHS/KIOSKS
Great Hall: Adjacent to Gate 6
Field Level: Section 128
Guest Relations Kiosks and Guest Relations Ambassadors are located in and around Yankee Stadium to assist Guests.

PLYMOUTH ROCK KIDS CLUBHOUSE
Yankee Stadium's children's area is located on the 300 Level in right field. It also includes a private space for nursing mothers.

RAMPS
Adjacent to Gates 2 and 6

Getting to Yankee Stadium

Yankee Stadium GPS Address:
One East 161st Street, Bronx, New York

Yankee Stadium is accessible from the Major Deegan Expressway (Interstate 87) at the following exits:

<u>Northbound I-87</u>: Exit 4 (East 149th Street/145th Street Bridge) and Exit 5 (East 161st Street/Macombs Dam Bridge).

<u>Southbound I-87</u>: Exit 6 (East 153rd Street/River Ave.) and Exit 5 (East 161st St./Macombs Dam Bridge).

BY SUBWAY The No. 4 train (East Side) and the D train (Sixth Avenue) make stops at the 161st Street/Yankee Stadium subway station, located on East 161st Street and River Avenue. B train (Sixth Avenue) service is also available, but only on weekdays. For more information, please visit www.mta.info or call the MTA at 511.

BY BUS Several New York City bus lines provide service to the Stadium. The Bx6 and Bx13 buses stop at East 161st Street and River Avenue; the Bx1 and Bx2 buses stop at East 161st Street and the Grand Concourse, a short walk from the Stadium; and the BxM4 bus stops at the Grand Concourse and East 161st Street (northbound) and East 158th Street (southbound). For more information, please visit www.mta.info or call the MTA at 511.

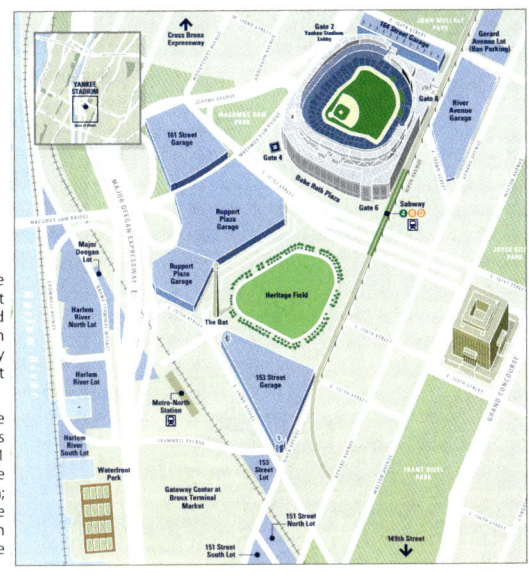

BY TRAIN Metro-North offers train service to the Stadium. For more information, please visit www.mta.info or call the MTA at 511.

Guests are encouraged to use public transportation in order to reduce CO_2 emissions.

FOR YANKEES TICKET INFORMATION, PLEASE VISIT YANKEES.COM OR CALL (212) YANKEES.

Time, opponent, date and team rosters and lineups are subject to change.

Game times listed as TBD are subject to determination by, among others, Major League Baseball and its television partners.

For the 2020 regular season, "Premium Games" are the following Games: (a) Opening Day; (b) Old Timer's Day; (c) all Games against the Boston Red Sox, Chicago Cubs and New York Mets; and (d) select Saturday games on June 6, 2020, July 11, 2020, August 8, 2020 and August 22, 2020.

All individual game ticket prices are subject to variable and dynamic pricing, which provide fans with more price options based on changing factors that affect market demand.

In no event will the Yankees be liable to the ticket holder and/or ticket purchaser for any direct, indirect, consequential, exemplary, incidental, special or punitive damages or for lost profits, revenues or business opportunities even if the Yankees have been advised of the possibility of such damages.

Be advised that the Yankees reserve the right to take appropriate action against individuals who fraudulently obtain wheelchair accessible and/or companion seats, including, without limitation, ejection and legal action.

Tickets may not be used for advertising, promotions of any kind (e.g., self-promotions, product promotions, ticket promotions, business promotions and/or commercial promotions) or any other commercial purposes, including, without limitation, contests, auctions, sweepstakes and giveaways, without the express written consent of the Yankees.

Please note that protective netting of varying heights is located between Section 011 on the 1st base/right field side of the Stadium and continues to Section 029 on the 3rd base/left field side of the Stadium.

WARNING: For the safety of everyone in Yankee Stadium, all Guests must stay alert and be aware of their surroundings at all times, as during all batting practices, fielding practices and warm-ups and throughout the course of all baseball games and the baseball game experiences, hard-hit baseballs and bats and fragments thereof may be thrown at or hit into the stands, concourses, walkways, concessions areas, Monument Park and all other publicly accessible areas within the Stadium. Further, Guests concerned with their original ticketed location by reason of the foregoing should, at any time before or during the baseball game or the baseball game experiences, proceed to a Yankee Stadium Ticket Window, located adjacent to Gate 6 in the Great Hall, adjacent to the Yankees Team Store behind home plate in the Great Hall, or adjacent to Section 320C on the Terrace/Grandstand Level; however, please remember that: (a) any requested relocation is subject to availability; (b) any alternate seat or standing location may be in a section and/or level of the Stadium and/or within a price category that is not in the same section and/or level and/or price category of the Guests' original ticketed location, regardless of their original ticketed location; and (c) any Guest requesting relocation is responsible for paying the incremental price increase, if any, of the ticket price for the available alternate location. Relocation to a seat or standing location at a lower price than the price of the original ticketed location will not result in a refund or credit.

WARNING: Guests may not transmit or aid in transmitting any photographs, images, videos, audio, livestreams or other accounts or descriptions (including play-by-play data), whether text, data or visual, in any media, now known or hereafter developed, of all or any part of the game or related events, without the express written consent of the Yankees.

NOTICE: For the safety of every Guest, all persons specifically consent to and are subject to (a) being screened by metal detectors; (b) bag/clothing inspections; and (c) physical pat-down inspections prior to entry. Any item or property that could affect the safety of Yankee Stadium, its occupants or its property shall not be permitted into the Stadium. Any person that could affect the safety of the Stadium, its occupants or its property shall be denied entry.

NOTICE: The Yankees reserve the right, with or without refunding any amount paid by the ticket holder, to refuse admission to and/or eject any person who: (a) is or appears to be impaired; (b) deliberately conceals alcohol, illegal substances and/or other prohibited items while attempting to enter Yankee Stadium; (c) acts in a manner that is unruly, disruptive or illegal; (d) uses derogatory, foul and/ or abusive language; (e) displays and/ or wears and fails to cover obscene, indecent and/ or inappropriate clothing; (f) exposes him/herself; or (g) otherwise violates the Stadium's Code of Conduct, ordinances, rules, requirements, directives, regulations. Ticket holders acknowledge and agree that the Yankees' ban on foul and/or abusive language and uncovered obscene, indecent and/or inappropriate clothing (i.e., clauses (d) through (f) above) does not violate their right to free speech and/or expression and that such time, place and manner of the restrictions are reasonable to maintain a family-friendly atmosphere for young Guests, ensure the safety of all Guests and sports or event participants, and preserve the enjoyment of the game or event for all Guests. In addition, ticket holders further acknowledge and agree that by entering the Stadium, they hereby consent to the ban on foul and/or abusive language and uncovered obscene, indecent and/ or inappropriate clothing and waive, to the fullest extent they may legally and effectively do so, any objection they may now or hereafter have to such ban and the penalties that the Yankees may impose for any violation of the same.

2020 New York Yankees Schedule

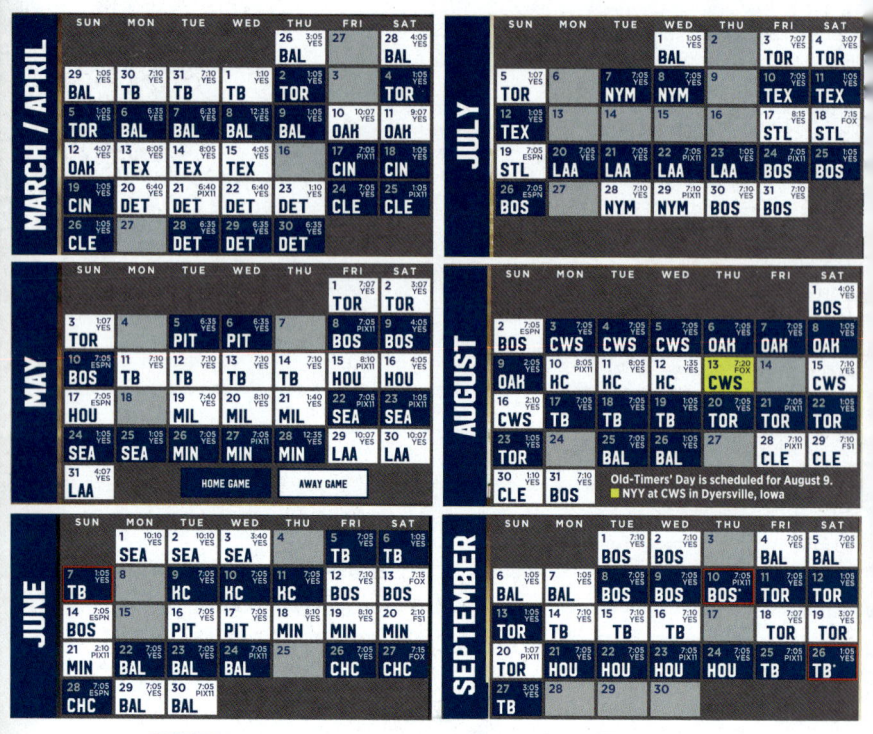

MARCH / APRIL

SUN	MON	TUE	WED	THU	FRI	SAT
				26 4:05 YES BAL	27 BAL	28 1:05 YES BAL
29 1:05 YES BAL	30 1:05 YES TB	31 7:10 YES TB	1 7:10 YES TB	2 1:10 YES TB	3 TOR	4 TOR
5 1:05 YES TOR	6 6:35 YES BAL	7 6:35 YES BAL	8 6:35 YES BAL	9 12:35 YES BAL	10 10:07 YES OAK	11 9:07 YES OAK
12 4:07 YES OAK	13 8:05 YES TEX	14 8:05 YES TEX	15 8:05 YES TEX	16 CIN	17 6:40 YES CIN	18 1:05 PIX11 CIN
19 1:05 YES CIN	20 6:40 YES DET	21 6:40 PIX11 DET	22 6:40 YES DET	23 1:10 YES DET	24 4:05 YES CLE	25 1:05 PIX11 CLE
26 4:05 YES CLE	27	28 6:40 YES DET	29 6:40 YES DET	30 6:35 YES DET		

MAY

SUN	MON	TUE	WED	THU	FRI	SAT
					1 7:07 YES TOR	2 1:07 YES TOR
3 1:07 YES TOR	4	5 6:35 YES PIT	6 6:35 YES PIT	7 7:05 PIX11 BOS	8 7:05 YES BOS	9 4:05 YES BOS
10 1:05 ESPN BOS	11 7:10 YES TB	12 7:10 YES TB	13 7:10 YES TB	14 7:10 YES TB	15 8:10 YES HOU	16 4:05 YES HOU
17 7:05 YES HOU	18	19 7:40 YES MIL	20 8:10 YES MIL	21 1:40 YES MIL	22 7:05 YES SEA	23 7:05 YES SEA
24 1:05 YES SEA	25 1:05 YES SEA	26 7:05 YES MIN	27 8:10 PIX11 MIN	28 1:10 YES MIN	29 10:05 YES LAA	30 10:07 YES LAA
31 4:07 YES LAA						

JUNE

SUN	MON	TUE	WED	THU	FRI	SAT
	1 10:10 YES SEA	2 10:10 YES SEA	3 3:40 YES SEA	4	5 7:10 YES TB	6 7:10 YES TB
7 1:05 YES TB	8	9 7:05 YES HC	10 7:05 YES HC	11 7:05 YES HC	12 7:05 YES BOS	13 7:05 FOX BOS
14 1:05 YES BOS	15	16 7:05 YES PIT	17 7:05 YES PIT	18 8:10 YES MIN	19 8:10 YES MIN	20 8:10 YES MIN
21 2:10 PIX11 MIN	22 7:05 YES BAL	23 7:05 YES BAL	24 7:05 YES BAL	25 YES CHC	26 7:15 YES CHC	
28 2:05 ESPN CHC	29 7:05 YES BAL	30 7:05 PIX11 BAL				

JULY

SUN	MON	TUE	WED	THU	FRI	SAT
			1 BAL	2	3 7:07 YES TOR	4 4:07 YES TOR
5 1:07 YES TOR	6	7 7:05 YES NYM	8 7:05 YES NYM	9	10 7:05 YES TEX	11 7:15 YES TEX
12 1:05 YES TEX	13	14	15	16	17 7:05 YES STL	18 7:15 YES STL
19 1:05 YES STL	20 7:05 YES LAA	21 7:05 YES LAA	22 7:05 YES LAA	23 7:05 YES LAA	24 7:05 PIX11 BOS	25 7:05 YES BOS
26 1:05 ESPN BOS	27	28 7:05 YES NYM	29 7:05 YES NYM	30 7:05 YES BOS	31 7:10 YES BOS	

AUGUST

SUN	MON	TUE	WED	THU	FRI	SAT
						1 4:05 YES BOS
2 7:05 ESPN BOS	3 7:05 YES CWS	4 7:05 YES CWS	5 7:05 YES CWS	6 7:05 YES OAK	7 7:05 YES OAK	8 7:05 YES OAK
9 OAK	10 8:05 YES HC	11 8:05 YES HC	12 1:35 YES HC	13 7:20 FOX CWS	14	15 7:05 YES CWS
16 7:05 YES CWS	17 7:05 YES TB	18 7:05 YES TB	19 7:05 YES TB	20 7:10 YES TOR	21 7:10 YES TOR	22 7:10 YES TOR
23 7:05 YES TOR	24	25 7:05 YES BAL	26 7:05 YES BAL	27	28 7:10 PIX11 CLE	29 7:10 FS1 CLE
30 CLE	31 7:10 YES BOS					

Old-Timers' Day is scheduled for August 9.
NYY at CWS in Dyersville, Iowa

SEPTEMBER

SUN	MON	TUE	WED	THU	FRI	SAT
		1 7:10 YES BOS	2 7:10 YES BOS	3	4 7:05 YES BAL	5 7:05 YES BAL
6 1:05 YES BAL	7 7:05 YES BAL	8 7:05 YES BOS	9 7:05 YES BOS	10 7:05 YES BOS*	11 7:05 YES TOR	12 7:05 YES TOR
13 1:05 YES TOR	14 7:07 YES HOU	15 7:05 YES HOU	16 7:05 YES HOU	17	18 7:07 YES TB	19 7:05 YES TB
20 1:05 YES TB	21	22	23	24	25	26 1:05 YES TB*
27 3:05 YES TB	28	29	30			

FOR YANKEES TICKET INFORMATION, PLEASE VISIT YANKEES.COM OR CALL (212) YANKEES.

Time, opponent, date and team rosters and lineups are subject to change.

Listings noted with a red border and asterisk (*) have game times subject to determination by, among others, MLB and its television partners. Any future start-time changes to these games will also be accompanied by a change in the television partner.

Game times listed as TBD are subject to determination by, among others, Major League Baseball and its television partners.

For the 2020 regular season, "Premium Games" are the following Games: (a) Opening Day; (b) Old Timer's Day; (c) all Games against the Boston Red Sox, Chicago Cubs and New York Mets; and (d) select Saturday games on June 6, 2020, July 11, 2020, August 8, 2020 and August 22, 2020.

All individual ticket prices are subject to variable and dynamic pricing, which provide fans with more price options based on changing factors that affect market demand.

In no event will the Yankees be liable to the ticket holder and/or ticket purchaser for any direct, indirect, consequential, exemplary, incidental, special or punitive damages or for lost profits, revenues or business opportunities even if the Yankees have been advised of the possibility of such damages.

Be advised that the Yankees reserve the right to take appropriate action against individuals who fraudulently obtain wheelchair accessible and/or companion seats, including, without limitation, ejection and legal action.

Tickets may not be used for advertising, promotions of any kind (e.g., self- promotions, product promotions, ticket promotions, business promotions and/or commercial promotions) or any other commercial purposes, including, without limitation, contests, auctions, sweepstakes and giveaways, without the express written consent of the Yankees.

Please note that protective netting of varying heights is located between Section 011 on the 1st base/right field side of the Stadium and continues to Section 029 on the 3rd base/left field side of the Stadium.

WARNING: For the safety of everyone in Yankee Stadium, all Guests must stay alert and be aware of their surroundings at all times, as during all batting practices, fielding practices and warm-ups and throughout the course of all baseball games and the baseball game experiences, hard-hit baseballs and bats and fragments thereof may be thrown or hit into the stands, concourses, walkways, concessions areas, Monument Park and all other publicly accessible areas within the Stadium. Further, Guests concerned with their original ticketed location by reason of the foregoing should, at any time before or during the baseball game or the baseball game experiences, proceed to a Yankee Stadium Ticket Window, located adjacent to Gate 6 in the Great Hall, adjacent to the Yankees Team Store behind home plate in the Great Hall, or adjacent to Section 320C on the Terrace/Grandstand Level; however, please remember that: (a) any requested relocation is subject to availability; (b) any alternate seat or standing location may be in a section and/or level of the Stadium and/or within a price category that is not in the same section and/or level and/or price category of the Guests' original ticketed location, regardless of their original ticketed location; and (c) any Guest requesting relocation is responsible for paying the incremental price increase, if any, of the ticket price for the available alternate location. Relocation to a seat or standing location at a lower price than the price of the original ticketed location will not result in a refund or credit.

WARNING: Guests may not transmit or aid in transmitting any photographs, images, videos, audio, livestreams or other accounts or descriptions (including play-by-play data), whether text, data or visual, in any media, now known or hereafter developed, of all or any part of the game or related events, without the express written consent of the Yankees.

NOTICE: For the safety of every Guest, all persons specifically consent to and are subject to: (a) being screened by metal detectors; (b) bag/clothing inspections; and (c) physical pat-down inspections prior to entry. Any item or property that could affect the safety of Yankee Stadium, its occupants or its property shall not be permitted into the Stadium. Any person that could affect the safety of the Stadium, its occupants or its property shall be denied entry.

NOTICE: The Yankees reserve the right, without refunding any amount paid by the ticket holder, to refuse admission to and/or eject any person who: (a) is or appears to be impaired; (b) deliberately conceals alcohol, illegal substances and/or other prohibited items while attempting to enter Yankee Stadium; (c) acts in a manner that is unruly, disruptive or illegal; (d) uses derogatory, foul and/ or abusive language; (e) displays and/or wears and fails to cover obscene, indecent and/or inappropriate clothing; (f) exposes him/herself; and/ or (g) otherwise violates the Stadium's Code of Conduct, ordinances, rules, requirements, directives, regulations. Ticket holders acknowledge and agree that the Yankees' ban on foul and/or abusive language and uncovered obscene, indecent and/or inappropriate clothing (i.e., clauses (d) through (f) above) does not violate their right to free speech and/or expression and that such time, place and manner of the restrictions are reasonable to maintain a family-friendly atmosphere for young Guests, ensure the safety of all Guests and sports or event participants, and preserve the enjoyment of the game or event for all Guests. In addition, ticket holders further acknowledge and agree that by entering the Stadium, they hereby consent to the ban on foul and/or abusive language and uncovered obscene, indecent and/or inappropriate clothing and waive, to the fullest extent they may legally and effectively do so, any objection they may now or hereafter have to such ban and the penalties that the Yankees may impose for any violation of the same.